The Encyclopedia of Early American Vocal Groups

100 Years of Harmony

1850 to 1950

Douglas E. Friedman and Anthony J. Gribin

Copyright © 2013 by Douglas E. Friedman and Anthony J. Gribin

ISBN 978-0-9713979-2-7

Library of Congress Control Number: 2013900533

Reproduction or translation of any part of this work beyond that allowed by the United States Copyright Act, without the written permission of the copyright holder, is not permitted. Any request for permission should be addressed to the publisher at defriedman@harmonysongs.com.

Published by HarmonySongs Publications, West Long Branch, New Jersey

Publisher website: www.harmonysongs.com

Printed in the United States of America.

First Edition

Cover design by Ken Wallace

Douglas E. Friedman dedication: To my brother, Ken Friedman, with thanks for his encouragement and support both with this book and throughout my life.

Anthony J. Gribin dedication: To my talented mother, Doris Tauber Gribin, who wrote the melody to the standard song "Them There Eyes" and handed down her love of music to me, among other things.

Both authors also dedicate this book to the memory of Ronald Italiano (Ronnie I.) who helped guide them through the world of vocal group harmony.

Contents

Acknowledgments vii

Introduction... ix

Chapter One: Before the Age of Recorded Sound...1

    The European Influence..3

    Minstrelsy 5

    The Chautauqua Movement 8

    Black Music Threads 10

Chapter Two 1890 to 1920: The Dawn of Recording..14

    The Advent of Recorded Sound 15

    Early Recording Groups 19

    Confluential Themes..25

    The 1910s...28

Chapter Three 1920 to 1939: The Dawn of the Radio Era 38

    The Influence of Instruments on the Sound of Vocal Groups 42

    The Male Groups...44

    The Female Groups...46

    Vocal Groups and the Big Bands 50

    Black Vocal Groups...52

    Gospel and Spiritual Group Singing 60

    Other Tributaries..63

Chapter Four 1940 to 1950: War and the Music Industry: The Birth of Rock and Roll 65

    The Economics of the Music Industry 66

    The Effects of World War II...67

    Technology 69

    Tape Recorder 70

    Soundies..70

    Transcriptions 71

- Record Charts 72
- The Jukebox 72
- Groups Whose Popularity Carried Over From the 1930s 73
- Black Groups Making Their Mark in the Early 1940s 79
- The White Pop Groups of the 1940s 82
- Gospel 85
- Black Groups of the Late 1940s 87
- Things To Come 90

Groupography 95
Discography 278
Technology and Vocal Groups 513
Sheet Music and Vocal Groups 515
Postcards and Vocal Groups 528
Lists 545
Bibliography 553
Photo Credits 558
Index 559

Acknowledgments

No one writes a book of this scope without a lot of help from others. For the early recording era, Dorothy Reuter at the Barbershop Harmony Society and Joseph Schlesinger provided assistance. Also, the works of the late Jim Walsh were critical to gaining an understanding of the early vocal groups. For the later groups, help was provided by Marv Goldberg, Tony Fournier and Karsten Lehl. Karsten is from Germany where there is a thriving (but somewhat small) community of vocal group enthusiasts. Marv Goldberg also read a fairly early draft of the text portion and provided valuable comments.

Mary Jo Grogan of the Moonmaids gave us insights into what it what was like breaking into the business. The late Deborah Chessler (real name, Shirley Reingold) recalled for us how she came to write "It's Too Soon To Know" and discovered the Orioles.

The late Ronald Italiano (Ronnie I.) provided both authors with guidance through the world of vocal group harmony and helped introduce them to the music beyond the charts.

Tim Hauser, founder of The Manhattan Transfer, and Terry Stewart, President and CEO of the Rock and Roll Hall of Fame and Museum, were gracious enough to provide cover blurbs.

Others who helped were Ina and Steve Kichen, Mitch Rand (who solved an unsolvable formatting issue with the Discography), Alan Sherman and Nick and Kevin from the Microsoft Store in Freehold who helped with the layout.

Doug's brother, Ken Friedman, was the primary editor and also provided support and advice. Doug's wife, Linda Lashbrook, read the manuscript several times and was a sounding board for ideas.

Introduction

Most people who grew up in the 1950s or 1960s have at least heard of vocal groups from the 1930s and 1940s such as the Mills Brothers, the Ink Spots and the Andrews Sisters, as well as 1950s white pop groups such as the McGuire Sisters, the Four Freshmen, the Four Aces and the Four Lads. But the less-celebrated great black groups of the 1940s such as the Delta Rhythm Boys, the Charioteers, the Four Tunes, the Golden Gate Quartet, the Four Vagabonds and the Four Knights are just about unknown. And, if we go back even further it just gets worse. Not one in 100,000 people under the age of fifty will have heard of the American Quartet, the Revelers or the Rhythm Boys. It's a shame because these people are missing out on a lot of great music.

We first became interested in the earlier vocal groups due to our involvement with the rhythm and blues vocal harmony groups of the 1950s. The main question that intrigued us was: How did vocal group music evolve from the days of minstrelsy to the Peerless Quartet and then on to the Boswell Sisters, the Mills Brothers, the Ravens and the Orioles? But, as we became more involved in the project, we were drawn to the beauty of the music itself and to the stories of the groups that gave us that music.

We had heard this music as kids – we both came from musical families – but we had lost touch with it over the years. There is precious little written about the early groups and certainly no one place where you can look to learn more about the pre-1950 period. Of course, the fact that there is not much source material out there made the research for this book even more formidable: It was not a matter of trying to choose from and then distill large amounts of information – it was trying to find any information at all and then bringing together the information that we found.

The Encyclopedia of Early American Vocal Groups consists of four parts: (1) a concise history, (2) a groupography, (3) a discography and (4) the illustrations – primarily sheet music and postcards. We compiled the groupography during years of research: Every time we came across a reference to a group, a recording or a piece of sheet music, we entered the name of the group into a database along with whatever information we found about the group. We compiled the discography in a similar way, although here we were helped by lists found on the internet as well as information contained in our own collections. Between us we own more than 1000 pieces of sheet music and other items that contain photos of early groups. We found most of this material on eBay or in antique shops and used bookstores.

Writing the history portion was not an easy task. For example, we can easily hear the difference between the Dinwiddie Colored Quartet in 1902 and the Four Vagabonds in 1947, but describing the nature of the change and how that change happened was much more challenging. As part of gaining an understanding of the musical evolution, we had to examine what were the things that influenced how the music developed. Influences that had an impact in the music itself and how and why it changed, were not always easy to identify and define, but that is what this book attempts to do.

The Encyclopedia of Early American Vocal Groups starts by tracing the evolution of the music from the minstrel shows, which featured group singing, up to the early gospel and secular groups. The post-Civil War era provided the beginnings of the group sound. This included contributions by freed slaves as well as waves of immigrants, both of whom offered novel approaches to shaping the popular music of the day. We then move on to the extremely popular groups of the late 19th and early 20th centuries, which brought together some of the best singers of the day. Sheet music also gained greater popularity and helped provide a market for popular music. The beginnings of Tin Pan Alley in New York fueled the growth of popular music, and that influence lasted until the birth of rock and roll in the early 1950s.

The beginnings of the Jazz Age ushered in what may have been the golden age of group singing: The groups that formed during this period were among the best and longest-lasting of any era. Their music can still be found in just about every music store. Groups such as the Boswell Sisters, the Andrews Sisters, and from Europe, the Comedian Harmonists. And, with the emergence of the Mills Brothers and the Ink Spots (featuring Bill Kenny, the first great lead of the "modern" era), black groups were able to gain a foothold with white audiences in a way that had not been seen since the Fisk Singers in the 19th century.

We then conclude by describing the transition from the pop sound that dominated the charts until the early 1950s to the R&B sound that took hold and ushered in the beginnings of the rock and roll era in the late 1940s and early 1950s.

Some information on gospel groups is included because of the tremendous influence of gospel on popular music; but we omitted any in-depth coverage of the gospel groups themselves due to space considerations and the fact that others have done this elsewhere (some of these works are listed in the body of this book). For the most part, we also excluded country and western and barbershop, primarily because these genres generally exist in worlds of their own.

Chapter One:

Before the Age of Recorded Sound

What do we know about group singing in the era before sound could be recorded? We know that men and women were singing in groups throughout the nineteenth century, both in America and in most parts of the world. We know that the options for types of entertainment were limited: there were no microphones; there were few instruments for popular music other than piano, guitar, banjo or harmonica; and orchestral music was only heard in the big cities — the music of the concert halls. The music of the masses was primarily vocal since the human voice is the most portable instrument of them all.

Nineteenth century audiences expected little, compared to today, and they got what they expected, and were quite pleased. Consider this passage about the performance of the apparently multi-talented George Swayne Buckley, given around 1836: "Some idea of Mr. Buckley's versatility may be gleaned from the fact that in one performance he sang a song and done a banjo solo in the first part, played a solo on the kitchen bellows in a burlesque on the Julien Concerts; gave Locust Hum in the third part; played a part in the burlesque opera; danced with two others in the finale, and gave his bone solo, which was a wonderful performance; with them he gave imitations of the drums, the march, the reveille, etc., concluding with imitations of two horses running a race. It must be understood that all these performances were given in an artistic manner . . . ."[1] In the 1830s, a performer's versatility and resourcefulness in creating rhythms by clacking bones together, imitating the sounds of insects and performing a song and dance routine must have seemed quite impressive.

In addition, we know that the geography and make-up of the population in the nineteenth century influenced the kind of entertainment that was heard. Serious vocal and instrumental music, presented by large and expensive-to-maintain organizations, that were similar to and derived from their European counterparts, could be heard in all of the large American cities. The country was largely agrarian, with the population spread out over millions of square miles. What could reach the far-flung masses were small, flexible groups of people who could and would travel light and reach the second-tier and smaller cities and towns. And, because there were no automobiles or buses, these groups were relegated to travel by horse and carriage, or were limited to stops along the existing railroad lines.

Furthermore, even in the large industrial cities, a majority of the people were poorly educated and musically unsophisticated. Much of the population did not appreciate opera or symphonic music. Without a method of recording or broadcasting, the only way to hear a symphony was to attend a concert. Open-air concerts were held occasionally, but for the most part classical music was for the better-off and better-educated. On the other hand, anyone could appreciate a good song and dance at the local theater, with a little humor thrown in to sweeten the pot.

We also have a good idea about the musical threads that contributed to what would, a century later, become our own American vocal music. Just as America itself was a melting pot, so too was its music. In the eighteenth century, the main contributors were (a) European popular music brought over to us by "singing families," (b) faux-black music called minstrelsy (that incorporated a white man's version of the African musical and

---

[1] Rice, Edward LeRoy. *Monarchs of Minstrelsy, 'Daddy' Rice To Date.* New York: Kenny Publishing Co., 1911, p. 18

cultural heritage of the plantations), (c) the Chautauqua movement, and (d) music created by blacks, both before and after the end of slavery, often done in a religious context.

These four main musical sources interacted with and influenced each other, and evolved throughout the nineteenth century. The absence of modern technology regulated the speed and manner in which these interactions could occur. Waiting eagerly for the new music, much as we do today, were the early twentieth-century Americans.

The European Influence

Four types of music made their way across the Atlantic; they were: (a) classical instrumental music and opera; (b) the vocal music of the formal singing societies (choruses), such as the Haydn and Handel Society of Boston; (c) the Austrian and German singing families that toured the United States beginning in the 1830s;[2] and (d) University Glee Clubs and the campus quartets they spun off. The informal quartets were less rigid and more creative, and it was clearly easier to get four people together for an impromptu session than it was to assemble a chorus.

The Melodeon Theatre, home of the Handel and Haydn Society from 1839 to 1853, It is the building with the pole on top. Illustration courtesy of the Handel and Haydn Society.

---

[2] Averill, Gage. *Four Parts, No Waiting: A Social History of American Barbershop Harmony.* New York: Oxford University Press, 2003, p. 22-23.

Small groups such as the Tyrolese Minstrels, the German Minstrels and the Alpine Minstrels, performed songs in three- and four-part harmony, as well as singing solos. Immensely popular and new to America, these singing troupes from overseas inspired home-grown American versions. By adding variety acts to the singing numbers to form what came to be known as minstrel troupes, producers hit upon the formula that would provide the main source of entertainment during the last half of the nineteenth century.

The Tyrolese Minstrels, composed of five members of the Austrian Rainer family, began touring in America in 1834 and appeared at the Melodeon concert hall on Boston in 1840. They helped to make the carol "Silent Night" popular by singing it in New York in 1839 at the site of Trinity Church, which had burned down: "American audiences were thrilled by the Rainers' precise enunciation and timing and by the impression they created of a harmony that was so well blended the audience could not determine which singer was singing which part. In the 1840s, groups of American singers, such as the Euterpean Quartette, the Hughes Family, Ossian's Bards, the Illsleys, the Boston Minstrels (also called the Ethiopian Serenaders), and the Alleghanians had formed quartets in their likeness, singing sentimental ballads, comic songs, martial airs, and patriotic and topical songs."[3] Black-and-white drawings of these groups can be found on sheet music from this period.

Alleghanians

The most famous of the American troupes was the Hutchinson family of New Hampshire (known early on as the Aeolian Vocalists), who were assembled in 1840 by John Hutchinson and were still going strong when they performed in 1893 at the Chicago World's Fair. There were sixteen (thirteen, by one account) children, most of them musicians. Various combinations of Hutchinsons toured, including some that featured their twelve-year-old sister, Abby, on the high part. Abby had joined the group when brother

---

[3] Averill, p. 23

Jesse decided to concentrate on songwriting and managing the group. In 1845, four of the Hutchinsons – Judson, John, Joshua and Abby – toured Europe as a vocal harmony group. They sang in standard tenor-tenor-baritone-bass form, with the lead usually being the second highest voice.

Although the twentieth century witnessed the insertion of political views into the music, this was still unusual around 1850, yet the Hutchinsons were ardent Abolitionists and their music reflected their beliefs. As the family members drifted apart, Judson's daughter, Kate Dearborn, carried on the tradition by performing with Joshua and John. Although the Hutchinson Family came to prominence during the Civil War, their likenesses appeared on sheet music as early as 1843.[4] Other musical families of the era were the Bakers (also New Hampshire), the Barkers, Blakeleys and Gibsons.

Hutchinson Family

Minstrelsy

The birth of minstrelsy came along at the same time as the popularity of the traveling vocal groups. Central to the idea of minstrelsy was the world of the plantation slave, introduced to the audience by imitating the slaves themselves. The minstrel shows began in the 1840s and usually featured black music made by white performers in blackface (burnt cork used as makeup). The blackface was to let the audience know that these shows were depicting black ways — at least, that is what they thought. Apart from the dancing and comedy, they featured choruses that sang in harmony. While the culture of black slaves had occasionally been depicted in popular entertainment as early as Revolutionary times, the most significant

---

[4] Averill, p. 24

influx of their culture into the white mainstream is traceable to Thomas Dartmouth Rice, when he first performed his "Jim Crow" song and dance in 1832. "Blacking-up" his face, Rice performed a routine that was supposed to portray a disabled slave named Jim Crow, a name that would live on in a different context long after Rice had been forgotten by all but a few enthusiasts. By the 1840s, groups of minstrels consisting of four or five entertainers produced a variety show that included song, instrumental music, dance and comedy. The main subject matter of these shows was the life of the Negro slave. "The plantation songs aroused enduring interest in white ears and minstrelsy developed to provide nationwide entertainment based on the imitation of slave and plantation music. Whites imitated blacks and later blacks imitated whites imitating blacks! Racial stereotypes provided jokes, music and dancing and the nationwide mass entertainment of the time."[5]

"In 1842, a group of four unemployed actors who had experience doing blackface routines in circuses banded together to present a full-length evening. Calling themselves The Virginia Minstrels (to spoof the popular Tyrolese Minstrels), their 'plantation songs' and shuffling dances were a sensation. This first minstrel show spawned a flurry of successful imitators."[6] The group, composed of Daniel Decatur Emmett, Frank Bower, Dick Pelham and Billy Whitlock, made its debut in 1843 at the Bowery Amphitheatre in New York.[7] (Emmett wrote "Dixie's Land," commonly known just as "Dixie," as well as "Turkey In The Straw," "The Blue Tail Fly" and many other famous songs). Groups such as the Virginia Minstrels, the Christy Minstrels (formed 1844), Bryant's Minstrels (1857) and Haverly's Minstrels (1877),[8] formalized the program of the minstrel show, and all incorporated blacking-up of their members. Edwin Christy of the Christy Minstrels wrote such classics as "Farewell Ladies" and "Merrily We Roll Along."

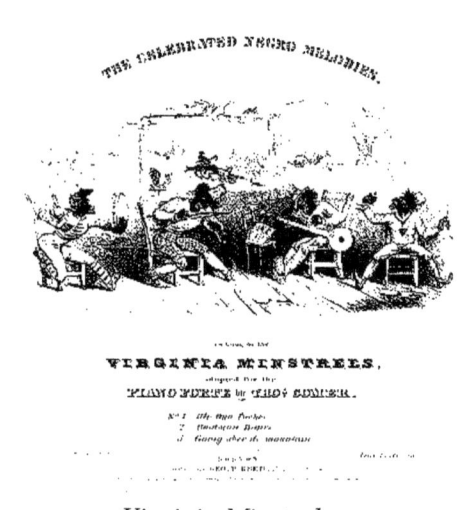

Virginia Minstrels

"The minstrel show had three parts. For the songs and jokes in the first part the performers stood in a semi-circle, Tambo and Bones as the end men with tambourine and

---

[5] http://www.meister.u-net.com/ (accessed January 3, 2007)
[6] Kenrick, John. "History of the Musical Stage 1700-1865: Musical Pioneers." On website: http://www.musicals101.com/ (accessed January 16, 2009)
[7] http://www.musicals101.com/minstrel.htm
[8] Haverly's was described in 1892, in the Columbus Daily Times, as "an all-white troupe employing burnt cork to achieve black faces . . ."

bone clackers[9] respectively; they would register noisy approval of a joke, signaling the audience to laugh (much like the canned laughter on today's sit-coms). The emcee in the centre was the boss, and the jokes were often at his expense, a touch of anti-authoritarianism; and there would also be a singer of sentimental ballads. The second part was comprised of specialty acts and novelties (called the 'olio', a term which survived in vaudeville, probably from the Spanish olla, or 'potpourri'), and the finale was a walk-around, or promenade. (A late invention was the cakewalk, in which members of the audience were invited to invent the most ridiculous strutting march, for which the prize was a cake.)"[10]

Cakewalk depiction on 1899 sheet music.

It was during the second part of the show, or the "olio," that the singers would assert themselves vocally as a group. Some of the early songs sung by groups or by ballad singers were the familiar "Oh Susanna," "Camptown Races," "Turkey In The Straw," "Old Black Joe," "I've Been Workin' On The Railroad," "Jeanie With The Light Brown Hair," "My Old Kentucky Home" and "Carry Me Back To Old Virginny." These shows were performed at both inside and outside venues. Concert halls, churches, bars, brothels and clubs provided adequate acoustics, since there was no electricity to provide amplification. Outside shows were better suited to porches and small parks for the same reason.

The quartet singing in the traveling minstrel shows made a smooth transition to quartet singing in vaudeville, when vaudeville became the rage in the last part of the nineteenth century. The difference between the minstrel shows and vaudeville is that the former were given by a fixed troupe of minstrel players who entertained in a standard format and traveled together from town to town, while the latter consisted of a series of acts, each involving a different set of people, doing what they did best at a fixed location — the vaudeville theater. Some would sing, some would dance, others would be comedians, or acrobats, or jugglers, or animal trainers. Vaudeville was a precursor to the variety show, which achieved popularity in the nascent television industry in the 1950s with shows such as "The Ed Sullivan Show."

---

[9] Bones was a rhythm instrument, originally made from animal bones, but later out of wood, that was held in the hand, similar to castanets.
[10] http://www.musicweb.uk.net/encyclopaedia/ (accessed January 3, 2007)

The Chautauqua Movement

Vocal quartets also performed in the "Chautauqua," or traveling shows that were given in tents and focused on teaching through lectures and dramatic or musical presentations. The history of the Chautauquas (Chautauqua is the name of a town in western New York State) can be traced to a Greek gymnasium, called the Lyceum, where Aristotle founded a school of philosophy.[11] Centuries later, in the early 1800s, the "Lyceum movement" attempted to further education for adults in England, and was then imported to the states as the "American Lyceum," which was founded by Josiah Holbrook in Milbury, Massachusetts in 1826. The word "Lyceum" is used to describe a public hall that is employed for educational lectures or concerts.[12] Before the Civil War, the likes of Henry Ward Beecher, DeWitt Clinton, Oliver Wendell Holmes and Abraham Lincoln lectured on the Lyceum "circuit," which by 1840 had grown to thousands of halls, constrained only by the reach of the rail lines. After the Civil War, Susan B. Anthony, William Cullen Bryant, Ralph Waldo Emerson and Julia Ward Howe were among those traveling and lecturing to eager adults.[13]

While the early Lyceum series were primarily lecture-driven, with religion, politics and the evils of alcohol being the most popular topics, the Chautauqua movement expanded the range of offerings to include entertainment. In 1874, Methodist minister John Heyl Vincent and businessman Lewis Miller established a summer program at a campsite on Chautauqua Lake in New York State. The meetings became popular with families, since they emphasized moral and clean, sometimes religious (but non-denominational) education. As the Chautauquas grew in popularity, they spread throughout the country, usually appearing in rural areas near bigger cities or near easily accessible rail lines. At the height of the movement, in the 1920s, several hundred permanent campsites or structures existed. In addition, beginning in 1904, traveling or "tent Chautauquas" were organized by Keith Vawter, a manager for the proprietary Redpath Lyceum Bureau (basically a booking and tour-arranging organization).[14] "In 1920, there were twenty-one companies operating ninety-three circuits in the United States and Canada. Programs were presented in 8,580 towns to 35,449,750 people."[15] Together with the traveling minstrel troupes, the Chautauquas provided most of the entertainment to rural America during this period.

---

[11] http://en.wikipedia.org/wiki/Lyceum (accessed January 16, 2009)
[12] http://en.wikipedia.org/wiki/Lyceum (accessed January 16, 2009)
[13] http://members.aol.com/AlphaChautauquan/lyceum.html (accessed January 3, 2007)
[14] http://www.lib.uiowa.edu/spec-coll/Bai/redpath.htm (accessed January 12, 2009)
[15] Homer, Charles F., *Strike the Tents, The Story of*. Philadelphia: Dorrance & Co., 1954

Music played an integral part in both the independent stationary organizations and the traveling tent versions of the Chautauquas. Bands, bell-ringers, folk music, singers, actors performing dramatic plays, light opera performances, orchestras and singing groups in all combinations (including spiritual singers) all found their way to the Chautauqua stage.

Chautauqua Tent, 1906

The performers at the Chautauquas were multi-talented. Often the bill included a male quartet that sang their own songs, played instruments on others, and played instruments behind the lead singer on still others. Some of the more popular groups to appear on the circuit were the Criterion Quartette from New York, the Deep River Singers, the Dunbar Male Quartette (who were also bell-ringers), the Schuberts (a mixed-gender quartet) and the Temple Quartette of Boston, which was formed in 1868 and lasted over forty years with changing membership.[16] Well over 150 vocal groups that appeared on the Chautauqua and Lyceum circuits are listed in the Groupography portion of this book.

---

[16] For more information on the content of their acts, see http://sdrcdata.lib.uiowa.edu/I (accessed January 12, 2009)

Black Music Threads

Singing helped black people to endure the trials of their days and years of enslavement and forced labor. Though initially the songs of their homeland, the lyrics that the African immigrant sang became increasingly English-based. With succeeding generations, the Euro-American styles of singing and rhythm patterns seeped into African-based arrangements. The songs and spirituals of the plantations provided an oral history of the lives of their residents that were heard by and influenced white performers and composers, and eventually were incorporated into the repertoires of American minstrel troupes that performed pastiches of black culture. The content of this entertainment would be patently offensive today, but regaled the population of America in the last half of the nineteenth century.

At the same time, black vocal group music, which had its start in black Baptist churches in the 1840s, was evolving. Slave owners did not allow certain forms of entertainment, but singing was acceptable, particularly at churches. Other forms, such as dancing, were alien and threatening, and could be done only in secret. Slaves would meet covertly, away from the plantation, and that was the beginning of what came to be called "camp meetings."

David Ewen, in *All The Years Of American Popular Music*,[17] says, "The slaves brought with them from Africa a gift for expressing their feelings in melody and rhythm." In 1851, Fredericka Bremer, the Swedish writer for whom Bremer County in Iowa is named, said, "I first heard the slaves, about a hundred in number, singing at their work ... they sang in quartettes... in such perfect harmony, and with such exquisite feeling that it was difficult to believe them self-taught."[18]

After the Civil War, minstrel companies were formed with black performers, some of whom also "blacked-up." Early troupes included the Hicks-Sawyer Colored Minstrels, which was owned by blacks,[19] but most black professional minstrel ensembles were owned by whites. This pattern was repeated frequently during the ensuing 100 or so years with all forms of popular music. Another famous black company was called Callender's Consolidated Spectacular Colored Minstrels, while a related group, the Callender-Haverly Colored Minstrels, toured Europe in 1881 with James Bland, a graduate of Howard University (his father attended law school there at the same time), the best known black

---

[17] Ewen, David. *All The Years Of American Popular Music*. Englewood Cliffs, NJ: Prentice-Hall, 1977, p.32.
[18] Gregory, Hugh. *A Century of Pop: A Hundred Years Of Music That Changed The World*. Chicago: A Cappella Books, 1998
[19] http://www.Britannica.com (accessed January 16, 2009)

songwriter of his day. "Oh Dem Golden Slippers" and "Carry Me Back To Old Virginny" are two of Bland's more famous compositions. Female singers who would become famous in their own right in the twentieth century, such as Bessie Smith and Ma Rainey, got their start in the minstrel shows when those groups later began to accept women.[20] [21]

Black colleges and universities were of paramount importance in sowing the seeds of the modern vocal group music that became so prevalent and popular by the middle of the twentieth century. The most important and famous of these groups was the Jubilee Singers, from what is now called Fisk University in Nashville, Tennessee. Fisk was established in an abandoned Union hospital barracks after the Civil War by the American Missionary Association,

James Bland

and was named the Fisk Free Colored School after the Union general, Clinton Bowen Fisk, who became the Assistant Commissioner of the Freedmen's Bureau in Tennessee and Kentucky during the Reconstruction period. General Fisk, who ran unsuccessfully for President under the banner of the Prohibitionist Party in 1888, believed in education for

Fisk Jubilee Singers, 1870s

---

[20] http://www.Britannica.com (accessed January 16, 2009)
[21] Some well-known black vocal groups in the 1850s were the Hyer Sisters and Wallace King and John Luca, the first known mixed-gender black quartet, the Lew Quartet and the first version of the Golden Gate Quartet. A secular group that was among the earliest to gain popularity was the Continental Vocalists that toured extensively, and performed solos as well as quartet arrangements. Other touring black vocal groups were the Continental Four, the Big Four, the American Four and the Hamtown Students, a group from the 1870s.

freed slaves and the missionary association named the school after him to gain his support for its endeavor.[22]

The Fisk Jubilee Singers were founded in 1867 by the school's Treasurer, George White. Although the student body was all black, White was Caucasian as was the entire faculty at that time. Four men and five women made up the initial group of singers. The institution was in dire need of money, so White took the group on tour to raise funds. Among other stops, they appeared at a festival in Boston in 1872 and met with surprising and gratifying success. For most Americans, the Fisk singers provided an introduction to the real music of the black people. Previously, Americans had heard only caricatures of black music, such as those performed by the white minstrels. The Fisk singers had a wide repertory, but soon learned that their most appealing pieces were the authentic black music, not the standard classic works. Many of the songs they sang are still known to us today: Examples are "Swing Low, Sweet Chariot," "Deep River," "Go Down, Moses," and "Sometimes I Feel Like A Motherless Child." Shortly after their tour, *Jubilee Songs As Sung By The Jubilee Singers* was published by Biglow and Main, which helped to solidify the group's place in history. They sang popular songs as well as spirituals and jubilee music: "spirituals" were said to come from the relationship of the music to the Holy Spirit while "jubilees" emanated directly from the person.

Songs of the Jubilee Singers

Jubilee singing became a link between nineteenth century black singing and the gospel music of the next century. Lynn Abbott says: "One of the most influential developments in the history of African-American music was the post-Civil War phenomenon called 'jubilee singing.' This was the vehicle through which the slave spirituals were transformed for future generations and through which the outside world gained its initial respect for African-American music and culture. More particularly, nineteenth-century jubilee singing troupes provided a working model for the explosion of grassroots vocal harmony groups that informed what is now called gospel music."[23] And gospel music in turn had a tremendous influence on secular vocal group music as well.

---

[22] Ward, Andrew. *Dark Midnight When I Rise*. New York: Farrar, Strauss and Giroux, 2000

[23] 'Do Thyself a' no Harm': The Jubilee Singing Phenomenon and the 'Only Original New Orleans University Singers,' in the Journal of the American Music Research Center, Volume 6 (1996)

Other well-known University-based groups of the era were the Hampton College Singers, the Tuskegee Institute Singers from Alabama, and the Tennessee Jubilee Singers. The Tuskegee Institute Singers from Alabama were founded in 1884 by Booker T. Washington. They began as the Tuskegee Quartet and were sent out by Washington to "promote the interest of Tuskegee Institute" – in other words, to raise money for the school. In various forms, the group continued to travel into the 1940s.[24] The Tennessee Jubilee Singers toured the West Indies in 1889 and featured Matilda Sissieretta Joyner Jones, who became known as the "Black Patti" (after the popular Italian opera singer, Adelina Patti) and was one of the earliest female stars of the entertainment world.

Matilda Sissieretta Joyner Jones

As the nineteenth century wound down, minstrelsy began to wane as the main source of entertainment for the masses, mainly due to the expense of sending large groups of men and women on the road or rails for an extended period of time. Minstrelsy was replaced by the variety show and vaudeville, both of which took place at fixed locations such as theaters and clubs. Now, instead of the entertainers going to the people, the people came to the entertainers. Vocal group and quartet singing, which adapted equally well to traveling or fixed-locale performances, continued to flourish. Also, by the 1880s, quartet singing was fully ingrained in the fabric of society. *White's Male Quartette Book* from 1884 set the standard for singers of the day. Music also entered politics as demonstrated by the *Garfield and Arthur Campaign Songs* as sung by the Central Quartette from the Presidential campaign of 1880.

White's Male Quartette   *Central Quartette*

---

[24] http://www.tuskegee.edu/ (accessed January 14, 2009)

Chapter Two

1890 to 1920: The Dawn of Recording

There was no way to record sound until the last quarter of the nineteenth century. Before that, the only way that music could be heard and spread was through live performances. Sheet music was the means by which music was standardized, so that the same piece could be played at different times in different places by different people, and still sound relatively the same.

By the nineteenth century, sheet music was the primary way for people to become familiar with popular music, especially after the upright piano began to appear in more and more homes. Sheet covers were decorated with black-and-white drawings and woodcuts. Likenesses of singing groups were common on sheet covers from about 1840 on. The artwork became more elaborate as the century progressed and photos of single artists and groups started to appear on the covers as advertisements towards the end of the 1890s, which helped sell even more copies.

Even after the first wax cylinders became available, sheet music remained popular because of its cheaper price: The cylinders were 25 cents and flat discs went for as much as a dollar, compared to only ten cents for a piece of sheet music around the turn of the century. The success of the sheet music to "After The Ball"[25] (1892) made many aware of the money to be made in this medium.[26] As cylinder and disc recordings came down in price, sheet music became less popular, but still held on to a significant share of the music market. However, when the radio became more popular in the 1920s, sheet music sales waned further.[27]

The Advent of Recorded Sound

In 1877, Thomas Alva Edison invented the phonograph, a machine that would forever change and empower the field of music by allowing professional performances to be heard by legions of people. This first phonograph, however, was not what most people think of as a "record player." This early machine played foil covered brass cylinders, which were the first medium on which music was recorded and sold, beginning in 1880. The machine consisted of a piece of tin foil wrapped around a cylinder on which electromechanical marks were made by a stylus during recording. When played, a needle "read" the marks made by the stylus and converted the impulses back into sound.[28] "When Edison built his first phonograph in 1877, he published an article proposing ten ways that his invention could be used, including preserving the last words of dying people, recording books for blind people, announcing clock time,

Early Edison Phonograph

---

[25] Although this song gained fame by its appearance in "Showboat," it did not originate in the show. It just appears there and was written in 1891 by Charles K. Harris, not Jerome Kern.
[26] http://www.gracyk.com/ (accessed January 14, 2009)
[27] Major collections of early sheet music can be found at the Library of Congress, National Museum of American History's Archive Center in Washington, D.C., Bagaduce Music Lending Library in Blue Hill, Maine, Brown University, Center For Popular Music at Middle Tennessee State University, University of Colorado, Duke University, Harvard Theatre Collection, University of Illinois at Urbana-Champaign Music Library, Lilly Library at Indiana University, Lester S. Levy Sheet Music Collection at Johns Hopkins University, University of Michigan, Templeton Music Museum at Mississippi State University and the University of North Carolina at Chapel Hill.
[28] Gregory

and teaching spelling. The reproduction of music was not high on Edison's list of priorities. A few years later Edison told his assistant that his invention had no commercial value. Within another few years Edison changed his mind and did start a business to sell phonographs—but only for use as office dictating machines. When other entrepreneurs created jukeboxes that allowed a phonograph to play popular music at the drop of a coin, Edison objected to this debasement, which he thought detracted from the serious office use of his invention. The foil cylinders were soon replaced by wax cylinders. Sizes of cylinders varied from four to eight inches in height and 1 5/16 to five inches in diameter. Only after about 20 years did Edison reluctantly concede that the main use of his phonograph was to record and play music."[29] Arthur Sullivan (of Gilbert & Sullivan) said in a letter to Edison in 1888: "I am ... terrified at the thought that so much hideous and bad music may be put on record forever."[30]

The flat discs that most of us think of as "records" were invented by Emil Berliner, who received a patent on his gramophone in 1887. Berliner also introduced a system for making multiple copies from one "master disc." A year later, his company began to mass-produce discs by grouping together a number of individual machines and made about 200 copies per day using this method.[31] The first master discs were made of rubber and used only one side; lyrics were often printed on the other side. Eventually, they began to use shellac made from crushed Malaysian beetles.[32] These two men, Edison and Berliner, who contributed so much to succeeding generations, had very little formal education: Berliner left school at age 14, and Edison quit even earlier. Berliner's German company would become Deutsche Grammophon, a label that still exists and specializes in classical music.

In 1888, the EMI (Electric & Musical Industries Ltd.) record company was formed by Berliner's interests in England and released recordings on the HMV (His Master's Voice) label. In 1900, EMI unveiled the now famous "Nipper" trademark of the small dog with his ears cocked toward a large speaker.

The story of Nipper is an interesting one. Nipper, a dog owned by Mark Barraud from Bristol, Great Britain, came by his name honestly, nipping at any convenient leg. When his master died, Nipper moved to the home of Barraud's brother, Francis, in London. Francis as

---

[29] Diamond, Jared. *Guns, Germs, And Steel: The Fates of Human Societies.* New York, NY: W. W. Norton & Co., 1997, page 243. Thank you to Marv Goldberg for providing this quote.
[30] http://www.bbc.co.uk/dna/h2g2/A30777438 (accessed October 19, 2010). Again, thank you to Marv Goldberg for providing this quote.
[31] http://nfo.net/usa/timeline.html (accessed January 16, 2009)
[32] In 1876, Berliner had also invented the microphone, which he intended, at least initially, for use with telephones. He sold the microphone patent to The Bell Telephone Company for $50,000. Edison was also working on a microphone and legal battles ensued over the patent, but these were eventually settled.

a painter and having noticed how intrigued the dog was by the sound coming from the cylinder machine, committed this scene to canvas in 1898, several years after Nipper's death. The painting, registered in 1899, as "Dog Looking At And Listening To A Phonograph," was renamed "His Master's Voice," but was turned down for exhibition and magazine reproduction because "no one would know what the dog was doing."[33]

Nipper Trademark

Having been advised to change the color of the horn on the player in the painting from black to gold, Barraud tried to borrow a horn from the Gramophone Company at 31 Maiden Lane in London so as to ensure the authenticity of his work. The Gramophone Company offered to buy the painting, but asked Barraud if he could re-do the scene to make the machine look like one of theirs. Barraud agreed and was paid £50 for the painting and another £50 for the copyright. Barraud would create 24 copies of the painting under commission from The Gramophone Company.

In 1893, Berliner formed a record company in the U.S., called the United States Gramophone Company. Discs were readily available to the public by the next year. This company would eventually become the Victor Talking Machine Company and then later, RCA Victor.[34]

---

[33] All from Erik Ostergaard's "The History of Nipper and His Master's Voice." See, http://www.erikoest.dk/nipper.htm. (accessed January 16, 2009)

[34] In 1889, a man named Louis Glass installed a coin slot on an Edison cylinder at the Palais Royale In San Francisco to create the first jukebox. The price was a nickel a song.

The recording process in these early years was primitive. Tim Gracyk, a leading authority on early recordings, provides invaluable information about the process and the use of the permanent master record that began in 1902:

> This made recording less lucrative for artists who in the 1890s had been paid to sing during any one session the same handful of songs over and over. Masters were used in the 1890s but they wore out after a few dozen duplicates were made. The gold-moulded cylinder process finally adopted in 1902 for commercially issued cylinders was revolutionary, and disc companies developed ways of creating identical negative stampers--a copper master would be made from the original wax master (a process that destroyed the fragile wax master), a mother shell would be made from the copper master, and several stamper shells would be made from the mother. The permanent master meant that once a song was successfully recorded, an artist rarely needed to cover it again for a company. Sessions for some artists became less frequent.[35]

The use of these permanent masters led to a series of unintended consequences. In previous years, recording artists were tied to the studio, having to sing the same songs over and over. Permanent masters meant less work for the older cadre of artists, but freed up time for the next generation of recording artists who, since they now had time for public appearances, were able to tour and become "stars."

These recordings were made in studios by singing into a horn that was wired to the recording device. Gracyk writes:

> The environment was 'strange' even in that singers heard their own voices differently than in a large auditorium. This was due to the size and acoustics of a studio but also to the voice being projected into a horn. Cupping a hand to the back of an ear helped a singer only a little in hearing his or her own voice. . . . Studios were bare and often stifling in these days before air conditioning. There was no audience to inspire brilliant performances unless one counts the studio pianist providing accompaniment. Soon after the turn of the twentieth century, a handful of house musicians provided accompaniment, and most were also near the horn, uncomfortably close to the featured artist (incidentally, accompanying musicians were seated in chairs of differing heights, some instruments being elevated so they would be recorded properly). . . . To perform take after take under these conditions required patience. Multiple takes were often needed since there was no way to edit blemishes from a performance, no way to splice together different takes. A mistake--or a cough

---

[35] Gracyk, Tim. *Popular American Recording Pioneers: 1895-1925*. Binghamton, NY: The Haworth Press, Inc., 2000, pages 15-16

or sneeze from an accompanying musician within range of the recording horn--usually meant beginning again.[36]

Early Recording Groups

Much of what we know about the early white vocal groups is due to the efforts of Ulysses "Jim" Walsh from Richmond, Virginia. From January 1942 to May 1985, Walsh wrote a monthly column for *Hobbies Magazine* on vintage recordings and recording artists. He had a massive collection of approximately 40,000 discs, 500 cylinders and 23 early phonographs that he left to the Library of Congress. All of us with any interest in this early music are deeply indebted to him. When we refer to chart positions, the information is taken from a series of books authored by Joel Whitburn. Although there were no official "charts" back then, Whitburn developed a formula to estimate the relative popularity of songs.[37] His method was not perfect but is the best we have. According to Whitburn's data, the first vocal group to have a Number One song was the Manhansett Quartette in 1892, with "The Picture Turned Toward The Wall." "Sally In The Alley" also charted later in the same year. Prior to this, artists singing in groups would simply be listed on the record label as "Quartette" or "Quintette," leaving subsequent generations in the dark about their provenance. The Manhansett Quartette was the first group to have its name featured on a

Bison City Quartette

---

[36] Gracyk
[37] *Joel Whitburn's Pop Memories, 1890-1954*. Menomonee Falls, Wisconsin: Record Research, Inc., 1986. For the 1890 to 1900 period, Whitburn cites a record publication called *The Phonoscope* that contained monthly lists of the most popular recordings. Whitburn used another publication, *The Phonogram*, and catalogs of leading record labels and put that together with sheet music sales data from ASCAP and the books of David Ewen, a well-known musicologist, to compile his charts. For the 1900 to 1920s, Whitburn cites the work of Jim Walsh in *Hobbies Magazine*. Also used was *Talking Machine World* which was provided with lists from the major record companies. By this time, *Billboard* and *Variety* also contained some information and ASCAP continued to help with its sheet music sales figures.

record label.[38] Another early group to record was the Bison City Quartet which appeared on cylinders on the New Jersey label in 1892.

It would be six years before a group reached Number One again. The Edison Male Quartette did it in 1898 on the Edison label with "My Old Kentucky Home." Next were the Haydn (later called Hayden) Quartette with "Because" and the Big Four Quartet with "Good-Bye, Dolly Gray," both in 1900, and Byron G. Harlan, Joe Belmont, Frank Stanley and the Floradora Girls with "Tell Me Pretty Maiden" in 1901. Of the twelve Number One songs of 1904, five were by vocal groups and six of the others were by individuals who were members of groups. The groups of the late nineteenth and early twentieth century were extremely popular, bringing together the best singers of the day.

Information about many of these early groups is scant. Sometimes the name of a group appears on a recording, but no photographs can be found. In fact, it can be much easier to hear a song by a particular group than to find a photo or get information about its members.[39] Other times a photo of the group appears on a piece of sheet music, but nothing else is known about them. The Empire City Quartette, whose picture appears on at least six pieces of sheet music from 1902 to 1909, belongs to this category.

Empire City Quartet, 1909

The first black group to record (with six titles to their credit) was the Unique Quartette in 1893. They sang a cappella and featured a pleasing lead and a strong bass. In "Mamma's Black Baby Boy Good" (1893), you can hear the voice separation that characterized their harmony. Tim Gracyk quotes a catalog from that era: "This quartette is composed of the best negro talent obtainable and their records are loud and distinct. To those who are fond of negro melodies, we can commend these productions of the genuine article."[40] Tim Brooks said, "It was a professional quartet with extensive stage experience and an interesting and distinctive repertoire."[41] In an unusual twist, at least for those days, Edison

---

[38] *Ibid*
[39] One good place to find recordings of these early white vocal groups is at http://www.gemm.com/catalog/gmv8264/agwco/, the website for American Gramophone & Wireless Co. (accessed January 14, 2009)
[40] http://www.gracyk.com/ (accessed January 14, 2009)
[41] Brooks, p. 75

had its white group, the Edison Male Quartette, cover⁴² six of the titles recorded by the Unique Quartette.⁴³

Another black group of that era was the Standard Quartette. They sang a cappella, but with less voice separation and some talking behind the lead, as heard in "Keep Movin" from 1894. The earliest example we found of a black group's photo on a piece of sheet music is W. H. Windom and his Quartette for the song "You'se Just A Little N****r, Still You'se Mine, All Mine," from 1898. The group was formed by William "Billy" Windom who had a minstrel troupe known as "The Forty Whites And Thirty Blacks."

One of the major black groups of the turn of the century was the Dinwiddie Colored Quartet which recorded for Victor in 1902. They were the first black group to record on flat disks; the Unique and Standard Quartettes recorded on cylinders. Formed at the John A. Dix Industrial School in Dinwiddie, Virginia, the word "colored" was added to their name so that audiences would know the race of the group members before purchasing a record. As others did before them, they sang in public to raise money for their school.

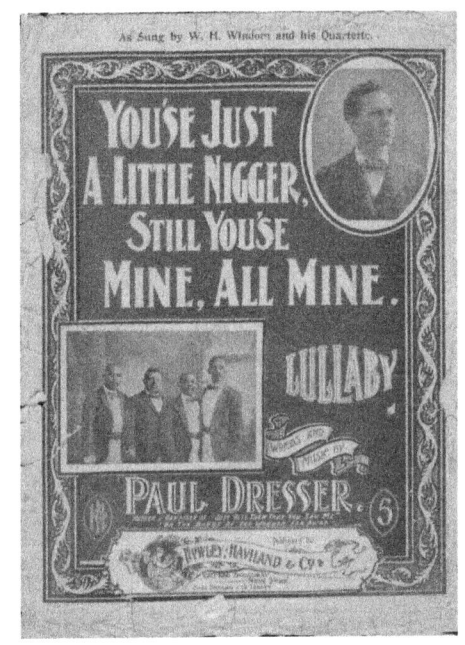

W.H. Windom and his Quartette, 1898

Dinwiddie Colored Quartet recording, 1902

Sterling Rex (first tenor), Clarence Meredith (second tenor), Harry B. Cruder (baritone) and James Mantell Thomas (bass) comprised the group. They sang a cappella, with a good lead, and often used "call and response" as part of their style. Call and response is when two different phrases are used, one after the other, to establish a kind of musical conversation. The leader sings

---
⁴² A "cover" is a new version of a previously recorded song, often where a better-known group seeks to capitalize on the creativity of a lesser-known group.
⁴³ For the early black groups, Document Records has the largest selection of their recordings. Their website is http://www.document-records.com/ (accessed January 14, 2009)

(calls) a line and there is a response, either from another singer or singers or, in some cases, by an instrument. The technique was an integral part of African music and was brought to this country by slaves. Used in churches and in the fields, it eventually found its way into American popular music. For example, in the Dinwiddie group's "Down On The Old Camp Ground" from 1902, the lead sings, "The little white stone came a rolling down," and the group follows with "way down the ole camp ground." This call and response technique is used in the verses with the choruses sung in full harmony. This form, with the lead's line being repeated, was popular in the churches because congregations often did not have the funds to buy hymnals. The preacher would sing a line and the congregation would repeat it.[44] The six sides Dinwiddie recorded in 1902 were the first jubilee records made by Victor[45].

With the turn of the century, popular music became somewhat less sentimental, at least by the standards of the day, and there were fewer waltzes, which had been a staple of the previous decade. The composers became more sophisticated and were able to provide the vocal groups of the era with an almost limitless amount of material. Lightness found its way into music with songs such as "Bill Bailey, Won't You Please Come Home?," "Oh, Didn't He Ramble?" and "In The Good Old Summertime." Tim Gracyk says that popular American music from 1895 to 1905 consisted of "Broadway show tunes, ragtime (and related 'coon songs'), marches [and] vocal numbers on sheet music ranging from sentimental ballads to comic songs . . . ."[46] Gracyk goes on to say that "Male quartet arrangements were popular, with tunes often sung by a vocal ensemble consisting of a first tenor (the highest pitch), second tenor (usually the leading voice) baritone, and bass."[47]

The Haydn Quartet reigned supreme among the male vocal groups of the 1900-1910 period. The group's founding members (there is some conflict among sources) probably were John

Haydn Quartet

---

[44] Brooks, p. 15
[45] Brooks, p. 156
[46] A "coon" song was a type of music that was popular in the late 18th and early 19th centuries that showed blacks in a stereotyped and racist manner.
[47] http://www.gracyk.com/ (accessed January 14, 2009)

Bieling, tenor, Jere Mahoney (replaced by Harry Macdonough and then Fred Rycroft), tenor, S. H. Dudley, baritone, and William F. Hooley, bass. When the Haydn Quartet sang for Edison, they were called the Edison Male Quartet. Famous tenor Billy Murray sang lead on some of their bigger hits, but Reinald Werrenrath replaced Dudley occasionally, especially in the later years of the group. After 1910, they changed the spelling of their name from "Haydn" to "Hayden." From 1898 to 1914, they had 62 hits that reached the charts, many of which are still well known today. These included, "Because" (in 1900 on Gram-o-Phone), "In The Good Old Summertime" (in 1903 on Victor), "Sweet Adeline" (in 1904 on Victor), "Dearie" (with Corrine Morgan in 1905 on Victor), "Take Me Out To The Ballgame" (in 1908 on Victor) and "By The Light Of The Silv'ry Moon" (in 1910 on Victor).

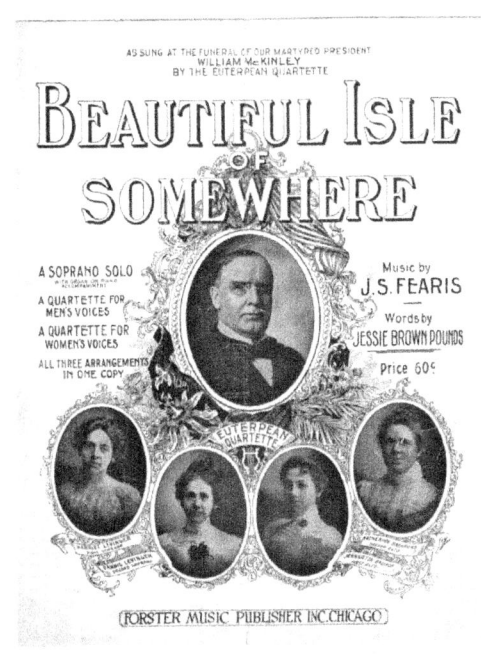

Recordings by females in groups (aside from duos) were scarce before 1910, but the first female group to be pictured on sheet music appears to have been the Euterpean Quartette in 1901 with "Beautiful Isle Of Somewhere." This group had the distinction of singing at the funeral of slain U.S. President,

Euterpean Quartette, 1901

William McKinley. (In September 1901, McKinley was assassinated at the Temple of Music in Buffalo, N.Y., which was built for the Pan-American Exposition of that year.)

Two mixed-gender groups, both octets, appeared in the first few years of the new century. The Beaux And Belles Octet was featured on a sheet of "My Magnolia Maid" in 1901, and the Williams Colored Singers, a black group founded by Charles Williams in 1904 in Chicago, had its photo on both a booklet and a postal

Williams Colored Singers

card. The Williams Colored Singers are said to be the first group to sell out the Philadelphia Academy of Music (in 1916).[48]

One of the more unusual groups for its day was the Old South Quartette, which had the uncommon configuration of a white lead named Polk Miller, a druggist prior to and an artilleryman for the Confederacy during the Civil War, and four black back-up men. Their "Watermelon Party" (1910) featured a banjo as backup instrumentation and an active lead. Tim Gracyk's website contains an article by Jas Obrecht that originally appeared in the *Victrola and 78 Journal* that says:

> Miller was daring enough to go on tour with four African Americans, the Old South Quartette, beginning around 1900 playing to both white and black audiences. In a *Richmond Journal* article dated January 3, 1912, Miller explained that the four, whom he referred to as his 'boys' or 'employees,' had been 'singing on the street corners and in the barrooms of this city at night to motley crowds of hoodlums and barroom loafers and handing around the hat . . . . I could get a dozen quartettes from the good singing material among the Negroes in the tobacco factories here.'[49]

Old South Quartette *Polk Miller*

Approximately twenty different men sang back-up with the group, but only two — James L. Stamper and Randall Graves — have been identified.

---

[48] Southern, Eileen. *Biographical Dictionary of Afro-American and African Musicians*. Westport: The Greenwood Encyclopedia of Black Music, Greenwood Press, 1982

[49] http://www.gracyk.com/ (accessed January 14, 2009)

Confluential Themes

The years around the turn of the century provided a hotbed of new musical styles that developed in parallel, including ragtime, coon songs, jazz and barbershop.

Ragtime music emerged at about the same time that the early white and black groups began to record. In 1895, Ben Harney came along with "You've Been A Good Old Wagon," which is said to have been the first ragtime song. This style extended well into the twentieth century. In *American Popular Music: A Reference Guide*[50] Mark Booth says: "It came from St. Louis and other cities and towns along the Mississippi, created by black piano players drawing on the rhythms of Afro-American folk tradition and accommodating those traditions to the compositional structures of western music."

Ragtime has no special significance to vocal group music, but it played a major part in the development of American popular music. Syncopation – a disturbance or interruption of the regular rhythm of a song – is the hallmark of ragtime music. Having started as folk music, it soon became a part of more traditional music. Ragtime, of course, is best known today from the songs of Scott Joplin brought to mainstream America by the song, "The Entertainer" in the popular 1973 movie *The Sting*, that featured Paul Newman and Robert Redford.

Coon songs became intertwined with ragtime, but are now known only to those who study the history of popular music, due in no small part to the pejorative nature of the term "coon" itself. During the age of minstrelsy, there were cakewalk contests and "coon shouting" matches. Coon songs came directly out of the tradition of minstrel shows, some of which featured a character called Zip Coon. There was actually a very popular song, known as "Zip Coon," that we

Example of sheet music for a Coon song

---

[50] Booth, Mark W. *American Popular Music: A Reference Guide*. Westport, Connecticut: Greenwood Press, 1983.

know today as "Turkey In The Straw." These songs were based on stereotypes of black culture and language. Ironically, many of the "coon" songs were written by black composers, including what might be the best known one, "All Coons Look Alike To Me," with lyrics by Ernest Hogan.

At roughly the same time, the uniquely American form of music that we call jazz (originally "jass") was evolving, incorporating the influence of African folk music, as well as songs sung by slaves on the plantations, spirituals, ragtime, blues and other sources. The city of New Orleans played a central role in its development, spawning musicians such as King Oliver, Louis Armstrong and Jelly Roll Morton. Jazz took hold around the turn of the twentieth century. Its influence on vocal groups of that era can be found in the freer style of the songs the groups sang, not in the performances themselves; at least, not until the Revelers came along. (More about the Revelers in the next chapter.)

Perhaps the greatest influence on the early vocal groups was barbershop. According to an article by Dr. Jim Henry on the Barbershop Harmony Society (formerly the Society for the Preservation and Encouragement of Barber Shop Quartet Singing in America, or SPEBSQSA) website, the earliest known reference to barbershop was in an article by a black commentator named Tom The Tattler in 1900. He associated it with black music, claiming that the barbershop singers were "stunting the growth of `legitimate,' musically literate black quartets in vaudeville." Dr. Henry goes on to state that the musical characteristics of (1) call and response, (2) rhythmic character and (3) harmony are essential to barbershop music and were also found almost exclusively in black music at that time.[51] The use of the adjectival term "barbershop," as applied to quartet singing as we know it today, did not become popular until the 1920s, but, as Jay Warner says, "By the 1890s the musical structure of barbershop harmony was set. The

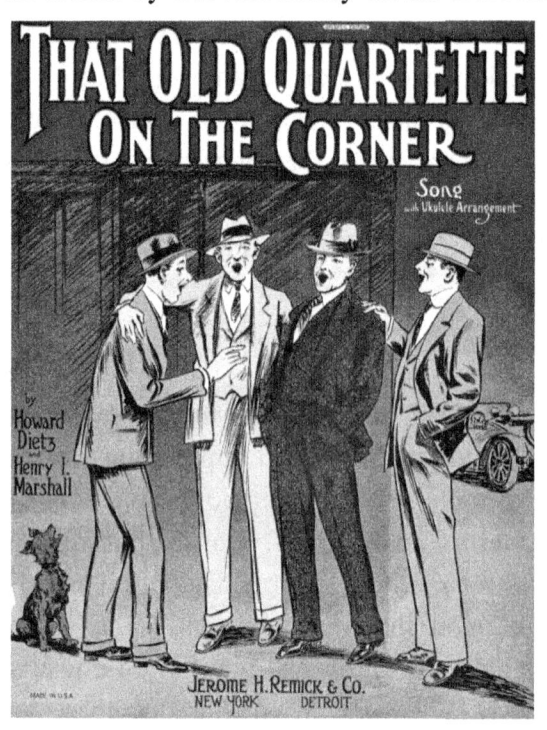

Barbershop singing on sheet music

---

[51] http://www.barbershop.org/ (accessed January 3, 2007)

lead, a second tenor, would sing the melody line, the first tenor sang above the lead and the baritone sang below; the bass would sing the root of the chord."[52]

Where did the term "barbershop" come from? Mark Axelrod, editor of "Blue Chip Chatter," says that "Barbershops, first in England, then here, were places of extemporaneous, amateur music making since Elizabethan times," and that, "A song written in 1910 and entitled '(Mister Jefferson Lord) Play That Barbershop Chord' iced the cake." Barbershop could first be heard in minstrel shows and later in vaudeville. Axelrod asserted that radio, more than any other factor "led to the rapid demise of vaudeville shows, barbershop's most important venue during the first third of the twentieth century."[53]

The term "barbershop" itself is linked to a revisionist view of the era. Gracyk says: "The phrase 'barbershop quartet' was not used in music trade journals or on sheet music a century [writing of the 1895 to 1905 period] ago. That term caught on in the 1920s and became widely used in the 1940s and later. In other words, during the period with which we now associate 'barbershop quartet' singing - - the 1890s through the World War I years or so - - no singers used that term and none wore barbershop uniforms."[54] Barbershop singing enjoyed a renaissance during the 1940s and has remained popular through the efforts of groups such as the Barbershop Harmony Society.

One of the most popular and well known songs of all-time has a distinct link to barbershop quartet singing. "You're The Flower Of My Heart, Sweet Adeline" (or just "Sweet Adeline") has been harmonized more times than any other song in history. The music was written in 1896 by Harry Armstrong but not published until 1903. According to author Sigmund Spaeth,[55] Armstrong was an 18-year-old working in a jewelry store and doing some amateur boxing, who also sang barbershop with a street corner group. He left Boston for New York where words were added to his composition by a postal clerk, Richard Gerard Husch. Initially, it was entitled "Sweet Rosalie," but the meter of the name "Rosalie" did not work well.

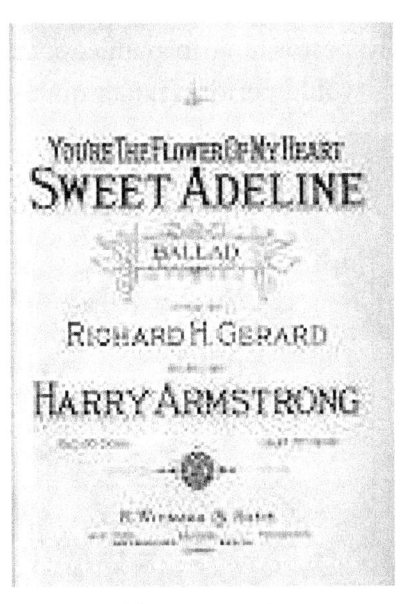

Sheet music for "Sweet Adeline"

---

[52] Warner, Jay. *The DaCapo Book of American Singing Groups, A History 1940 – 1990*. Cambridge: Da Capo Press, 2000
[53] http://www.harmonize.com/PROBE/aids/History/Quizzes/quiz1.html (accessed January 15, 2009)
[54] http://www.gracyk.com/century.shtml (accessed January 14, 2009)
[55] Spaeth, Sigmund. *A History Of Popular Music In America*. New York: Random House, 1948

The inspiration for the name "Adeline" came from Adelina Patti, a world-famous singer mentioned in the prior chapter. The last syllable of the name was changed to provide a note that sounded better being held while harmonizing went on behind it. "Sweet Adeline" became popular when sung by the Quaker City Four, and was also the theme song of John J. ("Honey") Fitzgerald, who was running the first of his two successful mayoral campaigns in Boston. (Fitzgerald's daughter, Rose, would gain fame as the matriarch of the Kennedy clan.) The song has become an unofficial theme song for barbershoppers. Sweet Adelines International is the name for the world-wide society of female barbershop singers.

The 1910s

The decade from 1910 to 1920 saw further changes in musical styles. The trend away from waltzes continued. Publishers wanted fox-trots, which had gained supremacy over other dance steps and many songs were either written in that form initially or would have fox-trot orchestration added to them later. The decade also saw a small number of dominant vocal groups that charted consistently.

Since the most prolific singers were studio-bound, rarely performing in public, some sleight-of-hand became possible — the same group of singers would perform under quite a few different names depending on the label for which they recorded.

The American Quartet, with featured soloist Billy Murray, was extremely popular during this time: They had 60 chart hits during this decade! It was a different group from the earlier one of the same name, with only the bass, William F. Hooley (who also sang with the Haydn Quartet) remaining. The other members were tenor, John Bieling and baritone, Steve Porter (replaced by John Young in 1914). Donald Chalmers took Hooley's place in 1918. When recording on the Edison label, they were called the Premier Quartet or the Premier-American Quartet. On Aeolian-Vocalion they called themselves the Murray Quartet. Some of their more famous numbers, all on the Victor label, were, "Casey Jones" (1910), "Come Josephine, In My Flying Machine" (1911), "Oh, You Beautiful Doll" (1911), "Moonlight Bay" (1912), "It's A Long Way To Tipperary" (1914), "Chinatown, My Chinatown" (1915), "Oh

Billy Murray

Johnny, Oh Johnny, Oh" (1917) and "Over There" (1917). They had six more Top 20 hits in the 1920s, with the last one in 1924. With counter-tenor[56] Will Oakland, they were billed as the Heidelberg Quintet and had a string of hits from 1911 through 1915. The American Quartet disbanded in 1925.

The Lyric Quartet was a mixed-gender group, featuring two men and two women, that had 111 chart songs from 1911-1917. The Lyric Quartet's membership changed several times but included Harry Macdonough, Frank Stanley, Corrine Morgan, Elise Stevenson and Reinald Werrenrath. Also hitting the charts at this time was the Orpheus Quartet with Harry Macdonough as its lead. The most popular all-female group of the time was the That Girl Quartet, featuring Harriet Keys, Allie Thomas, Precis Thompson and Helen Summers. They put five songs into the Top 10 from 1911 to 1913.

Record labels insisted that vocal groups record at the company's will. If a group left a label, a new quartet would be formed to take its place. That was how the Knickerbocker Quartet came into existence. When the members of the Edison Male Quartet left Edison to sign with Victor as the Haydn Quartet, the Knickerbocker Quartet took their place on Edison from 1909-1915. The same group hit it big on Columbia in 1917 with "Pack Up Your Troubles in Your Old Kit Bag (And Smile, Smile, Smile)."

Because of the inbred nature of the recording industry at the time, chart positions can be a little misleading. There was very little competition from unheard-of groups. Each record label would have its proprietary groups and those were few in number. The competition for chart spots came from the same artists (singing as soloists), who belonged to the groups. Because the groups were so few in number, they were extremely popular and well-known in their time.

Rivaling both the American and Haydn Quartets in stature was the Peerless Quartet. Originally called the Columbia Male Quartet, they achieved popular success from 1904 through 1928, hitting the charts 108 times in that span under various names. The Peerless Quartet's original members were tenors Henry Burr and Albert Campbell, Steve Porter (baritone who also sang with the American Quartet) and bass, Tom Daniels. Frank Stanley replaced Daniels in 1906. Stanley, from West Orange, New Jersey, managed the group until his untimely death from pneumonia in 1910 at the age of 41. Stanley was also involved with two precursor groups to the Peerless Quartet: the Columbia Male Quartet and the Invincible Quartet.

Later members of the Peerless also included Arthur Collins (baritone), John Meyer (bass) and Frank Croxton (baritone). They were best known for "You're The Flower Of My

---

[56] A range above tenor, often sung in falsetto

Peerless Quartet

Heart, Sweet Adeline" (1904, on Columbia as the Columbia Male Quartet), "Let Me Call You Sweetheart" (1911, on Columbia), "I Didn't Raise My Boy To Be A Soldier" (1915, on Columbia) and "The Lights Of My Home Town" (1916, for Victor). They were also called, at various times, the Invincible Four, Peerless Minstrels, U.S. Minstrels, Victor Minstrel Co. and the Victor Vaudeville Co. In England, the name Prince's Male Quartet was used on some of their Columbia recordings. Without Croxton, they also recorded as the Sterling Trio for the Victor label. Jim Walsh, writing in the December 1969 issue of *Hobbies Magazine*, says that the Peerless Quartet "was the most popular, successful and long-lived of all singing organizations that made records."

Many of the most popular groups of the early twentieth century were formed from the ranks of the successful popular singers of the days. In essence, they were "super groups." However, with some of the later groups, movement would be in the opposite direction: Stars emerged from the groups, rather than flowing into them. Bing Crosby had his first solo hit in 1931 with "Just A Gigolo," several years after charting as a group member of the Rhythm Boys with Paul Whiteman & His Orchestra. Connee Boswell's first solo hit came after the Boswell Sisters starting having hits. Jo Stafford's first solo hit came in 1944 with "Old Acquaintance," two years after she had joined the Pied Pipers. In the 1950s, Sam Cooke came out of the Soul Stirrers, Clyde McPhatter from the Dominoes and Drifters, and Jackie Wilson began with the Dominoes. Frankie Lymon had hit singles after he left the Teenagers, as did Dion after he left the Belmonts.

As an example of the reverse form of migration (where a singer began as a soloist and then later joined a group), Billy Murray had great success with "Tessie (You Are The Only,

Only)" and "Up On A Cocoanut Tree" as a single artist in 1903 before appearing on "You're The Flower Of My Heart, Sweet Adeline" in late 1904 with the Peerless Quartet. Albert Campbell, also a member of the Peerless Quartet, had nine solo hits, including "My Wild Irish Rose" (1899), before joining the group. The baritone from the quartet, Steve Porter, also had many earlier solo hits, such as "On The Banks Of The Wabash" (1898). Only the bass, Tom Daniels, did not have a hit record as a solo artist.

Murray was the most prolific of them all. In addition to 66 chart hits as part of the American Quartet, he hit the charts 169 more times either alone or with various partners. He soloed with "Meet Me In St. Louis, Louis" (1904, on Edison), "Give My Regards To Broadway" (1905, on Columbia), "Take Me Out To The Ballgame" (1908, on Victor with the Haydn Quartet) and "That Old Gang Of Mine" (1923, on Victor in a duo with Ed Smalle of the Revelers). The baritone of the American Quartet, Steve Porter, also charted 13 times on his own.

Not to be outdone, Henry Burr of the Peerless Quartet reached the charts 116 times, mostly as a soloist, but also as a duo with Albert Campbell (48 times). Campbell charted 16 times on his own, while Stanley charted 44 times alone and a dozen times as a duo with Burr. Arthur Collins charted 47 times alone and another 89 times with Byron Harlan as a comedy singing team. Frank Croxton had only three hits, one of them with Burr; and John Meyer had two hits as a single artist.

Aside from his work with the Haydn Quartet, Harry Macdonough had 99 chart hits on his own or with others, the biggest of which was "Down By The Old Mill Stream" (1911, on Victor). John Bieling, the second tenor of the Haydn (and later of the American Quartet), reached the charts eight times, S. H. Dudley 13 times and William F. Hooley once, but Hooley scored with a number one hit tune, "Gypsy Love Song" in 1899 on Edison.

Other popular white quartets were the Columbia Stellar Quartet and the Shannon Four. The Columbia group had 11 hits from 1912 to 1922. They reached number one on the charts with "The Battle Hymn Of The Republic" in 1918 on, of course, Columbia. The Shannon Four reached the charts 14 times between 1910-1920, but their real importance lies in the fact that in 1926 they evolved into the Revelers, one of the most important vocal

Shannon Four

groups of the next era. The original members were Charles Hart (tenor), Harvey Witherspoon (tenor), Elliott Shaw (baritone) and Wilfred Glenn (bass).

Most people who listen these pioneer groups that recorded between 1890 and 1920 have trouble distinguishing among them — they all sound pretty much alike. This holds true even for those of us who are accustomed to listening to music that was recorded before 1950. People who can easily distinguish among the sounds of the Ink Spots, Mills Brothers and Charioteers have great difficulty distinguishing the American, Haydn and Peerless Quartets from each other. The poor quality of many of the recordings makes the task even harder. Of course, we also know that the parents of teenagers in the 1950s said much the same thing about the groups of that era. A teenager in the 1950s could easily tell the difference between the Moonglows and the Flamingos, but to their parents, it was all "noise" that sounded the same. It is perhaps inevitable that we struggle to appreciate the music that came before us and even after us. We would guess that many baby boomers cannot tell the difference among any of the enormously popular groups from the previous generation.

Many of the early group records were either sung a cappella (such as the Manhansett Quartette) or used simple instrumental backing of just a piano or guitar. For most, the reason was simple: Bands cost money and the groups had none. The harmonies were good, but they got better as they went along. In some groups, such as the Haydn Quartet, the bass was a bit stronger and more active. Most, at least when compared to groups from only 20 years later, were quite stiff and formal in their presentation and not at all rhythmic.

Some groups, such as the Lyric Quartet, used instrumental accompaniment. Since they were a mixed-gender group, they used their soprano to take the part normally sung by a first tenor in an all-male group. The male and female leads alternated in singing parts of the chorus and there is a distinctly more rhythmic feel than in songs from the prior decade. Groups such as the Peerless Quartet used a strong lead that clearly stood out from the other three members, but they still sounded stiff and lacked the rhythmic quality that would begin to emerge in the 1920s.

The black groups that recorded in the 1910-1920 period tended to come out of the churches, so most of their output was spiritual. In 1912, the Apollo Male Quartette recorded "Swing Low Sweet Chariot," sung a cappella. The churches also produced chorus-type groups such as the Afro American Folk Song Singers, a mixed-gender group accompanied by piano, that recorded in 1914. Some of their leads were strong, as in "The Rain Song" (1914), where the lead sings alone and is followed by the chorus, and some leads were not, as in "Swing Along" (1914), a lively song that included softer female voices.

Another version of "The Rain Song" was recorded by the Right Quintette using "call and response" dialog between the lead and the rest of the group. This group also featured beautiful harmonies, as on "Exhortation" from 1915.

The Excelsior Quartette, recording slightly later, was one of the first black groups to direct its efforts to the black audience.[57] Of great significance was their "Coney Island Babe" in 1922, one of the first recordings where a group used their voices to imitate instruments that provided the background accompaniment for the lead singer.

Other innovations came from groups formed by Jim Europe and Noble Sissle. Europe's Singing Serenaders were a male, black chorus that recorded with his all-black orchestra in 1919. Europe featured a group, the Four Harmony Kings, with his orchestra. Their version of "Roll Jordan Roll" is a classic vocal group presentation. Europe was born into a musical family in Alabama in 1881. He was the first black to record as the leader of a band, and died while still a young man in 1919, after being stabbed in a fight with his percussionist.

Tim Brooks says of the Four Harmony Kings, "Arguably, they were the most prominent black quartet of their era, possibly the most popular prior to the debut of the Mills Brothers."[58] A black vaudeville quartet started by Will Hann in 1916, they also recorded on Pathé as "Lt. Jim Europe's Four Harmony Kings," and they appeared on Broadway in 1921 in "Shuffle Along." Their members were Ivan Harold Browning (tenor), William H. Berry (second tenor), Charles E. Drayton (baritone) (replaced by George Jones) and Hann (bass).[59] "In Bamville" and "Chocolate Dandies" were other shows in which they appeared in 1924. Hann left in 1925 to form the Emperors Of Song. The group toured Australia and England and lasted until the early 1930s.

Four Harmony Kings

Noble Sissle

---

[57] Romanowski, Ken. Liner notes for the CD, "The Earliest Negro Vocal Groups Vol. 2 (1893-1922)," Document Records - DOCD-5288
[58] Brooks, p. 18
[59] Other labels on which they appeared were Edison, Bell, Winner, Dominion and Black Swan, Emerson, Paramount and Vocalion.

In "Go Down Moses" (1919), Noble Sissle's Southland Singers offered one of the earliest uses of the high background tenor, a technique taken from African singing.[60] This foreshadowed the style of later background tenors in groups such as the Charioteers, Orioles and many 1950s groups. The Southland Singers were also one of the first groups to feature a strong bass. These innovations by the black vocal groups and musicians of this era should not surprise us. As Donald Clarke says in *The Rise And Fall Of Popular Music*: "The history of modern popular music may be seen as the repeated rescuing of a moribund scene by the music of African-Americans."[61] Tim Brooks discovered a great quote that summed up the unquestionably naïve feelings of at least one white writer of the era: "Pick up four colored boys or young men anywhere and the chances are ninety out of a hundred that you have a quartet. Let one of them sing the melody and the others will naturally find the parts. Indeed it may be said that all male Negro youth of the United States is divided into quartets."[62]

Novelty groups also reached the charts toward the latter part of the teens decade. Comedy groups, such as the Avon Comedy Four with Irving Kaufman, Harry Goodwin and the well-known comedy team of Joe Smith and Charles Dale (as "Smith and Dale"), became quite popular through the medium of vaudeville. The Avon group had several hits in the latter part of the decade. The Six Brown Brothers, consisting of five actual brothers and Harvey Finkelstein, were also popular in this era. They charted twice, first with "That Moaning Saxophone Rag," (1915), and then with "Darktown Strutters' Ball" (1917), both on Victor. While four versions of "Darktown Strutters' Ball" reached the charts in this decade, the Six Brown Brothers had the only vocal group hit. One of the earliest ethnic groups to achieve success was the mixed-gender Hawaiian Trio, which had a top 10 song in 1920 with "Alabama Moon" on Victor.

Avon Comedy Four, 1916

---

[60] Clarke, Donald. *The Rise And Fall Of Popular Music*. London: Penguin Books, 1995, p.56
[61] Brooks, p. 452-3
[62] Brooks, p. 463

Brox Sisters

The first of the sister groups to reach the charts was the Brox Sisters, who made their mark in the early 1920s.[63] Born in the United States, they grew up in Edmonton, Alberta, Canada. The family name Brock became Brox at the suggestion of a producer. The Brox featured Josephine (who changed her name first to Dagmar and then to Bobbe), Eunice (who became Lorayne) and Kathleen (later Patricia). Their career began on Broadway in Irving Berlin's "Music Box Revue." Berlin built a theatre, the Music Box, on West 45th Street in Manhattan to house his yearly musical revues. He produced four of these shows from 1921 through 1924. The sisters also appeared in movies such as "The Cocoanuts" in 1926 with the Marx Brothers. Bobbe, who was married to the songwriter Jimmy Van Heusen for over 30 years, died in 1999 at the age of 98.

By the end of the decade, the music business was stable and the rules for how composers were paid became established. The American Society of Composers, Authors and Publishers (ASCAP) was formed in 1914 — thanks in large part to the efforts of composer and conductor Victor Herbert — in order to protect composers' and artists' rights to "performance" royalties from the playing of their music in public settings, including over the radio. Organizations such as BMI[64] and SESAC[65] now compete with ASCAP in this area. These organizations pay royalties to songwriters based on the number of times a song is played on the radio, TV, in a concert, etc. Each organization uses a slightly different method of determining which songs have been played and how often. Composers also earn money from their work through "mechanical" royalties, collected by the publisher of the composition and paid for the recording of songs on media such as records, tapes or CDs.

The songwriting profession itself was alive and well by 1920. The beginnings of Tin Pan Alley in New York in about 1885 (then the area around West 28th Street between Broadway and Sixth Avenue) helped to fuel the growth of popular music, aided by the popularity of vaudeville. Author and songwriter Monroe H. Rosenfeld is believed to have

---

[63] The Farber Sisters hit the charts in 1918, but they were a duo and do not qualify as a vocal group
[64] Broadcast Music Incorporated. http://www.bmi.com/about/ (accessed January 16, 2009)
[65] http://www.sesac.com/ (accessed January 16, 2009)

been the first to call the neighborhood "Tin Pan Alley" and said that the name came from the sounds of the many pianos he heard in the studios there, saying it sounded like the banging of tin pans.[66] Tin Pan Alley is used as shorthand for the business under which people were retained by the publishing companies to create popular music. Its influence lasted until the birth of rock and roll in the 1950s. Followers of more recent music can make an analogy to the famous Brill Building of the 1950s and 1960s.

The most important harbinger of what was to come arrived over the airwaves. Although the first radio broadcast of music took place in 1906 (the year of the San Francisco earthquake), it was not until the Radio Corporation of America (RCA) was founded in 1919 that the influence of broadcast music began to be felt. The earliest daily commercial broadcasts occurred in Detroit in 1920 on what would become the station WWJ, but what really propelled the growth of radio was when the National Broadcasting Co. went on the air with 24 stations in 1926, followed by the Columbia Broadcasting System with 16 stations in 1927. Now, professionally performed music could be heard by just about anyone, anywhere.

---

[66] Paymer, Marvin E., General Editor. *Facts Behind The Songs: A Handbook Of American Popular Music From The Nineties To The '90s*. New York & London: Garland Publishing, Inc., 1993

The AABA Song Format

Almost all popular songs at the beginning of the twentieth century were written in the same pattern, or format, called "AABA." Once this format took hold, it held sway for the next 50 years.

In AABA, the chorus is normally divided into four parts, with the B-part serving as the bridge. The chorus was usually preceded by a verse that was often omitted on recordings. (Today, the verse has all but disappeared and many people refer to the A-parts as the verse and the B-part as the chorus.) An example of an AABA song is "Paper Doll" written by Johnny S. Black in 1915, which was a big hit for the Mills Brothers in 1943 on Decca. The song breaks down as follows:

Verse:
I guess I've had a million dolls or more,
I guess I've played the doll game o'er and o'er,
I just quarreled with Sue, that's why I'm blue:
She's gone away and left me just like all dolls do.
I'll tell you boys it's tough to be alone
And it's tough to love a doll that's not your own.
I'm through with all of them,
I'll never fall again,
'Cause this is what I'll do.

Chorus:
   First A-Part:
      I'm goin' to buy a paper doll that I can call my own,
      A doll that other fellows cannot steal.
   Second A-Part:
      And then the flirty, flirty guys with their flirty, flirty eyes,
      Will have to flirt with dollies that are real
   B-Part:
      When I come home at night she will be waiting,
      She'll be the truest doll in all this world
   Third A-Part
      I'd rather have a paper doll to call my own than have a fickle
      minded real live girl.

Chapter Three

1920 to 1939: The Dawn of the Radio Era

In the 1920s, significant changes occurred that strongly affected vocal group harmony, along with every other type of music. First, energized by the influence of jazz and ragtime and the emergence of the dance bands, a less formal, more rhythmic tone could be heard in all areas of singing. As the popularity of dance music grew, vocal groups and male and female solo vocalists became an important part of bands. Harmony groups also incorporated the replacement and imitation of musical instruments into their singing. In some cases, these techniques even eliminated or greatly reduced the need for background musicians.

Second, the advent of radio brought music to everyone — it allowed songs and the artists who performed them to be heard across the country soon after they were recorded, and this accelerated the cross-fertilization of all types of music. Other improvements in the realm of technology, such as better quality recording, spurred the growth of the entire music industry during this era. Radio also greatly helped to increase the popularity of dance bands.

Some of the music industry milestones in the 1920s were:

- Radios became a primary source of entertainment for most families. Although the medium was a novelty at the time — much like television sets in the 1950s — and even though money was scarce, every family just had to buy one. And once the set was purchased, the broadcasts were free!

- The first so-called "race" records appeared in 1920 beginning with Mamie Smith's "Crazy Blues." (Race records were music made by black artists and intended for black audiences.)

- The first commercial radio station, Pittsburgh's KDKA, went on the air in 1920.

- The first live radio broadcast of a band on radio took place in 1921 and featured the

- Vincent Lopez band.[67]

- A 1921 movie, "Gasoline Alley," with Fatty Arbuckle, contained an unidentified black vocal group. (Because it was a silent picture, no clues can be gained from listening to them.)

- Art Hickman and his pianist, Ferde Grofé, started the type of dance band that was such a central part of music from the 1920s to the rock and roll era. Many of the vocal groups of that period, particularly the white groups, sang with these bands. The first of the successful dance-bandleaders was Paul Whiteman. Some of the more popular black bands were Troy Floyd (San Antonio, Texas), Alphonso Trent (Dallas), Hayes Pillars who played in St. Louis for many years and, of course, Duke

---
[67] http://www.bigbandsandbignames.com/lopez.html (accessed January 16, 2009)

Ellington. The Fletcher Henderson band, which started in 1922 and featured musicians such as Coleman Hawkins and Louis Armstrong, used arrangements that were jazzier and gave a lot of leeway to their soloists.

- The microphone was invented in 1925 and acoustic recordings were quickly phased out. Electronic recording picked up subtleties of the human voice. Shrill, booming and penetrating voices had been preferred in the early years of recording because they recorded better, but were now relegated to the past (in much the same way that the silent film stars gave way to a new generation with the addition of sound to movies).

Martin Block

- In 1926, NBC built the first radio network that spanned the entire country. Music played in New York could now be heard in California within a short time. Dance bands became popular on radio stations, paving the way for the Big Band era.

- Microphones continued to evolve, making recordings more faithful to the source and adding bandwidth to the sound. "The ribbon or 'velocity' microphone was introduced by RCA in 1931, as the model 44A, and became one of the most widely used microphones in vocal recording. Many bands today hoping to achieve a more authentic 'vintage' sound still use the 44A. Another advance in recording sound came in 1933 when RCA introduced the 77A, cardioid pattern, dual ribbon microphone.[68] These advances in sound enabled subtle nuances in both playing and singing to be amplified for the first time and made for better live broadcasts. Until these advances, vocalists were required to get up and belt out a song with many of the subtleties in inflection and voice tone being lost."[69]

Records began to be played on the radio. Although radio played a huge role in disseminating music to the public, only live music was broadcast during the early years. The concept of playing recorded music over the radio has become so ingrained in our society over the last 75 years that it is hard to believe it was met with resistance when

---

[68] Cardioid refers to a microphone that picks up sound mainly from what is directly in front of it and a lesser amount from the sides (as opposed to omni- or uni-directional pickup).
[69] http://www.swingmusic.net (accessed September 17, 2006)

introduced. Al Jarvis, an announcer at station KFWB in Los Angeles, is usually credited with being the pioneer. Beginning in the 1930s, Jarvis called his radio show "The World's Largest Make Believe Ballroom," and played records over the air, but he was little known outside of the Los Angeles market. However, it was Jarvis' assistant, a young man named Martin Block, who would become the first of the superstar disk jockeys by changing established practice industry-wide.[70] Block began working at New York's WNEW in 1934, and in February, 1935, during the broadcast of the Lindbergh baby kidnapping trial, Block played some records when there was a break in the proceedings. This developed into a regular show in which, "Block created the illusion that he was broadcasting from a ballroom with the nation's top dance bands performing live. Block appropriated the name 'Make Believe Ballroom' and the show was an instant hit. 'Make Believe Ballroom' became so popular that when WNEW moved to a new studio on Fifth Avenue, they constructed a simulated ballroom—complete with chandelier and black linoleum—for Block's broadcasts."[71]

- The Wurlitzer company, which had been in the music business for several hundred years in Germany, began operations in the U.S. in the 1850s and became the largest instrument supplier in America. They also had piano stores and manufactured their own pianos. In the late 1800s, they put a coin slot on a player piano and started the coin-operated music boom.

- "In 1933 Homer Capehart sold the Simplex record changer mechanism to the Wurlitzer Company. The jukebox was to become an important tool in the popularity and accessibility of big band swing music. By the late 1930s, one could find them located in speakeasies, ice cream parlors, and even drugstores. The jukebox was at least part of the reason record sales began to show a tremendous increase toward the end of the decade."[72]

- The Apollo Theatre, on West 125th Street in New York, began as a music hall in 1913 and then became a burlesque theater. In 1934, the Apollo started its unparalleled run as the premier venue in the world for black entertainers.

---

[70] Some say the term "disk jockey" was coined by columnist Walter Winchell; others claim it was Decca record executive, Jack Kapp.
[71] http://www.radiohof.org/discjockey/martinblock.html ((accessed January 16, 2009)
[72] http://www.swingmusic.net/getset.html (accessed January 16, 2009)

- The proliferation of radios in homes had an enormous influence on the variety and quantity of music heard by the average citizen. By 1935, "the number of homes with radios was nearly 23 million, the total audience around 91 million."[73] [74] "Studio musicians made their money as background instrumentalists both for shows and commercials. Radio executives had learned in the 1920s that music shows were also successful. However, as far as nationally broadcast music shows in the years preceding 1934, dance and 'sweet' bands still dominated the airwaves. The general public was still only dimly aware of the great black jazz orchestras. Benny Goodman's 'Let's Dance' broadcasts, which aired regularly in 1934, were one of the first such weekly live radio broadcasts of hot jazz music to be aired by a national network on a steady, reoccurring basis."[75]

- Improvements in the materials used to make records also contributed to the improved quality of the sound. "By the late 1930s a limited use of vinyl resin to replace shellac pointed the way to quieter records. Lacquer-coated aluminum discs also came into use in the recording process. These had a quieter surface and for the first time allowed immediate playback in the studio for auditioning purposes. This enabled both engineers and musicians the ability to instantly make adjustments of microphone or personnel placement, further refining their recordings. These advances in disc recording, being honed during the Great Depression, had significant impact on the quality of recorded music during the big band era."[76]

The Influence of Instruments on the Sound of Vocal Groups

By the 1920s jazz — where you "played your feelings," instead of exactly what was written on the score — had gained widespread popularity and was influencing all facets of popular music. Musical instruments, the building blocks of jazz, found their way into the repertoires of vocal groups, with singers imitating or replacing the instruments with their voices.

Instrument *replacement* occurs when a group uses its voices to replace what the band would ordinarily provide as support for the vocal, without, however, actually trying to sound like the instruments. A good example can be found in the great Delta Rhythm Boys

---

[73] http://www.swingmusic.net/getset.html (accessed January 16, 2009)
[74] Out of a population of 127,000,000. http://www.infoplease.com/year/1935.html (accessed February 6, 2009)
[75] http://www.swingmusic.net/getset.html (accessed January 16, 2009)
[76] http://www.swingmusic.net/getset.html (accessed January 16, 2009)

song "Just A-Sittin' And A-Rockin'." Lee Gaines sings, "I don't go out walking." The group backup vocal follows with, "Voo da doo doo wah." Gaines continues, "I ain't for no talking." The group again follows with, "Voo da doo doo wah." Gaines: "My baby done left me." Group: "Rah da da dah." Gaines: "Just A-Sittin' And A-Rockin'." Group: "Doo doo doo dah." The use of this technique was widespread in the 1950s. The nonsense syllable "doo-wop" was meant to represent the sound that a horn would usually provide. A cappella renditions were punctuated by bass singers "bum-bumming" the equivalent of drums or stand-up basses.

Imitation of instruments occurs when the vocal group attempts to vocalize in a way that is designed to sound like an instrument, usually a trombone, trumpet or saxophone, or a stand-up bass. Examples of groups that used instrument imitation effectively are the Revelers ("Dinah"), Mills Brothers ("Caravan"), Comedian Harmonists ("Creole Love Song"), Golden Gate Quartet ("My Walking Stick") and Four Vagabonds ("Rosie The Riveter"). In 1985, an LP came out on the Clanka Lanka label called, "The Human Orchestra," which contained 16 vocal group cuts, in a variety of vocal group styles, that featured instrument imitation.[77]

The practice of both replacing and imitating instruments, starting in the 1920s, expanded the vocal repertoire of singing groups beyond merely singing lead and harmony. The result was a fuller, more diverse, more interesting sound, and stands as testimony to the flexibility of the human voice.[78]

Delta Rhythm Boys

---

[77] The LP has now been released by Jasmine Records on a CD with some bonus tracks.
[78] According to Opal Louis Nation's liner notes to the Four Aces CD (Flyright CD 62), in the late 19th century the Bell Quartet began the human orchestra sound that became so popular with vocal groups in the 1930s and 1940s.

Revelers

The Male Groups

The advent of instrumental jazz gave license to a freer approach to singing, breaking the mold set by the earlier, more formal-sounding groups. The first of the significant vocal groups of this era was the Revelers. As mentioned in the previous chapter, three of the four members came out of the Shannon Four. The importance of the Revelers stems from the way that they moved vocal group music forward by using more voice separation and a less formal style than the previous popular groups. They were also a pioneer in the use of instrument imitation. Franklyn Baur (first tenor), Lewis James (tenor), Elliott Shaw (baritone), Wilfred Glenn (bass) and Ed Smalle (piano) comprised the group. Their highest charting recordings were "Dinah" (1926-Victor), "Valencia" (1926-Victor) and "The Blue Room" (1926-Victor). Here is a view of them from the other side of the Atlantic:

> Popular music in America started to experience a subtle change in the middle of the twenties, which would inspire Wilfred Glenn. He would later say, that the character of the songs which the quartet would be requested to sing by the record companies at the beginning of 1925 increasingly displeased him. . . . more modern music was reserved for the instrumentalists. Glenn developed a new concept of arranging and presentation for his quartet at that time, supported by Franklyn Baur . . . The result was a new, more relaxed style of singing, closer to Jazz . . .[79]

---

[79] Czada, Peter and Günter Grosse. *Comedian Harmonists: Ein Vokalensemble erobert die Welt*. Berlin:

In his book, *Stardust Melodies,* Will Friedwald said: "This vocal quartet was harmonically quite innovative and was an important influence on such later groups as [Paul] Whiteman's own Rhythm Boys and the German Comedian Harmonists. Rhythmically, however, the Revelers were stiff beyond words and even the most rudimentary syncopation seems quite beyond them."[80] That, of course, is looking at them today. However, in the 1920s, what the Revelers were doing was revolutionary. The Rhythm Boys came a few years later and were from the same mold, but a little more rhythmic. While the Comedian Harmonists were greatly influenced by the Revelers, they were a much more polished unit and took the Revelers' innovations to another level.

The Rhythm Boys reversed a tradition that had been in place since the dawn of musical recording. Rather than the best singers coming together to form groups, the best singers came out of vocal groups in order to launch solo careers. The most famous group member turned soloist from this era was Bing Crosby, who got his start with the Rhythm Boys and Paul Whiteman's orchestra.

In the mid-1920s, two guys from Spokane, Washington, Crosby and Al Rinker, formed a singing duo. They travelled to California in 1925 and Rinker's sister, singer Mildred Bailey (group harmony fans may be familiar with the songs she recorded with the Delta Rhythm Boys), helped them get started. They were noticed, and in 1926 were asked to join the Paul Whiteman Orchestra. There, they joined with Harry Barris to form a trio called Paul Whiteman's Rhythm Boys. They were the first vocal trio to be regularly associated with a band. They also sang with the Gus Arnheim Band. In 1930, they left Whiteman to play clubs and appear in movies. Crosby began to get more and more solo work and in 1931 the group disbanded. Their manner of singing reflects the influence of the Revelers, but the Rhythm Boys did not break any new ground

Rhythm Boys

Edition Hentrich, 1993, 1998, p. 12 (English translation by Brita Schmitz.)
[80] Friedwald, Will. *Stardust Melodies, A Biography Of Twelve Of America's Most Popular Songs.* New York: Pantheon Books, 2002, p. 123

musically — certainly not in the way that we will see with the Boswell Sisters or the Mills Brothers.

Maple City Four

Vocal groups were springing up everywhere. Regional groups are exemplified by the Maple City Four, formed in 1924 in LaPorte, Indiana. They were favorites throughout the Midwest thanks to their long tenure (about 30 years) on radio. They were called the "Marx Brothers of radio," being known for their comedy as well as their singing.

The 1920s were years of transition, with new sounds coexisting with those of the past generations. As late as 1928 the Old South Quartette was still singing in the old, stiff style. They had continued performing after the death of Polk Miller in 1913 and were still at it into the 1930s. But most other groups were changing, filling the country's need for something different and more exciting to relieve the pressures caused by the Great Depression that followed the collapse of the New York Stock Exchange on October 29, 1929.

The Female Groups

Sister groups proliferated after the success of the Brox trio in the early 1920s. Although not many hit the charts before the Andrews Sisters in 1938, their pictures were often found on the covers of sheet music, including the Cambridge Sisters, De Marco Sisters, Doring Sisters, Five Locust Sisters, Four Aalbu Sisters, Giersdorf Sisters, LeBrun Sisters, Loomis Sisters, McQuade Sisters, Morin Sisters, Ozark Sisters, Pickens Sisters, Pickert Sisters, Starr Sisters, Stewart Sisters, Three Dennis Sisters, Three Ormand Sisters and Three X Sisters.

Then came the Boswell Sisters, one of the most innovative and influential groups — regardless of gender. Comprised of Connie (later Connee), Martha and Helvetia (Vet), they were one of the rare white groups to come out of New Orleans and preceded the Andrews Sisters by about 10 years. Each sister played an instrument (Connie, the cello, Martha, piano, and Vet, violin) and were members of the New Orleans Philharmonic Orchestra. They signed with Victor and made their first recording in 1925. In the early

1930s, they sang with the Dorsey Brothers Band. The group disbanded in 1936 and Connee continued with a successful individual career into the 1940s, charting 32 times as a solo. They were the first female group to break out of the stiff style of the 1920s and put some rhythm into their singing. Their hits included "You Oughta Be In Pictures" (1934, Brunswick) and "The Object of My Affection" (1935, Brunswick). Their "Rock and Roll" from 1934 is notable just for its title alone. Their harmony and rhythmic flair make their recordings eminently listenable even today, some 80 years later.

As an example of the influence of the Boswell Sisters and Connee in particular, consider this quote from the great Ella Fitzgerald speaking of Connee: "She was tops at the time. . . I tried so hard to sound just like her. . . . When I was a girl, I listened to records by all the singers, white and black, and I know that Connee Boswell was doing things that no one else was doing at the time."[81] In his book, *Classic Jazz*, Scott Yanow says that the Boswell Sisters "were on a completely different level altogether" when compared to the other sister groups of the era and that they were "the finest of all the sister groups of the past (20th) century . . ."[82] Will Friedwald said, "So quickly did the Boswell Sisters replace the Rhythm Boys that one suspects the three men disbanded just to avoid the competition."[83]

Boswell Sisters

Another popular female group from this era was the Pickens Sisters from Georgia (the family later moved to New York), consisting of Jane, Patti and Helen. They were originally known as the Three Little Maids From Pixie, but changed their name to the Pickens Sisters. Jane Pickens was a prominent Newport socialite, trained at the Curtis Institute of Music in Philadelphia as well as the Juilliard School of Music in New York.

---

[81] Nicholson, Stuart. *Ella Fitzgerald: A Biography of the First Lady of Jazz*. New York: Da Capo Press, New York, 1993, p. 10
[82] Yanow, Scott. *Classic Jazz: The Essential Listening Companion*. San Francisco: Backbeat Books, 2001, p. 36
[83] Friedwald, p. 61

Pickens Sisters

She also ran for Congress, losing to future New York mayor Ed Koch in 1972, and she had a TV show in the 1950s. The group is best known for "Did You Ever See A Dream Walking," recorded in 1934 for Victor.

Toward the end of the 1930s, two sister acts achieved enormous success: the King Sisters and, of course, the Andrews Sisters. The King Sisters came from a musical family in Oklahoma. Their real name was Driggs and the family consisted of six girls and two boys who performed as a family orchestra to help make ends meet. Eventually, Maxine, Luise and Alyce formed a vocal trio and sang locally while still in school, influenced by the Boswell Sisters. Their father, William King Driggs, was known as "King," so when it came time to change their name (at the suggestion of a radio station manager), they chose the King Sisters. Bandleader Horace Heidt heard them on the radio and asked them to join his band at an engagement in San Francisco in 1934. Two of the younger sisters, Yvonne and Donna, had formed a trio with a friend at about the same time. Heidt then added them to make the Six King Sisters (actually, five sisters and the friend, Anita). Alyce was fired by Heidt in a fit of temper in 1938 and sang for a while with Charlie Barnett. Yvonne also left, but Luise and Donna stayed on and sang as a trio with Peggy Pope. In 1939, the four sisters (Luise, Alyce, Yvonne and Donna) got back together and sang with Artie Shaw. They later sang with Alvino Rey, who had married Luise. In 1965, they had their own television show for one year — The King Family Show on ABC.

The Andrews Sisters — Patty, Maxene and La Verne — from Minneapolis, Minnesota, formed one of the most enduring and famous of the American vocal groups. Their names are still household words today, at least among older Americans. They began their professional career in 1932 when they went on tour with the Larry Rich Orchestra. Their second break came in 1936 when they joined Leon Belasco's orchestra. It was there they met Vic Schoen, who would become their musical director and arranger. They were singing on a radio program when Dave Kapp, the A&R man for

Decca Records, heard them.[84] Soon thereafter, Decca signed them to a contract. It would turn out to be a long-lasting relationship, with every one of the sisters' chart hits being released on Decca.

It is perhaps inevitable that the Andrews Sisters are compared to the Boswell Sisters and for the question to arise as to which group was more influential and which was better. Certainly, more people today are familiar with the Andrews than the Boswells, in part because the Andrews came later. However, most music historians would probably say that the Boswells were more influential and that they undoubtedly contributed more to the changing of music styles. In his book on the Andrews Sisters, John Sforza said, "The Andrews Sisters did indeed copy the Boswell style (both Patty and Maxene have admitted to this), and evidence of such emulation can be heard in such early Andrews Sisters hits as 'Says My Heart' and 'Where Have We Met Before?;' but with their first release, 'Jammin',' as well as with what immediately followed ('Bei Mir' and so on), their vocal style, perfect timing, harmonious blend and musical phrasing all showed that they were more than mere imitators."[85]

Andrews Sisters

From 1938, when the Andrews Sisters hit number one with the Yiddish song, "Bei Mir Bist Du Schoen," to 1951, they charted a remarkable 90 times! Six of those songs were number one, and they also had three R&B chart hits, two of them with Bing Crosby. This in an era with significantly more competition than the earlier groups had to face. (The king of the pop charts during the pre-1954 period was Bing Crosby, who placed 317 recordings there. He also charted an additional 23 times with the Andrews Sisters from 1939 to 1951.)

---

[84] "A&R" stands for artists and repertoire. The A&R man was the talent scout who found the groups and worked with them.
[85] Sforza, John. *The Andrews Sisters Story - Swing It!"* Lexington: The University Press of Kentucky, 2000, p. 51

Here's a teaser: Who is the most famous female ever to come out of a recognized vocal group? Answer: Dorothy Dandridge. The Dandridge Sisters included a young Dorothy Dandridge, her sister Vivian and a friend, Etta Jones. They worked at theaters in the Los Angeles area and eventually got a small part in the film "The Big Broadcast of 1936." The Dandridge Sisters performed successfully at the Cotton Club in New York and toured Europe until the start of World War II. When they returned, Dorothy became more interested in solo work and the group broke up — a familiar story.

Several influential groups featured female lead singers fronting male groups. The first of the three major groups in this category was the Merry Macs. Formed in Minneapolis, Minnesota, in the mid-1920s by brothers Ted, Judd and Joe McMichael, they added Cheri McKay and made their first recording in 1932 for Victor. They accompanied Bing Crosby on several numbers and charted twelve times from 1939 into the 1940s. The other two well-known groups with female leads and male backup were the Modernaires and the Pied Pipers, who made their marks with the big bands.

Dandridge Sisters

Vocal Groups and the Big Bands

The Swing Era is generally regarded to have occurred between the years 1935 and 1945. "It was the only time in history that the popularity of jazz music eclipsed all other forms of music in the U.S."[86] The first of the successful big bands was Benny Goodman's. He had been an arranger with the Ben Pollack band (along with another young arranger by the name of Glenn Miller). Goodman's "Let's Dance" broadcasts first aired in December of 1934, and some point to Goodman's appearance at the Palomar in Los Angeles in August, 1935, as the beginning of the Swing Era.

The Swing Era brought more and more bands onto the scene. Swing music has been defined as containing "a flowing, rhythmic pulse,"[87] and it was the greater emphasis on rhythm that made this new music so popular. The big bands were a major part of this

---

[86] http://www.swingmusic.net/getset.html (accessed January 16, 2009)
[87] Paymer

Babs and her Brothers

movement, turning out music that was both melodious and dance-friendly.

Following the trend started by Paul Whiteman and the Rhythm Boys in the late 1920s, more and more bands began to use vocal groups as part of their shows. Fred Waring, a bandleader who hit it big in radio with his Pennsylvanians on a show sponsored by Ford Motor Co., was a prime example. The most significant groups employed by Waring in the mid-1930s were Babs and her Brothers, Stella and the Fellas, Bea and the Bachelors and the V-8. "Babs" was Babs Ryan (nee Blanche Redwine) and the "brothers" were not hers but her husband Charlie Ryan and his brother, Little Ryan. They were also known as the Three Smoothies, because the sponsor of their show was Old Gold cigarettes, "the country's smoothest cigarette." They also sang with Hal Kemp's band as the Smoothies. When the show got a new sponsor, they changed their name to Babs and her Brothers. They were on the radio with Waring from 1933 to 1935, but disbanded when Babs and Charlie split up.

Stella Friend sang with Waring as one of the Three Waring Girls in 1930. She later joined first tenor Craig Leitch, second tenor Roy Ringwald and baritone Paul Gibbons to form Stella and the Fellas, who sang with Waring in 1935 and 1936. Ringwald was also one of Waring's arrangers.

Bea and the Bachelors featured Bea Swain, Al Rinker (of the Rhythm Boys), Ken Lane and Johnny Smedburg. These four combined with the four original Modernaires, Bill Conway, Hal Dickinson, Ralph Brewster and Chuck Goldstein (later a member of Four Chicks And Chuck), to form a group called the "V-8." According to the liner notes of the CD produced by the Fred Waring's America Collection at Penn State University, this was the first "vocal jazz/swing ensemble." They performed in 1936 on broadcasts by Waring of the Ford Dealers Show and took their name from the Ford V-8 engine.

All of the Waring groups were polished ensembles, including the first all-female choir to be featured on radio, Kay Thompson and the Girls' Choir, in 1935. Waring's success led some to copy his music off the air and a pirated transcription copy was sold to a radio station. Waring sued and won: It was an early success in the war against bootleg recordings. However, when Waring tried to stop others from playing even his commercially-made records without permission, he lost that case. Some suggest that this contributed to the demise of live music on radio.

The Modernaires started as a trio in Buffalo, New York, in the early 1930s. The members were Hal Dickinson, Bill Conway and Chuck Goldstein, and they added a fourth member, Ralph Brewster, in 1936 in time for the Waring broadcasts. When they left Waring and the V-8, they joined the Charlie Barnet Orchestra, with whom they recorded the classics "Make Believe Ballroom" and "The Milkman's Matinee" in 1936 on Bluebird. Ray Noble's band was next, but the Modernaires left him in 1939 to sing with a new ensemble being formed by Glenn Miller, who had also been with Noble. Their name came from a billboard Dickinson saw advertising a cleaning process called "Modernizing." Their chart hits all came in the 1940s and are covered in the next chapter.

Black Vocal Groups

While the Revelers came from the formal tradition of the early classic quartets, black groups followed a separate, but parallel evolution. Black groups were active in creating both popular and gospel music, but due to segregation in the music industry, these groups did not have much effect on the charts in the 1920s. This would begin to change in the late 1930s, and the popularity of the black groups grew enormously through the 1940s and 1950s as the country became exposed to their music.

The Norfolk Jazz and Jubilee Quartet is an interesting group to follow: They were active and recorded throughout the 1920s and 1930s, a period that saw great changes in music in general and in vocal group singing in particular. In 1923, the Norfolk group consisted of Otto Tutson (lead), J. "Buddie" Archer (tenor), Delrose Hollins (baritone) and bass Len Williams, but by the 1930s, the personnel had changed to Norman "Crip" Harris (lead & first tenor), Raymond Smith (second tenor), Melvin Colden

Norfolk Jazz and Jubilee Quartet

(baritone) and Williams (bass). They sang both secular (as the Norfolk Jazz Quartet) and spiritual numbers (as the Norfolk Jubilee Quartet) and recorded for Paramount, Okeh and Decca in the 1920s, and on Decca from 1937 to 1940. When Williams, the founder, died in 1940, the group disbanded.

The evolution of the Norfolk Quartet's sound — and perhaps the sound of many other singing groups — can be followed by listening to their recordings. In one of their early efforts, "Sad Blues" from 1923, you can hear the stiff, mainstream style of the early 1920s. In "He Just Hung His Head And Died" from 1927, the style is slightly looser and sounds slightly more modern. If you then fast forward to 1937, to "Beedle De Beedle De Bop Bop" or "Suntan Baby Brown," the music is more rhythmic and has a much more active bass. Founder Len Williams used the "walking bass" technique, where the singer vocalizes notes that would normally be created by plucking the strings of an upright bass.

Mills Brothers before the death of John, Jr. (far right), 1936

Mills Brothers with father, John, Sr., (second from bottom), 1943

There are few groups from this era, black or white, male or female, whose names are still widely recognized by non-collectors today. Among the black groups, there are two notable exceptions: the Mills Brothers, from Piqua, Ohio, and the Ink Spots. When the Mills Brothers began singing in church in the 1920s, it was the four brothers — John, Jr., Herbert, Harry and Donald. When John, Jr. died suddenly in 1936, he was replaced by their father, John, Sr.

Their father owned a barbershop and founded a barbershop quartet called the Four Kings of Harmony and the brothers' grandfather, Billy Mills, had sung with Stinson's Jubilee Singers in the 1880s. The brothers learned their close harmonies first-hand, and began performing around the area.[88] The Mills Brothers established themselves as a viable vaudeville act and even began broadcasting over a Cincinnati radio station during the late '20s. They would become the first black group to have a wide appeal to white audiences.

At one show early in their career, Harry Mills forgot his kazoo, the group's usual accompaniment, and ended up trying to emulate the instrument by cupping his hand over his mouth. The brothers were surprised to hear the sound of a trumpet coming from Harry's mouth, so they began to work the novelty into their act. John "played" tuba, Donald "trombone" and Herbert a second "trumpet." "Caravan" recorded in 1938, as an "instrumental," shows their uncanny ability to emulate the sound of real instruments.

Broadcasting executive William S. Paley, at CBS radio in New York, turned on his office speaker one day in September of 1930 at the urging of Ralph Wonders to listen to an audition of four young men that had been performing under different names in Cincinnati on WLW radio. They were billed as The Steamboat Four when they sang for Sohio (Standard Oil of Ohio). They were the Tasty Yeast Jesters when they sang for Tasty Yeast. They had been called the Four Boys and a Guitar, but on Sundays and for this audition, they went by their real name, the Mills Brothers. When Paley heard their performance, he immediately went downstairs and put them on CBS radio. The next day the Mills Brothers signed a three-year contract and became the first African-Americans to have a network show on radio.[89]

The Mills Brothers were prolific in their number of appearances on the pop charts. Eleven of their songs made it on the R&B charts and 70 hit the pop charts. They were also an enormous influence on many of the groups that followed, especially black groups that had witnessed the crossover of the Mills Brothers to the white pop charts. Their first hits were "Tiger Rag" and "Nobody's Sweetheart," both in 1931 on Brunswick.

---

[88] Close harmony is where all parts are sung in a narrow range, usually of an octave or octave and one-half.
[89] http://www.piquaoh.org/mills.htm (accessed January 16, 2009)

Ink Spots

The Ink Spots were a second extremely popular group that is regarded as being one of the primary influences on the rhythm and blues groups of the 1950s. Only the Mills Brothers rivaled them in their appeal to white audiences. They were founded in 1934 in Indianapolis by Deek Watson, Charles Fuqua (the uncle of Harvey Fuqua of the 1950s Moonglows), Orville "Hoppy" Jones and Jerry Daniels. Their first major performance was at the Apollo Theatre in Harlem, New York on August 9, 1934, and they had their first major hit in 1939 with the classic, "If I Didn't Care" on Decca. As J. C. Marion said: "[T]he musical world was stood on its collective ear when they heard this recording. The contrast of Bill Kenny's high tenor lead voice, and the deep bass recitation of 'Hoppy' Jones over the smooth harmonies was a sensation. . ."[90] At that time, the group members were lead Kenny (who had replaced Jerry Daniels), tenor and guitarist Fuqua, baritone and guitarist Watson, and bass and bassist (usually, a cello tuned as a bass) Jones.

Their style was characterized by Bill Kenny's high tenor lead and the talking bass bridges of Jones. Kenny's twin brother, Herb, said: "Bill painted a picture with every phrase. Some of his high notes would take your breath away."[91] In all, they reached the pop charts 46 times and the R&B charts 17 times. Marv Goldberg said: "If the Mills Brothers were primarily responsible for opening the airwaves to black artists in the early '30s, then the Ink Spots were the first black group to release records which consistently sold to white as well as black audiences."[92]

---

[90] http://home.earthlink.net/~jaymar41/Ten_Records_That_Shook_The.html (accessed September 13, 2010)
[91] Goldberg Marv. *More Than Words Can Say: The Ink Spots and Their Music*. Lanham, Maryland: Scarecrow Press, Inc., 1998, p. xiii
[92] Goldberg, p. 272

Aside from the Mills Brothers and Ink Spots, the music of very few black groups reached the ears of the vast majority of the white population, even though dozens of groups were recording and many of them were quite good. These groups generally fell into two categories – those that started from a religious background and those that were mainly secular and had a more jazz-based origin and sound.

From the first category, the Birmingham Jubilee Singers, from Jefferson County, Alabama, began recording in 1926. As was the custom, they recorded under different names, depending on what type of material they were performing. They recorded religious numbers as the Alabama Four and some secular material as the Mobile Four. Ken Romanowski said of them that they "were perhaps the most popular and influential black vocal quartet in the decade spanning 1926 . . . and 1936 . . . ."[93] They were an extremely professional-sounding group led by Charles Bridges, although they were not breaking any new ground in 1930 when they still had the sound of a 1920s group.[94]

One of the earliest black female groups was the Virginia Female Jubilee Singers who recorded in 1921. The most prominent female group was the Wheat Street Female Quartet from Atlanta, who recorded in 1925. They used call and response extensively in their recordings, which are in the old style and not nearly as advanced as some of the other groups of this period.

In 1927, the Utica Institute Jubilee Singers began a syndicated radio show on NBC, originating from New York. They were the first black group to break into radio syndication.[95] Two years later, a second black quartet — the Southernaires — also began a stint on a nationally syndicated radio show. The Southernaires' show lasted for eight years, and they were one of the few black groups of their era to appear on the cover of sheet music.

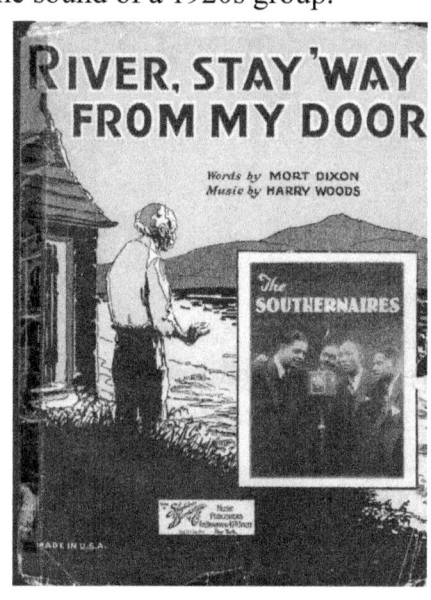

Southernaires

---

[93] Romanowski, Ken. Liner notes for the CD, "Hall Negro Quartette-Unissued Radio Programs-1936)," Document Records - DOCD-5415

[94] The Monarch Jazz/Jubilee Quartet of Norfolk may have been the same group as the Norfolk Jazz Quartet. This group recorded in the late 1920s in Richmond, Virginia, and New York.

[95] Romanowski, Ken. Liner notes for the CD, "Hall Negro Quartette-Unissued Radio Programs-1936)," Document Records – DOCD-5415

Another New York group, the Four Dusty Travelers, recorded on Columbia in the early 1930s, with their biggest hits being "Dinah" and "The Lonesome Road" (both in 1930) and as backup for the band of Ted Lewis, who was white. Their fairly traditional singing contrasted with a jazzy instrumental background.

An interesting — if somewhat mysterious — group from the mid-1930s was the Hall Negro Quartette; only six discs that were intended for radio broadcast survive. These recordings are among the earliest transcriptions of this type of music. The group is thought to have been the creation of Hall Johnson, a black, Juilliard-trained composer and arranger, who also formed the Hall Johnson Negro Choir,[96] but sadly, nothing else is known about them. The group had a polished sound and it is hard to believe that they have remained so anonymous. They used instrument imitation and several of their renditions included substantial speaking parts.

From Chicago came the Four Pods Of Pepper, a secular/jazz-oriented ensemble that recorded in the late 1920s, and Three Sharps And A Flat, a jive group that toured with Duke Ellington in 1936 and appeared on NBC radio.

Meanwhile, in St. Louis, there were the Three Peppers, featuring the lead of Oliver "Toy" Wilson and the Spirits of Rhythm, led by Leo Watson, whose scat singing was a trademark of the group. The Three Peppers were great musicians and apparently put on quite a show. A newspaper article from the period described the group as "plenty good."[97]

Three Peppers

The Palmer Brothers, a rare group from Rhode Island, were from Pawtucket and included Dick Palmer, Clarence Palmer (later of the Sparrows and the Jive Bombers in the 1950s) and Ernest Palmer as their members. They formed in the 1930s and sang with Cab Calloway as the Cabaliers, after which Dick carried on with the Beavers and the Blenders in the late 1940s and 1950s.

Palmer Brothers

---

[96] http://www.afrovoices.com/hjohnson.html (accessed February 6, 2009)
[97] Liner notes for the CD, "The Three Peppers – 1937-1940." Classics Records, 1141

Three Keys

From the Philadelphia area, the Three Keys featured George "Bon Bon" Tunnell as their lead. Tunnell started in the 1920s with a group called Bon Bon and his Buddies, a name to which he was to return in the early 1940s. The Three Keys charted with "Fit As A Fiddle" in 1933 on Brunswick. In 1937, Tunnell joined one of the big bands, Jan Savitt and His Top Hatters, becoming one of the first blacks to sing with a white band.[98] When Savitt's outfit played in the south, Tunnell had to register as the band's valet so he could stay in the same hotel as the other band members. Tunnell left Savitt in 1941 and went back to the Three Keys. They had a jazzy sound and Tunnell's leads presaged the style of later lead singers such as John Jordan of the Four Vagabonds.

A good example of the transition of vocal group singing from the stiff style of the 1920s into the looser style of the 1930s is provided by the Cole Brothers, as shown in their version of "Dinah," recorded in 1933. The tenor is occasionally active behind the lead in a way that would, through many permutations, lead to the great floating falsettos of the 1950s R&B era.

While the Mills Brothers and Ink Spots were the only black vocal groups that fully penetrated into the white entertainment world, there was another set of great black groups that never achieved the same level of chart success, although they appeared in films, on the radio and sang with some of the best talent of the era. Unlike the Mills Brothers and Ink Spots, these groups — the Charioteers, Delta Rhythm Boys and Deep River Boys — began on college campuses.

The Charioteers were formed at Wilberforce University in Ohio in the early 1930s as the Harmony Four, by Howard Daniel, a faculty member, and Billy Williams, a student. Williams sang tenor along with George Lubers (tenor), John Harewood (baritone), Daniel (bass) and Jimmy Sherman (pianist and arranger). The group took its name from the spiritual, "Swing Low, Sweet Chariot." They sang on WLW radio in Cincinnati from 1933 to 1935 and appeared with Bing Crosby on the radio show, Kraft

---

[98] In 1938, Billie Holiday joined Artie Shaw, becoming the first black female to sing with a white band.

Charioteers

Music Hall. They did quite a bit of backup work for singers such as Pearl Bailey, Frank Sinatra and Bing Crosby sang with the Eddy Duchin Band and appeared in the United Artists movie, "Road Show," in 1941.

The Delta Rhythm Boys came together at Langston University in Oklahoma in the mid-1930s. The school asked sophomore Otha Lee Gaines, a bass, to form a quartet and he picked Elmaurice Miller (tenor), Traverse Crawford (tenor) and Essie Atkins (baritone). They transferred to Dillard University in New Orleans in order to be with Frederick Hall, Dillard's Director of Music. They performed first as the New Orleans Quintet and then as the Frederick Hall Quintet and eventually added Rene DeKnight as their pianist. Someone connected with radio in Argentina heard the group and they performed in that country for nine months. Following that, they traveled to New York (where they lived in the same house as Eubie Blake), won the *Major Bowes Amateur Hour* radio show and appeared regularly on CBS radio. They toured with Bill "Bojangles" Robinson in 1940 and sang on the "Amos and Andy" radio show for two years. Clinton Holland and Kelsey Pharr replaced Miller and Atkins, and then were themselves replaced by Carl Jones and Hugh Bryant. "Just A-Sittin' And A-Rockin'" (on Decca) was a hit for the Delta Rhythm Boys in 1946, and "Don't Ask Me Why" (RCA, 1945) is considered to be one of their finer efforts. In all, they made over 70 recordings, including sessions with Ella Fitzgerald, Mildred Bailey and Johnny Mercer.

Hampton Institute in Virginia was where the Deep River Boys formed in 1934 as the Hampton Institute Quartet. Organized by Noah Ryder, director of the glee club and a student, the original members were Harry Douglas (baritone), James Lundy, Carter

Deep River Boys

Wilson and Ryder. They won the *Major Bowes Family Amateur Hour* radio show contest and changed their name to the Deep River Boys. As of 1939, the personnel were Vernon Gardner (tenor), George Lawson (tenor), Douglas and Edward Ware (bass). They appeared in the Broadway musical "Swingin' The Dream" in 1939 with Louis Armstrong. During the War, they performed for troops overseas on USO tours.

Gospel and Spiritual Group Singing

Gospel music and spirituals flourished during the 1920s and 1930s, and they became a major influence on secular groups, especially the black singing groups that made their mark in the 1940s and 1950s. The term "gospel" means "good news" and is designed to give a religious message. Spirituals used to be referred to as "Negro spirituals" and are songs originated by black Americans. Slaves would use the singing of spirituals as a way of communicating secretly, particularly when planning an escape. The link between the two is that they both use song to express religious thoughts or feelings.

Musicologist Randye Jones differentiates between the two:

> Spirituals often told stories about biblical characters and events. These folk songs were born in the rural regions of the American South, and their anonymous creators were inspired by the hardships of slavery. These songs were usually created at the moment using call-and-response between a leader and the group. They were accompanied only by the slaves' clapping hands or stamping feet. The steady, usually duple, rhythm was the driving force in the song, so words were often modified to fit the beat. Additionally, spirituals were lyrically simple so as to be easily passed orally from person to person.[99]

An example of a spiritual that is familiar to most people is "Swing Low, Sweet Chariot."

> In contrast, gospel music rose primarily from cities of the North. The songs were accompanied first by keyboard instruments, then by percussion and later electric and electronic instruments. The words tend to focus on spreading the "Good News" of salvation. Gospel songs provided solace to those who faced low-paying jobs, poor housing, inadequate education, and ill-treatment. Both singer and instrumentalist were expected to improvise within the song.[100]

---

[99] http://improvehomelife.com/2-The_Gospel_Truth_about_the_Negro_Spiritual-9923.htm (accessed February 2, 2009)

[100] http://improvehomelife.com/2-The_Gospel_Truth_about_the_Negro_Spiritual-9923 (accessed February 2, 2009)

A well-known example of a gospel song is "Amazing Grace." Gospel roots are clearly evident in 1950s groups such as the Orioles and Five Keys.

The most popular groups in the 1930s were male quartets or small groups such as The Golden Gate Quartet, who sang, usually unaccompanied, in jubilee style, mixing careful harmonies, melodious singing, playful syncopation and sophisticated arrangements to produce a fresh, experimental style far removed from the more somber hymn-singing. These groups also absorbed popular sounds from pop groups such as The Mills Brothers and produced songs that mixed conventional religious themes, humor and social and political commentary. They began to show more and more influence from gospel as they incorporated the new music into their repertoire.[101]

Thomas Dorsey (not the bandleader) is known as the father of gospel music. He was the son of a Baptist preacher. In the early 1930s he created gospel, "the African-American religious music which married secular blues to a sacred text."[102] When Dorsey's wife and child died during childbirth, he wrote his most famous composition, "Take My Hand Precious Lord." He co-founded the National Convention of Gospel Choirs and Choruses in 1933. In 1939, he joined with Mahalia Jackson and ushered in what was known as the "Golden Age of Gospel Music." Dorsey died in 1993, but many gospel vocal groups followed in his path.

The Golden Gate Quartet formed in the 1930s in the Norfolk, Virginia, area and was at least the second group to bear this name. By 1936, it was comprised of William Langford (tenor), Henry Owens (tenor), Willie Johnson (baritone) and Orlandus Wilson (bass). Their first recording was "The Golden Gate Gospel Train" in 1937 on Bluebird. Performances followed at Carnegie Hall, on radio and in night clubs.

Golden Gate Quartette

---

[101] http://en.wikipedia.org/wiki/Urban_contemporary_gospel (accessed January 16, 2009)
[102] http://www.pbs.org/thisfarbyfaith/people/thomas_dorsey.html (accessed January 16, 2009)

They went to Europe in 1955 and eventually spent most of their time there. Although primarily a gospel group, they could and did sing secular songs as well. Their influence can be seen in many of the groups that followed, including black groups such as the Jubalaires and white pop groups like the Four Lads. Listen, for example, to "Didn't It Rain" (1941) and you can even hear the roots of rap music.

Greenville, South Carolina was home to the Dixie Hummingbirds, one of the most significant gospel groups. They were formed by James Davis, who had known the famous singer, Josh White, when they were children. White helped them with their career, particularly in getting a recording deal. Members of their most well-known grouping were Ira Tucker (lead), James Walker (lead), Beechie Thompson (tenor), Davis (baritone) and Willie Bobo (bass). Tucker had a dramatic singing style that influenced many of the leads of the groups of the 1950s. They appeared regularly on radio in Philadelphia in the 1940s, and at the Newport Jazz Festival in 1966. A later version of the group backed Paul Simon on his 1973 hit "Loves Me Like A Rock," and they had a hit on the R&B chart that same year with their own version of the song on Peacock. Other names under which they sang were the Jericho Boys and the Swanee Quintet.

The Soul Stirrers were a gospel group that began in the mid-1930s in Trinity, Texas. Eileen Southern lists their gospel innovations as being the first to add a fifth member to the group, enabling the lead to sing with four-part harmony behind him, and as being one of the first groups to use instrumental accompaniment. While other groups also sang secular music, the Soul Stirrers sang gospel exclusively. Eileen Southern said: "The group's style was distinctive for its complex rhythms and syncopation and for its penchant for having the group chanting key words of the lyrics as a background for the lead-singers' verses."[103] They introduced a great deal of emotion into their performances and served as inspiration for many of the secular black groups (and, eventually, many white ones as well) that sang in the early days of R&B and into the soul era of the 1960s. Of their later members, Sam Cooke was clearly the most well-known.

Soul Stirrers

---

[103] Southern, p. 353

Other Tributaries

Although beyond the main focus of this book, vocal groups were singing in other styles and in other places. Country and Western groups sprang up wherever C&W solo artists could be heard. Of special note are the Sons Of The Pioneers, who formed in 1933 as the Pioneer Trio with Leonard Slye, Tim Spencer and Slumber Nichols, and then, in 1934, Hugh Farr was added. One night on a radio station the announcer introduced them as the Sons Of The Pioneers, saying later that they were not old enough to be pioneers. They decided to go with that name, especially as they were no longer a trio, and went on to become music legends, lasting for decades through many personnel changes. Their songs such as "Tumbling Tumbleweeds" (Decca, in 1934) were and are classics. Slye, of course, changed careers in 1938 when he replaced Gene Autry in a movie called "Under Western Stars," and changed his name to Roy Rogers.

Sons of the Pioneers

One foreign group is worthy of special mention. The Comedian Harmonists were a German sextet comprised of Ari Leschnikoff (lead tenor), Erich Collin (second tenor), Harry Frommermann (tenor), Roman Cycowski (baritone), Robert Biberti (bass) and Erwin Bootz (pianist). They began in 1928 in Berlin and modeled themselves after the American group, the Revelers, so much so that their first billings read, "The Comedian Harmonists, The German Revellers (sic)." But soon they far surpassed the Revelers and became the most popular vocal group in Europe and many places beyond.

Their voices were impeccable, blended beautifully and Frommermann's arrangements were masterpieces. Their all-too-short career lasted only until early 1935. Two of the members, Frommermann and Cycowski, were Jewish and Collin was considered Jewish by the Nazis because his parents had both been born as Jews. Because the three were non-Aryan, the group was at first restricted in what they could sing — no songs by Jewish composers or those published by Jewish-owned publishing houses, which constituted about three-quarters of their repertoire — and then prohibited from performing entirely.

Comedian Harmonists

The three non-Aryans left Germany found three new members and continued to perform as the Comedy Harmonists until the war broke out. The Aryans also found new members but were required to adopt an Aryan name, choosing the "Meistersextett." They too disbanded in 1941. Neither one of the new groups achieved the enormous critical or financial success of the original.

Marv Goldberg said, "What I've always found most relevant about them is their recording of "Ohne Dich" (Without You), a song that uses the melody of "Stormy Weather" (to which it has no lyrical connection whatever). Recorded in September 1933, it's almost pure R&B. As far as I know, no black American group would sing like that until the late 40s."[104]

American rock music critic for *Rolling Stone* magazine, Lester Bangs, said that the Comedian Harmonists' music sounded "like it was recorded in the ballrooms of Heaven."[105]

---

[104] Friedman, Douglas E. *The Comedian Harmonists: The Last Great Jewish Performers In Nazi Germany.* West Long Branch, New Jersey: HarmonySongs Publications, 2010

[105] Rockwell, John. *An Instant Fan's Inspired Notes: You Gotta Listen.* Previously unpublished liner notes on the Comedian Harmonists (written in 1981). *The New York Times*, September 5, 1999

Chapter Four

1940 to 1950: War and the Music Industry; The Birth of Rock and Roll

The music industry blossomed in the 1940s, affected by political and economic forces and spurred on by ever-improving technology. Aided by omnipresent radio broadcasts and clearer, cheaper recording capabilities, the income generated by the new industry grew astronomically, as did the financial rewards for the men and women who were in the right place at the right time. More and more people began to earn their living as performers, record company workers, studio musicians, composers and radio industry personnel, and they all wanted their share of the pie. In addition, the onset of the Second World War shaped the kind of music that existed and the way it was distributed. "The combination of world war and music business shenanigans caused profound changes in music itself."[106] The end of the decade saw the beginning of one of the biggest changes the music itself would ever undergo — the seeds for the rock and roll revolution were being sown.

The Economics of the Music Industry

In the early 1940s, the performing musicians and the record companies were engaged in a fierce economic struggle. As records were played more frequently on the radio and in jukeboxes, and as more records were sold, musicians began to lose some of the income that had previously been generated from live performances. James C. Petrillo, president of the American Federation of Musicians union, wanted the record companies to give a portion of their profits to the union in order to recompense its members. The record companies refused, leading to the famous headline in Downbeat Magazine, "All Recording Stops Today." Petrillo had ordered a ban on all recording by members of his union and August 1, 1942 became known as "the day the music died."

The recording ban lasted for a long time and had a significant negative impact on the type and quantity of music that was available to the public. Decca capitulated about a year later in September of 1943, but it was another 14 months before RCA and Columbia gave in. The ban likely played a large role in the demise of the big bands by removing them from the mix of new music being offered to the consuming public and, conversely, enhanced the role of singers and vocal groups since they required less overhead. The music industry was never the same.[107]

James C. Petrillo

A second set of economic struggles occurred between ASCAP (the American Society of Composers, Authors and Publishers), and both the radio industry and the body of have-not composers. Originally, much of ASCAP's revenue came from sheet music. As radio gained in popularity, the source of the revenue stream shifted to records as radio stations

---

[106] Clarke p. 250

[107] Another ban was imposed in 1948 that lasted a little less than a year and had less of an impact than the 1942 shutdown. This ban was resolved with the establishment of the Music Performance Fund which set aside a small part of the proceeds from the sale of records to compensate musicians who performed at free concerts.

began to play records. The stations resisted paying for the right to play these recordings, claiming that they were providing free advertising for ASCAP members.[108]

At the same time, ASCAP refused membership to composers of country and western or race music, at least in any significant numbers. So when, in 1940, ASCAP proposed increasing the fees for playing songs on the radio by 100%, the radio stations revolted and helped to establish Broadcast Music Incorporated (BMI)[109] as an alternative to ASCAP.

BMI filled the gap by licensing race music, including blues and rhythm and blues, in addition to country and western offerings. As ASCAP continued to demand higher payments from the radio stations, some stations actually banned ASCAP-licensed music. ASCAP and the stations eventually negotiated their differences, but by then BMI had established a strong foothold. By the end of 1940, 650 broadcasters had signed on with BMI, while ASCAP had only 200 left. BMI had cornered the market on country and western music and all but the most-acceptable-to-whites music created by blacks.[110]

The Effects of World War II

Unlike more recent wars, World War II enjoyed the almost unanimous support of the American public. The entertainment industry as a whole was supportive of the war effort and the singing groups played an important and observable role.

The most visible and photographed of the groups was the Andrews Sisters, who entertained the troops, helped to sell War Bonds and appeared in patriotic movies. The publicity photo of the Andrews Sisters for the movie, "Buck Privates," from 1941, showing them in uniform saluting, has become iconic; "Boogie Woogie Bugle Boy" came out of this movie and received an Oscar nomination. John Sforza said of this song, "It was vocal perfection for the sisters, and that sound became the definitive voice of the 1940s. Perhaps no other song or performance brings World War II to mind so quickly and unmistakably."[111]

---

[108] This is much the same argument that was used by independent record company executives in the 1950s to underpay the young and naïve members of vocal groups, telling them that they were gaining exposure that would lead to fame. Needless to say, the record company execs became wealthy and the groups did not.
[109] It was founded in 1939.
[110] http://jazzstandards.com/history/ (accessed January 16, 2009)
[111] Sforza, p.57

Andrews Sisters

The Andrews Sisters other war-related songs included "Any Bonds Today" (1941), "Don't Sit Under The Apple Tree" (1942), "Corns For My Country" (1944), and two with Bing Crosby — "Shoo-Shoo Baby" and "(There'll Be A) Hot Time in the Town of Berlin" (both from 1944).

Among the other groups that recorded war-related songs were the Five Red Caps with "Mama Put Your Britches On" (1943), the Charioteers with "We'll Meet Again" (1940), "A Slip Of the Lip Can Sink A Ship" (1943) and "The General Jumped At Dawn" (Kraft Music Hall Radio Show, June 29, 1944); the Four Vagabonds with "Hip Hip Hooray" (1942), "Comin' In On A Wing And A Prayer" (1943), "Jumpin" With A G.I. Gal" (1943), "Rose Ann Of Charing Cross" (1943), "Rosie The Riveter" (1943), "Stick To Your Knittin' Kitten" (1943) and "Ten Little Soldiers" (1943). The Song Spinners and Golden Gate Quartet both put out versions of "Comin' In On A Wing And A Prayer" in 1943.

The recording ban prevented much new music from reaching the troops. Lt. George Robert Vincent, who was in charge of distributing transcription recordings of radio shows to the troops, proposed a solution. He suggested that the Army make its own records that could be delivered to the men on a regular basis. James Petrillo gave his permission for the project.[112] "In July 1943, Petrillo seemed to loosen up a bit. He said the union would allow recordings to be made, provided that their only purpose was for Service Canteen jukeboxes. This wasn't as altruistic as it sounds. There were about 7.5 million servicemen at this time, and bandleaders must have been pressuring Petrillo to allow them to reach this concentrated captive audience. The war would be over someday, and these were the

V-Disc featuring the Ink Spots

---

[112] http://kzoo.edu/~ahilgart/vdisc.htm (accessed January 16, 2009)

listeners whose tastes would shape postwar music."[113] The first V-Discs (V for Victory) were shipped from Camden, New Jersey, in 1943. The result was a wealth of recordings that paint a vivid picture of the music scene of the time.

The combination of the ban and the war effort helped to bring an end to the Big Band era by the mid-forties. A tax was levied on all entertainment and that affected profitability for the labor-intensive big bands. Many band members left to join the armed forces, and their departures made producing consistently high-quality music difficult for the remaining core musicians. In 1946, the Benny Goodman, Jack Teagarden, Ina Ray Hutton, Tommy Dorsey, Woody Herman, Harry James and Benny Carter bands all folded.

The war also changed people's habits. They went out to dance less, spending more time at home in front of the family radio. During the ban, singers, either by themselves or in vocal groups, were the only ones still recording. By the time the war ended, the singers' popularity had eclipsed that of the bands.

Technology

As before, major advances in technology affected how people got their music. In 1940, regular FM radio broadcasting began in New York City.[114] The American Broadcasting Network (ABC) opened for business on June 14, 1945, after taking over the NBC Radio Blue Network.[115] The proliferation of the jukebox also contributed greatly to the growth of popular music, including that of the groups. And by the end of the decade, television was in full swing, replacing radio as the entertainment medium of choice.

The record industry itself was experiencing vast changes. With the Japanese controlling parts of Asia during World War II, there was a shortage of the shellac needed to make records. As a result, the first vinyl record was released by RCA in 1946. The first long playing, or "LP" record, a classical piece by violinist Yehudi Menuhin, was issued by Columbia in 1948. The LP played at 33 rpm and contained 25 minutes of recording on one side, an enormous improvement over the 78 rpm standard. Even so, it would be another ten years before the LP gained popularity.

In 1949, RCA countered with a 45 rpm record that featured a large hole in the middle.[116] The speed was arrived at by subtracting 33 from 78. These new smaller, lighter,

---

[113] Goldberg, p.110
[114] http://www.classicthemes.com/technologyTimeline.html (accessed January 16, 2009)
[115] http://www.classicthemes.com (accessed January 16, 2009)
[116] The large hole was to make it easier for jukebox mechanisms to handle the record. See, http://en.wikipedia.org/wiki/Gramophone_record (accessed January 16, 2009)

less fragile singles could hold about three minutes of recording per side. Songs would not routinely exceed that length until the 1960s. Being smaller and harder to break, 45s were the perfect medium for the teenage rush to rock 'n' roll that would occur in the 1950s.

Tape Recorder

Although reel-to-reel tape recording was not much of a factor until the end of the period covered by this book (1850-1950), it has an interesting origin. Modern tape recording was invented in Germany around 1930. After WWII, Jack Mullin, a member of the U.S. Army Signal Corps, and an audio engineer before the war, was able to acquire two Magnetophon recorders and proprietary tapes in Germany and ship them home. After coming stateside, Mullin developed similar machines for commercial use.[117]

After Mullin demonstrated his machine for MGM Studios in 1947, that resulted in a meeting with Bing Crosby, who realized that the invention might be able to be used to record radio broadcasts. "Crosby invested $50,000 in a local electronics company, Ampex, to enable Mullin to develop a commercial production model of the tape recorder. Using Mullin's tape recorders and with Mullin as his chief engineer, Crosby became the first American performer to master commercial recordings on tape and the first to regularly pre-record his radio programs on the medium. Ampex and Mullin subsequently developed commercial stereo and multitrack audio recorders, based on the system invented by musician Les Paul, who had been given one of the first Ampex Model 200 tape decks by Crosby in 1948."[118]

Soundies

Soundies were an early 1940s phenomenon that, while short-lived in their initial form, were actually a precursor to the music videos that are all-pervasive today. Soundies were two- or three-minute musical numbers on 16mm film, usually shown in groups of eight together on one reel, and played in a loop by a rear projector called a Panoram. They were viewed by putting a coin in a juke box-type device that caused the film to run. Minoco and RCM Productions (started by FDR's son, James Roosevelt) were the major companies

Panoram

---

[117] http://www.pavekmuseum.org (accessed January 16, 2009)
[118] http://en.wikipedia.org/wiki/Reel-to-reel_audio_tape_recording (accessed January 16, 2009)

producing Soundies, while nightclubs and other public places served as the primary venues for these films. The Soundies gave vocal groups such as the Ink Spots, Mills Brothers, Delta Rhythm Boys and the Deep River Boys the public exposure that would otherwise not have been available to them.

Transcriptions

Transcriptions were recordings of live performances that could be saved for later broadcast or distributed to radio stations; they represented the height of technology for archiving music before the advent of tape and digital media. The format was normally a 16" diameter record with either an aluminum core covered with lacquer, or a glass core covered with lacquer or vinyl. Frederic Ziv founded the first radio transcription service in 1937, when he recorded and distributed a Cincinnati radio show — "The Freshest Thing In Town" — for a local baker.[119] Some of the vocal groups that appeared in live performances on transcription recordings were the Charioteers, Delta Rhythm Boys, Deep River Boys, Fisk Jubilee Singers (obviously, not the original grouping!), Four Knights, Four Vagabonds, Ink Spots, Jubalaires and the Golden Gate Quartet. These live performances by vocal groups are available to us today only because of the transcription recordings that were made of them.

As an example of the impact of transcription recordings, consider this observation from Walter J. Beaupre, a professor of speech who started his working career in early radio:

> When I first began to work in a local broadcasting station in 1944, it was not what was there but what was missing that surprised me. Studio "A" was a floating, soundproof room complete with Hammond organ, Novachord, Steinway studio grand piano, and extensive sheet music files. Studio "B" also had a smaller piano which was tuned regularly for broadcast use. There were class "C" phone lines to the Yankee Network in Boston and the Mutual Broadcasting System in New York which provided "live" network music programs. . . .What I couldn't find anywhere at WCOU was a library of 78 rpm phonograph records! True, sitting on one of the cabinets in the control room were a dozen or so 10 inch records, each of which carried the warning, "Not licensed for broadcast." Of course, most of the time the record companies ignored the fact that their recordings were played on the air because this boosted sales. . . .The key pieces of furniture in the control room other than the RCA broadcast console and two RCA turntables were two oversized file cabinets which

---
[119] http://www.broadcastingcable.com (accessed January 16, 2009)

contained 16-inch discs. These electrical transcriptions were the extent of the station's library of recorded music.[120]

Record Charts

Tracking the popularity of various songs came to matter greatly to the public, the record companies and the artists themselves. *Billboard* began in 1894 as a magazine called "Billboard Advertising" that was concerned, strangely enough, with the billposting industry. The magazine made its first foray into the entertainment world in 1896 when it began covering fairs, and it first carried advertising for sheet music in 1902. In 1914, a feature called "Popular Songs Heard in Vaudevil" (sic) appeared and was quickly renamed "The Billboard's Song Chart." In 1936, "Chart Line," which covered the songs that were played most frequently by the three major radio networks, made its debut; however, it was not until 1940 that *Billboard* introduced the first comprehensive charts that tracked record sales.

In 1942, the magazine recognized the importance of black music with the establishment of the "Harlem Hit Parade" which later turned into the R&B charts.[121] Jerry Wexler, later of Atlantic Records, is credited with persuading the magazine to use the term "rhythm and blues" instead of "Race" records.[122]

In 1948, RCA Victor had begun to call the race records "blues and rhythm." Wexler reversed the order of the words.[123] He later joined Atlantic records, the premier R&B label of the early years. While R&B had its beginnings in the 1940s, it would reach its apex in the 1950s with groups such as the Drifters, Five Keys, Flamingos, Harptones, Moonglows, Teenagers and others.

The Jukebox

Coin-operated music devices (such as player pianos and phonographs) were around in the late nineteenth century. A primitive automatic record changer was invented in 1918, and by 1927 there was an automatic phonograph.

---

[120] http://otrsite.com/articles/artwb006.html (accessed January 16, 2009)
[121] http://www.billboard.com (accessed January 16, 2009)
[122] "It is important to point out that Race records (and the R&B follow-up) included anything by black artists: e.g., blues, big band, jazz, gospel. As long as the artist was black and not of a caliber of a Louis Jordan, it was Race." Email from Marv Goldberg, March 3, 2009
[123] http://www.newworldencyclopedia.org/entry/Rhythm_and_blues (accessed January 16, 2009)

In 1907, J. P. Seeburg, a Swedish immigrant, started a manufacturing company under his own name. The J. P. Seeburg Piano Co. began making automatic pianos called Orchestrions, but eventually they stopped making pianos and started to concentrate on the jukebox. Their first coin-op multiple record player appeared in 1928 and offered a choice of eight records. The company met with modest success until 1949 when they designed a machine that could play both sides of 50 records. In 1950, they became the first to manufacture a jukebox[124] to play 45 rpm records. As the jukebox market declined, they went out of business in the U.S. in the 1970s.

Wurlitzer, the other major brand, had been in the music business for several hundred years in Germany. In the 1850s, they began operations in the U.S. and became the largest instrument supplier in America. They also manufactured their own pianos and had piano stores. As mentioned, in the late 1800s, they put a coin slot on a player piano and started the coin-operated music boom:[125] "Jukeboxes and their ancestors were a very profitable industry from the 1890s on. They were most popular from the 1940s through the mid-1960s, particularly during the 1950s. Today jukeboxes are often associated with early rock and roll music, but were very popular in the swing music era as well. As a result, stores and restaurants with a retro theme, such as the Johnny Rockets chain, include jukeboxes."[126] By the middle of the 1940s, three-quarters of the records produced in America found their way into jukeboxes.

Groups Whose Popularity Carried Over From the 1930s

The Mills Brothers continued to be successful as the decades passed. The group had smash hits with "Paper Doll" (1943), "Till Then" (1944) and "Glow Worm" (1952), all on Decca. Truly a prolific and well-loved group, they appeared in eleven films, from "The Big Broadcast" in 1932 to "The Big Beat" in 1958. The Mills Brothers were the vocal group with longest span between first and last chart hits — 1931 to 1968. When their father died in 1956, the group continued on as a trio. Donald died in 1999, having performed in a duo with his son during the last years of his life.

Two of the most innovative items in the Mills Brothers repertoire were the imitation of instruments, described in the previous chapter, and the use of story songs . The story songs told a tale of an individual or event, as opposed to most popular songs, which dealt with

---

[124] The term jukebox came into usage around 1940, as did "juke joint," both stemming from a Gullah word for rowdy or wicked. See, http://en.wikipedia.org/wiki/jukebox (accessed January 16, 2009)
[125] http://www.nationaljukebox.com/home.htm (accessed January 16, 2009)
[126] http://www.dcwstore.com/ (accessed September 13, 2010)

some aspect of love or the loss of love. Examples of the group's story songs can be found in "Miss Otis Regrets" (1934), "Shoe Shine Boy" (1936), "Just A Kid Named Joe" (1938) and "Side Kick Joe" (1939). Some sample lyrics from "Just A Kid Named Joe" are:

> Just a kid named Joe
> What his second name is I don't know
> He sells the daily papers
> And so I buy all my papers from a kid named Joe.

and "Side Kick Joe" tells a story of betrayal:

> Then one evening
> While the coyotes were a howlin' in the dew
> Oh we happened to strike yellow
> And we split it 50-50 twixt the two.
> Now he was just my pal
> Man ain't never had a better pal
> [New voice] Oh oh, he stole your horse, your gal and all your dough
> Ain't never seen the likes of Sidekick Joe.

The Mills Brothers even tried a Hawaiian song in "My Little Grass Shack" (1934). Twenty-six years later, the Hi-Lo's released their own version, but had to fudge it on the Hawaiian words, "komo mai no kaua i ka hale welakahau." The Mills Brothers had no such trouble. They were truly a seminal group and not just for musical reasons. Jay Warner says: "The Mills Brothers' influence was pervasive: they made black music acceptable to a wide audience and encouraged other black vocalists to carry on what they had started. And lest we forget, they did it with dignity and grace in difficult racial times, carried forward by their warmth of character and mellow sound."[127]

The Andrews Sisters were far and away the most popular female group of the 1940s. Their hit recordings include, "Say Si, Si" (which reached number four on the charts), "The Woodpecker Song" (#6), "Ferryboat Serenade" (#1) and "Beat Me Daddy Eight To The Bar" (#2), all in 1940; "Boogie Woogie Bugle Boy" (#6), "I'll Be With You In Apple Blossom Time" (#5) (both from 1941); and "The Shrine Of St. Cecilia" (#3) and "Strip Polka" (#6) (both in 1942). In 1943, "Shoo-Shoo Baby" spent nine weeks at number one

---

[127] http://www.vocalgroup.org/inductees/mills_brothers.html (accessed January 16, 2009)

and 21 total weeks altogether on the charts, while "Rum And Coca-Cola" was number one for ten weeks and had 20 total weeks on the chart in 1945. "I Can Dream, Can't I?" was the Sisters' last Top Ten song, reaching number one for five weeks and remaining on the charts for 25 total weeks in 1949 and 1950.

In all, from 1938 to 1951, the Andrews Sisters charted 90 times! The versatile trio also appeared in 17 movies, including "In The Navy" (1941), "Buck Privates" (1941) and "Follow The Boys" (1944). In many of their films and in personal appearances the Sisters also performed dance routines. Amazingly, in the films they did for Universal, the company would not allow them to learn the dances on "company time," so they had to hire a private choreographer to teach them the steps.[128] LaVerne died in 1967 and Maxene in 1996. As of this writing, Patty is still alive.

The last of the "Big Three" groups of this era, especially in terms of their popularity with white audiences, was the Ink Spots, who reached the charts 46 times from 1939 to 1951, with six of their offerings hitting number one. Like the Mills Brothers and the Andrews Sisters, the Ink Spots also recorded for Decca. Their hits included "If I Didn't Care" (#2) and "Address Unknown" (#1) both in 1939; "When The Swallows Come Back To Capistrano" (#4), "Whispering Grass" (#10), "Maybe" (#2), "We Three" (#1) and "Java Jive" (#15) in 1940; "Do I Worry" (#8) and "I Don't Want To Set The World On Fire" (#4) in 1941; "Don't Get Around Much Anymore" (#2) in 1943; "I'm Making Believe" (#1) and "Into Each Life Some Rain Must Fall" (#1) in 1944; and "The Gypsy" (#1) and "To Each His Own" (#1) in 1946.

The Ink Spots appeared in two movies, "The Great American Broadcast" in 1941 and "Pardon My Sarong" in 1942. Their great bass, Hoppy Jones, died in 1944 and was replaced at first by Cliff Givens, and then by Bill Kenny's brother, Herb. The story goes that Herb stopped by to say hello while the Ink Spots were auditioning for a new bass. One of the applicants wasn't getting it right so Herb stepped into show him how and ended up getting the job. Over the years, Bill Kenny clashed with Deek Watson over the content of their act; Kenny preferred straight singing while Watson liked the comedy numbers. Watson soon left the Spots to form his own group with a derivative name: the Brown Dots.

The Charioteers featured Billy Williams, who many consider to have been one of the top lead voices of the day. Williams had a sweet high tenor, that like Bill Kenny's voice, was unmistakable. The group did quite a bit of backup work for singers such as Pearl Bailey, Frank Sinatra and Crosby, and also sang with the Eddy Duchin Band. Their song, "A Kiss And A Rose" (1949 on Columbia), made the Top 10 on the R&B charts and is a

---

[128] Sforza, p. 57

classic, characterized by Williams' beautiful high tenor lead. Williams left the group in 1949 and formed the Billy Williams Quartet; the Charioteers disbanded in the 1950s. Williams died penniless in Chicago in 1972 while living in a donated room in a church basement. As Jay Warner said, "Given the Charioteers' lack of hits, it was pure talent, performance popularity, and relatively stable membership that kept them together for 26 years..."[129]

The Billy Williams Quartet had a Top Ten Pop and R&B hit with "I'm Gonna Sit Right Down And Write Myself A Letter" in 1957 on Coral and appeared on television on Sid Caesar's "Your Show Of Shows."

The three major mixed-gender groups with female leads — the Merry Macs, Modernaires and Pied Pipers, all formed in the 1920s or 30s — continued to meet with success in the 1940s, both with big bands and on their own. The Merry Macs, who dated back to the mid-1920s, continued to perform through the 1960s, despite losing brother Joe McMichael (who was replaced by Lynn Allen) in the Second World War.

Billy Williams Quartet

The group's biggest hit was the novelty tune, "Mairzy Doats" (1944), but they also charted nine other times in the 1940s, including "Jingle Jangle Jingle" and "Praise The Lord And Pass The Ammunition" (both in 1942), "Pretty Kitty Blue Eyes" (1944), and "Laughing On The Outside" (1946), all on Decca. They also accompanied Bing Crosby on several numbers in the early 1940s.

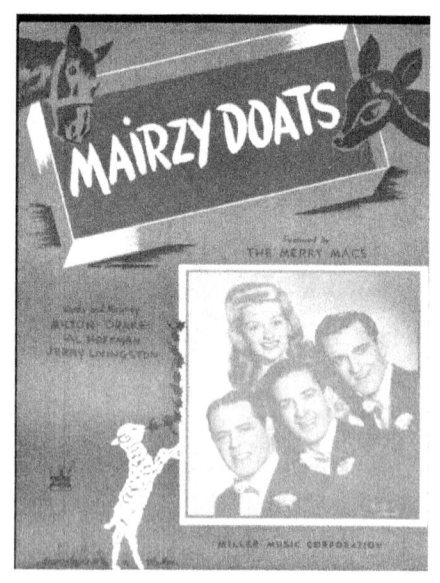

In 1941, the Modernaires joined the Glenn Miller Orchestra and stayed for two years. Paula Kelly, who had previously been with both Al Donahue and Artie

Merry Macs

---

[129] http://www.vocalgroup.org/inductees/the_charioteers.html (accessed January 16, 2009)

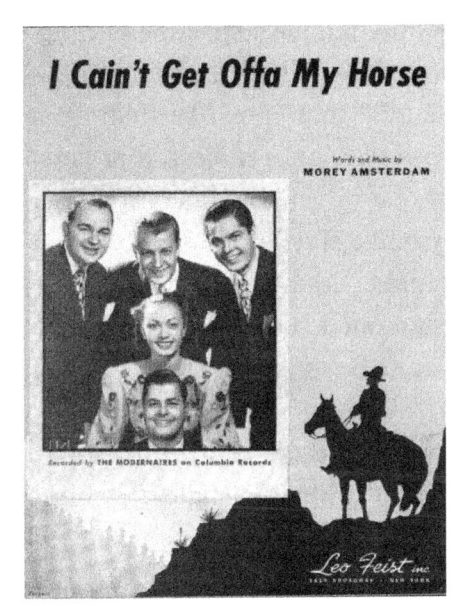

Modernaires

Shaw, joined Miller's band as a soloist. She became a member of the Modernaires and married Hal Dickinson. The group's hits included "Chattanooga Choo Choo" (1941, on Bluebird), "Don't Sit Under The Apple Tree (With Anyone Else But Me)" (1942, on Bluebird), "(I've Got A Gal) In Kalamazoo" (1942, on Victor) and "Juke Box Saturday Night" (1942, on Victor), all with Miller's orchestra. Aside from their work with Miller, they charted six other times in the 1940s.

The Pied Pipers had hits both with and without Tommy Dorsey, charting twelve times in the 1940s without the famous bandleader. The original group consisted of eight members, but Dorsey cut them back to a quartet that consisted of John Huddleston, Chuck Lowry, Billy Wilson and Jo Stafford. Wilson was replaced by Clark Yocum, and when Huddleston went into the armed forces, one of the original eight members, Hal Hopper, took his place. They were an immensely popular group that used innovative harmonies and charted with "Mairzy Doats" and "Trolley Song" (both in 1943) and "Dream" in 1945, all on Capitol. Stafford began to pursue a solo career while still with the Pipers and then left the group in 1944. June Hutton, the sister of female bandleader Ina Ray Hutton, replaced Stafford. June had previously sung in Charlie Spivak's band with the Stardusters. Author and record producer George T. Simon called her "the greatest lead voice ever to have sung with any vocal group,"[130] although the devotees of singers such as Bill Kenny and Billy Williams might have some quarrel with that blanket statement.

Other groups from the thirties that continued to make their mark were the King Sisters, Deep River Boys and the Delta Rhythm Boys. The King Sisters

Pied Pipers

---

[130] Simon, George T. *The Big Bands*. New York: The Macmillan Company, 1967, page 427

appeared on radio shows and in movies during the 1940s, and did guest spots on television in the 1950s. Finally, in 1965, they got their own TV show, "The King Family," on ABC, but it lasted for only one year. The King Sisters were one of the first, if not the first, female quartet to record in four-part close harmony with a jazzy style, not unlike a four-person version of the Boswells. Their biggest hit was "It's Love-Love-Love" for Bluebird in 1944. In the 1950s, they adopted a modern, unorthodox harmony in the style of the Hi-Lo's.

Many of the black groups still faced a lot of racial prejudice in the U.S. and some went to Europe, where race was not as much of an issue, and had good success. The three most prominent groups to travel that road were the Delta Rhythm Boys, Deep River Boys and Golden Gate Quartet.

The Delta Rhythm Boys appeared in more movies than any other singing group, black or white. They opened the decade of the 1940s by touring with Bill "Bojangles" Robinson and made regular appearances on the "Amos and Andy Show." The Deltas had hits in 1946 with "Just A-Sittin' And A-Rockin'" (Decca) and "Don't Ask Me Why" (RCA). Carl Jones, in a 2001 interview with Jason Gross, said that many of their vocals were patterned after orchestra arrangements. "If the trumpet [had] a solo, we kept the trumpet there and put words there and sang the trumpet part." Jones said his inspiration was the Merry Macs. What he liked about them was that they put their female voice on top as the lead — "rather than having the traditional quartet with the tenor over the top [of the lead] and baritone and bass underneath. That was basically how we did the Deltas' arrangements, especially after I joined the group." Jones also spoke about his impressions on meeting the group members when he was considering joining them: "I was quite impressed with them. They had the music all written out and everything. That impressed me too — in those days, most black quartets did head arrangements. They didn't know anything about writing music; they just got together and harmonized. But these guys were all musicians, they read music, they had the charts." Jones also confirmed that the Delta Rhythm Boys did some recording for Atlantic under the name of the Four Sharps.[131] Jay Warner said of the group's version of "Take The A Train" (in 1941 on Decca), that it started the vocalese style later used by many groups such as Manhattan Transfer.[132]

The Delta Rhythm Boys spent considerable time in Europe, particularly in London and Stockholm, where they were extremely popular. When their Lee Gaines died in 1987, former member Hugh Bryant sang at the funeral and, in what could have been a scene out of a movie, dropped dead as he finished his musical eulogy.

---

[131] All from interview by Jason Gross in 2001, http://www.furious.com/perfect/deltarhythmboys.html (accessed March 26, 2012)
[132] Warner p. 24

The Deep River Boys had only one chart hit, "Recess In Heaven" on RCA Victor in 1948. Like the Delta Rhythm Boys, the Deep River Boys toured with Bill "Bojangles" Robinson. They also made TV appearances on the Ed Sullivan and Milton Berle shows. After World War II, they spent a considerable time in London where they had a record-breaking ten-week stay at the London Palladium in 1953.

Black Groups Making Their Mark in the Early 1940s

Using a name that would become well-known about 20 years later, the Four Aces were a black group from Texas, as opposed to the white pop group that was popular in the 1950s. The original Four Aces had three members who served as entertainers during World War II. After the war, the group played clubs in the San Francisco area, did some traveling for gigs, and continued to record. Marv Goldberg said, "The Four Aces were one of the many transitional groups that took small-combo R&B into the 1950s. Possibly things would have been different for them had the white Four Aces not come along, but probably not. There were many, many of these small combos, some of which recorded, but almost completely without success (the only outstanding exceptions were the King Cole Trio and Johnny Moore's Three Blazers). However, they did manage to remain together for over 10 years (16, if you count the pre-war days), which is a tribute to their talent."[133]

The quintessential jive group was the Cats & The Fiddle,[134] who began their career in the late 1930s in Chicago with Austin Powell (lead), Jimmie Henderson (first tenor), Ernie Price (second tenor) and Chuck Barksdale (bass). A self-contained group that

Cats & the Fiddle

---
[133] http://home.att.net/~marvy42/4Aces/4aces.html (accessed January 16, 2009)
[134] "Jive" can mean a fast dance style to swing music or a slang, double-talk way of speaking. For our purposes, it refers to harmony a group that plays its own instruments with a lively type of music, using lyrics that usually made great use of the jive speech idioms.

played their own instruments, they credited the Spirits of Rhythm as being one of their biggest influences. "I Miss You So," written by Henderson and recorded in 1940 for Bluebird, was their biggest hit. Dave Penny called the song, "truly one of Doo Wop's seminal recordings."[135]

The Cats & The Fiddle appeared in several movies and recorded over 30 sides. The *All Music Guide* said: "If anything, the Cats & the Fiddle were ahead of their time, producing a bolder form of R&B than critics were prepared to accept at the time, such as 'That's All I Mean To You,' which likely would have slotted in perfectly a decade later, but in 1940 just seemed like style-less noise with a swing beat. They potentially offered a sound very different from the smooth model of the Mills Brothers, but found precious few positive notices to encourage them, though audiences at their performances were won over."[136]

Also out of Chicago was the Lewis Bronzeville Five, originally known as the Five Aces Of Rhythm, and featuring Royale Brent as lead. They played their own instruments, and recorded a number of appealing sides for Bluebird in 1940 in the jive idiom. Their songs included "Cotton Blossom Blues," "It Can Happen To You," "Laughing At Life," "Linda Brown," "Natchez Mississippi Blues," "Oh! Mabel, Oh!" and "Mississippi Fire Blues." The last song tells, in a haunting train-like rhythm, the story of a fire at the Rhythm Club in Natchez in 1940 where more than 200 people were killed, including most of the members of the Walter Barnes Orchestra. After a bad experience with a dishonest manager, the Lewis Bronzeville Five disbanded in 1941.

The Four Blazes, who were started by Paul Lindsley "Jelly" Holt in Chicago in 1940, added a member and changed their name to the Five Blazes in 1946. Each member of the group also played an instrument. They had R&B hits with "Please Send Her Back To Me" (1952) and "Perfect Woman" (1953) on United. As late as the mid-1950s they were still touring and were one of the bridge groups between the jive/blues combos of the 1940s and the more youthful R&B groups of the 1950s. The Four Blazes' most popular song was "Mary Jo" on United in 1952, with Tommy Braden on lead. Like many of the leads of this era, Braden's voice was sweet and husky, perfect for the group's repertoire. "Mary Jo" — "sly as a fox and dangerous as a grizzly bear" — provided the group with a number one R&B hit.

The Four Vagabonds began in St. Louis in 1933, but all of their significant recordings were made in the 1940s. The original members were lead John Jordan (lead) Robert O'Neal (first tenor), Norval Taborn (baritone) and Ray Grant, who sang bass and played guitar. When John Mills, Jr. died suddenly in 1936, the Four Vagabonds replaced the Mills

---

[135] Penny, Dave. Liner notes for the CD, "The Jive Is Jumpin'." WestSide 813
[136] http://www.allmusic.com/ (accessed January 16, 2009)

Brothers on a radio show, leading to a long string of appearances from 1936 to 1946 on Don McNeil's Breakfast Club radio show in Chicago. Their biggest hit was "P.S. I Love You" on Apollo in 1947, and they had an R&B chart hit with "It Can't Be Wrong" in 1943 on Bluebird. One of the most underrated groups of the era, the Four Vagabonds took the imitation of instruments to new heights. A remarkable example of this is found on "Rosie the Riveter" from 1943. Ray Grant began to grow blind in the mid-1940s, but he continued to appear at live performances without the audiences being aware of his condition. The group disbanded in 1952.

Four Vagabonds

The Jubalaires grew out of the Royal Harmony Quartet and were greatly influenced by the Golden Gate Quartet. The members were J. C. Ginyard (tenor), Theodore Brooks (baritone), Orville Brooks (tenor), John Jennings (tenor), George McFadden (bass) and Everett Barksdale (guitar), although perhaps not all at the same time. In the early 1940s, the group appeared on the Arthur Godfrey radio program. At one point Orville Brooks borrowed three singers from the Melody Kings and went on tour while the remaining three Jubilaires stayed behind to perform on the Godfrey show. They were also on the Phil Harris Show. Willie Johnson, formerly of the Golden Gate Quartet, joined them in 1948 and Ginyard left soon thereafter. The Jubalaires charted in 1946 with "I Know" on Decca, and in 1950 with "The Old Piano Roll Blues," on Capitol. Ginyard had a prolific career, also singing with the Dixieaires, Du Droppers and Golden Gate Quartet.

In 1943, The Five Red Caps were formed in Los Angeles from what had previously been members of the Four Toppers. The group featured two leads — Steve Gibson, a bass, and Jimmy Springs, a tenor.

Five Red Caps

Several members came from the Jones Boys Sing Band. The Red Caps had more than 30 releases on Beacon, four of which made the R&B Charts, including the beautiful "Just For You." Some of their novelty tunes are dated in style and content, and contain what are, today, unacceptable racial stereotypes. Examples are "Grand Central Station" (Beacon-1943) with its "It sure am" conclusion and "Tuscaloosa" (Beacon-1943) with its "It sure are" ending, both in "Stepin Fetchit"-style.[137] They charted with the ballad "I Learned A Lesson I'll Never Forget" (1944, on Beacon). In 1946 the group became known as Steve Gibson and The Red Caps, and they continued performing until the mid-1960s.

The White Pop Groups of the 1940s

After the success of the Boswell and Andrews Sisters in the 1930s, female groups continued to find new audiences. The Moon Maids were a female quartet (and sometimes, quintet) from Texas that sang with the Vaughn Monroe orchestra starting in 1946. The original members were Mary Jo Thomas, Maree Lee (of the Lee Sisters), Tinker Cunningham and June Hiett. Mary Jo Grogan (née Thomas) said: "We gals were lucky, in one sense, but we also worked to make it happen! We sang everywhere--and to anyone who would listen. We sang in bus stations, restrooms, walking down the street. Wherever we were — we sang. Sooner or later, doing that, you are bound to bump into an opportunity, which we did. Before we became the Moon Maids, we were a part of a USO tour —- singing to the WWII injured military men in hospitals. We were a college vocal group, known THERE as The Swingtet. Lots of opportunities to sing there . . . and to gain experience and confidence. It's such a kick to be part of a chord where everyone has his own note — often 5 different notes —- singing harmony a step apart often times."[138] The Moon Maids disbanded in 1952.

The Dinning Sisters came from an Oklahoma family of nine children, all but one of whom entered the music business. The group consisted of Jean and Ginger, who were twins, and Lou, who got married in

Dinning Sisters

---

[137] Stepin Fetchit was an actor whose real name was Lincoln Theodore Monroe Andrew Perry. On stage and in film he played a lazy, not-so-smart black man, offending many blacks in the process. Actually, Perry was intelligent and wrote articles for the *Chicago Defender*, the country's best known newspaper for blacks. http://www.imdb.com/name/nm0275297/bio (accessed January 16, 2009)

[138] Email, Mary Jo Grogan (nee Thomas) January 21, 2004

1946 and was replaced by non-family member Jayne Bundesen. In 1949, Bundesen left and Tootsie Dinning replaced her making them an all-family ensemble once again. The Dinning Sisters sang on NBC radio with their own daily show for seven years and recorded on Capitol, having an album that was number one on the national charts for 18 weeks. "My Adobe Hacienda" (1947), "I Wonder Who's Kissing Her Now" (1947), "Beg Your Pardon" (1948) and "Buttons And Bows" (1948) all charted. After the group disbanded in the early 1950s, Jean wrote the hit song "Teen Angel" for her brother, Mark Dinning, and Tootsie sang on the country and western television show, "Hee Haw."

From Sheboygan, Wisconsin, the Chordettes were a quartet consisting of Janet Ertel, Alice Buschmann, Jinny Lockard and Dorothy Hummitzsch that started out by singing barbershop. They appeared regularly on the Arthur Godfrey Show in the late 1940s and early 1950s. Their hits included "Mr. Sandman" (1954), "Born To Be With You" (1956), "Just Between You And Me" (1957) and "Lollipop" (1958), all on the Cadence label. The male voice on "Lollipop" was Archie Bleyer (Arthur Godfrey's band leader) who was married to Ertel.[139] The group disbanded in 1963.

The Clark Sisters — Peggy, Mary, Jean and Ann, from Minnesota — sang with the Blue Barron Band in the 1930s. In 1944, they joined the Tommy Dorsey Band (replacing the Pied Pipers), and Dorsey named them the "Sentimentalists" after his signature tune, "I'm Getting Sentimental Over You." They left Dorsey, but returned in 1947 to record, with Lillian Clark (who later married arranger Sy Oliver) replacing Mary.

Ed, Gene, Joe and Vic Urick from Malden, Massachusetts, formed a group and called themselves the Ames Brothers. Bandleader Russ Morgan helped them start their career when he featured them on his recording "Forever And Ever," a number one hit in 1949 on Decca. The Ames Brothers became a very successful pop group, charting over 20 times from the late 1940s through the mid-1950s. Their biggest hit was "The Naughty Lady of Shady Lane" on RCA Victor in 1954 and they had their own television

Ames Brothers

---

[139] Ertel's daughter was married to Phil Everly.

Mel Tormé and his Mel-Tones

series in 1955. Ed Ames had a successful solo career as a singer and actor, including a very famous moment in 1965 with a tomahawk on "The Tonight Show." Ed was showing Johnny Carson how to throw the tomahawk, using a rough drawing of a cowboy on some wood planks as a target. Ames threw the tomahawk and it hit the target square in the crotch!

Mel Tormé formed a mixed-gender backup group, the Meltones, with Betty Beveridge, Ginny O'Connor,[140] Les Baxter (the famous arranger and orchestra leader) and Bernie Parke, to complement his incomparable voice. Tormé said, "What I tried to do with the Meltones, really, was to think of them as a sax section, and write for them that way."

Tormé continued, "I had to admit candidly that, first of all, the Six Hits And A Miss had simulated the sound of a band with a lot of the things they did, long before I had the Meltones, and they were a big factor in the way I wrote for the Meltones. So were the Modernaires and a lot of vocal groups, as a matter of fact. We were only a departure because we did sing some band figures as if there were two saxophone sections with Artie Shaw, rather than one. We tried to do it that way—and it seemed to work. . . . The reason for breaking the group up was that I was getting offers to go out as a single. And also the fact that, tragically, the best vocal groups in the world just didn't make it."[141] Tormé talks about the group Six Hits And A Miss as if the group originated the use of voices to replace instruments. However, they recorded in the 1940s, long after the Revelers, Comedian Harmonists, Delta Rhythm Boys and many others had pioneered the use of instrument replacement and imitation. It is hard to believe that Tormé was unfamiliar with the seminal work of these earlier groups, or did not think to give them credit. As for his comment that vocal

Six Hits and a Miss

---

[140] She later married Henry Mancini.
[141] http://www.jazzprofessional.com/ (accessed January 16, 2009)

groups had trouble making it, while this may have been true in the jazz idiom, it was certainly not true in the genres of vocal group rhythm and blues and doo-wop.

Six Hits And A Miss recorded on various labels in the early 1940s. They charted with "You'd Be So Nice To Come Home To" on Capital in 1943 and appeared in more than 15 movies. After reducing their number and morphing into Four Hits And A Miss, they appeared on the Autolite radio show along with Dick Haymes and Helen Forrest.

The musicians' recording ban gave groups such as the Song Spinners an opportunity to provide backing for soloists. They recorded on Decca and backed singers such as Dick Haymes and Bill Kenny. On their own, they reached Number One on the charts in 1943 with "Comin' In On A Wing And A Prayer."

The Sportsmen Quartet was best known for its appearances on the Jack Benny radio show. The group joined the Benny show in September 1946 and stayed through at least 1963. Prior to that the Sportsmen sang with the Gus Arnheim Orchestra and then on the Mel Blanc Show in 1946-47. Thurl Ravenscroft was the original bass of the group, but he went into the service in 1942. When Ravenscroft returned from the war, he formed another group, the Mellomen. Ravenscroft became the voice of Tony The Tiger in the famous cereal commercials. The Sportsmen charted with "Woody Woodpecker" (1948) and appeared in movies and did guest spots on TV shows such as "My Three Sons," where they were featured as singing waiters.

Sportsmen Quartet

Gospel

Although gospel groups do not fall within the scope of this book and have been covered in detail by others,[142] any history of American vocal groups would be incomplete if we did not at least mention some of the great ones, their contributions to the body of vocal group recordings and their influence on the genre.

---

[142] See, for example, *Encyclopedia of American Gospel Music*, W. K. McNeil, Editor, Rutledge, Taylor & Francis Group, 2005; *Uncloudy Days: The Gospel Music Encyclopedia*, Bil Carpenter, Mavis Staples and Edin Hawkins. Backbeat Books, 2005; *Gospel Music Encyclopedia*, Robert Anderson and Gail North, Sterling Publishing, 1979.

In the 1940s, "the new gospel music composed by Dorsey and others proved very important among quartets, who began turning in a new direction. Groups such as the Dixie Hummingbirds, Pilgrim Travelers, Soul Stirrers, Swan Silvertones, Sensational Nightingales and Five Blind Boys of Mississippi introduced even more stylistic freedom to the close harmonies of jubilee style, adding ad libs and using repeated short phrases in the background to maintain a rhythmic base for the innovations of the lead singers. Individual singers also stood out more as jubilee turned to 'hard gospel' and as soloists began to shout more and more, often in falsettos anchored by a prominent bass. Quartet singers combined both individual virtuoso performances and jack off innovative harmonic and rhythmic invention — what Ira Tucker Sr. and Paul Owens of the Hummingbirds called 'trickeration' — that amplified both the emotional and musical intensity of their songs."[143]

Dixie Hummingbirds

The Swan Silvertones, who were particularly well known for Claude Jeter's soaring falsetto, began in the West Virginia coal mines in 1938 as the Four Harmony Kings. In the 1940s, they became the Silvertone Singers and then the Swan Silvertones, named after the Swan Bakery that sponsored the radio show on which the group appeared.

Finally, the Five Blind Boys of Mississippi were formed at the Piney Woods School For The Blind in Jackson, Mississippi, in 1939.[144] Like the Fisk Singers, the Blind Boys were sent out from the school for fundraising purposes, under the name the "Cotton Blossom Singers." Archie Brownlee was the lead with one of these traveling groups and when he left school he continued to tour with the Jackson Harmoneers. "They evoked a style in which the group sang a repeated phrase, building up the tension to highlight Brownlee's ecstatic

Swan Silvertones

---

[143] http://en.wikipedia.org/wiki/Urban_contemporary_gospel (accessed January 16, 2009)
[144] A fairly well-known female group, the International Sweethearts of Rhythm, was also based at the school.

falsetto which could provoke scenes of religious hysteria in church and concert audiences."[145] Eileen Southern credited Brownlee "with being the first to interject falsetto shrieks and screams in gospel-quartet style . . . singing."[146]

Black Groups of the Late 1940s

The last half of the 1940s witnessed another wave of black groups that, although not successful in the pop ratings, were appreciated by audiences that followed the R&B charts. These groups sang in a variety of idioms, from popular secular music to jazz, rhythm and blues, or gospel-influenced styles.

The Basin Street Boys were out of Los Angeles by way of Philadelphia. Ormande Wilson, who had sung with the Plantation Boys and was taught guitar by Steve Gibson of the Red Caps, formed the group. The Basin Street Boys had their biggest hit in 1946 on Exclusive with "I Sold My Heart To The Junkman." The song has a great lyric, "I gave my heart to you, the one that I trusted, you brought it back to me all broken and busted, so I've sold my heart to the junkman and I'll never fall in love again." "Voot Nay On The Vot Nay" from 1946, was a song about a new form of jive. The group made its last recording in 1948 and disbanded in 1951.

Basin Street Boys

In 1944, when Deek Watson formed the Brown Dots, he wanted to use the Ink Spots name but was prevented from doing so by litigation. The name "Brown Dots" was an obvious, but legal, takeoff on the Ink Spots' name. A talented group of musicians out of New York City, by far their biggest song was the 1945 classic on Manor, "For Sentimental Reasons," written by Pat Best, a member of the group. Watson received co-writing credit.

---

[145] Hardy, Phil and Dave Lang. *The Da Capo Companion to 20th-Century Popular Music*. New York: Da Capo Press, Inc., 1990, 1995, p. 320
[146] Southern, p. 134

When differences arose in the Brown Dots in 1948, Best, Gordon and Nabbie secretly formed a new group they called the Sentimentalists, adding Danny Owens to replace Watson. However, Tommy Dorsey objected to the use of that name, since he had used it for the Clark Sisters when they worked for him. The group again changed its name, this time to the Four Tunes. This talented group had hits on Jubilee in the early 1950s, including "Marie" (1953) and "I Understand Just How You Feel" (1954). With Savannah Churchill, they had a Number One R&B song in "I Want To Be Loved," in 1947 on Manor, on which they were credited as the Sentimentalists. As the Four Tunes, they also charted with Churchill on "I Want To Cry" (1948, on Manor). In all, they made the R&B Charts five times. The Four Tunes split up in 1963.

Brown Dots

Four Tunes

The Dozier Boys headlined at the Beige Room in the Pershing Hotel in Chicago for many years and appeared on the early TV show, "Spotlight Talent," hosted by Al Benson, a well-known Chicago deejay. The members also played instruments, as did many groups of that era. Of note was "In A Travelling Mood" from 1948 on Aristocrat.

Another talented New York group was Bill Johnson & his Musical Notes. They were described by Marv Goldberg as "One of the finest groups you probably know nothing about . . . . You may not be familiar with their music, but others were. They recorded 'Don't You Think I Ought To Know' six years before the Orioles, 'How Would You Know' four years before the Robins, and 'Dream Of A Lifetime' seven years before the Flamingos."[147]

---

[147] http://home.att.net/~freebizak/MusicalNotes/ (accessed January 16, 2009)

A mixed-gender, black quartet, the Ginger Snaps had four releases on RCA Victor between 1945 and 1947, including "Juke Box Joe," as well as two releases on University in 1944-45. A photo of the group from a Soundie shows the members as one male and three women, but the sheet music for "Two Many Irons In The Fire" shows only the female members They also sang with the Jimmy Mundy band in the mid-1940s.

A gospel group that transformed itself into a pop group was the Four Knights who began as the Southland Jubilee Singers in Charlotte, North Carolina, in 1943. The original members of the Four Knights were Gene Alford (lead), John Wallace (second tenor and guitar) and Oscar Broadway (bass) with Clarence Dixon (baritone) joining them in 1944. They appeared on the Carolina Hayride radio show, the Arthur Godfrey Show in 1945 and the Red Skelton Show in 1948. In 1946, they began to record for Decca and had their biggest success with "I Get So Lonely When I Think About You" (1954, on Capitol Records), a song sometimes known by the title "Oh Baby Mine." "If I May" (1955, on Capitol) was a Top Ten song. They also backed Nat King Cole on a number of his recordings. The group broke up in the early 1960s. Broadway sang bass lead on many of their songs.

Ginger Snaps

Four Knights

The Five Scamps can trace their lineage to a 1937 group in Kansas called The Scamps. The newer version of the group began in 1947 in Kansas City, Missouri.[148] Despite their success and longevity, they never charted. Their most well-known recording was "Red Hot" on Columbia in 1949. Some 70 years later, with many personnel changes, they are still performing. That has to be a record!

---

[148] They recorded for Modern as the Scamps, and for Columbia as the Five Scamps.

Things To Come

After World War II, the music industry began to change. Petrillo's recording ban and the struggle between ASCAP and the radio stations in the early 1940s created significant and irreversible differences in the musical landscape. Because musicians were not allowed to record, the singers and vocal groups became more popular than the instrumentalists. The Big Bands lost musicians to the war, and the enormous cost of maintaining and transporting a large number of band members forced many of the big bands to fold in the middle of the decade. At the same time, the ASCAP crowd that produced popular music — including the large record labels such as RCA, Decca and Capitol — lost ground to the fledgling labels that were allied with BMI. Small operations like Apollo, Savoy, National, King, DeLuxe, Specialty, Modern and Aristocrat were able to grab a toehold and then flourish. These new labels hired relatively young and obscure minority talent and country and western artists instead of the popular "white bread" performers that were allied with ASCAP and the major labels.

While the new music released by the new labels did not ensure economic success, the growing post-war power of teenagers and their craving for a new, more exciting kind of music, provided the final pieces of the puzzle. Just like the rabid teen following engendered by Benny Goodman's band, and the hordes of "bobby soxers" that swooned to a young Frank Sinatra, teenagers were irresistibly drawn to a vocal group from Baltimore called the Orioles.

"It's Too Soon To Know," released by the Orioles in 1948, unleashed a change in popular music that was to spawn the early rhythm and blues/rock and roll era. As J. C. Marion says on his "Doo Wop Nation" website, "This is the true kicker-offer, the real opener-upper of the age of vocal group harmony. It all evolves from this recording."[149] "It's Too Soon To Know" was the first R&B song to gain a high level of success with both black and white audiences, rising to Number One on the race chart and breaking into the Top 15 on the pop charts.

You could not have picked a more unlikely candidate to write the breakthrough song than a Jewish store clerk in her twenties from Baltimore named Deborah Chessler. Her most likely role in rock and roll history ordinarily would have been as a screaming audience member; but by the time Chessler met up with the Vibra-Naires, as the Orioles were first called, she had already written a song that had been recorded by Dinah Washington and Savannah Churchill, a beautiful ballad called "Tell Me So" that did not sell very well.

---

[149] http://home.earthlink.net/~jaymar41/Ten_Records_That_Shook_The.html (accessed January 16, 2009)

One day a friend called Chessler and asked her if she was interested in listening to a local singing group, the Vibra-Naires. She said, "When?" Her friend answered, "Now." He had them sing for her over the phone. They sang four songs, "I Cover The Waterfront," "Two Loves Have I," "Exactly Like You" and "At Night." Chessler was drawn to the talent she could feel coming through the wire. When she hung up and told her mother about the call, her mother asked, "Are they any good?" Chessler responded, "No, they're great!" She realized that their style was perfect for the type of songs that she was writing and believed she could help them. At that time, the groups that Chessler was listening to were the Ink Spots, Mills Brothers, Charioteers and Ravens.

At about that same time, a boy she was dating told her he loved her, but she had not known him very long. She told her mother what the boy had said and her mother asked Chessler how she felt about him. Chessler answered, "It's too soon to know," and the writing of the song followed. When she wrote "It's Too Soon To Know" she did not know how special it was: "It was just a thought that came into my mind." She continued, "People loved the lyrics – the words rang true to people. And the Orioles' rendition was very well accepted." She said that when she read write-ups about the song on the internet and elsewhere she thought, "I don't know what it changed. There have always been good songs. But it certainly changed my life. It was shocking how fast the song was taken up."[150]

Orioles

The Vibra-Naires were led by Erlington Tilghman, who obviously was highly motivated to come up with his stage name – "Sonny Til." Not only did the group record Chessler's song, but she also became their manager. The Vibra-Naires signed with Jubilee records and changed their name to the Orioles at the suggestion of Jubilee's owner, Jerry Blaine.

---

[150] All Chessler quotes are from a telephone interview on June 11, 2007 and a letter dated June 24, 2007.

The members of the Orioles were Til, Alexander Sharp (first tenor), George Nelson (second tenor and baritone), Johnny Reed (bass) and Tommy Gaither (guitar). They went on to record a string of hits, placing eleven songs on the R&B charts, including "Tell Me So" (1949) and "Crying In The Chapel" (1953), both Number One R&B songs.[151] "Tell Me So" was particularly important because of its use of Sharp's falsetto floating above the lead, a device that would be copied by countless groups over the next few decades.

Their performing style was a big part of the Orioles' success. The late Ronnie Italiano, founder and President of the United In Group Harmony Association,[152] said: "Their live performances greatly enhanced their acceptance and their appeal to the black audience. Til became a matinee idol."[153] Charlie Gillett said in his book, *The Sound Of The City*: "A guitar supplied the only accompaniment, played so quietly that its only purpose seemed to be to prevent the group from slowing down so much that they came to a complete stop. . . . In the background the group wailed one wordless melody together, concentrating attention on the voice of lead tenor Sonny Til, who seemed to try to withdraw himself from the situation, refusing to be involved, trying to be cool. . . .Til's voice was the sound of the streets, a strange echo of ghetto-experience." Gillett adds: "The overall impression was of impeccable purity. . . .The group . . . worked out an intricate pattern of movements around the microphone-bending, straightening up, turning away from the mike . . . ."[154] Til sang and millions of teens listened.

Ravens

The other late-1940s group that had a huge influence on the R&B groups that followed was the Ravens. While the Orioles' Til was the forerunner of teen-idol 1950s leads, the Ravens provided the next generation with a prototypical bass voice. The original quartet, formed in New York in 1945, was made up of Jimmy Ricks (bass and lead), Ollie Jones (lead and first tenor), Leonard Puzey

---

[151] Only "It's Too Soon To Know" and "Crying In The Chapel" reached the pop charts.
[152] At its peak, it had over 2000 members and UGHA was the premier organization in the world dedicated to preserving and promoting the pioneer group harmony sound. They can be found at http://www.ugha.org.
[153] Interview, August 26, 2006, Clifton, New Jersey
[154] Gillett, Charlie. *The Sound Of The City*. New York: Da Capo Press, Inc., 1996, p. 161

(second tenor) and Warren Suttles (baritone). In 1946, after several recordings on Hub, Ricks discovered Maithe Marshall, who had a (really) high tenor voice and brought Marshall into the group to replace Jones.

Unlike the Orioles, the Ravens aimed their music primarily at sophisticated adult audiences, both black and white; but because of Ricks' bass, their impact went well beyond. Ronnie Italiano said of their 1950 song "Count Every Star:" "What makes this song unique is the bass. This was the forerunner of the great basses that followed such as Gerald Gregory of the Spaniels and also the great bass intros such as heard in the Teenagers, 'Why Do Fools Fall in Love' with the intro by Sherman Garnes. 'Count Every Star' was not a great commercial success and the Ravens went back to their pop sound at which they were great."[155] Incidentally, the Ravens' cover of "It's Too Soon To Know"' reached #11 on the R&B charts.

As for Ricks' voice, it was unmatched. He could dominate a song, much in the same way as Lee Gaines of the Delta Rhythm Boys did before him. As Marv Goldberg said: "Ricks, and Ricks alone, was to influence an entire generation of aspiring bass singers; it's as simple as that."[156]

The strongest white vocal group presence came from the Four Freshmen, who would influence a host of white pop vocal groups in the 1950s. The group was formed in the mid-1940s in Indiana by Bob Flanigan, and the Barbour brothers, Don and Ross, who were cousins of Flanigan's. The three met Hal Kratzsch at music school in Indianapolis and formed a group they called Hal's Harmonizers. In 1948, at the urging of their agent, they changed their name to the Four Freshmen and came to the attention of the great bandleader, Stan Kenton, who helped them get a recording contract with Capitol Records. Ken Errair replaced Kratzsch in 1953 and was then himself replaced by Ken Albers in 1955. Don Barbour left the group for a solo career in 1960 and was replaced by Bill Comstock. There have been other changes

Four Freshmen

over the years and the group continues today — with all-new personnel. The Four Freshmen were the first major vocal jazz group to play their own instruments. More

---
[155] Interview August 26, 2006, Clifton, New Jersey
[156] http://home.att.net/~marvy42/Ravens/ravens01.html (accessed January 16, 2009)

important, however, their harmonies were unique and influenced many later groups such as the Beach Boys and Manhattan Transfer. Some of the Freshmen's more notable recordings on Capitol were "Day By Day" (1955), "Charmaine" (1955) and "Graduation Day," which broke into the Top 20 in 1956.

In the late 1940s and early 1950s young people became an even more significant factor in choosing the music that made the charts. By the mid-1950s their influence increased with the birth of rock & roll. The vocal group part of rock & roll, alternatively called doo-wop or rhythm and blues group harmony, was the first to emerge. Full-blown R&B group harmony contains not just harmony, but also a wide range of voice parts, nonsense syllables, simple and strong beats, instrumentation that remains in the background (except during the bridge of the song) and simple music and lyrics.

The characteristics of R&B group harmony appeared gradually over the last half of the 1940s. The Orioles provided the teen idol (in Sonny Til) and some harmony, the Ravens provided the bass voice (Jimmy Ricks) and more harmony, and the white groups threw in their own brand of close harmony allied with the barbershoppers. By 1950, "I'm Afraid the Masquerade Is Over" by the Blenders and "Just To See You Smile Again" by the Four Buddies followed the pattern. The Larks, Dominoes, Clovers, Swallows, Five Keys, Robins and Cardinals would all contribute songs with R&B group harmony characteristics by the end of 1951.

Within a few years, post-war relatively affluent white teen audiences, egged on by the driving rhythm of the music and hip deejays like Alan Freed, who plugged the music, helped vocal group harmony to gain unprecedented exposure and popularity. The music was new, it was energetic and it was by and for the young. Abby Hutchinson, the twelve-year-old member of the Hutchinson Family Singers from the mid-nineteenth century, would have been proud.

Groupography
With Contributions from Karsten Lehl, Andreas Wellen and Josef Westner

Aaron Sisters
Recorded on Columbia in 1932.

Acme Quartette
Sang at the turn of the 20th Century and were J. T. Fernando, C. Burton, B. Webster and C. Rue. *Reference*: Abbott and Seroff

Adanac Male Quartet
There were two groups that used this name, one from 1915 to 1919 and the other from 1921 to 1927. The members of the first grouping were Redferne Hollinshead (tenor), George Dixon (tenor), Arthur Blight (baritone) and H. Ruthven McDonald (bass). Tenor J. Elcho Fiddes also sang with them. The second group had McDonald with Riley Hallman (tenor), Ernest Bushnell (tenor), and Joseph O'Meara (baritone) and appeared on the Redpath Chautauqua circuit in 1927. Adanac is "Canada" spelled backwards. *Reference*: http://www.thecanadianencyclopedia.com/

Ad Club Quartette
Male group on the cover of sheet music of "At The Panama Pacific Fair" from 1914.

Adler, Weil & Herman
Appeared on several pieces of sheet music in 1924 and 1926, including "You Danced That Last Waltz With Me" in 1924.

Admirals
Edward Delbridge (tenor), Neil Evans (tenor), Chet Bree (baritone) and William Simon (bass). They recorded primarily on Columbia, Electron, Tri Ergon, Odeon, HMV, Zonophone and Polydor in the late 1920s and early 1930s in New York, London and Berlin. They were also known as the Four Admirals and Three Admirals. Norman Bartlett (baritone), Eddie Lee and Joe Lee (tenors) were later members. *Reference*: Lehl Discography

Aeolian Male Quartet
See, Criterion Quartet

Aeolian Mixed Quartet
Recorded on Vocalion.

Aeolian Quartette
Female group including Misses Puckney, Haeger, Edwards and Fisher, appear in a photograph from the spring of 1897. *Reference*: Cabinet photo taken in Wheaton, Illinois.

Aeolian Singers
See, Hutchinson Family Singers

Aeolian Vocalists
Trio containing John, Judson and Asa Hutchinson that performed in Wilton, MA for the first time in 1841. Approximately a year later they started performing under the name "The Hutchinson Family." *Reference*: Hamm

African Melodists
Early troupe performing in the 1840s after the success of the Virginia and Christy's Minstrels. *Reference*: http://mainemusicbox.library.umaine.edu/

Afro-American Folk Song Singers
Mixed-gender black group from Washington, D.C. that was formed in 1913. They were led by composer Will Marion Cook but their membership is unknown. *Reference*: ENVQ-2

Ah-Moors
Recorded on Rainbow in 1948.

Akins Birmingham Boys
Recorded on Columbia in 1928

Alabama Four
See, Birmingham Jubilee Singers.

Alabama Harmonizers
Recorded around 1930. *Reference*: VQ-1

Alabama Jubilee Quartet
Two men and two women, led by Luther J. Mason. Appeared on the Redpath circuit in the 1920s. *Reference*: Iowa

Alabama Magpie Trio
Recorded on Columbia in 1929. *Reference*: Lehl Discography

Alamo Quintette
Mixed group consisting of Ella and Mary St. Clair, Harold Dodds, Florence Doolen and Clarence Nash. Appeared in 1926 and 1927 on the Redpath-Chautauqua circuit. *Reference*: Iowa

Aldine Quartet
A double quartet (eight men), whose picture appears in W. T. Giffe's "Male Quartet and Chorus Books," from 1879. *Reference*: Averill

Alexander Brothers
Recorded on Champion in 1932 in Indiana. *Reference*: Lehl Discography

Nelson Alexander Trio
Nelson Alexander (piano, vocals), Edgar Rice (guitar, vocals) and Bill Reagan (bass, vocals) made up this jive group. *Reference*: Jive VG-2; http://www.eyeballproductions.com/

Alkahest Lady Quartette
Consisting of Effie C. Palmer, Florence M. Hobson, Flora R. Trein and Elizabeth Walker. Formerly known by the name of Lyceum Lady Quartette. A group that performed on the Chautauqua circuit from around 1903 to 1909. *Reference*: Iowa

Alleghenians
Early traveling minstrel group modeled after the Hutchinsons. Jesse Hutchinson, the Hutchinson's manager and composer, jumped ship and joined the Alleghenians in the early 1850s. Jesse died in 1853, while traveling with this group. *Reference*: Hamm

All Girl Quartette
Recorded somewhere between 1912 and 1929 on Edison Diamond Disc. *Reference*: http://members.aol.com/AGW1886/antique.htm

Almanac Singers
Mixed race group that, at times, included Josh White, Millard Lampell and Pete Seeger and Lee Hays of the Weavers. Other groupings consisted of those four and various combinations of Sam Gary, Carol White and Bess Lomax Hawes. Steve Tracy said of them, "Truly a super group of enormous importance." A seminal group in the folk music area. *Reference*: SVG-4

Alphabetical Four
Black group that was in the 1940 movie, "Paradise In Harlem." They sang mostly gospel. *Reference*: http://www.imdb.com/

Alpine Minstrels
A group of singers from Germany that gave concerts in the U.S. beginning in 1837. *Reference*: Averill

Amalu Trio
Recorded on Victor in 1934 in California. *Reference*: Lehl Discography

Ambassador Trio
Sang with the Gus Arnheim Orchestra in the 1930s and accompanied Kate Smith on several recordings. Also known as the Ambassadors Trio. *Reference*: Lehl Discography

American Comedy Four
Appeared on the sheet music "I Didn't Raise My Boy To Be A Soldier (A Mothers Plea For Peace)" in 1915.

American Four
The first of at least two groups with this name. They were a black group active in the 1870s.

American Four
Recorded on Decca in the early 1940s. *Reference*: Lehl Discography

American Glee Club
Male quartet featuring Lancelot Buftone (2nd tenor), Evard Servass (1st tenor), Anthony Dworak (basso) and Homer Wright (baritone). Appeared on the Ellison-White Bureau circuit around 1927. Another 1920s iteration of the same group included Francis Shor. *Reference*: Iowa

American Hawaiian Quartette
Appeared on sheet music of "On The Banks Of Honolulu Bay" in approximately 1915.

American Jubilee Singers
Black foursome from Knoxville (Presbyterian) College that appeared in the 1920s on the Redpath Circuit. There is also a promotional card for a European tour that shows a black, mixed gender group of eight people who claim to be the successors to the "Original 'Fisk' Group." It is not clear if both are versions of the same ensemble. On the latter, Daniel W. Brown is listed as Manager and claims that he was the former tenor of the original Fisk group. No Daniel Brown is listed in the definitive study of the Fisk group. *Reference*: Iowa

American Newsboy Quartette
Appeared on sheet music of "Somebody's Waiting For You" in 1906.

American Quartet (1)
The first of two classic groups with the same name, they sang at the turn of the 20th century and were comprised of Albert Campbell (1st tenor), W. T. Leahy (2nd tenor), S. H. Dudley (baritone) and W. F. Hooley (who was with both) (bass). They recorded on Victor from 1901 to 1904 and also did "A Night Trip To Buffalo" in 1900 on the Gramophone label. *Reference*: Walsh

American Quartet (2)
0The second classic group with this name, it began in 1909 and was also known as the Premier Quartet for recordings on the Edison label. Members were Billy Murray (tenor), John Bieling (tenor), Steve Porter (baritone) and William F. Hooley (bass). Bieling was replaced by John Young in 1914 and Hooley by Donald Chalmers in 1918. They reorganized in 1920 with Murray, Albert Campbell, John Meyer and Frank Croxton. The group broke up in 1925. Some of their more well-known recordings were "Casey Jones," "Oh, You Beautiful Doll" and "Moonlight Bay." They were also known as the Premier-American and Murray Quartets (Aeolian-Vocalion-1919). *Reference*: Walsh

American Quartet (3)
Male group that appeared on the Chautauqua and Lyceum circuits in the 1910s, and included J. M. Sawyer (1st tenor), Clayton Conrad (2nd tenor), Paul Fairchild (baritone) and L. E. Gilbert (bass). *Reference*: Iowa

American Ragtime Four
Male singers listed as Jenkins, Miller, Neff and Nedeau appearing on the cover of the sheet music to "Wedding Blossom Sue" from 1918.

American Singers
Began in 1927, lasted into the 1930s, and included Charles Harrison (1st tenor), Redferne Hollinshead (2nd tenor) (replaced by Lambert Murphy), Vernon Archibald (baritone) (replaced by Walter J. Preston in 1929) and Frank Croxton (bass). *Reference*: Walsh; Mainspring

Americus Quartette
Appeared on sheet music of "Will You Love Me In December As You Do In May" in 1905.

Ames Brothers
Brothers Ed, Gene, Joe and Vic Ames (real name, Urick) from Malden, Massachusetts were a pop group that charted over 20 times in the late 1940s through the mid-1950s. Their biggest hit was "The Naughty Lady of Shady Lane" (1954-RCA Victor). Bandleader Russ Morgan helped start their career when he featured them on his recording "Forever And

Ever," a number one hit in 1949 on Decca. They had a TV series in 1955 and Ed Ames had a successful solo career as a singer and actor. *Reference*: Whitburn-PM; Simon

Amherst Octette
Recorded on Columbia in 1912. *Reference*: Lehl Discography

Amory Brothers
See, Ames Brothers.

Amphion Glee Club
Community glee club from Washington, D.C., started in 1891 by Henry J. Lewis. Toured extensively and lasted into the 1930s. *Reference*: Southern

Amphion Quartette
See, Harmonizers Quartet.

Anderson's Minstrels of Boston
An article referred to them as, "Another short lived troupe was Anderson's Minstrels of Boston, which started in as opposition to the Morris Brothers. The Clipper at the time predicted an early dissolution and the collapse came as predicted. The fancy salaries and the gathering of so many minstrel stars settled the venture." The group apparently began and ended around 1859. *Reference*: Mainspring; http://www.circushistory.org/

Andrews Sisters
Patty, Maxene and La Verne Andrews, from Minneapolis, Minnesota, formed one of the most enduring of the American vocal groups. Their names are still household words today, at least among older Americans. They began their professional career in 1932 when they went on tour with the Larry Rich Orchestra. Their second break came in 1936 when they joined Leon Belasco's orchestra. It was there they met Vic Schoen who would become their musical director and arranger. They were singing on a radio program when they were heard by Dave Kapp who was Decca's A&R man. Soon thereafter, Decca signed them to a contract. It would turn out to be a long-lasting relationship with every one of the Sisters' chart hits being released on Decca. From 1938, when they hit number one with the Yiddish song, "Bei Mir Bist Du Schoen," to 1951, they charted a remarkable 90 times! Six of those songs were number one. They had three R&B chart hits, two of them with Bing Crosby. With Crosby, they charted 23 times in total. This in an era with significantly more competition than the earlier groups had to face. Some of their hit recordings were, "Say Si, Si" (#4), "The Woodpecker Song" (#6), "Ferryboat Serenade" (#1) and "Beat Me Daddy Eight To The Bar" (#2), all in 1940; and "The Shrine Of St. Cecilia" (#3) and "Strip Polka" (#6), both in 1942. "Rum And Coca-Cola" was number one for 10 weeks and had 20 total weeks on the chart in 1945. "I Can Dream, Can't I?" was their last Top 10 song but it was

number one for five weeks and on the charts for 25 in 1949 and 1950. Other hit recordings included "Hold Tight, Hold Tight" (1939) and "Beer Barrel Polka" (1939). They appeared in 17 movies, including "In The Navy" (1941), "Buck Privates" (1941) and "Follow The Boys" (1944). During the War they did USO tours. War-related songs of theirs included, "I'll Be With You In Apple Blossom Time" (#5 in 1941), "Boogie Woogie Bugle Boy" (#6 in 1941), "Don't Sit Under The Apple Tree" (1942), "Here Comes The Navy" (1942) and "Shoo-Shoo Baby" which spent nine weeks at number one and 21 total weeks on the charts in 1943. They left Decca in 1951 and split up in 1953. Patty went solo while Maxene and LaVerne continued together. The three reunited in 1956 and recorded on Dot Records in the 1960s. LaVerne became ill in 1966 and died in 1967. Maxene retired the next year and Patty went back to performing solo. In 1974, Maxene and Patty appeared in "Over There" on Broadway. Maxene died in 1996. *Reference*: Whitburn-PM

Angela Sisters
Foursome appearing on the cover of sheet music of "Susie-Ue" from 1898. Angela and Helen Morgan were two of the members. They also appeared as the Morgan Sisters. Their brother Albert was the manager of the group.

Anne, Judy & Zeke
Appeared on sheet music of "Sweet Violets" in 1932, "The Last Great Roundup" in 1935 and recorded on Okeh in 1933.

Anything Goes Foursome
Recorded on HMV and Victor in 1934. *Reference*: Lehl Discography

Apex Five
Appeared on sheet music of "Sweetheart Come Back To Me!" in 1919.

Apollo Jubilee Quartette
Made one record on Columbia in 1912 and their membership is unknown. *Reference*: Brooks

Apollo Minstrels
Black troupe appearing in Ohio in 1857. *Reference*: Averill

Apollo Quartet
Recorded on Berliner in 1898. *Reference*: Brooks

Apollo Quartet Of Boston
Recorded on Edison in 1916. Members were William Whittaker, Lyman Hemenway, John Smallman and Alexander Logan. *Reference*: Walsh

Apollo Three
Group that appears on the cover of the sheet music to "Luella Lee" in 1912.

Apollo Trio
See, Crescent Trio

Aragon Trio
Group that sang with the Wayne King Band around 1930. *Reference*: http://stevensorchestra.tripod.com/

Arcadian Quartette
Group on the cover of sheet music of "Back Home In Dixie Where I Long To Be" from 1916.

Arcadia Trio
Appear on sheet music of "Beautiful" in 1927.

Archibald Brothers Quartet
Recorded on Columbia in 1910.

Arion Quartet
Black secular concert quartet from Cincinnati performing in the 1870s. Members included Andrew D. Hart and John Lewis. *Reference*: Averill

Arion Quartette
White group pictured on the 1911 sheet music of "'Another' Rag (A Raggy Rag)" and "When Uncle Joe Plays A Rag On His Old Banjo" in 1912.

Aristocrats of Rhythm
Quintet featuring one woman and four men, featured on the cover of sheet music issued in 1940 of "De Camptown Races," the old song by Stephen C. Foster.

Aristokats
Bob Marshall was a member and they recorded with the Sy Oliver Orchestra on Decca in 1949. *Reference*: Fournier

Aristo-Kats
A Chicago group formed in 1946, its members were William "Lefty" Bates (guitar), Orlando Randolph (trumpet), Quinn Wilson (bass) and Julius Wright (piano). They are best known for their recording of "Jack, You're Dead!" on RCA Victor in 1947. They were not the same group as The Hollywood Arist-O-Kats. *Reference*: Fournier

Artists' Quartette
Male group that recorded on Columbia in 1911. *Reference*: Lehl Discography

Arlington's Minstrels
This troupe, around 1870, featured "Saxton, Lumbard, Charles Sutton, 'Fostelle,' Ike Withers, Johnny Booker, Dick Gorman, and 'Chang,' the Chinese giant." *Reference*: http://www.circushistory.org/Cork/BurntCork6.htm

Arlington Four
Appeared on sheet music of "Good-Bye Mister Greenback" in 1906 and "Think It Over Mary" in 1910.

Armstrong Quaker Quartet & Orchestra, etc.
Appeared on sheet music in 1930 of "An Armstrong's Quaker Rug In Every Home."

Stan Ashley's Harmoneers
From radio station WTIC, they appeared on sheet music of "The Four Years" in 1934.

Astor Four
Appeared on sheet music of "The Little House Upon The Hill" in 1915.

Atco Quartet
Recorded on Columbia in 1927. *Reference*: Lehl Discography

Athene Quartette
Female group, comprised of Lillian Louise Roberts (1st soprano), Emma Cecilia Hall (2nd soprano), Sadie Henshaw (Sarah) Whittemore (1st alto) and Lotta Winton (2nd alto), with Mr. F. Lyons (pianist) and Kate Brooks (accompanist). *Reference*: eBay auction

Atlanta University Quartette
Group included George A. Towns (1st tenor), Joseph T. Porter (2nd tenor), Robert W. Gadsden (1st basso) and James Weldon Johnson (2nd basso). After the fashion of the Fisk Jubilee Singers, this group toured New England raising money for their school. Johnson later became the first black man to pass the Florida Bar Exam. *Reference*: http://www.sc.edu/

Auber Quartet
Black secular concert quartet that featured, as of 1875, Messrs. Smith, Hill, Ruffin and Henry. *Reference*: Averill

Dolores Brown & the Auditones
Recorded at least four sides on Sterling in 1947.

Aunt Jemima Novelty Four
Mixed-gender vocal group that recorded in the late 1920s on Brunswick. *Reference*: BVG-10

Avon Comedy Four
Irving Kaufman (replaced by Eddie Miller) and Harry Goodwin with Joe Smith and Charles Dale (they were the famous comedy duo, Smith and Dale). They performed in Vaudeville. Jim Walsh noted that Arthur Fields also sang with them. They recorded from 1912 to 1924 on Victor, Emerson and Columbia. The quartet balanced comedy and harmony arrangements. *Reference*: Walsh

Babs And Her Brothers
From Chicago, they began as the Three Smoothies (the Fred Waring radio show on which they appeared was sponsored by Old Gold cigarettes, billed as the country's "smoothest cigarette," and thus their name) in 1933 with the Fred Waring Orchestra and changed their name to Babs and Her Brothers in 1934 (the show changed sponsors). The members were Babs Ryan (Blanche Redwine), her husband Charlie Ryan and his brother, Little Ryan. They also sang with Hal Kemp as the Smoothies. The group disbanded in 1935 when Charlie and Babs split up. *Reference*: Waring CD

Bachelor Four
Appeared on sheet music of "When You And I Were Seventeen" in 1924. The name "Kings Of Harmony" appears below the group name.

Bachelors
Sang with several orchestras, including Ted Lewis and recorded on Supertone, Gennett, Columbia, Mastertone and Brunswick from about 1927 to 1936. See also, Bea and the Bachelors. *Reference*: Lehl Discography

Bachelors
Formerly the Canaanites, the Bachelors were from Washington, D.C., and their members were Joe Van Loan (see, Ravens) (lead), Elijah Harvey (2d tenor), Jim Miller (baritone) and Allen Scott (bass). They recorded for Mercury and Carver (as the Joe Van Loan Quartet). *Reference*: Goldberg

Balladeers
Billy Mathews led this group that began recording on Mercury in 1947. *Reference*: http://www.jazzdisco.org/

Bill Matthews And The Ballardiers
Mixed-gender black quartet that recorded on Arlington in 1949. Also known as Billy Matthews And The Balladeers. *Reference*: Fournier

Barbecue Boys
Recorded with Norris The Troubador (likely Norris Mayhams) in 1936. *Reference*: BSVG-3

Barbour Plantation Singers
Recorded on Columbia in 1927.

Barry Sisters
Trio that sang with Wayne King. A posting on a website claims they also did Yiddish songs as the Bagelman Sisters. King began in 1927 but it is not clear when the Barrys sang with him. *Reference*: http://nfo.net/; http://mailman.xmission.com/

Basin Street Boys
Originally formed in 1934 with George Thompson, Sam Hucherson, Perry Anderson and Steve Gibson and recorded on Decca. A different group, sanctioned by Gibson, was formed by Ormand Wilson, who had sung with the Plantation Boys (and was taught guitar by Gibson), Gene Price, Reuben Saunders and Arthur Rainwater and began recording on Exclusive Records in 1946. They were out of Los Angeles by way of Philadelphia and had their biggest hit in 1946 with "I Sold My Heart To The Junkman." "I gave my heart to you the one that I trusted, you brought it back to me all broken and busted, so I've sold my heart to the junkman and I'll never fall in love again." They made their last recording in 1948 and disbanded in 1951. Songs such their "Voot Nay On The Vot Nay" (the flip side of Junkman), a song about a new form of jive, were the forerunners of the nonsense syllable numbers of the 1950s. *Reference*: Basin Street Boys-"Satchelmouth Baby." Night Train-NTICD7028; Warner;

Bea And The Bachelors
Quartet consisting of Bea Swain, Al Rinker (of the Rhythm Boys), Ken Lane and Johnny Smedburg. In 1936, they combined with the original Modernaires to form the V-8 on broadcasts by Fred Waring of the Ford Dealers Show. *Reference*: Waring CD

Beachcombers
Group that sang with the Johnny Long Band. *Reference*: http://www.parabrisas.com/

Beacon Four
Recorded on Decca in 1940-1941. *Reference*: Lehl Discography

Beacon Ladies Quartet of Boston
Included Marie Louise Campbell (1st soprano), Adalyn Dana Riley (2nd soprano), Izetta Ballou Holway (1st alto) and Louise Meek Corbett (2nd alto). Appeared for the White Entertainment Bureau in the 1909-1910 season. *Reference*: Iowa

Beale Street Boys
From Memphis, Tennessee, its members were William Barnes (1st tenor), Bob Davis (2d tenor), James Pugh (baritone) and David Pugh (bass). They recorded in 1948 and 1949 and were not heard from after then. *Reference*: RCM 18; Fournier

Beaux And Belles Octet
Mixed-gender white group that appeared on sheet music of "My Magnolia Maid" in 1901.

Beavers
Begun in 1949 by Joe Thomas, a teacher, in New York from among his students, members were Fred Hamilton (tenor), John Wilson (baritone), Raymond Johnson (bass) and Dick Palmer (tenor), whose brother was Clarence Palmer, lead singer of the Jive Bombers. They cut six sides, including "I'd Rather Be Wrong Than Blue" (1950-Coral). They backed Lionel Hampton on his recording of "Rag Mop" as his Hamptones. Palmer later sang with the Blenders; Johnson with the Blenders and the Dominoes. *Reference*: Goldberg; YM 1-2

Bel-Airs
Recorded on Cormac in 1949. *Reference*: Lehl Discography

Bel-Cantos
Recorded in the early 1930s mostly on Brunswick and Panachord and were Fred Shelton (tenor), T. K. Johnson (tenor), Marcel Jones (baritone) and Martin Thomas (bass). *Reference*: Lehl Discography

Bell Quartette
According to Opal Louis Nations' liner notes to the Four Aces CD (Flyright FLY CD 62), in the late 19th century, the Bell Quartette began the human orchestra sound that became so popular in the 1930s and 1940s and as perfected by groups such as the Mills Brothers and Four Vagabonds. *Reference*: Four Aces CD

Bell Serenaders
Recorded on Bell in 1923.

Belmont Garden Quartet
Recorded on Challenge in 1927.

Bennett College Quartet
19th-century group mentioned in Averill's book. *Reference*: Averill

Bennett Sisters
Maxine, Charlie Bell, and Marguerite Means joined the Clyde McCoy Band in 1936 as the Bennett Sisters. A fourth sister, Billie Jane, later joined them. Maxine married McCoy after the War. *Reference*: http://www.bigbandlibrary.com/

Ben Smith Quartet
Ben Smith (sax and drums), Ed Snead (bass), Lannie Scott (piano) and Artie Long (guitar) were its members. They recorded on Abbey in the late 1940s and early 1950s. *Reference*: Fournier; RCM

Bernhardt, Parker & Searles
Male trio on the cover of sheet music of "Another Rag" from 1911.

Bernie Trio
Recorded on Brunswick in 1928 and consisted of Dave Bernie, Maxwell Covert and Ray Covert. *Reference*: Lehl Discography

Bessemer Blues Singers
A Jefferson County, Alabama group. Bessie Smith recorded with them.

Bessemer Melody Boys
Another Jefferson County, Alabama group that recorded in 1930. *Reference*: BVG-1

Bethel Jubilee Quartet
Recorded on Victor in 1923. Members were A. C. Brogdon, H. S. Allen, J. C. Eubanks and T. H. Wiseman. *Reference*: Walsh

Betty, Jean and Jim
Trio appearing on the sheet music of the old Stephen Foster tune, "Oh! Susanna," in 1935.

Beulah Buck Quartet Company
Comprised of Beulah Buck (2nd soprano), Marjorie Paddock (1st soprano and accompanist), Wilma Whitacre (1st contralto) and Orlena Woodhouse (2nd contralto). Performed on the Coit Lyceum and Redpath circuits in the Midwest around 1914. *Reference*: Iowa

Biddle University Quartet
19th-century group mentioned in Averill's book. *Reference*: Averill

Big City Quartette
Appeared on sheet music of "That's A Picnic Called A Honeymoon" in 1910.

Big Four Minstrels
In operation between 1879 and 1880, they included "Harry Stanwood, James and Barney Kine, Harry Armstrong, Theodore Jackson, Charles Heywood, Edwin Stanley, Weston Brothers, Sam and Morris, and the proprietors." *Reference*: http://www.circushistory.org/

Big Four Quartet
Early group that recorded on Edison cylinders in 1900. Members were Byron G. Harlan (tenor), Joe Natus (tenor), Arthur Collins (baritone) and A. D. Madeira (bass). A simple piano background and a rather formal, subdued style of singing characterized their numbers. *Reference*: Walsh; Mainspring

Big Three Trio
Members of this Chicago group were Leonard Caston (lead), Bernardo Dennis (replaced by Ollie Crawford in 1947) and Willie Dixon. They began recording in 1946 and continued through the mid-1950s. Caston also was with the Five Breezes and the Four Jumps of Jive; his son sang with the Radiants (Chess-1962-1965). Dixon was also with the Four Jumps of Jive and the Five Breezes. They recorded numerous sides for Columbia ("You Sure Look Good To Me" hit the R&B charts in 1948) and later Dot and Okeh. *Reference*: Whitburn-RB

Bijou Comedy Trio
Two women and a man appearing on the sheet music for "Way Down Yonder In The Cornfield" from 1901.

Biltmore Rhythm Boys
Sang with the Bert Lown Band and probably took their name from the New York City hotel where the band played. Lown was active from 1929 to 1933. The members were Elmer Feldkamp, Paul Mason and Mac Ceppos. *Reference*: http://www.nfo.net/usa/voc1.html

Biltmore Trio
Recorded on Brunswick in 1928-1929 in Los Angeles and were led by Earl Burnett. *Reference*: Lehl Discography

Birmingham Jubilee Quartet
Recorded on Columbia from 1926-30.

Birmingham Jubilee Singers

From Jefferson County, Alabama, they began recording in 1926. Members were Charles Bridges (lead), Leo "Lot" Key (tenor), Dave Ausbrooks (baritone), Ed Sherrill (bass) (replaced by James Ricks in 1929). They also recorded as the Alabama Four and some of their secular numbers were issued under the name Mobile Four. Ken Romanowski in his liner notes to the Hall Negro Quartette CD said of them that they "were perhaps the most popular and influential black vocal quartet in the decade spanning 1926 . . . and 1936 . . . ."
Reference: Hall CD; Birmingham CD-II

Birmingham Quartet

See, Birmingham Jubilee Singers.

Bison City Four

Quartet whose photo appears on the cover of sheet music of "Honey Man," from 1911.

Bison City Quartette

One of the earliest groups to record. They were on New Jersey cylinders in 1892. Charles C. Miller, Ben R. Cook, Harry C. West and Lester L. Pike were its members. They appear on the sheet music of "His Only Boy" from 1893. *Reference*: Walsh

Black Arts Harmony Quartette

Black concert group from Nashville, Tennessee at around the turn of the 20th century.
Reference: Averill

Black Baby Boy Quartet

Black group that sang with Lew Johnson's Baby Boy Minstrels in the late 1880s.
Reference: Averill

Blackbirds of Harmony

Recorded on Columbia in 1926 in New York.

Black Cats And Kitten

Mixed-gender group whose members are not known. They recorded on Okeh in the 1940s.
Reference: That's Where My Jive Goes: The Best of Jive Vocal Groups, Vol. 2 - P-Vine Records

Blazes

See, Four Blazes.

Blenders
Ollie Jones from the Ravens formed the group in 1949, in New York, and sang lead. Other members were James DeLoach (bass), Abel DeCosta (tenor) and Tommy Adams (baritone). Jimmy Ricks helped them with their arranging so certain similarities to the Ravens' music can be heard. Their most popular song was "Don't Play Around With Love" (1953-Jay Dee) (there is a version with an alternate, less polite, title). In 1954, they played the Apollo in New York. Dick Palmer replaced Adams and Ray Johnson replaced DeLoach. After the group broke up, Jones and DeCosta formed the Cues. *Reference*: The Blenders CD - Famous Groove Records; Warner

William Blevin's Quartette
Recorded in 1937. *Reference*: VQ-1

Blue Bird Trio
Recorded on Champion in 1933 in New York. *Reference*: Lehl Discography

Blue Chips
Although mostly an instrumental group, they did some vocal recordings in New York in 1936. *Reference*: Lehl Discography

Blue Dandies
Quartet that appeared on sheet music, including "Sleepy Time Gal" and "Too Many Parties and Too Many Pals" in 1924 and 1925.

Blue Ribbon Quartet
See, Ritz Quartet.

Blue Ridge Mountain Singers:
Recorded on Columbia in 1927 and 1930. *Reference*: Lehl Discography

Blues
Male quartet with piano that appeared on sheet music of "Hawaiian Blues" in 1916.

Maggie Hathaway & her Bluesmen
Recorded at least two sides for Black & White in 1947.

Bob-O-Links
Vocal group originally called the Downbeats that sang with the Bob Crosby band in 1940 and 1941. Johnny Desmond was a member. Desmond later sang with Glenn Miller. *Reference*: Simon

Bodyguards
White male trio that sang with the Orrin Tucker Orchestra from 1939 to 1941. *Reference*: http://www.radioarchives.org/

Bonnie Laddies
Recorded with several orchestras including Jack Denny in the mid-1920s. Members were Jim Whelan, Charles Kenny and Lou Noll. *Reference*: Lehl Discography

Bon Ton Trio
Two men and a woman who appear on the 1899 sheet music of "The Song That My Mother Sang To Me."

Bostonian Four
Appeared on sheet music of "In The Heart Of The City That Has No Heart" in 1913.

Boston Minstrels
A mid-19th century group mentioned in Averill's book. *Reference*: Averill

Boswell Sisters
The Boswell Sisters, Connie (later Connee), Martha and Helvetia (Vet), were one of the rare white groups to come out of New Orleans. They preceded the Andrews Sisters by about 10 years, and helped pave the way for the numerous female groups that were to follow. Each played an instrument (Connie - cello, Martha - piano and Vet - violin) and were members of the New Orleans Philharmonic Orchestra. They signed with Victor and made their first recording in 1925. In the early 1930s, they sang with the Dorsey Brothers Band. The group disbanded in 1936 and Connee continued with a successful solo career into the 1940s. Their hits included "You Oughta Be In Pictures" (1934-Brunswick) and "The Object of My Affection" (1935-Brunswick). This was a number one song for them with the Jimmie Grier Orchestra and was in the film, "Times Square Lady." They had a rhythmic, bluesy style. *Reference*: BS-CD; Whitburn-PM

Bowery Boys Quartette
Appeared on sheet music of "Come Back To Connemara" in 1907. One of the four members is in blackface.

Bowman Sisters
Recorded in Tennessee in 1928 on Columbia. *Reference*: Lehl Discography

Boyce's Harlem Serenaders
Recorded on Decca in the early 1940s.

Bremer-Tully Trio/Quartet
Recorded in 1929 as part of the broadcasts for the Bremer-Tully Radio Show. *Reference*: Lehl Discography

Brevities Quartet
Recorded on Brunswick in 1930 in New York. *Reference*: Lehl Discography

Brian Sisters
Trio from Idaho, Betty, Doris and Gwen, who appeared in several movies in the 1930s and 1940s. "Swinging On A Star" on Capitol in 1944 was their only recording. When Betty married in 1945 the group disbanded. *Reference*: http://www.brian-sisters.org/index.shtml

Brick Morse Collegians
Recorded in 1931 in San Francisco. *Reference*: Lehl Discography

Brilliant Quartet
Recorded on Berliner in 1898 and 1899.

Broadway Quartette
Male group on the cover of sheet music of "Bye-Bye Dearie" from 1907. Members listed on sheet as Storm, Reals, Bennett and Pearl.

Broadway Quartette
See Columbia Stellar Quartet for the group on Columbia in 1916. *Reference*: Walsh

Broadway Quartette
See Criterion Quartet for the group on Vocalion in 1922. *Reference*: Walsh

Broadway Trio
Male group appearing on sheet music of "I Love Her Just The Same" from 1896. Members named as Edgar Turpen, Louis Powers and Eugene Smackels. Also on sheet music of "If You Only Had A Little Loving Left For Me" in 1914.

Brooker and Clayton's Georgia Minstrels
Organized in 1865, it was the first successful all-black minstrel troupe. Predecessor to Hick's Georgia Minstrels, and managed by Charles Hicks, a black man. *Reference*: Hamm; Averill

Brooks Brothers
Orville Brooks led this group that recorded on Decca in 1947. *Reference*: VG Archives-2

Bobby Brooks Quartet
Black group that appeared in several movies including, "Honeymoon Lodge" in 1943 and "This Is The Life" in 1944. They can also be seen in a music video, "Count Basie & Friends 1943-1945." *Reference*: www.imdb.com

Brown Brothers
Recorded in New York in 1927. *Reference*: Lehl Discography

Brown Dots
Formed in 1944 by Ivory "Deek" Watson, an original member of the Ink Spots. He left the Ink Spots to form his own group and wanted to call it the Ink Spots but litigation prevented that. The name "Brown Dots" was an obvious, but legal, takeoff on the Ink Spots name. They were a talented group of musicians out of New York City. Pat Best wrote their biggest song, "For Sentimental Reasons." (Watson received co-writing credit but had no part in writing the song.) Jimmy Gordon had sung in Broadway musicals and Jimmie Nabbie, who replaced Joe King, was a classically-trained tenor. Differences arose in the group in 1948 and Best, Gordon and Nabbie (along with Danny Owens) began singing and recording, behind Watson's back, with a group they named the Sentimentalists (later the Four Tunes) and that spelled the end of that version of the Brown Dots. Watson formed a second group in 1949 that lasted until 1951. They recorded for Manor and consisted of Watson, Donald "Junie" Cole (Cozy Cole's brother) and Danny Gibson (drums). *Reference*: Brown Dots CD

Brox Sisters
The Brox Sisters, Bobbe (Josephine), Patricia and Lorayne, were one of the earliest sister recording acts. Born in the U.S., they grew up in Edmonton, Alberta, Canada. Their family name was Brock and they changed it to Brox at the suggestion of a producer. They also changed their first names, Josephine to Dagmar and then Bobbe; Eunice to Lorayne and Kathleen to Patricia. They were featured on Broadway and appeared in films such as "The Cocoanuts" in 1926 with the Marx Brothers. Bobbe, who was married to songwriter Jimmy Van Heusen for over 30 years, died in 1999 at the age of 98. Patricia died in 1988 and Lorayne in 1993. *Reference*: www.dgarrick.com

Brunswick Male Chorus
Franklyn Baur (tenor), Charles Harrison (tenor), Billy Jones (tenor), Frank Munn (tenor), Elliott Shaw (baritone) and Wilfred Glenn (bass) were the members of this group that recorded for Brunswick in the 1920s. *Reference*: Mainspring

Brunswick Male Quartet
Audrey Hackett, Arthur Clough, Harry Wieting and A. Duncan Cornwall, made up this group that recorded on Columbia in 1911. *Reference*: Walsh

Tim Brymn's Black Devil Four
Male, black quartet that recorded in New York in the early 1920s, including "Aunt Hagar's Children Blues" in 1923. *Reference*: BSVG-1

Buccaneers
Octet that recorded in New York in 1934 on Columbia. *Reference*: Lehl Discography

Buckeye State Quartette
Group that appeared on sheet music of "Since Arrah Wanna Married Barney Carney" and "Two Blue Eyes" in 1907.

Buckingham Quartette
Male black group that appeared in the show "South Before The War" in New York in the 1890s. *Reference*: Brooks

Buckley's Serenaders
The Buckley family name was Burke. Troupe consisted of father James, Swaine Buckley, R. Bishop Buckley and Fred Buckley (also known as Master Ole Bull Buckley). Performed in the 1840s. See also, Congo Minstrels. *Reference*: Averill; Dumont (1914)

Verne Buck Trio
Bill Chandler was a member of this group that recorded in Chicago in 1928. *Reference*: Lehl Discography

Bon Bon & his Buddies
See, Three Keys.

Buford, Bennett & Buford
Female trio appearing on the cover of the 1915 sheet music of "To Lou." Also pictured are "The Three White Kuhns."

Burgess, Hughes, Prendergast & Donniker's Minstrels
Troupe with the longest name through the mid-1860s. Troupe members included Paul Berger, O. P. Sweet, Frank Bowles, Dion De Marbelle, Henry French, C. S. Fredericks, A. C. Stone, J. Saxton, Dave Thompson and an orchestra, presided over by John Donniker. *Reference*: Dumont (1915)

Luis Russell And His Burning Eight
Recorded on Okeh in 1929; Walter Pichon was one of the vocalists. *Reference*: Fournier

Eddie Bush Trio
Members were Eddie Bush, Bill Seckler and Paul Gibbons and they were active from 1928 to 1934. *Reference*: Lehl Discography

Cab Calloway & the Cabaliers
The famous Cab Calloway formed this group with the Palmer Brothers, Clarence, Dick and Ernest, in New York in 1942. See, Palmer Brothers. *Reference*: SU

Cabin Boys
Mixed-gender black group that recorded two sides on Decca in 1938. Delores Jackson (lead), Tyre Swanger, Raymond Nelson and Harold Waugh comprised the group. *Reference*: RCM 46

Cabineers (Cleveland)
Marv Goldberg found a reference to them that indicated they were from Cleveland and the members as of 1940 were Raymond Walker (1st tenor), Clarence Roberts (2nd tenor), Aaron Hopkins (baritone) and Emory Hopkins (bass). It is not believed that they ever recorded. *Reference*: Goldberg

Cabineers (New York)
William Westbrook (founder), Maggie Furman (alto), Count Cablo (baritone) and Matt McKinney (bass) made up this group that appears to have been formed in New York. They recorded on Decca in the 1940s. Herb Kenny and Adriel McDonald, who both also sang with the Ink Spots, were later members, as were James Peele and Samuel Copney. *Reference*: Goldberg

Cadets
Appeared on sheet music, including "Give My Love To Nell" in 1935. The original members of this white quintet were Al Stracke, Carl Schiebe, Sam Cowling, Lonnie _____ and Reo Fletcher (piano). Homer Allen (Snodgrass), Ken Morrow, Reo Fletcher, Bob Childe, Jack Halloran, Arnold Isolany, Ralph Nyland and Sam Thompson all appear on various lists as later members. They appeared on Don McNeil's Breakfast Club radio show in 1942. *Reference*: http://www.richsamuels.com/; http://otrrpedia.net/

Caldwells
Alex Caldwell (lead) lent his name to this mixed-gender quartet. Other members were Helen Stewart, Oleatha Grangel and John Dennis. They recorded primarily on RCA and Rainbow from 1947 to 1951. *Reference*: RCM 35, 47

California American Legion Quartet
Recorded on Vocalion in 1929.

California Humming-Birds
Male trio that recorded for several labels in 1928, including Cameo and Victor. Members were Charles Adler, Harry Weil and Oscar Herman (also piano). *Reference*: Sweetest Harmony

California Male Quartet
Male group with female accompanist (Mae Chandler). Members were John W. Lince (basso), George Thomas (1st tenor), James Ross McKenzie (baritone) and Earl S. Renner (2nd tenor). Appeared on the Lyceum and Chautauqua circuits in the 1910s. *Reference*: Iowa

Callender's Georgia Minstrels
Bought by Charles Callender from Charles Hicks around 1870. Featured the close harmony male quartet by the name of the Hamtown Students (whose last names were Little, Morris, Jones and Devonear). *Reference*: Averill

Calliope Quartette
Black group that was active in the 1880s. *Reference*: http://www.lib.unb.ca/

Cal Wagner's Pontoons
Minstrel troupe traveling around during the Civil War. Also called Cal Wagner's Minstrels. In the 1870s the troupe contained "Canfield and Booker, Cal Wagner, Sam Price, Lew Hallett, George Wilson, Milt Barlow, C. C. Templeton, and Harry Robinson." *Reference*: Dumont (1914)

Cambrian Quartette
Group appearing with their accompanist on the sheet music of "You Were A Wonderful Mother (Dear Little Mother Of Mine)" from 1916.

Cambridge Sisters
Trio (Hazel, Ruby and Jeanette) that appears on the cover of sheet music of "Sweetest Little Rose in Tennessee, a Lullaby" in 1920 and "How Do You Do" in 1924. The group was advertised as Chicago's favorite recording artists.

Cameo Male Quartet
Recorded on Cameo in 1924. *Reference*: Lehl Discography

Cameron Male Quartette
Appeared on the Redpath Lyceum and Chautauqua circuits in 1921. *Reference*: Iowa

Campbell's Minstrels
Also called the Original Campbell Minstrels. Formed in June, 1847 by John Campbell, a New York restaurateur. Included W. B. Donaldson, Jerry Bryant, John Rea, James Carter, Harry Mestayer and David Raymond. Rea left to join the Original Christy's Minstrels. *Reference*: Averill

Camp Meetin' Three
Recorded in 1926. *Reference*: BVG-3

Campus Boys
Recorded on Banner in 1928. *Reference*: Lehl Discography

Campus Glee Club
See, Shannon Four.

Campus Kids
Mixed-gender quintet - three women and two men - of the mid-1940s that recorded with Kay Kyser and his "Kollege Of Musical Knowledge." *Reference*: http://home.earthlink.net/

Campus Male Quartet
Recorded on Brunswick between 1923 and 1926. Members were Fred Vettle (tenor), Harold Land (tenor), Harvey Hindermeyer (baritone) and Donald Chalmers (bass). *Reference*: Lehl Discography

Campus Trio
Sang with Ted Wallace and were Norman Heyne, Harold Dennis and Lee Gillette and recorded on Columbia from 1929 to 1934. *Reference*: Lehl Discography

Canaanites
Philadelphia group with Joe Van Loan (lead), Elijah Harvey (2nd tenor), James Miller (baritone) and Alan Scott (bass). They started as a gospel group and did some unreleased secular tracks for Gotham. See, the Bachelors. *Reference*: Goldberg

Candy Makers
Recorded on Urban in 1946. Also recorded with Flora Washington in 1946 on United Artists. *Reference*: Fournier

Capitol City Four
Appeared on sheet music of "Would You Take Me Back Again" in 1913.

Cap-Tans
Washington, D.C. quintet that started as the Buddies and featured Sherman Buckner (lead), Floyd Bennett (1st tenor), Alfred Slaughter (tenor), Sherman Buckner (tenor) and Lester Fountain (baritone). Harmon Bethea from the Progressive Four joined in 1949. Raymond Reader replaced Fountain on 1951 and eventually, Fountain returned and was joined by Slaughter and Bradford Fenwick, Elmo Anderson and Lorenzo Miller. This grouping did not last long and Bethea joined the Progressivaires, a gospel quintet. After a seven year hiatus, they recorded again as L'Cap-Tans and continued until 1964. *Reference*: YM-8, Goldberg

Capitol City Singing Four
Male group on the cover of "Kentucky Four" from 1909.

Cardinal Quartet
White group that recorded on Black Swan in the 1920s and were also known as the Black Swan Quartette. They also recorded on Challenge in 1927. *Reference*: Mainspring

Cardinals
Ernie Warren (an underrated lead), Prince Brothers, Leon Hardy and Donald Jack Johnson were the original members of this Baltimore group that started as the Mellotones in 1946. They made their mark in the 1950s as the Cardinals. Sam Aydelotte was a later member and guitarist. They had three R&B charts hits on Atlantic, "Shouldn't I Know" (1951), "The Wheel Of Fortune" (1952) and "The Door Is Still Open" (1955). *Reference*: Warner

Carnival Four
Appeared on sheet music of "Just One Day" in 1916 and were Jack White, Chas. Smith, Andy Smith and Billy Lynch.

Carolina Carolers
Recorded in 1930. Listed as "Carolina Carolers (Dixie Harmonizers)." *Reference*: BVG-3

Carolon Quartet
White group from the 1930s. *Reference*: Warner

Carroll College Quartette
Male group from Carroll College in Waukesha, Wisconsin. Consisted of Edgar J. Best (1st tenor), Russell E. Oakes (basso), John S. Otten (baritone and reader), and Earl A. Lockman (tenor and manager). Appeared on the Redpath Chautauqua circuit around 1912. *Reference*: Iowa

Carroll Glees
Male group consisting of Burleigh E. Jacobs (1st tenor and pianist), Earl A. Lockman (2nd tenor), John S. Otten (bass) and Russell E. Oakes (2nd bass). Appeared on the Redpath Lyceum circuit in the 1910s. *Reference*: Iowa

Carroll Sisters
Trio that appeared on the Major Bowes' Original Amateur Hour radio show in 1943 and Ed Sullivan's TV show, "Toast of the Town" in 1950. They were also on sheet music of "Mairzy Doats" in 1943. *Reference*: www.imdb.com

Casion Four
Vaudeville quartette in which Al Jolson began his career. *Reference*: Averill

Castle Square Quartette
Two women and two men appearing on the cover of "One Little Soldier Man" from 1904.

Cathedral Quartet
See, Shannon Four

Cats and the Fiddle
This self-contained jive group began in the late 1930s in Chicago. Members were Austin Powell (lead), Jimmie Henderson (1st tenor), Ernie Price (2nd tenor) and Chuck Barksdale (bass) (Barksdale died in 1941 and was replaced by George Stainback). Powell went into the Armed Forces in 1941 and Hank Haslett took his place, followed by Herbie Miles until Powell returned after the war. Henderson became ill and was temporarily replaced by Miles; he returned and then died in 1941 and was replaced by Lloyd "Tiny" Grimes (see, Three Barons) who in turn was replaced by Pee Wee Branford. Branford gave way to Emmitt Slay in 1947 and then Johnny Davis. In 1948, a woman was added, Shirley Moore, who herself was replaced by Doris Knighton after four cuts. By 1949, the group consisted of Powell, Branford, Price and Stainback. Their biggest hit was "I Miss You So" (1940-Bluebird), written by Henderson. Dave Penny called the song, "truly one of Doo Wop's seminal recordings." They appeared in several movies and recorded over 30 sides. *Reference*: JJ-CD; Warner

Cats 'N' Jammer Three
From Chicago, they were Bill Samuels (lead), Sylvester Hickman and Adam Lambert (later with the Four Shades of Rhythm). They played their own instruments and later recorded on Miracle as the Bill Samuels Trio. *Reference*: RCM-8

Cavaliers
Recorded on CavaTone with the Jubilee Gospel Singers in 1949 and were led by Bob Geddin. *Reference*: Fournier

Cavaliers
They were part of the Victor Minstrels in 1929. *Reference*: Mainspring

Cecelian Quartet
Recorded on Victor in 1914.

Celebrated Oxford Quartette
Male group including W. Charles, A. H. Fulton, W. H. Voelker and W. F. Halpin that appears on the cover of sheet music of "Friends" from 1898.

Central Mississippi Quartet
Recorded on Vocalion and Okeh in 1930.

Central Quartette
Appear on the "Garfield and Arthur Book of Campaign Songs" in 1880 and are listed as F. E. Lansing (1st tenor), W. A. Paulsen (2nd Tenor), Jules Street (1st bass) and C. A. S. Herchelrode (2nd bass).

Frank Luther & the Century Quartet
Recorded on Decca in 1938, including "The Gay Parade." The group included Zora Layman. *Reference*: http://www.americanheritage.com/articles/magazine/l

Challenge Harmony Four
Recorded on Challenge in 1927-8.

Chanters
Not the same as the 1960s group from New York, this ensemble recorded in 1934 on Victor and Electrola with Don Bestor and possible personnel were Neil Buckley, Maurice Cross and Charles "Ducky" Yotz. *Reference*: Lehl Discography

Chapman Boys and their Seven Beautiful Fashionettes
The group was two men and seven women that appeared on sheet music of "For My Sweetheart" in 1926.

Charioteers
Formed at Wilberforce University in Ohio in the early 1930s as the Harmony Four or the Southern Black Birds, depending on which source you follow) by Howard Daniel, a faculty

member (bass) and Billy Williams (lead). The other members of the group were George Lubers (tenor) (replaced by Edward Jackson), John Harewood (replaced by Ira Williams) (baritone) and Jimmy Sherman (pianist and arranger). The group took its name from the spiritual, "Swing Low, Sweet Chariot." In Cincinnati, they sang on WLW radio from 1933 to 1935. They appeared with Bing Crosby on the Kraft Music Hall radio show. Billy Williams left the group in 1949 and formed the Billy Williams Quartet. Herbert Dickerson took Williams' spot in the Charioteers. Later members had included Robert Bowers, Peter Lubers and Henry King (for Eddie Jackson). They did quite a bit of backup work for singers such as Pearl Bailey, Frank Sinatra and Bing Crosby and sang with the Eddy Duchin Band. Their song, "A Kiss And A Rose" (1949-Columbia), made the Top 10 on the R&B charts and was #19 on the pop chart. Other songs included "Moanin' Low" (1929), "Walkin' My Baby Back Home" (1931) and "Basin St. Blues" (1931), all on Columbia. They appeared in the United Artists movie, "Road Show" in 1941. The Charioteers disbanded in the 1950s. Williams died penniless in 1972 in Chicago. *Reference*: Warner; Southern

Celestine Stewart & the Charmers
Recorded at least two sides for Hub in 1946.

Chase's Minstrels
Short-lived New York group from 1867, consisting of Hughey Dougherty, S. S. Purdy, C. C. Templeton, George H. Coes, J. W. Hilton, Charley Church, Dave Reed, J. W. Clark, Charley Fox, John Sivori, W. L. Hobbs, and Hi Melville. *Reference*: Dumont (1915)

Chautauqua Male Quartette
Appeared with Ethel Hinton on the Chautauqua circuit in the 1910s. *Reference*: Iowa

Chautauqua Preachers Quartet
Male group consisting of clergy. Members were Charles Alfred Briggs (basso and manager), Charles A. Gage (2nd tenor and director), Wesley J. Holland ("barytone") and Faye Arnold Moon (1st tenor). They recorded on Columbia in 1915 and toured the Chautauqua circuit. *Reference*: Walsh; Iowa

Chesterfieldians
Mixed-gender quartet that appeared on the Benny Goodman/Oscar Levant Show in New York on October 23, 1944. *Reference*: Lehl Discography

Chicago Five
They were billed both as Tampa Red and the Chicago Five and Bob Robinson and the Chicago Five and recorded on Bluebird in 1936. *Reference*: Lehl Discography

Chicago Lyceum Lady Quartette
Members were Myrtle Stitt (1st soprano), Emilie A. Compton (2nd soprano), Helen Dodge (1st Alto) and Mary K. O'Brien (2nd alto). Performed for the Chicago Lyceum Bureau around 1910 (date is a guess). *Reference*: Iowa

Chicago Male Quartet
Featured the baritone lead of Robert Herrick and were from the Redpath Chautauqua circuit, around 1927. Performed college and humorous material. *Reference*: Iowa

Chicago Male Quartet
Members listed only as Collins, MacMullen, Hedgcoxe and Smith. Appeared on the Lyceum circuit in 1926. *Reference*: Iowa

Hoagy Carmichael & the Chickadees
Quartet that recorded on Decca in the mid-1940s, including "Doctor, Lawyer, Indian Chief" in 1946.

Christy Minstrels
Founded by E. P. Christy in 1846, this group established the three-part construction of the typical minstrel show: the joking between the interlocutor (middle man) and the end-men, tambo and bones, the olio, or variety show (precursor to vaudeville), and a short skit about life on the plantation. They popularized such Stephen Foster standards as "Oh! Susanna" (1848), "Camptown Races" (1850) and "Old Folks At Home "(1851). First called The Original Christy Minstrels, and originating in Buffalo, N.Y., they consisted of E. P. Christy, George N. Christy, L. Durand, and T. Vaughn. When Enam Dickinson and Zeke Bachus were added, they changed their name to Christy's Minstrels. Performed in New York City from 1847 to 1854. *Reference*: Averill; White

Christy Minstrels (Billy Murray and the Haydn Quartet)
Recorded on Victor in 1907. *Reference*: http://www.denvernightingale.com/

Chuck, Ray and Gene (N.B.C.-WENR Artists)
Appeared on sheet music of "Sweet As Honey" in 1931. WENR was a Chicago radio station.

Chung Hwa Three
Appeared on sheet music, including "Just A Girl That Men Forget" in 1923.

Church City Four
Appeared on sheet music of "You Are The Ideal Of My Dreams" in 1910.

Clark Sisters
Peggy, Mary, Jean and Ann Clark made up the quartet. They started as the Sentimentalists with the Tommy Dorsey Band and were named after his signature tune, "I'm Getting Sentimental Over You." In 1947, they returned to Dorsey to record, with Lillian Clark replacing Mary (Lillian later married arranger Sy Oliver). They also sang with the Blue Barron Band in the 1930s. *Reference*: They Also Sang With Tommy Dorsey CD, Flyright EBCD-2186

Clayton, Jackson and Durante
Included Jimmy Durante and recorded in New York in 1929 on Columbia. *Reference*: Lehl Discography

Cleartones
See, Selah Jubilee Singers.

Clipper Quartette
Singing group that accompanied the McIntyre and Heath Minstrels in 1885. *Reference*: Dumont (1915)

Clipper Quartette
Male group on the cover of the sheet music to "When I Get You Alone Tonight" from 1912.

Clipper Trio
Three men in an informal pose on the cover of "Down Among The Sheltering Palms," from 1914. Group members are listed as Christie, Kennedy and Faulkner.

Cliquot Club Eskimo Quartet
Appeared on cover of sheet music of "I'm Lonely Without You" in 1926'

Clovers
Started out as a traditional post-war group and evolved into one that was more in tune with the R&B, rock and roll style of the 1950s groups. They formed in high school in Washington, D.C., in 1946 and were one of the great groups. They did extremely well on the R& B Charts (21 entries, 18 of them Top 10), but barely hit the Pop Charts. By 1950, the members were Harold Lucas (lead), Billy Shelton (bass) and Thomas Woods (tenor). Then John "Buddy" Bailey (lead) joined the group and Lucas switched to baritone, Matthew McQuater replaced Woods and Harold Winley took Shelton's place. Their songs included "One Mint Julep" (1952-Atlantic), "Fool, Fool, Fool" (1951-Atlantic), "Blue Velvet" (1954-Atlantic), "Devil Or Angel" (1956-Atlantic) and "Love Potion No. 9" (1959-

United Artists), which was a Lieber-Stoller song in which the Clovers adopted a Coasters-like style in an attempt to revive their popularity. *Reference*: Warner

Clubmen
Sang with Freddie Rich's Radio Orchestra and recorded on Decca and Brunswick in 1938. They also recorded on Victor. *Reference*: Lehl Discography

Club Trio
Male group (listed as Stevenson, Hayden and McIvor) that is featured on the cover of "If The Can Canny Cannibals Captured New York Town" in 1916.

Coakley, Hanvey & Dunlevy
Appear on sheet music of "In The Wee Small Hours Of The Morning" in 1915.

Cole Brothers
Recorded "Dinah" in 1933. *Reference*: Sweetest Harmony

Coleman Brothers
Began in 1917 in Montclair, New Jersey, and consisted of David, Lewis, Matthew and Levi Coleman. This group never recorded. Second and third groups were formed by other family members in the 1920s. Groups two and three eventually combined and consisted of Russell, Lander, Wallace and Melvin Coleman and Danny Owens (who also sang with the Melody Masters and the Four Tunes). Their first recording was "Low Down The Chariot" (1944-Decca). They appeared regularly on the radio and had their own conglomerate of Coleman Records, a hotel and restaurants and toured extensively. "I'll Always Be In Love With You" on the Coleman label was a Top 10 hit on the R&B charts in 1948 for them. *Reference*: Warner, Goldmine 36

College Girls
Four unnamed women who appeared at the Chautauquas in 1912. *Reference*: Iowa

College Singing Girls
There appear to have been two separate groups of this name on the Chautauqua and Lyceum circuits in the 1910s. One was a quartet including Henrietta Fraser, Ada Mary Porter, Bella Gerard and Madalyn Maier. *Reference*: Iowa

College Singing Girls
The second group of this name, they were a quintet comprised of Jean Warren, Katherine Galloway, Ethel Caween, Gertrude Crosby and an unknown fifth member. They sang on the Lyceum circuit in the 1910s. *Reference*: Iowa

Collegian Quartet of Olivet College
Male group including Crawford M. Rosebrugh (1st tenor), George O. Leonard (2nd tenor), Willis L. Osborn (1st bass) and Leon C. Maxey (2nd bass). Appeared on the Chautauqua circuit in the 1910s. *Reference*: Iowa

Collegians
Male quartet featuring Reid M. Strohm (1st tenor), E. A. Vir Den (2nd tenor), Rex S. Reynolds (baritone) and L. E. Spring (bass). Appeared for the Redpath Lyceum Bureau around 1919. *Reference*: Iowa

Collegiate Quartette
Mixed-gender group from New York City including Edith Chapman Gold (soprano), Corinne Welsh (contralto), John Young (tenor) and La Rue Boals (bass). Appeared for the White Entertainment Bureau in 1912. *Reference*: Iowa

Colonial Male Quartette
Male group whose picture appears on programs for a New York concert held in 1902. Singers are H. Wilson, W. A. Benjamin, Harland Buckmaster and W. Sedgwick Root. Their pianist is Miss Lucille Glover. *Reference*: eBay auction

Colonial Quartet
Recorded on a Zonophone disc in 1906.

Columbia Double Quartet
Also known as the Columbia Octette. They recorded in 1915. Walsh states they were likely the Columbia Stellar Quartet and Peerless Quartet members. *Reference*: Walsh

Columbia Ladies Quartet
Recorded for Columbia in 1913 and were Grace Kerns, Louise MacMahon, Mildred Potter and Clara Moister. *Reference*: Walsh

Columbia Male Quartet
There appear to have been two groups with this name. One included Tom Mabon (1st tenor), Elton Spicer (2nd tenor and accompanist), Stanley Heywood (baritone) and James H. Jackson (bass). Appeared on the Redpath Chautauqua circuit between 1900 and 1910 (date is a guess). The other group is listed immediately below. *Reference*: Iowa

Columbia Male Quartet
Started in the late 1890s and was made up of Albert Campbell (1st tenor), J. K. Reynard (2nd tenor) (replaced by Henry Burr in 1902 or 1903), Joe Belmont (baritone) and Joe

Majors (bass). Arthur Collins, Steve Porter, George Gaskin, Frank C. Stanley and "Big Tom" Daniels also sang in the group. See also, Peerless Quartet. *Reference*: Walsh

Columbia Male Trio
Recorded on Columbia in 1902. *Reference*: http://settlet.fateback.com/

Columbia Minstrels
Recorded in 1902 and were John Meyer, Arthur Collins, Albert Campbell and Henry Burr. *Reference*: www.archive.org/details.

Columbia Mixed Double Quartet
Columbia Mixed Quartet plus four other members. In 1915, they recorded on Columbia. *Reference*: Walsh.

Columbia Mixed Quartet
Members were Grace Kerns, Mildred Potter, Charles Harrison and Frank Croxton. They made two recordings for Columbia in 1912 and 1916. *Reference*: Walsh

Columbia Octette
See, Columbia Double Quartet.

Columbia Quartet
Original members were Albert Campbell, J. K. Reynard, Joe Belmont and Joe Majors. Henry Burr replaced Reynard in about 1902. *Reference*: Schlesinger

Columbia Sextet
Recorded on Columbia in 1902 and consisted of Bryon Harlan, Joe Belmont, Frank Stanley and three women from the Floradora Sextette (it is not known which three). *Reference*: Walsh

Columbia Sextette
Female group comprised of unnamed members. Appeared on the Lyceum and Chautauqua circuits between 1900 and 1910 (date is a guess). Their program consisted of "costumed songs, instrumental music for the entire orchestra, and vocal and instrumental solos, duets, trios and quartets." *Reference*: Iowa

Columbia Stellar Quartet
When formed in 1914, they were Charles Harrison, John Barnes Wells, Frank Croxton and Andrea Sarto. Wells was replaced by Henry Burr in 1915 and Burr by Reed Miller (himself occasionally replaced by Lewis James) shortly thereafter. Billy Jones sang lead on some of their recordings. Had a number one song with "Battle Hymn Of The Republic" (1918-

Columbia). They were also the Stellar Quartet and Broadway Quartet on Columbia. *Reference*: Whitburn – PM; Schlesinger

Columbia Tennesseans
Black sextette of four men and two women. Personnel included W. J. Williams (lyric tenor), D. Peyton (2nd tenor), Chas. Huggins (baritone), W. E. Fields (basso), Eva Bryant (soprano) and Belle E. Hocker (contralto). *Reference*: Iowa

Comedian Harmonists
German sextet comprised of Ari Leschnikoff (lead tenor), Erich Collin (tenor), Harry Frommermann (founder and tenor), Roman Cycowski (baritone), Robert Biberti (bass) and Erwin Bootz was their pianist. They began in 1928 in Berlin and modeled themselves after the American group, the Revelers, so much so that their first billings read, "The Comedian Harmonists, The German Revellers (sic)." But soon they far surpassed the Revelers and became the most popular vocal group in Europe and many places beyond. Their voices were impeccable, blended beautifully and Frommermann's arrangements were masterpieces. Their all too short career lasted only until early 1935. Two of the members, Frommermann and Cycowski, were Jewish and Collin was considered Jewish by the Nazis because his parents had both been born as Jews. Because three of them were non-Aryan, they were at first restricted in what they could sing (no songs by Jewish composers or those published by Jewish-owned publishing houses – these constituted about three quarters of their repertoire), and then prohibited from performing entirely. The three non-Aryans left Germany found three new members and continued to perform as the Comedy Harmonists until the war broke out. The Aryans also found new members but were required to adopt an Aryan name – they chose the Meistersextett. They too disbanded, in 1941. Neither new group achieved the enormous critical or financial success of the original.

Comedy Four
Male group on the cover of sheet music for "Good-By Betty Brown" from 1910.

Commanders
Sextette and orchestra that appeared on sheet music of "Oh Peter (You're So Nice)" in 1924.

Commonwealth Male Quartette Concert Company
Personnel included A. L. Hipson (1st tenor), E. S. Glines (2nd tenor), A. H. Carpenter (baritone) and A. H. Logan (basso). Boston group appearing for the Rochester Lyceum, probably around 1910. *Reference*: Iowa

Congo Minstrels
Later called the Negro Minstrels, this group was owned by George Swain Buckley and appeared at the Apollo Hall, on Broadway in New York City, in May of 1844. A drawing of

the group appears on the cover of "The Celebrated Congo Minstrels' Songs" published in Boston in 1844. By 1860, they were known as Buckley's New Orleans Serenaders. *Reference*: White; http://commons.wikimedia.org/

Connolly Sisters
Trio - May, Dolly and Belle - that appeared on sheet music of "Goodbye Eliza Jane" in 1903.

Consolidated Quartette
Male group that recorded on Consolidated in 1899. *Reference*: Lehl Discography

Continental Vocalists
Minstrel quartet of the mid-nineteenth century. *Reference*: Averill

Cook Sisters
Recorded on Brunswick in 1927.

Coquettes
Appear on sheet music of "That Naughty Waltz" from 1920.

Cotton Blossom Singers
See, Five Blind Boys Of Mississippi.

Cotton Pickers Quartet
Recorded in the late 1920s and early 1930s and sang with Jack Teagarden. *Reference*: BVG-3

Country Harmonizers
See, Harmonizers Quartet.

Counts and Countess
This Detroit group recorded on Melodisc in the mid-1940s and was a self-contained vocal/instrumental trio made up of Alma Smith (piano and vibes), John Faire (guitar) and Curtis Wilder (bass fiddle). *Reference*: Fournier

Cox Family Quartette
Appeared on Sheet music of "Dear Old Stars And Stripes Good-Bye" in 1902.

Crescent Trio
Charles Hart, Lewis James and Elliott Shaw recorded from 1918 to the late 1920s with slightly changing personnel. They were known as both the Apollo Trio and Orpheus Trio on Pathé Actuelle. *Reference*: Walsh

Crew Chiefs
Sang with the Tex Beneke Orchestra in the 1940s. Known members were Steve Steck, Murray Kane, Artie Malvin, James Lynn Allison and Gene Steck. They also sang with the Glenn Miller Air Force Band along with Johnny Desmond. *Reference*: http://www.bigbandlibrary.com/; http://mall.saleablegoods.com/

Criterion Glee Club
Members were Alvin L. Wilson (1st tenor), Frank W. Grover (2nd tenor), Cliff R. Cline (baritone) and Walter A. Wood (basso). Appeared on the Chautauqua circuit around 1910 (date is a guess). *Reference*: Iowa

Criterion Male Quartet/Criterion Quartette
The Criterion Male Quartet included, in 1905-1907, Robert R. Rainey, William A. Washburn, Reinald Werrenrath and Walter A. Downie. From 1916 to 1921 they were John Young, Horatio Rench, George W. Reardon and Donald Chalmers. In 1921 Frank Mellor replaced Young. At some point Frederic Thomas replaced Chalmers as bass. They recorded for Victor, Brunswick, Edison and Emerson and appeared on the Chautauqua circuit around 1915. They were also known as the Aeolian Male Quartet (on Vocalion), Strand Quartet (on Brunswick) and Broadway Quartet (on Vocalion). They sang at the Roxy Theater in New York in the late 1920s and became known as the Roxy Quartet. The sheet music for "Mine" dated 1912 lists the members as "Messrs. Quince, Snow, Noeker, Dumas." The sheet "Please Take Me Back To Dear Ohio" from 1920 shows the same members. A photo of them appears on a concert tour program from Maine, around 1915. The same group appears on a Midwest program, around the same year. *Reference*: Walsh; Averill; Iowa

Crooners
Recorded with several orchestras including Fred Rich and Ben Selvin, mostly on Columbia from 1926 to 1930. *Reference*: Lehl Discography

Crooning Cavaliers
Recorded on Cameo in 1927.

Crossman Trio
Male group appearing on the cover of the sheet music to "Captain Willie Brown" in 1907.

Phil Crow Trio
Recorded on Victor and Columbia in 1930 and 1931 and included Phil Crow, Frank Crow, Carson Robinson and Frank Luther at various times. *Reference*: Lehl Discography

Croxton Quartet
Agnes Kimball, Nevada Van Der Veer, Reed Miller and Frank Croxton made up the group in 1912. In 1918 on Gennett, it was Van Der Veer, Ines Barbour, Henry Burr and Croxton. *Reference*: Walsh

Croxton Trio
Ines Barbour, Henry Burr and Frank Croxton on Okeh in 1918 (according to Walsh). Mainspring lists Agnes Kimball, Reed Miller and Frank Croxton for Edison. *Reference*: Walsh; Mainspring

Crumit Quartet
Recorded in New York in 1920 and were Frank Crumit, William Davidson, H. Henke and Charles Laird. *Reference*: Lehl Discography

Cuatro Muchachos
Recorded in New York in 1942 on Columbia. *Reference*: Lehl Discography

Cuba Quartette
A late 19th-century group. Jake Powell was a member. *Reference*: Averill

C. W. Vreeland's Minstrels
Late 1800s troupe containing "George Hassall, soprano; Bassett and Cole, Arthur Deming, Harry Long, Hugh Franey, Billy Fries, Kennedy and Vonder, and George Dunbar." *Reference*: Dumont (1915)

Cyclone Quartette
Black concert quartet that performed at the Spokane, Washington Opera House in the early 1890s. *Reference*: Averill

Vernon Dalhart Trio
Recorded on Challenge in New York in 1927 and were Vernon Dalhart, Carson Robison and Hood. *Reference*: Lehl Discography

Dalton Boys
Appeared on sheet music of "Mike And Ike (The Twin Song)" in 1937.

Dandridge Sisters
Included a young Dorothy Dandridge, her sister Vivian and a friend, Etta Jones. They worked at theaters in the Los Angeles area and eventually got a small part in the film, "The Big Broadcast of 1936." They performed successfully at the Cotton Club in New York, sang with Jimmy Lunceford and toured Europe until the start of World War II. When they returned, Dorothy became more interested in solo work and the group broke up - a familiar story. *Reference*: http://en.wikipedia.org/wiki/Dandridge_Sisters

Dandies
White quartet that appeared on the cover of sheet music of "Down In Sleepy Hollow" from 1932.

Danford Sisters
Recorded with Ben Selvin in 1931. *Reference*: Lehl Discography

Davenny Festival Quintet
Contained Mr. and Mrs. Hollis Edison Davenny (baritone and soprano), John Siefert (tenor), Miss Mabel King (contralto) and Miss Elspeth Pritchard. At some point Louis Caton (tenor), Miss Marcella Geon (pianist) and Miss Clara Irene Gray (contralto) were members. *Reference*: Iowa

Davis Quartette
Included Robert J. Brown (tenor), Winona Davis (soprano), Edwina B. Wigent (contralto), Ralph W. Clark and Ethel Nimmons-Western (pianist). The appeared at Chautauquas in 1916. *Reference*: Iowa

Day Dawn And Dusk
Black trio made up of Bob Caver (also piano), Eddie Coleman and Gus Simmons The caption under a picture of them in the *Amsterdam News* in 1939 stated they had just returned from eight years in Europe. They recorded on several labels, including Herald. *Reference*: Fournier

Debonairs Quartette
Four men, on a national tour. Date unknown. *Reference*: Iowa

Debutantes
Trio consisting of Betty Noyes, Dorothy Compton and Marjorie Briggs that sang with the Ted Fio Rito Band from 1932 to 1938. *Reference*: http://www.collateralworks.com/

DeCastro Sisters
Trio from Cuba, Peggy, Babette and Cherie DeCastro, that came to the U.S. in 1945 and appeared in the film, "Copacabana." in 1947 (because all their recordings were after 1950, they are not in our Discography). Their greatest success came in the 1950s when they had a number two hit with "Teach Me Tonight" (1954-Abbott). *Reference*: http://home.earthlink.net/

Decca Band & The American Four
Recorded two sides on Decca in 1941. *Reference*: http://honkingduck.com/

Deep River Boys
Formed at Hampton Institute in Virginia in 1934 as the Hampton Institute Quartet by Noah Ryder, director of the glee club and a student. Members were Harry Douglas (baritone), Vernon Gardner (tenor), George Lawson (tenor) and Edward Ware (bass). They won the Major Bowes Family Amateur Hour radio show contest and changed their name to the Deep River Boys. Later members were James Lundy and Carter Wilson, both tenors, bass Al Bishop and second tenor Ray Beatty. Hugh Bryant, Ronnie Bright (of the Valentines and Coasters) and Rhett Butler also sang with them. They appeared in the Broadway musical, "Swingin' The Dream" in 1939 with Louis Armstrong and charted with "Recess In Heaven" (1948-RCA Victor). After World War II, they spent considerable time in London where they had a record-breaking ten week stay at the London Palladium. One of their more notable songs was "It Had To Be You" (1947-Victor). Douglas performed right up to his death in 1999 at the age of 84. *Reference*: Whitburn-PM; Southern

Deep River Plantation Singers
Five unnamed black males shown on an advertisement from 1942. An earlier version of this group, from the 1930s, featured only four males, and a brochure stated that they were successors to Jackson's Jubilee Singers. They recorded in Richmond in 1931. *Reference*: Iowa

Deep River Quintet
Recorded in 1927 with the Chicago Loopers, the Deep River Orchestra and Willard Robinson Orchestra. In 1931, they recorded as the Deep River Plantation Singers on Champion. *Reference*: Lehl Discography

Deep River Singers
Black ensemble group, formed in 1928, comprised of roughly twenty-five singers that performed in various combinations, from chorus to quartet to solo, in the 1930s. A quartet featured Albert Yarborough (tenor), Merton Smith (tenor), Albert Page (baritone) and John Burdette (bass). Burdette won the award given by the Chicago Tribune for the best male

vocalist in America. They appeared in a show in Chicago called the "Swing Mikado." Delano Obannion, of Fisk University, was their Director. *Reference*: Iowa

Deep Tones
New York group comprised of George Vereen (1st tenor), Ivy Floyd (tenor), Furman Hayes (2nd tenor), Calvin Williams (baritone) and Carroll Dean (bass). Vereen also sang with the Four Knights and the Stereos and Williams with the Four Knights. The group was later known as the Four Deeptones and then the HiLiters. *Reference*: Fournier; Goldmine 5/8/87

DeKoven Male Quartet
Members were Howard L. Baxter (1st tenor), Ivon H. Blackman (2nd tenor), Clifford A. Foote (baritone) and Robert von Zoll (basso). Active on the Midland Chautauqua Circuit in the 1910s. A second version featured Gerard S. Pell (1st tenor) and Walter G. Johnson replacing Blackman and von Zoll. *Reference*: Iowa

Del Mar Ladies Quartette
Members included Katharyn Bauder, Mildred Manville, Lois Wood and Edithe Trueblood. Toured the Midwest in the 1910s. *Reference*: Iowa

Delta Rhythm Boys
The Delta Rhythm Boys came together at Langston University in Oklahoma in the mid-1930s and then transferred to Dillard University in New Orleans (after a meeting with Dr. Horace Bond, father of politician Julian Bond) to be with Frederick Hall, the Director of Music at Dillard. Members were Otha Lee Gaines (bass), Elmaurice Miller (tenor), Traverse Crawford (tenor) and Essie Atkins (baritone). They performed first as the New Orleans Quintet and the Frederick Hall Quintet. Clinton Holland (soon replaced by Carl Jones) and Kelsey Pharr (replaced by Hugh Bryant in 1942) replaced Miller and Atkins. Rene DeKnight was their pianist. They were heard in New Orleans by someone connected with radio in Argentina, and went to that country for nine months. After Argentina, they traveled to New York where they lived in the same house as Eubie Blake. In New York they won the Major Bowes Amateur Hour radio show and appeared regularly on CBS radio. They toured with Bill "Bojangles" Robinson in 1940. "Just A-Sittin' And A Rockin'" (1946-Decca) was a hit for them and "Don't Ask Me Why" (1946-RCA) is considered by many to be one of their finer efforts. In all, they made over 70 recordings, three of which made the R&B Charts. Ella Fitzgerald, Mildred Bailey and Johnny Mercer were among those with whom they recorded. They were regulars on the "Amos and Andy Show." As with many of the Black groups of that era, spent much time in Europe, particularly in London and Stockholm where they were extremely popular. In an interview conducted by Bill Gardner on his Los Angeles radio show in the 1990s, Carl Jones said that many of their vocals were patterned after instrumental arrangements. Jones also said they did some recording for Atlantic as the Four Sharps. They, along with other groups of the era, made

film "Soundies" which were two or three minute musical numbers and were the forerunners of music videos. You would put a coin in a juke box type device and the film would run. They were in fifteen movies, probably more than any other vocal group. According to Jay Warner, their version of "Take The A Train" (1941-Decca) started the vocalese style later used by many groups such as Manhattan Transfer. When Lee Gaines died in 1987, Hugh Bryant sang at the funeral and, like a scene out of a movie, dropped dead as he finished his musical eulogy. *Reference*: The Delta Rhythm Boys Anthology CDs, Dee Jay; Whitburn–PM; Southern

De Luxe Artists-Singers
Mixed-gender sextette including Mary Krakowski (soprano), Alma King (contralto), Kenneth Morrow (tenor), Dan Leiner (bass), Luigi Pupillo (violinist) and Magdalen Massmann (pianist). Appeared for the Redpath Bureau in 1931. *Reference*: Iowa

DeMarco Sisters
A quintet, they appeared on Ed Sullivan's "Toast of the Town" television show four times from 1949 to 1953 and on other TV shows as well and were regulars on the Fred Allen radio show. They also appeared on sheet music of "On The Wrong Side Of The Fence" in 1934 as a trio, sang with Eddie Duchin and were in the movie "Skirts Ahoy" in 1952. *Reference*: www.imdb.com; http://www.courttv.com/

DeMille Quartet
Listed members were Hartwell DeMille (baritone), Alfred J. Atkinson (basso profundo), W. Edmond Capps (lyric tenor) and Gladstone Brown (tenor robusto), accompanied by Hilda Buckingham. Appeared on the Lyceum and Chautauqua circuits. Date estimated at 1905. *Reference*: Iowa

DeReszke Singers
Composed of Francis Luther (tenor), Floyd Townsley (tenor), Erwyn Mutch (baritone) and Harold Kellogg (basso). Appeared with Will Rogers on a program on November 23, 1926 at Orchestra Hall in Chicago. *Reference*: Iowa

W. C. Elkins & his Dextra Singers
Recorded in 1929. *Reference*: BVG-10

DeZunk Sisters
Recorded in 1939 on Conqueror.

Diamond Comedy Four
Len Spencer, Steve Porter, Billy Golden and Vess L. Ossman were the members. Date estimated at 1898 to 1900. *Reference*: Mainspring.

Diamond Four
Early group on Berliner in the mid-1890s. Members were Albert Campbell, James Kent Reynard, Steve Porter and Will C. Jones. *Reference*: Walsh

Diamond Quartette
A 19th-century black group. *Reference*: Averill

Doles Dickens and his Quintet
Recorded on Decca in 1949.

Dictators
Recorded in 1931 in New York on Brunswick.

Dinning Sisters
The Dinning Sisters came from an Oklahoma family of nine children and all but one was in the music business. The group consisted of Jean and Ginger, who were twins, and Lou. In 1946, Lou got married and left, to be replaced by non-family member Jayne Bundesen. In 1949, Bundesen left and Tootsie Dinning replaced her making it an all-family group once again. They sang on NBC radio with their own daily show for seven years and recorded on Capitol, having a national number one album for 18 weeks. "My Adobe Hacienda" (1947)," I Wonder Who's Kissing Her Now" (1947), "Beg Your Pardon" (1948) and "Buttons And Bows" (1948) also charted. After disbanding in the early 1950s, Jean wrote the hit song "Teen Angel" for her brother, Mark Dinning and Tootsie sang on the television show "Hee Haw." *Reference*: The Dinning Sisters Sing Their Tremendous Hits CD; Whitburn-PM

Dinwiddie Colored Quartet
This was the first black group to make a record (the Standard Quartette recorded earlier, but on cylinder). They formed at the John A Dix Industrial School in Dinwiddie, Virginia. The word "colored" was added to their name so that audiences would know the race of the group members. Their "Genuine Jubilee and Camp-Meeting Shouts" was captured by the Victor Talking Machine Company in 1892. Members were Sterling Rex (1st tenor), Clarence Meredith (2nd tenor), James M. Thomas (bass) and Harry Cruder (bass). They did six disks on Victor in 1902 and also cut six disks for Monarch, including "Down The Old Camp Ground" in 1902. *Reference*: Warner; RCM-49; ENVQ 1; ENVQ-2

Diplomats
Quartet that appeared on sheet music of "There's Something About A Rose (That Reminds Me Of You)" in 1928 and in George M. Cohan's "The Merry Malones" in 1927-28. Recorded on Columbia. *Reference*: Lehl Discography

Dipsy Doodlers
Sang with the Larry Clinton band in about 1947.

Dixieaires (Gotham)
The first of two groups with this name, this New York group sang mainly gospel. The members were Clyde Reddick, Conrad Frederick, Orlandus Wilson, Henry Owens and J. C. Ginyard. Ginyard had been with the Jubilaires, later was the lead of the Du Droppers and then joined the Golden Gate Quartet. Wilson, Owens and Riddick were all members of the Golden Gate Quartet. They had Top 10 R&B song with "Go Long" (1948-Gotham). *Reference*: Fournier

Dixieaires (Sunrise)
The second group of this name, they were J. C. Ginyard (he was with both), Joe Floyd, Johnny Hines and Jimmy Smith. Abe Green was their guitarist. They did mostly gospel and recorded on the Sunrise, Sittin In With, Prestige and Harlem labels. *Reference*: http://www.crossrhythms.co.uk/

Dixie Four
See, Four Dusty Travelers.

Dixie Girls
Appeared on sheet music of "It Took The Sunshine Of Old Dixieland" in 1917.

Dixie Hummingbirds
One of the more famous gospel groups, they began in 1928 in Greenville, South Carolina and were formed by James Davis, who had known Josh White when they were children. White helped them with their career, particularly in getting a recording deal. Members of their most well-known grouping were Ira Tucker (lead), James Walker (lead), Beechie Thompson (tenor), James Davis (baritone) and Willie Bobo (bass). Tucker had a dramatic singing style that influenced many of the leads of the 1950s groups. They appeared regularly on radio in Philadelphia in the 1940s, at the Newport Jazz Festival in 1966 and a later version of the group backed Paul Simon on his 1973 hit, "Loves Me Like A Rock." They charted (R&B) with their own version that same year on Peacock. They also sang as the Jericho Boys and the Swanee Quintet. *Reference*: Whitburn-RB; Southern.

Dixie Melody Masters
Members were Marion L. Kay (dramatic tenor), Harry D. Mickle (tenor), George Bizzelle (bass-baritone) and William Sanford (baritone). *Reference*: Iowa

Dixie Minstrels
Recorded in 1907 in Indestructible Cylinder.

Dixie Songsters
See, Charioteers.

Dixie Symphony Four
Also known as the Dixie Singers, they recorded in California, probably in the mid-1930s and their membership is unknown, except that Unice M. Townsend, Jr. was their director. *Reference*: BVG-9

Dixie Vagabond Quartet
Part of the Maryville College Glee Singers, the members were Chilton Bowles (1st tenor), Walter Matthews (2nd tenor), Jack Cotton (baritone) and Walter Courtenay (low bass). *Reference*: Iowa

Dr. Smith's Champion Hoss Hair Pullers
Recorded on Victor in 1928 and were Graydon Bone (tenor), Leeman Bone (tenor, guitar), Roosevelt Garner (tenor), Odie Goatcher (Bass), Hubert Simmons (bass), Clark Duncan, Bryan Lackey (violin) and Ray Marshall (mandolin). *Reference*: Lehl Discography

Dolce Sisters
This trio, Rosalie, Gertrude and Regina, was from New England and appeared on sheet music, including "Good-By Betty Brown" in 1910. They were primarily a vaudeville act. *Reference*:http://parlorsongs.com/issues/2006-1/thismonth/feature.asp

Donna & her Don Juans
Donna Wood led this group that sang with Horace Heidt. The Don Juans were probably George Jackson, Eddie Jones and Jimmy O'Brien. It is quite possible that Art Carney and Gordon McCrae as well as Charlie Jackson may have sung with them at times. Donna, who died at age 29, was the sister of singer Gloria Wood. *Reference*: http://nfo.net/

Donna Trio
White female group that appeared on sheet music of "That Old Girl Of Mine" in 1912.

Do Ray And Me
See, Do Re Mi Trio.

Do Re Mi Trio
From Los Angeles and first known as the Al Russell Trio, they were Al Russell (tenor), Joel Cowan (tenor) and William Joseph (bass). They sang with Rudy Vallee in 1934. Joe Davis replaced Joseph in 1947 and was followed by Curtis Wilder in 1948. They hit the R&B Chart in 1948 with "Wrapped Up In A Dream." In 1951, the group consisted of Russell,

Alton Buddy Hawkins and Al Moore and they stayed together until 1980. *Reference*: YM-12

Doric Quartette
Male group appearing on the cover to the sheet music of "Pride Of The Prairie Mary" from 1907.

Doring Sisters
White female trio that appeared on sheet music, including "Sweet And Low" in 1935. They also sang on Don McNeil's "Breakfast Club" radio show that same year. *Reference*: http://www.richsamuels.com/

Dot, Kay and Em
Sang with trumpeter Henry Busse in 1934. *Reference*: Lehl Discography

Downe Sisters
Sang with the Ray Miller Orchestra in the 1920s.

Downing Trio
Appeared on sheet music of "The Hung Up The Old Cordeen" in 1915.

Dozier Boys
They headlined at the Beige Room of the Pershing Hotel in Chicago for many years. They also appeared on the early TV show, "Spotlight Talent" hosted by Al Benson. The original members (as the Four Tones) were Lucius Teague (lead) (replaced by Bill Minor), Eugene Teague (baritone and guitar), Benny Cotton (bass) (replaced by Pee Wee Branford) and Cornell Wiley (1st tenor and string bass). As of 1957, Joe Boyce played vibes but did not sing with them. They also played instruments as did many groups of that era. The group was named after Wiley's stepfather, Cyrus Dozier, who helped them financially. Of note was "In A Travelling Mood" (1948-Aristocrat). *Reference*: WC-CD; http://hubcap.clemson.edu/

Dreamdusters
Tom Collins (tenor), Mel Johnson (tenor), Daniel Danforth (baritone) and John Avelis (bass) were individual performers that joined to form this Chicago quartet, active in the late 1940s. *Reference*: Iowa

Driscoll, Long and Hughes
Male group that appeared on the cover of sheet music of "Why Should I Cry Over You" in 1922.

Du Four Boys
Trio (despite the name) that appeared on sheet music of "By The Beautiful Sea" in 1914.

DuMond Male Quartet
Comprised of Ferdinand Nelson (1st tenor), Joe DuMond (2nd tenor), Pat Allison (baritone) and Lester Guyer (bass). Appeared for Redpath Vawter in the 1920s. *Reference*: Iowa

Dunbar Male Quartette
Group founded by Harry and Ralph Dunbar in 1898 that sang and rang bells after the tradition established by P. T. Barnum in the 1840s. This group, which performed more than 2800 concerts up to 1912, appeared on the Chautauqua circuit. Another version of this group, called the Dunbar Male Quartet and Bell Ringers, appeared in the 1920s, and included Reid M. Strohm (1st tenor), Earl A. Vir Den (2nd tenor), Geo. Aylsworth (baritone) and L. E. Spring (basso). Another foursome led by Ralph Dunbar appeared in the Midwest for the 1937-1938 season. Besides Dunbar, members were Albert Hindle, Jack Wood and Marvin Meiers. A group by this name appeared at the Second Annual Assembly of Monmouth Chautauqua in Monmouth, Illinois in August of 1905. This same meeting featured Wm. J. Bryan, Gov. Robert M. LaFollette and the Hon. Booker T. Washington. *Reference*: Iowa; eBay auction

Dunbar Singing Orchestra
Female sextette, members of which both sang and played instruments, appeared at Chautauquas in the early 1910s. *Reference*: Iowa

Dunham Jazz Singers
Led by Charlie Dunham, they recorded on several labels including Champion, Gennett, Supertone and Vocalion from 1928 to 1931. *Reference*: Lehl Discography

Duprez, Carle, Shorey and Green's Minstrels
Troupe traveling during the Civil War that later became Duprez and Green's Minstrels and Duprez and Benedict's Minstrels. Duprez and Benedict introduced the street parade, adding a brass band to the minstrel troupe around 1870. *Reference*: Dumont (1914 and 1915)

Eastern Glee Quartet
Male singers and bell ringers that toured the country on the Lyceum circuit in the early 1910s. *Reference*: Iowa

East Liberty Four
A 1930s group that had three white members and a black bass, Wilbur Gray. *Reference*: Warner

Ebonaires
Formed in Los Angeles in the late 1940s, they were James Bradley (leader and baritone), Charles Gross (tenor), Charles McCladdy (tenor) (replaced early on by Norman Brooks, who was replaced by Ray Wheaton) and John Dix (bass). They also recorded with Hadda Brooks in 1949 and Bill Day, both on Modern. Over the years they did quite a bit of backup work and appeared on TV on the Colgate Comedy hour *Reference*: *L.A. R&B Vocal Groups 1945-1965*, Propes & Gart (20010

Ebonaires
Male quartet formerly called the Deep River Singers that performed in concert, on stage and on the radio in the 1940s. *Reference*: Iowa

Ethel Waters & her Ebony Four
Recorded on Columbia in the mid-1920s.

Ebony Three
In 1939 they recorded on Decca.

Echo Quartette
Appeared on sheet music of "Oh Ho Lize With Those Great Great Big Eyes" in 1912 and recorded on Columbia in 1916. *Reference*: Lehl Discography

Eclipse Quartette
Black group that appeared in the show "South Before The War" in New York in the 1890s and sang with the Slavery Days Company in Brockton, Mass., in 1893. The Golden Gate Quartet also appeared. Also are on the 1914 sheet music of "In The Town Where I Was Born." *Reference*: Brooks

Edisongsters
Recorded in New York in 1929 on Edison. *Reference*: Lehl Discography

Edison Male Quartette
They began in 1894 and were known briefly as the American Quartet and then the Haydn Quartet after 1899. Members were Roger Harding (replaced by John Bieling in 1896), J. K. Reynard (replaced by Jere Mahoney in 1896), S. H. Dudley and William F. Hooley. Harry Macdonough took Mahoney's position in 1899. At the beginning, they made soft brown wax cylinders. See the Haydn Quartet entry for later details when they switched to discs. *Reference*: Walsh; http://www.collectionscanada.gc.ca/

Edison Minstrels
Recorded on Edison in 1903 and started as the Edison Modern Minstrels. In 1906 they became the Edison Minstrels. Members included Arthur Collins, Byron G. Harlan, Billy Murray, Len Spencer, Harry Macdonough, Will F. Denney, William F. Hooley, Edward Meeker, Dan W. Quinn and Steve Porter. *Reference*: http://cylinders.library.ucsb.edu/

Edison Mixed Quartet
Formed in 1906, they consisted of Florence Hinkle, Mary Porter Mitchell (replaced by Margaret Keyes in 1909), John Young and Frederick Wheeler. *Reference*: Walsh

Edison Mixed Sextet
Members were Corinne Morgan, Ada Jones, Grace Nelson, George Seymour Lenox, Bob Roberts and Frank C. Stanley. *Reference*: Walsh

Edison Mixed Trio
See, Metropolitan Trio.

Edison Modern Minstrels
See, Edison Minstrels.

Edison Sextet
Recorded as the Lucia Sextet in 1908 on Amberol and were Marie Stoddart, Margaret Keyes, John Young, George M. Stricklett, Frederick Wheeler and George Bemus. *Reference*: Walsh

Edmund Hall's Quintet
They did a recording with Duke Ellington in 1930 on Victor. *Reference*: Lehl Discography

Electric City Four
George Weaver, Jenkin Jonas, Martin Size and Joseph Wetter made up this group that recorded on Edison Blue Amberol in 1921. *Reference*: Walsh

Electric City Quartette
Appeared on sheet music of "Ireland Sweet Land Across The Sea" in 1915.

Electric City Trio
Appear on the 1914 sheet music of "In The Town Where I Was Born."

Eleo Quartet
Recorded a Demonstration Record for Chesterfield Cigarettes on Brunswick in 1930. *Reference*: Lehl Discography

Elk's Quartet of Spokane Lodge 228:
Recorded on Columbia in 1927. *Reference*: Lehl Discography

Elm City Quartet
First appeared in a 1917 revue in New York and then recorded on several labels including Brunswick and Vocalion in 1926 and Champion in 1934. The members were James F. Carty, Fred Lyon, Arthur Cardinal and Harry Morrisey. *Reference*: Lehl Discography

Embassy Boys
White quartet that appeared on sheet music of "Deep River" in 1935.

Emerson, Allen & Manning's Minstrels
Troupe that "borrowed" players from La Rue's Minstrels in 1868. Included Dr. Hanmer, C. S. Fredericks, E. S. Rosenthal, Charles Wheaton, Kelly and Holly, Master Eddie, Frank Bowles, C. A. Boyd, leader, and Willie Guy and later, Stevie Rogers. *Reference*: http://performingartsarchive.com/

Emperors Of Song
Group formed by Will Hann after he left the Four Harmony Kings in 1925. In 1926, they recorded an Edison Diamond Disk test pressing of "What Band Is This?" *Reference*: http://www.archive.org/

Empire City Four
Nineteenth century vaudeville act.

Empire City Quartette
Comedy vaudeville (and burlesque) quartet from Newark, N.J. in which George Burns began his career. Most prominent version included Harry Cooper, Irving Cooper, Harry Tally and Harry Mayo. They are found on the covers of at least six different pieces of sheet music from 1902 to 1907. *Reference*: Averill

Empire Comedy Four
Group that appears on the sheet music of "In Mobile Town" from 1913.

Empire Trio
Recorded on Columbia in 1916-7.

Empire Vaudeville Company
Recorded in 1910-11 on Edison and included the Premier Quartet. Byron G. Harlan and Arthur Collins were featured. *Reference*: http://cylinders.library.ucsb.edu/

Englewood Four
Recorded on Champion in 1927-8.

Escorts And Betty
Appear on at least two pieces of sheet music, including "Melody in F" from 1935. The group was comprised of three men and a woman. The original Betty was Betty Olsen who was replaced by Helen Nash. The Escorts were Cliff Petersen, Floyd Holm and Ted Clare, whose real name was Hansen. They appeared on Don McNeil's "Breakfast Club" radio show in 1942. *Reference*: http://www.richsamuels.com/

Eskimo Quartet
Recorded on Banner in 1928.

Ethiopian Serenaders
Boston group consisting of Frank Germon, M. Stanwood, Tony Winnemore, Quinn and others. They toured Europe in the late 1840s with a group containing F. Germon, G. Harrington, Moody Stanwood, G. Pelham and W. White. In London they were given rings by Queen Victoria. Another trip to Europe included J. A. Wells and Jerry Bryant. *Reference*: Dumont (1914); White

Ethiopian Serenaders
A second group of this name, they were a black quartet organized by Ralph Dunbar for appearances on the Redpath Lyceum Circuit around 1912. *Reference*: Iowa

Eton Boys
Recorded from 1930 to 1941 on various labels including Perfect, Melotone and Bluebird. Jack Day, Earl Smith, Art Gentry and Charles Day were the members. Ray Bloch (later of the Ed Sullivan and Jackie Gleason shows) was their accompanist and arranger. They were in the movie "The Gem Of The Ocean" in 1934 as singing bartenders. "Mirrors" (1934), "Wash Your Step" (1936), "Rhythm Café" (1938) and "Zero Girl" (1938) were other movies in which they appeared. *Reference*: http://www.78online.com/forum/

Etowah Quartet
Recorded on Columbia in 1928. *Reference*: Lehl Discography

Euclid Male Quartet
Members O. W. Beaver (2nd tenor), W. C. Shade (basso), H. E. Haines (1st tenor) and C. I. Beaver (baritone), all graduated from Antioch College. Appeared for the Mutual Lyceum Bureau of Chicago in the 1910s. Another brochure has K. M. Leith replacing O. W. Beaver. *Reference*: Iowa

Euphonium Glee Club
Comprised of Elmer Carr (1st tenor and soloist), Edgar Miehe (2nd tenor and reader), Clark Van Ausdall (baritone and accompanist) and Dan C. Funk (2nd bass and violin). On the Redpath Lyceum Circuit in the Midwest between 1900 and 1910. *Reference*: Iowa

Eureka Jubilee Singers
Mixed-gender black group whose members were Alpha Bratton (soprano), Lessie Brooks (mezzo), Inez Edmondson (contralto), H. Jones (1st tenor), J. Tucker (2nd tenor), L. McRae (1st bass and director), W. Cross (2nd bass) and Esther Gaskin (pianist). *Reference*: Iowa

Euterpean Quartette
Harriet Levinger, Fannie Levinger, Jeannette Bauhof, and Katherine Baehrens made up this all-female white group. They appeared on sheet music of "My Beautiful Isle Of Somewhere" in 1901 and sang at the funeral of slain President, William McKinley.

Eveready Mixed Quartet
Beulah Gaylord Young, Rose Bryant, Charles Harrison and Wilfred Glenn were the members of this late 1920s group. *Reference*: Walsh

Ewing Sisters
Recorded on Capitol in the late 1940s and early 1950s and sang with Jan Garber. *Reference*: http://www.bigbandmusic.com/

Timmie Rogers and the Excelsior Hep Cats
This 1940s jump group consisted of Timmie Rogers, Maxwell Davis, Jimmy Rowles, Barney Kessel (guitar), Red Callender and Lee Young. They recorded on Excelsior in the mid-1940s. *Reference*: Jive VG-2

Excelsior Norfolk Quartette
Recorded on Black Swan/Paramount in 1922.

Excelsior Quartette
Black group that toured with Hicks and Sawyer's Minstrels in the 1890s. Included William Coleman. *Reference*: Averill

Excelsior Quartette
According to Ken Romanowski, they were one of the first black groups to direct their efforts to the black audience. Members were Theodore Lee (lead), James C. Brown (tenor), Samuel Pierce (baritone) and William Gibson (bass). They recorded in 1922 in New York on Okeh. *Reference*: ENVQ-2

Fairchild Ladies Quartet
Featured Lela Fairchild (contralto), Mildred Fairchild (soprano), Bessie Fairchild (soprano) and Dorothy Fairchild (contralto). Appeared for the Redpath Lyceum Bureau. Date around 1915. *Reference*: Iowa

Famous Hillbillies
NBC radio quartet that appear on the sheet music of "Lazybones" in 1934. The four are named Annie, Judy, Zeke and Pete. "Judy" is Judy Canova, who later became a film star.

Famous Mundy National Jubilee Octet
Group of eight black singers, led by James A. Mundy. Appeared in the early to mid-1930s. *Reference*: Iowa

Fa Sol La Singers
Black group that recorded on Columbia in 1931. *Reference*: BVG-4

"Father" Robert Kemp's "Old Folks' Show"
Averill points to this troupe as one of the first in America to offer nostalgic songs. *Reference*: Averill

Fellows' Minstrels
In 1849, Earl Pierce left Christy's troupe and with J. B. Fellows founded Pierce and Fellows' Minstrels. Pierce retired in 1850 and the name changed to Fellows' Minstrels. *Reference*: Dumont (1914); White

Femina Quartette
Female group on the cover of the sheet music to "When Irish Eyes Are Smiling" from 1912. Two members of this group were named "Block" and "Hales."

Fidelis Male Quartette of Philadelphia
A photo of them survives from the 1910s.

Al G. Field's Minstrels
Organized in 1886 in Ohio. "It met with instant success and popularity and has been the leading troupe ever since. When the office of Klaw & Erlanger was called up and asked to name the best theatrical trade mark, the answer came, 'The Al G. Field Greater Minstrels.'" *Reference*: Fletcher; Dumont (1915)

Fields, Weston & Carroll
Male trio appearing on the sheet music of "Lady Angeline" from 1912.

Fire Department Quartette

Appeared on sheet music of "Meet Me At The Station Dear" from 1917. They were from the Fire Department City of New York and were Chas. McCormick (1st tenor), William Hall (2nd tenor), William H. Breuer (baritone) and William Schulz.

Fireside Quartet

Charles Harrison (tenor), Frederic Gunster (tenor), Elliott Shaw or Frank Mellor and Wilfred Glenn or Frederic Thomas (bass) made up this group. They recorded from 1923 to 1925 on Brunswick. Harrison, Shaw and Glenn were also with the Revelers. *Reference*: Mainspring

Fisk Jubilee Singers

One of the most significant groups in the history of American popular music. They were formed in 1867 at Fisk University in Tennessee. Fisk was one of the colleges formed after the Civil War by the American Missionary Association to educate former slaves. Their story is well known to followers of early black music. In 1871, the school needed money to continue and the white treasurer, George White, took the group on tour to raise funds - which they did. Original members were Georgia Gordon, Isaac P. Dickerson, Benjamin M. Holmes, Jennie Jackson, Julia Jackson, Mabel Lewis, Maggie Porter, Thomas Rutling, Ella Sheppard (piano), Minnie Tate and Edmund Watkins. This was the first time many white Americans had heard true black music. Unsuccessful at first, eventually the audiences grew to appreciate the unique sounds they were hearing. In late 1871, White began to refer to the group as Jubilee Singers, according to Eileen Southern, "after a favorite black folk-saying about 'the year of the jubilee.'" Southern claims that this helped the group become popular because the name was "catchy." They toured Europe several times and raised considerable sums for the school. In 1875, the school ceased sponsoring their tours and they became a private group under the leadership of Frederick J. Loudin. In 1910, they began recording on Victor, and James A. Myers, J. W. Work, N. W. Ryder and A. G. King (replaced by L. P. O'Hara) made up the group. They were led by Myers from 1916 to 1927 and then by his wife, Henrietta until 1947. *Reference*: Fisk-3; Southern; Walsh

Five Bars

Recorded on Bullet in 1947, including "I'm All Dressed Up With A Broken Heart." Jimmy Sweeney was the lead and he later sang with the Varieteers. *Reference*: Fournier

Five Best Niggers In The World

Dumont says that this group, composed of Jim Sanford, Master Diamond, Ole Bull Myers, Pickaninny Coleman and Master Chestnut, may have been the first legitimate group of minstrels to appear on stage, in June of 1842, in Philadelphia. *Reference*: Dumont (1914)

Five Blazes
See, Four Blazes.

Five Blind Boys Of Alabama
They began as the Happyland Jubilee Singers at the Talladega Institute For the Deaf and Blind in 1939. Original members were Johnny Fields, Clarence Fountain, George Scott, Olice Thomas and Velma Traylor. They left the school in 1945, began to sing professionally and changed their name in 1948 after the success of the Five Blind Boys of Mississippi. *Reference*: Southern

Five Blind Boys Of Mississippi
Formed at the Piney Woods School For The Blind in Jackson, Mississippi, in 1939. (A female group, International Sweethearts of Rhythm, was also based at the school.) Members included J. T. Clinkscales, Sam Lewis, Lawrence Abrams, Lloyd Woodard and Archie Brownlee (lead). Later members included Melvin Henderson, Joseph Ford, Isaiah Patterson, Roscoe Robinson and Big Henry Johnson. As had been the case with the Fisk Singers, groups were sent out from the school for fundraising purposes using the name the Cotton Blossom Singers. Brownlee sang with one of these groups and when he left school continued to tour using the Cotton Blossom Singers name for secular appearances and the Jackson Harmoneers for gospel. They became a quintet when Melvin Henderson joined. When the sighted Percell Perkins replaced Henderson in the mid-'40s, they became The Five Blind Boys. "They evoked a style in which the group sang a repeated phrase, building up the tension to highlight Brownlee's ecstatic falsetto which could provoke scenes of religious hysteria in church and concert audiences." Eileen Southern said of Brownlee, he was "credited with being the first to interject falsetto shrieks and screams in gospel-quartet style . . ." singing. They made their recording debut for Excelsior in 1946 and recorded for Coleman in 1948. "Our Father" was a Top Ten R&B hit in 1950. Brownlee died in 1960. *Reference*: Southern; Da Capo (p. 320); http://www.loc.gov/; http://www.allmusic.com/

Five Blue Flames
Led by Chris Powell, they recorded on Columbia (1949-1951) and Okeh (1951-1952). Other members were Johnny Leak (Johnny Echo), who had an extremely high voice, Vance Wilson (tenor), Harold "Duke" Wells (piano), Bill Jennings (guitar), James Johnson, bass and Eddie Lambert, guitar. *Reference*: Fournier

Five Breezes
From Chicago, they were Gene Gilmore, Leonard Caston, Willie Dixon (bass), Joseph "Cool Breeze" Bell and Willie Hawthorne. They recorded on Bluebird in the 1940s. Caston and Dixon later sang with the Big Three Trio. Gilmore and Dixon were with the Four Jumps Of Jive. *Reference*: Fournier; JIVE-CD

Five De Wolfes
Three young women and two young men appearing on the cover of sheet music for "Meet Me Tonight" from 1911.

Five Harmoniques
Recorded on See Bee in 1922.

Five Jinks
Male, black quintet that recorded in Charlotte, North Carolina in 1937 on Bluebird. Its membership is unknown. *Reference*: BSVG-2

Five Jones Boys
This 1930s Carbondale, Illinois group had as its members Jimmy Springs, Charles Hopkins, Louis Wood, Herman Wood and William Bartley. Springs later sang with the Five Red Caps. They recorded on Variety and Anchor and appeared in several movies. *Reference*: Fournier; Goldberg; Human Orch

Five Kings
Backed Savannah Churchill on several sides on Manor in 1947. *Reference*: Fournier

Sophie Tucker and her 5 Kings of Syncopation
Quintette featured with Tucker on the 1918 sheet music cover of "Ev'rybody Shimmies Now."

Five Locust Sisters
Appeared on sheet music of "Save Your Sorrow" in 1925 and recorded on Columbia. A film clip of them from 1928 appears in the review movie, "That's Entertainment! III." *Reference*: www.imdb.com

Five Pork Chops
Group from the late 1930s and early 1940s led by "Doctor Sausage" (Lucius) Tyson. "Doc Sausage" reappears in 1949/1950 for a few releases on Regal with "His Mad Lads." *Reference*: Fournier

Five Red Caps
They grew out of the Four Toppers in 1943 in Los Angeles. Members were Steve Gibson, Jimmy Springs (tenor and drums), David Patillo, Richard Davis, Doles Dickens (bass) and Romaine Brown (piano), the latter three having come from the Jones Boys Sing Band. They had more than 30 releases on Beacon (four of which made the R&B Charts) including a beautiful ballad called "Just For You." Some of the novelty tunes are dated in their style and would be unthinkable in today's world. In 1944, Emmett Mathews joined as a singer and

played saxophone. Charted with "I Learned A Lesson I'll Never Forget" (1944-Beacon). In 1946 the group became known as Steve Gibson and The Red Caps and lasted to the mid-1960s. *Reference*: FRC-CD, Whitburn-PM

Five Rocquettes
Recorded on Decca in 1941.

Five Scamps
The Five Scamps can trace their lineage to a 1937 group in Kansas called The Scamps. The more modern version of the group began in 1947 in Kansas City, Missouri. Members were Earl Robinson (lead), Terrence Griffin, James Whitcomb, Rudy Massingale, (piano and sax) and Wyatt Griffin (guitar). On their Modern recordings they were the Scamps and the Five Scamps on Columbia. Despite their success and longevity they never charted. Their most well-known recording was "Red Hot" on Columbia in 1949. As of the early 2000s, they were still performing. That has to be a record! *Reference*: RCM-42, Fournier

Flanagan Trio
Appeared on sheet music of "You May Not Think I Love You But I Do, Do, Do" in 1909.

Flennoy Trio
This black group recorded on Melodisc in 1945. Lorenzo Flennoy led and played piano. The other members may have been Gene Phillips on guitar and Winston Williams on bass. *Reference*: Fournier

Florida Four
Recorded on Edison in 1928.

Florida Jubilee Singers
A female quartet that recorded with Grace Outlaw in Chicago in 1926. *Reference*: BVG-10

Florida Normal and Industrial Quartet
College group from the 19th-century. *Reference*: Averill

Florie Le Vere Trio
A woman and two men, whose picture appears on the sheet music to "Welcome Home" in 1913.

Flower City Harmonists
Quartet from Rochester, New York, active around 1865. They were William Cowles, William Corkhill, John Boyd and J. Franuken. *Reference*: Averill

Flying Clouds Quintette
A photo survives of this black group of six from Detroit.

Fontane (Fontaine) Sisters
As the Three Sisters they appeared on several pieces of sheet music in the mid-1940s. Bea, Geri and Marge Fontane (family name Rosse) from New Jersey, comprised the group. They sang background with Perry Como and recorded for RCA Victor in the early 1950s (because virtually all their recordings were in 1950 or later, they are not in our Discography). They had a number one song with "Hearts of Stone" (1954-Dot) and charted numerous other times through 1958. *Reference*: Whitburn -PM

Forest City Trio
Appeared on sheet music of "I Wish You Were Jealous Of Me" in 1906.

Four Aalbu Sisters
Appeared on sheet music of "Roll On, Mississippi, Roll On" in 1931.

Four Aces (1920s)
The first of several groups (there were also an English group and a 1950s U.S. pop group, but they are outside the scope of this book) with the same name, they recorded in New York in the late 1920s and early 1930s. Personnel were Charlie Anderson, Al Perry, Joe Markese and Bennis Finnegan. Anderson played a Hawaiian guitar. *Reference*: Lehl Discography

Four Aces (Black)
Began in the I. M. Terrell High School in Fort Worth, Texas, in 1935. The original members were James Reuben Franks (1st tenor and guitar), Algia Pickett (2nd tenor), George Smith (baritone and pianist) and Otha Jackson (bass and bass fiddle). They toured with the Beckman and Garrity vaudeville road show and appeared on radio in Texas. Until a bass and piano were added in 1939, they sang a cappella. Three of the members of the Four Aces served in World War II in the entertainment field. After the war, they played clubs in the San Francisco area, did some traveling for gigs and continued to record. *Reference*: The Four Aces CD (Flyright FLY CD-62)

Four Aces (Champion Records)
The second of four groups with this name, they recorded on Champion Records in 1933. *Reference*: The Four Aces CD (Flyright FLY CD-62)

Four Aristocrats
Fred Weber, Bert Bennet, Ed Lewis and Tom Miller recorded on Victor and Edison from 1924 to 1928. Other members were Louis Monte, Harry Hill, George Harris, Jimmy Burns, Milt Hamilton and Webb Hahne. *Reference*: Walsh

Four Baldwins
Male group on sheet music of "That Baboon Baby Dance" from 1911.

Four Barons
See, Larks.

Four Bars
Mixed-gender group that appeared on the sheet music of "Carelessly" in 1936.

Four Belles
Female group that recorded in 1940 and 1941 in New York on Varsity and Bluebird and appeared on sheet music of "Maybe" in 1935. *Reference*: Lehl Discography

Four Blackamoors
Recorded on Decca in 1941 and backed Mabel Robinson on several sides.

Four Blackbirds
From Los Angeles, the members of this mixed-gender black group were David Patillo, Geraldine Harris, Leroy Hurte (baritone) and Richard Davis (bass). They, minus Harris, joined with the Five Jones Boys to form the Jones Boys Sing Band. Patillo also sang with the Four Toppers and the Red Caps. They appeared in several movies including "Harlem Rides The Range" and recorded on Vocalion, Brunswick and Melotone in the mid-1930s. *Reference*: Goldberg

Four Blazes (Chicago)
Started by Paul Lindsley "Jelly" Holt in Chicago in 1940 with Jimmy Bennett (replaced by Floyd McDaniels), William "Shorty" Hill and Prentice Butler. In 1946, Ernie Harper, a piano player, joined the group and they became the Five Blazes. Each member also played an instrument. In 1951, Tommy Braden became the lead and they had a hit in 1952 on United called "Mary Jo." Eddie Chamblee was a later member. They also had R&B hits with "Please Send Her Back To Me" (1952-United) and "Perfect Woman" (1953-United). They were touring as late as the mid-1950s and were one of the bridge groups between the jive/blues combos of the 1940s and the R&B groups of the 1950s. Braden had a combination sweet and husky voice that was perfect for the songs they did. "Mary Jo" was "sly as a fox and dangerous as a grizzly bear." *Reference*: WC-CD; http://hubcap.clemson.edu/

Four Blazes (Hollywood)
California based group that began in 1944 and consisted of George Crawford, Ulysses Livingston, LeGrand Mason, Dan Grisson and Connie Jordan. They recorded on

Lamplighter, Excelsior and AFRS Jubilee. Also recorded as the Four Blazers on Melodisc. *Reference*: http://hubcap.clemson.edu/~campber/blazes.html

Four Blue Birds
Recorded on Excelsior in 1949 with Bobby Nunn.

Four Blue Jackets
From Dayton, Ohio, they recorded on Mercury and were brothers Bill, Doc, Joe and Toby Bryant They were in the Navy together and made appearances at hospitals and other Navy-related locations. Nothing is known of them after their last recording in 1947. *Reference*: RCM-45, Fournier

Four Blues
Known members of this black Philadelphia group were Earl Plummer (lead), Arthur Davey and Carroll Jones (bass). They recorded in the 1940s in New York on DeLuxe and Apollo. Both Plummer and Davey later joined Steve Gibson's Red Caps. They did some religious recordings as the Golden Echo Quartet. [Best of Jive Groups CD lists Jones as lead tenor.]. *Reference*: 40s-50s-CD; BSVG-3

Four Bops
Recorded on Sittin' In in 1948.

Four Boys
Recorded on Brunswick in 1929 and were Gordon Reimers, Chappie Ryan, Bob Hartham and Roy Ringwald. *Reference*: Lehl Discography

Four Buddies
From Baltimore, they consisted of Leon "Larry' Harrison (1st tenor), John (Gregory) Carroll (2nd tenor) (his brother Charlie was a member of the Cats and the Fiddle), William Duffy (baritone) and Maurice Hicks (bass) and were originally known as the Metronomes. Vernon "Bert" Palmer replaced Duffy and William "Tommy" Carter replaced Hicks late in 1950. They changed the name of the group to the Four Buds and then, after their first recording session, to the Four Buddies. "I Will Wait" (Savoy) was released in late 1950 and was a Top 10 R&B hit in 1951. They added a fifth member, Alvin Bowen (guitar), in 1951. Also in 1951, Palmer left the group to be the lead of the Falcons (and Bowen added singing to his guitar playing) but soon returned to the Four Buddies. Carter left in 1952 and Hicks came back to the group. Carroll left in 1953 to join the Orioles. Harrison reformed the group as the Buddies with Roger Wainwright (2nd tenor), Luther Dixon (baritone) and Danny Ferguson (bass). They also recorded for Decca as the Barons with Hicks replacing Ferguson. *Reference*: The Four Buddies CD, Dipper Records-1998

Four Buzz Saws
Recorded in 1930, mostly on Vocalion and were Jimmy Yates, Moe Sigler, E. R. Smith and C.D. Linthicum. *Reference*: Lehl Discography

Four Chicks And Chuck
The Chuck in the group was Chuck Goldstein, formerly of the Modernaires and the V-8 and the Chicks were Sue Allen, Claire Frim, Gini McGurdy and Diane Carol. They recorded on Jubilee in the 1940s and made several appearances on the Philco Radio Hall Of Fame/Philco Summer Hours Show with host Paul Whiteman in 1944. *Reference*: "Band Leaders Magazine," March 1946.

Four Chords
Recorded on Sittin' In in 1949.

Four Clefs
This Chicago group had hits with "Dig Those Blues" and "4 Clefs Woogie" in the early 1940s and recorded on Bluebird and RCA Victor. They were a self-contained quartet whose members were Johnny Green (guitar), James Marshall (piano) and brothers Melvin (bass) and Willie (drums and lead singer) Chapman. *Reference*: Fournier

Four Chocolate Dandies
Black group that sang in vaudeville in the early 20th-century. *Reference*: Averill

Four Deeptones
See, Deep Tones.

Four Dots
See, Five Red Caps.

Four Dusty Travelers
Black group that consisted of Charles Emmett, William Emmett, Herbert Benson and Junior Dean. They recorded in the late 1920s and early 1930s in New York, including "Dinah" and "The Lonesome Road" (both 1930) with Ted Lewis (who was white) on Columbia in 1930. They were also billed as Ted Lewis & Four Dusty Travelers and were the same group as the Dixie Four. *Reference*: BSVG-3; Fournier

Four Embers
Group associated with the traveling Chautauquas around 1910. *Reference*: Averill

Four Esquires
Recorded on Brunswick and Trilon in 1935 and featured Joe Morrison. *Reference*: Lehl Discography

Four Freshmen
The group was formed in the mid-1940s in Indiana by Bob Flanigan, and the Barbour brothers, Don and Ross, who were cousins of Flanigan's. They met Hal Kratzsch at music school in Indianapolis and called themselves Hal's Harmonizers. In 1948, they changed their name to the Four Freshmen at the urging of their agent. They came to the attention of the great Stan Kenton who helped them get a recording contract with Capitol Records. Ken Errair replaced Kratzsch in 1953 and was himself replaced by Ken Albers in 1955. Don Barbour left the group for a solo career in 1960 and was replaced by Bill Comstock. There have been other changes over the years and the group continues today with all new personnel. They were the first major vocal jazz group to play their own instruments. More important, their harmonies were unique and influenced many groups such as the Beach Boys and Manhattan Transfer. Some of their more notable recordings on Capitol were "Day By Day" (1955), "Charmaine" (1955) and "Graduation Day" (1956), the latter breaking into the Top 20. *Reference*: http://www.fourfreshmen.com/

Four Gabriels
Recorded on World in 1948.

Four Harmonists
Appeared on sheet music of "I Wish I Was In Heaven Sittin' Down" in 1908. The names of the members are given as Pierson, Harold, Steinmann and Wood.

Four Harmony Kings
Black vaudeville quartet started by Will Hann in 1916. They appeared on Broadway in 1921 in "Shuffle Along." Personnel were Ivan Harold Browning (tenor), William H. Berry (2nd tenor), Charles E. Drayton (baritone) (replaced by George Jones) and W. A. Hann (bass). Hann was replaced by Roland Hayes in 1919. They also recorded on Pathé as "Lt. Jim Europe's Four Harmony Kings." Other labels on which they appeared were Edison Bell Winner, Dominion and Black Swan, Emerson, Paramount and Vocalion. "In Bamville" and "Chocolate Dandies" were other shows in which they appeared in 1924. Hann left in 1925 to form the Emperors Of Song and was replaced by John Crabbe. The group toured England. They lasted until the early 1930s. *Reference*: Mainspring.

Four Harmony Kings
See, Swan Silvertones.

Four Hawaiians
Recorded on Banner in 1927.

Four Hill Brothers
Recorded on Challenge in 1928.

Four Hits And A Miss
See, Six Hits And A Miss.

Four Hoosiers
Recorded on Challenge in 1927.

Four Jacks
California group that consisted of George Comfort, Bowling Mansfield, Buell Thomas and Ellison White. "I Challenge Your Kiss" was a Top 10 R&B hit on Allen in 1949. They also recorded in the 1950s, sometimes with female leads. *Reference*: RCM-46

Four Jumps Of Jive
From Chicago, its members were Ellis Hunter, Gene Gilmore, Bernardo Dennis and Willie Dixon (bass) and they recorded on Mercury. Dixon and Gilmore were also with the Five Breezes. *Reference*: http://www.allmusic.com/

Four Keys
"Slim" Furness (who also was with the Three Keys and the Furness Brothers) and Ernie Hatfield, Bill Furness and Peck Furness. Backed Ella Fitzgerald on four sides on Decca in 1942-1943. *Reference*: Fournier

Four Kings
Recorded in 1938 on Brunswick with Horace Heidt and his Brigadiers. *Reference*: Lehl Discography

Four Kings And A Queen
Group formed by Orville "Baggie" Hardiman that recorded on Comet in 1945, King in 1947 and Mercury in 1948 (as Orville "Baggie" Hardiman and the Kings). The Mercury group included Hardiman, Leroy Lovett, Stanley Gaines, Jake McKinney and Danny Turner. The "Queen" on the earlier recordings was Joanne Jones. It appears that she left the group and that is the reason for the different name on the Mercury recordings. They may have been from Kokomo, Indiana. *Reference*: Goldberg

Four Kings Of Rhythm
Recorded with Inez Washington in 1946.

Four Knights
A gospel group that transformed themselves into a pop group, they began in 1943 as the Southland Jubilee Singers in Charlotte, North Carolina. Original members were Gene Alford (lead), John Wallace (2nd tenor and guitar) and Oscar Broadway (bass). Clarence Dixon (baritone) joined them in 1944. They appeared on the Carolina Hayride radio show, the Arthur Godfrey Show in 1945 and the Red Skelton Show in 1948. Their first single was released on Decca in 1946 and they had their biggest recording success with "I Get So Lonely When I Think About You" in 1954 on Capitol Records, sometimes known by the title "Oh Baby Mine." "If I May" (1955-Capitol) was a Top 10 song for them. They also backed Nat King Cole on a number of his recordings. The group broke up in the early 1960s. *Reference*: The 4 Knights, Jivin' & Smoothin' CD, Orbital 346

Four Komical Kards
Male group that recorded on Edison Bell in 1908. *Reference*: Lehl Discography

Four Modernaires
See, Modernaires.

Four Mullen Sisters
Appeared on sheet music of "Roll On, Mississippi, Roll On" in 1931 and were in the film "The Big Benefit" in 1933. *Reference*: www.imdb.com

Four Musettes
Recorded on Musicraft in 1948.

Four Musical Colby's
A man, woman, boy and girl that appear on the sheet music of "Mama Number Two" in 1901.

Four Musketeers
From New Jersey, they recorded in 1933, including "The Girl In The Little Green Hat." *Reference*: Sweetest Harmony

Four New Yorkers
Recorded in New York in 1932 and were Carl Barron (tenor), Claude Reese (tenor), Jerry White (baritone) and August Wicke (bass). *Reference*: Lehl Discography

Four Notes
Recorded on Premier, Paradise and International from 1945 to 1947 and Gotham as Gotham's Four Notes in 1948. Members were Tommy Adams, Frederick Johnson, Gene Smith and James Sapp. Adams later sang with the Blenders. *Reference*: Fournier

Clarence Jackson And The Four Notes Of Rhythm
Recorded on Crystal Tone in 1948.

Four Novelty Aces
Recorded on Bluebird in 1933 in Chicago. *Reference*: Lehl Discography

Four Of Us
Appeared on sheet music of "No! No! Nora!" in 1923.

Four Of Us
Recorded on Modern in 1947. *Reference*: Fournier

Four Pals
Recorded in Camden, New Jersey, in 1929 and were Oscar E. Smith, Rube Myers, Tom Rowe and Tony Dooley. *Reference*: Lehl Discography

Four Pods Of Pepper
Black, male quartet that recorded in Chicago in the late 1920s and early 1930s. "Ain't Got No Mama Now" and "Queen Street Rag" were both recorded in 1929. They also recorded as the Pods of Pepper. *Reference*: BSVG-1

Four Rajahs
Recorded on various labels in the late 1920s, including with Nat Shilkret and the Victor Orchestra and were Louis Chicco, Martin Hurt, Art Gentry and Ted Roy. They are best known for "Too Busy" recorded in 1928. *Reference*: Lehl Discography; Sweetest Harmony

Four Recorders
Sang with the Henry Busse Band in the late 1920s and early 1930s and were W. Cleary, R. Moody, Alan Ray and D. Wells. *Reference*: Lehl Discography

Four Rockets
See, the Trumpeteers.

Four Serenaders
Recorded on Champion in 1927.

Four Shades
Recorded on the C. P. MacGregor label (date unknown). *Reference*: Lehl Discography

Four Shades Of Rhythm
From Cleveland, its members were Oscar Lindsay (baritone and cocktail drums), Willie Lewis (guitar) (replaced by Oscar Pennington), Sims London (piano) (replaced by Eddie McAfee) and Macon Sims (bassist) (replaced by June Cobb and then Eddie Meyers). Other replacements followed in the 1950s Their recording career began in 1949 on Old Swingmaster and lasted through 1958. *Reference*: RCM-8; Goldberg

4 Shannons
Group comprised of one boy and three girls that appears on the cover of "Good-Bye Mister Greenback" from 1906.

Foursome
They formed in Spokane in 1926 and were Marshall Smith, Dwight Snyder, Harry Isaacs (replaced by Jimmy Davis and then by Del Porter) and Kearney Walton (replaced by Raymond Johnson). They appeared in the film "The Wild Party" and also in "Girl Crazy" in 1930, where they hit it big with "Bidin' My Time" (it reached #9 on the charts). They also used an instrument called an ocarina that gave them a unique sound. After touring with Smith Ballew-Glenn Miller band they returned to Broadway in "Anything Goes" and were on WABC radio at the same time. In the late 1930s, they recorded on Decca, appeared often on the Kraft Music Hall radio show and backed Dick Powell. Bing Crosby, Ray Noble, Shirley Ross, Pinky Tomlin and Frances Langford. They disbanded in 1941 and reformed briefly after the war as the Sweet Potato Tooters for Capitol transcriptions and with other personnel as the Starlighters. *Reference*: http://www.allmusic.com/

Four Southerners
Recorded in Chicago in 1937 on Decca. *Reference*: Lehl Discography

Four Southern Singers
Mixed-gender, black quartet comprised of Robert Ward (lead), Annie Laurie Ward (tenor), James Ward (baritone) and Owen Ward (bass). They recorded in New York in the 1930s on Victor and Bluebird. *Reference*: BSVG-2

Four Spades
White group that changed its name in the 1950s to the Four Mascots. They were voted best new group by the Arthur Godfrey Talent Scout Show audience and recorded or Columbia. *Reference*: http://www.greenmesquite.net/

Four Squires
Recorded on Vocalion in 1938 and appeared in the movie "Swing It, Professor" in 1937. *Reference*: http://www.imdb.com/

Four Stars
Recorded on Variety in 1937 and Okeh in 1930.

Four Steps Of Jive
Recorded on Chord in 1948 and were Frank Ransom, Eddie Johnson, Benny Calloway and Mannie Whitlock on piano. Each of them played an instrument. *Reference*: Fournier

Four Tones
Los Angeles group whose members included Lucius "Dusty" Brooks, Leon Buck, Ira Hardin, Johnny Porter and Rudolph Hunter. Ray Wheaton also recorded with them in 1945. Appeared in the films "Harlem Rides The Range," "Harlem On The Prairie," "The Bronze Buckaroo" and "Two-Gun Man From Harlem." *Reference*: Fournier

Four Toppers
See, Five Red Caps

Four Tunes
When differences arose in the Brown Dots in 1948, William (Pat) Best, James Gordon and Jimmy Nabbie secretly formed a group they called the Sentimentalists, adding Danny Owens to replace Deek Watson. Owens had sung with the Coleman Brothers and the Melody Masters. Tommy Dorsey complained about the name since he had used it for his singers and they changed their name to the Four Tunes. As the Four Tunes, they had hits on Jubilee in the early 1950s such as "Marie" (1953) and "I Understand Just How You Feel" (1954). With Savannah Churchill, they had a number one R&B song in "I Want To Be Loved" (1947-Manor), credited as the Sentimentalists. They also charted with her as the Four Tunes on "I Want To Cry" (1948-Manor). In all, they made the R&B Charts five times. The original group broke apart in 1963 when Nabbie left and the other members dispersed. *Reference*: Whitburn-PM; Whitburn-RB; Goldmine 1989

Four Vagabonds
Began in St. Louis in 1933. The original members were John Jordan (lead), Robert O'Neal (1st tenor), Norval Taborn (baritone) and Ray Grant Jr. (bass and guitar). They got a break when they replaced the Mills Brothers on a radio show in 1936 due to the death of John Mills, Jr. Appearances followed on Don McNeil's Breakfast Club in Chicago from 1936 to 1946 and on numerous other radio shows. Ray Grant had begun growing blind in the mid-1940s but continued to appear live without the audiences knowing of his condition. Eventually, he was replaced by Bill Sanford in 1949. Sanford left in 1950 and Frank Houston replaced him. The group broke up in 1952. Their biggest hit was "P.S. I Love You" on Apollo in 1947 and they had an R&B chart hit with "It Can't Be Wrong" (1943-Bluebird). They used instrument imitation on many of their records and their technique was

truly remarkable. *Reference*: The Four Vagabonds, Yesterday's Memories CD, Relic Records; YM-7

Four Wanderers
Recorded in New York in 1929 for Victor and also with Fats Waller. Members were Herman Hughes, Charles Clinkscales (tenor), Maceo Johnson (baritone), Oliver Childs (bass) and W. W. Watson (director). They did both animal and banjo imitations. *Reference*: BVG-10

Fraternity Glee Club
Formed and managed by Ralph Dunbar (see Dunbar Male Quartette) around 1912. Performed on the Redpath-Slayton Lyceum Bureau tour in the Midwest. *Reference*: Iowa

Freshmen
Sang with Ray Noble in the mid-1930s. *Reference*: Lehl Discography

Frohne Sisters
Recorded in 1929 in New York and were Hilda, Leonora, Frieda and Alma Frohne. *Reference*: Lehl Discography

Frolickers
Recorded on Edison in 1926. Members were Arthur Hall, John Ryan and Ed Smalle. Smalle was the pianist for the Revelers. *Reference*: Walsh

Funnyboners
Recorded in 1932 in New York on Victor with Ruby Newman and his Orchestra. *Reference*: Lehl Discography

Furness Brothers
Started as a trio (Slim. Bill and Peck Furness) and became a quartet when brother Joe joined in 1950. Slim had been with the Three Keys and Four Keys. Bill, Peck and Joe Furness and Ernie Hatfield backed Ella Fitzgerald on four Decca releases (1942-43) as "Her Four Keys." *Reference*: Fournier

Gaiety Musical Comedy Chorus
See, Revelers.

Galli Sisters
Trio that appeared on sheet music of "Just For Me" in 1945 and also sang with the Art Mooney Orchestra. Norma Galli was one of the members. *Reference*: http://www.jazzology.com/

Ganus Brothers Quartet
Recorded on Columbia in 1928. *Reference*: Lehl Discography

Garden City Trio
Male group on the sheet music of "The Barn-yard Rag" from 1911.

Garland Brothers and Grinstead
Recorded on Columbia in 1928. *Reference*: Lehl Discography

Gates, Lucy & Quartet
Recorded with the Stellar Quartet in 1917 and on their own in 1922, both on Columbia.

Skeets Tolbert & his Gentlemen Of Swing
Black quartet that recorded on Decca in 1941 and played their own instruments. They were Skeets Tolbert (clarinet, alto sax), Carl Smith (trumpet), Otis Hicks (tenor sax), Red Richards (piano), John Drummond (bass), and Hubert Pettaway (drums). *Reference*: Fournier

George Christy's & Wood's Minstrels
Henry Wood took over J. B. Fellows' Minstrels in 1852. He joined with George Christy, who split from E. P. Christy to form this group in October, 1853. Wood retired in 1857 and George Christy left in 1854. *Reference*: White

Georgia Minstrels
Founded in 1866 by a man named Spragueland. In 1870, they were taken over by Orrin E. Richards and Charles W. Pringle and renamed Richards & Pringle's Georgia Minstrels. *Reference*: Dumont (1915)

Georgia Minstrels
Harry Macdonough (tenor), S. H. Dudley (baritone), William F. Hooley (bass) and Frank P. Banta (piano) were the members. They recorded on Victor and Monarch in the early 1900s. *Reference*: Mainspring

Giersdorf Sisters
Trio that appeared on sheet music, including "Back In Your Own Backyard" in 1928 and recorded on Columbia and other labels through 1935. *Reference*: http://www.honkingduck.com/

Gilbert's Male Quartette
Formed by Ellsworth Gilbert. Appeared on a Midwest Redpath circuit. Estimated date is 1920. *Reference*: Iowa

Gilbert's Singers and Bell Ringers
Made up of Earl Miller (bass and pianist), Mary Adaline Bradley (soprano), Tom Baldridge (tenor) and Mary Jane Rhea (contralto). Performed for the Redpath Lyceum Bureau around 1910. *Reference*: Iowa

Ginger Snaps
Mixed-gender, black quartet had four releases on (RCA) Victor between 1945 and 1947, including "Juke Box Joe." They also had two releases on University in 1944-45. A photo of them from a Soundie shows the members as Charles Ford, Ethel Harper, Leona Hemingway and Ruth Christian. They also sang with the Jimmy Mundy band in the mid-1940s. The sheet music of "Two Many Irons In The Fire" with a photo of the Ginger Snaps on the cover shows only the female members. *Reference*: http://www.group-harmony.com/

Girl Friends
Recorded on Columbia, Victor and Electrola from 1928 to 1932. See also The Three Waring Girls. *Reference*: Lehl Discography

Glendale Quartet
Male group appearing on the sheet music to "Gee! Ain't It Great To Be Home" from 1911.

G-Noters
Lillian Lane, Jerry Duane, Dave Lambert and Buddy Stewart made up this quartet that sang with the Gene Krupa Band in the 1940s. *Reference*: http://www.gkrp.net/1942-44.html

Golden Arrow Quartet
Recorded on Continental in 1947. *Reference*: Fournier

Golden Echo Quartet
Gospel group that made secular recordings as the Four Blues. *Reference*: Fournier

Golden Gate Quartet
The more well-known group of this name was formed in the 1930s in the Norfolk, Virginia, area. By 1936, it was comprised of William Langford (tenor), Henry Owens (tenor), Willie Johnson (baritone) and Orlandus Wilson (bass). Their first recording was "The Golden Gate Gospel Train" in 1937 on Bluebird. Performances followed at Carnegie Hall, on radio and in night clubs. Langford left in 1940 and was replaced by Clyde Riddick. Johnson left in 1948 and was replaced by Alton Bradley. They went to Europe in 1955 and eventually spent most of their time there. Although primarily a gospel group, they could and did sing in any style. J. C. Ginyard of the Du Droppers became a member in the 1950s as did Clyde Wright. Their influence can be seen in many of the groups that followed, including black

groups such as the Jubalaires and white pop groups like the Four Lads. *Reference*: Golden Gate Jubilee Quartet CD, Vol. 1 (Document Records DOCD-5472); Southern

Golden Gate Quartette
There has been more than one group to use this name. According to Eileen Southern, the first was probably from Baltimore in 1892 and consisted of Arthur "Dovey" Coates, Sherman Coates, Frank Sutton and Henry Winifred. They were on the vaudeville circuit and appeared in minstrel shows (Lady Africa Company, Sheridan and Flynn's Big Sensation Company, the Slavery Days Company, and the Metropolitan Burlesque Company) and variety shows. *Reference*: Southern; Averill.

Golden Gate Trio
White male group featured on sheet music of "Down By The Old Mill Stream" from 1910.

Golden Leaf Quartet
Recorded on Brunswick from 1928 to 1930 and were Archie Lee, "Pops" Melvin, Hoke Rice and Judge Lee. *Reference*: Lehl Discography

Goldin Quartet
Recorded on Columbia in 1905-9.

Gold Medal Four
Recorded on Champion in 1927.

Gondolier Trio
Recorded on Brunswick between 1919 and 1923. *Reference*: http://www.vitaphone.org/

Goodrich Silvertown Quartet
Recorded in 1927-9 on Columbia.

Lee Gordon Singers
In the late 1940s they included Lee Gotch and Sue Allen and may have been the same group as Four Hits And A Miss. They sang with Bing Crosby in 1950. *Reference*: http://www.geocities.com/BourbonStreet/

Gordon Trio
A male group that appeared on the cover of sheet music to "My Adobe Hacienda" in 1941.

Gorton's New Orleans Minstrels
In 1906 they featured Jake Welby, Sam Lee, Arthur Fulton, Fred Long, A. D. Roland, Welby and Pearl, C. T. Bell and R. J. Howland. *Reference*: Dumont (1915)

Gotham City Four
Male quartet featured on the sheet music of "When We Were Sweethearts" in 1911.

Gotham's Four Notes
See, Four Notes.

Gotham Trio
Recorded on Vocalion in 1922.

Gounod Mixed Quartet
Recorded on Okeh in 1922. *Reference*: http://settlet.fateback.com/OK4500.html

Graham Brothers
Recorded on Victor in 1932. *Reference*: Lehl Discography

Gramophone Quartet
Recorded on England circa 1906. They were Ernest Pike, Wilfred Virgo, Stanley Kirkby and Peter Dawson. Walsh states they were the Minster Singers on Gramophone and the Meister Singers on Edison Bell cylinders. *Reference*: Walsh

Grand Central Red Cap Quartet
Black group whose membership may have included William Robinson and people with the last names Smith and Garrison. Robert Cloud was the accompanist on piano. They recorded in New York in the early 1930s. "My Little Dixie Home" and "They Kicked The Devil Out Of Heaven" were both done in 1931 on Columbia. *Reference*: BSVG-2; Lehl Discography

Great American Four
Male group that appeared on the cover of sheet music to "When I Gathered The Myrtle With Mary" in 1910.

Greater City Four
Male quartet on sheet music of "Arizona Mary" from 1909.

Greater City Quartette
Male group pictured on the cover of "They're On Their Way To Frisco Fair" from 1914.

Greater London Quartette
Male group that traveled with I. W. Baird's Minstrel Troupe of 1881-1882, comprised of Edward Stanley, Will Smith and Chas. H. Bortel and E. B. Holmes. *Reference*: Advance Programme for I. W. Baird's Minstrels, 1881-1882

Greater New York Quartette
Roger Harding and Will C. Jones (tenors), Steve Porter (baritone) and ____ Hargrave (bass) comprised this group. Recorded on Columbia about 1900-01.

Great Lakes Sextette
Male group appearing in navy uniforms on the cover of the 1918 sheet music of "Pick A Little Four Leaf Clover (And Send It Over To Me)" and "As featured by The Great Lakes Sextette with John Philip Sousa's Great Lakes Band."

Great Northern Quartette
Male group on the cover of "Best Little Girl In The Wide Wide World" from 1898 and "The Tie That Binds" in 1901. There is a reference in a weekly newspaper to their appearance in Crookston, Minnesota in 1925. *Reference*: http://www.crk.umn.edu/

Great White Way Quartet
See, Harmonizers Quartet.

Greensboro Boys Quartet
Recorded in Johnson City, Tennessee in 1928 on Columbia. *Reference*: Lehl Discography

Greenville Trio
Recorded in 1926 in Atlanta on Columbia. *Reference*: Lehl Discography

Greenwich Villagers
Recorded on Brunswick in 1923 in New York. *Reference*: Lehl Discography

Grooveneers
Recorded on Decca in 1942.

Grosso Trio
Recorded on Gennett in New York in 1926. *Reference*: Lehl Discography

Guardsmen Quartet
Recorded in 1935 and 1936 with Bing Crosby on Brunswick and Decca. *Reference*: Lehl Discography

Gulf Coast Minstrels
Members of this black group were Clifford Ross, Perry Bradford and the rest are unknown. They did comedy recordings on Columbia in New York in 1923, including "Darktown Camp Meeting" and "I Ain't Skeered Of Work." *Reference*: BSVG-3

Gulf Coast Quartet
Originally called the Silvertone Four, its members were Sterling Green (lead), Cecil Rivers (tenor), Lemuel Jackson (baritone) and Archie Cross (bass). In 1921 and 1923 they recorded in New York. *Reference*: ENVG-4

Gumm Sisters
Mary Jane, Dorothy and Frances Gumm began as a child act in 1924 when Frances was only two. They appeared in vaudeville, movies and on radio. In 1934, they changed their name to the Garland Sisters, disbanded in 1935, and Frances went on to great fame as Judy Garland. Reference: http://songbook1.wordpress.com/

Hackberry Ramblers
Recorded in New Orleans on Bluebird in 1936. *Reference*: Lehl Discography

Hall Negro Quartette
Only six discs that were intended for radio broadcast in the mid-1930s survive from this black, male group. The group is thought to have been the creation of Hall Johnson, a black, Juilliard-trained composer and arranger, who also formed the Hall Johnson Negro Choir. Nothing else is known about them. They used instrument imitation and several of their renditions had substantial speaking parts in them. *Reference*: Hall CD

Hall Sisters
Recorded on Victor in 1947.

Don Hall Trio
White group of two women and one man that appeared on sheet music, including "Ole Faithful" in 1934. They recorded on Bluebird and Victor.

Hamlin Quartet
Recorded on Champion in 1927.

Hampton Institute Singers
In 1873, sixteen singers, performing four-part harmony, began to tour. A male quartet emerged later. *Reference*: Averill

Hamtown Students
Close harmony quartet that performed as part of Charles Callender's Georgia Minstrels in the 1870s. Members were named Little, Morris, Jones and Devonear. *Reference*: Averill

Handel Mixed Quartet
Made one disc on Victor in 1906. *Reference*: Gracyk

Hann's Jubilee Singers
Black septet, led by bass W. A. Hann, and consisting of four men and three women that toured the Redpath circuit around 1915. The Four Harmony Kings evolved out of this group. *Reference*: Mainspring; Iowa

Hann's Emperors Of Song
See, Emperors Of Song.

Mark Kel's Happy-Go-Luck Boys
Recorded with Nat Shilkret in 1929 on Victor. *Reference*: Lehl Discography

Happy Hikers
Male trio appearing on the 1914 sheet music of "Gee But I Like To Hike."

Happy Home Trio
Recorded on Harmony in New York in 1926. *Reference*: Lehl Discography

Happy Trio
Recorded on Victor.

Harden Brothers
Recorded on Decca in 1941. *Reference*: Fournier

Harlemaires
Black quartet that featured three men and a woman, they recorded on Atlantic in the late 1940s. Howard Lymon (father of Frankie and Louis), Jimmy Manning, Benjamin Peay (Brook Benton) and Dottie Smith were members. *Reference*: http://www.history-of-rock.com/atlantic_records.htm; http://www.amazon.com/

Harling Quartet
Recorded on Columbia in New York in 1917. *Reference*: Lehl Discography

Harmonaires
Group that recorded on Majestic in 1948. They formed in Columbus, Ohio and were George Boswell, Fugate Page and Walter Willis. At first they were the Curtiss-Wright Singers after the factory where they all worked but then became the Harmonaires. Subsequent members were Lawrence McGhee, J. Leroy Bowen, Dave Newlin, Edward Ritchie and J. Calvin Ward. After the War, they went to New York and were on the Carnation Hour, the Jack Smith Show, the Henry Morgan Show, the Arthur Godfrey Show, the Paul Whiteman Show and the Fred Allen Show radio programs. After three years of touring, they returned to Columbus, Reid retired and the group disbanded. In 1949, they

reformed as a quintet consisting of Bowen, Newlin, Page, Ritchie, Ward and pianist Harold Clark. They continued performing until 1974 when Clark and Ritchie died. *Reference*: http://genforum.genealogy.com/

Stan Ashley's Harmoneers
Appeared on sheet music of "The Four Years" in 1934.

Harmoneons
Formed in Boston and performed around the northeast in the 1840s. Members included L. V. Crosby, Frank Lynch, Pike and Powers. *Reference*: White; Averill

Harmonettes
Recorded on Bluebird in 1935 in New Orleans and were Miggy Felder, Dottye Inman and Louise Dupuy. *Reference*: Lehl Discography

Harmonians Quartet
Recorded in New York in 1933, including "At The Baby Parade," a novelty tune. Possible members were Jerry Cooper, Irene Collins and Fran Frey. *Reference*: Sweetest Harmony; Lehl Discography

Harmonious Four
Male group on the cover of sheet music of "Gee! But There's Class To A Girl Like You" from 1908.

Harmonizers
Recorded on Harmony in 1926-8.

Harmonizers Quartet
Charles Hart, Billy Jones, Steve Porter and Harry Donaghy were the members of this group that began recording on Edison in 1920. Also known as the Premier Quartet (after 1920), Amphion Quartet (on Brunswick), Great White Way Quartet (on Brunswick) and Country Harmonizers (on Pathé Actuelle). *Reference*: Walsh

Harmonizing Four
Richmond, Virginia, gospel group that started in the 1920s. Original members included Levi Handley and "Goat" Johnson (lead). Jimmy Jones (bass), "Gospel Joe" Williams, Ellis Johnson (Goat's son) and Lonnie Smith (baritone) were later members. They continued, with changing personnel, into the 1970s. *Reference*: http://www.sc.edu/

Harmony Brothers
Recorded on Columbia in 1925.

Harmony Four
Gladys Rice, John Young, George Wilton Ballard and Donald Chalmers made up this quartet that recorded for Edison in 1917. *Reference*: Walsh

Harmony Glee Club
Male quartet featuring Carl C. Brown (baritone and manager), Archer Ballantine (bass), Robert Jones (1st tenor) and Oliver Schmid (2nd tenor). Appeared on the Redpath Lyceum circuit around 1917. *Reference*: Iowa

Harmony Hounds
Recorded on Columbia in New York in 1925 and 1926. *Reference*: Lehl Discography

Harmony Kings
Recorded in New York in 1920 on Silvertone and may have been the Revelers. *Reference*: Lehl Discography

Harrison Quartet
Recorded in New York on Gennett in 1928. *Reference*: Lehl Discography

Harrison Sisters
Trio that appeared on sheet music of "By-U By-O" in 1941.

Ryman Hart & Barney's Minstrels
Troupe containing "Harry Norman, D. S. Vernon, Harry Saynor, Sam Ricky, and Master Barney, John Jennings and Add Weaver" around 1871. *Reference*: Dumont (1915)

Harvard Glee Club Double Quartet
Recorded on Columbia in 1911.

Haverly's Mastodons
Dumont lists their membership, around 1884, as "Carroll Johnson, Hughey Dougherty, Joe Garland, J. W. Meyers, Billy Richardson, Bobby Newcomb, Walter Hawkins, George Powers, Paul Vernon, the Three Gorman Brothers, Harry J. Armstrong, Dan Thompson, John S. Robinson, Seamon and Girard, W. H. Bishop and Charley Young." *Reference*: Dumont (1915)

Haverly's Genuine Colored Minstrels
Dumont lists them as Haverly Minstrels. (Dumont, 1914) In the early 1870s, the troupe contained "Charley Reynolds, Charley Pettingill, Sig. Brandisi, Gustave Bideaux, O. P. Sweet, Otis H. Carter and others." *Reference*: Dumont (1915)

Hawaiian Maarian Quintette
Appeared on sheet music of "I Want To Be In Dixie" in 1912. It shows five men with their guitars.

Hawaiian Quintette
Recorded on Victor between 1910 and 1929.

Hawaiian Trio
Sang in about 1918 and were Helen Louise Ferara, her husband, Frank Ferara and Irene Greenus. *Reference*: Walsh

Hayden Quartette
See, Haydn Quartet

Haydn Quartet
A true pioneer vocal group, they recorded from 1898 to 1914, mostly on Victor. Walsh states the first grouping was Fred Rycroft, Charles Belling, S. H. Dudley (baritone) and William F. Hooley (bass). Gracyk says it was John Bieling (tenor), Jere Mahoney (tenor) (replaced by Harry Macdonough), Dudley and Hooley. Gracyk's source is the publication, "The Phonoscope," and is likely to be more accurate. By June 1899, when they were on Victor, they were Rycroft, Bieling, Dudley and Hooley. Their most well-known songs included "Sweet Adeline" (1904), "Take Me Out To The Ballgame" (1908), "Put On Your Old Gray Bonnet" (1909) and "By The Light Of The Silv'ry Moon" (1910). When they recorded on Edison, they were known as the Edison Male Quartet. Members moved in and out - Billy Murray sang lead on some of the more popular recordings and Reinald Werrenrath sang baritone on some of their later work. According to Gracyk, they made several recordings as the Gramophone Minstrels on Berliner in 1900. In 1913, they changed the spelling of their name to the Hayden Quartet. When they broke up in 1914, three of the members formed the Orpheus Quartet with Lambert Murphy. *Reference*: Gracyk; Walsh

Hayward Trio
Appeared on sheet music of "What D'ye Mean You Lost Yer Dog" in 1913.

Cliff Weston and the Headliners
Recorded on 1935 and 1936 in New York on Banner and other labels. *Reference*: Lehl Discography

Heartbeats
Sang with the Russ Morgan Orchestra and were not the same as the great 1950s R&B group.

Heat Waves
Appeared on sheet music of "Footloose And Fanceyfree" in 1935.

Hedges Brothers and Jacobson
Trio appearing on the cover of sheet music of "Some Of These Days" from 1910.

Heidelberg Quintet
Consisted of members of the American Quartet (Billy Murray, John Bieling, Steve Porter and William F. Hooley), plus Will Oakland, a counter-tenor. They recorded for Victor from 1911 to 1915 and their most well-known songs were "Waiting For The Robert E. Lee" (1912) and "By The Beautiful Sea" (1914). *Reference*: Walsh

Ed Helton Singers
Recorded on Columbia in 1928. *Reference*: Lehl Discography

Hemstreet Singers
This female group recorded in New York in 1925 on Columbia. *Reference*: Lehl Discography

Goree Carter & his Hepcats
From Texas they recorded on Freedom and Blues Boy in the late 1940s and early 1950s.

Hewer's Quartet
Appeared on sheet music of "Old School Chums (or Shall I Meet My Lost Love In The High School Above)" in 1902.

Hicks' Georgia Minstrels
Black-owned troupe formed by Charles Hicks that began around 1865. Later toured Europe. Hicks eventually sold the troupe to Charles Callender. *Reference*: Averill

Hicks and Sawyer Colored Minstrels
Travelling black minstrel troupe that included the vocal group, the Magnolia Quartet. *Reference*: Averill

Higgins Sisters
Recorded in New York in 1930 on Victor and were Sally, Marie, Allie and Katherine Higgins. *Reference*: Lehl Discography

Hinshaw Lyric Glee Club
Male quartet featuring Lee Lewis (1st tenor), Henry Welton (2nd tenor), Andrew Dahlgren (baritone) and Thaddeus Haigler (basso). Active on the Lyceum and Chautauqua circuits in the 1920s. *Reference*: Iowa

Hipp Cats
Black group of unknown membership, except for Norris The Troubador. They recorded in the late 1930s in New York, including "It Must Be Jelly ('Cause Jam Don't Shake Like That)" and "Chippin' Rock Blues" (both 1938). *Reference*: BSVG-3

Hit Paraders
Recorded on Victor in New York in 1942 and sang on the television and radio show "Your Hit Parade." *Reference*: Lehl Discography; http://en.wikipedia.org/

Hoboken Four
This group, which included a young Frank Sinatra, performed on the Major Bowes and His Original Amateur Hour radio show in 1935. *Reference*: http://www.nj.com/sinatra/

Hodgers Quartet
Recorded in Johnson City, Tennessee in 1928 on Columbia. *Reference*: Lehl Discography

Holly Sisters
Quartet that sang with Frankie Masters in the late 1940s. Mary was one member and another was named Carol or Carolyn. *Reference*: Lehl Discography

Sol K. Bright's Hollywaiians
They did numerous recordings on Victor in Hollywood in the mid-1930s.

Hollywood Harmony Four
Recorded on Challenge in 1928.

Hollywood Harmony Quartet
Recorded on Banner in 1928.

Hollywood Trio
Recorded on Sunset in 1925.

Holy Trinity Male Quartette
Recorded on the Romeo label in 1928.

Homestead Trio
Began in 1917 and members were Gladys Rice (replaced by Elizabeth Spencer in 1921), Betsy Lane Shepherd and Amy Ellerman. They recorded on the Edison labels from 1917 to 1925. *Reference*: Walsh

Annisteen Allen & the Home Town Boys
Black group, they recorded on Queen (King) in 1946. In addition to Allen they included Harold "Money" Johnson, Bernie Peacock, Clarence "Bullmoose" Jackson, Sam "The Man" Taylor; Sir Charles Thompson; Bernard Mackey; Beverly Peer and Dave "Panama" Francis. Mackey had been with the Ink Spots. *Reference*: http://www.jazzdiscography.com/

Home Town Coolidge Club Quartette
Appeared on sheet music of "Keep Cool And Keep Coolidge" 1924. Picture on front has The Home Town Coolidge Club Quartette of Plymouth, Vermont, presenting to the President and Mrs. Coolidge the first certificates of membership in the Home Town Coolidge Club.

Honeydreamers
Began in the mid-1940s and the original members were Keith Textor, his wife Sylvia Textor, and Marion Bye, her husband, Bob Davis, and Lou Anderson. In 1947, they made their first recordings on the Vitacoustic label and then, in 1948, recorded for RCA Victor. Radio and television appearances followed on the Kay Kyser show and the Colgate Comedy Hour with Martin and Lewis. In 1951, the Textors left the group and Anderson left in 1955 to be Clarabell on the Howdy Doody Show (replacing Bob Keeshan, who became Captain Kangaroo). In 1955, they recorded on Capitol. They were last heard from in the late 1960s. *Reference*: http://home.earthlink.net/~v1tiger/Honeydreamers.html

Honolulu Honeys
Recorded on Columbia in 1931.

Hoosier Hot Shots
This group did both instrumental and vocal numbers and were Paul "Hezzic" Trietsch, Ken Trietsch, Charles "Gabe" Ward and Frank "Gil" Kettering Taylor. They recorded mostly in Chicago on Melotone, Columbia, Vocalion and other labels from 1934 to 1946. *Reference*: Lehl Discography

Howard Trio
Recorded in Cincinnati in 1930 on Victor. *Reference*: Lehl Discography

Howell, Horsley and Bradford
Recorded in New York in 1926 on Columbia and were Bert Howell, Gus Horsley and Perry Bradford. *Reference*: Lehl Discography

Hudson Male Quartet
See, Shannon Four.

Hudson Singers
Recorded in New York on Columbia in 1929 and may have included Ed Smalle from the Revelers. *Reference*: Lehl Discography

Hughes Family
Mid-19th century singing group. *Reference*: Averill

Hughes, Oxley & Sherwood
Male trio that are pictured on the sheet music of "I Got You Steve" in 1912.

Hun Hunters
Male quartet singing patriotic songs about the first World War in the late 1910s on the Lyceum circuit. Members not known. *Reference*: Iowa

Hutchinson Family Singers
Formed in 1840 in Massachusetts, and comprised of four (of twelve) brothers - John, Judson, Asa and Jesse Hutchinson. When Jesse stopped performing to concentrate on song writing the other three performed as the Aeolian Singers. In 1842 the three added twelve-year-old sister Abby as a high tenor to again form a quartet. They were also known as the Tribe of Jesse to reflect his songwriting status and to pay homage to the Tribe of Rainer who they emulated. The Hutchinsons were the first purely American popular singing group. Their signature song was "The Old Granite State," written by Jesse in 1843. The song, advertising their home state of New Hampshire, not only contained the names of the Hutchinson family members, but came to espouse emancipation of the slaves, temperance and women's suffrage. The Hutchinsons were ardent Abolitionists and their music reflected their beliefs. As family members drifted apart, Judson's daughter, Kate Dearborn, carried on the tradition and sang with Joshua and John. Asa and his family came to prominence during the Civil War. Their likenesses appeared on sheet music as early as 1843. Averill says of them: "There is good reason to believe that the singing Hutchinson Family had a strong influence on quartet singing of the early minstrel show." *Reference*: Averill; http://www.geocities.com/

Hyer Sisters and Wallace King and John Luca
They were the first known black, mixed-gender quartet and were active in the 1850s. *Reference*: Averill

Hylton Sisters
Recorded in 1929 in Los Angeles on Varsity. *Reference*: Lehl Discography

I. C. Glee Club Quartet
Recorded 20 songs on Okeh from 1928 to 1930 and sang both secular and spiritual music. They were sponsored by the Missouri Pacific and the Illinois Central Railroad. *Reference*: http://www.earlyblues.com/

I.G.A. Quartet
Male group in Chicago in 1930. *Reference*: Lehl Discography

Illseys
Singing family group in the mid-19th century. *Reference*: Averill

Imperial Quartet of Chicago
Comprised of Wallace Moody, C. R. Wood, Ben Q. Tufts and Oliver Johnson. Recorded "Perfect Day" in 1916 on Victor. Also known as the Imperial Quartette. *Reference*: Walsh

Imperial Quartette
Male group appearing on the sheet music of "By The Beautiful Sea" from 1914. See, Imperial Quartet of Chicago. *Reference*: Schlesinger

Indiana Male Quartet
They did some test recordings on Brunswick in Chicago in 1928. *Reference*: Lehl Discography

Ink Spots
An extremely popular group that is regarded as being one of the primary influences on the Rhythm and Blues groups of the 1950s. The original members were Charlie Fuqua, Orville "Hoppy" Jones and Jerry Daniels. They started as the Riff Brothers and the Percolating Puppies and also the Jesters. Their first major performance was the Apollo Theatre in Harlem, New York on August 9, 1934. Fortunately, they changed their name to the Ink Spots and had their first major hit in 1939 with the classic, "If I Didn't Care" on Decca. At that time, the group members were Bill Kenny (lead) (who had replaced Daniels), Fuqua (tenor and guitar), Ivory "Deek" Watson (baritone and guitar) and Jones (bass and string bass). They recorded for Decca records and had many other hits, including "Address Unknown" (#1) in 1939, "When The Swallows Come Back To Capistrano" (#4),

"Whispering Grass" (#10), "Maybe" (#2), "We Three" (#1) and "Java Jive" (#15) in 1940; "Do I Worry" (#8) and "I Don't Want To Set The World On Fire" (#4) in 1941. "Don't Get Around Much Anymore" hit number two in 1943. 1944 saw two number one songs – "I'm Making Believe" and "Into Each Life Some Rain Must Fall." "The Gypsy" and "To Each His Own" were both number one songs in 1946. Watson quit in 1944 and was replaced by Bill Bowen. Hoppy Jones died in 1944 and was replaced by Cliff Givens and then Herb Kenny, Bill's twin brother. Bill Kenny and Watson clashed over the content of their act; Kenny preferred straight singing while Watson liked the comedy bits. Watson quit in 1944 and founded the Brown Dots (later the Four Tunes) after leaving the group. Fuqua's nephew was Harvey Fuqua of the Moonglows. The Ink Spots were in two movies, "The Great American Broadcast" in 1941 and "Pardon My Sarong" in 1942. They reached the charts 46 times from 1939 to 1951, with six of their offerings hitting number one. Their style was characterized by Bill Kenny's high tenor lead and the talking bass bridges of Jones. *Reference*: Goldberg, Marv. *More Than Words Can Say*. Lanham, Maryland: Scarecrow Press, 1998; The Ink Spots, The Anthology CD, MCAD2-11728

International Association Quartet
Paul J. Gilbert, P. H. Metcalf, C. M. Keeler and Edward W. Peck made Edison cylinders in 1912. *Reference*: Walsh

International Sweethearts Of Rhythm
Recorded on Guild in 1945.

Invincible Male Quartet
Also known as the Invincible Four, early versions may have included Henry Burr, George J. Gaskin, Harry Macdonough (tenors), Arthur Collins, Steven Porter, Bob Roberts (baritones) and William J. Hooley (bass) on Climax and Columbia. When they recorded on Edison cylinders in 1904, members were Byron G. Harlan, George Seymour Lenox, Arthur Collins and Frank C. Stanley. On Columbia, Albert Campbell replaced Lenox. Walsh states that on Pathé sapphire discs some Peerless Quartet recordings were credited to the Invincible Four. *Reference*: Walsh; Mainspring

Invincible Quartet
Touring group from Rust College in the second half of the 19th century. *Reference*: Averill

Ivy, Verne & Von
Recorded with Floyd Ray in 1939 on Decca.

I. W. Baird's Minstrels
In 1888, this troupe contained "Billy McAllister; Bryant and Sharpley's musical act; Billy Melville; Major Gorman, military drill expert; Fred Russell; Bartell; Brassell; Thomas Prosho; Conway; and Gardner." *Reference*: Dumont (1915)

Jackson Harmoneers
See, Five Blind Boys Of Mississippi.

Jackson Jubilee Singers
Black group comprised of five men and two women, including Robert Jackson (pianist and director), Antoinette Jackson (soprano), Edgar Lee Shupee (1st tenor), Fred Fitchue (2nd tenor), Eleanor Taylor (contralto), Percy H. Lee (baritone) and Herbert S. Williams. *Reference*: Iowa

Ja-Da Trio
Male group whose last names were Carleton, Sobol and Rosenberg that appeared on sheet music of "Ja-Da" in 1918.

James Quintet
Recorded "Tell Me Why" on Coral in 1949. Danny Johnson was the lead. They also recorded on Derby and with Austin Powell of the Cats And The Fiddle in 1952 on Atlantic. *Reference*: Fournier

Jennie Eddy Trio
One man and two boys, one of the boys identified as a young Irving Kaufman, that appear on the cover of "Pliny, Come Kiss Your Baby" from 1899. Same group appears on the cover of "My Hannah Lady (Whose Black Baby Is You)" in 1899. *Reference*: Gracyk

Jersey City Police Quartet
Appeared on sheet music of "Cheer Up Mother It's All Right Now" in 1918.

Jesters
Red Latham, Wamp Carlson and Guy Bonham formed this group that sang novelty tunes in the 1930s and 1940s on Decca. At first they called themselves the Tasty Yeast Jesters after the sponsor of a radio show on which they sang. They backed Bing Crosby on sides on Decca in 1946 and 1947. *Reference*: Whitburn-PM; www.imdb.com

Jewel Male Quartet
Recorded on Challenge in 1928.

Jewel Trio
Appeared on sheet music of "The Little House Upon The Hill" in 1915.

Johnson Brothers and Johnson
Male trio, two boys and a man, featured on the cover of "I Believed Her Too" from 1910. The two boys are in blackface.

P. C. Johnson & his Singers
Black, mixed-gender sextet, comprised of P. C. Johnson (maybe J. L. Morris, according to Ken Romanowski in liner notes to the Black Vocal Groups, Volume 9 CD on Document Records), two other males and three females. They recorded in New York in 1929. *Reference*: BVG-10

Jolly Bakers
See, Singing Hoosier Quartet.

Jones Boys Sing Band
Formed by Leon René from members of the Four Blackbirds (minus Geraldine Harris) and the Five Jones Boys. Members were David Patillo, Jimmy Springs, Richard Davis, Louis Wood, Oscar Moore (guitarist), Herman Wood, Leroy Hurte, Charles Hopkins, and William Bartley. They appeared in five films (as the "Original Sing Band") and made one recording, all in the mid-1930s. *Reference*: Goldberg

Jones Brothers
Black trio made up of Max, Herb and Clyde Jones. They sang and played instruments and recorded on Majestic in 1946. *Reference*: Fournier

Jones, Grant and Jones
Black group of two men and a woman on sheet music of "Get Your Money's Worth (Instructions From The Boss)" from 1897.

Jordanaires
Group that formed in 1948 in Springfield, Missouri, but gained their real fame when in 1956 they began to sing backup for Elvis Presley. In 1949, they sang at the Grand Ole Opry. Original members were Bill and Monty Matthews, Bob Hubbard and Culley Holt. Gordon Stoker, Hoyt Hawkins, Neal Matthews (no relation) and Hugh Jarrett were later members. The Stoker, Hawkins, Matthews and Jarrett lineup was the one that backed Elvis on most of his sessions in the mid '50s. *Reference*: http://www.Jordanaires.net

Jubilaires (Jubalaires)
The Jubalaires grew out of the Royal Harmony Quartet and were greatly influenced by the Golden Gate Quartet. Its members were J. C. Ginyard (tenor), Theodore Brooks (baritone), Orville Brooks (tenor), John Jennings (tenor), George McFadden (bass) and Everett Barksdale (guitar), although perhaps not all at the same time. William Johnson joined in 1948 and Ginyard left. They charted in 1946 with "I Know" on Decca and in 1950 with "The Old Piano Roll Blues" on Capitol. They were on the Arthur Godfrey radio program. They also took three members of the Melody Kings and they, together with Brooks, toured as the Jubalaires while the others remained and performed on the Godfrey show. Ginyard, Johnson and Brooks also sang with the Golden Gate Quartet. They also were on the Phil Harris Show. Ginyard had a prolific career, also singing with the Dixieaires and Du Droppers. *Reference*: DISC-90, Goldmine 10/80, http://www.vocalgroupharmony.com/

Boone's Jumping Jacks
Recorded on Decca in 1942.

Lloyd Phillips' Jumping Jacks
Recorded on Decca in 1941.

Kalaluhi Honolulu Quartet
Recorded in Chicago in 1929 on Vocalion. *Reference*: Lehl Discography

Kalama's Quartet
Recorded from 1928 to 1935, mostly on Okeh and were Mikiel "Mike" Hanapi, William Kalama, Bob Nawahine and Dave Kaleipua Munson. They each also played instruments. *Reference*: Lehl Discography

Kanawha Singers
See, Ritz Quartet:

Kassel Trio
Group that sang with the Art Kassel Band. They recorded on Victor in the mid-1940s. *Reference*: http://www.parabrisas.com/

Kaydettes
Sang with the Sammy Kaye Band in the 1930s. *Reference*: http://www.radioarchives.org/

Kedroff Male Quartet
Recorded on Columbia in 1929.

Keep Shufflin' Trio
Recorded with the Jimmie Johnson Orchestra in 1929 on Victor. *Reference*: Lehl Discography

Keller Sisters & Brother Lynch
Trio that sang with Jean Goldkette and his Orchestra and Vincent Lopez in the 1920s. Although their names were Nan Keller, Taddy Keller and Frank Lynch, they were sisters and brother, the family name being Lynch. In some record listings, Lynch's first name is given as Al. They also recorded on Brunswick and Vocalion. *Reference*: http://en.wikipedia.org/

Kelly & Leon's Minstrels
Troupe active in New York around 1866. "In 1873, Kelly and Leon had Charles Lester, Sam Holdsworth, Dave Wilson, Frank Converse, H. T. Mudge, John Latour, Cool White, George Guy, Edwin Stanley, W. D. Corrister and Little Jake, a dwarf comedian." *Reference*: Dumont (1915)

Ken Darby Singers
Formed by Ken Darby, formerly of the King's Men. They backed Bing Crosby on several recordings in 1947 and 1949. *Reference*: www.imdb.com

Kenna Girls
Trio that appeared on sheet music of "Who Wouldn't Be Jealous Of You?" in 1928.

Kentucky Jubilee Singers
Brooks describes them as a chorus that began in the 1870s. As with other similar groups, they toured the country, including appearances in New York in 1877. Minnie Maurice may have been a member. They recorded for U.S. Phonograph Company of New Jersey in the 1890s. The name was used in 1928 for a group organized by Forbes Randolph and that did film shorts and recorded on Brunswick. *Reference*: Brooks; http://www.warrenfahey.com/; http://www.indiana.edu/

Kentucky Minstrels
Composed of Frank Lynch, T. G. Booth, H. Mestayer and Richardson in the mid-1840s. They later reorganized under the same name, but with members William Whitlock, T, G. Booth, Barney Williams, and Cool White. *Reference*: White

Kentucky Singers
Recorded on Pathé in 1933 and were Arthur Payne, Robert Carver, Edward Coleman, James Logan and Frank Riley. *Reference*: Lehl Discography

Kentucky Trio
Recorded in 1923. *Reference*: ENVG-3

Charley Kerr Trio
Group featured on the sheet music of "Honey" in 1928.

Dinah Washington & the Keynotes
Recorded on Mercury in 1947. It is not the same group that recorded on Apollo in the 1950s.

Keystone Quartette
Group of five (sic) men featured on the cover of sheet music of "I'm Tickled To Death (That Daddy Didn't Follow His Advice To Me)" from 1915.

Khorassan Four
Appeared on sheet music of "I'm Looking Over A Four Leaf Clover" in 1927.

Kidoodlers
Recorded on Okeh and Vocalion in 1939. *Reference*: Lehl Discography

Kiesewelter Quartet
Sang with Rudy Vallee in 1935 on Victor recordings. *Reference*: Lehl Discography

Kim Loo Sisters
Trio that sang with the Ina Ray Hutton band in 1943. They used the names Alice, Patricia and Margaret. Their mother came to America from Poland; their father from China. They were born in Minnesota and started as a dancing trio. They also appeared in the film, "Meet Miss Bobby Socks" in 1944. *Reference*: Simon; "Swingin Down The Lane" Message Board

Kinder Sisters
A trio that sang on KDKA radio in Pittsburgh in the 1940s.

King, Jack & Jester
Jerry Daniels, Charles Fuqua and Ivory "Deek" Watson were the members of this early 1930s group that preceded the Ink Spots, of which all three were original members. *Reference*: Lehl Discography

King Odom Four
Also known as the King Odom Quartet, members were David "King" Odom (lead), Isaiah Bing, Cleveland Bing and David ("Boots") Bowers (bass). In 1949, they were on the NBC radio show, Swingtime. In 1950, they recorded mostly for Derby Records. They disbanded

in 1952 and the Bings and Brooks joined the Larks. Bowers also was with the Ravens and Larks. *Reference*: Goldberg

King Sisters
The Driggs family was quite musical with the six girls and two boys performing as a family orchestra to help make ends meet. Eventually, Maxine, Luise and Alyce formed a vocal trio and performed locally while still in school, influenced by the Boswell Sisters. Their father, William King Driggs was known as King, so when it came time to change their name (at the suggestion of a radio station manager), they chose the King Sisters. Bandleader Horace Heidt heard them on the radio and asked them to join his band at an engagement in San Francisco in 1934. Two of the younger sisters, Yvonne and Donna, formed a trio with a friend at about the same time. Heidt then added them to make their act the Six King Sisters (actually, five sisters and the friend, Anita). At first, they did not sing in full harmony but in three-part or unison. When Heidt went east, he could only take four singers so sister Maxine and friend Anita stayed behind. Both were married and did not want to tour. Alyce was fired by Heidt in a fit of temper in 1938 and sang for a while with Charlie Barnett. Yvonne also left and Luise and Donna stayed and sang as a trio with Peggy Pope. In 1939, the four sisters (Alyce, Yvonne, Luise and Donna) got back together and sang with Artie Shaw. They later sang with Alvino Rey (who had married Luise) and had a TV series, "The King Family" on ABC. That lasted for one year, after which they continued with performances and recordings. Their biggest hit was "It's Love-Love-Love" (1944-Bluebird). In the 1950s, they adopted a modern style of harmony similar to the Hi-Lo's. *Reference*: King Sisters-2; www.danacountryman.com

King's Jesters
Quartet that sang with Paul Whiteman Orchestra in the 1930s. Sheet music of "Little Old Log Cabin in the Lane" from 1935 shows the "The Original King's Jesters" who were John Ravencroft, Ray McDonald, Francis Bastow and George Howard and they were likely the same group. *Reference*: http://www.the-forum.com/

Kings Men
Members were Bud Lin, John Dodson, Rad Robinson and arranger Ken Darby. They sang with Paul Whiteman from 1934 to 1937, on the Fibber McGee and Molly radio show during the 1940s and early 1950s and appeared in feature films. Darby later formed the Ken Darby Singers. They also backed Bing Crosby on four sides on Decca in the 1940s. *Reference*: http://www.otrchuck.com/; www.imdb.com

Orville Baggie Hardiman & the Kings
Recorded on Mercury in 1948.

Kiwanis Quartet
Sometimes listed as the Binghamton Kiwanis Quartet, they recorded on Columbia in 1924 and were Job L. Cogdon (tenor), Robert D. Truesdell (tenor), J. Fentmore Leonard (baritone) and Paul S. Sprout (bass). *Reference*: Lehl Discography

Knapp Trio
Recorded on Brunswick in 1938. *Reference*: Lehl Discography

Knickerbocker Four
In 1899 they appeared on sheet music of "The Girl I Loved In Sunny Tennessee." The members were Will B. Mitchell, F. E. Mitchell, Will Redmond and Frank Millard.

Knickerbocker Mixed Quartette
Recorded on Columbia in 1902. *Reference*: Lehl Discography

Knickerbocker Quartet
One of several groups with this name, they were on Edison from 1909 to 1915. Members were John Young, George M. Stricklett, Frederick Wheeler and Gus Reed. It had a fluid membership and Reinald Werrenrath, William F. Hooley, Royal Fish, Harvey Hindermyer, Robert D. Armour and John Finnegan also sang with them. Walsh states they were created to take the place of the Edison Male Quartet when its members moved to Victor. *Reference*: Walsh

Knickerbocker Quartet
This was a later group with this name. They had a hit with "Pack Up Your Troubles In Your Old Kit Bag" (1917-Columbia). Personnel were George Eldred, Lewis James, William Morgan and Glenn Howard. *Reference*: Walsh

Knickerbocker Quartette
Black concert group that toured with Billy Jackson's Minstrels in 1894 in New York and New Jersey. *Reference*: Averill

Knickerbocker Quintet
They made one Edison cylinder in 1905 and included Parvin White, Charles H. Bates, Geoffrey O'Hara, Walter C. White and Leon Parmett. *Reference*: Walsh

Knickerbockers
See, the Southern Sons.

Knites of Rhythm
Male quintet that recorded in New York in 1941 on Bluebird. *Reference*: Lehl Discography

Kunkel's Nightingale Opera Troupe
Dumont calls this group Kunkel's Nightingale Minstrels. Members included Tom Moxley ("Master Floyd"), Harry Lehr, William Penn Lehr and later Nelse Seymour. *Reference*: Averill; Dumont (1914)

Kay Kyser Group
Group that sang with the Kay Kyser Orchestra from 1938 to 1941 that consisted over time of Virginia "Ginny" Simms, Harry Babbitt, Merwin "Ish-Kabibble" Bogue, Sully Mason, Max Williams and Jack ???. They recorded mostly on Brunswick and Columbia. *Reference*: Lehl Discography

Lada's Louisiana Five
Male group featured on the cover of "Arkansas Blues (A Down-Home Chant)" from 1921.

Lady Entertainers
Quartet featuring Agnes Tully, Kathryn A. Reed, Kathryn Roberts and Mayfa M. Haines. Appeared on the Chautauqua circuit in the 1910-1911 season. *Reference*: Iowa

Lady Singers
Quartet featuring Merle Stevens (1st soprano), Helen Travis (2nd soprano), Lillian Madison (1st alto) and Marie Kelley (2nd alto). Performed on the Lyceum circuit around 1915. *Reference*: Iowa

Lady Washington Quartette
Group on the Lyceum and Chautauqua circuits around 1910. Members not known. *Reference*: Iowa

Lafayette Lyric Four
Male group on the cover of "Wait 'Till The Sun Shines, Nellie" from 1905.

Landt Trio and Howard White
The Landts were from Scranton, Pennsylvania and teamed with pianist Howard White in 1926. The appeared exclusively on the newly established NBC red and blue radio networks. For eight years beginning in 1941 they performed as a trio on the CBS "Sing Along" program, with a female singer, Carol Ames (who married their announcer, Bill Cullen). With the demise of live radio, they were gone from the scene by the early 1950s. *Reference*: http://landttrio.netfirms.com/

Lane Sisters
A trio, Rosemary, Priscilla and Lola Lane (whose real name was Mullican), that sang with the Fred Waring Orchestra in the mid-1930s. They had successful movie careers, each

appearing in more than 20 films in the late 1930s and 1940s. Rosemary and Priscilla were also part of Fred Waring's Glee Club. A fourth sister, Leota, sang with them at times. *Reference*: http://www.parabrisas.com/d_lanep.php

Lang's Gotham Four
Male group appearing on the sheet music of "When Winter Days Are Over" from 1907.

Larkin Sisters
Quartet that appeared on sheet music in the late 1940s and 1950s, including "Toolie Oolie Doolie" in 1948.

Larks
Another great group that never even hit the pop charts (they had two R&B Top 10 songs), the Larks came from North Carolina and grew out of the gospel group, the Selah Jubilee Singers. Thurmon Ruth, who was the original lead singer, put the Larks together with Gene Mumford as its new lead. Other members were Raymond "Pee Wee" Barnes (tenor), Allen Bunn (baritone) and David McNeil (bass). Mumford had one of the great voices and ranks at or near the top of virtually every list of best leads of the late 1940s-early 1950s era. He had been wrongly imprisoned, where he wrote the hauntingly beautiful, "When I Leave These Prison Walls" (1951-Apollo). He was eventually pardoned. "My Reverie" (1951-Apollo) was the Larks most successful recording. This group broke up in 1952 and Mumford began singing with the Golden Gate Quartet. In 1954, Mumford and Orville Brooks left the Golden Gate Quartet and formed a new Larks with David Bowers and Isaiah Bing, both of the King Odom Four. This new lineup sang more in the pop style than R&B and lasted less than one year. Mumford later sang lead on some of the top hits of Billy Ward & the Dominoes. McNeil also became a Dominoes member. Bunn formed the Wheels and Ruth continued as a gospel singer and disc jockey. *Reference*: The Larks, My Reverie CD, Relic 7124

La Rue's Carnival Minstrels
Troupe from the 1860s. For a year, featured Jerry Cohan, father of George M. *Reference*: Dumont (1915)

Lawrenceville Quartet
Male quartet that recorded on Columbia in 1924 in New York. *Reference*: Lehl Discography

LeBrun Sisters
Trio from Rochester, New York, sang with Glen Gray and the Casa Loma Orchestra in 1942. *Reference*: Simon; http://www.sealander.com/Letters.html

Lee Sisters
Miriam, Jean and Maree Lee and Virginia Halcombe made up this quartet that sang with Vaughan Monroe. Maree also sang with the Moonmaids. *Reference*: http://www.vaughnmonroesociety.org/

Le Maine, Keller & Turner
Two males and a female appearing on the sheet music of "Hitchy Koo" from 1912.

Lett Sisters & Louise
Trio that appeared on sheet music of "Coquette" in 1928. Louise was Louise Snav and one of the Letts was Mildred. They were later called the Premier Trio. *Reference*: http://www.samueljohnson.com/

Lewis Bronzeville Five
From Chicago, this black group, formerly known as the Five Aces Of Rhythm, featured Royale Brent (lead), Arthur Butler (tenor), Benny Holman (tenor), Alfred Elkins (baritone) and Clyde Townes (bass). They were a jive group that played their own instruments and recorded for Bluebird in 1940. Their "Natchez Mississippi Blues" tells the story of a fire in the Rhythm Club in Natchez in 1940. More than 200 people were killed, including most of the members of the Walter Barnes Orchestra. To avoid problems with their manager, they disbanded in 1941. *Reference*: JJ-CD; BSVG-3

Lewis Trio
Recorded in New York in 1930 on Banner and other labels. Sam M. Lewis was a member. *Reference*: Lehl Discography

Lew Johnson's Baby Boy Minstrels
The third and most successful of the groups led by Lew Johnson; they toured between 1887 and 1888. It featured the "Black Baby Boy Quartet." *Reference*: Averill

Lew Johnson's Minstrels
The first of several touring groups led by Lew Johnson that toured between 1866 and 1871. The quartet attached to this group included F. M. Proctor (a ballad singer), Mr. Hardey (tenor) and George Catlin (bass). *Reference*: Averill

Lew Johnson's Plantation Minstrels
The second touring group led by Lew Johnson, it toured between 1871 and 1896 and featured Alf Lindsey and O. T. Johnson (singers). *Reference*: Averill

Lew Male Quartet
Organized by black musician William Edward Lew in the 1880s in New England. Lew also formed the Lew Quintette. His vocal groups toured widely. Lew eventually became an academic. *Reference*: Southern; Cuney-Hare

Lew Johnson's Refined Minstrels
Another group led by Lew Johnson; they were active around 1890. *Reference*: Averill

Liberty Quartet
See, Shannon Four.

Lime Kiln Quartette
Black group that was featured in "Out of Bondage," staged by Lew Johnson's Refined Minstrels in 1890. *Reference*: Averill

Lions Quartet
Recorded on Columbia in 1927-8. *Reference*: Lehl Discography

Little Link Quartette
Toured with Allen's Minstrels in 1899. *Reference*: Abbott and Seroff

Livingston College Male Quartet
Formed in the 19th-century, they recorded as late as 1927 on Victor. *Reference*: Averill; Lehl Discography

Lloyd's Minstrels
Lloyd's Minstrels was organized by Lloyd, the map man. He took many of the famous stars of minstrelsy and promised them huge salaries. Among those he engaged were: Billy Birch, Charley Fox, Dave Wambold, Gustave Bideaux and Cool White. Philo A. Clark was the agent. When the members of the troupe called for their salaries, Lloyd sat at a table with a revolver and dared them to touch the money. He later organized Lloyd & Bideaux s Minstrels. *Reference*: Dumont (1914)

Locust Sisters
Trio that appeared on sheet music, including "When It's Night-time In Italy It's Wednesday Over Here" in 1923. In 1927, they were on Broadway in "Hit The Deck" as a quartet. As the Five Locust Sisters (four singers and a pianist) they were in a video in 1928 where they performed two songs. A cut from this was in the movie "That's Entertainment III." *Reference*: http://www.imdb.com/name/nm1708773/

Log Cabin Four
Recorded on Columbia in 1932.

Lombardi Quartette
Misses Crawford, Gladys McCoy Taylor, Rose Ann Carr and Burnett, and their pianist, appear in a photograph from 1935. *Reference*: http://virtuallymissouri.umsystem.edu/

Longacre Quartette
Appeared on sheet music of "That Fussy Rag" in 1910.

Longo Trio
Recorded on Pathé around 1920.

Loomis Sisters
Trio that appeared on the cover of sheet music of "Yearning" from 1925.

Lotus Glee Club of New York
Organized in 1881-1882, the original members were C. Frank Hunting (tenor), Nat. M. Brigham (tenor), Avon D. Saxon (baritone) and John K. Berry (bass). Members in the early 1910s included Harvey W. Hindermyer (1st tenor), G. Morgan Stricklett (2nd tenor), Charles L Lewis (baritone), Wilfred Glenn (later with the Revelers) (bass) and Frank J. Smith (conductor). *Reference*: Iowa

Lotus Male Quartet
Recorded on Columbia in 1908. A poster shows Robert Martin (1st tenor), William Hicks (2nd tenor), Nelson Raymond (baritone) and Frank Cannell (basso) as the members and indicates that they were from Boston. *Reference*: http://www.pawneecountyhistory.com/

Lotus Quartet
Made Edison cylinders in 1904. Members were George Seymour Lenox (tenor), George M. Stricklett (tenor), Charles Lewis (baritone) and Frank C. Stanley (bass). *Reference*: Walsh

Louisiana Boys
Recorded on Bluebird in 1936. *Reference*: Lehl Discography

Lovenberg Sisters and Neary Brothers
Mixed gender quartet that appeared on the cover of sheet music for "From Me To Mandy Lee" in 1917,

Lowland Singers
Recorded on Columbia in 1933. *Reference*: Lehl Discography.

Lubbock Texas Quartet
Recorded on Columbia in 1929. *Reference*: Lehl Discography

Luca Family Singers
Black group from New Haven, Connecticut, that was formed in the 1840s by John W. Luca. Other members were John's wife, Lisette, her sister, Diana Lewis, and sons John W., Jr., Simeon, Alexander and Cleveland. In 1850, they sang at an abolition convention in New York. *Reference*: Southern

Lunceford Trio
Sang with Jimmy Lunceford from 1934 to 1939 and were Sy Oliver, Willie Smith and Eddie Tompkins. *Reference*: Lehl Discography

Frank Luther Trio
Recorded mostly on Victor in the early 1930s and were Frank Luther, Mrs. Frank Luther and Leonard Stokes. *Reference*: Lehl Discography

Lyceum Trio
Appeared on sheet music of "Where Are The Scenes Of Yesterday" in 1909.

Lynch Trio
Three young people that appear on the cover of the sheet music to "If I Had You" from 1914.

Lyric Glee Club
Male foursome of Arthur Scott (1st tenor), Alvin Jones (2nd tenor), Paul Archibald (baritone) and Tom C. Polk (basso). Appeared for the Slayton Lyceum Bureau in the Midwest around 1910. *Reference*: Iowa

Lyric Male Quartet
See, Shannon Four.

Lyric Quartette
Mixed-gender group that was on Victor from 1906 to 1918 and featured an original line-up of Elise Stevenson, Corrine Morgan, Harry Macdonough and Frank Stanley. Stanley died in 1910, was replaced by Reinald Werrenrath and Olive Kline and Marguerite Dunlap replaced the two women. Dunlap in turn was replaced by Elise Baker. That grouping stayed intact until 1918 when they disbanded. Their biggest hit was "Down In The Sheltering Palms" (1915-Victor). *Reference*: Walsh

Lyric Trio
Mixed-gender group of the late 1890s that made Edison cylinders. They were Estella Louise Mann (soprano), John Hayes (tenor) and William F. Hooley (bass). In 1901 they switched to Victor and were Grace Spencer, Harry Macdonough and Hooley. *Reference*: Walsh

Lyric Trio
The second group of this name, it was not related to the earlier combination. Members were Will Oakland, Albert Campbell and Henry Burr. They recorded on Columbia in 1914 and 1915. *Reference*: Walsh

Macedonia Quartet
Recorded on Victor in 1928 and were Fred McPhail (tenor), Floyd Inman (tenor), Spencer Smith (baritone) and E. Henderson (bass). *Reference*: Lehl Discography

Mack Sisters
Black trio that recorded on Decca in 1939 and 1940 with Buddy Johnson. *Reference*: Fournier

Macon Quartet
Recorded on Columbia in 1927. *Reference*: Lehl Discography

Madam Rentz' Female Minstrels
Organized by M. B. Leavitt, they were the first all-female minstrel group. *Reference*: Dumont (1915)

Magnolia Quartette
Concert group featuring Will Wade, Fred Jones, Ollie Hall and L. Lucas. They toured with Fields' Negro Minstrels and the Canadian Jubilee Company in the 1890s. *Reference*: Averill

Maitland Entertainers
Trio comprised of Thomas Baldridge (1st tenor), Ralph Pearson (2nd tenor) and Walter Van Dyke (baritone). Appeared on the Midwest Lyceum circuit around 1923. *Reference*: Iowa

Majestic Quartette
Group featured on the cover of the sheet music to "Someone Thinks Of Someone" from 1905.

Male Quartette
Membership is unknown. They recorded on American, Edison Amberol, Busy Bee and Imperial, all in about 1906. *Reference*: ENVQ-1

Manhansett Quartette
They are believed to be the first vocal group to make commercial records in their own name. Members were George J. Gaskin, Gilbert Girard, Joe Riley and their bass, whose last name was Evans. John Bieling was a later member. They recorded cylinders for the New Jersey Record Co. label in 1892. Subsequently, they were John Bieling, Gaskin, Riley and Jim Cherry (replaced by Walter Snow). The Edison Male Quartet succeeded them. *Reference*: Walsh

Manhattan Harmony Four
Recorded in 1923. *Reference*: ENVG-5

Manhattan Ladies Quartet
Irene Cummings, Mabel Meade Davis, Annie Laurie McCorkle and Anne Winkoop made an Edison cylinder in 1912. *Reference*: Walsh

Manhattan Mixed Trio
Recorded on Edison in 1913 and Frank C. Stanley, Elise Stevenson and Henry Burr were its members. *Reference*: Gracyk

Manhattan Quartet
Made records for Edison and Victor from 1912 to 1929 and are said to have had both American and German members. Known members were H. Weimann, Albert Hall, N. C. Latterner and F. Schwarzkopf. *Reference*: Walsh; Lehl Discography

Manhattan Trio
See, Metropolitan Trio

Manhatters
Quartet that appeared on sheet music of "Dream Kisses" in 1927.

Maple City Four
White comedy quartet that performed in vaudeville in the 1910s. *Reference*: Averill

Maple City Four
Formed in 1924 LaPorte, Indiana, they were a different group from the one above and were favorites throughout the Midwest for many years thanks to their long tenure (about 30 years) on radio. According to an article on the Barbershop Harmony Society website by

Ruth Blazina-Joyce, they were called the "Marx Brothers of radio," being known for their comedy as well as their singing. Members were Art Janes, Fritz Meissner, Al Rice and Pat Petterson. Chuck Kerner was a later member, replacing Janes. *Reference*: http://www.barbershop.org/

Mariners
A mixed-race quartet with two black and two white members - Martin Karl, Jim Lewis, Tom Lockard and Nat Dickerson. They formed in 1942 in Manhattan Beach, New York, while in the Coast Guard, recorded on Columbia in the late 1940s and early 1950s and were regulars on the Arthur Godfrey TV show. *Reference*: Fournier

Mariners Trio
Recorded on Okeh in 1930.

Marlin Sisters
Had a hit with the song, "You Can't Be True, Dear" in 1948 with Eddie Fisher and reached the charts two other times that year, all on Columbia. In 1949, they were part of a hit that stayed on the charts for 26 weeks when they provided the vocals on "Blue Skirt Waltz" done by Frankie Yankovic and His Yanks, also on Columbia. In the 1950s, they recorded on Mercury, London, Decca and Coral. They also recorded some songs in Yiddish. Their real name was Malavsky. *Reference*: Whitburn-PM; http://home.earthlink.net/

Marshall, Dean & Reeves
Male trio that appeared on sheet music of "Tia-Da-Da Tia-Da-Da- My Croony Melody" in 1914.

Marshall Sisters
Recorded in 1929 on Electradisk. *Reference*: Lehl Discography

Martin-Aires Trio
Recorded on 1938 on Bluebird. *Reference*: Lehl Discography

Martinettes
White male trio that appeared on sheet music of "I Dreamt That I Dwelt In Marble Halls" in 1935.

Marvin Family:
Recorded on Columbia in 1929. *Reference*: Lehl Discography

Marx Brothers
The famous comedians and screen actors who began their career in vaudeville as a comedy/musical quartet called the Nightingales. *Reference*: Averill

Mask & Wig Male Quartet
Recorded on Victor in 1925.

Mason's Jubilee Singers
Black group with three women and two men that appeared on the Redpath Chautauqua circuit around 1928. Another version of the group featured four men and three women, around 1910. Managed by L. J. Mason. *Reference*: Iowa

Massanutten Military Academy Quartet
Directed by Jean Patrice Poulot, they recorded on Columbia in 1932. *Reference*: Lehl Discography

Master Keys
From Norfolk, they were Johnny Moore (tenor), Norman Harris (2nd tenor), Melvin Colden, previously with the renowned Norfolk Jazz/Jubilee Quartet and the Selah Jubilee Singers (baritone) and J. B. Nelson, also from the Selah group (bass). They were originally known as the Virginia Four. Nelson was killed in 1946 and Colden went back to the Selahs. Clarence Roberts and Robert White also sang with the group. *Reference*: Whiskey–9; Fournier

Masters Voices
Sang with the Frankie Masters Band in the 1940s. *Reference*: http://www.letrs.indiana.edu/

Matthes Trio
Trio of two boys and a girl, identified as "Those Klassy Kids" that appeared on sheet music of "Kentucky Home" in 1915.

Maxim's Cabaret Singers
Recorded on Columbia in 1913. *Reference*: Lehl Discography

Max Ritter Trio
Male group appearing on the cover of sheet music of "I'm Living On 5th Avenue" from 1901.

Maybelle Sunbeams
Appeared on sheet music of "Everybody's Doin' It Now" in 1911.

Mayfair Trio
Recorded on Vocalion in 1926.

McCarthy and Monroe Comedy Quartet
Group featured at Hyde & Behman's Music Hall, in Brooklyn, N.Y., around 1905. *Reference*: Advertisement by A. Windisch, N.Y.

McEnelly's Singing Orchestra
Featured on the cover of sheet music of "When The Leaves Come Tumbling Down" in 1922.

McIntyre and Heath Minstrel Company
Minstrel troupe that began in Atlanta, in 1878. The second version of this group was organized in St. Louis in 1880 and featured the San Francisco Quartette. The third iteration appeared in 1881, the fourth in 1885-1886 which included the Clipper Quartette. *Reference*: Dumont (1915)

Clayton McMichen and His Singing Sisters
Recorded on Columbia in 1927. *Reference*: Lehl Discography

McNish, Johnson & Slavin's Minstrels
Troupe launched in 1885, containing " Billy McAllister, George W. Powers, Bob Slavin, Frank E. McNish, Carroll Johnson, Frank Howard, Harry M. Morse, John Davis, W. W. Black, Raymond Shaw, George Hassell, Martin Hogan, Ernest Sinclair, William F. Holmes, Joseph Garland, Fox Samuels, Marcus Doyle, Willie Pickert, John Daly, Johnny Keegan, William Henry Rice, Henry Carmody, Larry McEvoy, Harry Long, John and Bob Morrissey, Mike Talbott and Dan Quinlan, master of transportation." *Reference*: Dumont (1915)

McQuade Sisters
Quartet of young girls that appeared on sheet music of "I Could Fall In Love With Someone Like You" in 1925.

McQueen Quartet
Recorded on Columbia in 1928. *Reference*: Lehl Discography

Meadowbrook Quartette
Black group around the turn of the 20th-century. *Reference*: Averill

Megetharian Minstrels
Started by Billy Emerson and R. M. Hooley and around 1880 included James A. Barney, E. M. Hall, Luke Schoolcraft, Arthur Cook, H. W. Frillman, Carl, Will and Rit Rankin, Harry Robinson, Seamon Summers and the Girard Brothers, Gibson and Binney, Walsh and King, Burt Haverly and Gibbs, Park and Donnavan, Lyons and Healey, Kelly and O Brien, John Oberist and V. Rigby. *Reference*: Dumont (1915)

Meigs Sisters Vocal Quartette
Appeared on a show bill in the 1880s promising "Unique Entertainment" and on the Chautauqua circuit. Reference: Meigs, Henry Benjamin. *Record of the Descendants of Vincent Meigs*. Baltimore: J. S. Bridges & co., 1901

Meister Singers
See, Gramophone Quartet.

Meister-Singers Quartette
Appeared on sheet music of "Rebecca Of Sunnybrook Farm" in 1914.

Mello Larks
White, mixed-gender group, they began in 1946 with Glenn Miller and recorded on RCA Victor. In 1947, they switched to United Artists. The members were Tommy Hamm, Bob Smith, Jack Bierman and Ginny O'Connor. O'Connor had sung with the Mel-Tones and later married Henry Mancini. Joan Loree (1949-51), Toni Southern (1951-52), Jamie Dina (1952-58) and Adele Castle (1958-60) in turn replaced O'Connor. Joe Eich replaced Bierman in 1951. They disbanded in 1960. *Reference*: Fournier; http://www.library.gsu.edu/

Mellomen
Max Smith (tenor) and Thurl Ravenscroft (bass) left the Sportsmen Quartet to form the Mellomen in 1948. Ravenscroft also did quite a bit of voiceover work in animated films and was the voice of Tony The Tiger in the cereal commercials. The other members were Bob Hamlin (1st tenor) (replaced by Bob Stevens in 1955) and Bill Lee (baritone). The group appeared on the Cavalcade of American Music radio show with Edgar Bergen. In the 1950s they did backup work for the likes of Peggy Lee and Elvis Presley. *Reference*: Goldberg; http://www.acappellanews.com/archive/000785.html

Melodeers
A 1940s group that included Herb Kenny and Jimmy Ricks (later of the Ravens). In 1945 Kenny left to join brother Bill and the Ink Spots as their bass. *Reference*: http://inkspots.ca/

Melodians
Trio from Chicago that appeared on the cover of sheet music for "Say Mister Have You Met Rosie's Sister" from 1926.

Hollis Smith and his Melodians
Recorded on Victor in New York in 1932. *Reference*: Lehl Discography

Melody Belles
Female quartet that performed on the Redpath Chautauqua circuit in 1929. *Reference*: Iowa

Melody Four
They included Jack Fenderson and Buck Franklin and recorded in 1931 in Camden, New Jersey on Bluebird and Victor. *Reference*: Lehl Discography

Melody Male Quartet
Recorded on Vocalion in 1922.

Melody Masters
Group from Newark, New Jersey, and featured Cliff Givens (bass). Although they recorded under the name Melody Masters, when they toured, they were known as the Southern Sons. Other members were Danny Owens (later with the Four Tunes), Pico Payne (tenor), James Waters (baritone) and Eric Miller (vocals and guitar). Givens also sang with the Ink Spots, Golden Gate Quartet and Dominoes. Owens also sang with the Four Tunes. *Reference*: 40s-50s-CD

Melody Monarchs
Appeared on sheet music of "The Ragtime Violin" in 1911.

Melody Musketeers
Male trio of NBC radio artists, Bill, Howe and Jim, that appeared on sheet music of "I Lost My Gal From Memphis" in 1930.

Murray & His Melody Men
See, Merry Melody Men.

Melody Monarchs
Appeared on the sheet music of "The Ragtime Violin" in 1911.

Melody Quartet
Recorded on Vocalion in 1922. *Reference*: Lehl Discography

Melody Three
Jack Parker, Will Donaldson and Phil Duey made up this group that also recorded as the Men About Town in the late 1920s. *Reference*: Walsh

Melo-Fellows
Recorded on Vocalion and Conqueror in 1939.

Mel Tormé & his Meltones
The Meltones were formed in 1944 by Mel Tormé who took a group called the Schoolkids and made them his Meltones. They were Sheldon Disruhd, Betty Beveridge, Ginny O'Connor and Bernie Parke. Disruhd was drafted and replaced by Les Baxter (the famous arranger and orchestra leader). Tormé broke up the group in 1946 but they regrouped in 1959 for some recordings with Sue Allen, Ginny O'Connor, Bernie Parke and Tom Kenny as members. O'Connor also sang with the Mellolarks. Tormé, of course, had about as good a solo career as one could want, gaining both critical and commercial success. *Reference*: Meltones CD; http://www.jazzprofessional.com/; http://www5.allusenet.org/

Men About Town
Trio that included Frank Luther and Scrappy Lambert and sang with Victor Young on Decca in the early 1930s. *Reference*: Lehl Discography

Mendelssohn Glee Club
From New York, they were organized in 1865. *Reference*: Averill

Mendelssohn Male Quartet
Recorded on Columbia in 1911.

Mendelssohn Mixed Quartet
Its members were Edith Chapman, Corrine Morgan, George Morgan Stricklett and Frank C. Stanley and they made Edison cylinders in the early 1900s. *Reference*: Walsh

Mendelssohn Quartette Co.
Male group including J. Lincoln Newhall (1st tenor), Maldwyn Evans (2nd tenor), Howard Stewart Barnett (baritone) and Urban Leo Alkire (basso). Appeared with Marguerite Smith ("of Famous Smith Sisters" and "the acknowledged Queen of Child Impersonators") for the Central Lyceum Bureau in Columbus, Ohio for the 1901-1902 season. A group by the same name appeared in 1929 with the Chicago Concert Company. *Reference*: Iowa

Mendelssohns
Foursome associated with the traveling Chautauquas around 1910. *Reference*: Averill

Men Of Notes
Appeared on sheet music of "Dark Eyes" in 1935.

Merrilees Entertainers
Female quartet including Gladys Ufford (soprano), Alta Burton (contralto and accompanist), Leila White (soprano and reader) and Ruth Edwards (contralto). Performed on the Redpath Chautauqua circuit for the 1917-1918 season. *Reference*: Iowa

Merrilees Ladies Quartette
Female quartet including Gladys Ufford (soprano), Bessie White (contralto), Leila White (soprano and reader) and Ruth Edwards (contralto). Performed for the Redpath Chautauqua circuit around 1918. *Reference*: Iowa

Merry Macs
Said to be the first mixed-gender harmony quartet to feature a female lead. The group was formed in Minneapolis, Minnesota in the mid-1920s by brothers Ted, Judd and Joe McMichael. They added Cheri McKay and made their first recording in 1932 for Victor. McKay was replaced in 1938 by Helen Carroll, and then, in turn, Mary Lou Cook and Marjory Garland. Joe was killed in World War II and replaced by Lynn Allen, but the group continued into the late 1960s. Their biggest hits were the novelty tune, "Mairzy Doats" and "Praise The Lord And Pass The Ammunition" both in 1942, "Pretty Kitty Blues Eyes" in 1944 and "Laughing On The Outside" in 1946, all on Decca. They also accompanied Bing Crosby on several numbers. *Reference*: The Merry Macs CD, Living Era 5393; Whitburn-PM

Merrymakers
See, Revelers.

Merry Melody Men
Billy Murray led this group that recorded on Vocalion in the 1920s. *Reference*: http://www.archive.org/details/BillyMurrayHisMerryMelodyMen

Metropolitan Entertainers
Elizabeth Spencer, Charles Harrison and Ernest Hare recorded on Edison in 1926. *Reference*: Walsh

Metropolitan Glee Club
Male foursome including F. M. Gates (1st tenor), N. F. Peters (2nd tenor), L. H. Waite (basso) and F. J. Tiernan (baritone and pianist). First performed in 1912; the group appeared in over 3500 programs for Lyceum and Chautauqua audiences. *Reference*: Iowa

Metropolitan Grand Quartet
Male group including Charles L. Neth (lyric tenor), Paul Chase (robust tenor), John Eberly (baritone) and Thomas Wade Lane (bass). Appeared on the Lyceum circuit in 1919. *Reference*: Iowa

Metropolitan Male Trio
Also known as the Metropolitan Entertainment Trio. Performed for the Lyceum Bureau of Chicago around 1915. *Reference*: Iowa

Metropolitan Mixed Chorus
Billy Murray, Frank Stanley and Ada Jones made up this trio. They recorded on Edison in 1916 and 1917, including "Dixie." *Reference*: http://www.archive.org/

Metropolitan Mixed Trio
In 1904, Corrine Morgan, George S. Lenox and Frank C. Stanley made cylinders for Edison. Later, Elise Stevenson, Henry Burr and Stanley comprised the group. They made some cylinders as the Manhattan Trio. *Reference*: Walsh

Metropolitan Quartet
Mixed-gender group made up of Florence Hinkle, Margaret Keyes, John Young and Frederick Wheeler. They made Edison cylinders in 1908. Walsh states that later, after Diamond Discs came into being, the personnel changed. Young, Wheeler and Elizabeth Spencer were frequent members and Mary Jordan sometimes was the contralto. *Reference*: Walsh

Metropolitan Quartette
Male group on the cover of sheet music of "Honey I Will Long For You" from 1910.

Mctropolitan Trio
Recorded on Columbia from 1908-11; the members were Frank Stanley, Henry Burr and Elise Stevenson. *Reference*: Walsh

Miami Valley Trio
Recorded on Champion in 1928.

Midland Jubilee Singers
Another W. A. Hann (basso, director and manager) group. Also included Willetta Campbell (soprano), Carolyn Dixon (contralto), Vreen Marshall (1st tenor), C. Dickerson (2nd tenor), Exodus (baritone and reader) and A. E. Sheppard (guitar and accompanist). *Reference*: Iowa

George Miller's Mid-Riffs
Recorded on Mercury in 1949.

Miles Bros. Quartette
Recorded in 1937. *Reference*: BVG-6

Military Quartet
Black group from San Francisco that appeared on sheet music of "When Winter Days Are Over" in 1907. *Reference*: Averill

Mille Martha & Sisters
They appear on the sheet music of "Rebecca of Sunnybrook Farm" in 1914.

Miller, Midge and the Callahan Brothers
A woman and two men on the cover of sheet music of "When Uncle Joe Plays His Piccolo" from 1919.

Mills Brothers
One of the most famous, enduring and influential vocal groups of any era. From Piqua, Ohio, when they began it was the four brothers - John, Jr. was born in 1910, Herbert in 1912, Harry in 1913, and Donald in 1915. They were the first black group to have wide appeal to white audiences. (In the previous century, the Fisk Jubilee Singers had great appeal to white audiences but it was necessarily limited because there was not yet recording or radios.) Their father owned a barber shop and founded a barbershop quartet called the Four Kings of Harmony. (Their grandfather, Billy Mills, had sung with Stinson's Jubilee Singers in the 1880s.) They learned their close harmonies first-hand, and began performing around the area. At one show, Harry Mills forgot his kazoo -- the group's usual accompaniment -- and ended up trying to imitate the instrument by cupping his hand over his mouth. The brothers were surprised to hear the sound of a trumpet coming from Harry's mouth, so they began to work the novelty into their act – with John taking tuba, Donald trombone and Herbert a second trumpet. Their version of "Caravan," recorded in 1938, as an "instrumental," shows their uncanny instrument imitation at its peak. When John died suddenly in 1935, he was replaced by their father, John, Sr. They had a huge number of hits (11 on the R&B Charts and 70 on the Pop Charts) and influenced many of the groups that followed. Biggest songs included "Tiger Rag" (1931-Brunswick), "Dinah" (1932-Brunswick), "Paper Doll" (1943-Decca), "Till Then" (1944-Decca) and "Glow Worm" (1952-Decca). The group continued as a trio when their father died in 1956. They had the longest tenure from first chart hit to last of any vocal group – 1931 to 1968. Donald died in 1999, having performed as a duo with his son during the last years of his life. They appeared in eleven films from "The Big Broadcast" in 1932 to "The Big Beat" in 1958 (as a trio without their father). As Jay Warner wrote of them: "The Mills Brothers' influence was

pervasive: they made black music acceptable to a wide audience and encouraged other black vocalists to carry on what they had started. And lest we forget, they did it with dignity and grace in difficult racial times, carried forward by their warmth of character and mellow sound." *Reference*: Whitburn – PM; Warner

Minnesota Ladies Quartette
Comprised of Alice Adrian Pratt (1st soprano), Grace Chadbourne (2nd soprano), E. W. French (1st alto), Florence Earle (2nd alto) and Margaret Hicks (pianist). Appeared at Chautauquas around 1920. *Reference*: Iowa

Minster Singers
Charles Alexander and the Minster Singers recorded on Zonophone in the early 1900s. *Reference*: http://www.normanfield.com/charlesalexander.htm

Minstrel Four
Group that appeared on sheet music of "Baby Please Don't Shake Me While I'm Gone" in 1912.

The Misses Dennis
See, Three Dennis Sisters.

Mississippi Mud Mashers
Black quintet of unknown membership. They recorded in New Orleans in the mid-1930s on Bluebird. *Reference*: BSVG-2

Missouri-Pacific Diamond Jubilee Quartette
Black quartet that recorded in St. Louis in 1927. Some railroad companies sponsored quartets that did local performances and also sang on trains. *Reference*: VQ-5

Mobile Four
See, Birmingham Jubilee Singers.

Mobile Revelers
Recorded on Grey Gull in 1929. *Reference*: Lchl Discography

Mocking Bird Minstrels
Black troupe that appeared around 1855 in Philadelphia. Averill thinks they were the first black group to call themselves "minstrels." *Reference*: Averill

Modernaires
Began in Buffalo, New York, in the early 1930s as a trio. The members were Harold Dickinson, Bill Conway and Chuck Goldstein. In 1936, they added Ralph Brewster in time for radio broadcasts with Fred Waring. With Waring they performed as part of the V-8 octet. When they left Waring and the V-8, they joined the Charlie Barnet Orchestra where they recorded in 1936 on Bluebird, including "Make Believe Ballroom" and "The Milkman's Matinee." They sang with Ray Noble's band and Paul Whiteman (1938-1940) and left him to sing with a new ensemble being formed by Glenn Miller, who had also been with Noble. In 1940, Paula Kelly, who had previously sung with the Al Donahue band and Artie Shaw, joined Miller's band as a soloist. She became a member of the Modernaires and married Hal Dickinson. They recorded "Chattanooga Choo Choo" (1941), "Don't Sit Under The Apple Tree (With Anyone Else But Me)" (1942-Bluebird) and "(I've Got A Gal) In Kalamazoo" (1942-Victor) with Miller. Marion Hutton also sang with them in 1941. In addition to their hits with Miller, they charted six other times in the 1940s including "Juke Box Saturday Night" (1946). Their name came from a billboard Dickinson saw advertising a cleaning process called "modernizing." *Reference*: The Modernaires with Paula Kelly CD, Sony A28191; Simon

Monarch Comedy Four
Male group that appeared on the cover of sheet music of "That Funny Oo-La-La" from 1912.

Monarch Jazz/Jubilee Quartet Of Norfolk
Male, black group, they may have been the same group as the Norfolk Jazz Quartet according to Steve Tracy in his liner notes to the CD, "Black Secular Vocal Groups - Volume 1" on Document Records (DOCD-5546). This group's recordings were in the late 1920s in Richmond, Virginia, and New York on Okeh. *Reference*: BSVG-1

Monarch Male Trio
Comprised of Frank McVey (tenor), William Kern (baritone) and (unknown first name) Allen. Performed on the Chautauqua circuit in 1920. *Reference*: Iowa

Monroe Quartet
Recorded on Okeh in 1927.

Monumental Quartette
Group featured at Hyde & Behman's Music Hall, in Brooklyn, N.Y., around 1905. *Reference*: Period advertisement

Moonlight Serenaders
Sang with the Tex Beneke Band in the 1940s. Their name came from the song, "Moonlight Serenade." *Reference*: Walker

Moonlight Trio
Gladys Rice, George Wilton Ballard and Donald Chalmers recorded on Edison in 1918. *Reference*: Walsh

Moon Maids
A female quartet (and sometimes, quintet) from Texas that was with the Vaughan Monroe orchestra starting in 1946. Members were Mary Jo Thomas, Maree Lee (of the Lee Sisters), Tinker Cunningham and June Hiett. Later members were Arlene Truax, Ruth Winston, Kathleen Carnes, Dee Laws, Ruth Wetmer, Lois Wilbur and Betty McCormick. They disbanded in 1952. *Reference*: Simon; http://www.vaughnmonroesociety.org/

Moon Men
After the success of his Moon Maids, Vaughan Monroe decided in 1948 to present a male vocal group as well. They were Johnny West, Walter Olsen, Bill Mustard and Nace Bernert. *Reference*: http://nfo.net/

Moore, O'Brien and Cormac
Male trio appearing on sheet music of "California And You" from 1914.

Phil Moore Four
Recorded on Victor in 1945.

Moore Sisters
Trio that appeared on sheet music of "Candy" in 1944. They recorded on Okeh.

Morehouse College Quartet
Began in 1870 at Morehouse College in Atlanta, Georgia. *Reference*: http://www.morehouse.edu/

Moreing Sisters
Sang with Anson Weeks and his Orchestra on Brunswick in 1932. *Reference*: Lehl Discography

Morganaires
Sang with the Russ Morgan Orchestra in the late 1940s. *Reference*: http://www.russmorganorchestra.com/

Morganton Trio
Recorded on Okeh in 1923. *Reference*: Lehl Discography

Loumell Morgan Trio
Recorded on Apollo in 1946.

Morgan Sisters
See, Angela Sisters

Morin Sisters
Trio that appeared on sheet music of "Come Back To Erin" in 1935. They were on Don McNeil's "Breakfast Club" radio show in 1934. *Reference*: http://www.richsamuels.com/

Morris Brothers, Al Jones, Edwin Kelly and Ambrose Thayer.
See, Ordway's Aeolians.

Morris Bros. Minstrels
Troupe from the 1860s featuring Jerry Cohan, the father of George M. Cohan. By 1872, they contained "Barnardo, Charles Sutton, J. C. Campbell, Barlow Brothers, Frank Campbell, J. W. McPhall, E. W. Prescott, Edwin Holmes, Sig Lavalee." *Reference*: Dumont (1915)

Morris Brown Quartet
Male black quartet that recorded in Atlanta in 1940 whose membership is not known. *Reference*: BVG-9; BVG-10

Morrow Brothers Quartette
F. E. (1st tenor), C. E. (2nd tenor), R. R. (baritone) and E. M. Morrow (basso) comprised the group. Managed by the Coit Lyceum Bureau in Cleveland. Toured around 1915. *Reference*: Iowa

Mound City Four
Appeared on sheet music of "Sahara, My Sweet Sahara Jane" in 1908.

Mound City Jubilee Quartette
Recorded in 1935, *Reference*: VQ-4

Mt. Vernon Singing Party
Mixed-gender quartet that performed on the Redpath Lyceum circuit around 1910. *Reference*: Iowa

Mount Zion Baptist Quartet
Male black quartet that recorded in New Orleans in 1927. They got to record through winning a local contest. *Reference*: VQ-5

Mozart Comedy Four
Group, some of whose members appear in blackface, on the cover of the sheet "Bill Bailey, Won't You Please Come Home?" from 1902.

Mozart Comedy Quartette
Male group whose picture appears on the 1899 sheet music of "Mandy Lee." Also appear on the cover of "Just Because My Face Ain't White" from 1901.

Mozart Four
Appeared on sheet music of "Melancholy" in 1911.

Mozart Male Quartet
Made Berliner discs in 1896. *Reference*: Gracyk

Mullens Sisters
They were with the Enric Madriguera orchestra. *Reference*: Simon

Mundy World's Fair Jubilee Octet
Black group featuring four men and four women. Managed and directed by James A. Mundy, they performed on the Redpath Lyceum Circuit around 1934. *Reference*: Iowa

Murphee Hartford Quartet
Recorded on Champion in 1930.

Murphy Sisters
Dottie, Muriel and Margie Murphy were a trio that sang with the Vaughan Monroe orchestra in the 1940s. *Reference*: Simon; http://www.vaughnmonroesociety.org/

Murray Quartet
See, American Quartet

Murray's Trio
Billy Murray, Carl Mathieu and Monroe Silver recording on Victor in 1927. *Reference*: Walsh

Musical Art Quartette
Male group made up of Hugh Aspinwall (1st tenor), W. P. Lovelass (2nd tenor), Fred K. Bollman (baritone) and Gustave Spaethe (bass) on the Chautauqua and Lyceum circuits around 1920. *Reference*: Iowa

Musical Maids
Sextette comprised of unknown women. Appeared on the Lyceum circuit in 1924. *Reference*: Iowa

Bill Johnson & his Musical Notes
Formed in New York and its members included Bill Johnson (vocals, alto sax and clarinet), Clifton "Skeeter" Best (vocals and guitar), Jimmy Robinson (vocals and bass), Gus Gordon (vocals and drums) and Egbert Victor (vocals and piano). Marv Goldberg said of them: "One of the finest groups you probably know nothing about is Bill Johnson and the Musical Notes. You may not be familiar with their music, but others were. They recorded 'Don't You Think I Ought To Know' six years before the Orioles, 'How Would You Know' four years before the Robins, and 'Dream Of A Lifetime' seven years before the Flamingos." *Reference*: Goldberg

Music Hour Quartet
Recorded on Victor in 1933.

Music Maids
Backed Bing Crosby on Decca in 1939 and 1941 and included Alice Sizer, Jeanne Darrell, Alice Ludes, Patt Hyatt, Dottie Messmer, Denny Wilson, Virginia Erwin and Bobbie Canvin. They appeared in several movies including "Kiss The Girls Goodbye" in 1941 and "Girl Crazy" in 1943 and were on the Kraft Music Hall radio show. *Reference*: http://www.imdb.com/

Music Makers
Male quartet appearing on the Lyceum circuit around 1912. Included Ray Temple (1st tenor), C. B. Huff (2nd tenor), Burwell Homes (baritone and pianist) and Frank Hallam, Jr. (basso). *Reference*: Iowa

Mystic Quartet
Recorded on Berliner in 1896.

Nassau Male Quartet
Recorded on Columbia in 1911.

National Cavaliers Quartet
Recorded in New York from 1927 to 1934, mostly on Victor. Members were Leo O'Rourke (tenor), Robert Stevens (tenor), John Seagle (baritone), Darrel Woodyard (bass) and David Buttolph (piano). In 1932, Henry Shope and Frank Parker and Elliott Shaw (of the Revelers, among other groups) replaced O'Rourke, Stevens and Woodyard and Lee Montgomery became the pianist. *Reference*: Sweetest Harmony

National Comedy Four
Male group billed as "The Premier Character Quartette" in a photo from the 1910s. Members were H. J. Genner, F. Krauskopf, J. B. Schaefer and W. W. Chamberlain.

National Male Quartet
Apparently a different group from the one listed immediately below, they included Lawrence Wickland (1st tenor), Stanley J. Graham (2nd tenor), Melvin Newquist (baritone) and Charles Cox (basso). Appeared for the Redpath Bureau in the Midwest in 1920. By 1922, Maurice Ivins had replaced Newquist. *Reference*: Iowa

National Male Quartet
Recorded on Pathé, Columbia, Victor and Edison in 1924 and 1925 and their personnel were Clarence DaSilva (replaced by Arthur Hall in 1926), Lloyd Wiley (replaced by John Ryan in 1926), Harry Jockin and Harry Donaghy. *Reference*: Walsh

Navy Girls
Female sextet including Ruth Bendell (contralto), Helen Stein (soprano and accompanist), Ruth Chapin (soprano), Marjorie Webster (soprano), Inez Smith (soprano) and Ethel Gwinn (contralto). Appeared on the Redpath Lyceum circuit in the Midwest around 1917. *Reference*: Iowa

Neapolitan Trio
Recorded on Victor in 1911.

The Negro Band
Appeared in New York in 1845, and were Barney Williams, Dan Rice, J. P. Carter, Howard and Jones. *Reference*: Dumont (1914)

Newcomb's Minstrels
Troupe from 1868 featuring "'Chang' the Chinese Giant, Carroll (Jim) Johnson, Dave Wilson, Harry Robinson, C. C. Palmer, Myron Calice, J. T. Gulick, Charles Hudson, J. R. Dudley, C. W. Millard, N. D. Roberts, manager." *Reference*: Dumont (1915)

New England Male Quartette
Only two of the four men are known: Thomas Blanchard (baritone) and Charles Gagnier (basso). Active on the Lyceum circuit in New England around 1922. *Reference*: Iowa

New England Singers
Recorded on Columbia in 1921 and were J. Sherman, Reed Miller (tenor), F. Cochran and T. MacPherson. *Reference*: Lehl Discography

New Orleans University Glee Club
Recorded in 1927. *Reference*: BVG-7

Newsboys' Quintette
Appeared on sheet music of "My Honolulu Lady" in 1895.

New South Jubilee Company
Members were E. F. Bennett (1st tenor), F. A. Nelson (2nd tenor), Alonzo Moor (magician), Walter Dean (baritone) and E. A. Nelson (bass). Active in the Chicago area Lyceum Bureau-Chautauqua circuit around 1902-1903. *Reference*: Iowa

New Stellar Quartet
Recorded on Vocalion in 1921.

New Yorkers
Quintet that in 1929 recorded on Edison. Its members were Ed Smalle (also with the Revelers), Colin O'More, Harry Donaghy and individuals whose last names were Shope and Preston. *Reference*: Walsh

New York Fire Quartet
Recorded on Okeh in 1923.

New York Serenaders
Toured California around 1850. *Reference*: White

Nifty Three
Recorded in New York on Columbia in 1928. *Reference*: Lehl Discography

Nightingales
Female quartet including Barbara Reynolds (1st soprano), Anna McCall (2nd soprano), Edna May Sharp (1st contralto) and Louise M. Corbett (2nd contralto). Appeared for the Slayton-Redpath Bureau in the 1926-7 season. *Reference*: Iowa

Nightingale Trio
Two boys (Eddie Malloney and Frankie Curtin) and a woman (Mae Mallahan) featured on the cover of sheet music of "Will You Love Me When The Golden Threads Are Gone?" from 1915.

Nitecaps
Recorded on Columbia in 1932. *Reference*: Lehl Discography

Nonpareil Jubilee Singers
Ten singers, six women and four men. Included Anna C. Acklen (1st soprano), Elexine Crawford (2nd soprano), Ellenette Hamilton (contralto), Gertrude Christian (alto), Daniel W. Brown (prime tenor and manager), Arthur C. Brown (2nd tenor), George W. Cole (1st bass), Harry T. Jackson (2nd bass), Mattie B. Malone (reader) and Cora Love Jeffers (pianist). Part of this group toured with the Fisk Jubilee Singers from 1899-1900 in the Canadian Provinces. This ten-person group is a later version, appearing on the Chautauqua circuit. *Reference*: Iowa

Nonpareil Trio
Male, black group whose membership is not known. They recorded in the late 1920s in New York on Columbia. *Reference*: BSVG-3

Nordstrom Sisters
Recorded on Columbia in New York in 1932. *Reference*: Lehl Discography

Norfolk Jazz/Jubilee Quartet
In 1923, this black group had as its members Otto Tutson (lead), J. "Buddie" Archer (tenor), Delrose Hollins (baritone) and Len Williams (bass). By the 1930s, they consisted of Norman "Crip" Harris (lead & first tenor), Raymond Smith (2nd tenor), Melvin Colden (baritone) and Williams. They did both secular and spiritual numbers and recorded for Paramount, Okeh and Decca in the 1920s and on Decca in New York in 1937-1940. Two of their better-known songs were "Just Dream Of You" and "Shim Sham Shimmie At The Cricket's Ball." When Williams, the founder, died in 1940, the group disbanded shortly thereafter. Smith later sang with the Cabineers, Colden with the Master Keys and Harris with Thurman Ruth's Selah Jubilee Singers. *Reference*: BSVG-2; Norfolk-6

Norris The Troubador
Membership unknown, but recorded in New York in the late 1930s. According to the liner notes for the CD, "Black Secular Vocal Groups, Vol. 3." Norris was likely Norris Mayhams who also recorded with the Barbecue Boys and the Blue Chips. He also sang with the Hipp Cats. *Reference*: BSVG-3

Norsemen
Recorded on Victor, Decca and Bluebird from 1934 to 1939. *Reference*: Lehl Discography

Norton Sisters
Trio (Dottie, Betty and Grace) that sang with the McFarland Twins band around 1940. They also sang, as a quartet (with Maree Lee), with Vaughan Monroe. *Reference*: Simon; http://www.vaughnmonroesociety.org/

Novak Girls
Trio that recorded on Brunswick in 1930 in Los Angeles. *Reference*: Lehl Discography

Novelty Four Quartet
Male black group that recorded in Chicago in 1928. *Reference*: VQ-5

Novelty Four
Male quartet featuring Samuel Nonneman (1st tenor), Milford Landis (tenor), Walter Collins (baritone) and Dale Shumaker (bass). Appeared on the Redpath Lyceum circuit in 1921 and 1922. *Reference*: Iowa

Novelty Quartet
Appeared on sheet music of "Down In Dear Old Dixieland" in 1915.

Oakland Quartet
Walsh states he was told by Oakland that he had no recollection of this group but Walsh speculates its members were Will Oakland, John Bieling, Steve Porter and William F. Hooley, the same as the Heidelberg Quintet, absent Billy Murray. They recorded in 1912 on Edison and U.S. Everlasting cylinders. *Reference*: Walsh

Oak Leaf Quartette
Black group active around the turn of the 20th century. *Reference*: Averill

Oak Mountain Quartet
Recorded on Champion in 1929.

Ohio Wesleyan Male Quartette
Represented Ohio Wesleyan University and Included H. C. Clase (1st tenor), G. S. Battelle (2nd tenor), E. H. Worth (baritone) and R. W. Parks (bass). Appeared on the Chautauqua circuit for the 1909-1910 season. For the 1910-1911 season, Battelle and Worth were replaced by C. E. Blume and W. I. Dumm. *Reference*: Iowa

Oklahoma City Quartett
Group that appeared on sheet music of "My Sweet Colleen" from 1921, They are listed as Jenkins, Light, Tillson and Crawford.

Old Apple Trio
Recorded in Chicago on Victor and Bluebird in 1933. *Reference*: Lehl Discography

Olden Time Minstrels
Recorded on Victor.

Old Glory Quartette
Four men that appeared on the Redpath Lyceum circuit around 1915. *Reference*: Iowa

Old Hickory Quartette
Horace Rushby was a member of this group that traveled with the McIntyre and Heath Minstrels of 1887-1888. *Reference*: Dumont (1915)

Old Home Singers
Quintet of three women and two men that appeared on the Redpath Lyceum circuit in 1916. Ruth Martin was their pianist. A quartet with the same name and comprised of two women and two men was on the Redpath Lyceum circuit around 1917. *Reference*: Iowa

Old National Male Quartette
Group that appeared on the Redpath Lyceum circuit in 1914. *Reference*: Iowa

Old South Quartette
Originally called Polk Miller and his Old South Quartette, known members were Polk Miller (tenor), James L. Stamper (bass) and Randall Graves. Miller appears on their earlier recordings but not on those from 1928 that were done in Long Island City, New York. Miller was white and the group was black, a rarity in those days. Tim Gracyk's website contains an article by Jas Obrecht that originally appeared in the Victrola and 78 Journal that says of them: "Miller was daring enough to go on tour with four African Americans, the Old South Quartette, beginning around 1900. In a Richmond Journal article dated January 3, 1912, Miller explained that the four, whom he referred to as his 'boys' or 'employees,' had been 'singing on the street corners and in the barrooms of this city at night to motley crowds of hoodlums and barroom loafers and handing around the hat . . . . I could get a dozen quartettes from the good singing material among the Negroes in the tobacco factories here.' The clipping indicates that Polk and his quartet played colleges and military schools, as well as the 'most exclusive social clubs' in New York, Boston, Baltimore, Washington, Pittsburgh, and Cleveland. Their two-hour show featured dialect stories and

recitations, coon songs, and displays of Polk's prowess on fiddle and banjo." *Reference*: Gracyk; ENVQ-1; Walsh

Old Time Jubilee Singers
Mixed-gender black quartet that recorded in New York in 1924. *Reference*: VQ-5

Old Town Quartette
Appeared on sheet music of "I'm On My Way To Mandalay" in 1913.

Oleanders
Nothing is known about this black group but two transcription cuts from 1939 survive, "Mama Don't Allow It" and "Ol' Man Mose." *Reference*: BSVG-2

Olympia Ladies Quartette
Black group that appeared on the Chautauqua and Lyceum circuits around 1905. Comprised of Dazalia Underwood (1st soprano), Hester O. Brown (contralto), Anna Smith (soprano) and Crealea Peyton (1st alto). *Reference*: Iowa

Olympian Quintette
Black group that performed on Keith's vaudeville (variety) show in 1883 in Boston. *Reference*: Averill

Lowe Stokes and His Organ Grinders:
Recorded on Columbia in 1929. *Reference*: Lehl Discography

Orange Grove Trio
Men appearing in high hats on the cover of sheet music of "Mary Lou" from 1926.

Ordway's Aeolians
Minstrel troupe from Boston organized around 1845 by J. P. Ordway. Group included Johnny Pell, Warren White, Jack Huntley, the Morris Brothers, Al Jones, Edwin Kelly and Ambrose Thayer. This company also called themselves the Cow-bell-o-gians, burlesquing the Swiss bell ringers, who had created a furor throughout the country and especially in Boston. The minstrels performed tunes on the cowbells. After Pell's death the troupe became known as the Morris Brothers Minstrels. It was with this troupe that Fred Wilson introduced the clog dance for the first time with a minstrel troupe. *Reference*: White; Dumont (1914)

Oriental Quartette
Male group featuring C. H. Ogden (1st tenor), F. B. Newton (2nd tenor), E. T. Clissold (baritone) and W. A. Ward (bass). Appeared on the Chautauqua circuit in 1908. *Reference*: Iowa

Original Bison City Quartette
Male group on the cover of sheet music of "Come Back My Love" from 1893. Members pictured are Frank A. Girard (1st Tenor), Ben R. Cook (2nd Tenor), Harry C. West (Baritone) and Lester L. Pike (Basso).

Original Dunbar Sisters
Female trio pictured on the cover of sheet music of "Tillie Tootie (The Coney Island Beauty)" from 1898.

Original Five Blind Boys
See, Five Blind Boys Of Mississippi.

Original Honeyboys
Appeared in a caricature in blackface on sheet music of "Get Out And Get Under The Moon" in 1928.

Original Lyric Trio
In 1899 its members were John C. Havens, Estella Louise Mann and William F. Hooley. The Library and Archives Canada states that Harry Macdonough was a member in 1899. They recorded on cylinders for National Phono Co. in 1899. *Reference*: Gracyk; http://www.gracyk.com/; http://www.collectionscanada.ca/

Original Melody Boys
Trio that appeared on sheet music of "I Still Get A Thrill (Thinking Of You)" in 1930.

Original Nashville Students
Their full title was: "Original Nashville Students Colored Concert Company, H. H. Thearle, proprietor." A group of black singers that toured the U.S. supported by Christian, Temperance and Aid societies. The group is pictured on the booklet entitled "Jubilee Songs and Plantation Melodies" from 1884 and published by the Redpath Lyceum Bureau of Boston and Chicago.

Original Newsboys Quintette
Five young men, four white and one black, on the cover of sheet music of "My Honolulu Lady" from 1898.

Original Outcast Newsboy's Quintette
Appeared on sheet music of "On A Starry Night" in 1903.

Original Tennesseans
A group from Central Tennessee College formed in 1873. *Reference*: Averill

Original Valentin Choral Club Quintette
Recorded in New Orleans in 1924. *Reference*: BVG-1

Orioles
The Orioles were one of the earliest, best and most influential of the R&B groups. Members were Earlington "Sonny Til" Tilghman (lead), Alexander Sharp (1st tenor), George Nelson (2nd tenor), Johnny Reed (bass) and Tommy Gaither (guitar). Formed in 1947 in Baltimore, they were originally called the Vibra-Naires and changed their name in 1948. Their "It's Too Soon To Know" (1948-Jubilee) (number one R&B) is considered a seminal R&B recording. The song was written by Deborah Chessler who went on to manage the group. In 1950, Gaither was killed in an auto accident and replaced by Ralph Williams. The group had a string of great recordings (11 R&B chart songs) on Jubilee such as "Tell Me So" (1949), "A Kiss And A Rose" (1949), (number one R&B), "Crying In The Chapel" (1953) (number one R&B) (a cover of a country song recorded by Darrell Glenn), "Hold Me Thrill Me Kiss Me" (1953) and "In The Chapel In The Moonlight" (1954). "Tell Me So" was important because of its use of Sharp's falsetto floating above the lead. This device would be copied by countless groups over the next few decades. Their performing style was a big part of their success and Til became a matinee idol to the black audience. *Reference*: The Orioles, For Collectors Only CD, Collectibles COL-CD-8801

Orphean Music Club
Male quartet that in 1908 consisted of W. G. Laye (1st tenor), E. H. Dennis (2nd tenor), E. W. Crumbaker (baritone) and Victor F. Henry (basso). Appeared on the Central Lyceum Bureau circuit in from the early 1900s to at least 1916. In 1909, E. V. Williams replaced Laye. Also called the Orpheans and the Orpheans Musical Club. By 1916, A. H. Richardson performed as first tenor. *Reference*: Iowa

Orpheus Four
Male quartet featuring Samuel B. Glasse (1st tenor), Paul S. Breckenridge (2nd tenor), Verner A. Campbell (baritone) and Houston M. Dudley (basso). Advertised as the "Official Quartet of the Orpheus Club of Los Angeles, winners of the International Grand Prize of $3,000 for male Chorus at the Panama Pacific Exposition." Appeared on the Lyceum and Chautauqua circuits in the 1910s. *Reference*: Iowa

Orpheus Male Quartette
Comprised of T. Stanley Perry (first tenor), Frank Scherer (second tenor), J. Clarence Hoekstra (baritone) and Victor Harold Vogel (basso), with H. Glen Henderson (accompanist). Active in 1916. *Reference*: Iowa

Orpheus Male Quartette
Another group, also in 1916, with the same name as above, was advertised as Canada's Finest and Most Versatile Entertainers. Members included Arthur Davies (tenor), William Fisher (tenor), Bobby Powner (baritone) and Arthur Fisher (basso profundo). *Reference*: Iowa

Orpheus Quartet
Three of the original members, Harry Macdonough (tenor), Reinald Werrenrath (baritone) and William F. Hooley (bass) came out of the Hayden Quartet. Lambert Murphy (tenor) completed the group. They recorded on Victor from 1914 to 1919 (and were sometimes known as the Victor Male Quartet). Their highest charting song was "Turn Back The Universe And Give Me Yesterday" (1916). *Reference*: Whitburn – PM; Schlesinger

Orpheus Quartette
Black male group that travelled with McAdoo's Original Jubilee Singers and Virginia Concert Company in the 1890s. O. M. McAdoo sang bass for the group, which featured the comic song "B.I.N.G.O." An unknown female quartet also traveled with this company. *Reference*: Averill

Orpheus Trio
Recorded in New York in 1920-1921 on Gennett and Pathé. *Reference*: Lehl Discography

Ossian's Bards
A 19th century group mentioned in Averill. *Reference*: Averill

Otterbein Male Quartette and Bell Ringers
Personnel included R. H. Richards (1st tenor), Lloyd Miller (2nd tenor and pianist), A Rae Condit (baritone and whistler) and H. U. Engle (bass and manager). Appeared in the Midwest around 1910-1912. Also known as the Otterbein Male Quartette Company. *Reference*: Iowa

Ottumwas Male Quartette
Featured Edw. Weeks, B. B. Brock, E. W. Peterson and Geo. H. Lott ("the Great American Basso"). Performed for the Central Lyceum Bureau for the 1900-1901 season. *Reference*: Iowa

Oxford Quartette
Appeared on cover of sheet music for "Friends" in 1898. Members were W. Charles, A. H. Fulton, W. H. Voelker and W. F. Halpin.

Ozark Sisters
Trio that appeared on sheet music of "Way Down Yonder In The Cornfield" in 1938.

Pacific Comedy Four
Appeared on sheet music of "Lonesome And Sorry" in 1926.

Palace Trio
Recorded on Brunswick and Okeh in 1919 and 1920.

Palm Beach Boys
Trio that recorded on Okeh in 1927 and as the Harmonizers on British Parlophone. *Reference*: Lehl Discography

Palmer Brothers
Dick, Clarence and Ernest Palmer from Pawtucket, Rhode Island made up this group. They formed in the 1930s and sang with Cab Calloway as the Cabaliers. Dick also was with the Beavers and the Blenders and Clarence was with the Sparrows and Jive Bombers. *Reference*: The Blenders CD - Famous Groove Records; SU-7, YM-8

Palmer's Lyceum Ladies Quartette
Members were Maude Harkleroad (coloratura soprano), Lila Alton (2nd soprano), Florence M. Hobson (alto) and Effie C. Palmer (contralto). Toured the Lyceum circuit in the 1920s. *Reference*: Iowa

Palmer's Lyceum Quintette
Female group led by Effie C. Palmer (contralto). The group also included Jessie Carter (soprano and pianist), Ruby McIntyre (1st soprano), Julia Hastings (mezzo-soprano) and Ethel Shoemaker (alto). Toured with the Coit Lyceum bureau in the Midwest in the 1920s. *Reference*: Iowa

Palmetto Jazz Quartette
Recorded in New York in 1921 on Okeh. *Reference*: ENVG-4

Palmolive Revelers
See, Revelers.

Palmo's Burlesque Opera Company
A troupe from the mid-19th century. *Reference*: Averill

Panama Singers
Foursome associated with the traveling Chautauquas around 1910. Pictures of the group were featured in brochure from a Redpath performance in 1917. *Reference*: Averill; Iowa

Pan-American Quartet
Recorded in New York in 1927 and were Joseph E. Loomis (tenor), Walter Hilliard (tenor), Charles Downs (baritone) and John W. Turner (bass). *Reference*: Lehl Discography

Paradise Islanders
A Hawaiian trio that recorded in New York on Victor in 1932. *Reference*: Lehl Discography

Paramount Jubilee Singers
Mixed-gender quartet that recorded in New York in 1923. *Reference*: BVG-10

Park Avenue Jesters
Recorded on Claude in 1947. Their tenor was Ray Reynolds. *Reference*: Fournier

Park Avenue Promenaders
Recorded in New York in 1932 on Columbia. *Reference*: Lehl Discography

Parker Sisters
Female trio appearing on the cover of sheet music of "Daydream Island" in 1943 and "Dance With A Dolly" in 1944.

Park, Rome and Francis
Male trio on the cover of sheet music of "I'm Going Back To Texas (And The Silvery Rio Grande)" from 1916.

Pastels
Quintet that sang with the Stan Kenton Orchestra in 1946-7. Membership varied slightly and included Dave Lambert, Jerry Duane, Wayne Howard, Margaret Dale, Jimmy Borland, Don McLeod and Jerry Packer. *Reference*: http://memory.loc.gov/

Paulette Sisters
Appeared on sheet music of "Paper Doll" in 1942. They recorded on Capitol and Decca and did several records with Connee Boswell. *Reference*: Lehl Discography

Paupers
Group that recorded on Melford in 1949.

Peabody Trio
Recorded on Columbia in Atlanta in 1926 and 1927. Members possibly included Ralph Bennett and Shucks Park. *Reference*: Lehl Discography

Peerless Four
See, Shannon Four.

Peerless Princess Quartet
Female group including Gertrude M. Johnston (contralto and pianist), Ruth N. Keller (contralto), Mabel P. Cochran (2nd soprano) and Bertha K. Miller (1st soprano). Appeared for the Central Lyceum Bureau in the 1920s. *Reference*: Iowa

Peerless Quartet
Beginning as the Columbia Male Quartet, they recorded from 1904 to 1926 and had an enormous number of popular recordings on Columbia and Victor. Some of their more well-known songs were "Sweet Adeline" (1904-Columbia), "Let Me Call You Sweetheart" (1911-Columbia), "Over There" (1917-Columbia) and "I Don't Know Where I'm Going But I'm On My Way" (1918-Victor). Members were Henry Burr (tenor), Albert Campbell (tenor), Steve Porter (baritone) and Tom Daniels (bass). In 1906, Frank Stanley replaced Daniels and the group took the Peerless name. Arthur Collins replaced Porter in 1909 and John Meyer replaced Stanley in 1910. Frank Croxton took Collins' place in 1918. The group had further changes (Carl Mathieu replaced Campbell, Stanley Baughman replaced Meyer and James Stanley replaced Croxton) in 1925 and dissolved in 1928. They also recorded as the Lakeshore Club Quartet, Invincible Four, Peerless Minstrels, U.S. Minstrels, Victor Minstrel Co. and Victor Vaudeville Co. In England, the name Prince's Male Quartet was used on some of their Columbia records. *Reference*: Walsh; Whitburn-PM; Schlesinger

Peerless Serenaders
Recorded on Okeh in the mid-1920s. *Reference*: http://settlet.fateback.com/

Peerless Trio
Billy Murray, Byron G. Harlan and Steve Porter were the members of this group that recorded cylinders on Indestructible in 1907 and 1908. *Reference*: Walsh

Perham's Minstrels
Short-lived New York troupe in the late 1850s. A drawing of them appears on the sheet music of "Gems Of The Minstrelsy: Opera Vocalists," songs written by H. S. Cartee for Perham's troupe. *Reference*: Dumont (1914)

Philadelphia Male Quartette
Composed of Charles Stahl (tenor), Philip Warren Cooke (tenor), Harold Albert Simonds (baritone) and John Vandersloot (bass). Appeared in the 1920s on the Chautauqua circuit and recorded on Victor. *Reference*: Iowa

Philips Jenkins Singers
A female quintet that recorded in Camden, New Jersey in 1927. *Reference*: Lehl Discography

Bonnie Davis & the Piccadilly Pipers
Black group that recorded on Savoy in 1942 and later on Coral and Chart. On Savoy the personnel were Clem Moorman, Ernie Ransom, Henry Padgett and Bonnie Davis. Their name came from the Piccadilly Club in Newark where they played in 1940. *Reference*: http://repository.upenn.edu/

Pickens Sisters
Sisters Jane, Patti and Helen were from Georgia. The family later moved to New York. First known as the Three Little Maids From Pixie, they changed that to the Pickens Sisters. Jane Pickens was a prominent Newport socialite, trained at the Curtis Institute of Music in Philadelphia as well as the Juilliard School of Music in New York. She also ran for Congress (and lost to Ed Koch) in New York in 1972, and had a TV show in the 1950s. They are best known for "Did You Ever Hear A Dream Walking" (Victor-1934). *Reference*: http://www.janepickens.com/

Pickert Sisters
Trio that appeared on the cover of sheet music of "Melody Chimes" in 1912.

Pied Pipers
The original group had eight members – Jo Stafford, John Huddleston, Hal Hopper, Chuck Lowry, Bud Hervey, George Tait, Woody Newbury and Dick Whittinghill. In the late 1930s, they began to sing with Tommy Dorsey who reduced the group to a quartet – Stafford, Huddleston, Lowry and Billy Wilson. (Whittinghill became a well-known disk jockey in California.) Wilson was replaced by Clark Yocum in 1939 and when Huddleston went into the service, Hal Hopper (one of the original eight) took his place. They were an immensely popular group that used innovative harmonies. They charted with "Mairzy Doats" and "Trolley Song" in 1943 and "Dream" in 1945, all on Capitol. They also appeared in movies such as "Jam Session" in 1941. In addition to their hits with Dorsey, the Pied Pipers charted 12 times in the 1940s. Stafford began pursuing a solo career while still with the Pied Pipers and left the group in 1944. June Hutton, female bandleader Ina Ray Hutton's sister, replaced Stafford. Hutton previously sang with the Stardusters in Charlie Spivak's band. *Reference*: http://en.wikipedia.org/; Simon

Pierce and Fellows' Minstrels
In 1849, Earl Pierce left Christy's troupe and with J. B. Fellows founded this one. Pierce retired in 1850 and the name changed to Fellows' Minstrels. *Reference*: Dumont (1914)

Pig Footers
Recorded on Mercury in 1949.

Pilgrim Travelers
The Pilgrim Travelers were begun by Joe Johnson and Willie Davis in Houston in the early 1930's. By 1942, this gospel group had relocated to Los Angeles with cousins Kylo Turner and Keith Barber. In 1945, J. W. Alexander joined the group and became their manager. In 1947, they were signed by Specialty Records and also got a new baritone, Jesse Whitaker, who replaced Davis. They used flamboyant showmanship in their performances. Eventually, the floor was miked to pick up their percussive foot tapping which was marketed as walking rhythm spirituals. The group enjoyed immense popularity as a result. Between 1947 and 1956, the Pilgrim Travelers recorded over one hundred sides on Specialty. Lou Rawls was a member of a later version of the group. *Reference*: http://www.singers.com/gospel/; http://afgen.com/pilgrim.html

Pioneer Quartet
Male group that recorded on Edison from 1927 to 1929. *Reference*: Lehl Discography

Plantation Male Trio
Recorded on Okeh in 1924.

Pauline Wells & her Plantation Quartette
Appeared on sheet music of "Alexander Don't You Love Your Baby No More?" in 1904.

Plantation Singers
Mixed-gender black group whose membership is unknown, but that recorded in New York in 1939. *Reference*: BVG-10

Plink, Plank & Plunk
Wilson "Serious" Myers, "Tiger" George Haynes and Bob Mosley (replaced by Paul Curry) comprised the group and were from Chester, Pennsylvania. They were active in the late 1930s and early 1940s. Myers had been with the Spirits of Rhythm. Hayes joined the Three Flames in 1945. *Reference*: Goldmine 4/80; http://www.allmusic.com/

Ponce de Leon Quartet
Group that performed at a San Francisco Minstrel show in 1897 and featured W. C. Handy ("St. Louis Blues"). *Reference*: Averill

Premier-American Quartet
Recorded on Okeh, Emerson, Pathé, Aeolian, Vocalion, Gennett and Medallion in 1919-20.

Premier Quartet
See, American Quartet and Harmonizers Quartet.

Premier Quartet Minstrels
Recorded on Edison from 1918 to 1922.

Premier Trio
See, Lett Sisters & Louise.

Norman Price Trio
Recorded on Bluebird in New York in 1934. *Reference*: Lehl Discography

Primrose Four
White quartet that named themselves the "Thousand Pounds of Harmony." Performed in the early 1910s. *Reference*: Averill

Progressive Four
Group began in Washington, D.C. in 1932 and members were Wilbur Griffin (lead), Heartwell Mouton (tenor), Doug Sommers (baritone) (replaced by Harmon Bethea) and Johnny Allen (bass) (replaced by Oliver Armstead). Linsay Wilson later was added to the group. They recorded on the D.C. label and in 1949 became the Corinthian Singers. They sang both spiritual and secular songs. By 1950, they had become the Cap-Tans. *Reference*: Goldberg

Pro-Phy-Lac-Tic Playboys
Appeared on sheet music of "You're The First Thing I Think Of In The Morning" in 1928.

Psi Upsilon Quartet
Recorded on Columbia in 1930 and were Harald E. Winston (tenor), John Barnes Wells (tenor), Reinald Werrenrath (baritone) and Cyrille Carreau (Bass).
Reference: Lehl Discography

Pullman Four
Recorded on Challenge in 1926. Charles Hart was a member. *Reference*: http://settlet.fateback.com/Challenge1.htm

Pullman Porters Quartette
Black group that recorded in Chicago in the late 1920s, including "Good News Chariot's Coming," "Every Time I Feel The Spirit," "Jog-A-Long Boys" and "Pullman Passenger Train" (all 1927). *Reference*: BSVG-1

Don & his Q-Tones
Recorded on Bullet in 1949.

Quaker City Four
Introduced the classic "Sweet Adeline" in New York in 1903. *Reference*: Ewen

Quaker City Quartet
Mentioned in Averill. *Reference*: Averill

The Quartette
Recorded on Edison, Columbia, U.S. Everlasting and Indestructible between 1904 and 1911.

Quartones
They backed Billy Eckstein on MGM in 1948-1950. *Reference*: Fournier

Queen City Quartette
Black group that traveled with the integrated Washburn's Double Minstrels in the late 1890s. Members included James Thomas Fernando (baritone) and J. H. Bailey (bass). Also toured with Allen's Minstrels in 1900. *Reference*: Averill; Abbott/Seroff

Queens Vocal Trio
Appeared in a Soundie with Phil Spitalny in 1932. *Reference*: Lehl Discography

Quinteto Yucatan
Recorded on Vocalion in 1930 in Los Angeles. *Reference*: Lehl Discography

Quintones
Quintet of four men and a woman that recorded on Vocalion in 1938 and 1939 and is best known for "Fool That I Am" that was done with an orchestra led by Buck Ram who would later manage the Platters. They also did some recordings as late as 1950 with Johnny Desmond. *Reference*: Lehl Discography

Radio Kittens
Jean, Henriette and Kate Ellen Murtagh appear on sheet music of "Everywhere You Go" in 1927.

Radiolites
Sang with the Ben Selvin Orchestra in the early 1930s. *Reference*: http://ds.dial.pipex.com/jazzitoria/selvin.htm

Radio Revelers
Recorded in New York in 1947 and London in 1951-1952 on Columbia. *Reference*: Lehl Discography

Radio Trio
Appeared on the sheet music of "I'm Trying To Coax The Smiles To Come Back" in 1924.

Rambler Minstrel Company
Quartet comprised of Byron G. Harlan, Billy Murray, Arthur Collins and Steve Porter. They were known as the Colonial Quartet and the Zonophone Quartet for their recordings on Zonophone in about 1906. They also recorded as the Victor Minstrel Company. *Reference*: Walsh

Ramblers
Recorded on Decca in 1939.

Ranch Boys
Cowboy trio consisting of Ken Carson, Jack Ross and Curley Bradley that appeared on sheet music including "The Lost Chord" in 1935. They recorded on Decca. *Reference*: http://www.dagmar-anita-binge.de/

Ravens
One of the great transition groups that moved vocal group harmony from the pop music of the 1940s into the R&B/Rock and Roll music of the 1950s. The original quartet was formed in New York in 1945 and consisted of Jimmy Ricks (bass lead), Ollie Jones (1st tenor) Leonard Puzey (2nd tenor) and Warren Suttles (baritone). In 1946, Ricks discovered Maithe Marshall (Maithe Williams) and brought his high tenor voice into the group replacing Jones. Howard Biggs was their musical arranger and wrote some of their songs. They recorded on Hub in 1946 and began on National in 1947. Later labels included King, Columbia, Okeh, Mercury and Argo. Numerous personnel changes followed with some members floating in and out. They included Richie Cannon, Joe Medlin, Bill Sanford, Louis Heyward, Jimmy Stewart, Louis Frazier, Joe Van Loan and Tommy Evans. Their "Write Me A Letter" (1948-National) was the first R&B song to make the pop charts. They continued into the late 1950s with entirely different personnel, including former members of the Du-Droppers. The new lineup had several recordings on Argo. Ricks is regarded by many as the finest bass of the era. *Reference*: Goldberg; Warner

Raynor's Serenaders
Active around 1850, they toured California. *Reference*: White

Ray-O-Vacs
New York black quartet that began in the late 1940s and featured Lester Harris as its lead (later replaced by Herb Milliner). They had three Top 10 R&B songs - "I'll Always Be In Love With You" (1949-Coleman), "Besame Mucho" (1950-Decca) and its flip, "You Gotta Love Me Baby Too." Joel Whitburn described them as having a "unique 'stop-time' rhythm delivery." *Reference*: Fournier; Whitburn – RB

Record Boys
Recorded on Columbia in 1926.

Recorders
Trio consisting of Mildred Berri, Ham Masden and Dale Jones that recorded in 1928 in New York. *Reference*: Lehl Discography

Red Caps
Began in California as the Four Toppers and included Steve Gibson and Jimmy Springs. David Patillo then joined them followed in 1943 by Emmett Matthews and Romaine Brown in New York. Patillo had been with the Four Blackbirds and Springs with the Jones Boys and Jones Boys Sing Band. They played instruments and various members sang lead, with Springs on most of the ballads. They changed their name to Steve Gibson and the Red Caps in 1947 when they began recording for Mercury. The membership changed over the years and included Doles Dickens, Ormande Wilson (Gibson's stepbrother and lead of the Basin Street Boys), Arthur Davey, Andre D'Orsay and many others into the later 1950s. Damita Jo DuBlanc, Gibson's wife and a terrific singer, was with them in 1951 as was Gloria Smith. *Reference*: The Five Red Caps 1943-1945 CD, Flyright 60; YM-4

Redpath Grand Quartet
Male group including Cecil James (1st tenor), Dr. Ion Jackson (2nd tenor), Dr. Carl Duft (baritone) and Frederick Martin (basso). Performed on the Redpath circuit in 1909-1910. *Reference*: Iowa

Republic Male Quartet
Members were Raymond Simonds (1st tenor), Paul Thayer (2nd tenor), Alfred Halverson (1st bass) and Edwin Mitchell (2nd bass and pianist). Appeared for the Affiliated Lyceum Bureaus of America in the 1910s. *Reference*: Iowa

Revelers
An extremely popular group in the 1920s and early 1930s. They were one of the forerunners in using instrument imitation and had a less formal style than the previous popular groups. Members were Franklyn Baur (1st tenor) (replaced by Frank Luther, Charles Harrison, Frank Parker, Robert Simmons and James Melton), Lewis James (tenor), Elliott Shaw (baritone) (replaced by Phil Duey), Wilfred Glenn (bass) and Ed Smalle (piano) (replaced by Frank Black). James, Shaw and Glenn came from the Shannon Four after parting ways with Charles Hart. Highest charting recordings were "Dinah" (1926-Victor), "Valencia" (1926-Victor) and "The Blue Room" (1926-Victor). They were also known as the Singing Sophomores (on Columbia), Gaiety Musical Comedy Chorus (on Brunswick), and the Merrymakers. They appeared on radio on the Palmolive Hour (as the Palmolive Revelers) and House of Wrigley, and as the Seiberling Singers on a program sponsored by Seiberling
Tires. In the mid-1930s, they were on the Will Rogers radio program and also sang with Jean Goldkette. *Reference*: Walsh; Breezin' Along With The Revelers, Living Era AJA5278

Rhythmaires
A group that began in 1938 and continued into the 1950s. They sang with many famous artists including Bing Crosby, Hoagy Carmichael, Frankie Laine, Ella Fitzgerald and Louis Armstrong. They also sang with the Russ Morgan, Spike Jones, Tommy Dorsey, Les Brown, Billy May, Lew Raymond and Ziggy Elman bands. Jud Conlon was a member. They appeared in four movies. *Reference*: Lehl Discography

Rhythmasters
See, Rhythm Kings.

Rhythm Boys
Bing Crosby and Al Rinker began as a duct act in Spokane, Washington. They went to California in 1925 and Rinker's sister, singer Mildred Bailey (group harmony fans know her from the songs she recorded with the Delta Rhythm Boys), helped them get started. They were noticed, and in 1926 were asked to join the Paul Whiteman Orchestra. There, they teamed up with Harry Barris and became a trio called Paul Whiteman's Rhythm Boys. They were the first vocal trio to be regularly associated with a band. They also sang with the Gus Arnheim Band. In 1930, they left Whiteman and played clubs and appeared in movies. Crosby began to get more and more solo work and in 1931 the group disbanded. Rinker was later with the V-8 group that sang with Fred Waring. Barris composed the popular standards, "Mississippi Mud" and "I Surrender, Dear." His daughter, Marti, was on the "Howdy Doody Show" and his nephew Chuck Barris is best known for "The Gong Show." Of course, Crosby went on to become one of the most popular singers of the century. (In 1932, Whiteman featured George McDonald, Al Dary, Ray Kulz and Jim Noel as his

Rhythm Boys.) *Reference*: The Rhythm Boys CD, Blue Lantern Electrical Records 103; Pitts, Michael and Frank Hoffmann. *The Rise of The Crooners*. Lanham, Maryland: Scarecrow Press, 2001

Rhythmettes
Recorded in 1935 and 1940 on Victor and Decca. *Reference*: Lehl Discography

Rhythm Kings
Members were Cecil Murray, Leonard Thomas, Howard Scott, James Riley and Isaac Royal. They did some backup work as the Four Students and may also have been the Rhythmasters. They did two Christmas songs on Apollo, released in 1950. *Reference*: 40s-50s-CD

Rhythm Quads
Recorded in 1938 on Bluebird. *Reference*: Lehl Discography

Richmond Starlight Quartette
Black group that recorded in New York in the late 1920s. *Reference*: BSVG-1

Riffers
Group that included Lil Armstrong and Clarence Williams, they recorded on Columbia in 1932. They also backed singer Eva Taylor. *Reference*: http://www.mp3.com/albums/

Right Harmony Four
Appeared on the cover of sheet music of "It Takes Me Back To The Old Folks At Home" in 1909.

Right Quintette
New York group founded in 1912 by James E. Lightfoot (bass). They performed in the Williams and Walker stage shows. Other members were James Mantell Thomas (bass) (formerly of the Dinwiddie Colored Quartet), James W. Loguen (1st tenor) and Clarence Tisdale (2nd tenor). They recorded on Columbia. *Reference*: ENVQ-1

Rigoletto Quartet of Morris Brown University
Black mixed-gender quartet that recorded in New York in 1926. *Reference*: VQ-5

Ritz Four
Appeared on sheet music of "Bye Bye Blackbird" in 1926 and "I'll Take Care Of Your Cares" in 1927.

Ritz Quartet
Recorded on Vocalion and Brunswick from 1926-30 and were Arthur Herbert (1st tenor), Alex Mason (2nd tenor), Neil Evans (baritone) and Jesse Phillips (bass). They also recorded as the Blue Ribbon Quartet and the Kanawha Singers. *Reference*: Lehl Discography

Rivals
Group from Camden, New Jersey, that began as gospel singers in the mid-1940s. Members were Johnny Smith (lead-baritone), Chandler Tribble (tenor), Booker Weeks (tenor) and Ira Mumford (bass). Mumford was the brother of Gene Mumford of the Larks and Dominoes. They recorded two sides on Apollo in 1950. *Reference*: 40s-50s-CD

Riversiders Quartet
Recorded on Bluebird in 1937.

Robert Edmond's Sunny South Ladies' Quartet
Black group appearing in vaudeville in the 1910s. *Reference*: Averill

Robert Edmond's Sunny South Male Quartet
Black group appearing in vaudeville in the 1910s. *Reference*: Averill

Robert's Trio
Two girls and a boy formed this children's group that appeared on sheet music of "Do I Know What I'm Doing" in 1926.

Robinson Brothers & Wilson
Trio that appeared on sheet music of "When I Lost You" in 1912.

Robinson Trio
Two black men and one black woman on the cover of sheet music of "Any Old Place In Yankee Land Is Good Enough For Me" from 1908.

Carson Robison Trio
Included Frank Luther and Carson Robison and they recorded in New York on Perfect in 1929-1930 *Reference*: Walsh; Lehl Discography

Robinson Brothers and Wilson
Appeared on sheet music of "When I Lost You" in 1912.

Rob Roy Quartet
Male group including Victor F. Henry (bass), George Brower (baritone) and Harvey B. Dunn (2nd tenor). Appeared on the Lyceum and Chautauqua circuits in 1916. Henry was joined by members Quinn, Armstrong and Hughes in 1917. *Reference*: Iowa

Rockets
See, the Trumpeteers.

Rockwell's Sunny South Company
Black minstrel variety show that featured two quartets around 1910. *Reference*: Averill

Herb Morris' Rocky Mountain Quartet
Appeared on sheet music of "I'm Longing For My Rocky Mountain Home" in 1924 and "(Gee! But I Was Lucky) Down In Old Kentucky" in 1926. Comprised of Frank Ridner Morris (1st tenor), Herb Morris (2nd tenor), Fred Herbert Morris (baritone) and J. Courtland Morris (basso). They were a male family group on the Redpath circuit in 1926. *Reference*: Iowa

Roe Brothers and Morrell
Recorded on Columbia in 1927. *Reference*: Lehl Discography

Rogers Brothers
The cover of sheet music of "My Starlight Queen" in 1902 shows a trio of one woman and two men, presumably the Rogers Brothers. The woman is not identified. It is advertised as "Coon Song & Chorus."

Rollickers
Sang with the Freddie Rich Orchestra. Rich was active in the late 1920s and early 1930s. They also sang with Ben Selvin. Members were Victor Hall, Randolph Weyant, Norman LeMoyne and A. R. McAdams. *Reference*: http://www.collateralworks.com/

Rollin Smith's Rascals
Recorded on Perfect in the early 1930s and known members were Roland Smith, John Anderson and Dr. Doug Speaks. *Reference*: Fournier

Rollins Trio
Recorded on Challenge in 1920/1921. *Reference*: Lehl Discography

Romancers
A group that sang with Paul Whiteman in 1931 and included Jack Fulton, Bill Seckler and Craig Leitch. *Reference*: Lehl Discography

Romeos
White trio that sang on Don McNeill's "Breakfast Club" radio show in 1942. The originals were Sam Cowling, Gil Jones and Louie Perkins. Jones and Perkins left for the service and Carl Chase and Boyce Smith replaced them. *Reference*: http://www.richsamuels.com/

Rondoliers
Group that recorded on Columbia in 1930 and may have included Jack Fulton, Milt Coleman, Paul Small and Orlando Roberson. They also sang with Ben Selvin, Paul Whiteman and others. *Reference*: Lehl Discography

Ross Sisters
Trio, Aggie, Maggie and Elmira, who appeared on sheet music of "Candy" in 1944. They were in the movie, "Broadway Rhythm" in 1944 in which they both sang and performed amazing acrobatic feats.

Rounders
From 1927 to 1931 they recorded on Victor and sang with Ben Black and Henry Halstead. They also backed Jeanette MacDonald in 1930 on "Beyond The Blue Horizon." Members were Dudley B. Chambers (tenor), Ben McLaughlin (tenor), Otto Plotz (tenor), Richard C. Hartt (baritone), Armand Girard L'Ecuyer (bass) and William Cowles (piano). *Reference*: Lehl Discography

Rountowners
Made several recordings in 1931 on Clarion and Columbia and may have included Bradford Reynolds and Larry Murphy. *Reference*: Lehl Discography

Roxy Male Quartet
Formerly the Criterion Quartet, they recorded on Banner and Conqueror in 1931-2. Members were John Young (1st tenor), Frank Mellor (2nd tenor), George Reardon (baritone) and Donald Chalmers (bass) (replaced by Fred Thomas). *Reference*: Gracyk

Royal Greek Quartet
Recorded on Columbia in 1908-9.

Royal Harmony Quartet
Beginning in the mid-1930s, they were the group from which the Jubilaires evolved. They had a Top 10 R&B song in 1942 with "Praise The Lord And Pass The Ammunition" (Keynote). Caleb "J, C," Ginyard (lead), Orville Brooks (tenor), Theodore Brooks (baritone) and George McFadden (bass) were the members. In later years, John Jennings (1st tenor) and Elijah Wright (bass) were with them. After the Jubilaires, Ginyard was with the Dixieaires, Du Droppers and the Golden Gate Quartet. *Reference*: Whitburn-RB

Royal Hawaiian Sweethearts
Sister trio whose family name was Bray; they sang with the Harry Owens Band in 1934 and took their name from the Royal Hawaiian Hotel on Waikiki where the band had its longest engagement. (Owens's daughter, Leilani, inspired the song "Sweet Leilani."). *Reference*: Walker; http://www.archive.org/

Royalists
Recorded in 1937 on Variety. *Reference*: Lehl Discography

Royal Rhythm Boys
Recorded on Decca in the late 1930s and early 1940s and also backed Slim Gaillard. *Reference*: Fournier

Royal Sons Quintet
Gospel group formed in 1942 in Winston-Salem, North Carolina, that evolved into the Five Royales R&B group. *Reference*: http://www.rockabilly.nl/

Royal Sumner Quartet
Recorded in 1927 on Clarion. *Reference*: Lehl Discography

Runaway Four
Male group on the cover of sheet music of "(When It's) Moonlight On The Alamo" from 1914.

Al (Stomp) Russell Trio
Began in 1942 and the members were Al "Stomp" Russell, Joel Cowan and William "Doc Basso" Joseph. They recorded on Coast, Excelsior, 20th Century, DeLuxe and Sapphire. *Reference*: Goldberg

Sterling Russell Trio
Recorded with Bennie Moten and his Kansas City Orchestra in 1932 and were Sterling Russell, Hamilton Stewart and Clifton Armstrong. *Reference*: Lehl Discography

Russians
Recorded on Apollo.

Rust College Quartet
Black mixed-gender group that recorded in Memphis in 1927. They also had an all-male quartet, the Invincible Quartette of Rust College that recorded in Memphis in 1928. *Reference*: VQ-5

Ryan Sisters
Recorded in Camden, New Jersey in 1929 on Victor. *Reference*: Lehl Discography

Sable Brothers
Consisting of Evans, Turpin and Cleveland among others. Performed in New York City around 1847. *Reference*: Dumont (1914)

Sable Harmonists
Formed in 1846 and traveled the South and West. Comprised of Plumer, Archer, J. Farrell, W. Roark, Nelson Kneas, J. Murphy, among others. Also performed in New York in June, 1847. *Reference*: White

St. Claire Four Sisters
Featured Ella (soprano), Mary (2nd soprano), Velma (1st alto) and Lillian (contralto) St. Claire. Appeared for the Redpath Lyceum Bureau in 1919. *Reference*: Iowa

St. Felix Sisters
Trio drawn on the cover sheet music of "Roses And Violets," from 1882.

St. Louis Metropolitan Police Quartette
Appeared on the cover of sheet music to "Officer Kelly Don't You Think It's Time To Wake Up?" in 1924. They were St. Louis policemen in uniform, named Reede, Valleroy, Buechart and Sanders.

St. Marks Chanters
Recorded in 1926. *Reference*: VQ-6

Dick Sanford Trio
Recorded in New York in 1933 on Bluebird, Electradisk, Victor and Sunrise. *Reference*: Lehl Discography

San Francisco Minstrels
Troupe active in New York starting around 1865. Included men named Birch, Wambold, Bernard and Backus. In 1880, the group included Arthur Cook, W. F. Bishop, T. B. Dixon, Frank Dumont, Harry Wyatt, H. W. Frillman, Arthur Moreland, Johnson and Powers, George Thatcher, Edwin French, Harry Kennedy, Ricardo, Charles Gibbons, Carl Rudolph, W. S. Mullaly (leader) and others. *Reference*: Dumont (1914); Dumont (1915)

San Francisco Quartette
John Hall Greaves (1st tenor), Charley Ukon (2nd tenor), Tom Ross (baritone) and Frank Meader (bass). Toured with the McIntyre and Heath Minstrel Company in the 1880s. *Reference*: Dumont (1915)

Sans Souci Quartette
Black group that appears on an 1893 San Francisco playbill advertising Cleveland's Colored Minstrels. *Reference*: Averill

Sappho Quartette
Female group featuring Estelle Solon (1st soprano), Helene Paulson (2nd soprano), Lucie Scheibe (1st alto) and Ida May Paulson (2nd alto). Appeared on the Chautauqua circuit in 1906. *Reference*: Iowa

Helen Carroll & the Satisfiers
Made up of Helen Carroll (replaced by DeLoris Randall) and three men — Ted Hanson (replaced by Loren Welch), Art Lambert and Bob Lange — they sang backup for Perry Como on his radio show in the 1940s and recorded on RCA Victor and then on Coral. They also backed Connee Boswell, Vaughn Monroe, Jo Stafford and Guy Mitchell and sang with Charlie Barnet and Tommy Dorsey. *Reference*: http://kokomo.ca/; Satisfiers CD, Jasmine 502

Savoy Girl Quartet
Recorded on Columbia in 1911.

Savoy Quartette
Appeared on sheet music of "Good-Bye Eyes Of Blue" in 1905.

Schiller Male Quartette
Featuring Cecil C. James (1st tenor), Charles T. Paterson (2nd tenor), George B. Gookins (baritone) and Harry T. Butterworth (basso). Appeared on the Chautauqua circuit in 1901. *Reference*: Iowa

Schubert Ladies Quartet
Included Corelli Carter (soprano), Helen Trover, Grace Dye and Ruth Holden. Appeared at Chautauquas around 1910. *Reference*: Iowa

Schubert Male Quartette
Chicago group that performed at the Patchogue, Long Island (N.Y.) Methodist Episcopal Church in 1892. Members unknown. *Reference*: eBay

Schubert Male Quartette of Chicago
Members were George H. Lott, Jirah D. Cole, John G. Anderson and Frank Barnard and they were accompanied by Gertrude Canfield. Appeared on the Chautauqua circuit around 1909. *Reference*: Iowa

Schubert Quartette
Male group from the late nineteenth century comprised of R. C. Martin, C. W. Swaine, W. W. Walker and Dr. G. R. Clark that advertised an address of 149A, Tremont Street, Boston. *Reference*: eBay auction

Schubert Quartette
Male group including Thomas A. Pritchard (tenor and manager) and Carlton Neville (2nd tenor and pianist) that appeared on the Acme Chautauqua circuit in the 1910s. *Reference*: Iowa

Schubert Quartette of New York
Mixed-gender group, consisting of Mildred Graham Reardon (soprano), Florence La Salle Fiske (contralto), Forrest Robert Lamont (tenor) and George Warren Reardon (baritone). Appeared on the Chautauqua circuit in 1911. *Reference*: Iowa

The Schuberts
Mixed-gender quartet, featuring Caroline Neumont (contralto), Louis H. Kennedy (baritone), Jean Bohannan (soprano) and Ord Bohannon (tenor). Appeared for the Coit Lyceum Bureau in Cleveland around 1910. Another group (or the same with different personnel?) has its members listed as Glenn Wells (basso), Mara W. Conover (soprano), Ella M. Clark (contralto) and John G. Hedgcoxe (tenor and pianist). *Reference*: Iowa

Schubert Trio
Mixed-gender group consisting of Elise Stevenson, Harry Macdonough and Frank C. Stanley. They recorded on Victor in 1907. *Reference*: Walsh

Schuster Family
Female sister quartet featuring Genevieve (soprano), Imogene, Adrienne and Chloris Schuster. Appeared on the Chautauqua circuit around 1916. *Reference*: Iowa

Scranton Quintette
Appeared on sheet music of "Scranton Diamond Jubilee And Booster Song" in 1941.

Second Battalion of the Massachusetts Infantry
Little is known about this quartet that popularized the anti-slavery song "John Brown's Body." *Reference*: Averill

Sedelia Quartette
Group formed by Scott Joplin in the late 19th-century. *Reference*: Averill

Seiberling Singers
Male quartet that recorded in New York in 1928 on Columbia. *Reference*: Lehl Discography

Selah Jubilee Singers
A gospel group with Thurmon Ruth as its lead that eventually became the Larks. They also recorded as the Cleartones for Signature in 1948. *Reference*: Warner

Sentimentalists
See, Clark Sisters.

Sentimentalists
See, Four Tunes.

Serenaders
Recorded on Columbia in 1948.

Serenaders
Recorded on Victor in 1922.

Seven Musical Magpies
Henry Ford (1st tenor), Joseph Cisco (2nd tenor), Thomas Davis (baritone) and George Early (bass) were the members of this black group. They did comic numbers and imitations of instruments in the mid-1920s and recorded in New York. *Reference*: BSVG-3

Sextette From Lucia
Group of four men and two women that appeared on sheet music of "Voom Voom (Moaden On The Gayen)" in 1926.

Shadows
New Haven, Connecticut group that started as the Melody Kings, was also the "touring" Jubalaires (see, Jubalaires) and had a Top 10 R&B hit with "I've Been A Fool" in 1949 on Lee. Members were Scott King (lead), Raymond Reid (tenor), Sam McClure (baritone) and Jasper Edwards (bass). Reid, McClure and Edwards had been part of the Jubalaires. *Reference*: Whitburn – RB; Disc90

Shannon Four
They began in 1917 on Victor and were comprised of Charles Hart, Harvey Hindermyer, Elliott Shaw and Wilfred Glenn. In 1918, Lewis James replaced Hindermyer. They became the Shannon Quartet in 1923 with the same basic makeup, except that Hart left and they had no fixed lead tenor. Soon after, they became the Revelers. Other names by which they were known included Acme Male Quartet (on Pathé), Campus Glee Club (on Cameo), Cathedral Quartet (on Emerson), Hudson Male Quartet (on Pathé), Liberty Quartet (on Emerson), Lyric Male Quartet (on Edison and Harmony) and the Peerless Four (on Okeh and Gennett). *Reference*: Walsh

Shannon Quartet
Male group consisting of Cecil McMahan (baritone and pianist), Benjamin Hill (2nd tenor), J. L Greenup (bass) and an unknown fourth member. Another version of this same group featured McMahan and Hill, as well as Earl Miller (bass) and Joseph Thackeray (second tenor). Appeared on the Redpath circuit in the 1920s. *Reference*: Iowa

Shannon Quartette
See, Shannon Four.

Shell Creek Quartet
Recorded on Columbia in 1928. *Reference*: Lehl Discography

Shelly Quartet
Black group from Danville, Virginia, they recorded on Harlem in 1945.

Sherry Sisters
Trio made up of Jane, Paula and Carolyn Manthey from South Dakota. They sang with the Dean Hudson band in the 1940s. *Reference*: http://archiver.rootsweb.com/

Shumate Brothers
Paul (1st tenor), Lewis (2nd tenor), Don (baritone) and Raymond (bass) comprised this family group that also played instruments. Appeared on the Redpath circuit in 1928-1929. *Reference*: Iowa

Shumway Male Quartet
Four unnamed males appearing on the Chautauqua circuit in 1915. *Reference*: Iowa

Silveraires
Recorded on Gotham in 1949.

Silver City Harmony Four
White group from about 1910.

Silver Lake Quartette
Group featured on the cover of "Silver Tones: A New Temperance and Prohibition Song Book" from 1892. Songs compiled by Rev. C. H. Mead and G. E. Chambers. "As sung by the Silver Lake Quartette for use in W.C.T.U....." *Reference*: eBay auction

Silver Leaf Quartette
Mentioned in Averill. *Reference*: Averill

Silvertone Quartet
Male, black vocal group that recorded one track in Southern California around 1940. *Reference*: BVG-9

Silver-Tone Quintette
Black group featuring three men and two women. Included Helen White (soprano), Nellie Hartman (contralto), Lewis White (basso), J. De Koven Killingsworth (pianist and manager) and J. Maceo Jackson (tenor). Organized by Chas. P. Williams, who earlier sponsored Williams World Famous Singers and started the Williams Lyceum Bureau. *Reference*: Iowa

Simmons and Slocum's Minstrels
Active between 1872-1874, and contained "Billy Manning, William Henry Rice, Primrose and West, William Hamilton, Shattuck, J. H. Stout, Matt Wheeler, Fred Walz, J. J. Kelly, Charles Stevens, Justin Robinson, Billy Sweatnam, J. L. Woolsey, William Dwyer, Welch and Rice, Charley Reed, George Thatcher, James G. Russell (the ventriloquist), Alexander Davis and others." *Reference*: Dumont (1915)

Hank Simmon's Show Boat Quartet
Male group that recorded on Edison in 1928. *Reference*: Lehl Discography

Singing Bachelors
Recorded on Cameo in 1923. *Reference*: http://settlet.fateback.com/

Singing Bakers
Male quartet that sang on WORK radio in York, Pennsylvania in the 1940s.

Singing Hoosier Quartet
Recorded on Challenge in 1926.

James Reese Europe's Singing Serenaders
Male, black chorus that recorded with James Reese Europe's all-black orchestra in 1919. (Europe was the first black to record as the leader of a band and was killed when he was stabbed during a fight in 1919.). *Reference*: ENVQ-1; Da Capo

Singing Sisters
Quartet that sang on WORK radio in York, Pennsylvania in the 1940s

Singing Sophomores
See, Revelers.

Singing Sweethearts
Recorded on Columbia in 1931.

Singing Troubadours
Quartet that recorded in New York in 1926 on Pathé Actuelle. *Reference*: Lehl Discography

Six Bips And A Bop
Recorded on Manor in 1948.

Six Black Dominoes
Recorded on Columbia in 1928.

Six Hits & A Miss
Recorded on various labels and charted with "You'd Be So Nice To Come Home To" on Capital in 1943. They reduced their number by two and became Four Hits And A Miss. In this formation, they were on the Autolite radio show that also included Dick Haymes and Helen Forrest and appeared in more than 15 movies. Members included Martha Tilton (1930s), Pauline Byrne and Sue Allen. By 1946, they were William Seckler, Mac McLean, Lee Gotch (also with the Lee Gordon Singers), Marvin Bailey and Beverly Mahr. Other members were Clark Yocum (who also sang with the Pied Pipers) and Rex Dennis. It seems as if they sang with everyone – Johnny Mercer, Judy Garland, Jimmy Durante and Bing Crosby among them. *Reference*: The Groups Sing CD-Jasmine Records-JASCD 393; http://bigband-era.com/

Six Musical Cuttys
Three men and three women who appeared on sheet music of "Sighing" in 1911.

Sizzlers
Recorded on Victor and Bluebird in 1932 and 1933 and were Paul Cordner, Johnny Russell, William Kearns and Henry E. Lloyd (piano). *Reference*: Lehl Discography

Skiff and Gaylord's Minstrels
Troupe extant during the Civil War – "There was Skiff and Gaylord's Minstrels, organized by Johnny Steele (Coal Oil Johnny), who spent thousands buying hotels, diamonds, race horses, etc., etc., but the troupe long survived the spendthrift that organized it." *Reference*: White

Skippet, Kennedy & Reeves
Appeared on the sheet music of "When I First Met You" in 1912.

Skylarks
Met in the Panama Canal Zone while in the Army during WWII and were Bob Sprague (1st tenor), Harry Gedicke (2nd tenor), Harry Shuman (baritone) and George Becker (arranger). When the War was over they regrouped in Detroit and Gilda Maiken joined them as lead. They toured with Woody Herman as the Velvetones. After the Herman band broke up, they recorded a few sides with Bing Crosby as the Skylarks. In 1948, they sang with Jimmy Dorsey and then Harry James and Russ Morgan. In the 1950s, the members were Maiken, Becker, Joe Hamilton, Earl Brown and Jacki Gershwin (replaced by Carol Lombard). They disbanded in 1979. *Reference*: http://www.vocalhalloffame.com/

Skyliners
Sang with the Ray Anthony orchestra in the late 1940s and should not be confused with the 1950s group of the same name. *Reference*: http://home.earthlink.net/~jaymar41/

Slayton Jubilee Singers
Black group of four (or five, depending on the program) men and three women that appeared on the Redpath circuit in 1906-1909. *Reference*: Iowa

Slayton Tennesseans
Black jubilee troupe, advertised as the "Sweet Singers of the Sunny South," consisting of three men and three women on the Redpath circuit in the 1920s. *Reference*: Iowa

Sleepy Hollow Quartet
Sang with Dick Powell in 1940 on several Decca recordings. *Reference*: Lehl Discography

Ben Smith Quartet
Recorded with Nellie Hill on Abbey in 1949 and on Coleman in 1950. *Reference*: Fournier

Smoothies
See, Babs & Her Brothers.

Snowflakes
Group that sang with Claude Thornhill and got their name from his theme song, "Snowfall." Original members in 1942 were Buddy Stewart, Lillian Land and Martha Wayne. Later members included Nancy Clayton, Joe Derise, Jim Preston and Hugh Baker. Jazz singer Chris Connor was also a member in 1949. *Reference*: http://www.parabrisas.com/; http://www.jazzdiscography.com/

Roy Milton And His Solid Senders
Recorded on Specialty in 1949.

Solitaire Cowboys Quartette
Appeared on sheet music of "Meet Me In Cheyenne For Old Frontier Days" in 1934. Although they are called a quartet, there are five men in the inset picture. NBC Station KOA is mentioned on the cover.

Song Fellows
Recorded on Banner, Conqueror and Perfect in 1932 and 1933. *Reference*: Lehl Discography

Buddy Hawkins And The Songmasters
Recorded on Commodore in 1948.

Songopators
Recorded on Bluebird and Victor in 1933 and 1934 and sang with Red Nichols. Members were Jack Wilcher, George Bacon and Russell Crowell. They made one recording with the Aaron Sisters. *Reference*: Lehl Discography

Songsmiths
Sang with Victor Young and made recordings that spanned 1933 to 1950. *Reference*: Lehl Discography

Song Spinners
Quartet of two men and two women that was on Decca and was one of those that backed soloists (such as Dick Haymes) during the Musician Union's recording ban that occurred from 1942 to 1944. Essentially, they used voices to replace instruments (not to imitate them). They also hit number one on the charts on their own with "Comin' In On A Wing And A Prayer" (1943-Decca) and recorded with Ella Fitzgerald, Bing Crosby and Bill Kenny of the Ink Spots. *Reference*: The Groups Sing CD-Jasmine Records-JASCD 393

Sonnysiders
A group that sang with the Sonny Dunham band and included Harold Grogan. *Reference*: http://www.vaughnmonroesociety.org/

Sons Of The Pioneers
Formed in 1933 as the O-Bar-O Cowboys consisting of Leonard Slye, Tim Spencer and Bob Nolan. In 1934, Hugh Farr was added and they became the Pioneers. One night on a radio station the announcer introduced them as the Sons Of The Pioneers, saying later that they were not old enough to be pioneers. They decided to go with that name and went on to become music legends, lasting for decades through many personnel changes. Their songs such as "Tumbling Tumbleweeds" (Decca-1934) were and are classics. Slye, of course, changed careers in 1938 when he replaced Gene Autry in a movie called, "Under Western Stars" and changed his name to Roy Rogers. *Reference*: The Sons of the Pioneers CD, Castle PLS CD 4456

Sophisticates
Sang with the Bernie Cummins band in the 1930s. *Reference*: http://nfo.net/usa/

Sorority Singers
Female quartet from the 1920s. Appeared on the Chautauqua circuit. *Reference*: Iowa

Soul Stirrers
Gospel group that began in the mid-1930s in Trinity, Texas. Its original members were Rebert Harris (lead), Silas Roy Crain (tenor), T. L. Bruster (tenor), R. B. Robinson (baritone) and Jesse Farley (bass). Eileen Southern lists their gospel innovations as being the first to add a fifth member to the group enabling the lead to sing with four-part harmony behind him. They sang gospel exclusively (others also sang secular music) and were one of the first to have instrumental accompaniment. Southern said: "The group's style was distinctive for its complex rhythms and syncopation and for its penchant for having the group chanting key words of the lyrics as a background for the lead-singers' verses." Of their later members, Sam Cooke was clearly the most well-known. *Reference*: Southern.

South Carolina Quartette
Recorded in New York in 1928.

Southernaires
Black quartet formed in 1929 in New York and consisting of Lowell Peters (lead), Homer Smith (tenor), Jay Stone Toney (baritone) and William Edmondson (bass). They sang on radio and were one of the few black groups of their era to appear on sheet music ("River Stay 'Way From My Door"-1931). They were also one of, if not the, earliest black groups to

appear on a nationally syndicated radio show - one that lasted for eight years. *Reference*: Southern

Southern Blues Singers
Recorded on Gennett in 1929; "Cow Cow" Davenport was on piano and vocal. *Reference*: Fournier

Southern Four
See, Fisk Jubilee Quartet

Southern Jubilee Singers and Players
Octet comprised of the Tennesseans, a black male quartet and the Olympia Ladies, a female black quartet. Members were Dazalia Underwood (soprano and manager of the Olympia Ladies), Hester O. Brown (contralto), Anna Smith (soprano), Crealea Peyton (alto), E. S. Thomas (bass and manager of the Tennesseans), C. W. Glass (first tenor), Chas. W. Boyd (baritone) and W. P. Talbert (second tenor). Appeared for the Coit Lyceum Bureau in 1914. *Reference*: Iowa

Southern Male Quartet
Recorded on Brunswick in 1939-40.

Southern Male Quartet
Male, black group, they made a few recordings, but nothing more is known about them; not even where or exactly when. *Reference*: BVG-10

Southern Melody Artists
Recorded on Okeh in 1927.

Southern Negro Quartette
Recorded "Anticipatin' Blues" for Columbia in the 1920s. Rick Whitesell, writing in Record Exchanger, said "the style of the recording clearly fits the R&B genre." See, Southern Quartette. *Reference*: Record Exchanger, Volume 4, Number 3

Southern Pacific Quartette
Appeared on sheet music of "Days Of '49" in 1922.

Southern Plantation Singers
Recorded in 1928. *Reference*: BVG-8

Southern Quartette
Male black group that appeared in the show "South Before The War" in New York in the 1890s. Members were Johnny Johnson (tenor), Sherman Kelly (tenor), Albert Johnson (baritone) and Beecher Davis (bass). They recorded from 1921 to 1927 as the Southern Quartette, the Southern Negro Quartette and the Southern Four. *Reference*: Brooks

Southern Sons
Willie "Highpockets" Langford, previously with the Golden Gate Quartet, began this group; the other members were James Baxter, Wesley Hill, Charles Wilson and Clifford Givens. They hit the R&B Top 10 with "Praise The Lord And Pass The Ammunition" (1942-Bluebird). The Knites Of Rhythm was another name under which they recorded. *Reference*: Whitburn-RB

Southern University Quartet
Recorded in 1935. *Reference*: BVG-8

Southland Jubilee Singers
Formed in 1943, they evolved into the Four Knights. They were also known as the Old Southland Jubilee Singers and the Old Southland Sextet. Some of the time they performed as a mixed-gender double quartet. They made recordings in New York in 1921 and 1924. *Reference*: ENVG-4

Southland Quartet
Recorded on Challenge in 1927 and Decca in 1938.

Southland Singers
Black group comprised of eight singers, half male. Members were Irene Jackson (soprano), Nettie Cartman (mezzo soprano), Betty Mae Stevens, Beulah Brandon (accompanist), Leonard Napper (baritone), Calvin Delph (tenor), Curtis Jackson (2nd tenor) and Oscar Bragg (basso). Appeared for the Lyceum Redpath Bureau in the 1930s. Another version, from 1938, included Jackson, Mary Johnson (mezzo soprano), Inez Edmondson (contralto), Brandon, Merton Smith (lyric tenor), Delph, Jackson and Edward R. Fraction. *Reference*: Iowa

Southland Singers
Black male quartet led and managed by John Douglass (basso). Appeared for the Coit Lyceum Bureau of Cleveland in the 1920s. *Reference*: Iowa

Noble Sissle's Southland Singers
Mixed-gender group of unknown membership that recorded in New York in 1919. Sissle was a well-known song writer (he was Eubie Blake's partner) and band leader. *Reference*: BVG-10

Sparkling Four Quartette
From the Norfolk, Virginia area, its members were Joe Key (lead), Dick Bell (tenor), someone known as "Spark" (baritone) and Walter Casson (bass). They recorded in New York in 1928 and in Richmond, Virginia in 1929. *Reference*: VQ-7.

Spencer Trio
Len Spencer, Billy Golden (he was a yodeler and did blackface comedy) and Steve Porter. They made cylinders as early as 1897. Others who likely sang with them were George P. Watson, George W. Johnson and Billy Williams (not the one from the Charioteers). Billy Murray sang with them on remakes of their Columbia records. *Reference*: Walsh

Buddy Spencer Trio
Recorded on Perfect in 1932. *Reference*: Lehl Discography

Spiders
They were primarily a 1950s group that got its start in 1947 in New Orleans as the Zion City Harmonizers. By 1950, its members were Chuck Carbo (lead), Joe Maxon (tenor), Matthew West (baritone), Oliver Howard (bass) and Chick Carbo (Chuck's brother) (bass and sometimes lead). *Reference*: Goldberg

Spirits of Rhythm
Founded in St. Louis in the late 1920s and as of its first recording in 1932 (as the Washboard Rhythm Kings) its members were Leo Watson, Dave Page, Ben Smith, Jimmy Shine, Carl Wade, Eddie Miles, Wilbur Daniels and Frank Benton. In 1933, they recorded as the Five Cousins with Watson, W. Daniels, Douglas Daniels, Teddy Bunn, Wilson Myers and Virgil Scoggins. They also cut four sides as the Five Spirits of Rhythm that same year. As Red McKenzie with The Spirits of Rhythm in 1934, they consisted of McKenzie, Watson, W. Daniels, D. Daniels, Bunn, Wellman Braud and Scoggins for four sides and then, the same group, minus McKenzie, as The Spirits of Rhythm for five cuts. They did some recordings that year with Ella Logan on vocal and one record in 1934 on Brunswick as the Nephews. The scat singing of Leo Watson was featured by the group. Several members played the tipple, a small stringed instrument. *Reference*: Spirits of Rhythm CD. Retrieval Records 79004

Sportsmen Quartet
Best known for their appearances on the Jack Benny radio show when the members were Bill Days (1st tenor), Max Smith (2nd tenor), Marty Sperzel (baritone), and Gurney Bell (bass). John Rarig (baritone) had been a prior member and their arranger. Thurl Ravenscroft was the original bass of the group until he went into the service in 1942. When he returned, Bell retained his spot and Smith and Ravenscroft founded the Mellomen. Ravenscroft was also the voice of Tony The Tiger in the cereal commercials. Prior to the Benny show, they sang with Gus Arnheim and then on the Mel Blanc Show in 1946-47. They charted with "Woody Woodpecker" (1948-Capitol), were in some movies and did guest spots on TV shows such as My Three Sons (as singing waiters). *Reference*: http://www.jackbenny.com/

Stafford Sisters
Recorded with Louis Prima in 1936 on Brunswick. *Reference*: Lehl Discography

Stamps Ozark Quartet
Male group and pianist that appeared on KWFT radio in Wichita Falls, Texas. Members were Henry Slaughter, Pat Garner, Ford Keith, Charles Bartlett and Russell Richardson.

Stamps Quartet
Recorded on Columbia in 1927 and were the Owen Brothers and Ellis. *Reference*: Lehl Discography

Standard Minstrels
San Francisco group that in 1884 contained "Carroll Johnson, Al. Holland, Franz Wetter, Charley Reed, W. J. Morant, Harry Wyatt, William Henry Rice, John Robinson, Tommy Bree, Hooley Thompson, Keegan and Wilson." *Reference*: Dumont (1915)

Standard Quartette
Black group from Chicago that recorded on cylinders for New York Phonograph, Columbia Phonograph, Ohio Phonograph and U.S. Phonograph Co. of New Jersey as early as 1891. Members are thought to have been H. C. Williams, Ed DeMoss, William Cottrell and Rufus L. Scott (bass). They toured with the "South Before The War" stage show. *Reference*: ENVQ-1; ENVQ-2; Brooks

Stanford Four
Male group on the cover of sheet music of "By The Beautiful Sea" from 1914.

Stardusters
Quartet that sang with the Charlie Spivak band in 1942 and featured June Hutton, who later replaced Jo Stafford in the Pied Pipers and who was female bandleader Ina Ray Hutton's sister. Author and record producer George T. Simon called June Hutton, "the greatest lead

voice ever to have sung with any vocal group." Other members were Dick Wylden, Glenn Gaylord and Curt Purnell. *Reference*: Simon; http://www.nfo.net/usa/

Starlighters
Backed Jo Stafford on several recordings and had four chart singles in the late 1940s. *Reference*: Whitburn-PM

Starr Sisters
Trio that appeared on sheet music of "Melody In F" in 1935 and sang with Paul Page in the 1940s. Kay Starr was one of them and went on to a very successful solo career. *Reference*: http://www.wfmu.org/LCD/18/ppage.html

Stella And The Fellas
Sang with Fred Waring in 1935 and their members were Stella Friend (she was one of the Three Waring Girls in 1930), Craig Leitch (1st tenor), Roy Ringwald (2nd tenor) and Paul Gibbons (baritone). Ringwald was also an arranger for the Pennsylvanians and sang with the Four Boys. *Reference*: Waring CD

Stellar Quartette
See, Columbia Stellar Quartet

Sterling Quartette
Male group that recorded on Okeh in 1918. *Reference*: Lehl Discography

Sterling Trio
Sang on various labels from 1916 to 1920 and solely on Victor from 1920 to 1925. Also made up 3/4ths of the Peerless Quartet. Members were Henry Burr, Albert Campbell and John Meyer. *Reference*: Walsh

Sterling Young Trio
Recorded in 1936 on Melotone. *Reference*: Lehl Discography

Stevenson, Hayden & McIvor "The Club Trio"
Comedy threesome on the cover of sheet music of "If The Can Canny Cannibals Captured New York Town" from 1916.

Stewart Harmony Singers
Recorded on Champion in 1932.

Stewart Sisters
Trio that appeared on sheet music of "Throwin' Stones At The Sun" in 1934 and recorded that same year with Rudy Vallee.

Still City Quartette
Appeared on sheet music of "That Mesmerizing Mendelssohn Tune" in 1909.

Stinson's Jubilee Singers
Known today only because Billy Mills, grandfather of the Mills Brothers, was a member in the 1880s. *Reference*: Southern

Strand Quartet
See, Criterion Quartet.

Strasser Family
Family of European singers who, like the Rainers, toured the U.S. in the early 1840s. *Reference*: Averill

Striders
New York group that did considerable backup work for Savannah Churchill. Members were Gene, Charles and Jim Strider and Al Martin. Other members are listed as E. Williams and F. Thomas. Their most popular song on their own was "Hesitating Fool" (1955-Apollo) (that was actually recorded in 1949). They also recorded with Dolores Martin in 1949 on Mystery. *Reference*: 40s-50s-CD; Rex-19

Strollers Quartette
Male group featuring Alfred Humfeld, David Whitehead, Harry Longstreet and Hayden Thomas. Appeared for the Redpath Lyceum Bureau in 1910. *Reference*: Iowa

Strollers Quartette
Appeared on sheet music of "The Yankee Boys From Yankee Land Are On Their Way To France" in 1918 and recorded on Challenge, Banner and Conqueror in 1930-1. It is not clear if they are a different group from the one listed above. *Reference*: Lehl Discography

Stroup Quartet
Recorded on Columbia in 1928.

Sun-Beam Quartette
Appear on a postcard mailed from Indiana in 1916

Richard Huey & his Sundown Singers
Recorded on Decca in 1943.

Sunny Southern Four
Appeared on sheet music of "Deep Henderson" in 1926.

Sunny South Ladies' Quartet
Black group that sang in vaudeville in the early 20th-century. *Reference*: Averill

Sunny South Men's Quartet
Black group that sang in vaudeville in the early 20th-century. *Reference*: Averill

Sunset Four
Recorded in Chicago in 1924 and 1925 on Paramount and were Hosy Crawford, Andy Bryant, Leonard Burton and Fred Vaughan. *Reference*: Lehl Discography.

Swanee Jubilee Company
Four men and two women. including James C. Prosser (tenor), Ida G. Slaughter (soprano), Susie M. Boyd (alto), Clarence H. Graham (baritone and pianist), Calvin J. Prosser (2nd tenor) and Andrew C. Smith (bass). The four men comprised the Swanee Jubilee Male Quartet. The group appeared on the Redpath circuit around 1920. *Reference*: Iowa

Roy Campbell's Swanee Singers
Recorded in 1935 on Victor. *Reference*: Lehl Discography

Swan Silvertones
Began in the coal mines in West Virginia in 1938 as the Four Harmony Kings and were led by Claude Jeter. By the 1940s, the members of this gospel group were Jeter, John Myles, John Manson and Henry Bossard. They became the Silvertone Singers and then the Swan Silvertones after the Swan Bakery which sponsored the radio show on which they appeared. They were particularly known for Jeter's falsetto. Jeter died in 2009 at the age of 94. *Reference*: Southern

Swan Singers
Black quintet and guitarist that recorded on King in the 1940s.

Del Casino & the Swantones
Recorded on Manor in 1948. *Reference*: http://settlet.fateback.com/Manor.htm

Swedish Ladies Trio
Appeared on the sheet music of "When Summer With It's [sic] Roses Comes Again" in 1912.

Eddie Cantor's Sweethearts
Appeared on sheet music of "I'd Love To Call You My Sweetheart' in 1924.

Sweet Potato Tooters
See, Foursome.

Sweet Violet Boys
Recorded on Columbia and Vocalion in from 1935 to 1938, Conqueror in 1938-40 and Okeh in 1941. *Reference*: Lehl Discography

Swing Masters
Sang with the Frankie Masters band. *Reference*: http://www.bigbandlibrary.com/

Syncopators
Washington, D.C. quintet that recorded on National in 1949. Members were James Pinkney (lead tenor), George Summers (2nd tenor), Howard "Ghostie" Smith (baritone), his brother, Theodore Smith (bass, baritone and second lead), and Edmond Johnson (bass, baritone and guitar). *Reference*: Goldberg

Tampa Boys
Recorded on Decca in 1941.

Taskiana Four
Recorded on Bluebird and Victor in from 1926 to 1929 and were Daniel Johnson (tenor), Norman Allen (tenor), Edward Foster (baritone) and James Ricke (bass). *Reference*: Lehl Discography

Tasty Yeast Jesters
Trio that appeared on sheet music in the 1930s, including "Dream A Little Dream Of Me" in 1931.

Taylor-Parsons-Hawks
Appeared on sheet music of "Bam Bam Bamy Shore" in 1925.

Taylor Trio
Recorded on Columbia in 1915-17 and Champion in 1922-3.

T.C.I. Women's Four
Female quartet whose membership is not known. They and their affiliated groups, Sister Cunningham and T.C.I. Sacred Singers, Famous Jubilee Singers and the Famous Myers Jubilee Singers, all recorded in Chicago in 1927 and 1928. *Reference*: VQ-7

Temple Quartet
There were at least three groups with the same or a very similar name. It is not clear if they were related so they are presented separately. This one was a male group including R. M. Strahan (1st tenor), H. H. Ferner (2nd tenor), C. A. Risser (baritone) and L. E. Spring (basso). They also played instruments and appeared at Lyceum Bureaus as the Dunbar Bell Ringers and toured in 1908. *Reference*: Iowa

Temple Quartette
The first traveling Chautauqua appeared in Iowa in 1904 and featured the Temple Quartette. The movement featured "clean and inspirational entertainment." The group was so named because it opened a Masonic temple in Boston. *Reference*: Averill

Temple Quartette
Group on the covers of the sheet music to "I Want To Go Back To Michigan (Down On The Farm)," and "When It's Night Time Down In Dixieland" from 1914. Also appear on sheet music of "Smile Awhile."

Temple Quartette
Group formed from a Masonic Temple choir in 1868. First members were D. F. Fitz (1st tenor), W. H. Fessenden (2nd tenor), H. A. Cook (baritone) and A. C. Ryder (basso). After that, they had numerous changes in membership through at least 1905. *Reference*: Iowa

Temple Quartette Concert Company
Male group touring for the 1905-1906 Redpath Lyceum season. Included H. G. Tripp (1st tenor), F. P. Baker (baritone), A. C. Steele (bass) and E. F. Webber (2nd tenor). *Reference*: Iowa

Temple Singers
Mixed-gender quartet featuring Lucille Buzzo (soprano), Katherine Strong (contralto), Edwin Delbridge (tenor) and Dimetrie Styop (baritone). Accompanied by Bernice Coughill. Appeared on the Chautauqua circuit in the 1920s. *Reference*: Iowa

Tennesseans
Black septet of four men and three women. The men apparently also sang as a quartet around 1910 on the Chautauqua circuit. They featured E. S. Thomas, "The Great Afro-American Basso." *Reference*: Iowa

Texas Comedy Four
Male group on the cover of sheet music of "I've Got The Rumatiz (Oh Gee Whiz I've Got The Rumatiz All Over Me)" from 1918.

Texas Medley Quartette
Formed in 1894 by Scott Joplin, it was comprised of eight singers (double quartet) including two of Joplin's brothers, Will and Robert. The group also featured Emmet Cook, a drummer with the Queen City Cornet Band. *Reference*: Averill

Texas Rangers
Male quartet that appeared on sheet music of "Who Threw The Overalls in Mistress Murphy's Chowder" in 1937.

That Bostonian Four
White male group that appeared on sheet music of "In The Heart Of The City That Has No Heart" in 1913.

Thatcher, Primrose & West
Large troupe from the late 1870s and 1880s led by musical director, Charles F. Warner. *Reference*: Dumont (1915)

That Girl Quartet
Harriet Keys, Allie Thomas, Precis Thompson and Helen Summers were the members. They recorded in 1911 and 1912 on Victor, Columbia, Edison and U.S. Everlasting and appeared on the covers of sheet music including "Motor King," from 1910. *Reference*: Walsh

That Quartette
Led by Geo. W. "Poodles" Jones, whose specialty number was "Down Where The Wurzburger Flows," this group also featured Frank Morrell, Harry Sylvester and Aubrey Pringle. Appeared on sheet music of "I Miss You More And More Every Day" in 1906 and "Why Did You Break My Heart" in 1908. *Reference*: Averill

That Singing Four
Recorded on Edison in 1925.

Theise's Harmonists
Quartet that appeared on sheet music of "Honey Boy" in 1907.

Theremin Vocal Group
Recorded on Capitol in 1949.

Those Four Boys
Appeared on sheet music of "Another Rag" in 1911.

Those Three Boys
Male trio on the cover of sheet music of "Red Moon" from 1908.

Those Three Fellows
Male group on the cover of sheet music of "Alexander's Ragtime Band" from 1911.

Three Australian Boys
Male group on the cover of sheet music of "Ev'rything's Gonna Be All Right" from 1926.

Three Barons
A 1930s and 1940s group featuring Tiny Grimes (guitar and vocals). Joe Springer (piano and vocals), Bass Robinson (bass and vocals) and Doc West (drums and vocals) were the other members. Also known as the Three Riffs. Grimes was also with the Cats And The Fiddle. *Reference*: Jive VG-2

Three Barons
A different group from the one listed above, they sang with the Sammy Kaye Orchestra in the late 1930s and early 1940s. Members were Jimmy Brown, Charlie Wilson and Tommy Ryan. *Reference*: Lehl Discography

Three Beaus And A Peep
Sang with the Shep Fields band in the late 1940s and appeared on the Colgate Comedy Hour TV show in the early 1950s. *Reference*: http://en.wikipedia.org/wiki/Shep_Fields; http://www.imdb.com/name/nm2271628/

Three Beaux
Recorded on Okeh in 1940. *Reference*: Lehl Discography

Three Bees And A Honey
Sang with Fred Waring in 1944 and recorded on Savoy in 1949. Margaret Ann Anderson was a member. *Reference*: http://www.libraries.psu.edu/waringcollections/; http://pqasb.pqarchiver.com/

Three Bips And A Bop
Babs Gonzales (vocal) led this black group that included at various times Rudy Williams (saxophone), Tadd Dameron (piano, vocals), Pee Wee Tinney (guitar, vocal), Art Phipps (bass), Charles Simon (drums) and Walter Davis (piano). Babs' real name was Lee Brown

and he was from Newark, NJ. *Reference*: Jive VG-2; http://www.musicweb-international.com/

Three Bits Of Rhythm
Recorded on Decca and Modern Music in the 1940s and were Theodore "Fate" Rudolph (bass), Bruce Williams and Solomon Laugenour (guitars). They added Johnny Creach on violin and as a quartet, called themselves the Bits of Rhythm. Creach would gain fame years later as "Poppa" John Creach of Jefferson Starship/Hot Tuna. *Reference*: Fournier; http://home.earthlink.net/~jaymar41/index.html

Johnny Moore's Three Blazers
Trio from Los Angeles that began in the mid-1940s. Members were Johnny Moore, Charles Brown and Eddie Williams. They later added a fourth in Moore's brother Oscar who had been with Nat King Cole. They had many R&B hits (19 on the charts) including "Drifting Blues" (1946-Philo) and "New Orleans Blues" (1947-Exclusive). Brown left in 1949 to go on his own. It panned out as he had 13 songs that made the R&B charts between 1949 and 1960. *Reference*: Whitburn-RB

Three Blue Notes
Sang with the Blue Barron band in the late 1930s and early 1940s. *Reference*: http://www.findvinylrecords.com/

Three Cheers
Recorded in 1936 and 1938 on Brunswick and Bluebird and accompanied Bing Crosby in 1936. *Reference*: Lehl Discography

Three Chips
Recorded with the Bert Block Orchestra in 1935 on Melotone. *Reference*: Lehl Discography

Three Dennis Sisters
They are identified as Ruth, Ann and Cherie on sheet music of "Dreamy Melody" in 1922. They also appeared on sheet music of "Just Lonesome" in 1925 and in a 1928 movie "The Crowd." *Reference*: http://movies2.nytimes.com/

Three Dixie Girls
Appeared on sheet music of "Years, Years Ago" in 1911.

Three Du For Boys
Appeared on the sheet music of "I'm On My Way To Mandalay" in 1913.

Three Dynamites
Recorded on Columbia in 1947-8.

Three Earbenders
Sang with the Eddie Duchin Band in the 1930s. *Reference*: http://catalog.berklee.edu/

Three E's
Female trio that appeared on sheet music of "Take Me To Roseland, My Beautiful Rose" in 1913.

Three Esquires
Vocal trio that sang with Tommy Dorsey in 1935 made up of Jack Leonard, Axel Stordahl and Joe Bauer, all of whom came out of the Bert Block band. Stordahl was also an arranger for Dorsey and Bauer played trumpet. *Reference*: Simon

Three Flames
Tiger Haynes and Roy Testamark (replaced by Loumell Morgan in 1954) from St. Croix and Averill "Rill" Pollard from Barbados made up this group that formed in New York. Haynes had sung with Plink, Plank and Plunk. The Three Flames had a number one hit with "Open The Door, Richard" (1947-Columbia) and appeared on TV series "Washington Square." During the 1950s and 1960s, Haynes appeared in several major Broadway musicals. *Reference*: Whitburn–PM; Jive VG-2; Goldmine-4/80

Three Georgia Crackers
Recorded on Columbia in 1930. *Reference*: Lehl Discography

Three Girl Friends
Sang with Fred Waring and charted with Waring, together with Stuart Churchill, with "So Beats My Heart For You" on Victor in 1930. *Reference*: Whitburn-PM

Three Grouch Killers
Male group on the cover of sheet music of "The Good Ship Mary Ann" from 1914.

Three Hokum Kids
Recorded in Chicago in 1929 on Brunswick. *Reference*: Lehl Discography

Three Horsemen
Sang with Jimmy Green in 1930 on Columbia. *Reference*: Lehl Discography

Three Jacks
Recorded in 1930 in New York on various labels including Clarion and Harmony. Rodney Rodgers and Bill Coty may have been members. *Reference*: Lehl Discography

Three Jazz Aces
Recorded in New York in 1926 on Champion and Porter Grainger may have been a member. *Reference*: Lehl Discography

Porter Grainger's Three Jazz Singers
Recorded in New York in 1926 and were Bert Howell, Gus Horsly and Perry Bradford, with Grainger on piano. *Reference*: Lehl Discography

Three Kaufields
Recorded in New York from 1919 to 1921 and were Irving Kaufman (tenor), Arthur Fields (tenor) and Jack Kaufman (baritone). Irving Kaufman was also with the Avon Comedy Four. *Reference*: Lehl Discography

Three Kaydets
Sang with Sammy Kaye Orchestra in the 1940s. *Reference*: http://www.bigbandlibrary.com/

Three Keys
From the Philadelphia area, its members were George "Bon Bon" Tunnell (lead), Bob Pease (tenor) and "Slim" Furness (baritone) (also an accomplished guitarist). Tunnell started in the 1920s with a group called Bon Bon and his Buddies, a name to which he was to return in the early 1940s. They charted once with "Fit As A Fiddle" (1933-Brunswick). In 1937, Tunnell joined one of the big bands, Jan Savitt and His Top Hatters, and was one of the first blacks to sing with a white band. When they played in the south, Tunnell had to register as the band's valet so he could stay in the same hotel as the other band members. (In 1938, Billie Holiday joined Artie Shaw, becoming the first black female to sing with a white band.) Tunnell left Savitt in 1941 and went back to the Three Keys (he also cut six sides on Decca as Bon Bon and his Buddies). Furness also sang with the Furness Brothers and the Four Keys. *Reference*: Whitburn – PM; Simon; The Three Keys CD, Classics Records 1141

Three Kuhns
Listed as Paul, Charles and Robert. They were on the covers of several pieces of sheet music, including "Someone Thinks Of Someone," from 1905 and "Good-Night Little Girl Good-Night" in 1906. As the Three White Kuhns, they appeared on sheet music of "Underneath The Cotton Moon" in 1913. In 1915, they were on sheet music (in a picture with a female trio named Buford, Bennett & Buford) of "To Lou," billed as "Atlantic City's Favorites."

Three Leightons
Male trio on the cover of "Frankie And Johnny (You'll Miss Me In The Days To Come)" from 1912.

Three Little Maids
Recorded on Bluebird in 1933 and were Eva, Evelyn and Lucille Overstake. *Reference*: Lehl Discography

Three Little Playmates
They were three not so little men identified on sheet music of "You Told Me To Go" from 1925 as Haynes, Kaiser and Lehmann.

Three Little Sachs
Appeared on sheet music of "A Little Street Where Old Friends Meet" in 1932. A photo identifies them as "How," "Jim" and "Bill."

Three Little Words
Female group appearing on the cover of sheet music of "Moon Over Miami" from 1935. They also were billed as Herb Cook and his Three Little Words in 1933 recordings on Victor, Bluebird and Elektradisk. *Reference*: eBay; Lehl Discography

Three Melodians
Recorded with Ben Selvin in 1928 on Columbia. *Reference*: Lehl Discography

Three Minute Men
Recorded on Brunswick in 1931. *Reference*: Lehl Discography

Three Mitchells
Trio on the cover of sheet music of "Any Rags" from 1902. One girl, one woman and one man comprise the group.

Three Moaxes
Sang with Charlie Barnet band in 1940. *Reference*: http://www.jazzconnectionmag.com/

Three Musketeers
Recorded in Charlotte, North Carolina in 1936 on Bluebird and were Tommy Bowles, Paul Ennis and James Jones. *Reference*: Lehl Discography

3 Musketeers
Male group that appeared on sheet music of "Underneath The Cotton Moon" in 1918.

Three Night Caps
Recorded on Velvet Tone in 1932.

Three O'Connor Sisters
Female group on the cover of sheet music of "When That Midnight Choo Choo Leaves For Alabam'" from 1912.

Three Ormand Sisters
Appeared on sheet music of "In A Little Spanish Town" in 1926.

Three Peppers
St. Louis, Missouri, group that was comprised of Oliver "Toy" Wilson, Robert Bell (also guitar) and Walter Williams (also played bass). Ray Branca was a later member. Producer Irving Mills gave them a recording contract on the Variety label in 1937. Sally Gooding sang lead on four of their recordings in 1937. They charted with "Love Grows On The White Oak Tree" (1939-Decca) and their last recording was made in 1949. *Reference*: The Three Peppers CD, Classics Records 889; http://www.allmusic.com/

Three Peppers
Trio that appeared on the cover of sheet music of "I Get The Blues When It Rains" from 1929. One of two groups with this name.

Three Peters Sisters
A black trio comprised of Mattye, Anne and Virginia. Their career extended from the 1930s to the 1960s. In 1937, they appeared in the movie, "Ali Baba Goes To Town." *Reference*: Fournier

Three Pickert Sisters
Female group on the cover of sheet music of "When Uncle Joe Plays A Rag On His Old Banjo" from 1912 and "Bobbin' Up And Down" from 1913.

Three Rascals
Recorded in 1933 on Columbia. Possible members were Tommy Green, John Ingram and Charlie Palloy. *Reference*: Lehl Discography

Three Reasons
A female group that recorded on Bluebird in the late 1930s. *Reference*: Lehl Discography

Three Rhythm Rascals
Recorded with Gus Arnheim in 1933 and were Robert Harthun, Freddy Fritsch and Robert Keith. *Reference*: Lehl Discography

Three Riffs
From Cleveland, the members were Howard Green (replaced by Bunnie Walker), Edward Parton and Joe Seneca (also known as Joe McGhee). They recorded on Decca, Atlantic, Jubilee and Apollo from 1939 to 1950. *Reference*: Fournier

Three Ripples
Recorded on Bluebird in 1938. *Reference*: Lehl Discography

Three Scamps
Recorded on Victor in 1934. *Reference*: Lehl Discography

3 Shades of Blue, Jean Goldkettes'
Female group that appeared of sheet music of "Little Black Sheep" in 1927.

Three Shades Of Rhythm
Members were Sleepy Williams, Lucius Smith, Alyce Haynes Marcus and Louise Harris. Effie Smith was a later member. They were in the 1943 movie "Hoosier Holiday." In an Excelsior release in 1944, they were listed as Herb "Flamingo" Jeffries and the Three Shades of Rhythm. *Reference*: http://www.imdb.com/; Fournier

Three Sharps & A Flat
This jive group started in Chicago in the early 1930s as the Three Flats and was comprised of Jimmy Turner (lead), Thurman "Red' Cooper (1st tenor) and Arvid Garrett (2nd tenor). They were singing on NBC radio, but left to tour with Duke Ellington (and were replaced on NBC by the Four Vagabonds). Leonard Bibbs (bass) was added to the group at that time and they became the Three Sharps & A Flat. In 1939, Turner and Bibbs left and Leroy Morrison replaced Bibbs. They stayed with only three members for most of their career, but retained the name Three Sharps and A Flat. They joined the Navy in 1942 and performed together while in the service. A female singer, Kiki Williams, sang with them for a while after the war. They recorded on Decca, Okeh, Tower and Hamptone and disbanded in 1952. *Reference*: Goldmine, March 1980, with help from Marv Goldberg

Three Sisters
See, Fontane Sisters.

3 Sisters Hawthorne
Group on the cover of "They All Love Nellie Tracy (This Dainty Girl Of Mine)" from 1897.

Three Songies
Recorded with Red Nichols in 1937 on Variety. *Reference*: Lehl Discography

Three Spades
Recorded on Vocalion in 1937.

Three Star Singers
Recorded with Sam Lanin in 1928 on Okeh. *Reference*: Lehl Discography

Three Strikes
Group that sang with the Henry Busse Band in the 1930s. *Reference*: Walker

Three Top Hatters
Sang with the Jon Savitt Band. *Reference*: Walker

Three Toppers
Recorded in the late 1930s. *Reference*: http://www.lordisco.com/index.html

Three T's
Recorded on Victor in 1936.

Madeline Green & her Three Varieties
Recorded on Bluebird in 1941. *Reference*: Fournier

3 Varsity Fellows
Group whose picture appears on the sheet music of 'When It's Night Time Down In Dixieland" in 1914.

Three Voices
Recorded on Bluebird in 1933.

Three Wainwright Sisters
Appeared on sheet music of "The Little Red School House" in 1922 and recorded on Edison in 1925.

Three Waring Girls
They hit number one on the charts with Fred Waring with "I Found A Million Dollar Baby (In A Five-And-Ten-Cent Store)" on Victor in 1931 and charted three additional times with him. *Reference*: Whitburn-PM

Three White Kuhns
See, Three Kuhns.

Three X Girls
Appeared on sheet music in the 1930s, including "Hold Me" in 1933.

Three X Sisters
Appeared in vaudeville as The Hamilton Sisters & Fordyce. On radio they became "the mysterious singing sisters of the air who wore eye masks for their publicity shots." The sisters were Jesse, Pearl and Violet Hamilton. They also were the voices of musical cartoon characters during the early period of sound, were on sheet music of "Colorado Moon" in 1933 and appeared in the movies "The Audition" in 1933 and "All Aboard" in 1937. Recorded on Victor. *Reference*: http://vaudeville.org

Tietge Sisters
Recorded on Victor from 1926 to 1929 and were Elsie, Florence and Martha Tietge. *Reference*: Lehl Discography

Tiffany Male Quartet
Group of unknown composition that appeared for the Wm. King agency in the 1920s. *Reference*: Iowa

Tip-Top Four
Two women and two men on the cover of "When It's Night Time Down In Dixieland" from 1914.

Tivoli Quartette
This group appears on the cover of the 1911 sheet music to "You'll Never Know The Good Fellow I've Been ('Till I've Gone Away)." Also pictured on the sheet cover is Sophie Tucker.

Todrank Quartette
Ellen, Gus, Frances and Ray appear on the sheet music of "When Grand-Pa Courted Grand-Ma" from 1939.

Tom, Dick and Harry
Trio featured on the cover of the sheet music to "Turn Me Loose At The Ballgame" from 1936. They recorded on Vocalion, Brunswick and Victor from 1929 to 1931. *Reference*: eBay

Tone Performers
Recorded for Columbia in 1912. *Reference*: Lehl Discography

Tones
Recorded on Baton in 1949.

Top Hatters
Trio that was active in the mid-1930s. They may have recorded on Decca. *Reference*: http://www.lordisco.com/

Toppers
See, Five Red Caps.

Town Criers
A family group that started as the Four Polks and were Lucy Ann, Alva, Gordon and Vernon Polk. From 1942-1944, as the Town Criers, they sang with Les Brown, from 1944-1946 with Kay Kyser, with Lionel Hampton also in 1944, Jimmie Lunceford in 1945, Bob Crosby in 1945, Earl Hines in 1946 and with the Tommy Dorsey band in 1947. When Elva married in 1948, the group broke up. Gordon stayed with Dorsey, sang with Harry James, worked as an actor, had a brief stint in the Modernaires and then played guitar with Les Brown's band. Lucy also stayed with Dorsey and charted several times and then sang with Les Brown and Kay Kyser. *Reference*: http://www.advancedpoetx.com/

Trail Blazers Male Quartet
Recorded on the Trailblazer label in 1928. *Reference*: Lehl Discography

Trainmen's Trio
Jeff Skinner, Matty Balling and Charles Burton were its members and they appeared on sheet music of "Somewhere Along The Sunrise Trail" in 1926. They worked for the Long Island Railroad. *Reference*: http://sbiii.com/d-keller/

Tremaine Brothers
Recorded on Gennett in 1925.

Trevette Quartette
Appeared on sheet music of "Down By The Old Mill Stream" in 1910.

Triangle Quartette
Male, black quartet that recorded in Chicago in the late 1920s. *Reference*: BSVG-1

Trinity Mixed Quartette
Recorded on National in 1921.

Trio Del Mar - Gilbert
Recorded songs in Spanish in Los Angeles in 1928 and 1929. *Reference*: Lehl Discography

Trio Dominguez De La Vega
Recorded songs in Spanish in Chicago in 1929. *Reference*: Lehl Discography

Trio Jaliciense
Recorded songs in Spanish in Chicago in 1928 and were Daniel Ramirez and individuals with the last names of Del Prado and Gonzalez. *Reference*: Lehl Discography

Trio Tamaulipeco
Recorded songs in Spanish in San Antonio in 1929. *Reference*: Lehl Discography

Trocadero Quartette
Appeared on sheet music of "She Was Bred in Old Kentucky" in 1898 and members were Chas. Lomier, Steve Prideau, Jack Sample and Joe Birnes. *Reference*: http://digitalgallery.nypl.org/nypldigital/

Troubadour Four
Male group featured on sheet music of "She's Kentucky's Fairest Daughter" from 1901.

Troy Comedy Four
In 1912, this musical comedy group featured characters called "Messenger Boy," "Tough Kid," "Brokendown Actor" and "Dutch" (played by Fred Stein). They called themselves the "Little Men with Big Voices" and sang songs such as "Roll Dem Bones" and "When I First Met Kate Down By The Golden Gate." *Reference*: Averill

Bobby Tucker Singers
They backed Frank Sinatra on several recordings during the recording ban of the early 1940s.

Tuft's College Octette
Recorded on Columbia in 1914. *Reference*: Lehl Discography

Tune Twisters
Recorded on Vocalion in the 1930s.

Tuskegee Institute Singers
Founded in 1884 by Booker T. Washington at his Tuskegee Institute. First known as the Tuskegee Quartet, it members were Hiram H. Thweatt, John F. McLeMore, Warren Logan

and leader, Robert H. Hamilton. They traveled to "promote the interest of Tuskegee Institute" and continued to do so into the 1940s. *Reference*: http://www.tuskegee.edu/

Tuskegee Quartet
See, Tuskegee Institute Singers.

Twilight Quartette
Black group including Isaac Hines, Joseph Hodges, Robert Martin and Billy Moore (bass) that performed with Cleveland's Colored Minstrels in the early 1890s and McCabe's Minstrels in 1894. They appeared in the show "South Before The War" in New York in the 1890s. *Reference*: Averill; Brooks

Twin City Foursome
Three men and a woman formed this group that appeared on sheet music of "If We Never Meet Again" in 1936.

Twin City Quartette
Appeared on sheet music of "That Italian Rag" in 1910.

Twin Tones
Quartet that sang with the Jan Garber Orchestra in the 1940s after the war. Members were Bob Parker, Bette Bligh, Doris Brian (of the Brian Sisters) and Alan Copeland.

Two Tones
Recorded on Cosmo in 1946.

Tyrolese Minstrels
Composed of members of the Rainer family from Europe - Anton, Franz, Maria, Felix and Joseph. They performed German part-songs and folk songs in solos, trios and quartets, while touring the U.S. beginning in 1834. A second group by the same name, with family members Margaretta, Ellena, Lewis and Semir toured between 1839 and 1843. This second group introduced America to "Silent Night" (Stille Nacht), and was the most influential of the touring European vocal groups. Also known as the Rainer Family or the Tribe of Rainer. American audiences were "thrilled by the Rainers' precise enunciation and timing and by the impression they created of a harmony that was so well blended the audience could not determine which singer was singing which part." *Reference*: Averill

Uncle Sam Trio
Three sailors in uniform pictured on the cover of sheet music of "Tom, Dick And Harry And Jack" from 1917.

Unique Quartette
The earliest known black vocal group to record, with "Mama's Black Baby Boy" being the only remaining track. Joseph M. Moore was the lead and also managed the group. Others were William H. Tucker (tenor), E. J. Carsons (baritone) and Samuel G. Baker. J. E. Settles and basses Burt Lozier, Thomas (?) Craig and Frank (?) DeLyons were also members. Recorded cylinders for New York Phonograph Co. in 1890. Later, they recorded for Edison and New Jersey. As well as performing on stage on their own, they also toured with various minstrel shows and had a theatrical career. *Reference*: ENVQ-2; Brooks

Universal Quartet
Walsh states this may be a group that recorded on Zononphone in 1905 made up of Geoffrey O'Hara (tenor), Reinald Werrenrath (baritone) and Walter MacPherson (bass). Walsh says O'Hara remembered the lead only as "Skutty." *Reference*: Walsh

University Four
Male group on the cover of sheet music of "That International Rag" from 1913.

University Four
Female quartet, with unnamed members, appearing on the Midland Lyceum circuit in the 1920s. *Reference*: Iowa

University Girls
Female quartet whose only known members were Linda Mohrman and Mildred M. Morrison. Appeared on the Chautauqua circuit for the Midland Lyceum Bureau in 1913. *Reference*: Iowa

University Male Quartet
Recorded on Brunswick in 1921.

University of Pennsylvania Quartette
Recorded on Columbia in 1914. *Reference*: Lehl Discography

Uptowners Quartet
Accompanied Frances Langford in 1936 on Brunswick. *Reference*: Lehl Discography

Utica Institute Jubilee Singers
Formed in 1925 by Dr. William H. Holtzclaw, the founder of the Utica Normal and Industrial Institute for the Training of Young Men and Women. As with the Fisk group they too toured to raise money for their school. They were the first black group to be syndicated on the radio when in 1927 they had a show originating from an NBC station in New York. *Reference*: Hall-CD; http://lrc.hindscc.edu/

Utica Jubilee Singers
Black male quintet. Appeared at the Chautauquas in 1932. *Reference*: Iowa

V-8
Vocal ensemble featured on the 1936 broadcasts by Fred Waring of the Ford Dealers Show. It was a mixed-gender combination of two groups, the first consisting of Bea Swain, Al Rinker (of the Rhythm Boys), Ken Lane and Johnny Smedburg of Bea and the Bachelors and the second, the early Modernaires: Bill Conway, Hal Dickinson, Ralph Brewster and Chuck Goldstein (later in Four Chicks And Chuck). The group took their name from the auto engine. According to the liner notes of the CD produced by the Fred Waring's America Collection at Penn State University, this was the first "vocal jazz/swing ensemble." *Reference*: Waring CD

Vagabonds
Although there were several groups with this or a similar name, this one was formed in 1928 by Harold Goodman, Dean Upson and Curt Poulton. They sang both pop and country songs and appeared on WLS in Chicago and at the Grand Old Opry in Nashville. They recorded on Victor and Bluebird through 1933. *Reference*: https://music.msn.com/

Valdosta Rotary Double Quartet:
Recorded on Columbia in 1924. *Reference*: Lehl Discography

Jimmy Valentine Quintet
Recorded on Varsity in 1948.

Valley Inn Quartet
Recorded on Champion in 1926-7.

Vardon, Perry and Wilber
Appeared on sheet music of "Wish Me Good Luck On My Journey" in 1907.

Variety Four
Black, male quartet that recorded in Chicago in 1927 on Brunswick. Members were Chester Jones, Harold DeMund, Frederic McCoy and Raymond Giles. *Reference*: BSVG-1

Variety Girls
Sang with Ted Dahl in 1932. *Reference*: Lehl Discography

Vassar Girls Quartet
Katherine Armstrong, Lovira Taft, Florence Fiske and E. Eleanor Patterson comprised this group that made Edison cylinders in 1910. *Reference*: Walsh

Velvetones
A 1940s black group from Chicago made up of Toggo Smythe, Wallace Caldwell, Herman Bell and Danny Gibson. They recorded on Columbia. *Reference*: Fournier

Velvetones
Black group from Newark, New Jersey, that began in 1943. Marv Goldberg lists Enoch Martin, Madison Flanagan, Walter Dawkins and Sam Rucker as its members. They recorded on Decca, Coronet, Sonora, Super Disc, among others. *Reference*: Goldberg

Velvetones
See, Skylarks.

Verne, Lea and Mary
Appeared on the cover of sheet music to "Down By The Old Birch Tree" in 1936.

Versatile Sextette
Group on the sheet music to "Just A Little Love Song" from Bessie Clayton's Revue "The Box Party," from 1922.

Versatile Three
Members were A. Haston, A. Tuck and W. Vesey and they recorded in 1926 on Vocalion. *Reference*: Lehl Discography

Victor Ladies Quartet
According to Walsh, they likely were Elizabeth Wheeler, Olive Kline, Elsie Baker and Marguerite Dunlap and recorded in about 1915. *Reference*: Walsh

Victor Male Quartet
See, Orpheus Quartet.

Victor Minstrels
Recorded on Victor in the early 1900s and by 1929 were Billy Murray, Henry Burr and Frank Crumit (tenors), James Stanley (baritone) and the Cavaliers male quartet. *Reference*: Mainspring; http://www.meloware.com/category/vaudeville.htm

Victor Mixed Chorus
Harry Macdonough (tenor) was a member. They recorded on Victor in 1915. *Reference*: http://www.collectionscanada.ca/4/4/m2-3000-e.html

Victor Opera Trio, Quartet and Sextet
Harry Macdonough (tenor) was a member. They recorded on Victor in 1915. *Reference*: http://www.collectionscanada.ca/4/4/m2-3000-e.html

Victor Vaudeville Company
In addition to recordings under this name done by the Peerless Quartet, some were done in 1908 by Byron G. Harlan, Billy Murray and Steve Porter. *Reference*: Walsh

Victory Four
Recorded on Pathé, probably around 1920. *Reference*: http://settlet.fateback.com/

Village Choir
Quartet of two men and two women that appeared on the cover of sheet music of "If I Should Fall In Love With You" from 1907.

Village Singers
Male quartet comprised of Howard L. Baxter (1st tenor), Ivon H. Blackman (2nd tenor and manager), Clifford A. Foote (baritone and accompanist) and John J. Odbert (basso and accompanist). Often accompanied by a soprano, Anna Florence Smith. They appeared on the Lyceum circuit in 1906. *Reference*: Iowa

Virginia Female Jubilee Singers
Female quartet that recorded in New York in 1921 on Okeh. *Reference*: ENVG-4

Virginia Four
From Norfolk, Virginia, they recorded in New York in 1929. Known members were Norman Harris (2nd tenor), Melvin Colden (baritone) and Len Williams (bass). They grew out of the Norfolk Jazz Quartet. Colden also sang with the Master Keys. *Reference*: RCM-5/91

Virginia Girls
Female sextet billed as a "singing orchestra." Appeared on the Chautauqua circuit around 1910. *Reference*: Iowa

Virginia Minstrels
Formed in 1843 by Daniel Decatur Emmet from a quartet of out-of-work actors, they took the name "Minstrels" from the touring European families of the time. This group incorporated the emulation of slave culture and language into their repertoire and introduced what was later to be the standard minstrel repertoire of tambo and bones, olio and promenade. Their most recognizable song was "Buffalo Gal (Won't You Come Out Tonight)," written by Cool White (John Hodges) in 1844. *Reference*: Averill

Virginians
Mixed-gender black quartet including George Day (tenor), R. L. Ferguson (baritone), Irene Howard (contralto) and Arlie Payne (soprano). Another group by the same name featured Hester O. Brown (contralto), Carrie M. Ross (soprano), Floyd Henry Lacy (tenor) and James M. Ross (baritone). Appeared on the Lyceum and Chautauqua circuits in the 1910s. *Reference*: Iowa

Virginia Serenaders
Philadelphia group containing of James Crawford, Cool White, Richard Myers and Robert Edwards, among others. They performed all over the northeast in the 1840s. Dumont claims that they organized in 1840 and included Jim Sanford, Eph Horn, Old Bull Myers, Ed. Deaves, Tony Winnemore and P. Solomons on accordion. Harriet Phillips appeared as the first blacked-up woman with this group in 1848 in Philadelphia. Dumont also lists George Kunkel as the bass of this group. *Reference*: White; Dumont (1915)

Vocalaires
Recorded with Slim Coates on Crystal in 1949. *Reference*: Fournier

Vocardians
Recorded in 1934 with Paul Whiteman. *Reference*: Lehl Discography

Voices Four
Sang with the Tommy Tucker Orchestra in the 1940s. They were also known as the Voices Three. *Reference*: http://www.parabrisas.com/d_tuckert.php

Walker's Fisk Jubilee Singers
A brochure advertising this troupe said that "There are only two Jubilee companies in the world representing Fisk University." They were named as "Fisk University Jubilee Singers, Managed by Prof. John W. Work, Jr." and "Walker's Fisk Jubilee Singers, Under the Management of M. Eliza Walker Crump." *Reference*: Iowa

Wallace Sisters
Trio that recorded on Decca in 1937. *Reference*: Lehl Discography

Wallace Trio
Recorded in 1931 on Clarion. *Reference*: Lehl Discography

Wanderers
Recorded on Bluebird in 1935.

Washington's Kentucky Quartet
Male black group that recorded in Richmond, Indiana in 1925. A. F. Ferguson, Perry Gray, Good J. Johnson and Howard C. Washington were the members. *Reference*: VQ-7

Washington Trio
Two men and a woman who appeared on sheet music of "Carolina Rolling Stone" in 1921.

Watson, Baker & Saville
Two men and a woman (Baker) appearing on the cover of sheet music of "I've Got Your Number" from 1910.

Weary Willie Trio
Billy Murray, Edward Meeker and Donald Chalmers made up this group that recorded on Edison from 1916 to 1919. *Reference*: Walsh

Weatherwax Brothers
Foursome from Iowa associated with the traveling Chautauquas around 1910. *Reference*: Averill

Weavers
Legendary folk group that began as the Almanac Singers in the 1940s. Members included Pete Seeger, Lee Hays and Woody Guthrie. Seeger and Hays then formed the Weavers with Fred Hellerman and Ronnie Gilbert and helped popularize folk music in the US. Hits included "Tzena, Tzena, Tzena" (1950), "Goodnight Irene" (1950),"So Long, It's Been Good To Know Ya" (1951), "On Top Of Old Smoky" (1951) and "Wimoweh" (1952), all on Decca. *Reference*: Whitburn-PM

Webb, Dolan & Frazer
Male trio that appeared on the cover of sheet music to "Those Good Old Days Back Home" in 1916.

We Girls Quartet
Gladys Rice, Betsy Lane Shepherd, Marion Evelyn Cox and Amy Ellerman made up this group that recorded on Edison in 1918. *Reference*: Walsh

Wesley Female Quartet/Trio
Recorded in 1926. *Reference*: BVG-8

West Brothers
Recorded in 1935 for Clarion and were Philip, David and Billy West. Some of their numbers were instrumental. *Reference*: Lehl Discography

Westinghouse Quartette
On Am. Gramophone tapes of 1900-1926.

Ray West Trio
Recorded on Columbia in Los Angeles in 1930. *Reference*: Lehl Discography

West Virginia Collegiate Singers
Recorded in 1927. *Reference*: BVG-8

West, Will and his Original "Picks"
Octet, including what look like some children, on the cover of sheet music of "The Pick-A-Ninny" from 1902.

Harry Wham Quartette
White group that appeared on cover of sheet music of "Old Man Happiness" from 1948.

Wheat Street Female Quartet
Black group that recorded in Atlanta in 1925-1925. *Reference*: VQ-7

Whippoorwill Four
Recorded on Brunswick in 1930. *Reference*: http://settlet.fateback.com/

White's Serenaders
Formed in New York City in 1846, and performed at White's Melodeon, White's Varieties and White's Opera House, all in the Bowery, for eleven years. Consisted of C. White, R. White, F. Stanton, W. Smith, H. Neil and Master Juba. *Reference*: White

White Way Male Quartet
Recorded on Brunswick in 1922.

William Reese & the White Way Quartet
Recorded on Brunswick in 1922.

Whitmore & Clarke's Minstrels
Eastern troupe of the 1860s in which "the first triple clog dance was introduced by Stiles, Phelps and Johnny Armstrong." Included Andy Wyatt, Johnny Armstrong, Thomas Maynard, Hank White, G. M. Clark, Boyle Brothers, and J. B. Porter. *Reference*: Dumont (1915).

Whitney Brothers Quartet
Alvin, Edwin, William and Yale Whitney comprised this group on Victor and Edison in 1908. They were associated with the traveling Chautauquas around 1910. *Reference*: Walsh; Averill

Wiedoft-Wadsworth Quartet
Recorded on Brunswick and Vocalion in the early 1920s.

Billy Williams Quartet
Founded in New York in 1949 by Billy Williams of the Charioteers, one of the great lead voices of his era. Other members were John Bell (tenor), Claude Riddick (baritone) and Eugene Dixon (bass). They had a Top 10 R&B hit with "I'm Gonna Sit Right Down And Write Myself A Letter" (1957-Coral) and appeared on the TV show, "Your Show Of Shows" with Sid Caesar. Williams was the first guest on the American Bandstand national telecast. When he died in 1972, he was living in a donated room in the basement of a church in Chicago, and no one claimed his body. *Reference*: Whitburn-RB, Marion

Williams Brothers
Quartet from Iowa that started in the late 1930s and included Andy Williams and his brothers Bob, Dick and Don. They sang with Bing Crosby on "Swingin On A Star" in 1944 which hit number one on the charts. Andy went solo in 1952. *Reference*: http://www.allmusic.com/; http://en.wikipedia.org/

Williams Colored Singers
Mixed-gender black group also known as the Williams Jubilee Singers. Charles Williams founded the group in 1904 in Chicago. There were eight men and eight women in the original ensemble. They performed for black and white audiences alike and are said to be the first group to sell out the Philadelphia Academy of Music. In 1908 its members included G. L. Johnson (1st tenor), C. P. Williams (2nd tenor), J. H. Johnson (baritone), J. S. Crabbe (basso), Pearl M. Crawford (soprano) and Clara K. Williams (contralto). Anna Highwarden was the accompanist. Eight of them toured Europe as the Williams Jubilee Singers. They recorded in Atlanta in 1926. *Reference*: VQ-7; Southern; Iowa

Jack Williams Quartet
Recorded on Specialty with Betty Cobbs in 1949. *Reference*: Fournier

Williams Original Dixie Jubilee Singers
See, Williams Colored Singers

Williams Trio
Sang with the Griff Williams Band in the 1940s. *Reference*: http://nfo.net/usa/w4.html

Clarence Williams Trio
Mixed-gender group consisting of Eva Taylor, Clarence Williams and Clarence Todd that recorded on Okeh in 1925. *Reference*: Lehl Discography

Willing Four
Black group that featured Walter Holden (tenor), Joseph Thomas (baritone), George Thomas (baritone) and Vincent Simpson (bass). *Reference*: VQ-7

Doris Wilson Trio
A female group on the cover of sheet music to "On The Shores Of Italy" in 1914.

Wilson's Minstrels
Minstrel troupe containing "Shattuck, Will Walling, W. E. Nankeville, John Davis, Tommy Donnelly, Fulton Brothers, Andy Rankin, Dan Quinlan, William Henry Rice" around 1878. *Reference*: Dumont (1915)

Wilson Quartet
Recorded on Columbia and Clarion in 1930. Their names possibly were Touchette, Cornell, Hendrie and Ehler. *Reference*: Lehl Discography

Wingmen Quartet
Recorded on Down Beat in 1948.

Windom Quartette
Formed by William "Billy" Windom who had a minstrel troupe known as "The Forty Whites And Thirty Blacks." He was a black tenor who also wrote many songs, including "She May Have Seen Better Days." They appeared on the cover of sheet music of "You'se Just A Little N*****, Still You'se Mine, All Mine" from 1898, and were likely the first black group to have their photograph on a piece of sheet music. *Reference*: Hare

Windy City Four
Recorded on Vocalion in 1931.

Edward Clark & his Winning Widows
A man and six women who appeared on the cover of sheet music to "Say Sis! Give Us A Kiss!" in 1907.

WMBI Announcers
Recorded in 1928 in Chicago on Victor and were Wendell P. Loveless (tenor), H. Hermansen (baritone and piano) and William E. King (bass). *Reference*: Lehl Discography

Wolverine Four
Appeared on sheet music of "I'll Take You Home Again Pal O'Mine" in 1923. The biography for Clint H. O'Reilly on www.imdb.com states he was their accompanist from 1920 to 1931. *Reference*: www.imdb.com

Wolverine Quartette
Male group from Michigan featuring Ralph Thomas (1st tenor), Harry Clifford (2nd tenor), Arnold Lovejoy (bass) and Ward A. French (baritone and pianist). Appeared on the Chautauqua circuit in the 1920s. *Reference*: Iowa

Wonder State Harmonists
Recorded on Vocalion in 1928.

Woodland Quartette
Male group with unnamed members featured on the Chautauqua circuit around 1920. They also recorded on Gennett. *Reference*: Iowa

Woods Bros. G.O.P. Quartette
Appeared on sheet music titled "Republican Rally Song: Republicans Will Win This Fall" in 1934. The sheet states it is from "Republican State Convention, Sprinfield [sic], Ill. Aug, 9. 1934."

Wood's Minstrels
A troupe from the mid-19th century. *Reference*: Averill

Woodyard Trio
Recorded on Brunswick in 1931 in New York. *Reference*: Lehl Discography

Wynken - Blynken - Nod
A female group that recorded in Chicago in 1928 and 1929 on Brunswick and Victor with Jean Goldkette. *Reference*: Lehl Discography

Xentrique Male Quartette
Group from Mt. Vernon, Ohio that included Walter J. Sperry (2nd bass), George B. Kelly (1st tenor), Wm. G. Gower (2nd tenor) and Harry O. Mitchell (1st bass). Appeared on the Chautauqua circuit around 1915. *Reference*: Iowa

X-Rays
Recorded on Savoy and Coral from 1948 to 1952. Members were Milton "Tippy" Larkin, Willie Moore, Alfred "Chippy" Outcalt, Hal Singer, George Rhodes, Walter Page and Bobby Donaldson. *Reference*: http://www.group-harmony.com/

Yacht Club Boys
Recorded on Brunswick and Columbia from 1926 to 1934 and were Billy Mann, Tom Purcell, Chick Endor (replaced by Eddie Thomas) and George Walsh. *Reference*: Lehl Discography

Yale Trio
Recorded in 1928 on Brunswick. *Reference*: Lehl Discography

Yellow Jacket Four
Recorded on Columbia in 1925. *Reference*: Lehl Discography

Yellow Jackets
They were from Georgia Tech and recorded in Atlanta in 1930 on Brunswick. *Reference*: Lehl Discography

Ye Olde Towne Quartette
Male group featuring T. E. Hutchinson (lyric tenor), W. A. Greene (tenor), T. F. Kanatzar (baritone) and Ralph Stolz (basso). Appeared for the Coit Lyceum Bureau in the 1910s.

Young American Quintette
Mixed-gender group of four men and a woman that appeared on sheet music of "Let's Go Home" in 1908.

Zonophone Quartet
See, Rambler Minstrel Company. Also, some recordings originally listed as by the Colonial Quartet were later issued under this name. *Reference*: Walsh

Notes:

   Groups that had their leader's name in the title are listed under the group, not the leader. For example, Johnny Moore's Three Blazers are listed alphabetically under the "Ts."

   Lehl Discography   This indicates that the source of the information is the Discography compiled by Karsten Lehl. Lehl is a German collector of early vocal group music and is the baritone for the great German vocal group Ensemble Six - http://www.ensemblesix.de/. German collectors Andreas Wellen (also of Ensemble Six) and Josef Westner also contributed to this Discography.

   Gospel groups, except for the 20 or so top groups in terms of influence and excellence are not included in this book. Where there was doubt as to whether a group was strictly gospel or also sang secular music, it was included.

For the most part, this book references only American groups. A few foreign groups are mentioned either because of their influence (the Comedian Harmonists) or to differentiate them from an American group of a similar name; for example, the British Four Aces.

Country and Western groups are generally not included except for the Sons of the Pioneers because of their great fame and longevity.

Where there was doubt as to whether a group was vocal or instrumental, it was included.

CD References
Birmingham CD-II: Birmingham Jubilee Singers – Vol. 2. Document Records DOCD-5346
BSB: Basin Street Boys, Satchelmouth Baby CD, Night Train NTICD7028
BSVG-1: Black Secular Vocal Groups Vol. 1. Document Records: DOCD-5546
BSVG-2: Black Secular Vocal Groups Vol. 2. Document Records: DOCD-5550
BSVG-3: Black Secular Vocal Groups Vol. 3. Document Records: DOCD-5604
BVG-1: Black Vocal Groups Vol. 1 (1924-1930). Document Records DOCD-5340
BVG-3: Black Vocal Groups Vol. 3 (1925-1943). Document Records DOCD-5551
BVG-4: Black Vocal Groups Vol. 4 (1927-1939). Document Records DOCD-5552
BVG-6: Black Vocal Groups Vol. 5 (1926-1943). Document Records DOCD-5554
BVG-7: Black Vocal Groups Vol. 7 (1927-1941). Document Records DOCD-5555
BVG-8: Black Vocal Groups Vol. 8 (1926-1935). Document Records DOCD-5556
BVG-9: Black Vocal Groups Vol. 9 (1929-1942). Document Records DOCD-5606
BVG-10: Black Vocal Groups Vol. 9 (1919-1929). Document Records DOCD-5632
ENVG-3: The Earliest Negro Vocal Groups Vol. 3. Document Records DOCD-5531
ENVG-4: The Earliest Negro Vocal Groups Vol. 4. Document Records DOCD-5355
ENVG-5: The Earliest Negro Vocal Groups Vol. 5. Document Records DOCD-5613
ENVQ-1: The Earliest Negro Vocal Quartets Vol. 1 (1894-1928). Document Records DOCD-5061
ENVQ-2: The Earliest Negro Vocal Quartets Vol. 2 (1893-1922). Document Records DOCD-5288
Fisk-3: Fisk University Jubilee Singers Vol. 3. Document Records DOCD-5535
40s-50s-CD: Goodbye 40's Hello 50's CD, Relic Records
Hall CD: Hall Negro Quartette, Unissued Radio Programs – 1936. Document Records DOCD-5415
Human Orch: Human Orchestra LP, Clanka Lanka 144.003
JJ-CD: The Jive Is Jumpin': RCA & Bluebird Vocal Groups, 1939-1952. West Dise
Jive VG-2: That's Where My Jive Goes-The Best of Jive Vocal Groups 2. PCD-5779
Norfolk-6: Norfolk Jazz & Jubilee Quartets Vol. 6. Document Records DOCD-5386
SVG-4: Secular Vocal Groups Vol. 4 (1926-1947). Document Records DOCD-5615

Sweetest Harmony: Sweetest Harmony CD – Living Era CD AJA 5216
VQ-1: Vocal Quartets Vol. 1. Document Records DOCD-5537
VQ-4: Vocal Quartets Vol. 4. Document Records DOCD-5540
VQ-5: Vocal Quartets Vol. 5. Document Records DOCD-5541
VQ-6: Vocal Quartets Vol. 6. Document Records DOCD-5542
VQ-7: Vocal Quartets Vol. 7. Document Records DOCD-5543
Waring CD: Fred Waring's America Collection, The Pennsylvania State University
WC-CD: Rare Windy City R&B CD, U-114

Books

Abbott/Seroff: Abbott, Lynn and Doug Seroff. *Ragged But Right: Black Traveling Shows, "Coon Songs," and the Dark Pathway to Blues and Jazz.* Jackson: University Press of Mississippi, 2007

Averill: Averill, Gage. *Four Parts, No Waiting.* Oxford and New York: Oxford University Press, 2003

Brooks: Brooks, Tim. *Lost Sounds: Blacks And The Birth Of The Recording Industry 1890-1919.* Urbana and Chicago: University of Illinois Press, 2004

Cuney-Hare: Cuney-Hare, Maud. *Negro Musicians and Their Music.* New York: Da Capo, 1974

Da Capo: Hardy, Phil and Dave Laing. *The Da Capo Companion To 20th-Century Popular Music.* New York: Da Capo Press, 1990

Dumont (1914): Dumont, Frank. *The Golden Days of Minstrelsy.* "New York Clipper," December 19, 1914

Dumont (1915): Dumont, Frank. *The Younger Generation in Minstrelsy and Reminiscences of the Past.* "New York Clipper," March 27, 1915

Ewen: Ewen, David. *All the Years of American Popular Music.* Englewood Cliffs, New Jersey: Prentice-Hall, 1977

Fletcher: Fletcher, Tom. *One Hundred Years of the Negro in Show Business.* New York: Burdge & Company Ltd., 1954, pp. 9-14

Gracyk: Gracyk, Tim. *Popular American Recording Pioneers 1895-1925.* Binghamton, New York: The Haworth Press, 2000

Hamm: Hamm, Charles. *Yesterdays: Popular Song in America*. New York: W. W. Norton, 1979

Marion: http://home.earthlink.net/~jaymar41/doowopTP.html

Schlesinger: Schlesinger, Joseph. *Turn Of The Century Quartets*. SWD Roundup. Volume 46, Number 3, August 1999

Simon: Simon, George T. *The Big Bands*. New York: The Macmillan Company, 1967

Southern: Southern, Eileen. *Biographical Dictionary Of Afro-American And African Musicians*. Westport-London: Greenwood Press, 1982

Walker: Walker, Leo. *The Big Band Almanac*. New York: Da Capo Press, 1989

Warner: Warner, Jay. *The Da Capo Book of American Singing Groups*. New York: Da Capo Press, 1992, 2000

Whitburn-PM: Whitburn, Joel. *Joel Whitburn's Pop Memories 1890-1954*. Menomonee Falls, Wisconsin: Record Research Inc., 1986

Whitburn-RB: Whitburn, Joel. *Joel Whitburn's Top R&B Singles 1942-1995*. Menomonee Falls, Wisconsin: Record Research Inc., 1996

White: White, Charles. *Negro Minstrelsy: Its Starting Place Traced Back Over Sixty Years, Arranged and Compiled from the Best Authorities*. "New York Clipper," April 28, 1860

Periodicals

DISC: Discoveries Magazine
Goldmine: Goldman Magazine
Walsh: Walsh, Jim. *Favorite Pioneer Recording Artists-The First Ten Years*. Hobbies Magazine, May 1952; *A Directory Of Pioneer Recording Groups*. Hobbies Magazine, October 1962; *History Of The Peerless Quartet*. Hobbies Magazine, December 1969; The (Premier) American Quartet. Hobbies Magazine, February 1970.
RCM: Record Collector's Monthly
Rex: Record Exchanger
SU: Story Untold
Whiskey: Whiskey, Women, and . . . .
YM: Yesterday's Memories

Other References

Fournier: Tony Fournier's website - http://www.vocalgroupharmony.com/
Goldberg: Marv Goldberg's website - http://home.att.net/~marvy42/marvart.html
Iowa: http://sdrcdata.lib.uiowa.edu/libsdrc/
Mainspring: http://www.mainspringpress.com/
Marion: J. C. Marion's website - http://home.earthlink.net/~jaymar41/doowopTP.html

Introduction to the Discography

This discography has been compiled by culling information from a number of sources (the main ones are listed below). The culling process, the nature of the early methods of phonographic recording, as well as the variety of ways that some groups marketed themselves, leads to a number of minor problems. While it is likely that the great majority of information contained in the discography is fully accurate as to group name, song title, year released and label(s), it is also likely that there are many small discrepancies in the data.

As an example, one source may list a group as the "Eponymous Quartet," while another uses "Eponymous Quartette." The two versions may occur because the group used both names, because the same song by this group was released on two separate labels (each choosing different spelling), the group recorded the same song at different times for the same label and released it under two separate spellings, or it could simply be an oversight by one of the discographers listing this group. Further, the names of a group may differ depending on the audience targeted by the record company. Thus the Golden Gate Quartet recorded music meant for the general public, while the Golden Gate Jubilee Quartet released religious music. Also, there are occasionally "families" of names for a given group of singers - Steve Gibson & the Redcaps, the Redcaps, the Red Caps, the Five Red Caps and the Original Redcaps were composed of identical or nearly identical group members, and had different names appear on different media (78, 45, LP, CD, etc.).

The same lack of certainty extends to song titles. Titles can vary, for example, "Get On Board Little Chillun'," versus "...Little Children,"; "Git On Board..." versus "Get On Board..." Also, for example, "Goin'..." versus "Going...." As with group names, the titles may have actually appeared differently on different issues, or may have been changed by a discographer intentionally or by mistake. The Mills Brothers released "Just A Dream Of You, Dear" in 1940, 1946 and 1950, all on Decca, but with different label numbers.

The sheer number of recordings and lack of access to all versions, make it nearly impossible for us to know whether they are the same or different. For the same reasons, we also have no easy way of knowing if identical songs by identical groups are the same version, or are iterations caused by multiple takes or the re-recording that was necessary during the early years of the recording era. Frequently a song was released on both a label and sub-label, such as Decca and Brunswick, or on a flat disc or amberol cylinder, or with and without an "announcer." For some groups we do not know whether all of a group's recordings are vocal group only, solo artist or even instrumental as, for example, with Johnny Moore's Three Blazers.

Despite these caveats, the listing below will prove quite accurate and virtually complete for vocal group recordings that were released in the U.S. between the dawn of recorded sound through roughly 1950. Foreign releases are not included, nor are vocal group recordings released in a foreign language by an American label.

Abbreviations Used: 2mincyl=2 minute cylinder
4BA= 4 minute Blue Amberol cylinder
DD= Diamond Disk

Sources:

Karsten Lehl's Discography, graciously provided to us and compiled by him over many years of research and collecting.

Abrams, Steven. The Online Discographical Project at http://www.78discography.com/

Hoffman, Frank, Dick Carty & Quentin Riggs. *Billy Murray: The Phonograph Industry's First Great Recording Artist.* Lanham, Maryland: Scarecrow Press, 1997.

Konig, Henry. *http://www.musiktiteldb.de/musiktitel.html*

Warner: Warner, Jay. *The Da Capo Book of American Singing Groups.* New York: Da Capo Press, 1992, 2000.

While some gospel recordings are included, no attempt was made to search for them. If gospel recordings presented themselves to us in connection with other research or if there was doubt about whether recordings were gospel, they were included.

Where there was doubt as to whether a group was vocal or instrumental, it was included.

Due to some formatting issues, we were unable to fix all "widows and orphans," but the information is there – even if it looks a bit lonely at times.

Group Title	Year	Label
Aaron Sisters		
How'm I Doin'! (with the Song-O-Pators)	1932	Columbia 2699-D
Oh! Mo'nah!	1932	Columbia 2689-D
St. Louis Blues, The (with the Song-O-Pators)	1932	Columbia 2699-D
Abernathy Quartet		
Don't Forget To Pray	1932	Victor 2366360
Redeemed	1932	Victor 23663
Aeolian Male Quartet		
Medley Of Plantation Songs	1920	Vocalion 14081B
Aeolian Male Quartet, Lewis James & the		
First Noel, The	1922	Vocalion 14438A
Aeolian Mixed Quartet		
Blest Be The Tie That Binds	1922	Vocalion 14470B
Excerpts From Pinafore Pt. 1	1923	Vocalion 14615A
Excerpts From Pinafore Pt. 2	1923	Vocalion 14615B
It Came Upon A Midnight Clear	1922	Vocalion 14437B
Joy To The World	1922	Vocalion 14443B
O Little Town Of Bethlehem	1922	Vocalion 14438B
Safe In The Arms Of Jesus	1922	Vocalion 14425B
Shall We Gather At The River	1922	Vocalion 14470A
Silent Night - Hark The Herald Angels Sing	1922	Vocalion 14438B
Aeolian Shannon Quartet		
Crossing The Bar	1922	Vocalion 14398B
Afro-American Folk Song Singers		
Rain Song, The	1914	Columbia A-1538
Swing Along	1914	Columbia A-1538
Ah-Moors		
Honey Honey Honey	1948	Rainbow 10060
Airport Boys		
Bad Girl	1940	Bluebird B-10939
You Are My Sunshine	1940	Bluebird B-10939
Akins Birmingham Boys		
I Walked And Walked	1928	Columbia 15348-D
There Ain't No Flies On Auntie	1928	Columbia 15348-D
Alabama Four		
Goodbye, My Alabama Babe	1928	Victor 21136
His Troubles Was Hard	1930	Piccadilly 569
How Beautiful Heaven Must Be	1927	Broadway 8209
Jerusalem Mornin'	1930	Piccadilly 569
Looking This Way	1927	Broadway 8209
Queen Street Rag	1928	Victor 21136
Rollin' Down To Jordan	1928	Victor 21197
What You Gonna Do When The World's On Fire	1928	Victor 21197
Alabama Magpie Trio (with Marion Handy & his Alabamians)		
Georgia Pines	1929	Columbia 2034-D
Song Of The Bayou	1929	Columbia 2034-D
Alabama Sacred Harp Singers		
Christian's Hope, The	1928	Columbia
Cuba	1928	Columbia 15349-D
Present Joys	1928	Columbia 15274-D
Religion Is A Fortune	1928	Columbia 15349-D
Rocky Road	1928	Columbia 15274-D
Victoria	1928	Columbia
Albertville Quartet		
I Hold His Hands	1929	Columbia 15666-D
Workers For Jesus	1929	Columbia 15666-D
Alcoa Quartet		
Shall We Gather At The River	1925	Columbia 15022-D
Throw Out The Life Line	1925	Columbia 15022-D
Alexander Brothers		
Goodnight Irene	1950	Mercury 5465
Limehouse Blues	1932	Champion 16493
Mood Indigo	1932	Champion 16499
St. Louis Blues	1932	Champion 16499
Tiger Rag	1932	Champion 16493
Alexander Brothers Quartette		
Hear Dem Bells & Shepherd's Chorus	1910	Columbia A-942
Hunter's Farewell, The	1910	Columbia A-916
I Love To Tell The Story	1910	Columbia A-914
I Need Thee Every Hour	1910	Columbia A-914
Love Divine, All Love Excelling	1910	Columbia A-1115
May, Dearest May	1910	Columbia A-942
Soldier's Farewell, The	1910	Columbia A-913/Columbia A-3007
Alexander Trio, The Nelson		
Drink-Up, Light-Up	1997	Specialty CD 9065 (recorded in 1947)
Allen Quartet		
Beautiful River	1927	Okeh 45196
God's Children Are Gathering Home	1927	Okeh 45168
Life's Railway To Heaven	1927	Okeh 45196
My Mother's Bible	1927	Okeh 45168
My Old Cottage Home	1927	Okeh 45130
My Precious Savior	1927	Okeh 45130
Redeemed	1920	Okeh 40797
Try To Win Some Soul To Him	1927	Okeh 45109
We Are Going Down In The Valley	1927	Okeh 40797
When The Sweet By And By Is Ended	1927	Okeh 45109
Almanac Singers		
All I Want	1941	Keynote K303
Ballad Of October 16th	1941	Almanac 1103
Billy Boy	1941	Almanac 1101
C For Conscription/Washington Breakdown	1941	Almanac 1102
Get Thee Behind The Me	1941	Keynote K302
Lisa Jane	1941	Almanac 1102
Plow Under	1941	Almanac 1103
Strange Death Of John Doe	1941	Almanac 1101

Talking Union	1941	Keynote K301
Union Maid	1941	Keynote K303
Union Train	1941	Keynote K301
Which Side'	1941	Keynote K302

Alphabetical Four

Book Of The Seven Seas, The	1940	Decca 7712
Do Not Pass Me By	1940	Decca 7734
Get On Board, Little Children	1938	Decca 7594
Go Down Jonah And Serve The Lord	1940	Decca 7712
Go Where I Send Thee	1940	Decca 7704
Harlem Blues	1938	Movie transcription from
Have You Heard About The World'	1940	Decca 7752
He Sees All We Do And Hears All We Say	1940	Decca 7774
He Was Nailed To The Cross	1938	Decca 7601
I Can't Feel At Home In This Any More	1941	Decca 7840
I Don't Care Where They Bury My Body	1940	Decca 7774
I Just Can't Help From Crying Sometimes	1941	Decca 7840
I Want To Veil My Face	1938	Decca 7507
My Mother's Prayers Have Followed Me	1938	Decca 7594
Noah, God's Gonna Ride On The Rainy Tide	1940	Decca 7704
Old Ark's A-Moverin', The	1938	Decca 7546
Precious Lord, Hold My Hand	1938	Decca 7546
Rock My Soul	1940	Decca 7734
Shake My Mother's Hand	1940	Decca 7752
Shepherd, Go Feed My Sheep	1941	Decca 7845
Sleep On, Darling Mother	1941	Decca 7854
Valley Of Time, The	1941	Decca 7854
We Will Understand It Better Bye And Bye	1941	Decca 7845
What A Friend We Have In Jesus	1938	Decca 7610
When The Moon Goes Down In The Valley Of Time	1938	Decca 7507
Will The Circle Be Unbroken'	1938	Decca 7601
Live Humble	1938	Decca 7610

Amalu Trio (with Charles Amalu & his Troupe)

I Strolled Along The Shore	1934	Victor 24685
Soft Green Seas	1934	Victor 24685

Ambassador Trio

I'm Doin' That Thing	1930	Victor 22505

Ambassador Trio (Loyce Whiteman & male trio)

Put Your Little Arms Around Me	1931	Victor 22853

Ambassadors Trio (as Kate Smith & the Ambassadors)

When The Moon Shines Over The Mountain	1937	Victor 25760

Ambassadors Trio (with Kate Smith & her Swanee Music)

College Rhythm	1934	Brunswick 01937/Decca 277
Continental, The	1934	Brunswick 01931/Decca 288
Let's Give Three Cheers To Love	1934	Brunswick 01937/Decca 277

Amber Sisters

Cherokee Eyes	1953	Capitol 2538
I've Waited Too Long	1952	Capitol 2394
Lonesome Road Blues	1952	Capitol 2289
Look What Followed Me Home Last Night	1953	Capitol 2684
One More Time	1952	Capitol 2394
So Tired Of Your Running Around	1953	Capitol 2684
Useless	1953	Capitol 2538
When I Want Lovin' Baby	1952	Capitol 2289

American Four

Any Bonds Today'	1941	Decca 3962A
Arms For The Love Of America	1941	Decca 3962B
Wings Over The Navy	1942	Decca 4308

American Four (Dick Powell assisted by the)

Captains Of The Clouds	1942	Decca 4174
Over There	1942	Decca 4174

American Four, Dick Robertson & the

Ev'ryone's A Fighting Son Of That Old Gang Of Mine	1941	Decca 4117
Eyes Of The Fleet	1942	Decca 4308
Goodbye Mama (I'm Off To Yokohama)	1941	Decca 4116
I May Stay Away A Little Longer	1941	Decca 4116
We Did It Before (And We Can Do It Again)	1941	Decca 4117

American Quartet

And The Green Grass Grew All Around	1913	Victor 17344
Any Girl Looks Good In The Summer Time	1911	Edison BA 1777/Victor 16879
Army Blue	1913	Victor 17500
Billy	1905	American 031178/Zonophone 163/Zonophone 163 (1906)
Bring Back Those Minstrel Days	1926	Victor unreleased BVE-36856
Cut Yourself A Piece Of Cake (And Make Yourself At Home)	1923	Victor 19155
Darling Nellie Gray	1902	Lambert 630 (2 mincyl)
Denver Town	1909	Victor 5683/Edison 10155 (1909)/Victor 16524 (1910)
Down In Dear Old New Orleans	1912	Victor 17248

Down On The Mississippi	1910	Victor 35143//Edison 626 (4mincyl) (1911)	Farmyard Medley	1902	Lambert 560 (2mincyl)
Good Night, Mr. Moon	1912	Victor 17046	Finnegan's Birthday Surprise Party	1902	Lambert 591 (2mincyl)
Grizzly Bear, The	1911	Victor 16681	Holy City	1902	Lambert 526 (2mincyl)
I've Got The Sweetest Girl In Maryland	1917	Victor 18294	I Can't Think Of Nothing Else But You, Lulu	1903	Edison Bell 5520
Jingle Of Jungle Joe, The	1911	Victor 5808			
Melodious Jazz	1920	Canadian Victor 216144	Kentucky Babe	1902	Lambert 595 (2mincyl)
Negro Medley	1910	Victor 16463	Killarney	1903	Edison Bell 5518
Nellie Kelly, I Love You	1922	Zonophone 3571	Lead Kindly Light	1902	Lambert 622 (2mincyl)
Night Trip To Buffalo	1910	Edison 4mincyl 492			
Red Rose Rag, The	1911	Victor 16965	Louisiana Lou	1902	Lambert 519 (2mincyl)
'Round Her Neck She Wears A Yeller Ribbon (For Her Lover Who Is Fur, Fur Away)	1918	Victor 18436	Meeting Of The Limekiln Club, A	1902	Lambert 590 (2mincyl)
She's Dixie All The Time	1917	Victor 18257	Nearer, My God, To Thee	1902	Lambert 623 (2mincyl)
Siam	1916	Victor 17993			
Soldier's Farewell, A	1902	Lambert 521 (2mincyl)	Nellie Gray	1902	Lambert 630 (2mincyl)
Summer Days	1911	Zonophone 5759	Night Trip To Buffalo, A	1902	Gram-o-Phone 43/Lambert 522 (2mincyl) (1902)
That Certain Party	1926	Victor unissued			
That College Rag	1912	Victor 17067			
That Coontown Quartet	1912	Victor 17128	Onward, Christian Soldiers	1902	Lambert 646 (2mincyl)
That Fellow With The 'Cello Rag	1911	Victor 5844			
That Slippery Slide Trombone	1912	Victor 17090	Plantation Songs: De Ole Banjo	1903	Edison Bell 5522
That Syncopated Boogie-Boo	1912	Victor 17250	Sally In Our Alley	1903	Edison Bell 5516
There Is Silver Now Where Once There Was Gold	1911	Victor 17107	Steamboat Leaving The Wharf At New Orleans	1902	Lambert 568 (2mincyl)
Tomorrow Morning	1925	Victor unissued	Vacant Chair, The	1902	Lambert 600 (2mincyl)
War Song Medley	1915	Victor 17823			
What Do You Do Sunday, Mary'	1923	Victor 19188	Way Down Yonder In The Cornfield	1903	Edison Bell 5517
You Can't Get Away From The Blarney	1917	Victor 18377	When The Harvest Days Are Over	1902	Lambert 565 (2mincyl)
You're A Grand Old Flag	1917	Victor 18358	Where Do We Go From Here	1908	Victor
Turkestan	1919	Aeolian/Vocalion 12123/Emerson 7498/Emerson 9174	**American Quartet (2)**		
			Alabamy Bound	1925	Victor 19680
			All Aboard For Chinatown	1916	Victor 17993
American Quartet & Ada Jones			All Aboard For Dixieland	1914	Victor 17535
Come Josephine In My Flying Machine	1911	Victor 16953	Along The Rocky Road To Dublin	1916	Edison BA 2817/Victor 17900
American Quartet (1)			America, I Love You	1915	Victor 17902
Almost Persuaded	1902	Lambert 623 (2mincyl)	Another Rag (A Raggy Rag)	1911	Victor 17027
			Any Little Girl That's A Nice Little Girl Is The Right Little Girl For Me	1910	Victor 16560
Annie Laurie	1903	Edison Bell 5519			
As Your Hair Grows Whiter	1903	Edison Bell 5515			
Church Scene From The Old Homestead	1902	Lambert 514 (2mincyl)	Anything Is Nice If It Comes From Dixieland	1919	Victor 18589/Edison DD 50537 (1919)
Coon Wedding In Southern Georgia, A	1902	Lambert 520 (2mincyl)	At The Mississippi Cabaret	1914	Victor 17650
Dinah, De Moon Am Shinin'	1903	Edison Bell 5521	Baby Rose Darky Ballad	1911	Victor 16859
Dixie Land	1902	Lambert 524 (2 mincyl)	Back To Dixieland	1915	Victor 17783
			Beautiful Doll, Goodbye	1913	Victor 17244

Title	Year	Label/Number
Because You're Irish	1917	Victor 18279
Benny Havens, Oh!	1913	Victor 17500
Billy (She Always Dreams Of Bill)	1911	Victor 16965
Breeze (Blow My Baby Back To Me), The	1919	Victor 18605/Zonophone 3223 (1919)
Bring Back The Kaiser To Me	1917	Victor 18414
Carolina In The Morning	1922	Victor 19006
Cheer Up Liza	1917	Victor 18400
Childhood Days	1922	Victor 18959
Chinatown, My Chinatown	1915	Victor 17684
Circus Day In Dixie	1915	Victor 17838
College Rag	1912	Victor 17067
Come Over To Dover	1915	Victor 17751
Coontown Quartet	1912	Victor 17128
Curse Of An Aching Heart	1913	Victor 17372
Daddy	1912	Victor 17089
Dixie Gray	1911	Victor 16866
Dixie Is Dixie Once More	1919	Victor 18610
Dixie Volunteers, The	1918	Victor 18429
Do You Take This Woman For Your Lawful Wife' - "I Do, I Do"	1914	Victor 17554
Emmett's Lullaby	1912	Victor 17217
Everybody Loves An Irish Song	1916	Victor 18198
Everybody Rag With Me	1915	Victor 17769
Everybody Two-Step	1912	Victor 17171
Everything Is Peaches Down In Georgia	1918	Victor 18497
Farmyard Medley	1910	Victor 16676/Victor 35124
Floatin' Down To Cotton Town	1919	Victor 18628
Floating Down The River ('Cause It's Moonlight Now In Dixieland)	1913	Victor 17438
Gasoline Gus And Jitney Bus	1915	Victor 17838
Good-Bye Broadway, Hello France	1917	Victor 18335
Goodnight Mr. Moon	1912	Victor 17046
Grand Old Flag	1917	Victor 18358
Green Grass Grew All Around, The	1913	Victor 17344/Victor 19265 (1924)
Here's A Typical Tipperary	1920	Okeh 4128
Hitchy-Koo	1912	Victor 17196
Honey Man (My Little Lovin' Honey Man)	1911	Victor 16979
Honeymoon Bells	1915	Victor 17853
Honolulu America Loves You	1916	Victor 18192
Honolulu Hicki Boola Boo	1917	Victor 18235
How's Every Little Thing In Dixie	1917	Victor 18225
If You Ever Get Lonely	1916	Victor 18224
I Knew Him When He Was All Right	1914	Victor 17684
I'll Be Glad To Get Back To My Home Town	1922	Victor 18847
I Love It	1911	Victor 16953/Victor 16953 (1911)
I Love The Land Of Old Black Joe	1920	Vocalion 14080A/Okeh 4129
I'm Missin' My Mammy's Kissin'	1920	Victor 18751
In The Land Of Harmony	1911	Victor 16896/Edison 10524 (1911)
In The Little Red School House	1922	Victor 18904
It's A Long, Long Way To Tipperary	1914	Victor 17639
It's A Long Way To Berlin, But We'll Get There!	1917	Victor 18386
I've Got The Nicest Little Home In D-I-X-I-E	1917	Victor 18378
I Would Like To Try It But I'm Just Afraid	1912	Victor 17070
Keep Your Head Down Fritzi	1918	Victor 18467
Let's All Be Americans Now	1917	Victor 18256
Let's All Do Something	1917	Victor 18320
Little Red Schoolhouse	1922	Victor 18904
Little Willie	1909	Victor 16359/Edison 10186 (2 mincyl) (1909)
Loading Up The Mandy Lee	1916	Victor 17947
Lullaby Blues (In The Evening)	1919	Emerson 7513/Emerson 9176/Columbia A-2725/Victor 18553
Mammy's Shufflin' Dance	1912	Victor 17082
Mandy 'N' Me	1922	Victor 18832
Marry A Yiddisher Boy	1912	Victor 17028/Edison 949 (4mincyl) (1912)
Medley Of Negro Songs	1910	Victor 16463
Mickey Donahue	1924	Victor 19280
Mocking Bird Rag, The	1912	Victor 17204
Monkey Doodle	1924	Victor 19321
Moonlight Bay	1912	Victor 17034/Edison 10550 (2mincyl) (1912)
My Little Lovin' Sugar Baby	1912	Victor 17236
Nellie Kelly, I Love You	1922	Victor 18957
Nestle In Your Daddy's Arms	1921	Victor 18751
Night Trip To Buffalo (Two Irishmen In A Sleeping Car)	1910	Victor 16524
No One But Your Dear Old Dad	1916	Victor 17985
Ogalalla	1910	Victor 16497
Oh Johnny, Oh Johnny, Oh!	1917	Victor 18279
Old McDonald Had A Farm	1924	Victor 19265
On Her Neck She Wears A Yellow Ribbon	1918	Victor 18436
On The 5:15	1915	Victor 17704
On The Banks Of The Wabash	1913	Victor 17397

On The Mississippi	1912	Victor 17237
Over There	1917	Victor 18333
Paddy Duffy's Cart	1912	Victor 17056
Parisienne	1912	Victor 17239
Polly Put The Kettle On	1924	Victor 19322
Pucker Up Your Lips Miss Lindy	1912	Victor 17099
Ragtime Dream, The	1914	Victor 17535
Ragtime Violin	1912	Victor 17025/Edison 1806
Rebecca Of Sunny-Brook Farm	1914	Victor 17534
Rolling Stones (All Come Rolling Home Again)	1917	Victor 18215
Rosa Lee (or: Don't Be Foolish, Joe)	1911	Victor 16964
Row! Row! Row!	1913	Victor 17295
Sailin' Away On The Henry Clay	1917	Victor 18353
Sailing Down The Chesapeake Bay	1913	Victor 17411
She Gave Them All To Me	1910	Victor 16477
Siam	1916	Victor 17993
Since I Am The Man They Are Looking For	1910	Victor 16648
Skeleton Rag, The	1912	Victor 17041
Slippery Slide Trombone	1912	Victor 17090
Somebody Else, It's Always Somebody Else	1910	Victor 16707Victor 16956
Some Of These Days	1911	Victor 16834
Some Sunny Day	1922	Victor 18903
Songs Of Colleges: Army Blue	1913	Victor 17500
Stop! Look! Listen!	1921	Victor 18732
Stop That Rag	1911	Victor 16787
Strut, Miss Lizzie	1921	Victor 18799
Summer Days	1911	Victor 16879
Swanee Babe	1909	Victor 16433
Syncopated Boogie Boo	1913	Victor 17248
Tennessee, I Hear You Calling Me	1915	Victor 17666
Tennessee Moon	1912	Victor 17207
Texas Tommy Swing	1912	Victor 17079
That Hypnotizing Man	1911	Victor 17031
That Mysterious Rag	1911	Victor 16982
That Old Girl Of Mine	1912	Victor 17264
That Soothing Symphony	1916	Victor 17972
There's A Typical Tipperary Over Here	1920	Vocalion 14076A
There's Silver Now Where Only Gold Used To Be	1912	Victor 17107
They All Had A Finger In The Pie	1915	Victor 17704
Those Good Old Days Back Home	1916	Victor 17972
Toot, Toot, Tootsie Goodbye	1923	Victor 19006
Turkestan	1919	Columbia A-2728
Valley Flower	1910	Victor 16806
Washington Waddle, The	1911	Victor 16971
Way Down East Tonight	1915	Victor 17751
When I First Met You	1913	Victor 17426
When I'm Alone I'm Lonesome	1911	Victor 16884
When I Was Twenty-One And You Were Seventeen	1912	Victor 17057
When I Was Twenty-One And You Were Sweet Sixteen	1912	Edison 4mincyl 784
When You Wore A Tulip And I Wore A Big Red Rose	1914	Victor 17652
Where Do We Go From Here	1917	Victor 18335
Yanks Are At It Again, The	1918	Victor 18495
You Need A Rag	1913	Victor 17501
You're My Baby	1912	Victor 17114

American Quartet (2) & Byron G. Harlan

They Gotta Quit Kickin' My Dawg Aroun'	1912	Edison 1023 (4mincyl)/Victor 17065 (1912)

American Quartet (2) (with Walter Van Brunt)

Mary Was My Mother's Name	1912	Victor 17130

American Quartet (2), Billy Murray & Edna Brown with the

When You're Away	1912	Victor 17139

American Quartet (2), Billy Murray & the

Casey Jones	1910	Victor 16483
(Dance Of The) Grizzly Bear	1911	Victor 16681
He's A College Boy Now	1910	Victor 16492

American Quartet (2), Will Oakland &

Way Down South	1912	Victor 17146

American Quartet, Ada Jones & the

I'm Looking For A Nice Young Fellow Who Is Looking For A Nice Young Girl	1910	Victor 5811

American Quartet, Cal Stewart & the

Evening Time At Punkin Center	1919	Columbia A-2789/Emerson 10253 (1920)
Meeting Of The Hen Roost Club, A	1919	Columbia unissued
Pick 'Em Up Silas, Lay 'Em Down Zeke	1919	Perfect 11000/Silvertone 1205
Train Time At Pun'Kin Centre	1919	Columbia A-3851/Perfect 11001/Victor 18595

American Singers

Auld Lang Syne	1927	Columbia 1417-D/Conqueror 9101 (1938)
Darling Nellie Gray	1927	Edison DD 52636
Dear Old Girl	1930	Victor 22387
First Noel, The	1927	Columbia 1128-D
How Can I Leave Thee'	1927	Columbia 1703-D
I Need Thee Every Hour	1927	Columbia 1163-D
It Came Upon The Midnight Clear	1927	Columbia 1128-D
Mug Song, The	1930	Victor 22424
My Old Kentucky Home	1927	Columbia 1417-

Title	Year	Label/Number
On The Banks Of The Wabash	1930	D/Conqueror 9101 (1938) Victor 22387
On The Banks Of The Wabash Far Away	1927	Edison DD 52636
Rescue The Perishing	1927	Columbia 1163-D
Song Of The Navy, The	1930	Victor 24075
When The Little Ones Say 'Goodnight'	1927	Edison DD 52179
Why Adam Sinned	1927	Edison DD 52179

American Singers (with Rudy Vallee & his Connecticut Yankees)

Title	Year	Label/Number
To The Legion	1930	Victor 24075

Ames Brothers

Title	Year	Label/Number
Absence Makes The Heart Grow Fonder	1952	Coral 60804
Addio	1954	RCA Victor 47-5897/Coral 5897 (1954)
Adeste Fideles	1950	Coral 60268
Al-Lee-O', Al-Lee-Ay!	1952	Coral 60846
Always In My Dreams	1953	Coral 61005
And So I Waited Around	1952	Coral 60680
At The End Of The Rainbow	1953	Coral 60967
Auf Wiederseh'n Sweetheart	1952	Coral 60773
Barroom Polka	1949	Coral 60052/Coral 60400 (1951)
Because	1951	Coral 60339
Blind Barnabas	1952	Coral 60636
Blue Prelude	1950	Coral 60173
Boogie Woogie Maxixe	1953	RCA Victor 47-5530
Break The Bands That Bind Me	1952	Coral 60773
Bring Her Out Again (Fifi)	1950	Coral 60164
Bye Bye Blackbird	1948	Coral 24319/Decca 24319 (1949)
Can Anyone Explain' (No, No, No!)	1950	Coral 60253
Candy Bar Boogie	1953	Coral 60967
Can't I'	1953	Coral 60926
Christopher Sunday	1969	Coral 7566
Clancy Lowered The Boom	1949	Coral 60035/Coral 60154 (1950)/Coral 60399 (1951)
Crazy Cause I Love You	1952	Coral 60731
Cruising Down The River	1949	Coral 60035
Dancin' In The Streets	1959	RCA Victor 47-7474/Coral 7474 (1959)
Deep River	1952	Coral 60633
Did You Ever Get The Roses	1956	RCA Victor 47-6821/Coral 6821 (1957)
Do Nothin' Till You Hear From Me	1952	Coral 60870
Don't Believe A Word They Say	1954	Coral 61145/Coral 61127 (1954)
Don't Leave Me Now	1958	Coral 7167
Don't Lie To Me	1954	Coral 61145
Dorm! Dorm! (Sleep, Sleep)	1950	Coral 60185
Dry Bones	1952	Coral 60633
Everything's Gonna Be Alright	1951	Coral 60549
Far Away Places	1948	Coral 60016
Favorite Song, A	1952	Coral 60846
Forever Darling	1956	RCA Victor 47-6400/Coral 6400 (1956)
49 Shades Of Green	1956	Coral 6608
Game Of Love, The	1956	Coral 6720
Go Down Moses	1952	Coral 60635
God Rest Ye Merry Gentlemen	1950	Coral 60270
Good Fellow Medley, Etc.	1949	Coral 60017/Coral 60114 (1949)
Gotta Be This Or That	1955	RCA Victor 47-6177/Coral 6117 (1955)
Hark The Herald Angels	1950	Coral 60269
Hawaiian War Chant (Ta-Hu-Wa-Hu-Wai)	1951	Coral 60510
Helen Polka	1954	Coral 61127
Hoop-Dee-Doo	1950	Coral 60209/Coral 60397 (1951)
Hopelessly	1954	RCA Victor 47-5840
I Can't Believe That You're In Love With Me	1953	RCA Victor 47-5530
I Didn't Kiss The Blarney Stone	1950	Coral 60154
I Don't Mind Being All Alone	1950	Coral 60300
If I Live To Be A Hundred	1948	Decca 24447/Coral 24447 (1948)
If You Had All The World	1948	Decca 24329/Coral 24329 (1948)
If You Wanna See Mamie Tonight	1956	RCA Victor 47-6481/Coral 6481 (1956)
If You Want My Heart	1953	RCA Victor 47-5404
I Got A Cold For Xmas	1954	RCA Victor 47-5929/Coral 5929 (1954)
I Know Only One Way To Love You	1956	RCA Victor 47-6821/Coral 6821 (1957)
I'll Still Love You	1952	Coral 60617
I Love Her Oh! Oh! Oh!	1950	Coral 60153
I Love You Much Too Much	1951	Coral 60404
I'm Gonna Love You	1956	RCA Victor 47-6400/Coral 6400 (1956)
I'm Just Wild About Harry	1949	Coral 60017

Song	Year	Label/Number
I'm Looking Over A Four Leaf Clover	1948	Decca 24319/Coral 24319 (1948)
In Love	1958	RCA Victor 47-7142/Coral 7142 (1958)
In The Evening By The Moonlight	1951	Coral 60336
I Saw Esau	1956	Coral 6720
It Came Upon The Midnight Hour	1950	Coral 60269
It Only Hurts For A Little While	1956	RCA Victor 47-6481/Coral 6481 (1956)
I Wanna Love You	1952	Coral 60617
Jolly Old St. Nicholas	1951	Coral 60572
Joshua Fit De Battle Of Jericho	1952	Coral 60635
Just A Dream Of You Dear	1950	Coral 60336
Lazy River	1953	Coral 61060
Leave It To Your Heart	1954	RCA Victor 47-5764
Let's Walk And Talk	1954	RCA Victor 47-5764
Lingering Down The Lane	1949	Coral 60091
Little Gypsy	1958	RCA Victor 47-7142/Coral 7142 (1958)
Little Serenade	1958	Coral 7268
Lonely Wine	1953	Coral 60926
Lorelei	1948	Coral 60016
Lovely Lady Dressed In Blue	1952	Coral 60628/Coral 61723 (1952)
Love's Old Sweet Song	1951	Coral 60339
Loving Is Believing	1951	Coral 60352
Man, Man, Is For Woman Made	1954	RCA Victor 47-5644/Coral 5644 (1954)
Man On Fire	1957	RCA Victor 47-6851/Coral 6851 (1957)
Man With The Banjo, The	1954	RCA Victor 47-5644/Coral 5644
Marianna	1950	Coral 60185/Coral 60398 (1951)
Mason-Dixon Line	1959	RCA Victor 47-7526/Coral 7526 (1959)
Meet Me Tonight In Dreamland	1950	Coral 60338
Melodie D'Amour	1957	Coral 7056
Merci Beaucoup	1955	RCA Victor 47-6165/Coral 6165 (1955)
Moonlight Bay	1950	Coral 60338
More Beer	1948	Coral 60015/Coral 60399 (1951)
More Than I Care To Remember	1951	Coral 60363
Mother, At Your Feet Is Kneeling	1952	Coral 60628/Coral 61723 (1952)
Music By The Angels	1950	Coral 60333/Coral 60352 (1951)
My Bonnie Lassie	1955	RCA Victor 47-6208/Coral 6208 (1955)
My Favorite Song	1952	Coral 60846
My Love, My Life, My Happiness	1953	RCA Victor 47-5404/RCA Victor 47-6323 (1955)
My Love Serenade	1951	Coral 60404
My Love, Your Love	1955	Coral 6323
Naughty Lady Of Shady Lane, The	1954	RCA Victor 47-5897/Coral 5897
Next Time It Happens, The	1955	RCA Victor 47-6323/Coral 6323
Noah's Ark	1949	Coral 60092/Coral 60400 (1951)
No Moon At All (with Les Brown)	1953	Coral 60870
No One But You (In My Heart)	1958	Coral 7315
Now Hear This	1959	RCA Victor 47-7565/Coral 7567 (1959)
Now It's Me	1959	RCA Victor 47-7565/Coral 7567 (1959)
Oh Babe!	1950	Coral 60327
Oh Little Town Of Bethlehem	1950	Coral 60270
Oh, You Sweet One	1949	Coral 60065
Once Upon A Time	1953	RCA Victor 47-5325
One More Time	1954	RCA Victor 47-5840
Only, Only You	1951	Coral 60549
Only Your Love	1959	RCA Victor 47-7474
On The Street Of Regret	1948	Coral 24411/Decca 24422 (1948)
Pussy Cat	1958	RCA Victor 47-7315/Coral 7315 (1958)
(Put Another Nickel In) Music! Music! Music!	1950	Coral 60153
Rag Mop	1950	Coral 60140/Coral 60397 (1951)
Red River Rose	1958	RCA Victor 47-7413/Coral 7413 (1958)
Rockin' Shoes	1957	RCA Victor 47-6930/Coral 6930 (1957)
Sentimental Journey	1951	Coral 60566
Sentimental Me	1950	Coral 60140/Coral 60173 (1950)/Coral 65510 (1951)

Shadrack	1952	Coral 60634	Tree In The Meadow, A	1948	Coral 24411/Decca 24422B (1949)
Sheik Of Araby, The	1952	Coral 60680			
Silent Night	1950	Coral 60268	Twelve Days Of Christmas	1950	Coral 60267
Sing A Song Of Santa Claus	1952	Coral 60861	Undecided	1951	Coral 60566/Coral 65510 (1951)
Sing Until The Cows Come Home	1950	Coral 60164/Coral 60398 (1951)			
			Very Precious Love, A	1958	Coral 7167
Sittin' 'N Starin' 'N Rockin'	1950	Coral 60253	Wang Wang Blues	1951	Coral 60489
So Little Time	1957	Coral 7046	Wassail Song	1950	Coral 60267
Someone To Come Home To	1959	RCA Victor 47-7526/Coral 7526 (1959)	We'll Still Be Honey-Mooning	1949	Coral 60052
			What Do I Hear	1960	Coral 7566
			When Summer Comes Again	1958	RCA Victor 47-7413/Coral 7413 (1958)
Somewhere There Must Be Happiness	1951	Coral 60452			
Southern Cross	1955	RCA Victor 47-6177/Coral 6117 (1955)	When The Apple Blossoms Fall	1948	Coral 24447
			White Christmas	1949	Coral 60113
			Who Built The Ark	1952	Coral 60636
So Will I	1955	RCA Victor 47-6208/Coral 6208 (1955)	Who'll Take My Place	1951	Coral 60489
			Winter's Here Again	1952	Coral 60861
			Winter Wonderland	1949	Coral 60113
St. Bernard Waltz	1949	Coral 60065	Wrong Again	1955	RCA Victor 47-6165/Coral 6165 (1955)
Star Dust	1952	Coral 60751/Coral 61060 (1953)			
Stars Are The Windows Of Heaven	1950	Coral 60209	Yeah, Yeah, Yeah (It's So Good)	1957	RCA Victor 47-6851/Coral 6851 (1957)
Stay	1958	Coral 7268			
Still Waters And Green Pasture	1949	Coral 60091	(Yes I Need) Only Your Love	1959	Coral 7474
String Along	1952	Coral 60804	You Tell Me Your Dream I'll Tell You Mine	1951	Coral 60337
Summer Sweetheart	1956	Coral 6608			
Sweet Brown Eyed Baby	1955	RCA Victor 47-6044/Coral 6044 (1955)	You You You	1953	RCA Victor 47-5325
			You, You, You Are The One	1948	Coral 60015
Sweet Leilani	1951	Coral 60510	**Amherst Octette**		
Swing Low Sweet Chariot	1952	Coral 60634	Cheer For Old Amherst	1912	Columbia A-1182
Sympathetic Eyes	1955	RCA Victor 47-6044/Coral 6044 (1955)	Lord Jeffrey Amherst	1912	Columbia A-1182
			Amory Brothers (Ames Brothers)		
			Moonlight And Roses	1948	Majestic 1196
Take Me Along	1959	Coral 7604	Winter Song	1948	Majestic 1196
Tammy	1957	RCA Victor 47-6930/Coral 6930 (1957)	**Amory Male Quartet**		
			Keep Your Eyes On Jesus	1928	Okeh 45288
			We're Drifting On	1928	Okeh 45288
Tears Of Happiness	1949	Coral 60092	**Amphion Quartet**		
Tell Me A Story	1948	Decca 24329/Coral 24329 (1948)	Apple Blossom Time	1921	Brunswick 2057
			Feather Your Nest	1920	Brunswick 2063
There'll Always Be Xmas	1954	RCA Victor 47-3929/Coral 3929 (1954)	I Want To Be The Leader Of The Band	1921	Brunswick 2068
			My Mammy	1921	Brunswick 2068
Thing, The	1950	Coral 60333	**Andrews Sisters**		
Thirsty For Your Kisses	1950	Coral 60300	Adios	1952	Decca 28342
This Is Fiesta	1953	Coral 61005	Alexander's Ragtime Band	1948	Decca 24424
Three Dollars & Ninety Nine Cents	1951	Coral 60363	All The World To Me	1951	Decca 27878
			Amelia Cordelia McHugh-McWho'	1949	Decca 24536
Till We Meet Again	1951	Coral 60337			
Ting-A-Ling-A Jingle	1951	Coral 60572	Any Bonds Today'	1941	Decca 4044
Too Many Women	1951	Coral 60452	Atlanta Georgia	1946	Decca 18833
To Think You've Chosen me	1950	Coral 60327	At Sonya's Caf	1942	Decca 18312

Title	Year	Release
Aurora	1941	Decca 3732/Decca 25096 (1947)
Avocado	1946	Decca 18840
Azusa	1946	Decca 18899
Beat Me Daddy, Eight To The Bar	1940	Decca 3375/Decca 23607 (1946)
Beer Barrel Polka	1939	Decca 2462/Decca 23609 (1946)
Beer Barrel Polka (Roll Out The Barrel)	1940	Radio Broadcast 1/18/40
Begin The Beguine	1939	
Begin The Beguine	1940	Radio Broadcast 1/13/40
Bei Mir Bist Du Schoen	1937	Decca 1562/Decca 23605 (1946)
Bei Mir Bist Du Sch	1939	Radio Broadcast 12/27/39
Bella Bella Marie	1948	Decca 24499
Between Two Trees	1951	Decca 27421
Billy Boy	1938	Decca 2214/Decca 23606 (1946)
Blond Sailor, The	1945	Decca 18700/Decca 27878 (1951)
Blossoms On The Bough, The	1949	Decca 24822
Boogie Woogie Bugle Boy	1941	Decca 3598
Booglie Wooglie Piggy, The	1941	Decca 3960
Boolee Boolee Boon	1942	Decca 18319
Bounce Me Brother With A Solid Four	1941	Decca 3598
Bride And Groom Polka, The	1948	Decca 24406
Brighten The Corner	1951	Decca 14539
Buckle Down Winsocki	1996	Magic CD 49
Bushel And A Peck, A	1950	Decca 27252
Can't We Talk It Over'	1950	Decca 27115
Carioca, The	1951	Decca 27757
Carmen's Boogie	1952	Decca 28342
Chattanooga Choo Choo	1941	Decca 4094
Chico's Love Song	1939	Decca 2756
Chico's Love Song	1940	Radio Broadcast 1/16/40
Choo'N Gum	1950	Decca 24998
Christmas Candles	1949	Decca 24748
Christmas Island	1946	Decca 23722/MCA 65020 (1946)
Christmas Tree Angel, The	1950	Decca 27251
Coax Me A Little Bit	1946	Decca 18833
Cock-Eyed Mayor Of Kaunakakai, The	1940	Decca 3245/Decca 28295 (1952)
Coffee Song, The	1946	Decca 23740
Comes Love	2002	Capitol/EMI CD 538416
Come To Baby Do	1996	Magic CD 49
Count Your Blessings	1950	Decca 14502
Daddy	1941	Decca 3821/Decca 27757 (1951)
Dimples And Cherry Cheeks	1951	Decca 27652
Do I Love You'	2003	BMG Heritage CD
Donkey Serenade, The	1940	Radio Broadcast 3/21/40
Don't Blame Me	1948	Decca 23827
Don't Rob Another Man's Castle	1949	Decca 24592
Don't Sit Under The Apple Tree	1942	Decca 18312
Don't Worry 'Bout Strangers	1948	Decca 24533
Down By The O-hi-o (O My O!)	1940	Decca 3065
Down In The Valley	1943	Decca 18572/Decca 27894 (1951)
Dreams Come Tumbling Down	1952	Decca 28116
East Of The Rockies	1943	Decca 18533
East Of The Sun	1953	Decca 28482
Elmer's Tune	1941	Decca 4008
Ethelena	1943	Decca 18563
Every Time I Fall In Love	1996	Magic CD 49
Farewell Blues	2003	BMG Heritage CD
Ferdinand The Bull	1938	
Ferryboat Serenade	1940	Decca 3328
For All We Know	1941	Decca 4094
From The Land Of The Sky Blue	1938	Decca 1912
Fugue For Tinhorns	1953	Decca 28680
Gimme Some Skin, My Friend	1941	Decca 3871
Girl And A Sailor, A	1996	Magic CD 49
Glory Of Love, The	1950	Decca 27202
Goodbye Darling, Hello Friend	1951	Decca 27834
Guys And Dolls	1950	Decca 27252
Hang Your Head In Shame	1949	Decca 28163
Heat Wave	1948	Decca 24425
He Bought My Soul At Calvary	1949	Decca 14566
Helena	1943	Decca 18563
Her Bathing Suit Never Got Wet	1946	Decca 18840
Here Comes The Navy	1942	Decca 18497
He Rides The Range (For Republic)	1949	Decca 24809
He Said-She Said	1942	Decca 4153
His Feet Too Big For De Bed	1947	Decca 23860
Hit The Road	1940	Decca 3328
Hohokus, New Jersey	1949	Decca 24645
Hold Tight, Hold Tight	1938	Decca 2214/Decca 23606/
Hold Tight, Hold Tight	1940	Radio Broadcast 2/27/40
Homework	1949	Decca 24660
Honey	1941	Decca 4008
Hooray For Love	2002	Capitol/EMI CD 538416
How Lucky You Are	1947	Decca 24171
How Many Times'	1948	Decca 24426
Hula Ba Luau	2007	WTNTS CD
Hummingbird, The	1942	Decca 18464
Hurry! Hurry! Hurry!	1949	Decca 24613
I Can Dream, Can't I	1949	Decca 24705
I Could Write A Book	1957	Capitol LP T-790

100 Years of Harmony: 1850 to 1950

Title	Year	Release
I Didn't Know The Gun Was Loaded	1949	Decca 24613
Idle Chatter	1952	Decca 28276
I'd Like To Hitch A Ride With Santa Claus	1950	Decca 27251
I Don't Know Why (I Just Do)	1946	Decca 18899
If I Had A Boy Like You	1953	Decca 28481
I Hate To Lose You	1948	Decca 24380
I'll Be With You In Apple Blossom Time	1941	Decca 3622
I'll Pray For You	1942	Decca 4153
I'll Walk Alone	2003	Sepia CD 1020
I Love To Tell The Story	1950	Decca 14509
I Love You Much Too Much	1940	Radio Broadcast 1/30/40
I Love You Much Too Much	1943	Decca 18563
I Married An Angel	1938	Decca 1912
I'm Bitin' My Fingernails And Thinking Of You	1949	Decca 24592
(I'm Getting) Corns For My Country	1944	Decca 18628
I'm Gonna Paper All My Walls	1950	Decca 24998
I'm In A Jam	1951	Decca 27432
I'm In A Jam (With Baby)	1944	Decca 18628
I'm In Love Again	1951	Decca 27635
I'm On A Seesaw Of Love	1951	Decca 27910
In The Mood	1939	Radio Broadcast 12/27/39
In The Mood	1953	Decca 28482
I Remember Mama	1951	Decca 27537
It Is No Secret	1949	Decca 14566
It Never Entered My Mind	1951	Decca 27635
It's A Blue World	2003	BMG Heritage CD (recorded 1940)
It's All Over But The Memories	2003	Sepia CD 1020 (recorded 1951)
It's Easier Said Than Done	1938	Decca 1691
It's Fun Learning Music	1952	Decca 28042
It's The Talk Of The Town	1996	Magic CD 49
I Used To Love You	1951	Decca 27700
I've Got A Guy In Kalamazoo	1942	Decca 18464
I've Got No Strings	1940	Radio Broadcast 2/13/40
I've Just Got To Get Out Of The Habit	1950	Decca 27007
I Wanna Be Loved	1950	Decca 27007
I Want My Mama (Mama Yo Quiero)	1940	Decca 3310
I Want To Go Back To Michigan (Down On The Farm)	1948	Decca 24424
I Wish I Had A Dime (For Ev'ry Time I Missed You)	1941	Decca 3966
I Wish I Knew	1951	Decca 27421
I, Yi, Yi, Yi, Yi (I Like You Very Much)	1941	Decca 3622
Jack, Jack, Jack	1947	Decca 23860
Jack Of All Trades	1941	Decca 4097
Jammin'	1937	Brunswick 7863
Jealous	1941	Decca 4019/Decca 25303 (1948)
Jitterbug's Lullaby, A Part 1	1938	
Johnny Fedora And Alice Blue	1945	Decca 23474
Johnny Peddler	1940	Decca 3553
Jolly Fella Tarantella	1950	Decca 24965
Joseph! Joseph!	1938	Decca 1691/Decca 23605 (1946)
Jumpin' Jive (Jim Jam Jump), The	1939	Decca 2756
Just A Simple Melody	1937	Decca 1496
Lady From 29 Palms, The	1947	Decca 23976
Let A Smile Be Your Umbrella	1949	Decca 24548
Let's Have Another One	1940	Decca 3013
Let's Pack Our Things	1940	Decca 3245
Let The Lower Lights Be Burning	1951	Decca 14539
Let There Be Love	2002	Capitol/EMI CD 538416
Lily Belle	1945	Decca 18700
Little Brown Jug	2003	BMG Heritage CD (recorded in 1940)
Little Red Fox, The (N'ya N'ya Ya Can't Catch Me)	2003	BMG Heritage CD (recorded 1940)
Little Sally Waters	2003	BMG Heritage CD (recorded 1940)
Lonesome Mama	1941	Brunswick 03156
Long Time No See	1939	
Love Is Here To Stay	2003	Sepia CD 1020 (recorded 1951)
Love Is Such A Cheat	1951	Decca 27760
Love Is Where You Find It	1938	Decca 2016
Lovely Night	1949	Decca 24717
Love Sends A Little Gift Of Roses	1954	Decca 28929
Lullabye To A Little Jitterbug	1938	Decca 2082
Lullaby Of Broadway	1947	Decca 23824
Lying In The Hay	1951	Decca 27760
Malaguena	1949	Decca 24645
Massachusetts	1942	Decca 18497
Mean To Me	1940	Decca 3440/Decca 25303 (1948)
Merry Christmas Polka	1949	Decca 24748
Mister Five By Five	1942	Decca 18470
Money Is The Root Of All Evil	1945	Decca 23474
Money Song, The	1948	Decca 24499
More Beer!	1949	Decca 24548
Music Lessons	1952	Decca 28116
Music Makers	1941	Decca 3732
Muskrat Ramble	1950	Decca 24981
My Dearest Uncle Sam	1947	Decca 23824
My Love, The Blues And Me	1954	Decca 29149
My Love Went Without Water	1940	Decca SA 1873
My Mom	1951	Decca 27537
My Romance	1957	Capitol LP T-860

Title	Year	Label/Number
Near You	1947	Decca 24171
Nevertheless	2002	Capitol/EMI CD 538416
Nice Work If You Can Get It	1937	Decca 1562
Nickel Serenade, The	1941	Decca 3960
Ninety And Nine, The	1950	Decca 14521
Nobody's Darling But Mine	1951	Decca 27834
No Deposit No Return	1952	Decca 28492
Now That I'm In Love	1953	Decca 28680
Of Thee I Sing	2002	Capitol/EMI CD 538416
Oh! Faithless Maid	1938	Decca 1875
Oh! Ma-Ma! (The Butcher Boy)	1938	Decca 1859
Oh He Loves Me	1940	Decca 3310
Oh Johnny, Oh Johnny, Oh!	1940	Decca 2840
Oh Johnny, Oh Johnny, Oh!	1940	Radio Broadcast 2/8/40
Old Don Juan	1953	Decca 28483
One For The Wonder	1952	Decca 28276
One Meat Ball	1944	Decca 18636
One O'Clock Jump	1940	Radio Broadcast 2/29/40
One, Two, Three O'Leary	1938	Brunswick 02837
Only For Americans	1949	Decca 24660
On The Avenue	1947	Decca 24102
Ooooo-Oh Boom	1938	Decca 1744
Open Door, Open Arms	1949	Decca 24822
Pagan Love Song	1938	Decca 1859
Pennsylvania 6-5000	1940	Decca 3375
Pennsylvania Polka	1942	Decca 18398/Decca 23608 (1946)
Penny A Kiss - A Penny A Hug, A	1951	Decca 27414
Piccolo Pete	1953	Decca 28481
Play Me A Hurtin' Tune	1952	Decca 27910
Poor-Whip-Poor-Will	1952	Decca 27979
Pross-Tchai (Goodbye)	1939	Decca 2082
Put That Ring On My Finger	1945	Decca 18726
Rainy Day Refrain, A	1950	Decca 27202
Rainy Night In Rio, A	1946	Decca 23740
Rancho Pillow	1941	Decca 4019
Red River Valley	1946	Decca 18780/Decca 25149 (1947)/Decca 27894 (1951)
Rhumboogie	1940	Decca 3097
Rock Rock-A-Bye Baby	1939	Decca 2414
Rum And Coca Cola	1944	Decca 18636/Decca 25096 (1947)/Decca 29995 (1957)
Rumba Jumps, The	1940	Radio Broadcast 1/25/40
Runnin' Wild (An Ebony Jazz Tune)	2003	BMG Heritage CD (recorded in 1940)
Run, Rabbit, Run!	2003	BMG Heritage CD (recorded in 1940)
Run, Run, Run	1948	Decca 23827
Sabre Dance	1948	Decca 24427
Say "Si Si" (Para Vigo Me Voy)	1940	Decca 3013
Say 'Si Si' (In Spain They Say 'Si Si')	1940	Radio Broadcast 1/3/40
Says My Heart	1938	Decca 1875
Scrub Me Mama With A Boogie Beat	1941	Decca 3553/Decca 23607 (1946)/Brunswick 03157
Shall We Gather At The River	1950	Decca 14521
Sha-Sha	1938	Decca 1974
Shoo-Shoo Baby	1943	Decca 18572
Short'nin' Bread	1938	Decca 1744
Shrine Of St. Cecilia, The	1941	Decca 4097
Sing A Tropical Song	1944	Decca 18581/Decca 25095 (1947)
Six Jerks In A Jeep	1942	
Sleepy Serenade	1941	Decca 3821
Sleigh Ride	1950	Decca 27310
Softly And Tenderly	1950	Decca 14509
Some Sunny Day	1948	Decca 24426
Song Is You, The	2008	EMI CD
Sonny Boy	1941	Decca 3871
South American Way	1940	Decca 2840/Decca 25095 (1947)
South Of The Border (Down Mexico Way)	2003	BMG Heritage CD (recorded in 1940)
Stars Are The Windows Of Heaven	1950	Decca 24965
Straighten Up And Fly Right	1944	Decca 18606
Strip Polka	1942	Decca 18470
Sweet Marie	1947	Decca 24102
Sweet Molly Malone	1940	Decca 3440
Sweet Potato Piper	2003	BMG Heritage CD (recorded in 1940)
Tea For Two	1957	Capitol LP T-860
Tegucigalpa	1953	Decca 28773
That Ever Lovin' Rag	1952	Decca 28042
That's A-Plenty	1950	Chesterfield Radio Show 3/23/50
That's The Chance You Take	2003	Sepia CD 1020 (recorded in 1952)
That's The Moon, My Son	1942	Decca 18398
There'll Be A Jubilee	1944	Decca 18581
There's A Rainbow In The Valley	1954	Decca 29149
There Was A Night	1951	Decca 27652
There Will Never Be Another You	1950	Decca 27115
This Little Piggie Went To Market	1954	Decca 28929
Three Bells, The	1951	Decca 27858
Three Little Sisters	1942	Decca 18319
Three O'Clock In The Morning	1951	Decca 27432
Tica-ti Tica-Ta	1941	Brunswick 03337

100 Years of Harmony: 1850 to 1950

Tico Tico	1944	Decca 18606/Decca 25098 (1947)
Ti-Pi-Tin	1938	Decca 1703/Decca 25097 (1947)
Too Fat Polka	1947	Decca 24268
Toolie Oolie Doolie (The Yodel Polka)	1948	Decca 24380
(Toy Balloon) Boolee Boolee Boo	1942	Decca 18319
Tu-Li-Tulip Time	1938	Decca 1974
Turntable Song, The	1947	Decca 23976
Tuxedo Junction	1940	Decca 3097
Tuxedo Junction	1940	Radio Broadcast 2/27/40
Underneath The Arches	1948	Decca 24490
Underneath The Linden Tree	1949	Decca 24560
Victory Polka		V-Disc 232
Waiting For The Train To Come In	1996	Magic CD 49
Wake Up And Live	1937	Brunswick 7872
Walk With A Wiggle	1950	Decca 24981
Wedding Of Lili Marlene, The	1949	Decca 24705
Wedding Samba, The	1950	Decca 14502
We Just Couldn't Say Good-Bye	1948	Decca 24406
Welcome Song, The	1945	Decca 18726
Well, All Right	1946	Decca 23606
Well All Right (Tonight's The Night)	1939	Decca 2462/Decca 23609 (1946)
What To Do	1942	Decca 4182
When A Prince Of A Fella Meets A Cinderella	1938	Decca 2016
When Johnny Comes Marching Home	1943	Decca 18533
When The Midnight Choo Choo Leaves For Alabam	1948	Decca 24425
Where Have We Met Before'	1938	Decca 1703
Why Don't We Do This More Often	1941	Decca 3966
Why Talk About Love	1937	Decca 1496
Windmill Song, The	1951	Decca 27858
Winter Wonderland	1946	Decca 23722/MCA 65020 (1946)
With Every Breath I Take	2002	Capitol/EMI CD 538416
Wondering	1952	Decca 27979
Woodpecker Song, The	1940	Decca 3065
Yes, My Darling Daughter	1941	Decca 3599
Yodelin' Jive	1940	Radio Broadcast 1/4/40
You Call Everybody Darling	1948	Decca 24490
You Don't Know How Much You Can Suffer	1939	Decca 2414
You Do Something To Me	1957	Capitol LP T-860
Younger Than Springtime	2003	EMI CD 5813482
You're A Lucky Fellow	1941	Decca 3599
You're Just A Flower From An Old Bouquet	1942	
You're Off To See The World	2002	Jasmine CD 387
Your Red Wagon	1947	Decca 24268
You Too, You Too'	1953	Decca 28680
You Was	1949	Decca 24560
Zing Zing-Zoom Zoom	1951	Decca 27414
Zoot Suit (For My Sunday Gal), A	1942	Decca 4182
Back In Your Own Back Yard	1958	Capitol ED 26 0417
Barney Google	1958	Capitol ED 26 0417
Collegiate	1958	Capitol ED 26 0417
Don't Bring Lulu	1958	Capitol ED 26 0417
In The Garden	1950	Decca 14502
Japanese Sandman, The	1958	Capitol ED 26 0417
Keep Your Skirts Down, Mary Ann	1958	Capitol ED 26 0417
Last Night On The Back Porch	1958	Capitol ED 26 0417
Me Too	1958	Capitol ED 26 0417
Show Me The Way To Go Home	1958	Capitol ED 26 0417
Smile Will Go A Long Long Way, A	1958	Capitol ED 26 0417
Telephone Song, The	1950	Decca 27310
That Naughty Waltz	1958	Capitol ED 26 0417
When Francis Dances With Me	1958	Capitol ED 26 0417

Andrews Sisters (with Al Jolson)

Old Piano Roll Blues, The	1950	Decca 27024
'Way Down Yonder In New Orleans	1950	Decca 27024

Andrews Sisters (with Alfred Apaka)

Cockeyed Mayor Of Kannakakai, The	1950	Decca 28295
Fair Hawaii	1950	Decca 28296
Goodnight Aloha	1952	Decca 28297
Ke Kali Nei Au	1950	Decca 28296
King's Serenade	1952	Decca 28295
Malihini Mele	1952	Decca 28297
My Isle Of Golden Dreams	1952	Decca 28294
Nalani	1952	Decca 28294

Andrews Sisters (with Billy May)

No, Baby	1957	Capitol 3658

Andrews Sisters (with Bing Crosby & Dick Haymes)

Anything You Can Do	1947	Brunswick 03809/Decca 40039
There's No Business Like Show Business	1947	Brunswick 03809/Decca 40039

Andrews Sisters (with Bing Crosby & Nat King Cole)

May The Good Lord Bless And Keep You	1951	Chesterfield Radio Show 2/28/51

Andrews Sisters (with Bing Crosby)

Ac-Cent-Tchu-Ate The Positive	1945	Decca 23379
Along The Navajo Trail	1945	Decca 23437
Apalachicola, Fla.	1948	Decca 24282
Ask Me No Questions	1950	Decca 24942
At The Flying "W"	1948	Decca 24481

Song	Year	Label/Number
Betsy	1949	Decca 24718/Decca 27555 (1951)
Black Ball Ferry Line	1951	Decca 27631
Ciribiribin	1939	Decca 2800
Cool Water	1952	Decca 28419
Don't Fence Me In	1944	Decca 23364/Decca 23484 (1946)
Forsaking All Others	1951	Decca 27477
Freedom Train, The	1947	Decca 23999
Get Your Kicks On Route 66	1946	Decca 23569
Good, Good, Good	1945	Decca 23437
Go West, Young Man	1947	Decca 23885
Have I Told You Lately That I Love You'	1950	Decca 24827
Here Comes Santa Claus	1950	Decca 24658
High On The List	1950	Decca 27173
Hot Time In The Town Of Berlin, A	1944	Decca 23350
Hundred And Sixty Acres, A	1948	Decca 24481
If I Were A Bell	2003	Sepia CD 1020 (recorded in 1950)
I'll Si-Si Ya In Bahia	1952	Decca 28256
Is You Is, Or Is You Ain't, My Baby'	1944	Decca 23350
Jing-A-Ling Jing-A-Ling	1950	Decca 27242
Jingle Bells	1943	Decca 23281
Life Is So Peculiar	1950	Decca 27173
Live Oak Tree, The	1952	Decca 28256
Lock, Stock And Barrel	1950	Decca 24942
Mele Kalikimaka	1950	Decca 27228
Parade Of The Wooden Soldiers	1950	Decca 27242
Pistol Packin' Mama	1943	Decca 23277/Decca 23484 (1946)
Poppa Santa Claus	1950	Decca 27228
Quicksilver	1950	Decca 24827
Santa Claus Is Coming To Town	1943	Decca 23281
South America, Take It Away	1946	Decca 23569
South Rampart Street Parade	1952	Decca 28419
Sparrow In The Tree Top	1951	Decca 27477
Tallahassee	1947	Decca 23885
There's A Fellow Waiting In Poughkeepsie	1945	Decca 23379
Three Caballeros, The	1944	Decca 23364
Twelve Days Of Christmas	1950	Decca 24658
Vic'try Polka	1943	Decca 23277
Weddin' Day	1949	Decca 24718/Decca 27555 (1951)
Yodeling Ghost, The	1951	Decca 27631
Yodelin' Jive	1939	Decca 2800
You Don't Have To Know The Language	1948	Decca 24282

Andrews Sisters (with Bob Cats)

Song	Year	Label/Number
Begin The Beguine	1939	Decca 2290/Decca 25097 (1947)
Long Time To See	1939	Decca 2290

Andrews Sisters (with Burl Ives)

Song	Year	Label/Number
Blue Tail Fly	1948	Decca 24463
I'm Going Down The Road	1948	Decca 24463

Andrews Sisters (with Carmen Miranda)

Song	Year	Label/Number
Ca-Room' Pa Pa	1950	Decca 24979
Cuanto La Gusta	1948	Decca 24479
I See, I See (Asi, Asi)	1950	Decca 24841
Matador, The	1948	Decca 24479
Wedding Samba, The	1950	Decca 24841
Yipsee-I-D	1950	Decca 24979

Andrews Sisters (with Dan Dailey)

Song	Year	Label/Number
I Had A Hat (When I Came In)	1949	Decca 24610
In The Good Old Summertime	1949	Decca 24605
Take Me Out To The Ball Game	1949	Decca 24605
When Clancy Lowered The Boom	1949	Decca 24610

Andrews Sisters (with Danny Kaye)

Song	Year	Label/Number
Amelia Cordelia McHugh	1949	Decca 24536
Beatin', Bangin' 'N Scratchin'	1949	Decca 24536
Big Brass Band From Brazil	1948	Decca 24361
Bread And Butter Woman	1947	Decca 23940
Ching-Ara-Sa	1950	Decca 27261
Civilization (Bongo, Bongo, Bongo)	1947	Decca 23940
It's A Quiet Town	1948	Decca 24361
Merry Christmas At Grandmother's, A	1950	Decca 24769
Old Piano Roll Blues, The	1950	Decca 27024
Put 'Em In A Box Tie 'Em With	1948	Decca 24462
Songs From Mr. Music	1950	Decca 27261
'Way Down Yonder In New Orleans	1950	Decca 27024
Woody Woodpecker, The	1948	Decca 24462

Andrews Sisters (with Desi Arnaz)

Song	Year	Label/Number
Mambo Man, The	1953	Decca 28483

Andrews Sisters (with Dick Haymes)

Song	Year	Label/Number
Adieu	2007	WNTS CD (recorded in 1949)
Great Day	1946	Decca 23412
Here In My Heart	1952	Decca 28213
I'd Love To Call You My Sweetheart	1948	Decca 24504
I'm Sorry	1952	Decca 28213
I Ought To Know More About You	2003	Sepia CD 1020 (recorded in 1950)
Love Sends A Little Gift	1953	Decca 28929
My Sin	1948	Decca 24320
Pack Up Your Troubles	1946	Decca 23412
Teresa	1948	Decca 24320
This Little Piggie	1953	Decca 28929
What Did I Do'	1948	Decca 24504

Andrews Sisters (with Eddy Heywood)

Song	Year	Label/Number
House Of Blue Lights, The	1946	Decca 23461
Man Is A Brother To A Mule, A	1946	Decca 23461
Them That Has, Gets	1946	Decca 23656

Andrews Sisters (with Les Paul)
Rumors Are Flying　　　　　　　1946　Decca 23656
Andrews Sisters (with Ray Eberle)
Indian Summer　　　　　　　　　1940　Radio Broadcast 1/16/40
Andrews Sisters (with Red Foley
She'll Never Know　　　　　　　1954　Decca 29222
Andrews Sisters (with Red Foley)
Baby Blues　　　　　　　　　　　2003　Sepia CD 1020 (recorded in 1951)
Bury Me Beneath The Willow　　　1954　Decca 29222
I Want To Be With You Always　　1951　Decca 27609
Lonely Night　　　　　　　　　　1949　Decca 24717
Satins And Lace　　　　　　　　　1951　Decca 27609
Unless You're Free　　　　　　　　1953　Decca 28767
Where Is Your Wandering Mother Tonight　1949　Decca 28163
Whispering Hope　　　　　　　　1949　Decca 24717
Andrews Sisters (with Russ Morgan)
Charley My Boy　　　　　　　　　1949　Decca 24812
Linger Awhile　　　　　　　　　　1952　Decca 28143
Now! Now! Now! Is The Time　　　1949　Decca 24664
Oh, You Sweet One　　　　　　　1949　Decca 24664
She Wore A Yellow Ribbon　　　　1949　Decca 24812
Wabash Blues　　　　　　　　　　1952　Decca 28143
Andrews Sisters (with Skip Martin)
Don't Be That Way　　　　　　　　1953　Decca 28480
Sing Sing Sing　　　　　　　　　　1952　Decca 28480
Andrews Sisters (with the Harmonica Gentlemen)
Heartbreaker　　　　　　　　　　1948　Decca 24427
Andrews Sisters and Curt Massey
Christmas Candles　　　　　　　　1996　Magic CD 49
I Wish I Were In Michigan　　　　1996　Magic CD 49
Patience And Fortitude　　　　　　1946　Decca 18780
Andrews Sisters and Curt Massey & the Ambassadors
Symphony　　　　　　　　　　　1996　Magic CD 49
Andrews Sisters, Leon Belasco & the
There's A Lull In My Life　　　　　1937　Brunswick 7872
Andrews, Patti and Curt Massey
Baby Won't You Please Come Home　1996　Magic CD 49
I'm Gonna Love That Girl　　　　　1996　Magic CD 49
That's For Me　　　　　　　　　　1996　Magic CD 49
Anne, Judy and Zeke
Ain't Gonna Grieve My Lord And More　1933　Okeh (unreleased)
Don't Let My Mother Know　　　　1933　Okeh 45578
Me And My Still　　　　　　　　　1933　Okeh 45576
Mississippi Waters　　　　　　　　1933　Okeh 45578
My Old Model T　　　　　　　　　1933　Okeh (unreleased)
When The Sun Goes Down The Hill (And The Moon Begins To Rise)　1933　Okeh 45576

Antlers
In The Hills Of Old Kentucky　　　1952　Decca 28831
Antlers of Miami
I Don't Mind Being All Alone　　　1951　Artists 1260
Just In Case You Change Your Mind　1951　Artists 1260
Anything Goes' Foursome
Gypsy In Me　　　　　　　　　　1934　Victor 24817
Lady Fair　　　　　　　　　　　　1934　Victor 24817
Apollo Jubilee Quartet
Swing Low Sweet Chariot　　　　　1912　Columbia A-1169
Apollo Male Quartet
Shout All Over God's Heaven　　　1912　Columbia A-1169
Apollo Male Trio
Medley Of Old Time Songs, Part 3　1923　Perfect 11033
Medley Of Old Time Songs, Part 4　1923　Perfect 11033
Apollo Quartet
Tenting On The Old Campground　189'　Berliner 4264
When The Corn Is Waving　　　　1911　Victor 16858
Apollo Quartette
Camp Meeting　　　　　　　　　1912　Columbia
Little David　　　　　　　　　　　1912　Columbia
Aragon Trio
If I'm Dreaming　　　　　　　　　1929　Victor
Put A Little Salt On The Bluebird's Tail　1929　Victor
To Be Forgotten　　　　　　　　　1929　Victor 22236
Archibald Brothers Quartette
Juanita　　　　　　　　　　　　　1910　Columbia A-0903
That Beautiful Land　　　　　　　1910　Columbia A-5232
Two Roses　　　　　　　　　　　1910　Columbia A-0903
Work For The Night Is Coming　　1910　Columbia A-5232
Arden, Victor, Phil Ohman & their Orchestra (with Revelers)
Funny Face　　　　　　　　　　　1927　Victor
Aristocrats
Baby, Oh Where Can You Be　　　1929　Banner 2439
I've Got A Feeling I'm Falling　　　1929　Banner 2338
Singing In The Rain　　　　　　　1929　Banner 2435
Aristo-Kats
Ain't That Gravy Good　　　　　　1947　RCA Victor 20-2243
Boogie In 'C'　　　　　　　　　　1946　RCA Victor 20-1954
It Makes Me Blue　　　　　　　　1946　RCA Victor 20-2066
Jack, You're Dead!　　　　　　　　1947　RCA Victor 20-2243
Lady Be Good　　　　　　　　　　1946　RCA Victor 20-2066
Like I Need A Hole In The Head　　1947　RCA Victor 20-2299
Spider And The Fly, The　　　　　1947　RCA Victor 20-

Watch Yourself Baby	1946	RCA Victor 20-2299 1954
Artists' Quartette		
Come My Soul	1911	Columbia
Hark, Hark My Soul	1911	Columbia A-1097
Holy Ghost With Light Divine	1911	Columbia A-992
Prayer Of Thanksgiving	1911	Columbia A-992
Stars Of The Summer Night	1911	Columbia A-1019
Stein Song, A	1911	Columbia
'Vira	1911	Columbia A-1019
Ash, Sam & the Crescent Trio		
Leave Me With A Smile	1921	Okeh 4526
Ash, Samuel & Quartet		
My Lady Of The Telephone	1916	Columbia A-1921
Ash, Samuel with Knickerbocker Quartet		
I Wasn't Born To Be Lonesome	1917	Columbia A-2221
Ashford Quartet		
Out On The Ocean	1929	Brunswick 456
Ready To Go I'll Be	1929	Brunswick 402
Where Is Your Boy Tonight	1929	Brunswick 402
You Can't Make A Monkey Out Of Me	1929	Brunswick 456
Atco Quartet		
Don't Be Knocking	1928	Columbia 15312-D
Rich Young Ruler, The	1928	Columbia 15312-D
Atlanta Harmony Singers		
Alone	1928	Champion 15634
In The Morning	1928	Champion 15616
Join That Band	1928	Champion 15634
Old Ark's A-Moverin', The	1928	Champion 15616
Auditones		
As Years Go By	1947	Rainbow 10025
Near To You	1947	Rainbow 10025
Audrey Male Quartet		
Hold To God's Unchanging Hand	1928	Okeh 45210
Oh Beautiful City	1928	Okeh 45210
Aunt Jemima Novelty Four		
Go Down Moses - Medley	1929	Brunswick
Joshua Fought De Battle Of Jericho	1929	Brunswick
Judge For A Day	1929	Brunswick 7055
Minstrel, The	1929	Brunswick
Nobody Knows De Trouble I Seen	1929	Brunswick
Nobody Knows You When You're Down And Out	1929	Brunswick 7056
Po-Mona	1929	
You're Going To Leave The Old Town Jim	1929	Brunswick 7056
Avoca Quartet		
He Lives On High	1927	Okeh 45182
My Precious Mother	1927	Okeh 45182
Avon Comedy Four		
Clancy's Minstrels	1924	Victor 35750
Cohen's Wedding	1916	Victor 35602
Come On Papa	1918	Columbia A-2692
Gila Galah Galoo	1916	Victor 18125/Emerson 7119 (1916)
Ginsberg's Stomp Speech	1916	Victor 35606
Hungarian Restaurant Scene	1916	Victor 35602
I'm Crazy Over Every Girl In France	1917	Columbia A-2399
I'm Going Way Back Home And Have A Wonderful Time	1916	Victor 18088
My Mother's Rosary	1916	Victor 18081
New School Teacher, The	1924	Victor 35750
Oh What A Time For The Girlies When The Boys Come Marching Home	1918	Columbia A-2692
On A Summer Night	1916	Victor 18129
Professor's Birthday, The	1916	Victor 35606
Songs Of Yesterday	1916	Victor 18126/Emerson 7134 (1916)
Sweetest Melody Of All, The	1916	Emerson 7138
Way Out Yonder In The Golden West	1916	Victor 18133
When I Get Back To Loveland And You	1917	Columbia A-2433
When The Black Sheep Returns To The Fold	1916	Victor 18126
Yaaka Hula Hickey Dula	1916	Victor 18081
You're A Dangerous Girl	1916	Victor 18088
You're Just As Dear To Me As Dixie Was To Lee	1917	Columbia A-2433
Avondale Mills Quartet		
Rejoicing On The Way	1928	Victor 40211
Stilling The Tempest	1928	Victor 40211
Babs And Her Brothers		
Breeze Is Bringing My Baby Back To Me, The	1934	From the Old Gold and Ford radio broadcasts of Fred Waring and the Pennsylvanians, 1933-1935.
Dancing On A Rooftop	1934	From the Old Gold and Ford radio broadcasts of Fred Waring and the Pennsylvanians, 1933-1935.
Double Trouble	1935	Decca 518B/Brunswick 02059
Hands Across The Table	1934	From the Old Gold

Title	Year	Source
Keep On Doin'	1934	From the Old Gold and Ford radio broadcasts of Fred Waring and the Pennsylvanians, 1933-1935.
Let's Swing It	1935	Decca 505A
Little Bit Independent, A	1935	Decca 634A
Lookie, Lookie, Here Comes Cookie	1935	From the Old Gold and Ford radio broadcasts of Fred Waring and the Pennsylvanians, 1933-1935.
Moonglow	1934	From the Old Gold and Ford radio broadcasts of Fred Waring and the Pennsylvanians, 1933-1935.
My Very Good Friend The Milkman	1935	Decca 505B/Brunswick 02059
No Other One	1935	Decca 635A
Object Of My Affections, The	1934	From the Old Gold and Ford radio broadcasts of Fred Waring and the Pennsylvanians, 1933-1935.
Oh What A Little Love Can Do	1934	From the Old Gold and Ford radio broadcasts of Fred Waring and the Pennsylvanians, 1933-1935.
Put On Your Glasses	1934	From the Old Gold and Ford radio broadcasts of Fred Waring and the Pennsylvanians, 1933-1935.
Shuffle Off To Buffalo	1933	From the Old Gold and Ford radio broadcasts of Fred Waring and the Pennsylvanians, 1933-1935.
Solitude	1934	From the Old Gold and Ford radio broadcasts of Fred Waring and the Pennsylvanians, 1933-1935.
Sweetie Pie	1934	From the Old Gold and Ford radio broadcasts of Fred Waring and the Pennsylvanians, 1933-1935.
Theme and Commercial	1935	From the Old Gold and Ford radio broadcasts of Fred Waring and the Pennsylvanians, 1933-1935.
There's Gonna Be A Wedding In The Band	1934	From the Old Gold and Ford radio broadcasts of Fred Waring and the Pennsylvanians, 1933-1935.
Two Tickets To Georgia	1933	From the Old Gold and Ford radio broadcasts of Fred Waring and the Pennsylvanians, 1933-1935.
Were Your Ears Burning Baby	1934	From the Old Gold and Ford radio broadcasts of Fred Waring and the Pennsylvanians, 1933-1935.
What Have We Got To Lose	1933	From the Old Gold and Ford radio broadcasts of Fred Waring and the Pennsylvanians, 1933-1935.
When A Great Love Comes Along	1936	Decca 634B
Wild Honey	1934	From the Old Gold and Ford radio broadcasts of Fred Waring and the Pennsylvanians, 1933-1935.
Yankee Doodle Never Went To Town	1936	Decca 635B
You're An Old Smoothie	1933	From the Old Gold and Ford radio broadcasts of Fred Waring and the Pennsylvanians, 1933-1935.

You're OK	1934	From the Old Gold and Ford radio broadcasts of Fred Waring and the Pennsylvanians, 1933-1935.
You're So Darn Charming	1935	Decca 518A

Babs And Her Brothers (with Johnny Davis)

Suntan Charlie	1934	From the Old Gold and Ford radio broadcasts of Fred Waring and the Pennsylvanians, 1933-1935.

Bachelors

Headin' For Better Times	1931	Columbia 2378-D/Columbia 2721-D

Bachelors (with Joe Van Loan)

Hereafter	1949	Mercury 8159
Yesterday's Roses	1949	Mercury 8159

Bacon, Trevor & Ensemble

Hey Huss!	1942	Decca 4146

Bailey, Mildred & the Delta Rhythm Boys

All Too Soon	1940	Decca 25462
Everything Depends On You	1940	Decca 25462

Balladeers, Billy Matthews & the

Goodbye Little Girl	1952	RCA 47-4612
If You Only Knew	1950	Jubilee 5024
I Love You, Yes I Do	1948	Mercury 8073
I Never Knew I Loved You	1950	Jubilee 5024
It Ain't Right	1950	Jubilee 5021
I Wish I Was Single Again	1952	RCA 47-4612
Red Sails In The Sunset	1950	Jubilee 5021
Smooth Sailing	1948	Mercury 8073

Balladiers

Keep Me With You	1949	Aladdin 3008
Please Don't Deceive My Heart	1949	Aladdin 3008
What Will I Tell My Heart	1952	Aladdin 3123
Forget Me Not	1952	Aladdin 3123

Balladiers, Billy Matthews & the

Please Give My Heart A Break	1949	Arlington 201
Rock And Roll	1949	Arlington 201

Banner Quartet

Hark, The Herald Angels Sing	1919	Banner 2066
Holy Night, Peaceful Night	1919	Banner 2066
Joy To The World	1919	Banner 2065

Banner Sacred Quartet

Silent Night	1923	Banner 2123

Barber Shop Quartet

When You Were Sweet Sixteen	1940	Decca 3448A

Barbour's Plantation Singers

Doan Let Satan Git You	1927	Columbia 14253-D
In-A-De-Mornin'	1927	Columbia 14253-D

Barnes, John & the Haydn Quartet

Sweet Genevieve	1910	Victor 16440

Barnes, William & Quartet

Girl Who Wears A Red Cross, The	1916	Victor 18052

Barons

Believe In Me	1951	Modern 818
Forever	1951	Modern 818

Basin Street Boys

Ain't Got No Loot	1947	Exclusive 245
Evening Swing	1938	Movie transcription from
Exactly Like You	1947	Exclusive 247/Flame 1002
For You	1947	Exclusive 245
I'll Get Along Somehow	1947	Exclusive 247
I'm Gonna Write A Letter To My Baby	1947	Exclusive 239
I Need A Knife, A Fork, And A Spoon	1946	Exclusive 229
I Sold My Heart To The Junkman	1946	Cash 1052/Exclusive 225 (1946)/Exclusive 39x (1948)/Flame 1002
Josephine	1947	Exclusive 239
Jumpin' At The Jubilee	1945	Exclusive 220
Near To You	1947	Exclusive 21x
Nothin' Ever Happens To Me	1945	Exclusive 220
Satchelmouth Baby	1947	Exclusive 19x
Summertime Gal	1947	Exclusive 19x
This Is The End Of A Dream	1946	Exclusive 229
Thursday Evening Swing	1938	From soundtrack of the movie
Voot Nay On The Vot Nay	1946	Exclusive 225/Exclusive 39x (1948)
You're Mine Forever	1947	Exclusive 21x

Basin Street Boys (singing with Bob Crosby)

It's My Night To Howl - Part 1	1934	Decca 112
It's My Night To Howl - Part 2	1934	Decca 112

Basin Street Boys, Judy Carol & The

Changes	1945	Exclusive 215
I Want To Love And Be Loved	1945	Exclusive 215

Basin Street Boys, Ormond Wilson & the

Come To Me	1948	Mercury 8106
If I Can't Have You	1948	Mercury 8106
Please Give My Heart A Break	1948	Mercury 8120
To Make A Mistake Is Human	1948	Mercury 8120

Bateman Sacred Quartet

Nothing But Old-Time Religion	1929	Columbia 15608-D
Some Day	1929	Columbia 15608-D

Bayou Boys

Dinah	1952	Checker 765

Jambalaya	1952	Checker 765
Bea & the Bachelors		
Hot Spell	1936	Brunswick 7606
Beachcombers, Marion Morgan & the		
Sierra Nevada	1952	Atlantic 936
Take My Love	1952	Atlantic 936
Beacon Four (Barbershop Quartet)		
Honey That I Love So Well/Sweetness	1940	Decca 3651A
Mandy Lee/Somebody Stole My Gal	1940	Decca 3651B
Beale Street Boys		
Baby Don't Be Mad At Me	1948	MGM 10197
Home	1948	MGM 10273
I've Kept Everything The Same For You	1949	MGM 10505
I Wish I Had A Dime	1949	MGM 10505
Next Christmas	1960	OBA 101
Teach Me, Teach Me Baby	1948	MGM 10141
There's Nothing Greater Than A Prayer	1960	OBA 102
Wait'll I Get You In My Dreams Tonight	1948	MGM 10273
Wedding Bells	1948	MGM 10197
Why Does It Have To Rain On Sunday	1948	MGM 10141
Beale Street Boys, Bob Davis & the		
As High As My Heart	1960	OBA 109
Beale Street Gang		
Back Alley Blues	1950	Savoy 731
Beavers		
Big Mouth Mama	1950	Coral 65026
I'd Rather Be Wrong Than Blue	1950	Coral 65026
If You See Tears In My Eyes	1949	Coral 65018
I Gotta Do It	1949	Coral 65018
Beavers (as Herb Lance)		
That Lucky Old Sun	1949	Sittin In 524
Beavers (as Lionel Hampton & the Hamptones)		
Rag Mop	1950	Decca 24855
Bel-Canto Quartet		
Bow Down	1930	Panachord 25181
Get Away, Jordan	1932	Victor 22952
Honey, I Wants Yer Now	1930	Panachord 25181
I Am Wandering Down (Life's Short Path)	1930	Brunswick 6072/Panachord 25088
Jesus Savior Pilot Me	1930	Brunswick 6072/Panachord 25088
Nearer My God To Thee	1930	Brunswick 6011/Panachord 25063
Rigoletto Quartet Travesty	1932	Victor 22952
Softly And Tenderly	1930	Brunswick 6011/Panachord 25063
Until The Dawn	1930	Brunswick 6115/Panachord 25181
Winding Trail, The	1930	Brunswick 6115/Panachord 25181
Bell Hops		
For The Rest Of My Life	1951	Decca 48208
I'm All Yours	1951	Decca 48239
It Would Take A Million Years	1951	Decca 48208
Where Is Love	1951	Decca 48239
Bell Quartet		
Sunday	192'	Bell 471
Bell Record Quartet		
Hinky Dinky Parlez Vous	1924	Bell 285
Bell Serenaders		
Love	1923	Bell 235
That Old Gang Of Mine	1923	Bell 235
Two Blue Eyes	1924	Bell 265
Belltones		
Way Up In North Carolina	1951	Mercury 5692
Belmont Garden Quartet		
Sam, The Old Accordion Man	1927	Challenge 242
When I First Met Mary	1927	Challenge 266
Belt Sacred Quartet		
I Have Another Building	1929	Victor 38587
My Lord Is On High	1929	Victor 38587
Beltona Male Quartet		
When I'm Gone You'll Soon Forget	1925	Beltona 922
When You're Gone I Won't Forget	1925	Beltona 922
Beltones, Little Esther & the		
Cupid's Boogie	1950	Savoy 750
Just Can't Get Free	1950	Savoy 750
Bennett Sisters		
Bugles In The Sky (with Dick Lee)	1940	Decca 3581
Don't Look Now	1939	Decca 2630
Lost My Rhythm, Lost My Music, Lost My Man	1935	Bluebird B-6049
Love Can Do The Darndest Things	1940	Decca 3581
Sittin' Around On Sunday	1935	Bluebird B-6048
Sugar Plum	1935	Bluebird B-6115
Tom Tom The Piper's Son (with Wayne Gregg)	1938	Decca 2217
Why Stars Come Out At Night	1935	Bluebird B-6049
Ya Got Me	1938	Decca 2149
Bernie Trio		
Crazy Rhythm	1928	Brunswick 3913
Dream Kisses	1928	Brunswick 3771/ Brunswick 03718
Imagination	1928	Brunswick 3913/Brunswick

I Told Them All About You	1928	Brunswick 3774/Brunswick 03724
It Was The Dawn Of Love	1928	Brunswick 3951/Brunswick 03834
There's Something About A Rose	1928	Brunswick 3921/Brunswick 03807/Brunswick A 7790
(What Are You Waiting For) Mary'	1928	Brunswick 3774/Brunswick 03724

Bessemer Blues Singers

Louisiana Babe	1930	Columbia 14583-D
My Mammy's Baby Child	1930	Columbia 14583-D

Bessemer Blues Singers, Bessie Smith & the

Moan, You Mourners	1930	Columbia 14538-D
On Revival Day (A Rhythmic Spiritual)	1930	Columbia 14538-D

Bessemer Quartet

In The Valley Of Peace	1929	Supertone S 2245
Lord, I'm Troubled	1929	Supertone S 2245
You Can Hear Those Darkies Sing	1927	Champion 15327

Bessemer Singers

Louisiana Babe	1930	Columbia 14583D

Bessemer Sunset Four

Adam And Eve	1929	Vocalion
Are You Ready'	1930	Vocalion 1681
Climbing Jacob's Ladder	1930	Vocalion 1639
Don't You Want That Stone'	1930	Vocalion 1581
Ham And Eggs	1928	Vocalion 1260
Heaven Is In My View	1928	Vocalion 1233
He Brought Joy To My Soul	1930	Vocalion 1488
I Feel Like My Time Ain't Long	1930	Vocalion 1650
I'm A Child Of God	1929	Vocalion 1451
I'm Climbing Up Zion Hill	1929	Vocalion 1681
I'm Going Home To Rest	1930	Vocalion 1625
In The Valley Of Peace	1929	Vocalion 1427
I've Got A New Name	1930	Vocalion 1524
I Want To Go Home To See My Lord	1930	Vocalion 1650
I Will Ever Stand	1929	Vocalion 1451
John The Revelator	1929	Vocalion
Lord, I'm Troubled	1929	Vocalion 1427
Lord's Been Good To Me, The	1930	Vocalion 1581
Mighty Day	1928	Vocalion 1260
My Lord's Coming Soon	1930	Vocalion 1639
Rollin' Down To Jordan	1928	Vocalion 1233
Take This Ring With You	1929	Vocalion 1293
We're Going To Walk The Golden Streets	1930	Vocalion 1524
What A Wonderful Love The Father Has	1929	Vocalion 1293
When I Lay My Burden Down	1930	Vocalion 1488
You're Going To Need That Pure Religion	1930	Vocalion 1625

Beta Octette

Psi Upsilon Songs	1915	Columbia

Bethel Jubilee Quartet

Ain't It A Shame To Work Sundays	1924	Victor 19289
Golden Slippers	1910	Victor 16453
Hard Trials	1924	Victor 19289
Hush Somebody Calls My Name	1923	Victor 19119A
I Couldn't Hear Nobody Pray	1910	Victor 16448
You Must Come In At The Front Door	1923	Victor 19119B

Bethel Quartet

Brother Cain Struck Abel	1928	Victor 38530
Moses Gonna Chunk Dat Melon Down	1928	Victor 38530
On My Knees	1928	Victor 38510
Walk Through The Valley In Peace	1928	Victor 38510

Biddleville Quartet

As I Live Let Me Live	1930	Paramount 13092
Blessed Be The Tie That Binds	1930	Paramount 12969
Coming To Christ	1927	Paramount 12480
Day Is Past And Gone, The	1929	Paramount 12847/Champion 50035 (1929)/Paramount 13144 (1930)
Didn't It Rain	1929	Paramount 12848
Fight On, Your Time Ain't Long	1926	Paramount 12396
Got Heaven Is My View	1926	Paramount 12406/Paramount 12847 (1929)
Handwriting On The Wall	1929	Paramount 12903/Paramount 13092 (1930)
Holy Is My Name	1929	Paramount 12846
I Feel My Time Ain't Long	1929	Champion 50035
I Heard The Voice Of Jesus Say	1926	Paramount 12396/Paramount 12845 (1929)
I'm Going To Live With The Lord	1930	Paramount 12969
I'm Tormented In The Flame	1927	Paramount 12506
In The Garden Of Gethsemanie	1927	Paramount 12462
I Stretch My Hand To Thee	1929	Paramount 12937
Jacob Sent Joseph	1927	Paramount 12448
Jesus Gonna Shake My Righteous Hand	1927	Paramount 12506/Paramount 13144 (1930)
Jesus Is A Rock In The Weary Land	1929	Paramount 12937
Jesus Is Gonna Shake My	1929	Paramount 12849

Righteous Hand		
Judas And Jesus Walk Together	1929	Paramount 12903
Lord Giveth, The	1929	Paramount 12849
Oh Why Not Tonight	1926	Paramount 12393
Pharaoh's Army Got Drowned	1929	Paramount 12848
Prodigal Son	1927	Paramount 12462
Receiving The Message	1927	Paramount 12480
This Train Is Bound For Glory	1927	Paramount 12448
Wasn't That A Mighty Day'	1926	Paramount 12393/Paramount 12845 (1929)
Way Down In Egyptland	1926	Paramount 12406/Paramount 12846 (1929)
Whosoever Will May Com	1927	Broadway 5007

Big City Four

When The Boys From Dixie Eat The Melon On The Rhine	1918	Pathe 20308

Big Four

Sweet Jennie Lee!	1931	Sampler 0641

Big Four Quartet

Good-Bye, Dolly Gray	1901	Edison 7728
Kentucky Babe	1922	Cameo 235
Little Cotton Dolly	1922	Cameo 235
Little Sunshower	1922	Cameo 249
Mary Dear, Someday We'll Meet	1922	Cameo 249

Big Four Quartet (Peerless Quartet)

In My Gondola	1926	Champion 15071
Prisoner's Sweetheart	1926	Champion 15082
Tamiami Trail	1926	Champion 15071

Big Seven, Dickie Wells'

Bedrock	1949	Aladdin 3019
We're Through	1949	Aladdin 3019

Big Three Trio, Rosetta Howard & the

After Awhile	1947	Columbia 30103/Columbia 37983 (1947)
Appetite Blues	1949	Delta 208/Columbia 30239 (1951)
Baby, I Can Go On Without You	1947	Columbia 30103/Columbia 37983 (1947)
Be A Sweetheart	1953	Okeh 6944
Big Three Boogie	1948	Columbia 30125
Big Three Stomp	1949	Columbia 30166
Blip Blip	1951	Columbia 30239
Blue Because Of You	1952	Okeh 6863
Cigareets, Whiskey, And Wild Women	1949	Delta 208
Come Here Baby	1953	Okeh 6944
Don't Let That Music Die	1949	Delta 202/Columbia 30190 (1950)
Ebony Rhapsody	1947	Columbia 30053/Columbia 37573 (1947)/Columbia 40494 (1955)
88 Boogie	1948	Columbia 30110/Columbia 38093 (1948)
Evening	1948	Columbia 30125
Get Her Off Of My Mind	1949	Columbia 30174
Get Up Those Stairs, Mademoiselle	1947	Bullet 274
Goodbye Mr. Blues	1950	Columbia 30222
Got You On My Mind	1952	Okeh 6863
Hard Notch Boogie Beat	1949	Columbia 30156
Help Me Baby	1947	Columbia 30105/Columbia 38029 (1947)
I Ain't Gonna Be Your Monkey Man No More	1949	Columbia 30166
I Feel Like Steppin' Out	1949	Columbia 30156
If The Sea Was Whiskey	1947	Columbia 30019/Columbia 37358 (1947)
I Keep On Worrying	1948	Columbia 30127
I'll Be Right Some Day	1948	Columbia 30142
It Can't Be Done	1948	Columbia 30108/Columbia 38064 (1948)
It's All Over Now	1951	Okeh 6842
It's Hard To Go Thru Life Alone	1948	Columbia 30113/Columbia 38145 (1948)
Just Can't Let Her Be	1948	Columbia 30144
Lonely Roamin'	1947	Bullet 274/Columbia 30055 (1947)/Columbia 37584 (1947)
Lonesome	1951	Okeh 6807
Money Tree Blues	1947	Columbia 30055/Columbia 37584 (1947)
My Love Will Never Die	1952	Okeh 6901
No More Sweet Potatoes	1948	Columbia 30108/Columbia 38064 (1948)
No One To Love Me	1949	Columbia 30174
Practicing The Art Of Love	1950	Columbia 30190
Reno Blues	1948	Columbia 30142
Signifying Monkey	1947	Bullet 275/Columbia 30019 (1947)/Columbia 37358 (1947)/Dot 1124
Since My Baby's Been Gone	1948	Columbia 30144
Tell That Woman	1951	Okeh 6842

There's Something On My Mind	1950	Columbia 30228
Till The Day I Die	1949	Delta 202/Columbia 30222 (1950)
Too Many Drivers	1947	Columbia 30105/Columbia 38029 (1947)
Violent Love	1951	Okeh 6807
When I Been Drinking	1947	Columbia 30053/Columbia 37573 (1947)
Where Shall I Go	1948	Columbia 30113/Columbia 38145 (1948)
Why Be So Blue	1948	Columbia 30127
Why Do You Do Me Like You Do	1950	Columbia 30228
You Don't Love Me No More	1952	Okeh 6901
You Sure Look Good To Me	1947	Bullet 275/Columbia 30110 (1948)/Columbia 38093 (1948)/Dot 1124

Biltmore Rhythm Boys

Bye-Bye Blues	1930	Columbia 2258-D
Crying Myself To Sleep	1930	Victor 22583
Here Comes The Sun	1930	Victor 22541
I'm Yours (Soy Tengo)	1930	Victor 22541
Loving You The Way I Do	1930	Victor 22568
Only A Rose	1930	Harmony 1111-H/Publix 2005-P
Under A Texas Moon	1930	Harmony 1088-H
Under The Sun It's Anyone, Under The Moon It's You	1930	Columbia 2258-D
You're Simply Delish	1930	Victor 22568

Biltmore Trio

Heartaches	1931	Victor 22612
I've Found What I Wanted In You	1931	Victor 22653
I Wanna Sing About You	1931	Victor 22689
June Time Is Love Time	1931	Victor 22740
Never	1931	Victor 22725
To Whom It May Concern	1931	Victor 22603
When Your Lover Has Gone	1931	Victor 22652

Binghamton Kiwanis Quartet

My Lady Chlo!	1924	Columbia 229-D
Swing Along!	1924	Columbia 229-D

Binghamton Kiwanis Quartet

Kiwanis	1924	
Sylvia	1924	
Winter Song	1924	

Birmingham Jubilee Quartet

Whosoever Will May Come	1926	Broadway 5007/Paramount 12464

Birmingham Jubilee Singers

Ain't That Good News	1929	Columbia 14408-D
All Over This World	1930	Vocalion 1629
Birmingham Joys	1926	Columbia 14154D
Crying To The Lord	1926	Columbia 14140-D
Dixie Bobo	1930	Vocalion 1495
Don't You Want That Stone'	1927	Columbia 14252-D
Do You Call That Religion'	1926	Columbia 14163-D
Every Time I Feel The Spirit	1926	Columbia 14176-D
Four And Twenty Elders	1926	Columbia 14176-D
Gamblin' Man	1930	Vocalion 1563
Glory Hallelujah	1929	Columbia 14467-D
God Is Love	1929	Columbia 14515-D
Gonna Raise Ruckus Tonight	1927	Columbia 14263D
Great Gittin' Up Mawnin'	1930	Vocalion 1537
He Died On Calvary	1927	Columbia 14467-D
He Took My Sins Away	1926	Columbia 14140-D
Home In The Rock	1926	Columbia 14163-D
Hope I'll Join That Band	1929	Columbia 14408-D
Hymn With Prayer By Brother Sherrill, A	1927	Columbia 14236-D
I Heard The Preachin' Of The Elders	1927	Columbia 14345-D
I'm A Pilgrim	1926	Columbia
I'm Going To Serve God Till I Die	1930	Vocalion 1599
I'm Going To Sit At The Welcome Table	1930	Vocalion 1599
I've Done What You Told Me To Do	1930	Vocalion 1629
I Want God's Bosom To Be Mine	1930	Vocalion 1644
Join The Band	1930	Vocalion 1644
King Jesus Is My Captain	1927	Columbia 14252-D
My Love Pie (Dixie Lullaby)	1930	Vocalion 1495
Pharaoh's Army Got Drowned	1926	Columbia 14203-D
Run Mary	1930	Brunswick 1509/Vocalion 1509
See The Lion Of Judgement	1926	Columbia 14203-D
They Crucified My Lord	1930	Brunswick 1509/Vocalion 1509
Wade In The Water	1930	Vocalion 1563
Walk In Jerusalem, Just Like John	1927	Columbia 14236-D
Way Down In Egyptland	1930	Vocalion 1537
We Will Leave	1929	Columbia 14515-D

Birmingham Jubilee Sinners

Where Are You Running, Sinner'	1928	Columbia 14345-D

Birmingham Quartet

Birmingham Boys	1926	Columbia 14154-D
Fight On, Your Time Ain't Long	1926	Broadway 5003
How Come You Do Me Like You Do	1926	Columbia 14190-D
I Heard The Voice Of Jesus Say Come Unto Me	1926	Broadway 5003
Louisiana Bo-Bo	1927	Columbia 14224-D

Queen Street Rag	1927	Columbia 14311-D
Raise A Ruckus Tonight	1927	Columbia 14262-D
Show Pity Lord	1926	Paramount 12424/Broadway 5007 (1926)
South Bound Train	1926	Columbia 14154-D
Steamboat, The	1927	Columbia 14224-D
Stop That Band!	1928	Columbia 14311-D
Sweet Mama, Tree Top Tall	1926	Columbia 14190-D
Watermelon On The Vine	1927	Columbia 14263-D
Way Back Home	1926	Columbia 14567-D
Yodel	1926	Columbia 14567-D

Black Cats And The Kitten

I'm The Winder	1941	Okeh 5972
My Boogie Woogie Daddy	1940	Okeh 5882
Step It Up And Go	1940	Okeh 5882
You Better Ask Somebody	1941	Okeh 5972

Black Devil Four, Tim Brymn's (Tim Brymn's Devils)

Aunt Hagar's Children Blues	1920	Okeh 8011

Blackbirds Off Harmony (with Perry Bradford and his Gang)

Just Met A Friend	1926	Columbia 14142-D
So's Your Old Man	1926	Columbia 14142-D

Blenders

All I Gotta Do Is Think Of You	1951	Decca 27587
Busiest Corner In My Hometown, The	1951	Decca 27587
Come Back Baby Blues	1949	National 9092
Count Every Star	1950	Decca 48158
Don't Play Around With Love	1953	Jay-Dee 780
Gone	1950	Decca 48156
Honeysuckle Rose	1950	Decca 48156
I Can Dream, Can't I	1949	National 9092
I'd Be A Fool Again	1952	Decca 28092
I Don't Miss You Anymore	1953	MGM 11488
If That's The Way You Want It Baby	1953	MGM 11488
I'm So Crazy For Love	1950	Decca 48183
Isn't It A Shame	1953	MGM 11531
Just A Little Walk With Me	1952	Decca 28092
Little Small Town Girl	1951	Decca 27403
Masquerade Is Over, The	1951	Decca 27403
Memories Of You	1952	Decca 28241
My Heart Will Never Forget	1951	Decca 48244
Never In A Million Years	1952	Decca 28241
Please Take Me Back	1953	MGM 11531
Tell Me What's On Your Mind	1961	Decca 31284
What About Tonight	1950	Decca 48183
When I'm Walkin' With My Baby	1961	Decca 31284
Would I Still Be The One In Your Heart	1950	Decca 48158
You Do The Dreamin'	1951	Decca 48244
You'll Never Be Mine Again	1953	Jay-Dee 780

Blenders, Vivian Gary & the

Tenderly	1948	Miltone 5220

Blue Bird Trio

Mickey Mouse And Minnie's In Town	1933	Champion 16706
Sing A Little Lowdown Tune	1933	Champion 16706
Where The River Swanee Flows	1933	Champion 16725

Blue Moon Melody Boys

In My Bouquet Of Memories	1928	Champion 15492
Louisiana	1928	Champion 15492

Blue Ribbon Quartet

Adorable	1926	Vocalion 15361B
Breezin' Along With The Breeze	1926	Vocalion 15391
Honey Bunch	1926	Vocalion 15350
Hum Your Troubles Away	1926	Vocalion 15473
I Can't Believe That You're In Love With Me	1927	Vocalion 15521
If I Knew I'd Find You	1926	Vocalion 15361
I'll Fly To Hawaii	1926	Vocalion 15458B
I'm Looking Over A Four Leaf Clover	1927	Vocalion 15521B
Just A Bird's Eye View (Of My Kentucky Home)	1926	Vocalion 15473B
Lonesome And Sorry	1926	Vocalion 15350B
Oriental Moonlight	1927	Vocalion 15567
Shanghai Dream Man	1927	Vocalion 15567
Sweet Genevieve	1927	Vocalion 15572
There's A Long, Long Trail	1927	Vocalion 15572
Tonight You Belong To Me	1926	Vocalion 15458
When The Red Red Robin Comes Bob Bob Bobbin' Along	1926	Vocalion 15391B

Blue Ribbon Trio

Aggravatin' Papa	1923	Okeh 4824
Childhood Days	1922	Okeh 4710
First Waltz, The	1923	Okeh 4796
Goodnight Waltz	1923	Okeh 4900
Love's Ship	1923	Okeh 4796
Sweet Annabelle	1923	Okeh 4900
That Da Da Strain	1923	Okeh 4824
Who Loves You Most Of All	1922	Okeh 4710

Blue Ridge Gospel Singers

I'm Alone In This World	1927	Brunswick 152
I'm Going Home To Die	1927	Brunswick 152
My Loved One Is Waiting For Me	1927	Brunswick 151
Oh Why Not Tonight	1927	Brunswick 151
On The Hills Over There	1927	Brunswick 150
Twill Be Glory Bye And Bye	1927	Brunswick 150

Blue Ridge Singers

Christine Le Roy	1930	Columbia
Engineer's Last Run, The	1930	Columbia 15647-D
Give My Love To Nell	1930	Columbia 15580-D
Glory Is now Rising In My Soul	1927	Columbia 15228-D
I'll Remember You In My Prayers	1930	Columbia 15550-D
I Want To Go There, Don't You'	1927	Columbia 15228-D
I Wish I'd Never Met You	1930	Columbia
Letter That Never Came, The	1930	Columbia 15580-D
Lorena	1930	Columbia 15550-D

Mansion Of Aching Hearts	1930	Columbia 15678-D
Sinful To Flirt	1930	Columbia 15678-D
Tramp Song, The	1930	Columbia 15647-D

Bluebirds, Ann Nichols & the

I Wonder What It Takes To Make Me Happy'	1950	Sittin' In With 561
Let Me Know	1950	Sittin' In With 552
Lost In A Fog Over You	1950	Sittin' In With 552

Bluesmen, Maggie Hathaway & the

Here Goes A Fool	1946	BW 555
Too Late To Be Good Blues	1946	BW 556

Bodyguards

All Alone And Lonely (with Orrin Tucker)	1941	Columbia 36172
Autumn On The Campus	1940	Columbia 35925
Drifting And Dreaming	1939	Columbia 35332
Drink The Barrel Dry	1941	Columbia 36192
Georgia On My Mind (with Orrin Tucker)	1941	Columbia 36049
I Want To Live (As Long As You Love Me)	1940	Columbia 35813
Keep An Eye On Your Heart (with Bonnie Baker)	1941	Columbia 36016
La Rosita	1939	Columbia 35722
Li'l Abner	1940	Columbia 35792
Oh, Lady Be Good (with Bonnie Baker)	1939	Columbia 35576
Sh! Baby's Asleep (with Bonnie Baker)	1939	Columbia 35405
Some Must Win (Some Must Lose)	1941	Columbia 36223

Bodyguards, Bonnie Baker & the

If You Love Me	1940	Columbia 35489
It'll Come To You	1940	Columbia 35528
Strawberry Lane	1939	Columbia 35858
What Are Little Girls Made Of'	1939	Vocalion 4805

Bodyguards, Orrin Tucker & the

Irene	1940	Columbia 35440
Powder Your Face With Sunshine	194'	Double Feature DF
Whispering Grass	1940	Columbia 35639

Bon Bons

Chocolates And Chewing Gum	1948	Apollo 170
You Know Baby	1948	Apollo 170

Bonnie Laddies

'Deed I Do	1927	Brunswick 03454/Brunswick A245
'Deed I Do	1927	Vocalion 15517
Hello Bluebird	1926	Brunswick A235/Vocalion 15480
High-High-High Up In The Hills (Watching The Clouds Roll By)	1927	Brunswick 03452
I Love You But I Don't Know Why	1927	Brunswick 03454/Brunswick A245
I Love You But I Don't Know Why	1927	Vocalion 15516
Moonlight On The Ganges	1926	Brunswick 20587/Brunswick 03371/Brunswick A208
Moonlight On The Ganges	1926	Vocalion 15489
Short An' Sweet	1926	Brunswick A235/
Short An' Sweet	1926	Vocalion 15480
Some Day	1926	Brunswick 20589/Brunswick 03371

Bonnie Laddies (with the Six Hayseeds)

Crazy Words, Crazy Tune (Vo-Do-De-O)	1927	Vocalion 15520
I Love College Girls	1927	Vocalion 15514

Bonnie Laddies (with the Six Jumping Jacks)

Crazy Words, Crazy Tune (Vo-Do-De-O)	1927	Brunswick 03434/Brunswick A247
I Love College Girls	1927	Brunswick 03434/Brunswick A247

Booker Male Quartet

Shout All Over God's Heaven	1926	Silvertone 3294
Swing Low, Sweet Chariot	1926	Silvertone 3294

Boone's Jumping Jacks

Messy	1942	Decca 8644

Boston Male Vocal Quartet

Catastrophe - Humoresque, The	1910	Odeon A 47218
Kentucky Babe	1910	Odeon A 47216

Boston Quintet

Mighty Lak A Rose/Sweet And Low	1917	Victor 18375

Boswell Sisters

Ain't Misbehavin'	1931	Brunswick Test
Alexander's Ragtime Band	1934	Brunswick 7412/Brunswick 01893/Brunswick A 9688/Brunswick A 500528/Okeh 4239/Vocalion 4239 (1938)
At The Darktown Strutters Ball	1934	Brunswick 15255 A
Betty Lou/It Looks Like Love	1931	Brunswick Test
Between The Devil And The Deep Blue Sea	1932	Brunswick 6291/Brunswick 01306/Brunswick A 9244
California, Part 2	1932	Brunswick 20107 N/Brunswick A 5112
Charlie Two-Step	1932	Brunswick

100 Years of Harmony: 1850 to 1950

Title	Year	Release
Cheek To Cheek	1935	6418/Brunswick 6418/Brunswick A 9317 Decca 574/Brunswick 02067/Brunswick A 9854
Clouds	1935	Brunswick 7363
Coffee In The Morning And Kisses In The Night	1933	Brunswick 6733/Brunswick 01711/Brunswick A 9512
Concentratin' On You	1931	Decca
Crazy People	1932	Brunswick 6847/Brunswick 01416/Brunswick A 9390
Crazy Rhythm	1930	Brunswick
Crying Blues	1925	Victor 19639
Dad	1925	Victor
Darktown Strutter's Ball, The	1934	Unreleased (from Vintage CD VMP 0011)
Darktown Strutter's Ball, The	1934	Columbia DO 1255
Dinah	1935	Brunswick 7412/Brunswick 01926/Brunswick A 9688/Brunswick A 500528/Okeh 4239/Rex 8873/Vocalion 4239 (1938)
Does My Baby Love'	1930	Brunswick unreleased (from Vintage CD VMP 0011)
Doggone! I've Done It Again	1932	Brunswick 6335/Brunswick 01362/Brunswick 01893/Brunswick A 9285
Don't Let Your Love Go Wrong	1934	Brunswick 6929/Brunswick 01832/Brunswick A 9616/Columbia DS 1462/Odeon A 272287/
Don't Tell Him What Happened To Me	1930	MGM
Down Among The Sheltering Palms	1932	Brunswick 6418/Brunswick A 9299/Columbia 36522
Down On The Delta	1932	Brunswick 01403//Brunswick A 9392
Down On The Delta	1932	Brunswick 6395
Down The River Of Golden Dreams	1930	Brunswick
Everybody Loves My Baby (But My Baby Don't Love Nobody But Me)	1932	Brunswick 6271/Brunswick 01295/Brunswick A 9232
Every Little Moment	1935	Brunswick 7454/Brunswick 02033/Brunswick A 9800
Fare Thee Well, Annabelle	1935	Brunswick 02043/Brunswick A 9823/Brunswick A 500594
Farewell Blues	1930	Brunswick
Forty-Second Street	1933	Brunswick 6545/Brunswick 01516/Brunswick A 9416/Brunswick 500241
Gee, But I'd Like To Make You Happy	1930	Okeh 41470/Odeon A 221321/Odeon A 286029/Odeon O-25200
Gee, But I'd Like To Make You Happy	1930	Decca
Goin' Home	1934	Brunswick 6951/Brunswick 01791/Brunswick A 9600
Gold Diggers' Song, The	1933	Brunswick 6596/Brunswick 01556/Brunswick A 9443/Brunswick A 500271
Got The South In My Soul	1932	Brunswick 6302/Brunswick 01330/Brunswick A 9262
Hand Me Down My Walkin' Cane	1932	Brunswick 6335/Brunswick 01362/Brunswick 01893/Brunswick A 9285
Heebie Jeebies	1930	MGM
Heebie Jeebies	1931	Brunswick 6173/Brunswick 01218/Brunswick 80013/Brunswick A 9143
Here Comes The Sun	1930	Brunswick
If I Had A Million Dollars	1934	Brunswick 7302/Brunswick

Song	Year	Release
If It Ain't Love	1932	Brunswick 6302/Brunswick 01330/Brunswick A 9262
I Found A Million Dollar Baby (In A Five And Ten Cent Store)	1931	Brunswick 6128/Brunswick 01193
I Hate Myself (For Being So Mean To You)	1934	Brunswick 6798/Brunswick 01751/Brunswick A 9575
I'll Never Have To Dream Again	1932	Unreleased (from Vintage CD VMP 0011)
I'm All Dressed Up With A Broken Heart	1931	Decca
I'm Gonna Cry (Cryin' Blues)	1925	Victor 19639
I'm Gonna Sit Right Down And Write Myself A Letter	1936	Decca 671/Brunswick 02142/Brunswick A 9923
I'm In Training For You	1930	Unreleased (from Vintage CD VMP 0011)
I'm On A Diet Of Love	1930	Unreleased (from Vintage CD VMP 0011)
I'm Putting All My Eggs In One Basket	1936	Decca 709/Brunswick 02165/Brunswick A 9959
I'm Yours	1930	
I Surrender Dear (with Frank Munn)	1931	Brunswick 0102/Brunswick 20100/Brunswick A 5106
It Don't Mean A Thing (If It Ain't Got That Swing)	1932	Brunswick 6442/Brunswick 01436/Brunswick A 9350/Columbia DB 1994/Okeh 4546/Rex 8873/Vocalion 4546 (1938)
I Thank You, Mr. Moon	1931	Brunswick 6231/Brunswick 01272/Brunswick A 9208
It's Sunday Down In Caroline	1933	Brunswick 6596/Brunswick 01556/Brunswick A 9443
It's The Girl!	1931	Brunswick 01957/Brunswick A 9672
It's Written All Over Your Face	1934	Brunswick 7348//Brunswick A 9702/Brunswick 01961/Columbia 36523
It's You!	1931	Brunswick 6151/Brunswick 80014/Brunswick 01181/Brunswick A 9112
I've Lost You	1930	Unreleased (from Vintage CD VMP 0011)
Let Me Sing And I'm Happy	1930	Continental Transcriptions 4132
Let Yourself Go	1936	Decca 709/Brunswick 02165/Brunswick A 9959
Life Is Just A Bowl Of Cherries	1931	Decca
Liza Lee	1930	Continental Transcriptions 4129
Lonesome Road	1934	Brunswick 6951/Brunswick 01791/Brunswick A 9600
Louisiana Hayride	1932	Brunswick 6470/Brunswick 01625/Brunswick A 9378/Brunswick A 9507/Brunswick A 500230
Lullaby Of Broadway	1935	Brunswick 02043/Brunswick A 9823/Brunswick A 500594
(Meet Me Tonight Dear Old) Pal O' Mine	1925	Victor
Me Minus You	1932	Unreleased (from Vintage CD VMP 0011)
Minnie The Moocher's Wedding Day	1932	Brunswick 6442/Brunswick 01436/Brunswick A 9350/Okeh 4546/Vocalion 4546 (1938)
Mood Indigo	1932	Brunswick 6470/Brunswick

It's You! 1931 Brunswick 6151/Brunswick 80014/Brunswick 01181/Brunswick A 9112

100 Years of Harmony: 1850 to 1950

Title	Year	Release
		01543/Brunswick A 9378/Brunswick A 500230/Columbia 36521/Columbia DB 1960/Rex 8910
Music Goes 'Round And Around, The	1936	Decca 671/Brunswick 02142/Brunswick A 9923
My Future Just Passed	1930	Davis
My Mad Moment	1930	Unreleased (from Vintage CD VMP 0011)
My Mammy	1930	Continental Transcriptions 4132
Nights When I'm Lonely	1925	Victor 19639
Nights When I'm Lonely	1925	Decca
Night When Love Was Born, The	1932	Unreleased (from Vintage CD VMP 0011)
Nothing Is Sweeter Than You	1931	Brunswick 6231/Brunswick 01272/Brunswick A 9208
Object Of My Affection, The	1934	Brunswick 7348//Brunswick A 9702/Brunswick 01961/Columbia 36523
OK America, Part 1 (with Carmen Lombardo and Fran Frey)	1932	Brunswick 20112/Brunswick A 5114
OK America, Part 2 (with Mills Brothers, Fran Frey and Frank Munn)	1932	Brunswick 20112/Brunswick A 5114
Old Man Of The Mountain, The	1932	Decca
Old Yazoo	1932	Brunswick 6360/Brunswick 01379/Brunswick A 9317
One I Love Just Can't Be Bothered With Me, The	1930	Unreleased (from Vintage CD VMP 0011)
Put That Sun Back In The Sky	1932	Lucky 60128 (Brunswick)
Puttin' It On	1933	Brunswick 6625/Brunswick 01576/Brunswick A 9440
Rainy Days	1931	Broadcast for Bakers Chocolate
Rarin' To Go	1930	Unreleased (from Vintage CD VMP 0011)
River, Stay Away From My Door (with the Dorsey Brothers, Joe Venuti and Eddie Lang)	1931	Brunswick 6218/Brunswick 01251/Brunswick 80014/Brunswick A 9191
Rock And Roll	1934	Brunswick 7302/Brunswick 01957/Brunswick A 9672/Columbia 36523/Columbia DS 1462/Odeon A 272287
Roll On, Mississippi, Roll On	1931	Brunswick 6109/Brunswick 01136/Brunswick 80012/Brunswick A 9081
Sentimental Gentleman From Georgia, The	1932	Brunswick 6395/Brunswick 01379/Brunswick A 9392/Columbia 36522/Rex 8910
Sharing	1930	Unreleased (from Vintage CD VMP 0011)
Shine On, Harvest Moon	1931	Brunswick 6173/Brunswick 01218/Brunswick 80013/Brunswick A 9143
Shout, Sister, Shout	1931	Brunswick 6109/Brunswick 01136/Brunswick 1416/Brunswick 6783/Brunswick 80012/Brunswick A 9081/Brunswick A 9390
Shuffle Off To Buffalo	1933	Brunswick 6545/Brunswick 01516/Brunswick A 9416/Brunswick 500241
Sing A Little Jingle (English vocal)	1931	Brunswick 01193
Sing A Little Jingle (scat vocals)	1931	Brunswick 6128/Brunswick A 9076
Sleep, Come On And Take Me	1932	Brunswick unreleased (from Vintage CD VMP 0011)
Song Of Surrender	1933	Brunswick 6733/Brunswick

Song Of The Dawn	1930	Brunswick unreleased (from Vintage CD VMP 0011)
Sophisticated Lady	1933	Brunswick 6650/Brunswick 01592/Brunswick A 9484
St. Louis Blues	1935	Brunswick 7467/Brunswick 02044/Brunswick A 9811/Brunswick A 500577/Columbia DB 1944/Okeh 4495/Vocalion 4495 (1938)
Star Dust	1931	Brunswick 0102/Brunswick 20100/Brunswick A 5106
Stop The Sun, Stop The Moon (My Man's Gone)	1932	Brunswick 6271/Brunswick 01295/Brunswick A 9232
Strange As It Seems	1932	Decca
Swanee Mammy	1933	Brunswick 6625/Brunswick 01576/Brunswick A 9440
That's How Rhythm Was Born	1933	Brunswick 6650/Brunswick 01592/Brunswick A 9484/Columbia DB 1960
That's Love	1931	Brunswick
That's What I Like About You	1930	National
There'll Be Some Changes Made	1932	Brunswick 6291/Brunswick 01306/Brunswick A 9244/Columbia 36521
There's A Wah Wah Girl In Agua Caliente	1930	Brunswick unreleased (from Vintage CD VMP 0011)
This Is The Missus	1931	Brunswick
Through	1930	Brunswick
Time On My Hands	1931	Brunswick
Top Hat, White Tie And Tails	1935	Decca 574/Brunswick 02067/Brunswick A 9854
Trav'lin' All Alone	1935	Brunswick 7467/Brunswick 02044/Brunswick A 9811/Brunswick A 500577/Okeh 4495/Vocalion 4495 (1938)
Washboard Blues	1932	Decca
Was That The Human Thing To Do'	1932	Brunswick 6257/Brunswick 01284/Brunswick A 9226
'Way Back Home	1935	Brunswick 7454/Brunswick 02033/Brunswick A 9800
We Just Couldn't Say Goodbye	1932	Brunswick 6360/Brunswick 01347/Brunswick A 9299
We're On The Highway To Heaven (Caminito Del Cielo)	1930	Victor 22500
(We've Got To) Put That Sun Back In The Sky	1932	Brunswick 6257/Brunswick 01284/Brunswick A 9226
Wha'd Ja Do To Me'	1931	Brunswick 6083/Brunswick 01113/Brunswick 80011/Brunswick A 9066
What Is It'	1931	Unreleased (from Vintage CD VMP 0011)
What Is It'	1931	Brunswick
When I Take My Sugar To Tea	1931	Brunswick 6083/Brunswick 01113/Brunswick 80011/Brunswick A 9066
When The Little Red Roses Get The Blues For You	1930	Unreleased (from Vintage CD VMP 0011)
Why Don't You Practice What You Preach'	1934	Brunswick 6929/Brunswick 01832/Brunswick A 9616
You Can Call Me Baby All The Time	1925	Victor
You Oughta Be In Pictures	1934	Brunswick 6798/Brunswick 01751/Brunswick A 9575

Boswell Sisters (as the Three Boswell Sisters)

Don't Tell Her (What's Happened	1930	Okeh 41470/Odeon

To Me)		A 221321/Odeon O-25200
Heebie Jeebies	1930	Okeh 41444/Odeon 41444/Odeon A 221310/Odeon O-25223
My Future Just Passed	1930	Okeh 41444/Odeon A 221310/Odeon O-25223

Boswell Sisters (with Bing Crosby)
Lawd You Made The Night Too Long	1932	Biltmore 1013/Brunswick 20109 N/ Brunswick 0107/Brunswick A 5113

Boswell Sisters (with New Yorkers)
Makin' A Face At The Man In The Moon	1931	Brunswick 6170/Brunswick 01221/ Brunswick A9141
(With You On My Mind I Find) I Can't Write The Words	1931	Brunswick 6170/Brunswick 01221/Brunswick 01395/Brunswick A9141

Boswell Sisters, Bing Crosby, Mills Bros.
Gems From "George White's Scandals"	1931	Brunswick

Bowen, Billy & the Butterball Five
Diamond Mine In Madagascar	1952	MGM 11271
I'll Remember	1960	X-Tra 101

Bowen, Billy & the Butterball Four
You Broke My Heart	1952	MGM 11271

Bowman Sisters
My Old Kentucky Home	1928	Columbia 15473-D
Old Lonesome Blues	1929	Columbia 15621-D
Railroad Take Me Back	1929	Columbia 15621-D
Swanee River	1928	Columbia 15473-D

Boy Friends, The
It Happened In Monterey	1930	Perfect 11300
When It's Springtime IN The Rockies	1930	Perfect 11300

Boyce's Harlem Serenaders
Get In The Groove	1941	Decca 8585
Harlem After Midnight	1942	Decca 8602

Breckenridge, Paul & the Four Heavenly Knights
I Shall Not Be Moved	1947	King 4192

Brevities Quartet
Woman In The Shoe, The	1930	Brunswick 4737
Wrapped In A Red Red Rose	1930	Brunswick 4737

Brian Sisters
Swinging On A Star	1944	Capitol

Brick Morse Collegians
Big C	1931	Victor 22832
Hail To California	1931	Victor 22832

Bright Moon Quartet
Dying Gambler, Spare Me Lord	1936	Bluebird 6497
Good News, The Chariot Is Coming	1936	Bluebird 6497
If I Could Hear My Mother Pray Again	1936	Bluebird 6674
I See The Sign Of Judgement	1936	Bluebird 6743
Lord, I'm Goin' Through	1936	Bluebird 6743
Lord Send Thee	1936	Bluebird 6613
Pray Unto Thy Father	1936	Bluebird 6674
You Can't Go Wrong And Get By	1936	Bluebird 6613
You're Gonna Need That Pure Religion	1936	Bluebird 6544
Your Name Signed Down	1936	Bluebird 6544

Brilliant Quartet
Grandfather's Birthday	1898	Berliner 0853W
Imitation Of A Steam Calliope	1899	Berliner 0653N
I'se Gwine Back To Dixie	1899	Berliner 0658

Broadway Quartet, Andrea Sarto & the
If The Tango Should Change To A March, Little Girl	1917	Columbia A-2242

Broadway Quartet, Charles W. Harrison & the
Yankee Doodle	1917	Columbia A-2277

Broadway Quartet, Edgar Stoddard & the
Dixie	1917	Columbia A-2277
Three Cheers For The Army And Navy	1917	Columbia A-2294

Broadway Quartet, Henry Burr & the
Come Along Ma Honey	1918	Columbia A-2621

Broadway Quartette
America Prepare!	1916	Columbia A-2046
Any Old Time At All	1924	Banner 1370/Regal 9662
Can't Yo' Heah Me Collin' Caroline	1916	Columbia A-2055
Fair Hawaii	1920	Columbia A-2109
Georgia Rose	1921	Columbia A-3513
Hinky Dinky Parlez Vous	1924	Banner 1382/Regal 9678
Home Again (That's The Song Of The World To Me)	1918	Columbia
Honolulu, My Home	1917	
If Shamrocks Grew Along The Swanee Shore	1921	Columbia A-3438
It's A Long, Long Way To The U.S.A.	1917	Columbia A-2361
I Wonder If You Still Care For Me	1921	Columbia A-3476
Kentucky Home	1921	Columbia
Little Bit Of Heaven	1916	Columbia A-1916
Mammy Lou	1922	Vocalion 14283A

Mammy's Little Coal Black Rose	1916	Columbia A-2114
Murmuring Zephyrs	1916	Columbia A-1941
My Last Cigar	1916	Columbia A-1942
My Sunny Tennessee	1921	Columbia A-3465
On The Banks Of The Wabash	1915	Columbia A-1893
She Sang 'Aloha' To Me	1916	Columbia A-2109
That Old Gang Of Mine	1923	Banner 1257
There's A Long, Long Trail	1916	Columbia A-2055
What's Today Got To Do With Tomorrow'	1924	Banner 1370/Regal 9662
When Evening Shadows Fall	1916	Columbia A-2164
When I Come Back To You (We'll Have A Yankee Doodle Wedding)	1918	Columbia
When Shall We Meet Again	1921	Vocalion 14270B
Where The River Shannon Flows	1916	Columbia A-1916
Winter Medley: Jingle Bells/Aunt Dinah	1916	Columbia A-2125
You Can Have Every Light On Broadway	1922	Vocalion 14312A

Broadway Quartette & Vernon Dalhart
Bull Dog, The	1916	Columbia A-1942

Broadway Quartette (with Oscar Seagle)
When They Ring The Golden Bells For You And Me	1921	Columbia A-3518

Broadway Quartette, Albert Wiederhold & the
We'll Never Let The Old Flag Fall	1916	Columbia A-2023

Broadway Quartette, Charles Harrison & the
When Your Boy Comes Back To You	1916	Columbia A-2312

Broadway Quartette, Hugh Donovan & the
Goodbye Dolly Gray	1918	Columbia A-2476

Bronzeville Five, The Lewis
Cotton Blossom Blues	1940	Bluebird 8433/Montgomery Ward 8898 (1940)
It Can Happen To You	1940	Bluebird 8480/Montgomery Ward 8901 (1940)
Laughing At Life	1940	Bluebird 8433/Montgomery Ward 8898 (1940)
Linda Brown	1940	Bluebird 8460/Montgomery Ward 8899 (1940)
Low Down Gal Blues	1940	Bluebird 8460/Montgomery Ward 8899 (1940)
Mississippi Fire Blues	1940	Bluebird 8445/Montgomery Ward 8900 (1940)
Natchez Mississippi Blues	1940	Bluebird 8445/Montgomery Ward 8900 (1940)
Oh! Mabel, Oh!	1940	Bluebird 8480/Montgomery Ward 8901 (1940)

Brooklyn Boys
If She Should Call	1956	Fenis 902

Brooks Brothers
Fool That I Am	1947	Decca 48049
Is It Too Late	1947	Decca 24267
Mickey	1947	Decca 24267
St. Louis Blues	1946	Diamond 2006
Things You Want Most Of All, The	1948	Decca 24287
Who Were You Kissing	1948	Decca 24287
You're Gonna Make A Wonderful Sweetheart	1947	Decca 48049

Brooks, Dusty (with Four Tones)
Chili Dogs	1951	Bullet 346
Whoa Mule	1951	Bullet 346

Brooks, Orville (the Jubalaires)
I've Waited All My Life For You	1948	Coral 65000
Since Things Got Tough Again	1948	Coral 65000

Brown Brothers
At Sundown	1927	Cameo 1199/Romeo 0427
How Could Jack Horner Just Fit In A Corner		Cameo 8305
Rosy Cheeks	1927	Cameo 1200/Romeo 0428
Yes She Do		Cameo 8306

Brown Dots, Deek Watson & the
As Though You Don't Know	1949	Manor 1166
At Our Fireplace	1949	Manor 1170
Bow-Wow-Wow	1949	Manor 1170
Darktown Strutter's Ball	1949	Manor 1166
Devil Was Beatin' His Wife, The	1949	Varsity 5015
Escuchame (Listen To Me)	1946	Manor 1016
For Sentimental Reasons	1945	Manor 1009/Manor 1041 (1946)
How Can You Say I Don't Care'	1946	Manor 1044/Arco 1253 (1950)/Kayron 1000 (1954)
I Don't Know From Nothin', Baby	1947	Manor 1057
If I Can't Have You	1946	Manor 1027
I'm Loving You For You	1946	Manor 1027
Is It Right'	1945	Manor 1017
It's A Pity To Say Goodnight	1946	Manor 1041
I've Got The Situation Well In Hand	1948	Majestic 1244/Varsity 5015 (1949)
Just In Case You Change Your Mind	1945	Manor 1015/Manor 1163 (1949)

Let's Give Love Another Chance	1945	Manor 1005/Manor 1163 (1949)
Long Legged Lizzie	1946	Manor 1044
My Bonnie Lies Over The Ocean	1949	Manor 1179
Patience And Fortitude	1945	Manor 1017
Please Give A Broken Heart A Break	1946	Manor 1032
Pray For The Lights To Go Out	1948	Majestic 1244
Rumors Are Flying	1946	Manor 1040
Satchelmouth Baby	1946	Manor 1026
Shout, Brother, Shout	1947	Manor 1057
Surrender	1946	Manor 1026
That's What She Gets	1946	Manor 1016/Manor 1075 (1947)
Thirty-One Miles For A Nickel (Subway Serenade)	1945	Manor 1005
Well, Natch!	1946	Manor 1032
You Better Think Twice	1949	Manor 1179
You're A Heartache To Me	1945	Manor 1015
You're Heaven Sent	1945	Manor 1009
You Took All Of My Love	1946	Manor 1040

Brown Dots, Deek Watson & the (as the Sentimentalists)

I'll Close My Eyes	1946	Manor 1047
I Want To Be Loved (with Savannah Churchill)	1947	Manor 1046
Save Me A Dream	1946	Manor 1047

Brown Dots, Gwenn Bell & the

After Awhile	1949	Manor 1171
If I Could Be With You	1949	Manor 1171

Brown Quartet, The Morris

Ain't That Good News	1940	Bluebird 8428
Climbing Up The Mountain	1939	Bluebird 8260
De Blind Man Stood On De Road And Cried	1939	Bluebird 8260
Drink To Me Only With Thine Eyes	1940	Bluebird 8398
I Can Tell The World About This	1939	Bluebird 8275
I'm In His Care	1939	Bluebird 8296
Just A Wearying For You	1940	Bluebird 8398
Rock Of Ages	1940	Bluebird 8479
Rollin' Down To Jordan	1939	Bluebird 8316
Swing Low Sweet Chariot	1939	Bluebird 8275
That Old Time Religion	1940	Bluebird 8428
There's A Great Camp Meeting	1939	Bluebird 8296
Wade In De Water	1939	Bluebird 8316
You Got To Walk That Lonesome Valley	1940	Bluebird 8479

Brox Sisters

Away Down South	1922	Brunswick 2305
Bench In The Park, A (with Rhythm Boys)	1930	Columbia 2164-D/Columbia CB 86/Columbia 07037
Bring On The Pepper	1922	Brunswick 2360
Broken-Hearted Sue	1926	Victor 20325/Zonophone 2883
Come On Home	1922	Brunswick 2360
Cover Me Up With The Sunshine Of Virginia	1924	Victor 19298
Do I'	1922	Brunswick 2330
Down Among The Sleepy Hills Of Tennessee	1923	Brunswick 2247
Early In The Morning Blues	1922	Brunswick 2330
How Many Times'	1926	Victor 20123
I'm Lonely Without You	1926	Victor 20232/Zonophone 2867
Iyone, My Own Iyone	1926	Victor 20123
Kentucky's Way Of Saying "Good Morning"	1926	Victor 19921
Kicky-Koo	1922	Brunswick 2305
Lay Me Down To Sleep In Carolina	1926	Victor 20232/Zonophone 2867
Lazy	1924	Victor 19298
Learn To Do The Strut	1923	Brunswick 2538
Little Boy Blues	1923	Brunswick 2427
Mandy, Make Up Your Mind	1924	Victor 19510
Nobody Loves You Like I Do	1924	Victor 19478
Pretty Cinderella	1926	Victor 20325/Zonophone 2883
Red Hot Mama	1924	Victor 19510
School House Blues, The	1922	Brunswick 2268
Sittin' In A Corner	1923	Brunswick 2538
Some Sunny Day	1922	Brunswick 2268
Sweetest Little Rose In Tennessee	1924	Victor 19478
Tie Me to Your Apron Strings Again	1926	Victor 19921
Tokyo Blues	1925	Victor 19631
Who'	1925	Victor 19631

Brunswick Male Chorus

Homeland	1925	Brunswick 2901
Serenade from 'Student Prince'	1925	Brunswick 2901

Brunswick Male Quartet

Sally	1911	Columbia A-1047
Sing Me A Song Of The South	1909	Columbia A-0798

Brunswick Quartet

I'm Looking For A Nice Young Fellow Who's Looking For A Nice Young Girl (with Ada Jones)	1911	Columbia A-1000/Brunswick
My Wild Irish Rose	1910	Columbia A-0895

Brunswick Quartet (Strand Quartet)

Peck's Bad Boy	1921	Brunswick 2123

Brunswick Quartet, Frank Coombs & the

Seeing Nellie Home	1910	Columbia A-0921

Bryant's Jubilee Quartet
I'll Be Satisfied	1933	Vocalion 2615/Conqueror 8456 (1934)
I'm Going Through	1933	Vocalion 2615

Bryant's Jubilee Singers
Everytime I Feel The Spirit	1934	Conqueror 8358
Hold The Wind	1934	Conqueror 8357
King Jesus Is Listening	1933	Vocalion 25019
Let Jesus Lead You	1931	Conqueror 7799
Oh Rocks Don't You Fall On Me	1934	Conqueror 8357
Shine On Me	1934	Conqueror 8358
Sinner You Better Get Ready	1934	Conqueror 8456
South Bound Passenger Train	1931	Conqueror 7749
When This World's On Fire	1933	Vocalion 25019
Who Stole De Lock'	1931	Conqueror 7749

Brymm's Quartet, Tim (Tim Brymm's Black Devil Four)
Aunt Hagar's Blues	1923	Okeh 8011/Okeh 8054 (1923)

Bubbling Over Five
Don't Mistreat Your Good Boyfriend	1929	Okeh 8737
Get Up Off That Jazzophone	1929	Okeh 8737

Buccaneers
There's Something About A Soldier	1934	Columbia 2911-D
Wagon Wheels	1934	Columbia 2911-D

Buck Trio, Verne
What A Girl! What A Night!	1928	Columbia 1651-D

Buckley, Eugene & Quartet
K-K-Katy	1918	Columbia A-2530

Buddies, Billy Bunn & his
I'm Afraid	1951	RCA Victor 47-4483
I Need A Shoulder To Cry On	1951	RCA Victor 47-4483
That's When Your Heartaches Begin	1952	RCA Victor 47-4657
Until The Real Thing Comes Along	1952	RCA Victor 47-4657

Buddies, Bob Camp & his
Between You And Me	1949	Decca 48118
My Little Rose	1949	Decca 48112
Reading Blues	1949	Decca 48112
When You Surrender To Me	1949	Decca 48118

Buddies, Bon Bon & his
Rickety Rockin' Chair	1942	Decca 8628
Seeing You Again Did Me No Good	1942	Decca 8603
Sleepy Old Town	1942	Decca 8603

Buddies, Bon Bon & the
All That Meat And No Potatoes	1941	Decca 8567
Blow, Gabriel Blow	1941	Decca 8567
I Don't Want To Set The World On Fire	1941	Decca 3980
I'm Not Much On Looks	1942	Decca 8622
Sweet Mama Papa's Getting Mad	1941	Decca 3980

Burke, C. & Three Shades/Four Dreamers
From Twilight 'Till Dawn	1943	Excelsior

Burnett, Rev. J. C. & his Quartet
Rejected Stone	1928	Columbia 14385-D
Will The Circle Be Unbroken	1928	Columbia 14385-D

Burr Octet, The Henry
Lass O'Mine	1927	Victor 37388
Swing Along	1927	Victor 37387

Burr, Henry & Quartet
I Am Praying For You	1908	Columbia A-0241
Silver Threads Among The Gold	1923	Victor 19112

Burr, Henry (with Columbia Stellar Quartet)
Carry Me Back To Old Virginia	1915	Columbia A-1820
Heidelberg Stein Song	1920	Columbia A-1852
My Wild Irish Rose	1920	Columbia A-1852
Old Oaken Bucket, The	1915	Columbia A-1820

Burr, Henry (with Peerless Quartet)
Cows May Come, Cows May Go, But The Bull Goes On Forever	1915	Columbia A-1696
I'se Gwine Back To Dixie	1920	Columbia A-1881
Kentucky Home	1921	Victor 18821
Over There	1917	Columbia A-2306
Submarine Attack Somewhere At Sea, The	1918	Columbia A-2626

Burt, Virginia & the Shannon Four
Hymns Of The Old Church	1923	Okeh 4768

Burtnett's Biltmore Trio, Earl
Garden In The Rain, A	1929	Brunswick 4336
Love Boat	1928	Brunswick 4232/Brunswick 03965
Love Me Or Leave Me	1929	Brunswick 4336
Old Plantation	1928	Brunswick 4350/Brunswick A8879
Song Of The Islands	1928	Brunswick 4350/Brunswick A8879

Burton, Billy & Quartet
Have A Heart: Napoleon	1917	Columbia A-2307
Have A Heart: Napoleon (Part 2)	1917	Columbia A-2307

Bush Brothers
Complete For All The World	1928	Columbia 15287-D
Does Your Path Seem Long	1928	Columbia 15287-D
Endless Glory To The Lamb	1929	Columbia 15500-D
Happy Pilgrims	1929	Columbia
I'll Make It My Home	1930	Columbia 15649-D
I'm No Stranger To Jesus	1930	Columbia 15696-D
In A Little While	1930	Columbia

Keep Your Light Shining	1929	Columbia 15524-D	**Bush Trio, Eddie (as Earl Burtnett's Biltmore Trio)**		
Look Inside The Glory Gate, A	1930	Columbia 15649-D	How Are You Tonight In Hawaii'	1930	Brunswick
My Happiest Day	1929	Columbia 15500-D	If I Can't Have You (If You Can't Have Me)	1929	Brunswick 4619
On The Glory Road	1928	Columbia 15263-D			
Pathway, The	1929	Columbia 15524-D	If I'm Dreaming (Don't Wake Me Too Soon)	1930	Brunswick 4715/Brunswick A 8700
Redeeming Love	1929	Columbia			
Singing Along The Way	1930	Columbia			
What Love!	1930	Columbia 15696-D	I'm Sorry Sally	1928	Brunswick 4185
When The Gates Of Glory Open	1928	Columbia 15263-D	Look What You've Done To Me	1929	Brunswick 4605
Bush Brothers Sacred Singers			Moonlight On The Colorado	1930	Brunswick
Called Home	1927	Columbia 15368-D	Out Of The Past	1929	Brunswick 4619
Hallelujah! He Is Mine	1927	Columbia 15235-D	Stairway Of Dreams	1928	Brunswick 4105
He Pardoned Me	1927	Columbia 15203-D	Steppin' Along	1929	Brunswick 4522
Mother Dear Is Waiting	1927	Columbia 15368-D	Swingin' In A Hammock	1930	Brunswick
Oh Wonderful Day	1927	Columbia 15235-D	Tired Of Love	1930	Brunswick
Saved By His Sweet Grace	1927	Columbia 15203-D	Truthful Parson Brown	1931	Brunswick
Bush Trio, Eddie			What Do I Care'	1929	Brunswick 4605
At Last I'm In Love	1929	Brunswick 4607	Where Is The Song Of Songs For Me'	1928	Brunswick 4105
Go Home And Tell Your Mother	1930	Brunswick 4872/Brunswick 01024/Brunswick A 8829			
			Where The Golden Daffodils Grow	1930	Brunswick 4825
Here Comes The Sun	1930	Brunswick 4861/ Brunswick A 8819	Where The Shy Little Violets Grow	1928	Brunswick 4185
			With A Song In My Heart	1929	Brunswick 4522
I'm A Dreamer - Aren't We All'	1929	Brunswick A 8531/Brunswick 4573	Year From Today, A	1930	Brunswick 4715/Brunswick A 8700
I'm Doin' That Thing	1930	Brunswick 4872/Brunswick 01024/Brunswick A 8829	You Will Come Back To me	1930	Brunswick 4825
			Across The Sea	1929	Brunswick 4338/Brunswick A 8664
Just A Little Dance, Mam'selle	1930	Brunswick 4927/Brunswick 01074	Avalon Town	1929	Brunswick 4262
			I'm In Love With You	1929	Brunswick 4511
			I'm That Way About Baby	1929	Brunswick 4407
Lila	1928	Columbia	May Day Is Lei Day In Hawaii	1929	Brunswick 4338/Brunswick A 8664
Now I'm In Love	1929	Brunswick 4443			
Parade Of The Blues	1929	Brunswick 4634			
Singing A Song To The Stars	1930	Brunswick 4830		1929	Brunswick 4407
Song Of The Dawn	1930	Brunswick 4756/Brunswick A 8724	This Is Heaven		
			Web Of Love, The	1929	Brunswick 4511
			Bush Trio, Eddie (as the Biltmore Trio)		
Stay Out Of The South	1928	Columbia 1361-D	Do You Ever Think Of Me'	1929	Brunswick 4217
Sweet Sue - Just You	1928	Columbia 1361-D	I Gotta Feelin' For You	1929	Brunswick A 4376/Brunswick A 8287
That's What I Call Sweet Music	1929	Brunswick 4443			
There's A Religion In Rhythm	1931	Brunswick			
Tune In On My Heart	1929	Brunswick 4599	Neighbors (with Stanley Hickman)	1934	Columbia 2922-D
Was I Just Another Love Affair To You	1931	Brunswick			
			Orange Blossom Time	1929	Brunswick 4375
What Do I Care'	1929	Brunswick 4599	Ridin' Around In The Rain	1934	Columbia 2921-D
When The Little Red Roses Get The Blues For You	1930	Brunswick 4716/Brunswick A 8684	Waitin' At The Gate For Katy	1934	Columbia 2922-D
			Your Mother And Mine	1929	Brunswick A 4377/Brunswick A 8283
With You	1930	Brunswick 4679/Brunswick A 8678	You Were Meant For Me	1929	Brunswick 4231/Brunswick

Bush Trio, Eddie (as vocal quartet)
Happy	1928	Brunswick 4104/Brunswick A 8041
Sally Of My Dreams	1928	Brunswick 4104/Brunswick A 8041

Bush Trio, Eddie (s Eddie Bush's Biltmore Trio)
I Can't Go On Like This	1934	Victor 24565

C. & M.A. Gospel Quintette
Jesus Remembered You	1925	Columbia 79-P
Shine For Jesus	1925	

Cabin Boys, Delores Jackson & the
Carelessly	1938	Decca 7396
Cloudy	1938	Decca 7396

Cabineers
Baby Mine	1952	Prestige 917
Baby, Where'd You Go'	1951	Prestige 902
Each Time	1951	Prestige 904
How Can I Help It'	1949	Abbey 3001
How Was I To Know	1941	Decca 7835
Let The Party Go On	1941	Decca 7873/Clanka Lanka CL-144.033
Lindy	1941	Decca 7835
Lost	1951	Prestige 904
My, My, My	1951	Prestige 902
Sweet Louise	1941	Decca 7872
Tell Me Now	1949	Abbey 3001
What's The Matter With You'	1952	Prestige 917
Whirlpool	1949	Abbey 3003/Abbey 72 (1949)
You're Just A Great Big Heartache To Me	1949	Abbey 3003/Abbey 72 (1949)

Caldwells
I Don't Hurt Anymore	1947	RCA 20-2613
I Gotta Move	1947	RCA 20-2613

California Aeolians
Little Close Harmony, A	1931	Columbia
Lord Is My Shepherd, The	1931	Columbia
Moonlight On The Lake	1931	Columbia
Old Rugged Cross, The	1931	Columbia 15699-D
Rose Of Sharon, The	1931	Columbia 15699-D
What Did He Do'	1931	Columbia

California American Legion Quartet
In Rest Camp	1929	Vocalion 15816B
In The Trenches	1929	Vocalion 15816

California Humming Birds
Ain't She Sweet	1927	Cameo 1129
Constantinople	1928	Victor 21477
Could I' I Certainly Could!	1926	Cameo 962
Counting The Days	1926	Cameo 1009
Crazy Words, Crazy Tune (Vo-do-de-o)	1927	Cameo 1099/Lincoln 2614
Down On The Florida Shore	1926	Cameo 909
Everything's Gonna Be Alright	1926	Cameo 909
For My Sweetheart	1926	Cameo 1008
Get Out Of That Aeroplane, Jane	1928	Victor BVE-43312
Her Beaus Are Only Rainbows	1926	Cameo 948
Horses	1926	Cameo 930
Hot Henry!	1926	Cameo 930
How Many Times'	1926	Cameo 1008/Romeo 269
If I Didn't Know Your Husband	1927	Cameo 1100
I Just Roll Along (Havin' My Ups And Downs)	1928	Victor 21309
I'm Just Wild About Animal Crackers	1926	Cameo 949
(I'm Sitting Here, You're Sitting Here) What Are We Waiting For'	1926	Cameo 1002/Romeo 267
It Goes Like This	1928	Victor 21766
Let's Talk About My Sweetie	1926	Cameo 943
Lonesome And Sorry	1926	Cameo 949
My Dream Of The Big Parade	1926	Cameo 960
Nesting Time	1927	Cameo 1101
She Don't Wanna	1927	Victor 20753
She Knows Her Onions	1926	Cameo 1009
She's A Great, Great Girl	1928	Victor 21309
She's Got It	1927	Cameo 1186/Romeo 0413
Somebody Is Sweet On Me	1928	Victor 21477
Ten Little Miles From Town	1928	Victor 21766
Thanks For The Buggy Ride	1926	Cameo 920
That's A Good Girl	1926	Cameo 1026
There's A Trick In Pickin' A Chick, Chick, Chicken	1927	Cameo 1202/Romeo 0430
There's Something Nice About Everyone But) There's Everything Nice About You	1927	Cameo 1099/Lincoln 2614
When The Red, Red, Robin Comes Bob, Bob, Bobbin' Along	1926	Romeo 267
Whisper Song, The (When The Pussy Willow Whispers To The Catnip)	1927	Victor 20753
Why Can't A Fella Like Me Get A Girl Like You	1926	Cameo 920
Why Don't You Marry The Girl	1926	Cameo 948
Would Anybody Like To Have A Car	1928	Victor
Ya Gotta Know How To Love 'Em	1926	Lincoln 2561

Cameo Male Quartet
College Days Medley	1924	Cameo 529
Old Time Medley	1924	Cameo 529

Campbell Quartet
My Lord What A Morning	1931	Okeh 8900
There Is A Balm In Gilead	1931	Okeh 8900

Campbell's Sacred Singers (Criterion Quartet)
Old Rugged Cross (with chimes), The	1926	Aurora 22034

Campbell's Sacred Singers (Old Southern Sacred Singers)
Safe In The Arms Of Jesus	1927	Aurora 22035
What A Friend We Have In Jesus	1927	Aurora 22035

Campbell's Swanee Singers, Roy
Cradle And The Music Box, The	1935	Victor 24842
I Was Lucky	1935	Victor 24845

Campbell's Swanee Singers, Roy (as Jack Ericson & Trio)
Tiny Little Fingerprints	1935	Victor 24842

Campus Boys
I Faw Down An' Go Boom!	1928	Banner 6257

Campus Four
Cuddle Closer	1927	Columbia 959-D

Campus Male Quartet
Drinking Song	1925	Brunswick 2944
Homeland	1925	Brunswick
I Like Pie, I Like Cake, But I Like You Best Of All	1925	Brunswick 2868
We're Gonna Have Weather (Whether Or Not)	1925	Brunswick 2868

Campus Trio
Absence Makes The Heart Grow Fonder (For Somebody Else)	1930	Columbia 2238-D
By A Lazy Country Lane	1931	Columbia 2441-D
Come To Me	1931	Columbia 2514D
Don't Tell Her What's Happened To Me	1930	Columbia 2275-D
Guilty	1931	Columbia 2523D
Have You Forgotten'	1931	Columbia 2471-D
Hello! Beautiful	1931	Columbia 2376D
Here Comes The Sun	1930	Columbia 2238-D
Hot Choc'late Soldiers	1934	Victor 24623
Hittin' The Bottle	1930	Columbia 2254D
I'm An Unemployed Sweetheart (Looking For Somebody To Love)	1931	Columbia 2493D
It's A Lonesome Old Town (When You're Not Around)	1931	Columbia 2402-D
It's The Girl	1931	Columbia 2493D
I Want You For Myself	1931	Columbia 2402-D
Life Is Just A Bowl Of Cherries	1931	Columbia 2523D
Little Things In Life, The	1930	Columbia 2334D
Little White Lies	1930	Columbia 2254D
Lonesome Rover	1930	Columbia 2363D
Mary Jane	1931	Columbia 2441-D
My Baby Just Cares For Me	1930	Columbia 2301-D
One Little Raindrop	1931	Columbia 2413D
One More Kiss, Then Goodnight	1932	Columbia 2613D
Reaching For The Moon	1930	Columbia 2363D
Shine On, Harvest Moon	1931	Columbia 2514D
Star Dust	1931	Columbia 2471-D
Stein Song (University of Maine)	1930	Columbia 2151-D
Sweetheart Of My Student Days	1930	Columbia 2334D
Sweetheart Trail	1930	Columbia 2140-D
Sweet Jennie Lee	1930	Columbia 2301-D
Three Little Piggies Are Pork	1934	
Chops Now, The (with Adele Girard)		
Thrill Me	1931	Columbia 2413D
Tomorrow Is Another Day	1930	Columbia 2275-D
Where Have You Been'	1931	Columbia 2376D

Candy Makers
And So Tomorrow	1946	Urban 124

Capitol City Four
By The Watermelon Vine	1940	Victor 26631
Dear Old Girl	1940	Victor 26630
Down By The Old Mill Stream	1940	Victor 26632
I've Been Working On The Railroad	1940	Victor 26630
Just A Dream Of You Dear	1940	Victor 26631
Sweet Adeline	1940	Victor 26632

Cap-Tans
Asking	1951	Coral 65071
Chief, Turn The Hose On Me	1950	Dot 1018
Crazy About My Honey Dip	1950	Dot 1009
I Love You So	1951	Flyright
I'm So Crazy For Love	1950	Dot 1009/Dot 15114 (1953)
My, My, Ain't She Pretty	1950	Gotham 233
Never Be Lonely	1950	Gotham 233
Satchelmouth Baby	1948	D.C 8048
Waiting At The Station	1951	Gotham 268
Who Can I Turn To'	1951	Coral 65071
With All My Love	1950	Dot 1018/Dot 15114 (1953)
Yes	1948	D.C. 8048
Yes, I Thought I Could Forget	1951	Gotham 268

Cap-Tans, Paul Chapman & the
Coo-Coo Jug-Jug	1948	D.C. 8054
Goodnight Mother	1948	D.C. 8064
Let's Put Our Cards On The Table	1948	D.C. 8064
You'll Always Be My Sweetheart	1948	D.C. 8054

Cardinal Quartet (Jolly Bakers)
I've Got The Girl	1926	Challenge 241

Carolina Gospel Singers
He Bore It All	1929	Champion 15901/Champion 45177 (1929)
In Gesemalne Alone	1929	Champion 15901
Jesus Paid It All	1929	Champion 15856/Champion 45177 (1929)
My Prayer	1929	Champion 15833
My Redeemer Lives	1929	Champion 15833
We Will Rise And Shine	1929	Champion 15856

Carolina Ladies Quartet
Don't Put Off Salvation Too Long	1929	Champion 15879
It Won't Be Long	1931	Champion 16319
I've Got A Home In The Rock	1931	Champion 16662

Life Boat, The	1931	Champion 16319
My Loved Ones Are Waiting For Me	1929	Champion 15879
Sitting At The Feet Of Jesus	1931	Champion 16644
Under His Wings	1931	Champion 16644

Carolina Quartet

His Name Is Jesus	1927	Okeh 45189
Is It Well With Your Soul'	1927	Okeh 45175
Saved By His Sweet Grace	1927	Okeh 45175
Twilight Is Stealing	1927	Okeh 45189

Carollers

Come All Ye Faithful/Good King Wenceslas	1941	Bluebird 11352
Hark The Herald Angels Sing/Christmas Carols	1941	Bluebird 11352
Joy To The World/Oh Holy Night	1941	Bluebird 11350
While Shepherds Watched Their Flocks	1941	Bluebird 11350

Carols

Call For Me If You Want Me		Savoy 989
Drink Gin	1950	Columbia 30210
Fifty Million Women	1953	Savoy 896
If I Could Steal You From Somebody Else	1950	Columbia 30217
I Got A Feelin'	1953	Savoy 896
I Should Have Thought	1950	Columbia 30217
Mighty Like A Rose		Savoy 989
Please Believe In Me	1950	Columbia 30210

Cathedral Quartet

Abide By Me	1925	Harmony 12-H/Velvet Tome 1014-V
Dinah	1925	Victor 19796
Holy Holy Holy	1925	Harmony 14-H
Lohengrin Wedding March	1922	Vocalion 14321B
Oh, Miss Hannah!	1925	Victor 19796

Cats & the Fiddle

Another Day	1942	Bluebird 8902/RCA Victor 47-4393 (1951)
Blue Skies	1941	Bluebird 8847
Chant Of The Rain	1940	Bluebird 8402/Montgomery Ward 8521 (1940)/RCA Victor 20-2795 (1948)
Crawlin' Blues	1941	Bluebird 8705
Darling, Can't We Make A Date	1947	Manor 1086
Do You (Really) Love Me	1950	Gotham 239
Gang Busters	1939	Bluebird 8248/RCA Victor 20-2794 (1948)
Gone	1940	Bluebird 8465/Montgomery Ward 8769 (1940)
Hep Cat's Holiday	1940	Bluebird 8519
Honey, Honey, Honey	1948	Manor 1112
Hush-A-Bye Love	1940	Bluebird 8585/Montgomery Ward 8905 (1941)
I Don't Want To Set The World On Fire	1941	Bluebird 8847
I'd Rather Drink Muddy Water	1940	Bluebird 8402/Montgomery Ward 8521 (1940)/Manor 1045 (flip is
If I Dream Of You	1941	Bluebird 8665/RCA Victor 20-3260 (1948)
I'll Always Love You Just The Same	1941	Bluebird 8639
I'll Never, Never Let You Go	1949	Gotham 197
I'm Afraid Of You	1948	Manor 1112
I'm Gonna Pull My Hair	1941	Bluebird 8665/Manor 1078 (1947)/RCA Victor 20-3260 (1948)
I Miss You So	1940	Bluebird 8429/Regis 6000 (1946)/Manor 6000 (1947)/Montgomery Ward 8767 (1940)/RCA Victor 20-2072 (flip is
I'm Singing (So Help Me)	1941	Bluebird 8685
I'm Stuck With You	1947	Manor 1067
In The Midst Of A Dream	1940	Bluebird 8519
Just A Roamer	1940	Bluebird 8489/Montgomery Ward 8770 (1940)
Killer Diller Man From The South	1939	Bluebird 10484/Montgomery Ward 8519 (1940)
Killin' Jive	1939	Bluebird 8216
Lawdy-Clawdy	1941	Bluebird 8870
Left With The Thought Of You	1940	Bluebird 8443/Montgomery Ward 8768 (1940)
Life's Too Short	1942	Bluebird 8932/Manor 1023 (1946)
Lover Boy	1950	Decca 48151
Mister Rhythm Man	1940	Bluebird 8465/Montgomery Ward 8769 (1940)
Movin' Out Today	1950	Gotham 239
My Darling	1941	Bluebird 8685
My Sugar's Sweet To Me	1946	Regis 6000/Manor

Title	Year	Label
New Look Blues, The	1948	Manor 1140
Nothing	1940	Bluebird 8535
Nuts To You	1939	Bluebird 8216
One Is Never Too Old To Swing	1941	Bluebird 8639
Out In The Cold Again	1950	Decca
Part Of Me	1942	Bluebird 8932
Pig's Idea	1940	Bluebird 8560/Montgomery Ward 8904 (1941)
Please Don't Leave Me Now	1939	Bluebird 8248/Manor 1037 (1946)/RCA Victor 20-2794 (1948)
Public Jitterbug No. 1	1940	Bluebird 8429/Montgomery Ward 8767 (1940)
Romance Without Finance	1946	Manor 1023
Shorty's Got To Go	1946	Manor 1037
Sighing And Crying	1941	Bluebird 8870
Start Talking Baby	1949	Gotham 197
Stomp, Stomp	1942	Bluebird 8902
Swing The Scales	1940	Bluebird 8585/Montgomery Ward 8905 (1941)
That's All I Mean To You	1940	Bluebird 8535
That's My Desire	1947	Manor 1064
That's On, Jack, That's On	1940	Bluebird 8489/Montgomery Ward 8770 (1940)
That's What I Thought You Said	1948	Manor 1140
They Don't Understand	1947	Manor 1067
Thursday Evening Swing	1939	Bluebird 10484/Montgomery Ward 8519 (1940)
Till The Day I Die	1939	Bluebird 10547/Montgomery Ward 8520 (1940)
Until I Met You	1941	Bluebird 8705
We Cats Will Swing For You	1939	Bluebird 10547/Montgomery Ward 8520 (1940)
When Elephants Roost In Bamboo Trees	1947	Manor 1064
When I Grow Too Old To Dream	1940	Bluebird 8443/Montgomery Ward 8768 (1940)
Where Are You	1947	Manor 1078
Wine Drinker	1950	Decca 48151
You're So Fine	1940	Bluebird 8560/Manor 1086 6000 (1947)/Arco 1265 (1950)

Cats & the Fiddle, June Davis & the

Title	Year	Label
Gin Misery Blues	1946	Manor 1038
J.D. Blues	1946	Manor 1038

Cats 'N' Jammer Three, Bill Samuels & the

Title	Year	Label
Candy Store Stomp	1947	Mercury 8029
For You	1947	Mercury 8033
Ghost Of A Chance	1947	Mercury 8012
I Cover The Waterfront	1946	Mercury 2003
If I Had Another Chance	1947	Mercury 8064
I Know What You're Puttin' Down	1947	Mercury 8037
I'm Coming Home To Stay	1946	Mercury 2021
I'm Falling For You	1946	Mercury 8006
I Surrender Dear	1947	Mercury 8021
Jockey Blues	1946	Mercury 2003
Lilacs In The Rain	1947	Mercury 8037
My Baby Didn't Even Say Goodbye	1947	Mercury 8033
My Bicycle Tillie	1947	Mercury 8021
One For The Money	1947	Mercury 8064
One Hundred Years From Today	1946	Mercury 2021
Open The Door, Richard!	1947	Mercury 8029
Port Wine	1947	Mercury 8012
That Chick's Too Young To Fry	1946	Mercury 8006

Cavendish Three

Title	Year	Label
Shakespeare In Rhythm	1940	

Cecelian Quartet

Title	Year	Label
Heart Of Oak	1914	Victor 17698

Cecilian Arcadian Quartet

Title	Year	Label
Girl I Left Behind Me, The	1911	Victor 16874

Central Mississippi Quartet

Title	Year	Label
Angels Please Tell Mother	1930	Okeh 45534
Far Away In The South	1930	Vocalion 5415
God's Children Are Gathering Home	1930	Okeh 45514
I'll Wear A White Robe	1930	Okeh 45525
My Heart's In Mississippi	1930	Vocalion 5415
Safe In The Homeland	1930	Okeh 45514
Shake Hands With Mother	1930	Okeh 45534
Sweetest Mother	1930	Okeh 45525

Century Quartet, Frank Luther & the

Title	Year	Label
Ah, May The Red Rose Live Always	1940	Decca 3499A
Comrades, Fill No Glass For Me	1940	Decca 3497B
Gentle Annie/Dolly Day	1940	Decca 3498A
Glendy Burk/Under The Willow/Way Down To Cairo	1940	Decca 3496B
Hour For Thee And Me/My Brudder Gum	1940	Decca 3495A
Laura Lee/Angelina Baker	1940	Decca 3495B
Mother Thou'rt Faithful To Me	1940	Decca 3496A
Open They Lattice, Love	1940	Decca 3497A
Our Bright Summer Days Are	1940	Decca 3498B

Gone Medley		
Sweetly She Sleeps, My Alice Fair	1940	Decca 3499B

Century Quartet, Frank Luther, Zora Layman & the

Adelita/Four Little White Doves (Songs Of Old California)	1939	Decca 2473B
America (Patriotic Songs For Children)	1939	Decca 2476A
America The Beautiful (Patriotic Songs For Children)	1939	Decca 2476B
As Your Hair Grows Whiter/Cat Came Back Medley (Songs Of The Gay Nineties)	1939	Decca 2460A
At Buffalo/Somebody Loves Me Medley (Songs Of The Gay Nineties)	1939	Decca 2461A
Ballad Of Henry Green/Siege Of Plattsburg (Songs Of Old New York Pt. 5)	1939	Decca 2431A
Buffalo Gals/Perry's Victory/By The Lake (Songs Of Old New York Pt. 6)	1939	Decca 2431B
Christmas In Song Medley (Pt. 10)	1939	Decca 2867B
Christmas In Song Medley (Pt. 3)	1939	Decca 2864A
Christmas In Song Medley (Pt. 4)	1939	Decca 2864B
Christmas In Song Medley (Pt. 5)	1939	Decca 2865A
Christmas In Song Medley (Pt. 6)	1939	Decca 2865B
Christmas In Song Medley (Pt. 7)	1939	Decca 2866A
Christmas In Song Medley (Pt. 8)	1939	Decca 2866B
Christmas In Song Medley (Pt. 9)	1939	Decca 2867A
Christmas In Song Pt. 1: Christmas In The Morning	1939	Decca 2863A
Christmas In Song Pt. 2:	1939	Decca 2863B
Christmas In Song Vol II	1939	Decca 2868A
Christmas In Song Vol II	1939	Decca 2869A
Christmas In Song Vol II	1939	Decca 2869B
Christmas In Song Vol II	1939	Decca 2870A
Christmas In Song Vol II	1939	Decca 2870B
Christmas In Song Vol II	1939	Decca 2871A
Christmas In Song Vol II	1939	Decca 2871B
Christmas In Song Vol II	1939	Decca 2872A
Christmas In Song Vol II	1939	Decca 2872B
Cielito Lindo/The Night Is Serene (Songs Of Old California)	1939	Decca 2472B
Clementine/Abalone (Songs Of Old California)	1939	Decca 2475B
Columbia, The Gem Of The Ocean (Patriotic Songs For Children)	1939	Decca 2477B
Dutch Company/Dutch Lullaby Medley (Songs Of Old New York Pt. 3)	1939	Decca 2430A
Erie, The/Niagara Falls/Low Bridge (Songs Of Old New York Pt. 4)	1939	Decca 2430B
Faded Coat Of Blue/Battle Hymn, The	1939	Decca 2428B
Flag Around Me, Boys Medley, The	1939	Decca 2428A
Hail Columbia (Patriotic Songs For Children)	1939	Decca 2477A
Hammock, The/Teamster's Song/White Hawk (Songs Of Old California)	1939	Decca 2474B
Hello My Baby/White Wings/Kathleen Medley (Songs Of The Gay Nineties)	1939	Decca 2457B
In The Bright Mohawk Valley/Sparkling And Bright (Songs Of Old New York Pt. 2)	1939	Decca 2429B
Joe Bowers/Santy Ana (Songs Of Old California)	1939	Decca 2473A
Just As The Sun Went Down/Take Back Your Gold (Songs Of The Gay Nineties)	1939	Decca 2462B
Kiss Me Honey Do/Keep A Place At The Table (Songs Of The Gay Nineties)	1939	Decca 2460B
Life On The Vicksburg Bluff, A/Lilly Dale (Songs Of The South Pt. 6)	1939	Decca 2423B
Linen Clothes/Seeing The Elephant (Songs Of Old California)	1939	Decca 2474A
Michael Roy/A Little More Cider Medley	1939	Decca 2432B
My Pearl's A Bowery Girl/Two Sides To Every Story (Songs Of The Gay Nineties)	1939	Decca 2458A
New York, Oh What A Charming City/Jim Fiske (Songs Of Old New York Pt. 1)	1939	Decca 2429A
On The Banks Of The Sacramento Medley (Songs Of Old California)	1939	Decca 2472A
On The Benches In The Park/I Waited Long Medley (Songs Of The Gay Nineties)	1939	Decca 2459B
Pt. 1:Battle Cry Of Freedom/Marching Along	1939	Decca 2425A
Pt. 2:We Are Coming Father Abraham	1939	Decca 2425B
Pt. 3: Tenting Tonight On The Old Camp Ground	1939	Decca 2426A
Pt. 4:Before The Battle, Mother Medley	1939	Decca 2426B
Pt. 5:When Johnny Comes Marching Home Again Medley	1939	Decca 2427A

Pt. 6:The Vacant Chair/Tramp Tramp Tramp	1939	Decca 2427B
Rose Of Alabama/Bonnie Eloise (Songs Of The South Pt. 5)	1939	Decca 2423A
Songs Of The South (Songs Of The South Pt. 2)	1939	Decca 2421B
Stonewall Jackson's Way/Cavaliers Of Dixie (Songs Of The South Pt. 8)	1939	Decca 2424B
Sweet Betsy From Pike/Little Ah Sid (Songs Of Old California)	1939	Decca 2475A
Ta-Ra-Ra-Boom-Der-E/In Good Old New York Again (Songs Of the Gay Nineties)	1939	Decca 2457A
Throw Him Down, McLoskey/She May Have Seen Bette	1939	Decca 2458B
When This Cruel War Is Over (Songs Of The South Pt. 7)	1939	Decca 2424A
While Strolling Through The Park One Day Medley (Songs Of The Gay Nineties)	1939	Decca 2459A
Woodman Spare That Tree/Benny Havens (Songs Of Old New York Pt. 7)	1939	Decca 2432A

Challenge Four (Jolly Bakers)
High, High, High Up In The Hills	1927	Challenge 241

Challenge Harmony Four
Juanita	1928	Challenge 419
Old Oaken Bucket, The	1928	Challenge 418
When You're Gone I Won't Forget	1927	Challenge 417

Challenge Quartet
Annie Laurie	1919	Challenge 170
Do Your Best Then Wear A Smile	1928	Challenge 430
Home Sweet Home	1919	Challenge 171/Challenge 249 (1921)
Kentucky Babe	1923	Challenge 174
Little Cotton Dolly	1923	Challenge 173
Long, Long Ago	1923	Challenge 174
Old Oaken Bucket, The	1923	Challenge 173
On The Banks Of The Wabash	1921	Challenge 171/Challenge 249 (1921)/Challenge 350
Riding On The Glory Waves	1928	Challenge 430
Sam, The Old Accordion Man	1927	Challenge 266
When I First Met Mary	1927	Challenge 266

Challenge Quartette (Criterion Quartette)
Old Black Joe	1922	Challenge 170

Challenge Trio (Sterling Trio)
Always	1926	Challenge 203
In My Gondola	1926	Challenge 204
In The Middle Of The Night	1926	Challenge 204
Someone To Love	1926	Challenge 203

Champion Gospel Quartet
Church In The Wildwood	1928	Champion 45113

Champion Quartet (Criterion Quartet)
First Noel, The	1922	Champion 15041
God Rest Ye Merry Gentlemen	1923	Champion 15043
Hark The Herald Angels	1924	Champion 15045
Jingle Bells	1923	Champion 15042
Silent Night	1923	Champion 15044
There's A Light In The Valley	1923	Gennett 5273

Champion Quartette
Silent Night	1922	Champion 15044

Champion Sacred Quartet
O Come All Ye Faithful	1928	Champion 40048 (1927)/ Champion 16052 (1928)/Champion 16123 (1928)Champion 16675 (1928)
Silent Night	1928	Champion 15601/Champion 16123 (1928)/Champion 16675 (1928)
Silent Night, Holy Night	1927	Champion 40048/Champion 16502 (1928)

Chanaclairs
See See Rider	1949	Coleman 1056
Yuletide Love	1949	Coleman 1056

Chanters
Charming	1934	Victor 24559
Inka Dinka Doo	1934	Victor 24503/Electrola EG 2998
Like Me A Little Bit Less	1934	Victor 24506
Party's Over, The	1934	Victor 24523
Throw Another Long On The Fire	1934	Victor 24523
What's Good For The Goose (Is Good For The Gander)	1934	Victor 24556

Chapel Bells Trio
Face To Face	1934	Brunswick 7475
God Be With You	1934	Brunswick 7475
Lead Kindly Light	1934	Brunswick 7476
Nearer My God To Thee	1934	Brunswick 7476

Chapel Quartet
Beautiful Isle Of Somewhere	1937	Decca 1148
Come, Ye Thankful People	1937	Decca 1055
God Be With You Till We Meet Again	1937	Decca 1148
Hark! The Herald Angels Sing	1937	Decca 1055
It Came Upon A Midnight Clear	1937	Decca 1054
Oh Little Town Of Bethlehem	1937	Decca 1054

Charioteers
All Alone And Lonely	1941	Okeh 6220

Title	Year	Label/Number
All God's Chillun Got Shoes	1939	Brunswick 8468/Columbia 35741 (1939)
All I Need Is You		Standard Program Library U-17
Along Tobacco Road	1935	Decca 420A
Amen		
Bagel And Lox	1946	Columbia 37195
Between Friends	1941	Columbia 35981
Bob White		Standard Program Library U-17
Braggin'	1941	Columbia 36027
Brother Bill		Standard Program Library U-17
By And By		War Department H3 290 Personal Album
By The Light Of The Silvery Moon		Standard Program Library U-17
Calling Romance	1940	Columbia 35736
Calliope Jane	1940	Columbia 35779
Call It Anything, It's Love	1941	Okeh 6424
Call Of The Canyon, The	1940	Columbia 35811
Cancel The Flowers	1941	Okeh 6509
Cancel The Flowers		V-Disc 431
Candles, The	1957	MGM 12569
Careless Love	1941	Okeh 6220
Carry Me Back To Old Virginny	1940	Columbia 35887
Chi-Baba, Chi-Baba (My Bambina Go To Sleep)	1947	Columbia 37384/Columbia C 889
Cottage In Old Donegal, A	1948	Columbia 38438
Cowboy Serenade, The	1941	Okeh 6310
Daddy	1941	Okeh 6247
Damn The Torpedoes	1943	Kraft Music Hall Transcription from 8/12/43
Darktown Strutter's Ball	1942	
Darling, Je Vous Aime Beaucoup	1940	Columbia 35736
Dinah		
Don't Cry Baby		War Department H3 290 Personal Album
Don't Cry, Cry Baby		Standard Program Library U-17
Don't Cry Pretty Baby	1943	Kraft Music Hall Transcription from 8/26/43
Don't Play No Mambo	1955	Josie 787
Don't Talk Too Much	1943	Kraft Music Hall Transcription from 12/30/43
Don't You Notice Anything New'	1945	Columbia 36792
Down, Down, Down	1941	Okeh 6247
Down In Chicazola Town	1950	Ramsdell 76158
Dream For Sale, A	1941	Columbia 36094
Elmer's Tune	1941	Okeh 6390
Forget If You Can	1939	Okeh 5025/Vocalion 5025 (1939)/Tuxedo 892 (1955)
G.I. Jive		War Department H3 290 Personal Album
Gaucho Serenade, The	1940	Columbia 35424/Columbia 37519 (1947)
General Jumps At Dawn, The		
GI Jive	1944	Kraft Music Hall Transcription from 1/27/44
Go Down Moses	1939	Columbia 35718
Golden Slippers		
Goodnight, Mother	1940	Columbia 35851
I Can't Get Started	1947	Columbia 37915
I Didn't Mean To Be Mean To You	1957	MGM 12569
I Don't Want To Cry Anymore	1940	Columbia 35765
I Don't Want To Set The World On Fire	1941	Okeh 6332
I Dug A Ditch		Standard Program Library U-17
If I Could Be With You (One Hour Tonight)	1947	Columbia 37914
I Got It Bad, And That Ain't Good	1941	Okeh 6509
I Heard Of A City Called Heaven	1941	Okeh 6292
I'll Forget	1941	Columbia 35981
I'm A Stranger	1955	Tuxedo 891
I'm Gettin' Sentimental Over You	1939	Columbia 35229/Columbia 37518 (1947)
I'm In His Care	1939	Columbia 35741
I'm In The Mood For Love	1947	Columbia 37912
I Miss You So	1947	Columbia 37546/Columbia C 909
I'm The World's Biggest Fool	1952	Keystone 1416
I Should Have Known You Years Ago	1940	Columbia 35779
It Doesn't Cost You Anything To Dream	1945	Columbia 36792
It's Too Soon To Know	1948	Columbia 38329//Columbia C 1184
I Understand	1941	Columbia 36094
I've Got My Heart On My Sleeve	1955	Josie 787
Jeepers Creepers		
Jesus Is A Rock In A Weary Land	1939	Columbia 35787
Jesus Is A Rock In The Weary		War Department H3

Title	Year	Label/Number
Land		
Kiss And A Rose, A	1948	Columbia 38438
Last Thing I Want Is Your Pity, The	1947	Columbia 38187
Laughing Boy Blues	1938	Okeh 4125/Vocalion 4125 (1938)
Let's Get Lost	1943	Kraft Music Hall Transcription from 6/10/43
Little David, Play On Your Harp	1935	Decca 421A
Love's Old Sweet Song	1940	Columbia 35749
Mairzy Doats	1944	Kraft Music Hall Transcription from 1/20/44
Mairzy Doats		Standard Program Library U-17
Man Who Cares (with Penny Wise), The	1938	Brunswick 8237
May I Never Love Again	1941	Columbia 35942
Me And My Shadow	1943	Kraft Music Hall Transcription from 6/10/43
Milk Man Keep Those Bottles Quiet		
Moonlight Bay		Standard Program Library U-17
My Fate Is In Your Hands	1947	Columbia 37913
My Gal Sal	1939	Okeh 5025/Vocalion 5025 (1939)
My Gal Sal	1943	Kraft Music Hall Transcription from 3/11/43
My Heart's On Ice	1940	Columbia 35851
My Lord, What A Mornin'		V-Disc 673/V-Disc 729
Nobody's Sweetheart	1943	Kraft Music Hall Transcription, 10/7/43
No Soup!	1946	Columbia 36903
Nothin'	1941	Okeh 6424
Old Folks At Home	1940	Columbia 35887
One More Dream (And She's Mine)	1945	Columbia 36903
One, Two, Three O'Leary (Oh! My! Whoa! Mary!)	1941	Okeh 6332
Only Forever	1940	Columbia 35765
On the Boardwalk (In Atlantic City)	1946	Columbia 37074
On The Sunny Side Of The Street	1947	Columbia 37914
Oooh! Look-A-There, Ain't She Pretty'	1947	Columbia 38065
Oooh, Look-A There, Ain't She Pretty'		V-Disc 839
Open The Door, Richard!	1946	Columbia 37420
Pistol Packin' Mama		War Department H3 290 Personal Album
Red River Valley		Standard Program Library U-17
Ride, Red, Ride	1947	Columbia 37399/Columbia C 894
Ridin' Around In The Rain	1935	Decca 420B
Rogue River Valley	1946	Columbia 37195
Runnin' Wild		Standard Program Library U-17
Run, Run, Run	1948	Columbia 38261
Say No More	1947	Columbia 37384/Columbia C 889
Shoo Shoo Baby	1943	Kraft Music Hall Transcription 12/16/43
Silver Threads Among The Gold	1940	Columbia 35749
Sing A Song Of Sixpence	1938	Vocalion 3923
Sleepy River Moon	1955	Tuxedo 892
Sleepy Time Gal	1947	Columbia 37913
Snowball	1935	Decca 421A
So Long	1940	Columbia 35424/Columbia 37399 (1947)/Columbia C894
Song Of The Volga Boatman	1938	Okeh 4015/Vocalion 4015 (1938)
Speak To Me Of Love (Parlez-Moi D'Amour)	1938	Okeh 4068/Vocalion 4068 (1938)
S'posin'	1952	Keystone 1416
Star Dust		
Steal Away To Jesus	1939	Brunswick 8459/Columbia 35787 (1940)
Stormy Weather		
Sweet Georgia Brown		
Sweet Lorraine	1947	Columbia 37912
Sweet Marie	1947	Columbia 37915
Swing For Sale	1943	Kraft Music Hall Transcription from 10/28/43
Swing Low, Sweet Chariot	1939	Brunswick 8468/Columbia 35693 (1939)
Sylvia	1941	Columbia 36730/Columbia 37518 (1947)

Song	Year	Label
Tain't So, Honey, Tain't So		
Taking A Chance On Love	1943	Kraft Music Hall Transcription from 6/3/43
Thanks For Yesterday	1955	Tuxedo 891
Them There Eyes	1943	Kraft Music Hall Transcription from 8/19/43
This Side Of Heaven	1944	Columbia 36730/Columbia 38602 (1949)
Tica-Tee, Tica-Ta	1941	Okeh 6589
Tourist Trade, The	1948	Columbia 38261
Train Song, The	1941	Okeh 6589
Train Song, The		V-Disc 431
Tremble, Tremble, Tremble	1955	RCA Victor 47-6098
Until	1948	Columbia 38329/Columbia C 1184
Water Boy	1939	Brunswick 8459/Columbia 35693 (1939)
Way Down Yonder In New Orleans	1938	Vocalion 3923/Kraft Music Hall Transcription from 1/4/45
We'll Meet Again	1940	Columbia 35811/Columbia 37519 (1947)
Were You There'	1939	Columbia 35718
What Did He Say' (The Mumble Song)	1947	Columbia 38065
When I Grow Too Old To Dream	1948	Columbia 38187
Why Is A Good Gal So Hard To Find'	1941	Columbia 35942
Why Should I Complain'	1939	Columbia 35229
With Every Breath I Take	1942	
Words That Are Breaking My Heart		V-Disc 893
Wrap Your Troubles In Dreams	1941	Okeh 6292
Yes, Indeed!	1941	Okeh 6310
You Can't See The Sun When You're Crying	1946	Columbia 37420
You Make Me Feel So Young	1946	Columbia 37074
You're Breaking In A Brand New Heart (While You're Breaking Mine)	1947	Columbia 37546/Columbia C 909
You Walk By	1941	Columbia 36027
Easy Does It	1955	RCA Victor 47-6098
Hawaiian Sunset	1941	Okeh 6390/Columbia 38602
Aloutette (with Bob McCoy)	1938	Brunswick 8216
Dust (with Larry Cotton)	1938	Brunswick 8129/Brunswick A 81772
I Wish I Could Shimmy Like My Sister Kate		
Let's Have Harmony	1938	Brunswick 8237
Sing, You Sinners	1938	Okeh 4125/Vocalion 4125 (1938)

Charioteers (with Bing Crosby)

Song	Year	Label
I've Got A Home In That Rock Medley From		V-Disc 729
Kentucky Babe	1943	Kraft Music Hall Transcription from 8/26/43
One More Dream		V-Disc 673
Pistol Packin' Mama	1943	
Shoo Shoo Baby	1943	
What Do You Do In The Infantry	1944	Kraft Music Hall Transcription from 1/20/44

Charioteers (with Buddy Clark)

Song	Year	Label
Now Is The Hour (Maori Farewell Song)	1947	Columbia 38115
Peculiar	1948	Columbia 38115

Charioteers (with Frank Sinatra)

Song	Year	Label
Don't Forget Tonight Tomorrow	1945	Columbia 36854
I've Got A Home In That Rock	1945	Columbia 37853
Jesus Is A Rock In A Weary Land	1945	Columbia 37853
Lily Belle	1945	Columbia 36854

Charioteers (with Gladys Patrick)

Song	Year	Label
Somebody Please	1956	MGM 55015

Charioteers (with intro by Bing Crosby)

Song	Year	Label
Slip Of The Lip Can Sink A Ship, A	1944	Kraft Music Hall
Straighten Up And Fly Right	1943	Kraft Music Hall Transcription from 7/22/43

Charioteers (with Maxine Sullivan)

Song	Year	Label
Brown Bird Singing, A	1938	Okeh 4068/Vocalion 4068 (1938)
Dark Eyes	1938	Okeh 4015/Vocalion 4015 (1938)

Charioteers (with Mildred Bailey)

Song	Year	Label
Ain't That Good News'	1939	Vocalion
Don't Dally With The Devil	1939	Okeh 5209/Vocalion 5209 (1939)
Sometimes I Feel Like A Motherless Child	1939	Okeh 5209/Vocalion 5209 (1939)

Charioteers (with Pearl Bailey)
Don't Ever Leave Me	1947	Harmony 1059
Who	1948	V-Disc 865
Who'	1947	Harmony 1059

Charmers, Celestine Stewart & the
If I Didn't Have You	1946	Hub 3006
Waitin' For The Train To Come In	1946	Hub 3006

Chautauqua Preachers Quartet
Better Land, The	1917	Columbia
Church In The Wildwood, The	1914	Columbia A-1586
De Brewer's Big Horses	1916	Columbia
Flag Without A Stain, The	1916	Columbia
Glorious Things Of You Are Spoken	1914	Columbia A-1582
Hold The Fort	1914	Columbia A-1585
In The Sweet Bye-And-Bye	1917	Columbia
I Want My Life To Tell	1914	Columbia A-1583
Kings Business, The	1916	Columbia A-2120
Layendo Del Beso: Boys Of The Old Brigade	1914	Columbia A-1586
Let The Lower Lights Be Burning	1914	Columbia A-1584
My Anchor Holds	1917	Columbia
Nearer To Thee	1917	Columbia
Old Flag That Never Touched The Ground, The	1917	Columbia
Remember Me Oh Mighty One	1914	Columbia A-1610
Softly Now The Light Of Day	1914	Columbia A-1584
Still Still With Thee	1914	Columbia A-1610
Valley Of Peace	1916	Columbia A-2120
Wayside Cross, The	1914	Columbia A-1585
What A Friend Thou Are To Me	1914	Columbia A-1582
Why Did He Die'	1914	Columbia A-1583

Chautauqua Preachers Quartet
When The Roll Is Called Up Yonder	1918	Columbia A-2667

Chautauqua Preachers Quartet
Come Spirit Come	1917	Columbia A-2396
That Beautiful Land	1917	Columbia A-2396

Chicago Methodists Preachers Quartette
Remember Me, Oh Mighty One	1911	Columbia A-1082
Still, Still With Thee	1911	Columbia A-1082

Chickadees, Hoagy Carmichael & the
For Every Man There's A Woman	1947	Decca 24331
Gonna Get A Girl	1947	Decca 24299
Huggin' And Chalkin'	1946	Decca 23675
I May Be Wrong	1946	Decca 23675
I'm Comin' A Courtin', Corabelle	1947	Decca 24307
Ok'I Baby Dok'I	1947	Decca 24331
That Feathery Feeling	1947	Decca 24299

Churchill, Savannah & her Group (The Four Tunes)
Can Anyone Explain' (No, No, No)	1950	Arco 1259A
Devil Sat Down And Cried, The	1950	Arco 1259B

Churchill, Savannah (with Four Tunes)
Time Out For Tears	1948	Manor 1116

Churchill, Savannah (with King Odom Four)
I'm So Lonesome I Could Cry	1952	RCA Victor 4583

Churchill, Savannah (with Quartet)
Gypsy Was Wrong, The	1954	Decca 29262
I Cried	1954	Decca 29194
Just Whisper	1954	Decca 29262
My Memories Of You	1954	Decca 29194

Churchill, Savannah (with Ray Charles Singers)
Last Night I Cried Over You	1954	Decca 28973

Churchill, Savannah (with unnamed group)
If I Didn't Love You So	1952	RCA Victor 5031
Let Me Be The First One To Know	1956	Argo 5251
They Call Me A Fool	1956	Argo 5251
Walking By The River	1952	RCA Victor 5031

Clan-Tones
If You Were Mine	1959	Ebony 1021

Clark, Helen & the Peerless Quartet
Man In The Silvery Moon	1911	Edison 4mincyl 570

Classic City Quartet
Hold Thou To Me	1929	Columbia 15566-D
I'll Be Singing Round The Throne Some Day	1929	Columbia 15566-D

Clayton, Jackson and Durante
Can Broadway Do Without Me'	1929	Columbia 1860-D
So I Ups To Him!	1929	Columbia 1860-D

Clefs
Ride On	1952	Chess 1521
We Three	1952	Chess 1521

Cloister Singers
Our God, Our Help In Ages Past	1936	Decca 1030A
Rock Of Ages	1936	Decca 1030B

Clough, Arthur & the Peerless Quartet
Let's Make Love Among The Roses	1910	Edison 787 (4mincyl)
Little Annie Rooney	1911	Edison 4mincyl 654

Clough, Arthur (with Brunswick Quartet)
Down By The Old Mill Stream	1911	Columbia

Clubmen
Heigh-Ho (Dwarfs Marching Song)	1938	Decca 1632
One Song	1938	Decca 1633
Someday My Prince Will Come	1938	Decca 1632
Whistle While You Work	1938	Decca 1631
With A Smile And A Song	1938	Decca 1633

Clubmen Trio, Ben Alley & the
I'm Just A Dancing Sweetheart	1931	Hit Of The Week L 1

Clubmen, Frank Luther & the
Introduction And Heigh-Ho	1938	Decca

Clubmen, Zora Layman & the
Snow White And The Seven Dwarfs	1938	Decca 1700

Coats Sacred Quartet
Heaven For Me	1940	Vocalion 5525
I'd Rather Have Jesus	1936	Conqueror 8801
I'm Feeling Love Waves	1940	Vocalion 5525
Just Wear A Smile	1940	Vocalion 5451
Oh What A Joy To Sing	1935	Vocalion 3129
On The Royal Glory Road	1935	Vocalion 3129
We'll Soon Be Done With Troubles	1936	Conqueror 8801
Won't We Be Happy'	1940	Vocalion 5451

Cole Brothers
Dinah	1933	

Coleman Brothers
End Of The Journey, The	1945	Manor 100
Get Away, Mr. Satan, Get Away	1946	Decca 8673
Goodnight Irene	1950	Regal 3281
His Eye Is On The Sparrow	1944	Decca 8662/Coral 65003 (1949)
I Can See Everybody's Mother But Mine	1945	Manor 102/Manor 1003 (1945)/Arco 1208 (1949)
It's My Desire	1945	Manor 100
Low Down The Chariot	1944	Decca 8662/Coral 65003 (1949)
My Eye Is On The Sparrow	1947	Manor 1065
New Milky White Way	1945	Manor 101
Noah	1947	Manor 1065
Now What A Time	1947	Manor 1055
Ooh La La	1950	Regal 3281
Plenty Of Room In The Kingdom	1945	Manor 102/Manor 1003 (1945)/Arco 1208 (1949)
Raise A Ruckus Tonight	1946	Decca 8673
Seek	1947	Decca 48051
Sending Up My Timber	1947	Decca 48041
We'll Understand	1945	Manor 101
We're Living Humble	1947	Decca 48051
When The Saints Go Marching In	1947	Manor 1055
Where Shall I Be	1947	Decca 48041

Colemans
I Ain't Got Nobody	1950	Regal 3308
I Don't Mind Being All Alone	1950	Regal 3297
If You Should Care For Me	1950	Regal 3308
You Know I Love You, Baby	1950	Regal 3297

Collins, Arthur (with Peerless Quartet)
My Croony Melody	1914	Edison BA 2456

Columbia Double Male Quartet
Land Sighting	1915	Columbia A-5742

Columbia Double Mixed Quartet
Radiant Moon	1916	Columbia A-5935

Columbia Double Mixed Quartette
America (My Country 'Tis Of Thee)	1916	Columbia A-2012
Battle Hymn Of The Republic	1916	Columbia A-2012
King All Glorious	1916	Columbia A-5935

Columbia Double Quartet
Heidelberg Stein Song	1915	Columbia A-1852
Musical Trust	1915	Columbia A-1816

Columbia Ladies Quartet
Golden Ring	1914	Columbia A-1667
Little Alabama Coon	1913	Columbia A-1475
Lullaby	1915	Columbia A-1753
Mighty Lak A Rose	1915	Columbia A-1753
Rockin' In De Win'	1913	Columbia A-1475

Columbia Light Opera Company
Desert Song - Vocal Gems, The	1927	Columbia 50031-D
Lucky - Vocal Gems	1927	Columbia 50039-D
Oh, Kay! - Vocal Gems	1927	Columbia 50031-D
Rio Rita - Vocal Gems	1927	Columbia 50039-D

Columbia Male Chorus
America (My Country 'Tis Of Thee)	1927	Columbia 50041-D
Star-Spangled Banner, The	1927	Columbia 50041-D
Your Land And My Land	1927	Columbia 897-D

Columbia Male Octette
America (My Country 'Tis Of Thee)	1915	Columbia A-1155
In Vocal Combat	1915	Columbia A-5742
Land Sighting	1915	Columbia A-5742
Musical Trust, The	1915	Columbia A-1816
When The Boys Come Home	1918	Columbia

Columbia Male Quartet
Arrival Of The American Troops In France	1917	Columbia A-2354
Artillerist's Oath, The	1909	Columbia A-0798
Bulldog: Old College Song	1910	Columbia A-0822
Come Where My Love Lies Dreaming	1909	Columbia A-0774
Coon Wedding In Southern Georgia, A	1908	Columbia A-0370
Departure Of The American Troops For France	1917	Columbia A-2354
Dixie Gray	1911	Columbia A-1029
Don't Blame Me For Lovin' You	1911	Columbia A-1045
Emmalina Lee	1911	Columbia A-0988
Festival Te Deum	1914	Columbia A-5538
God Be With You Till We Meet Again	1909	Columbia A-0757
How Can I Leave Thee	1911	Columbia A-1060
If You Were Mine	1908	Columbia A-5085
I'll Go With You To The End Of The World And Then To The World Beyond	1911	Columbia A-1075
In Grandma's Day	1908	Columbia A-0622
Kentucky Babe	1908	Columbia A-0369
Let's Go Back To Those Baby Days	1909	Columbia A-0729
Liza	1909	Columbia A-0727

Mandy Lou	1911	Columbia A-1045	Battle Hymn Of The Republic, The	1916	Columbia 2012
Ma Pretty Chloe From Tennessee	1908	Columbia A-0292/Columbia A-0579	**Columbia Mixed Quartet**		
			Adeste Fideles	1915	Columbia A-1858
Medley Of Plantation Songs	1910	Columbia A-0958	Adore And Be Still	1913	Columbia A-5514
Meeting Of The Hen Roost Club, A	1908	Columbia A-0491	Araby	1915	Columbia A-1830
			Auld Lang Syne	1912	Columbia A-1238
Morning	1914	Columbia A-5538	Battle Hymn Of The Republic	1916	Columbia A-2012
Mrs. Sippi You're A Grand Old Girl	1914	Columbia A-1624	Battle Hymn Of The Republic, The	1902	Columbia 1155
My Bonnie Rose	1908	Columbia A-0378	Beautiful Isle Of Somewhere	1910	Columbia A-0935
My Creole Sunshine Sue	1910	Columbia A-0866	Brightest And Best	1913	Columbia A-1415
My Dinah	1908	Columbia A-0500	Christmas Anthem	1915	Columbia A-1858
Nearer, My God, To Thee	190'	Columbia 9012 (2mincyl)	Christmas Bells	1913	Columbia A-5514
			Christmas Carols	1911	Columbia A-1076
Oh, You Beautiful Doll	1911	Columbia A-1104	Crossing The Bar	1915	Columbia A-1891
Old Time Religion	1910	Columbia A-0827	Day Of God	1914	Columbia E-5052
Onward Christian Soldiers	1917	Columbia A-2220	Forever With The Lord (O Mother Dear Jerusalem' by Frank Croxton & Henry Burr)	1912	Columbia A-1254
Rosary, The	1913	Columbia A-1265			
Wedding Bells	1909	Columbia A-0767			
Winter Song	1908	Columbia A-0504/Columbia A-0958 (1910)	Goodbye Sweet Day	1915	Columbia A-1741
			Good Night, Good Night, Beloved	1903	Columbia 1138/Columbia A-494
Columbia Male Quartet (with Arthur Collins)					
Way Down Yonder In The Cornfield	1908	Columbia A-0473	Hark! The Herald Angels Sing	1916	Columbia 2104/Columbia 465-D (1925)
Columbia Male Quintette					
Maid Of The Valley, The	1916	Columbia A-1941	Holy City, The	1926	Columbia 782-D
Parson Pinkney Discourses On Adam And Eve	1905	Columbia 3111/Columbia A-438	Holy God, We Praise Thy Name	1916	Columbia A-2030
			Home Of The Soul	1916	Columbia A-2048
Columbia Male Trio			Home Over There	1910	Columbia A-0900
			How Can I Leave Thee'	1911	Columbia A-1060
Camp Meeting	1908	Columbia A-0386/Columbia A-0873 (1910)	How Fair Art Thou	1911	Columbia A-0985
			I'll Meet You When The Sun Goes Down	1911	Columbia A-1089
In Front Of The Old Cabin Door	1909	Columbia A-0389/Columbia A-0652/Diamond A-389/Peerless 652/Peerless 652	I'm A Pilgrim	1915	Columbia A-1713
			In The Glory Of The Moonlight (with Henry Burr)	1915	Columbia A-1849
			In The Sweet Bye And Bye	1913	Columbia A-5518/Columbia A-6074 (1918)
Columbia Minstrels					
De Golden Wedding/Bye Bye Ma Eva/Angel Gabriel	1913	Columbia A-5497	Jerusalem	1910	Columbia A-0833
			Juanita	1915	Columbia A-1793
Old Log Cabin	1902	Columbia	Lift Up Your Heads	1915	Columbia A-1713
Columbia Mixed Chorus			Medley Of Christmas Carols - Part 1	1917	Columbia A-2392
Abide With Me	1927	Columbia 1224-D			
Holy, Holy, Holy	1927	Columbia 1224-D	Medley Of Christmas Carols - Part 2	1917	Columbia A-2392
Home Sweet Home	1927	Columbia 1518-D/Conqueror 9102 (1938)			
			Medley Of Old Popular Songs	1915	Columbia
			Medley Of Old Time Songs	1915	Columbia A-1811
Sweet And Low	1927	Columbia 1518-D/Conqueror 9102 (1938)	Meet Me By Moonlight	1914	Columbia A-1491
			Moonlight On The Lake	190'	Columbia 9008 (2 min cyl)
Columbia Mixed Double Quartet					
			Mother Dear O Pray For Me	1916	Columbia A-2030
America	1916	Columbia 2012	O Come Ye All Faithful	1910	Columbia A-0922

The Encyclopedia of Early American Vocal Groups

Oh Canada	1913	Columbia A-1369
Oh Come All Ye Faithful	1915	Columbia A-1859/Columbia A-2104
Oh Come All Ye Faithful & Adeste Fidelis	1910	Columbia A-0922
Oh Happy Day	1916	Columbia
O Holy Night (with Charles Harrison)	1916	Columbia A-5888
O Holy Night (with Royal Dadmun)	1912	Columbia A-5384
O Little Town Of Bethlehem	1917	Columbia A-2391/Columbia 465-D (1925)
O Lord, I Am Not Worthy & Sweet Saviour, Bless Us	1916	Columbia
O My Father	1916	Columbia A-2073
On Christmas Eve - Medley (Old Santa Claus, Tree Of Fir, The Night Before Christmas, God Rest You Merry Gentlemen)	1912	Columbia
On The Banks Of The Wabash	1915	Columbia
Queen Of Heaven (in Latin)	1915	Columbia A-5713
Refuge (Jesus, Love Of My Soul)	1903	Columbia 1139/Columbia A-246
Regina Coeli	1915	Columbia A-5713
Silent Night, Holy Night	1926	Columbia 782-D
Silent Night, Holy Night (Heilige Nacht)	1915	Columbia A-1859
Snowtime	1911	Columbia A-1088
Softly Floating On The Air	1914	Columbia A-1668
So Great Therefore (in Latin)	1915	Columbia A-5713
Sweet And Low	1908	Columbia A-0495
Tantum Ergo In F	1915	Columbia A-5713
Te Deum No 7 in B-Flat	1914	Columbia A-5538
Temple Bells	1912	Columbia A-1232
Thousand Years, A	1913	Columbia A-5518/Columbia A-6074 (1918)
To Jesus Heart All Burning	1916	Columbia
Viderunt & Aleluia	1915	Columbia A-1858
Welcome Happy Morning	1912	Columbia A-1130
While Shepherds Watched By Night	1917	Columbia A-2391

Columbia Quartet

Ain't You Comin' Back To Old New Hampshire	1908	Columbia A-0501
Ain't You Coming Back To Old New Hampshire, Molly'	1906	Columbia 3547/Columbia 33048 (2mincyl)
Alamo Rag	1911	Columbia A-1000
Alice, Where Art Thou Going' (with Billy Murray)	1906	Columbia 3533/Columbia 33049 (2mincyl)
Annie Laurie	1908	Columbia A-0384
Annie Laurie	190'	Columbia 9014 (2mincyl)
Annie Laurie	190'	Columbia 716/Harvard 716
Any Girl Looks Good In The Summer Time	1911	Columbia A-1033
Artillerist's Oath, The	1906	Columbia 3492
At The Telephone	1911	Columbia A-5309
Barbecue In Old Kentucky, A	1902	Columbia 891/
Battle Hymn Of The Republic	1912	Columbia A-1155
Black Jim	1907	Columbia 3750/Columbia A-0423 (1908)
Bring Back The Kaiser To Me	1917	Columbia
By The Light Of The Silvery Moon	1909	Columbia A-0799
Call To Arms	1908	Columbia A-0363
Carry Me Back To Old Virginia	1908	Columbia A-0375
Carry Me Back To Old Virginny	190'	Columbia 9068 (2mincyl)
Carry Me Back To Old Virginny	190'	Columbia 511/Climax 511/Marconi 0346/Columbia A-375
Characteristic Negro Medley, A	1908	Columbia A-0352
Characteristic Negro Medley, A	190'	Columbia 890/Standard 890
Christmas Morning At Flanigan's	1906	Columbia 3512
Christmas Morning At The Flanagan's	1908	Columbia A-0457
Church Scene: Old Homestead	1908	Columbia A-0382
Come Rise With The Lark	1908	Columbia A-0390
Come Rise With the Larks	1906	Columbia 3407
Coon Wedding In Southern Georgia, A	190'	Columbia 456/Climax 456/Standard 456
Darling Nellie Gray	1905	Columbia 32836 (2mincyl)/Busy Bee 326
Day Of The Game, The	1909	Columbia A-0698
Denver Town	1909	Columbia A-0673
Descriptive Medley	1906	Columbia 3480/Standard A 355
Descriptive Medley	1908	Columbia A-0355
Did He Run	1909	Columbia A-0664
Dixie Land	1908	Columbia A-0381
Dixie Land (Emmet)	190'	Columbia 451/Harvard 451/Climax 451
Down Among The Sheltering Palms	1915	Columbia A-1770
Down In Chinkapin Lane (A	1905	Columbia 32907

100 Years of Harmony: 1850 to 1950

Title	Year	Release
Lover's Wooing) (with Bob Roberts)		(2mincyl)/Busy Bee 352/Columbia 3349 (1906)
Down On The Farm	1908	Columbia A-0356/Columbia 822
Down Where The Sweet Potatoes Grow (with George O'Connor)	1917	Columbia A-2411
Dreaming Of Mother And Home Sweet Home	1909	Columbia A-0756
Dublin Bay	1912	Columbia A-1148
Dublin Daisies	1909	Columbia A-0731
Evening In The Camp - Part 1	1917	Columbia
Evening In The Camp - Part 2	1917	Columbia
Everybody's Doing It Now	1911	Columbia A-1148/Columbia A-1123 (1912)
Every Mother's Son There Sang 'The Wearing Of The Green'	1908	Columbia A-0409
Fairy Moon	1911	Columbia A-1008
Farm Yard Medley	1908	Columbia A-0367
Farmyard Medley	190'	Columbia 455/Harvard 455/Climax 455
For Dixie And Uncle Sam	1916	Columbia A-2084
For Every Boy Who's Lonely There's A Girl Who's Lonely, Too (with Beulah Gaylord Young)	1911	Columbia A-5304
Forsaken	1904	Columbia 32759 (2mincyl)/Busy Bee 284
Frisco Frizz, The	1911	Columbia
Funeral Service Over President McKinley	190'	Columbia 31654 (2mincyl)
Good Bye, Dolly Gray	1901	Columbia 513/Climax 513
Goodbye, My Love, Goodbye	1911	Columbia A-1072
Goodnight Moonlight	1909	Columbia A-0713
Hail Glorious Apostle	1913	Columbia A-1269
Hear The Pickaninny Band	1912	Columbia A-1136
Henpecks: June	1911	Columbia A-1009
Home Sweet Home	1908	Columbia A-0387
Honey Boy	1907	Columbia 33188 (2mincyl)
Honey Boy	1907	Columbia 3669
Honey Boy	1908	Columbia A-0497
Honey You'se My Lady Love	190'	Columbia 9053 (2mincyl)
Honolulu America Loves You	1916	Columbia A-2148
Hymns And Prayer From The Funeral Of President McKinley	1908	Columbia A-0251
Hymns And Prayer From The Funeral Service Over President McKinley	190'	Columbia 31651 (2mincyl)
Hymns And Prayer From The Funeral Service Over President McKinley	190'	Columbia 453/Harvard 453/Climax 453
Hymns Of The Old Church Choir, The	1907	Columbia 3693/Columbia A-0254 (1908)
In Old Madrid	1906	Columbia 3382
In The Evening By The Moonlight	1918	Columbia A-2683
In The Golden Afterwhile	1912	Columbia A-1111
In The Shade Of The Old Apple Tree	1904	Columbia 32764 (2mincyl)/Busy Bee 308
In The Shadow Of The Pyramid	1905	Columbia 3216
In The Wildwood Where Bluebells Grow	1908	Columbia A-0496
In The Wildwood, Where The Bluebells Grew	1907	Columbia 3648
I'se Gwine Back To Dixie	1902	Columbia 753/Climax 753/Standard 753
I'se Gwine Back To Dixie	1908	Columbia A-0376
Isle Of Somewhere	1910	Columbia A-0935
It's A Long Lane That Has No Turning	1912	Columbia A-1141
I Want A Girl (Just Like The Girl That Married Dad)	1911	Columbia A-1034
Jesus Lover Of My Soul	1908	Columbia A-0246
Kentucky Babe	1904	Columbia 3055/Columbia A-0866 (1910)
Lady Love	1909	Columbia A-0744
Laughing Quartette, The	1901	Columbia 31693 (2mincyl)
Lead Kindly Light	1908	Columbia A-0249
Lead Kindly Light	190'	Columbia 510/Climax 510/Oxford 510
Let Me Call You Sweetheart	1911	Columbia A-1057
Little Alabama Coon	190'	Columbia 9015 (2mincyl)
Little Boy Called 'Taps' - Medley, A	1905	Columbia 3225
Little Boy Called Taps	1908	Columbia A-0458
Little Darling, Dream Of Me	1901	Columbia 519/Climax 519
Look Out For Jimmy Valentine	1911	Columbia A 1043
Lord's Prayer/Gloria Patria	1908	Columbia A-0252
Louisiana Lou	1899	Columbia 9022 (2mincyl)
Maggie Murphy's Lawn Party	1906	Columbia 3481
Mah Pretty Chloe From Tennessee	1905	Columbia 32906 (2mincyl)/Columbia 3317/ (1905)/Busy Bee 351
Mandy Lane	1909	Columbia A-0627

Title	Year	Release
Mandy Lee	1908	Columbia A-0498
Mandy Lee	190'	Columbia 749/Standard 749/Climax 749
Manzanillo	1914	Columbia A-1603
Medley Of Old Plantation Songs	1908	Columbia A-0361
Medley Of Patriotic Airs	1902	Columbia 651/Climax 651
Medley Of Patriotic Songs	1908	Columbia A-0470
Medley Of Plantation Songs (Carry Me Back To Old Virginny/In The Evening By The Moonlight/My Old Cabin Home/Massa's In The Cold, Cold Ground)	1903	Columbia 32241 (2mincyl)
Medley Of Popular Choruses	1908	Columbia A-5069
Meeting Of The Hen Roost Club, A	1906	Columbia 85111 (3mincyl)/Columbia 3609 (1907)
Moonlight On The Lake	1904	Columbia 1801
Moonlight On The Lake	1908	Columbia A-0379
My Baby Sue	1905	Columbia 3252/Harmony 3252
My Bonnie Rose	1905	Columbia 3316
My Country Tis Of Thee	1912	Columbia A-1155
My Creole Sue	1902	Columbia 750/Climax 750
My Creole Sue	1908	Columbia A-0366
My Dinah	1903	Columbia 32192 (2mincyl)
My Dinah	190'	Columbia 452/Climax 452/
My Heart's Desire & Nellie Dean	1906	Columbia 85089 (3mincyl)
My Louisiana Lou - Coon Song	1908	Columbia A-0499
My Louisiana Lou (Madden-Edwards)	190'	Columbia 448/Climax 448
My Old Kentucky Home	1902	Columbia 9019 (2mincyl)/Busy Bee 142
My Old Kentucky Home	190'	Columbia 512/Climax 512/Standard 512/Columbia A-371
My Old Town	1911	Columbia A-1094
Nationality Medley	1901	Columbia 650/Oxford 650/Climax 650
Nationality Medley	1908	Columbia A-0503/Columbia A-0869 (1910)
Nearer My God, To Thee	1901	Columbia 518/Harvard 518/Climax 518/Oxford 518/Harvard A-250
Nearer My God To Thee	1908	Columbia A-0250
Nellie Dean, You're My Heart's Desire	1908	Columbia A-0377
New Parson At Darktown Church, The	1907	Columbia 3629
New Parson At The Darktown Church	1908	Columbia A-0490
Night Trip To Buffalo	1908	Columbia A-0448
Night Trip To Buffalo, A	190'	Columbia 458/Harvard 458/Climax 458/Standard 458
Old Black Joe	1906	Columbia 30038
Old Black Joe	1906	Columbia A-5032
Old Homestead, The (Church Scene)	190'	Columbia 449/Harvard 449/Oxford 449/Columbia A-382/Harmony A 382
Old Oaken Bucket, The	1899	Columbia A-9018 (2mincyl)
Old Oaken Bucket, The	1901	Columbia 521/Climax 521
Old Oaken Bucket, The	1908	Columbia A-0372
Old Uncle Ned	1904	Columbia 32583 (2mincyl)/Busy Bee 165
On The Sandwich Isles	1916	Columbia A-2148
Onward, Christian Soldiers	1902	Columbia 754/Climax 754
Onward Christian Soldiers	1908	Columbia A-0244
Over The Top	1917	Columbia A-2423
Owl And The Pussy Cat, The	190'	Columbia 751/Climax 751
Owl And The Pussy, The	1908	Columbia A-0398
Perfect Day, A	1914	Columbia A-1622
Plantation Song Medley	1902	Columbia 752/Climax 752
Plantation Songs Medley	1910	Columbia A-0869
Pride Of The Prairie	1907	Columbia 3769/Columbia A-0433 (1908)
Prince Of Pilsen: Heidelberg Stein	1908	Columbia A-0380
Rescue By The Life Boat Crew	1908	Columbia A-0353/Standard A 353/
Rescue By The Lifeboat Crew, A	1905	Columbia 3248
Ring In The Bells Of Heaven	1910	Columbia A-0888
Ring The Bells Of Heaven	1906	Columbia 33032 (2mincyl)/Columbia 3511

Title	Year	Label/Number
Roses Bring Dreams Of You	1909	Columbia A-0641
Sabbath Day, The	1906	Columbia 3482/Columbia A-0248 (1908)
Sally In Our Alley	1908	Columbia A-0357
Sally In Our Alley	190'	Columbia 715
Sidewalks Of New York, The	190'	Climax 459
Sleigh Ride Party	190'	Columbia 9040 (2mincyl)
Sleigh Ride Party, The	1908	Columbia A-0365
Sleigh Ride Party, The	190'	Columbia 450/Harvard 450/Climax 450/Standard 450
Society Bear, The	1912	Columbia
Soldiers Farewell	1908	Columbia A-0346
Soldier's Farewell, A	1900	Columbia 31548 (2mincyl)
Soldier's Farewell, A	1901	Columbia 520/Climax 520
So Long Mother	1917	Columbia A-2383
Southern Girl	1907	Columbia 3692
Southern Girl	1908	Columbia A-0481
St. Patrick's Day At Clancy's	190'	Columbia 3082
Steamboat Leaving The Wharf At New Orleans (Steamboat Medley)	190'	Busy Bee 120
Steamboat Medley	1908	Columbia A-0374
Steamboat Medley (Steamboat Leaving The Wharf At New Orleans)	190'	Columbia 454/Oxford 454/Climax 454
Summertime	1907	Columbia 3771
Summertime	1908	Columbia 33229 (2mincyl)
Summertime	1908	Columbia A-0422
Sunday School Picnic At Pumpkin Center (with Ada Jones & Cal Stewart)	1905	Columbia 32926 (2mincyl)/Busy Bee 371
Sunday School Picnic At Pumpkin Center (with Mr. & Mrs. Cal Stewart)	1906	Columbia 3345
Suwannee River (The Old Folks At Home)	190'	Columbia 818/Oxford 818/Harmony 818
Sweetheart Days	1907	Columbia 3772
Sweetheart Days	1908	Columbia A-0427
Sweetheart's A Pretty Name When It's Y-O-U	1909	Columbia A-0731
Sweetness	1910	Columbia A-0943
Take Me Back To The Garden Of Love (with Charles W. Harrison)	1912	Columbia A-1141
Tell Mother I'll Be There	1907	Columbia (1906)/Columbia A-2043 (1908)/Busy Bee 410
Tell Mother I'll Be There	1908	Columbia A-0264
Tenting On The Old Camp Ground	190'	Columbia 9048 (2mincyl)
Tenting Tonight On The Old Camp Ground	1901	Columbia 514/Climax 514/Peer 514
Tenting Tonight On The Old Camp Ground	1908	Columbia A-0360/Columbia A-1808 (1915)
This Is The Sabbath Day	1906	Columbia 32987
Trip To The Country Fair, A	190'	Columbia 457/Climax 457
Trip To The County Fair, A	1908	Columbia A-0505
Uncle Josh's Barn Dance (with Cal Stewart)	1909	Columbia A-0697
Vacant Chair, The	190'	Columbia 9062 (2mincyl)
Waltz Me Around Again, Willie	1906	Columbia 3450
Waltz Me Around Again, Willie	1908	Columbia A-0359
War Song Hits #1 (It's A Long Way To Berlin/Keep The Home Fires Burning/Where Do We Go From Here/Pack Up Your Troubles In Your Old Kit Bag And Smile)	1917	Columbia A-2428
War Song Hits #2 (For Your Country And My Country/Goodbye Broadway/I Don't Know Where I'm Going But I'm On My Way/Over There)	1917	Columbia A-2428
Way Down East	1911	Columbia A-0970
Way Down Yonder In The Cornfield	190'	Columbia 9029 (2mincyl)/Busy Bee 121
Way Down Yonder In The Cornfield	190'	Columbia 714/Harvard 714/Oxford 714/United A 473
When Daddy Sings The Little Ones To Sleep	1906	Columbia A-5029
When Daddy Sings The Little Ones To Sleep	1910	Columbia 33070 (2mincyl)
When Daddy Sings The Little Ones To Sleep (with Albert Campbell)	1906	Columbia 30046
When Other Hearts Have Closed Their Doors	1909	Columbia A-0663
When Sweet Marie Was 16	1908	Columbia A-5069
When The Bloom Is On The Heather	1910	Columbia A-0895
When The Bluebirds Nest Again, Sweet Nellie	1908	Columbia A-0474
When The Bluebirds Nest Again,	1907	Columbia 3677
		3751/Standard A 264

Sweet Nellie Gray		
When The Roll Is Called Up Yonder	1907	Columbia 3752
When The Roll Is Called Up Yonder	1908	Columbia A-0260
When The Sheep Are In The Fold	1908	Columbia A-0420
When The Sheep Are In The Fold, Jennie Dear	1907	Columbia 33187 (2mincyl)
When The Sheep Are In The Fold, Jennie Dear	1907	Columbia 3711
When The Summer Days Are Gone	1908	Columbia A-0612
Where Is My Wandering Boy To-Night'	190'	Columbia 9061 (2mincyl)/Busy Bee 150
While The Old Mill Wheel Is Turning	1906	Columbia 3453
Widow Wood, The	1911	Columbia A-1024
Winter	1911	Columbia A-0970
Winter Song	1905	Columbia 3071
Women (Lovely Women)	1907	Columbia 3762
Yankee Doodle's Come To Town (with Billy Murray)	1908	Columbia 33281 (2mincyl)
You're The Flower Of My Heart, Sweet Adeline	1905	Columbia 3166/Standard 3166
You're The Flower Of My Heart, Sweetheart	1908	Columbia A-0385

Columbia Quartet & M. Ames

Run Home And Tell Your Mother	1911	Columbia A-1042

Columbia Quartet (as Billy Murray & Chorus)

Yankee Doodle's Come To Town	1908	Columbia A-583

Columbia Quartet (as Prince's Male Voice Quartette)

Nellie Dean (You're My Heart's Desire, I Love You)	1905	Columbia 3174

Columbia Quartet (with Albert Campbell)

Call To Arms, A	1906	Columbia 3381

Columbia Quartet with Amparito Farrar

When Johnny Comes Marching Home	1919	Columbia A-2716

Columbia Quartet, A. Campbell & H. Burr & the

While The Old Mill Wheel Is Turning	1908	Columbia A-0508

Columbia Quartet, Ada Jones & the

In Old Madrid	1908	Columbia A-0502
Pussy Cat Rag	1913	Columbia A-1457

Columbia Quartet, Henry Burr & the

Golden Land Of My Dreams	1909	Columbia A-0642

Columbia Quartet, Hugh Donovan & the)

Melody Land	1917	Columbia A-2394

Columbia Quartet, James F. Harrison & the

Cheer Up Liza	1917	Columbia A-2394

Columbia Quartette

Lead Kindly Light	1902	Columbia 31668
Rocked In The Cradle Of The Deep	190'	Columbia 9011 (black2mincyl)

Columbia Stellar Male Quartet

My Old Kentucky Home	1908	Columbia A-0371/Columbia A-0812 (1910)

Columbia Stellar Quartet

Absent	1915	Columbia A-1891
Alexander	1918	Columbia A-2534
All Erin Is Calling	1917	Columbia A-2407
All Through The Night	1915	Columbia A-1718
Aloha Oe	1917	Columbia A-5960
Annie Laurie	1914	Columbia A-1491
Artillerist's Oath, The	1917	Columbia
Ashore	1917	Columbia A-2407
Auld Lang Syne	1918	Columbia
Beautiful Isle Of Somewhere	1916	Columbia A-2048
Blue Bells Of Scotland	1917	Columbia
Bridge, The	1915	Columbia A-1751
Bring Back My Bonnie To Me	1918	Columbia A-2504
Can't Yo' Heah Me Callin', Caroline	1919	Columbia A-1919
Carry Me Back To Old Virginny	1915	Columbia A-1820/Columbia A-6091 (1918)
Come Back To Erin	1915	Columbia A-1751
Come Where My Love Lies Dreaming	1920	Columbia
Crossing The Bar	1915	Columbia A-1891
Crossing The Bar	1919	Columbia
Dreams Of Galilee	1915	Columbia A-1782
Eileen Alanna	1916	Columbia A-2010
Fare The Well, Love, Fare Thee Well	1921	Columbia A-3460
From Greenland's Icy Mountains	1917	Columbia
Gem Of The Ocean, The	1914	Columbia A-1548
Girl I Left Behind Me, The	1913	Columbia A-1440/Columbia A-2549 (1918)
Hard Times	1918	Columbia A-5012
Hark The Herald Angels Sing	1916	Columbia A-2104
Henry's Barn Dance	1917	Columbia A-2427
Holy City, The	1915	Columbia A-5744
Holy God, We Praise Thy Name	1919	Columbia
Home Sweet Home	1917	Columbia A-2465
Illinois	1918	Columbia A-2586
In Arcadia	1919	Columbia
I Need Thee Every Hour	1916	Columbia A-1961
In The Sweet Bye And Bye	1917	Columbia A-2220
Irish Have A Great Day Tonight, The	1917	Columbia A-2247
John Peel	1917	
Just As I Am	1916	Columbia A-1997
Just A-Wearyin' For You	1916	Columbia A-1958

Title	Year	Label/Number
Just Before The Battle, Mother	1916	Columbia A-2246
Kathleen Mavourneen	1916	Columbia A-5899
Lamp In The West, The	1915	Columbia A-1871
Larboard Watch, The	1918	Columbia A-2504
Last Night	1916	Columbia A-2010
Lead Kindly Light	1917	Columbia A-3469
Loch Lomond	1916	Columbia A-5899
Long Day Closes, The	1915	Columbia A-1871
Lost Chord, The	1915	Columbia A-5744
Mary Of Argyle	1918	Columbia
Medley Of Brahms Songs	1915	Columbia A-1811
Medley Of Children's Songs - Part 1	1917	Columbia A-2369
Medley Of Children's Songs - Part 2	1917	Columbia A-2369
Medley Of Old Songs	1919	Columbia A-1958
Medley Of Patriotic Airs	1916	Columbia A-2065
Mighty Fortress, A	1916	Columbia A-2146
Mighty Lak A Rose	1918	Columbia A-2535
Molly O	1917	Columbia
Mother Dear, Oh Pray For Me	1919	Columbia
Murmuring Zephyrs	1916	Columbia A-1941
My Gal Sal	1921	Columbia A-3436
My Mammy	1921	Columbia A-3377
My Old Kentucky Home	1918	Columbia A-6059
My Old Kentucky Home	1919	Columbia A 8127
My Own United States	1917	Columbia A-2246
My Wild Irish Rose	1915	Columbia A-1852
My Wild Irish Rose	1919	Columbia A-2052
Nearer My God To Thee	1921	Columbia A-3469
Nellie Dean	1919	Columbia A-1881
Noah's Ark	1918	Columbia A-2534
Now The Day Is Over	1916	Columbia A-1961
Oft In The Stilly Night	1917	Columbia
Oh Come All Ye Faithful	1919	Columbia A-2788
On The Banks Of The Wabash Far Away	1916	Columbia A-1893
Onward, Christian Soldiers	1918	Columbia A-2706
Owl And The Pussy Cat	1915	Columbia A-1816
Patriotic Medley #1: Girl I Left Behind Me	1917	Columbia A-2269
Patriotic Medley #2: When Johnny Comes Home	1917	Columbia A-2269
Robin Adair	1916	Columbia A-1958
S.R. Henry's Barn Dance (Down At The Huskin' Bee)	1917	Columbia A-2427
Sailing	1918	Columbia A-2549
Sally In Our Alley	1913	Columbia A-1440
Santa Lucia	1917	Columbia A-2465
Sing Me To Sleep	1916	Columbia A-1912
Soft And Low	1921	Columbia
Stand Up For Jesus	1919	Columbia A-2706
Still, Still With Me	1916	Columbia A-1997
Swanee River Moon	1921	Columbia A-3432
Sweet And Low	1915	Columbia A-1741/Columbia A-2535 (1918)
Sweet Genevieve	1918	Columbia A-2591
Sweetheart Of Mine	1915	Columbia A-1791
That Old Oaken Bucket	1915	Columbia A-1820
There Was A Little Man	1915	Columbia A-1892
Torpedo And The Whale, The	1918	Columbia A-2534
Two Roses, The	1915	Columbia A-1793
Way Down Yonder In The Corn Field	1917	Columbia A-2427
When It's Night-Time Down In Burgundy	1914	Columbia A-1625
When Johnny Comes Marching Home Again (Passing The Reviewing Stand)	1918	Columbia
When The Boys Come Home	1919	Columbia A-2694
When The Corn Is Waving, Annie Dear	1920	Columbia A-1961
When You Feel A Little Longing In Your Heart	1918	Columbia A-2581
When You Wore A Tulip And I Wore A Big Red Rose	1915	Columbia A-1683
Ye Olden Yuletide Hymns #1	1920	Columbia A-2993
Ye Olden Yuletide Hymns #2	1920	Columbia A-2993
You're The Flower Of My Heart, Sweet Adeline	1918	Columbia A-2591
Battle Cry For Freedom	1917	Columbia A-2357
Columbia Gem Of The Ocean	1917	Columbia A-2341
Hail Columbia	1917	Columbia A-2341
How Can I Leave Thee	1917	Columbia A-2325
Stars Of The Summer Night	1917	Columbia A-2325

Columbia Stellar Quartet (with Barbara Maurel)

Title	Year	Label/Number
Old Black Joe	1918	Columbia A-6091

Columbia Stellar Quartet (with Charles Harrison)

Title	Year	Label/Number
Battle Hymn Of The Republic, The	1918	Columbia 2367
Tramp, Tramp, Tramp (The Boys Are Marching)	1917	Columbia A-2357

Columbia Stellar Quartet (with Henry Burr)

Title	Year	Label/Number
Break The News To Mother	1917	Columbia A-2436
Little Bit Of Heaven, A	1919	Columbia A-1916

Columbia Stellar Quartet (with Lucy Gates)

Title	Year	Label/Number
My Old Kentucky Home	1918	Columbia 6059

Columbia Stellar Quartet (with Margaret Keyes)

Title	Year	Label/Number
Some Day I'll Wander Back Again	1916	Columbia A-5785

Columbia Stellar Quartet (with Margaret Romaine)

Title	Year	Label/Number
In The Evening By The Moonlight	1920	Columbia A-3312

Columbia Stellar Quartet (with Oscar Seagle)

Title	Year	Label/Number
Jesus Savior Pilot Me	1919	Columbia A-2808

Columbia Stellar Quartet, Barbara Maurel with the

Title	Year	Label/Number
Star O The East, The	1919	Columbia A-2790

Columbia Stellar Quartet, Charles Harrison & the

Title	Year	Label/Number
Oh Holly Night	1919	Columbia A-2801
Ring Out, Sweet Bells Of Peace	1918	Columbia A-2694

Columbia Stellar Quartet, Charles Harrison with the
Men Of The North, The	1920	Columbia
My God Preserve Thee, Canada	1920	Columbia

Columbia Stellar Quartet, Charles W. Harrison
Battle Hymn Of The Republic	1917	Columbia A-2367
Star Spangled Banner	1917	Columbia A-2367

Columbia Stellar Quartet, Graham Marr & the
Brown October Ale	1916	Columbia A-5879
Stein Song	1916	Columbia A-5879
Uncle Ned	1916	Columbia A-5855

Columbia Stellar Quartet, Lucy Gates & the
Carry Me Back To Old Virginny	1917	Columbia A-6015
Come, Come, Ye Saints	1918	Columbia
Darling Nellie Gray	1918	Columbia A-6059
Massa's In The Cold, Cold Ground	1917	Columbia A-6015
O Ye Mountains High	1918	Columbia

Columbia Stellar Quartet, Marie Morrissey & the
Memories Of Easter - Part 1	1919	Columbia A-2693
Memories Of Easter - Part 2	1919	Columbia A-2693

Columbia Stellar Quartet, Oscar Seagle & the
Freedom For All Forever	1928	Columbia
Keep The Home Fires Burning	1918	Columbia A-6028
Life's Railway To Heaven	1921	Columbia A-3420
Massa's In The Cold, Cold Ground	1918	Columbia A-6082
Nazareth	1920	Columbia A-6169
Ol' Car'lina	1921	Columbia A-3448
Old Folks At Home	1918	Columbia A-6082
Pack Up Your Troubles In Your Old Kit Bag	1918	Columbia A-6028
Voice Of The Chimes, The	1920	Columbia A-6169

Columbia Stellar Quartet, Oscar Seagle with the
I Love To Tell The Story	1920	Columbia A-3354
Nearer, My God, To Thee	1920	Columbia A-3354

Columbia Stellar Quartet, Rosa Ponselle & the
Keep The Home Fires Burning	1919	Columbia A-7038

Columbia Stellar Quartet, Vernon Stiles & the
We'll Never Let The Old Flag Fall	1918	Columbia A-2609

Columbia Stellar Quartette
Beauty's Eyes	1917	Columbia A-2174
Calling Me Home	1914	Columbia A-1661
Creation's Hymn (Beethoven)	1916	Columbia A-2146
I's Gwine Back To Dixie	1916	Columbia
Jesus, Refuge Of My Soul	1914	Columbia A-5568
Mona	1916	Columbia A-2174
My Mother's Bible	1916	Columbia
Old Black Joe	1919	Columbia A-2051
On The Old Bob Sled	1916	Columbia A-2125
Tenting Tonight On The Old Camp Ground	1915	Columbia A-1808
Vacant Chair (We Shall Meet But We Shall Miss Him), The	1915	Columbia A-1808
When The Corn Is Waving, Annie Dear	1916	Columbia A-2051

Columbia Stellar Quartette, Lucy Gates & the
Aloha Oe	1916	Columbia
Juanita	1915	Columbia A-1793/Columbia A-5960
Listen To The Mocking Bird	1916	Columbia

Columbia Trio
At The Post Office	1908	Columbia A-0472
Attila: Praise Ye	1915	Columbia A-5731

Columbians (Lewis James, Franklyn Baur, Elliott Shaw)
Your Land And My Land	1927	Columbia 975-D

Comedy Harmonians
Creole Love Call	1935	Victor 24876 (German)
Night And Day	1935	Victor 24876 (German)

Comets, Herb Kenny & the
Only You	1952	Federal 12083
When The Lights Go On Again All Over The World	1952	Federal 12083

Commanders
I'd Like To Know You Better Than I Do	1948	Modern 567
Lonesome Road	1948	Modern 567

Commonwealth Quartet
Deep River	1927	Banner 1955/Conqueror 7014 (1928)
I Ain't Gonna Grieve No More	1927	Banner 1955/Conqueror 7014 (1928)
I'm Going To Shout All Over God's Heaven	1926	Banner 2145
Little David Play On Your Harp	1926	Banner 2145

Commuters Barbershop Quartet
Sweet Adeline	1940	Decca 3583A
You Tell Me Your Dream, I'll Tell You Mine	1940	Decca 3583B

Congo Rhythm Boys
One Way Ticket	1950	Hamptone International 611
Please Don't Cry	1949	Hamptone International 611
Please Don't Cry	1950	Hamptone International 611
Weekend Blues	1950	International 607

Consolidated Male Quartette
My Old New Hampshire Home	1899	Consolidated 9614

Continentals
Handful Of Stars	1951	Capitol 1877
It Can't Be Wrong	1951	Capitol 1877
My Heart Sings	1951	Capitol 1844

Contractors, Helen Humes & the

Title	Year	Label
Take Me Back	1952	Capitol 1951
Violets For Your Furs	1952	Capitol 1989
Walk The Lonesome Night	1952	Capitol 1989
Where Was I'	1952	Capitol 1951
You Go To My Head	1951	Capitol 1844

Contractors, Helen Humes & the

Title	Year	Label
Free	1949	Mercury 8119
I've Got The Strangest Feeling	1949	Mercury 8119

Cook Sisters

Title	Year	Label
Shady Tree, A	1927	Brunswick 3668
Where The Cot-Cot-Cotton Grows	1927	Brunswick 3668

Cook, Herb & his Three Little Words

Title	Year	Label
Got That Old-Fashioned Love In My Heart	1933	Bluebird B-5135
There's A Wild Rose That Grows On The Side Of The Hill	1933	Bluebird B-5135
When The Day-Time Meets The Night-Time Down In Dixie	1933	Victor 23851
When You're Looking Through The Window	1933	Victor 23851

Coombs, Frank & Quartet

Title	Year	Label
Hard Times Come Again No More	1911	Columbia A-1052

Copperhill Male Quartet

Title	Year	Label
Crossing The Bar	1927	Columbia
There Is A Fountain Filled With Blood	1927	Columbia 15164-D

Cornfed Four

Title	Year	Label
Let The Church Roll On	1930	Okeh 8841
Waiting At The Gate	1930	Okeh 8841

Corsairs

Title	Year	Label
Four Letters	1950	Columbia 38700
Jonathan	1950	Columbia 38715
On The Motor Boat	1950	Columbia 38700
Subway Boom-De-Ay, The	1950	Columbia 38715

Cote, Emile & Serenaders

Title	Year	Label
Tea Leaves	1948	Columbia 38230

Cotton Belt Quartet

Title	Year	Label
Give Me That Old Time Religion	1926	Vocalion 1022
Go Down Moses	1926	Vocalion 1024
Golden Slippers, The	1926	Vocalion 1005
I Couldn't Hear Nobody Pray	1926	Vocalion 1023
I'm Gonna Shout All Over God's Heaven	1926	Vocalion 15263/Vocalion 1001 (1926)
In My Heart	1926	Vocalion 1022
Lord I've Done What You Told Me To	1926	Vocalion 1005
Steal Away To Jesus	1926	Vocalion 1024
Swing Low Sweet Chariot	1926	Vocalion 1023
We'll Be Ready When The Great Day Comes	1926	Vocalion 15263/Vocalion 1001 (1926)

Cotton Pickers Quartet

Title	Year	Label
All God's Children Got Wings	1931	Okeh 8917/Conqueror 8360 (1932)
Joshua Fit De Battle Of Jericho	1931	Okeh 8878
Listen To The Lambs	1931	Okeh 8868/Conqueror 8359 (1932)
Mammy's Angel Child	1932	Conqueror 8361
Nobody Knows The Trouble I've Seen	1932	Conqueror 8360
Pore Mourner	1931	Okeh 8868
Steal Away To Jesus	1931	Okeh 8878/Conqueror 8359 (1932)
Swing Low Sweet Chariot	1931	Okeh 8917/Conqueror 8360 (1932)

Cotton, Sammy

Title	Year	Label
I Live The Life I Love	1953	Okeh 7043

Cottonbelt Quartet

Title	Year	Label
Hallelujah	1927	Paramount 12530
Talk About Dixie	1927	Paramount 12530

Craven, James & Male Trio

Title	Year	Label
That's How I Believe In You	1922	Brunswick 2185

Crescent Mixed Trio

Title	Year	Label
Old Kentucky Moonlight	1922	Okeh 4734

Crescent Trio

Title	Year	Label
All By Myself (with Ernest Hare)	1921	Brunswick 2108
Arabian Yogi Man, The	1920	Pathe 22495
Brazilian Chimes	1920	Okeh 4149/Edison Blue Amberol 4033 (1920)
Bungalow Of Dreams	1928	Victor 21230
Chahotka - Three O'Clock In The Morning	1922	Okeh 4681
Drowsy Head	1921	Vocalion 14191A
For Every Boy Who's On The Level There's A Girl Who's On The Square	1920	Columbia A-3318/Columbia A-3323
Georgia	1922	Okeh 4643
Hallelujah!	1927	Columbia 998-D
Homesick	1922	Okeh 4751
I Can't Sleep Without Dreaming	1920	Brunswick 2016
I'll Be In My Dixie Home Again Tomorrow	1922	Okeh 4734
I'm Missin' My Mammy's Kissin'	1921	Okeh 4270
In The Heart Of Dear Old Italy	1920	Okeh 4246/Vocalion 14152A
Jane	1921	Edison DD 50831/Edison Blue Amberol 4434/Vocalion

The Encyclopedia of Early American Vocal Groups

		14215A/Okeh 4411A			2098 (1921)/Okeh 4314 (1921)
Japanese Sandman	1920	Vocalion 14102	Sunny Southern Smiles	1920	Okeh 4126
Kentucky Home	1921	Edison DD 50849/Edison Blue Amberol 4420	Sweet And Low	1920	Okeh 4073
			Sweet Bells Of San Jose	1921	Okeh 4313/Hydrola 4313
Little Grey Sweetheart Of Mine	1922	Edison DD 50935	To-Morrow (I'll Be In My Dixie Home Again)	1922	Okeh 4728/Okey 4751
Lullaby Blues	1920	Okeh 4076	Under A Mulberry Tree	1922	Okeh 4602
Mammy's Good-Night Lullaby	1920	Edison DD 50698/Edison Blue Amberol 4118 (1920)	Waiting For The Sun To Come Out	1920	Pathe 22452
			Wandering Home	1921	Okeh 4313/Hydrola 4313
Mammy's Little Sunny Honey Boy	1921	Vocalion 14187B/Edison DD 50786/Okeh 4341	We'll Have A new Home (In The Mornin')	1927	Columbia 1274-D
			When I Look Into Your Wonderful Eyes	1920	Okeh 4173
Margie	1921	Cardinal 2005	Whispering	1920	Edison Blue Amberol 4178
Marion	1920	Victor 18671			
Mollie O (with James Sheridan)	1921	Brunswick 5058	Who'll Take The Place Of Mary'	1920	Victor 18671/Okeh 4108B (1920)
My Old Hawaiian Home	1922	Okeh 4723			
Now I Lay Me Down To Sleep	1920	Pathe 22483	You're The Only Girl That Made Me Cry	1920	Vocalion 14113A
Old Time Medley - Part 3		Pathe 7531			
Old Time Medley - Part 4		Pathe 7531	**Crescent Trio, Elisabeth Lennox & the**		
One Two Three Four	1920	Okeh 4243	Rosary, The	1921	Brunswick 2696/Brunswick 5041/
Orange Blossoms	1921	Brunswick 2110/Vocalion 14205A			
			Crescent Trio, Jane Audrey (Irene Williams) & the		
Pickaninny Blues	1918	Lyric 5212/Okeh 4067 (1919)/Edison DD 50664 (1920)/Edison Blue Amberol 4039 (1920)	I Cannot Sleep Without Dreaming Of You	1920	Brunswick 2046
			Crescent Trio, Sam Ash & the		
			Love Me With A Smile	1921	Okeh 4526
			Mary O'Brien	1921	Okeh 4472
			Crescent Trio, Theo Karle & the		
Plantation Lullaby	1921	Edison DD 50855/Edison Blue Amberol 4447	I'll Take You Home Again, Kathleen	1921	Brunswick 5106/Brunswick 13021/Brunswick 13069
Rose Of Virginia	1920	Edison DD 50902/Edison Blue Amberol 4092 (1920)	**Criterion Male Quartet**		
			Bridge (I Stood On The Bridge At Midnight), The	1905	Columbia 3240/Columbia A-362 (1908)/Standard A 362/Harvard 3240
Sighing	1921	Okeh 4270/Vocalion 14121 (1920)/Edison Blue Amberol 4201 (1920)			
			Brighten The Corner Where You Are	1920	Brunswick 2223/Brunswick 5042 (1920)
Silver Threads Among The Gold	1920	Okeh 4140	Carmen Ohio	1921	Gennett 10045
So Blue	1927	Columbia	Church In The Wildwood	1926	Brunswick 3292
Somebody's Mother	1921	Vocalion 14175B/Edison DD 50773 (1921)/Edison Blue Amberol 4315 (1921)/Brunswick	Cotton Dolly	1922	Vocalion 14338B
			De Sandman	1922	Vocalion 14376B
			Dixie	1921	Brunswick 2699/Brunswick 5055 (1921)
			Far From My Heavenly Home	1906	Excelsior 1210

Forgive And Forget	1927	Bell 478/Emerson 3107		Colleen	1920	Edison
Heidelberg Stein Song, The	1908	Columbia 3284/Columbia A-380/Lakeside 70518/Marconi Velvet Tone 0353/Standard 3284		Come Where The Lilies Bloom	1923	Columbia
				Daddy	1904	Edison Bell 6182
				Darling	1920	Brunswick 2211/Brunswick 5024 f(1920)
				Day Of The Lord, The	1927	Brunswick 3691/Melotone M 12254/Brunswick 2726
I'd Love To Call You Sweetheart	1927	Bell 478/Emerson 3107		Dear Lord Remember Me	1924	Brunswick 2659/Brunswick 3293 (1926)/Supertone S 2111 (1926)
Kentucky Babe	1922	Vocalion 14338A/Brunswick 3642 (1927)				
Ohio And Across The Field	1921	Gennett 10045				
Old Rugged Cross	1926	Brunswick 3293		De Coppah Moon	1923	Victor 19042
Sally In Our Alley	1921	Medallion 8314/Brunswick 3642 (1922)		De Sandman	1920	Brunswick 2218/Brunswick 5032/Brunswick 3688 (1927)
Some Blessed Day	1919	Brunswick 2216/Brunswick 5030		Down At The Husking Bee	1921	Brunswick 2236/Brunswick 5062 (1921)
Sometime Somewhere	1920	Brunswick 2216/Brunswick 5030 (1920)		Drifting Down	1920	Brunswick 2232/Brunswick 5057 (1920)/Columbia A-3748 (1922)
Stand Up, Stand Up For Jesus	1921	Gennett 10047				
Wayside Cross, The	1919	Brunswick 5001/Brunswick 2196 (1920)				
				Drum, The	1919	Brunswick 2028
When The Roll Is Called Up Yonder	1921	Gennett 10047		Faded Love Letters	1923	Vocalion 14578B
				Fate	1923	Edison DD 51158
Criterion Male Quartette				Faust Soldier's Chorus	1922	Vocalion 14321A
Church In The Wildwood, The	1919	Brunswick 5001/Brunswick 2196 (1920)		First Noel, The	1923	Columbia A-3998
				Gospel Train, The	1922	Vocalion 14352B/Brunswick 2232/Brunswick 5057
Darling Nellie Gray	1922	Vocalion 14392				
I'll Take Care Of Your Cares	1927	Bell 502/Emerson 3129		Honey, Dat's All	1923	Brunswick 2449
Little Cotton Dolly	1922	Vocalion 14338		Honey, I Wants Yer Now	1922	Vocalion 14376A.Victor 19042 (1923)
Sally King	1922	Vocalion 14378				
Sunset Trail Of Gold, The	1922	Vocalion 14454				
Sweet And Low	1922	Vocalion 14454/Victor 19042		Indiana	1925	Brunswick 3065/Brunswick 3058 (1925)
There Is A Green Hill Far Away	1927	Bell 1130		In The Garden	1922	Brunswick 2266/Vocalion 14606B (1923)
When I First Met Mary	1927	Bell 502/Emerson 3129				
When The Roll Is Called Up Yonder	1927	Bell 1130		In The Sweet Bye And Bye	1925	Brunswick 2869
				Ireland Is Heaven To Me	1924	Vocalion 14863B
Criterion Quartet				I'se Gwine To Sing In The Heavenly Choir	1923	
Beside A Babbling Brook	1923	Edison 51174				
Bridge, The	1905	Columbia 3240/Columbia A-362		It Came Upon A Midnight Clear	1923	Columbia A-3998/Clarion 5097-C/Harmony 518-H/Velvet Tone
Church In The Wildwood, The	1922	Vocalion 14352A				

Song	Year	Release
Jerusalem Morning & Little Tommy	1919	Brunswick 2028
Just Outside The Door	1922	Brunswick 2266
Kentucky Babe	1927	Brunswick 2228/Brunswick 5050
Life's Railway To Heaven	1925	Brunswick 2931/Supertone S 2111
Lindy Lady	1924	Edison DD 51295
Little Close Harmony, A	1921	Brunswick 2236/Brunswick 5062 (1921)
Little Cotton Dolly	1920	Brunswick 2228/Brunswick 5057 (1920)/Brunswick 430920)/Brunswick 3642 (1927)/Brunswick 4300 (1927)
Little David, Play On Your Harp	1923	Brunswick 2543
Lucky Jim	1920	Brunswick 2220/Brunswick 5035 (1920)
Mammy's Lullaby	1922	Brunswick 2287
Medley Of Southern Songs	1922	Champion 15162
Memories Of Galilee	1919	Brunswick 2199/Brunswick 5009 (1919)
My Cradle Melody	1922	Columbia A-3667
My Mammy	1921	Columbia
My Old Kentucky Home	1924	Vocalion 14783A
Nearer, My God, To Thee	1906	Excelsior X 1203
No Night There	1924	Brunswick 2720/Brunswick 5198
Oh Miss Hannah	1925	Brunswick 2944
Oh Susannah	1923	Edison DD 51295
Old Black Joe	1919	Brunswick 2001/Brunswick 2384 (1919)/Champion 15162 (1922)/Vocalion 14783B (1924)/Brunswick 5004
Old Rugged Cross	1924	Brunswick 2659
Old Time Favorites Pt. 1	1923	Vocalion 14721A
Old Time Favorites Pt. 2	1923	Vocalion 14721B
Ole Uncle Moon	1920	Brunswick 2220/Brunswick 5035 (1920) 1518-V
On The Banks Of The Wabash, Far Away	1925	Brunswick 3065/Brunswick 3058 (1925)
Open Up De Gates Of Glory	1923	Brunswick 2449
Sauntering Along With Susan	1921	Brunswick 2099
Silver Threads Among The Gold	1919	Bell 001
Some Blessed Day	1919	Victor 18808
Sometime, Somewhere	1922	Columbia A-3748
Son Of God Goes Forth To War, The	1919	Brunswick 2230/Brunswick 5053 (1919)
Still Sweeter Every Day	1920	Brunswick 2223/Brunswick 5042 (1920)
Still, Still With Thee	1919	Brunswick 2230/Brunswick 5053 (1919)
Sweeter As The Years Go By	1919	Brunswick 2199/Brunswick 5009 (1919)/Brunswick 5009/Vocalion 14606A (1923)
Sweet Rose O'Sharon	1924	Vocalion 14863A
Swing Along	1922	Brunswick 2287
Swing Low, Sweet Chariot	1923	Brunswick 2543
Tell Mother I'll Be There	1925	Brunswick 2869
Unclouded Day, The	1925	Brunswick 2931/Supertone S 2121
Voodoo Man	1923	Edison DD 51158
Wayside Cross	1921	Victor 18808
When The Roll Is Called Up Yonder	1924	Brunswick 2772
When They Ring The Bells (For You)	1924	Brunswick 2772
When You And I Were Young Maggie	1919	Bell 001
While The Years Roll By	1922	Columbia A-3686
Church In The Wildwood, The (with chimes)	1926	Brunswick 3292/Supertone S 2119
Nearer My God To Thee	1925	Brunswick
Old Rugged Cross (with chimes), The	1926	Brunswick 3293/Supertone S 2120
Some Blessed Day	1926	Brunswick 3296
Sweeter As The Years Go By	1926	Brunswick 3296
Wayside Cross, The	1926	Brunswick 3292/Supertone S 2119
When The Roll Is Called Up Yonder	1926	Brunswick 3295/Supertone S 2121
When They Ring The Golden	1926	Brunswick

Bells For You And Me　　　　3295/Supertone S 2121

Criterion Quartet (Alice Nielsen with)
Always Do As People Say You Should　1922　Columbia

Criterion Quartet (Arthur Fields & the)
Hail Chicago　1921　Columbia

Criterion Quartet (as Allen McQuhae & male trio)
La Rosita　1924　Brunswick

Criterion Quartet (as Allen McQuhae & Trio)
Dreamy Melody　1923　Brunswick 2492
When Clouds Have Vanished And Skies Are Blue　1923　Brunswick 2492

Criterion Quartet (as Brunswick Concert Orchestra with Male Quartet)
In A Monastery Garden　1928　Brunswick 20067/Brunswick A 5055

Criterion Quartet (as Claire Dux & Male Trio)
Somewhere A Voice Is Calling　1925　Brunswick

Criterion Quartet (as Dorothy deBeau & Male Trio)
Holy Night (Cantique De Noel)　1927　Supertone S 2124
Silent Night (Christmas Hymn)　1927　Supertone S 2124

Criterion Quartet (as Edith Mason & Male Trio)
Ancora Un Passo (Butterfly's Entrance)　1924　Brunswick 15096
Carry Me Back To Old Virginny　1928　Brunswick 10242/Brunswick 010263
My Old Kentucky Home　1928　Brunswick 10242/Brunswick 010263

Criterion Quartet (as Florence Easton & Male Trio)
Holy Night (Cantique De Noel)　1927　Brunswick 10296
Silent Night (Christmas Hymn)　1927　Brunswick 10296

Criterion Quartet (as Florence Easton & Trio)
O Holy Night (Cantique De Noel)　1923　Brunswick 10113/Brunswick 15058
Silent Night (Stille Nacht, Heilige Nacht)　1923　Brunswick 10113/Brunswick 15058

Criterion Quartet (as Frank Munn & Male Trio)
Silver Threads Among The Gold　1926　Brunswick 2978/Supertone S 2113
I'll Take You Home Again, Kathleen　1927　Brunswick 4167/Brunswick 01124
My Wild Irish Rose　1927　Brunswick 3711/Brunswick 01123/Brunswick 03802
Somewhere A Voice Is Calling　1927　Brunswick 4167/Brunswick 01124/Supertone S 2114 (1927)

Criterion Quartet (as Frank Whalen & Male Trio)
I'll Take You Home Again, Kathleen　1927　Supertone S 2114

Criterion Quartet (as James Sheridan & Male Trio)
La Rosita　1924　Brunswick 2597

Criterion Quartet (as John Charles Thomas & Male Trio)
Little Old Log Cabin In The Lane, The　1927　Brunswick
Where Is My Boy Tonight'　1927　Brunswick 15152/Brunswick 010261/Supertone S 2106

Criterion Quartet (as Marie Morrisey with Male Trio)
Rosary, The　1928　Brunswick A 8038

Criterion Quartet (as Marie Tiffany & Male Trio)
Carry Me Back To Old Virginny　1928　Brunswick 15218
My Old Kentucky Home　1928　Brunswick 15176

Criterion Quartet (as Marie Tiffany & Trio)
I'se Gwine Back To Dixie　1923　Brunswick
Ol' Car'lina　1928　Brunswick 15179

Criterion Quartet (as Mario Chamlee & Male Trio)
Absent　1927　Brunswick
Perfect Day, A　1927　Brunswick 10104

Criterion Quartet (as Ruth Pierson & Male Trio)
Carry Me Back To Old Virginny　1928　Supertone S 2104
My Old Kentucky Home　1928　Supertone S 2104

Criterion Quartet (Campus Male Quartet)
Day Of The Lord　1924　Brunswick 2726/Vocalion 7

Criterion Quartet (Harry C. Browne &)
Angelina　1922　Columbia A-3769

Criterion Quartet (Irving Kaufman &)
Little Rover　1923　Vocalion 14520

Criterion Quartet (Marie Tiffany &)
Sweet And Low　1923　Brunswick 13094

Criterion Quartet (with Franklyn Baur, Frank Munn, Elliott Shaw)
Song Of The Volga Boatmen　1926　Brunswick 3127/Supertone S 2142/Brunswick 40632

Criterion Quartet (with Merrymakers)
Goin' Home　1926　Brunswick 3127/Brunswick A 138

Criterion Quartet with Ferrera Trio
Coral Sands Of My Hawaii　1923　Vocalion 14700A
One Two Three Four　1923　Vocalion 14700B

Criterion Quartet, Vernon Dalhart & the
Weep No More (My Mammy)　1921　Columbia A-3500

Criterion Quartette

Title	Year	Release
Alma Mater	1922	Gennett 10052
Americans Come!, The	1918	Edison
Annie Laurie	1916	Edison DD 80519/Champion 15161 (1919)
Besides A Babbling Brook	1923	Edison DD 51174
Carry Me Back To Old Virginny	1916	Edison DD 82191/Edison DD 30005/Edison 12042-N
Church In The Wildwood, The	1921	Gennett 9145
Crossing The Bar	1921	Edison DD 80728/Edison BA 4566
Dear Old Tech	1922	Gennett 10052
De Sandman/The Drum	1916	Edison DD 80358/Edison BA 2903
Dixie Kid, The	1924	Edison DD 80802/Edison BA 4923
Favorite Sig Songs, Part 1	1922	Fraternity
Favorite Sig Songs, Part 2	1922	Fraternity
He Included Me	1918	Edison
He Will Hold Me Fast	1908	Victor 16239
Home Sweet Home	1919	Champion 15161
Honey Babe	1920	Edison DD 80651/Edison BA 4261
Honey, I Wants Yer Now	1916	Edison DD 80323/Edison BA 2862/
Humming	1921	Edison DD 50817
I'm A Pilgrim, I'm A Stranger	1924	Edison DD 80788
In The Sweet Bye And Bye	1921	Gennett 9145
Iowa Corn Song	1921	Gennett 4798/Edison DD 51123 (1923)
Last Night On The Back Porch	1923	Vocalion 14646
Lead Kindly Light (a cappella)	1922	Gennett 4811
Little Cotton Dolly - Plantation Lullaby	1916	Edison DD 80323/Edison BA 2872
Little Tommy Went A-Fishing	1918	Edison DD 80483/Edison BA 3600
Lucky Jim	1921	Edison DD 80742/Edison BA 3092/Brunswick 5001
Mammy Lou	1922	Edison DD 50915
Mammy's Lullaby	1922	Vocalion 14482
Oh My Father	1921	Edison DD 80719
Oh The Banks Of The Wabash	1921	Gennett 4798
Old Black Joe	1916	Edison DD 80358/Edison BA
Ole Aunt Mary's Chile	1924	Edison DD 80802/Edison BA 4920
Ole Uncle Moon	1921	Edison DD 80635/Edison BA 4784/Vocalion 14482 (1922)
Rock Of Ages (a cappella)	1922	Gennett 4811
Silent Night, Holy Night	1923	Gennett 5228
Soldier's Chorus	1922	Vocalion 14321
Soldier's Farewell	1910	Zonophone 72
Still, Still With Thee	1923	Edison DD 80748/Edison BA 4771
Sunset	1918	Edison
That Old Gang Of Mine	1923	Vocalion 14646
Things Are Never Quite So Bad	1916	Edison
Voice Of The Chimes, The	1923	Vocalion 14683
We'll Never Let The Old Flag Fall	1918	Edison
When The Corn Is Waving, Annie Dear	1919	Edison DD 80514
Winter Song	1916	Edison BA 2952
You Left Me Out In The Rain	1924	Edison

Criterion Quartette (Anna Case with)

Title	Year	Release
Come Where My Love Lies Dreaming	1918	Edison DD 83078/Edison Purple Amberol
It Is Well With My Soul	1919	Edison DD 83085

Criterion Quartette (as Clarence Whitehill & Quartet)

Title	Year	Release
Massa's In The Cold Cold Ground	1919	Victor

Criterion Quartette (Christine Miller with)

Title	Year	Release
Battle Hymn Of The Republic	1918	Edison
When You Come Home	1918	Edison

Criterion Quartette (Elisabeth Spencer with)

Title	Year	Release
Honey, Dat's All	1923	Edison DD 80754

Criterion Quartette (Frieda Hempel with)

Title	Year	Release
Aloha Oe	1918	Edison DD 82551/Edison Purple Amberol
Emmett's Lullaby	1917	Edison DD 82550/Edison Purple Amberol
My Old Kentucky Home	1918	Edison DD 82551/Edison Purple Amberol
There's A Long, Long Trail A-Winding	1918	Edison DD 82145

Criterion Quartette (Helen Clark with)

Title	Year	Release
Each Stitch Is A Thought Of You, Dear	1918	Edison BA 3496

Criterion Quartette (Marie Rappold with)

Title	Year	Release
Love's Old Sweet Song	1918	Edison 82553/Edison

Criterion Quartette (with Mabel Garrison)
Jingle Bells	1919	Edison Purple Amberol

Criterion Quartette (with Mrs. Asher & Homer Rodeheaver)
Old Rugged Cross, The	1922	Silvertone 4894/Rainbow 1015 (1922)

Criterion Quartette (with Oscar Seagle)
Little Old Log Cabin In The Lane, The	1921	Columbia A-3582/Columbia 64-M
Uncle Ned	1921	Columbia A-3582/Columbia 64-M

Criterion Quartette, Anna Case & the
Where My Love Lies Dreaming	1919	Edison 29022 (Royal Purple Amberol Cyl)

Criterion Trio (as Marie Tiffany & Trio)
Sweet And Low	1923	Brunswick

Criterion Trio (Marie Tiffany &)
Carry Me Back To Old Virginny	1923	Brunswick 13091
My Old Kentucky Home	1923	Brunswick 13091

Crooners
Clap Yo' Hands	1926	Columbia 802-D
Cross Your Fingers	1929	Columbia 2077-D
Happy Days Are Here Again	1930	Columbia 2118-D
Happy Days Are Here Again	1930	Columbia
Just A Little Longer	1926	Columbia 773D
One Girl, The	1930	Columbia 2118-D
Stein Song, The	1930	Champion 15975
That's A Good Girl	1926	Columbia 773D
Why'	1929	Columbia 2077-D

Crooners (with the Columbia Photo Players)
Rogue Song, The	1929	Columbia 2080-D
When I'm Looking At You	1929	Columbia 2080-D

Crooners (with the Knickerbockers)
March Of The Old Guard	1929	Columbia 2120-D
Parting The Clouds With Sunshine	1929	Columbia 2018D

Crooners Quartet
Stein Song, The	1930	QRS 1046

Crooning Cavaliers
Coming Home From School	1927	Cameo 1287
Moonlit Waters	1927	Cameo 1271
Pretty Girl, A Pretty Tune, A	1927	Cameo 1263
Sunshine Follows The Rain	1927	Cameo 1263
Talkin' And Rollin' Home	1927	Cameo 1286

Crosby, Bing & Foursome
When The Bloom Is On The Sage	1938	Decca 25000

Crosby, Bob & Vocal Group
Shally-Go-Shee	1949	Harmony 1065
Toot, Toot, Tootsie!	1949	Harmony 1065

Crow Trio, Phil
Bidin' My Time	1930	Victor 23036
I'm A-Gittin' Ready To Go	1930	Victor 23504/Columbia 15627-D
In The Cumberland Mountains	1931	Columbia 2619-D

Croxton Quartette
Good-Bye, Sweet Day	1918	Okeh 1053
Praise Ye, Attila	1918	Okeh 1019
Sweet And Low	1918	Okeh 1018

Croxton Trio
Battle Hymn Of The Republic	1918	Okeh 1057
O Holy Night	1919	Okeh 1163
Star Spangled Banner	1918	Okeh 1057

Croxton Trio`
Medley Of Hymns	1919	Okeh 1163

Croxton, Frank & Ladies Quartet
List The Cherubic Host	1916	Columbia A-5784

Croxton, Frank Quartet
Abide With Me	1912	Edison 1545 (4BA)
Rigoletto-Quartet	1913	Edison 1528 (4BA)

Crumit Quartet
Lindy	1920	Columbia

Dadmun, Royal & the Metropolitan Quartet
Oh Holy Night	1911	Columbia A-5384

Dalhart Trio, Vernon
Oh Susanna	1927	Challenge 559
Old Plantation Melody	1927	Challenge 570/Jewel 5229

Dalhart, Vernon (with Kaplan's Melodists)
Bringing Home The Bacon	1924	Edison 4890 (4BA)/Edison 51351 (1925)
I'll Take You Home Again, Kathleen	1925	Edison 5126 (4BA)/Edison 5`1666 (1925)
My Best Girl	1924	Edison 1924 (4BA)/Edison 51439 (1924)
Oh! Those Eyes	1925	Edison 51520
Prisoner's Song		Edison 5105 (4BA)/Edison 51666 (1925)

Dalhart, Vernon (with Premier Quartet)
From Me To Mandy Lee	1917	Edison 3316 (4BA)

Dalhart, Vernon with Vocal Trio
In The Baggage Coach Ahead	1925	Victor 19627
Many, Many Years Ago	1925	Victor 19681

Dandridge Sisters
Minnie The Moocher Is Dead	1940	Columbia 35700
Red Wagon	1940	Columbia 35782
Undecided	1939	
You Ain't Nowhere	1940	Columbia 35782

Danford Sisters
Do The New York	1931	Columbia 2499-D
My Sweet Tooth Says I Wanna (But My Wisdom Tooth Says No)	1931	Columbia 2501-D
Nobody Loves No Baby Like My Baby Loves Me	1931	Columbia 2501-D

Davis Bible Singers
Daniel Saw The Stone	1929	Columbia 14525-D
Do You Want To Be A Lover Of The Lord'	1929	Columbia 14525-D

Deacon Utley Smile Awhile Quartet
Hear Me When I Pray	1948	Columbia 30122
I've Got That Old Time Religion	1948	Columbia 30122

Dean Boys
That Little Boy Of Mine	1936	Conqueror 8753

Debutantes
Cabin On A Hilltop	1936	Decca
Hawaiian Hospitality	1937	Decca 1176/Brunswick A 81475
King Kamehameha	1938	Decca 1909/Decca 1257A
La Estrellita	1938	Decca/Brunswick A 81975
La Paloma	1938	Decca/Brunswick A 81975
My Little Grass Shack In Kealakekua, Hawaii	1938	Decca 1909/Decca 1256A
Never Gonna Dance (with Muzzy Marcellino)	1936	Decca 894
Sweet Leilani (with Muzzy Marcellino)	1937	Decca 1176

Debutantes (Ted Rito's), Muzzy Marcellino & the
What's Good For The Goose Is Good For The Gander	1933	Brunswick 6736

Debutantes and Muzzy Marcellino
Mickey Mouse's Birthday Party	1936	Decca 954
There's 'Yoo-Hoo' In Your Eyes	1936	Decca 954

Debutantes, Muzzy Marcellino & the
Broken Record, The	1936	Decca
Cielo Lindo	1937	Decca 1614
Cling To Me (without Marcellino)	1936	Decca 679
Cross-Eyed Cowboy On The Cross-Eyed Horse, The	1937	Brunswick 81402
Donkey Serenade, The	1937	Decca 1614/Brunswick A 81402
How Many Rhymes Can You Get	1937	Brunswick A 81409
It's Been So Long	1936	Decca 697
(I Went Hunting) And The Big Bad Wolf Was Dead	1934	Brunswick A 9631
Just One Of Those Things	1936	Decca
(Lookie Lookie) Here Comes Cookie	1935	Brunswick 7380/Brunswick A 9777
Love Song Of Tahiti	1935	Brunswick 7446
Lulu's Back In Town	1935	Brunswick 7452C
More Beautiful Than Ever	1932	Brunswick 6422/Brunswick 01413
Vieni, Vieni	1937	Decca 6529/Brunswick A 81344
(Where Were You) On The Night Of June The Third'	1935	Brunswick 7399
Willow, Weep For Me	1932	Brunswick 6422/Brunswick 01413
You Can Be Kissed	1935	Brunswick 7452C/Brunswick C 967

Debutantes, Rudy Vallee & the
Ha-Cha-Cha	1934	Victor 24722

Debutantes, Stanley Hickman & the
Indian Love Call	1936	Decca 694/Brunswick A 9942

Deep River Boys
Ain't Misbehavin'	1948	RCA Victor 20-2998
All I Need Is You	1952	Beacon 9146
All My Love Belongs To You	1956	Vik 0205
Are You Certain	1961	Wand 117
Ashes of Roses	1950	
Bewitched	1950	
Biggest Fool, The	1953	RCA Victor 47-5268
Bird In The Hand, A	1940	Bluebird B-10847
Bloop Bleep	1947	RCA Victor 20-2397
Body And Soul	1946	Associated Program Transcription 60927
Bullfrog And The Toad, The	1940	Bluebird B-10676
Carry Me Back To Old Virginny	194'	Lang-Worth Transcription
Charge It To Daddy	1947	RCA Victor 20-2157
Cherokee	1941	Bluebird B-11178
Chloe	194'	Lang-Worth Transcription
City Called Heaven	194'	Lang-Worth Transcription
Clouds Before The Storm, The	1965	Michelle 1001
Cousin Jedidah	194'	Lang-Worth Transcription 768
Cry And You Cry Alone	1949	RCA Victor 22-0013
De Band Of Gideon	194'	Lang-Worth Transcription

Title	Year	Label
Deep Water	1952	
Doesn't Make Sense To Me	1952	Beacon 9143
Don't Ask Me Why	1949	RCA Victor 22-0003
Don't Blame Me	1946	Associated Program Transcription 60927
Don't Trade Your Love For Gold	1952	
Down In The Glen	1949	
Dream Street	1947	RCA Victor 20-2305
Eili Eili	1952	
Ev'ry Sunday Afternoon	1940	RCA Victor 26533
Farewell Farewell	194'	Lang-Worth Transcription
Feel Grace	1950	RCA Victor 22-0078
Foolishly Yours	1946	RCA Victor 20-1990
Get Up Those Stairs, Mademoiselle	1947	RCA Victor 20-2305
Git On Board, Little Children	1946	Pilotone 5147
Git On Board, Little Chillun'	194'	Lang-Worth Transcription
Glad Rag Doll	1952	
Go Down Moses	1946	Pilotone 5150
Grandfather's Clock	1941	
Heads Up Win, Tails I Lose	1947	RCA Victor 20-2517
(Home) How Dear Can It Be	1956	Vik 0224
Honey, Honey, Honey	1946	Pilotone 5152
Honey, Honey, Honey	194'	Lang-Worth Transcription
I Am Seekin' For A City	194'	Lang-Worth Transcription
I Didn't Know About You	1946	Associated Program Transcription 60927
I Don't Know Why	1959	Gallant 2001/Seeco 6046 (1960)
I Feel My Time Ain't Long	1938	Decca 7428
If You Love God, Serve Him	1950	RCA Victor 22-0078/RCA Victor 50-0078 (1950)
I Got A Home In Dat Rock	194'	Lang-Worth Transcription
I Know I'd Like To Read	194'	Lang-Worth Transcription
I Left Myself Wide Open	1947	RCA Victor 20-2397
I'll Be Around	194'	Lang-Worth Transcription
I'm Confessin'	1958	
I'm Sorry I Didn't Say I'm Sorry (The Mumble Song)	1947	RCA Victor 20-2610
I'm Trampin'	1946	Pilotone 5154
I'm Troubled In Mind	194'	Lang-Worth Transcription 699
I'm Trying	194'	Lang-Worth Transcription
In Dat Great Gittin' Up Mornin'	194'	Lang-Worth Transcription
Indiana	1946	Associated Program Transcription 60927
I Need Somebody To Love	194'	Lang-Worth Transcription
In The Kingdom	194'	Lang-Worth Transcription
I Still Love You	1951	
Itchy Twitchy Feelin'	1958	
It Had To Be You	1947	RCA Victor 20-2517
(It's No) Sin	1952	
It's Too Soon To Know	1948	RCA Victor 20-3203
I Wanna Sleep	1948	RCA Victor 20-2808
I Was A Fool To Let You Go	1940	Bluebird B-10676
I Wish I Had Died In My Cradle	1941	Bluebird B-11217
I Wonder Why	1955	
I Won't Cry Anymore	1952	
Jealous	1947	RCA Victor 20-2157
Jersey Bounce	194'	Lang-Worth Transcription
Jerusalem Morn	194'	Lang-Worth Transcription
Just A Little Bit More	1956	
Just A-Sittin' And A-Rockin'	1945	Majestic 1023
Keep Me In Mind	194'	Lang-Worth Transcription
Kiss And A Cuddle Polka, A	1954	
Kissin'	1959	Gallant 102
Lament To Love	194'	Lang-Worth Transcription AS-871 B
Live Humble	1947	RCA Victor 20-2265
Live Humble	194'	Lang-Worth Transcription
Lord's Prayer, The	194'	Lang-Worth Transcription
Lord, Until I Reach My Home	194'	Lang-Worth Transcription
Lucky Black Cat	1954	
May The Good Lord Bless And Keep You	1951	
Mine Too	1950	RCA Victor 20-3699

Title	Year	Label/Number	Title	Year	Label/Number
Mister And Mississippi	1951				3203
Moon Nocturne	194'	Lang-Worth Transcription	Ride On Jesus	194'	Lang-Worth Transcription
More 'N' More Amour	1965	Michelle 1001	Rock A Beatin' Boogie	1956	
My Castle On The Nile	1946	Pilotone 5153	Roll Jordan Roll	194'	Lang-Worth Transcription
My Heart At Thy Sweet Voice	1941	Bluebird B-11178			
My Old Home Town	1952	Select R-177-S	Romance A La Mode	1954	
My Old Kentucky Home	194'	Lang-Worth Transcription	Said He Would Calm The Ocean	194'	Lang-Worth Transcription
My Way's Cloudy	194'	Lang-Worth Transcription	See If I Care	1946	Associated Program Transcription 60927
My Yiddisher Momma	1952				
Necessity	1947	RCA Victor 45-0013	Seen Four And Twenty Elders	1947	Victor 20-2265
			September Song	1951	
Night Is Young & You're So Beautiful	194'	Lang-Worth Transcription	Shake Rattle And Roll	1955	
			Shortnin' Bread	1946	Associated Program Transcription 60927
Nola	1959	Gallant 101			
No One Else Will Do (recorded in 1951)	1954	Jay-Dee 788	Sleepy Little Cowboy	1952	Beacon 9146/Beacon 104
No One Sweeter Than You	1949	RCA Victor 22-0013	Slow Train To Nowhere	1958	
			Smack Dab In The Middle	1955	
Nothing But You	1940	RCA Victor 26533	Somebody Got Lost In The Storm	194'	Lang-Worth Transcription
Not Too Old To Rock And Roll	1958				
Oh, Freedom	1950	Pilotone S 45			
Oh, Freedom	194'	Lang-Worth Transcription	Stars Are The Windows Of Heaven, The	1951	X 1019
Oh, Susanna	194'	Lang-Worth Transcription	St Louis Blues	1955	
			Story Of Ee-Bobba-Lee-Bob	1946	RCA Victor 20-1863
Oh Tell Me Gypsy	1949				
Oh The Rocks & the Mountains	194'	Lang-Worth Transcription	Summertime	194'	Lang-Worth Transcription
Oh Wasn't That A Wide River	194'	Lang-Worth Transcription	Sweet Canaan	194'	Lang-Worth Transcription
Oh Yes! Oh Yes!	194'	Lang-Worth Transcription	Sweet Mama Tree Top Tall	1954	
			Swinging At The Seance	1941	
Old Devil Moon	1947	RCA Victor 45-0013	Swing Low, Sweet Chariot	1946	Pilotone 5149/Pilotone S 45 (1950)
Old Folks At Home	194'	Lang-Worth Transcription			
			Swing Low Sweet Clarinet	1948	RCA Victor 20-2622
Ole Time Religion	194'	Lang-Worth Transcription	Swing Out To Victory	1942	Bluebird 11569
Ol' Sheep Done Know De Road, The	194'	Lang-Worth Transcription	Talkin' To The Lawd	194'	Lang-Worth Transcription 699
On Freedom	1946	Pilotone 5151	Tennessee News Boy	1952	
Only Fascination	1952		That Chick's Too Young To Fry	1946	Victor 20-1863/Victor 20-2135
Oo-Shoo-Be-Do-Be	1953	RCA Victor 47-5268			
Opportunity	1950	RCA Victor 20-3825	That Lucky Old Sun	1949	
			That's Right	1956	
Poor Priscilla	1946	Associated Program Transcription 60927	That's What You Need To Succeed	1946	Associated Program Transcription 60927
Purgatory	1948	RCA Victor 20-2622	That's What You Need To Succeed	1948	RCA Victor 20-2998
Recess In Heaven	1948	RCA Victor 20-	There's A Goldmine In The Sky	1956	

100 Years of Harmony: 1850 to 1950

These Foolish Things	1945	Majestic 1017
They Look Like Men Of War	194'	Lang-Worth Transcription
This Chick's Too Young To Fry	1946	RCA Victor 20-1863
This May Be The Last Time	194'	Lang-Worth Transcription
Timber's Gotta Roll	1959	Gallant 2001/Seeco 6046 (1960)
Tis The Old Ship Of Zion	194'	Lang-Worth Transcription
Too-Whit, Too-Whoo	1949	
Too Young	1951	
Truthfully	1952	Beacon 9143/Jay-Dee 788 (1954)
Trying	1952	
Tuxedo Junction	1950	RCA Victor 20-3825
Tween Four And Twenty Elders	1947	RCA Victor 20-2265
Two Blocks Down, Turn To The Left	1948	RCA Victor 20-2808
Utt-Da-Zay	1941	Bluebird B-11217
Vanishing American, The	1961	Wand 117
Violins Were Playing	194'	Lang-Worth Transcription
We Are Walking In The Light	1946	Pilotone 5148
We're Almost Home	194'	Lang-Worth Transcription
What Did He Say	1947	RCA Victor 20-2610
What Kind Of Shoes You Gwine To Wear	194'	Lang-Worth Transcription
Wheel In A Wheel, A	194'	Lang-Worth Transcription
When Your Lover Has Gone	1946	Associated Program Transcription 60927
When Your True Love Forgets	194'	Lang-Worth Transcription
Who Built De Ark	194'	Transcriptions 1941 to 1943
Whole Lotta Shakin' Goin' On	1956	
Whole Wide World	1956	Vik 0205
Who'll Jine De Union	194'	Lang-Worth Transcription
William Didn't Tell	1946	RCA Victor 20-1990
Wrapped Up In A Dream	1949	RCA Victor 22-0003
You Better Mind	194'	Lang-Worth Transcription
You Don't Know Nothin'	1940	Bluebird B-10847
You'll Never Know	1943	Lang-Worth AS-27
You Must Be Losing Your Mind	1946	Associated Program Transcription 60927
You're Not Too Old	1956	Vik 0224

Deep River Boys (with Thelma Carpenter)

Hurry Home	1945	Majestic 1023

Deep River Boys, Bea Wain & the

God Bless The Child	1941	RCA 27579
Sometimes I Feel Like A Motherless Child	1941	RCA 27579

Deep River Boys, Basie & the)

Solid As A Rock	1950	Victor 20-3699/Victor DJ 925/RCA Victor 47-3235

Deep River Boys, Fats Waller & the

By The Light Of The Silvery Moon	1942	Bluebird 11569/RCA 20-2448 (1947)

Deep River Boys, Thelma Carpenter & the

My Guy's Come Back	1945	Majestic 1017

Deep River Plantation Singers

I Feel My Time Ain't Long	1931	Champion 16463/Champion 50039 (1931)
Joshua Fit De Battle Of Jericho	1931	Champion 16378
Lonesome Road	1931	Champion 16730/Champion 50010 (1931)
Look Away Into Heaven	1931	Champion 16730/Champion 50010 (1931)
Roll Jordan Roll	1931	Champion 16463
Train's A-Comin'	1931	Champion 16378/Champion 50039 (1931)

Deep River Quintet (with Chicago Loopers)

Clorinda	1927	Perfect 14910
I'm More Than Satisfied	1927	Perfect 14905

Deep River Quintette

My Blue Heaven	1927	Perfect 14875

Deep River Singers

I Feel Like My Time Ain't Long	1937	Decca 7428
Train's A-Comin'	1931	Decca 7428

Deep South Boys

Holy Ghost Getting Us Ready	1948	Columbia 30114
I Bowed On My Knees And Cried Holy	1948	Columbia 30114
In The Garden	1949	Columbia 30171
Just A Little Talk With Jesus	1948	Columbia 30117
My Soul Is A Witness	1949	Columbia 30171
One Morning Soon	1948	Columbia 30117
Over In Zion	1948	Columbia 30131
Take Hold The Life Line	1949	Columbia 30165

Uncluded Day, The	1948	Columbia 30131
Until I Found The Lord	1949	Columbia 30165

Delta Big Four

God Won't Forsake His Own	1930	Paramount 12987
I Know My Time Ain't Long	1930	Paramount 12948
I'll Be Here	1930	Paramount 13095
Jesus Got His Arms Around Me	1930	Paramount 13095
Moaner, Let's Go Down In The Valley	1930	Paramount 13009
We're All Gonna Face The Rising Sun	1930	Paramount 13009
Where Was Eve Sleeping	1930	Paramount 12948

Delta Four

Farewell Blues	1936	Decca 737B/Decca 3864A (1940)
Swingin' On The Famous Door	1936	Decca 737A/Decca 3526B

Delta Rhythm Boys

Ain't Gonna Worry 'Bout A Soul All Alone	1947	RCA 20-2588
All The Things You Are	1951	Metronome B 575
All The Things You Are	1952	Mercury 1409/London 1145 (1952)
Alouette, Gentille Alouette	1952	Metronome B 630
Are You For It'		World Feature LJ-18B
Ark Is Movin', The	1959	Coral LP
A-Sittin' & A-Rockin'	194'	AFRS 202
Baby, Are You Kiddin"	1945	Decca 23451
Babylon	1955	Decca 29528
Baseball Boogie	1952	Metronome B 612
Begin The Beguine	1950	Metronome B 521Mercury LP 25153 (1953)
Bewitched Bothered & Bewildered	1957	Elektra LP 138
Black Is The Color	1953	Metronome MEP 316
Blow Out The Candle	1952	London 1145
Blues Ain't News To Me, The	1952	Metronome B 612
Blue Skies	1957	Elektra LP 138
Blues My Naughty Sweetie Gives To Me	1941	
Bugle Woogie	1941	Doctor Horse LP 809
But She's My Buddy's Chick	1946	Decca 18911
Bye, Bye, Alibi Baby	1947	Victor 20-2183
Certainly Lord	1941	Doctor Horse LP 809
Cha Cha Joe	1957	Elektra LP 138
Charmaine	1952	Metronome B 616
Chilly 'N' Cold	1941	Decca 8514
Chloe		
Come In Out Of The Rain	1947	RCA 20-2365
Conversation At Midnight	1941	
Dancin' With Someone	1953	RCA Victor 47-5217
Darktown Strutter's Ball		World Feature LJ-21B
Do Nothin' Till You Hear From Me	1944	Decca 4440A
Do Nothin' Till You Hear From Me		World Feature LJ-21B
Don't Ask Me Why	1949	Atlantic 875/Musicraft 597 (1949)
Don't Even Change A Picture On The Wall	1955	Decca 29582
Don't Knock It	1945	Decca 18739
Dormaredansen	1950	Doctor Horse LP 809
Down On The Delta Shore	1941	Decca 8584
Do You Care	1941	Decca 8561
Dry Bones	1941	Decca 8522/Decca 4406 (1942)/Decca 25019 (1941)/Decca 30466 (1957)
Dry Bones	1947	Victor 20-2460/Victor 47-2826 (1949)
Early Autumn		
East Of The Sun	194'	AFRS California Melodies 21
East Of The Sun, West Of The Moon	1947	RCA 20-2461/Victor 47-2827 (1949)
Emphatically No	1952	Metronome B 618
Every So Often	1947	RCA 20-2365
Ev'rytime We Say Goodbye	1947	RCA 20-2462/'Victor 47-2828 (1949)
Ev'ry Time We Say Goodbye		World Feature LJ-19B
Ezekiel Saw De Wheel	1941	
Fan Tan Fannie	1950	Decca 48148
Fantastic	1949	Musicraft 597
Get On Board Little Children		World Feature LJ-19B
Gimme Some Skin	1941	Decca 8514
Give Me Some Skin	1941	Decca 8530
Give Me Some Skin	194'	AFRS
Gotta Be This Or That	1945	Live Transcription
Gypsy In My Soul, The	1950	Metronome B 522/Odeon DK 1117/Mercury 1407 (1952)
Have A Hope, Have A Wish, Have A Prayer	1954	Decca 29273

100 Years of Harmony: 1850 to 1950

Title	Year	Label
Headin' For The Bottom	1955	Decca 29528
Hello, Goodbye, Forget It	1946	Decca 23771
Hey, John!		World Feature LJ-21B
Hey, John! (Keep Your Glasses On)	1947	Victor 20-2271
Honeydripper, The	1945	Decca 23451
How High The Moon	194'	AFRS California Melodies 21
I Can't Tell A Lie To Myself	1948	RCA 20-3007
I Do, Do You (Believe In Love)'	1941	Decca 8554
I'd Rather Be Wrong Than Blue	1950	Decca 48140
I Dreamt I Dwelt In Harlem	1941	
If I Knew Then		
If You Are But A Dream	1947	RCA 20-2463/Victor 47-2829 (1949)
If You See Tears In My Eyes	1950	Atlantic 900
I'll Never Get Out Of This World Alive	1952	Victor 47-5094
I'm Awfully Strong For You	1947	Victor 20-2271
I'm Beginning To See The Light	1944	Jubilee 143
I'm Beginning To See The Light		World Feature LJ-20B
I'm In Love With A Gal (Who's In Love With A Guy Who Looks Like Me But Ain't)	1947	RCA 20-2436
I'm Used To You	1952	Victor 47-5094
Indiana		
It Ain't Necessarily So	1957	Elektra LP 138
It Had To Be You		
It's All In Your Mind	1950	Decca 48148
It's Alright With Me	1957	Elektra LP 138
It Was Wonderful Then	1941	
I've Got You Under My Skin	1950	Metronome B 522/Odeon DK 1117/Mercury 1407 (1952)
Jenny Kissed Me	1947	Victor 20-2183
Jersey Bounce		World Feature LJ-20B
Joshua Fit De Battle Of Jericho	1941	Decca 8522/Decca 25019 (1941)/Decca 30466 (1957)
Just A-Sittin' And A-Rockin' (fast)	1945	Decca 18739/Brunswick 82717/Decca 23541 (1946)
Just Squeeze Me (But Don't Tease Me)	1946	Decca 23771
Keep On To Galilee	1941	
Keep Smilin', Keep Laughin', Be Happy	1942	Decca 4266
Kiss Crazy Baby	1954	Decca 29329
Knock Me A Kiss	1943	Jubilee Transcription 61 (AFRS MER-2)
Kullerullvisan	1950	Doctor Horse LP 809
La Cucaracha	1941	
Laugh's On Me, The	1949	Atlantic 889
Let Me Off Uptown	1941	Decca 8578
Little Lize I Love You	1941	
Little Small Town Girl (With The Big Town Dreams)	1947	RCA 20-2588
Long Gone Baby	1953	RCA Victor 47-5217
Lover Come Back To Me	1951	Metronome B 568/Mercury 1409/Doctor Horse LP 809 (1952)
Lullabye Of Birdland		
Mad About Her, Sad Without Her, How Can I Be Glad Without Her Blues	1942	Decca 4266
Midnight Sun		
Mighty Day	1941	
Miss Me	1952	Metronome B 618
Mood Indigo	1954	Decca 29273
More I Go Out With Somebody Else, The		World Feature LJ-18B
My Blue Heaven	1941	Decca 8542/RCA 20-3007 (1948)
My Future Just Passed	1947	RCA 20-2436
My Imaginary Love	1941	Decca 8542
My Own True Love	1962	Philips 40023
My Sacrifice		World Feature LJ-20B
Never Underestimate The Power Of A Woman	1948	RCA 20-2855
9:20 Special	1951	Metronome B 575/Doctor Horse LP 809
Nobody Knows	1950	Atlantic 900
No Greater Love	1941	Varieton
No Pad To Be Had	1946	Decca 23541/Brunswick 82717
Old Black Magic	1943	Jubilee Transcription 61 (AFRS DEL-7)
Old Man River		
One O'Clock Jump	1947	Victor 20-2463/Victor 47-2829 (1949)
One O'Clock Jump		World Feature LJ-20B
On The Sunny Side Of The Street	1950	Metronome B 521/Mercury 1408

		(1952)	Walk It Off	1946	Decca 18911
Oo Wee Baby	1952	Metronome B 580	Watermelon On The Vine	1941	
Paper Doll	194'	AFRS California Melodies 21	When I'm Gone You'll Soon Forget	1941	Decca 4128
Perdido			When You're Gone I Won't Forget	1941	Decca 4128
Playin' The Game	1941	Decca 8584	Whiffenpoof Song		
Poor Boy	1957	Elektra LP 138	Without A Song	1952	Metronome B 580
Praise The Lord And Pass The Ammunition	1942	Decca 4406	Work Song	1962	Philips 40023
			Would It Be Asking Too Much	1941	Decca 8530/Decca 25395 (1948)
Railroad Song, The	1941				
Riddle Song, The	1957	Elektra LP 138	You Are Closer To My Heart	1950	Decca 48140
Saturday Night Fish Fry	1957	Elektra LP 138	You Go To Your Church, I'll Go To Mine Beyond The Sunset	1950	Decca 48138
Scandalize My Name	1941				
September Song	1947	RCA 20-2460/Victor 47-2826 (1949)	Young Man With A Horn	1957	Elektra LP 138
			You're Mine, You!	1948	RCA 20-2855
			Delta Rhythm Boys (Gulf Coast Five)		
Shadrack			Gee, Baby Ain't I Good To You	1945	Decca 18650
She Believed A Gypsy	1941	Decca 8561	Is There Somebody Else	1945	Decca 18650
Shoes	1954	Decca 29329	**Delta Rhythm Boys (with Ella Fitzgerald)**		
Shoe Shoe Baby	194'	AFRS California Melodies 21	Cry You Out Of My Heart	1945	Decca 23425
			For Sentimental Reasons	1946	Decca 23670/Decca 29136 (1954)
Should You Go First	1950	Decca 48138			
Side By Side	1957	Elektra LP 138	It's A Pity To Say Goodnight	1946	Decca 23670
Snoqualimie Jo Jo		World Feature LJ-21B	(It's Only A) Paper Moon	1945	Decca 23425/Decca 29136 (1954)
So High So Wide So Low	1959	Coral LP	**Delta Rhythm Boys (with Fred Astaire)**		
Something I Dreamed Last Night	1957	Elektra LP 138	Since I Kissed My Baby G'Bye	1941	Decca 18187//Brunswick 03287
St. Louis Blues	1947	Victor 20-2462/'Victor 47-2828 (1949)			
			Wedding Cake Walk, The	1941	Decca 18188/Brunswick 03288
St. Louis Blues		World Feature LJ-18B			
Star Dust	1941	Decca 8530/Decca 25395 (1948)	**Delta Rhythm Boys (with Les Paul Trio)**		
			One-Sided Affair, A	1946	Decca 24193
Star Dust		World Feature LJ-19B	What Would It Take'	1946	Decca 24193
Sweetheart Of Mine	1949	Atlantic 889	**Delta Rhythm Boys (with Mildred Bailey)**		
'S Wonderful	1957	Elektra LP 138	Bugle Woogie	194'	AFRS
Take Me	1960	Vega EP	Ev'rything Depends On You	1941	Decca 3888/Decca 25462 (1950)
Take The "A" Train	1941	Decca 8578/Victor 20-2461 1947)/Victor 47-2827 (1949)	It's So Peaceful In The Country	1941	Decca 3953A/Brunswick 80109/Decca 27920 (1952)
Texas Polka		World Feature LJ-19B			
			Jenny	1941	Decca 3661
That's Just The Way I Feel	1955	Decca 29582	Rockin' Chair & There'll Be Some Changes Made	1943	'Transcription, Dubs & Tests' CD
There'll Be Some Changes Made	1957	Elektra LP 138			
They Didn't Believe Me	1951	Metronome B 568/Mercury 1408 (1952)	When That Man Is Dead And Gone	1941	Decca 3661
			Delta Rhythm Boys (with Mildred Bailey) (as Mildred Bailey with Delta Four)		
Things I Love, The	1941	Decca 8554			
Travelin' Light	1944	Decca 4440	Georgia On My Mind	1941	Decca 3691/Decca 11083 (1946)/Decca 27919
Tre Trallande Jantor	1951	Metronome			
Undecided	1952	Metronome B 616			
Wait Till I Put On My Crown	1941				

Rockin' Chair	1941	Decca 3755/Decca 11083 (1946)/Decca 27918/Brunswick 03198/Brunswick 82699
Sometimes I'm Happy	1941	Decca 3755/Decca 27918/Brunswick 03198/Brunswick 82699

Delta Rhythm Boys (with Mildred Bailey) (as Mildred Bailey with Delta Four))
I'm Afraid Of Myself	1941	Decca 3691

Delta Rhythm Boys (with Ruth Brown)
(I'll Come Back) Someday	1950	Atlantic 899
It's All In Your Mind	1954	Atlantic 1023
Sentimental Journey	1950	Atlantic 905/Atlantic 1023 (1954)
Why	1950	Atlantic 899

DeMarco Girls (Five Demarco Sisters)
Mickey Mouse And Minnie's In Town	1933	Victor 24410
Who's Afraid Of The Big Bad Wolf	1933	Victor 24410

DeMarco Sisters (Five DeMarco Sisters)
Easy Come, Easy Go	1934	Victor 24611
Riptide (with Lew Sherwood)	1934	Victor 24613
When A Woman Loves A Man	1934	Victor 24611

Dempsey Quartet
Face To Face	1928	Columbia
With Joy We Sing	1928	Columbia

Dennis Sisters
Just Like That	1946	Musicraft 395
Listen	1946	Musicraft 395
Send Back My Honeyman		Edison 51088

Denson Parrish Harp Singers
Mount Zion	1934	Bluebird 5977

Denson Quartet
Christian Soldier	1928	Columbia 15526-D
I'm On My Journey Home	1928	Columbia 15526-D

Denson Sacred Harp Singers
Christian Hope, The	1934	Bluebird 5977
Concord	1934	Bluebird 5978
Exhortation	1934	Bluebird 5980
Happy Sailor, The	1928	Brunswick 302
Passing Away	1934	Bluebird 5980
Protection	1928	Brunswick 302
Ragan	1934	Bluebird 5976
Raymond	1934	Bluebird 5976
Resurrected	1934	Bluebird 5979
Reverential Anthem	1934	Bluebird 5979
Sing To Me Of Heaven	1934	Bluebird 5978

DeZurik Sisters
Arizona Yodeler, The	1939	Conqueror 9253
Birmingham Jail	1939	Conqueror 9251
Go To Sleep My Darling Baby	1939	Conqueror 9251
Guitar Blues	1939	Conqueror 9252
I Left Her Standing There	1939	Conqueror 9253
Sweet Hawaiian Chimes	1939	Conqueror 9252

Diamond Four
Palms, The	1898	Berliner 0898Y
Star Spangled Banner	189'	Berliner 4258

Diamond Four (with J. Reynard)
Little Darling Dream Of Me	1898	Berliner 0892X
Moonlight Medley	1898	Berliner 4250Z

Dictators
Look In The Morning Glass	1931	Brunswick Test
Road To Mandalay	1931	Brunswick Test

Dinning Sisters
And Mimi	1947	Capitol B 466
And Then It's Heaven	1951	Capitol 281
Ask Me	1951	Capitol 1766
As Long As I'm Dreaming	1954	Decca 28833
As Time Goes By		
Aunt Hagar's Children Blues	1943	Capitol 20018
Beg Your Pardon	1947	Capitol 490
Better Not Roll Those Blue, Blue Eyes	200	Jasmine CD 384
Brazil	1943	Capitol 938/Capitol 20020 (1946)/Capitol 1653 (1949)
Bride And Groom Polka, The		
Bury Me Not On The Lone Prairie		Jasmine CD 3551
Buttons And Bows	1947	Capitol 15184
Christmas Island	1947	Capitol 1258
Clancy		
Down In The Diving Bell		
Do You Love Me	1946	Capitol 241
Dreamy Melody	1951	Capitol 1743
Drop Me A Line		
Easy Talk	1951	Capitol 1577
Echo Said No	1947	Unreleased
Farther Along		Jasmine CD 3551
Fun And Fancy Free	1947	Capitol B 466
Goofus		Essex 388
Gospel Cannonball		Jasmine CD 3551
Harlem Sandman	1947	Capitol 15339
Hawaiian War Chant		
Heartbreak Hill	1951	Capitol 1858
He Like It! She Like It!	1946	Capitol 353
He's Just A Sentimental Gentleman From Georgia	2001	Jasmine CD 384
Hold Everything ('Til I Get Back To You)		
Home On The Range		Jasmine CD 3551
Homesick - That's All	1945	Capitol 209/Victor

I Called But Nobody Answered		5095 Jasmine CD 3551
I Can't Forget	1951	Capitol 1726
I Don't Know Why		
I Don't Stand A Ghost Of A Chance	1951	Capitol 1792
If I Had My Life To Live Over	1947	Capitol 389
I Get Along Without You Very Well		
I Get The Blues When It Rains	1947	Capitol B 20131
Iggity Song, The	1946	Capitol 261
I Love My Love	1951	Capitol 281
I'm Lost	1952	Capitol 2082
I'm Sorry Now		Jasmine CD 3551
In All Of My Dreams	1951	Capitol 1770
In The Pines		Jasmine CD 3551
I Only Want A Buddy Not A Sweetheart		Jasmine CD 3551
I Wonder Where You Are Tonight		Jasmine CD 3551
I Wonder Who's Kissing Her Now	1947	Capitol 433
Keep Your Promise, Willie Thomas	1954	Decca 28833
Kissing Song, The	1950	Capitol 1429
Kiss Me Goodbye, Love	1951	Capitol 1743/Capitol 1770 (1951)
Last Thing I Want Is Your Pity, The		Jasmine CD 3551
Let's Draw Straws		Jasmine CD 3551
Lilac Tree, The		
Little Brown Gal	1952	Capitol 2004
Little Te-Long		
Lolita Lopez	1947	Capitol 433
Louisiana Hayride		Jasmine CD 3551
Love Letters	1945	Capitol 209
Love Me Blues	1951	Capitol 1792
Love Me Sweet, Love Me Long	1952	Capitol 2082
Love On A Greyhound Bus	1945	Capitol 261
Mama, He Treats Your Daughter Mean		Essex 388
Melancholy	1947	Capitol 490
Molly Malone		
Morning On The Farm		Jasmine CD 3551
My Adobe Hacienda	1947	Capitol 389
No! No! No! Not That	1951	Capitol 1858
No Letter Today		Jasmine CD 3551
Oh! Mo'nah	1947	Capitol 15539/Jasmine CD 3551
Oklahoma Hills	1951	Capitol 1766
Old Music Master, The		
Once In A While	1943	Capitol 20019/Capitol 938
Pig Foot Pete		
Please Don't Talk About Me When I'm Gone		
Pretty Girl Milking Her Cow, A		
Pretty Little Busybody		
Ridin' Down The Canyon		Jasmine CD 3551
San Antonio Rose	1946	Capitol 15184/Jasmine CD 3551
Santa Catalina (Island Of Romance)	1947	Unreleased
Shenandoah Waltz	1950	Capitol 1429
Shine On Harvest Moon		
Somebody	1951	Capitol 1511
Sometimes I'm Happy		
Statue In The Park, The		
Steel Guitar Rag	1954	Decca 28980
Strawberry Tears	1951	Capitol 1577
Sweethearts Or Strangers		Jasmine CD 3551
Tennessee Blues	1951	Capitol 1726
Thanks For The Buggy Ride		Jasmine CD 3551
There's A Rainbow 'Round My Shoulder		
They Didn't Believe Me	1954	Decca 28980
They Just Chopped Down The Old Apple Tree		
Three-Quarter Boogie		
Till We Meet Again		Jasmine CD 3551
Trail Of The Lonesome Pine, The		Jasmine CD 3551
Trouble In Mind		Jasmine CD 3551
Turn Your Radio On		Jasmine CD 3551
Very Good Advice	1951	Capitol 1511
Wave To Me My Lady	1946	Capitol 241
Way You Look Tonight, The	1943	Capitol 20020
We'll Meet Again		
Whatsa Malla You	1952	Capitol 2004
When The Bloom Is On The Sage		Jasmine CD 3551
Where Or When	1943	Capitol 20018
Winter Wonderland		
Years And Years Ago	1946	Capitol 353
You Are My Sunshine		Jasmine CD 3551
You'll Be Sorry		Jasmine CD 3551
You're A Character, Dear	1943	Capitol 20019

Dinning Sisters (with Tennessee Ernie Ford)

Rock City Boogie	1951	Capitol 1911
Streamlined Cannonball	1951	Capitol 1911

Dinwiddie Colored Quartet

Down On The Old Camp Ground	1902	Monarch 1714
Gabriel's Trumpet	1902	Monarch 1725
My Way Is Cloudy	1902	Monarch 1724
Poor Mourner	1902	Monarch 1715
Steal Away	1902	Monarch 1716
We'll Anchor Bye-And-Bye	1902	Monarch 1726

Diplomats

Can't We Be Friends'	1929	Columbia
Come On And Make Whoopee	1928	Columbia 1641-D
Diga Diga Doo	1928	Columbia 1534-D

Doin' The New Low-Down		1928	Columbia 1534-D	Sharp Mama	1948	Continental 6076
Down Among The Sugar Cane		1929	Columbia 1796-D	Swing Down Chariot	1948	Sunrise 2117
From Sunrise To Sunset		1929	Columbia 1796-D	Swing Low Sweet Chariot		Melojazz 7008
Just A Little Blue For You		1928	Columbia 1495-D	Thee Governor	1952	Prestige 2001
Melancholy		1929	Columbia	Things Got Tuff Again	1948	20th Century 20-60/Gotham 167 (1948)
Oh! You Sweet Watcha May Call It		1928	Columbia 1641-D			
Dixiaires (Dixie-Aires/Dixieaires)				Traveling All Alone	1954	Harlem 2326
Bloodstained Banner		1952	Prestige 2001	Until You Say You Are Mine	1948	Continental 6067/Lenox 518 (1949)
Buckle My Shoe			Spirituals 5000			
Casey Jones			Exclusive 116x			
Christ ABCs			Exclusive 117x/Sittin' In With 2019	Wade In The Water	1948	Sunrise 2117/Melojazz 7008
Coming Of The King, The			Sittin' In With 2003	Way Down In Egypt	1948	Lenox 506
Don't Let That Worry You		1950	Sittin' In With 553	Well Done		Harlem 1012
Doomed		1949	Lenox 530	When That Great Ship Went Down	1949	Sittin' In With 2013
Down By The Riverside		1948	Continental 6072			
Feed Me Jesus			Sittin' In With 2020	You Better Get Ready	1949	Lenox 531
Friends Let Me Tell You About Jesus		1949	Exclusive 98x	You Better Run	194'	Sunrise 319
Gabriel Sound Your Trumpet			Harlem 1012	You Can't Cure The Blues	1948	Continental 6067/Lenox 518 (1949)
Gamblin' Man		1949	Lenox 530			
God Is The Greatest Creator			Sittin' In With 2017	Your Red Wagon	1948	Continental 1227
Go Long		1948	Gotham 163	**Dixie Four**		
He Never Said A Mumblin' Word			Spirituals 5000	Blue Star Has Turned To Gold, A	1951	Gospel 519
I Can See My Saviour Standing There			Exclusive 117x	Kneel At The Cross	1951	Gospel 519
				Dixie Four, Ted Lewis & the		
If You See My Saviour		1948	Continental 6071	Dinah	1930	Columbia 2181-D
I Got A Home In That Rock		1949	Exclusive 98x	Lonesome Road, The	1930	Columbia 2181-D
I Got To Stand		1948	Continental 6071	**Dixie Hummingbirds**		
I'm Going To Shoulder Up My Cross		1949	Sittin' In With 2012	God's Got Your Number	1939	Decca 7646
				I'll Live Again	1952	Okeh 6864
I'm Not Like I Used To Be		1954	Harlem 2326	I'll Never Forget	1952	Okeh 6864
Joe Louis Is A Fightin' Man		1949	Sittin' In With 2012	I Looked Down The Line	1939	Decca 7688
Joshua		1949	Lenox 514	I'm Leaning On The Lord	1939	Decca 7677
Just A Closer Walk With Thee		1951	Sittin' In With 2020	Joshua Journeyed To Jericho	1939	Decca 7645
Just Getting Ready		1949	Sittin' In With 2013	Just A Closer Walk With Thee	1947	
Keep Me With You		1948	20th Century 20-60/Gotham 167 (1948)	Little Wooden Church	1939	Decca 7667
				Lord If I Go	1939	Decca 7646
Little Wooden Church		1948	Sunrise 2118	Moving Up That Shining Way	1939	Decca 7677
Long, Lean And Lanky		1948	Gotham 163	Sleep On, Mother	1940	Decca 7715
Loose The Man			Sittin' In With 2019	Soon Will Be Done With The Troubles Of This World	1940	Decca 7746
My Dungeon Shook		1949	Lenox 531			
My God Called Me		1948	Continental 6072	Walking On The Water	1940	Decca 7715
My God Call Me This Morning		1948	Sunrise 319	What A Time	1939	Decca 7688
My Time Ain't Long		1949	Lenox 514	When The Gates Swing Open	1939	Decca 7645
Playing With Fire			Exclusive 116x	Where Was Moses	1940	Decca 7746
Pray		1950	Sittin' In With 553	Wouldn't Mind Dying	1939	Decca 7667
Precious Memories		1948	Lenox 506	**Dixie Jubilee Quartet**		
River Stay Away From My Door		1948	Continental 6076	Climbin' Up The Mountain Chain	1926	Brunswick 3150
Rock In The Harbor			Sittin' In With 2003	Good News	1926	Brunswick 3150
Run On For A Long Time		1948	Sunrise 2118	**Dixie Jubilee Quintet**		
Send Me Jesus			Sittin' In With 2017	So I Can Write My Name	1926	Brunswick 3209
				Stand Steady	1926	Brunswick 3209

Dixie Jubilee Singers
Don't You Scandalize My Name	1926	Cameo 914
Ezekiel Saw The Wheel In The Middle Of The Air	1928	Banner 7261
Give Me That Old Time Religion	1928	Banner 7237
Golden Slippers	192'	Brunswick 2645
His Trouble Was Hard	1928	Columbia 14329-D
I Ain't Gonna Study War No More	1928	Banner 7237
I Couldn't Hear Nobody Praying	192'	Brunswick 2773
In My Heart	1928	Champion 15473
Joshua Fit The Battle Of Jericho	1928	Columbia 14329-D
Let The Lower Lights Be Burning	1925	Columbia 537-D
My Father's House	1928	Champion 15473
My Lord's Gonna Move This Wicked Race	192'	Brunswick 2645
Roll, Jordan, Roll	192'	Brunswick 2773
Send One Angel Down	1928	Columbia 14376-D
Steal Away And Pray	1927	Champion 15249
Sun Don't Set In The Mornin'	1928	Columbia 14376-D
There's Enough Room In Heaven For Us All	1927	Champion 15249
Were You There When They Crucified My Lord	1927	Gennett 6092
What's You Gonna Do When The World's On Fire'	1928	Banner 7261
Whiter Than Snow	1925	Columbia 537-D
Who Is That Yonder'	1926	Cameo 914

Dixie Jubilee Singers, Hamilton Hamtree & the
Elder Lowdown At The Camp Meeting	192'	Brunswick 2655

Dixie Minstrels
Dixie Minstrels #1	1907	Indestructible Cylinder 654
Dixie Minstrels #2	1907	Indestructible Cylinder 655

Dixie Quartette
His Troubles Was Hard	1930	Van Dyke 84312
Jerusalem Mornin'	1930	Van Dyke 84312

Dixie Sacred Quartet
Bringing In The Sheaves	1927	Champion 15448
Nearer My God, To Thee	1927	Champion 15448
Tell Mother I'll Be There	1927	Champion 15411
They Crucified My Savior	1927	Champion 15411

Dixie Sacred Singers
Are You Washed In The Blood Of The Lamb'	1927	Vocalion 5158
Bear Me Away On Your Snowy Wings	1927	Vocalion 5160
In The Sweet Bye And Bye	1927	Vocalion 5162
Maple On The Hill	1927	Vocalion 5158
Nearer My God To Thee	1927	Challenge 339
Shall We Gather At The River	1927	Vocalion 5162
Walking In The Sunlight	1927	Vocalion 5160
You Can't Make A Monkey Out Of Me	1927	Champion 15431

Dixie Songsters
Dinah		Associated Transcriptions
Down South		Associated Transcriptions
Sing A Song Of Sixpence		Associated Transcriptions
Sweet Georgia Brown		Associated Transcriptions

Dixieaires (Dixiaires/Dixie-Aires)
Elijah	1948	Exclusive 50x
Handwriting On The Wall	1948	Exclusive 37x
He Is Coming Again Soon	1949	Exclusive 87x
Hide Me In Thy Bosom	1948	Exclusive 38x
Just A Closer Walk With Thee	1948	Exclusive 37x
Loose The Man	1948	Exclusive 38x
Movin' Up The King's Highway	1949	Exclusive 82x
My Trouble Is Hard	1948	Exclusive 50x
Poor And Needy	1949	Exclusive 66x
Soon Now	1948	Coleman 102
Sun Will Shine, The	1948	Coleman 102
Time's Winding Up	1949	Exclusive 87x
When The Moon Goes Down	1949	Exclusive 82x
Will The Circle Be Unbroken	1949	Exclusive 66x

Dixie-Aires (Dixieaires/Dixiaires)
Elijah		Dot 1034
My Trouble Is Hard		Dot 1034

Dixieaires (Jubalaires) (with Muriel Gaines)
After All	1945	Queen 4111
I Know We Will Never Meet Again	1945	Queen 4111

Dixieland Four (Ritz Quartet)
Down By The Old Mill Stream	1927	Brunswick 4114
Moonlight Bay	1927	Brunswick 3522/Brunswick 01115
Put On Your Old Grey Bonnet	1927	Brunswick 4114
When You Wore A Tulip And I Wore A Big Red Rose	1927	Brunswick 3522/Brunswick 01115

Dixon Brothers Quartet
Daniel In De Lion Den	1926	Okeh 8327
Ezekiel Saw De Wheel	1926	Okeh 8327

Dixon, Raymond & the Orpheus Quartet
Hail Columbia	1917	Victor 18316

Dixon's Quartet, Raymond
Blow Thou Winter Wind	1915	Victor 17717

Do Ray And Me (Do Ray Me Trio/Do-Ray-Mi Trio/Do Re Me Trio/Do-Re-Me Trio/Do Re Mi Trio)
Cabaret		Commodore 7550
Darling You Make It So	1948	Commodore 7550
How Can I Smile		Commodore 7549
Teresa	1947	Commodore 7504

Title	Year	Label/Number
There's A Man At The Door	1947	Commodore 7504
Wise Old Man, The	1947	Commodore 7505
Wrapped Up In A Dream	1947	Commodore 7605
You Can't Love Two		Commodore 7549

Do Ray Me Trio (Do Ray And Me/Do-Ray-Mi Trio/Do Re Me Trio/Do-Re-Me Trio/Do Re Mi Trio)

Title	Year	Label/Number
Holding Hands		Reet 101
I		Reet 101
I Couldn't Help It	1949	Ivory 754
I Don't Want To Set The World On Fire	1954	Coral 61184
I'll Never Fail You	1954	Coral 61184
I'll Never Stop Being Yours	1953	Brunswick 80218
I'm Only Human	1953	Brunswick 80218
Only One Dream		Ivory 750
Rhumba Blues	1949	Ivory 754
Tell Me You Love Me		Ivory 750

Do Re Me Trio, Buddy Hawkins & the (Do Ray And Me/Do Ray Me Trio/Do-Ray-Mi Trio/Do-Re-Me Trio/Do Re

Title	Year	Label/Number
How I Love My Baby	1958	Carlton 460
That's The Way Life Goes	1958	Carlton 460

Do Re Mi Trio (Do Ray And Me/Do Ray Me Trio/Do-Ray-Mi Trio/Do Re Me Trio/Do-Re-Me Trio)

Title	Year	Label/Number
Holding Hands		Variety 1001
I'm Used To You	1952	Rainbow 181/Variety 1002
Oo-Wee		Variety 1002
She Would Not Yield	1952	Rainbow 181
Tell Me You Love Me		Variety 1001

Doctor Sausage & his Five Pork Chops

Title	Year	Label/Number
WHAM	1940	Decca 7736

Doctor Sausage And his Five Pork Chops

Title	Year	Label/Number
Doctor Sausage's Blues	1940	Decca 7736

Don Hall Trio

Title	Year	Label/Number
I'm Sure Of Everything But You	1932	Victor
Just Because You're You	1932	Victor

Don Hall Trio (as George's Hot Shots)

Title	Year	Label/Number
We Do It Just The Same	1932	Victor 23739

Don Hall Trio (as Hannah's Hot Shots)

Title	Year	Label/Number
Why Should I (Fight About What)	1932	Bluebird B-6414

Don Hall Trio (Donaldson Trio)

Title	Year	Label/Number
I'm Twisting Loops In Pretzels, Just To Pass The Time Away	1933	Victor 23799
It Makes No Difference	1933	Victor 23797
Little Mother Of The Hills	1933	Victor 24305
When I Take My Vacation In Heaven	1933	Victor 24305
When The Wild, Wild Roses Bloom	1933	Victor 23799/Bluebird B-5060/Electradisk 1986/Sunrise S-3145
You're My Dream (That Came True)	1933	Victor 23797/Bluebird B-5060/Electradisk 1986/Sunrise S-3145

Don Hall Trio (Donaldson Trio/Rose Family)

Title	Year	Label/Number
Answer To Twenty-One Years, The	1933	Victor 23782/Bluebird 1834/Bluebird B-5004/Electradisk 1962/Sunrise S-3108
Hills Of Tennessee Are Calling Me, The	1933	Victor 23782/Bluebird 1833/Bluebird B-5003/Electradisk 1961/Sunrise S-3108
Keep It To Yourself	1933	Victor 23784/Bluebird 1834/Bluebird B-5004/Electradisk 1962/Sunrise S-3108
Sidewalk Waltz	1933	Victor 24252
When It's Lamp Lightin' Time In The Valley	1933	Victor 24252/Bluebird 1833/Bluebird B-5003/Electradisk 1961/Sunrise S-3107

Don Hall Trio (George Donaldson Trio)

Title	Year	Label/Number
Absolutely Free	1933	Victor 23836/Bluebird B-5221/Electradisk 2107/Sunrise S-3304
It I Had Somebody To Love	1933	Victor 24371/Bluebird B-5166/Electradisk 2063/Sunrise S-3247
Little Locket Of Long Ago	1933	Victor 24371/Bluebird B-5134/Electradisk 2040/Sunrise S-3215
Old Nebraska Moon	1933	Victor 24838/Bluebird B-5134/Electradisk 2040/Sunrise S-3215
Shepherd Of The Air	1933	Victor 24838/Bluebird B-5166/Electradisk 2063/Sunrise S-3247
That's A Lot Of Nonsense (with	1933	Victor

Dick Roberts)		23841/Bluebird B-6250
When The Fog Of Merry Old London Gets In Your Hair	1933	Victor 23836/Bluebird B-5221/Electradisk 2107/Sunrise S-3304
You Never Saw A Saw Fish Like The Saw Fish That I Saw (with Dick Roberts)	1933	Victor 23841

Don Hall Trio (The Spiritual Singers)

An Old Lullaby	1934	Bluebird B-5422
Carry Me Back To The Lone Prairie	1934	Bluebird B-5422
Death Is No More Than A Dream	1934	Bluebird B-5396
Dream Of Me, Darling Tonight	1934	Bluebird B-5392
How Beautiful	1934	Bluebird B-5396
Strawberry Roan, The	1934	Bluebird B-5392

Don Hall Trio, Dick Robertson & the (Dixon Trio/Donaldson Trio/Donaldson Quartet/Rose Family)

Carolina Lullaby	1933	Victor 23790/Bluebird B-5035/Electradisk 1967/Sunrise S-3133
Hannah From Panama	1933	Victor 23788/Bluebird B-5074/Electradisk 1997/Sunrise S-3155
Oh! How I'd Love To Own A Fish Store	1933	Victor 23787/Bluebird B-5036/Electradisk 1968/Sunrise S-3134
Oh! Look At The Rain - Part 1	1933	Victor 23790
That Means You're Falling In Love	1933	Victor 23788/Bluebird B-5016/Electradisk 1968/Sunrise S-3134
What Are We Gonna Use For Money'	1933	Victor 23787/Bluebird B-5035/Electradisk 1967/Sunrise S-3133

Don Hall Trio, Don Robertson & the

At The Close Of A Long, Long Day	1932	Victor 23754
I'm So Happy When The Sun Is Shining	1932	Bluebird B-5557/Victor 23762
Lonesome Valley Sally	1932	Bluebird B-5557
Oh! Look At The Rain - Part 1	1932	Bluebird B-5074
Oh! Look At The Rain - Part 2	1932	Bluebird B-5074
Old Bill Smith	1932	Victor 23764
Pumpkin Has No Pump, A	1932	Victor 23764
She's Still Got It	1932	Victor
There Ain't No Man In The Moon	1932	Victor 23752
When I Played Peek-A-Boo With Daddy	1932	Victor 23762
When The Wandering Boy Comes Home	1932	Victor 23754

Do-Ray-Mi Trio (Do Ray And Me/Do Ray Me Trio/Do Re Me Trio/Do-Re-Mi Trio/Do Re Mi Trio)

On A Slow Boat To China	1959	Stereocraft 112
Saturday Night Fish Fry	1959	Stereocraft 112

Do-Re-Me Trio, Al Russell & the (Do Ray And Me/Do Ray Me Trio/Do-Ray-Mi Trio/Do Re Me Trio)

How Can You Say You Love Me	1951	Okeh 6806
I Couldn't Help It	1951	Okeh 6831
I Don't Want To Be Alone For Christmas	1951	Okeh 6845
I'll Be Waiting	1951	Okeh 6831
I Love Each Move You Make	1951	Okeh 6845
I Want To Be With You Always	1951	Columbia 39385
May That Day Never Come	1951	Okeh 6806
No More Dreams	1951	Columbia 39385

Do-Re-Mi Trio

Hold My Hand (with Cavaliers)	1934	Victor 24581
Nasty Man	1934	Victor 24581

Dornberger, Charles & his Orchestra (with Franklyn Baur, Lewis James, Elliott Shaw)

One Sweet Letter From You	1927	Victor 20823

Dot, Kay and Em (with Henry Busse and his Music)

Fool That I Am	1934	Columbia 2932-D
Little Dutch Mill	1934	Columbia

Down Home Jubilee Quartette (Sunset Four Jubilee Quartette)

Hand Me Down My Silver Trumpet	1925	Herwin 92008
Oh Lord What A Morning	1925	Herwin 92008

Down South Boys (Norfolk Jubilee Quartet)

Wonder Where Is The Gamblin' Man	1927	Varsity 6011

Down Town Trio

Down Town Shuffle	1948	Down Town 2017
Make Love To Me, Baby	1948	Down Town 2017

Dozier Boys

All I Need Is You	1950	Aristocrat 409
Big Time Baby	1949	Aristocrat 3002
Cold, Cold Rain (Is Falling)	1953	United 163
Do You Ever Think Of Me'	1953	Unreleased
Early Morning Blues	1953	United 163/Janie 457 (1953)/Fraternity 767 (1957)
I Keep Thinking Of You	1953	United 143
I'm So In Love With You	1958	Apt 25014
Laughing In Rhythm	1953	Unreleased

Linger Awhile	1953	United 143
Music Goes 'Round And 'Round	1949	Aristocrat 3002
My Heart Is Yours	1958	Apt 25014
Pretty Eyes	1950	Chess 1436
She Only Fools With Me	1949	Aristocrat 3001
She's Gone	1950	Aristocrat 409
Special Kind	1953	Janie 457
Special Kind Of Lovin'	1957	Fraternity 767
St. Louis Blues	1949	Aristocrat 3001
Woke Up Early One Morning	1953	Unreleased
You Got To Get It	1950	Chess 1436

Dr. Smith's Champion Hoss Hair Pullers

Going Down The River	1928	Victor 21711
In The Garden Where The Irish Potatoes Grow	1928	Victor 21711
Just Give Me The Leavings	1928	Victor V-40124
Nigger Baby	1928	Victor V-40124
Save My Mother's Picture From The Sale	1928	Victor V-40059
Up In Glory	1928	Victor V-40059

Drifters

And I Shook	1950	Coral 65040
Honey Chile	1951	Excelsior 1314
I Had To Find Out For Myself	1950	Coral 65040
I'm The Caring Kind	1950	Coral 65037
Mobile	1951	Excelsior 1315
Wine Headed Woman	1950	Coral 65037

Duncan Sisters

Argentines, Portuguese And The Greeks	1923	Victor 19113
Aunt Susie's Picnic Day	1924	Victor 19311
Baby Sister Blues	1923	Victor 19050
Bullfrog Patrol	1924	Victor 19352
Crossword Puzzle Blues	1924	Victor 19527
Happy Go Lucky Days	1926	Victor 19987
I Never Had A Mammy	1923	Victor 19206B
Kinky Kids Parade	1926	Victor 19987
Mean Cicero Blues	1924	Victor 19527
Music Lesson, The	1923	Victor 19050
Rememb'ring	1923	Victor 19206A
Stick In The Mud	1923	Victor 19113
Tomboy Blues	1924	Victor 19352
Um Um Da Da	1924	Victor 19311

Dunham Jazz Singers

Honey Turn Your Damper Down A	1927	Champion 15378/Gennett 6259

Dunham Jubilee Singers

Angel Child	1931	Columbia 14676-D
Calvary	1928	Gennett 6723
Do What The Lord Say Do	1928	Gennett 6723/Supertone 9532
Ephraim Got The Coon	1931	Columbia 14609-D
Get On Board	1931	Columbia 14676-D
Got Heaven In My View	1928	
Go With Me To Paradise	1931	
Holy Is My Name	1928	Gennett 6625/Supertone 9303
I Dreamed Of The Judgment Morning	1930	Columbia 14540-D
If Men Go To Hell, Who Cares'	1931	Columbia 14643-D
I've Been Rebuked And Scorned	1928	
Light Of The World	1931	Columbia 14658-D
Lord, Hear My Pray	1928	
Old Account Was Settled Long Ago, The	1931	Columbia 14605-D
See How They Did My Lord	1931	Columbia 14605-D
See My Friends Again	1931	Columbia 14636-D
When The Moon Vanishes Away	1931	Columbia 14658-D
Who Stole The Lock'	1931	Columbia 14609-D
Wide Wide World	1931	
Will He Welcome Me There	1930	Columbia 14540-D
Wouldn't Mind Dying	1928	
You Can Tell The World	1928	Gennett 6625/Supertone 9303

Eagle Jubilee Four

Good Lord I Can't Turn Back	1938	Vocalion 4534
In My Father's House	1938	Vocalion 4613
Maybe The Last Time	1940	Vocalion 5503
No More Weeping And Wailing	1938	Vocalion 4613
On Calvary Mountain	1938	Vocalion 4534
When The Trumpet Sounds	1940	Vocalion 5503

Eagle Trio

Herd Girl's Dream, The	1926	Columbia 731-D
Love's Dream After The Ball	1926	Columbia 731-D

Earle-Aires (Richard Dunbar & the)

Number One Baby	1954	JOB 1154

Easton, Florence & Male Trio

Croon, Croon, Underneat' De Moon	1925	Brunswick 10211

Ebonaires

Sleepy Time Gal	1949	Modern 656
Song Of The Wanderer	1949	Modern 656

Ebonaires, Bill Day & the

Baby You're The One	1953	Aladdin 3211
Bye, Bye, Bye, Bye	1949	MGM 10361
Come In, Mr. Blues	1949	MGM 10361
Hey, Baby, Stop	1956	Money 220
How Long Can A Heart Go On Loving'	1949	Modern 711
Lawd, Lawd, Lawd	1954	Aladdin 3212
That Lucky Old Sun	1949	Modern 711
Three O'Clock In The Morning	1953	Aladdin 3211
Very Best Luck In The World, The	1956	Money 220
You're Nobody Till Somebody	1954	Aladdin 3212

Loves You
Ebonaires, Johnnie Lee & the
  You Can't Lose A Broken Heart   1949 Columbia 30172
Ebonaires, Monette Moore & the
  Peace, Sister, Peace   1949 Columbia 30173

Ebony Aires (Bill Lacey)
  Cowboy Santa Claus   1955
Ebony Three
  Go Down Moses   1938 Decca 7527
  Heartbroken Blues   1938 Decca 7503
  Mississippi Moan   1938 Decca 7503
  Swing Low, Sweet Chariot   1938 Decca 7527
Echo Quartette
  Annie Laurie   1916 Par-O-Ket 25 A
  Nearer, My God, To Thee   1916 Par-O-Ket 25 B
Eckstein, Billy & the Quartones
  Bewildered   1948 MGM
Edison Male Quartet
  Carry Me Back To Old Virginny   1898 Edison 2237 (2mincyl)
  First Noel, The
  I'se Gwine Back To Dixie   1897
  Mandy Lee   Edison 7551 (2mincyl)
  Medley Of Plantation Songs   1901 Edison 7857 (2mincyl)
  My Old Kentucky Home   1898
  Nearer My God To Thee   1904 Edison 7267
  Owl And The Pussycat, The   Edison 7531 (2mincyl)
  Vesper Service   Edison 7581
  Where The Southern Roses Grow   Edison 8976 (2mincyl)

Edison Minstrels
  Dixie Minstrels   1907 Edison 9672
  Jubilee Minstrels   1908 Edison 9953 (2mincyl)

Edison Mixed Quartet
  Crossing The Bar   Edison 1924 (4BA)
  Dreams Of Galilee   Edison 2204 (4BA)
  Gloria From The 12th Mass   Edison 1898 (4BA)
  I Love To Tell The Story   Edison 1913 (4BA)
  Lead Us, Heavenly Father, Lead Us   Edison 1936 (4BA)
  My Mother's Prayer   Edison 9827 (2mincyl)
  Rock Of Ages   Edison 1633 (4BA)
  What A Friend We Have In Jesus   Edison 1855 (4BA)
  When The Roll Is Called Up Yonder   Edison 9879 (2mincyl)/Edison 1811 (4BA)
  Where Is My Wandering Boy Tonight'   Edison 2125 (4BA)

Edison Modern Minstrels
  Alabama Minstrels   1904 Edison 2min 8631
  Edison Modern Minstrels   1909 Edison 10135 (2mincyl)
Edison Quartet
  Old Oaken Bucket, The   1902 Edison 8807 (black2mincyl)
  Rocked In The Cradle Of The Deep   1899 Edison 2217 (brown2mincyl)
Edisongsters
  I Want To Meander In The Meadow   1929 Edison 14028
  Peace Of Mind   1929 Edison 14028
  Red Hair And Freckles   1929 Edison 14043
  Red Hot Trumpet, The   1929 Edison 14043
  Sorrows   1929 Edison DD 52601
  'Tain't Nobody's Fault But My Own   1929 Edison DD 52601
Edisonians
  Just A Memory   Edison 52143
  Song Is Ended, The (But The Melody Lingers On)   Edison 52233
  Among My Souvenirs   1928 Edison 52233
Electric City Four
  Beela Boola   1920 Edison Blue Amberol 4210
Eleo Quartet
  They Satisfy (Demonstration record for Chesterfield Cigarettes)   1930 Brunswick
Elkins' Jubilee Singers, William C.
  Great Day   1929 Brunswick 4600
  Without A Song   1929 Brunswick 4600
Elkins Mixed Quartet
  Christians Awake   1927 Paramount 12418
Elkins Negro Ensemble
  Go Down, Moses   Gennett
  Goin' Home   Gennett
Elkins Sacred Singers
  Christians Hold Your Light Up High   1925 Cameo 830
  Couldn't Hear Nobody Pray   1925 Cameo 808
  I Got A Robe   1925 Cameo 808
Elkins Sacred Singers, W.C.
  Nobody Knows The Trouble I've Seen   1925 Cameo 830
Elkins, W.C. & his Dextra Singers
  Climbing Up The Mountain   1928 QRS R 7045
  Downward Road Is Crowded, The   1928 QRS R 7066
  Eloi   1928 QRS R 7063
  Hail, Hail, Hail   1928 QRS R 7046
  Joshua Fit De Battle Of Jericho   1928 QRS R 7068
  My Lord Delivered Daniel   1928 QRS R 7045
  Oh Mother, Don't You Weep   1928 QRS R 7046
  Pickin' On The Harp Wid De   1928 QRS R 7063

Golden Strings
Ride On, Moses	1928	QRS R 7066
Roll, Roll, Chariot	1928	QRS R 7047
We Are Climbing Jacob's Ladder	1928	QRS R 7047
Wheel In A Wheel, A	1928	QRS R 7068

Elkins-Payne Jubilee Quartette (Alberta Hunter with the)
If The Rest Of The World Don't Want You (Go Back To Your Mother And Dad)	1924	Paramount 12093
Old-Fashioned Love	1924	Paramount 12093

Elkins-Payne Jubilee Singers
Be Ready When Your Jesus Comes	1925	Okeh 40268
Down By The Riverside	1923	Paramount 12071
Elder Take It All - Part 1 (See Me Fo' You Go)	1924	Paramount 12079
Elder Take It All - Part 2 (On Dancing)	1924	Paramount 12079
Ezekiel Saw De Wheel	1924	Okeh 40250
Gonna Shout All Over God's Heaven	1923	Paramount 12071
Standing In The Need Of Prayer	1923	Paramount 12070
When The Saints Go Marching In	1925	Okeh 8170
You Must Shun Old Satan	1924	Okeh 40250

Elkridge, Roy & Others
Honeysuckle Rose

Elks Male Quartet
I'm A Soldier Of The Cross		Edison 52160
Nobody Knows The Trouble I've Seen		Edison 52160

Elks Quartet Of Spokane Lodge 228
Vacant Chair, The	1927	Columbia 1144D
Who Knows'	1927	Columbia 1144D

Ellington Sacred Quartet
Bringing In The Sheaves	1928	Challenge 402
While The Years Roll On	1928	Challenge 402

Elliott, Lu & Joe Van Loan Group
Joog-Joog	1948	Columbia

Elm City Four (assisting Harry Richman)
Birth Of The Blues, The	1926	Vocalion 15412/Brunswick 01/Brunswick 03501
Lucky Day	1926	Vocalion 15412/Brunswick 01/Brunswick 03523

Elm City Quartet
Tree Song, The	1934	Champion 16827/Champion 45109 (1934)
Twenty Five Years From Now	1934	Champion 16827/Champion 45109 (1934)

Emerson Quartet
Everything Made For Love	192'	Bell 471

Empire Jubilee Quartet
Get Right Church	1929	Victor 38534
God's Gonna Move All My Troubles Away	1929	Victor 38534
Wade In De Water	1932	Victor 23340
Where Shall I Go	1932	Victor 23340

Empire Staters Quartet (Wilson Quartet)
Beggar For Blues	1930	Clarion 5198-C
Singing Away The Blues	1930	Clarion 5207-C

Empire Trio
I'll Wed The Girl I Left Behind	1916	Columbia A-2107
I'm Coming Back To California (That's Where I Belong)	1917	Columbia A-2171
I'm Proud To Be The Mother Of A Boy Like You	1917	Columbia A-2227
Somewhere In Dixie	1917	Columbia A-2188
Those Hawaiian Melodies	1917	Columbia
'Twas Only An Irishman's Dream	1916	Columbia A-2151
Ukalou	1916	Columbia A-2160

Empire Vaudeville Company (including the Premier Quartet)
Mother Goose Days	1910	Edison 4mincyl 685
Mrs. Clancy's Boarding House	1911	Edison 4mincyl 471
Mrs. Clancy's Boarding House	1911	Edison BA 2059/Edison 471 (4mincyl) (1911)

Enchanters
Today Is Your Birthday	1952	Jubilee

Englewood Four
Green Grass Grew All Around, The	1927	Champion 15451
Old McDonald Had A Farm	1927	Champion 15451
Silver Threads Among The Gold	1928	Champion 15487
Sweet Elaine	1928	Champion 15487

Eskimo Quartet
Behind The Clouds	1926	Banner 1721
Comin' Home From School	1926	Banner 1770
In My Gondola	1926	Banner 1721
Valencia	1926	Banner 1770

Esquire Boys
Caravan	1952	Rainbow 188
We Drifted Apart	1952	Rainbow 188

Esquire Boys, Kay Karol & the
Forgetting You	1952	Rainbow 178

Esquires
If I Had Wings	1951	Jubilee 5067

Eton Boys
I Don't Blame You	1931	Perfect 15547
I Want A Girl (Just Like The Girl That Married Dear Old Dad)	1941	Victor 27696
Meet Me Tonight In Dreamland	1941	Victor 27698

My Castle On The Nile	1941	Victor 27697
Oh! Leo	1934	Columbia 2968-D
Polly Wolly Doodle & Kemo Kimo	1941	Victor 27698
Potatoes Are Cheaper - Tomatoes Are Cheaper, Now's The Time To Fall In Love	1931	Banner 32327/Oriole 2387/Perfect 15550
Rock And Roll	1934	Columbia 2968-D
Roll Dem Bones	1941	Victor 27696
She's So Nice	1931	Banner 32327/Oriole 2387/Perfect 15550
Sweet Genevieve	1941	Victor 27695
Wait Till The Sun Shines, Nellie	1941	Victor 27697
When Uncle Joe Plays A Rag On His Old Banjo	1941	Victor 27695
Who's Your Little Who-zis'	1931	Perfect 15547

Eton Boys (The Four Eton Boys with Abe Lyman & his Californians)
Let's Put The Axe To The Axis	1941	Bluebird B-11410

Eton Boys (with Clevelanders)
Where Can You Be'	1930	Oriole 2078/Perfect 15350

Eton Boys (with the Piano Twins)
Ooh That Kiss	1931	Banner 32321/Oriole 2378/Perfect 11329

Eton Boys (with Ukulele Ike (Cliff Edwards))
Love Is Just Around The Corner	1934	Melotone M 13254
Old-Fashioned Love	1934	Melotone M 13331/Perfect 13118/Romeo 2475
One Little Kiss	1934	Melotone M 13254
St. Louis Blues	1934	Melotone M 13331/Perfect 13118/Romeo 2475

Etowah Quartet
Back In The Years	1930	Vocalion 5465
For Me	1928	Columbia 15635-D
Walking With My Lord	1930	Vocalion 5465
Who Is That	1928	Columbia 15635-D

Evangelist Singers Of Alabama
Walk In The Light	1951	Chess 1486

Evening Four
Don't Drive Me Away	1937	Bluebird 6906
Don't Feel No Way Tired	1937	Bluebird 6871
I've Got A Mother Over Yonder	1937	Bluebird 6906
Oh Link Oh Link	1937	Bluebird 6871

Ewing Sisters
Fiddle Faddle	1950	Capitol 1421
Ventura Boulevard Boogie		Capitol 1733
You've Been So Good To Me Daddy	1950	Capitol 1421

Excelsior Hep Cats, Timmie Rogers & the
Bring Enough Clothes For Three Days	1945	Excelsior TR-107

Excelsior Norfolk Quartette
Coney Island Babe	1922	Black Swan 2060/Paramount 12131 (1925)
Jelly Roll Blues	1922	Black Swan 2060/Starr 9250 (1922)/Paramount 12131 (1925)

Excelsior Quartette (1)
Reception Medley	189'	Berliner 0874X

Excelsior Quartette (2)
Down By The Old Mill Stream	1923	Okeh 8035
Going Up To Live With God (Golden Slipper)	1922	Okeh 4619
Good-Bye, My Coney Island Baby	1922	Okeh 8038
Good Lord, I Done Done	1922	Okeh 4701
I Am The King Of The Sea	1922	Okeh 4701
If Hearts Win Tonight, You Lose	1922	Okeh 8038
Jelly Roll Blues	1922	Gennett 4881/Starr 9250/Okeh 4481
Kitchen Mechanic Blues	1922	Gennett 4881/Starr 9250/Okeh 4481/Okeh 8033
Nobody Knows The Trouble I See	1922	Okeh 4636
Over The Green Hill	1922	Okeh 8035
Roll Them Bones	1922	Okeh 8033
Sinners Crying, Come Here Lord	1922	Okeh 4636
Walk In Jerusalem Just Like John	1922	Okeh 4619

Excelsis Trio
Take Time To Be Holy (with the Metropolitan Quartet)	1928	Edison DD 52398-L

Fa So La Singers
Happy On The Way	1931	Columbia 14638-D
I'll Stay On The Right Road Now	1931	Columbia 14638-D
Jesus Walks With Me	1931	Columbia 14658-D
Rejoicing On The Way	1931	Columbia 14658-D

Fairfield Four
Better Leave That Liar Alone	1947	Bullet 253
Don't Let Nobody Turn You 'Round	1948	Bullet 284
Standing In The Safety Zone	1948	Bullet 284
Who Stole My Old Shoes	1947	Bullet 253

Famous Bluejay Singers
Brother Jonah	1932	Paramount 13139/Champion 50025 (1932)
Children Wade In The Water	1932	Paramount 13128/Champion 50026 (1932)
I Declare My Mother Ought To Live Right	1932	Paramount 13128/Champion

I'm Leaning On The Lord	1932	Champion 50056
Lead Me On	1932	Paramount 13135
Oh My Lord, Didn't It Rain	1932	Paramount 13126
Sleep, Baby, Sleep	1932	Paramount 13139/Champion 50025 (1932)
Standing By The Bedside Of A Neighbor	1932	Paramount 13126/Champion 50056 (1932)
Who Cares	1932	Paramount 13135
Famous Garland Jubilee Singers		
Didn't It Rain	1931	Banner 32175
Hold The Wind	1931	Banner 32249
I'll Be Satisfied	1931	Banner 33084
I Want To Be Ready	1931	Banner 32267
Let Jesus Lead You	1931	Banner 32174
Oh Lord How Long	1931	Banner 32175
Oh Rocks Don't You Fall On Me	1931	Banner 32249
Sinner You Better Get Ready	1931	Banner 33084
South Bound Train	1931	Banner 32173
This Train	1931	Banner 32267
Were You There	1931	Banner 32174
Who Stole De Lock	1931	Banner 32173
Famous Jubilee Singers		
Ezekiel Prophesized To The Dry Bones	1928	Paramount 12667
He Locked A Lion's Jaw	1928	Paramount 12667
There's No Hiding Place	1927	Paramount 12542
Wait Til I Put On My Robe	1927	Paramount 12542
Famous Rising Star Singers		
While The Blood (Is Running In Your Veins)	1949	Cava-Tone 256
Farber Sisters		
Goodbye Alexander	1918	Columbia A-2599
How'd You Like To Be My Daddy	1918	Columbia A-2525
I Can't Let 'Em Suffer	1918	Columbia A-2573
If He Can Fight Like He Can Love	1918	Columbia A-2556
I'm So Glad Mama Don't Know Where I'm At	1918	Columbia A-2573
I Want A Daddy Like You	1918	Columbia A-2544
Won't You Be A Dear, Dear Daddy	1918	Columbia A-2544
Farmer Sisters		
I Love You Best Of All	1935	Vocalion 3153
Little Home In Tennessee	1935	Vocalion 3104
Maple On The Hill	1935	Vocalion 3104
You're As Welcome As Flowers In May	1935	Vocalion 3153
Favor, Edward M. with American Quartet		
Dublin Rag, The	1910	Victor 16728
Favor, Edwin & the Peerless Quartet		
Paddy Duffy's Cart	1911	Edison 4mincyl 317
Fireside Male Quartet		
I Wonder How The Old Folks Are At Home	1925	Brunswick 2792
Fireside Quartet		
Annie Laurie	1923	Brunswick 2519
Home Sweet Home	1923	Brunswick 2519
When I'm Gone You'll Soon Forget	1925	Brunswick 2886
When You're Gone I Won't Forget	1925	Brunswick 2886
Fireside Quartet (Criterion Quartet)		
When The Sunset Turns The Ocean's Blue To Gold	1924	Brunswick 2676
Where The Silvery Colorado Wends Its Way	1924	Brunswick 2676
Fireside Quartet (Alan McQuahac & Male Trio)		
Where The River Shannon Flows	192'	Brunswick 2748
Fireside Quartet (James Sheridan & Male Trio)		
Drifting To You	1924	Brunswick 2635
Fireside Quartet (Marie Morrisey & Male Trio)		
Rosary, The	1924	Brunswick 10154/Brunswick 010154
Fisk University Jubilee Quartet		
Band Of Gideon	1911	Victor 16864
Done What You Told Me	1911	Victor 16895
Good News/Wasn't The River Wide'	1911	Victor 16856
Great Camp Meeting	1910	Victor 16487
I Know My Lord Laid His Hands Upon Me	1911	Victor 16895
In Bright Mansions Above	1911	Victor 16856
Little David, Play On Yo' Harp/Shout All Over God's Heaven	1910	Victor 16448
My Soul Is A Witness	1911	Victor 16864
Old Ark/Brethren, Rise And Shine	1911	Victor 16840
Old Black Joe	1915	Columbia
O Mary, Don't You Weep For Me	1915	Columbia
Po' Mo'ner Got A Home At Last	1911	Victor 16843/Columbia (1920)
Roll Jordan Roll	1910	Victor 16466
Shout All Over God's Heaven	1915	Columbia A-1883
Steal Away To Jesus	1926	Columbia 562-D (1926)
Swing Low, Sweet Chariot	1915	Columbia A-1883
There Is A Light Shining For Me	1915	Columbia A-1895
There's A Balm In Gilead	1910	Victor 16487
Fisk University Jubilee Singers		
Do Lord Remember Me	1924	Columbia
Everytime I Feel The Spirit	1926	Columbia 562-D
Hope I'll Join The Band	1924	Columbia 163D
I Done What You Told Me To Do	1923	Columbia A-3919
In-A That Mornin' Oh My Lord	1920	Columbia 2-D
I Wonder If The Light Will Ever	1920	Columbia

Shine On Me'

Nobody Knows The Trouble I See	1926	Columbia
What Kinda Shoes You Goin' To Wear'	1924	Columbia
Where Shall I Go To Ease My Trouble In Mind	1924	Columbia
You Better Get Somebody On Your Bond	1924	Columbia 163D
You May Carry Me, You May Bury Me In The Coming Day	1921	Columbia 2-D

Fisk University Male Quartet

Brethren Rise	1917	Columbia A-2342

Fisk University Quartet

Couldn't Hear Nobody Pray	1916	Columbia A-1932
Ezekiel Saw De Wheel	1920	Columbia A-3370/Columbia 818-D (1926)
I Know The Lord Has Laid His Hand On Me	1922	Columbia A-3657
In That Great Gettin' Up Mawnin'	1917	Columbia A-2342
Little David Play On Your Harp	1919	Columbia A-2803
River Of Jordan	1916	Columbia A-1932
Roll, Jordan, Roll	1922	Columbia A-3657
Steal Away To Jesus	1919	Columbia A-2803
Swing Low Sweet Chariot	1910	Victor 16453
You're Going To Reap Just What You Sow	1920	Columbia A-3370

Fisk University Singers

Give Way Jordan	1923	Columbia A-3819
Good News, Chariot's Coming	1916	Columbia A-2072
Great Camp Meeting, The	1916	Columbia A-2072
I Ain't Goin' Study War No More	1922	Columbia A-3596
I Know I Have Another Building	1922	Columbia A-3726
I Want To Be Ready	1922	Columbia A-3726
Keep A'Inchin' Along	1926	Columbia 658-D
Little David	1926	Columbia 818-D
'Most Done Travelling	1920	Columbia A-2901
My Soul Is A Witness For My Lord	1923	Columbia A-3819
Oh Reign Mass Jesus, Reign	1920	Columbia A-2901
Shout All Over God's Heaven	1926	Columbia 658-D
Were You There	1923	Columbia A-3919
You Hear De Lambs A-Cryin'	1922	Columbia A-3596

Fitzgerald, Ella & the Delta Rhythm Boys

I'll Cry You Out Of My Heart	1946	Decca 23425
It's A Pity To Say Goodnight	1946	Decca 23670

Fitzgerald, Ella & the Four Keys

All I Need Is You	1942	Decca 18347
Four Leaf Clover In Your Pocket	1942	Decca 18472
He's My Guy	1942	Decca 18472
I'm Gettin' Mighty Lonesome For You	1942	Decca 4315A
Mama Come Home	1942	Decca 18347
My Heart And I Decided	1942	Decca 18530
When I Come Back Crying	1942	Decca 4315B

Fitzgerald, Ella & the Song Spinners

And Her Tears Flowed Like Wine	1944	Brunswick 03566/Decca 18633
Confessin'	1944	Brunswick 03566/Decca 18633

Fitzgerald, Ella with Andy Love Quartet

Sunday Kind Of Love, A	1954	Decca 28993
That's My Desire	1954	Decca 28993

Fitzgerald, Ella with Song Spinners

My Happiness	1948	Decca 24446
Tea Leaves	1948	Decca 24446

Five Bars

I'm All Dressed Up With A Broken Heart	1947	Bullet 1009

Five Blazes

All My Geets Are Gone	1947	Aristocrat 202
Chicago Boogie	1947	Aristocrat 201
Dedicated To You	1947	Aristocrat 201
Every Little Dream	1947	Aristocrat 202

Five Blue Flames, Chris Powell & the

Blue Boy	1952	Okeh 6900
Blues In My Heart	1950	Columbia 30216
Break It Up	1955	Groove 0105
Chinatown	1955	Groove 0128
Country Girl Blues	1951	Columbia 39272
Dance Til The Break Of Dawn	1950	Columbia 30216
Darn That Dream	1952	Okeh 6875
Down In The Bottom	1950	Columbia 30205
Goodbye Little Girl	1955	Groove 0128
Hauntin' Pinochle Blues	1950	Columbia 30205
Hot Dog	1949	Columbia 30162
I Come From Jamaica	1952	Okeh 6900
Ida Red	1952	Okeh 6875
I'm Still In Love With You	1950	Columbia 30180
In The Cool Of The Evening	1951	Columbia 39407
I've Made A Big Mistake	1949	Columbia 30169
Last Saturday Night	1949	Columbia 30162
Love Ya Like Crazy	1955	Groove 0105
Man With The Horn, The	1951	Columbia 39272
Masquerade Is Over, The	1951	Okeh 6818
My Love Has Gone	1951	Columbia 39407
On The Sunny Side Of The Street	1949	Columbia 30175
Rock The Joint	1949	Columbia 30175
Something's Got To Give	1955	Groove 0111
Sunday	1949	Columbia 30169
Swingin' In The Groove	1950	Columbia 30180
Talkin'	1951	Okeh 6818
That's Right!	1951	Okeh 6850
Twilight	1951	Okeh 6850
Uh Uh Baby	1954	Grand 108
Unchained Melody	1955	Groove 0111

Five Breezes
Just A Jitterbug	1941	Bluebird 8710
Laundry Man	1941	Bluebird 8710
Minute And Hour Blues	1940	Bluebird 8590/Clanka Lanka CL-144.033
My Buddy Blues	1941	Bluebird 8614
Return, Gal O' Mine	1941	Bluebird 8614
Sweet Louise	1940	Bluebird 8590
Swingin' The Blues	1941	Bluebird 8679
What's The Matter With Love'	1941	Bluebird 8679

Five DeMarco Sisters
Blue	1946	Majestic 7166
Chico, Chico (From Puerto Rico)	1945	Majestic 7151
Chiquita Banana (The Banana Song)	1946	Majestic 7194
Doin' What Comes Natur'lly	1946	Majestic 7193
Dreamboat	1955	Decca 29470
Flat River, Missouri	1945	Majestic 7160
Hop, Skip And Jump!	1945	Majestic 7160
Hot Barcarolle, The	1955	Decca 29607
I Don't Know Why (I Just Do)	1945	Majestic 7194
I Fall In Love With You Ev'ry Day	1946	Majestic 7174
It's Been A Long, Long Time	1945	Majestic 7157
Just A Girl That Men Forget	1954	Decca 29299
Love Me	1954	Decca 29299
One-zy Two-zy	1946	Majestic 7174
Romance Me	1957	Decca 29758
Sailor Boys Have Talked To Me	1955	Decca 29607
Say You Care	1957	Decca 29758
Sweet I've Gotten On You (The Pennsylvania Dutch Song)	1946	Majestic 7166
That Wonderful Worrisome Feeling	1946	Majestic 7193
Two Hearts, Two Kisses	1955	Decca 29470

Five Harmoniques
Blue Sunday Blue Law Blues	1922	See Bee 200
Hallelujah To The Lamb	1922	See Bee 200

Five Jinks
Cushion Foot	1937	Bluebird 6905/Savoy
Dirt-Dishing Daisy	1937	Bluebird 6951
Found A Baby Down Dixie Way	1937	Bluebird 6857
I'm Moaning All Day For You	1937	Bluebird 6857
There Goes My Headache	1937	Bluebird 6951
Za Zu Swing	1937	Bluebird 6905

Five Jones Boys
Ace In The Hole	1936	Anchor A 24
Anytime, Anyday, Anywhere	1937	Standard ET 97128
Day You Get Away, The	1937	Standard ET 97584
Doin' The Suzie-Q	1937	Variety 522
Don't Count Your Chickens Before They Hatch	1937	Variety 579
Everything Stops For Tea	1937	Standard ET 97584
Honeysuckle Rose	1935	
How Am I Doin'	1937	Standard ET 97128
I Gotta Feelin' Your Foolin'		
I Heard	1937	Standard ET 97584
It's Been So Long	1937	Standard ET 97584
Love Is The Reason	1937	Standard ET 97128
Melody From The Sky	1937	Standard ET 97584
Mister Ghost Goes To Town	1937	Varsity 522/Clanka Lanka CL-144.033
Mood Indigo	1937	Standard ET 97127
My Dear	1937	Standard ET 97127
My Gal Mezzanine	1937	Variety 579
Nagasaki	1936	Allied Radio Transcription B-3048
Rose Room	1937	Standard Electrical Transcription 97127
Rosetta	1937	Standard Electrical Transcriptions 97127
Shoeshine Boy	1937	Standard ET 97584
Tiger Rag	1937	Standard ET 97128
When Your Old Wedding Ring Was New	1936	Anchor A 24
You're So Appealing	1937	Standard ET 97127

Five Kings
Meet Me At No Special Place	1947	Manor 1062
That's How Much I Love You	1947	Manor 1062

Five Kings, Savannah Churchill & the
I Can't Get Up The Nerve To Miss You	1947	Manor 1061
I'm Too Shy	1947	Manor 1066
Let's Call A Spade A Spade	1947	Manor 1061
Sincerely Yours	1947	Manor 1066

Five Locust Sisters
You Gotta Know How To Love	1926	Columbia 736D

Five Pennies
Let It Rain		

Five Red Caps
After I've Spent My Best Years On You	1945	Beacon 7128
Am I To Blame'	1950	RCA 47-3986
Are You Lonesome Tonight'	1950	Mercury 8174
Atlanta, G.A.	1946	Davis 2102
Big Game Hunter	1953	RCA 47-5130
Bless You	1947	Mercury 5011
Bobbin'	1952	RCA 47-4835/RCA 47-6345 (1955)
Boogie Beat'll Getcha If You Don't Watch Out, The	1945	Beacon 7135
Boogie Woogie Ball	1944	Beacon 7121/Gennett 7121
Boogie Woogie On A Saturday Night	1945	Beacon 7133/Joe Davis 7133/MGM

Title	Year	Label/Number
		10285 (1948)/RCA 47-4294 (1951)
Confused	1946	Beacon 7141
Destination Unknown	1944	Beacon 7125
Dirt Dishin' Daisy	1950	Mercury 8186
Do I, Do I, Do	1952	RCA 47-5130
Don't Fool With Me	1943	Beacon 117/Beacon 7116 (1943)
Don't Say We're Through	1944	Beacon 7125
Don't You Know	1944	Beacon 7122
D'Ya Eat Yet, Joe'	1951	RCA 47-4076
Gabriel's Band	1944	Beacon 7124
Give Me Time	1948	Mercury 8093
Grand Central Station	1943	Beacon 118/Beacon 7118 (1943)
Have A Heart For Someone Who Has A Heart For You	1946	Beacon 7141
How Do I Cry	1952	RCA 47-4835/RCA 47-6345 (1955)
I Didn't Mean To Be Mean To You	1945	Beacon 7127
I'd love To Live A Lifetime For You	1948	Mercury 8069
I Don't Want To Set The World On Fire	1947	Mercury 8052
If I Can't Have You	1945	Beacon 7128/MGM 10285 (1948)
I Learned A Lesson I'll Never Forget	1943	Beacon 7120MGM 10330(1948)/Mercury 8109 (1948)
I'll Remind You	1946	Beacon 7136
I Love An Old Fashioned Song	1945	Davis 2102
I Love You	1949	Mercury 8146
I Made A Great Mistake	1943	Beacon 116/Beacon 7115 (1943)/Gennett 7115
I May Hate Myself In The Morning	1952	RCA 47-4670
I'm Crazy 'Bout You	1945	Beacon 7130
I'm Glad I Waited For You	1946	Davis 2101
I'm Going To Try To Live My Life Alone	1943	Beacon 7119/Gennett 7119
I'm The One	1943	Beacon 115/Beacon 7115 (1943)/Gennett 7115
I'm To Blame	1945	Beacon 7133/Joe Davis 7133/MGM 4001 (1948)/RCA 50-0127 (1951)
In The Quiet Of The Dawn	1945	Beacon 7134
It Hurts Me But I Like It	1954	Jay-Dee 796
It's So Good Good Good	1945	Beacon 7129
I've Been Living For You	1949	Mercury 8157
I've Learned A Lesson I'll Never Forget	1944	Beacon 7120
I Wake Up Every Morning	1950	Mercury 8165
I Was A Fool To Let You Go	1945	Beacon 7131
Jack! You're Dead	1947	Mercury 8038
Just For You	1943	Beacon 7119/Gennett 7119
Lenox Avenue Jump	1944	Beacon 7121/Gennett 7121
Little White Lies	1948	Mercury 8085
Mama, Put Your Britches On	1943	Beacon 117/Beacon 7117 (1943)
Mary Had A Little Jam	1945	Beacon 7132
Money Is Honey	1948	Mercury 8093
My Everlasting Love For You	1946	Beacon 7136
Never Give Up Hope	1944	Beacon 7126/Joe Davis 7126
No Fish Today	1943	Beacon 118/Beacon 7118 (1943)
No One Else Will Do	1945	Beacon 7130
'Nuff Of That Stuff	1955	RCA 47-6096
Ouch	1954	Jay-Dee 796
Petunia	1949	Mercury 8157
Pleasant Dreams	1945	Beacon 7132
Red Caps Ball	1945	Beacon 7127
San Antonio Rose	1947	Mercury 8038
Scratch And You'll Find It	1948	Mercury 8091
Second Hand Romance	1954	Mercury 70389
Seems Like Old Times	1946	Davis 2101
Sentimental Me	1950	Mercury 8174
Shame	1951	RCA 47-4294
Somebody's Lyin'	1944	Beacon 7123
Spellbound	1945	Beacon 7129
Steve's Blues	1950	Mercury 8186
Strictly On The Safety Side	1944	Beacon 7122/Beacon 7142 (1946)
Sugar Lips	1944	Beacon 7124/MGM 10330 (1948)
Tables Have Turned On Me, The	1944	Beacon 7126/Joe Davis 7126
There's A Light On The Hill	1943	Beacon 116/Beacon 7116 (1943)
They Ain't Gonna Tell It Right	1950	Mercury 8165
Thing, The	1950	RCA 47-3986
Thinking	1945	Beacon 7131
Three Dollars And Ninety-Eight Cents	1951	RCA 47-4076
Through Thick And Thin	1945	Beacon 7134
Thru Thick And Thin	1948	Davis 7134/MGM 4001
Turnip Greens	1948	Mercury 8085
Tuscaloosa	1943	Beacon 115/Beacon 7115 (1943)
Two Little Kisses	1952	RCA 47-4670

Walkin' Through Heaven	1947	Mercury 8059	That's My Desire		Harmony CD 1001
Was It You	1944	Beacon 7123	They All Say I'm The Biggest Fool		Harmony CD 1001
Wedding Bells Are Breaking Up That Old Gang Of Mine	1948	Mercury 8069/Mercury 70389 (1954)	We'll Meet Again (unissued)		Harmony CD 1001
			With All My Heart	1949	Columbia 30158/Okeh 7049 (1954)
When You Come Back To Me	1951	RCA 50-0138			
Why Don't You Love Me	1952	RCA 47-5013			
Win Or Lose	1955	RCA 47-5987	Worry (Over You Like I Do)		Harmony CD 1001
Words Can't Explain	1943	Beacon 7120/Davis 7120/Beacon 7142 (1946)	Yes My Baby		Harmony CD 1001
			Five Scamps (with Evelyn Twine)		
			Fishing Song, The	1949	Columbia 30168
Would I Mind	1951	RCA 50-0138	**Five Spirits Of Rhythm**		
You Can't See The Sun When You're Crying	1947	Mercury 5011	Dr. Watson And Mr. Holmes	1934	Brunswick 01944
			I Got Rhythm	1933	Brunswick 9583/Parlophone R 262
You Made Me Love You	1948	Mercury 8109			
You Never Miss The Water Till The Well Runs Dry	1947	Mercury 8052	I'll Be Ready When The Great Day Comes	1933	Brunswick 6728
You're Driving Me Crazy	1947	Mercury 8059	Junk Man	1934	Brunswick 01944
You Thrill Me	1945	Beacon 7135	My Old Man	1933	Brunswick 6728
Five Red Caps (Bon Bon & the Red Caps Trio)			Rhythm	1933	Brunswick 9583/Parlophone R 262
Truthfully	1945	Joe Davis 7192/RCA 47-5013 (1952)			
			Shootin' In That Amen Corner	1934	Brunswick 02058
Five Rocquettes			That's What I Hate About Love	1934	Brunswick 02058
Dearie	1941	Decca 7848	**Flames**		
Lord's Prayer, The	1941	Decca 7842	Baby, Baby, Baby	1953	7-11 2106
Reminiscing	1941	Decca 7848	Baby, Pretty Baby	1953	7-11 2107
Sometimes I Feel Like A Motherless Child	1941	Decca 7842	Cryin' For My Baby		Spin 101
			Flam Mambo	1950	Aladdin 3349
Five Scamps			Keep On Smiling	1953	7-11 2106
Baby Don't You Cry (unissued)		Harmony CD 1001	Please Tell Me Now	1950	Selective 113
Bye Bye Boogie		Harmony CD 1001	So Alone	1950	Aladdin 3349
Chicken Shack Boogie	1949	Columbia 30157	Strange Land Blues		Spin 101
Dance Boogie	1951	Columbia 30242	Together	1953	7-11 2107
Don't Blame Me (unissued)		Harmony CD 1001	Young Girl	1950	Selective 113
Don't Cry Baby		Harmony CD 1001	**Flames, Patty Anne & the**		
Fine Like Wine	1949	Columbia 30163	Midnight	1952	Aladdin 3162
Gone Home	1949	Columbia 30157	My Heart Is Free Again	1952	Aladdin 3162
Gonna Buy Myself A Mule	1951	Columbia 30242	**Flames, Tommy "Mary Jo" Braden &**		
Good Lover Blues	1949	Columbia 30168	Did You Ever See A Monkey Play A Fiddle	1954	United 177/
How Nice	1949	Columbia 30163			
If I Didn't Care (unissued)		Harmony CD 1001	Do The Do	1954	United 177
I'll Never Smile Again		Harmony CD 1001	**Flat Creek Sacred Singers**		
I'll See You In My Dreams		Harmony CD 1001			
I Love The Way You Walk	1949	Columbia 30177	Home On The Banks Of The River	1928	Brunswick 265
I'm Gonna Cry	1949	Columbia 30177/Harmony CD 1001	Is It Far	1928	Vocalion 5232
			Look Away To Calvary	1928	Brunswick 236
More Than You Know		Harmony CD 1001	Mother, Tell Me Of The Angels	1928	Brunswick 236
Red Hot	1949	Columbia 30158/Okeh 7049 (1954)	Tell It Everywhere You Go	1928	Brunswick 265
			When We Go To Goryland	1928	Vocalion 5232
			Florida Four		
Solitude		Harmony CD 1001	I'm Tired Of Everything But You		Edison 51630
Stormy Weather (unissued)		Harmony CD 1001	Miami		Edison 51650
Sweet Slumber		Harmony CD 1001	My Kintucky Kinfolks		Edison 51747

Nobody But Fanny		Edison 51630
No Foolin'		Edison 51747
Roll 'Em Girls (Roll Your Own)		Edison 51650

Florida Normal & Industrial Quartette

Dis Train	1922	Okeh 40010
Tree, The	1922	Okeh 40010
Welcome Tablet, The	1922	Okeh 40079

Florida Normal Quartet

Oh! My Soul Is A Witness	1924	Okeh 40079

Fontaine Sisters

My Fickle Eye	1946	Musicraft 15067

Forrest, Helen & the Chickadees

I Like Mike	1946	Decca 18886
Linger In My Arms A Little Longer, Baby	1946	Decca 18908
Somewhere In The Night	1946	Decca 18886
Whatta Ya Gonna Do'	1946	Decca 18908

Foster Brothers (Ray Pettis)

Revenge

Foundation Quartet

I Love To Tell The Story	1928	Okeh 45309
No One Knows	1928	Okeh 45293
Softly And Tenderly Jesus Is Calling	1928	Okeh 45271
Sweet And Low	1928	Okeh 45271
When The Sunset Turns The Ocean Blue To Gold	1928	Okeh 45309
When They Ring Those Golden Bells For Me	1928	Okeh 45293

Four Aces

Aces Swing	1949	4-Star 1292/ET-20 (Radio Transcription)
Ain't It A Crying Shame	1947	Trilon 180
Amor	1954	Decca 29036
Because I'm In Love With You	1950	4-Star 1408
Charlie Was A Boxer	1957	Decca 29889
Cherie	1947	Trilon 178
Christmas Song, The	1956	Decca 29702
Don't Forget Me	1953	Decca 28744
Dream	1954	Decca 29217
Dreamer	1957	Decca 29989
False Love	1953	Decca 28744
Gal With The Yaller Shoes, The	1957	Decca 29809
Gang That Sang 'Heart Of My Heart'	1954	Decca 28843
Garbage Man	1946	Trilon 144
Garden In The Rain, A	1952	Decca 27860
Girl With The Dreamy Eyes, The	1935	Champion 40029
Gumbo	1947	Trilon 180
Heart	1955	Decca 29476
Heart And Soul	1951	Decca 28390
Heaven Can Wait	1951	Decca 28392
If You Can Dream	1957	Decca 29809
If You Take My Heart Away	1952	Decca 28560
I'll Be With You In Apple Blossom Time	1955	Decca 29344
I'll Never Let You Go Again	1947	Trilon 178
I'll Never Smile Again	1951	Decca 28391
I'm Crying All The Time	1947	Trilon 179
I'm Walkin' The Chalk Line	1935	Champion 40029
I'm Yours	1949	Decca 28162
In The Shade Of The Old Apple Tree	1934	
I Only Know I Love You	1957	Decca 29217
It's A Woman's World	1955	Decca 29269
I Understand	1949	Decca 28162
I've Been Waiting A Lifetime	1954	Decca 28843
I Wonder, I Wonder, I Wonder	1946	Trilon 143
Jingle Bells	1956	Decca 29702
Jumpin' Out	1949	4-Star 1324
Just Squeeze Me	1951	Decca 28390
Katie May		ET-20 (Radio Transcription)
La Rosita	1951	Decca 28393
Laughing On The Outside	1954	Decca 28843
Lazy Navaho		ET-20 (Radio Transcription)
Lazy Navajo	1949	4-Star 1292
Love Is A Many Splendored Thing	1955	Decca 29625
Melody Of Love	1955	Decca 29295
Mister Sandman	1955	Decca 29344
My Devotion	1951	Decca 28391
My Hero	1948	Decca 28073
New Jig Rhythm	1935	Champion 40028
Of This I'm Sure	1956	Decca 29725
O Holy Night	1956	Decca 29712
Put Your Cards On The Table	1946	Trilon 144
Rhythm Is Our Business	1935	Champion 40028
Richard Ain't Gonna Open That Door	1947	Trilon 153
Shine On Harvest Moon	1955	Decca 29625
Should I	1950	Decca 28323
Silent Night	1956	Decca 29712
Sluefoot	1955	Decca 29476
So Long	1954	Decca 29036
Spring Is A Wonderful Thing	1948	Decca 28073
Stranger In Paradise	1954	Decca 28927
Take Me In Your Arms	1951	Decca 28393
Tell My Why	1952	Decca 27860
There Goes My Heart	1955	Decca 29435
There Is A Tavern In The Town	1955	Decca 29295
There's A Rumor Going Around	1946	Trilon 145
There's Only One Tonight	1950	Decca 28323
This Little Chick Went To Market	1947	Trilon 179
Three Coins In The Fountain	1954	Decca 29123
Till I Go Dreaming Of You		ET-20 (Radio

100 Years of Harmony: 1850 to 1950

Ti-Pi-Tin	1951	Decca 28392
To Love Again	1957	Decca 29889
Too Late	1949	4-Star 1324
Too Late		ET-20 (Radio Transcription)
Wedding Bells Are Breaking Up That Old Gang Of Mine	1954	Decca 29123
Who Is There To Blame	1950	4-Star 1408
Who Was There To Blame (tense change accurate)		ET-20 (Radio Transcription)
Woman In Love, A	1956	Decca 29725
You Fooled Me	1952	Decca 28560
You'll Always Be The One	1955	Decca 29435

Four Aces (as the Cardinal Trio)

Gee But I'd Like To Make You Happy	1930	Broadway 1403L
Go Home And Tell Your Mother	1930	Broadway 1402L
Have You Forgotten Waikiki	1930	Broadway 1402L
Moonlight On The Colorado	1930	Broadway 1403L
Two Hearts In 3/4 Time	1931	Broadway 1454L

Four Aces (Four Boys and a Guitar)

Copper Coloured Gal	1937	Decca F6265

Four Aces (old)

All I Can Do (Is Think Of You)	1931	Clarion 5448C/Harmony 1305H/Velvet Tone 2508V
As Long As You Love Me	1930	Harmony 1254H
Blue Hawaii	1929	Diva 2897G/Harmony 897H/Velvet Tone 1897V
Broadway Melody	1929	Harmony 931H/Velvet Tome 1931V
Cabin In The Hills	1930	Harmony 1231H
Dark Eyes	1931	Harmony 1267H
Honey	1929	Diva 2897G/Harmony 897H/Publix 1020P/Velvet Tone 1897V
I'll Always Be In Love With You	1929	Harmony 969H/Velvet Tone 1969V
I Never Dreamt You'd Fall In Love With Me	1930	Harmony 1158H
It Can't Matter Now	1930	Harmony 1208H
Love Me	1929	Harmony 1019H/Clarion 530C
Michigan Waltz, The	1929	Harmony 1060H/Velvet Tone 2060V
Mississippi Moon	1930	Harmony 1101H/Velvet Tone 2101V
Moonlight On The Colorado	1930	Clarion 5079/Harmony 1208H/Velvet Tone 2208V
My Yesterdays With You	1930	Harmony 1254H
Singin' In The Bathtub	1929	Harmony 1060H/Velvet Tone 2060V
Someone Sang A Sweeter Song To Mary	1931	Clarion 5208C/Harmony 1267H
Song Of The Moonbeams	1929	Harmony 969H/Velvet Tone 1969V
Song Without A Name The	1930	Harmony 1158H
Under A Texas Moon	1930	Harmony 1101H/Publix 2009P/Velvet Tone 2101V
When My Dreams Come True	1929	Harmony 931H/Velvet Tome 1931V
When You're Looking For Tulips (To Kiss Your Troubles Away)	1931	Clarion 5449C/Harmony 1305H/Velvet Tone 2508V
Who Was The Lady'	1927	Brunswick 23847
Witchee Kitchee Koo	1929	Harmony 1019H/Clarion 530C
Yes She Do!	1927	Brunswick 23844
You'll Never Know, Sweetheart	1930	Clarion 5208C/Harmony 1231H

Four Amory Brothers, Thelma Carpenter & the

Joshua Fit De Battle Of Jericho	1947	Majestic 1104

Four Aristocrats

Bells Of Hawaii	1927	Victor 20587
Don't Sing Aloha When I Go		Edison 51858/Victor 20311
Everybody Loves My Girl	1927	Victor 21104
Hello! Swanee - Hello	1926	Columbia 808-D
I Gotta Get Myself Somebody To Love	1927	Victor 20465
I Told Them All About You	1927	Columbia 1227-D
It's O.K., Katy, With Me	1927	Electrola
I Wish I Was In Dixie	1927	Columbia 1061-D
Just Like A Melody Out Of The Sky	1928	Banner 7204
Little Music In The Moonlight, A		Edison 51858

Me And My Shadow	1927	Edison DD 52027/Edison BA 5361
Mountain Trail In Old Hawaii, A	1928	Banner 2439
Our Bungalow Of Dreams	1927	Columbia 1278-D
Schultz Is Back Again	1927	Victor 20465
She's Still My Baby	1926	Columbia 808-D/Victor 20314
Sixty Seconds Every Minute	1927	Columbia 1061-D
That's My Weakness Now	1928	Regal 8602
That's The Reason Why I Wish I Was In Dixie	1927	Edison DD 52027/Edison BA 5361
That's What The Lei Said To Me	1928	Victor 21499
Voom Voom (Maiden On The Gayden)	1927	Electrola/Victor 20587
Was It A Dream'	1928	Conqueror 7119
What Aloha Means	1928	Victor 21499
You Can Tell Her Everything Under The Sun (When You Get Her Under The Moon)	1927	Columbia 1278-D
Your Smile	1928	Banner 7209

Four Aristocrats (as the Aristocrats)

Egyptian Echoes	1924	Edison DD 51539
Hello, Aloha! How Are You'	1926	Edison DD 51759
Please	1924	Edison

Four Aristocrats (as the Hollywood Harmony Four)

Get Our And Get Under The Moon	1928	Banner 7148
Sunnyside Lane	1928	Challenge 671/Banner 7148 (1928)

Four Bachelors

Darling Nellie Gray	1927	Gennett/Supertone 9144
Hush-a-bye	1927	Gennett 6058
In The Evening By The Moonlight		Gennett/Supertone 9144
Someday	1927	Gennett 6058

Four Barons

Got To Go Back Again	1950	Regent 1026
Lemon Squeezer	1950	Regent 1026

Four Bars And A Melody

It Shouldn't Happen To A Dream	1948	Savoy 657
Near You	1948	Savoy 657

Four Bars, Mr. Google Eyes & his

Poppa Stoppa's (Bebop Blues)		Coleman 118
Young Boy		Coleman 118

Four Bars, Roy Lewis & the

Don't You Wanna Marry Me	1951	Imperial 5154
I Can't Go Home	1951	Imperial 5154
Jealous Blues	1951	Imperial 5136
When You Were Mine	1951	Imperial 5136

Four Belles

It Was Wonderful Then (And It's Wonderful Now)	1941	Bluebird B-11112
Just A Little Bit South Of North Carolina	1941	Bluebird B-11091
Rushin' Around On Rush Street	1941	Bluebird B-11112
We Go Well Together	1941	Bluebird B-11091

Four Belles (with Olsen & Johnson)

Boomps-A-Daisy	1940	Varsity 8318
My Heartzapoppin'	1940	Varsity 8308
My Mommy Sent Me To The Store	1940	Varsity 8318
Oh! Gee Oh! Gosh, Oh! Golly I'm In Love	1940	Varsity 8308

Four Blackamoors

Break It Up Charlie	1940	Decca 7850
Darling You Can't Have Five Take Fifty	1940	Decca 8512

Four Blackamoors, Mabel Robinson & the

Don't Give Up Your Old Love	1941	Decca 8568
Romance In The Dark	1941	Decca 8512
Search Your Heart And See	1941	Decca 8568
Somebody's Getting My Love	1941	Decca 8580
You Don't Know My Mind	1941	Decca 8580

Four Blackbirds

Basin Street Blues	1935	Brunswick A 86015/Vocalion 2981
Black-Eyed Susan Brown	1935	Vocalion A 86015
Dixie Rhythm	1935	Vocalion 2895
Hunkadola	1935	Melotone M 13347
I Got Shoes - You Got Shoosies	1935	Melotone M 13403
It's An Old Southern Custom	1935	Melotone M 13347
I Was Born Too Late	1935	Melotone M 13403
Louisville Lady	1935	Vocalion unreleased
Miss Otis Regrets	1935	Vocalion 2895
Moonglow	1935	Vocalion unreleased transcription

Four Blazes

Air Mail Special	1953	Delmark CD DE-542
All Night Long	1953	United 168
Boogie Woogie Billy	1945	AFRS Jubilee 136/AFRS Jubilee 222/P-Vine CD 5779
Caravan	1953	Delmark CD DE-542
Chicago Blues	194'	Jubilee 234
Did You Ever See A Monkey Play A Fiddle'	1954	United 177
Done Got Over	1955	United 191
Don't Lose Your Cool	1954	Delmark CD DE-

100 Years of Harmony: 1850 to 1950

Do The Do	1954	United 177	Bell Bottom Trousers	1945	De Luxe 1000
Drunken Blues	1954	Delmark CD DE-704	Bluer Than Bluer Than Blue	1942	Decca 8637
Ella Louise	1953	United 158	Blues Can Jump, The	1945	De Luxe 1004/De Luxe 3195 (1948)
It Ain't Necessarily Blues	1953	Delmark CD DE-542	Chitins And Pigs Feet	1945	De Luxe 1001
Lovin' Man	1953	Delmark CD DE-704	Easy Does It	1940	Decca 8517
Man, That's Groovy	1945	AFRS Jubilee 136/AFRS Jubilee 222/P-Vine CD 5779	Honey Chile	1940	Decca 8637/Apollo 398 (1948)
			I Couldn't Hear Nobody Pray	1945	De Luxe 1003
			I'm Gone	1945	De Luxe 1000
			I Need You	1950	
			It Takes A Long Tall Brown Skinned Gal	1948	Apollo 398
Mary Jo	1952	United 114	Jitterbug Sadie	1940	Decca 8517
Mood Indigo	1952	United 114	Missing You	1950	Apollo 1160
My Great Love Affair	1953	United 168	Noah And The Ark	1945	De Luxe 1005
My Hats On The Side Of My Head	1953	United 146	Re-Bop-De-Boom	1950	Apollo 1145
			Study War No Mo'	1945	De Luxe 1005
Never Start Living	1953	Delmark CD DE-704	Things You Want The Most Of All, The	1945	De Luxe 1002
Night Train	1952	United 125	Vegetable Song	1950	Apollo 1145
Not Any More Tears	1953	United 146	When The Old Gang's Back On The Corner	1945	De Luxe 1004
Oh Boy! That's Where My Money Goes	194'	Jubilee 234	**Four Blues, Ann DuPont & the**		
Perfect Woman	1953	United 158	Oh Daddy, Please Bring That Suitcase In	1945	De Luxe 1002
Please Send Her Back To Me	1952	United 127	**Four Bops**		
Raggedy Ride	1953	Delmark CD DE-704	Bop In B Flat	1948	Sittin' In With 503
			Prelude To A Kiss	1948	Sittin' In With 503
Rug Cutter	1952	United 125	**Four Buddies**		
She Needs To Be Loved	1955	United 191/Delmark CD DE-704	Close To You	1951	Savoy 959 (bootleg)
			Don't Leave Me Now	1951	Savoy 779
			Got Everything I Need But You	1953	Savoy 955 (bootleg)
			Heart And Soul	1951	Savoy 817
Snag The Britches	1953	Delmark CD DE-704	I Love You, Yes I Do	1951	Savoy 951 (bootleg)
			I'm Yours	1951	Savoy 809 (bootleg)
Stop Boogie Woogie	1952	United 127	It Could Have Been Me	1951	Savoy 951 (bootleg)
Women, Women	1955	Delmark CD DE-704	It's No Sin	1951	Savoy 817
			Just To See You Smile Again	1950	Savoy 769
Four Bluebirds (with Bobby Nunn)			Moonlight In Your Eyes	195	Unreleased
My Baby Done Told Me	1949	Excelsior 540	My Mother's Eyes	1953	Savoy 888
Four Bluejackets			My Summer's Gone	1951	Savoy 789
Baby, Baby Please Come Home	1947	Mercury 8017	Nothin' Shakin' Baby	1952	
I Know Who Threw The Whiskey In The Well	1947	Mercury 8017	Ooh-Ow	1953	Savoy 888
Jezebel	1947	Mercury 8031	Simply Say Goodbye	1951	Savoy 823
Little David And I	1947	Mercury 8019	Sin	1951	Savoy 817
Moses Smote The Water	1946	Mercury 8004	Stop Your Hittin' On Me	1951	Savoy 959 (bootleg)
Rip, Somebody Done Snagged Their Britches	1947	Mercury 8019	Story Blues	1952	Savoy 845
			Sweet Slumber	1951	Savoy 779
Rock-A-My Soul	1946	Mercury 8004	Sweet Tooth For My Baby	1952	Savoy 866
Weep No More My Children	1947	Mercury 8031	What's The Matter With Me'	1952	Savoy 866
Four Blues			Why At A Time Like This'	1950	Savoy 789
As Long As I Live	1950	Apollo 1160	Window Eyes	1951	Savoy 823
Baby, I Need A Whole Lot Of Everything	1945	De Luxe 1001	You Left Me Blue	1953	Savoy 955 (bootleg)
			You're Part Of Me	1952	Savoy 845

Four Buddies (as the Four Buds)
I Will Wait	1950	Savoy 769

Four Buddies (The Buddies)
I Stole Your Heart	1955	Glory 230
I Waited	1955	Glory 230

Four Buddies, Dolly Cooper & the
I'd Climb The Highest Mountain	1953	Savoy 891

Four Buds (Four Buddies)
Just To See You Smile Again	1950	Savoy 769

Four Buzz Saws
Baptising Sister Lucy Lee	1930	Vocalion 1652
Elevator Blues	1930	Vocalion 1652
Farewell Blues	1930	Vocalion 5471
I'm forever Blowing Bubbles	1930	Melotone M 12105
Three O'clock In The Morning	1930	Melotone M 12105
Tree Song, The	1930	Vocalion 5471

Four Chicks & a Chuck
Are You Livin' Old Man'	1948	Cosmo 453
Body And Soul	1948	Cosmo 465
Ghost Of Barrelhouse Joe	1948	Cosmo 465
In The Middle Of May	1948	Cosmo 467
Jose Gonzalez	1948	Cosmo 453
Surprise Party	1948	Cosmo 467

Four Chicks and a Chuck
I Go In When The Moon Comes Out (Turntable Song)	1947	MGM 10070
Kate, Have I Come Too Early, Too Late	1947	MGM 10048
Kokomo Indiana	1947	MGM 10070
My Best Girl	1947	MGM 10319
My Little Grass Shack (In Kealakekua, Hawaii)	1947	MGM 10319B
Wait'll I Get My Sunshine In The Moonlight	1947	MGM 10048

Four Chicks and Chuck
Foolin'	1953	Rainbow 226
3 O'Clock In The Morning	1953	Rainbow 226

Four Chorders
Rose Of Tralee	1953	Decca 28829
Whiffenpoof Song, The	1953	Decca 28830

Four Chords
Again	1949	Sittin' In With 516
You Had The Blues	1949	Sittin' In With 516

Four Clefs
Am I Still Your Baby	1948	Bullet 268
Blue 'Lude #2	1940	Bluebird 8484
Blue Lude In C Sharp Major	1939	Bluebird 8311
Blue Paradise	1941	Bluebird 8859
Dig These Blues	1946	RCA 20-2072/RCA 20-2072 (1946)
Down In My Heart	1940	Bluebird 8332
Fair Enough	1941	Bluebird 8809
First Thing In The Morning, The	1948	Bullet 268
Four Clefs Woogie	1942	Bluebird 11587/RCA 20-4507 (1952)
Get Together	1941	Bluebird 8859
Hiding All My Cares	1939	Bluebird 8311
Honey Dear	1941	Bluebird 8670
I Guess I'll Be On My Way	1941	Bluebird 8624/RCA 20-0098 (1950)
I Like Pie, I Like Cake	1941	Bluebird 8884
I'm In Love With You	1941	Bluebird 8809
I Must Have Been Dreaming	1941	Bluebird 8832
Inspiration Of Love	1941	Bluebird 8670
It's Heavenly	1941	Bluebird 8655
Jive Is Jumpin', The	1939	Bluebird 8297
Losing My Mind Over You	1939	Bluebird 8195/Montgomery Ward 8531
Love Has Come My Way	1944	Bluebird 34-0719
My Tiny Bundle Of Love	1942	Bluebird 11541
New Shanghai Honeymoon	1940	Bluebird 8484
Put On Your Old Grey Bonnet	1939	Bluebird 8232
Returning	1941	Bluebird 8690
Shanghai Honeymoon	1939	Bluebird 8281
Spo-De-O-Dee	1940	Bluebird 8332
Swanee River Swing	1939	Bluebird 8281
Take It And Git	1942	Bluebird 11492
These Blues Come On	1941	Bluebird 8832
Until I Return	1941	Bluebird 8884
V-Day Stomp	1945	Bluebird 34-0726/RCA 20-1656 (1945)
Watching My Ships Go Drifting By	1941	Bluebird 8624
We Love To Swing	1939	Bluebird 8195/Montgomery Ward 8531
When I'm Low I Get High	1945	
When The Clouds Roll By	1942	Bluebird 11587
Why Be So Blue	1945	Bluebird 34-0726/RCA 20-1656 (1945)
Why Pretend	1942	Bluebird 11541/RCA 20-3234 (1948)
Why Should I Care	1939	Bluebird 8297/RCA 20-3234 (1948)
You'll Always Dwell In My Heart	1941	Bluebird 8690
You're My Secret Desire	1942	Bluebird 11492
You Should Be Satisfied	1944	Bluebird 34-0719
You Tore Up My Heart	1939	Bluebird 8232/RCA 20-0098 (1950)

Four Deals
Ain't No Bears In The Forest	1950	Capitol 1313
It's Too Late Now	1950	Capitol 1313

Four Deep Tones
Castle Rock	1951	Coral 65061
Just In Case You Change Your Mind	1951	Coral 65061
Night You Said Goodbye, The	1951	Coral 65062
When The Saints Go Marching In	1951	Coral 65062

Four Dots
My Dear	1951	Dot 1043
You Won't Let Me Go	1951	Dot 1043

Four Dusty Travelers
Great Gittin' Up Mornin'	1929	Columbia 14499-D
March On Down To Jordan	1929	Columbia 14499-D
Me An' Mah Pardner	1929	Columbia 14477-D
Po' Mourner	1929	Columbia 14477-D

Four Dusty Travelers, Ted Lewis & the
Dinah	1930	Columbia 2181-D/Okeh 41585
Lonesome Road, The	1930	Columbia 2181-D

Four Esquires
Honeysuckle Rose	1935	Trilon 12455
Lazy Bones Gotta Job Now	1935	Brunswick 7574

Four Gabriels
Gloria	1948	World 2505
Recess In Heaven	1948	World 2505

Four Gospel Singers
Angels Shouting Glory, Just To Tell The Story	1931	Bluebird 5705/Victor 23924 (1932)
Do You Want To Be A Worker For The Lord	1931	Bluebird 5311/Victor 23312 (1932)
Dry Bones	1931	Bluebird 5311/Victor 23312 (1932)
New Jerusalem	1931	Bluebird 5705/Victor 23924 (1932)

Four Harmony Kings
My Lord's Gonna Move This Wicked Race	1924	Vocalion 14941A
When The Saints Come Marching In	1924	Vocalion 14941B

Four Harmony Kings, Jim Europe's
Swing Low Sweet Chariot	1919	Perfect 11056/Pathe 020851

Four Hawaiians
Honolulu Moon	1927	Banner 1926
Rio Nights	1927	Banner 1926

Four Hearsemen
Charmaine	1955	Decca 29238

Four Hill Brothers
Perfect Day, A	1928	Challenge 418

Four Hits And A Miss
Sixpence	1950	Columbia 38967/Columbia DW 5283
Coney Island Washboard	1954	Decca 28951

Four Hits And A Miss (with Charles La Vere)
Have A Little Sympathy	1948	Decca 24584

Four Hits And A Miss (with Ella Fitzgerald)
I Don't Want The World (With A Fence Around It)	1950	Decca MU 60490
M-I-S-S-I-S-S-I-P-P-I	1950	Decca MU 60490

Four Hits And A Miss (with Evelyn Knight)
It's Too Late Now	1949	Decca 24636
You're So Understanding	1949	Decca 24636

Four Hits And A Miss (with Johnny Mercer)
Bob White (What You Gonna Sing Tonight)	1937	Brunswick 7988/Harmony 1009
Jamboree Jones	1937	Harmony 1010
Last Night On The Back Porch	1937	Brunswick 8011/Harmony 1009/Vocalion 578
Murder Of J.B. Markham, The	1937	Brunswick 8011/Harmony 1010/Vocalion 578

Four Hits And A Miss (with Michael Douglas)
She's A Home Girl	1948	Decca 24584

Four Hits And A Miss (with Toni Harper and Mannie Klein's Dixie)
Dish Rag (Rub A Dub Dub), The	1950	Columbia 38917

Four Hits And A Miss, Bing Crosby with Jane Wyman &
In The Cool Cool Of The Evening	1951	Brunswick 82581/Brunswick 04760/Decca 27678/Decca Y 6332
Misto Christoforo Columbo	1951	Brunswick 82581/Brunswick 04760/Decca 27678/Decca Y 6332

Four Hits And A Miss, Debbie Reynolds and
Oogie Oogie Wa Wa	1951	MGM 30493/

Four Hits And A Miss, Dick Haymes with
Old Master Painter, The	1949	Decca 24801

Four Hits And A Miss, Doris Day and
Very Good Advice (From 'Alice In Wonderland')	1951	Columbia 39295/Columbia DS 2016

Four Hits And A Miss, Frank Sinatra and
It's The Same Old Dream	1946	Columbia 37288/Columbia DS 1675

Four Hits And A Miss, Stumpy Brown and
Be-Bop Spoken Here	1949	Columbia 38499/Columbia

Four Hoosiers
		DS 1832
Gypsy Love Song	1927	Challenge 347
Love's Old Sweet Song	1927	Challenge 347
Memories	1927	Challenge 417
Old Black Joe	1927	Challenge 346

Four Jacks
Becky Ann		Rebel 1313
Careless Love	1949	Allen 21001
Darling I'm Lonesome For You	1952	MGM 11179
Forever Begins Today		Sharp 44
Goodbye Baby	1952	Federal 12075
I Ain't Coming Back Anymore (with Cora Williams)	1952	Federal 12079
I Can't Forget		Rebel 1313
I Challenge Your Kiss	1949	Allen 21000
I Cry My Heart Out	1950	Gotham 219
I'll Be Home Again	1952	Federal 12087
Last Of The Good Rocking Men, The	1952	Federal 12087
Love Lies		Sharp 44
Sure Cure For The Blues (with Shirley Haven)	1952	Federal 12079
Swing Low, Sweet Chariot	1949	Allen 21000
Take Me	1950	Gotham 219
You Met A Fool	1952	Federal 12075
You're In Love With Someone Else	1952	MGM 11179

Four Jacks & the Four Kings (with Horace Heidt & his Brigadiers)
Dardanella	1938	Brunswick 8248/Brunswick A 81871
Do You Ken John Peel	1938	Brunswick A 81585

Four Jacks, Janet Shay & the
Busy Bee	1960	Alcar 1502
If And When	1960	Alcar 1502

Four Jacks, Lil Greenwood & the
Grandpa Can Boogie Too	1952	Federal 12093
Monday Morning Blues	1952	Federal 12082
My Last Hour	1952	Federal 12082
Never Again	1952	Federal 12093

Four Jacks, Mac Burney & the
Let Me Get Next To You	1956	Hollywood 1058
This Is My Last Affair	1954	Aladdin 3274
Tired Of Your Sexy Ways	1954	Aladdin 3274
Walking And Crying	1956	Hollywood 1058

Four Jacks, Shirley Haven & the
Stop Foolin' Around	1952	Federal 12092
Troubles Of My Own	1952	Federal 12092

Four Jumps Of Jive
Boo Boo Fine Jelly	1946	Mercury 2015
It's Just The Blues	1946	Mercury 2001
Satchel Mouth Baby	1946	Mercury 2001
Streamline Woman Blues	1946	Mercury 2015

Four Kings & the Four Jacks (with Horace Heidt & his Brigadiers)
Do You Ken John Peel	1938	Brunswick A 81585

Four Kings (& the Four Jacks with Horace Heidt & his Brigadiers)
Dardanella	1938	Brunswick A 81871

Four Kings (with Horace Heidt & his Brigadiers)
Ferdinand The Bull	1938	Brunswick A 81623
Sugar Blues	1938	Brunswick A 81662
Who Do You Think I Saw Last Night'	1938	Brunswick A 81612

Four Kings And A Queen
Hands Across The Table	1948	King 4199
How Could We Ever Have Been Strangers	1948	King 4199

Four Kittens, Fat Man Mathews & the
Later Baby	1952	Imperial 5211
When Boy Meets Girl	1952	Imperial 5211

Four Knights
After	1955	Capitol 3250
Anniversary Song	1953	Capitol 2403
Baby Doll	1953	Capitol 2517
Believing You	1955	Capitol 3192
Bibbady Bobbady Boo		
Blossom Fell, A	1955	Capitol 3095
Blue Tail Fly	1959	Lang-Worth Transcription 1458
Bottle Up The Moonlight	1956	Capitol 3386
Brother Bill	1947	Lang-Worth Transcription AS-416
Charmaine	1951	Capitol 1875
Chi-Baba Chi-Baba (My Bambino Go To Sleep)	1947	Lang-Worth AS-364
Cry	1951	Capitol 1875
Crystal Gazer	1949	Coral 60072
Crystal Gazer	1949	Lang-Worth Transcription AS-570
Dark Town Strutters Ball	1945	Lang-Worth Transcription AS-161
Doll With The Sawdust Heart, The	1952	Capitol 1998
Don't Be Ashamed To Say I Love You`	1946	Decca 11003/Decca 48026 (1947)
Don't Count Your Dreams	1947	Lang-Worth Transcription 1287
Don't Cry, Cry Baby	1949	Coral 60046
Don't Depend On Me	1956	Capitol 3494

Title	Year	Label/Number
Don't Sit Under The Apple Tree	1955	Capitol 3192
Don't You Love Me Anymore	1947	Lang-Worth Transcription AS-399
Doo Wacka Doo	1952	Capitol 2127
Dreams Are A Dime A Dozen	1947	Lang-Worth Transcription AS-365
Easy Street (recorded in 1952)	1954	Capitol 2894
Fantastic	1949	Coral 60072
Fantastic	1949	Lang-Worth Transcription AS-570
Few Kind Words, A	1953	Capitol 2403
15 Hugs After Midnight 20 Kisses To One	194'	Lang-Worth Transcription
Five Foot Two, Eyes Of Blue	1951	Capitol 1914
Foolishly Yours	1955	Capitol 3093
Foolish Tears	1958	Coral 62045
Four Minute Mile, The	1958	Coral 61936
Funny How You Get Along Without Me	1946	Decca 48014
Georgia On My Mind	1945	Lang-Worth Transcription 1148
Georgia On My Mind	1954	Previously unreleased
Glory Of Love, The	1951	Capitol 1806
Got Her Off My Hands (But I Can't Get Her Off My Mind)	1951	Capitol 1787
Grandfather's Clock	1949	Lang-Worth Transcription 1458
Gratefully Yours	1955	Capitol 3155
Guilty	1955	Capitol 3279
Hands Across The Table	194'	Lang-Worth Transcription
Happy Birthday Baby	1956	Capitol 3339
Heartaches	194'	Lang-Worth Transcription
He'll Understand And Say Well Done	1947	Decca 48018/Decca 14524 (1950)
Honey Bunch	1955	Capitol 3024
Honeyfoglin' Time	1946	Lang-Worth Transcription AS-330
How Can You Not Believe Me	1957	Capitol 3689
How Wrong Can You Be	1954	Capitol 2847
I Ain't Got Nobody	1954	Previously unreleased - demo
I Couldn't Stay Away From You	1949	Lang-Worth Transcription 1458
I Couldn't Stay Away From You	1953	Capitol 2654
Ida! Sweet As Apple Cider	1954	
Ida Sweet As Apple Cider	194'	Lang-Worth Transcription
I Don't Wanna See You Cryin'	1954	Capitol 2938
I Don't Want To Set The World On Fire	194'	Lang-Worth Transcription
If I Had My Life To Live Over	194'	Lang-Worth Transcription
If You Ever Change Your Mind	1958	Coral 61981
I Get So Lonely (When I Dream About You)	1953	Capitol 2654 (second pressing)
I Go Crazy	1951	Capitol 1787
I Love That Song	1957	Capitol 3730
I Love The Sunshine Of Your Smile	1951	Capitol 1587
I Love You For Sentimental Reasons	1946	Lang-Worth Transcription 1254
I Love You Still	1956	Capitol 3339
I'm A 12 O'Clock Guy In A 9 O'Clock Town	194'	Lang-Worth Transcription
I'm Falling For You	1946	Lang-Worth Transcription AS-330
I'm Falling For You	1947	Decca 24139
I'm The World's Biggest Fool	1952	Capitol 2087
Inside Out	1955	Capitol 3093
In The Chapel In The Moonlight	1951	Capitol 1840/Capitol 2894 (1954)
It Doesn't Cost Money	1957	Capitol 3689
It Had To Be You		
It's A Good Day	1946	Lang-Worth Transcription AS-330
It's A Sin To Tell A Lie	1952	Capitol 2087
It's So Nice To Be Nice To Your Neighbor	1947	Lang-Worth Transcription 1287
I Wanna Say Hello	1951	Capitol 1840
I Was Meant For You (The Wah-Wah Song)	1954	Capitol 2782
I Wish I Had A Girl	1952	Capitol 1930
Jezebel	194'	Lang-Worth Transcription
Just In Case You Change Your Mind	1946	Decca 11003/Decca 48026 (1947)
La La		Triode 104
Lead Me To That Rock	1947	Decca 48018/Decca 14524 (1950)
Let Me Off Uptown	194'	Lang-Worth Transcription
Lies	1952	Capitol 2234
Lonesome	1947	Lang-Worth Transcription 1294
Look Up	1949	Lang-Worth Transcription 1458
Love Is Gone	194'	Lang-Worth Transcription
Man Who Paints The Rainbow, The	1947	Lang-Worth Transcription AS-

Song	Year	Label
Marshmallow Moon	1951	Capitol 1914
Me	1955	Capitol 3155
Million Dollar Baby		Coral LP 57309
Million Tears, A	1952	Capitol 2315
Mistaken	1956	Capitol 3386
More I Go Out With Somebody Else, The	1952	Capitol 1998
My Dream Sonata	1956	Capitol 3456
My Favorite Friend	194'	Lang-Worth Transcription
My Melancholy Baby	1947	Lang-Worth Transcription AS-416
No Baby No	194'	Lang-Worth Transcription
O' Falling Star	1958	Coral 62045
Oh Baby, I Get So Lonesome	1953	Capitol 2654
Oh, Happy Day	1952	Capitol 2315
Oh, Miss Hannah	1954	
Old Dan Tucker	194'	Lang-Worth Transcription
One Way Kisses	1952	Capitol 2234
Perdido	1955	Capitol 3250
Period	1954	Capitol 2847
Peter Cotton Tail		
Put Another Chair At The Table	194'	Lang-Worth Transcription ep 42A
Ridin' Down The Canyon	1946	Lang-Worth Transcription 1273
Saw Your Eyes	1954	Capitol 2938
Say No More	1952	Capitol 2195
Send For Me	1957	Capitol 3737
Sentimental Fool	1951	Capitol 1587
Sentimental Journey	1954	
Sin (It's No Sin)	1951	Capitol 1806
Sleepy Time Gal	1954	
So Soon	1947	Decca 24139
Speaking Of Angels	194'	Lang-Worth ep 17A
Sugar Foot Rag	194'	Lang-Worth Transcription
Take Me Right Back To The Track	194'	Lang-Worth Transcription
Tennessee Train	1953	Capitol 2517
Texas Is So Big		VGOR
That Feeling In The Moonlight	194'	Lang-Worth ep 42B
That's The Way It's Gonna Be	1952	Capitol 2195
There Are Two Sides To Ev'ry Heartache	1952	Capitol 1971
They Say It's Wonderful	1946	Lang-Worth AS-277
They Tell Me	1954	Capitol 2782
Things To Do Today	1959	Coral 62110
Tic Toc		Triode 104
		364
Till Then	1954	Lang-Worth Transcription
Walkin' And Whistlin' Blues	1951	Capitol 1707
Walkin' And Whistlin' Blues	1957	Capitol 3730
Walkin' In The Sunshine	1952	Capitol 1971
Walkin' With My Shadow	1946	Decca 48014
Walkin' With My Shadow	1946	Lang-Worth Transcription 1216
Way I Feel, The	1952	Capitol 1930
What Are You Doing New Years Eve	1947	Lang-Worth Transcription ep 17B/Lang-Worth AS-399
When My Baby Smiles At Me	1954	
When Tonight Is Just A Memory	1949	Lang-Worth ep 17B/ Lang-Worth AS-399
When Your Lover Has Gone	1958	Coral 61936
When Your Old Wedding Ring Was New	194'	Lang-Worth Transcription ep 42A
Where Is The Love	1959	Coral 62110
Who Am I'	1951	Capitol 1707
Who's Sorry Now	194'	Lang-Worth Transcription
Why Did It Have To End So Soon	1947	Lang-Worth Transcription AS-399
Win Or Lose	1952	Capitol 2127
Wrapped Up In A Dream	1949	Coral 60046
Wrapped Up In A Dream	1949	Lang-Worth Transcription AS-546
Write Me, Baby	1955	Capitol 3024
Yes I Do (The Wedding Song)	1958	Coral 61981
You	1955	Capitol 3279
You're A Honey	1956	Capitol 3494
You Tell Me Your Dream	194'	Lang-Worth Transcription

Four Knights (with Nat King Cole)

Song	Year	Label
If I May	1955	Capitol 3095
My Personal Possession	1957	Capitol 3737
That's All There Is To That	1956	Capitol 3456

Four Komical Kards

Song	Year	Label
Dr. Whackem's Academy	1908	Edison Bell 20098

Four Men Only

Song	Year	Label
When Buddha Smiles	1941	

Four Modernaires

Song	Year	Label
Mandy	1939	

Four Musettes

Song	Year	Label
Azusa, Cucamonga and Anaheim	1948	Musicraft 582
Beside A Bubbling Brook	1948	Musicraft 582
Daddy Surprise Me	1948	Musicraft 555
Everybody Loves My Baby	194'	Musicraft 542
Oh, What I Know About You	194'	Musicraft 542

Title	Year	Label
Papa, Won't You Dance With Me'	194'	Musicraft 537
Swinging Down The Lane	194'	Musicraft 537
Yearning	1948	Musicraft 555

Four Musketeers

Title	Year	Label
Girl In The Little Green Hat, The	1933	

Four New Yorkers

Title	Year	Label
Darktown Strutter's Ball, The	1932	
Rock Me In A Cradle of Kalua	1932	

Four Notes

Title	Year	Label
Auld Lang Syne	1948	Paradise 113
Coffee Five, Doughnuts Five		Premier 29002
Deep River		International 453/454
Eileen		International 453/454
Foolishly Yours		International 216
House I Live In, The		International 455/456
Jungle Twilight		Premier 29002
May It Be Christmas	1948	Paradise 113
Moonlight Bay		International 455/456
Re-Bop		International 451/452
Rockin' Chair	1948	Paradise 115
St. Louis Blues		International 215
When Day Is Done		International 451/452
Whiffenpoof Song	1948	Paradise 115

Four Novelty Aces

Title	Year	Label
Drifting In A Lover's Dream	1933	
Get Away Jordan	1933	Bluebird B-5561
Honey	1933	
Standing In The Need Of Prayer	1933	Bluebird B-5561

Four Of Us

Title	Year	Label
Lift Up The Latch	1947	Modern 222

Four Pals

Title	Year	Label
Hello Everybody	1929	
If I Can't Have The One I Love	1955	Royal Roost 610

Four Pods Of Pepper

Title	Year	Label
Ain't Got No Mama Now	1929	Brunswick 7103
Queen Street Rag	1929	Brunswick 7103

Four Pods Of Pepper (as Bethlehem Four)

Title	Year	Label
Doubting Thomas	1929	Vocalion

Four Pods Of Pepper (as Montana Taylor & the Jazoo Boys)

Title	Year	Label
Hayride Stomp	1929	Vocalion 1275
Whoop Holler And Stomp	1929	Vocalion 1275

Four Pods Of Pepper (with Banjo Ikey Robinson)

Title	Year	Label
Gee, I Hate To Love That Girl	1931	Columbia 14664-D
Get Off Your Stuff	1931	Columbia 14590-D
I Was A Good Loser Until I Lost You	1931	Columbia 14664-D
You've Had Your Way	1931	Columbia 14590-D

Four Rajahs

Title	Year	Label
After I See The Sandman	1928	Brunswick
Blue Waters	1928	Victor 21822
Broadway Melody	1929	Victor 21886
Gotta Be Good	1928	Victor 21772
I Want A 'Yes' Girl	1928	
Lend Me Your Eyes, Pretty Baby	1928	
My Gal Sal	1928	
Sweet Dreams	1928	Victor 21792
Sweetest Little Honey	1928	
Sweet Sue - Just For You	1928	
Too Busy!	1928	Victor 21550
Waitin' For Katie	1928	Brunswick 21550

Four Recorders

Title	Year	Label
One Step To Heaven	1928	Victor 21674

Four Riffs

Title	Year	Label
Tormented	1949	Atlantic unreleased
You've Got To Reap What You Sow	1949	Atlantic unreleased

Four Rockets

Title	Year	Label
Little Brown Jug	1948	Aladdin 3017
Little Red Wagon	1948	Aladdin 3007
Loch Lomond	1948	Aladdin 3017
Travelin' Light	1948	Aladdin 3007

Four Serenaders

Title	Year	Label
Everything's Made For Love	1927	Champion 15221
High High Up In The Hills	1927	Champion 15208
Thinking Of You	1927	Champion 15208

Four Shades Of Rhythm

Title	Year	Label
Baby, I'm Gone	1949	Old Swingmaster 13
Ghost Of A Chance		Mad 1202
Howie Sent Me	1947	Vitacoustic 1005
Hundred Years From Today, A	1960	Apex 967
I Can Dream	1949	Old Swingmaster 23
Life With You	1960	Apex 967
Master Of Me	1949	Old Swingmaster 23
My Blue Walk	1949	Old Swingmaster 13
One Hundred Years From Today	1947	Vitacoustic 1005
So There	1952	Chance 1126
Yesterdays	1952	Chance 1126

Four Sharps (Delta Rhythm Boys)

Title	Year	Label
Don't Ask Me Why	1949	Atlantic 875
I Can Hardly Wait	1949	Atlantic 875

Four Southern Singers

Title	Year	Label
Be Ready	1935	Victor 24264
Careless Love	1935	Bluebird B-8392
Hambone Am Sweet	1935	Victor 24328
Mammy Lou	1935	Victor 24264
Old Man Harlem	1935	Bluebird B-8392
You're Sweet To Your Mammy & Mudder Knows	1935	Victor 24328

Four Southerners
Dan The Back Door Man	1937	Decca 7291
Trouble In Mind	1937	Decca 7291

Four Spades
Making Up Blues	1924	Columbia 14028-D
Squabblin' Blues	1924	Columbia 14028-D

Four Squires
Aren't The Funnies Funny'	1938	Vocalion 4057
Baby Won't You Please Come Home	1938	Vocalion 5389
Blue Skies	1938	Vocalion 4096
Old Black Joe	1938	Vocalion 5389
Prisoner's Song, The	1938	Vocalion 4057
Put On Your Old Grey Bonnet	1938	Vocalion 4096

Four Stars
As Long As You Love Me	1930	Okeh 41457
If You're Ever In My Arms Again	1937	Variety VA 621
My Yesterdays With You	1930	Okeh 41457

Four Steps Of Jive (Bernie Calloway & the)
Oshkosh-Beb-A-Losh	1948	Chord 656

Four Tones
Goodnight Baby Goodnight	1941	Bluebird B-11408/Make Believe Ballroom 2358
Hey, What You Say'	1945	Preview 666/667
Lullaby Of The Lonesome Trail	1939	D&S 158
Muggin With A Swing	1939	D&S 153
My Island Love		Keystone S171
Please Don't Rush Me	1945	Memo 1003/Memo 7001 (1948)
Put Your Cards On The Table	1945	Memo 1005/Memo 7001 (1948)
Satchelmouth Baby	1945	Preview 668/669
Someone Over Here Loves Someone Over There	1945	Preview 666/667
Someone's Rocking My Dreamboat	1941	Bluebird B-11408/Make Believe Ballroom 2358
Swingin' In Rhythm		Keystone S171
Two Hearts To Beat Tonight	1941	Ebony 100
Two Tears Met	1945	Preview 668/669
Uptown Rhythm	1945	Memo 1002
What A Fool Was I	1941	Ebony 100

Four Tones (with Herb Jeffrey)
I'm A Happy Cowboy	1939	D&S 154

Four Tones, Dusty Brooks & the
Chili Dogs	1952	Dootone 306
Cream Of Wheat	1950	Majestic 123
Cryin' To Myself	1951	Columbia 30236
Do! Do! Baby	1944	A-1 1001/Lamarr's Star 101 (1945)
I Ain't Gonna Worry No More	1951	Columbia 30241
I Didn't Cry	1950	Majestic 127
I'll Follow You	1944	A-1 1001/Lamarr's Star 101 (1945)
Liddy	1950	Columbia 30230
Little Chum	1945	Lamarr's Star 103/Memo 1002 (1945)
'Ol Man River	1950	Majestic 123
Once There Lived A Fool	1951	Columbia 30236
Play Jackpot	1945	Lamarr's Star 103/Memo 1001 (1945)
Seclusion	1945	Lamarr's Star 102/Memo 1003 (1945)/Memo 1005 (1945)
Shadow Of The Blues	1951	Columbia 30241
Shoo Boogie Mama	1950	Columbia 30230
Shuffle Board Boogie	1950	Majestic 127
Thank You For The Lies	1945	Lamarr' s Star 102/Memo 1001 (1945)
You Never Told A Lie	1952	Dootone 306

Four Toppers
Carry Me Back To Old Virginny	1940	Ammor 100
Jumpin' Jive	1940	Ammor 101

Four Tunes
All My Dreams	1948	Manor 1116/Arco 1257 (1950)
All Torn Up		Jubilee (unreleased)
Am I Blue'	1950	RCA Victor 50-0072
At The Steamboat River Ball	1955	Jubilee 5218
Ballad Of James Dean, The	1956	Jubilee 5255
Brooklyn Bridge	1955	Jubilee 5212
Can I Say Anymore'	1952	RCA Victor 47-4663
Careless Love	1949	RCA Victor 50-0008
Carry Me Back To The Lone Prairie	1951	RCA Victor 50-0131
Come What May	1952	RCA Victor 20-4489/RCA Victor 47-4489 (1952)
Confess	1948	Manor 1131
Cool Water	1950	RCA Victor 47-3967/Jubilee 5276 (1957)
Dancing With Tears In My Eyes	1956	Jubilee 5245
Darling You Make It So	1947	Manor 1076
Do-Do-Do-Do-Do-Do It Again	1954	Jubilee 5135
Do Do Do It Again	1954	Jubilee 5135
Do I Worry'	1950	RCA Victor 47-3881

Song	Year	Label/Number
Don't Blame My Dreams	1950	Arco 1246
Don't Cry Darling	1954	Jubilee 5165
Don't Get Around Much Anymore	1953	RCA Victor 47-5532
Don't Know	1948	Manor 1131
Don't You Ever Mind	1948	Manor 1141
Don't You Run Away	1958	Crosby 3
Dreams	1947	Manor 1087
Du Bist Mein Wiener Tzatzkellah	1947	Manor 1076
Early In The Morning	1951	RCA Victor 47-4305
Far Away Places	1956	Jubilee 5245
Good News (Chariot's Comin')	1954	Jubilee 5174
Greatest Feeling In The World, The	1954	Jubilee 5152
Greatest Song I Ever Heard, The	1952	RCA Victor 20-4489/RCA Victor 47-4489 (1952)
Help Me		
Hold Me Closer	1956	Jubilee 5239
How Can I Make You Believe In Me	1948	Manor 1141
How Can You Say I Don't Care'	1950	RCA Victor 47-3967
I Close My Eyes	1955	Jubilee 5183
I Cried		
I Don't Want To Set The World On Fire	1952	RCA Victor 47-4968
I'd Rather Be Safe Than Sorry (also released as by the Sentimentalists)	1946	Manor 1049
I Gambled With Love	1953	Jubilee 5128
I Gotta Go	1956	Jubilee 5239
I Hope	1955	Jubilee 5183
I'll Always Say I Love You (also released as by the Sentimentalists)	1946	Manor 1050
I'll Be Waiting For You (also released as by the Sentimentalists)	1946	Manor 1049
I'll Close My Eyes (also released as by the Sentimentalists)	1946	Manor 1047
I'll See You In My Dreams	1951	RCA Victor 47-4427
I'll Try		
I Married An Angel	1951	RCA Victor 47-4241
I'm Gonna Ride Tillie Tonight	1949	Manor 1154
I'm Just A Fool In Love	1949	RCA Victor 50-0042/RCA Victor 22-0058 (1949)
I'm The Guy	1949	RCA Victor 50-0016
I Sold My Heart To The Junkman	1955	Jubilee 5174
I Understand	1947	Manor 1093
I Understand Just How You Feel	1954	Jubilee 5132/Kay-Ron 1005 (1954)
I Want My Baby To Come Home		
I Wonder	1952	RCA Victor 47-4663
(I Wonder) Where Is My Love	1948	Columbia 30145/Columbia 40132
Japanese Farewell Song (Sayonara)	1956	Jubilee 5255
Just In Case You Change Your Mind	1954	Kay-Ron 1005
Kentucky Babe	1950	RCA Victor 50-0085
L'Amour Toujours L'Amour	1954	Jubilee 5165
Last Round-Up, The	1951	RCA Victor 47-4102
Let Me Go Lover	1955	Jubilee 5174
Let's Give Love Another Chance	1952	RCA Victor 47-4968
Little On The Lonely Side, A	1957	Jubilee 5276
Lonesome	1954	Jubilee 5152
Lonesome For You	1954	Jubilee 5154
Lonesome Road	1950	RCA Victor 50-0042
Love Is Calling		
Marie	1953	Jubilee 5128
Marquita	1957	Jubilee JLP 1039
May That Day Never Come	1951	RCA Victor 50-0131
Mister Sun	1949	Manor 1173
My Buddy	1951	RCA Victor 47-4305
My Muchacha	1949	Manor 1154
My Wild Irish Rose	1954	Jubilee 5135
Never Look Down	1958	Crosby 3
Old Fashioned Love	1950	RCA Victor 50-0085
Our Love	1956	Jubilee 5232
Prisoner's Song, The	1951	RCA Victor 47-4241
Rock 'n' Roll Call	1956	Jubilee 5232
Rock And Egg Roll		
Rose Marie	1957	Jubilee JLP 1039
Save Me A Dream (also released as by the Sentimentalists)	1946	Manor 1047
Sayonara	1956	Jubilee 5255
Say When	1950	RCA Victor 47-3881
Sheik Of Araby, The	1949	Manor 1173
Someday	1948	Manor 1129
Sometime Someplace Somehow	1947	Manor 1077
Starved For Love	1958	Crosby 4
Sugar Lump	1954	Jubilee 5132
Take My Lonely Heart	1948	Columbia

Song	Year	Label
Tell Me Why	1951	RCA Victor 47-4427
There Goes My Heart	1950	RCA Victor 50-0072
They Don't Understand	1952	RCA Victor 47-4828
Three Little Chickens	1955	Jubilee 5212
Time Out For Tears	1955	Jubilee 5200
Tired Of Waitin'	1955	Jubilee 5200
Too Many Times (also released as by the Sentimentalists)	1946	Manor 1050
True Love		
Twinkle Eyes	1958	Crosby 4
Water Boy	1953	RCA Victor 47-5532
Where Is My Love	1947	Manor 1077
Why Did You Do This To Me'	1952	RCA Victor 47-4828
Wishing You Were Here Tonight	1951	RCA Victor 47-4102
Wrapped Up In A Dream	1947	Manor 1083
Yellow Moon Sailing By, A		
You Are My Love	1955	Jubilee 5218
You Don't Love Me No More		Previously unreleased
You're An Angel		Previously unreleased - demo
You're Heartless	1949	RCA Victor 50-0008
You're My Love	1950	Arco 1246
Four Tunes (with Betty Harris)		
Chillicothe, Ohio	1947	Manor 1087
Four Tunes (with Juanita Hall)		
I'm In The Mood For Love	1950	RCA Victor 20-3633/RCA Victor 47-3149 (1950)
Old Bojangles Is Gone	1950	RCA Victor 20-3633/RCA Victor 47-3149 (1950)
Four Tunes (with Savannah Churchill)		
All Of Me	1949	Manor 1168
How Could I Know	1948	Manor 1152
I Don't Believe In Tomorrow	1951	RCA Victor 47-4280
I'll Never Be Free	1949	Arco 1202
I'll Never Belong To Anyone Else	1948	Manor 1142A
Is It Too Late	1947	Manor 1093A
(It's No) Sin	1951	RCA Victor 47-4280
It's Raining Down In Sunshine Lane	1948	Manor 1152A
I Want To Cry	1948	Manor 1129A/Arco 1220 (1950)
		30145/Columbia 40133
Little Jane	1948	Manor 1123
My Last Affair	1949	RCA Victor 50-0016
Tell Me So	1948	Manor 1123
Time Out For Tears	1948	Manor 1116/Arco 1257 (1950)
Would You Hurt Me Now	1949	Manor 1168A
Four Tunes, Pat Best & the		
Karen Lynn	1949	Manor 1195
Someday	1949	Manor 1195
Four Tunes, Savannah Churchill & the		
Best Of Friends, The	1948	Columbia 30146
Daddy Daddy	1950	Arco 1222
Don't Cry Darling	1950	Arco 1236
Don't Try To Explain	1949	Manor 1180/Arco 1229 (1950)
Foolishly Yours	1946	Manor 1046/Arco 1253 (1950)
In Spite Of Everything You Do	1951	RCA 47-4448
I Want To Be Loved	1946	Manor 1046/Arco 1253 (1950)/Kay-Ron 1000 (1954)
My Baby-Kin	1950	Arco 1220
Savannah Sings The Blues	1949	Manor 1180/Arco 1229 (1950)/Kay-Ron 1000 (1954)
Things You Do To Me, The	1948	Columbia 30146
Four Vagabonds (with Memphis Slim)		
Mother Earth	1950	Premium 867
Four Vagabonds		
Ask Anyone Who Knows	1947	Apollo 1060
Big Fat Mama	1942	PMS 076336-Standard X-126
Cabin In The Sky	1943	D3MM-2227-Standard X-132 (Radio Transcription)
Can't Get Stuff In Your Cuff	1943	D3MM-2086-Standard X-128 (Radio Transcription)
Choo-Choo	1947	Apollo 1075
Comin' In On A Wing And A Prayer	1943	Bluebird 30-0815
Dinah		
Don't Get Around Much Anymore	1943	D3MM-2086-Standard X-128 (Radio Transcription)
Do You Know What It Means To Miss New Orleans	1946	Apollo 1039
Dreams Are A Dime A Dozen	1946	Apollo 1055
Duke Of Dubuque, The	1942	Bluebird 11519
Four Buddies	1943	D3NN-2198-Standard X-131

100 Years of Harmony: 1850 to 1950

Title	Year	Label/Number
Freckle Song, The	1946	Apollo 1057
G. I. Wish, A	1945	RCA 20-1677
Gang That Sang Heart Of My Heart, The	1947	Apollo 1076
Hasta Luego	1942	PMS 2035-Standard X-127 (Radio Transcription)
Hey Good Lookin'	1943	D3MM-2086-Standard X-128 (Radio Transcription)
Hip Hip Hooray	1942	PMS 2034-Standard X-127 (Radio Transcription)
Hit That Jive, Jack	1943	D3MM-2227-Standard X-132 (Radio Transcription)
Hoe Cake, Hominy And Sassafras Tea	1946	Apollo 1030
I Can't Make Up My Mind	1946	Atlas 111
I Don't Want Anybody	1943	D3NN-2198-Standard X-131 (Radio Transcription)
If I Were You	1945	RCA 20-1677
I Had The Craziest Dream	1943	Bluebird 30-0810
I Had The Craziest Dream	1943	PMS 076336-Standard X-126 (Radio Transcription)
I Lost My Sugar In Salt Lake City	1942	PMS 2035-Standard X-127 (Radio Transcription)
I'm Thinking Tonight Of My Blue Eyes	1943	D3MM-2290-Standard X-134 (Radio Transcription)
It Can't Be Wrong	1943	Bluebird 30-0815
I Wonder Who's Kissing Her Now'	1946	Apollo 1055
Juke Box Saturday Night	1942	PMS 076336-Standard X-126 (Radio Transcription)
Jumpin' With A G.I. Gal	1943	D3NN-2198-Standard X-131 (Radio Transcription)
Just A Dream Of You	1943	D3MM-2227-Standard X-132 (Radio Transcription)
Kentucky Babe	1946	Apollo 1030
Lazy Countryside	1947	Apollo 1075/Lloyds 102 (1953)
Massachusetts	1942	PMS 076336-Standard X-126 (Radio Transcription)
Mighty Hard To Go Thru Life Alone	1949	Miracle 141
Moonlight Mood	1942	PMS 2035-Standard X-127 (Radio Transcription)
Move It Over	1942	PMS 076335-Standard X-126 (Radio Transcription)
Murder He Says	1943	D3NN-2198-Standard X-131 (Radio Transcription)
My Heart Cries	1949	Miracle 141
Object Of My Affection, The	1951	Mercury 5759
Oh My Achin' Heart	1947	Apollo 1060
Oh, What A Polka	1946	Atlas 111
Old Man Romance	1943	D3MM-2227-Standard X-132 (Radio Transcription)
On The Alamo	1943	D3MM-2227-Standard X-132 (Radio Transcription)
P. S. I Love You	1946	Apollo 1057/Lloyds 102 (1953)
Pleasure's All Mine, The	1946	Apollo 1039
Rose Ann Of Charing Cross	1943	Bluebird 30-0811
Rosie The Riveter	1943	Bluebird 30-0810
Rosie The Riveter	1943	PMS 076335-Standard X-126 (Radio Transcription)
Sharp As A Tack	1943	D3MM-2086-Standard X-128 (Radio Transcription)
Sho 'Nuff	1943	D3MM-2290-Standard X-134 (Radio Transcription)
Sing Baby Sing		VGOR
Slender Tender And Tall	1942	PMS 2034-Standard X-127 (Radio Transcription)
Slow And Easy	1942	Bluebird 11519
Sorry That We Say Goodbye	1949	

Steam Is On The Beam	1942	PMS 076335-Standard X-126 (Radio Transcription)	In The Blue Of The Evening	1943	D3MM-2252-Standard X-133 (Radio Transcription)
Stick To Your Knittin' Kitten	1943	D3MM-2086-Standard X-128 (Radio Transcription)	Lonesome	1943	D3MM-2252-Standard X-133 (Radio Transcription)
Stop Telling Lies	1942	PMS 076335-Standard X-126 (Radio Transcription)	Lonesome Mama Blues	1943	D3MM-2228-Standard X-132 (Radio Transcription)
Tain't A Fit Night Out	1943	D3MM-2290-Standard X-134 (Radio Transcription)	More Than Anything In The World	1943	D3MM-2252-Standard X-133 (Radio Transcription)
Take It From There	1942	PMS 2034-Standard X-127 (Radio Transcription)	On Time	1943	D3MM-2228-Standard X-132 (Radio Transcription)
Taking My Chance With You	1946	Mercury 2050			
Ten Little Soldiers (On A Ten Day Leave)	1943	Bluebird 30-0811	Right Kind Of Love, The	1943	D3MM-2228-Standard X-132 (Radio Transcription)
That Old Gang Of Mine	1947	Apollo 1076			
There Are Such Things	1942	PMS 076335-Standard X-126 (Radio Transcription)	St. Louis Blues	1943	D3MM-2252-Standard X-133 (Radio Transcription)
There's A Ray Of Sunshine	1943	D3NN-2198-Standard X-131 (Radio Transcription)	You'll Never Know	1943	D3MM-2228-Standard X-132 (Radio Transcription)
Thru The Darkness	1943	D3MM-2290-Standard X-134 (Radio Transcription)			

Four Vagabonds (with Patti Clayton)

			Can't Get Out Of This Mood	1942	PMS 2034-Standard X-127 (Radio Transcription)
When The Old Gang's Back On The Corner	1946	Mercury 2050	Could It Be You'	1943	D3MM-2085-Standard X-128 (Radio Transcription)
When Will I See You Again	1949				
Yeah Man	1942	PMS 076336-Standard X-126 (Radio Transcription)	Hit The Road To Dreamland	1943	D3MM-2085-Standard X-128 (Radio Transcription)
You Linger Near	1943	D3MM-2290-Standard X-134 (Radio Transcription)	It Can't Be Wrong	1943	D3MM-2085-Standard X-128 (Radio Transcription)

Four Vagabonds (with Janette)

Between The Devil And The Deep Blue Sea	1943	D3MM-2252-Standard X-133 (Radio Transcription)	I've Heard That Song Before	1942	PMS 2035-Standard X-127 (Radio Transcription)
I Never Mention Your Name	1943	D3MM-2228-Standard X-132 (Radio Transcription)	Saving Myself For Bill	1943	D3MM-2085-Standard X-128 (Radio Transcription)

Three Dreams	1942	PMS 2034-Standard X-127 (Radio Transcription)
Why Don't You Fall In Love With Me	1942	PMS 2035-Standard X-127 (Radio Transcription)
You'd Be So Nice To Come Home To	1942	PMS 2035-Standard X-127 (Radio Transcription)

Four Wanderers
Animals Coming In	1929	Victor 23370
Farmer's Life For Me	1929	Victor V-38540
Fault's In Me, The	1929	Victor 23370
I Ain't Got Nothin' To Lose	1929	Victor V-38533
In My Father's House	1929	Victor 38545
Make A Country Bird Fly Wild	1929	Victor V-38107
Preaching Of The Elders	1929	Victor 38545
Street Urchin	1929	Victor 38540
You'se My Lady Love	1929	Victor V-38533

Four Wanderers (with Fats Waller & his Buddies)
I Need Someone Like You	1929	Victor V-38086
Lookin' Good But Feelin' Bad	1929	Victor V-38086

Foursome, Dick Powell with the
Good Fellows Medley	1939	Decca 2760/
I Like Mountain Music	1939	Decca 2655/Decca F 7307
Jingle Bells	1939	Decca 2760/Decca F 7307
(They Would Wind Him Up) And He Would Whistle	1939	Decca 2655/Decca F 7413

Foursome, Jack Teagarden & the
On Revival Day, Part 1	1930	Brunswick A 9008
On Revival Day, Part 2	1930	Brunswick A 9008

Foursome, June Arthur & the
Doin' What Comes Natur'lly		Black & White 774

Foursome, Shirley Ross & the
Mine	1939	Brunswick 02990/Decca 2878
That Certain Feeling	1939	Decca 2878

Foursome, The
Bidin' My Time	1930	Brunswick 4996/Decca 2880 (1939)
Blue	1937	Decca 1867
Bungalow, A Piccolo, And You, A	1932	Columbia 2709-D
Chinatown, My Chinatown	1937	Decca 1595
Honey's Lovin' Arms	1937	Decca 1867
I Guess I'll Have To Change My Plan (The Blue Pajamas Song)	1932	Columbia 2709-D
I'm Telling The Birds, I'm Telling The Bees How I Love You	1926	Columbia 828-D/Columbia 4323
In Ole Oklahoma	1938	Brunswick 02716/Decca 2014/Decca 25296
It's The Gypsy In Me	1934	Victor 24817
My Honey's Lovin' Arms	1938	Decca 1867
My Pretty Girl	1946	Victor 20-2023
Nobody's Sweetheart	1937	Decca 1480
Oh, Lady Be Good	1939	Decca 2880
Ragtime Cowboy Joe	1938	Brunswick 02716/Decca 2014/Decca 25296
Sweet Georgia Brown	1937	Decca 1595
Sweet Potato Swing	1937	Decca 1480
Take In The Sun, Hang Out The Moon	1926	Columbia 828-D
There Ain't Not Maybe In My Baby's Eyes	1926	Columbia 839-D
There'll Be Some Changes Made	1938	Decca 1529
Walkin' My Baby Back Home	1930	Brunswick 4996
When That Midnight Choo Choo Leaves For Alabam	1938	Decca 1529

Foursome, The (as Kenny Sargent & the Boresome Foursome)
Don't Do It, Darling	1942	Decca 18479

Foursome, The (as the Kahn-A-Sirs Vocal Trio)
Fit As A Fiddle	1932	Columbia 2726D
Sheltered By The Stars, Cradled By The Moon	1930	Columbia 2696D
You've Got Me In The Palm Of Your Hand	1930	Columbia 2695-D

Foursome, The (assisting Bing Crosby with John Scott Trotter's Frying Pan Five)
Alla En El Rancho Grande (My Ranch)	1939	Brunswick 1671/Brunswick 02873/Decca 2494 (1939)/Decca 23914 (1947)/Decca Y 5384
Down By The Old Mill Stream	1939	Brunswick 1635/Brunswick 02807/Decca 2447/Decca Y 5369/Decca 25492
Ida Sweet As Apple Cider	1939	Brunswick 02890/Brunswick 05273/Decca 2494/Decca 25492/Decca Y 5384
Poor Old Rover	1939	Brunswick 02873/Decca 2385/Decca Y 5362
Sweet Potato Piper	1939	Brunswick 02974/Decca 2999/Decca Y

Title	Year	Label/Number
When The Bloom Is On The Sage (Round Up Time In Texas)	1938	5462/Decca 11030 Brunswick 02809//Decca 2237/Decca 25000/Decca Y 5342
Foursome, The (with Dick Powell)		
Eyes Of Texas Are Upon You, The	1938	Decca 2013/Decca 25248
In My Little Red Book	1938	Decca 1782/Decca F 6694
On, Wisconsin!	1938	Decca 2013/Decca 25248
Rambling Wreck From Georgia Tech (Georgia Institute Of Technology)	1938	Decca 2025/Brunswick 03994
Stein Song (University Of Maine)	1938	Decca 2024/ Decca F 7097
Victory March (University Of Notre Dame)	1938	Decca 2025/Brunswick 03994
We're Loyal To You, Illinois	1938	Decca 2024
Foursome, The (with Frances Langford)		
Dream Girl Of Pi K A	1937	Decca 1454
Little Fraternity Pin	1937	Decca 1454/Brunswick A 81406
Frank Luther Trio		
Buck Jones Rangers Song	1932	Elektradisk 1903
Going Back To The One I Love	1932	Victor 23741
I'll Meet You In Loveland	1932	Victor 23744
I'm Laughin'	1934	Melotone M 12989
I Wouldn't Trade The Silver In My Mother's Hair	1932	Victor 23741
Just Around The Bend	1932	Victor 23740
My Ivy-Coloured Cabin Home	1932	Victor 23740
Old River Valley	1932	Bluebird 1823/Bluebird B-5009/Elektradisk 1903/Sunrise S-3109
She's 'Way Up Thar & Broadway's Gone Hill-Billy	1934	Melotone M 12989
Silver-Haired Mother	1932	Victor 23744
When The Leaves Turn Red And Fall	1932	Elektradisk 1918
Freeman Quartet		
All Praise Our King	1930	Vocalion 5410
Fly Away And Sing	1929	Vocalion 5368
Happy Song Of Praise	1930	Vocalion 5416
I'll Ride On The Clouds With My Lord	1929	Vocalion 5376
I'm Only On A Visit Here	1928	Vocalion 5289
I'm On The Right Side Now	1930	Vocalion 5429
It's Just Like Heaven	1930	Vocalion 5461
I Want My Life To Testify	1929	Vocalion 5357
Jesus Knows How	1928	Vocalion 5275
King I Love, The	1929	Vocalion 5368
Living For Jesus	1930	Vocalion 5400
Master Of The Storm	1930	Vocalion 5429
My Glorious Savior	1930	Vocalion 5449
My Troubles Will Be Over	1928	Vocalion 5289
O Blessed Day	1929	Vocalion 5357
O Lights Of Home	1930	Vocalion 5449
Right Will Win	1929	Vocalion 5376
Sing Hallelujah And Hosanna	1930	Vocalion 5400
Walking With My Savior	1928	Vocalion 5316
We Shall Reach Home	1930	Vocalion 5461
With Joy We Sing	1928	Vocalion 5275
Freshmen		
Double Trouble	1935	Victor 25105
I'm The Fellow Who Loves You (with Al Bowlly)	1935	Victor 25190
Let's Swing It	1935	Victor 25070
Let Yourself Go (with Al Bowlly)	1935	Victor 25241
Life Begins At Sweet Sixteen	1935	Victor 25190
Top Hat	1935	Victor 25094
We Saw The Sea	1935	Victor 25240
Friendship Quartet		
Abide With Me	1928	Okeh 45233
Great Judgement Morning	1928	Okeh 45233
I Surrender All	1928	Okeh 45204
Jesus Savior Pilot Me	1928	Okeh 45265
Lead Me Gently Home, Father	1928	Okeh 45204
Lead Me Savior	1928	Okeh 45265
Frohne Sisters		
Singin' In The Rain	1929	Victor 22057
Funnyboners		
Am I Wasting My Time'	1932	Victor 24042
Because I Worship You	1932	Victor 22931
Can't We Talk It Over'	1932	Victor 22931
If I Could Call You Sweetheart	1932	Victor 24048
I Send My Love With These Roses	1932	Victor 24043
Laffin' At The Funnies	1932	Victor 22934
My Heart's At Ease	1932	Victor 24073
Three Guesses	1932	Victor 24043
Till The Shadows Retire	1932	Victor 24074
Winnie The Wailer	1932	Victor 22934
Ganus Brothers Quartet		
Have A Sunny Smile	1928	Columbia 15390-D
Jesus Knows The Way	1928	Vocalion 5271
Just A Thought Of Mother	1928	Vocalion 5312
Rejoice In God	1928	Columbia 15390-D
Row Us Over The Tide	1928	Vocalion 5312
Sometime We'll Say Goodbye	1928	Columbia 15331-D
Wondrous Love	1928	Columbia 15331-D
Garland Brothers and Grinstead		
Beautiful	1928	Columbia 15679-D

Just Over The River	1928	Columbia 15679-D
Garland's Negro Quintet		
Darkies Jubilee	1924	Vox 4166
Swanee River/I Got A Robe	1924	Vox 4166
Gates, Lucy & Quartet		
Chiming Bells Of Long Ago	1922	Columbia A-3749
Gates, Lucy & the Stellar Quartet		
Blue Danube Waltz	1917	Columbia A-5948
Juanita	1917	Columbia A-5960
Gates, The (Golden Gate Quartet)		
I'm Just A Dreamer	1948	Columbia 30149/Columbia 40131 (1948)
She's Gonna Ruin You, Buddy	1948	Columbia 30149/Columbia 40131 (1948)
Gentry Family Quartet		
Jog Along, Boys	1928	Victor 40013
You Can't Make A Monkey Out Of Me	1928	Victor 40013
Georgia Sacred Singers		
Lord I Don' Care Where They Bury My Body	1927	Broadway 5047
Moanin' In The Land Will Soon Be Over	1929	Broadway 5049/Herwin 92037
Georgia Sacred Singers (Norfolk Jubilee Quartet)		
Daniel In The Lion's Den	1927	Broadway 5051
He Just Hung His Head And Died	1927	Broadway 5047/Herwin 93025
His Eye Is On The Sparrow	1927	Broadway 5048/Herwin 93028
I'm Going Through	1927	Paramount 12749
I'm Nearer My Home	1927	Herwin 93026
I Want To Cross Over To See The Other Side	1926	Herwin 93026
I Wouldn't Mind Dying If Dying Was All	1927	Broadway 5048/Herwin 93028
Lord, I Don't Care Where They Bury My Body	1927	Broadway 5047/Herwin 93025
When The Moon Goes Down	1927	Broadway 5049/Herwin 92037
Gibson Sisters		
I Wish I Was In Dixie	1927	Champion 15328
Giersdorf Sisters		
Blue Skies	1927	Columbia 878-D
Chant Of The Weed	1934	Victor 36161
In A Little Spanish Town	1927	Columbia 878-D
Revenge With Music - Part 1	1934	Victor 36142
Revenge With Music - Part 2	1934	Victor 36142
Rosy Cheeks	1927	Columbia 1008-D
Rumba Fantasy	1934	Victor 36161
Swanee River Trail	1927	Columbia 1008-D
Ginger Snaps		
Gang That Sang Heart Of My Heart, The	1945	RCA Victor 20-1738
Grandfather's Clock	1945	University 510
I Left My Heart In Mississippi	1946	RCA Victor 20-1960
Juke Box Joe	1945	RCA Victor 20-1738
Low Down River Blues	1945	University 510
Muddy Waters	1944	University 509
Shrimp Man, The	1945	RCA Victor 20-1735
There's A Big Rock In The Road	1947	RCA Victor 20-2170
Tico Tico	1945	RCA Victor 20-1735
Too Many Irons In The Fire	1946	RCA Victor 20-1960
Turnpike Turn	1947	RCA Victor 20-2170
You've Got My Heart	1944	University 509
Girl Friends		
Lila	1928	Columbia 1489-D
Waitin' For Katy	1928	Columbia 1489-D
Girl Friends, The (as Clare Hanlon & the Three Waring Girls)		
Elisabeth	1931	Victor 22655
Girl Friends, The (as The Three Waring Girls)		
Dancing In The Dark	1932	Victor 22708/Victor 25080
High And Low	1932	Victor 22708
Let's Have Another Cup O' Coffee (with Chick Bullock)	1932	Victor 22936
Soft Lights And Sweet Music	1932	Victor 22936
Girl Friends, The (Three)		
Dancing Dominoes	1929	Victor 22268
Good For You, Bad For Me	1930	Victor 22326
I Found A Million-Dollar Baby (In A Five And Ten Cent Store) (with Clare Hanlon)	1932	Victor 22706
I'm Only Guessin'	1931	Victor 22900
It Seems To Be Spring (It Must Be Spring)	1930	Victor 22470
Love For Sate	1930	Victor 22598
Piccolo Pete	1929	
Picnic For Two, A (with Nelson Keller & Clare Hanlon)	1932	Victor/Electrola EG 26797
Ramona	1928	Columbia 1387-D

Sing A Little Jingle	1931	Victor/Electrola EG 24686
Thank Your Father (with Wilbert Morgan)	1930	Victor 22326
There Must Be A Silver Lining	1928	Columbia 1387-D
Wasn't It Beautiful While It Lasted' (with Stuart Churchill)	1930	Victor 22325
Well! Well! Well!	1932	Victor 24186/Electrola EG 27687
Where Have You Been'	1930	Victor 22598

Girl Friends, The Three & Clare Hanlon

Little White Lies (Mentiras)	1930	Victor 22492

Girl Friends, The Three & Stuart Churchill

(Across The Breakfast Table) Looking At You	1930	Victor 22340
So Beats My Heart For You	1930	Victor 22486
Tea For Two	1930	Victor 22292/Electrola EG 1596

Girl Friends, The Three & Tom Waring

Let Me Sing And I'm Happy	1929	Victor 22340
My Sweeter Than Sweet	1929	

Girl Friends, The Three & Wilbert Morgan

Thank Your Father	1930	Victor 22326

Girls (Kate Smith & the)

There's A Gold Mine In The Sky	1937	Victor 25752

Girls Of The Golden West

By The Grave Of Nobody's Darling	1938	Conqueror 9009
Cowboy's Love Call	1938	Conqueror 9114
I Love Her Just The Same	1938	Conqueror 9114
I Want To Be A Real Cowboy's Girl	1938	Conqueror 9010
Oh Darlin' You're Breakin' My Heart	1938	Conqueror 8998
Only One Step More	1938	Conqueror 8997
On The Sunny Side Of The Rockies	1938	Conqueror 9009
Roamin' In The Gloamin'	1938	Conqueror 9115
Roundup In Cheyenne, The	1938	Conqueror 9010
Texas Moon	1938	Conqueror 9115
There's A Silver Moon On The Golden Gate	1938	Conqueror 8998
Will There Be Any Yodeling In Heaven'	1938	Conqueror 8997

Gluck, Alma (with the Orpheus Quartet)

Aloha Oe (Farewell To Thee) (one-sided)	1917	Victrola 74534
Lane, The	1918	Victrola 64809
Little Old Log Cabin, The	1918	Victrola 64809

Gold Medal Four

Can't Yo' Heah Me Callin'	1927	Champion 15289
Gypsy Love Song	1927	Champion 15327
Indiana	1927	Champion 15351
Love's Old Sweet Song	1927	Champion 15309
Memories	1927	Champion 15309
Old Black Joe	1927	Champion 15289

Golden Bell Quartet

Low Down Chariot	1946	RCA Victor 20-1939
Who's That Hammerin'	1946	RCA Victor 20-1939

Golden Crown Quartet

Scandalize My Name	1929	Okeh 8739
Sign Of Judgment, The	1929	Okeh 8739

Golden Echo Quartet

Golden Slippers	1927	Columbia 14228-D
Good News - The Chariot's Coming	1927	Columbia 14228-D
Noah And The Ark	1945	De Luxe 1005
Study War No Mo'	1945	De Luxe 1005
This World Is Not My Home	1930	Columbia 14572-D
Witness	1930	Columbia 14572-D

Golden Gate Jubilee Quartet

Alone	1939	Bluebird 8286/Montgomery Ward 8774
Anyhow	1941	Okeh 6238/Columbia 37477 (1947)/Columbia 30044 (1948)
Bedside Of A Neighbor	1937	Bluebird 7278/RCA Victor 20-3308 (1948)/Montgomery Ward 7441
Behold The Bridegroom Cometh	1937	Bluebird 7154/Victor 20-3308 (1948)/Montgomery Ward 7440
Bonnett	1937	
Born Ten Thousand Years Ago	1937	Bluebird 7205
Carolina In The Morning	1938	Bluebird 7415
Change Partners	1939	Bluebird B 10154
Cheer The Weary Traveler	1939	Bluebird 8019/Montgomery Ward 7867
Daniel Saw The Stone	1941	Okeh 6204
Dese Bones Gonna Rise Again	1939	Bluebird 8123/Montgomery Ward 7869
Dipsy Doodle, The	1938	Bluebird 7415
Dip Your Fingers In The Water	1942	Okeh 6712
Everything Moves By The Grace Of God	1939	Bluebird 8087/Montgomery Ward 7868
Every Time I Feel The Spirit	1939	Bluebird

100 Years of Harmony: 1850 to 1950

Title	Year	Release
Gabriel Blows His Horn	1937	Bluebird B 7126
Golden Gate Gospel Train	1937	Bluebird B 7126/Montgomery Ward 7493
Go Where I Send Thee	1937	Bluebird 7340
He Said He Would Calm The Ocean	1939	Bluebird 8328/Montgomery Ward 8776
Hide Me In Thy Bosom	1940	Bluebird 8362/Montgomery Ward 8778
If I Had My Way	1939	Bluebird 8306/Montgomery Ward 8775
I Heard Zion Moan	1938	Bluebird B 7962/Montgomery Ward 7865
I Looked Down The Road And I Wondered	1940	Bluebird 8348/Montgomery Ward 8777
I'm A Pilgrim	1940	Bluebird 8362/Montgomery Ward 8778
I've Found A Wonderful Savior	1937	Bluebird B 7278/Montgomery Ward 7441
I Was Brave	1938	Bluebird 7513/Montgomery Ward 7495/Bluebird 7564
Job	1937	Bluebird 7376/Victor 27323
John The Revelator	1938	Bluebird 7631/Victor 27324 (1941)/Montgomery Ward 7912
Jonah In The Whale	1937	Bluebird 7154/Victor 27322/Montgomery Ward 7440
Lead Me On And On	1938	Bluebird 7617/Montgomery Ward 7494 (1938)
Let That Liar Alone (a cappella)	1938	Bluebird B 7835
Lis'n To The Lambs	1939	Bluebird 8123/Montgomery Ward 7869
Lord, Am I Born To Die	1939	Bluebird 7994/Montgomery Ward 7866
Massa's In The Cold, Cold Ground	1937	Bluebird 7264
Motherless Child	1938	Bluebird B 7463/Montgomery Ward 7496
My Lord Is Waiting	1938	Bluebird B 7804/Montgomery Ward 7596
My Prayer	1940	Bluebird 10569
Noah	1939	Bluebird 7962/Bluebird 8160 (1939)/Montgomery Ward 7865
Old Man River	1939	Bluebird 8190
Ol' Man Mose	1939	Bluebird B 10154
Our Father	1939	
Packing Up- Getting Ready To Go	1939	Bluebird 8019/Montgomery Ward 7867
Preacher And The Bear (That Ol' Time Religion), The	1937	Bluebird 7205/Victor 27322 (1941)
Precious Lord	1939	Bluebird 8190
Put On Your Old Grey Bonnet	1937	Bluebird 7264
Rock My Soul	1938	Bluebird B 7804/Montgomery Ward 7596
Run On	1942	Okeh 6713
Samson And Delilah	1938	Bluebird 7513/Montgomery Ward 7495
Stand In The Test In Judgment	1938	Bluebird B 7376
Stormy Weather	1939	Bluebird 8579/Montgomery Ward 8779
Swanee River	1938	Bluebird 7676
Sweet Adeline	1938	Bluebird 7676
Take Your Burdens To God	1938	Bluebird 7617/Montgomery Ward 7494 (1938)
This World Is In A Bad Condition	1939	Bluebird 8160
Timber	1939	Bluebird 8620/Montgomery Ward 8781
Time's Winding Up	1941	Okeh 6238/Columbia 37477 (1947)/Columbia 30044 (1948)
To The Rock	1938	Bluebird B 7835
Travelin' Shoes	1938	Bluebird B 7463/RCA 20-2073 (1946)/Montgomery Ward 7496
Troubles Of The World	1939	Bluebird

Song	Year	Label
Way Down In Egypt's Land	1939	Bluebird 8087/Montgomery Ward 7868
What Are They Doing In Heaven Today'	1939	Bluebird 8306/Montgomery Ward 8775
What A Time	1939	Bluebird 7994/Montgomery Ward 7866
What's New'	1940	Bluebird 10569
When The Saints Go Marching In	1938	Bluebird B 7897/Montgomery Ward 7864
When They Ring The Golden Bells	1938	Bluebird B 7897/Montgomery Ward 7864
Won't There Be One Happy Time	1937	Bluebird 7340
You'd Better Mind	1940	Bluebird 8348/Montgomery Ward 8777/Bluebird 8548 (1940)

Golden Gate Quartet

Song	Year	Label
Abdullah	1947	Columbia 30128
Atom And Evil	1946	Columbia 37236
Basin Street Blues		
Blessed Jesus	1950	Mercury 8164
Blind Barnabas	1941	Okeh 6345/Columbia 37476 (1941)/Columbia 37834 (1941)/Columbia 30043 (1948)
Blue Suede Shoes		
Bones, Bones, Bones	1946	Columbia 36937/Sittin' In 2026 (1952)
Broodle-Oo, Broodle-Oo (Said The Pigeon)	1947	Columbia 30128
Brother Bill	1941	
Bye And Bye Little Children	1938	Bluebird 7848/Montgomery Ward 7594 (1938)
C'est Si Bon		
Clopin Clopan		
Comin' In On A Wing And A Prayer	1943	Okeh 6713
Darling Nellie Gray	1940	Bluebird 8565/Montgomery Ward 8783
Devil With The Devil, The	1940	Bluebird 8594/Montgomery Ward 8780
Didn't It Rain	1941	Okeh 6529/Columbia 37475 (1947)/Columbia 30042 (1948)
Didn't Old Pharaoh Get Lost	1942	
Didn't That Man Believe	1950	Mercury 5385
Dock Of The Bay, The		
Douce France		
Do Unto Others	1947	Columbia 30136
Down By The Riverside		
Do You Think I'll Make A Soldier	1941	
End Of My Journey, The		
Et Maintenant	194'	Film Soundtrack
Ezekiel Saw The Wheel	1960	
Fare You Well, Fare You Well	1947	Columbia 30160
For The Rest Of My Life	1960	
Frankie And Johnny		
G.E. FM Radio Commercial	1941	
Gabriel Blows His Horn	1948	RCA 20-2921
General Electric FM Advert	1941	
General Jumped At Dawn, The	1946	Okeh 6741
General Rolls, The	1942	Film Soundtrack
Get On Board	1960	
Glory Hallelujah!		
God Almighty Said	1938	Bluebird 7848/Montgomery Ward 7594 (1938)
God's Gonna Cut You Down	1947	Columbia 37835
Golden Slippers	1960	
Goodbye Mister Froggie	1960	
Good News	1960	
Gospel Train	1941	
Go Where I Send Thee	1947	RCA 20-2134
Great Pretender, The		
Handwriting On The Wall		
He Never Said A Mumblin' Word	1941	Okeh 6529/Columbia 37475 (1947)/Columbia 30042 (1948)
He's My Rock, My Sword, My Shield	1941	
He Walks And He Talks Like No Other		
High, Low And Wide	1947	Columbia 37499
His Eye Is On The Sparrow	1952	Sittin' In 2025
Hit The Road To Dreamland		
Hold The Wind		
Honey Pie		
Hush	1946	Columbia 30136
Hymne A L'Amour		
I Just Telephone Upstairs	1952	Okeh 6897
I Looked Down The Road And I	1948	Victor 20-3159

100 Years of Harmony: 1850 to 1950

Title	Year	Label
Wondered		
I'm On My Way		
I'm So Glad, That Troubles Don't Last Always		
I'm Troubled		
In That Great Getting Up Morning	1941	
Invisible Hands	1955	
I Pitched My Tent	1955	
I Want To Know		
I Will Be Home Again	1946	Okeh 6741/Columbia 37832 (1947)
J'ai Deux Amours		
Jesus Met The Woman At The Well	1949	Mercury 8124
Jezebel	1941	Okeh 6204/Columbia 37835 (1947)/Jubilee
Job	1941	RCA 27323/RCA 20-2134 (1947)
John Saw The Number	1949	Mercury 8142
Jonah	1941	RCA 27322/RCA 20-2073 (1946)
Jonah In The Whale	1941	Bluebird 8620/Montgomery Ward 8781
Joshua Fit De Battle Of Jericho	1946	Columbia 37833/Columbia BF 332
Julius Caesar	1940	Bluebird 8594/Montgomery Ward 8780
Kansas City		Jubilee
King Of Kings, The		Jubilee
La Vie En Rose		
Les Copains D'Abord		
Let That Liar Alone	1938	Montgomery Ward 7595
Let Us Cheer The Weary Traveler		
Listen To The Lambs	1951	Columbia 39216
Little Wheel A Turning In My Heart	1941	
Look Away From Heaven, A	1941	
Look Up!	1949	Mercury 5242
Lord Have Mercy	1950	Mercury 8164
Lord I Am Tired And Want To Go Home	1949	Mercury 8142
Lord I Want To Be A Christian	1951	Mercury 8243
Lord I Want To Walk With Thee	1949	Mercury 8158
Mack The Knife		
Mary Mary	1949	Mercury 8124
Me And Brother Bill		
Mene Mene Tekel	1948	Mercury 8118
Michael		
Midnight Train		
Mister Blue	1959	
Moses Smote The Waters	1946	Columbia 36937
Mother's Love	1952	Sittin' In 2024
My Heart Is An Open Book	1959	
My Lord Is Ridin' All The Time	1941	
My Lord, What A Morning!		
My Walking Stick	1940	Bluebird 8565/Montgomery Ward 8783
Nelly Was A Lady	1941	
Nicodemus	1951	Columbia 39216
Noah (Didn't It Rain)	1941	RCA 27323
Nobody Knows The Trouble I've Seen		
No, No, No		
No Restricted Signs	1946	Columbia 37832
Oh Happy Day		
Oh Why' (Mon Amour Oublie)	1960	
Ol' Dan Tucker	1944	Jubilee
Only You		
On The Sunny Side Of The Street		
On Top Of Old Smokey	1952	Sittin' In 2022
Poor Little Jesus	1960	
Pray For The Lights To Go Out	1947	Columbia 37499
Prendre Un Enfant Par La Main		
Primrose Lane	1959	
Prodigal Son, The	1941	
Pure Religion	1938	Montgomery Ward 7493
Rain Is The Teardrops Of Angels	1952	Okeh 6897
Religion Is Fortune	1949	Mercury 8155
Remember Me	1938	Bluebird 7631
Ride On Moses	1950	Mercury 8162
Ride Up In The Chariot	1941	
Rock My Soul	1948	RCA 20-2921
Roll Jordan, Roll	1960	
Round The Bay Of Mexico		
Round The Great White Throne	1952	Sittin' In 2026
Rudolph, The Red Nose Reindeer	1960	
Saint Louis Blues		
Same Train	1950	Mercury 8162
Samson	1938	Bluebird B 7564/Victor 27324 (1941)
Satisfied	1949	Mercury 8155
See How They Done My Lord	1938	Bluebird 7631/Montgomery Ward 7912
Seven Angels And Seven Trumpets	1951	Mercury 8243
Shadrack	1946	Columbia 37236
Shoo Shoo Baby	1943	
Show Me The Way	1942	
Sittin' In With Mother's Love	1952	Sittin' In 2022

Song	Year	Label
Sometimes I Feel Like A Motherless Child	1958	
Soon, I Will Be Done		
Stalin Wasn't Stallin'	1943	Okeh 6712
Stand In The Test Of Judgment	1948	RCA 20-2797 (1948)
Steal Away	1958	
Steal Away And Pray	1952	Sittin' In 2025
Straighten Up And Fly Right	1943	Argo
Sun Didn't Shine, The	1941	Okeh 6345/Columbia 37476 (1941)/Columbia 30043 (1948)
Swing Down, Chariot	1946	Columbia 37834/Columbia BF 332
Swing Low, Sweet Chariot		
Talkin' Jerusalem To Death	1948	Mercury 8118
There Is No Greater Love	1960	Arco
There's A Man Going Round Taking Names	1950	Mercury 5385
This World Is In A Bad Condition	1948	Victor 20-3159/Victor DJ 588
Toll The Bell Easy Tonight	1941	Columbia 30160
To The Rock	1938	Montgomery Ward 7595
Turn Back Pharaoh's Army	1942	
Valley Of Time, The	1940	Bluebird 8388/Montgomery Ward 8782
Wade In The Water	1946	Columbia 37833
Waillie-Waillie	1960	
Walk In Jerusalem Just Like John	1941	
We'll Stand The Storm	1942	
What Did Jesus Say	1940	Bluebird 8388/Montgomery Ward 8782
When The Saints Go Marching In	1948	RCA Victor 20-2797
White Christmas	1975	
Whoa Babe	1940	Bluebird 8579/Montgomery Ward 8779
Will I Find My Love Today	1949	Mercury 5242
World Outside(Warsaw Concerto), The	1960	
Wrestlin' Jacob	1941	
You Ain't Got Faith (Til You Got Religion)		
You Ain't Got Religion	1949	Mercury 8158
You Better Mind	1952	Sittin' In 2024
You'll Never Walk Alone	1955	
You Scandalized My Name		

Golden Gate Quartet (with Jeri Sullivan & Louis Armstrong)

Song	Year	Label
Song Is Born, A - Part I	1947	Capitol 10172
Song Is Born, A - Part II	1947	Capitol 10172

Golden Gate Quartet, Huddie Ledbetter (Lead Belly) & the

Song	Year	Label
Alabama Bound	1941	RCA 27268
Can't You Line 'Em'	1941	
Didn't Ole John Cross The Water'	1941	
Gray Goose	1941	RCA 27267
Ham And Eggs	1941	RCA 27266
Julianne Johnson	1941	
Midnight Special	1941	RCA 27266
Pick A Bale Of Cotton	1941	RCA 27268
Rock Island Line	1941	
Stew-Ball	1941	RCA 27267
Take This Hammer	1941	
Whoa Back, Buck	1941	
Yellow Gal	1941	

Golden Hour Mixed Quartet

Song	Year	Label
Joy To The World	1927	Okeh 40924
O! Little Town Of Bethlehem	1927	Okeh 40924

Golden Leaf Quartet

Song	Year	Label
Alabama Camp Meeting	1930	Brunswick 7032
Beautiful Lamb	1930	Brunswick 7228
Central Georgia Blues	1930	Brunswick 7150
Ding Dong Bell	1930	Brunswick 7032
Give Me That Old Time Glory	1930	Brunswick 7221
I Sing Because I'm Happy	1930	Brunswick 7221
Let God Use You	1930	Brunswick 7228
Let Me Ride	1930	Brunswick 7169
Send The Angels Down	1930	Brunswick 7169
Shake My Righteous Hand	1930	Brunswick 7176
Sleep Baby Sleep	1930	Brunswick 7150
Soldier On The Battlefield	1930	Brunswick 7176

Golden Leaf Quartette

Song	Year	Label
Every Time I Feel The Spirit	1928	Brunswick 7050
I Wouldn't Mind Dying (But I Gotta Go By Myself)	1928	Brunswick 7050

Golden Light Jubilee Quartet

Song	Year	Label
Sit Down Child	1939	Bluebird 8196
You Better Run	1939	Bluebird 8196

Golden Light Jubilee Singers

Song	Year	Label
I Am In His Care	1939	Bluebird 8049
I Can Tell The World	1939	Bluebird 8212
Take My Hand And Lead Me On	1939	Bluebird 8049
What Are They Doing In Heaven Today'	1939	Bluebird 8212

Goodman Sacred Singers

Song	Year	Label
Do Your Best And Wear A Sunny Smile	1928	Champion 15713
Give The World A Smile	1928	Champion 15612

Glory Land Way	1928	Champion 16100
Glory Now Is Riding In My Soul	1928	Champion 15673
Hallelujah He's Mine	1928	Champion 15813
Happy Band, A	1928	Champion 15813
He'll Tell Us All About It	1928	Champion 15612
I Am Happy With My Savior	1929	Champion 15878
I Am Redeemed At Last	1928	Champion 15547
Keep Holding On	1929	Champion 15773
Love Enough For Me	1927	Champion 15431/Challenge 342 (1927)
Nearing My Long Sought Home	1928	Champion 15673
Oh Declare His Glory	1928	Champion 15504
Riding On The Glory Wave	1928	Champion 15713
Right Will Always Win	1929	Champion 15878
Rocking On The Waves	1928	Champion 15547
Singing On The Journey Home	1928	Champion 16100
That Beautiful Land	1928	Champion 15504
Where We'll Never Grow Old	1929	Champion 15773
Working For The Master	1927	Champion 15330/Challenge 342 (1927)

Goodrich Silvertown Quartet (Rollickers)

Blue Shadows	1928	Columbia 1647-D
Old Pals Are The Best Pals After All	1928	Columbia 1435-D
Ol' Man River	1928	Columbia 1304-D
Pals, Just Pals	1928	Columbia 1647-D
Roam On My Little Gypsy Sweetheart	1927	Columbia 1142-D
There's A Cradle In Carolina	1927	Columbia 1142-D
Thou Swell	1928	Columbia 1294-D
Under The Clover Moon	1928	Columbia 1382-D
Weary River	1929	Columbia 1743-D
Wedding Bells (Are Breaking Up That Old Gang Of Mine)	1929	Columbia 1743-D
Who's Blue Now'	1928	Columbia 1382-D

Gordon Quartet

Beyond The Clouds Is Light	1930	Columbia 15713-D
Walking In The King's Highway	1930	Columbia 15713-D

Gospel Camp Meeting Singers

Come And Go To That Land	1929	Vocalion 1283
Hold Onto His Hand	1929	Vocalion 1283

Gospel Four

Church In The Wildwood	1928	Champion 15568
Since Jesus Came Into My Heart	1928	Champion 15527
World Sees Jesus In You, The	1928	Champion 15527

Gospeleers

Devil's Gonna Get You, The	1941	Decca 7851
I'm Going To Glory	1941	Decca 7851

Gotham Trio

Carolina Rolling Stones	1922	Vocalion 14283B

Gotham's Favorite Quartet

Nearer My God To Thee	1923	Cameo 239
Onward Christian Soldiers	1923	Cameo 239

Gothams Four Notes

Away	1949	Gotham 164
East Side, West Side	1949	Gotham 164

Gounod Mixed Quartet

Home Sweet Home	1922	Okeh 4653

Graham Brothers

Bobby Boy - Part 1	1932	Victor 23664
Bobby Boy - Part 2	1932	Victor 23690
Don't Hang Me In The Morning	1932	Victor 23690
Embers	1932	Victor 23668
Gene, The Fighting Marine	1932	Victor 23664
It Ain't No Fault Of Mine	1932	Victor 23667
Mobiloil Theme Song	1932	
Ninety-Nine Years - Part 1	1932	Victor 23654
Ninety-Nine Years - Part 2	1932	Victor 23654
Spring's Tornado	1932	Victor 23668
Under The Old Umbrella	1932	Victor 23667

Graham Brothers (Grant Trio)

I Hear The Voice Of An Angel	1932	Victor 23657/Victor 23743
Say A Prayer For Mother's Baby	1932	Victor 23657

Grainger's Jubilee Singers, Porter (Porter Grainger's Three Jazz Songsters)

I'm On The Right Road Now	1926	Gennett 2249/Silvertone 3837
Wish I Had In Egypt Land	1926	Gennett 2249/Silvertone 3837

Grainger's Three Jazz Songsters, Porter

Baa-Baa Blues	1926	Buddy 8051/Gennett 3323
Where Did You Get That Hat	1926	Genett 3323
Ground Hog Blues	1926	Gennett 3317
It Makes No Diff'rence To Me	1926	Buddy 8051/Gennett 3317

Grand Central Red Cap Quartet

My Little Dixie Home	1931	Columbia 14621-D
They Kicked The Devil Out Of Heaven	1931	Columbia 14621-D

Great Day New Orleans Singers

Shout On	1929	Okeh 8755
You've Got To Be Modernistic	1929	Okeh 8755

Greater New York Quartette

Blue And The Grey, The	1899	Columbia 9071 (2mincyl)
Every Other Day Will Be Sunday	1899	Columbia
Farmyard Medley	1902	Columbia 9037/Busy Bee 149
Little Alabama Coon	1900	Columbia 9015
My Old Kentucky Home	1902	Columbia 9019
Nearer, My God, To Thee	1900	Columbia 9032
Old Black Joe	1899	Columbia 9050
Old Homestead, The	1899	Columbia 9039

Owl And The Pussy Cat, The	1900	Columbia 31583
Rock Of Ages	1900	Columbia
Steamboat Leaving The Wharf At New Orleans (Steamboat Medley)	1899	Columbia 9041

Green, Madeline & the Boys

Ev'rything Depends On You	1941	Bluebird 11036

Green, Madeline & the Three Varieties

It Had To Be You	1941	Bluebird 11308/Bluebird 30-0825 (1944)

Greene y Singers, Bela Lam & the

Crown Him	1929	Okeh 45407
Glory Bye And Bye	1929	Okeh 45407
If Tonight The World Should End	1929	Okeh 45456
Tell It Again	1929	Okeh 45456

Greene, Gene & Quartet

From Here To Shanghai	1917	Victor 18242

Greensboro Boys Quartet

Sing Me A Song Of The Sunny South	1928	Columbia 15507-D
Sweet Little Girl Of Mine	1928	Columbia 15507-D

Greenville Trio

Bulldog, The	1926	Columbia
Tipperary Moonlight	1926	Columbia

Greenwich Villagers (possibly the Revelers)

Sunset Valley	1923	Brunswick 2387

Grisham's Quartet

My Prayer	1929	Victor 40238 (1929)/Bluebird 5405
Redeeming Star	1929	Victor 40295
Some Day We'll Meet Our Mother	1929	Victor 40238 (1929)/Bluebird 5405
When The Mighty Trumpet Sounds	1929	Victor 40295

Grooveneers

I'm Not That Way Anymore	1941	Decca 7883

Grosso Trio

If Tears Could Bring You Back To Me	1926	Gennett 6002

Grove Quartet (with Sister Sallie Sanders)

Got Right With God	1926	Columbia
I've Gotta Ride To The Tree Of Life	1926	Columbia 14185-D
Shall Our Checks Be Dried'	1926	Columbia

Guardsmen Quartet (with Bing Crosby)

Adeste Fideles	1935	Brunswick 1847/Brunswick 02054/Decca 621/Decca FM 5001/Decca Y 5080/Brunswick 02054
Empty Saddles	1936	Brunswick 022070/Decca 870/Decca 11008/Decca 25346/Decca Y5109
Silent Night, Holy Night	1935	Brunswick 1847/Brunswick 02054/Decca 621/Decca FM 5001/Decca Y 5080/Brunswick 02054

Gulf Coast Minstrels

Darktown Camp Meeting	1923	Columbia 14004-D
I Ain't Skeered Of Work	1923	Columbia 14004-D

Gulf Coast Quartet

Alabama Blues	1923	Columbia 14012-D
Happy Boy Blues	1923	Columbia 14012-D

Hadacol Boys, Elmore Nixon & his

Foolish Love	1950	Sittin' In With 546
It's A Sad Sad World	1950	Sittin' In With 546

Hagan, Cass & his Park Central Hotel Orchestra (with Lewis James, Elliott Shaw, Frank Luther)

Manhattan Mary	1927	Columbia 1138-D

Hagan, Cass & his Park Central Hotel Orchestra (with Lewis James, Elliott Shaw, Franklyn Baur)

Varsity Drag, The	1927	Columbia 4966/Columbia 1114-D

Hall Sisters

Money, Money, Money	1948	Victor 20-2728
Teach Me, Teach Me, Baby	1948	Victor 20-2728

Hall's Quintet, Edmund

Three Little Words	1930	Victor

Hamilton, Edw. & the Orpheus Quartet

Battle Cry Of Freedom, The	1917	Victor 18316

Hamlin Quartet

My Old Kentucky Home	1927	Champion 15351/Challenge 346 (1927)
O Come All Ye Faithful	1927	Champion 15374
Old Oaken Bucket, The	1927	Champion 15433
Silent Night	1927	Champion 15374
When The Roll Is Called Up Yonder	1927	Champion 15330
When You're Gone I Won't Forget	1927	Champion 15433

Hamlin Sacred Quartet

Beautiful Side Of Somewhere	1927	Challenge 338
O, Come, All Ye Faithful	1927	Challenge 337
Rock Of Ages	1927	Challenge 338
Roll Is Called Up Yonder, The	1927	Challenge 337
Tell Mother I'll Be There	1927	Challenge 339

Hammond, Walter & Male Trio

Silver Threads Among The Gold	1920	Brunswick

Hampton Institute Quartet
De Ole Ark A-Moverin' Along	1939	Harmony 234
Ezekiel Saw De Wheel	1939	Harmony 232
Goin' To Shout All Over God's Heaven	1939	Harmony 230
In Bright Mansions Above	1939	Harmony 231
I Want To Be Ready	1939	Harmony 233
I Want To Go To Heaven When I Die	1939	Harmony 234
Little David Play On Your Harp	1939	Harmony 231
Mary And Martha Jes Gone	1939	Harmony 232
Ole Time Religion	1939	Harmony 233
Reign Massa Jesus, Reign	1939	Harmony 230

Hamptones (Beavers)
Rag Mop	1950	Decca 24885

Handy's Sacred Singers
Aframerican Hymn	1929	Paramount 12719
Let's Cheer The Weary Traveler	1929	Paramount 12719

Happy Four
Climbing Up The Golden Stairs	1927	Columbia 15225-D
Come And Dine	1927	Columbia 15225-D
He Knows How	1927	Columbia 15164-D

Happy Home Trio
I Still Believe In You	1926	Harmony 285-H
Just A Little Longer	1926	Harmony 273-H

Happy Trio
Dear Granny	1922	Victor 73608
Veronica	1922	Victor 73608

Hardin Brothers
Don't You Want Me Anymore	1941	Decca 8511
I Miss You So	1941	Decca 8511

Hare, Ernest & Quartet
My Buddy	1922	Brunswick 2320

Harlan, Byron & Quartet
Bobby The Bomber	1918	Columbia A-2587

Harlem Hamfats
You Got The Devil To Pay	1937	Decca 7382

Harlemaires
If You Mean What You Say	1948	Atlantic 856
Oo Dot En Pow	1948	Atlantic unreleased
Pretty Eyes	1948	Atlantic unreleased
Rose Of The Rio Grande	1948	Atlantic 856
Yes, Ma'm	1948	Atlantic unreleased

Harling Mixed Quartet
Nancy Lee	1917	Columbia
Thy Dear Voice	1917	Columbia

Harling Quartet
Comin' Thro' The Rye	1917	Columbia
Midshipmite, The	1917	Columbia

Harmonaires
Deep River	1948	
Dream	1948	
I'll Get Along Somehow	1948	Majestic 2006/Brunswick 5007 (1920) 1242/Varsity 78-LP 6915
Runnin' Wild	1948	Majestic 1242
You Can Depend On Me	1948	

Harmoneers
Weep Below Children	1948	King 4233

Harmonettes
Object Of My Affection, The	1935	Bluebird B-5833
That's A Plenty	1935	Bluebird B-5833

Harmonians
I'll Be Hard To Handle	1933	Columbia 2847-D
My Galveston Gal	1933	Columbia 2840-D
One Alone	1928	Velvet Tone 1654-V

Harmonians Quartet
At The Baby Parade	1933	

Harmonizer Quartet
Christmas Carols Part 2	1927	Harmony 516
I Told Them All About You	1927	Harmony 507
Medley Of Christmas Carols	1927	Harmony 516
Shady Tree, A	1927	Harmony 507

Harmonizers
Adorable	1926	Harmony 200
Baby Your Mother	1927	Harmony 472
Barcelona	1926	Harmony 218
Behind The Clouds	1926	Harmony 139
Blue River	1927	Harmony 448
Breezin' Along With The Breeze	1926	Harmony 218
Bye Bye Blackbird	1926	Harmony 167
Cherie I Love You	1926	Harmony 309
Dixie Vagabond	1927	Harmony 335
Everything's Made For Love	1926	Harmony 317
Give Me A Ukulele	1926	Harmony 290
Honey Bunch	1926	Harmony 167
Hum Your Troubles Away	1926	Harmony 252H
Hush-A-Bye Baby	1928	Harmony 618H
If I Can't Have You (I Want To Be Lonesome - I Want To Be Blue)	1928	Harmony 618H
I Know The Reason Why		Operaphone 21190
I'm Gonna Meet My Sweetie Now	1927	Harmony 419
I'm Looking Over A Four Leaf Clover	1926	Harmony 290
I'm Missin' Mammy's Kissin'	1921	Columbia A-3377
In My Gondola	1926	Harmony 139
I've Got The Girl	1926	Harmony 290
Just A Bird's Eye View Of My Old Kentucky Home	1926	Harmony 252H
Lane In Spain, A	1927	Harmony 419
Mary	1927	Harmony 541
Medley Of Marching Songs	1920	Columbia
My Blue Ridge Mountain Queen	1928	Harmony 576
My Connecticut Girl	1927	Harmony 359

My Mammy	1920	Columbia
My Regular Gal	1927	Harmony 377
Plenty Of Sunshine	1927	Harmony 541
Sa-Lu-Ta	1927	Harmony 423
Side By Side	1927	Harmony 401H
Sometimes I'm Happy	1927	Harmony 448
Sunday	1927	Harmony 335
Take In The Sun And Hang Out The Moon	1926	Harmony 309
Valencia	1926	Harmony 200
When The Red Red Robin Comes Bob Bob Bobbing	1926	Harmony 194
Whisper Song (When The Pussy Willow Whispers To The Catnip), The	1927	Harmony 401H
Ya Gotta Know How To Love	1926	Harmony 194
Yankee Rose	1927	Harmony 377

Harmonizers (as Billy Jones & Male Trio)

Mandy 'N' Me	1921	Brunswick 2168

Harmonizers (Harmonizers Quartet)

Lindy	1921	Brunswick 2058
Something	1921	Brunswick 2061

Harmonizers Quartet (Harmonizers)

Ain't We Got Fun	1921	Brunswick 2114
Aunt Jemima's Jubilee	1920	Vocalion 14152B
Down On The Farm	1921	Brunswick 2114
For Every Boy Who's On The Level (There's A Girl Who's On The Square)	1920	Victor 18709
Gone Are The Days	1920	Vocalion 14123B
Hi Yo	1920	Vocalion 14150A
I Ain't Nobody's Darling	1921	Brunswick 2135
I Lost My Heart To The Meanest Girl In Town	1921	Vocalion 14174A
In The Heart Of Dear Old Italy	1921	Brunswick 2089
I've Got The Blues For My Old Kentucky Home	1920	Vocalion 14131A
I Want To Be The Leader Of The Band	1920	Vocalion 14141A
I Was Born In Michigan	1921	Brunswick 2093
I Wish I Had Been Born In Borneo	1920	Vocalion 14141B
Lindy	1920	Vocalion 14131B
Melon Time In Dixieland	1921	Vocalion 14216A
My Home Town Is A One Horse Town	1921	Brunswick 2058
My Town Is A One Horse Town	1920	Vocalion 14123A
Nightmare Blues	1921	Vocalion 14223B
Pucker Up And Whistle	1921	Brunswick 2093
Quartet Rehearsal, A	1922	Vocalion 14306A
Sally Green (The Village Vamp)	1920	Vocalion 14104A
Scandinavia	1920	Vocalion 14161A/Brunswick 2089 (1921)

Harmonizers, Gladys Rice & the

All Night Long	1920	Columbia

Harmonizers, Harry C. Browne & the

Come Along, Sinners	1920	Columbia
Dar's A Lock On De Chicken Coop Door	1920	Columbia A-3622

Harmony Brothers

Just A Bundle Of Sunshine	1925	Columbia 399-D

Harmony Double Mixed Quartet

Oh Little Town Of Bethlehem	1926	Harmony 274
While Shepherds Watched	1926	Harmony 274

Harmony Four

He's A Wonderful Savior To Me	1929	Okeh 45399
I Have To Raise My Voice In Song	1929	Okeh 45441
I Hold His Hand	1929	Okeh 45441
I'll Know Him	1929	Okeh 45419
I'm Sailing On	1929	Okeh 45399
My Friend Divine	1929	Okeh 45419
Smiles		Edison 3613 (4BA)

Harmony Hounds

Done Got De Blues	1925	Columbia 14119-D
I'm So Glad Trouble Don't Last Always	1926	Columbia
I've Got A Gal And She Ain't No Good	1925	Columbia 14119-D
I've Opened My Soul To You, My Lord	1926	Columbia
That Dog O'Mine	1926	Columbia 14131-D
Up North Blues	1926	Columbia 14131-D

Harmony Kings (possibly the Revelers)

Doan You Cry Ma Honey	1921	Silvertone 2805
Sweet And Low	1920	Silvertone 2805

Harmony Quartet (Ritz Quartet)

Down By The Old Mill Stream	1927	Supertone S 2105
Medley Of Barbershop Ballads	1929	Supertone S 2110
Medley Of Songs Of Old New York	1929	Supertone S 2110
Put On Your Old Grey Bonnet	1927	Supertone S 2105

Harmony Quartet, Charles Hilton & the

Oh Holy Night	1919	Clarion 5119-C/Velvet Tone 1275-V

Harris, Marion & the American Quartet

Maiden's Prayer, The	1917	Victor unissued
Some Sweet Day	1917	Victor unissued

Harris, Wynonnie & the Harlemaires

I Don't Stand A Ghost Of A Chance	1947	Aladdin

Harrison Quartette

Sidewalks Of New York	1928	Gennett 6528

Harrison, Charles & Quartet

Funiculi Funicula	1915	Columbia A-1851

Harrison, Charles & the Broadway Quartet

When Your Boy Comes Back To	1917	Columbia A-2312

You
Harrison, Charles (with Columbia Quartet)
  Take Me Back To The Garden Of Love   1912   Columbia 1141
Harrison, Charles (with Edison Mixed Quartet)
  Tell Mother I'll Be There   Edison 1533 (4BA)
Harrison, James & Quartet
  Cheer Up Liza Jane   1917   Columbia A-2394
Harrison, James F. (with Knickerbocker Quartet)
  Pack Up Your Troubles In Your Old Kit Bag And Smile, Smile, Smile   1917
Harrod's Jubilee Singers
  Hallelu   1925   Paramount 12117
  Jacob's Ladder   1924   Paramount 12116
  Joshua Fought The Battle Of Jericho   1924   Paramount 12116
  Live Humble   1925   Paramount 12117
  Rise And Shine   1925   Paramount 12118
  Way Over Jordan   1925   Paramount 12118
Hart Sisters
  Honey Lou   1922   Columbia A-3606
  Little Red Schoolhouse   1922   Columbia A-3588
  Sleepy Little Village (Where Cotton Grows)   1922   Columbia A-3650
Hart, Charles & Male Trio
  Time After Time   1922   Brunswick 2252
Hart, Charles & the Shannon Four
  What Are You Going To Do To Help The Boys   1918   Victor 18467
Hart, Charles & the Shannon Quartet
  Paul Revere Won't You Ride   1918   Victor 18481
Hartford Quartet
  I Am Going Home   1930   Vocalion 5431
  March Along With Christ   1930   Vocalion 5431
Harvard Glee Club Double Quartette
  Annie Laurie   1911   Columbia A-5318
  Fair Harvard   1911   Columbia
  Football Song Medley   1911   Columbia A-1049
  Hawaiian Love Song   1911   Columbia
  Here's To The Health Of King Charles   1911   Columbia A-1048
  Johnny Harvard & Australia   1911   Columbia A-1048
  Old Friends Medley   1911   Columbia A-5318
  Sparkling Piper Heidsock   1911   Columbia A-1049
  Up The Street   1911   Columbia
Hawaiian Quintet
  Aloha Oe   1913   Victor 18577
  Kuu Home   1913   Victor 18577
Hawaiian Troubadours
  Lei Lani (Wreath Of Heaven)   1928   Banner 7150
Hawkins, Buddy (Keynotes)
  I Shouldn't Love You But I Do
Hayden Quartet
  Almost Persuaded   189'   Berliner 4278
  Christ Arose (Easter Hymn)   Victor Victrola 782
  Where Is My Boy Tonight   1908   Victor 16412
Hayden Quartet (with S. H. Dudley)
  Buck Robin Adair   189'   Berliner 4291
Haydn Quartet
  Adeste Fideles - Come All Ye Faithful   1909   Victor 16197
  At The Chapel   189'   Berliner 4287
  Auld Lang Syne   1899   Berliner 0115N
  Because   1900
  Bedelia   1904
  Beulah Land   1909   Victor 16166
  Blue Bell   1904
  Blue Bell March   1909   Victor 16179
  Bridge, The   1909   Victor 16217
  Bring Back My Bonnie To Me   1908   Victor 16105
  Budweiser's A Friend Of Mine   1907   Victor 5320
  By The Saskatchewan - Pink Lady   1912   Victor 17225
  Christ Arose   1908   Victor 16008
  Christ Receiveth The Sinful Men   1907   Victor 16038
  Come Back To Erin   1909   Victor 16289
  Coon Medley   189'   Berliner 4272
  Cornfield Medley   1909   Victor 16218
  Cross The Great Divide, I'll Wait For You   1914   Victor 17545
  Darling Nellie Gray   1909   Victor 16174
  Dear Old Girl
  Dear Old Yale/Eli Yale   1911   Victor 16713
  Don't Be An Old Maid, Molly   1909   Victor 16360
  Down Where The Silvery Mohawk Flows   1909   Victor 16256
  Down Where The Swanee River Flows   1908   Victor 16165
  Eternal Father, Strong To Save   1910   Victor 16541
  Evening Breeze Is Sighing Home Sweet Home   1909   Victor 16257
  Girl Of My Dreams   1912   Victor 17230
  Glory Song (one-sided)   1905   Victor 4398
  Grandfather's Clock   1909   Victor 16198
  Hail Columbia   1910   Victor 16495
  Hard Times   1908   Victor 16142/Victor 16915 (1911)
  Hat My Father Wore On St. Patrick's Day, The   1909   Victor 16365
  I'll Love You While The Music's Playing   1912   Victor 17124
  I'll Make A Ring Around Rosie   1910   Victor 16498
  I'm Happy When The Band Plays Dixie   1907   Victor 5330
  In Dear Old Georgia   1909   Victor 16220
  In The Evening By The Moonlight   1913   Victor 17305
  In The Good Old Summertime   1908   Victor 16125
  In The Sweet Bye And Bye   1910   Victor 16532
  I'se Going Back To Dixie   1908   Victor 16104

I'se Gwine Back To Dixie		
Jesus Christ Is Risen	1909	Victor 16178
Just A Dream Of You, Dear	1913	Victor 17365
Lady Love	1909	Victor 16366
Last Rose Of Summer	1909	Victor 16213
Lead Kindly Light	1909	Victor 16394
Leaf By Leaf The Roses Fall	1909	Victor 16198
Little Alabama Coon	1898	Berliner 0870Z
Little Annie Rooney	1908	Victor 16078
Man In The Silvery Moon	1911	Victor 16832
Massa's In The Cold, Cold Ground	1909	Victor 16218
Meet Me Where The Lanterns Glow	1910	Victor 16509
Mollie Darling	1911	Victor 16915
My Faith Looks Up To Thee	1900	Berliner 1128N
My Old Kentucky Home		Victor
My Wild Irish Rose	1911	Victor 16741
Nearer My God To Thee	1899	Berliner 0021
Nearer My God To Thee	1911	Victor 16742
New Year's At Old Trinity	1904	
Old Black Joe	189'	Berliner 4294
Old Oaken Bucket, The	1899	Berliner 0023
Old Time Religion	1911	Victor 16743
Only A Message From Home	1911	Victor 16801
Orange And Black	1911	Victor 16873
Owl And The Pussycat	1908	Victor 16105
Put On Your Old Grey Bonnet	1909	Victor 16377
Rain In The Face	1908	Victor 16153
Rest For The Weary	1909	Victor 16261
Robin Adair	1907	Victor 16039
'Round The Campfire	1904	
Sailing	1908	Victor 16014
Sally In Our Alley	1899	
Schoolmates	1910	Victor 16548
Shall We Gather At The River'	1909	Victor 16261
Ship Of My Dreams	1913	Victor 17398
Silent Night, Hallowed Night	1909	Victor 16286
Soldier's Farewell	1907	Victor 16039
Sunbonnet Sue	1910	Victor 16548
Sweet Adeline You're The Flower Of My Heart	1911	Victor 16803
Sweetheart Town	1908	Victor 5624
Take Me Up With You Dearie	1909	Victor 5718/Victor 16769 (1911)
Tell Mother I'll Be There	1910	Victor 16414
Tenting On The Old Camp Ground	1909	Victor 16404
Up Up Up In My Aeroplane	1909	Victor 16340
Vacant Chair, The	1909	Victor 16361
Vesper Service	1909	Victor 16166
Vesper Service (one-sided)		Decca
When I Marry You	1909	Victor 16433
When The Bees Are In The Hive	1909	Victor 16256
When The Flowers Bloom In The Spring	1909	Victor 16318
When The Summer Days Are Gone	1908	Victor 16002
Where Is My Boy Tonight	1909	Victor 16412
Where The Ivy's Clinging	1910	Victor 16478
Where The Southern Roses Grow	1909	Victor 16167
Will There Be Any Stars In My Crown'	1909	Victor 16286
Winter	1911	Victor 5814/Victor 16927
Woman Thou Gavest Me, The	1914	Victor 17544
Yale Boola Song	1911	Victor 16860
You're The Same Old Girl	1913	Victor 17388
Haydn Quartet & Billy Murray		
American Idea - Sullivan	1910	Victor 16664
Haydn Quartet & Corinne Morgan		
So Long Mary	1910	Victor 16549
Haydn Quartet & Harry MacDonough		
When The Old Folks Were Young	1912	Victor 17139
Haydn Quartet & S. Dudley		
My Old Kentucky Home	1898	Berliner 0871X
Old Oaken Bucket, The	1898	Berliner 0873
Haydn Quartet (with S. H. Dudley)		
Cornfield Medley	1899	Berliner 0416N
Farm Yard Medley	1899	Berliner 0422N
Hosanna In The Highest	189'	Berliner 4290
Lead Kindly Light	189'	Berliner 4265Z
Massa's In The Cold, Cold Ground	189'	Berliner 4253Y
Old Folks At Home	189'	Berliner 4251
Soldier's Farewell	189'	Berliner 4292Z
Haydn Quartet with Harry MacDonough		
When The Roll Is Called Up Yonder	1911	Victor 16749
Haydn Quartet with Henry MacDonough		
Teasing	1909	Victor 16179
Haydn Quartet, Rycroft & the		
Doan Ye Cry, Mah Honey	1900	Berliner 01304
Haydn Quartet, S. H. Dudley & the		
Massa's In De Cold, Cold Ground	1899	Berliner 0413
Haymes, Dick & the Song Spinners		
Cradle Song Of The Virgin	1944	Decca 18629
First Noel, The	1944	Decca 18629
Headliners, Cliff Weston & the		
(If I Had) Rhythm In My Nursery Rhymes	1935	Banner 6-02-07/Conqueror 8619/Melotone 6-02-07/Oriole 6-02-07/Perfect 6-02-07
I'm Gonna Clap My Hands	1936	Banner 6-04-04/Melotone 6-04-04/Perfect 6-04-04
I Wanna Woo	1935	Imperial 17055
Music Goes 'Round And Around	1935	Banner 6-02-07/Conqueror

Polly Wolly Doodle	1935	8619/Melotone 6-02-07/Oriole 6-02-07/Perfect 6-02-07 Imperial 17055
Wah-Hoo!	1936	Banner 6-04-04/Melotone 6-04-04/Perfect 6-04-04

Heavenly Gospel Singers

Ain't That Good News	1939	Bluebird 8047
Angels Drooped Their Wings	1936	Bluebird 6650
Cheer The Weary Traveler	1938	Bluebird 7969
Don't You Want That Stone	1937	Bluebird 7301
Ezekiel Saw The Wheel	1938	Bluebird 7590
Forgive Me Lord	1938	Bluebird 7590
Going Back With Jesus	1937	Bluebird 7046
Goin' To Shake My Hand	1937	Bluebird 7177
Go Where I Send Thee	1938	Bluebird 7656
Handwriting On The Wall	1938	Bluebird 7953
Have You Any Time For Jesus'	1936	Bluebird 6650
Have You Got Good Religion	1935	Bluebird 6113
Heavenly Gospel Train	1937	Bluebird 6887
How We Got Over	1938	Bluebird 7907
I Can't Straighten Them	1939	Bluebird 8156
If It Wasn't For The Lord	1938	Bluebird 7486
I Got Heaven On My Mind	1938	Bluebird 7907
I Got My Ticket Ready	1937	Bluebird 6887
I Just Got Over	1937	Bluebird 7254
I'm A Pilgrim And A Stranger	1936	Bluebird 6317
I'm Going To Telephone To Glory	1936	Bluebird 6389
I'm Living Humble	1935	Bluebird 6168
I'm The Light Of The World	1938	Bluebird 7427
Inching Along	1937	Bluebird 7133
I Open My Mouth	1937	Bluebird 7254
It Is God's Love	1938	Bluebird 7537
I've Been Buked	1939	Bluebird 8047
I Want To Be More Like Jesus	1938	Bluebird 7427
Jesus Is Mine	1937	Bluebird 7046
John Wrote A Revelation	1936	Bluebird 6708
Lead Me On	1939	Bluebird 8156
Lord's Prayer, The	1937	Bluebird 7133
Moving Up The King's Highway	1936	Bluebird 6296
My Lord Heard Jerusalem When She Moaned	1936	Bluebird 6708
My Lord Is Writing All The Time	1940	Bluebird 8494
Nobody's Fault But Mine	1939	Bluebird 8077
Old Death	1941	Bluebird 9011
Old Time Religion	1939	Bluebird 8077
Old World's In Bad Condition	1937	Bluebird 7301
On The Battlefield	1936	Bluebird 6527
Prayer Wheel	1936	Bluebird 6296
Precious Lord Take My Hand	1937	Bluebird 6846
Prodigal Son	1935	Bluebird 6168
Rock My Soul	1937	Bluebird 7177
Run On	1941	Bluebird 9011
Singers Oh Jonah	1939	Bluebird 8206
So High I Can't Get Over	1938	Bluebird 7486
Something On My Mind	1935	Bluebird 6113
Somewhere To Lay My Head	1938	Bluebird 7953
Standing By The Bedside	1938	Bluebird 7656
Sun Didn't Shine, The	1936	Bluebird 6317
Time's Windin' Up	1940	Bluebird 8494
Travel This Road	1939	Bluebird 8206
Two Wings	1937	Bluebird 6846
Walk In The Light	1936	Bluebird 6389
Walk With Me	1938	Bluebird 7537
Watery Grave	1936	Bluebird 6427
When The Gate Swings Open	1938	Bluebird 7969
When The Moon Goes Down	1936	Bluebird 6527
You Better Run	1937	Bluebird 6928
You Can Tell The World	1936	Bluebird 6427
You Go And I Go With You	1937	Bluebird 6928

Heidelberg Quintet

Across The Rio Grande	1914	Victor 17599
Boom-Tum-Ta-Ra-Zing-Boom	1913	Victor unissued B-13371
By The Beautiful Sea	1914	Victor 17560
Emmett's Lullaby	1912	Victor 17217
Give Me Your Hand	1913	Victor 17334
Harmony Bay	1914	Victor 17602
In Apple Blossom Time (Down On The Farm)	1913	Victor 17390
In The Heart Of The Kentucky Hills	1913	Victor 17378
I Want To Love You While The Music's Playing	1912	Edison BA 1565/Edison Amberol 1156/Victor 17124 (1912)
My Little Lovin' Sugar Babe	1912	Victor 17236
On A Beautiful Night With A Beautiful Girl (flip is	1912	Victor 17152
Roll Them Cotton Bales	1914	Victor 17633
Tennessee Moon	1912	Victor 17207
That Tinkling Tango Tune	1913	Victor unissued
They're On Their Way To Mexico	1914	Victor 17599
Under The Love Tree	1912	Edison Amberol (4mincyl) 1131/Victor 17082 (1912)
Waiting For The Robert E. Lee	1912	Victor 17141
Way Down South	1912	Edison BA 1531/Victor 17146

Heidelberg Quintet (with Will Oakland)

Floatin' Down The River On The Alabam'	1913	Victor 17360
Give Me Your Hand	1913	Victor 17347
Ragtime Regiment Band	1913	Victor 17360
Teasing Moon	1912	Victor 17365
You're A Great Big Blue-Eyed Baby Doll	1913	Victor 17344

Hemstreet Singers
Come Where My Love Lies Dreaming	1925	Columbia
Love's Old Sweet Song	1925	Columbia

Hendersonville Double Quartet
I Want My Life To Testify	1929	Columbia 15443-D
Onward, Ye Soldiers	1929	Columbia 15443-D

Hendersonville Quartet
Blue Galilee	1929	Victor 40250
Take Time To Be Holy	1929	Victor 40213
That Beautiful Land	1929	Victor 40213
Under His Wings	1929	Victor 40250

Hepcats, Coree Carter & his
Hoy Hoy	1949	Freedom 1516
Rock Awhile	1949	Freedom 1506

Higgins Sisters
Don't You Love Your Daddy Too'	1930	Victor 22318
Have Thine Own Way, Lord	1930	Victor 22312
Nailed To The Cross	1930	Victor 22312
Old-Fashioned Cabin, The	1930	Victor 22318

Highland Lads
My Love She's Just A Lassie	1913	Victor 17408

Highlander Laddies
Farewell Gibraltar	1913	Victor 17408

Hilton, Charles & the Harmony Quartet
Oh Holy Night	1926	Harmony 275

Hipp Cats
It Must Be Jelly ('Cause Jam Don't Shake Like That)	1938	Decca 7518

Hipp Cats (Norris The Troubador)
Chippin' Rock Blues	1938	

Hit Paraders
Ti-Pi-Tin	1942	Victor 27865

Hodgers Quartet
I'll Go Flipping Through The Pearly Gates	1928	Columbia
You Can't Make A Monkey Out Of Me	1928	Columbia

Hollywood Harmony Four
Get Out And Get Under The Moon	1928	Challenge 671
Sunnyside Lane	1928	Challenge 671

Hollywood Harmony Four (Four Aristocrats)
Get Out And Get Under The Moon	1928	Banner 7148

Hollywood Harmony Quartet
Sunnyside Lane	1928	Banner 7148
That's My Weakness Now	1928	Banner 7172
Was It A Dream'	1928	Banner 7150

Hollywood Trio
Cecilia	1925	Sunset 1122
You Told Me To Go	1925	Sunset 1122

Hollywood's Four Blazes (Four Blazers)
As Long As I Live	1946	Lamplighter 103
As Long As You're Mine	1945	Excelsior 112
Big Leg Mama's Fine, The	1945	Excelsior 111
I Never Had A Dream To My Name	1945	Excelsior 110
Let's Do And Say We Didn't	1945	Excelsior 113
Love Will Bloom In Paris This Spring	1945	Excelsior 108
That's A Good Little Old Deal	1945	Excelsior 109

Holy Ghost Sanctified Singers
Jesus Throwed Up The Highway For Me	1930	Brunswick 7148
Sinner I'd Make A Change	1930	Brunswick 7148
Thou Carest Lord For Me	1930	Brunswick 7162
When I Get Inside The Gate	1930	Brunswick 7162

Holy Trinity Quartet
Abide With Me	1923	Cameo 371
Christmas Eve At Grandma's	1923	Cameo 413
Christ The Lord Is Risen	1925	Cameo 689
Church In The Wildwood	1924	Cameo 614
Nearer My God To Thee	1923	Cameo 371
Old Rugged Cross	1925	Cameo 689
Onward Christian Soldiers	1923	Cameo 486
Rock Of Ages	1923	Cameo 486
Tell Mother I'll Be There	1924	Cameo 614
Yuletide Echoes	1923	Cameo 413

Home Town Boys, Anisteen Allen & the
She Lost Her Rebop	1946	King

Homestead Trio
Aloha Sunset Land	1917	Edison DD 80514/Edison BA 3984
Amazon ('River Of Dreams')	1923	Edison DD 51121
Carolina Lullaby	1921	Edison DD 50796/Edison BA 4361
Dixie Lullaby	1919	Edison DD 80521/Edison BA 3962
Dusky Lullaby, A	1918	Edison DD 80469/Edison BA 3684
Granny (You're My Mammy's Mammy)	1921	Edison DD 50915/Edison BA 4488
Hearts	1919	Edison DD 50612
Hush-A-Bye-Bay	1923	Edison DD 80755
Indiana	1917	Edison DD 80334/Edison BA 3249
Just A Baby's Prayer At Twilight (For Her Daddy Over There)	1918	Edison DD 80406/Edison BA 3504
Just An Old Love Song	1923	Edison DD 51119
Keep The Home Fires Burning ('Till The Boys Come Home)	1918	Edison DD 82149/Edison BA

Laddie In Khaki	1918	Edison DD 82149
Little Tin Soldier, The	1921	Edison DD 50770/Edison BA 4567
Memory Isle	1923	Edison DD 51272/Edison BA 4831
Moonlight In Mandalay	1920	Edison DD 50699
Ole Virginny Days	1917	Edison DD 80411/Edison BA 3355
There's A Mother Always Waiting For You At Home, Sweet Home	1921	Edison DD 50860
Thine Eyes So Blue And Tender	1918	Edison
Thinking Of You (I've Grown So Lonesome)	1921	Edison DD 50788/Edison BA 4504
Wandering Home	1921	Edison DD 50773/Edison BA 4313

Homestead Trio (with Elisabeth Spencer)
Two Little Eyes	1923	Edison DD 80754

Homestead Trio (with J. Harold Murray)
Faded Love Letters (Of Mine)	1922	Edison DD 51110

Homestead Trio (with Thomas Chalmers)
Do They Think Of Me At Home'	1921	Edison DD 80677

Homestead Trio (with Walter Scanlan)
Pal Of My Cradle Days	1925	Edison DD 80839

Honey Boys
Vippity Vop

Honey Jumpers, Oscar McLollie &
Be Cool My Heart		
Dig That Crazy Santa Claus	1954	
Fallin In Love With You		
God Gave Us Christmas	1953	
Love Me Tonight		

Honolulu Honeys
Blue Kentucky Moon	1931	Columbia 2545-D
Kiss That You've Forgotten, The	1931	Columbia 2545-D

Hooley, William F. & Quartet
Rolling Stone, The	1911	Victor 16982

Hornsby Novelty Quartet, Dan
Has Anybody Here Seen Kelly'	1928	Columbia 1637-D
Hinky Dinky Dee	1929	Columbia 15444-D
Oh! By Jingo	1928	Columbia 1637-D
Take Me Out To The Ball Game	1929	Columbia 15444-D
Vamp, The	1929	Columbia

Hornsby Trio, Dan
Banquet In Misery Hall, The	1927	Columbia
Can't Yo' Heah Me Callin' Caroline'	1928	Columbia 15381-D
Cubanola Glide	1927	Columbia 1268-D
Dear Old Girl	1927	Columbia 15769-D
Goodbye Alexander	1928	Columbia
I Want A Girl (Just Like The Girl That Married Dear Old Dad)	1928	Columbia 15276-D
Oceana Roll	1928	Columbia
Oh Susannah	1927	Columbia 1268-D
On Mobile Bay	1928	Columbia 15276-D
She Was Bred In Old Kentucky	1928	Columbia 15381-D

Howard Trio
Here Comes Emily Brown	1930	Victor 22476

Howell, Horsley and Bradford
Harry Wills The Champion	1926	Columbia 14168-D
Wasn't It Nice'	1926	Columbia 14168-D

Hudson Singers
I'm Feathering A Nest (For A Little Bluebird)	1929	Columbia 1880-D
Where The Bab-Bab-Babbling Brook (Goes Bub-Bub-Bubbling By)	1929	Columbia 1880-D

Huff Quartet
I'm Led By Love	1930	Vocalion 5410
Wonderful King	1930	Vocalion 5410

Huff's Quartet
Hail To The King	1929	Vocalion 5383
I Found This Love In Calvary	1929	Vocalion 5383

Hylton Sisters
End Of The Rainbow, The	1939	Varsity 8155
Piggy Wiggy (Pichi Pichi Wool)	1939	Varsity 8069
Seven Little Oranges	1939	Varsity 8155
Shoo Fly	1939	Varsity 8069
Three Little Maids	1939	Varsity 8071
Tin Roof Blues	1939	Varsity 8071
What Used To Was, Used To Was	1939	Varsity 8146
Willie, The Chilly Troubadour	1939	Varsity 8146

Imperial Quartet
Beautiful Isle Of Somewhere	1915	Victor 17914
Cross Bow ('Robin Hood'), The	1915	Victor 17873
Forsaken	1916	Victor 18169
I'm A Pilgrim, I'm A Stranger	1916	Victor 18199
Lead Kindly Light	1915	Victor 17914
Love's Old Sweet Song	1916	Victor 18169
My Ain Folk	1915	Victor 17872
My Lady Chlo	1916	Victor 18158
Perfect Day, A	1915	Victor 17872
Pickaninny Lullaby	1916	Victor 18158
Remember Now Thy Creator	1917	Victor 18264
Some Blessed Day	1916	Victor 18199
Speed Our Republic	1915	Victor 17906
That Flag Without A Stain	1915	Victor 17906
Way Down Yonder In The Cornfield	1915	Victor 17873
When They Ring The Golden Bells For You And Me	1915	Victor 17982
When We Stood Before The King	1917	Victor 18264

Imperial Quartet, Lewis James & the
Home Sweet Home For You	1917	Columbia
We're Fighting		

Imperial Quartette
By Order Of The King	1916	Columbia
I'll Be A Long, Long Way From Home	1916	Columbia

Independent Quartet
In The Bible There's A Story	1929	Columbia 14486-D
Let The Church Roll	1929	Columbia 14486-D

Indiana Male Quartet
Evening Brings Memories Of You	1928	Brunswick
When The Golden Rod Is Blooming	1928	Brunswick

Ink Spots
Address Unknown	1939	Decca 2707/Decca 23757 (1946)
Alabama Barbecue	1937	Decca 1154
Aladdin's Lamp	1948	Decca 24496
All My Life	1952	Decca 27996/Decca 25533 (1961)
Always	1947	Decca 24140
Am I Asking Too Much	1948	Decca 24517
And Then I Prayed	1951	Decca 27494
Ask Anyone Who Knows	1947	Decca 23900
As You Desire Me	1949	Decca 24585
Baby Brown	1935	Victor unreleased
Best Things In Life Are Free, The	1948	Decca 24327/Decca 30058 (1956)
Bewildered	1949	Decca 24566/Decca 29991 (1956)
Bless You (For Being An Angel)	1939	Decca 2841/Decca 23757 (1946)
Blueberry Hill		
Bow Wow Wow		
Brown Gal	1938	Decca 2044
Can You Look Me In The Eyes And Say We're Through	1947	Decca 23900
Careless Love	1962	Ford 115
Castles In The Sand	1951	Decca 27464
Christopher Columbus	1936	Decca 883
Coquette	1940	Decca 3077/Decca 25240 (1947)
Did You Tell Me A Lie	1952	unreleased
Do I Worry'	1940	Decca 3432/Decca 23633 (1946)/Decca 11050 (1952)/Grand Award 1001 (19560
Don't 'Low No Swingin' In Here	1935	RCA Victor 24876
Don't Believe Everything You Dream	1944	Decca 18583
Don't Be Sorry	1947	unreleased
Don't Ever Break A Promise	1940	Brunswick 04183
Don't Get Around Much Anymore	1942	Decca 18503
Don't Leave Now	1942	Decca 4303/Decca 25378 (1948)
Don't Let Old Age Creep Up On You	1938	Decca 1731
Don't Put Off Till Sunday	1954	Decca 28982
Don't Tell A Lie About Me, Dear	1942	Decca 18383
Do Something For Me	1951	Decca 27493
Do You Feel That Way, Too'	1947	Decca 24111
Dream Awhile	1950	Decca 27259
Driftwood	1941	Decca 3872/Decca 29957 (1956)
Echoes	1949	Decca 24741
Either It's Love Or It Isn't	1946	Decca 23695
Either It's Love Or It Isn't	1947	AFRS P-685
Every Night About This Time	1956	Decca 29957
Everyone Is Saying Hello Again	1946	Decca 18817/Decca 23936 (1947)
Ev'ry Night About This Time	1942	Decca 18461
Foo-gee	1942	Decca 4303
Fool Grows Wise, A	1951	Decca 27493
Friend Of Johnny's, A	1951	Decca 27391
Give Her My Love	1939	Decca 2790
Gypsy, The	1946	Decca 18817/Decca 23936 (1947)
Hawaiian Wedding Song	1962	Ford 115
Heartaches And Tears		
He's Got The Whole World In His Hands		
Hey, Doc	1941	Decca 3987
Home Is Where The Heart Is	1947	Decca 24192
Honest And Truly	1952	Decca 27996
I Can't Stand Losing You	1943	Decca 18542
I Could Make You Care	1940	Decca 3346
I Cover The Waterfront	1946	Decca 18864
I'd Climb The Highest Mountain	1945	Decca 18711/Decca 25239 (1947)
I Don't Stand A Ghost Of A Chance With You	1951	Decca 27742/Decca 30058 (1956)
I Don't Want Sympathy, I Want Love	1939	Decca 2841
I Don't Want To Set The World On Fire	1941	Decca 3987/Decca 25431 (1949)
If	1951	Decca 27391
If I Cared A Little Bit Less	1942	Decca 18528
If I Didn't Care	1939	Decca 2286/Decca 23632 (1946)/Decca 11050 (1952)
If I Didn't Care	1944	AFRS 78/AFRS P-167 (1945)
If You Had To Hurt Someone	1949	Decca 24672
I Get The Blues When It Rains	1946	Decca 23695
I Get The Blues When It Rains	1947	AFRS P-685

100 Years of Harmony: 1850 to 1950

Title	Year	Label
I Hope To Die If I Told A Lie	1945	Decca 18657
I'll Be Listening For A Knock On The Door		
I'll Be Seeing You		
I'll Get By	1945	AFRS 100
I'll Get By (As Long As I Have You)	1944	Decca 18579/Decca 25238 (1947)
I'll Lose A Friend Tomorrow	1947	Decca 24261
I'll Lose A Friend Tomorrow	1948	AFRS P-956
I'll Make Up For Everything	1948	AFRS P-956
I'll Make Up For Everything	1948	Decca 24286
I'll Never Make The Same Mistake Again	1943	Decca 18542
I'll Never Smile Again	1940	Decca 3346/Decca 23635 (1946)
I Love You Truly		
I Love You When		
I'm Confessin'		
I'm Getting Sentimental Over You	1940	Decca 3077/Decca 25239 (1947)
I'm Gonna Sit Right Down And Write Myself A Letter		
I'm Gonna Turn Off The Teardrops	1946	Decca 18755/Decca 25344 (1948)
I'm Lucky To Have You	1951	Decca 27742
I'm Not The Same Old Me	1942	Decca 18461
I'm Only Human	1940	Decca 3468
I'm Still Without A Sweetheart, I'm Still In Love With You	1941	Decca 3806
I'm Through	1940	Decca 2966
I Must Say Goodbye	1952	Decca 28078
In A Shanty In Old Shanty Town		
I Never Had A Dream Come True	1946	Decca 23615
Information Please	1947	Decca 24111
In The Doorway		Unreleased (recorded 08/21/40)
In The Shade Of The Old Apple Tree		
Is It A Sin'	1942	Decca 4112
It Isn't A Dream Anymore	1942	Decca 4194
It Only Happens Once	1949	Decca 24585
It's All Over But The Crying	1948	AFRS P-956
It's All Over But The Crying	1948	Decca 24286
It's A Sin To Tell A Lie	1942	Decca 4112/Decca 25505 (1952)
It's Been A Long, Long Time		
It's Funny To Everyone But Me	1939	Decca 2507
It's Funny To Everyone But Me	1955	Decca 29750
It's Nothin'		
I've Got A Bone To Pick With You	1941	20th Century Fox 57
I've Got The World On A String		
I Want To Thank Your Folks	1947	Decca 23851
I Was Dancing With Someone	1950	Decca 27102
I Was Looking At You		
I Wasn't Made For Love	1947	Decca 23851
I Wish I Could Say The Same	1940	Brunswick 03673
I Wish You The Best Of Everything	1938	Decca 1870
I Woke Up With A Teardrop In My Eye	1948	Decca 24327
Java Jive	1940	Decca 3432/Decca 23633 (1946)
Java Jive	1944	AFRS 78/AFRS P-167 (1945)
Johnnie		
Just As Though You Were Here	1942	Decca 18466
Just For A Thrill	1939	Decca 2507/Decca 25238 (1947)
Just For Me	1947	Decca 24173
Just For Now	1948	Decca 24461
Just Plain Love	1947	Decca 24173
Keep Away From My Doorstep	1936	Decca 1036
Keep Cool, Fool	1941	Decca 3958
Kiss And A Rose, A	1949	Decca 24611
Knock Kneed Sal	1939	Decca 2286
Knock Me A Kiss		Unreleased (recorded 06/23/42)
Land Of Love	1949	Decca 24741
Let's Call The Whole Thing Off	1937	Decca 1251
Little White Lies		
Lost In A Dream	1950	Decca 24887
Love Is Strange		
Lovely Way To Spend An Evening, A	1944	AFRS 78/AFRS P-167 (1945)
Lovely Way To Spend An Evening, A	1944	Decca 18583
Mamma Don't Allow It	1935	
Marie		
Maybe	1940	Decca 3258/Decca 23634 (1946)
Maybe It's All For The Best	1945	Decca 18657
Memories Of You	1940	Decca 2966/Decca 29750 (1955)
Mine All Mine, My My	1942	Decca 18528
More Of The Same Sweet You	1951	Decca 27632
My Baby Didn't Even Say Goodbye	1948	Decca 24496
My Blue Heaven		
My Greatest Mistake	1940	Decca 3379/Decca 25237 (1947)
My My My		
My Prayer	1939	Decca 2790/Decca 29991 (1956)
My Reward	1950	Decca 24933
My Wild Irish Rose		
No Orchids For My Lady	1949	Decca 24566
Nothin'	1941	Decca 4045

Song	Year	Label
No Wonder	1939	
Oh, Red	1938	Decca 1789
Old Joe's Hittin' The Jug	1936	Decca 883
Please Take A Letter, Miss Brown	1941	Decca 3626
Pork Chops And Gravy	1938	Decca 2044
Prisoner Of Love	1946	Decca 18864
Puttin' And Takin'	1940	Decca 3468
Recess In Heaven	1948	Decca 24517
Remind Me Of You		
Right About Now	1950	Decca 27214
Ring, Telephone, Ring	1941	Decca 3626/Decca 25378 (1948)
Rock And Roll Rag	1956	Grand Award 1001
Say Something Sweet To Your Sweetheart	1948	Decca 24507
Shine On Harvest Moon		
Shout, Brother, Shout	1942	Decca 4194
Sincerely Yours	1947	Decca 24192
Slap That Bass	1937	Decca 1251
Somebody Bigger Than You And I	1951	Decca 27494
Someday I'll Meet You Again	1944	Decca 18579
Someday I'll Meet You Again	1945	AFRS 100
Someone's Rocking My Dreamboat	1941	Decca 4045/Decca 25431 (1949)
Sometime	1950	Decca 27102
So Sorry	1941	Decca 3806
Stairway To The Stars	1939	
Stars Fell On Alabama		
Stompin' At The Savoy	1936	Decca 1036
Stop Pretending (So Hep You See)	1940	Decca 3288
Street Of Dreams	1942	Decca 18503
Sweetest Dream, The	1946	Decca 18755
Sweet Sue, Just You		
Swing, Gate, Swing	1935	RCA Victor 24876
Swing High, Swing Low	1937	Decca 1236
Swingin' On The Strings	1935	RCA Victor 24851/Bluebird 6530 (1936)
'Tain't Nobody's Biz-ness If I Do	1936	Decca 817
Tell Me You Love Me	1951	Decca 27464
That Cat Is High	1938	Decca 1789
That's When Your Heartaches Begin	1941	Decca 3720/Decca 25505 (1952)
That's Where I Came In	1947	Decca 23809
That's Where I Come In	1947	AFRS P-742
There Goes My Heart		
This Is Worth Fighting For	1942	Decca 18466
Thoughtless	1945	Decca 18711
Tiger Rag	1939	
Time Out For Tears	1950	Decca 27259
To Each His Own	1946	Decca 23615
To Make A Mistake Is Human		
To Remind Me Of You	1949	Decca 24672
Turn Off The Teardrops		
Until The Real Thing Comes Along	1941	Decca 3958/Decca 23625 (1946)
Wanting You		Unreleased (recorded 11/24/47)
Way It Used To Be, The	1950	Decca 27214
We'll Meet Again	1941	Decca 3656/Decca 25237 (1947)
We'll Meet Again	1944	V-Disc 118-A/V-Disc 205-A
We Three (My Echo, My Shadow And Me)	1940	Decca 3379/Decca 23634 (1946)
What Can I Do'	1940	Decca 3195
What Can You Do	1951	Decca 27632
What Good Would It Do'	1941	Decca 3720
When The Sun Goes Down	1938	Decca 1870
When The Swallows Come Back To Capistrano	1940	Decca 3195/Decca 25240 (1947)
When You Come To The End Of The Day	1947	Decca 24261
When You Come To The End Of The Day	1948	AFRS P-956
When You Were Sweet Sixteen		
Where Are You	1941	20th Century Fox 56
Where Flamingoes Fly	1948	Decca 24461
Whispering Grass (Don't Tell The Trees)	1940	Decca 3258/Decca 23632 (1946)
White Christmas	1947	Decca 24140
Whoa, Babe	1937	Decca 1236
Who Do You Know In Heaven	1949	Decca 24693
Who Wouldn't Love You'	1942	Decca 18383
Why Did It Have To Be Me		
Why Didn't You Tell Me'	1941	Decca 3872
Why Must We Say Goodbye		
With My Eyes Wide Open, I'm Dreaming	1950	Decca 24887
With Plenty Of Money And You	1937	Decca 1154
Yes-suh!	1937	Decca 1731
You Always Hurt The One You Love		
You Bring Me Down	1939	Decca 2707
You Can't See The Sun When You're Crying	1947	AFRS P-742
You Can't See The Sun When You're Crying	1947	Decca 23809
You Left Me Everything But You	1950	Decca 24933
You're Breaking My Heart	1949	Decca 24693
You're Breaking My Heart All Over Again	1940	Decca 3288
You're Looking For Romance, I'm Looking For Love	1941	Decca 3656
Your Feet's Too Big (rec. 01/04/35)	1935	RCA Victor 24851/Bluebird

Ink Spots, Bill Kenny with the

Title	Year	Label
You Were Only Fooling	1948	Decca 24507/Decca 25533 (1961)

Ink Spots, Bill Kenny with the

Title	Year	Label
You May Be The Sweetheart Of Somebody Else	1952	Decca 28164

Ink Spots, Charlie Fuqua's

Title	Year	Label
Am I Too Late	1954	King 1336
Changing Partners	1954	King 1304
Command Me	1955	King 4857
Darling, Don't Cry	1957	Verve 10071
Doin'		Unreleased (recorded 07/11/54)
Don't Laugh At Me	1955	King 1512
Ebb Tide	1953	King 1297
Flowers, Mister Florist, Please	1953	King 4670
Here In My Lonely Room	1953	King 4670
If I'd Only Known You Then	1957	Verve 10094
If You Should Say Goodbye	1953	King 1297
I'll Walk A Country Mile	1955	King 4857
Keep It Movin'	1955	King 1512
Little Bird Told Me, A	1959	Verve 10198
Melody Of Love	1954	King 1336/King 1429 (1954)
Planting Rice	1954	King 1378
Secret Love	1959	Verve 10198
Someone's Rocking My Dreamboat	1955	King 1425
Stranger In Paradise	1954	King 1304
There Is Something Missing	1954	King 1429
Very Best Luck In The World, The	1957	Verve 10094
When You Come To The End Of The Day	1955	King 1425
Yesterdays	1954	King 1378
You Name It	1957	Verve 10071

Ink Spots, Ella Fitzgerald & the

Title	Year	Label
Cow-Cow Boogie	1944	Decca 18587/Decca 25047 (1947)
I'm Beginning To See The Light	1945	Decca 23399
I'm Making Believe	1944	Decca 23356
Into Each Life Some Rain Must Fall	1944	Decca 23356
Into Each Life Some Rain Must Fall	1945	V-Disc 365-A
I Still Feel The Same About You	1951	Decca 27419
Little Small Town Girl	1951	Decca 27419
That's The Way It Is	1945	Decca 23399/Decca 25047 (1947)
That's The Way It Is	1947	AFRS P-742

Ink Spots

Title	Year	Label
Knock On The Door, A	1949	Decca 24611
		6530 (1936)/Decca 817 (1936)

Invincible Four

Title	Year	Label
Ting Ling Toy	1919	Pathe 22239

Invincible Male Quartet

Title	Year	Label
Nearer My God To Thee	1910	Columbia A-5188

Invincible Quartet

Title	Year	Label
Fireman's Duty	1902	Edison (2mincyl)
High Old Time, A	1905	American Record Company 030798
My First Nowell	1910	Columbia A-0918
My Old Kentucky Home	1905	American Record Company 030793
Nellie Dean	1905	American Record Company 031297
St. Patrick Day At Clancy's	1905	American Record Company 030800

Invincible Quartette

Title	Year	Label
Characteristic Negro Medley, A	1905	American Record Company 030796/Columbia 890
Coon Wedding In Southern Georgia, A	1903	Columbia 33242/Busy Bee 130/American Record Company 030794 (1905)
Farmyard Medley	1904	Columbia 455
Hoosier Hollow Quilting Party, The (with Cal Stewart)	1903	Columbia 32237/Universal Zonophone 5608/Columbia 1515
Kentucky Babe	1900	Columbia 9054
Medley Of Plantation Songs (In The Evening By The Moonlight; Massa's In The Cold, Cold Ground, Carry Me Back To Old Virginny)	1903	Columbia 33241/Columbia 890
My Creole Sue	1905	Columbia 750
My Dinah	1904	Columbia 452/Standard A 500
Night Trip To Buffalo, A	1904	Columbia 458
Old Black Joe	1900	Columbia 9050
Old Homestead: Church Scene, The	1904	Columbia 449
On Board The Battleship Oregon	1902	Edison 8012 (2mincyl)
Sleigh Ride Party, The	1904	Columbia 450
Steamboat Medley (Steamboat Leaving The Wharf At New Orleans)	1904	Columbia 454
Way Down Yonder In The Cornfield	1905	Columbia 714

Invincible Quartette of Rust College (Rust College Quartet)

Title	Year	Label
Bye And Bye	1928	
Climbing Up The Mountain,	1928	Okeh 8561

Children
   King Jesus Is A Listening 1928 Okeh 8561
   Who'll Be A Witness' 1928

Ipana Troubadours
   I'll Get By 1928

Ipana Troubadours
   Rose Of Mandalay 1928

Jacob Quartet
   Lord I'm Troubled 1925 Broadway 5024
   This Train Is Bound For Glory 1925 Broadway 5024

James Brothers Quartet
   Ain't It A Shame 1931 Okeh 8925
   I'm In My Savior's Care 1931 Okeh 8925

James Quintet
   Bewildered 1949 Coral 60018/Coral 65002 (1949)
   Don't Worry 1950 Derby 732
   Drop A Penny In The Wishing Well 1951 Decca 48237
   I Could Make You Care 1951 Decca 48237
   I'm Just A Fool 1949 Derby 726
   Let's Put Our Hearts On The Table 1950 Derby 732
   Neighborhood Affair, A 1951 Decca 48218
   Oo Bop Choo Bop 1949 Coral 60022
   Paw's In The Kitchen 1949 Derby 726
   Pleasing You 1949 Coral 60018/Coral 65002 (1949)
   Remember When' 1949 Coral 65016
   Tell Me Why 1949 Coral 60022/Coral 65016 (1949)
   You Make Too Much Noise When We Kiss 1951 Decca 48218

James Quintet, Ruth Brown & the
   Daddy Daddy 1952 Atlantic 973
   Have A Good Time 1952 Atlantic 973

Jenkins Sacred Singers
   Church In The Wildwood, The 1927 Okeh 45113
   Glory Land Way, The 1927 Okeh 40795
   If I Could Hear My Mother Pray Again 1927 Okeh 45113
   Only A Prayer 1927 Okeh 45134
   Pictures From Life's Other Side 1927 Okeh 45134
   When I See The Blood 1927 Okeh 40795

Jenkins Singers, Philip
   Kentucky Babe 1927
   Rock-A-Bye Baby Mine 1927
   Song Of Kisses 1927

Jesters, The
   Bugle Call Rag/Had But Fifty Cents 1932
   McNamara's Band 1932 Victor 24052
   Sipping Cider/The Jester's Jiffy Feet/Cuckoo Song 1932 Victor 24052

Jesters (with Bing Crosby)
   Feudin' And Fightin' 1947 Decca 23975
   Goodbye My Lover, Goodbye 1947 Decca 23975
   Sioux City Sue 1946 Decca 23508
   You Sang My Love Song To Somebody Else 1946 Decca 23508

Jesters, The (Pep, Vim & Vigor)
   Bolshevich 1931 Brunswick Test

Jesters, The (Red Latham, Wamp Carlson, Guy Bonham)
   Hut-Hut Song - A Swedish Serenade, The 1941 Decca 3778
   'Round Her Neck She Wears A Yellow Ribbon (For Her Lover Who Is Fur, Fur Away) 1941 Decca 3778

Jewel Jubilee Singers
   Who Shall Walk Through Gethsemane 1949 King 4301

Jewel Male Quartet
   Give Me That Old Time Religion 1928 Challenge 937
   I Ain't Gonna Study War No More 1928 Challenge 937

Jim Europe's Singing Serenaders/Four Harmony Kings
   Ev'rybody Dat Talks 'Bout Heaven Ain't Goin' There 1919 Pathe 22105
   Exhortation (Jubilee Shout) 1919 Pathe 22084
   Little David Play On Your Harp 1919 Pathe 22084
   One More Ribber To Cross 1919 Pathe 22187
   Roll Jordan Roll 1919 Pathe 22105
   Swing Low, Sweet Chariot 1919 Pathe 22187

Johnson Brothers Quartet
   Living In Glory Divine 1928 Vocalion 5283
   Oh, Declare His Glory 1928 Vocalion 5283

Johnson Jubilee Singers
   Heavy Load 1943 King Solomon 1006
   Humble Yourself 1943 King Solomon 1006

Johnson, Bill & his Musical Notes
   All Dressed Up With A Broken Heart 1948 RCA Victor 20-2749
   Believe Me, My Beloved 1948 RCA Victor 20-3037
   Chickasaw Limited 1947 RCA Victor 20-2498
   Don't You Think I Oughta Know' 1947 RCA Victor 20-2225/Harlem 1011 (1947)
   Elevator Boogie 1948 RCA Victor 20-3108/AFRS Transcription Vol P-1171
   For Once In Your Life 1947 RCA Victor 20-2427
   Half A Love 1947 RCA Victor 20-2362
   How Would You Know' 1949 King 4286
   I Learned To Cry 1947 RCA Victor 20-

Title	Year	Label
Leave It To Fate, Gate	1947	RCA Victor 20-2362
Let's Be Sweethearts Again	1947	RCA Victor 20-2591
Let's Walk		Tru-Blue 414
Mama, Mama, Mama	1947	RCA Victor 20-2591
My Baby Likes To Be-Bop	1948	RCA Victor 20-2749
My Baby's Giving Me The Brush	1948	RCA Victor 20-3108/AFRS Transcription Vol P-1171
My Little Redhead	1947	RCA Victor 20-2427
Pretty Eyed Baby	1947	RCA Victor 20-2235
Roselle	1949	King 4286
Say Something Nice About Me	1948	RCA Victor 20-3037/AFRS Transcription Vol P-1171
Sharkie's Boogie	1947	RCA Victor 20-2298
Shorty's Got To Go	1947	RCA Victor 20-2225
So Tired	1947	RCA Victor 20-2618
That Night We Said Goodbye	1947	RCA Victor 20-2298/AFRS Transcription Vol P-1171
When Your Hair Has Turned To Silver	1954	Tru-Blue 414
You Didn't Have To Say I Love You	1947	RCA Victor 20-2235
You're The Dream Of A Lifetime	1947	RCA Victor 20-2498

Jolly Bakers

Title	Year	Label
Thinking Of You	1926	Challenge 262/Challenge 267/Gennett 6018

Jolly Bakers (Challenge Four)

Title	Year	Label
High, High, High Up In The Hills	1927	Challenge 264

Jolly Bakers (Singing Hoosier Quartet)

Title	Year	Label
You Know - I Know Everything's Made For Love	1926	Challenge 262/Challenge 267

Jolson, Al & the Mills Brothers

Title	Year	Label
Down Among The Sheltering Palms	1948	Decca 24534

Jones & Farr Quartette

Title	Year	Label
Annie Laurie	1898	Edison Bell 3006
As Your Hair Grows Whiter	1898	Edison Bell 3001
Dinah, De Moon Am Shinin'	1898	Edison Bell 3010
I Can't Think Of Nothing Else But You	1898	Edison Bell 3007
Killarney	1898	Edison Bell 3004
Plantation Songs: De Ole Banjo	1898	Edison Bell 3012
Sally In Our Alley	1898	Edison Bell 3002
Way Down Yonder In The Cornfield	1898	Edison Bell 3003

Jones Boys

Title	Year	Label
Alone In The Night		DC unreleased
Jones Bones	1954	S&G 5008
Mood Indigo		Electrical Transcription 97127
You Got A Lot To Learn	1955	S&G 5009
You Make Me Feel Like A Penny Waiting For Change	1953	S&G 5007
You're So Appealing		Electrical Transcription 97127

Jones Boys Sing Band

Title	Year	Label
Pickin' A Rib	1937	Decca 1439

Jones Boys Sing Band (with Otis Rene)

Title	Year	Label
Sleepy Time In Hawaii	1937	Decca 1439

Jones Brothers

Title	Year	Label
Ain't She Pretty'	1946	Majestic 1038
Every Night	1954	Sun 213
Hundred Years From To-Day, A	1946	Majestic 1038
I Wanna Be Loved Like A Baby	1946	Majestic 1039
Look To Jesus	1954	Sun 213
Them There Eyes	1946	Majestic 1039

Jones, Ada & Male Quartet

Title	Year	Label
By The Light Of The Silvery Moon	1909	Edison 4mincyl 421/Edison BA 1521 (1912)

Jones, Ada & Quartet

Title	Year	Label
Christmas Time At Pumpkin Center	1919	Columbia A-2789

Jones, Ada & the American Quartet

Title	Year	Label
Nora Malone	1912	Victor 16486
Tickle Toes	1911	Victor 16683

Jones, Ada & the American Quartet (2)

Title	Year	Label
Call Me Up Some Rainy Afternoon	1910	Victor 16508
Come Josephine In My Flying Machine	1911	Victor 16844

Jones, Ada & the Premier Quartet

Title	Year	Label
Call Me Up Some Rainy Afternoon	1910	Edison 4mincyl 485
You Can Tell I'm Irish	1916	Edison unissued

Jones, Ada & Trio

Title	Year	Label
You Can Tell I'm Irish	1916	Edison unissued ED-501

Jones, Billy & Male Quartet (Shannon Four)
Mary Dear	1922	Brunswick 2321

Jordanaires
Be Prepared	1954	Capitol 2915
Bugle Call From Heaven	1954	Capitol 2815
David And Goliath	1947	Capitol 1363
He Bought My Soul At Calvary	1950	Capitol 1499
In My Savior's Loving Arms	1953	Capitol 2725
I Want To Rest	1947	Capitol 1254
My Journey To The Sky	1947	Capitol 1363
Noah	1954	Decca 29188
Read That Book	1950	Capitol 1499
Rock My Soul In The Bosom Of Abraham	1954	Decca 29188
Tattler's Wagon	1953	Capitol 2725
This Ole House	1954	Capitol 2815/Capitol 2915 (1954)
Working On The Building	1947	Capitol 1254

Jordanaires, Mervin Shiner & the
Lord I'm Coming Home	1955	Decca 29363
Pass Me Not	1955	Decca 29363

Jubalaires
As Summer Turns To Fall	1951	Capitol 1779
Before This Time Another Year	1944	Decca 8666/Decca 48085 (1948)
David And Goliath	1951	Capitol 1888
Dream Is A Wish Your Heart Makes, A	1950	Capitol 845
Ezekiel Saw The Wheel A-Rollin'	1948	Decca 48085
Get Right With God	1950	Decca 48103/Decca 48166 (1950)
Get Together With The Lord	1946	Decca 18782/Decca 23934 (1947)
Go Down Moses	1950	Decca 48166
I Don't Know What I'd Do Without You	1946	Decca 18916
I Know	1946	Decca 18782/Decca 23934 (1947)
I'm Movin' Up The King's Highway	1947	Decca 48031
I'm On My Way To Canaan Land	1947	Decca 48031
I'm So Lonesome I Could Cry	1946	Decca 18916
It Ain't What You Want That Does You Good	1949	Capitol 70040
I've Done My Work	1951	Capitol 1888
I've Waited	1949	King 4325
Keep On Doin' What You're Doin'	1951	Capitol 1715
Little Mr. Big	1950	Capitol 1054
Living Is A Lie	1951	Capitol 1779
Mene, Mene, Teckel	1949	Capitol 683
Pianola	1950	Capitol 1054
Rain Is The Teardrops Of Angels	1951	Capitol 1715
Somebody Broke My Dolly	1949	Capitol 683
St. Louis Blues	1949	Capitol 70040
That Old Pianola	1950	Capitol 1054
That Old Piano Roll Blues	1950	Capitol 845
They Put John On The Island	1950	Decca 48103
When It's All Over But The Shoutin'	1944	Decca 8666

Jubalaires (as by Kay Starr)
Game Of Broken Hearts, A	1949	Capitol 792
Tell Me How Long The Train's Been Gone	1949	Capitol 792

Jubalaires, Johnny Smith & the (Jubilaires)
Blue Ribbon Gal	1950	Capitol 821
Home, Home, Home	1949	Capitol 784
I Wish I Had A Sweetheart	1949	Capitol 784
Pal That I Loved Stole The Gal That I Loved, The	1950	Capitol 821

Jubilaires
Again		Standard Transcription U-264
All Alone And Feeling Mighty Blue		Standard Transcription U-264
Chattahoochee Lullabye	1950	King 15040
Day Is Mine, The	1949	King 4303
Get Lost	1949	King 4290
Git On Board, Little Children		Standard Transcription U-287
Go Down Moses	1947	Queen 4167
Got Almighty's Gonna Cut You Down	1947	Queen 4167
Hey Lawdy Mama	1944	CBS Radio Transcription, 6/7/44
Icky, Yacky	1947	Queen 4172/King 4172
It Ain't What You Want That Does You Good		Standard Transcription U-264
It's Breaking My Heart To Say Goodbye		Standard Transcription U-264
I've Waited All My Life For You	1947	Queen 4166/King 4325 (1949)
Jean	1949	King 4290
Jube's Blues	1947	Queen 4166
Keep On Doing What You're Doing		Standard Transcription U-264
Let It Rain	1949	King 4325
Lilliette		Standard Transcription U-264
My God Called Me This Morning	1949	Queen 4168/King 4168

Title	Year	Label
Piccolo Polka		Standard Transcription U-264
Pray	1947	Queen 4163
Ring That Golden Bell	1949	Queen 4168/King 4168
Somebody Stole My Rose Colored Glasses		Standard Transcription U-264
St. Louis Lou	1949	King 4303
Sunday Kind Of Love, A	1947	Queen 4163
Tara Talara Tala		Standard Transcription U-264
Twelve O'Clock And All Is Well	1950	King 15040
You're Gonna Make A Wonderful Sweetheart	1947	Queen 4172/King 4172

Jubilaires, Original

Title	Year	Label
Dreaming Of The Ladies In The Moon	1954	Modern
You Better Stop	1954	Modern

Jubilee Gospel Singers

Title	Year	Label
I'm A Pilgrim	1924	Broadway 5000
I Want Jesus To Walk With Me	1929	Paramount 13113
Jesus Is Mine	1929	Paramount 13113
These Bones Are Goin' To Rise Again	1929	Paramount 12835

Jubilee Gospel Singers (Bob Geddins' Cavaliers)

Title	Year	Label
I'm Just A Stranger	1949	Cava-Tone 101/Gilt-Edge 5022 (1951)
Nobody's Business If I Do	1949	Cava-Tone 101/Gilt-Edge 5022 (1951)

Jubilee Gospel Team

Title	Year	Label
Don't Know When Death Will Come	1929	Paramount 12837
Dry Bones In The Valley	1929	Paramount 12835
I Have Crossed The Separating Line	1929	Paramount 12838
I Know The Lord Has Laid His Hand Upon Me	1929	Paramount 12837
Let Jesus Lead The Way	1929	Paramount 12836
Station Will Be Changed	1929	Paramount 12836
You've Got To Meet Your God Somewhere	1929	Paramount 12838

Jubilee Male Quartet (Norfolk Jubilee Quartet)

Title	Year	Label
You're Goin' to Need That Pure Religion	1927	Varsity 6008

Jubilee Quartet

Title	Year	Label
Father Prepare Me	1923	Paramount 12054
My Lord's Gonna Move This Wicked Race	1923	Paramount 12054/Banner 1550 (1925)
Old Time Religion	1925	Banner 1550

Jubilee Singers

Title	Year	Label
Couldn't Hear Nobody Pray	1928	Bluebird 5032
O Mary, Don't You Weep	1928	Bluebird 5032

Judson Sisters

Title	Year	Label
Bungalow Of Dreams	1927	Champion 15406
Together We Two	1927	Champion 15405

Kalaluhi Honolulu Quartet

Title	Year	Label
Wyoming Lullaby (Go To Sleep, My Baby)	1929	Vocalion 15842

Kaltenborn Quartet

Title	Year	Label
Beautiful Milleress	1911	Columbia A-0991
Winter Tales	1911	Columbia A-0991

Kanawha Singers

Title	Year	Label
Brighten The Corner Where You Are	1929	Brunswick 328
Climbing Up De Golden Stairs	1928	Brunswick 205/Brunswick 3801 (1928)/Brunswick 01127/Brunswick 03798/Brunswick A 7656/Supertone S 2125
Climb Up, Ye Chillun, Climb Up	1929	Brunswick 459
De Camptown Races	1929	Brunswick 337
Early In The Mornin'	1929	Brunswick 365
Ella Rae (Carry Me Back To Tennessee)	1929	Brunswick 459
Golden Slippers	1927	Brunswick 189/Supertone S 2040/Vocalion 5173
Goodbye, My Lover, Goodbye	1928	Brunswick 242/Brunswick 3991/Brunswick 03859
Gospel Train, The	1929	Brunswick 365
Hail West Virginia	1927	Brunswick 158/Vocalion 5142
High Silk Hat And A Walking Cane, A	1929	Brunswick 347/Brunswick 01097/Superson S 2050
If Your Heart Keeps Right	1929	Brunswick 472
Indiana	1928	Brunswick 255
Keep In The Middle Of De Road	1929	Brunswick 337
Mountains Ain't No Place For Bad Men	1929	Brunswick 347/Brunswick 01097/Superson S 2050
Oh, Dem Golden Slippers	1927	Vocalion 5173
On The Banks Of The Wabash Far Away	1928	Brunswick 255
Shall We Gather At The River	1929	Brunswick 328

Swing Low, Sweet Chariot	1928	Brunswick 205/Brunswick 3801 (1928)/Brunswick 01127/Brunswick 03798/Brunswick A 7656/Supertone S 2125			3368/Brunswick A 190
			I'm Proud Of A Baby Like You	1926	Victor 20469
			In The Evening	1924	Brunswick 2608
			Just A Little Longer	1926	Gennett 3404
			Lane In Spain, A	1927	Brunswick 3517/Brunswick A 417
That Good Old Country Town (Where I Was Born)	1928	Brunswick 242/Brunswick 3991 (1928)/Brunswick 03859	Let's Make Believe	1927	Brunswick 3586/Vocalion 15579
			Me And My Shadow	1927	Challenge 652/Domino 3979
Them Golden Slippers	1927	Brunswick 189	Morning Won't You Ever Come'	192'	Brunswick 2653
There Is Sunshine In My Soul Today	1929	Brunswick 472	Nesting Time	1927	Brunswick 3516/Brunswick A 416/Vocalion 15558
West Virginia Hills	1927	Brunswick 158/Vocalion 5142			
Kansas City Police Quartet			Only You And Lonely Me	1926	Vocalion 15365
Bringin' Home The Bacon	1940	Decca 3690A	Petrushka	1926	Brunswick 3308
I Want To Linger/Somebody Knows/Ma!	1940	Decca 3744B	Red Lips, Kiss My Blues Away	1927	Perfect 12344
			Roses	1926	Brunswick 3217
Kaufman, Irving & his Quartet			She's Still My Baby	1926	Brunswick 3308
Hail! Hail! The Gang's All Here (What The Deuce Do We Care)	1917	Columbia A-2443	She's Still My Baby	1926	Vocalion 15437/Brunswick A 160
Kaye, Danny & the Skylarks					
Best Things Happen While You're Dancing, The	1955	Decca 29290	Somebody and Me!	1927	Brunswick 3586/Vocalion 15580
Choreography	1955	Decca 29290			
			Sunday	1926	Victor 20273/Electrola EG 35736
Kedroff Male Quartet					
Church Bells Of Novgorod	1929	Columbia 1778-D			
Russian Folk Songs	1929	Columbia 1778-D	Together, We Two	1927	Brunswick 3685/Brunswick A 7549
Keep Shufflin' Trio					
You Don't Understand	1929	Victor V-38099			
You've Got To Be Modernistic	1929	Victor V-38099	What'll I Do	192'	Brunswick 2608
			When The Red, Red Robin Comes Bob Bob, Bobbin' Along	1926	Brunswick 3213
Keller Sisters & Lynch					
Don't Sing Aloha When I Go	1926	Gennett 3404	Where The Dreamy Wabash Flows	192'	Brunswick 2653
Hallelujah	1927	Domino 3979/Perfect 12344	Why Did You Say Goodbye'	1926	Gennett 3389
Hello Bluebird	1926	Brunswick 3368/Brunswick A 190	**Keller Sisters & Lynch (as the Vaudeville Trio)**		
			I'm Walking Around In Circles	1926	Vocalion 15427
I Found A Round-A-Bout Way To Heaven	1926	Brunswick 3217	Lay Me Down To Sleep In Carolina	1926	Vocalion 15432
			Meet Me In The Moonlight	1926	Vocalion 15432
I'll Just Go Along	1927	Brunswick 3517/Brunswick A 417	Nobody Worries 'Bout Me	1926	Vocalion 15427
			Keller Sisters & Lynch (with the Clevelanders)		
I Love Her	1926	Brunswick 3201/Brunswick A 116E	Side By Side	1927	Brunswick
			Keller Sisters & Lynch (with the Ipana Troubadours)		
			Give Me A Ukulele	1926	Columbia 772-D
I'm Forever Dreaming Of You	1926	Gennett 3389	Just A Bird's Eye View (Of My Old Kentucky Home)	1926	Columbia 772-D
I'm On My Way Back Home	1926	Brunswick			
I'm On My Way Home	1926	Brunswick			

Kel's Happy-Go-Lucky Boys, Mark
That Wonderful Something	1929	Victor 22203

Kenny, Bill (with Ink Spots)
At The End Of The Day	1951	Decca 14588
Ave Maria	1950	Decca 14538
Bundle From Heaven, A	1952	Decca 28289
Don't Mind The Rain	1953	Decca 28738
Don't Put It Off Till Sunday	1954	Decca 28982
Do You Know What It Means To Be Lonely	1953	Decca 28738
Forgetting You	1952	Decca 28462
Gentle Carpenter Of Bethlehem, The	1951	Decca 14562
Hand Of God, The	1952	Decca 28219
His Eye Is On The Sparrow	1951	Decca 14562
I Believe In The Man In The Sky	1953	Decca 28868
I Counted On You	1952	Decca 28462
If I Forget You	1952	Decca 27946
I Hear A Choir	1950	Decca 27326
I Keep Thinking Of You	1953	Decca 28677
I'm Heading Back To Paradise	1952	Decca 28078
I See God	1951	Decca 14588
It's No Secret	1950	Decca 27326
Just For Today	1954	Decca 28982
Keep On The Sunny Side Of Life	1951	Decca 14593
Lord's Prayer, The	1950	Decca 14538
Moonlight Mystery	1952	Decca 28412
My First And Last Love	1951	Decca 27844
Once	1951	Decca 27844
Our Lady Of Fatima	1950	Decca 27256
Please Mr. Sun	1952	Decca 27946
Precious Memories	1951	Decca 14547
Rose Of Roses, The	1954	Decca 29070
Sentimental Baby	1954	Decca 29163
Soldier's Rosary, A	1952	Decca 28219
Sorry You Said Goodbye	1952	Decca 28289
Stranger In The City	1950	Decca 27256
These Things Shall Pass	1951	Decca 14593
Under The Honeysuckle Vine	1952	Decca 28164
Vision Of Bernadette, The	1951	Decca 3958
Vows	1954	Decca 29070
What More Can I Do	1954	Decca 29163
When The Chimes Ring (At Evening)	1953	Decca 28868
Who's To Blame	1953	Decca 28677
You Are Happiness	1952	Decca 28412

Kenny, Herb & Trio
Key To My Heart	1950	Aladdin 3048
Why Do I Love You	1950	Aladdin 3048

Kentucky Jubilee Quartet
Do You Call That Religion'	1927	Okeh 8509
I'm Going To Lay Down My Heavy Load	1927	Okeh 8509

Kentucky Jubilee Quartet, The F. Randolph
Deep River	1928	Brunswick 4063
I'll Be Ready When The Great Day Comes	1928	Brunswick 4063

Kentucky Jubilee Singers
I'm Gonna Shout All Over God's Heaven	1928	Brunswick 4285

Kentucky Trio
Do You Want To Go There	1923	Okeh 4982
God's Gonna Set The World On Fire	1924	Okeh 8120
Lord I Want To Be A Christian	1923	Okeh 4982
Mother's Religion	1925	Okeh 8239
Old Account Was Settled, The	1925	Okeh 8239
Shine For Jesus	1924	Okeh 8120

Kerns, Grace & Male Quartet
Ring Out Wild Bells (with Grace Kerns)	1915	Columbia A-5745

Keynotes, Dinah Washington & the
Evil Gal Blues	1947	Mercury 8043
Homeward Bound	1947	Mercury 8043
I Know How To Do It	1947	Mercury 8044
Salty Papa Blues	1947	Mercury 8044

Keys
Key To My Heart, The	1950	London 30101
Stairway To The Stars, A	1950	London 698

Kidoodlers
In The Old Country Jail	1939	Okeh 05027
Ivan, The Ice Cream Man	1939	Vocalion 04907
Maybe	1939	Okeh 05027
Rumpel-Stilts-Kin	1939	Vocalion 04907

Kiesewelter Quartet (with Rudy Vallee & his Connecticut Yankees)
Goodbye, Bronco Bill	1935	Victor
Vallee Medley - Part 2, The	1935	Victor 36171

King Sisters
Ac-Cent-Tchu-Ate The Positive	1945	Victor 20-1631
All Of Me	1947	
Aloha Oe	1957	Capitol 1476
Army Air Corps Song, The	1942	Bluebird B-11476
Arthur Murray Taught Me Dancing In A Hurry	1941	Bluebird B-11431
At Sundown	1947	
Back In Your Own Backyard	1947	
Basin Street Blues		
Between The Devil And The Deep Blue Sea	1947	
But Beautiful	1958	
Button Up Your Overcoat	1947	
By The River Sainte Marie	1947	
Call Of The Canyon	1940	Bluebird 10834
Chop Fooey	1939	Bluebird 10660
Cielito Lindo (Beautiful Sky)	1940	Bluebird 10690
Crazy Rhythm	1947	

Day You Came Along, The		
Deep Purple	1958	Capitol British F3933
Don't Take Your Love From Me	1941	Bluebird B-11272
Don't Worry 'Bout Me	1947	
Early Autumn	1957	
East Of The Sun	1947	
Everybody Loves My Baby	1947	
Ferryboat Serenade	1940	Bluebird 10856
Fifteen Minute Intermission	1940	Bluebird 10834
For You	1947	
Four Brothers	1959	Capitol 6055
Give A Little Whistle	1939	Bluebird 10590
Gobs Of Love	1942	Bluebird 11576
Happy Feet	1950	Mercury 5449
Hey Zeke	1942	Bluebird 11472
Holy Smoke	1939	Bluebird 10590
Hot Gavotte	1939	Bluebird 10603
How Long Has This Been Going On'	1958	
I Came Here To Talk For Joe	1942	Bluebird 11576
I Don't Know Why	1947	
If I Could Only Play A Concertina	1942	Bluebird 11444
I Hadn't Anyone Till You	1958	
I'll Get By	1940	Bluebird 10856
I'll Never Forget	1942	Bluebird 11444
Imagination	1957	Capitol F3713
I May Be Wrong	1947	
Impossible	1959	
It's Easy To Remember	1947	
It's The Natural Thing To Do	1937	Brunswick 7927
(I've Got A Gal In) Kalamazoo	1942	Bluebird B-11566
I've Had My Moments	1947	
Just Squeeze Me	1947	
Little Haven Of The Seven Seas	1937	Brunswick 7946
Love Is In The Air To-Night	1937	Brunswick 7939
Mama, That Moon Is Here Again	1937	Brunswick 8013/Brunswick A 81324
Man I Love, The	1947	
Memories Of You	1947	
Moonglow	1941	Bluebird B-11279
Music 'Til Dawn	1942	Bluebird B-11517
My Wubba Dolly	1939	Bluebird 10512
Nearness Of You, The	1958	
Nice Work If You Can Get It	1947	
Oh, How I Miss You Tonight	1942	Bluebird B-11511
Oh Marie - Oh Marie	1937	Brunswick 7920
Old Guitar And An Old Refrain, An		
Pagan Love Song	1947	
Red Sails In The Sunset	1947	
Run, Rabbit Run	1939	Bluebird 10603
Sailor With Navy Blue Eyes	1940	Bluebird 10690
Slap-Slap (That's The Way You Say Hello)	1941	Bluebird B-11279
Some Days There Just Ain't No Fish	1950	Mercury 5431
Sometimes I'm Happy	1939	Bluebird 10660
Sophisticated Lady	1947	
Spring Is Here	1958	
Star Dust	1947	
Stars Fell On Alabama	1947	
Stomping At The Savoy	1947	
Strip Polka	1942	Bluebird B-11573
Sweetheart Of All My Dreams	1945	Victor 20-1672
Take Me In Your Arms	1945	Victor 45-0000
Take The "A" Train	1957	
That Old Feeling	1957	
That's All	1959	
There Is No Greater Love	1958	
'Tis Autumn	1941	Bluebird B-11431
What's New	1957	
What's The Use	1947	
When My Dreamboat Comes Home	1947	
When The Roses Bloom Again	1942	Bluebird 11472
When The Swallows Come Back To Capistrano	1947	
You Made Me Love You		
Zing! Went The Strings Of My Heart	1947	

King Sisters (as the Four King Sisters)

Heavenly Hide-Away	1942	Bluebird B-11522
In The Mood	1939	Bluebird B-10545
Irish Washerwoman	1939	Bluebird B-10545
Jersey Bounce	1942	Bluebird B-11522
Music Makers	1941	Bluebird B-11154

King Sisters (Four King Sisters)

Back In Your Own Back Yard	1941	Bluebird 11184
Bee Gezind, A	1939	Bluebird 10512
Bells Of St. Mary's, The	1937	Brunswick A 81347
Bibi	1941	Bluebird 11317
Candy	1945	Victor 20-1633
Daybreak	1942	Bluebird 11582
Don't Go In The Lion's Cage Tonight	1940	Bluebird 10930
Heigh-Ho!	1938	Brunswick A 81508
History Of Sweet Swing (Stompin' At The Savoy), The	1937	Brunswick 8048
Hot Lips	1937	Brunswick A 81347
Hut Hut Song, The	1941	Bluebird 11154
I Dreamt I Dwelt In Harlem	1941	Bluebird 11184
I'm Looking For Someone's Heart	1940	Bluebird B-10958
It's Love-Love-Love	1944	Bluebird 30-0822
I Understand	1941	Bluebird 11122
Jack And Jill	1941	Bluebird 11349
Java Jive	1940	Bluebird 10746
Kalamazoo	1942	Bluebird 11566
Kille Kille-Indian Love	1942	Bluebird 11582

Title	Year	Label
Love Me A Little, Little Man	1941	Bluebird 11209
Lover's Lullabye, A	1940	Bluebird 10746
Mairzy Doats And Dozy Doats (Mares Eat Oats And Does Eat Oats)	1944	Bluebird 30-0822
Milkman, Keep Those Bottles Quiet	1944	Bluebird 30-0824
Minka	1941	Bluebird 11317
Miss Otis Regrets	1941	Bluebird 11055
My Sister And I	1941	Bluebird 11122
On Behalf Of A Visiting Fireman	1940	Bluebird 10764
Over The Rainbow	1942	Bluebird 11566
Perspicacity	1941	Bluebird 11099
Poi, My Boy, Will Make A Man Of You	1940	Bluebird 10764
Rose O'Day	1941	Bluebird 11349
Sadie Hawkins Day	1940	Bluebird 10733
Sand In My Shoes	1941	Bluebird 11209
San Fernando Valley	1944	Bluebird 30-0824
Saturday Night (Is The Loneliest Night In The Week)	1945	Victor 20-1633
Six Lessons From Madama La Zonga	1940	Bluebird 10733
There's A Brand New Picture In My Picture Frame	1938	Brunswick A 81681
Used To Love You (But It's All Over Now)	1940	Bluebird 10930
Voice In The Old Village Choir, The	1940	Bluebird B-10958
Whatcha Know, Joe'	1941	Bluebird 11055
Where The Mountains Meet The Moon	1941	Bluebird 11099
Bless 'Em All	1940	Victor 27407
Coffee Song (They've Got An Awful Lot Of Coffee In Brazil), The	1946	Victor 20-1943
Divorce Me C.O.D.	1946	Victor 20-2018
It's A Pity To Say Goodnight	1946	Victor 20-2018
It's Yours	1941	Bluebird B-11196
Keep Smilin', Keep Laughin', Be Happy	1942	Victor 27936
Kiss The Boys Goodbye	1941	Bluebird B-11196
Rose Room	1941	Bluebird B-11002
Row, Row, Row Your Boat	1940	Bluebird B-10948
Santa Claus Is Comin' To Town	1941	Bluebird B-11353
Sing Your Worries Away	1942	Bluebird B-11420
Smile For Me (Until We Meet Again)	1942	Bluebird B-11461
St. Louis Blues	1940	Bluebird B-10948
Stone Cold Dead In The Market (He Had It Coming)	1946	Victor 20-1943
Tell Me Pretty Maiden	1940	Victor 27407
Tender Word Will Mend It All, A	1945	Victor 20-1672
Tiger Rag	1941	Bluebird B-11002
When It's Moonlight On The Blue Pacific (with Bill Schallen)	1942	Victor 27948

King Sisters (Four King Sisters) (with the Rhythm 'Reys')

Title	Year	Label
Conchita, Marquita, Lolita, Pepita, Rosita, Juanita Lopez	1942	Bluebird B-11555
Don't Sit Under The Apple Tree (With Anyone Else But Me)	1942	Bluebird B-11511
Having A Lonely Time	1941	Bluebird B-11252
He's 1-A In The Army And He's 1-A In My Heart	1941	Bluebird B-11252
How Do You Fall In Love'	1942	Bluebird B-11420
My Devotion	1942	Bluebird B-11555
Rose And A Prayer, A	1941	Bluebird B-11239
Someone's Rocking My Dreamboat	1941	Bluebird B-11398
Te Amo, Oh! Baby	1941	Bluebird B-11239
We're The Couple In The Castle	1941	Bluebird B-11398

King Sisters and Hal Derwin

St. Louis Blues

King's Men

Title	Year	Label
Alexander's Ragtime Band	1941	Decca 4119
Awake In A Dream (with Ramona Davies)	1936	Victor 25265
Blue-Tail Fly	1947	MGM 30086
Cindy	1947	MGM 30085
I'm The Echo	1935	Victor 25198
Jubilee - Medley Part 1 (with Ramona Davies)	1935	Victor 36175
Lamp Is Low, The	1939	Vocalion 4878
Little Toot	1947	MGM 10178
Look For The Silver Lining	1936	Victor 25278
Me And Marie	1935	Victor 25135
My Grandfather's Clock	1947	MGM 30086
Oh My Darling Clementine	1947	MGM 30087
Old Dan Tucker	1947	MGM 30087
Pecos Bill	1947	MGM 10178
Red River Valley	1947	MGM 30085
Roundup Lullaby, A	1947	MGM 30088
Saddle Your Blues To A Wild Mustang (with Bob Lawrence)	1936	Victor 25251
Skip To My Lou	1947	MGM 30088
Someone I Love	1935	Victor 25023
Stairway To The Stars	1939	Vocalion 4878
Top Hat - Medley Part 1 (with Durelle Alexander and Johnny Hauser)	1935	Victor 36174
Top Hat - Medley Part 2 (with Ramona Davies)	1935	Victor 36174
Wah-Hoo!	1936	Victor 25252
Waltz Was Born In Vienna, A	1936	Victor 25274
'Way Back Home (with John Hauser)	1935	Victor 25022
When I Grow Too Old To Dream	1934	Victor 24844/Electrola EG 3403
You're A Grand Old Flag	1941	Decca 4119

King's Men & Pearl Carr
Shepherd Of The Hills	1952	Decca F9872

King's Men (with Bing Crosby)
De Camptown Races	1940	Brunswick 1860/Brunswick 03190/Decca 18803/Decca 25139
Did Your Mother Come From Ireland'	1940	Brunswick 1849/Brunswick 03651/Decca 3609/Decca 23787
Don't Ever Be Afraid To Go Home	1948	Decca 28061/Brunswick 04938 (1952)
My Old Kentucky Home	1940	Decca 3886/Decca 18803/Brunswick 1860/Brunswick 04101
Open Up Your Heart	1952	Brunswick 05070/Decca 28470
Rosaleen	1948	Decca 28061/Brunswick 04938
Two Shillelagh O'Sullivan	1952	Brunswick 04921/Decca 28048/
Where The River Shannon Flows	1940	Brunswick 1849/Brunswick 03651/Decca 3609/Decca 23787
You Don't Know What Lonesome Is	1952	Brunswick 05070/Decca 28470

King's Men (with Rudy Vallee)
Lazy Rolls The Rio Grande	1940	Varsity 8211
Whiffenpoof Song	1940	Varsity 8211

King's Men, John Hauser & the
Star Dust	1934	Victor 36159

King's Men, Judy Garland & the
I Don't Care	1947	MGM 30206/MGM 50026
Last Night When We Were Young	1947	MGM 30432
Play That Barbershop Chord	1947	MGM 30206/MGM 50026/MGM 30432

King's Men, Ramona [Davies] & the
I Feel A Song Comin' On	1935	Victor 25091

King's Jesters
After You've Gone	1933	Bluebird B-5149/Electradisk 2048/Sunrise S-320
China Boy	1933	Bluebird B-5184/Electradisk 2077/Sunrise S-3264
Dance Of The Little Dutch Dolls	1931	Victor 22870
Fly Outflew The Flea, The	1938	Decca 1826
I Can't Give You Anything But Love	1933	Bluebird B-6517
Shine	1933	Bluebird B-5184/Electradisk 2077/Sunrise S-3264
Some Of These Days	1933	Bluebird B-6517
Yeah Man!	1933	Bluebird B-5149/Electradisk 2048/Sunrise S-320

King's Jesters & Louise
I Surrender Dear	1933	Vogue R-708
S'Posin'	1933	Vogue R-708

King's Jesters (with Mildred Bailey)
Dear Old Mother Dixie	1932	Bluebird B-7873/Victor 24137
When It's Sleepy Time Down South	1931	Victor 22828

King's Jesters (with Red McKenzie and Frank Luther)
Face The Music - Medley	1932	Victor 36050

Kings, Orville Baggie Hardiman & the
Diane	1948	Mercury 8108
Great Day	1948	Mercury 8108

Kirk, Andy And his Clouds Of Joy
Little Joe From Chicago	1940	Decca 3385

Kiwanis Quartette (Binghamton Kiwanis Quartet)
Builders	1924	Columbia

Kline, Olive & the Lyric Quartet
Chin Chin: Love Moon - Waltz Song	1914	Victor 17665

Knapp Trio
Everything Stops For Tea	1936	Brunswick 7649

Knickerbocker Trio
Carry Me Back To Old Virginny	1917	Gennett 10031
Darling Nellie Gray	1917	Gennett 10031

Knickerbocker Male Quartet
Hush A Bye Baby	1928	Harmony 618
If I Can't Have You	1928	Harmony 618

Knickerbocker Mixed Quartette
Refuge	1902	Columbia 32075

Knickerbocker Quartet
America, Here's My Boy	1917	Columbia A-2225
Anchored	1915	Edison (2mincyl)
Annie Laurie	1909	Edison (cyl)
Bridge, The	1911	Edison 1901 (4BA)/Edison 708 (4BA)

100 Years of Harmony: 1850 to 1950

Come Where My Love Lies Dreaming	1908	Edison 1933 (4BA)
Elks' Funeral Odes	1914	Edison (cyl)
Fading, Still Fading	1910	Edison (cyl)
Goodnight Farewell	1913	Edison (4BA)
Home Sweet Home	1910	Edison (cyl)
Honolulu Hicki Boola Boo	1916	Columbia A-2160
Indiana	1917	Columbia A-2221
I've Got The Sweetest Girl In Maryland	1917	Columbia A-2207
Lead Kindly Light	1909	Edison (cyl)
Let's All Be Americans Now	1917	Columbia A-2225
Lighthouse By The Sea, The	1913	Edison (cyl)
Memories Of Galilee	1909	Edison (cyl)
Moonlight On The Lake	1910	Edison 2278 (4BA)
My Old Kentucky Home	1909	Edison (cyl)
Nearer, My God To Thee		Edison 1557 (4BA)
Oft In The Stilly Night	1910	Edison (cyl)
Old Black Joe	1913	Edison 1865 (4BA)
Old Fashioned Girl, An	1922	Columbia
Old Oaken Bucket, The	1915	Edison 2046 (4BA)
Pack Up Your Troubles In Your Old Kit Bag	1917	Columbia A-2181
Passing Show Of 1917: Meet Me At The Station Dear	1917	Columbia A-2229
Sally In Our Alley	1915	Edison (cyl)
Seven Favorite College Songs	1909	Edison (cyl)
Silver Bay	1917	Columbia A-2187
So Do I	1908	Edison (cyl)
Songs Of Yale	1911	Edison (cyl)
Songs Of Yesterday	1916	Columbia A-2129
Sweet Elaine	1928	Harmony 587
Sweetheart Of Sigma Chi	1928	Harmony 587
Sword Of Bunker Hill, The	1908	Edison (cyl)
Tramp! Tramp! Tramp! (The Boys Are Marching)	1914	Edison 2432 (4BA)
We're Tenting Tonight	1913	Edison 1881 (4BA)
When The Corn Is Waving	1913	Edison 2138 (4BA)/Edison 658 (4BA)
When The Ebb-Tide Flows	1914	Edison (cyl)
Winter Song	1911	Edison (cyl)
Yaddie Kaddie Kiddy Koo	1916	Columbia A-2151

Knickerbocker Quartet, Elizabeth Spencer & the

I Love You, California		Edison 80138
Rosary, The		Edison 1525 (4BA)
Summer Days		Edison 80138

Knickerbocker Quartet, Elizabeth Spencer with the

I Love You California	1913	Edison (cyl)

Knickerbocker Quartet, James Harrod & the

I'll Come Back To You	1917	Columbia

Knickerbocker Quartette

Honolulu, America Loves You (We've Got To Hand It To You)	1916	Columbia A-21484
When Grandma Sings The Songs	1916	Columbia
She Loved At The End Of A Perfect Day		

Knickerbocker Quartette (with Harry C. Browne)

Dar De Ole Serpent Was A-Crawlin'	1916	Columbia
De Gospel Train Am Comin'	1916	Columbia A-22554
Keep In De Middle Ob De Road	1916	Columbia A-2116
Meet Me At The Station, Dear	1917	Columbia A-22294
Oh! Dem Golden Slippers	1916	Columbia A-2116

Knickerbocker Quintet

Rosary		Edison 9052 (2mincyl)

Knickerbocker Serenaders

After The Ball/Medley	1947	Decca 28019
Bill Bailey/Medley	1947	Decca 28018
Daisy Bell/Medley	1947	Decca 28017
In The Good Old Summertime	1947	Decca 28016
Meet Me In St. Louis, Louis	1947	Decca 28017
On The Benches In The Park	1947	Decca 28019
Sidewalks Of New York, The	1947	Decca 28016
Tammany Medley	1947	Decca 2808

Knickerbocker Trio

Silver Threads Among The Gold	1920	Champion 15157

Knickerbockers

Somewhere, Somehow, Sweetheart	1953	It's A Natural 3000
You Must Know	1953	It's A Natural 3000

Knites Of Rhythm

Baby Won't You Fall In Love	1941	Bluebird B-8882
Chattanooga Choo Choo	1941	Bluebird B-8882

Lakeshore Club Quartet (Peerless Quartet)

Sam The Old Accordion Man	1927	Champion 15221
Take In The Sun, Hang Out The Moon	1926	Champion 15206

Landt Trio

Whippoorwill	1930	Victor 22408

Landt Trio (and White)

Animal Trainer, The	1934	Victor 24804
No! No! A Thousand Times No!	1934	Victor 24804

Landt Trio (with Mildred Hunt)

Sleepy Valley	1929	Victor 22102
S'Posin'	1929	Victor 22102

Langford, Frances & Male Quartet

Carry Me Back To Ole Virginny	1938	Decca 15040
Little Grey Home In The West	1938	Decca 15040

Laurel Fireman Quartet

Great Redeemer, The	1936	Conqueror 8746
You Gotta Live Your Religion Every Day	1936	Conqueror 8746

Laurel Firemen's Quartet

Because I Love Him	1929	Okeh 45437
Give The World A Smile	1929	Okeh 45404
He's Calling All	1929	Okeh 45426
Jesus Is The Light	1929	Okeh 45426

My Friend Divine	1929	Okeh 45437
When I Reach Home	1929	Okeh 45404

Lawrence, Brian & his Quartet

Ain't She Sweet	1935	Champion 40034
Dinah	1935	Champion 40058
Shine	1935	Champion 40046
Singing In The Rain	1935	Champion 40046
Somebody Stole My Gal	1935	Champion 40034
Tiger Rag	1934	Champion 40058

Le Brun Sisters

Don't Get Around Much Anymore	1942	Decca 10072/Decca 18479

Leatherman Sisters

Home Coming Week	1936	Bluebird 6598
Just A Little While	1936	Bluebird 6598

Lennox, Elizabeth & the Crescent Trio

Cradle Song, The	1927	Brunswick 2696/Brunswick 3598
Rosary, The	1927	Brunswick 2696/Brunswick 3598

Lewis Trio

Happy Days Are Here Again	1930	Banner 0610/Challenge 874/Jewel 5867/Oriole 1867/Romeo 1230
Have A Little Faith In Me	1930	Banner 0610/Oriole 1867/Conqueror 7490/Romeo 1230
Smiles Are Making The World Go Around	1930	Banner 0699/Oriole 1955/Romeo 1319
Tell Me You Care	1930	Banner 737/Romeo 1351
Under A Texas Moon	1930	Banner 0699/Conqueror 7546/Domino 4563/Jewel 5955/Romeo 1319

Liberty Quartet

Abide With Me	1919	Banner 2074
Adeste Fideles	1919	Banner 2065
Holy, Holy, Holy	1919	Banner 2073
Nearer My God, To Thee	1919	Banner 2071
Onward Christian Soldiers	1919	Banner 2070

Limber Quartet

Brother Noah Built An Ark	1924	Victor 19451

Lincoln Quartet

I Hope I Join The Band	1928	Paramount 12621
Wade In The Water	1928	Paramount 12621

Lions Quartet

Deep River	1927	Columbia 1167-D
Moanin' Lady	1927	Columbia 1167-D

Lions Quartet Of Seattle

Hear Dem Bells	1928	Columbia 1527-D
How Can I Leave Thee	1928	Columbia 1597-D
I See My Love At The Window & Calliope	1928	Columbia 1503-D
Oh! Dem Golden Slippers	1928	Columbia 1527-D/Columbia 5292
Sweet Genevieve	1928	Columbia 1597-D
Vere Is Mein Leetle Dog Gone	1928	Columbia 1503-D

Livingston College Negro Male Quartet

Good Old Songs - Medley	1927	Victor 20824
Gospel Train	1927	Victor 20949
Mosquito	1927	Victor 20949
Quartet Rehearsal	1927	Victor 20824

Log Cabin Four

Bugle Call Rag	1932	
Cabin In The Cotton	1932	Columbia 2664D
Minnie The Moocher's Weddin' Day	1932	Columbia 2664D
Now's The Time To Fall In Love	1932	
Sing That Thing	1932	
Slappin' The Bass	1932	
Some Of These Days	1932	Columbia
So Sweet	1932	
So The Bluebirds And The Blackbirds Got Together (with Ruth King)	1932	Victor
Tiger Rag	1932	

Longo Trio

Mighty Lak' A Rose	1920	Pathe 22277
Somewhere A Voice Is Calling	1920	Pathe 22277

Lotus Male Quartet

I Can't Think Of Nothin' Else But You	1902	Columbia 820
Little Darling, Dream Of Me		Columbia 519
Mandy Lee	190'	Columbia 749
My Creole Sue	190'	Columbia 750
Old Oaken Bucket, The		Peer 521
Suwanee River	1902	Columbia 818/Columbia A-0368 (1908)

Louisiana Boys

Every Man A King	1935	Bluebird B-5840
Follow Long (The Louisiana Song)	1935	Bluebird B-5840

Lowland Singers

High Society	1933	Columbia 2806-D
Shim Sham Shimmy Dance, The	1933	Columbia 2806-D

Lubbock Texas Quartet

O Mother How We Miss You	1929	Columbia 15510-D
Turn Away	1929	Columbia 15510-D

Lucy Smith Jubilee Singers

No Room At The Hotel	1928	Vocalion 1222
Seeking For Me	1928	Vocalion 1222

Lunceford Trio
Babs	1935	Brunswick A 81016
Chillun, Get Up (with Henry Wells)	1934	Victor 24522
Me And The Moon	1936	Decca 915
Muddy Water	1936	Decca 1219/Brunswick 02491/Brunswick A 81299
My Blue Heaven	1935	Brunswick 81031/Decca 712
Slumming On Park Avenue	1937	Decca 1128
'Taint Good (Like A Nickel Made Of Wood)	1936	Brunswick A 81097

Lunceford Trio & James Young
Ain't She Sweet	1939	Okeh 4875/Vocalion 4875/Brunswick A 82174/Odeon A 272253

Lunceford Trio with James Young
Cheatin' Me	1939	Okeh 4582/Okeh 6894/Vocalion 4582/Odeon A 272292/Odeon O-31768
'Taint What You Do	1939	Columbia/Odeon A 272292/Odeon O-31768

Lunceford Trio, Sy Oliver & the
I'll Take The South	1935	Brunswick 81031/Decca 805

Lyn Murray Quartet, Frank Luther & the
Back'd Car, The/Kerry Dance	1939	Decca 2298B
Beautiful Dreamer	1938	Decca 1996
Believe Me, If All Those Endearing Young Charms	1939	Decca 2299A
Come Where My Love Lies Dreaming	1938	Decca 1999
De Camptown Races	1938	Decca 1998
Handful Of Earth From My Mother's Grave, A	1939	Decca 2296B
Harp That Once Thro' Tara's Halls	1939	Decca 2300
I Dream Of Jeannie With The Light Brown Hair	1938	Decca 1997
I'll Take You Home Again, Kathleen	1939	Decca 2297A
Kathleen Mavourneen	1939	Decca 2296A
Killarney	1939	Decca 2300
Little Town In Ould County Down	1939	Decca 2297B
Massa's In De Cold, Cold Ground	1938	Decca 2000
My Old Kentucky Home	1938	Decca 1996
Nelly Bly/Hard Times Come Again	1938	Decca 2000
Oh Boys Carry Me 'Long	1938	Decca 1999
Old Black Joe	1938	Decca 1998
Old Folks At Home	1938	Decca 1997
Rose Of Tralee, The	1939	Decca 2298A
Where The River Shannon Flows	1939	Decca 2299B

Lyric Male Quartet
Broadway Rose	1921	Edison DD 7617
Down In The Old Neighborhood	1927	Harmony 423-H
Hallelujah	1927	Harmony 423-H
Medley Of Old Favorites	1927	
Sometimes I'm Happy	1927	

Lyric Male Quartet, Frieda Hempel & the
Vesper Hymn		Edison 8972

Lyric Quartet
Asleep In Jesus	1913	Victor 17389
Come And Trip It As You Go	1916	Victor 18123
Down Among The Sheltering Palms	1915	Victor 17778
For Every Boy Who's Lonely	1912	Victor 17230
Funiculi Funicula	1922	Victor 18968
God Is A Spirit	1907	Victor 16038
God Is Love	1912	Victor 17096
Haste Thee Nymph	1916	Victor 18123
Home Again	1916	Victor 18222
How Lovely Are The Messengers	1912	Victor 17208
I'm Looking For Someone's Heart	1915	Victor 17754
In The Night When The Moon Slyly Winks	1914	Victor 17546
In The Time Of The Roses	1913	Victor 17351
In Zion's Sacred Gates	1899	Berliner 0767
I Want To Go To Tokyo	1915	Victor 17754
Lo How A Rose Ever Blooming	1915	Victor 17870
Lord's Prayer/Gloria Patria	1911	Victor 16877
Loving	1913	Victor 17250
Martha: Goodnight Quartet	1912	Victor 17226
Mikado Madrigal: Bright Dawning	1912	Victor 17226
My Bonne Lass She Smileth	1916	Victor 18146
My Boy	1913	Victor 17434
My Dreamy China Lady	1916	Victor 18034
Nazareth	1914	Victor 17647
Oh Cecilia	1914	Victor 17546
Oh Hush Thee My Baby	1917	Victor 18441
Old Refrain, The	1913	Victor 17370
One Wonderful Night	1915	Victor 17811
On The Bay Of Old Bombay	1915	Victor 17831
Psalm 100: The Mear	1914	Victor 17646
Psalm 107: Dundee	1914	Victor 17646
Rock Of Ages	1909	Victor 16269
Sleep Noble Hearts	1913	Victor 17310
Sweet And Low	1917	Victor 18417

Sweet Is True Love	1916	Victor 18146
Temple Bells/Under Many Flags	1912	Victor 17219
There's A Girl In Havana	1911	Victor 16985
Vacant Chair	1911	Victor 16984
When The Angelus Is Ringing	1914	Victor 17587
Where The Edelweiss Is Blooming	1912	Victor 17194
You For Me In Summertime	1915	Victor 17778

Lyric Quartet & Edward Hamilton

Land Of Hope And Glory	1914	Victor 17698

Lyric Quartet & Mr. & Mrs. Wheeler

Girl Like Me, A	1912	Victor 17095

Lyric Quartet with Harry Macdonough

Funiculi Funicula	1912	Victor 17208
I Love Love	1913	Victor 17250
You're In Love	1917	Victor 18260

Lyric Trio

Everything Reminds Me Of That Old Sweetheart Of Mine	1915	Columbia A-1684

Lyric Trio & William Hooley

Adeste Fideles	1899	Berliner 0771O
God Be Merciful Unto Us	1899	Berliner 0768O

Lyric Trio (with Will Oakland)

Dear Love Days	1914	Columbia A-1577

Macdonough, H. & the Haydn Quartet

Your Picture Says Remember	1908	Victor 16032

Macdonough, Harry & Quartet

Home Over There	1909	Victor 16197

Macdonough, Harry & the Haydn Quartet

Garden Of Roses	1910	Victor 16467
My Heart Has Learned To Love You	1910	Victor 16503
Throw Out The Life Line	1909	Victor 16431

Macdonough, Harry with American Quartet

Here's To The Friend In The Stormy Seas	1912	Victor 17058

MacDowell Sisters

Baby Sister Blues	1924	Edison 51368
One, Two, Three, Four		Edison 51368

Macedonia Quartet

House By The Side Of The Road, The	1928	Victor 21293
I Have Been Redeemed	1928	Victor 21576
Sweet Little Girl Of Mine	1928	Victor 21293
Who'll Be To Blame'	1928	Victor 21576

Mack Sisters

Jammin' In Georgia	1939	Decca 7684
Stop Pretending (So Hip You See)	1939	Decca 7684

Macon Quartet

Uncle Joe	1927	Columbia 15211-D
Yodel	1927	Columbia 15211-D

Magichords

Cherry Tree	1949	Regal 3237
Darling	1949	Regal 3238
Doubt In Your Mind	1950	Domino 360
Game Of Broken Hearts, The	1949	Regal 3237
I Beeped When I Should Have Bopped	1949	Regal 3238
If I Didn't Love You Like I Do	1950	Marlow 101
It's Over Because We're Through	1950	Domino 360
Parrot And The Rooster, The	1950	Marlow 101
Why Feel This Way About You	1949	Tritone

Magichords, Hot Lips Page & Sylvia Vanterpool & the

Chocolate Candy Blues	1950	Columbia 30220

Magichords, Madeline Greene & the

Be Sure	1950	Domino 311
I've Got A Right To Be Blue	1950	Domino 311

Magichords, Sylvia Vanterpool & the

I Was Under The Impression (That You Loved Me)	1950	Columbia 30227

Majestic Male Quartet

Coming	1935	Bluebird 6833
I Love To Raise My Voice	1935	Bluebird 6833
Jericho Road	1936	Bluebird 6580
Jesus Holds My Hand	1936	Bluebird 6580

Majestic Quartet

He Said I'd Be Lifted Up	1939	Bluebird 8154
Holy Be Thy Name	1939	Bluebird 8255
I'll Meet You In The Morning	1939	Bluebird 8255
In The Shadow Of The Cross	1939	Bluebird 8051
Little Talk With Jesus, A	1939	Bluebird 8154
Oh Happy Day	1939	Bluebird 8051

Majestic Quartette

America	1922	Banner 2099
Star Spangled Banner	1922	Banner 2099

Majors

At Last	1951	Derby 763
Come On Up To My Room	1951	Derby 779
Laughing On The Outside, Crying On The Inside	1951	Derby 779
You Ran Away With My Heart	1951	Derby 763

Male Quartet

Alone In The Deep		Edison 2616 (4BA)
Sleigh Ride Party, The	1906	Imperial 44686/Imperial 44686 (1906)/Busy Bee 1324 (1906)
Steamboat Medley	1906	American 031298

Male Quartet with Tuxedo Orchestra

Song Of The Vagabonds	1925	Vocalion 15162

Male Trio (Charles Hart, Elliott Shaw and Everett Clark)

Granny	1922	Columbia A-3556

Male Trio, Tenor &

Mocking Bird Medley	1908	Columbia A-0392

Manhansett Quartette

Annie Laurie	1894	North American 2

Little Alabama Coon | 1897 | Columbia 9015
Moonlight On The Lake | 1897 | Columbia 9008
My Old Kentucky Home | 1902 | Columbia 9019
Nearer, My God, To Thee | 1897 | Columbia 9012
Old Oaken Bucket, The | 1897 | Columbia 9018
Picture Turned Toward The Wall | 1892 | North American
Sally In Our Alley | 1896 | min. cyl/Columbia 9014 (1897)/Columbia 85097 (1906)

Manhattan Brothers
Amazin' Ananbi (Honey Be My Honey Bee) | 1951 | Gallotone 1277
Malayisha | 1951 | Gallotone GB-1278
Wami-Wami (Satchel Mouth Baby) | 1951 | Gallotone 1277

Manhattan Harmony Four
Lift Every Voice And Sing | 1924 | Paramount 12106
My Way Is Clouded | 1924 | Paramount 12106

Manhattan Mixed Trio
Do They Think Of Me At Home' | | Edison 1973 (4BA)

Manhattan Quartet
Good Night | 1924 | Edison
Juanita | 1928 | Champion 15786
Kentucky Babe - Negro Lullaby | 1916 | Edison DD 80313/Edison BA 2399
Passing Regiment, The | 1917 | Starr 7614
Pickaninny Lullaby | 1923 | Edison DD 51214

Maple City 4
Angry | 1934 | Conqueror 8302
Beautiful Isle Of Somewhere | 1934 | Conqueror 8301
Old Wooden Rocker, The | 1934 | Conqueror 8301
Take Me Back To Col-Ler-Rad-Da | 1934 | Conqueror 8302

Maple City Four
Aura Lee | 1946 | Mercury A-1031
Green Grass Grew All Around, The | 1928 | Silvertone 5195/Supertone 9213
Heart Of My Heart | 1946 | Mercury A-1029
Just A Dream Of You Dear | 1946 | Mercury A-1031
Missouri Waltz | 1946 | Mercury A-1030
Oh Monah! | 1931 | Banner 32770/Melotone 12699/Perfect 15774/Conqueror 8167
Old MacDonald Had A Farm | 1928 | Silvertone 5195/Supertone 9213
Rockin' Alone In The Old Rockin' Chair | 1931 | Conqueror 8165
Shine On Harvest Moon | 1946 | Mercury A-1029
Stephen Foster Medley | 1946 | Mercury A-1030
Tell My Mother I'm In Heaven | 1931 | Banner 32774/Conqueror 8165
Tiger Rag | 1931 | Banner 32770/Perfect 15774/Conqueror 8167
Two Little Pretty Birds | 1933 | Conqueror 8166
Will The Angels Play Their Harps For Me' | 1931 | Banner 32774/Melotone 12703/Conqueror 8166

Maples
I Must Forget You | 1954 | Blue Lake 111

Mariners
And Then I Prayed | 1951 | Columbia 39332
Angels Watchin O'er Me | 1950 | Columbia 38667
Beautiful Isle Of Somewhere | 1952 | Columbia 39655
Be The Good Lord Willing | 1950 | Columbia 38667
Beyond The Reef | 1950 | Columbia 38966
Castles In The Sand | 1951 | Columbia 39193
Chee Chee-oo Chee | 1955 | Columbia 40514
Come To The Casbah | 1952 | Columbia 39655
Do As You Would Be Did By | 1955 | Columbia 40439
Everyone Is Welcome In The House Of The Lord | 1951 | Columbia 39422
Gentle Carpenter Of Bethlehem, The | 1952 | Columbia 39606
Good Luck, Good Health, God Bless You | 1951 | Columbia 39445
Hello Sunshine | 1951 | Columbia 39445
Hey, Mabel! | 1955 | Columbia 40405
How Near To My Heart | 1951 | Columbia 39073
I Didn't Come To Say Hello | 1955 | Columbia 40439
I Don't Know Whether To Laugh Or Cry Over You | 1950 | Columbia 38677
I Just Want You | 1952 | Columbia 40047
In The Chapel In The Moonlight | 1954 | Columbia 40271
I See God | 1952 | Columbia 39606
I See The Moon | 1952 | Columbia 40047
It Is No Secret | 1951 | Columbia 39073
It's All Over But The Memories | 1952 | Columbia 39607
Jambo | 1954 | Columbia 40318
Jeannine | 1952 | Columbia 39718
Leprechaun Lullaby | 1949 | Columbia 38724
Light In The Window | 1951 | Columbia 38219
Loving Is Believing | 1951 | Columbia 38219
Mariners' Song, The | 1951 | Columbia 39515
Mighty Navy Wings | 1951 | Columbia 39515
Minnequa | 1950 | Columbia 38966
My Little Grass Shack | 1951 | Columbia 39101

Oh Mo'Nah	1954	Columbia 40271
Old Beer Bottle, An	1955	Columbia 40405
Old Friend Is The Best Friend, An	1951	Columbia 39101
One Love	1952	Columbia 39718
Only, Only You	1951	Columbia 39422
On The Island Of Oahu	1949	Columbia 38724
Our Lady Of Fatima	1950	Columbia 39042
Poison Ivy	1950	Columbia 38677
Red, Red Robin, A	1953	Columbia 40104
Rosary, The	1950	Columbia 39042
Rusty Old Halo, A	1955	Columbia 40514
Sentimental Eyes	1954	Columbia 40157
Shannon, The Shamrocks And You, The	1951	Columbia 39332
Sometime	1950	Columbia 38781
Stars	1950	Columbia 38781
Steam Heat	1954	Columbia 40241
Sweet Mama, Tree Top Tall	1953	Columbia 40104
Take Me Home	1952	Columbia 39607
They Call The Wind Maria	1951	Columbia 39568
They Don't Play The Piano Anymore	1954	Columbia 40157
They'll Forget About You	1954	Columbia 40318
Tinkle Song, The	1951	Columbia 39568
When I Needed You Most	1954	Columbia 40241
With These Hands	1951	Columbia 39193

Mariners (with Ipana Troubadours) (Mariners Trio)

Promises	1930	Columbia 2220-D
Sing (A Little Happy Thing)	1930	Columbia 2220-D

Mariners Trio

Down The River Of Golden Dreams	1930	Okeh 41433/Odeon A 221280
Hangin' On The Garden Gate	1929	Victor 22301
Happy Feet	1930	Okeh 41433/Odeon A 221280
I Don't Mind Walkin' In The Rain	1930	Okeh 41449
Just A Little Dance Mam'selle	1930	Okeh 41449

Marr, Graham & the Stellar Quartet

Stein Song	1916	Columbia A-5879

Marshall Brothers

I Didn't Know	1951	Savoy 986 (unreleased bootleg)
It All Comes (Back To Me Now)	1951	Savoy 986 (unreleased bootleg)
Just A Poor Boy In Love	1952	Savoy 833
Mr. Santa's Boogie	1951	Savoy 825
My Life Is My Life		Savoy 977 (unreleased bootleg)
Who'll Be The Fool From Now On'	1951	Savoy 825
Why Make A Fool Out Of Me'	1952	Savoy 833

Marshall Brothers, William Cook & the

Just Because	1951	Savoy 828
Soldier's Prayer	1951	Savoy 828

Marshall Sisters

Underneath The Harlem Moon	1932	Electradisk 1922

Martin-Aires Trio

Yes, There Ain't No Moonlight	1938	Bluebird B-7406

Marvin Family

Life On The Ocean Wave	1929	Columbia 15474-D

Mask & Wig Male Quartet

Joan Of Arkansas	1925	Victor 19626

Maskat Shriners Quartet

Absent	1926	Brunswick 3115
Goodnight Beloved	1926	Brunswick 3115
I Couldn't Hear Nobody Pray	1926	Brunswick 3116
Lord It Is I	1926	Brunswick 3114
O Holy Father	1926	Brunswick 3114
Standing In Need Of Prayer	1926	Brunswick 3116

Massanutten Military Academy Quartet

Drink To Me Only With Thine Eyes	1932	Columbia 15751-D
Nancy Lee	1932	Columbia 15751-D

Master Keys

I Got The Blues In The Mornin'	1949	Jubilee 5004
When Will I Know	1945	Top 1147
You're Not The Only Apple (On The Apple Tree)	1945	Top 1147/Jubilee 5004 (1949)

Masterkeys

Don't Talk Darling	1949	Abbey 2017
Mr. Blues	1949	Abbey 2017

Maurel, Barbara & Male Quartet

O Come All Ye Faithful	1921	Columbia A-6196

Maurel, Barbara & the Stellar Quartet

Hark The Herald Angels Sing	1921	Columbia A-6196

Mayfair Trio

Always	1926	Vocalion 15259A
I Wish I Had My Old Gal Back Again	1926	Vocalion 15355B
Just A Cottage Small	1926	Vocalion 15229B
Moon Deer	1926	Vocalion 15229
My Heart Will Tell Me So	1926	Vocalion 15406B
Night Of Love, A	1926	Vocalion 15259B
Put Your Arms Where They Belong	1926	Vocalion 15406
Whispering Trees	1926	Vocalion 15355

Mayfield, Percy

Please Send Me Someone To Love	1950	

McCarthy Sisters

Tia Da Tia Dee	1920	Okeh 4153
You'll See The Day	1920	Okeh 4168

McDonald Quartet

Christ Is Mine, Forever Mine	1930	Okeh 45517
Do Your Best And Wear A Sunny	1928	Champion 45150

Smile
Give The World A Smile	1932	Conqueror 8007
Glad Bells, The	1930	Okeh 45503
Grandmother's Bible	1932	Conqueror 8051
He Keeps My Soul	1930	Okeh 45530
I'm No Stranger To Jesus	1930	Okeh 45530
In The Hills Of Arkansas	1932	Conqueror 8064
Living For Jesus	1930	Okeh 45538
Love Enough For Me	1932	Conqueror 8050
My Faith Is Clinging To Thee	1932	Conqueror 8052
My Friend	1930	Okeh 45538
My Redeemer Lives	1932	Conqueror 8050
Precious Memories, The	1930	Okeh 45517
Riding On The Glory Waves	1928	Champion 45150
Rocking On The Waves	1932	Conqueror 8053
Singing An Old Hymn	1932	Conqueror 8007
Singing To Victory	1930	Okeh 45503
Trying To Be Happy	1932	Conqueror 8051
Tune Jesus Into Your Heart	1935	Conqueror 8502
Way Down In Georgia	1932	Conqueror 8064/Banner 32589 (1932)
We'll Never Say Goodbye	1932	Conqueror 8052
We'll Reap What We Sow	1932	Conqueror 8053

McDonald Quartette
Gypsy Love Song	1932	Banner 32590/Conqueror 8065 (1932)
I'm Happy With Him	1932	Banner 32591/Conqueror 8008 (1932)
I'm Working For The Master	1932	Banner 32591/Conqueror 8008 (1932)
Living For Jesus	1932	Banner 33342/Conqueror 8502 (1935)
Love Lifted Me Up	1932	Banner 32592/Conqueror 8009 (1932)
Precious Memories	1932	Banner 32592/Conqueror 8009 (1932)
Rocking On The Waves	1932	Banner 33342
Roll On Blue Moon	1932	Banner 32590/Conqueror 8065 (1932)

McDonough, Harry (with Haydn Quartet)
Dreaming On The Ohio (one-sided)	1905	Victor 2836
In The Wildwood Where The Bluebells Grow (one-sided)	1907	Victor 5168

McDonough, Harry (with Orpheus Quartet)
Someday They're Coming Home Again	1918	Victor 18468
There's A Little Blue Star In The Window	1918	Victor 18468

McIntyre, Lani & the Bush Quartet
Aloha Angel	1939	Decca 2704B
At Waikiki	1939	Decca 2706A
Clouds Across The Moon	1939	Decca 2706B
Next Door To Heaven	1939	Decca 2705B
Sweet Little Sweetheart	1939	Decca 2704A
Way Down In Hawaii	1939	Decca 2705A

McLaurin, Bette & Her Friends
I May Hate Myself In The Morning	1952	Derby 790

McMichen, Clayton & his Singing Sisters
Mister Moon	1927	Columbia
Old Black Joe	1927	Columbia

McMillan Quartet
Glory Is Coming	1927	Columbia 15194-D
I Love To Tell His Story	1928	Columbia 15681-D
No Stranger Yonder	1927	Columbia 15194-D
Singing On The Journey Home	1928	Columbia 15681-D

McQuahae, Allen & Male Trio
Where The River Shannon Flows	192'	Brunswick 2748

McQueen Quartet
Liza Jane	1928	
Lovesick Blues	1928	Columbia

McQuire Quintet, The Mac
I'm Gonna Dry Every Tear	1950	Capitol 1314
Place Where I Worship, The	1950	Capitol 1314

Mello Larks
Fat Man Blues	1947	United Artist 2004

Mellomen
His Arms Are Open To Everyone	1951	Decca 28371
I Walk Into The Garden	1951	Decca 28371
Lady	1956	Decca 29627

Mello-Tones
Cool By The River Banks	1951	Okeh 6828
Rough And Rocky Road	1951	Okeh 6828

Mellowmen
That Old Time Religion	1948	Decca 28081
There's A Light Burning Brightly For Me	1948	Decca 28081

Mcl-O-Dots
Baby Won't You Please Come Home	1952	Apollo
Just How Long	1952	Apollo
One More Time	1952	Apollo
Rock My Baby	1952	Apollo

Melody Four
Because I'm Yours Sincerely	1931	Victor 23289
Call Of The Freaks	1931	Bluebird 1848/Bluebird B-5028/Sunrise S 3114/Victor 23279

Title	Year	Label/Number
I'm Crazy 'Bout My Baby	1931	Victor 23289
Melody Male Quartet		
Sweet Genevieve	1922	Vocalion 14419B
Melody Masters		
Don't You Ever Mind Them	1946	Apollo 383
Fox And The Crow	1948	Apollo R-1093
If I Only Knew You Were Mine	1948	Apollo R-1093
My Baby	1946	Apollo 379
Subway Cutie	1946	Apollo 383
Wig Blues	1946	Apollo 379
Melody Three		
Beggars Of Life (with Daniel Woodyard)	1928	Victor
Blue Grass	1928	Brunswick 4002/Brunswick 03855
Bye And Bye, Sweetheart	1929	Victor 21911
California Here I Come	1928	Victor 21673
Deep In The Arms Of Love	1929	Victor 22197
Don't Hold Everything	1928	Victor 21791
Fioretta	1928	Victor 21894
Get Happy	1930	Victor 22444
Goodnight	1928	Victor 21726
Hail! Hail! The Gang's All Here	1928	Victor 21673
If You're Not Kissing Me	1930	Victor 22450
I'll Close My Eyes To The Rest Of The World	1929	Victor 22197
I'm Forever Blowing Bubbles	1929	Victor 35995
Lazy Lou'siana Moon	1930	Victor 22334
Lonesome In The Moonlight	1928	Victor 21643
Love (All I Want Is Love)	1928	Victor 21746
Love Tale Of Alsace-Lorraine, A	1929	Victor
My Song Of The Nile	1929	Victor 22028
Pals Forever	1929	Victor 22028
Pals, Just Pals	1928	Victor 21754
Remember Me To Mary (If She Still Remembers Me)	1928	Victor 21754
Sonny Boy	1928	Victor 35945
There'll Never Be Another You	1928	Victor 21601
Waiting At The End Of The Road	1929	Victor 22073
You Tell Me Your Dream	1928	Victor 21726
Melody Three (with Jesse Crawford)		
Out Of The Dawn	1928	Victor 21666
Ten Little Miles From Town	1928	Victor 21666
Melody Three (with Joe Schenk)		
He's That Kind Of A Pal	1930	Victor
Melody Three (with the Troubadours)		
Memories Of France	1928	Victor 21590
Melo-Fellows		
I'll See You In My Dreams	1939	Vocalion 5101/Conqueror 9509 (1940)
I Used To Love You	1939	Vocalion 5101
I Wonder Who's Kissing Her Now	1939	Vocalion 5226/Conqueror 9508 (1940)
Meet Me Tonight In Dreamland	1939	Vocalion 5226/Conqueror 9508 (1940)
Meltones, Mel Torme & the		
Ah, But It Happens	1948	Sounds Great SG5012/Mr. Music CD MMCD-7006
Am I Blue'	1945	Decca 18707
Back In Your Own Backyard	1948	Sounds Great SG5012/Mr. Music CD MMCD-7006
Bless You	1949	Capitol 791
Blues In The Night	1948	Mr. Music CD MMCD-7006
Brahm's Lullaby	1948	Sounds Great SG5006/Mr. Music CD MMCD-7005
California Suite	1949	Capitol P200/Discovery DS910
Everything Happens To Me	1948	Sounds Great SG5012/Mr. Music CD MMCD-7005
Fairmont College (Dear Old Fairmont)	1948	Sounds Great SG5006/Mr. Music CD MMCD-7005
Fine And Dandy	1948	Sounds Great SG5006/Mr. Music CD MMCD-7006
Fine Romance, A	1948	Sounds Great SG5012/Mr. Music CD MMCD-7006
Four Winds And The Seven Seas, The	1949	Capitol 57-671/Rhino CD R2-71589
French Lesson, The	1948	Sounds Great SG5006/Mr. Music CD MMCD-7005
Friendship	1948	Mr. Music CD MMCD-7006
Geometric Blues (Pythagoras How You Stagger Us)	1948	Mr. Music CD MMCD-7005
Get Out And Get Under	1948	Sounds Great SG5012/Mr. Music CD MMCD-7006
Got The Gate On The Golden Gate	1949	Capitol P200/Discovery DS910/Rhino CD R2-71589
Here I'll Stay	1948	Mr. Music CD MMCD-7005

Hooray For Love	1948	Mr. Music CD MMCD-7005		P200/Discovery DS910
How High The Moon	1948	Rhino R2-71589 CD	Stranger In Town, A	1944 Decca 18653/Coral 60071
I Fall In Love Too Easily	1945	Decca 18707	Sunday Night In San Fernando	1949 Capitol
I Get Along Without You Very Well	1948	Sounds Great SG5012/Mr. Music CD MMCD-7006	That Old Black Magic	1948 Mr. Music CD MMCD-7005 P200/Discovery DS910
I Gotta Right To Sing The Blues	1948	Mr. Music CD MMCD-7005	That's Where I Came In	1946 Musicraft
I'm Down To My Last Dream	1945	Decca	There's No One But You	1946 Musicraft 363
Isn't It Romantic	1948	Sounds Great SG5012/Mr. Music CD MMCD-7006	They Go To San Diego	1949 Capitol P200/Discovery DS910
It's A Most Unusual Day	1948	Sounds Great SG5006/Mr. Music CD MMCD-7005	This Is The Moment	1948 Mr. Music CD MMCD-7006
It's Dark On Observatory Hill	1948	Mr. Music CD MMCD-7005	We Think The West Coast Is The Best Coast In The Land	1949 Capitol P200/Discovery DS910
It's Magic	1948	Mr. Music CD MMCD-7006	What Is This Thing Called Love'	1948 Sounds Great SG5012/Mr. Music CD MMCD-7006
It's The Sentimental Thing To Do	1948	Sounds Great SG5012/Mr. Music CD MMCD-7006	When The Red, Red Robin Comes Bob, Bob, Bobbin' Along	1948 Sounds Great SG5006/Mr. Music CD MMCD-7005
It's Too Late Now	1949	Capitol 57-671/CDP0777-7-89941-2	Where Or When Willow Road	1944 Jewel 4000 1946 Musicraft 363
I've Got The Sun In The Morning	1948	Sounds Great SG5006/Mr. Music CD MMCD-7005	Wish I May, Wish I Might	1948 Sounds Great SG5006/Mr. Music CD MMCD-7005
Let's Fall In Love	1948	Sounds Great SG5012/Mr. Music CD MMCD-7006	Wrap Your Troubles In Dreams	1948 Sounds Great SG5012/Mr. Music CD MMCD-7006
Lover's Delight (Malt Shop Special)	1948	Sounds Great SG5006/Mr. Music CD MMCD-7006	You're Driving Me Crazy	1948 Sounds Great SG5006/Mr. Music CD MMCD-7005
Maybe You'll Be There	1948	Mr. Music CD MMCD-7005	You're The Cream Inn My Coffee	1948 Sounds Great SG5012/Mr. Music CD MMCD-7006
Miami Waltz, The	1949	Capitol P200/Discovery DS910	You're The Top	1948 Sounds Great SG5006/Mr. Music CD MMCD-7005
Money Song, The	1948	Sounds Great SG5012/Mr. Music CD MMCD-7006	You've Laughed At Me For The Last Time	1944 Decca 18653/Coral 60071
Mountain Desert Theme	1949	Capitol P200/Discovery DS910	**Meltones, Mel Torme & the (with Bing Crosby** Day By Day	1945 Decca 18746
Mountain Greenery	1948	Mr. Music CD MMCD-7005	Prove It By The Things You Do **Memphis Pullman Singers**	1945 Decca 18746
Night Must Fall	1945	Decca	Somebody's Knocking At Your Door	1930 Victor 38626
Old Master Painter, The	1949	Capitol 791	There Is Joy In The Land	1930 Victor 38626
On A Slow Boat To China	1948	Sounds Great SG5006/Mr. Music CD MMCD-7005	**Men About Town** Christmas Party - Part 1 Christmas Party - Part 2	1934 Decca 303 1934 Decca 303
Poor Little Extra Girl	1949	Capitol	Christmas Party - Part 3	1934 Decca 304

Christmas Party - Part 4	1934	Decca 304
Let's Drift Away On Dreamer's Bay	1931	Brunswick 6188

Mendelsohn Male Quartet

Prayer Of Thanksgiving	1911	Columbia A-0992

Mendelsohn Mixed Quartette

Blest Be The Tie That Binds	1907	Columbia 3777/Columbia A-265 (1908)
Good Night, Good Night, Beloved	1903	Columbia 1138
Holy Ghost With Light Divine	1911	Columbia A-0992
Home Sweet Home	1903	Columbia 1621/Columbia A-387
Lord's Prayer And Gloria Patria	1903	Columbia 1516
Refuge (Jesus, Love Of My Soul)	1903	Columbia 1139
Ring The Bells For Christmas Morn	1908	Columbia A-0616/Harmony A 616
Sweet And Low	1902	Columbia 1137
Where Are You Goin' My Pretty	1908	Columbia A-0595/Columbia 33298

Mendelssohn Male Quartet

Hark Hark My Soul	1911	Columbia A-1097
Stars Of The Summer Night	1911	Columbia A-1019
Vira	1911	Columbia A-1019

Merry Macs

Annabella	1941	Decca 4074A
A-Ruble A-Rhumba	1939	Decca 2404A
Beside The Rio Tonto		Universal 6252
Breathless	1942	Decca 4265A/Decca F 8206
Breezin' Along With The Breeze	1940	Decca 3025B
By-U, By-O (The Lou'siana Lullaby)	1941	Decca 4023B/Decca F 8064
Cheatin' On The Sandman	1942	Decca 18361
Chinatown, My Chinatown	1939	Decca 2471
Choo Choo Polka	1945	Decca 18684
Chopsticks	1939	Decca 2333B
Clap Yo' Hands	1939	Decca 2877A
Cuckoo In The Clock	1939	Decca 2334A
Deep In The Heart Of Texas	1941	Decca 4136A/Decca F 8131
Down On Ami Ami Oni Oni Isle	1941	Decca
Do You Know Why'	1940	Decca 3483A/Decca F 7887
Drowning In Your Deep Blue Eyes	1947	Majestic 7260
Dry Bones	1940	Decca 3390B
Ferdinand The Bull	1939	Decca 2238A
Forties, The	1960	DL-4007
Hello Frisco	1939	Decca 2471
Hey Mabel	1942	Decca 4265B/Decca F 8211
Hiawatha's Lullaby	1933	Victor 23806
Ho! Sa Bonnie	1940	Decca 3088A
Honk Honk	1941	Decca 3930
Honk, Honk (The Rumble Seat Song)	1941	Decca 3930/Decca F 8017
Hut-Sut Song (A Swedish Serenade), The	1941	Decca 3810A/Decca F 8131
Idaho	1942	Decca 4313A/Decca F 8211
I Get The Blues When It Rains	1940	Decca 3347A
Igloo	1939	Decca 2506A
I Got Rhythm	1939	Decca 2877B
I Got Rings On My Fingers	1939	Decca 2238B
I Got Ten Bucks And Twenty Four Hours Leave	1943	Decca 18588
I Love My Love	1947	Decca 24262
I'm Forever Blowing Bubbles	1939	Decca 2506B
I'm Ridin' For A Fall	194'	
In A Little White Church On The Hill	1933	Victor 23806
In The Mood	1939	Decca 2842A
Isn't That Just Like Love'	1940	Decca 3483B/Decca F 7887
It Just Isn't There	1941	Decca 3690A
It Just Isn't True	1941	Decca 2380
It's Easy To Say You're Sorry	1947	Decca 24262
I Wanna Go Back To West Virginia	1942	Decca 18527
Jingle, Jangle, Jingle	1942	Decca 18361/DL-4007 (1960)
Jingle Jangle Jingle	1942	Decca 18361/Decca F 8206
Johnson Rag	1940	Decca 3088B
Just A Blue Serge Suit	1945	Decca 18715
Kimaneero Down To Cairo (A Frog Went A-Courting)	1941	Decca 4136/Decca F 8131
Kiss The Boys Goodbye	1941	Decca 3930/Decca F 8017
La Paloma	1939	Decca 2404B
Laughing On The Outside	1946	Decca 18811
Lazy River	1937	Decca 2397
Let's Sing A Song About Susie	1944	Decca 18622
Little Bit Independent, A	1936	
Little Guppy, The	1941	Decca 4074B
Long As You Got Your Health	1937	Victor 25504/Electrola EG 3978

Song	Year	Label
Looking At The World Through Rose-Colored Glasses	1944	Decca 18715
Love Song Of The Nile	1933	Victor 24313
Ma! He's Making Eyes At Me	1940	Decca 3025A
Mairzy Doats	1943	Decca 18588
Mary Lou	1941	Decca 3810B/Decca F 8131
Monkey And The Organ Grinder, The	1949	Harmony 1067
Moon Country	1937	Decca 2397
My Cat Fell In The Well	1939	Decca 2759B
Natch	1947	Majestic 7260
Olivia	1942	Decca 4313B
On The Bumpy Road To Love	1938	Decca 1969A
Pass The Biscuits, Mirandy	1942	Decca 18478/Decca F 8278
Patty Cake, Patty Cake	1939	Decca 2334B
Pop Goes The Weasel	1938	Decca 1968B/Decca 25191 (1947)
Poppa, Don't Preach To Me All The Time	1947	Majestic 1134
Praise The Lord And Pass The Ammunition	1942	Decca 18498/Decca F 8249
Pretty Kitty Blue Eyes	1944	Decca 18610
Put On Your Old Grey Bonnet	1942	Decca 18436
Red Wing	1940	Decca 3390A
Rolleo-Rolling Along (The Bicycle Song)	1942	Decca 18436/Decca F8211
Rose O'Day (The Filla-Ga-Dusha Song)	1941	Decca 4023/Decca F 8064
Rosie O'Day	1941	Decca 4023A
Rumpel-Stilts-Kin	1939	Decca 2495A
Sentimental Journey	1945	Decca 18684
Shoot The Sherbet To Me, Herbert	1939	Decca 2842B
Sing Me A Song Of Texas	1944	Decca 18610
Slumming On Park Avenue	1937	Victor 25507/Electrola EG 4009
Stop Beatin' 'Round The Mulberry Bush	1938	Decca 1968A
Sunday	1942	Decca 18527
Ta-Hu-Wa-Hu-Wa-I	1939	Decca 2333A/Decca 25191 (1947)
Tee-Oli-Ee-Go	1941	
Ten Days With Baby	1944	Decca 18630
Thank Dixie For Me	1944	Decca 18630
There's Honey On The Moon Tonight	1938	Decca 1969B
Too Tired	1939	Decca 2496B
Tweedle O'Twill	1942	Decca 18498
Under A Strawberry Moon	1942	Decca 18478/Decca F 8278
Up, Up, Up	1944	Decca 18622
Vol Vistu Gaily Star	1939	Decca 2759A
Way You Look Tonight, The	1940	Decca 3347B
We Knew It All The Time	1947	Majestic 1134
We're Together Again	1933	Victor 24313
You'll Never Get Rich	1941	Decca 3690B

Merry Macs (with Bing Crosby)

Song	Year	Label
Dolores	1941	Decca 23599/Brunswick 1897/Decca 3644A (1940)
Do You Ever Think Of Me'	1940	Brunswick 04104/Decca 25424
Pale Moon	1940	Decca 25399/Brunswick 04115/Decca 3887A (1941)
You Made Me Love You	1940	Decca 3423A/Decca 25424 (1940)
You Made Me Love You (I Didn't)	1940	Brunswick 04104/Decca 25424

Merry Macs, Judy Garland & the

Song	Year	Label
If I Had You	1945	Decca 23436
On The Atchison, Topeka and the Santa Fe	1945	Decca 23436

Merry Macs, Lynn Martin & the

Song	Year	Label
And The Great Big Saw Came Nearer And Nearer	1937	Variety VA 578
Big Three Medley, The 'Margie - Mary Lou - Bright Eyes'	1937	Variety VA 570
Dear, Dear, What Can The Matter Be	1937	Variety VA 578
Let's All Sing Like The Birdies Sing	1937	Variety VA 570

Merry Melody Men

Song	Year	Label
I Call You Sunshine	1921	Vocalion 14178A
In The Devil's Garden	1921	Vocalion 14178B

Merrymakers (Revelers)

Song	Year	Label
Baby Face	1926	Brunswick 3289/Brunswick A 175
Barcelona	1926	Brunswick 3289/Brunswick A 175
Blue Skies	1927	Brunswick 3441/Brunswick A 433
Clap Hands, Here Comes Charlie!	1926	Brunswick 3049/Brunswick A 174
Down On The Banks Of The Old Yazoo	1926	Brunswick 3312

Song	Year	Label
Honey, Be Mine	1926	Brunswick
Honey Bunch	1926	Brunswick 3148/Brunswick A 114
How D'Y'Do Miss Springtime	1926	Brunswick 3154/Brunswick A 153
I Never Knew	1925	Brunswick 3004/Brunswick A 173
Keep On Croonin' A Tune	1925	Brunswick 3004/Brunswick A 173
Mah Lindy Lou	1926	Brunswick 3154/Brunswick A 153
Merrymaker's Carnival, Part 1	1926	Brunswick 20044/Brunswick A 5000
Merrymaker's Carnival, Part 2	1926	Brunswick 20044/Brunswick A 5000
Merry Makers In Hawaii, The (with Frank Ferrera)	1926	Brunswick 20049/Brunswick A 5003
Merry Makers In Spain, The (with Virginia Rea)	1926	Brunswick 20049/Brunswick A 5003
Mine	1927	Brunswick 3441/Brunswick A 433
My Castle In Spain	1926	Brunswick 3059/Brunswick A 152
Sunny Disposish	1926	Brunswick 3312/Brunswick A 189
Sweet Child (I'm Wild About You)	1926	Brunswick 3059/Brunswick A 152
That Certain Party	1926	Brunswick 3049/Brunswick A 174

Metropolitan Mixed Trio

Song	Year	Label
In The Gloaming	1909	Columbia A-0774
Jack And Jill	1908	Columbia A-0590
Long, Long Ago	1909	Columbia A-0747

Metropolitan Quartet

Song	Year	Label
Modern Woodmen Of America	1913	Victor 17244
Past Master Ode	1913	Victor 17484

Metropolitan Trio

Song	Year	Label
Along The River Of Time	1909	Victor 16348
Attila Praise Ye	1909	Columbia A-0671
Baby's Sweetheart Serenade	1909	Columbia A-661
Do They Think Of Me At Home'	1909	Victor 16355
Dreaming	1909	Victor 16439
Give Alms Of They Goods	1909	Columbia A-0779
I'll Be Home At Harvest Time	1909	Columbia A-0663
Knocking, Knocking Who's There	1907	Columbia A-0259/Columbia 33189/ Columbia A-259
Nothing But The Blood Of Jesus	1908	Columbia A-5089
Praise Ye	1909	Columbia A-677/Columbia A-844
Prayer	1909	Columbia 30217/Columbia A-5097
Sacred Prayer	1909	Columbia A-5097
Silent Night	1909	Columbia A-5135/Columbia A-5384 (1911)
Won't You Be My Playmate'	1909	Columbia A-0646/Victor 16442 (1910)

Metropolitan Trio

Song	Year	Label
Nothing But Leaves	1908	Columbia 3753/Columbia A-0257

Miami Valley Trio

Song	Year	Label
Someone To Love	1926	Champion 15082

Midnight Four (Elkins-Payne Jubilee Singers)

Song	Year	Label
Down By The Riverside	1923	Silvertone 3569
Gonna Shout All Over God's Heaven	1923	Silvertone 3569
I'm Gonna Make Heaven My Home	1925	Silvertone 3575
Throw Out The Lifeline	1925	Silvertone 3575

Miles Brothers Quartet

Song	Year	Label
Do Lord, Remember Me	1937	Conqueror 8931
Leaning On The Lord	1937	Conqueror 8931

Miller's Quartette, Reed

Song	Year	Label
Oh, Come Ye All Faithful	1920	Paramount 33070
Voice Of The Chimes	1920	Paramount 33070

Millionaires (Blenders)

Song	Year	Label
Kansas Kapers	1956	Davis 441
Somebody's Lying	1956	Davis 441

Mills Brothers

Song	Year	Label
Across The Alley From The Alamo	1947	Decca 23863/Decca 25516 (1948)
After All	1952	Decca 28384
After You	1947	Decca 24180
Ain't Misbehavin'	1939	Brunswick 02892
All The Way	1955	Decca 29781
And The Angels Sing	1939	Brunswick 02823/Decca 630
Anytime, Anyday, Anywhere	1933	Brunswick 6490/Harmony

100 Years of Harmony: 1850 to 1950

Around The World	1951	1001 (1949) Decca 27400			(1934)/Perfect 13061
Asleep In The Deep	1939	Decca 2804			(1934)/Banner 33215 (1932)
Autumn Leaves					
Baby Clementine	1958	Dot 15858/Dot 16234 (1961)	Chum Chum Chittlum Chum	1965	Dot 16733
			Cielito Lindo	1947	Decca 25046/V-Disc 452
Baby, Don't Be Mad At Me	1948	Decca 24441			
Baby Won't You Please Come Home	1932	Brunswick 6225/Oriole 3034 (1934)/Perfect 13081 (1934)/Banner 33254 (1934)	Come Summer	1972	Paramount 0147
			Coney Island Washboard	1932	Brunswick 6377/Melotone 13178 (1934)/Oriole 3006 (1934)/Perfect 13057 (1934)/Banner 33211 (1934)/Rainwood 1054 (1976)
Ballerina	1961	Dot 16258			
Barbershop Quartet, The	1958	Decca 30546			
Basin Street Blues	1939	Brunswick 02844			
Beaver	1959	Dot 15909			
Bells Of San Raquel, The	1941	Decca 4070			
Be My Life's Companion	1951	Decca 27889	Confess	1948	Decca 24409
Between Winston-Salem And Nashville, Tennessee	1970	Paramount 0046/Rainwood 1020 (1975)	Cottage With A Prayer, A	1951	Decca 27683
			Daddy's Little Boy	1950	Decca 27236/Decca 29564 (1955)
Beware	1953	Decca 28818	Daddy's Little Girl	1950	Decca 24872
Beyond The Stars	1942	Decca 4251	Daisies Never Tell	1975	Rainwood 1042
Big City	1963	Dot 16451	Darktown Strutter's Ball	1936	
Bird In The Hand, A	1940	Decca 3486	Darling Nellie Gray	1941	Decca 3705
Blue And Sentimental	1952	Decca 28309	Delilah	1941	Decca 4108
Brazilian Nuts	1941	Decca 3789	Did Anyone Call	1940	Decca 3567
Break The News To My Mother	1941	Decca 3705	Diga Diga Doo	1933	Brunswick 6519
Bugle Call Rag	1932	Brunswick 6357/Melotone 13182 (1934)/Perfect 13061 (1934)/Banner 33215 (1932)/Rex 8896	Dinah	1933	Brunswick 6485
			Dirt Dishin' Daisy	1932	Brunswick 6340/Perfect 13082 (1934)/Banner 33255 (1934)
			Doin' The New Low-Down	1933	Brunswick 6517
			Don't Be A Baby, Baby	1946	Decca 18753/Decca 25516 (1948)
But For Love	1968	Dot 17162	Don't Be Afraid To Tell Your Mother	1935	Decca 402
Buy On The Go	1969	Dot 17235			
Bye Bye Blackbird	1965	Dot 16733	Don't Blame Me	1964	Dot 16579
By The Watermelon Vine, Lindy Lou	1940	Decca 3545	Don't Get Caught	1956	Decca 30024
			Don't Let Me Dream	1953	Decca 28736
Cab Driver	1967	Dot 17041/Rainwood 961 (1973)	Donut And A Dream, A	1972	Paramount 0181
			Down, Down, Down	1941	Decca 3763
			Dream	1969	Dot 17198
Can't You Heah Me Callin' Caroline	1940	Decca 3455/Decca 23625 (1946)/Decca 24763 (1950)	Dream, Dream, Dream	1947	Decca 23863
			Dream Of You	1956	Decca 29853
			Dreamsville, Ohio	1942	Decca 4251
Caravan	1938	Decca 1876B	El Paso	1975	Rainwood 1040
Carnival In Venice	1954	Decca 29115	End Of The World	1963	Dot 16451
Change For A Penny	1957	Decca 30430	Every Second	1954	Decca 29276
Chinatown, My Chinatown	1932	Brunswick 6305/Melotone 13182	F.D.R. Jones	1939	Brunswick 02832
			Fiddlin' Joe	1933	Brunswick 6490/Perfect 13082 (1934)/Banner

Title	Year	Label/No.
Flower Road, The	1968	Dot 17096
Fourtuosity	1967	Dot 17041
Funiculi Funicula	1938	Decca 2029
Funny Feelin'	1950	Decca 27267
Gather Your Dreams	1949	Decca 24656
George White's Scandals	1931	Brunswick 20102
George White's Scandals Part 1	1947	Brunswick 85001
George White's Scandals Part 2	1947	Brunswick 85001
Georgia On My Mind	1939	Brunswick 02892/Decca 3688 (1941)
Get A Job	1958	Dot 15695
Git Along	1932	Brunswick 6340
Gloria	1948	Decca 24509/Atlantic
Glow-Worm, The	1952	Decca 28384/Dot 16037 (1959)/Rainwood 107 (1974)/MCA 60125 (1974)
Go In And Out Of The Window	1954	Decca 29115
Goodbye Blues	1932	Brunswick 6278/Melotone 13179 (1934)/Perfect 13058 (1934)/Banner 33212 (1932)/Romeo 2381
Good-Bye Blues	1939	Decca 2441
Got Her Off My Hands	1951	Decca 27762
Gum Drop	1955	Decca 29686
Happy Songs Of Love	1971	Paramount 0095
He Gives Me Love	1974	Rainwood 974
He'll Have To Go		
Help Yourself To Some	1969	Dot 17321
High And Dry	1952	Decca 28021
Highways Are Happy Ways	1960	Dot 16091
Honey, Dat I Love So Well	1949	Decca 24757
Honey In My Pockets	1934	Brunswick 6894
Honeysuckle Rose Blues Bossa Nova	1966	Dot 16972
How Am I Doing Hey, Hey	1932	Brunswick 6269/Melotone 13179 (1934)/Perfect 13058 (1934)/Banner 33212 (1932)Rex 8896/Romeo 2381
How Blue	1954	Decca 29185
How Did She Look	1940	Decca 3567
I Believe In Santa Claus	1955	Decca 29754
I Can't Give You Anything But Love	1933	Brunswick 6517/Brunswick 6519 (1933)
I Couldn't Call My Baby	1948	Decca 24441
I Cried Like A Baby	1950	
Ida, Sweet As Apple Cider	1934	Decca 165
I Don't Know Enough About You	1946	Decca 18834
I Don't Mind Being All Alone	1950	Decca 27267
If I Had My Way	1949	Decca 24756
If I Lived To Be A Hundred	1950	Decca 24872
If It's True	1941	Decca 3901/Decca 25284 (1947)
I Found A Million Dollar Baby In A Five And Ten Cent Store	1958	Dot 15695
I Found The Only Girl For Me	1962	Dot 16360
I Found The Thrill Again	1936	
If You Didn't Cry	1950	
I Got You	1960	Dot 16091
I Guess I'll Be On My Way	1941	Decca 4070
I Guess I'll Get The Papers	1946	Decca 23638
I Had To Call You Up To Say I'm Sorry	1954	Decca 29019
I Heard	1932	Brunswick 6269/Melotone 13180 (1934)/Perfect 13059 (1934)/Banner 33213 (1932)Conqueror 8400
I'll Be Around	1942	Decca 18318/Jubilee (1942)/V-Disc 495/Decca 27157 (1950)
I'll Never Be Without My Dream	1948	Decca 24472
I'll Never Forgive Myself	1969	Dot 17285
I'll Never Make The Same Mistake Again	1947	Decca 24252
I'll See You In My Dreams		
I'll Take Care Of Your Cares	1961	Dot 16258
I Love You So Much It Hurts	1948	Brunswick 04073/Decca 24550
I'm Afraid To Love You	1946	Decca 25713/Decca 27184 (1950)/Rainwood 974 (1974)
I Met Her On Monday	1942	Decca 18473
I'm Happy Being Me	1949	Decca 24621
I Miss You So	1960	Dot 16049
I'm Sorry I Answered The Phone	1971	Paramount 0095
I'm Sorry I Didn't Say I'm Sorry	1947	Decca 24252
I'm The Guy	1956	Decca 29977

I'm With You	1953	Decca 28670	King Porter Stomp	1956	Decca 29897
In A Mellow Tone	1956	Decca 29853	Kiss Me And Kill Me With Love	1955	Decca 29511
In De Banana Tree	1957	Decca 30224	Knocked Out Nightingale, The	1957	Decca 30224
I Need Thee Every Hour	1950	Decca 14536	Lambeth Walk, The	1938	Decca 2008
In Old Champlain	1942	Decca 18473	Lazybones	1934	Decca 176
In The Sweet By And By	1950	Decca 14503	Lazy River	1941	Decca 4187/Decca 25046 (1947)/Decca 28458 (1952)MCA 60125 (1974)
I Ran All The Way Home	1951	Decca 27762			
I Still Get A Thrill					
I Still Love You	1950	Decca 27236			
It Ain't No Big Thing	1969	Dot 17321			
It Don't Mean A Thing	1945	V-Disc 365-A	Lazy River		V-Disc 465
It Don't Mean A Thing (If It Ain't Got That Swing)	1932	Brunswick 6377/Decca 2982 (1939)	Let Me Dream		
			Limehouse Blues	1934	Decca 267
			Little House That Love Built, The	1936	Decca 1093
It Hurts Me More Than It Hurts You	1964	Dot 16579	Little Old Lady	1937	
			London Rhythm	1936	Decca 1082
I've Been In Love Before	1940	Decca 3545	Long About Midnight	1936	Decca 1360
I've Changed My Mind A Thousand Times	1955	Decca 29781	Long Long Ago	1949	Decca 24758
			Lora-Belle Lee	1949	Decca 24679
I've Found A New Baby	1934	Brunswick 6785/Oriole 3034 (1934)/Perfect 13081 (1934)/Banner 33254 (1934)Decca 228 (1934)	Lord Ups And Downs	1951	Decca 27683
			L-O-V-E	1971	Paramount 0117
			Love Bug Will Bite You, The	1937	Decca 1227
			Love Is Fun	1948	Decca 24382
			Loveless Love	1932	Brunswick 6305/Melotone 13180 (1934)/Perfect 13059 (1934)/Banner 33213 (1932)
I've Got My Love To Keep Me Warm	1949	Decca 24550			
I've Shed A Hundred Tears	1950	Decca 24994			
I Want Someone To Care For	1953	Decca 28586			
I Want To Be The Only One	1948	Decca 24509	Love Lies	1951	Decca 27889
I Want You To Want Me	1949	Decca 24749	Love Me	1951	Decca 27615
I Wish I Could Afford The Life I'm Livin'	1952		Love's Old Sweet Song	1940	Decca 3455/Decca 24758 (1949)
I Wish I Had A Brand New Heart	1945	Decca 18663	Love You So Much It Hurts	1949	Decca 24550
I Wish I Knew The Name	1948	Decca 24333	Lullabye In Ragtime	1959	Dot 15950
I Yi Yi Yi Amigo	1941	Decca 3789	Lulu's Back In Town	1935	MB/CHRON-3
Jeepers Creepers	1939		Manana	1948	Decca 24333
Jesus, Savior, Pilot Me	1950	Decca 14525	Marie	1940	Decca 3291
Jimtown Road, The	1969	Dot 17198	Me And My Shadow	1958	Dot 15827
Jones Boy, The	1953	Decca 28945	Meet Me Tonight In Dreamland	1938	Decca 2804/Decca 23625 (1946)/Decca 24763 (1950)
Julius Caesar	1938	Decca 1964			
Jungle Fever	1934	Brunswick 6785/Melotone 13177 (1934)/Banner 33210 (1934)			
			Mi Muchacha	1955	Decca 29621
			Miss Otis Regrets	1934	Decca 166
			Mister And Mississippi	1951	Decca 27579
Just A Dream Of You, Dear	1940	Decca 3225/Decca 23624 (1946)/Decca 24762 (1950)	Mister Sandman		
			Moanin' For You	1935	Decca 497
			Money In My Pockets	1934	Brunswick 6894/Brunswick 01756/Brunswick A 9573
Just A Kid Named Joe	1938	Decca 2029			
Just Tell Me Your Dreams, I'll Tell You Mine	1939	Decca 2285			
			Mood Indigo		
Just When We're Falling In Love	1952	Decca 28309	Moonlight Bay	1940	Decca 3331/Decca

Song	Year	Label
(Mr. Paganini...) You Will Have To Swing It	1939	Brunswick 02741/Brunswick A 82033
Music Maestro, Please!	1958	Dot 15827
My Christmas Song For You	1949	Decca 24768
My Gal Sal	1934	Decca 165/Decca 3225 (1940)/Decca 23624 (1946)/
My Honey's Lovin' Arms	1933	Brunswick 6525/Columbia 4304 (1944)/Harmony 51227 (1952)
My Little Grass Shack In Kealakekua Hawaii	1934	
My Shy Violet	1968	Dot 17096
My Troubled Mind	1957	Decca 30299
Nagasaki	1934	Decca 176
Never Make A Promise In Vain	1946	Decca 18753
Nevertheless	1950	Decca 27253/Rainwood 1054 (1976)
Ninety-Eight Cents	1956	Decca 29977
Nobody's Sweetheart	1931	Brunswick 6197
Now The Day Is Over	1951	Decca 14550
Oh! Ma-Ma	1960	Dot 16049
Oh! My Aching Heart	1947	Decca 23979
OK America Part 1	1932	Brunswick 20112
OK America Part 2	1932	Brunswick 20112
Old Black Joe	1940	Decca 3132
Old-Fashioned Love	1934	Decca 166
Old Man Of The Mountain, The	1932	Brunswick 6357
Old Rugged Cross, The	1950	Decca 14503
On A Chinese Honeymoon	1949	Decca 24694/Rainwood 1003 (1974)
On The Banks Of The Wabash	1940	Decca 3331/Decca 23626 (1946)/Decca 24759 (1949)
On This Christmas Eve	1949	Decca 24768
Open The Gates Of Dreamland	1950	Decca 24994
Opus 1	1974	Rainwood 105
Opus One	1955	Decca 29496
O'Race Track, The	1968	Dot 17162
Organ Grinder's Swing		
Out Of Love	1949	Decca 24679
Paper Doll	1942	Decca 18318/Decca 27157 (1950)/Decca 23626 (1946)/Decca 24759 (1949)/Decca 24762 (1950)
Paper Doll		V-Disc 495
Paper Valentine	1955	Decca 29382
Pennies From Heaven	1937	Decca 1147
Please Don't Talk About Me When I'm Gone	1951	Decca 27447
Poor Butterfly		
Pretty As A Picture	1952	Decca 28180
Pretty Butterfly	1953	Decca 28736
Put Another Chair At The Table	1945	Decca 18663
Put On Your Old Grey Bonnet	1934	Brunswick 6913/Decca 2982 (1939)/Harmony 1002 (1949)
Queen Of The Senior Prom	1957	Decca 30299/Dot 16360 (1962)
Rhythm Saved The World	1936	Decca 961
Rig A Jig Jig	1941	Decca 3763
Rockin' Chair	1932	Brunswick 6278/Melotone 13181 (1934)/Perfect 13060 (1934)/Banner 33214 (1932)Decca 167 (1934)
Rockin' Chair Swing	1937	Decca 1227
Sally Sunshine	1972	Paramount 0147
Sawdust Heart	1975	Rainwood 1042
Say Si Si	1953	Decca 28670
She Was Five And He Was Ten	1953	Decca 28945
Shine	1939	Brunswick 02844/Decca 3688/Decca 24382
S-H-I-N-E	1941	Decca 3688/Decca 24382 (1948)
Shoe Shine Boy	1936	Decca 961
Shoulder To Weep On, A	1952	Decca 28459
Side Kick Joe	1939	Decca 2599
Since We Fell Out Of Love	1937	Decca 1495
Single Saddle	1949	Decca 24656
627 Stomp	1941	Decca 4187
Sixty Seconds Got Together	1938	Decca 1964
Sleepy Head	1934	Brunswick 6913/Melotone 13177 (1934)/Banner 33210 (1934)
Sleepy Time Gal	1940	Decca 3291
Smack Dab In The Middle	1955	Decca 29511/Dot 16972 (1966)
Small Town Girl	1950	

Paper Doll 1951 Dot 11051 (1952)/Dot 16037 (1959)/Rainwood 107 (1974)

Title	Year	Label/Number
Smile Away Each Rainy Day	1970	Paramount 0046
Smoke Rings	1933	Brunswick 6525/Harmony 1002 (1949)
Solitude	1936	Decca 1082
Someday	1949	Decca 24694
Some Of These Days	1934	Decca 228
Someone Cares	1948	Decca 24409
Someone Loved Someone	1952	Decca 28459
South Of The Border (Down Mexico Way)	1939	Brunswick 02823/Decca 630
St. Louis Blues	1932	Brunswick 6330/Melotone 13178 (1934)/Oriole 3006 (1934)/Perfect 13057 (1934)/Banner 33211 (1932)/Conqueror 8400/Harmony 1001 (1949)
Standing On The Corner	1956	Decca 29897
Star Dust	1939	Brunswick 02741
Stardust	1939	
Star For Everyone To Love, A	1950	Decca 27184
Stop Beatin' 'Round The Mulberry Bush	1939	Brunswick 02725/Brunswick A 82006
Strawberry Fair	1939	Brunswick A 82206
Strollin'	1971	Paramount 0117
Suddenly There's A Valley	1955	Decca 29686
Summer Night	1936	Decca 1093
Swanee River	1940	Decca 3132
Sweet Adeline	1939	Decca 2285/Decca 23623 (1946)/Decca 24761 (1950)
Sweet And Slow	1935	
Sweeter Than Sugar	1934	Decca 267
Sweet Genevieve	1949	Decca 24756
Sweet Georgia Brown	1934	Decca 380
Sweet Lucy Brown	1935	Decca 497
Sweet Sue, Just You	1932	Brunswick 6330/Melotone 13181 (1934)/Perfect 13060 (1934)/Banner 33214 (1932)/Decca 2441 (1939)
Swing For Sale	1937	Decca 1147
Swing Is The Thing	1936	
Swing It, Sister	1934	Brunswick 6894
Take Me Along	1959	Dot 15987
Tea For Two		
Tell Me More	1956	Decca 30136
Te Quiero	1959	Dot 15950
That's All I Ask Of You	1955	Decca 29621
That's All I Need	1956	Decca 30136
That's Georgia	1933	Brunswick 01531/Brunswick A 9410
That's Right	1956	Decca 30024
There Goes My Heartache	1934	Decca 380
There's No Life On The Moon	1972	Paramount 0181
There's No One But You	1946	Decca 18834
Thirsty For Your Kisses	1950	Decca 27253
This One Day, That One Tomorrow	1951	
Three Little Fishies (Itty Bitty Poo)	1939	Brunswick 02800/Brunswick A 82206
Tiger Rag	1931	Brunswick 6197/Decca 167 (1934)/Decca 11051 (1942)/Rainwood 1003 (1974)
Till Then	1944	Decca 18599/Decca 23930 (1947)/Rainwood 105 (1974)/Rainwood 1040 (1975)
Till Then		V-Disc 465
Till We Meet Again	1949	Decca 24757
Too Many Irons In The Fire	1946	Decca 23638
Truck Stop	1973	Rainwood 961
Tunnel Of Love, The	1950	Decca 27104
Twice As Much	1953	Decca 28586
Two Blocks Down, Turn To The Left	1948	Decca 24472
Two Minute Tango	1957	Decca 30430
Up To Maggie Jones	1969	Dot 17285
Urge, The	1955	Decca 29382
Very Thought Of You, The	1941	Decca 3901/Decca 25284 (1947)
Way Down Home	1939	Decca 2599/Decca 4348 (1942)/Decca 23627 (1946)/Decca 24764 (1950)
Welcome Home	1965	Dot 16705
What Have I Done For Her Lately	1969	Dot 17235
What's The Reason (I'm Not Pleasin' You')	1935	Decca 402
What You Don't Know Won't Hurt You	1947	Decca 23979

When I See An Elephant Fly	1942	
When The Lights Are Low	1936	
When The Roll Is Called Up Yonder	1950	Decca 14525
When You Come Back To Me	1952	Decca 28180
When You Said Goodbye	1940	Decca 3486
When You Were Sweet	1942	Decca 4348
When You Were Sweet Sixteen	1940	Decca 3381/Decca 23627 (1946)/Decca 24764 (1950)
Who Knows Love	1951	Decca 27615
Who'll Be The Next One	1949	Decca 24749
Who Put The Devil In Evelyn's Eyes	1953	Decca 28818
Why Do I Keep Lovin' You	1954	Decca 29185
Why Fight The Feeling	1950	Decca 27104
Will There Be Any Stars	1951	Decca 14550
Window Washer Man	1941	Decca 4108
Wish Me Good Luck Amigo	1952	Decca 28458
Wonderful Wasn't It	1951	Decca 27579
Wonderful Words Of Love	1950	Decca 14536
Words	1949	Decca 24621
Yam, The	1938	Decca 2008
Yellow Bird	1958	Dot 15858/Dot 16234 (1961)
Yes You Are	1955	Decca 29496
You Always Hurt The One You Love	1944	Decca 18599/Decca 23930 (1947)/Dot 15987 (1959)/Rainwood 106 (1974)
You Always Hurt The One You Love		V-Disc 495
You Are My Sunshine	1975	Rainwood 1020
You Broke The Only Heart That Ever Loved You	1946	Decca 23713
You Can't Be True Dear	1959	Dot 15909
You Didn't Want Me When You Had Me	1954	Decca 29019
You Don't Have To Be A Santa Claus	1955	Decca 29754
You Don't Have To Drop A Heart To Break It	1951	Decca 27400
You Know You Belong To Somebody Else	1951	Decca 27447
You Never Miss The Water Till The Well Runs Dry	1947	Decca 24180
You Only Told Me Half The Story	1958	Decca 30546
You Rascal, You	1931	Brunswick 6225
You're Making The Wrong Guy Happy	1965	Dot 16705
You're Nobody Till Somebody Loves You	1954	Decca 29276/Rainwood 106 (1974)
You're Not Worth My Love	1952	Decca 28021
You're Not Worth My Tears	1952	Decca 28021
You Tell Me Your Dreams		V-Disc 452
You Tell Me Your Dreams, I'll Tell You Mine	1946	Decca 23623/Decca 24761 (1950)

Mills Brothers (Harry & Donald Mills of the)

Shuffle Your Feet (And Just Roll Along)	1933	Brunswick 6520

Mills Brothers (Harry & Donald Mills)

Shuffle Your Feet/Bandanna Babies	1933	

Mills Brothers (with Al Jolson)

Down Among The Sheltering Palms	1949	Decca 24534
Is It True What They Say About Dixie	1948	Decca 24534

Mills Brothers (with Bing Crosby)

Can't We Talk It Over'	1932	Brunswick 6240
Dinah	1932	Brunswick 6240
Please	1944	Columbia 4304
Shadows On The Window	1932	Brunswick 6276
Shine	1933	Brunswick 6485/Columbia 4305 (1944)/Columbia 4421-M (1947)/Harmony 51226 (1952)
Some Of These Days	1944	Columbia 4305/Columbia 4421-M (1947)

Mills Brothers (with Dick Powell)

Out For No Good	1934	MB/CHRON-3

Mills Brothers (with Ella Fitzgerald)

Big Boy Blue	1937	Decca 1148/Decca 25361 (1948)
Dedicated To You	1937	Decca 1148/Decca 25361 (1948)
Fairy Tales	1949	Decca 24813
I Gotta Have My Baby Back	1949	Decca 24813
Shine	1936	

Mills Brothers (with Louis Armstrong and Harry Mills)

Elder Eatmore's Sermon On Generosity	1938	
Elder Eatmore's Sermon On Throwing Stones	1938	

Mills Brothers (with Louis Armstrong)

Boog It	1940	Decca 3180
Carry Me Back To Old Virginny	1937	Decca 1245
Cherry	1940	Decca 3180/Decca 25536 (1948)
Darling Nellie Gray	1937	Decca 1245
Flat Foot Floogee	1938	Decca 1876A

In The Shade Of The Old Apple Tree	1937	Decca 1495	Say Mister! Have You Met Rosie's Sister!	1926	
Marie	1940	Decca 3151/Decca 25536 (1948)/Decca 28984 (1953)	Study War No More	1927	Okeh 8472
			Where Shall I Be When The First Trumpet Sounds	1927	Okeh 8472
			Mitchell Christian Singers		
My Walking Stick	1938	Decca 1892A/Decca 28984 (1953)	Angels Will Roll The Stone Away	1934	Conqueror 8497/Banner 33390 (1934)
Old Folks At Home, The	1937	Decca 1360	Are You Living Humble	1939	Vocalion 4844
Once Upon A Dream	1939	Brunswick 03139/Decca 3381 (1940)	Are You Working On The Building'	1934	Banner 33196
			Brother Come On In	1938	Vocalion 4472
Song Is Ended, The	1938	Decca 1892B	Drinkin' Of The Holy Wine	1939	Vocalion 4844
W.P.A.	1940	Decca 3151	Here Am I	1934	Banner 33434
Mills Brothers (with Peggy Lee)			Homey Homey	1934	Banner 33434
It Must Be So	1954	Decca 29359	How About You'	1934	Banner 33433/Conqueror 8431 (1934)/Vocalion 4394 (1934)
Straight Ahead	1954	Decca 29359			
Mississippi Jubilee Singers					
Jesus Said If You Go	1927	Paramount 12495			
You Belong To The Funeral Train	1927	Paramount 12495			
Mississippi Juvenile Quartet			I'm Gonna Do What My Lord Says	1938	Vocalion 4964
Memories Of Galilee	1928	Okeh 45216			
Wandering Child, Oh Come Home	1928	Okeh 45216	I'm On My Way	1934	Banner 33390
			I Need To Be More Like Jesus	1938	Vocalion 5097
Mississippi Mud Mashers			Jesus Goin' To Make Up My Dying Bed	1938	Vocalion 4357
Bring It On Home To Grandma	1935	Bluebird 5845			
Don't 'Low No Quartet Singin' In Here	1935	Bluebird 5899	Jesus Hear Me Praying	1939	Vocalion 4913
			Lean Your Head Out The Window	1934	Banner 33283/Conqueror 8414 (1934)
Let's Go To Dinner	1935	Bluebird 5845			
Moonglow	1935	Bluebird 7316			
Take My Seat And Sit Down	1935	Bluebird 5899	Lord Have Mercy	1938	Vocalion 4418
Tiger Rag	1935	Bluebird 7316	Mother Where Was You'	1934	Banner 33195/Conqueror 8457 (1934)
Mississippi Sheiks					
Do Right Blues	1935	Bluebird 5847			
Fingerin' With Your Fingers	1935	Bluebird 5949	My Mother's Gone To Glory	1938	Vocalion 4273
I Can't Go Wrong	1935	Bluebird 5881	On My Way	1934	Conqueror 8497
It's Back Firing Now	1935	Bluebird 5881	They Scandalized My Name	1934	Banner 33195/Conqueror 8457 (1934)
I've Got Blood In My Eyes For You	1931	Columbia 14660-D			
Kind Treatment	1931	Columbia 14672-D	Traveling Shoes	1934	Banner 33196
Lean To One Woman	1935	Bluebird 5949	Way Down In Egyptland	1938	Vocalion 5097
New Sittin' On Top Of The World	1932	Broadway 5109	What Are They Doing In Heaven'	1934	Banner 33433/Conqueror 8431 (1934)
New Stop And Listen	1932	Broadway 5109			
Please Don't Wake It Up	1931	Columbia 14672-D			
World Is Going Wrong, The	1931	Columbia 14660-D	When A Man Feels Discouraged	1934	Banner 33283/Conqueror 8414 (1934)
World Roundup, The	1935	Bluebird 5847			
Missouri Pacific Lines Quartet					
One At Last	1928	Victor 40051	While He's Passing By	1938	Vocalion 4472
When The Home Gates Swing Open	1928	Victor 40051	You Got To Make A Change	1938	Vocalion 4176
			You Got To Stand Judgment	1938	Vocalion 4964
Missouri-Pacific Diamond Jubilee Quartette			**Mitchell Jubilee Singers**		
I've Been Working On The Railroad	1927	Okeh 40868	I Ain't Gonna Lay My Receiver Down	1939	Vocalion 4783
Medley Of Southern Songs	1927	Okeh 40868	I Got A Letter From Jesus	1938	Vocalion 4418

I Have A Home In Yonder City	1939	Vocalion 4913			61949/Coral 61949 (1958)
I Heard The Preachin' Of The Elders	1938	Vocalion 4593	At Last	1942	Victor 27934
Judgment Is Coming	1938	Vocalion 4273	At My Front Door	1955	Columbia 61513/Coral 61513 (1955)
Lord's Gonna Trouble The Water, The	1938	Vocalion 4176			
My Poor Mother Died A-Shouting	1939	Vocalion 4720	At The President's Birthday Ball (with Marion Hutton)	1942	Bluebird B-11429
Rock My Soul In The Bosom Of Abraham	1939	Vocalion 4720	Autumn Serenade		
Saints Are Marching, The	1938	Vocalion 4357	Back In Your Own Back Yard	1952	Coral 60946
Up On The Mountain	1938	Vocalion 4593	Beautiful Blonde From Bashful Bend, The	1949	Columbia 38505
What Are The Doing In Heaven	1938	Vocalion 4394			
Won't I Be Glad When I Get To Heaven	1939	Vocalion 4783	Bicycle Built For Two, A (Daisy Bell)		
Mitchell Quartet			Bidin' My Time	1947	Columbia 38904
Beautiful Isle Of Somewhere	1928	Champion 40052	Big Movie Show In The Sky, The	1949	Columbia 38692
			Billy Boy		
Mixed Quartet			Birds And Puppies And Tropical Fish	1953	Columbia 61348/Coral 61348
Jerusalem		Edison 124 (4BA)			
Sleepy Time, Mah Honey	1913	Victor 17351	Blow, Gabriel, Blow	1956	Coral
Mixed Quartette			Boogie Woogie		
In Heavenly Love Abiding		Edison 91 (4BA)	Boogie Woogie/I'll Never Smile Again/Oh! Look/On The Sunny Side Of The Street/Once In A While	1956	Coral 61779
Mixed Vocal Quartet					
Goodnight, Goodnight Beloved	1908	Columbia A-0494			
Mobile Four (Birmingham Quartet)			Booglie Wooglie Piggy, The	1958	Coral 62037
Bohunkus And Josephus	1927	Columbia 14370-D	Booglie Wooglie Piggy, The (with Tex Beneke and Paula Kelly)	1941	Bluebird B-11163
Eliza	1927	Columbia 14357-D			
Goodbye, My Alabama Babe	1927	Columbia 14370-D	Bugle Call Rag	1952	Columbia 60726/Coral 60726 (1952)
Toot Toot Dixie Bound	1927	Columbia 14357-D			
Mobile Four (Norfolk Jubilee Quartet)					
I'm Gonna Do All I Can For My Lord	1926	Herwin 92030	Busy Doing Nothing	1947	Columbia 38416
			Bye Bye Blues		
Jesus Lay Your Head In The Window	1926	Herwin 92030	Calypso Melody	1957	Columbia 61837/Coral 61837 (1957)
Mobile Revelers					
St. Louis Blues	1929	Grey Gull 4287/Van Dyke 5122	Caribbean Clipper		
			Chattanooga Choo Choo		
			Chattanooga Choo Choo (with Tex Beneke)	1941	Bluebird B-11230/Electrola EG 7905/Victor 20-2410/Victor 20-2972
Modernaires					
Act Your Age	1958	Columbia 61949/Coral 61949 (1959)			
			Close Your Eyes/How Important Can It Be'/I'm Always Hearing Wedding Bells	1954	Columbia 61378/Coral 61378 (1954)
Adios	1961				
Ain't Misbehavin'	1947	Columbia 38403			
Ain't She Sweet	1956	Columbia 61555	Conchita, Marquita, Lolita, Pepita, Rosita, Juanita Lopez (with Marion Hutton, Tex Beneke and Ernie Caceres)	1942	Victor 27943
Alice In Wonderland	1951	Columbia 60439/Coral 60439 (1951			
			Coquette		
Alright, Okay, You Win	1955	Columbia 61513	Dear Arabella (with Marion Hutton and Tex Beneke)	1941	Bluebird B-11326
Alright, Okay, You Win	1955	Coral 61513			
Angels Of Mercy (with Ray Eberle)	1942	Bluebird B-11429	Dear Old Girl	1958	Columbia 59141
As Long As I Have You	1958	Columbia	De Camptown Races		

Title	Year	Label/Number
Delilah (with Tex Beneke)	1941	Bluebird B-11274
Dig-Dig-Dig For Your Dinner	1950	Columbia 38904
Dipsy Doodle, The	1951	Coral 60658/Columbia 60658 (1952)
Dolores/Rosalie/Begin The Beguine/You Must Have Been A Beautiful Baby/If I Had You	1949	Standard Transcription U-274
Don't Sit Under The Apple Tree (With Anyone Else But Me) (with Marion Hutton and Tex Beneke)	1942	Bluebird B-11474/Victor 68-1344
Down By The Station/Ollie Ollie Outs In Free/Johnny Get Your Girl/That Certain Party/Old MacDonald Had A Farm/McNamara's Band	1949	Standard Transcription U-273
Down The Lane	1950	Columbia 38791
Dreamsville, Ohio (with Ray Eberle)	1941	Bluebird B-11342
Dry Bones/On Accounta Because I Love You/The New Ashmolean Marching Society/The Law Is Comin' For Your Paw/An Old Fashioned Christmas	1949	Standard Transcription U-284/United 287
Elmer's Tune		
Elmer's Tune (with Ray Eberle)	1941	Bluebird B-11274/Victor 20-3185
Foggy Day, A	1957	Columbia 61873/Coral 61873 (1957)
Four Or Five Times	1952	Columbia 60824/Coral 60824 (1952)
Glenn Miller Story Part 1, The	1953	Coral C 91074
Glenn Miller Story Part 2, The	1953	Coral C 91074
Goody Goody	1952	Columbia 60726/Coral 60726 (1952)
Goofus		
Gotta Be This Or That	1952	Columbia 60881/Coral 60881 (1952)
Grandfather's Clock		
Great Pretender, The	1956	Columbia 57063
Harmony Is The Thing	1957	Columbia 57141/Columbia 59141 (1958)
Here Come The Modernaires	1957	Columbia 57140
He Who Has Love	1953	Columbia 60982/Coral 60982 (1953)
Home Town Band	1949	Columbia 38688
Honeymoon	1953	Columbia EC81031
How Important Can It Be	1955	Columbia 61378
Humming-Bird, The	1942	Victor 27933
I Cain't Get Offa My Horse	1947	Columbia 37485
I Can't Carry A Tune (If I Had) Wings On My Wishes	1951	Coral
I Guess I'll Have To Dream The Rest (with Ray Eberle)	1941	Bluebird B-11187
I Had Too Much To Dream Last Night	1947	Columbia 37485
I Know Why	1954	Columbia 61199/Coral 61199 (1954)
I Know Why (with Paula Kelly)	1941	Bluebird B-11230/Electrola EG 7541
I'll Always Be Following You	1951	Coral 60658/Columbia 60658 (1952)
I'll Be Hanging Around	1952	Coral 60946
I'll Never Smile Again		
I'm Always Hearing Wedding Bells	1955	Columbia 61378
I'm Getting Sentimental Over You		
I'm Late	1951	Coral 60439/Columbia 60439 (1951)
In A Little Spanish Town		
In The Mood		
Irving	1951	Coral 60514
It Happened In Sun Valley (with Paula Kelly, Ray Eberle and Tex Beneke)	1941	Bluebird B-11263
It May Sound Silly	1955	Columbia 61378
It Must Be Jelly ('Cause Jam Don't Shake Like That)	1942	Victor 20-1546
It's A Lonesome Old Town (When You're Not Around) (Salute To Ben Bernie)	1947	Columbia 38402
(I've Got A Gal In) Kalamazoo (with Marion Hutton and Tex Beneke)	1942	Victor 27934
I Wanna Hug You, Squeeze You, Kiss You/It May Sound Silly/Pledging My Love	1954	Coral 61378/Columbia 61378 (1955)
I Want A Girl	1953	Columbia 81032
Ja Da		
Java Jive	1950	Columbia 38883
Jingle Bells (with Tex Beneke and Ernie Caceres)	1941	Bluebird B-11353/Victor 20-2510
Johnny Get Your Girl	1949	Columbia 38416
Juke-Box Saturday Night (with Marion Hutton and Tex Beneke)	1942	Electrola EG 7787/Victor 20-1509/Victor 20-3185/Victor 42-0035

Title	Year	Label/Number
Just For Laughs	1947	Columbia
Just Like You Used To Do	1955	Columbia 61449
Kiss Polka, The (with Paula Kelly and Ernie Caceres)	1941	Bluebird B-11263
Knit One, Purl Two (with Marion Hutton)	1942	Victor 27894
La Festa	1955	Coral 61449/Columbia 61449 (1955)
Lamplighter's Serenade, The (with Ray Eberle)	1942	Bluebird B-11474
Let's Have Another Cup O' Coffee (with Marion Hutton and Ernie Caceres)	1942	Bluebird B-11450
Let The Rest Of The World Go	1953	Columbia 81032/Columbia 57141 (1957)
Little Brown Jug		
Little Old Church In England, A (with Ray Eberle and Dorothy Claire)	1941	Bluebird B-11069
Loch Lomond		
Love Happy	1949	Columbia 38589
Lovely Is The Evening	1951	Coral 60408/Columbia 60408 (1951)
Lullaby Of The Rain (with Ray Eberle)	1942	Victor 27894
Makin' Whoopee	1957	Coral 61873/Columbia 61873 (1957)
Ma-Ma-Maria (Fee-dle, Fee-dle, Ed-dle-La) (with Ray Eberle)	1941	Bluebird B-11299
Man On The Flying Trapeze, The		
Margie	1947	Columbia 38403
Margie/Just Can't Say I Love You/I'm A Little Cuckoo/Love Happy/I'll String Along With You	1949	Standard Transcription U-284
Marie		
Milkman's Matinee, The	1954	Coral 61490
Milkman's Matinee, The	1955	Columbia 61490/Columbia CRL57051
Mine! Mine! Mine!	1954	Coral 61348/Columbia 61348 (1954)
Mm-Mm Good	1947	Columbia 38208
Molly O'Reilly	1949	Columbia
Mood Indigo	1954	Coral 61265/Columbia 61265 (1954)
Moonlight Becomes You (with Skip Nelson)	1942	Victor 20-1520/
Moonlight Serenade		
My Friend Irma	1949	Columbia 38589
Never Again	1951	Columbia 60521
Never Again (with Harry Babbitt)	1951	Coral 60521
New Ashmolean Marching Society, The	1949	Decca 24810
New Juke Box Saturday Night	1952	Coral 60899/Columbia 60899 (1953)
Night We Called It A Day, The		
Noah	1956	Columbia 61764
October 2nd, 1992	1951	Columbia 60609
Oh, Dem Golden Slippers		
Oh, How I Miss You Tonight	1953	Columbia 81032
Old MacDonald Had A Farm		
O'Leary Is Leary	1949	Columbia
Ollie Ollie Outs In Free	1949	Columbia 38688
On Accounta Because I Love You	1949	Columbia 38588
Once In A While		
One Rose, The	1953	Columbia EC81031
Only You (And You Alone)	1956	Columbia 57063
On The Old Assembly Line (with Tex Beneke and Marion Hutton)	1942	Bluebird B-11480
On The Sunny Side Of The Street		
Opus #1		
Out Of Breath	1951	Coral 60522/Columbia 60522 (1951)
Papa Niccolini (The Happy Cobbler) (with Ray Eberle and Tex Beneke)	1941	Bluebird B-11342
Peekaboo To You (with Paula Kelly)	1941	Bluebird B-11203
Pennsylvania 6-5000		
Perfidia (with Dorothy Claire)	1941	Bluebird B-11095/Victor 27-0157
Pledging My Love	1955	Columbia 61378
Put Some Money In The Juke Box	1953	Coral 61037/Columbia 61037 1953)
Rainbow Rhapsody	1942	
Red Wing		
Rock-A-Bye Boogie	1953	Coral 61037/Columbia 61037 (1953)
Rock It For Me (Salute To Chick Webb)	1947	Columbia 38401
Rubber Knuckle Sam	1950	Columbia 38791
Runnin' Wild	1952	Coral 60899
Salute To Glenn Miller, A - Pt. 1	1953	Coral 61110
Salute To Glenn Miller, A - Pt. 2	1953	Coral 61110/Coral 69044
Salute To Glenn Miller (new version)	1954	Columbia 61110
Salute To Tommy Dorsey	1956	Coral 61779
Santa's Little Sleigh Bells	1955	Coral

Title	Year	Release
Says Who' Says You, Says I! (with Marion Hutton and Tex Beneke)	1941	61547/Columbia 61547 (1955) Bluebird B-11315
Say You're Mine Again	1953	Coral 60982/Columbia 60982 (1953)
Schenectady	1950	Columbia 38883
School Days		
Senora	1949	Columbia 38505
Serenade In Blue (with Ray Eberle)	1942	Victor 27935/Victor 20-2889
Shanghai (with Harry Babbitt)	1951	Coral 60522
She'll Always Remember (with Ray Eberle)	1942	Bluebird B-11493
Shhh, It's A Military Secret (with Marion Hutton and Tex Beneke)	1942	Bluebird B-11493
Sleepy Little Space Cadet	1955	Coral 61547/Columbia 61547 (1955)
Sleepy Time Train		
Slewfoot (recorded in 1955)		Columbia 61412
Sluefoot	1955	Coral 61412
Something In The Wind	1947	Columbia 37569
Song Of India		
St. Louis Blues March		
Stardust (Salute To Jack Denny)	1947	Columbia 38401
Stompin' At The Savoy	1951	Coral 60609/Columbia 60609 (1951)
Stop, Look And Listen	1952	Coral 60928
String Of Pearls, A		
Sunrise Serenade		
Swanee River		
Sweet Sue		
Swing Low, Sweet Chariot		
Teach Me Tonight	1954	Coral 61265/Columbia 61265 (1954)
That Old Black Magic (with Skip Nelson)	1942	Electrola EG 7447/Victor 20-1523/Victor 20-1560/Victor 42-0035/Victor 42-0089
That's You, That's Me, That's Love	1954	Coral 61199/Columbia 61199 (1954)
There Are Such Things		
There's Something About A Hometown Band		
Turntable Song, The	1947	Columbia 37569
Tuxedo Junction		
Wake Up The Place	1954	Coral
When Johnny Comes Marching Home (with Tex Beneke and Marion Hutton)	1942	61490/Columbia 61490 (1955)/Columbia CRL57051 Bluebird B-11480
When My Love Comes Back To Me	1952	Coral 60824/Columbia 60824 (1952)
When That Man Is Dead And Gone (with Tex Beneke)	1941	Bluebird B-11069
Whoo-Loo-Ed-Siana	1951	Coral 60525
Whoo-loo-ee-siana	1951	Columbia 60525
Why Did I Tell You I Was Goin'	1951	Columbia 60521
Wildflower	1952	Coral 60881/Columbia 60881 (1952)
Wine, Women And Gold	1955	Coral 61412/Columbia 61412 (1955)
Wishing Star	1949	Columbia 38588
Wishing You Were Here Tonight	1951	Coral 60408/Columbia 60408 (1951)
Yes Indeed		
Yesterday's Gardenias	1942	Victor 27933
Yodel Blues, The	1949	Columbia 38692
You Call It Madness (But I Call It Love) (Salute To Ross Columbo)	1947	Columbia 38402
You'll Always Be My Sweetheart	1951	Coral 60525
You'll Always Be The Sweetheart	1951	Columbia 60525
You'll Never Be Mine	1953	Coral 61086/Columbia 61086 (1953)
You'll Never Be Mine, Part 2	1953	Coral 61086

Modernaires & the Skylarks

Title	Year	Release
Brush Those Tears From Your Eyes	1948	Columbia 38364
Gloria	1948	Columbia 38352
Money Song, The	1948	Columbia 38352
One Sunday Afternoon	1948	Columbia 38364

Modernaires (Alan Freed, Steve Allen, Al 'Jazzbo' Collins & the)

Title	Year	Release
Space Man, The	1956	Coral 61693

Modernaires (as Dolly Dawn & the Four Modernaires)

Title	Year	Release
Old Plantation	1937	Variety VA 547

Modernaires (as Paul Whiteman's Four Modernaires)

Title	Year	Release
At The Story Book Ball	1940	Decca 3137
Broom Dance	1939	Decca 2844
Hoiriger Schottische, The	1939	Decca 2921
Hot Gavotte, The	1939	Decca 2921
Piggy Wiggy Woo	1939	Decca 2844
Ragtime Cowboy Joe	1940	Decca 3038B

Song	Year	Label
Rain	1940	Decca 3137
Wham (Wham, Re, Bop, Boom, Bam)	1940	Decca 3038

Modernaires (as Paula Kelly & the Four Modernaires)

Song	Year	Label
Sweeter Than The Sweetest	1941	Bluebird B-11183/Electrola EG 7432/Victor 20-1546

Modernaires (as the Barnet Modern-Aires)

Song	Year	Label
Bye-Bye Baby	1936	Bluebird B-6504
Make Believe Ballroom	1936	Bluebird B-6504
Milkman's Matinee, The	1936	Bluebird B-6593

Modernaires (as the Four Modernaires)

Song	Year	Label
Alexander's Ragtime Band	1939	Decca 2695
All Ashore	1938	Decca 2075/Brunswick A 81862
Aunt Hagar's Blues (with Jack Teagarden)	1938	Decca 2145/Brunswick 02693/Brunswick A 81905/Brunswick A 82544/Decca 3522
(Be It Ever So Thrilling) There's No Place Like In Your Arms	1938	Decca 2076/Brunswick A 81861
Darn That Dream	1939	Decca 2937
Hello Hawaii - How Are You	1937	Variety VA 534
Hooray For Spinach	1939	Decca 2418/Brunswick A 82109
I Go For That	1938	Decca 2283/Brunswick A 82094
I'm Coming Virginia (with Jack Teagarden)	1938	Decca 2145/Decca 3943/Brunswick A 81905/Brunswick A 82544
It's Swell Of You	1937	Variety VA 526
I Used To Be Color Blind	1938	Decca 2073/Brunswick A 81860
Jamboree Jones	1938	Decca 2074/Brunswick 82041
Jeepers Creepers (with Jack Teagarden)	1938	Decca 2222/Brunswick A 82020
Lazy	1939	Decca 2696
Love Bug Will Bite You, The	1937	Variety VA 530
Make Believe Ballroom Time	1940	Bluebird B-10913
Mandy	1939	Decca 2696
Mutiny In The Nursery (with Joan Edwards and Jack Teagarden)	1938	Decca 2222/Brunswick A 82020
Never Felt Better, Never Had Less	1938	Decca 2283/Brunswick A 82094
Nobody Knows	1939	Decca 2695
Now And Then	1939	Decca 2417/Brunswick 82108
Okolehao	1937	Variety VA 534
Peelin' The Peach	1938	Decca 2073/Brunswick A 82041
Rose Room	1939	Decca 2466/Decca 3943
Shoemaker's Holiday, The	1939	Decca 2505
Sing A Song Of Sixpence	1938	Decca 2074/Brunswick A 81860
Step Up And Shake My Hand	1939	Decca 2418/Brunswick A 82109
There's A Lull In My Life	1937	Variety VA 526
Three Little Fishies	1939	Decca 2417/Brunswick 82018

Modernaires (with Frank Sinatra)

Song	Year	Label
When The Sun Goes Down	1950	Columbia 38790

Modernaires with Hal Dickinson

Song	Year	Label
Jingle Bell Polka, The	1947	Columbia 37980
Whistler, The	1947	Columbia 37980

Modernaires with Paula Kelly

Song	Year	Label
Autumn Serenade	1945	Columbia 36878
Coffee Five, Doughnuts Five (Coffee And Doughnuts Ten)	1945	Columbia 36878
Connecticut	1946	Columbia 37220
Dummy Song, The	1946	Columbia 38305
Holiday For Strings	1945	Columbia 35123
Hoodle Addle	1947	Columbia 37266
How Do You Do'	1946	Columbia 37170
It's Lovin' Time	1946	Columbia 37122/Columbia 37266 (1947)
I Want To Be Loved (But Only By You)	1947	Columbia 37328
Jog Along	1945	Columbia 36847
Juke Box Saturday Night	1946	Columbia 36992
La Cucaracha	1946	Columbia 38305
La Cucaracha	1946	AFRS Jubilee 200/AFRS Jubilee 293
Laughing On The Inside	1946	AFRS Jubilee 200/AFRS Jubilee 293
Mission Of The Rose, The	1946	Columbia 37170
My Heart Goes Crazy	1946	Columbia 37220

Night Is Young And You're So Beautiful, The	1945	Columbia 36847
Pennies From Heaven (without Paula Kelly)	1946	Columbia 38208
Salute To Glenn Miller	1946	Columbia 36992
Santa Catalina (Island Of Romance)	1947	Columbia 37328
Sweet I've Gotten On You	1946	Columbia
There, I've Said It Again	1945	Columbia 36800
To Each His Own	1945	Columbia 35123
To Each His Own	1946	Columbia 37063
Too Many Irons In The Fire	1946	Columbia 37147
You Belong To My Heart	1945	Columbia 36800
Zip-A-Dee-Doo-Dah	1946	Columbia 37147

Modernaires, Charles Wolcott & the

Glooby Game, Part 1, The	1949	Columbia 90053
Glooby Game, Part 2, The	1949	Columbia 90053
Glooby Game, Part 3, The	1949	Columbia 90054
Glooby Game, Part 4, The	1949	Columbia 90054

Modernaires, Dinah Shore & the

Bongo, Part 1	1947	Columbia 37898
Bongo, Part 2	1947	Columbia 37899
Bongo, Part 3	1947	Columbia 37900
Bongo, Part 4	1947	Columbia 37900
Bongo, Part 5	1947	Columbia 37899
Bongo, Part 6	1947	Columbia 37898
I'm Out To Forget Tonight	1947	Columbia 37850
Lazy Countryside	1947	Columbia 37884
So Dear To My Heart	1947	Columbia 38299
Stanley Steamer, The	1947	Columbia 37850

Modernaires, Doris Day & the

It's A Quiet Town	1947	Columbia 38159
Thoughtless	1947	Columbia 38079

Modernaires, Frank Sinatra with the

Kisses And Tears (with Jane Russell)	1950	Columbia 38790
Old Master Painter, The	1949	Columbia 38650
Sorry	1950	Columbia 38662/Columbia C 1425
Why Remind Me	1949	Columbia 38662/Columbia C 1425

Modernaires, Harry Babbitt & the (with George Cates)

I Can't Say I Love You	1951	Coral

Modernaires, Marion Hutton & the

Johnny Zero	1943	V-Disc 4

Modernaires, Martha Tilton & the

Please Don't Cry	1951	Coral 60522/Columbia 60522 (1951)

Modernaires, Paula Kelly & the

Ain't She Sweet	1955	Coral 61555
April In Paris	1956	Columbia 61599/Columbia 57140 (1957)
Ask For Joe	1956	Columbia 61674/Coral 61674 (1956)
Bye Bye Blues/Rain/Coquette/Red Wing/Ja Da/In A Little Spanish Town	1947	Lang-Worth Transcription AS-346
Go On With The Wedding	1955	Coral 61555/Columbia 61555 (1956)
Grandfather's Clock/De Camptown Races/The Man On The Flying Trapeze/Loch Lomond/Billy Boy/Old MacDonald Had A Farm	1946	Lang-Worth Transcription 1256
Hi-Diddlee-I-Di	1956	Columbia 61599/Coral 61599 (1956)
I'm On The Level With You	1945	Columbia 35162
Let's Dance Medley - Pt. 1 (The Benny Goodman Story)	1955	Coral 61568
Let's Dance Medley - Pt. 2 (The Benny Goodman Story)	1955	Coral 61568
Listen To The Mockingbird/Little Brown Jug/Swing Low, Sweet Chariot/Bicycle Built For Two/Golden Slippers	1946	Lang-Worth Transcription 1253
Livin' Western Style	1945	Columbia 35162
Ninety-Eight Cents	1956	Coral 61674/Columbia 61674 (1956)
Oh Frenchy	1944	V-Disc
Sweet Sue/Stompin' At The Savoy/String Of Pearls/In The Mood/School Days/Goofus	1947	Lang-Worth Transcription AS-336
Tabby The Cat	1944	

Modernaires, Ray Eberle

Below The Equator	1941	Bluebird B-11235
Day Dreaming	1941	Bluebird B-11382
Dear Mom	1942	Bluebird B-11443
It Happened In Hawaii	1941	Bluebird B-11416/Victor 20-2536
Moonlight Cocktail	1941	Bluebird B-11401/Victor 20-2536
One I Love (Belongs To Somebody Else), The	1941	Bluebird B-11110
Sleep Song	1942	Victor 27879
Soldier, Let Me Read Your Letter	1942	Victor 27873
Spring Will Be So Sad (When She Comes This Year)	1941	Bluebird B-11095
Sweet Eloise	1942	Victor 27879

You Stepped Out Of A Dream	1941	Bluebird B-11042

Modernaires, Skip Nelson & the

Dearly Beloved	1942	Victor 27953
Moonlight Mood	1942	Victor 27953/Victor 20-1520/V-Disc 12

Modernaires, Steve Allen & the

Cinderella Baby	1956	Columbia 61837/Coral 61837 (1956)
I'm Ready To Love Again	1956	Coral 61764/Columbia 61764 (1956)

Modernaires, Virginia Maxey & the (with Lou Bring)

Our Hour	1947	Columbia 37876
Say It With A Slap	1947	Columbia 37876

Modernaires, Whiteman's

Wham	1940	Decca 3038A

Monarch Jazz Quartet (Norfolk Jubilee/Jazz Quartet)

Four Or Five Times	1929	Okeh 8736
I Ain't Got Nobody (And Nobody Cares For Me)	1929	Okeh 8761
Just Too Late	1929	Okeh 8931
Mean To Me	1929	Okeh
Pleading Blues	1932	Okeh 8931
Somebody's Wrong	1929	Okeh 8761
What's The Matter Now'	1929	Okeh 8736

Monarch Jubilee Quartet Of Norfolk (Norfolk Jubilee/Jazz Quartet)

King Jesus, Stand By Me	1930	Okeh 8797
Somebody's Always Talking About Me	1929	Okeh 8778
When Death Shall Shake This Frame	1930	Okeh 8797
When I Was A Moaner	1929	Okeh 8778

Monarch Quartet (Criterion Quartet)

When I'm Gone You'll Soon Forget	1926	Vocalion 15128
When You're Gone I won't Forget	1926	Vocalion 15128

Monroe Quartet

Beautiful Land	1927	Okeh 40794
Bruddah Brown	1927	Okeh 45141
Bulldog, The	1927	Okeh 45134
Just Before The Battle, Mother	1927	Okeh 45133
Old Folks At Home	1927	Okeh 45133
Whispering Hope	1927	Okeh 40794

Montgomery Quartet

In The Garden	1934	Decca 147B
Life's Railway To Heaven	1934	Decca 146A
Little Brown Church, The	1934	Decca 147A
Old Rugged Cross, The	1934	Decca 146B

Moody Quartet

I Believe In God	1930	Vocalion 5448
Kneel At The Cross	1930	Vocalion 5448

Moody's Bible Trio

Grace Greater Than Our Sin	1928	Victor 40015
I Cannot Get Beyond His Love	1928	Victor 40015

Moonlight Serenaders

Sometime	1925	Harmony 13
You Forgot To Remember	1925	Harmony 13

Morehouse Quartet

Down By The Riverside	1923	Okeh 4887
Every Time I Feel The Spirit	1923	Okeh 40268
Swing Low Sweet Chariot	1923	Okeh 4887

Moreing Sisters

Everyone Says 'I Love You'	1932	Brunswick 6391

Morgan, Corrine & the Haydn Quartet)

Toyland	1904	Victor 2721/Victor 31203 (1904)

Morgan, Corrine (with Haydn Quartet)

Dearie	1905	
How'd You Like To Spoon With Me	1906	

Morgan, Frank & the Sportsmen Quartet

Gay Caballero, A	1946	Decca 23540
Man That Broke The Bank At Monte Carlo, The	1946	Decca 23540

Morgan, Rev. William H. (with Edison Mixed Quartet

St. Luke & Calvary	Edison 1641 (4BA)
St. Mark & Peace! Be Still	Edison 1642 (4BA)

Morganton Trio

Fate Of Gladys Kincaid, The	1927	Columbia
Two Little Girls In Blue	1927	Columbia

Morris Sacred Quartet, J. L.

Bound For The Promised Land	1929	Columbia
Sweeping Through The Gates	1929	Columbia

Moultrie Georgia Quartet

Rock Of Ages	1926	Columbia
'Tis The Old-Time Religion	1926	Columbia

Mound City Jubilee Quartet

Dry Bones In The Valley	1935	Decca 7158
Hand Writin' On The Wall	1935	Decca 7057
I Heard The Voice	1935	Decca 7110
I'm A Pilgrim	1935	Decca 7110
Lead Me To The Rock	1935	Decca 7134
Let That Liar Alone	1935	Decca 7058
Old Ship Of Zion	1935	Decca 7057
Seven Seas, The	1935	Decca 7058
Sleep On, Darling	1935	Decca 7158
Standing By The Bedside Of A Neighbor	1935	Decca 7134

Mount Sinai Jubilee Quartette

Tell Me Who Built The Ark	1927	Gennett
You Must Have That True Religion	1927	Gennett 6338

Mount Vernon Quartet

New Jerusalem Way, The	1927	Columbia 15245-D
Sweet Bye And Bye	1934	Bluebird 5693

Tenting Tonight On The Old Camp Ground	1927	Columbia 15245-D	Lead Kindly Light	1902	Edison Bell 9014 (2mincyl)
When I Take My Vacation On Heaven's Bright Shore	1934	Bluebird 5693	Louisiana Lou	1902	Edison Bell 9059 (2mincyl)/Edison Bell 5532 (2mincyl) (1903)
Mount Zion Baptist Quartet					
Hard Trials, Great Tribulation	1927	Victor 21350			
I Shall Not Be Moved	1927	Victor 21350	Medley Of Coon Songs	1902	Edison Bell 9051 (2mincyl)/Edison Bell 5524 (2mincyl) (1903)
Let The Church Roll On	1927	Victor 20562			
They Called Me A Liar	1927	Victor 20562			
Mountain Singers Male Quartet					
Bringing In The Sheaves	1929	Okeh 45315	Old Black Joe	1902	Edison Bell 9060 (2mincyl)/Edison Bell 5533 (2mincyl) (1903)
Stand Up For Jesus	1929	Okeh 45364			
Throw Out The Life Line	1929	Okeh 45315			
Whosoever Meaneth Me	1929	Okeh 45364			
Mountain View Quartet			Robin Hood: The Owl And The Pussy Cat	1902	Edison Bell 9055 (2mincyl)/Edison Bell 5528 (2mincyl) (1903)
On The Glory Road	1928	Columbia			
Willing Workers	1928	Columbia			
Moylan Sisters					
Freckles	1941	Decca 3916B	Sleigh Ride Party	1903	Edison Bell 5526 (2mincyl)
Huckleberry Finn	1941	Decca 3916A			
I Don't Want To Play In Your Yard/Smarty	1941	Decca 3915B	Sleigh Ride Party, The	1902	Edison Bell 9053 (2mincyl)
Lazy Lack-A-Daisy Melody, A	1940	Decca 3301A	Steamboat Leaving The Wharf At New Orleans, A	1902	Edison Bell 9054 (2mincyl)/Edison Bell 5527 (2mincyl) (1903)
Little Sweetheart Of The Valley	1940	Decca 3301B			
M-I-S-S-I-S-S-I-P-P-I	1941	Decca 3917A			
School Days/Little Red School House	1941	Decca 3915A			
Six Times Six Is Thirty Six	1941	Decca 3917B	Sweet And Low	1902	Edison Bell 9062 (2mincyl)/Edison Bell 5535 (2mincyl) (1903)
Mozart Quartet					
Annie Laurie	1902	Edison Bell 5523 (2mincyl)/Edison Bell 9050 (2mincyl) (1902)			
			While Shepherds Watched	1903	Edison Bell 5935 (2mincyl)
			Munn, Frank & Male Chorus		
Auld Lang Syne	1902	Edison Bell 9052 (2mincyl)	Nazareth	1925	Brunswick 2959
			Oh, Come Ye All Faithful (Adeste Fidelis)	1925	Brunswick 2959
Auld Lang Syne	1903	Edison Bell 5525 (2mincyl)			
			Murphee Hartford Quartet		
Camp Meeting Scene	1902	Edison Bell 9061 (2mincyl)/Edison Bell 5534 (2mincyl) (1903)	I Know My Lord Will Keep Me	1930	Champion 16056
			I'm Always Out Of Luck	1930	Champion 16074
			It Won't Be Very Long	1930	Champion 16056
			Oh How It Hurt	1930	Champion 16033
Christians, Awake!	1903	Edison Bell 5936 (2mincyl)	That's What Ruined Me	1930	Champion 16033
			You Can't Keep A Good Man Down	1930	Champion 16074
Good-Bye Dolly Gray	1902	Edison Bell 9057 (2mincyl)/Edison Bell 5530 (2mincyl) (1903)	**Murray & his Merry Melody Men**		
			Gay Caballero, A	1928	Edison BA 5668/Edison DD 52518-R (1928)
Hot Corn Medley	1902	Edison Bell 9056 (2mincyl)/Edison Bell 5529 (2mincyl) (1903)	**Murray & his Merry Melody Men (with Ermine Calloway)**		
			Ever Since The Movies Learned To Talk	1928	Edison DD 52518-L
Just Break The News To Mother	1902	Edison Bell 9058 (2mincyl)/Edison Bell 5531 (2mincyl) (1903)	**Murray, Billy & his Melody Men**		
			If I'm Wrong, Sue Me	1929	Edison DD 52611-R

Murray, Billy & his Merry Melody Men
In Old Tia Juana	1929	Edison DD 52609-R/Edison Lateral 14014R (1929)

Murray, Billy & Quartet
Nellie Dean	1906	Busy Bee 1297

Murray, Billy & the American Quartet
High Brown Blues	1922	Victor 18904
Melon Time In Dixieland	1921	Victor 18794
Oh That Navajo Rag	1911	Victor 17000/Edison 917
Oh, You Beautiful Doll	1911	Victor 16979
Play That Barber-Shop Chord (Mister Jefferson Lord)	1910	Victor 5799
Way Down In Cotton Town	1910	Victor 5801

Murray, Billy & the Haydn Quartet
Budweiser's A Friend Of Mine	1907	Victor 16049
By The Light Of The Silvery Moon	1910	Victor 16460
Harrigan	1910	Victor 16664
Lazy Moon	1905	Victor 4471/Victor 16153 (1908)
Lily Of The Prairie	1909	Victor 16353
So What's The Use	1907	Victor 16049

Murray, Billy (with Haydn Quartet)
Take Me Out To The Ball Game	1908	

Murray, Billy and Ada Jones with Haydn Quartet
Taffy	1908	Victor 5592/Victor 16824 (1911)

Murray, Billy assisted by the Haydn Quartet
Come Take A Swim In My Ocean	1909	Victor 16334

Murray, Billy with Edison Male Quartet
Lazy River	1905	Edison 9204 (2mincyl)

Murray, Billy with Edison Male Quartette
Ida-Ho!	1907	Edison 9250 (2mincyl)

Murray, Billy with Hayden Quartet
Old Dog Tray	1910	Victor 16686

Murray, Billy with Haydn Quartet
Arrah Wanna	1906	Victor 4907/Victor 16223 (1918)
Dinner Bells	1905	Victor unissued
Don't Be Cross	1906	Victor unissued C-2995
Down In Sunshine Alley	1910	Victor 16450
Goodbye Flo	1904	Victor 4545
Homesick Yankee, The	1907	Victor 5095/Brunswick 4293 (1907)
I'd Rather Float Through A Dreamy Waltz With You	1908	Victor 16076
It's Allus De Same In Dixie	1905	Victor 4434
Keep On Smiling	1907	Victor 5379/Victor 16158 (1908)
Meet Me Down At Luna, Lena	1905	Victor 4369
Meet Me In Rose Time, Rosie	1909	Victor 5676/Victor 16665 (1910)
Molly Lee	1909	Victor 16437
Only One, The	1906	Victor unissued
Rainbow	1908	Victor 5571/Victor 17233 (1912)
Sullivan	1908	Victor 5617/Victor 16664 (1908)
Take Me Out For A Joy Ride	1909	Victor 5732/Victor 16780 (1911)
Take Me Where There's A Big Brass Band	1907	Victor 5216
Waiting For A Certain Girl	1906	Edison 2 mincyl 9496 /Victor unissued (1907)
Waltz Me Around Again, Willie	1906	Victor 4738/Victor 16770 (1911)
When Love Is Young In Springtime	1906	Victor 31535
When Tommy Atkins Marries Dolly Gray	1906	Victor 4898
Yankee Doodle	1910	Victor 16495

Murray, Billy with Male Quartet
(You're The Flower Of My Heart) Sweet Adeline	1905	American 031225/Aretino A-1081 (1905)/Busy Bee 1225 (1905)/Concert 7699 (1905)/Imperial 44699 (1905)

Murray, Billy with Male Quartet Chorus
Good Luck, Mary	1909	Edison 4mincyl 314

Murray, Billy with Merry Melody Men
Kansas City Kitty	1929	Edison BA 5716/Edison DD 52559-L/Regal 8745
She's Got Great Ideas!	1929	Edison DD 52559-R

Murray, Billy with Premier Quartet & New York Military Band
Yankee Doodle	1911	Edison 4mincyl 745

Murray, Billy with Premier Quartette
Frenchy, Come To Yankee Land	1919	Edison BA 3783/Edison DD 50555

Murray, Billy, with the Peerless Quartet
I'm Goin' To Settle Down Outside Of London Town	1919	Columbia A-2702

Murray, Pete & the Peerless Quartet
Lily Of The Prairie	1910	Edison 207

100 Years of Harmony: 1850 to 1950

Murray's Trio, Billy
We're The Sunday Drivers	1926	Victor 20517

Music Hour Quartet
Dawn At Carmel/Music In The Air/Yankee Doodle	1933	Victor 24272
Home Sweet Home/Nightingale/God Speed	1933	Victor 24272
Merry Life, A/Stars Of A Summer Night/O Susanna	1933	Victor 24273
Old Black Joe/Swing Low Sweet Chariot	1933	Victor 24271

Music Maids (with Bing Crosby)
Blues In The Night	1942	Brunswick 03313/Decca 4183
Bombardier Song, The	1942	Decca 10042/Decca 18432/Decca Y 5795
Clementine	1939	Brunswick 1984/Brunswick 04108/Decca 4033/Decca 25020/Decca Y 5781
Happy Holiday	1942	Brunswick 03381/Decca 10060/Decca 18424/Decca 23820/Decca Y 5792
In My Merry Oldsmobile	1939	Brunswick 02881/Decca 2700/Decca Y 5392
It Must Be True (You Are Mine - All Mine)	1939	Brunswick 1671/Brunswick 03396/Decca 2535/Decca 25229/Decca Y 5404
Little Sir Echo	1939	Brunswick 1622/Brunswick 02753/Brunswick A 82054/Decca 2385/Decca Y 5369
Medley Of Gus Edwards Song Hits	1939	Brunswick 02841/Decca 2700/Decca 11021
Old Oaken Bucket, The	1939	Brunswick 1984/Brunswick 04108/Decca 4343/Decca 25020/Decca Y 5781
S'posin'	1939	Brunswick 1623/Brunswick 02779/Decca 2413/Decca 3542/Decca 25368/Decca Y 5393

Mystic Quartet
Carry Me Back To Ole Virginny	1896	Berliner 0855Z
When De Big Bell Rings	1896	Berliner 0852

Nassau Male Quartet
Princeton Cannon Song	1911	Columbia A-1053
Princeton Steps Song	1911	Columbia A-1053

National Cavaliers
Am I Blue'	1929	
Beautiful	1928	Victor 21516
Bluebird, Sing Me A Song	1928	Victor
Cheerful Little Earful	1931	Victor 22609
Dear, On A Night Like This	1927	Victor 21112
Do I Hear You Saying (I Love You)	1928	
Down By The Old Mill Stream	1928	Victor 21399
Face On The Barroom Floor, The	1932	
Here Comes The Sun	1930	Victor 22559
I Ain't Got Nobody	1929	
I Told Them All About You	1927	Victor 21112
Lonesome, That's All	1929	Victor 22347
My Blackbirds Are Bluebirds Now	1928	Victor 21759
My Isle Of Golden Dreams	1929	Victor 22347
Pale Moon (An Indian Love Song)	1928	Victor 21399
Perfect Day, A	1929	Victor 21926
Sing (A Happy Little Thing)	1930	Victor 22559
Slumber Boat, The	1929	Victor 21926
Song I Love, The	1928	Victor 21759
Sweet Jennie Lee	1931	Victor 22609
Volunteer Organist, The	1932	
William Tell, The Apple Vendor	1932	

National Cavaliers (as Fred Hillebrand assisted by the Cavaliers)
Drunkard Song - Part 1, The	1934	Decca 216
Drunkard Song - Part 2, The	1934	Decca 216
Home, James, And Don't Spare The Horses - Part 1	1934	Decca 215/Decca F 5723
Home, James, And Don't Spare The Horses - Part 2	1934	Decca 215/Decca F 5723
Man On The Flying Trapeze - Part 1, The	1934	Decca 217
Man On The Flying Trapeze - Part 2, The	1934	Decca 217

National Cavaliers (as The American Singers with Orchestra)
Dear Old Girl	1929	Victor 22387
On The Banks Of The Wabash	1929	Victor 22387

National Cavaliers (as the Cavaliers & Everett Marshall)
Let Me Be Born Again	1934	Decca 15002/Decca K 746

National Cavaliers (as the Cavaliers with Rudy Vallee, the Do-Re-Mi Trio & Rudy Vallee & his Connect
Hold My Hand	1934	Victor 24581

National Male Quartet
Barnyard Medley	1923	Banner 2096
Old Folks At Home	1923	Okeh 40032
Southern Medley	1923	Banner 2096
Street Corner Quartette, A	1924	Okeh 40122
Unky Unky Sextette Band, The	1924	Okeh 40122
Yes, We Have No Bananas	1923	Okeh 40032
You Can Take Me Away From Dixie	1924	Okeh 40103

National Quartet
College Songs-Medley	1923	Banner 2102
Jubilee Days	1925	Harmony 40-H
O'Toole's Weddin'	1925	Columbia 394D
Scotch Medley	1924	Pathe 021118
Song Of The Sod	1925	Columbia 394D
Songs Of The Past	1924	Columbia 243D
Songs Of The South	1924	Columbia 243D
Street Corner Medley	1924	Pathe 021118
When I'm Gone You'll Soon Forget	1925	

Nazareth Jubilee Quartette (Norfolk Jubilee Quartet)
Down By The Riverside	1927	Herwin 93003
Swing Low, Sweet Chariot	1927	Herwin 93003

Neapolitan Trio
Happy Days	1911	Victor 16967
Herd Girl's Dream	1911	Victor 16967

New England Singers
Somebody's Mother	1921	Columbia

New Orleans Humming Four (Hawks)
I'm Satisfied	1952	Imperial 5200

New Orleans Jubilee Singers
Calvary	1928	Champion 15655
Holy Is My Name	1928	Champion 15655

New Rhythm Boys
Mississippi Mud	1954	Coral 61336
Then And Now	1954	Coral 61336

New Stellar Quartet
Wait Until You See My Madeline	1921	Vocalion 14187A
When The Autumn Leaves Begin To Fall	1921	Vocalion 14173A

New York Fire Quartet
Fire Laddie	1923	Okeh 4851

New York Police Department Quartet
Little Close Harmony, A	1940	Decca 3448B

New Yorkers
I'm Feathering A Nest (For A Little Bluebird)	1929	Edison DD 52642

Nic Nacs
Gonna Have A Merry Christmas	1950	RPM 313/RPM 342 (1951)
You Didn't Want My Love	1951	RPM 316

Nic Nacs (with Mickey Champion)
Found Me A Sugar Daddy	1950	RPM 313/RPM 316 (1951)/RPM 342 (1951)

Nichols, Ann (with Bluebirds)
Those Magic Words	1950	Sittin' In With 561

Nifty Three
Anything Your Heart Desires	1928	Columbia 1591-D
Dog-Gone!	1928	Columbia 1591-D
From Midnight Till Dawn	1928	Columbia 1423-D
Sleepy Town	1928	Columbia 1423-D

Nightingales
My Life Is In His Hands	1950	King 4348
One Of These Days	1950	King 4348

Nite Owls
Do You Ever Think Of Me'	1948	Columbia 20295
Married Man Blues	1948	Columbia 20295

Nitecaps (with Johnny Mercer)
Sizzling One-Step Medley	1932	Columbia

Nitecaps (with Rhythm Boys)
If It Ain't Love	1932	Columbia 2648-D
Keepin' Outa Mischief Now	1932	Columbia 2648-D

Non Pareil Trio
Susianna	1929	Columbia 14403-D
Yellow Dog Blues, The	1929	Columbia 14403-D

Nordstrom Sisters
Let's Put Out The Light (And Go To Sleep)	1932	Columbia
Medley, Part 1	1932	Columbia
Medley, Part 2	1932	Columbia
Say It Ain't So	1932	Columbia

Norfolk Jazz Quartet
Ain't It A Shame	1923	Paramount 12032
Beedle De Beedle De Bop Bop (Adi Eedi Idio)	1937	Decca 7443
Big Fat Mama	1921	Okeh 4380
Blues That Drove Man To Ruins	1921	Okeh 4391
Cornfield Blues	1921	Okeh 4380
Dixie Blues	1923	Paramount 12055
Every Ship Must Find A Harbor	1921	Okeh 8034
Get Hot	1921	Okeh 8022
Going Home Blues	1921	Okeh 4391
He Ha Shout	1937	Decca 7383
Honey, God Bless Your Heart	1921	Okeh 8019
I Could Learn To Love You	1921	Okeh 8028
Jelly Roll Blues	1921	Okeh 4318
Jelly Roll's First Cousin	1924	Paramount 12218
Just Dream Of You	1937	Decca 7349
Monday Morning Blues	1921	Okeh 4345
My Mammy	1921	Okeh 8007
Over The Green Hill	1923	Okeh 8035

Pleading Blues	1924	Paramount 12218
Preacher Man Blues	1921	Okeh 4366
Quartette Blues	1923	Paramount 12055
Raise R-U-K-U-S Tonight	1923	Paramount 12032
Sad Blues	1923	Paramount 12054
Shim Sham Shimmie At The Cricket's Ball	1937	Decca 7349
Southern Jack	1921	Okeh 4318
Standing On The Corner	1921	Okeh 4345
Stop Dat Band	1923	Paramount 12054
Strut Miss Lizzie	1921	Okeh 8007
Suntan Baby Brown (Suntan Lady)	1937	Decca 7443/Clanka Lanka CL-144.033
Tell That Broad (You Came Too Late)	1937	Decca 7333
Wang Wang Blues	1921	Okeh 8022
What Is The Matter Now	1929	Paramount 12844/Decca 7383 (1937)
When I Walked Up I Was Sharp As A Tack	1921	Okeh 8019
Wide Wide World	1921	Okeh 4366

Norfolk Jazz Singers

Swinging The Blues (Ever Had The Blues)	1937	Decca 7333

Norfolk Jubilee Quartet

Come On! Let's Go To Heaven	1938	Decca 7572
Crying Holy Unto The Lord	1924	Paramount 12217/Broadway 5077/Paramount 13146 (1932)
Daniel In The Lion's Den	1927	Paramount 12499
Down By The Riverside	1927	Paramount 12445
Do You Want To Be A Lover Of The Lord'	1926	Paramount 12421
Every Time I Feel The Spirit	1925	Paramount 12268
Ezekiel Saw De Wheel	1924	Paramount 12217/Broadway 5077/Paramount 13146 (1932)
Father Prepare Me	1927	Paramount 12035
Get On Board, Little Children, Get On Board	1925	Paramount 12268
Gonna Serve The Lord Till I Die	1932	Paramount 13151
Great Change	1938	Decca 7595
Great Jehovah	1926	Paramount 12342
He Just Hung His Head And Died	1927	Paramount 12734/Champion 50005/Paramount 13155
His Eye Is On The Sparrow	1927	Paramount 12630
How Is It With Me	1927	Paramount 12785
I Don't Care Where They Bury My Body	1932	Paramount 13155
If Anybody Asks You Who I Am	1927	Paramount 12468/Paramount 13147 (1932)
I Have Anchored My Soul	1927	Paramount 12589/Paramount 13148 (1932)
I Heard The Voice Of Jesus Say	1930	Paramount 12993
I Hope I May Join The Band	1921	Okeh 4400
I'm A Pilgrim	1924	Paramount 12225/Broadway 5074
I'm Going To Meet My Mother	1924	Paramount 12233
I'm Gonna Build Right On Dat Shore	1927	Paramount 12234
I'm Gonna Do All I Can For My Lord	1926	Paramount 12356
I'm Gonna Make Heaven My Home	1925	Paramount 12267
I'm Gonna Serve God Till I Die	1929	Paramount 12785/Paramount 12818/Paramount 13154 (1932)
I'm Nearer My Home	1927	Paramount 12694
I'm Pressing On To That City	1930	Paramount 12993
I Want To Cross Over To See My Lord	1927	Champion 50020
I Want To Cross Over To See The Other Side	1926	Paramount 12694/Paramount 13145 (1932)
I Want To Know Will He Welcome Me There	1927	Paramount 12785
I Will Guide Thee	1927	Paramount 12515
I Wouldn't Mind Dying If Dying Was All	1927	Paramount 12630/Champion 50006/Paramount 13154 (1932)
Jesus Is Making Up My Dying Bed	1938	Decca 7481
Jesus Lay Your Head In The Window	1926	Paramount 12356
Job	1938	Decca 7481
Jonah In The Belly Of The Whale	1938	Decca 7472/Decca 48004
King Jesus Stand By Me	1927	Paramount 12589/Paramount 13148 (1932)
Let The Church Roll On	1927	Paramount 12468/Paramount 13147 (1932)
Lord, I Don't Care Where They Bury My Body	1927	Paramount 12734/Champion 50006/Paramount 13155
Louisiana Bo Bo	1927	Paramount 12453
Moanin' In The Land Will Soon Be Over	1929	Paramount 12890

Song	Year	Label
My Lord's Gonna Move This Wicked Race	1927	Paramount 12035
No Hiding Place	1938	Decca 7582
Oh The Shoes That My Lord Gave Me	1926	Paramount 12421
Oh What A Beautiful City	1929	Paramount 12929
Old Account Was Settled Long Ago, The	1927	Paramount 12499
Our Father	1927	Paramount 12669/Paramount 13149 (1932)
Pharaoh's Army Got Drowned	1926	Paramount 12342
Please Give Me Some Of That	1929	Paramount 12844
Queen Street Rag	1927	Paramount 12453
Revival Day	1926	Paramount 12371
Ride On King Jesus	1927	Paramount 12669/Paramount 13149 (1932)
Roll Jordan Roll	1924	Paramount 12233
See The Sign Of Judgment	1926	Paramount 12371
Shepard Where Is Your Little Lamb	1927	Paramount 12515
Shine For Jesus	1939	Decca 7635
Sinner You Can't Hide	1927	Paramount 12749
Sit Down, Sit Down, I Can't Sit Down	1925	Paramount 12301
Somebody's Always Talking About Me	1925	Paramount 12301
Standing By The Bedside Of A Neighbor	1938	Decca 7472/Decca 48004
Swing Low Sweet Chariot	1924	Paramount 12225/Broadway 5000 (1924)/Champion 50020 (1927)/Paramount 12445 (1927)/Paramount 13145 (1932)
Tell Me What You Say	1929	Paramount 12929
This Old World Is In Bad Condition	1939	Decca 7635
Way Down In Egyptland	1929	Paramount 12818/Paramount 13151 (1932)
'Way Down In Egyptland	1937	Decca 7421
When The Moon Goes Down	1927	Paramount 12890
When The Train Comes Along	1938	Decca 7533
Where Shall I Be	1924	Paramount 12234/Broadway 5074
Who Built The Ark'	1921	Okeh 4400
Wonder Where Is The Gamblin' Man	1927	Paramount 12715/Crown 3328/Paramount 13150 (1932)
You Got To Live So God Can Use You	1937	Decca 7359
You're Goin' To Need That Pure Religion	1927	Paramount 12715/Paramount 13150 (1932)/Joe Davis 7000

Norfolk Jubilee Quartette

Song	Year	Label
I'm Gonna Open My Mouth To The Lord	1924	Paramount 12957
There Will Be Glory	1929	Paramount 12957/Champion 50006
Throw Out The Lifeline	1925	Paramount 12267
What You Gonna Do When The World's On Fire	1925	Paramount 12266
When I Was A Moaner	1925	Paramount 12266

Norfolk Jubilee Singers

Song	Year	Label
Death Train Is Coming, The	1940	Decca 7758
You Better Run	1939	Decca 7758

Norfolk Quartet

Song	Year	Label
Believe In Jesus	1937	Decca 7533
Didn't It Rain	1937	Decca 7359
Free At Last	1937	Decca 7402
He Just Hung His Head	1927	Champion 50005
He's Mine, Yes He's Mine	1938	Decca 7559
I	1927	Champion 50006
I Can't Stay Away	1937	Decca 7595
I Wouldn't Mind Dying	1927	Champion 50006
King Jesus Stand By Me	1938	Decca 7572
Lord I Don't Care Where	1927	Champion 50005
My Feet Been Taken Out The Mirey Clay	1937	Decca 7421
My Lord's Gonna Move This Wicked Race	1937	Decca 7336
Pure Religion	1937	Decca 7336
Sit Down, Sit Down, I Can't Sit Down	1937	Decca 7402
Stand By Me	1937	Decca 7559
Where's That Gambling Man Gone'	1938	Decca 7582

Normanaires

Song	Year	Label
My Greatest Sin	1953	MGM 11622
Wrap It Up	1953	MGM 11622

Norris Quartet

Song	Year	Label
I've Been Redeemed	1928	Columbia
Precious Memories	1928	Columbia

Norris The Troubador

Song	Year	Label
Talk About Jerusalem Mornin'	1938	
Winter Will Soon Be Over	1938	

Norsemen

Song	Year	Label
Moonbeams	1939	Bluebird 10535
My Creole Sue	1939	Bluebird 10535
Shenanigans	1938	Regal Zonophone G 23424

100 Years of Harmony: 1850 to 1950

Norsemen (with Rudy Vallee & his Connecticut Yankees)
Fare Thee Well, Annabelle (with Stewart Sisters)	1935	Victor 24833
Good Green Acres Of Home, The	1934	

Norsemen, Dick Powell & the
Army Air Corps, The	1939	Decca 2975
Marine's Hymn, The	1939	Decca 2975
On, Brave Old Army Team	1939	Decca 3267
Semper Paratus	1939	Decca 3267/Decca F 7413

North Canton Quartet
I'm Bound For Home	1930	Columbia 15643-D
I Want To Live Beyond The Grave	1930	Columbia 15643-D

Novak Girls
After I Say I'm Sorry	1930	Brunswick Test

Novelty Four Quartet
Blood Done Sign My Name, The	1928	Vocalion 1212
Little Wheel Rolling In My Heart	1928	Vocalion 1212

Oak Mountain Quartet
Down South Everybody's Happy	1929	Champion 15966
Sailin' Away On The Henry Clay	1929	Champion 15966

Oakland, Will & the American Quartet (2)
Don't Go Away	1914	Victor 17605
In The Gloaming	1910	Victor 16646/Victor 16829 (1910)/Victor 16928 (1910)
Stick To Your Mother, Tom	1911	Edison BA 2380/Edison Amberol (4mincyl) 783

O'Connell, Margaret & Quartet
Everybody Loves An Irish Song	1916	Columbia A-2129

Odom, King 4
All Of Me	1951	Derby 757
My Heart Cries Out For You	1951	Derby 754
Rain Is The Teardrops Of Angels	1951	Derby 757
What A Wonderful Feeling	1951	Derby 754

Odom, King Four
Don't Trade Your Love	1952	Abbey 15064
If He Didn't Love Me	1950	Derby 743
I'm Glad I Made You Cry	1950	Derby 736
Lover Come Back To Me	1950	Derby 736
Lucky	1952	Abbey 15064
Walkin' With My Shadow	1950	Derby 743

Odom, King Quartet
Basin Street Blues (8/11/48 NBCs Swingtime Radio Show)	1948	Best of King Odom CD
Hand Me Down My Walking Cane (8/4/48 NBCs Swingtime Radio Show)	1948	Best of King Odom CD
I Found A Twinkle	1948	Musicraft 579
I Got It Bad (And That Ain't Good)	1948	Musicraft Unissued (Best of King Odom CD)
I'll Dance At Your Wedding (2/7/48 WOR Harlem Hospitality Show with Willie Bryant and Bill Robinson)	1948	Best of King Odom CD
I'm Livin' Humble	1948	Musicraft 544
I'm Looking Over A Four Leaf Clover	1948	Musicraft 543
Mary Lou	1948	Musicraft 543
Moonlight Frost	1948	Musicraft 575
Pickin' A Chicken (2/7/48 WOR Harlem Hospitality Show with Willie Bryant	1948	Best of King Odom CD
Route 66	1948	Musicraft Unissued (Best of King Odom CD)
She's A Beauty	1948	Musicraft Unissued (Best of King Odom CD)
So Long	1948	Musicraft Unissued (Best of King Odom CD)
They Put John On The Island	1948	Musicraft 554

Odom, King Quartette
Amazin' Willie Mays	1954	Perspective 5001
Basin Street Blues	1954	Perspective 5001
I Found A Twinkle	1948	Musicraft 579

Odum, King Quartet
Pickin' A Chicken	1948	Musicraft 579
Who Struck John	1948	Musicraft 575

O'Keefe, Dennis & Quartet
Songs Of Long Ago	1920	Brunswick 2046

Okeh Sacred Quartet (Peerless Quartet)
Onward, Christian Soldiers	1927	Okeh 40790

Old Apple Trio
Clover Blossoms	1933	Victor 24311/Bluebird B-5120/Electradisk 2030/Sunrise S-3201
Darktown Strutter's Ball	1933	Bluebird B-5649
Smile For Me	1933	Bluebird B-5649
Twelfth Street Rag	1933	Victor 24311/Bluebird B-5120/Electradisk 2030/Sunrise S-3201

Old Harp Singers
Barnyard Song, The/On Springfield Mountain	1937	Musicraft 222
Frog Went A-Courtin'/Sourwood Mountain	1937	Musicraft 222
Old Ship Of Zion, The	1937	Musicraft 221

Poor Wayfaring Stranger	1937	Musicraft 221
Old Pal Smokeshop Quartet		
Black Cat Blues	1926	Vocalion 1046
Surprised Blues	1926	Vocalion 1046
Old South Quartette		
Bohunkus And Josephus	1928	Broadway 5031
No Hiding Place Down Here	1928	QRS R 7025
Oh What He's Done For Me	1928	QRS R 7025
Oysters And Wine At 2 A.M.	1928	Broadway 5031/QRS R 7006
Pussy Cat Rag	1928	Broadway 5031/QRS R 7006
Watermelon Party	1928	QRS R 7029
When De Corn Pone's Hot	1928	QRS R 7029
Old South Quartette, Polk Miller & his		
Bonnie Blue Flag, The	1909	Edison 2175 (4BA)
Jerusalem Mornin'	1909	Standard 10334 (cylinder)
Laughing Song	1909	Edison 2176 (4BA)
Old Time Religion, The	1909	Standard 10333 (cylinder)
Rise And Shine	1909	Standard 10332 (cylinder)
Watermelon Party, The	1909	Edison 2178 (4BA)
What A Time	1909	Edison 2177 (4BA)
Old Southern Sacred Singers		
Going Down The Valley One By One	1927	Brunswick 166/Supertone S 2102
Home Over There, The	1927	Brunswick 172
I'll Go Where You Want Me	1929	Brunswick 471
I'll Live On	1929	Brunswick 486
I'm Bound For The Promised Land	1927	Brunswick 161/Supertone S 2096
Just Before The Battle Mother	1927	Brunswick
Just Break The News To Mother	1927	Brunswick 165/Supertone S 2097
Lord I'm Coming Home	1929	Brunswick 390
My Mother's Prayers Have Followed Me	1927	Brunswick 165/Supertone S 2097
Nothing Between	1927	Brunswick 159
Nothing But The Blood Of Jesus	1929	Brunswick 389
Old Time Religion	1927	Brunswick 161
Only Trust Him	1929	Brunswick 471
Onward Christian Soldiers	1927	Brunswick 166/Supertone 2100
Picture From Life's Other Side	1932	Brunswick 115
Precious Name	1929	Brunswick 389
Safe In The Arms Of Jesus	1927	Brunswick 159/Supertone S 2100
Soul Winner For Jesus, A	1927	Vocalion 5185
Take The Name Of Jesus With You (The Precious Name)	1927	Brunswick 162
There Is A Fountain	1927	Brunswick
Tis So Sweet To Trust In Jesus	1929	Brunswick 486
Unclouded Day, The	1927	Brunswick 160/Vocalion 5185
What A Friend We Have In Jesus	1927	Brunswick 172/Supertone S 2117
Where The Gates Swing Outward Never	1929	Brunswick 357
Where We Never Grow Old	1932	Brunswick 115
Will My Mother Know Me There'	1929	Brunswick 357
Will There Be Any Stars In My Crown'	1927	Brunswick 162
Will There Be Any Stars In My Crown'	1929	Brunswick 390/Vocalion 5176
Old Time Jubilee Singers		
That Old Time Religion	1924	Ajax 17041
When The Saints Go Marching In	1924	Ajax 17041
Olden Time Minstrels		
Darky Shout (Get Happy)	1905	Victor 4599
Oleanders		
Mama Don't Allow It	1939	
Ol' Man Mose	1939	
Olympic Quartet (Old Southern Sacred Singers)		
Take The Name Of Jesus With You (The Precious Name)	1927	Melotone M 12076/Polk P 9052 (1927)
Will There Be Any Stars In My Crown'	1927	Melotone M 12076/Polk P 9052 (1927)
Organ Grinders, Lowe Stokes & his		
Back Up And Push	1929	Columbia 15394-D
Charming Betsy	1929	Columbia 15445-D
Four Thousand Years Ago	1929	Columbia 15445-D
Smoke Behind The Clouds	1929	Columbia 15394-D
Sweet Sixteen Next Sunday	1929	Columbia
Original Four Aces		
I Can See An Angel	1955	Big Town 118
I Can See Angel (DJ copy with different artists doing the same song)		Big Town (unnumbered)
Release	1954	Big Town 112
Whose Arms Are You Missing	1954	Big Town 112
You Were My First Affair	1955	Big Town 118
Original Jubilaires		
Drinkin' And Dreamin'		
Little Church Of Capistrano	1954	
Waiting All My Life For You	1954	Crown 111
You Won't Let Me Go	1954	
Original Valentine Quartet		
Give Me That Old Time Religion	1924	Okeh 8574

100 Years of Harmony: 1850 to 1950

Sing On	1924	Okeh 8574
Orioles		
Along About Sundown	1952	Jubilee (unreleased)
Angel	1956	Jubilee 5231
At Night	1950	Jubilee 5025
Baby, Please Don't Go	1951	Jubilee 5065
Bad Little Girl	1953	Jubilee 5115
Barbra Lee	1948	It's A Natural 5000/Jubilee 5000 (1948)
Barfly	1952	Jubilee 5084
Blame It On Yourself	1951	Jubilee (unreleased)
Bring The Money Home	1955	Jubilee (unreleased)
Can't Seem To Laugh Anymore	1950	Jubilee 5040
Cigareetos	1955	Jubilee (unreleased)
Count Your Blessings Instead Of Sheep	1954	Jubilee 5172
Crying in The Chapel	1953	Jubilee 5122
Dare To Dream	1948	Jubilee 5001
Deacon Jones	1949	Jubilee 5005
Dem Days	1953	Jubilee 5115
Didn't I Say	1957	Vee Jay 244/Abner 1016 (1958)
Donkey Serenade	1949	Jubilee 5008
Don't Cry Baby	1952	Jubilee 5092
Don't Go To Strangers	1954	Jubilee 5137/Jubilee 5231 (1956)
Don't Keep It To Yourself	1952	Jubilee (unreleased)
Don't Stop	1952	Jubilee (unreleased)
Don't Tell Her What Happened To Me	1951	Jubilee 5065
Don't You Think I Ought To Know'	1953	Jubilee 5122
Drowning Every Hope I Ever Had	1954	Jubilee 5143
Every Dog-Gone Time	1950	Jubilee 5025
Everything They Said Came True	1950	Jubilee 5028
Fair Exchange	1955	Jubilee 5177
Feeling Low	1952	Jubilee (unreleased)
For All We Know	1956	Vee Jay 228
Forgive And Forget	1949	Jubilee 5016
Gettin' Tired, Tired, Tired	1952	Jubilee 5084
Good Looking Baby	1952	Jubilee (unreleased)
Goodnight Irene	1950	Jubilee 5037
Happy Go Lucky Local Blues	1951	Jubilee 5055
Happy Till The Letter	1956	Vee Jay 196
Hey Little Woman	1962	
Hold Me! Squeeze Me!	1951	Jubilee 5061
Hold Me, Thrill Me, Kiss Me	1953	Jubilee 5108
How Blind Can You Be	1951	Jubilee 5071
I Challenge Your Kiss	1949	Jubilee 5008
I Cover The Waterfront	1953	Jubilee 5120
I Cross My Fingers	1950	Jubilee 5040
I Don't Want To Take A Chance	1952	Jubilee 5102
I'd Rather Have You Under The Moon	1950	Jubilee 5031
If You Believe	1954	Jubilee 5161
I Had To Leave Town	1950	Jubilee (unreleased)
I Just Got Lucky	1956	Vee Jay 196
I Love You Mostly	1955	Jubilee 5177
I May Be Wrong	1951	Jubilee (unreleased)
I'm Beginning To Think You Care For Me	1952	Jubilee (unreleased)
I Miss You So	1951	Jubilee 5051/Jubilee 5107 (1953)
I'm Just A Fool In Love	1951	Jubilee 5061
I Need You, Baby	1955	Jubilee 5189
I Need You So	1950	Jubilee 5037
In The Chapel In The Moonlight	1954	Jubilee 5154
In The Mission Of St. Augustine	1953	Jubilee 5127
I Promise You	1952	Jubilee (unreleased)
Is My Heart Wasting Time	1950	Jubilee 5018
It's A Cold Summer	1949	Jubilee 5009
It Seems So Long Ago	1949	Jubilee 5002
It's Over Because We're Through	1952	Jubilee 5082
It's Too Soon To Know	1948	It's A Natural 5000/Jubilee 5000 (1948)
I Wonder When'	1950	Jubilee 5026
Kiss And A Rose, A	1949	Jubilee 5009
Lonely Christmas	1948	Jubilee 5001/Jubilee 5017 (1949)
Longing	1954	Jubilee 5161
Lord's Prayer, The	1950	Jubilee 5045
Maybe You'll Be There	1954	Jubilee 5143
Moody Over You	1955	Jubilee 5221
Moonlight	1950	Jubilee 5026
My Baby's Gonna Get It	1952	Jubilee (unreleased)
My Loved One	1951	Jubilee (unreleased)
Never Leave Me, Baby	1956	Vee Jay 228
Oh, Holy Night	1950	Jubilee 5045
Once Upon A Time	1952	Jubilee (unreleased)
One More Time	1953	Jubilee 5120
Pal Of Mine	1951	Jubilee 5055
Please Give My Heart A Break	1949	Jubilee 5002
Please Sing My Blues Tonight	1955	Jubilee 5221
Pretty, Pretty Rain	1952	Jubilee (unreleased)
Robe Of Calvary	1954	Jubilee 5134
Runaround	1954	Jubilee 5172
Secret Love	1954	Jubilee 5137
See See Rider	1952	Jubilee 5092
Shrimp Boats	1952	Jubilee 5074
So Much	1949	Jubilee 5016
Sugar Girl	1957	Vee Jay 244/Abner 1016 (1958)
Teardrops On My Pillow	1953	Jubilee 5108
Tell Me So	1949	Jubilee 5005/Herald (second version)

Title	Year	Label/Number
Thank The Lord! Thank The Lord!	1954	Jubilee 5154
That's When The Good Lord Will Smile	1955	Jubilee 5189
There's No One But You	1954	Jubilee 5134
Till Then	1953	Jubilee 5107
To Be With You	1948	Jubilee 5001
Trust In Me	1952	Jubilee 5074
Waiting	1952	Jubilee 5082
Walking By The River		
Wanted	1952	Jubilee (unreleased)
We're Supposed To Be Through	1950	Jubilee 5031
What Are You Doing New Year's Eve	1949	Jubilee 5017
When You're A Long, Long Way From Home	1951	Jubilee 5057
When You're Not Around	1951	Jubilee 5071
Why Did You Go	1952	Jubilee (unreleased)
Would I Love You (Love You, Love You)	1951	Jubilee 5057
Would You Still Be The One In My Heart	1950	Jubilee 5018
Write And Tell Me Why	1953	Jubilee 5127
You Are My First Love	1951	Jubilee 5051
You Belong To Me	1952	Jubilee 5102
You're Gone	1950	Jubilee 5028

Orioles, Sonny Til & the

Title	Year	Label/Number
At Night (with chorus)	1959	Jubilee 5363
Back To The Chapel Again	1962	Charlie Parker 213
Come On Home (with the Helen Way Singers)	1960	Jubilee 5384
Crying In The Chapel	1964	Lana 109
Crying In The Chapel (with chorus)	1959	Jubilee 6001
Don't Mess Around With My Love	1962	Charlie Parker 214
Don't Tell Her What Happened To Me	1963	Charlie Parker 216
First Of Summer (with chorus), The	1960	Jubilee 5384
Forgive And Forget (with chorus)	1959	Jubilee 6001
Hey! Little Woman	1962	Charlie Parker 212/Charlie Parker 219 (1963)
I Miss You So	1963	Charlie Parker 215/Charlie Parker 219 (1963)
In The Chapel In The Moonlight	1962	Charlie Parker 212
It's Too Soon To Know	1963	Charlie Parker 215/Sutton (unreleased)
Lonely Christmas	1962	Charlie Parker 213
Over The Rainbow		Sutton (unreleased)
Secret Love	1962	Charlie Parker 211/Sutton (unreleased)
Tell Me So (with chorus)	1959	Jubilee 5363
What Are You Doing New Year's Eve	1962	Charlie Parker 214/Lana 109
Wobble, The	1962	Charlie Parker 211
Write And Tell My Why	1963	Charlie Parker 216

Orphans

Title	Year	Label/Number
Baby, I'll Be Waitin'	1955	Decca 29237
Stephen Foster Medley	1955	Decca 29236
Sweetheart Of Sigma Chi, The	1955	Decca 29236
When You're A Long, Long Way From Home	1955	Decca 29237

Orpheus Quartet

Title	Year	Label/Number
Ain't You Comin' Back To Dixie	1917	Victor 18235
Carry Me Back To Ole Virginny (take 1)	1916	Victor 18195
Chu Chin Chow	1917	Victor 18336
Darling Nellie Gray	1916	Victor 18195
Fair Harvard	1913	Victor 17413
Girl In The Gingham Gown	1913	Victor 17468
God Be With You Till We Meet Again	1909	Victor 16399
Harvard University Song	1913	Victor 17413
Ho Holly Jenkin	1912	Victor 17053
I Can Hear The Ukuleles Calling Me	1917	Victor 18282
If All My Dreams Were Made Of Gold	1912	Victor 17057
Just A Voice To Call Me	1917	Victor 18399
Long Day Closes, The	1912	Victor 17053
Lovely Night	1911	Victor 16902
Mammy's Little Coal Black Rose	1916	Victor 18183
Molly Dear, It's You I'm After	1915	Victor 17900
More And More	1911	Victor 16902
My Hawaii, You're Calling Me	1917	Victor 18326
Our Country's In It Now	1918	Victor 18470
Pretty Baby	1916	Victor 18162
Sing Me The Rosary	1913	Victor 17467
Some Day They're Coming Home	1918	Victor 18468
Stein Song, A	1915	Victor 17899
Swing Along	1915	Victor 17899
They Kissed, I Saw Them Do It	1911	Victor 16888
Though I'm Not The First To Call You Sweetheart	1917	Victor 18239
When Evening Shadows Fall	1908	Victor 18183
When I Carved Your Name On A Tree	1913	Victor 17334
Where Would I Be	1913	Victor 17370
Whose Pretty Baby Are You	1917	Victor 18238

Orpheus Quartet & Harry Macdonough

Title	Year	Label/Number
For Freedom Of The World	1917	Victor 18337

Orpheus Quartet with Harry Macdonough

Title	Year	Label/Number
Letter That Never Reached Home	1916	Victor 18030

Orpheus Quartet, Harry McDonough & the

Title	Year	Label/Number
Turn Back The Universe And	1916	Victor 18112

Give Me Yesterday 5414/Victor 38543 (1929)

Orpheus Quartet, Raymond Dixon & the
When You Come Back	1918	Victor 18494

Orpheus Trio
Arabian Nights	1921	Pathe 22096
Who'll Take The Place Of Mary	1920	Gennett 9036

Ozark Mountain Sacred Singers
Jesus Is Mine	1929	Champion 15926
Serving The Master	1929	Champion 15926
What Is He Worth To The Soul	1928	Champion 15793
Where The Soul Never Dies	1929	Champion 15793

Pace Jubilee Singers
Certainly Lord	1927	Black Patti 8043/Paramount 12678 (1927)
Cryin' Holy Unto The Lord	1929	Victor 38573
Everytime I Feel De Spirit	1928	Bluebird 5414
Every Time I Feel The Spirit	1928	Victor 38019
Going Through Jesus	1927	Victor 20225
Gonna Reap What You Sow	1927	Victor 20310
Hark From The Tomb	1927	Black Patti 8042
Haven Of Rest, The	1928	Victor 38510
Heaven's Door Gonna Close	1928	Black Patti 8012/Paramount 12678 (1928)
He's Got His Eye On The Sparrow	1927	Black Patti 8042
Holy Ghost With Light Divine	1929	Victor 38573/Victor 23412 (1932)
I Can't Stay Away	1929	Victor 38591
I Do	1927	Victor 20226
I'll Be Satisfied	1927	Paramount 12485
I'm Going Through Jesus	1926	Bluebird 5079/Black Patti 8031 (1927)
I'm Going To Do All I Can	1928	Victor 38019
In That City	1929	Victor 38543
Is It Well With My Soul	1932	Victor 23412
It Pays To Serve Jesus	1927	Paramount 12485
I've Done My Work	1928	Victor 38029
Jesus Is A Rock In The Weary Land	1929	Victor 38631
Lawdy, Won't You Come By Home	1927	Brunswick 7009/Vocalion 1168 (1927)
Life Is Like A Mountain Railroad	1932	Victor 23350
Little Talk With Jesus, A	1932	Victor 23350
Lonesome Valley	1927	Victor 20310
Mammy's Child	1927	Black Patti 8032
My Lord Is My Writin'	1927	Victor 20226
My Lord What A Morning	1927	Victor 20225
My Lord Will Deliver	1927	Brunswick 7009/Vocalion 1168 (1927)
My Task	1928	Victor 38029
No Night There	1928	Bluebird
Old Ship Of Zion	1928	Black Patti 8022
Old Time Religion	1929	Bluebird 5811
Prayer Meetin' In Hell	1927	Black Patti 8031
Roll Jordan Roll	1929	Victor 38622
Sing Sing Ethiopia Sing	1927	Black Patti 8032
Steal Away And Pray	1928	Victor 38510/Black Patti 8011 (1928)
Take Your Burden To The Lord And Leave It There	1928	Bluebird 5477
There's Room Enough In Heaven For You And Me	1927	Black Patti 8011
Throw Out The Lifeline	1929	Victor 38622
Walk In The Light Of God	1927	Brunswick 7008/Vocalion 1167 (1927)
Walk With Me	1929	Victor 38591
Were You There	1928	Black Patti 8012
What A Friend We Have In Jesus	1926	Bluebird 5079
What Are They Doing In Heaven Today'	1929	Victor 38631
When The Saints Go Marching In	1928	Bluebird 5477
You Belong To The Funeral Train	1927	Paramount 12495
You'd Better Mind	1927	Paramount 12495
You Got To Run, Run, Run	1929	Bluebird 5811

Pace Jubilee Singers (with H. Parker)
It Pays To Serve Jesus	1929	Victor 38522
It's A Precious Thing	1929	Victor 38522

Pace Jubilee Singers, Hattie Parker & the
Don't You Want To Meet Your Mother Over There	1927	Brunswick 7021
His Eye Is On The Sparrow	1927	Brunswick 7008/Vocalion 1167 (1927)
Is It Well With Your Soul Today	1927	Brunswick 7001
I've Started And I'm Going All The Way	1927	Brunswick 7021
We Will Walk Through The Valley Of Peace	1927	Brunswick 7001

Palace Trio
I've Got My Captain Working For Me Now	1919	Brunswick 2016
I Want A Daddy Who Will Rock Me To Sleep	1919	Brunswick 2027
Lone Star	1920	Okeh 4086
Missy	1920	Okeh 4086
Where The Lanterns Glow	1919	Brunswick 2014
You'll Be Sorry (But You'll Be Sorry Too Late)	1919	Brunswick 2017

Palm Beach Boys
Just A Memory	1927	Parlophone E 5946
Magnolia	1927	Okeh 40878
Under The Moon	1927	Okeh 40878

Palmer Brothers
Big Boy Blue	1937	Variety 531
Disappointed In Love	1935	Decca 389
Rhythm Lullabye	1935	Decca 389
Rip Van Winkle	1939	Varsity 8106

Palmer Brothers (with Larry Wynn)
You Appeal To Me	1938	Regal Zonophone G 23424

Palmetto Jazz Quartet
Baseball Blues	1921	Okeh 8023
Home Again Blues	1921	Okeh 8023
My Jazz Gal	1921	Okeh 8011
Norfolk Religion	1921	Okeh 8034
Old Pal Why Don't You Answer Me	1921	Okeh 8016
Sweet Mamma (Papa's Getting Mad)	1921	Okeh 8016
'U' Need Some Loving	1921	Okeh 8028

Palmetto Quartet
God's Love	1931	Champion 16731
I Love To Raise My Voice	1931	Champion 16731
I'm Not Satisfied Here	1931	Champion 16250
O'er Shadowed By God's Love	1931	Champion 16250

Pan-American Quartet
Swanee River Melody	1927	

Paramount Jubilee Singers
I Couldn't Hear Nobody Pray	1923	Paramount 12070
My Soul Is A Witness For My Lord	1923	Paramount 12072
Steal Away To Jesus	1923	Paramount 12072
That Old Time Religion	1923	Paramount 12073
When The Saints Come Marching In	1923	Paramount 12073

Paramount Lady's Four
God's Gonna Set The World On Fire	1926	Paramount 12415
Shine For Jesus	1926	Paramount 12415

Paramount Quartet
Heaven Is My Home	1925	Columbia 15020-D
What Did He Do'	1925	Columbia 15020-D

Paramount Sacred Four
Beautiful Land, The	1927	Broadway 8182
Echoes From Glory Shore	1927	Broadway 8105
Get Away Jordan	1927	Paramount 12557
Heaven	1927	Paramount 12557
How Wonderful Heaven Must Be	1927	Broadway 8133
Ridin' Billows For Home	1927	Broadway 8133
Right Will Always Win	1927	Broadway 8105
Unclouded Day	1927	Broadway 8182

Paramount Singers
You've Got To Bow Down Before God	1952	Coral 65100

Park Avenue Promenaders
Love Me Tonight	1932	Columbia
'Twas Only A Summer Night Dream	1932	Columbia 2717-D

Park Avenue Trio, Bon Bon & the
If You Cared For Me	1945	Joe Davis 7196

Parker Brothers
I Can't Help From Cryin' Sometimes	1950	Atlantic 908
Separating Line, The	1950	Atlantic 908

Parker Trio, Charlie
Where Shall I Be'	1927	Columbia
While Eternal Ages Roll	1927	Columbia

Paulette Sisters
Bluebird Singing In My Heart, A		Spotlite 505
Cruising Down The River		Spotlite 505
Dreamy Melody		Broadway BR 1088
Ev'rybody Loves Saturday Night	1953	Columbia 40115
Far Away Places		Spotlite 500
Following The Leader	1953	Philips B 21060
Kalamazoo To Timbuktu	1951	Columbia 39679
Longing For You		Broadway BR 1088
Love Makes The World Go Round	1951	Columbia 39617
Never Smile At A Crocodile	1953	Philips B 21060
Oh, Johnny, Oh Johnny, Oh	1952	Columbia 39697
(That Is Where A Man He) Put The Foot Down	1952	Columbia 39697
What Should I Do'		Broadway 1013

Paulette Sisters, Connee Boswell & the
I Fall In Love With You Every Day	1946	Decca 18793
I'm Gonna Make Believe (I've Got Myself A Sweetheart)	1946	Decca 18881
I'm In Love With Two Sweethearts	1946	Decca 18793
There Must Be A Way	1945	Decca 18689
Who Told You That Lie'	1946	Decca 18881

Paupers
Blue Sunday Morning	1949	Melford 258
Prettiest Gal In Town	1949	Melford 258

Peabody Trio (with the Seven Aces)
Have You Forgotten'	1926	Columbia 863-D
There's Everything Nice About You	1927	Columbia 1001-D
Who'll Be The One'	1926	Columbia 863-D

Peck's Male Quartette
Going Down The Valley	1930	Banner 32100/Conqueror 7798 (1931)
No Stranger Yonder	1930	Banner 32097
Oh! I Want To See Him	1930	Banner 32100/Conqueror 7798 (1931)

Unclouded Day, The	1930	Banner 32097
Peerless Four		
Dixie Vagabond, The	1927	Okeh 40780
Roses For Remembrance	1927	Okeh 40780
Peerless Quartet		
Ain't You Coming Out, Malinda'	1921	Victor 18812
Alabama Blacksheep	1923	Victor 19180
Alagazam (To The Music Of The Band)	1915	Columbia A-1865/Victor 17904 (1915)
All Aboard For Dixie (with Ada Jones)	1914	Columbia A-1481
All For The Love Of A Girl	1915	Columbia A-1707
Aloha Oe (with Marie Morrisey)	1918	Brunswick 15243
Along The Silvery Colorado	1922	Victor 19029
Along The Way To Waikiki	1917	Victor 18326
America, Here's My Boy	1917	Victor 18256
America (My Country 'Tis Of Thee)	1919	Okeh 1116
Any Old Time At All	1918	Columbia A-2658
A.O.H.'s Of The U.S.A., The	1914	Columbia A-1664
Are You Coming Out Matilda	1921	Victor 18812
Are You From Dixie	1916	Columbia A-1921
Arrah Go On, I'm Gonna Go Back To Oregon	1916	Victor 18046
Artillerist's Oath, The	1908	Victor 16142/Victor 16957 (1911)
At The Bully Woolly Wild West Show	1913	Victor 17514
At The Devil's Ball	1913	Victor 17315
At The Midnight Masquerade	1913	Columbia A-1437/Victor 17480 (1913)
At The Ragtime Ball	1912	Victor 17191/Columbia A-1261 (1913)
Auld Lang Syne	1918	Victor 18792
Au Revoir But Not Goodbye	1918	Victor 18438
Away Down South	1922	Victor 18942
Bachelor Days	1916	Columbia A-2062/Victor 18120 (1916)
Back To Dixieland	1915	Columbia
Back To The Carolina You Love	1914	Victor 17666
Back To The Old Folks At Home	1913	Columbia A-1335
Batter Up	1918	Columbia
Battle In The Air, A	1918	Columbia A-2626
Beautiful Isle Of Somewhere	1925	Victor 19883/Montgomery Ward 4808/Timely Tunes C-1568
Bells, The	1914	Victor 17539/Columbia
Beyond The Smiling And Weeping	1910	Victor 16500
Big Bass Viol	1910	Victor 16507
Big Bass Violin	1909	Everlasting 253 (2mincyl)
Blue Jeans	1921	Victor 18740
Bobbin' Up And Down	1913	Columbia A-1298/Victor 17335 (1913)
Bounce Me John, I've Rubber Heels On	1915	Columbia A-1847
Bring Back My Golden Dreams	1912	Victor 17124
Broadway Rose	1920	Columbia A-3333
Buddha	1920	Pathe 22334
Buddha	1920	Victor 18653
Buddy Boy - How's Every Little Thing With You'	1919	Columbia A-2703
Buffalo Baby Rag	1914	Columbia A-1496
By The Campfire	1919	Victor 18540
By The Old Cathedral Door	1912	Victor 17175
By The Saskatchewan	1912	Phono-Cot 5099
California For Mine	1912	Columbia A-1233
Call Me Back Again	1922	Victor 19228
Calm On The Listening Ear Of Night	1925	Victor 19794
Carolina, I'm Coming Back To You	1918	Victor 18497/Columbia A-2540 (1918)
Carry Me Back To Old Virginny	1910	Everlasting 1076 (4mincyl)
Casey Jones	1910	Everlasting 1106 (4mincyl)
Characteristic Negro Medley, A	1910	Edison BA 1876/Edison 431 (4mincyl) (1910)/Indestructible 3042 (4mincyl) (1910)
Cheer Up Father, Cheer Up Mother	1918	Columbia A-2597/Okeh 1075 (1918)
Cheer Up The Old Folks At Home	1924	Victor 19333
Chimes Of Trinity, The	1925	Victor 19716
Chin Chin Chinaman	1918	Brunswick 5200
Christmas Light, Behold	1913	Victor 35335
College Days	1916	Victor 18168
Come Along To Toy Town	1918	Columbia A-2664/Okeh 1134 (1919)
Come Back To Dixie	1915	Victor 17836
Come My Honey	1913	Victor 17497
Come Where My Love Lies Dreaming	1908	Victor 16663
Come Where My Love Lies Dreaming	1909	Everlasting 343 (2mincyl)
Cost Of Loving, The	1914	Victor 17622

Title	Year	Label/Number
Dancing 'Neath The Irish Moon	1915	Columbia A-1773
Darling Nellie Gray	1916	Victor 18195/Victor 19887 (1925)
Day With The Soldiers, A	1913	Columbia A-5497
Dear Old Dreamy Honolulu Town	1916	Victor 18101
Dear Old Girl	1921	Columbia A-3436/Meteor 1104
Dear Old Moon Light	1909	Everlasting 252 (2mincyl)
Dear Rose Marie	1913	Victor 17467
De Gospel Train Am Comin'	1919	Columbia
Did He Run	1909	Victor 16324
Dinah	1913	Victor 17494/Edison 2167 (4BA)
Ding Dong	1918	Columbia A-2647/Okeh 1135 (1919)
Dixie Days	1913	Columbia A-1439
Dixie Land	1915	Columbia A-1764
Dixie's Land		Busy Bee 123 (2mincyl)
Dixie Volunteers, The	1917	Columbia A-2447
Don't Be Afraid To Come Home	1926	Victor 34194
Don't Blame It All On Broadway	1913	Victor 17539/Columbia A-1497 (1914)
Don't Blame Me For Loving You	1911	Victor 16991/Columbia (1916)
Don't Forget The Salvation Army (with Arthur Fields)	1919	Columbia
Don't Go Away	1914	Columbia A-1564
Don't Stop	1914	Columbia A-1482
Don't Take My Darling Boy Away	1915	Victor 17736
Down At The Husking Bee	1916	Victor 18206
Down De Lover's Lane	1912	Victor 17097
Down Old Harmony Way	1913	Victor 17372
Down On The Farm	1920	Columbia A-356
Down Where The Swanee River Flows	1916	Victor 17983
Down Yonder	1921	Victor 18775
Do Your Little Bitty-Bit (Right Now)	1918	Columbia A-2602
Drifting	1920	Victor 18679/Columbia A-2984 (1920)
Emaline Lee	1911	Victor 16852/Victor 16956 (1911)
Everybody Loves A Chicken	1913	Columbia A-1283
Everybody's Crazy Over Dixie	1919	Columbia
Everybody Two-Step	1912	Columbia A-1261
Everything Is Hunky Dory In Honky Tonk Town	1918	Columbia A-2659
Ev'ryone In Town Loves My Girl	1914	Columbia A-1523
Farmyard Medley	1915	D&R 3681
Father, Dear Father, Come Home With Me Now	1925	Victor 19716
Fiddle-De-Dee (with Lew Dockstader)	1912	Columbia A-1200
Firefly (My Pretty Firefly)	1915	Victor 17836/Columbia A-1790 (1915)
Fires Of Faith	1919	Columbia A-2731
Follow The Swallow	1924	Victor 19455
Follow Up The Big Brass Band	1914	Columbia A-1532
For Your Boy And My Boy	1918	Victor 18494/Columbia A-2635 (1918)
For Your Country And My Country	1917	Columbia A-2273
France, We'll Rebuild Your Towns For You	1918	Columbia A-2567
Georgia	1922	Victor 18876
Georgia Land	1913	Victor 17349/Columbia A-1278 (1913)
Ghost Of The Terrible Blues, The	1916	Victor 17944/Columbia A-1925 (1916)
Ghost Of The Ukulele	1917	Victor 18254
Ghost Of The Violin	1912	Columbia A-1244
Girl From Saskatchewan	1911	Indestructible (4mincyl)
Girl I Loved In Sunny Tennessee, The	1924	Victor 19390
Goodbye Barney Boy	1918	Columbia A-2529/Brunswick 5199 (1918)
Goodbye Boys	1913	Columbia A-1301
Goodbye Broadway, Hello France	1914	Columbia A-1552
Goodbye Broadway, Hello France (with Arthur Fields)	1917	Columbia A-2333
Goodbye Frenchy	1918	Victor 18514
Good-bye Summer! So Long Fall! Hello Winter Time!	1913	Victor 17430/Columbia A-1403 (1913)
Goodnight Angeline	1919	Columbia A-2888/Okeh 4028 (1919)
Goodnight (I'll See You In The Morning)	1926	Victor 20012
Green Fields Of Virginia, The	1924	Victor 19390
Hail Pennsylvania	1913	Victor 17384
Happy Days In Dixie	1919	Columbia A-2900
Harmony Bay	1914	Columbia A-1536
Harmony Joe	1913	Victor 17354/Columbia A-1327 (1913)
Hear That Orchestra Rag	1912	Victor

Title	Year	Label/Number
Hear The Pickaninny Band	1912	Victor 17052
Hearts Of The World Love Canada, The	1918	Columbia 17099/Columbia A-1185 (1912)
Hello! Swanee - Hello!	1926	Okeh 40722
Hello Bill: Elk Song	1914	Columbia A-1544
Here's Love And Success To You	1912	Victor 17131
He's A Rag Picker	1914	Victor 17655/Columbia A-1628 (1914)/Edison BA 2513
He's Had No Lovin' For A Long Long Time	1919	Columbia
High Cost Of Living	1914	Victor 17622
Hike Hike Hike! (Along The Old Turn Pike)	1918	Columbia A-2540
Hits Of Days Gone By (von Tilzer Medley) Part 1	1920	Columbia A-2926
Hits Of Days Gone By (von Tilzer Medley) Part 2	1920	Columbia A-2926
Home-Coming Of The American Troops, The - Part 1	1919	Columbia
Home-Coming Of The American Troops, The - Part 2	1919	Columbia
Home Over There, The	1927	Victor 20669
Homeward Bound	1918	Victor 18247
Hong Kong	1917	Victor 18295
Honolulu, America Loves You	1919	Columbia
Honolulu Blues	1916	Victor 18068/Columbia A-2000
How Could I Know'	1913	Columbia A-1343
How Sorry You'll Be	1919	Vocalion 14005A
Hunting Scene, A	1919	Columbia
I Can Always Find A Little Sunshine In The Y.M.C.A.	1918	Columbia A-2647
I Didn't Raise My Boy To Be A Soldier	1915	Columbia A-1697
I'd Love To Fall Asleep And Wake Up In My Mammy's Arms	1920	Victor 18692/Vocalion 14059B (1920)
I Don't Know Where I'm Going But I'm On My Way	1917	Victor 18383/Columbia A-2329 (1917)
I Don't Want The Bacon	1918	Columbia A-2620
If I Had My Way	1914	Victor 17534
If I Had Someone Like You At Home	1914	Victor 17589
If You Only Had My Disposition	1915	Victor 17912
If You See Sally	1927	Victor 20571
I Gave My Heart And Hand To Someone In Dixie Land	1916	Victor 18024/Columbia A-1952 (1916)
I'll Always Be Waiting For You	1919	Victor 18642
I'll See You In The Morning	1927	Victor 20012
I'll Take You Home Again, Kathleen	1921	Victor 18781
I Loved You Just Like Lincoln Loved...		Edison 2312 (4BA)
I Love Her Oh Oh Oh	1913	Columbia A-1348
I Love The Moonlight	1927	Victor
I Love To Fall Asleep And Wake Up In My Mother's Arms	1920	Victor 18692
I Love You California	1913	Columbia A-1384
I Love You Just The Same, Sweet Adeline	1919	Columbia A-2810/Okeh 4074 (1920)
I May Be Gone For A Long, Long Time	1917	Columbia A-2306
I May Stay Away A Little Longer	1918	Victor 18469
I'm Coming Back To California	1916	Victor 18204
I'm Coming Back To Dixie And You	1914	Victor 17685/Columbia A-1547 (1914)
I'm Gonna Pin My Medal On The Girl I Left Behind	1918	Victor 18486
I'm Gonna Spend My Honeymoon In Dixie	1920	Columbia
I'm Missin' My Mammy's Kissin'	1921	Victor 18751
I'm On My Way To Dublin Bay	1915	Victor 17736
I'm Proud To Be A Mother Of A Boy Like You	1915	Victor 17758
I'm San Francisco Bound	1913	Columbia A-1333
In Alabama Dear, With You	1915	Victor 17875/Columbia A-1828 (1915)
In Banjo Land	1913	Victor 17264
In Blinky, Winky, Chinky Chinatown	1915	Victor 17875
Indiana	1919	Columbia A-2221
I Never Knew How Wonderful You Were	1925	Victor
In Grandma's Day	1908	Victor 16128
In San Domingo	1917	Victor 18393
In The Candle Light	1924	Victor 19412
In The Days Of Old Black Joe	1916	Victor 18225
In The Evening By The Moonlight	1926	Victor 20055
In The Golden Afterwhile	1911	Victor 16991
In The Heart Of Dear Old Italy	1921	Victor 18795
In The Light Of The Same Old Moon	1908	Victor 16262
In The Palace Of Dreams	1914	Columbia A-1579
In The Sweet Bye-And-Bye	1926	Victor 20669
In The Y.M.C.A.	1919	Okeh 1135
Irish Tango, The	1914	Victor 17571/Columbia A-1515 (1914)
I'se Gwine Back To Dixie	1915	Columbia A-1881

Is There Still Room For Me'	1915	Victor 17927
I Think I'll Wait Until They All Come Home	1919	Emerson (Blue Label) 9146
I Think We've Got Another Washington (Wilson Is His Name)	1915	Columbia A-1864
It Must Be Love	1925	Victor 19827
It's A Long Lane That Has No Turning	1912	Victor 17030/Phono-Cut 5099 (1912)
It's Always Orange Day In California	1916	Victor 18103
It's Time For Every Boy To Be A Soldier	1917	Columbia A-2242
I've Got The Nicest Little Home In D-I-X-I-E	1917	Columbia A-2356
I Want A Man Just Like Dad	1913	Columbia A-1380
I Want My Mammy	1922	Victor 18832
I Want To Go Home	1913	Columbia A-1300
I Want To Sleep And Wake Up In My Mammy's Arms	1920	Okeh 4127
Jane	1915	Victor 17813
Jazz Babies' Ball	1920	Vocalion 14029B
Jean	1920	Columbia A-2915
Jerusalem Morn	1925	Victor/Brunswick (1929)
Jimmy Valentine	1912	Victor 17036
Jolly Tars Medley, The	1915	Columbia A-1749
June	1910	Everlasting 381 (2mincyl)
Just A Dream Of You Dear	1913	Columbia A-1379
Just A Little Longer	1927	Victor 20335
Just As The Sun Went Down	1917	Columbia A-2436
Just One Day	1916	Victor 18129/Columbia A-2083 (1916)
Keemo Kimo	1919	Columbia A-2853
Keep The Trench Fires Going For The Boys Out There	1918	Columbia A-2522
Keep Your Eye On The Girlie	1916	Victor 18204
Keep Your Eye On Uncle Sam	1914	Columbia A-1581
Kentucky Babe	1918	Okeh 1017
Kentucky Days	1912	Columbia A-1223
Kentucky Lullaby	1927	Victor 37696
Lantern Of Love	1926	Victor 20012
Last Long Mile, The (with Arthur Fields)	1918	Columbia A-2601
Lay Me Down In Dixieland	1922	Victor 18884
Lead, Kindly Light	1908	Indestructible 850 (2mincyl)
Lead Kindly Light	1920	Okeh 4190
Lead Me, Saviour	1925	
Let Me Call You Sweetheart	1911	
Let Me Linger Longer In Your Arms	1925	Victor 19827
Let's Go Back To The Baby Days	1909	Victor 16341
Liberty Bell (It's Time To Ring Again)	1918	Victor 18434/Columbia A-2473 (1918)
Lights Of My Home Town	1916	Victor 17943
Lindy Lady	1923	Victor 19194
Little Boy Blue	1926	Victor
Little Cotton Dolly		Busy Bee 134 (2mincyl)
Little Old Log Cabin In The Lane, The	1910	Indestructible (4mincyl)
Little White Church In The Valley	1915	Victor 17810
Liza	1909	Victor 16336
Louana Lou	1916	Victor 17992
Love Me While The Lovin's Good	1913	Victor 17421/Columbia A-1378 (1913)
Love's Old Sweet Song	1926	Okeh 40647/Busy Bee 249 (2mincyl)
Low Bridge, Everybody Down Or Fifteen Years On The Erie Canal	1913	Columbia A-1296
Lucille Love (flip is 'Zudora' by Harry Macdonough)	1915	Victor 17734
Lucky Boy	1913	Columbia A-1405
Makin's Of The U.S.A., The	1918	Columbia A-2522
Mammy Lou	1921	Victor 18884
Mammy's Good Night Lullaby	1920	Vocalion 14087A
Man Behind The Hammer And Plow	1917	Victor 18320
Mandalay	1924	Victor 19418
Mandy And Me	1918	Columbia
Mandy Lou	1910	Everlasting 1179 (4mincyl)
Mandy Lou	1911	Victor 16904/Columbia (1916)
Medley of Foster Songs: My Old Kentucky Home, Old folks At Home, Old Black Joe, I'se Gwine Back To Dixie, Carry Me Back To Old Virginny, Massa's In The Cold Cold Ground	1929	Victor 35095
Medley Of Popular Songs	1909	Indestructible 1033 (2mincyl)
Medley Of Sea Chanties	1914	Columbia A-1559
Melodious	1920	Okeh 4084
Melodious Jazz	1920	Vocalion 14050B
Memories Of Virginia	1923	Victor 19168
Men Of Harlech	1912	Victor 17180
Merrily We Roll Along	1918	Columbia A-2659
Mid The Green Fields Of Virginia	1924	Victor 19390
Mississippi Days	1916	Victor 18134
Moonlight Bay	1912	Everlasting 1570 (4mincyl)
Moonlight On The Lake	1908	Victor 16149

Title	Year	Label/Number
Morning	1914	Columbia
Musical Sam From Alabam'	1918	Victor 18350/Columbia A-2533 (1918)
Music Of Wedding Chimes, The	1919	Columbia A-2749
My Bird Of Paradise	1915	Victor 17770/Columbia A-1760 (1915)
My Cradle Melody	1922	Victor 18935
My Daddy Long Legs	1915	Columbia A-1681
My Dixie Rosary	1920	Columbia
My Dream Of The Big Parade	1926	Victor 20098/New World Records 222 (1926)
My Dream Of The Big Parade - Part 1	1926	Victor 35498
My Gal Sal	1922	Victor 18905
My Grandfather's Girl (She Was A Grand Old Girl)	1916	Columbia A-2019
My Hidden Treasure	1914	Columbia
My Little Persian Rose	1912	Columbia A-1247
My Lovin Melody Man	1913	Victor 17453
My Mammy (with Fred van Eps)	1921	Victor 18730
My Old Kentucky Home	1907	Indestructible 694 (2mincyl)
My Old Kentucky Home	1910	Everlasting 1077 (4mincyl)
My Old New Hampshire Home	1924	Victor 19508
My Pony Boy	1909	Indestructible 1198 (2mincyl)
My Rose Of Argentine	1915	Columbia A-1758
My Sahara Rose	1920	Vocalion 14059A
My Sunny Tennessee	1921	Victor 18812
My Swanee Home	1922	Victor 18905
My Tallahassee Flo	1912	Victor 17235
My Turkish Opal From Constantinople	1913	Victor 17367/Columbia A-1318 (1913)
Nationality Medley		Busy Bee 207 (2mincyl)
Nautical Medley	1915	Columbia A-1749
Navy Will Bring Them Back, The	1918	Victor 18514
Nearer My God To Thee		Everlasting 1393
Negro Wedding In Southern Georgia, A	1910	Victor 16526
Nellie Was A Lady		Busy Bee 236 (2mincyl)
New Parson At The Darktown Church	1908	Victor 16186
Night Alarm, The	1920	Columbia
Night Scene In Maxims	1913	Columbia A-1509
Norinne Maureen	1922	Victor 19228
Now You'll Be Sorry	1919	Okeh 4027
Oh, Joe, With Your Fiddle And Bow	1916	Victor 18046
Oh My Redeemer	1911	Everlasting 1257 (4mincyl)
Oh You Bundle Of You	1915	Victor 17827
Oh You Million Dollar Doll	1913	Columbia A-1443
Oh You Silv'ry Bells	1912	Victor 17202/Columbia A-1251 (1912)/Aretino D 741
Old Black Joe	1909	Victor 16531
Old Black Joe (a cappella)	1916	Rex 5069
Old Home Down On The Farm, The	1925	
Old Names Of Old Flames	1927	Victor 21079
Old Oaken Bucket, The	1908	Victor 16780/Victor 16217 (1909)
On A Beautiful Night With A Beautiful Girl	1912	Columbia A-1240
On A Good Old Time Sleigh Ride	1913	Victor 17482/Columbia A-1452 (1913)
On A Little Farm In Normandie	1919	Columbia A-2715
One And Two And Three And Four, Rockabye	1919	Columbia A-2714
On Honolulu Bay (with Hawaiian Guitars)	1916	Victor 18212
On The Old Dominion Line	1916	Victor 18067/Columbia A-2041
On The Sandwich Isles	1916	Victor 18227/Columbia (1919)
Open Up De Gates Of Glory	1927	Victor 37365
Our American Girl	1927	Victor 21026
Over There	1917	Columbia A-2306
Over There	1917	Indestructible 1556
Perfect Day, A	1926	Okeh 40647
Pick Me Up And Lay Me Down In Dear Old Dixieland	1922	Victor 18884
Picture Without A Frame, A	1922	Victor 18975
Piney Ridge	1915	Columbia A-1827
Pull For Shore	1914	Victor 17667
Pussy Cat Rag	1913	Victor 17514
Quilting Party, The	1925	Victor 19791
Raggedy Rag	1913	Victor 17341
Ragtime Dream, The	1914	Columbia A-1515
Rah Rah Rah	1908	Victor 16066
Railroad Section Gang	1910	Victor 16727
Rainbow From The U.S.A., A	1918	Victor 18484/Columbia A-2598 (1918)/Okeh 1090 (1918)/Brunswick 5244 (1918)
Red Lips, Kiss My Blues Away	1927	Victor

Title	Year	Label/Number
Red, White And Blue, The	1913	Victor 17384/Columbia A-1630 (1914)/Victor 17652 (1914)
Rejoice, Ye Pure In Heart	1927	Okeh 40790
Rockabye Lullaby Mammy	1920	Victor 18707
Rocked In The Cradle Of The Deep		Busy Bee 122 (2mincyl)
Rock Me In My Swanee Cradle	1922	Victor 18908
Rock Me To Sleep, Mother	1926	Victor 34696
Rolling	1913	Victor 17377/Columbia A-1326 (1913)
Rose Of The Mountain Trail	1914	Victor 17590
Rube Quartette, The	1915	Columbia A-1803
Sailor Song	1915	Columbia A-1803
Sally's Not The Same Old Sally	1926	Victor 20057
Salvation Nell	1913	Victor 17410/Columbia A-1403 (1913)
San Francisco Bound	1913	Victor 17367/Columbia A-1333 (1913)
Say A Prayer For The Boys Out There	1917	Victor 18411
Schmaltz's German Band	1916	Columbia A-1918
Shadows	1920	Pathe 22359
Silver Bell	1910	Victor 16646/Victor 16927 (1910)
Since Mother Goes To Movie Shows	1916	Victor 17959/Columbia A-1955 (1916)
Sleepyhead	1921	Victor 18786
Sleepy Moon	1915	Columbia A-1709
Smile Will Go A Long, Long Way, A	1924	Victor 19281
Soldier's Chorus (from 'Faust')		Busy Bee 230 (2mincyl)
Somebody Knows	1915	Victor 17779/Columbia A-1695 (19150
Somebody's Mother	1921	Victor 18746
Somebody's Waiting For Someone	1919	Victor 18554
Somewhere In France Is Daddy	1917	Columbia A-2336
Southern Hospitality	1915	Victor 17748
Spirit Of '17	1917	Columbia A-2301
Steam Boat Leaving Wharf At New Orleans	1909	Indestructible 1080 (2mincyl)
Stop! Look! Listen!	1920	Columbia
Sunset Valley	1922	Victor 18999
Sunshine And Roses	1913	Columbia A-1343
Swanee	1920	Victor 18688/Vocalion 14087B (1920)
Swanee River Trail	1927	Victor 37697
Sweet Adeline	1927	Victor 20055
Sweet Cider Time, When You Were Mine	1916	Victor 17969
Sweet Cookie Mine	1917	Victor 18350
Sweet Emalina My Gal	1917	Victor 18377
Sweet Genevieve	1927	Victor 20283
Sweetheart Days	1908	Indestructible 782 (2mincyl)
Sweetheart's A Pretty Name When It's You	1909	Victor 16352
Sweet Little Buttercup		Pathe 20309
Take In The Sun, Hang Out The Moon	1926	Okeh 40722
Take Me To My Alabam	1916	Victor 18167
Tell That To The Marines	1918	
Tennessee Moon	1912	Columbia A-1223
Tenting Tonight On The Old Camp Ground	1917	Pathe 40032
Texico	1913	Columbia A-1302
That Aeroplane Glide	1912	Victor 17113/Columbia A-1197 (1912)/Columbia A-1600 (1914)
That Is The Time For Sweethearts	1912	Columbia A-1196
That Mellow Melody	1912	Columbia A-1222
That Naughty Melody	1913	Columbia A-1407
That Raggedy Rag	1912	Victor 17052/Columbia A-1177 (1912)
That Wonderful Woodland Band	1913	Columbia A-1335
There's A Little White Church In The Valley	1915	Columbia A-1726
There's A Typical Tipperary Over Here	1920	Columbia A-2937
There's One In A Million Like You (with Manuel Romain)	1913	Columbia A-1336
There's Ragtime In The Air	1913	Columbia A-1441
There's Yes! Yes! in Your Eyes	1924	Victor 19418
They're On Their Way To Germany	1918	Columbia
Thinking Of You	1921	Victor 18762
This Is The Life	1914	Columbia A-1509
Those Hawaiian Melodies	1917	Victor 18254
Those Ragtime Melodies	1913	Victor 17320/Keen-O-Phone 5035
Throw Out That Mason Dixon Line	1920	Vocalion 14050A/Columbia (1920)
Ting Ling Toy	1919	Okeh 4029
Tip-Top Tipperary Mary	1914	Victor 17678
To Lou	1915	Columbia A-1828/Victor 17877 (1915)

Title	Year	Label/Number
Virginia Lee	1915	Victor 17723
Wait'll You See	1919	Columbia A-2850
Walla Walla Man, The	1914	Columbia A-1557
Watchin' The Moon Rise	1924	Victor 19262
Watch Your Step: That Syncopated Walk	1915	Victor 17748
'Way Back Home	1913	Columbia A-1314
Way Down In Tampa Bay	1915	Victor 17708
Way Down South	1913	Columbia A-1279
Way Down Upon The Swanee River	1927	Victor 37366
Way Down Yonder In New Orleans	1922	Victor 18942
Way Down Yonder In The Cornfield	1918	Okeh 1016
Wedding Of Uncle Josh And Aunt Nancy, The	1919	Columbia A-1717
We Don't Want The Bacon (What We Want Is A Piece Of The Rhine)	1918	Victor 18505/Columbia A-2620 (1918)
Wee Little Drop Of The Cruiksheen Lawn	1912	Victor 17148
Weep No More My Mammy	1922	Victor 18847
Welcome Home	1913	Victor 17322/Columbia A-1285 (1913)
Welcome, Honey, To Your Old Plantation Home	1916	Victor 18120/Columbia A-2039 (1916)
We'll Do Our Share	1918	Victor 18480
We'll Have A Jubilee In The Old Town	1915	Victor 17825
We Must Have A Song To Remember	1919	Columbia A-2888/Vocalion 14011A (1919)/Empire 413 (1920)
We're Going Over	1917	Victor 18383/Columbia A-2399 (1917)
We Stopped At The Marne	1918	Columbia A-2540
We Take Our Hats Of To You Mr Wilson	1914	Columbia A-1664
Whadya Mean Ya Lost Ye Dog	1913	Victor 17481
What A Friend We Have In Mother	1924	Victor 19305
What Are You Going To Do To Help The Boys'	1918	Columbia A-2545
What Kind Of American Are You'	1917	Victor 18300
What'll We Do With Him Boy	1918	Columbia A-2539
What's Today Got To Do With Tomorrow'	1924	Victor 19300
What Yankee Doodle Says He'll Do, He'll Do	1918	Columbia A-2587
When Evening Shadows Fall	1920	Meteor 1104
When I'm Gone You'll Soon Forget	1919	Columbia A-2810/Victor 18609A (1920)/Okeh 4143 (1920)/Okeh 4969 (1923)
When I Send You A Picture Of Berlin	1918	Victor 18474
When It's Moonlight In Mayo	1915	Columbia A-1727
When It's Moonlight On The Alamo	1914	Victor 17591
When It's Night Time Down In Dixieland (with Sam Ash)	1915	Columbia
When It's Orange Blossom Time In Loveland	1915	Victor 17924
When My Golden Hair Has Turned To Silver Gray	1925	
When Old Bill Bailey Plays The Ukulele	1915	Victor 17904/Columbia A-1865 (1915)
When The Angelus Is Ringing	1917	Columbia A-1533
When The Bees Are In The Hive		Busy Bee 224 (2mincyl)
When The Corn Is Waving, Annie	1921	Victor 18781
When The Old Boat Heads For Home	1919	Columbia
When The Roll Is Called Up Yonder	1913	Columbia A-1305/Victor 22945 (1926)
When The Summer Days Are Gone	1908	Indestructible 900 (2mincyl)
When The Sun Goes Down In Dixie	1917	Victor 18272
When The War Is Over I'll Return To You	1918	Columbia A-2558
When They Christened Brother Johnson's Child	1914	Columbia A-1534
When Uncle Sammy Leads The Band	1916	Victor 18139
When We Wind Up Our Watch On The Rhine	1917	Columbia A-2382
When You And I Were Young, Maggie	1920	Columbia
When You're Five Times Sixteen	1916	Victor 18170
When You're Gone I Won't Forget	1920	Victor 18705
When You Wore A Tulip And I Wore A Big Red Rose	1919	Columbia
Where Is My Wandering Boy Tonight'	1920	Paramount 33010
Where The Dreamy Wabash Flows	1924	Victor 19455
Where The Red, Red Roses Grow	1914	Columbia A-1613
Where The Silvery Colorado Wends Its Way	1926	Victor 19885
Where The Sunset Turns The	1923	Victor 19029/Victor

Ocean's Blue To Gold		19885
Where The Wabash Waters Flow	1920	Columbia
While They Were Dancing Around	1914	Victor 17571/Rex 5120 (1916)
Whistling Jim	1912	Everlasting 1606 (4mincyl)
Whistling Jim	1912	Victor 17239/Columbia A-1271 (1913)
Who'll Take The Place Of Mary'	1920	Columbia A-2913
Will There Be Any Stars In My Crown'	1925	Victor
Winter Nights	1915	Columbia A-1680
Winter Song	1910	Victor 16476/Victor 16957 (1911)
Without You, The World Don't Seem The Same	1910	Victor 16689
Women	1908	Victor 5392
Women - The Merry Widow	1909	Victor 16424
Worst Is Yet To Come, The	1918	Columbia A-2672
Yaddie Kaddie Kiddie Kaddie Koo	1920	Columbia
Years, Years Ago	1912	Columbia A-1209
Yellow And The Blue	1916	Victor 18168
You Can't Go Wrong With A Girl From Dixieland	1920	Vocalion 14074B
You Know You Won't	1913	Columbia A-1326
Young America (We're Strong For You)	1916	Victor 17967/Columbia A-2023 (1916)
Your Country Needs You Now	1917	Columbia A-2361
You're A Great Big Blue-Eyed Baby	1913	Columbia A-1300
You're The Flower Of My Heart, Sweet Adeline	1926	Victor 20055
You're The Greatest Little Mother In The World	1918	Columbia A-2638
Christy Mathewson Memorial Song	1926	Victor

Peerless Quartet & Ada Jones
All Night Long	1913	Columbia A-1297

Peerless Quartet & Billy Murray
Everybody Loves Chicken	1913	Victor 17286

Peerless Quartet (Ada Jones & the)
All Night Long	1913	Columbia A-1297
Whistle It	1912	Columbia A-1185

Peerless Quartet (Ada Jones and Cal Stewart & the)
Uncle Josh's Husking Bee Dance	1919	Columbia A-697

Peerless Quartet (Amparito Farrar & the)
By The Camp Fire	1919	Columbia 2716

Peerless Quartet (Arthur Fields & the)
Flying	1918	Columbia
I Ain't Got Weary Yet!	1918	Columbia A-2669
Johnny's in Town	1919	Columbia A-2703
Just Like Washington Crossed The Delaware, General Pershing Will Cross The Rhine	1918	Victor 18469/Columbia A-2545
There'll Be A Hot Time In The Old Town Tonight	1917	Columbia A-2476

Peerless Quartet (Arthur Fields, Henry Burr & the)
Any Old Place The Gang Goes (I'll Be There)	1918	Columbia A-2514

Peerless Quartet (as Male Quartette)
Push Dem Clouds Away/Goodbye Manhattan Isle	1916	Little Wonder 53

Peerless Quartet (as Sam Ash & Quartette)
Goodbye, Virginia	1915	Columbia A-1697

Peerless Quartet (as the Victor Minstrels)
Minstrels #10 - Bye Bye Sailor	1908	Victor 16149

Peerless Quartet (Billy B. Van & the)
Have A Heart, Napoleon - Part 1	1917	Columbia A-2307
Mike's The Boy	1917	Columbia

Peerless Quartet (Billy Murray & the)
I Love The Land Of Old Black Joe	1920	Victor 18677B
Johnny's In Town	1919	Columbia A-2702

Peerless Quartet (Byron G. Harlan & the)
Round Her Neck She Wears A Yellow Ribbon	1918	Columbia

Peerless Quartet (Cal Stewart & the)
Uncle Josh's Birthday	1919	Columbia

Peerless Quartet (Cal Stewart and Ada Jones & the)
Christmas Time At Pumpkin Center	1919	Columbia A-2789
Evening Time At Pumpkin Center	1919	Columbia A-2789

Peerless Quartet (Clara Moister & the)
Just For Tonight	1914	Columbia A-1561

Peerless Quartet (Eddie Morton with)
I'm A Member Of The Midnight Crew	1909	Victor 16324

Peerless Quartet (Frank Sterling &)
That Fussy Rag	1912	Victor 17235

Peerless Quartet (Harry C. Browne & the)
Carve Dat Possum	1917	Columbia A-2590
Climb Up! Ye Chillun, Climb!	1917	Columbia A-2590
Gwine To Get A Home Bye And Bye	1919	Columbia A-2218
Li'l Liza Jane	1918	Columbia A-2622
Oh! Susannah!	1916	Columbia 2218
Oh Susanna	1917	Columbia A-2218
Shine On	1918	Columbia
Uncle Ned	1919	Columbia 1-H

Peerless Quartet (Henry Burr & the)
Broadway Rose	1920	Victor 18710
I'd Love To Meet That Old Sweetheart Of Mine	1926	Victor 20165
My Own Dear Canada	1917	Columbia

Peerless Quartet (Idelle Patterson & Quartette)
Maxim Girl, The	1912	Columbia A-1248

Peerless Quartet (Marie Morrisey & the)
I Think I'll Wait Until They All Come Home	1918	Columbia

Peerless Quartet (Maurice Burkhart & the)
Going Up With The Elevator Man	1912	Columbia A-1188
Ragtime Jockey Man, The	1912	Columbia A-1188

Peerless Quartet (Ned La Rose & the)
Follow The Crowd	1914	Columbia A-1513

Peerless Quartet (Raymond Hitchcock & the)
Sometime	1916	Victor 55080

Peerless Quartet (Rene Dietrich & the)
I Hate To Lose You	1918	Victor 18458

Peerless Quartet (Robert Lewis (Lewis James) with the)
Hello, America, Hello	1917	Columbia

Peerless Quartet (Walter J. Van Brunt with quartet)
You're Just As Sweet At Sixty As You Were At Sweet Sixteen	1912	Victor 17202

Peerless Quartet (with Ada Jones)
Pussy Cat Rag (Kitty, Kitty, Kitty, Kitty), The	1914	Edison 2197 (4BA)

Peerless Quartet (with Billy Murray)
My Dream Of The Big Parade	1926	Victor 35499

Peerless Quartet (with Henry Burr)
Call To Arms	1915	Columbia A-1835/Emerson 7138 (1917)
Down Honolulu Way	1916	Columbia A-2060
Hymns Of The Old Church Choir, The	1924	Columbia A-1763
There's A Quaker Down In Quaker Town	1916	Columbia A-2005
When You And I Were Young, Maggie (with Henry Burr)	1920	Okeh 4191
You'll Be There!	1915	Victor 17902/Columbia A-1898 (1915)

Peerless Quartet, Ada Jones & the
Pussy Cat Rag (Kitty, Kitty, Kitty)	1913	Columbia A-1457
Wall Street Girl	1912	Columbia A-1185

Peerless Quartet, Arthur Fields & the
Good Morning Mr. Zip Zip	1918	Columbia A-2530/Victor 18510 (1918)
I Wonder What They're Doing Tonight (Your Girl And Mine)	1918	Columbia A-2557
Keep Your Head Down, Fritzy Boy	1918	Columbia A-2600
Navy Will Bring Them Back, The	1918	Columbia A-2677
Oh Frenchy	1918	Columbia A-2569
We're All Going Calling On The Kaiser	1918	Columbia A-2569
When I Send You A Picture Of Berlin	1918	Columbia A-2580
Where Do We Go From Here'	1917	Columbia A-2299
Yanks Are At It Again, The	1918	Columbia A-2620

Peerless Quartet, Byron G. Harlan & the
Long Boy	1917	Columbia A-2409

Peerless Quartet, Ernest Ball & the
Across The Rio Grande	1916	Columbia A-2085

Peerless Quartet, Frank Stanley & the
Bulldog, The	1910	Edison 10378
Sweetness	1910	Edison 10454
Way Down East	1911	Edison 10489

Peerless Quartet, Frederic H. Potter & the
Goodbye, Betty Brown		Edison 10452 (2mincyl)
Red Clover	1911	Edison 4mincyl 447
Red Wing	1911	Edison BA 1543/Edison 4mincyl 541 (1911)
Valley Flower	1911	Edison 4mincyl 562

Peerless Quartet, Harry C. Browne & the
Hear Dem Bells	1919	Columbia A-2853
Hi Jenny, Ho Jenny Johnson	1920	Columbia A-2922
Keep Those Golden Gates Wide Open	1920	Columbia A-2992
Meet Me On De Golden Shore	1920	Columbia A-2992
Razors In The Air	1920	Columbia A-2922

Peerless Quartet, Henry Burr & the
While You're Away	1918	Columbia A-2642

Peerless Quartet, Len Spencer & the
Cowboy's Romance, A	1910	Edison 4mincyl 552

Peerless Quartet, M.J. O'Connell & the
Faugh A Ballan	1918	Columbia A-2514

Peerless Quartet, Romain Manuel & the
There's One In A Million Like You	1913	Columbia A-1346

Peerless Serenaders
I've Lost My Dog	1926	Okeh 40729
You Broke My Heart	1926	Okeh 40729

Peerless Trio
At The Village Post Office	1907	Columbia 3704/Columbia A-472/Indestructible 652
Do You Miss Me Tonight'	1934	Bluebird 5350
I'll Have The Last Waltz With Mother	1934	Bluebird 5354
Memory Waltz	1934	Bluebird 5354
My Little Grass Shack In Kahulalaluhi Hawaii	1934	Bluebird 5349
Sweetheart Of Red River Valley	1934	Bluebird 5350
Three Rubes Seeing New York		Indestructible 680
Village Constable, The		Indestructible 738
Wish I Could Dance Forever	1934	Bluebird 5349

Perfect Harmony Quartet
My Good Lord's Done Been Here	1927	Okeh 8448

There's A Meeting Here Tonight	1927	Okeh 8448

Philadelphia Male Quartet

Mah Lindy Lou	1925	Victor 19765
Musical Trust, The	1925	
Ole Uncle Moon	1925	Victor 19765
Wake, Miss Lindy	1925	

Philips, Joseph & the Shannon Four

Samoa	1920	Okeh 4149
Wishing Moon	1920	Okeh 4152

Phillip's, Lloyd's Jumping Jacks

Bogey Bottom Blues	1941	Decca 7860
Sally Long	1941	Decca 7860

Piccadilly Pipers

I Loved Only You	1956	Chart 615
Let Me Play With Your Poodle	1946	Savoy 5525
Lonely Lover's Prayer, A	1956	Chart 619
My Butterball	1956	Chart 619
So Near And Yet So Far	1954	Melmar 100
Toy Piano Man	1950	Columbia 30215
Where's My Baby	1956	Chart 615
You're Not Doing Your Homework	1944	Savoy 5531

Piccadilly Pipers, Bonnie Davis & the

How Could You	1954	Groove 0032
(I'm Not Cryin' Over You) I'm Peelin' Onions	1950	Columbia 30219
Since You're Gone	1954	Groove 0032
Your Fool Again	1950	Columbia 30219

Pickens Sisters

Back In Old Sunday School	1932	Victor 24180
Beat Of My Heart, The	1934	Victor 24625
Be Still, My Heart	1934	Victor 24751
Blue Kentucky Moon	1931	Columbia
China Boy	1932	Victor 24355
Darktown Strutter's Ball	1932	Victor 24355
Did You Ever See A Dream Walking'	1933	Victor 24468
Do The New York (with Rondoliers)	1931	Columbia 2499-D
Dream Sweetheart	1932	Victor 22975
Good Morning, Glory	1933	Victor 24468
Goodnight, Moon	1932	Victor 22929
Happiness Ahead	1934	Victor 24751
Kiss That You've Forgotten, The	1931	Columbia
Lawd, You Made The Night Too Long	1932	Victor 22975
Little Man, You've Had A Busy Day	1934	Victor 24630
Love Is Just Around The Corner	1934	Victor 24815
Many Moons Ago	1933	Victor 24471
May I'	1933	Victor 24625
Medley Of Cole Porter Hits (with Ramona Davies and the Rollickers)	1933	Victor 36085
My Sweet Tooth Says 'I Wann' (But My Wisdom Tooth Says 'No')	1931	Columbia 2501-D
Night And Day (with Phil Dewey)	1933	Victor 36085
Nobody Love No Baby (Like My Baby Loves Me)	1931	Columbia 2501-D
Riptide	1934	Victor 24630
San	1932	Victor 24025
Sentimental Georgia From Georgia	1932	Victor 24190
Somebody Loves You	1932	Victor 22965
Sweet Georgia Brown	1932	Victor 24025
Thief Of Bagdad, The	1934	Victor 24753
Too Many Tears	1932	Victor 22965
Was That The Human Thing To Do'	1932	Victor 22929
When Mother Played The Organ (And Daddy Sang A Hymn)	1932	Victor 24180
You're Such A Comfort To Me	1933	Victor 24471

Pied Pipers

Come Rain Or Come Shine		
Come To Baby Do		
Deacon Jones	1943	Capitol 140
Doctor, Lawyer And Indian Chief		
Doin' What Comes Natur'lly		
Easy Street		
Friendship	1940	
Girl Of My Dreams	1947	Capitol 766
Gotta Be This Or That	1945	
Heat Wave	1957	
Huggin' And A Chalkin'	1946	Capitol 334
I'll Buy That Dream		
I'll Close My Eyes	1946	Capitol 342
I'm Getting Sentimental Over You	1957	
In A Little Spanish Town	1939	RCA Victor 26364
It's Only A Paper Moon		
I've Got The Sun In The Morning		
Just A Sittin' And A Rockin'		
Linger In My Arms A Little Longer, Baby	1946	
Mamselle	1947	
Marie	1957	
My Gal Sal		
Nine Old Men	1941	
Oh, Look At Me Now	1941	RCA Victor 27274
Once In A While	1957	
Penny	1947	Capitol 478
Polly Wolly Doodle All Day	1939	RCA Victor 26320
Ragtime Cowboy Joe		
Remember Me'	1946	Capitol 264
Rendezvous With A Rose	1949	Capitol 15216
Route 66		
Sentimental Journey		
Sugar Foot Stomp	1939	RCA Victor 26320
Surprise Party	1945	Capitol 217
Sweet Potato Piper	1940	Victor 26500

Tabby The Cat	1944	Capitol 185
Taking A Chance On Love	1957	
Tampico		
There's A Boat Dat's Leavin' Soon For New York	1947	
There's Good Blues Tonight		
Ugly Chile (You're Some Pretty Doll)	1946	Capitol 268
What A Deal		
What Is This Thing Called Love'	1939	RCA Victor 26364
What Ya Gonna Do'		
Whiffenpoof Song, The	1947	Capitol 766
Why Does It Get Late So Early		
Won't Be Satisfied		Decca
You Grow Sweeter As The Years Go By	1943	
Avalon	1947	Capitol 10087
Charming Little Faker	1940	Victor 26581
Cuddle Up A Little Closer	1943	Capitol 168
Do I Worry' (with Frank Sinatra)	1941	RCA Victor 27338
Dream	1945	Capitol 185
Dream	1948	Capitol 1628
Either It's Love Or It Isn't	1946	Capitol 306
Embraceable You	1941	Victor 27638/Victor 20-2007
Embraceable You	1946	Capitol 10065
Everybody Loves My Baby	1946	Capitol 279
Funny Little Pedro	1940	Bluebird B-10771
Goodbye Romance	1947	Capitol 15142
Highway To Love	1947	Capitol 15094
I Have But One Heart	1947	Capitol 460
I'll See You In My Dreams	1948	Capitol 495
I Love It So	1941	Victor 27392
In The Moon Mist	1946	Capitol 243
It's Dreamtime	1956	Capitol 342
It's The Same Old Dream	1947	Capitol 396
It's Watcha Do With Watcha Got	1947	Capitol 15233
I Wanna Be A Friend Of Yours	1947	Capitol 456
Journey To A Star, A	1943	Capitol 148
Judaline	1947	Capitol 15103
Just Around The Corner	1947	Capitol 456
Just Plain Love	1947	Capitol 429
Lady From 29 Palms, The	1947	Capitol 460
Lily Belle	1945	Capitol 207
Love Sends A Gift Of Roses (with K. Curtis)	1941	Victor 27782
Madame Butterball	1951	Capitol 243
Mairzy Doats	1944	Capitol 148
Make Me Know It	1956	Capitol 344
Mam'selle	1947	Capitol 396
Mary Lou	1947	Capitol 489
Mind If I Love You	1944	Capitol 15216
My! My!	1940	RCA Victor 26535
My Happiness	1948	Capitol 15094
My Happiness	1948	Capitol 1628
Night We Called It A Day, The	1941	Victor 20-1553
Ok'l Baby Dok'l	1948	Capitol 495
Ol' Man River	1946	Capitol 279
Open The Door, Richard	1947	Capitol 369
Pistol Packin' Mama	1943	Capitol 14083
Remember Me	1952	Capitol 264
Riddle Song, The	1947	Capitol 429
Should I	1946	Capitol 10063
Skunk Song (Part 1), The (with Chuck Peterson)	1941	Victor 27621
Skunk Song (Part 2), The (with Chuck Peterson)	1941	Victor 27621
Smile	1947	Capitol 15103
Somebody Loves Me	1941	Victor 27690
Star Dust (with Frank Sinatra)	1941	RCA Victor 27233
Trolley Song, The	1944	Capitol 168
Walkin' Away With My Heart	1946	Capitol 306
Walk It Off	1946	Capitol 264
We'll Be Together Again	1945	Capitol 207
What Can I Say After I Say I'm Sorry	1940	Victor 26518
Whatcha Know Joe'	1941	Victor 27359
When Am I Gonna Kiss You Good Morning'	1947	Capitol 369
Whiffenpoof Song, The	1947	Capitol B 20131
Who'	1946	Capitol 10072
Winter Weather	1941	Victor 27749
With All My Heart (I Give My Heart To You)	1946	Capitol 15142
Yes, We Have No Bananas	1947	Capitol 15233
You And Your Love	1943	Capitol 10003
You Can't See The Sun When You're Crying	1956	Capitol 344
You Grow Sweeter (As The Days Go By)	1943	Capitol 10003
You Say The Sweetest Things, Baby (with Connie Haines)	1940	
You've Got Me This Way	1941	RCA Victor 26770

Pied Pipers (2), King Perry & the

Blue And Lonesome	1950	Specialty 398
Day And Night Blues	1950	Specialty 412
Everything Gotta Be Alright	1950	Specialty 367
I Ain't Got A Dime To My Name	1950	Specialty 412
Mellow Gate Blues	1950	Specialty 367
Natural Born Lover	1950	Specialty 398

Pied Pipers (Connie Haines)

Isn't That Just Like Love	1940	

Pied Pipers (F. Sinatra, C. Haines)

Let's Get Away From It All	1941	

Pied Pipers (with Billy Eckstine)

Careless Lips	1955	MGM 11998
La De Do De Do (Honey Bug Song)	1955	MGM 12105

Pied Pipers (with Frank Sinatra and Connie Haines)
Oh! Look At Me Now	1941	Victor 27274/Victor 20-1578
You Might Have Belonged To Another	1941	Victor 27274

Pied Pipers (with Frank Sinatra)
Ain'tcha Ever Comin' Back	1947	Columbia 37554
Could 'Ja'	1946	Columbia C 1389
Dum Dot Song (I Put The Penny In The Gum Slot), The	1946	Columbia 37996
How Am I To Know'	1940	Victor
I'll Never Smile Again	1940	RCA Victor 26628/Victor 27521/V-Disc 582
One I Love (Belongs To Somebody Else), The	1940	RCA Victor 26660/Victor 20-2446

Pied Pipers (with Johnny Mercer & Jo Stafford)
Blues In The Night	1943	Capitol 10001

Pied Pipers (with Johnny Mercer)
Brer Rabbit And The Tar Baby (Part 1) (Tales Of Uncle Remus)	1946	Capitol 10071
Brer Rabbit And The Tar Baby (Part 2) (Tales Of Uncle Remus)	1946	Capitol 10071
Dixieland Band	1943	Capitol 10004
I'm Gonna See My Baby	1945	Capitol 183
Jamboree Jones	1943	Capitol 10004
On The Nodaway Road	1943	Capitol 10001
Tuscaloosa Bus	1946	Capitol 15285

Pied Pipers, Andy Russell & the
If We Can't Be The Same Old Sweethearts (We'll Just Be The Same Old Friends)	1949	Capitol 15281
It's Too Soon To Know	1949	Capitol 15281
Just For Me	1949	Capitol 15183
Underneath The Arches	1948	Capitol 15183

Pied Pipers, Frank Sinatra & the
Dig Down Deep	1942	Victor 20-1539
Dolores	1941	RCA Victor 27317
Free For All	1941	Victor 27532
I Guess I'll Have To Dream The Rest	1941	RCA Victor 27526
I'll Take Tallulah	1942	Victor 27869
It Started All Over Again	1943	RCA Victor 20-1522
Just As Though You Were Here	1942	RCA Victor 27903
Last Call For Love, The	1942	Victor 27849
Neiani	1941	Victor 27508
Snootie Little Cutie (with Connie Haines)	1942	Victor 27876
Street Of Dreams	1942	RCA Victor 27903
There Are Such Things	1942	RCA Victor 27974/Victor 42-0151
Whispering	1940	Bluebird B-10771/Victor 20-1597

Pied Pipers, Frank Sinatra, Connie Haines & the
Let's Get Away From It All - Part 1	1941	Victor 27377
Let's Get Away From It All - Part 2	1941	Victor 27377

Pied Pipers, Jo Stafford & the
I Didn't Know About You	1944	Capitol 171
On The Sunny Side Of The Street	1944	Capitol 199
Tumbling Tumbleweeds	1944	Capitol 171

Pied Pipers, Johnny Mercer & the
Ac-Cent-Tchu-Ate The Positive	1944	Capitol 180
Alexander's Ragtime Band	1945	Capitol 10064
Aren't You Glad You're You	1945	Capitol 225
Camptown Races	1944	Capitol 217
Cecilia	1947	Capitol 422
Down Among The Sheltering Palms	1948	Capitol 15241
Everybody Has A Laughin' Place	1946	Capitol 323
Ev'rybody Has A Laughing Place	1946	Capitol 323
Gal In Calico, A	1945	Capitol 316
Goofus	1947	Capitol 15051
Hills Of California, The	1947	Capitol 15051
Hooray For Love	1947	Capitol 15028
If I Knew Then	1945	Capitol 230760
In The Middle Of May	1946	Capitol 225
I've Been Hit	1947	Capitol 15412
Jingle Bells	1947	Capitol 15004
Let's Fly	1947	Capitol 15337
Limehouse Blues	1947	Capitol 15134
Love That Boy	1947	Capitol 15152
Memphis Blues	1945	Capitol 15218
Memphis Blues	1951	Capitol 10063
Movie Tonight	1946	Capitol 367
My Gal Is Mine Once More	1947	Capitol 15025
My Sugar Is So Refined	1946	Capitol 268
On The Atchison, Topeka, And The Santa Fe	1945	Capitol 195/Capitol 10156
Personality	1945	Capitol 230
Rhode Island Is Famous For You (without Mercer)	1947	Capitol 489
Santa Claus Is Comin' To Town	1947	Capitol 15004
School Days	1947	Capitol B 21028
St. Louis Blues	1945	Capitol 1618
Sugar Blues	1947	Capitol 448
Sweetie Pie	1948	Capitol 15096
Take Me Back To Little Rock	1946	Capitol 334
Tallahassee	1947	Capitol 422
That's The Way He Does It	1947	Capitol 15016
Why Should I Cry Over You	1947	Capitol 448
Winter Wonderland	1947	Capitol 316
Winter Wonderland	1949	Capitol 1285

Would Ya' (Eyah-Eyah-Eyah)	1948	Capitol 15337	
You Don't Have To Know The Language	1947	Capitol 15025	
Zip-A-Dee-Doo-Dah	1946	Capitol 323	

Pied Pipers, Johnny Mercer, Jo Stafford & the
Candy	1944	Capitol 183

Pied Pipers, June Hutton & the
There's A Fellow Waiting In Poughkeepsie	1944	Capitol 180

Pied Pipers, Margaret Whiting & the
God Bless America	1947	Capitol 15003

Pied Pipers, Vic Damone & the
In The Cool, Cool, Cool Of The Evening	1951	Mercury 5670/Metronome B 577

Piedmont Melody Boys
Tell Him Now	1932	Victor 23660

Pig Footers
Even, Evans, Even	1949	Mercury 8135
Hucklebuck, The	1949	Mercury 8130
Neck Bones	1949	Mercury 8130
Strollin'	1949	Mercury 8135

Pilgrim Jubilee Singers
Goodnight, The Lord's Coming	1927	Vocalion 1126
I'm In His Care	1927	Vocalion 1118
King Of Kings	1927	Vocalion 1119
Lord's Prayer, The	1927	Vocalion 1119
My Lord's Gonna Move This Wicked Race	1927	Vocalion 1118
My Soul Looked Back	1927	Vocalion 1126

Pioneer Quartet
Southern Jingles	1927	Edison DD 53202
Southern Songs	1927	Edison DD 53202

Plantation Male Trio
Chicken Opera	1924	Okeh 8131
Oh! What A Time	1924	Okeh 8131

Pound Hounds
Home, Sweet Home	1956	Decca 29627

Powell Quintet The Austin (Cats 'n' the Fiddle)
Wishing Well	1951	Decca 48251

Powell, Austin (with James Quintet)
I Surrender Dear	1952	Atlantic
There I Go, There I Go	1952	Atlantic
What More Can I Ask'	1952	Atlantic 968
Wrong Again	1952	Atlantic 968

Powell, Austin Quintet The (Cats
All This Can't Be True	1951	Decca 48206
Please Consider Me	1951	Decca 48251
Some Other Spring	1951	Decca 48206

Powell, Dick & Foursome
Old Shep	1940	Decca 3389B
Tumble Down Ranch In Arizona	1940	Decca 3389A

Praetorian Quartet
At Sunset I'm Going Home	1928	Columbia 15384-D
Is It Well With Your Soul'	1928	Columbia 15384-D

Premier American Quartet
Dixie Is Dixie Once More	1919	Okeh 1226
Jazzola	1919	Okeh 1224
Lullabye Blues	1919	Okeh 1214
Turkestan	1919	Okeh 1205/Pathe 22125 (1919)

Premier Quartet
I'm On My Way To Dublin Bay	1914	Edison DD 50245/Edison BA 2610 (1915)
I've Got The Blues For My Old Kentucky Home	1918	Edison BA 4219/Edison DD 50737 (1920)
Jazzola	1919	Edison DD 50555/Columbia 78420 (unissued)
My Little Lovin' Sugar Babe	1912	Edison BA 1590
Nightingale	1911	Edison 10484 (2mincyl)
Oh, By Jingo! By Gee! (You're The Only Girl For Me)	1920	Edison 4041

Premier Quartet & Inez Barbour
Patriotic Songs Of America	1910	Edison 4mincyl 457/Edison BA 1626 (1910)

Premier Quartet (as Anna Chandler with male quartette)
I Want Everyone To Love Me	1911	Edison 4mincyl 770

Premier Quartet, Ada Jones & Billy Murray with the
I'm Looking For A Nice Young Fellow Who Is Looking For A Nice Young Girl	1911	Edison 1853

Premier Quartet, Billy Murray & the
There's A Typical Tipperary Over Here	1920	Edison BA 4087/Edison DD 50683

Premier Quartet, Cal Stewart with the
Train Time At Pun'Kin Centre	1919	Edison BA 3904/Edison DD 50654-R (1919)

Premier Quartette
Alexander's Band Is Back In Dixieland	1919	Edison BA 3901/Edison DD 50601
Along The Rocky Road To Dublin	1915	Edison DD 50328
And The Green Grass Grew All Around	1913	Edison BA 1808
Angel Eyes	1910	Edison 10444 (2mincyl)
Another Rag (A Raggy Rag)	1911	Edison 937 (4BA)
Any Little Girl That's A Nice Little Girl Is The Right Little Girl For Me	1910	Edison 4mincyl 548
Anything Is Nice If It Comes	1919	Edison BA 3748

Title	Year	Release
From Dixieland		
Aunt Jemima's Jubilee	1921	Edison
Baby Rose	1911	Edison 10507 (2mincyl)/Edison 719 (4mincyl) (1911)
Battle In The Air, A - Descriptive	1918	Edison BA 3618
Bing! Bang! Bing 'Em on The Rhine	1918	Edison BA 3494/Edison DD 50489
Blacksmith Rag, The	1920	Edison BA 4540
Blue Jeans	1921	Edison DD 50771/Edison BA
Breeze (Blow My Baby Back To Me)	1919	Edison BA 3888/Edison DD 50584
Carry Me Back To Old Virginny	1910	Edison 4mincyl 512
Casey Jones	1921	Edison DD 50747
Characteristic Negro Medley, A	1918	Edison DD 50570
Chong (He Come from Hong Kong)	1919	Edison BA 3769/Edison DD 50538/Pathe 22113
Circus Day In Dixie	1915	Edison BA 2716/Edison DD 50283
Comrades In Arms	1922	Pathe 92271
Cross The Mason-Dixon Line	1913	Edison 2082 (4BA)
Daddy, I Want To Go	1917	Edison BA 3453
Darkies Jubilee		Edison 4mincyl 361
Darktown Quartette Rehearsal, A	1922	Edison DD 50917
Darktown Strutter's Ball	1918	Edison BA 3476/Edison DD 50468
Denver Town	1909	Edison 10155 (2mincyl)
Dixie Is Dixie Once More	1919	Edison BA 3839/Edison DD 50583
Dixie Volunteers, The	1918	Edison BA 3479/Edison DD 50474
Down In Chinatown	1920	Edison BA 4185
Down In Dear Old New Orleans	1912	Edison 1645 (4BA)
Down In Midnight Town	1921	Edison BA 4479/Edison DD 50897
Down On The Mississippi	1910	Edison BA 1944
Down Yonder	1921	Edison DD 50790
Everybody's Doing It Now	1912	Edison 10570 (2mincyl)/Edison 4mincyl 1030 (1912)
Farmyard Medley	1910	Edison 4mincyl 451/Edison BA 3488
		(1918)/Edison DD 50485 (1918)
Floatin' Down To Cotton Town	1919	Edison BA 3910/Edison DD 50607
Floating Down The River (Cause It's Moonlight Now In Dixieland)	1913	Edison BA 2133
Goodbye Summer!	1913	Edison BA 2031
Good Bye Summer! So Long Fall		Edison 2031 (4BA)
Good Night, Mr. Moonlight	1909	Edison 10174 (2mincyl)
Hey, Paw!	1921	Edison DD 50771
Hippity Hop	1920	Edison BA 3978/Edison D 50644
How's Every Little Thing In Dixie	1917	Edison BA 3143
Huckleberry Finn	1917	Edison BA 3322/Edison DD 50944
I'll Always Keep A Corner In My Heart For Tennessee	1920	Edison BA 4061
I Love You Just The Same, Sweet Adeline	1919	Edison BA 3914/Edison DD 50621
In Good Time Town	1911	Edison 4mincyl 713
In The Land Of Harmony	1911	Edison 10524 (2mincyl)
In The Land Of Plankity-Plank	1913	Edison BA 2143
I've Got The Sweetest Girl in Maryland	1917	Edison BA 3217
I Want To Be The Leader Of The Band	1920	Edison DD 50769
I Was Born In Michigan	1921	Edison DD 50782/Edison BA
I Would Like To Try It But I'm Just Afraid	1912	Edison 10565 (2mincyl)
Jazz Babies' Ball	1920	Edison
Jingle Of Jungle Joe, The	1911	Edison 4mincyl 638
Keep Your Eye On The Girlie You Love	1916	Edison BA 3114/Edison DD 50420
Lindy	1920	Edison BA 4207
Little Church, The	1922	Pathe 92310
Loading Up The Mandy Lee	1916	Edison BA 2827/Edison DD 50333
Mammy's Lullaby	1919	Edison BA 3729/Edison 50528
Medley Of Popular Choruses (Includes: 'To The End Of The World With You,' 'Keep A Little Feeling In Your Heart For Me,' 'The Longest Way 'Round Is The Sweetest Way Home,' 'No One Knows' and 'In Old Vienna.'	1909	Edison 4mincyl 213

Title	Year	Release
Melon Time In Dixieland	1921	Edison DD 50818
Moonlight Bay	1912	Edison 10550 (2mincyl)/Edison 962 (4mincyl) (1912)/Edison BA 1848 (1915)/Edison DD 50258 (1915)
Musical Sam From Alabam'	1917	Edison BA 3397
My Mammy	1920	Edison BA 4227/Edison DD 50741
Nightmare Blues, The	1921	Edison
Night Trip To Buffalo, A - Descriptive Scene	1911	Edison 492 (4minAmberol)
Oh, By Jingo! By Gee! (You're The Only Girl For Me)	1920	Edison DD 50666
Oh Johnny, Oh Johnny, Oh!	1917	Edison BA 3237/Edison DD 50442
Oh, That Navajo Rag	1911	Edison 4mincyl 917
Oh, You Beautiful Doll	1911	Edison 10545 (2mincyl)/Edison 921 (4mincyl) (1911)
Pocahontas	1920	Edison BA 4232/Edison DD 50754
Polly	1920	Edison BA 4112
Put Me To Sleep With An Old-Fashioned Melody	1915	Edison
Ragtime Violin, The	1912	Edison 10560 (2mincyl)/Edison 966 (4mincyl) (1912)/Edison BA 1806 (1912)
Red Rose Rag, The	1912	Edison 10535 (2mincyl)
Roll Them Cotton Bales	1914	Edison BA 2448
Sailing Down The Chesapeake Bay	1913	Edison 2039 (4BA)
Send Me A Curl	1917	Edison BA 3507
She's Dixie All The Time	1917	Edison BA 3211
Skeleton Rag, The	1912	Edison 1064 (2mincyl)/Edison 10575 (2mincyl) (1912)
Submarine Attack, A - Descriptive	1918	Edison BA 3497/Edison DD 50490
Sunny Southern Smiles	1920	Edison BA 4126
Swanee Babe	1909	Edison 10262 (2mincyl)
Tennessee, I Hear You Calling Me	1915	Edison BA 2581/Edison DD 50233
Texas Tommy Swing	1912	Edison 4mincyl 1017
That Coontown Quartet	1912	Edison 4mincyl 996
That Hypnotizing Man	1911	Edison 4mincyl 1001
That Mysterious Rag	1912	Edison 10539 (2mincyl)/Edison 893 (4mincyl) (1912)
That Slippery Slide Trombone	1912	Edison 4mincyl 1083
That Syncopated Boogie-Boo	1912	Edison BA 1646
Then You'll Know You're Home	1919	Edison
They're Wearing 'Em Higher In Hawaii	1916	Edison BA 3125/Edison DD 50420
Those Good Old Days Back Home	1916	Edison
Trip To The County Fair	1910	Edison 4mincyl 538
Turkestan	1919	Edison BA 3782/Edison DD 50545
Uncle Sammy	1918	Edison BA 3602
Wait For The Wagon Medley	1910	Edison 4mincyl 411
Wedding Bells	1910	Edison 10294 (2mincyl)
We're Going Over!	1917	Edison BA 3367/Edison DD 50449
We Stopped Them At The Marne	1918	Edison BA 3525
When You Come Back (And You Will Come Back)	1918	Edison BA 3597/Edison DD 80425
You Need A Rag	1913	Edison BA 2188
You're A Great Big Blue-Eyed Baby	1913	Edison BA 1792
You're My Baby	1912	Edison 4mincyl 1119

Premier Quartette Minstrels

Title	Year	Release
Land Of Minstrelsy, The	1918	Edison BA 3755/dison DD 50750-R (1918)

Premier Quartette, Billy Murray & the

Title	Year	Release
Washington Waddle, The	1911	Edison 10530 (2mincyl)/Edison 827 (4mincyl) (1911)

Premier-American Quartette

Title	Year	Release
Afghanistan	1919	Emerson 10153/Medallion 8166
Alexander's Band Is Back In	1919	Vocalion

Dixieland		12207Emerson 1075 (1919)/Medallion 8134 (1920)
Anything Is Nice If It Comes From Dixieland	1919	Pathe 22128
Breeze (Blow My Baby Back To Me)	1919	Pathe 22177
Christmas Eve In The Old Homestead	1919	Aeolian/Vocalion 12221
Dixie Is Dixie Once More	1919	Aeolian/Vocalion 12140/Gennett 4541 (1919)
Floatin' Down To Cotton Town	1920	Vocalion 12225/Pathe 22240 (1920)
Himalaya	1919	Aeolian/Vocalion 12177/Emerson 7509 (1919)/Pathe 22141 (1919)
In Cleopatra's Land	1919	Aeolian/Vocalion 12177
I've Lost My Heart In Dixieland	1919	Vocalion 12225/Emerson 7509 (1919)/Pathe 22141 (1919)
Jazzola	1919	Aeolian/Vocalion 12104/Emerson 9189 (1919)
Lullaby Blues (In The Evening)	1919	Vocalion 12123
Premier-American Quartette (Cal Stewart, Ada Jones & the)		
Christmas Time At Pun'kin Center	1919	Emerson 1096/Medallion 8141 (1919)
Price Family Sacred Singers		
I Went Down Into The Valley To Pray	1927	Okeh 40796
Ship Of Glory	1927	Okeh 40796
Price Trio, Norman (The Peerless Three')		
Sweetheart Of Red River Valley	1934	Bluebird B-5350
Price Trio, Norman ('The Peerless Three')		
Do You Miss Me Tonight'	1934	Bluebird B-5350
I'll Have The Last Waltz With Mother	1934	Bluebird B-5354
I Wish We Could Dance Forever	1934	Bluebird B-5349
Memory Waltz, The	1934	Bluebird B-5354
My Little Grass Shack In Kealakekua, Hawaii	1934	Bluebird B-5349
Primrose Quartet		
Seven Last Words Of Christ	1915	Victor 17800
Progressive Four		
Beautiful Land, The	1930	Columbia 14552-D
Darling Nellie Gray	1948	D.C. 8037
Ding Dong Bells	1931	Columbia 14601-D
Farther Along	1948	D.C. 8057
I Ain't Ready To Go	1948	D.C. 8042/Savoy 4006
I Cried Holy	1948	D.C. 8038/Savoy 4001
I Want A Little Girl	1947	D.C. 8036
Lord's Been Good To Me, The	1931	Columbia 14601-D
New Name	1930	Columbia 14552-D
Old Time Religion	1948	D.C. 8042/Savoy 4006
Ring Those Golden Bells	1948	D.C. 8052
Satchelmouth Baby	1948	D.C. 8048
Vale Of Time	1948	D.C. 8052
Yes	1948	D.C. 8048
You Can Run On	1948	D.C. 8038/Savoy 4001
Propes Quartet		
Overshadowed By His Love	1934	Bluebird 5672
Rocking On The Waves	1934	Bluebird 5612
Springtime In Glory	1934	Bluebird 5672
On The Jericho Road	1934	Bluebird 5612
Psi Upsilon Quartet		
Brothers, The Day Is Ended	1930	Columbia 145-P
Psi U. Doxology	1930	Columbia 145-P
Pullman Four		
Sleepy Head	1926	Challenge 192
Valencia	1926	Challenge 192
Pullman Porters Quartette		
Every Time I Feel De Spirit	1927	Paramount 12580
Good News Chariot's Coming	1927	Paramount 12580
Jog-A-Long Boys	1927	Paramount 12607
Pullman Passenger Train	1927	Paramount 12607
Q-Tones, Don Q & the		
Baby I Don't Need You Now	1949	Bullet 330
Private Property	1949	Bullet 330
Quartette		
Dear Old Moonlight	1908	U.S. Everlasting 252 (2minindestructcyl)
Dreaming On The Ohio	1904	Edison 8807 (black2mincyl)
God Be With You Till We Meet Again	1911	Indestructible 1472 (2minindestructcyl)
My Old New Hampshire Home	190'	Columbia 9045 (black2mincyl)
Since Nelly Went Away	1906	Edison 9408 (black2mincyl)
Queens Vocal Trio (with Phil Spitalny)		
Dinah	1932	
Quintones		
Chew Chew Chew (Chew Your Bubble Gum)	1939	Vocalion V 4928
Five Little Quints	1940	Vocalion 5409
Harmony In Harlem	1940	Vocalion 5596

Heaven Will Protect The Working Girl	1940	Vocalion 5509
Honey Bunny Boo	1940	Vocalion 5596
Lonesome Trail Ain't Lonesome Anymore, The	1938	Vocalion V 4230
Midnight Jamboree	1940	Vocalion 5409
Nami-Nami	1938	Vocalion V 4230
Sly Mongoose	1940	Vocalion 5509
Utt-Da-Zay (The Tailor Song)	1939	Vocalion V 4928
When My Sugar Walks Down The Street	1939	Vocalion 5172
With My Eyes Wide Open, I'm Dreaming	1950	MGM 287
You're Breaking My Heart	1950	MGM 10478

Quintones, Bob Carroll & the

I'll Never Let A Day Pass By	1941	Bluebird B 11202
Wasn't It You'	1941	Bluebird B 11223

Quintones, Buck Ram's

Fool That I Am	1939	Vocalion 5172

Quintones, Johnny Desmond with the

C'est Si Bon (It's So Good)	1950	MGM 10613

Radars

I Need You All The Time	1950	Abbey 3025
I Want A Little Girl		Prestige 478
Too Bad		Prestige 478
You Belong To Me	1950	Abbey 3025

Radio Revellers

Ciribiribin On The Mandolin	1947	Columbia DB 2976
I Love The Sunshine Of Your Smile	1947	Columbia DB 2976
I'm Afraid To Love You ('Fraid I Might Like It)	1947	Columbia 38209
Shoemaker's Serenade (Ticky Ticky Tee), The	1947	Columbia 38209

Rainbow Quartette

Don't Be Knocking	1929	Columbia
'Twas Love Divine	1929	Columbia
When Jesus Comes	1928	Columbia
When The Sweet Bye And Bye Is Ended	1928	Columbia

Ramblers

T'Ain't What You Do	1939	Decca 2470

Rangers Quartet

Beyond The Clouds	1941	Okeh 6569/Conqueror 9879 (1941)
Glory Special, The	1941	Okeh 6578/Conqueror 9881 (1941)
Goodbye Sin	1941	Okeh 6513/Conqueror 9878 (1941)
If Heaven's Any Better	1941	Okeh 6578/Conqueror 9881 (1941)
I've Changed My Mind	1941	Okeh 6513
I Will Slip Away From Home	1941	Okeh 6658/Conqueror 9880 (1941)
Keep A Happy Heart	1941	Okeh 6445/Conqueror 9877 (1941)
Let Jesus Convoy You Home	1941	Okeh 6445/Conqueror 9877 (1941)
Mighty The Lord	1941	Okeh 6569/Conqueror 9879 (1941)
Somebody Knows	1941	Conqueror 9880
Where He Leads Me	1941	Okeh 6658/Conqueror 9880 (1941)

Ravens

Always	1948	National 9064
Ashamed	195'	Jubilee (unreleased)
Begin The Beguine	1952	Mercury 5800
Be I Bumblebee Or Not	1947	National 9040
Bells Of San Raquel, The	1955	Jubilee 5203
Be On Your Merry Way	1948	National 9056
Boots & Saddles	1956	Jubilee 5237
Bye, Bye, Baby Blues	1946	Hub 3033
Bye, Bye, Baby Blues	1948	King 4234
Bye, Bye, Baby Blues	1955	Jubilee 5184
Calypso Song, The	1952	Okeh 6888
Careless Love	1949	National 9085
Chloe-E	1952	Mercury 5853
Come A Little Bit Closer	1953	Mercury 70119
Count Every Star	1950	National 9111
Dear One	1957	Argo 5276/Checker 871 (1957)
Deep Purple	1949	National 9065
Don't Look Now	1950	Columbia 6-903/Columbia 1-903 (1950)
Don't Mention My Name	1952	Mercury 70060
Escortin' Or Courtin' (by Jimmy Ricks)	1954	Mercury 70307
Everything But You	1951	Okeh 6843
Fool That I Am	1947	National 9040
For You	1947	National 9034/National 9039 (1947)
Get Wise, Baby	1949	National 9098
Going Home	1954	Mercury 70330
Gotta Find My Baby	1951	Columbia 39194
Green Eyes	1955	Jubilee 5203
Happy Go Lucky Baby	1955	Jubilee 5184
Honey	1946	Hub 3030
Honey	1949	King 4272

Title	Year	Label/Number
Honey I Don't Want You	1951	Columbia 39408
House I Live In, The	1949	National 9073
How Could I Know	1948	National 9059
I Can't Believe	1956	Argo 5255
I Don't Have To Ride No More	1949	National 9101
I Don't Know Why I Love You Like I Do	1948	National 9059
If I Love Again	1950	Columbia (unreleased)
If You Didn't Mean It	1949	National 9089
I Get All My Lovin' On A Saturday Night	1951	Okeh 6825
I'll Always Be In Love With You	1956	Jubilee 5237
I'll Be Back	1952	Mercury 70060
I'm Afraid Of You	1949	National 9098
I'm Gonna Paper All My Walls With Your Love Letters	1950	National 9111
I'm Gonna Take To The Road	1950	National 9131
I'm So Crazy For Love	1950	Columbia 6-925/Columbia 1-925 (1950)
It's The Talk Of The Town	194'	National (unreleased)
It's Too Soon To Know	1948	National 9056
I've Been A Fool	1949	National 9101
I've Got The World On A String	194'	National (unreleased)
I've Got You Under My Skin	1954	Mercury 70413
Kneel And Pray	1956	Argo 5255
Leave My Gal Alone	1949	National 9065
Lilacs In The Rain	1951	National 9148
Lonesome Road, The	1954	Mercury 70330
Looking For My Baby	1952	Mercury 5800
Love Is No Dream	1954	Mercury 70413
Love Is The Thing	1952	Mercury 8296
Lullaby	1946	Hub 3030
Mahzel	1947	National 9034
Mam'selle	1952	Okeh 6888
Marie	1951	Rendition 5001
Midnight Blues	1951	Columbia 39112
Moonglow	194'	National (unreleased)
My Baby's Gone	1950	Columbia 6-925/Columbia 1-925 (1950)
My Sugar Is So Refined	1946	Hub 3032
My Sugar Is So Refined	1949	King 4293
No More Kisses For Baby	194'	National (unreleased)
Old Man River	1955	Mercury 70554
Ol' Man River	1947	National 9035
Once And For All	1946	Hub 3033
Once And For All	1948	King 4234
Once In A While	1948	National 9053
On Chapel Hill	1955	Jubilee 5217
Out Of A Dream	1946	Hub 3032/King 4260 (1948)
Phantom Stage Coach	1950	National 9131
Please Believe Me	1950	National (previously unreleased)
Ricky's Blues	1949	National 9073
Rockin' At The Record Hop	195'	Jubilee (unreleased)
Rock Me All Night Long	1954	Mercury 8291
Rooster	1948	National 9064
Rough Ridin'	1953	Mercury 70213
Searching For Love	1947	National 9039
Send For Me If You Need Me	1948	National 9045
September Song	1948	National 9053/Mercury 70307 (1954)
She's Got To Go	1953	Mercury 70119
Silent Night	1948	National 9062/Mercury 70505 (1954)/Savoy 1540 (1958)
Simple Prayer, A	1956	Argo 5261
Someday	1949	National 9089
Summertime	1947	National 9038
Sylvia	194'	National (unreleased)
Tea For Two	194'	National (unreleased)
That'll Be The Day	1957	Argo 5276/Checker 871 (1957)
That Old Gang Of Mine	1951	Okeh 6843
There's Nothing Like A Woman In Love	1949	National 9085
There's No Use Pretending	1951	Mercury 5764/Mercury 8259 (1951)
There's No You	1948	National 9042
Time Is Marching On	1951	National 9148
Time Takes Care Of Everything	1950	Columbia 6-903/Columbia 1-903 (1950)
Together	1948	National 9042
Too Soon	1952	Mercury 8296
Until The Real Thing Comes Along	1948	National 9045
Wagon Wheels	1951	Mercury 5764/Mercury 8259 (1951)
Walkin' My Blues Away	1953	Mercury 70240
Walkin' With The Blues (with the Benny Goodman Sextet)	1950	Columbia 39045
We'll Raise A Ruckus Tonight	1955	Jubilee 5217
Whiffenpoof Song, The	1951	Okeh 6825
White Christmas	1948	National

Who'll Be The Fool	1953	9062/Mercury 70505 (1954)/Savoy 1540 (1958) Mercury 70213
Who's Sorry Now	194'	National (unreleased)
Why Did You Leave Me	1952	Mercury 5853
Without A Song	1953	Mercury 70240
Would You Believe Me	1947	National 9035
Write Me A Letter	1947	National 9038/Rendition 5001 (1951)/Mercury 70554 (1955)
Write Me One Sweet Letter	1954	Mercury 8291
You Don't Have To Drop A Heart To Break It	1951	Columbia 39112
You Foolish Thing	1951	Columbia 39408
You're Always In My Dreams	1951	Columbia 39194
You're Gonna Lose Your Gal (with the Benny Goodman Sextet)	1950	Columbia 39045
Water Boy	1956	Argo 5261

Ravens (Nancy Reed)

Oh Babe! (with the Benny Goodman Sextet)	1950	Columbia 39045

Ravens, Dinah Washington & the

Hey, Good Lookin'	1951	Mercury 8257
Out In The Cold Again	1951	Mercury 8257

Ray-O-Vacs

Besame Mucho (Kiss Me Much)	1950	Decca 48162
Charmaine	1950	Decca 48260
Crying All Alone	1956	Kaiser 384/Atco 6085 (1957)
Darling	1954	Josie 763
Goodnight My Love	1951	Decca 48197
Got Two Arms	1951	Decca 48181
Hands Across The Table	1950	Decca 48260
Hong Kong	1957	Kaiser 784
Hot Dog	1951	Regent 1039
If You Should Ever Leave Me	1951	Decca 48211
I'll Always Be In Love With You	1948	Coleman 100/Sharp 103
I'm The Baby Now	1948	Coleman 112
I Still Love You Baby	1950	Decca 48234
Kiss In The Dark, A	1951	Decca 48181
Let's	1951	Decca 48221
My Baby's Gone	1950	Decca 48221
Once Upon A Time	1950	Decca 48141
Outside Of Paradise	195'	Jubilee
Party Time	1957	Atco 6085
Sentimental Me	1950	Decca 48141
She's A Real Lovin' Baby	1953	Decca 48274
Take Me Back To My Boots And Saddle	1951	Decca 48197
What Can I Say	1952	Jubilee 5098
What's Mine Is Mine	1950	Decca 48234
When The Swallows Come Back To Capistrano	1953	Decca 48274
Wine-O (as by Bill Walker)	1957	Kaiser 874
You Can Depend On Me	1951	Decca 48211
You Gotta Love Me, Baby, Too	1950	Decca 48162
You Know	195'	Jubilee

Ray-O-Vacs, Flap McQueen & the

All About Daddy	1955	Josie 781
I Still Love You	1955	Josie 781

Rea, Virginia & Male Quartette

Good-Bye, Beloved, Good-Bye		Edison 4919 (4BA)

Record Boys

Hokum Smokum Yodel Indian	1926	Columbia 655-D
Oo-Long's In Wrong In Hong-Kong Now	1926	Columbia 655-D

Recorders

Religion	1928	Victor
Sleepy Now	1928	Victor
Who's Blue Now	1928	Columbia
Wouldn't That Be Too Bad	1928	Columbia

Red Caps (Damita Jo)

A'Fussin' And A'Fightin'	1952	Mercury
Always	1955	Mercury
Freehearted	1955	Mercury
Wait	1952	RCA 47-4835

Red Caps (with Damita Jo)

I Went To Your Wedding	1952	RCA 47-4835
Sleepy Little Cowboy	1952	Mercury

Red Caps Trio

Get Off Of That Kick	1945	Beacon 7220
It's Got A Hole In It	1945	Beacon 7220
Monkey And The Baboon	1945	Beacon 7221
That's The Stuff	1945	Beacon 7221

Red Caps, Steve Gibson & the

Bless You	1959	Rose 5534/Hunt 326 (1959)
Blueberry Hill	1946	Mercury 8146/Stage 3001 (1959)
Boogie Woogie On A Saturday Night	1951	Victor 20-4294
Cheryl Lee	1959	Hunt 326
Danny Boy	1948	Mercury 8091
Flamingo	1957	ABC 9856
Forever 'N' A Day	1958	Hi Lo 103
Gaucho Serenade	1956	ABC 9750
How I Cry	1955	RCA Victor 47-6345
I-Bitty-Bitty	1958	Hi Lo 101
I'd Love To Live A Lifetime With You	1948	Mercury 8069
I Lived A Lifetime For You	1951	Mercury LP 25116

I'll Never Love Anyone Else	1950	Mercury 5380	Evenin'	1928	Victor 21807
I Miss You So	1959	Rose 5534	Every Sunday Afternoon (with Carson Robison)	1925	Victor 19731
It's Love	1958	Hi Lo 103			
I Want A Roof Over My Head	1950	Mercury 5380	Gems From 'Tip Toes' (with Gladys Rice)	1926	Victor 35772
I Want To Be Loved	1958	Hi Lo 101			
I Went To Your Wedding	1960	ABC 10105	Ginger-Bread Parade, The	1934	Victor
Let The Rest Of The World Go By	1951	Mercury LP	Grandfather's Clock	1934	Victor
			Hallelujah!	1927	Victor 20609
Love Me Tenderly	1956	ABC 9702	Happy Feet	1930	Victor 22547
My Tzatskele (My Little Darling)	1955	RCA Victor 47-5987	Honeybunch	1926	Brunswick
			Honolulu Moon	1927	Victor 20719
Poor Me, Poor Me	1959	Stage 3001	Hosanna	1931	Victor
Rock And Roll Stomp	1956	ABC 9702	I Know That You Know	1927	Victor 20380
San Antone Rose	1959	Hunt 330/Casa Blanca 5505	I Love to Tell The Story	1938	Decca 1752
			I'm Gonna Charleston Back To Charleston	1925	Victor 19778
Silhouettes	1957	ABC 9856			
Together	1960	ABC 10105	I'm In Love Again	1927	Victor 20678
Where Are You	1959	Hunt 330/Casa Blanca 5505	I'm Looking Over A Four-Leaf Clover	1927	Victor 20678
Write To Me	1956	ABC 9750	In A Little Spanish Town	1927	Victor 20457
You May Not Love Me	1957	ABC 9796	Jesus Savior, Pilot Me	1937	Decca 1741
You've Got Me Dizzy	1957	ABC 9796	Jingle Bells	1928	Victor 19791
Red Caps, Steve Gibson & the (with Damita Jo)			Just A Bundle Of Sunshine (with Carnon Robison)	1925	Victor 19731
Feelin' Kinda Happy	1955	RCA Victor 47-6096			
			Just A Little Drink	1925	Victor 19666
Red Caps, The Original			Just Around The Corner	1926	Victor 19968
Sidewalk Shuffle	1951	RCA Victor 50-0127	Kentucky Babe	1929	Victor 22249
			King's Horses (And The King's Men), The	1931	Victor
Regal Quartet					
Onward Christian Soldiers	1919	Banner 2122	Lady Play Your Mandolin	1931	Victor 22622
Revelairs			Last Round-Up, The	1934	Victor
Just That Way	1946	De Luxe 1048	Little Cotton Dolly (Plantation Lullaby)	1929	Victor 22249
Rumors Are Flying	1946	De Luxe 1048			
Revelers			Love Your Spell Is Everywhere	1929	Victor
Ah! Ha!	1925	Victor 19666	Lucky Day	1926	Victor 20111
All Alone Monday	1927	Victor 20417	Mammy Is Gone	1928	Victor 21448
Among My Souvenirs	1927	Victor 21100	Mary Lou	1927	Victor 20380
Bam Bam Bammy Shore	1925	Victor 19848	Moonlight On The Ganges	1926	Victor 20140
Beautiful Isle Of Somewhere	1937	Decca 1741	More We Are Together, The	1927	Victor 20603
Birth Of The Blues, The	1926	Victor 20111	Narcissus	1928	
Blue Again	1931	Victor 22622	Nola	1927	Victor 21100
Blue River	1927	Victor 20920	Oh! Lucindy	1927	Victor 21241
Blue Room, The	1926	Victor 20082/Victor 24707	Oh Miss Hannah	1925	Victor 19796
			Ol' Man River	1928	Victor 21241
Blue Shadows	1928	Victor 21765	Ploddin' Along	1929	Victor 22036
Canzone Amoroso	1928	Victor	Quilting Party, The	1928	Victor 19791
Chant Of The Jungle	1930	Victor 22270	Raquel	1929	Victor 21911
Comin' Home	1928	Victor 21807	Riff Song, The	1926	Victor 20373
Cottage For Sale, A	1930	Victor 22382	Roam On, My Little Gypsy Sweetheart	1927	Victor 20920
Dancing In The Dark	1931	Victor 22772			
Dinah	1926	Victor 19796/Jubilee	Singing A Vagabond Song	1930	Victor 22401
			Sing Something Simple	1930	Victor 22547
Don't Wait Too Long	1926	Victor 19949	Sing, You Sinners	1930	Victor 22422
Dream River	1928	Victor 21448	Snowball Men, The	1930	Victor
Dusky Stevedore	1928	Victor 21765	So Beats My Heart For You	1930	

100 Years of Harmony: 1850 to 1950

So Blue	1927	Victor 20564
Strike Up The Band!	1930	Victor 22401
Swinging On The Gate	1926	Victor
Talking To The Moon	1926	Victor 20046
Tentin' Down In Tennessee	1926	Victor
Valencia	1926	Victor 20082
Varsity Drag, The	1927	Victor 21039
Waiting At The End Of The Road	1930	Victor 22270
Wake Up! Chillun, Wake Up	1929	Victor 22036
Was It A Dream'	1928	Victor 21316
When Yuba Plays The Rumba On The Tuba	1931	Victor 22772
Where Is My Rose Of Waikiki	1926	Victor 19949
Who'	1925	Vocalion 15183/Brunswick 2997
Woman In The Shoe, The	1930	Victor 22382
Yankee Rose	1927	Victor 20564
Yesterday	1927	Victor 20597
You Remind Me Of A Naughty Springtime Cuckoo	1926	Victor

Revelers (as male quartet with Carl Fenton's Orchestra)

Song Of The Vagabonds	1925	Brunswick 2995/Brunswick 4734/Brunswick A 8695
There Ain't No Flies On Auntie	1925	Vocalion 15157/Vocalion X 9761/Vocalion 9778

Revelers (as male quartet with Tuxedo Orchestra)

Tie Me To Your Apron Strings Again	1926	Brunswick 3045

Revelers (as unnamed group with Paul Whiteman & his Orchestra)

No Foolin'	1926	Victor 20064/Victor 20019

Revelers (Gladys Rice & the)

Oh, Kay! Vocal Gems	1927	Victor 35811

Revelers (Jeanette MacDonald & the)

March Of The Grenadiers	1929	Victor 22247

Revelers (Merrymakers)

My Castle In Spain	1926	Brunswick

Revelers (Singing Sophomores)

Collegiate	1925	Victor 19978/Electrola EG 199
My Ohio Home	1928	

Revelers (with Ed Smalle)

Breezin' Along With The Breeze	1926	Victor 20140

Revelers (with Troubadours)

Baby Feet Go Pitter-Patter	1927	Victor 20967

Revelers Male Quartet

Blessed Assurance	1940	Decca 3494A
Church In The Wildwood, The	1938	Decca 2064B
I Love To Tell The Story	1937	Decca 1752B
Rock Of Ages	1938	Decca 1752A
Sweet Bye And Bye	1938	Decca 2064A

Revelers, Wilfred Glenn & the

When Mother Wields The Shingle	1930	Victor 24111

Revellers

Nearer My God To Thee	1938	Decca 1943B
Old Rugged Cross, The	1938	Decca 1943A

Revillon Trio

Rosary, The	1915	Columbia A-1815
Somewhere A Voice Is Calling	1915	Columbia A-1856

Rhythm Boys

Among My Souvenirs	1927	Victor
Because My Baby Don't Mean 'Maybe' Now	1928	Columbia 1441-D/Columbia 5007/Columbia 07007
Bench In The Park, A	1930	Columbia 2223-D/Columbia DB 282
Broken-Hearted	1927	Victor 20757
Bunch Of Happiness	1926	Victor
Calinda, The	1927	Victor 20882
Cinderella's Fella	1933	Columbia 2851-D
Collette	1927	Victor 20757
C-O-N-S-T-A-N-T-I-N-O-P-L-E	1928	Columbia 1402-D/Columbia 4951/Columbia 07002
Dancing Shadows	1928	Victor 21341/Victor 27687
Do I Hear You Saying'	1928	Victor 21398
Don't Somebody Need Somebody'		Columbia
Evening Star	1928	Columbia 1401-D/Columbia 4950/Columbia 07001
Everything's Agreed Upon	1930	Columbia
Fallen Leaf	1927	Victor 20683
Five Step, The	1927	Victor 20883/Electrola EG 700
From Monday On	1928	Victor 21274/Victor 27-0136
Georgianna	1926	Victor 20017
Georgie Porgie	1928	Columbia 1491-D/Columbia 5040/Columbia 07011
Get Out And Get Under The Moon	1928	Columbia 1402-D/Columbia 4951/Columbia 07001
Gold Digger's Song (We're In The Money Now), The	1933	Victor 24322

Song	Year	Label/Number
Happy Feet	1930	Columbia 2164-D/Columbia CB 86/Columbia 07031
I'd Rather Cry Over You	1928	Columbia 1496-D/Columbia 4980/Columbia 07005
If You See Sally	1927	Victor
I Know That You Know	1926	Victor
I Like The Things You Do	1930	Columbia 2170-D/Columbia LB 87/Columbia 07038
I Like To Do Things For You	1930	
I'll Take An Option On You	1933	Victor 24304
I'm Coming Virginia	1927	Victor/Electrola EG 614
I'm In Love Again	1927	Victor 20646
I'm On The Crest Of A Wave	1928	Columbia 1465-D/Columbia 5241/Columbia 07012
I'm Wingin' Home	1928	Victor 21365
Indian Cradle Song (with Mildred Hunt)		
Inka Dinka Doo	1933	Columbia 2858-D
In My Bouquet Of Memories	1928	Victor 21388
In The Evening	1928	Columbia 1484-D
It Was The Dawn Of Love	1928	Victor 21453
It Won't Be Long Now	1927	Victor 20883
I've Got The Girl	1926	Columbia 824-D/Columbia 4310/Columbia 0688
La Golondrina	1928	Columbia 50070-D/Columbia 9459/Columbia 07501
La Paloma	1928	Columbia 50070-D/Columbia 9495/Columbia 07501
Let's Do It	1928	Columbia 1701-D/Columbia 5331/Columbia 07028
Lonely Eyes	1926	Victor 20418
Lonesome In The Moonlight	1928	Columbia 1448-D/Columbia 5039/Columbia 07010
Louisiana	1928	Victor 21438/Victor 25369/Biltmore 1030
Love Nest, The	1928	Victor 24105
Manhattan Mary	1927	Victor 20874
Marching Along Together	1933	Victor 24364
March Of The Musketeers	1928	Victor 21315
Metropolis (Part 3)	1928	Victor 35934
Mississippi Mud	1928	Victor 21274/Biltmore 1029
Missouri Waltz	1927	Victor 20973
(Mix The Lot - What Have You Got') Magnolia	1927	Victor 20679/Electrola EG 582/Decatur 505
My Angel	1928	Victor 21388
My Blue Heaven	1927	Victor 20828
My Heart Stood Still	1928	Victor 35883
My Pet	1928	Victor 27686/Victor 21389
Night At The Biltmore, A	1932	Victor 67-2000
Night At The Biltmore, A - Part 1	1932	Victor 39000
Night At The Biltmore, A - Part 2	1932	Victor 39000
Night Owl	1933	Victor 24400/Electrola EG 2903
No More Worryin'	1926	Victor 20007
Ooh! Maybe It's You	1927	Victor 20885
Pettin' In The Park	1933	Victor 24322
Poor Butterfly	1928	Victor 24078
Precious	1926	Victor 20139
Pretty Lips	1927	Victor 20627
Ramona	1928	Victor 21214/Victor 25436
Shanghai Dream Man	1927	Victor 20683
Side By Side	1927	Victor 20627/Decatur 505/Electrola EG 708
Sittin' On A Backyard Fence	1933	Victor 24403
Smile	1928	Victor 21228
Song Of The Dawn	1930	Columbia 2163-D/Columbia LB 87/Columbia 07036
Sunshine	1928	Victor 21240
Sweet Dreams	1928	Columbia
Tentin' Down In Tennessee	1926	Victor 20017
That Saxophone Waltz	1927	Victor 20513
That's My Weakness Now	1928	Columbia 1444-D/Columbia 5006/Columbia 07008
Them There Eyes (Esos Tus Ojitos)	1930	Victor 22580
There Ain't No Sweet Man That's Worth The Salt Of My Tears	1928	Victor 21464/Biltmore

Three Little Words	1930	1031 Victor 25076/Electrola EG 2428/Victor 22528/Victor 27-0031/Victor 42-0031
Trudy	1926	Victor 20177
When	1928	Victor 27681
When The Red, Red Robin Comes Bob-Bob Bobbin- Along	1926	Victor 20177
Whiteman Medley - Part 2	1930	Victor 36199
Why Do Ya Roll Those Eyes'	1926	Victor 20197
Wistful And Blue	1926	Victor 20418
You're Telling Me	1932	Victor 24140
Your Land And My Land	1927	Victor
You Took Advantage Of Me	1928	Victor 21398/Victor 25369/Biltmore 1030

Rhythm Boys (with Bing Crosby)

You Took Advantage Of Me	1930	Victor unissued

Rhythm Boys (with Three Brox Sisters)

Bench In The Park, A	1930	

Rhythm Boys, Bing Crosby & the

Changes	1927	Victor 25370/Victor 21103/Biltmore 1032
From Monday On	1928	Victor 25368
There Ain't No Sweet Man That's Worth The Salt Of My Tears	1928	Victor 25675

Rhythm Boys, Paul Whiteman's

Ain't She Sweet/Mississippi Mud	1933	Victor 24240
At Twilight	1929	Columbia 1993-D/Columbia 5655/Columbia 07028
Bahama Mamas	1932	Victor 24095
Christmas Melodies	1928	Columbia 50098-D/Columbia 9561/Columbia 07511
From Monday On	1928	Victor 24349/Victor 21302//Victor 27688 (1928)
Great Day (with Jack Fulton)	1929	Columbia 2023-D/Columbia CB 116/Columbia 07034
I'm A Dreamer, Aren't We All' (with Jack Fulton)	1929	Columbia 2010-D/Columbia 07031
I'm In Seventh Heaven	1929	Columbia 1877-D/Columbia 5544/Columbia 07023
Jig Time	1932	Victor 24190
Just A Sweetheart	1928	Columbia 1630-D/Columbia 5305
Lost In Your Arms	1932	Victor 24095
Louise	1929	Columbia 1819-D/Columbia 5457
Makin' Whoopee	1928	Columbia 1683-D/Columbia 5556/Columbia 07019
Miss Annabelle Lee	1927	Victor 21104/Electrola EG 865
Mississippi Mud/I Left My Sugar Standing In The Rain	1927	Victor 20783/Electrola EG 728
My Suppressed Desire	1928	Columbia 1629-D/Columbia 5240/Columbia 07016
Out O' Town Gal	1928	Columbia 1505-D/Columbia 5039/Columbia 07011
Rhythm King	1928	Columbia 1629-D/Columbia 5240/Columbia 07016
Silent Night, Holy Night	1928	Columbia 50098-D/Columbia 9561/Columbia 07511
So The Bluebirds And The Blackbirds Got Together	1929	Columbia 1819-D/Columbia 5457
Sweet Lil/I Left My Sugar Standing In The Rain	1933	Victor 24240
Sweet Lil/Ain't She Sweet	1927	Victor 20783/Victor 24240
That's Grandma	1927	Victor 27688/Columbia 1455-D (1928)
Wa-Da-Da	1928	Columbia 1455-D/Columbia 5006/Columbia 07009
What Price Lyrics'	1928	Victor 24349/Citro 21302
When You're Counting The Stars Alone	1929	Columbia 1993-D/Columbia 5675
Your Mother And Mine	1929	Columbia 1845-D/Columbia 5560

Rhythm Boys, The Original

Mississippi Mud	1928	Victor 25366

Rhythm Boys, Whiteman's

Basin Street Blues	1932	Victor

Her Majesty (My Sugar)	1932	Victor
Milenberg Joys	1932	Victor 24095

Rhythm Kings
Christmas Is Coming At Last	1950	Apollo 1171
I Gotta Go Now	1951	Apollo 1181
I Shouldn't Have Passed Your House		Ivory 751
Merry Christmas One And All	1950	Apollo 1171
Night After Night		Ivory 751
Pop! Goes Your Heart	1934	Victor 24706
Talkin' To Myself	1934	Victor 24703
Why, My Darling Why'	1951	Apollo 1181

Rhythm Maniacs, Delores Jackson & the
I Know Now	1938	Decca 7407
My Cabin Of Dreams	1938	Decca 7407

Rhythm Quads
College Humor	1938	Bluebird B-7505

Rhythmaires
Baby Buggie Boogie	1950	RCA Victor 20-3939
Barroom Polka	1949	Decca 24608
Hi-Yo, Silver!	1938	Vocalion 4193
My Margarita	1938	Vocalion 4193
Put Your Shoes On, Lucy	1949	Decca 24608

Rhythmaires (with Bing Crosby)
Ballerina	1947	Decca 24278
Everywhere You Go	1949	Decca 24612
Golden Earrings	1947	Decca 24278
Headless Horseman, The	1949	Decca 24702
Ichabod	1949	Decca 24702

Rhythmaires (with Ella Fitzgerald)
Baby Doll	1951	Decca 27900
Lady Bug	1951	Decca 27900

Rhythmaires (with Hoagy Carmichael)
Put Yourself In My Place, Baby	1947	Decca 24247
Tune For Humming, A	1947	Decca 24247

Rhythmaires, Bob London & the
Everything I Have Is Yours	1951	Decca 27691

Rhythmaires, Bob London and Frances Irvin & the
Oh! Look At Me Now	1951	Decca 27733

Rhythmaires, Frances Irvin & the
Hula Hula Boogie, The	1951	Brunswick 82560

Rhythmaires, Jud Conlon's
If You Go (Si Tu Partais)	1951	Coral 60647
Manhattan	1951	Coral 60612/Coral 65513
Please, Mr. Sun	1951	Coral 60647
Solitaire	1951	Coral 60612

Rhythmaires, Judd Colon's (sic) (with Frankie Laine)
Satan Wears A Satin Gown	1949	Mercury 5316
That Lucky Old Sun	1949	Mercury 5316

Rhythmettes
City Called Heaven, A	1947	Capitol 1199
Got Me Doin' Things	1935	Victor 24866
Lord Is Coming Bye And Bye, The	1947	Capitol 1130
Moment In Sorrento, A	1940	Decca 3315
Roll On, Jordan	1947	Capitol 1199
South Of Pago Pago	1940	Decca 3315
Television	1947	Capitol 1130

Richmond Starlight Quartette
Gone Jazz Crazy	1928	QRS R 7028
Gone Pretty Mama	1929	
Jazz Crazy Blues	1929	
Mary, Don't You Weep	1929	
Monkey Man Blues	1928	QRS R 7028
Mother, You'll Surely Be Late	1929	
Oh, You Better Mind	1928	QRS R 7056
Won't Be Worried No More	1928	QRS R 7056

Ricks, Jimmy (Rickateers)
Same Sweet Wonderful One, The		Prev. unreleased
She's Fine, She's Mine	1956	
Unbeliever, The	1956	

Riffers
Rhapsody In Love	1932	Columbia 14677-D
Say It Isn't So/Papa De-Da-Da	1932	Columbia 14677-D

Right Quintette
Exhortation	1916	Columbia A-1987
My Old Kentucky Home	1916	Columbia
Rain Song	1916	Columbia A-1987
Swing Along	1916	Columbia

Rigoletto Quartet Of Morris Brown University
I Couldn't Hear Nobody Pray	1926	Okeh 8400
In Some Lonesome Graveyard	1926	Okeh 8386
I've Got A Home In That Rock	1926	Okeh 8386
Standing In The Need Of Prayer	1926	Okeh 8400

Riley Cole Quartet
I Am Happy With My Saviour	1928	Columbia
That City Of Rest	1928	Columbia

Ritz Quartet
Aggie War Hymn, The	1928	Brunswick 3924
Away To Rio!	1929	Brunswick 4905
Come West, Little Girl, Come West	1928	Brunswick A 8301/Brunswick 4328 (1929)
Down In The Old Neighborhood	1927	Brunswick 3546
Eyes Of Texas	1928	Brunswick 3924
Grass Grows Greener (	1928	Brunswick 3962
Hurry On!	1928	Brunswick
I'm Bringing A Red, Red Rose	1928	Brunswick A 8301/Brunswick 4328 (1929)
In A Persian Market - Intermezzo Scene	1928	Brunswick 20067/Brunswick A 5055
Medley Of Barbershop Ballads	1929	Brunswick 4894/Supertone S 2110

Medley Of Old Ballads, Part 1	1929	Brunswick 4598
Medley Of Old Ballads, Part 2	1929	Brunswick 4598
Medley Of Songs Of Old New York	1930	Brunswick 4894/Supertone S 2110
Old Man Noah	1929	Brunswick 4905
On Candle Light Lane	1928	Brunswick
Oriental Moonlight	1927	Brunswick 3525/Brunswick A 491
Shanghai Dream Man	1927	Brunswick 3525/Brunswick A 491
Sweet Elaine	1928	Brunswick 3962
That's What I Call A Pal	1927	Brunswick 3546
Your Land And My Land	1927	Brunswick 3537/Brunswick A 424

Ritz Quartet (with Grace Moore)
Home Sweet Home	1928	Brunswick

Ritz Quartet (with Lew White)
Just Like A Butterfly (That's Caught In The Rain)	1927	Brunswick

Ritz Quartette
Darktown Strutter's Ball, The	1928	Brunswick 20066/Brunswick A 5057

Ritz Trio (Angelo-Persians with vocal trio)
Down South	1927	Brunswick 3612/Brunswick A 487

Ritz Trio (Marie Tiffany with Male Trio)
Darling Nellie Gray	1928	Brunswick 15179

Rivals
Don't Say You're Sorry Again	1950	Apollo 1166
Rival Blues	1950	Apollo 1166

River Rovers (with Lydia Larson)
Bald-Headed Daddy	1951	Apollo 432
Delta Drag	1951	Apollo 432

Riverboat Four, Peach Tree Logan & the
Heap Sees And Few Knows	1950	MGM 10655
That's All Brother, That's All	1950	MGM 10655

Riversiders Quartet
For Me And My Gal	1937	Bluebird 6956/Montgomery Ward M-7275
Girl Of My Dreams	1937	Bluebird 6977
Lonesome And Sorry	1937	Bluebird 6977
Mary Lou	1937	Montgomery Ward M-7275
Mickey	1937	Bluebird 6956/Montgomery Ward M-7274
Oh! What A Pal Was Mary	1937	Bluebird 6969
Old Pal Why Don't You Answer Me'	1937	Bluebird 6930/Montgomery Ward M-7269
Radio In Heaven	1937	Bluebird 6930/Montgomery Ward M-7269
Who's Sorry Now	1937	Bluebird 6969

Robbins
All I Do Is Rock	1954	Crown 120
Key To My Heart	1954	Crown 120

Robbins, Bobby Nunn & the
Rockin'	1951	Modern 807
That's What The Good Book Says	1951	Modern 807

Robins (with Maggie Hathaway)
Bayou Baby Blues		Recorded In Hollywood 112
When Gabriel Blows His Horn		Recorded In Hollywood 121

Robinson Quartet
Church In The Wildwood	1922	Champion 15087
Jesus Savior Pilot Me	1922	Champion 15087
Lead Kindly Light	1922	Champion 15086
What A Friend We Have In Jesus	1922	Champion 15086

Robinson Quintet
Bye, Bye, Roberta	1950	Decca 48130
Was I Right	1950	Decca 48130

Robinson Trio, Carson
Moonlight On The Colorado	1930	Perfect 12630
She Was Bred In Old Kentucky	1930	Perfect 12630

Robinson, Mabel & the Four Blackamoors
Romance In The Dark	1941	Decca 8512

Rockets, Herb Kenny & the
But Always Your Friend	1953	MGM 11487
Calling You	1952	MGM 11360
Do I Have To Tell You I'm Sorry'	1953	MGM 11648
Don't Take My Word (Take My Heart)	1953	MGM 11648
I Don't Care	1952	MGM 11360
I Miss You So	1953	MGM 11397
Let's Make Memories Tonight		Unreleased
My Song	1952	MGM 11332
Star-Spangled Dawn	1953	MGM 11487
Take A Little, Leave A Little	1953	MGM 11397
You Never Heard A Word I Said	1953	MGM 11332

Roe Brothers and Morrell
Goin' Down The Road Feelin' Bad	1927	Columbia 15199-D
Little Sweet Lillie	1927	Columbia
Meet Me In St. Louis, Louis	1927	Columbia
My Little Mohi	1927	Columbia 15199-D
She'll Be Coming Around The Mountain	1927	Columbia 15156-D
Ship That Never Returned, The	1927	Columbia 15156-D

Rollickers

Dixie Jamboree	1929	Columbia 2043-D
Dream Avenue	1930	Columbia 2195-D
For You	1930	Columbia 2195-D
He's So Unusual	1929	Columbia 2043-D
I Don't Want Your Kisses	1929	Columbia 1979-D
I Kiss Your Hand, Madame	1929	Columbia 1778-D
Nobody But You	1929	Columbia 1838-D
Revolutionary Rhythm	1929	Columbia 1965-D
Singin' In The Rain	1929	Columbia 1838-D
Strike Up The Band!	1930	Columbia 2132-D
Tip-toe Thru' The Tulips With Me	1929	Columbia 1924-D
Until The End	1929	Columbia 1979-D
Used To You	1929	Columbia 1878-D
When The Real Thing Comes Your Way	1929	Columbia 1965-D
Why Can't You	1929	Columbia 1878-D
Wishing And Waiting For Love	1929	Columbia 1924-D
Yours Sincerely	1929	Columbia 1778-D

Rollickers (Goodrich Silvertown Quartet)

Bird Songs At Eventide	1930	Columbia 2204-D
Clorinda	1927	Edison DD 52121
Comin' Home	1928	Brunswick 4159
Dawn Brought Me Love And You, The	1930	Columbia 2353-D
I'm In Heaven When I See You Smile Diane	1927	Edison DD 52150
In The Silence Of The Night (Rachmaninoff)	1930	Columbia 2353-D
It Was Only A Sun Shower	1927	Edison DD 52121
I've Got Religion	1928	Edison DD 52331
Japansy	1928	Edison DD 52211
Lonely Little Cinderella	1929	Edison DD 52600
Oh Miss Hannah	1928	Edison DD 52246
Ready For The River	1928	Edison DD 52331
Sea Rapture	1930	Columbia
Song Of The Sands	1929	Edison DD 52600
Spirit Flower, A	1930	Columbia 2204-D
We'll Have A New Home (In The Morning)	1928	Brunswick 4159
When Love Comes Stealing	1928	Edison DD 52211
You're What I Need	1928	Edison DD 52246

Rollickers (with Cavaliers)

I'll Always Be In Love With You	1929	Columbia 1832-D
My Dear	1929	Columbia 1832-D

Rollickers (with Pickens Sisters)

Medley Of Cole Porter Hits	1933	Victor 36085

Rollickers Quartet

I'll Tell The World	1929	Columbia 1751-D
Wedding Bells (Are Breaking Up That Old Gang Of Mine)	1929	Columbia 1740-D

Rollickers, Johnny Ealker & his

Give Yourself A Pat On The Back	1930	Columbia 2201-D
Mug Song, The	1930	Columbia 2201-D

Rollin Smith's Rascals

Kickin' The Gong Around		Clanka Lanka CL-144.033

Rollins Trio

That Tumble Down Shack In Athlone	1920	Challenge 206

Romain, Manuel & the Peerless Quartet

Under Southern Skies		Edison BA 1894/Edison 4A 810

Romancers

Gettin' Sentimental	1931	Victor 22876

Romancers, Jack Fulton & the

Cuban Love Song	1931	Victor 22834/Electrola EG 2485
Faded Summer Love, A	1931	Victor 22827/Electrola 22873-B
Tango Americano	1931	Victor 22913
Tell Me With A Love Song	1931	Victor 22834
There's A Blue Note In My Love Song	1931	Victor 22873/Electrola 22873-A
Vilia	1931	Victor 22885/Victor 24728

Romancers, Mildred Bailey, Jack Fulton & the

I'm Sorry Dear/Old Playmate/Good Night Sweetheart	1931	Victor L 16002

Rondoliers

Auld Lang Syne	1933	Avalon 573
Behind The Big White House	1932	Columbia 15761
Charlie Cadet	1931	Columbia 2554-D
Cheer Up (Good Times Are Comin')	1930	Columbia 2253-D
Chidlins'	1931	Columbia 2435-D
Do The New York (with the Pickens Sisters)	1931	Columbia 2499-D
Faded Summer Love, A	1931	Columbia 2555-D
Father Of The Land We Love	1932	Columbia 2599-D
Happy Birthday Friend	1933	Avalon 573
Happy Days Are Here Again	1930	Columbia 2123-D
Here Comes The Sun	1930	Columbia 2253-D
High And Low (I've Been Looking For You)	1931	Columbia 2473-D
Hikin' Down The Highway	1931	Columbia 2499-D
I Miss A Little Miss (Who Misses Me In Sunny Tennessee)	1930	Columbia 2356-D
In My Heart It's You	1930	Columbia 2289-D
It's Great To Be In Love	1931	Columbia 2526-D
Lazy Lou'siana Moon	1930	Columbia 2145-D
Let 'Em Eat Cake	1933	Columbia 2831-D
Let's Drink A Drink To The Future!	1931	Columbia 2487-D

Little Mary Brown	1931	Columbia 2554-D
Lo-Lo	1930	Columbia 2234-D
Medley Of Washingtonian Songs	1932	Columbia 2599-D
Mine	1933	Columbia 2831-D
Moonlight On The Colorado	1930	Columbia 2266-D
Nobody To Love	1932	Columbia 15760
Sad Song, The	1932	Columbia 15761
Should I'	1930	Columbia 2145-D
Sittin' On A Rainbow	1930	Columbia 2224-D
Something To Remember You By	1930	Columbia 2297-D
Somewhere In Old Wyoming	1930	Columbia 2266-D
Song Of The Fool (with Irving Kaufman), The	1930	Columbia 2345-D
Songs We Love To Sing - Part 1	1933	Columbia 2903-D
Songs We Love To Sing - Part 2	1933	Columbia 2903-D
Stein Song (University Of Maine)	1930	Columbia
Syracuse	1933	Columbia
Tears	1930	Columbia 2361-D
Trees	1931	Columbia 2524-D
Voice In The Old Village Choir, The	1932	Columbia 15760
When Yuba Plays The Rumba On The Tuba	1931	Columbia 2483-D
Who's Calling You Sweetheart Tonight'	1930	Columbia 2345-D
Yours Is My Heart Alone	1931	Columbia 2524-D

Rondoliers (as Johnny Falker & his Rollickers)

Betty Co-Ed	1930	Columbia 2247-D
Kitty From Kansas City	1930	Columbia 2247-D

Rondoliers (as the Columbia Photo Players)

Live And Love Today (with Irving Kaufman)	1930	Columbia 2256-D

Rondoliers (with Art Gillham)

Shine On, Harvest Moon	1931	Columbia 2374-D

Rondoliers (with the Cavaliers)

I'm Alone Because I Love You	1930	Columbia 2339-D
Masquerade	1932	Columbia 2670-D
Sylvia	1932	Columbia 2670-D
Waiting By The Silv'ry Rio Grande	1930	Columbia 2239-D

Rondoliers (with the Columbia Photo Players)

Dark Night	1930	Columbia 2196-D
Dust	1930	Columbia 2196-D

Rondoliers (with the Knickerbockers)

Of Thee I Sing	1932	Columbia 2598-D
Who Cares (So Long As You Care For Me)	1932	Columbia 2598-D

Rondoliers and their Piano Pals

I Need Lovin'	1931	Columbia 2456-D
Lady Of Spain	1931	Columbia 2456-D
My Old Kentucky Home	1931	Columbia

Rondoliers Quartet, Dick Robertson & the

Paradise Waltz Medley	1932	Columbia 18001

Rondoliers, Charles Lawman with the

Prairie Skies	1931	Columbia 2420-D

Rondoliers, Helen Richards & the

Around The Corner	1930	Columbia 2221-D

Rosettes

I'll Be Satisfied	1951	Decca 48223
I'm So Glad	1951	Decca 48223

Rotary Club Quartette

Oh Listen To The Lambs	1923	Gennett
Sweet Genevieve	1923	Gennett

Rounders

Chloe (Song Of The Swamp)	1928	Victor 21382
Coquette	1928	Victor 21505
Coronado Nights	1927	Victor 20697
Deep Night	1929	Victor 22002
Dixie Vagabond	1927	Victor 20696
Doughboy's Lullaby	1929	
Faded Blue Prints	1931	
Hello Cutie	1927	Victor 20696
I Got Rhythm	1931	
Molly	1929	Victor 22286
My Idea Of Heaven	1927	Victor 20689
Persian Rug	1928	Victor 21505
Ready For The River	1928	Victor 21382
Singin' In The Rain	1929	Victor 22002
There'll Never Be Another Mary	1929	
When You Dream, Dream Of Me	1927	Victor
Winding Trail, The	1927	Victor 20697
Wrapped In A Red, Red Rose	1929	

Rounders (assisting Jeanette MacDonald)

Beyond The Blue Horizon	1930	Victor 22514

Rounders (John Boles with the)

Song Of The Dawn, The	1930	Victor 22372

Rounders (with Van and Schenk)

Ten Mammas	1929	

Rountowners

Little Sweetheart Of The Mountains	1931	Columbia 2429-D

Rountowners Quartet

I'm The Last One Left On The Corner (Of That Old Gang Of Mine)	1931	Clarion 5255-C/Harmony 1290-H/Velvet Tone 2321-V/Odeon 221345
King's Horses (And The King's Men), The	1931	Clarion 5255-C/Harmony 1289-H/Velvet Tone 2318-V/Odeon O-4119
One-Man Band, The	1931	Clarion 5253-C/Harmony 1289-H/Velvet Tone 2319-V/Clarion 5253-C/Harmony 1289-V

Roxy Male Quartet

Abide With Me	1932	Conqueror 8212

I Love To Tell The Story	1931	Banner 32207/Conqueror 7752 (1931)	Drop Another Nickel In The Jukebox		Excelsior 136
			Fla-Ga-La-Pa		Excelsior 136
I Need Thee Every Hour	1931	Banner 32207/Conqueror 7752 (1931)	Holiday Blues	1947	Queen 4162
			I Must Forget About You		Excelsior 174
			Mellow Jelly Blues		Excelsior 176
It Is Well With My Soul	1931	Banner 32266/Conqueror 7849 (1931)	More Than You Know		Excelsior 180
			Shy Ann		De Luxe 5002
			What Kind Of Love Is That		Excelsior 175
Lead Kindly Light	1932	Conqueror 8212	World War Two Blues	1947	Queen 4162
Rock Of Ages	1931	Conqueror 7805	**Russell Trio, Sterling**		
When The Roll Is Called Up Yonder	1931	Banner 32266/Conqueror 7849 (1931)	Imagination	1932	Bluebird B-5078/Sunrise S-3159/Victor 23378
Royal Greek Quartet					
May Song, The	1908	Columbia A-0444/Columbia A-0665 (1909)	Only Girl I Ever Loved, The	1932	Bluebird B-5078/Sunrise S-3159/Victor 23378
Two Nightingales (Laughing Song), The	1908	Columbia A-0471/Columbia A-0665 (1909)	**Russians**		
			Along The Highway		Apollo 127
			Driver, Don't Hurry The Horses		Apollo 130
Royal Harmony Quartet			No, No, I Don't Want		Apollo 129
Praise The Lord And Pass The Ammunition	1942	Key 101	Of These Beautiful Dark Eyes		Apollo 129
			Quick, Quick, A Bottle Of Beer		Apollo 127
We'll Be Singing Hallelujah Marching Through Berlin	1942	Key 101	Thank You My Heart		Apollo 130
			What Do I Care		Apollo 128
			Withered Chrysanthemums		Apollo 128
Royal Rhythm Boys			**Rust College Quartet**		
Beat It Out Bumpin' Boy	1939	Decca 2830	Hallelujah	1928	Columbia 14615-D
Blue Skies	1941	Decca 7759	Oh How He Lied	1928	Columbia 14307-D
In A Shanty In Old Shanty Town	1939	Decca 2830	Old McDonald Had A Farm	1928	Columbia 14307-D
Peace, Brother, Peace	1941	Decca 7759	Train To Glory	1928	Columbia 14615-D
Royal Sons			**Ryan Sisters, H. Lamar & the**		
Bedside Of A Neighbor	1948	Apollo 253	You Never Did That Before	1929	Victor V-40130
Come Over Here	1948	Apollo 266	**Sacred Harp Singers**		
Journey's End	1948	Apollo 253	Blooming Youth	1934	Bluebird 5599
Let Nothing Separate Me	1948	Apollo 266	Conversion	1934	Bluebird 5598
Royal Summer Quartet			Fillmore	1934	Bluebird 5597
Be A Man	1927	Columbia 15233-D/Clarion 15233-D/Velvet Tone 7109-V	Good Old Way	1934	Bluebird 5599
			Heavenly Port	1934	Bluebird 5598
			New Britain	1934	Bluebird 5597
Fight To Win	1927	Columbia 15233-D/Clarion 15233-D/Velvet Tone 7109-V	**Sacred Quartet**		
			In The Morning	1941	Okeh 6560
			Sanderson Quartet		
			Onward Christian Soldiers	1928	Champion 40052
Royalists, Roy Campbell's			**Sanford Trio, The Dick**		
Jamboree	1937	Variety 505	Boarder That Stole My Dear Wife, The	1933	Bluebird B-5125/Elektradisk 2035
Royals, Chuck Willis & the					
Dreams Of You	1951	Okeh 6832			
If You Love Me	1951	Okeh 6832	Don't Be Ashamed To Walk Beside Your Mother	1933	Bluebird B-5123/Elektradisk 2033
Russell Trio, Al					
Cement Mixer		Excelsior 174			
Cynthia		Excelsior 176	Down The Mountain, Thru' The Valley To The Sea	1933	Bluebird B-5125/Elektradisk 2035
Dig, Mister K. Kay Kay		Excelsior 180			
Down The Road Apiece		De Luxe 5002			

Husband's Lament, The	1933	Bluebird B-5246/Elektradisk 2129
I Can't Find My Poor Mother's Grave	1933	Bluebird B-5227
I'm Lonely Tonight (Beside The Wishing Well)	1933	Bluebird B-5227
Just A Whoop And A Holler (Doo-Da Doo-Da Day)	1933	Bluebird B-5246/Elektradisk 2129
Prisoner's Confession, The	1933	Bluebird B-5123/Elektradisk 2033
When The Bible Was The Best Book In The Land	1933	Bluebird B-5190/Elektradisk 2083

Satisfiers

As Long As I Live	1951	Capitol 228
One More Dream (And She's Mine)	1951	Capitol 228
Rickety Tickety Melody	1949	Rainbow 270

Satisfiers Foursome (with Louise Carlyle)

Old Rusty Trunk	1949	King 15007
Stargazer	1949	King 15007

Satisfiers, Connee Boswell & the

When I Come Back Crying (Will You Be Laughing At Me)	1945	Coral 60040
Who'll Lend Me A Rainbow'	1945	Decca 18689
You Can't Say I Didn't Try	1945	Coral 60040

Satisfiers, Frances Irving & the

It's A Lovely Day Today	1950	Decca 27313

Satisfiers, Phil Barton & the

Tell It To A Star	1945	Decca 18736

Savoy Girl Quartet

Don't Wake Me Up, I'm Dreaming	1911	Columbia A-1001
Let Me Live And Stay In Dixieland	1911	Columbia A-1001

Scamps

Chica Biddie Boogie	1947	Modern 550
Don't Cry, Baby	1947	Modern 512
I'll Never Smile Again	1948	Modern 561
I'm Falling For You	1948	Modern 521
I Wonder, I Wonder, I Wonder	1947	Modern 516
More Than You Know	1947	Modern 512
Solitude	1947	Modern 550
Sweet Slumber	1948	Modern 521
That's My Desire	1947	Modern 516
Worry	1948	Modern 561

Seagle, Oscar & Quartet

Old Carolina	1921	Columbia A-3448

Seagle, Oscar & the Columbia Quartet

Nearer My God To Thee	1916	Columbia A-5766

Seagle, Oscar & the Columbia Stellar Quartet

There's A Long, Long Trail A-Winding	1917	Columbia A-2452

Seagle, Oscar & the Stellar Quartet

Calling Me Home To You	1917	Columbia A-2452

Seale & Quartet

Sin Is To Blame	192'	Vaughan 850

Seale & Vaughan & Quartet

Face To Face At Last	192'	Vaughan 875

Second Zion Four

On Flowery Beds Of Ease	1929	Columbia 14495-D
Praise His Shining Angels	1929	Columbia 14495-D
Second Zion Four We Are, The	1930	Columbia 14547-D
Trust In God	1930	Columbia 14547-D

Seiberling Singers

At Dawning	1928	Columbia 1475-D
Japanese Sunset, A	1928	Columbia 1475-D

Selah Jubilee Six Of St. Mark's Holy Church

Dry Bones	1931	Columbia
God Done Curse That Lamb	1931	Columbia
I'm Going Home On A Holy Train	1931	Columbia
That's What's The Matter With The Churches Today	1931	Columbia
Waiting For The Boatman	1931	Columbia
What Shall We Call Him'	1931	Columbia

Selvin, Ben and his Orchestra (with Lewis James, Elliott Shaw, Franklyn Baur)

Wherever You Are	1927	Columbia 1133-D

Senior Chapel Quartet

Great Judgment	1929	Vocalion 1475
In My Saviour's Care	1929	Vocalion 1475
Lonesome Road	1929	Vocalion 1437
Way Down Home	1929	Vocalion 1437

Sentimentalists

Chicago Z(with Sy Oliver)	1945	Victor 20-1773/Victor 20-2008
Door Will Open, A (with Stuart Foster)	1945	Victor 20-1728
Down By The Station (with Lucy Ann Polk and Denny Davis)	1945	Victor 20-3317/Electrola EG 7464
Foolishly Yours	1948	Manor 1046A
I'd Rather Be Safe Than Sorry	1946	Manor 1049
I'll Be Waiting For You	1946	Manor 1049
I'll Close My Eyes	1946	Manor 1047
In The Valley (Where The Evenin' Sun Goes Down)	1945	Victor 20-1682
It Still Suits Me (with Sy Oliver)	1945	Victor 20-1784
I Want To Be Loved (By Only You)	1948	Manor 1046A
Moment I Met You, The	1945	Victor 20-1761
Moon Love (with Town Criers)	1945	Victor 20-2871
Nevada (with Stuart Foster)	1945	Victor 20-1710
Never Too Late To Pray (with Stuart Foster)	1945	Victor 20-1773

O Come, All Ye Faithful	1946	Manor 8002
On The Atchison, Topeka & Santa Fe	1945	Victor 20-1682
On The Sunny Side Of The Street	1944	Victor 20-2005
Save Me A Dream	1946	Manor 1047
Silent Night	1946	Manor 8003
That Went Out With Button Shoes	1945	Victor 20-1761
Tonight We Love (with Town Criers)	1945	Victor 20-2869
Where Did You Learn To Love (with Stuart Foster)	1945	Victor 20-1819
White Christmas	1946	Manor 8003
Why Do I Love You (with Stuart Foster)	1945	Victor 20-1787
You're Drivin' Me Crazy	1945	Victor 20-1614

Sentimentalists (Presented by Billy Cotton)

I'm Confessin' (That I Love You)	1945	Decca F 8545
Lonely Footsteps	1945	Decca F 8589
No Need For Words (I'll Understand)	1945	Decca F 8589
Waiting In Sweetheart Valley	1945	Decca F 8545

Sepianaires

All I Can Do Is Dream	1950	Spinit 0101
By The Deep End Of The River	1950	Spinit 0101

Serenaders (1)

Kiss In The Dark, A	1922	Victor 18972
Waltz Is Made For Love	1922	Victor 18972

Serenaders (2)

I Want Some Money	1948	Columbia 38274
Underneath The Arches	1948	Columbia 38274

Seven Musical Magpies

Calliope, The	1924	Victor 19544
Laughing Song	1924	Victor 19544

Seven Stars Quartet

Departed Neighbors	1938	Vocalion 4558
God Called John	1940	Vocalion 5564
Here Am I	1938	Vocalion 4558
I'm Going To Work On The Battlefield	1938	Vocalion 4746/Conqueror 9287 (1938)
Little Black Train	1940	Vocalion 5477
Lord I'm Troubled	1940	Vocalion 5564
Walking Down The Lonesome Road	1940	Vocalion 5477
We'll All Rise Together	1938	Vocalion 4746/Conqueror 9287 (1938)

Shadows

Beans	1951	Sittin' In With 590
Better Than Gold	1954	Decca 48322
Big Mouth Mama	1954	Decca 48322
Coon Can Annie	1952	Sittin' In With 627
Don't Be Bashful	1953	Decca 48307
Don't Be Late	1951	Sittin' In With 590
Don't Blame My Dreams	1950	Lee 207
I'd Rather Be Wrong Than Blue	1950	Lee 202
I'll Never Never Let You Go	1950	Sittin' In With 583
I'm Crying	1950	Lee 207
It's Too Bad	1952	Sittin' In With 627
I've Been A Fool	1949	Lee 200
Jitterbug Special	1950	Sittin' In With 583
Love Me Baby		Hub 556
Nobody Knows	1949	Lee 200
No Use	1953	Decca 28765
Peter		Hub 556
Stay	1953	Decca 28765
Tell Her	1953	Decca 48307
You Are Closer To My Heart	1950	Lee 202

Shady Grove Quartet (with Sister Sallie Sanders)

Shall Our Cheeks Be Dried	1926	Columbia 14185-D

Shand Jubilee Singers

Silver Slippers	1928	Vocalion 1265
True Religion	1928	Vocalion 1265

Shannon Four

Adeste Fideles	1920	Emerson 1087/Pathe 29219
Ain't You Coming Out, Malinda'	1921	Vocalion 14215B
All By Myself	1921	Vocalion 14189A
All Hail The Power Of Jesus	1922	Okeh 4651
All Thro' The Night	1926	Vocalion 15151
America	1923	Okeh 4834
Annie Laurie	1920	Okeh 4248/Okeh 4653 (1922)
Any Old Time At All	1924	Columbia 133-D/Okeh 40126 (1924)
At Dawning	1919	Okeh 4014
Auld Lang Syne	1921	Brunswick 2219/Brunswick 5034
Back In The Old Neighborhood	1923	Columbia 42-D
Bonnie Lassie	1920	Okeh 4244
Break The News To Mother	1917	Victor 18358
Bring Back Those Rock-A-Bye Baby Days	1924	Columbia 222-D
California Here I Come	1924	Columbia 86-D
Carolina Mammy	1922	Columbia A-3763
Casey Jones	1921	Federal 5117/Resona 75117/Silvertone 2117
Chili Bom Bom	1924	Okeh 40039
Chiming Bells Of Long Ago	1922	Columbia 19-M/Columbia A-3749
Ching-A-Ling's Jazz Bazaar	1920	Vocalion X-9040/Vocalion 14044A/Okeh 4094 (1920)

Christmas Tidings - Part 1	1922	Columbia A-3707	Lindy Lou	1923	Columbia A-3854
Christmas Tidings - Part 2	1922	Columbia A-3707	Linger Awhile	1924	Columbia 86-D
Colleen	1921	Pathe 22481	Lot Of Blue Eyed Marys Down In Dixie	1919	Victor 18631
College Days	1921	Victor 18792			
Come Thou Almighty King/Hymn Medley	1921	Vocalion 14171B	Mansfield Hail	1924	Columbia 40-P
			Maryland, My Maryland	1922	Columbia
Cornfield Medley	1921	Vocalion 14203A	Medley of Harvard Songs Part 1: Gridiron King/Soldier's Field	1922	Columbia A-3780
County Kerry Mary	1920	Okeh 4244			
Daisy Days	1921	Okeh 4414	Medley of Harvard Songs Part 2: Australia/Rhine Wine	1922	Columbia A-3780
Darling Nellie Gray	1921	Silvertone 2114/Federal			
			Medley Of Old Timers Part 1: Daisy Bell/Annie Rooney	1922	Columbia A-3797
Dear Heart	1920	Okeh 4142			
Do You Ever Think Of Me'	1921	Okeh 4324	Medley Of Old Timers Part 2: Old Apple Tree/Rosie Grady	1922	Columbia A-3797
Dreamy Melody	1923	Columbia A-3985			
Drinking Song	1925	Columbia 281-D	Melody Land	1917	Victor 18400
Ev'ry Sunday Afternoon	1925	Columbia 452-D	Melon Time In Dixieland	1921	Okeh 4410
Follow The Swallow	1924	Columbia 193-D	Mickey Donohue	1924	Columbia 66-D
Forsaken	1921	Pathe 20608	Mother Here's Your Boy	1918	Victor 18517
Gypsy Love Song	1922	Columbia	Moxie	1921	Vocalion 14250
Hail! Hail! The Gang's All Here	1917	Victor 18414	Music Of Wedding Chimes, The	1919	Victor 18596
Hello Aloha Hello	1917	Victor 18401	Nearer My God To Thee	1920	Okeh 4144/Emerson 1039 (1920)
Holy Night, Peaceful Night	1920	Emerson 1087			
Homeland	1925	Columbia 357-D			
Humming	1921	Okeh 4354	Oh Come All Ye Faithful	1923	Okeh 4972
Hymn Medley Pt. 2	1921	Vocalion 14211B	Old Man Jazz	1920	Okeh 4093
I'll Be Good	1920	Okeh 4173	Old Oaken Bucket, The	1920	Okeh 4191
I'll Take You Home Again, Kathleen	1925	Okeh 40302	Old Time Medley - Part 1	1921	Pathe 020691
			Old Time Medley - Part 2	1921	Pathe 020691
I Love You Just The Same, Sweet Adeline	1920	Emerson 10108/Symphonola 4190	On The Old Bob Sled	1921	Okeh 4493
			Onward Christian Soldiers	1920	Okeh 4106/Emerson 1039 (1920)
I May Be Gone For A Long, Long Time	1917	Victor 18333			
			Paul Revere (Won't You Ride For Us Again)	1918	Victor 18481
I'm Drifting Back To Dreamland	1923	Columbia 14D			
I'm On My Way	1920	Okeh 4148	Plantation Lullaby	1921	Okeh 4456/Vocalion 14248B (1921)/Okeh 4643 (1921)
In The Evening By The Moonlight	1921	Silvertone 2124/Federal			
In The Gloaming	1922	Okeh 4724			
In The Old Neighborhood	1923	Columbia 42-D			
I Want To Be Happy	1924	Columbia 222-D	Polly Put The Kettle On	1924	Columbia 93-D
Jesus Savior, Pilot Me	1920	Vocalion 14054B	Princeton Medley - Part 1	1922	Columbia A-3691
Juanita	1922	Okeh 4724/Silvertone 2124/Federal	Princeton Medley - Part 2	1922	Columbia A-3691
			Ring The Bells Of Heaven	1923	Columbia
			Rock Me In My Swanee Cradle	1922	Columbia A-3641
Just A Little Cottage In The Country Calling 'Come Back Home'	1917	Victor 18391	Rose Of Old Castile	1924	Okeh 40048
			Save Your Sorrow (For To-Morrow)	1925	Columbia 404-D
Ka-Lu-A	1922	Columbia A-3552	Scotch Songs Medley No. 1	1921	Okeh 4484
Kentucky Babe	1920	Okeh 4141/Emerson 10208 (1920)/Cleartone T 34	Scotch Songs Medley No. 2	1921	Okeh 4484
			Show Me The Way To Go Home	1925	
			Sing A Little Song	1924	Columbia 193-D
			Soldier's Farewell	1922	Okeh 4747
			Southern Medley Part 1: Way Down Yonder/Kentucky Babe	1923	Columbia A-3848
Last Night On The Back Porch	1923	Columbia A-3976			
Lindy	1920	Okeh 4247	Southern Medley Part 2: Old	1923	Columbia A-3848

Black Joe/O Susanna Star Spangled Banner	1923	Okeh 4834
Swanee River Rose	1924	Okeh 40126
Sweet Adeline	1922	Okeh 4748
Sweet And Low	1919	Okeh 4008/Phonola 4008 (1919)
Sweet Bells Of San Jose	1921	Vocalion 14167B
Swingin' Down The Lane	1923	Columbia A-3938
Ten Thousand Times	1922	Okeh 4651
Tenting On The Old Campground	1922	Okeh 4747
That Old Gang Of Mine	1923	Columbia A-3976
There Is Only One Pal After All	1921	Okeh 4314
There's A Lot Of Blue-Eyed Marys Down In Maryland	1919	Victor 18631
There's A Rainbow In The Sky	1923	Columbia A-3810
There's A Service Flag Flying At Our House	1917	Victor 18434
Tom, Dick and Harry and Jack (Hurry Back)	1918	Victor 18438
Tripping Along (With You And Me)	1924	Columbia 66-D
Tuck Me To Sleep In My Old Kentucky Home	1921	Vocalion 14236A
Underneath The Mellow Moon	1923	Columbia A-3938
Voice Of The Chimes, The	1920	Okeh 4209/Okeh 4972 (1923)
Wait'll You See My Gal	1924	Columbia 133-D
Wake Up Little Girl	1922	Columbia A-3606
Washington And Lee Swing	1923	Columbia A-3890
Way Down Home	1925	Columbia 281-D
Way Down Yonder In De Cornfield	1921	Okeh 4319
Weep No More	1921	Vocalion 14256A
West Virginia Hills/Hail, West Virginia, The	1923	Columbia A-3890
When Lights Are Low	1923	Columbia 68-D
When Mother Sings 'Sweet And Low'	1923	Columbia 42-D
When The Corn Is Waving	1922	Okeh 4748
When They Ring The Golden Bells For You And Me	1925	Okeh 40302
When You're Gone I Won't Forget	1920	Columbia A-3318/Vocalion 14142A (1920)/Emerson 10311 (1920)/Okeh 4969 (1923)
Where The Dreamy Wabash Flows	1924	Columbia 180-D
Winter Song	1922	Vocalion 14505A
Wond'ring	1920	Brunswick 2039
Yale Songs: Wake Freshmen/Brave Mother Yale	1922	Columbia A-3723
Yale Songs: Yale Boola/Whoop It Up/Eli Yale	1922	Columbia A-3723
You're A Million Miles From Nowhere	1920	Okeh 4091
Open Your Arms My Alabamy	1922	Columbia A-3763

Shannon Four & Lewis James

Do You Ever Think Of Me'	1921	Okeh 4319

Shannon Four (Alice Nielson & the)

Little Coon's Prayer, A	1924	Columbia 30007-D
Nebber Min', Mah Honey	1924	Columbia 30007-D

Shannon Four (Charles Harrison & the)

All Thro' The Night	1921	Brunswick 2219/Brunswick 5034

Shannon Four (Charles Hart & the)

Mandy	1919	Brunswick 2022
Oh! What A Pal Was Mary	1919	Brunswick 2022
Oh What A Pal Was Mary	1919	Brunswick 2022

Shannon Four (Elisabeth Spencer & the)

My Sweet Little Buttercup	1917	Victor 18427

Shannon Four (Harry C. Browne & the)

Marsa' Joe	1923	Columbia 53-D
Shinbone Alley	1923	Columbia 53-D

Shannon Four (Harry Macdonough & the)

Goodbye Mother Machree	1918	Victor 18488

Shannon Four (Helen Clark & the)

Any Old Time At All	1918	Victor 18487

Shannon Four ('Lasses White, Al Bernard, Vernon Dalhart & the)

'Lasses White Minstrels: Levee Scene	1923	Columbia A-3871
'Lasses White Minstrels: Plantation Scene	1923	Columbia A-3871
Old-Time Minstrels - Part 1	1923	Columbia A-6231
Old-Time Minstrels - Part 2	1923	Columbia A-6231

Shannon Four (Lewis James & the)

Dolly	1921	Okeh 4356
Just Keep A Thought For Me	1921	Okeh 4354
When The Autumn Leaves Begin To Fall	1921	

Shannon Four (Lucy Gates & the)

Sweet And Low	1922	Columbia A-3749

Shannon Four (Oscar Seagle with the)

Brown October Ale	1922	Columbia A-3768
I'se Gwine Back To Dixie	1922	Columbia A-3824

Shannon Four (Sam Ash & the)

Oh Me! Oh My!	1921	Okeh 4356

Shannon Four (with Charles Hart)

Last Long Mile, The	1918	Victor 18455
Little Bit Of Sunshine, A	1918	Victor 18453
What Are You Doing To Help The Boys'	1918	Victor 18467

Shannon Four (with Jane Nielson)

Beautiful Savior	1921	Okeh 4273
When The Cathedral Bells Ring At Twilight	1921	Okeh 4273

100 Years of Harmony: 1850 to 1950

Shannon Four (with Lewis James)
All Aboard For Home	1918	Victor 18441

Shannon Four with Sam Ash
Peggy O'Neill	1921	Okeh 4329

Shannon Four, H.C. Brown & the
Mars' Joe	1923	Columbia 53D

Shannon Four, Wilfred Glenn & the
When Good Fellows Get Together	1923	Vocalion 14505B

Shannon Quartet
All Aboard For Home Sweet Home	1918	Victor 18441
All Through The Night	1924	Victor 19413
America The Beautiful	1923	Victor 19242
Annie Lisle	1924	Victor 19466
Asleep In The Deep	1928	Columbia 1643-D
Beautiful Isle Of Somewhere	1929	Columbia 1703-D
Beyond The Smiling And The Weeping	1928	Columbia 1643-D
Blest Be The Tie That Binds	1928	Columbia 1438-D
Bonny Eloise	1924	Victor 19466
Break The News To Mother	1926	Columbia 739-D
Bring Me A Letter From My Home Town	1918	Victor 18481
By The Watermelon Vine (Lindy Lou)	1923	Victor 19142
Calling Me Back Home	1917	Victor 18391
Calm On The Listening Ear Of Night	1925	Victor 19794
Carry Me Back To Old Virginny	1925	Victor 19887/Columbia 745-D (1926)
Cheer For A.T.O.	1922	University Records 722
Cheer Up: Melody Land	1917	Victor 18400
Christ Arose!	1925	Victor 19883
Come Back To Erin	1924	Victor 19583
Cowboy Song - Whoopee Ti Yi Yo	1923	Victor 19059
Hail, Hail, The Gang's All Here	1917	Victor 18414/Edison DD 50460 (1917)/Edison Blue Amberol 3375 (1917)
Hark!, The Herald Angels Sing	1926	Columbia 740-D
Heidelberg (Stein Song)	1926	Columbia 730-D
Honey I Wants Ya Now	1922	Victor 19042
I May Be Gone A Long Long Time	1917	Victor 18333
In My Gondola	1926	Vocalion 15237/Brunswick 3041/Brunswick A 379
In The Evening By The Moonlight	1926	Columbia 747-D
In The Sweet Bye And Bye	1926	Columbia 748-D
I Wonder What's Become Of Sally'	1924	Victor 19415
Jesus, Lover Of My Soul	1928	Columbia 1438-D
Jingle Bells	1925	Victor 19791/Columbia 1576-D (1928)
Just Around The Corner	1926	
Just As The Sun Went Down	1926	Columbia 739-D
Katy Malone	1917	Edison DD 80436/Edison Blue Amberol 3425 (1917)
Keep Smiling At Trouble	1925	Victor 19588
Keep Your Skirts Down, Mary Anne	1926	Brunswick 3041/Brunswick A 379/Vocalion 15238
Kentucky Babe	1923	Victor 19013/Columbia 978-D (1927)
Killarney	1924	Victor 19583
Lead, Kindly Light	1926	Columbia 744-D
Let Me Call You Sweetheart	1926	Victor 19941
Levee Song: I've Been Workin' On The Railroad	1923	Victor 19059
Little Alabama Coon	1924	Victor 19343
Little Bit Of Heaven, A	1926	Columbia 746-D
Little Cotton Dolly (Plantation Lullaby)	1923	Victor 19013/Columbia 978-D (1927)
Louisiana Lou	1923	Victor 19142
Maggie Murphy's Home	1924	Victor 19336/Victor 20128 (1926)
Mandy	1919	Victor 18605A
Mandy Lee	1924	Victor 19508
Medley Of Stephen Foster's Songs	1926	Victor
Mighty Lak' A Rose	1917	Victor 18375
My Creole Sue	1924	Victor 19343
My Wild Irish Rose	1926	Columbia 730-D
Nearer, My God, To Thee	1926	Columbia 744-D
Nellie Dean	1926	Columbia 592-D
Now I Know	1919	Victor 18642
Oft In The Stilly Night	1924	Victor 19413
Oh! Susanna	1924	Victor 19290/Gramophone 19290
Oh, Come, All Ye Faithful	1926	Columbia 740-D
Old Familiar Faces	1924	Victor 19412
Old Oaken Bucket, The	1926	Columbia 745-D
One I Love, The	1924	Victor 19281
On The Banks Of The Wabash, Far Away	1928	Columbia 1358-D
Onward, Christian Soldiers	1926	Columbia 748-D
Phi Marching Song	1922	University Records 583

475

Song	Year	Label
Please Be Good To My Old Girl	1925	Victor 19605
Quilting Party, The	1925	Victor 19791/Columbia 1576-D (1928)
Rainbow	1924	Victor 20173
Red Wing	1924	Victor 20173
Riff Song, The	1926	Columbia 835-D/Columbia 1824-D
Rose Of The Old Castile	1920	Okeh/Odeon 312887 (1920)/Odeon O-3245 (1920)
Shy Phi Delt	1922	University Records 950
Sidewalks Of New York, The	1924	Victor 19336/Victor 20128 (1926)/Columbia 1358-D (1928)
Silent Night, Hallowed Night	1925	Victor 19794
Someone Is Waiting For You	1917	Edison DD 50477/Edison Blue Amberol 3427
Stars Of A Summer Night	1923	Victor 19242/Victor 20895 (1927)
Sweet Adeline	1926	Columbia 592-D
Sweet Elaine (with Ed Smalle)	1928	Victor 21324
Sweet Rosie O'Grady	1926	Victor 20072
Tales Of Hoffman Barcarolle (Oh, Night Of Love)	1917	Victor 18375
There's Another Angel Now In Old Killarney	1917	Edison
There's A Vacant Chair In Every Home Tonight	1918	Victor 18428
Wake Up, Virginia	1917	Edison BA 3380/Victor 18355 (1917)
When You're Gone, I Won't Forget You	1920	Okeh/Odeon 312886 (1920)/Odeon O-3244 (1920)
Where The River Shannon Flows	1926	Columbia 746-D
Where The Silvery Colorado Wends Its Way	1926	Columbia 747-D
Will You Love Me In December'	1926	Victor 20072

Shannon Quartet (and Lewis James)

Song	Year	Label
I Wonder How The Old Folks Are Back Home	1923	Victor 19266
There's Mother Always Waiting	1923	Victor 19266

Shannon Quartet (assisting Corinne Rider Kelsey)

Song	Year	Label
Massa's In The Cold, Cold Ground	1926	Columbia 119-M
My Old Kentucky Home	1926	Columbia 119-M

Shannon Quartet (Gladys Rice & the)

Song	Year	Label
Sweet Little Buttercup, or My Mother's Eyes	1917	Edison

Shannon Quartet (Helen Clark & the)

Song	Year	Label
Lullaby	1917	Edison DD 80836

Shannon Quartet (Lawrence Tibbett & the)

Song	Year	Label
Old Black Joe	1927	Victor 1265
Uncle Ned	1927	Victor 1265

Shannon Quartet (Oscar Seagle with the)

Song	Year	Label
Stein Song	1922	Columbia A-3768

Shannon Quartet (Wendell Hall with the)

Song	Year	Label
Gwine To Run All Night	1924	Victor 19290/Gramophone 19290

Shannon Quartette

Song	Year	Label
I May Be Gone For A Long, Long Time	1917	Edison DD 50451 (1917)/Edison Blue Amberol 3319 (1917)

Shamrock Trio

Song	Year	Label
Arabian Nights	1919	Okeh 1225

Shaw, Elliott and Male Trio

Song	Year	Label
Say It With Music	1922	Brunswick 2184

Shelby Gospel Four

Song	Year	Label
How About You	1938	Decca 7501
Lord Have Mercy	1938	Decca 7501
New Burying Ground	1938	Decca 7471
Take Your Burden To The Lord	1938	Decca 7471

Shell Creek Quartet

Song	Year	Label
Back Where The Old Home Stands	1928	Columbia 15355-D
My Boyhood Days	1928	Columbia 15355-D

Sheridan, James & Female Quartet

Song	Year	Label
Rosita	192'	Brunswick 2597
Until Tomorrow	192'	Brunswick 2597

Shilkret, Nat & the Victor Orchestra (with Johnny Marvin, Ed Smalle, Elliott Shaw)

Song	Year	Label
Are You Thinking Of Me Tonight'	1927	Victor 20899
Dawn Of Tomorrow	1927	Victor 20659

Silver Echo quartette

Song	Year	Label
Moses Smote The Water	1945	Regis 122

Silver Leaf Quartet

Song	Year	Label
I Am A Pilgrim	1928	Okeh 8594
I Can Tell The World	1928	Okeh 8594

Silver Leaf Quartet Of Florida

Song	Year	Label
Rock, Sword And Shield	1946	Gotham 142

Silver Leaf Quartet Of Norfolk

Song	Year	Label
Beautiful Lamp, The	1930	Okeh 8783
Daniel Saw The Stone	1931	Okeh 8914
God Has Promised To Provide For Me	1931	Okeh 8914
Hope I'll Join The Band	1928	Okeh 8628
I Am A Pilgrim	1938	Vocalion 4395
I'm Going Through With Jesus	1928	Okeh 8628
Jesus Is All In All	1931	Okeh 8874
Jesus Is Mine	1930	Okeh 8814

Lord I'm Troubled	1930	Okeh 8814
Lord Is Walking With Me	1931	Okeh 8874
Lover Of The Lord	1930	Okeh 8783
My Soul Is Witness For The Lord	1928	Okeh 8655
One Happy Time	1930	Okeh 8793
Our Father	1928	Okeh 8644
Savior Let Me Press Thy Hand	1930	Okeh 8793
Ship Is At The Landing	1929	Okeh 8777
Sittin' In A Circle With The Saints	1930	Okeh 8803
Sleep On Mother	1928	Brunswick 7056/Okeh 8644 (1928)
There Will Be Glory	1930	Okeh 8803
What's The Matter With The Church	1928	Okeh 8667
When Jesus Comes	1928	Okeh 8655
Will The Circle Be Unbroken'	1938	Vocalion 4395/Okeh 8777 (1929)
You Better Let That Liar Alone	1928	Okeh 8667

Silvertone Jubilee Quartet

Ain't Nobody's Fault But Mine	1938	Conqueror 9439/Vocalion 5429 (1940)
All Over This World	1938	Conqueror 9439/Vocalion 5429 (1940)
Bible Is Right, The	1940	Vocalion 5515
I Feel Like Shoutin'	1938	Vocalion 4501/Conqueror 9773 (1940)
I'm Done With Trouble	1928	Vocalion 4605
I'm Gonna Sit Down Beside King Jesus	1938	Conqueror 9283/Vocalion 4799 (1939)
In Beulah Land	1938	Vocalion 4507
In That Land	1928	Vocalion 4605
I've Been Down To Jordan	1938	Vocalion 4501/Conqueror 9773 (1940)
Oh Lord You Know	1938	Conqueror 9438
Oh My Lordy Lord	1938	Vocalion 4507
Old Rugged Cross, The	1938	Conqueror 9283/Vocalion 4799 (1939)
Old Ship Of Zion	1940	Vocalion 5515
Wait On The Rising Sun	1938	Conqueror 9438

Silvertone Quartet

Oh Lord You Know	1939	Vocalion 5234
Wait On The Rising Sun	1939	Vocalion 5234

Simmon's Show Boat Quartet, Hank

Melodies Of Long Ago (In The Gloaming, Sunbonnet Sue, Dear Old Girl, Star Of The Summer Night, Sweet Genevieve, Red Wing, Wail Till The Sun Shines Nellie)	1928	Edison DD 52441

Simms, Jean and Griffins

Love Like You, A	1954	

Sing-Copates

When The Mobile Boy Sings	1953	Decca 28830

Singing Bachelors

I Wouldn't Care	1923	Cameo 468

Singing Hoosier Quartet (Jolly Bakers)

Take In The Sun And Hang Out The Moon	1926	Challenge 235
You Know - I Know Everything's Made For Love	1926	Challenge 235

Singing Serenaders, Jim Europe's (Four Harmony Kings)

Roll, Jordan, Roll	1919	Perfect 11056

Singing Sophomores

All I Want To Do Is Be With You	1926	Columbia 682-D/Columbia 4102 (1926)
Barcelona	1926	Columbia 732-D
Breezin' Along With The Breeze	1926	Columbia 4235
Chloe	1928	Columbia 1257-D/Columbia 4866 (1927)
Clap Yo' Hands	1926	Columbia 838-D/Columbia 4619 (1926)
Collegiate Blues	1925	Columbia 530-D
Cornfield Medley	1927	
Georgianna	1926	Columbia 625-D/Columbia 4001
Girl Friend -Medley, The (The Blue Room, Mountain Greenery)	1927	Columbia 4564
Good News	1927	Columbia 1237-D
Hear In My Arms	1926	Columbia 4193
Hello, Aloha! How Are You'	1926	Columbia 652-D/Columbia 4025 (1926)
Hit The Deck Medley: Sometimes I'm Happy/Hallelujah	1927	Columbia 4504/Columbia 4620 (1927)
Hollywood Rose	1928	Columbia 1435-D
Honey Bunch	1926	Columbia 652-D/Columbia 4025
Honey Mine	1926	Columbia 625-D/Columbia 4001
I'd Love To Meet That Old Sweetheart Of Mine	1926	Columbia 732-D/Columbia 4193 (1926)
I'd Rather Be Alone In The South	1925	Columbia 485-D
I'm Coming Virginia	1927	Columbia 1178-D
In My Gondola	1926	Columbia 4235
Just A Memory	1927	Columbia 1178-D
Just Like A Butterfly (That's	1927	Columbia 1032-

Caught In The Rain)		D/Columbia 4690 (1927)
Lay Me Down To Sleep In Carolina	1926	Columbia 756-D/Columbia 4272
Mother	1927	Columbia 897-D
My Blue Heaven	1927	Columbia 1203-D
My Ohio Home	1928	Columbia 1257-D/Columbia 4866
One Darn Thing After Another - Medley (Birth Of The Blues - My Heart Stood Still)	1927	Columbia 4541
Peggy Ann - Medley	1927	Columbia 4504/Columbia 4541 (1927)
Russian Lullaby	1927	Columbia 985-D
Show Me The Way To Go Home	1925	Columbia 485-D
Sing	1927	Columbia 927-D/Columbia 4346 (1927)
Slow River	1927	Columbia 1032-D/Columbia 4619 (1927)
Somebody Else	1927	Columbia 985-D
Sweet And Low Down	1926	Columbia 568-D/Columbia 4081 (1926)
Sweet Marie	1927	Columbia 1057-D
Take In The Sun, Hang Out The Moon	1926	Columbia 838-D/Columbia 4346
Then I'll Be Happy	1925	Columbia 530-D
When The Red, Red, Robin Comes Bob, Bob, Bobbin' Along	1926	Columbia 682-D/Columbia 4081
Where's That Rainbow'	1927	Columbia 927-D/Columbia 4620
Who'	1926	Columbia 568-D/Columbia 4081 (1926)/Columbia 4102 (1926)
Why Do Ya Roll Those Eyes'	1926	Columbia 756-D/Columbia 4272
Ya Gotta Know How To Love	1926	Columbia 4168

Singing Sophomores (with Ipana Troubadours)

Good Night (I'll See You In The Morning)	1926	Columbia 609-D/Columbia 3962 (1926)
Sunny	1926	Columbia 595-D/Columbia 4100 (1926)

Singing Sophomores (with Vaughn De Leath)

When Honey Sings An Old-Time Song	1927	Columbia 1203-DE

Singing Sweethearts

My Little Mountain Home	1931	Champion 16441
Plodding Along	1931	Champion 16441
Wabash Moon	1931	Champion 16267

Singing Wanderers

Don't Drop It	1954	Decca 29230
Say Hey, Willie Mays	1954	Decca 29230
Three Roses	1955	Decca 29298
Wrong Party Again, The	1955	Decca 29298

Six Bips And A Bop

Choice Taste, A	1948	Manor 1159
Honeysuckle Rose	1948	Manor 1153
Lesson In Bopology, A	1948	Manor 1159
Loop-Plu-E-Du	1948	Manor 1153

Six Black Dominoes

You Took Advantage Of Me	1928	Columbia 1389-D

Six Hits & A Miss

Sheik Of Araby	1940	Okeh 5776
Bye Bye Blackbird	1942	Capitol 135
Carioca, The	1940	Vocalion 5571
Carry Me Back To Old Virginny	1940	Okeh 5776
Dance With A Dolly	1940	Vocalion 5571
Dry Bones	1940	Okeh 5689
I Never Took A Lesson In My Life	1940	Okeh 5689
It Had To Be You	1940	Vocalion 5532
I've Got The World On A String	1940	Okeh 5876
Karlstad Ball	1940	Okeh 5926
Ramona	1940	Okeh 5926
Relax	1940	Vocalion 5532
Sheik Of Araby	1940	Okeh 5776
Two Dreams Met	1940	Okeh 5876
Two On A Bike	1942	Capitol 135
Would You Rather Be A Colonel With An Eagle On Your Shoulder Or A Private With A Chicken On Your Knee'	1943	Capitol 127

Six Hits & A Miss (with Bing Crosby)

On The Atchison, Topeka, And The Santa Fe	1945	Decca 18690

Six Hits & A Miss (with Gordon Jenkins)

You'd Be So Nice To Come Home To	1942	Capitol 127

Sizzlers

Baby	1932	
Campin' On Your Doorstep	1933	Bluebird B-5070/Electradisk 1993/Sunrise S-3152
Farmer's Daughter's Wedding Day, The	1933	Bluebird B-5070/Electradisk 1993/Sunrise S-3152
Forty-Second Street	1933	Bluebird 1841/Bluebird B-5017/Electradisk 1949/Sunrise S-3101

Title	Year	Label
Gotta Go Places And Do Things	1933	Bluebird B-5071/Electradisk 1994
Here It Is Monday And I've Still Got A Dollar	1932	
I Dreamed		radio transcription on 'Transcriptions, Dubs & Tests' CD
It Don't Mean A Thing (If It Ain't Got That Swing)	1932	Victor
I've Got My Fingers Crossed ('Til You Come Home)	1933	Bluebird B-5071/Electradisk 1994
Scat Song, The	1932	
Shuffle Off To Buffalo	1933	Bluebird 1841/Bluebird B-5017/Electradisk 1949/Sunrise S-3101

Skylarks (Starlings)

Title	Year	Label
Glory Of Love, The	1951	Decca 48241
You And I	1951	Decca 48241

Skyscrapers

Title	Year	Label
Certain Other Someone	1947	Miracle 119
Don't Cry	1956	Mercury 70795
I Thought You'd Care	1956	Mercury 70795
Last Call	1947	Miracle 119

Skyscrapers, Browley Guy & the

Title	Year	Label
Blue Train	1952	States 107
Knock Me A Zombie	1949	Miracle 137
That Gal Of Mine	1949	Miracle 137
Watermelon Man	1954	Checker 779
You Ain't Gonna Worry Me	1952	States 107
You Look Good To Me	1954	Checker 779

Skyscrapers, Ted Lawrence & the

Title	Year	Label
Ska-Doodle	1954	Rama 16

Sleepy Hollow Quartet, Dick Powell & the

Title	Year	Label
I Wonder How The Old Folks Are At Home	1940	Decca 3662
Life's Railway To Heaven	1940	Decca 3784
When They Ring The Golden Bells	1940	Decca 3784
Where The Morning Glories Twine Around The Door	1940	Decca 3662

Smeck's Trio, Roy

Title	Year	Label
Can Love Like Ours Be Wrong	1932	Conqueror 8056
I'm Still Without A Sweetheart (With Summer Coming)	1932	Conqueror 8057
In A Shanty In Old Shanty Town	1932	Conqueror 8054
Let Me Dream	1932	Conqueror 8055
Lullaby Of The Leaves	1932	Conqueror 8056
Masquerade	1932	Conqueror 8055
My Mom	1932	Conqueror 8058
That Silver Haired Daddy Of Mine	1932	Conqueror 8058
Voice In The Old Village Choir, The	1932	Conqueror 8057
While We Danced At The Mardi Gras	1932	Conqueror 8054

Smith Quartet, Ben

Title	Year	Label
Be The Candle Glow	1951	Coleman 110
Big Fat Lips	1953	Rama 17
Blues Got Me Walking, Talking To Myself	1950	Abbey 3012
Cadillac Song, The	1953	Rama 17
Don't Worry Me No More	1950	Abbey 3008
I Ain't Fattenin' Frogs For Snakes	1950	Abbey 3008
Leave That Dog Alone	1950	Columbia 30208
She Knows How The Drops Will Fall	1950	Columbia 30214
Where Did She Go'	1950	Columbia 30208
You Are Closer To My Heart	1950	Abbey 3012
You've Got Me Crying My Heart Out	1950	Columbia 30214

Smith Quartet, Homer

Title	Year	Label
Go Down With Moses	1927	Paramount 12432
I Want Jesus To Talk To Me	1927	Paramount 12432

Smith, Hollis & his Melodians

Title	Year	Label
I Ain't Got Nobody	1932	Victor 22930
Somebody Stole My Gal	1932	
Some Of These Days	1932	Victor 22930
St. Louis Blues Somebody Stole My Gal	1932	

Smith's Sacred Singers

Title	Year	Label
Are You Washed In The Blood Of The Lamb'	1929	Columbia 15430-D
Beautiful Life, A	1927	Columbia 15671-D
Beyond The Stars Is Home	1934	Bluebird 5611
Calvary	1934	Bluebird 5670
Child At Mother's Knee, A	1927	Columbia 15671-D
Church In The Wildwood, The	1930	Columbia 15551-D
City Of Gold	1927	Columbia 15195-D
Climbing Up The Golden Stairs	1927	Columbia 15195-D
Deliverance Will Come	1928	Columbia 15329-D
Drifting Down	1928	Columbia 15257-D
Eastern Gate, The	1926	Columbia 15110-D
Echoes From The Glory Shore	1929	Columbia 15579-D
Endless Joy Is Waiting Over There	1929	Columbia 15471-D
From The Cross To The Crown	1934	Bluebird 5943
Gathering Home	1930	Columbia 15708-D
God's Children Are Gathering Home	1934	Bluebird 5606
Good Morning In Glory	1935	Bluebird 6137
Gospel Waves	1927	Columbia 15208-D
Have Thine Own Way Lord	1934	Bluebird 5883
He Bore It All	1927	Columbia 15208-D
He Holds Me By The Hand	1929	Columbia 15579-D
He Is Coming Back	1927	Columbia 15173-D

Title	Year	Label
He Is Everything To Me	1935	Bluebird 6092
He Lives On High	1927	Columbia
He Will Set Your Fields On Fire	1927	Columbia 15144-D
His Picture Is In My Heart	1929	Columbia 15494D
Hold On To God's Unchanging Hands	1928	Columbia 15308-D/Bluebird 5943 (1934)
Home On The Banks Of The River	1934	Bluebird 5671
Home Over There, The	1928	Columbia 15329-D
How Firm A Foundation	1930	Columbia 15619-D
I Am Going That Way	1927	Columbia 15389-D
I'd Rather Be An Old Time Christian	1934	Bluebird 5614
If I'm Faithful To My Lord	1926	Columbia 15128-D
I Have Found The Way	1929	Columbia 15739-D
I'll Be Singing Round The Throne Someday	1935	Bluebird 6206
I'll Go	1927	Columbia
I'm Only On A Visit Here	1926	Columbia
In A Little While	1930	Columbia 15683D
In Our Happy Home Sweet Home	1935	Bluebird 6121
In The Happy Land Over Yonder	1934	Bluebird 5614
In The Happy Long Ago	1927	Columbia
Is It Well With Your Soul'	1930	Columbia 15708-D
It Won't Be Long	1930	Columbia 15683D
I Want To Go To Heaven	1927	Columbia 15230-D
I Will Sing Of My Redeemer	1927	Columbia 15144-D
Jesus Died For Me	1929	Columbia 15430-D
Jesus Is All The World To Me	1934	Bluebird 5972
Jesus Is Calling	1934	Bluebird 5883
Jesus, Lover Of My Soul	1930	Columbia 15593D
Jesus Prayed	1927	Columbia 15159-D/Vocalion 2921 (1935)
Keep On Climbing	1927	Columbia 15351-D
Keep The Sunlight In Your Sky	1929	Columbia 15772-D
Labor On	1929	Columbia 15517-D
Let The Lower Lights Be Burning	1928	Columbia 15257-D/Bluebird 5611 (1934)
Life Boat	1927	Columbia
Life's Railway To Heaven	1927	Columbia 15159-D/Vocalion 2921 (1935)
Lord I'm Coming Home	1935	Vocalion 2941/Columbia 15371
Love Lifted Me	1930	Columbia 15619-D
Meet Me There	1929	Columbia 15401-D
My Latest Sun Is Sinking Fast	1928	Columbia 15281-D
My Redeemer Lives	1930	Columbia 15639-D
My Saviour's Train	1929	Columbia 15749-D
No Stranger Yonder	1934	Bluebird 5809
Old Time Religion For Me	1930	Columbia 15639-D
Over In The Glory Land	1927	Columbia
Pictures From Life's Other Side	1926	Columbia 15090-D/Bluebird 5606 (1934)/Vocalion 2949 (1935)
Prepare To Meet Thy God	1928	Columbia 15281-D
Prodigal's Return, The	1926	Columbia 15137-D
Saved By Grace	1934	Bluebird 5854
Shouting On The Hills	1926	Columbia 15110-D
Since Jesus Came Into My Heart	1934	Bluebird 5721
Sing All Your Troubles Away	1930	Columbia 15659-D
Smile Your Troubles Away	1935	Bluebird 6092
Stand Up For Jesus	1934	Bluebird 5809
Tell Mother I'll Be There	1934	Bluebird 5671
There Is A Fountain Filled With Blood	1930	Columbia 15551-D
Trace The Footsteps Of Jesus	1927	Columbia 15173-D/Bluebird 6183 (1935)
Unclouded Day, The	1928	Columbia 15351-D
Vain World Adieu	1934	Bluebird 5670
Waiting On The Golden Shore	1928	Columbia 15308-D
Walking Along With Me	1927	Columbia
Wayside Wells	1930	Columbia 15659-D
We'll Be Happy Bye And Bye	1935	Bluebird 6121
We'll Understand It Better By And By	1934	Bluebird 5750
We'll Work Till Jesus Comes	1934	Bluebird 5854
We're Going Down The Valley One By One	1926	Columbia 15128-D
We're Living For Jesus	1935	Bluebird 6137
What A Gathering That Will Be	1929	Columbia 15471-D
What A Happy Time	1935	Bluebird 6183
When Jesus Comes	1935	Vocalion 2941/Columbia 15371-D
When Our Lord Shall Come Again	1929	Columbia 15772-D
When Our Saviour Comes Again	1935	Bluebird 6273/Columbia 15494D
When The Happy Morning Breaks	1928	Columbia 15389-D
When They Ring The Golden Bells	1934	Bluebird 5972
Where We'll Never Grow Old	1926	Columbia 15090-D/Bluebird 5721 (1934)/Vocalion 2949 (1935)
Will You Meet Me Up There'	1935	Bluebird 6206
Wonderful City	1935	Bluebird 6273
Work, For The Night Is Coming	1930	Columbia 15593D
Working For The Crown	1929	Columbia 15401-D
You Can't Do Wrong And Get By	1934	Bluebird 5750Columbia 15517-D

Smith's Sacred Singers, Frank
We Shall Rise	1927	Columbia 15230-D

Smoothies
Ain't She Sweet	1939	Bluebird B-10310
Alabamy Bound	1939	Bluebird 10279
Beautiful Buxom Barmaid	1939	Bluebird 10542
Breezin' Along With The Breeze	1939	Bluebird B-10295
Chew-Chew-Chew (Chew Your Bubble Gum)	1939	Bluebird B-10295
Down By The Ohio (O, My, O)	1940	Bluebird 10710
Friendship	1940	Bluebird 10616
Goody Goodbye	1939	Bluebird B-10501
If I Had My Way	1939	Bluebird 10228
I Love To Watch The Moonlight	1940	Bluebird 10742
Meet The Sun Half Way	1940	Bluebird 10742
No Mama No	1939	Bluebird B-10501
Pretty Baby	1940	Bluebird 10640
Say Si Si (Para Vigo Me Voy)	1940	Bluebird 10616
Sh! The Baby's Asleep	1940	Bluebird 10710
Show You Linen, Miss Richardson	1939	Bluebird 10228
Starlit Hour, The	1939	Bluebird 10542
Steamboat Bill	1939	Bluebird B-10310
You're An Old Smoothie	1939	Bluebird 10279
Blue Skies	1946	Apollo 1015
Confucius Say	1939	Victor 26452
Girl With The Pigtails In Her Hair, The	1939	Victor 26385
Give A Little Whistle	1940	Victor 26466
Green Eyes	1941	Victor 27501
Happy Birthday To Love	1939	Victor 26403
I'm Sorry For Myself	1939	Victor 26272
I Must Have One More Kiss Kiss Kiss (Before We Say Goodnight)	1939	Victor 26347
Let's Do It (Let's Fall In Love)	1939	Victor 26300
Little Red Fox, The (N'ya, N'ya Ya Can't Catch Me)	1939	Victor 26416
Love For Sale	1939	Victor 26278/Victor 27285 (1939)
Love Grows On The White Oak Tree	1939	Victor 26349
Love Never Went To College	1939	Victor 26368
Ma-Ma-Maria	1941	Victor 27612
Nickel Serenade, The (The Coin Machine Song)	1941	Victor 27571
Ooh! What You Said	1939	Victor 26449
Playmates	1940	Victor 26469
Roll Me Over	1946	Apollo 1015
Rose O'Day (The Filla-Ga-Dusha Song)	1941	Victor 27620
Shepherd Serenade	1941	Victor 27527
Speak Your Heart	1941	Victor 27285
Three Little Fishies	1939	Victor 26203/Electrola EG 6929

Smoothies (Babs, Charlie and Little)
Easy Does It	1940	Bluebird 10640

Soft Notes
Can Anyone Explain	1950	Mercury 5464

Song Fellows
It Don't Mean A Thing	1932	Banner 32594/Melotone M 12508
Me Minus You	1932	Conqueror 8045
Sentimental Gentleman From Georgia	1932	Banner 32594
So Ashamed	1932	Conqueror 8045/Melotone M 12508

Song Spinners
Bring Me A Letter From My Old Home Town	1947	Decca 24348
Christmas	1951	Decca 27331
Comin' In On A Wing And A Prayer	1943	Brunswick 03469/Decca 18553
Don't Forget To Write	1947	Decca 24348
Faded Letter	1947	Decca 24349
First Letter	1947	Decca 24350
God Bless My Darling, He's Somewhere	1942	Decca 4430B
Have I Stayed Away Too Long'	1942	Decca 4430A
I Am Sending Criss Cross Kisses	1947	Decca 24351
Johnny Zero	1943	Brunswick 03469/Decca 18553
Jumpin' Jimmy Christmas	1951	Decca 27331
Letter Edged In Black	1947	Decca 24350
Little Rosewood Casket	1947	Decca 24349
Mister Five By Five	1944	Musicraft 15009
Praise The Lord And Pass The Ammunition	194'	Musicraft 15008
Send Me A Line	1947	Decca 24351
Stalin Wasn't Stallin'	1943	Decca 18554
(Watch Out) Love Is Goin' To Be Rationed	1943	Decca 18554
When The Lights Go On Again	1944	Musicraft 15009
White Christmas	194'	Musicraft 15008

Song Spinners (Bob Eberly & the)
Don't Cry, Little Girl, Don't Cry	1947	Decca 23945
I Wish I Could Say The Same	1947	Decca 23945

Song Spinners (Dick Haymes with the)
Nature Boy	1948	Decca 03905
You Can't Be True, Dear	1948	Decca 03905

Song Spinners (with Bing Crosby)
Mighty Lak' A Rose	1945	Brunswick 03939/Decca 23482/Decca FM 5428/Decca Y 5989

Sweetest Story Ever Told, The	1945	Brunswick 03939/Decca 23482/Decca FM 5428/Decca Y 5989
Song Spinners, Bryer, Dick & the		
Over There	194'	Musicraft 15011
You'd Be So Nice To Come Home	194'	Musicraft 15011
Songcopators		
I'm Hummin', I'm Whistlin', I'm Singin'	1934	Bluebird B-5552
In The Vine Covered Church 'Way Back Home	1933	Victor 23842
Jungle Fever	1934	Bluebird B-5547
Keep A Light In Your Window Tonight	1933	Bluebird 5379
Let Me Call You Mine	1934	Bluebird B-5549
Old White's Whiskers	1934	Bluebird B-5583
Rollin' Home	1934	Bluebird B-5548
Runnin' Wild	1934	Bluebird B-5533
Shine	1934	Bluebird B-5533
Ten Hours A Day -Six Days A Week	1933	Victor 23842
When It's Moonlight Down In Lover's Lane	1933	Bluebird 5379/Sunrise S-3460
Songfellows		
I'm So Ashamed	1932	Banner 32566
Me Minus You	1932	Banner 32566
Songmasters, Buddy Hawkins & the		
I'm Just A Dreamer	1948	Commodore 7556
Song-O-Pators		
Oh! Mo'Nah! (with the Aaron Sisters)	1932	Columbia 2689-D
Old Man Of The Mountain, The	1932	Columbia 2689-D
St. Louis Blues (with the Aaron Sisters)	1932	Columbia 2699-D
Songsmiths		
Dancing With You	1950	Rondo R 233
Last Round-Up, The	1933	Brunswick 6651/Brunswick A 9490
Old Injun Trail In The Valley	1950	Rondo R 233
Who's Afraid Of The Big Bad Wolf	1933	Brunswick 6651/Brunswick A 9490
Songsmiths (John Brownlee assisted by the)		
It's A Long, Long Way To Tipperary	1941	Decca 3770
Oh! Susanna	1941	Decca 3769
(Pack Up Your Troubles In Your Old Kit Bag And) Smile Smile Smile	1941	Decca 3770
There's A Long, Long Train Awinding	1941	Decca 3769
Sophomores		
After All	1956	Decca 29669
Big Joke	1956	Decca 29669
South Carolina Quartet		
Church Is Rolling On, The	1928	QRS
I Heard My Mother Call My Name	1929	Paramount 12834
Paul And Silas	1929	Paramount 12834
Southern Alabama Chorus		
Little David, Play Yo' Harp	1926	Champion 15104
Wheel In A Wheel (Ezekiel Saw Da Wheel)	1926	Champion 15104
Southern Blues Singers		
Light House Blues	1929	Gennett 6828
Southern Fall Coloured Quartet		
Ukulele Lady	1925	Victor 19690
Southern Four, The		
Shout All Over God's Heaven/Standin' In The Need O' Prayer	1921	Edison 51364
Swing Low, Sweet Chariot	1921	Edison 51364
Southern Jubilee Singers		
Couldn't Hear Nobody Pray	1927	Black Patti 8036/Paramount 12711 (1928)
Listen To The Lambs	1927	Paramount 12711 (1928)
Southern Male Quartet (1)		
Songs Of The Past-Medley	1923	Banner 2102
Southern Male Quartet (2)		
Carry Me Back To Old Virginny	1940	Brunswick 8501
De Glory Road- Part 1	1927	Brunswick 8475/Brunswick 8475 (1939)
De Glory Road- Part 2	1927	Brunswick 8475/Brunswick 8475 (1939)
Go Down Moses	1939	Brunswick 8479
I'm In His Care	1939	Brunswick 8487
Jesus Is A Rock In A Weary Land	1939	Brunswick 8479
Love's Old Sweet Song	1940	Brunswick 8495
Old Folks At Home/Swanee River	1940	Brunswick 8501
Silver Threads Among The Gold	1940	Brunswick 8495
Were You There	1939	Brunswick 8487
Southern Melody Artists		
I'll Be With You When The Roses Bloom Again	1927	Okeh 40865
My Carolina Home	1927	Okeh 40865
Southern Negro Quartet		
I'm Wild About Moonshine	1921	Columbia A-3444
Southern Negro Quartet (Southern Quartette)		
I Ain't Givin' Nothin' Away	1921	Columbia A-3450

Southern Negro Quartette
- Anticipatin' Blues — 1921 — Columbia A-3444
- Daddy, Won't You Please Come Home' — 1921 — Columbia
- Nightmare Blues — 1921 — Columbia

Southern Plantation Singers
- De's Bones Gwine Rise Again — 1928 — Vocalion 1219
- Don't You Want That Stone — 1928 — Vocalion 1250
- Get On Board Little Children — 1928 — Vocalion 1414
- My Lord Delivered Daniel — 1928 — Vocalion 1219
- This Train Is Bound For Glory — 1928 — Vocalion 1250
- Throw Out The Lifeline — 1928 — Vocalion 1414

Southern Quartet
- Charleston Charlie — 1924 — Columbia
- Gonna Raise Ruckus Tonight — 1924 — Columbia 14048-D
- Hampton Road Blues — 1924 — Columbia 14038-D/Diva 6029-G/Velvet Tone 7055-V
- Hard Trials And Great Tribulations — 1924 — Columbia 14035-D
- Hey Hey And Hee Hee (I'm Charleston Crazy) — 1924 — Columbia 14043-D
- I'm Going To Build Right On That Shore — 1924 — Columbia
- Jesus Christ I Want To Find — 1924 — Columbia
- Listen To The Lambs — 1927 — Black Patti 8036
- Lullaby Blues — 1924 — Columbia 14038-D/Diva 6029-G/Velvet Tone 7055-V
- Moanin' Groanin' Blues — 1924 — Columbia 14043-D
- My Lord's Gonna Move This Wicked Race — 1924 — Columbia 14035-D
- My Man Rocks Me (With One Steady Roll) — 1924 — Columbia 14048-D
- Oh Lord Have Mercy — 1927 — Columbia 14245-D
- Sweet Mama, Papa's Gettin' Mad — 1921 — Columbia A-3450

Southern Quartette
- He Took It Away From Me — 1921 — Columbia A-3489
- I'll Be Good But I'll Be Lonesome — 1921 — Columbia A-3489

Southern Railroad Quartet
- God Is Love — 1928 — Victor 40002
- Life's Railway To Heaven — 1928 — Victor 40002

Southern Sanctified Singers
- Soon We'll Gather At The River — 1929 — Brunswick 7074
- Where He Leads Me I Will Follow — 1929 — Brunswick 7074

Southern Serenaders
- Alone At Last — 1925 — Harmony 5

Southern Sons
- Praise The Lord And Pass The Ammunition — 1942 — Bluebird 30-0806

Southern University Quartet
- All Over This World — 1935 — Bluebird 5846
- Hold The Wind — 1935 — Bluebird 5846
- I'm Tired Of Living In The Country — 1935 — Bluebird 5932
- Let The Church Roll On — 1935 — Bluebird 6142
- Little David Play Your Harp — 1935 — Bluebird 5932

Southern Wonders Jubilee Quartet
- I Will Ever Stand — 1927 — Columbia 14245-D

Southernaires
- Abide With Me — 1941 — Decca 3921A
- Beautiful Isle Of Somewhere — 1941 — Decca 3919A
- Hang Your Hat In Harlem — 1937 — Movie transcription, from
- Holy Ghost With Light Divine — 1941 — Decca 3918B
- Jesus, Saviour, Pilot Me — 1941 — Decca 3920B
- Lord's Prayer, The — 1941 — Decca 3918A
- Old Rugged Cross, The — 1941 — Decca 3922A
- Rock Of Ages — 1941 — Decca 3920A
- Softly And Tenderly — 1941 — Decca 3922B
- Sweet Hour Of Prayer — 1941 — Decca 3919B
- Yield Not To Temptation — 1941 — Decca 3921B

Southernaires Male Quartet
- Couldn't Hear Nobody Pray — 1939 — Decca 2856A
- Ezekiel Saw De Wheel — 1939 — Decca 2858A
- Go Down Moses — 1939 — Decca 2855B
- Gonna Shout All Over God's Heaven — 1939 — Decca 2859A
- Joshua Fit De Battle Of Jericho — 1939 — Decca 2858B
- Little David, Play On Your Harp — 1939 — Decca 2857A
- Nobody Knows De Trouble I've Seen — 1939 — Decca 2859B
- Roll, Jordan, Roll — 1939 — Decca 2857B
- Steal Away To Jesus — 1939 — Decca 2856B
- Swing Low, Sweet Chariot — 1939 — Decca 2855A

Southernaires Quartette
- Live Humble — 1931 — Brunswick Test
- Medley Of Negro Shout Songs — 1931 — Brunswick Test

Southland Jubilee Singers
- Creep Along, Moses — 1928 — Champion 15488
- Do You Call That Religion' — 1928 — Champion 15508
- Ezekiel Saw De Wheel — 1928 — Champion 15508
- Great Camp Meeting — 1921 — Okeh 4271
- Little David Play On Your Harp — 1921 — Okeh 4271
- My Lord's Gonna Move This Wicked Race — 1924 — Okeh 8170
- My Lord's Writing All The Time — 1921 — Okeh 4390
- Shout All Over God's Heaven — 1921 — Okeh 4390
- South Bound Passenger — 1928 — Champion 15543
- This Old World Can't Stand Much Longer — 1928 — Champion 15488
- We're Walking In The Light — 1921 — Okeh
- Who Stole De Lock Off De Henhouse Door — 1928 — Champion 15543

Southland Jubilee Singers (Norfolk Jubilee Quartet)
Get On Board, Little Children, Get On Board	1925	Herwin 92009

Southland Ladies Quartet
Don't Put Off Salvation Too Long	1929	Challenge 426
My Loved Ones Are Waiting For Me	1929	Challenge 426

Southland Quartet
Waiting For The Boatman	1938	Decca 5570
When Spring Roses Are Blooming	1938	Decca 5570
You Can Hear Those Darkies Singing	1927	Challenge 348/Challenge 419 (1927)

Sparkling Four Quartet
Hold The Wind	1929	Okeh 8741
Keep On To Galilee	1929	
Shepherd, Feed My Sheep	1929	
They Won't Believe In Me	1929	Okeh 8741

Sparrows, All Sears & the
Brown Boy	1950	Coral 65023
125th Street, New York	1950	Coral 65029
Shake Hands	1950	Coral 65023
Tan Skin Lad	1950	Coral 65029

Spartanburg Famous Four
John Wrote The Revelations	1938	Decca 7543
Lily Of The Valley	1938	Decca 7543

Spartanburg Four
Anybody In Heaven That You Know'	1938	Decca 7478
Can You Make It To The City'	1937	Decca 7467
Do You Call That Religion'	1937	Decca 7467
Go Where I Send Thee	1937	Decca 7468
Graveyard Is Waiting On Poor Me	1937	Decca 7468
How Can You Talk About Other People	1940	Decca 7821
I Know My Time Ain't Long	1938	Decca 7517
John, Don't You Write No More	1938	Decca 7478
Satan, Your Kingdom Must Come Down	1940	Decca 7821
When That First Trumpet Sounds	1938	Decca 7517

Spencer Trio
Alpine Specialty	1897	Columbia 7708/Columbia 648 (1902)
Camp Meeting Jubilee	1898	Columbia 7707 (brown2mincyl)
In Front Of The Old Cabin Door	1902	Columbia 652
Mocking Bird (with bird imitations), The	1897	Columbia 7705/Columbia 653 (1902)
Our Sunny Southern Home	1898	Columbia 7712 (brown2mincyl)

Spencer Trio, Buddy
Rockin' Alone	1932	Perfect 12863/Lucky 60222
When The Mellow Moon Is Shining	1932	Perfect 12863/Lucky 60222

Spencer, Elizabeth & the Peerless Quartet
Any Girl Looks Good In The Summer Time	1911	Edison 4mincyl 775

Spencer, Len & Company
Mamma's Boy	1910	Edison 4mincyl 529/Kalamazoo 6820

Spencer, Len & the Edison Male Quartet
South Carolina Minstrels	1905	Edison 9024 (2mincyl)

Spencer, Len & the Peerless Quartet
Rescued From The Flames		Edison 4mincyl 506

Spencer, Len, Billy Murray & the Edison Male Quartet
Louisiana Minstrels	1904	Edison 8920 (2mincyl)

Spencer, Len, Harry Macdonough, Billy Murray & the Edison Male Quartet
Tennessee Minstrels	1904	Edison 8951 (2mincyl)

Spindale Quartet
Face To Face	1929	Columbia 15488-D
God Will Take Care Of You	1929	Columbia 15514-D
Lift Him Up	1929	Columbia 15488-D
Sweet Peace, The Gift Of God's Love	1929	Columbia 15514-D

Spirits Of Rhythm
As Long As I Live	1934	Decca 302
Dr. Watson And Mr. Holmes	1934	Decca 160B
From Monday On	1934	Decca 186
It's All Forgotten Now	1934	Decca 243
I've Got The World On A String	1934	Decca 302
Junk Man	1934	Decca 160A
Tutti Frutti	1943	
Way Down Yonder In New Orleans	1934	Decca 186
What's The Use Of Getting Used To You	1934	Decca 243

Spiritual Singers
How Beautiful	1934	Bluebird 5396

Spiritualaires
Every Day Will Be Sunday	1953	Capitol 2714
He Will Surely Make It Right	1954	Capitol 2837
Meet You By The River	1953	Capitol 2714
Seek Ye The Lord	1954	Capitol 2837

St. Mark's Chanters
'Buked And Scorned	1926	Columbia 14198-D
Live Humble	1926	Columbia 14149-D
My Lord's Gonna Move This Wicked Race	1926	Columbia 14149-D

So High	1926	Columbia 14198-D

Stafford Sisters, Louis Prima & the (with Louis Prima & his New Orleans Gang)

Let's Get Together And Swing	1936	Brunswick 7740

Stamps All Star Quartet, Frank

Dreaming Alone In The Twilight	1932	Bluebird 5785
Dreams Of The Past	1932	Bluebird 5785
Great Redeemer, The	1932	Victor 23753
His Love Leads Home	1929	Victor 40301
Homeward Bound	1932	Victor 23854
I Ain't Gonna Let Satan Turn Me Around	1932	Victor 23729
I'm Finding Glory	1932	Victor 23854
I'm Only Here On Vacation	1929	Victor 40228
I'm On The Right Road Now	1929	Victor 40245
In The Master's Presence	1929	Victor 40279
I Want To Hear Him Call My Name	1932	Victor 23753
Living For Jesus	1929	Victor 40245
Oh Declare His Glory	1929	Victor 40279
Reapers Be True	1929	Victor 40228
Singing In My Soul	1929	Victor 40320
Skies Will Be Blue	1932	Victor 23702
There's Springtime In My Soul	1932	Victor 23702
Troubles All Will End	1932	Victor 23660
With Joy We Sing	1929	Victor 40301
Wonderful Love Divine	1932	Victor 23729
Working For The Master	1929	Victor 40320

Stamps Quartet

Beautiful Prayer, A	1938	Columbia 20337/Vocalion 4176 (1938)/Conqueror 9105 (1938)Conqueror 9592 (1940)
Because I Love Him	1928	Victor 40078
City Of Gold	1929	Brunswick 418
Cling To The Cross	1929	Brunswick 408
Come To The Savior	1928	Victor 40062
Coming	1928	Columbia 15347-D
Delighting In The Name Of God	1928	Columbia 15434-D
Don't Forget To Pray	1929	Okeh 45359
Do Your Best	1928	Victor 40122
Farther Along	1938	Columbia 20337/Vocalion 4236 (1938)
Follow Jesus	1930	Brunswick 583
Give The World A Smile	1927	Bluebird 6038/Vocalion 5414 (1940)
Glad Bells, The	1929	Brunswick 408
Go On, We'll Soon Be There	1928	Columbia 15347-D
Heavenly Chorus, The	1928	Victor 40029
He Keeps My Soul	1929	Brunswick 447
He's Calling All	1929	Columbia 15655-D
He's Calling You	1929	Columbia 15560-D
Holy Be Thy Name	1938	Bluebird 6038/Conqueror 9105 (1938)/Conqueror 9592 (1940)
I Am O'ershadowed By Love	1929	Columbia 15605-D
I'll Be Happy	1928	Victor 40029
I'm Going Over There	1927	Columbia 15242-D
I'm In The Way	1929	Brunswick 447
In Christ Our Lord	1930	Brunswick 500
In The City Where There Is No Night	1927	Columbia 15242-D
It Will Not Be Long	1929	Okeh 45385
I Want To Do My Best	1929	Columbia 15502-D
I Worship The Lord	1929	Columbia 15502-D
Jesus Is Coming, It May Be Soon	1928	Victor 40078
Jesus Taught Me To Smile	1930	Brunswick 508
Just A Little Talk With Jesus	1938	Vocalion 4329/Conqueror 9668 (1940)
Launch Out To The Sea Of The Gods	1930	Brunswick 500
Like The Rainbow	1928	Victor 40122
Longer I Know Him, The	1930	Brunswick 555
Lord Is With Me, The	1938	Vocalion 4329/Conqueror 9668 (1940)
Love Leads The Way	1927	Bluebird 6038
My Friend	1930	Brunswick 569
Old Time Religion For Me	1930	Brunswick 569
On The Cross	1929	Okeh 45385
Singing While Ages Roll	1928	Bluebird 5274
There's A Little Pine Log Cabin	1940	Vocalion 5414
Thou Art My Strength	1929	Brunswick 418
Walking At My Side	1930	Brunswick 555
Way To Glory Land, The	1929	Okeh 45359
We Shall Reach Home	1928	Victor 40062
We Will March Along	1930	Brunswick 583
Who'	1938	Vocalion 4160
Won't We Be Happy'	1930	Brunswick 508
Working For The King Of Kings	1928	Columbia 15434-D
You Shall Reap What You Sow	1929	Columbia 15560-D

Stamps Quartet, Frank

Endless Joy Is Coming	1932	Victor 23572
It Won't Be Long	1932	Victor 23519
I Will Never Give Up	1930	Bluebird 5487
I Will Walk With My Savior	1930	Bluebird 5487
Lord Let Me Serve	1930	Bluebird 5544
Oh Such Wondrous Love	1932	Victor 23519
Singin' Of Wonderful Love	1930	Bluebird 5487
Song Of Jesus' Love Bring Heaven Down, A	1932	Victor 23572

Stamps Quartet, Original
He Will Be With Me	1929	Brunswick 375
Little While Then Glory, A	1929	Brunswick 375

Standard Quartette
Every Day'll Be Sunday Bye And Bye	1894	Co Cylinder unnumbered
Keep Movin'	1894	Co Cylinder unnumbered

Stanley, Frank & the Columbia Male Quartet
In The Wildwood Where The Bluebirds Grew		Columbia 496

Star Sacred Singers
Death Is No More Than A Dream	1927	Broadway 8087
Near The Cross	1927	Broadway 8087
There is No Disappointment In Heaven	1927	Broadway 8127
Where We'll Never Grow Old	1927	Broadway 8127

Starlighters
Honeymoon Hill	1951	Capitol 1547
Thousand Goodnights, A	1951	Capitol 1547

Starlings
Dream	1951	Regent 1037

Statesman
That Old Gang Of Mine	1955	Decca 29239

Statesman Quartet
Bound For The Kingdom	1952	Capitol 2016
Happy Rhythm	1947	Capitol 1211
How Many Times'	1953	Capitol 2469
I'm Gonna Take A Ride	1952	Capitol 1917
I Want To Be Ready To Meet Him	1951	Capitol 1582
Led Out Of Bondage	1947	Capitol 1189
Listen To The Bells	1951	Capitol 1582
Love Of God, The	1952	Capitol 2303
One Of These Mornings	1953	Capitol 2566
On Revival Day	1952	Capitol 2016
Peace In The Valley	1949	Capitol 1489
Rockin' My Soul	1952	Capitol 2115
Sho' Do Need Him Now	1949	Capitol 1489
Someone To Care	1953	Capitol 2469
Something To Shout About	1947	Capitol 1211
Standing Outside	1952	Capitol 1917
Sunday Meetin' Time	1952	Capitol 2115
Trouble	1952	Capitol 2303
Wait Till You See Me In My New Home	1947	Capitol 1189
When I Get Saved	1947	Capitol 1211
When You Travel All Alone	1953	Capitol 2566
You're Gonna Reap What You Sow	1947	Capitol 1211

Statesmen
Hello My Baby	1952	Decca 28831

Steelman Sisters
Cowgirl's Prayer, The	1936	Conqueror 8762
I'm Drifting Back To Dreamland	1936	Conqueror 8753
Lonesome Valley Sally	1936	Conqueror 8762

Stehl-Lufsky-Schuetze Trio
Oh Fair Sweet And Holy	1914	Columbia A-1622

Stehl-Taylor-Bergh Trio
I Hear You Calling Me	1915	Columbia A-1815

Stella & the Fellas
Alabamy Bound	1935	Fred Waring's Ford radio broadcasts, 1935-1936. From The Archive Series, Pennsylvania State University.
Avalon Town	1935	Fred Waring's Ford radio broadcasts, 1935-1936. From The Archive Series, Pennsylvania State University.
Blue Moon	1935	Fred Waring's Ford radio broadcasts, 1935-1936. From The Archive Series, Pennsylvania State University.
Dardanella	1935	Fred Waring's Ford radio broadcasts, 1935-1936. From The Archive Series, Pennsylvania State University.
Great Day	1935	Fred Waring's Ford radio broadcasts, 1935-1936. From The Archive Series, Pennsylvania State University.
Hallelujah	1935	Fred Waring's Ford radio broadcasts, 1935-1936. From The Archive Series, Pennsylvania State University.
I Feel A Song Comin' On	1935	Fred Waring's Ford radio broadcasts, 1935-1936. From The Archive Series, Pennsylvania State

Isle Of Capri	1935	Fred Waring's Ford radio broadcasts, 1935-1936. From The Archive Series, Pennsylvania State University.	Summertime	1935	Fred Waring's Ford radio broadcasts, 1935-1936. From The Archive Series, Pennsylvania State University.
Japanese Sandman	1935	Fred Waring's Ford radio broadcasts, 1935-1936. From The Archive Series, Pennsylvania State University.	Swing Waltz	1935	Fred Waring's Ford radio broadcasts, 1935-1936. From The Archive Series, Pennsylvania State University.
My Romance	1935	Fred Waring's Ford radio broadcasts, 1935-1936. From The Archive Series, Pennsylvania State University.	You And The Night And The Music	1935	Fred Waring's Ford radio broadcasts, 1935-1936. From The Archive Series, Pennsylvania State University.
Night And Day	1935	Fred Waring's Ford radio broadcasts, 1935-1936. From The Archive Series, Pennsylvania State University.			
Nobody's Sweetheart Now	1935	Fred Waring's Ford radio broadcasts, 1935-1936. From The Archive Series, Pennsylvania State University.			
Oh Miss Hannah	1935	Fred Waring's Ford radio broadcasts, 1935-1936. From The Archive Series, Pennsylvania State University.			
Program Closing	1935	Fred Waring's Ford radio broadcasts, 1935-1936. From The Archive Series, Pennsylvania State University.			
Soon	1935	Fred Waring's Ford radio broadcasts, 1935-1936. From The Archive Series,			

Stellar Male Quartet

Little Bit Of Heaven	1928	Harmony 594-H
Where The River Shannon Flows	1928	Harmony 594

Stellar Male Quartette

Artillerist's Oath, The	1915	Columbia
Carry Me Back To Old Virginny	1919	Columbia A-1820
Come Back To Erin	1915	Columbia A-1751
Medley Of Harrigan-Braham Songs	1915	Columbia A-1811
Mrs. Sippi, You're A Grand Old Girl	1914	Columbia A-1624
Old Oaken Bucket, The	1915	Columbia A-1820
Owl And The Pussy Cat, The	1915	Columbia A-1816
Songs My Mother Taught Me	1915	Columbia
Sweet And Low	1915	Columbia A-1741

Stellar Male Quartette (Columbia Stellar Quartet)

Are You The O'Reilly'	1915	Columbia A-1783

Stellar Quartet

All Erin Is Callin Mavourneen	1916	Columbia A-2407
Down Around The 'Sip 'Sip 'Sippy Shore	1921	Columbia
I Need Thee Every Hour	1920	Columbia A 2051
Oh Come All Ye Faithful	1927	Harmony 517
Somebody's Mother	1921	Columbia

Stellar Quartet & Margaret Romain

In The Evening By The Moonlight	1920	Columbia A-3312

Stellar Quartet (Amparito Farrar with the)

Sweet And Low	1918	Columbia A-2535

Stellar Quartet (as Dolly Vernon & male quartet)

Star Of The East	1920	Clarion 5119-C/Harmony 518-H/Velvet Tone

Stellar Quartet (Henry Burr, Andrea Sarto & the)
Sons Of Liberty	1917	Columbia A-2312

Stellar Quartet, Alice Nielsen & the
Star-Spangled Banner, The	1917	Columbia

Stellar Quartet, Andrea Sarto & the
Hats Off To The Flag And The King	1917	Columbia
It's A Long, Long Way to The U.S.A.	1917	Columbia A-2361

Stellar Quartet, Charles W. Harrison & the
Battle Cry Of Freedom, The	1917	Columbia A-2357

Stellar Quartet, Cyrena van Gordon & the
Bring Back My Bonnie To Me	1921	Columbia

Stellar Quartet, Margaret Woodrow Wilson & the
My Old Kentucky Home	1917	Columbia A-2416

Stellar Quartette
Absent	1915	Columbia A-1891
Annie Laurie	1913	Columbia A-1491
At Parting	1915	Columbia A-1912
Beautiful Isle Of Somewhere	1919	Columbia A-2048
California	1922	Banner 1081
Columbia, The Gem Of The Ocean	1914	Columbia A-1548
Come Along, Ma Honey (Down Upon The Swanee River) (With Henry Burr)	1918	Columbia 2621
Favorites Of Other Days - Part 1	1917	Columbia
Favorites Of Other Days - Part 2	1917	Columbia
Hark, The Herald Angels Sing	1919	Vocalion 14111/Harmony 517 (1927)
Heidelberg	1919	Columbia A-1852
Home, Sweet Home	1919	Columbia A-2465
Hong Kong Romance, A	1915	Columbia A-1892
In The Gloaming	1921	Banner 2004
Joy To The World	1919	Vocalion 14111A
Just A-Wearyin' For You	1919	Columbia A-1958
Lamp In The West, The	1915	Columbia A-1871
Love's Old Sweet Song	1921	Banner 2004
Medley Of Old Songs	1919	Columbia A-1893
Oh Come All Ye Faithful	1919	Columbia A-2788/Clarion 5096-C/Harmony 517-H Velvet Tone 1517-V
Old Oaken Bucket, The	1919	Columbia A-1820
Onward, Christian Soldiers	1915	Columbia A-2220
Sally In Our Alley	1913	Columbia A-1440
Swanee River Moon	1922	Banner 1055
We'll Never Let The Old Flag Fall (with Vernon Stiles)	1917	
Hark! The Herald Angels Sing	1919	Columbia A-2788/Clarion 5097-C/Harmony 517-H Velvet Tone 1517-V
Marching Through Georgia	1916	Columbia A-107/Columbia A-2065/Columbia A-3015

Sterling Quartette
One For All, And All For One	1918	Okeh 1069

Sterling Trio
Alice, I'm In Wonderland (Since The Day That I First Met You)	1918	Columbia A-2560/Brunswick 5220 (1918)/Okeh 1059 (1918)
Aloha Oe (Farewell To Thee)	1918	Okeh 1046
Always	1926	Gennett 3246
Avalon, I'll Travel To You	1917	Victor 18365/Brunswick 5038 (1917)
Back To Mother And Home Sweet Home	1917	Brunswick 5202
Beautiful Isle Of Somewhere	1917	Perfect 11019
Bye Lo	1916	Emerson 10113/Vocalion 14051B (1920)
By The Camp Fire	1919	Columbia A-2718/Okeh 1192 (1919)
Cairo Land	1919	Okeh 4063
Captain Of The Toy Brigade, The	1918	Columbia A-2584
Carolina Mammy	1923	Victor 19126
Carolina Sunshine	1919	Victor 18612/Columbia A-2770 (1919)/Paramount 33019 (1920)
Caroline I'm Coming Back To You	1918	Columbia A-2640
Chimes Of Normandy	1917	Brunswick 5172/Okeh 1060 (1918)
Dear Old Lady	1923	Victor 19194
Deep Down In An Irishman's Heart	1925	Victor 19749
Don't Try To Steal The Sweetheart Of A Soldier	1917	Columbia A-2447
Do What Your Mother Did (I'll Do The Same As Your Dad)	1916	Victor 18079/Columbia A-2020 (1916)
Down Deep In An Irishman's Heart	1925	Victor 19749
Dreaming Of Home Sweet Home	1918	Columbia A-2668
Dreams	1919	Columbia A-2717
Dreamy Melody	1923	Victor 19150

Egyptland	1919	Okeh 1153	Longing	1919	Columbia A-2725
Everybody's Crazy 'Bout The Doggone Blues, But I'm Happy	1918	Brunswick 5217	Louisiana	1920	Victor 18726
Everything Is Peaches Down In Georgia	1918	Columbia A-2623/Emerson 973 (1924)	Mammy O'Mine	1919	Columbia A-2718/Okeh 1197 (1919)
			Mandy	1926	Symphonola 4144
Friends	1919	Columbia A-2744/Okeh 1231 (1919)	Manyana	1920	Vocalion 14068
			Merrily We'll Roll Along	1918	Okeh 1058
			Mother, Dixie And You	1917	Victor 18325/Columbia A-2275 (1917)
Georgia Moon	1915	Victor 17927			
Georgia Rose	1922	Victor 18837			
Girl Of Mine	1917	Victor 18302	Mother, Here's Your Boy	1918	Columbia A-2677
Give Me The Right To Love You All The While	1917	Columbia A-2415/Victor 18435 (1918)	Mother's Lullaby	1920	Victor 18710/Columbia A-3333 (1920)
Golden Hours	1917	Brunswick 5039	Mummy Mine	1919	Victor 18525
Have A Smile	1918	Victor 18518	My Dixie Rosary	1920	Vocalion 14085B/Okeh 4150 (1920)
Hawaiian Butterfly	1917	Victor 18272			
Hearts	1919	Pathe 22159			
Hiawatha Melody Of Love	1920	Victor 18660	My Isle Of Golden Dreams	1920	Vocalion 14010
I'd Rather Cry Over You (Than Smile At Somebody Else)	1928	Brunswick	My Little Sunshine	1925	Emerson 9197
			My Lonely Lola Lo (In Hawaii)	1916	Victor 18171/Columbia A-2131 (1916)
I Found A Rose In The Devil's Garden	1921	Victor 18746			
I'll Take You Home Again, Kathleen	1918	Brunswick 5251	My Pretty Little Rainbow	1919	Victor 18624/Columbia
I Lost My Heart In Honolulu	1916	Columbia A-2045	My Sunshine Jane (Down By The Weeping Willow Tree)	1917	Victor 18403/Brunswick 5156 (1917)
I'm Aching For The Sight Of You	1919	Okeh 1230			
I Miss That Mississippi Miss That Misses Me	1918	Victor 18496			
			My Swanee Home	1919	Columbia A-2755
Indiana	1917	Victor 18251	Not So Very Far From Zanzibar	1916	Columbia A-2083
In Florida Among The Palms	1916	Victor 18138	Oh My Lady	1920	Vocalion 14045B/Okeh 4095 (1920)
In The Glory Of Moonlight	1916	Victor 17953			
In The Heart Of Dear Old Italy	1921	Victor 18795			
In The Middle Of The Night	1926	Gennett 3246	Old Irish Mother Of Mine	1920	Okeh 4174
In The Shadow Of The Desert Palm	1918	Columbia A-2661	Old Kentucky Moonlight	1922	Victor 18908
			One For All, All For One	1918	Okeh 1069
			One The Road To Home Sweet Home	1918	Pathe 20353
In The Sweet Long Ago	1916	Victor 18212			
It's A Long Way Back To Mother's Knee	1917	Victor 18349/Brunswick 5157 (1917)	On Lake Champlain	1916	Victor 18101/Columbia A-2062 (1916)/Pathe 20082
It's A Small World After All	1919	Columbia			
It's Never Too Late To Be Sorry	1919	Columbia A-2690	On The South Sea Isle	1916	Victor 18113/Columbia A-2045 (1916)
I Want Him Back Again	1918	Columbia A-2546			
Just Before The Battle Mother	1918	Brunswick 5224			
Just For Me And Mary	1920	Okeh 4076			
Just Like A Gypsy	1919	Victor 18696/Okeh 4175 (1920)	On Your Next Birthday	1920	Vocalion 14051A
			Out Of The Cradle, Into My Heart	1916	Victor 18170/Columbia A-2123 (1916)
Just Like The Rose	1919	Vocalion 14005B			
K-K-K-Katy	1918	Brunswick 5217			
Let Me Dream	1920	Victor 18653	Over There	1918	Okeh 1007
Little Birch Bark Canoe And You, A	1918	Columbia A-2655/Brunswick 5255/Okeh 1160 (1919)	Pickaninnies Paradise, The	1918	Victor 18512B/Columbia A-2623 (1918)/Okeh 1095

Title	Year	Release
Pickaninny Blues	1920	Emerson 10159
Pretty Little Rainbow	1919	Emerson 1068
Ring Out, Liberty	1918	Okeh 1107
Shades Of Night	1916	Victor 18028/Columbia A-2002 (1916)
She'll Be Waiting When You Come Back Home	1918	Okeh 1092
She's Just Like Sal	1920	Vocalion 14045A
Silver Threads Among The Gold	1918	Okeh 1016
Smile Again, Kathleen Mavourneen	1924	Victor 19444
Some Day I'll Make You Glad	1919	Victor 18529/Columbia A-2713 (1919)
Statue Of Liberty Is Smiling, The	1919	Okeh 1154
Sweetest Little Girl In Tennessee	1917	Victor 18355
That Girl Of Mine	1917	Victor 18302
That Long, Long Trail Is Getting Shorter Now	1919	Okeh 1203
That Old Irish Mother Of Mine	1920	Victor 18696
That Tumble Down Shack In Athlone	1919	Columbia A-2698/Okeh 1173 (1919)/Okeh 4613 (1922)/Little Wonder 1128 (1919)/Victor 18545 (1919)/Gennett 455 A (1920)
There's A Little Blue Star In The Window	1918	Brunswick 5220
There's A Service Flag Flying At Our House	1918	Columbia A-2493
Tomorrow Land	1922	Victor 18837
Tumble Down Shack In Athlone	1919	Victor 18545/Champion 15164 (1919)
'Twas Only An Irishman's Dream	1920	Columbia
Wait'n For Me	1920	Okeh 4184
Watch, Wait And Hope, Little Girl (Till I Come Back To You	1918	Columbia A-2656
We'll Do Out Share	1918	Okeh 1063
When I Look In Your Wonderful Eyes	1920	
When Sweet Susie Goes Steppin' By	1928	Brunswick
When The Harvest Moon Is Shining	1920	Okeh 4091
When The Sun Goes Down In Romany	1916	Victor 18079
When We Meet In The Sweet Bye And Bye	1918	Victor 18484/Columbia A-2582 (1918)/Okeh 1088 (1918)
When Will The Sun Shine For Me'	1923	Victor 19126
When You And I Were Young, Maggie	1918	Okeh 1017
When You Come Back	1918	Okeh 1073
When You Play With The Heart Of A Girl	1918	Columbia A-2519
When You Sang 'Hush-A-Bye Baby' To Me	1918	Victor 18493
Where The Morning Glories Grow	1922	Brunswick 5156
Wonderful Pal	1919	Victor 18631
Yearning	1919	Okeh 4007
You'll Find Dixie Looking Just The Same	1918	Columbia A-2640
You're Going To Fall In Love With California	1918	Okeh 1115
You're My Little Indian Rose	1917	Columbia A-2440
You're Still An Old Sweetheart Of Mine	1919	Columbia A-2698
Your Wife	1916	Victor 18027/Columbia A-1983 (1916)
Yukaloo - My Pretty South Sea Island Lady	1917	Victor 18227
I Am Always Building Castles In The Air	1920	Paramount 30052
Venetian Moon	1920	Vocalion 14029A
When The Sun Goes Down In Sleepy Hollow (That's The Time I Think Of Home Sweet Home)	1918	Columbia

Sterling Trio (with Elisabeth Spencer)

Title	Year	Release
Where The Morning Glories Grow	1917	Victor 18403

Sterling Trio (with Frank Banta)

Title	Year	Release
Miniature Concert, A	1925	Victor 35753

Sterling Trio (with Henry Burr)

Title	Year	Release
My Sweetheart Is Somewhere In France	1917	Columbia A-2355

Sterling Trio, Henry Burr & the

Title	Year	Release
Down By The Old Red Mill	1917	Columbia A-2440/Brunswick 5157 (1922)
It's A Long Way Back	1922	Brunswick 5157

Sterling Trio, Henry Burr with the

Title	Year	Release
Mickey	1919	Columbia A-2662

Sterling Trio, with Henry Burr

Title	Year	Release
Just A Little Cottage (I'll Call It 'Home Sweet Home')	1918	Columbia A-2512/Brunswick 5251 (1918)

Stevens' Dance Quartet

Title	Year	Release
Bring Back The Sunshine You Took Away		Edison 51126
Lady Of The Lake		Edison 51126

Once In A Lifetime		Edison 51240
Steven's Trio		
Baby Blue Eyes		Edison 51104
Chicago (That Toddling Town)		Edison 51120
Chick, Chick, Chick, Chick, Chicken (Lay A Little Egg For Me)		Edison 51120
Dumbbell		Edison 51104
Falling	1923	Edison 51141
Like A Rose		Edison 51234
Love (My Heart Is Calling You		Edison 51258
Tell Me With Smiles		Edison 51120
World Is Waiting For The Sunrise, The		Edison 51234
Stevens' Trio, Ernest		
Hesitation Waltz		Edison 51042
If I Had My Way Pretty Baby		Edison 51026
Magic Mirror Waltzes		Edison 51042
Red Moon	1922	Edison 51026
Tinkle Tune		Edison 51240
Stevens' Trio, Ernest L.		
Hot Lips	1922	Edison 51026
Love Sends A Little Gift Of Roses		Edison 51037
Stewart Harmony Singers		
Carry Me Back To The Mountains	1932	Champion 16527
Do Not Wait Till I'm Under The Ground	1932	Champion 16538
I Only Want A Buddy	1932	Champion 16538
My Renfro Valley Home	1932	Champion 16527
Stewart Sisters (with Rudy Vallee & his Connecticut Yankees)		
Fare Thee Well, Annabelle	1935	Victor 24833
On The Good Ship Lollipop	1934	Victor 24838/Electrola EG 3414
Plain Old Me	1935	Victor 25109
Sweet Flossie Farmer	1934	
Strand & Male Trio (Billy Jones &)		
Tuck Me To Sleep (In My Old 'Tucky Home)	1921	Brunswick 2127
Strand Male Quartet		
Adeste Fideles	1922	Cameo 278
Banks Of Newfoundland		Brunswick 2176
Holy Night, Peaceful Night	1922	Cameo 278
Peck's Bad Boy	1921	Brunswick 2123
Strand Male Quartet (Criterion Quartet)		
Kentucky Babe	1921	Brunswick 2099
Strand Male Trio		
Drowsy Head	1921	Brunswick 2099
Strand Quartet		
Behind The Clouds	1926	Cameo 929
Bells Of Shandon	1920	Brunswick 2166
College Medley, A	1921	Banner 2092
Drum, The	1923	Cameo 490
I Used To Love Her But It's All	1921	Brunswick 2121
Over Now		
Just Around The Corner	1926	Cameo 929
Mamie	1925	Cameo 729
Mammy Lou	1922	Brunswick 2189
Massa's In De Cold Ground	1924	Cameo 718
Mother Goose	1923	Cameo 490
My Cradle Melody	1922	Vocalion 14390
Newfoundland		Brunswick 2176
Old Black Joe	1924	Cameo 718
Owl And The Pussy Cat	1921	Banner 2092
Sally In Our Alley	1921	Brunswick 2166
Striders		
Baby Don't You Cry	1950	Apollo (unreleased)
Come Back To Me Tomorrow	1954	Derby 857
Cool Saturday Night	1950	Apollo 1159
Five O'Clock Blues	1950	Apollo 1159
Hesitating Fool	1955	Apollo 480
If I Only Knew	1950	Apollo (unreleased)
I Wonder	1955	Apollo 480
Pleasin' You	1948	Capitol 15306
Rollin'	1954	Derby 857
Somebody Stole My Rose Colored Glasses	1948	Capitol 15306
Vamoose	1950	Apollo (unreleased)
Striders, Bette McLaurin & the		
I Won't Tell A Soul I Love You	1952	Derby 804
My Heart Belongs To Only You	1952	Derby 804
Striders, Dolores Martin & the		
I'm The Lonesomest Girl In Time	1953	Mystery 526
Striders, Savannah Churchill & the		
Aint'cha Glad I Love You	1950	Arco 1263
And So I Cry	1951	Regal 3313
Changeable You	1950	Arco 1263
Don't Grieve, Don't Sorrow, Don't Cry	1951	RCA 47-4448
Don't Worry 'Bout Me	1952	RCA Victor 4773
My Affair	1952	RCA Victor 4583
Once There Lived A Fool	1950	Regal 3309
Waiting For A Guy Named Joe	1952	RCA Victor 4773
Wedding Bells Are Breaking Up That Old Gang Of Mine	1951	Regal 3313
When You Come Back To Me	1950	Regal 3309
Stringfellow Quartet		
I Want To Hear Him Call My Name	1931	Columbia 15726 D
Just A Little Nearer Home	1931	Columbia
My Heavenly Homecoming	1931	Columbia
We'll Reap What We Sow	1931	Columbia 15726-D
Strollers Quartet		
Bub, Bub, Baby Of Mine	1930	Banner 0604/Jewel 5860/Oriole 1860/Romeo 1219
Egypt Moon	1930	Banner 0601/Jewel 5055/Romeo 1225

Hallelujah	1930	Banner 0584/Domino 4485/Jewel 5840/Perfect 15268	Sun Shines Once Again, The	1951	Okeh 6814
			They Said It Couldn't Happen	1951	Onyx 2008
			Today Is Your Birthday	1951	Onyx 2007/Okeh 6877 (1952)
Hello Baby	1929	Banner 0563/Domino 4479	Wishin'	1952	Okeh 6877
			Your Fool Again	1951	Okeh 6814
I Apologize	1931	Conqueror 7850	**Sultans**		
I Don't Know Why (I Just Do)	1931	Conqueror 7850	Baby Don't Put Me Down	1954	Duke 133
I'm Keeping Company	1931	Banner 32230/Oriole 2310/Conqueror 7826	Blues At Dawn	1952	Jubilee 5077
			Boppin' With The Mambo	1954	Duke 135
			Don't Be Angry	1952	Jubilee 5077
			Good Thing Baby	1954	Duke 125
It's The Girl	1931	Banner 32230/Oriole 2310/Conqueror 7826	How Deep Is The Ocean	1954	Duke 125
			I Cried My Heart Out	1954	Duke 133
			If I Could Tell	1954	Duke 178
			Lemon Squeezing Daddy	1951	Jubilee 5054
I Want To Be Happy	1930	Banner 0567/Domino 4484/Perfect 15267	My Love Is High	1954	Duke 178
			What Makes Me Feel This Way	1954	Duke 135
			You Captured My Heart	1951	Jubilee 5054
Lane Of Forgotten Dreams	1930	Challenge 871/Banner 0642	**Sundown Singers, Richard Huey & his**		
			Blues Boogie Woogie, The	1943	Decca 8656
She Stole My Heart	1930	Banner 0623/Oriole 1882/Romeo 1243	Hurry Sundown	1943	Decca 8656
			Sunset Four Jubilee Quartette		
Sweetheart	1930	Banner 0632/Challenge 892/Oriole 1888/Romeo 1252	Barnum's Steam Calliope	1924	Paramount 12241
			Didn't He Ramble'	1924	Paramount 12241
			Do You Call That Religion'	1924	Paramount 12221
			Jerusalem Morning	1924	Paramount 12221
Under A Texas Moon	1930	Banner 0570/Oriole 1825/Perfect 15267/Romeo 1190	Wade In The Water	1925	Paramount 12273
			Walk In Jerusalem	1925	Paramount 12292
			When I Came Out Of The Wilderness	1925	Paramount 12314
When The Moon Shines Down On Sunshine And Me	1930	Banner 0570/Oriole 1825/Romeo 1190	You Must Come In At The Front Door	1925	Paramount 12314
Where The Golden Daffodils Grow	1930	Banner 0658/Conqueror 7520/Regal 8977/Perfect 15294	You Must Have That Old Time Religion	1925	Paramount 12292
			Sunset Four Jubilee Quartette, The Grace Outlaw		
			Hand Me Down My Silver Trumpet	1925	Paramount 12285
Why Make A Promise	1930	Challenge 860/Banner 0602/Romeo 1220	Plantation Days - Part 1	1925	Paramount 12309
			Plantation Days - Part 2	1925	Paramount 12309
Strollers' Quartette			**Sunset Quartet**		
What Am I To Do'	1930	Banner 643	Good News, Chariot's Comin'	1925	Paramount 12273
Stroller's Quartette			Oh Lord What A Morning	1925	Paramount 12285/
Sing You Sinners	1930	Challenge 871/Banner 0642/Regal 8970	**Sunshine Four**		
			Beautiful Land, The	1926	Columbia 15119-D
Stroup Quartet			Broder Jonah	1926	Columbia
Dreaming	1928	Columbia 15299-D	Hypocrite	1926	Columbia
Man Behind The Plough, The	1928	Columbia 15299-D	In My Heart	1926	Columbia 15119-D
Sugartones			**Swanee Four**		
Annabelle	1951	Onyx 2007	His Troubles Was Hard	1930	Goodson 222
Buzzard And The Hawk, The	1951	Onyx 2008	Jerusalem Mornin'	1930	Goodson 222
I Just Want To Dream	1952	Okeh 6837/Okeh 6992 (1953)	**Swanee Jubilee Singers**		
			I've Opened My Soul	1927	Vocalion 1066
I Know You Gotta Go	1953	Okeh 6992	My Good Lord's Done Been Here	1927	Vocalion 1066
It's Over	1952	Okeh 6837			

Swanee Melodists
Title	Year	Label/Number
Crooning	1921	Vocalion 14181A
Pucker Up And Whistle	1921	Vocalion 14181B

Swantones, Del Casino & the
Title	Year	Label/Number
I've Lost All My Love For You	1948	Manor 1063
You Only Want Me When You're Lonesome	1948	Manor 1063

Sweet Violet Boys
Title	Year	Label/Number
Back Yard Stomp	1938	Columbia 20350/Columbia 37773/Vocalion 4528
Boy Take Your Time	1939	Vocalion 5162
Chiselin' Mam	1939	Columbia 20351/Columbia 37774/Vocalion 5229
Down By The Old Mill Stream	1935	Columbia 37615
Down On The Farm	1936	Columbia 20284/Columbia 37705/Vocalion 3327
Father Put The Cow Away (with Gale Ryan)	1940	Conqueror 9445/Vocalion 5461
Fly Butterfly	1939	Conqueror 9224/Vocalion 4756
Fly Butterfly #2	1940	Conqueror 9445/Vocalion 5461
Gee, But It's Great To meet A Friend	1937	Columbia 20345/Columbia 37768/Conqueror 9443/Vocalion 3766
Gee, But It's Great To Meet A Friend	1938	Conqueror 9066/Conqueror 9443 (1939)
Hinky Dinky Parley Voo	1938	Columbia 20283/Columbia 37704/Conqueror 9067
Hinky Dinky Parlez Vous No. 2	1936	Columbia 20284/Columbia 37705/Vocalion 3327
Hurry, John, Hurry	1935	Columbia 20220/Columbia 37621/Vocalion 3402
I Give In So Easy (with Gale Ryan)	1940	Columbia 20352/Columbia 37775/Conqueror 9446 (1940)/Vocalion 5368
I Haven't Got A Pot To Cook In	1936	Columbia 20220/Columbia 37621/Vocalion 3402
I Love My Fruit	1939	Vocalion 5162
I'm Gonna Fix Your Wagon	1939	Vocalion 5412
I'm Wasting My Time	1940	Okeh 5681
I Wish I'd Never Been Born	1938	Conqueror 9099/Vocalion 4428
Jim's Windy Mule	1935	Columbia 20341/Columbia 37764/Vocalion 3587
Let's All Get Good And Drunk	1941	Okeh 6482
Lulu From Honolulu	1940	Vocalion 5498
Medley Of Bar Room Songs	1936	Columbia 20283/Columbia 37704/Vocalion 3281
My Head Went Round And Round	1941	Okeh 6482
On Mexico's Beautiful Shore	1940	Vocalion 5412
Put On Your Old Grey Bonnet	1935	Columbia 20208/Columbia 37609/Conqueror 8600/Vocalion 3110
Round And Round	1936	Columbia 20344/Columbia 37767/Vocalion 3663
Sally Let Your Bangs Hang Down	1939	Columbia 20351/Columbia 37774/Vocalion 5229
Scarecrow Son	1940	Okeh 5681
She Came Rolling Down The Mountain	1936	Vocalion 3219
Show Me A Man That Won't	1940	Conqueror 9446
Show Me A Man That Won't Want Women	1940	Columbia 20352/Columbia 37775/Conqueror 9446/Vocalion 5368
Stamp Collector	1939	Conqueror 9224/Vocalion 4756
Sweet Birds	1936	Vocalion 3218
Sweet Violets	1935	Columbia 20208/Columbia 37609/Vocalion 3110

Sweet Violets No. 2	1936	Columbia 20214/Columbia 37615/Vocalion 3218			20184/Bluebird B-5264/Montgomery Ward 4841/Sunrise 3354
Sweet Violets No. 3	1937	Columbia 20341/Columbia 37764/Conqueror 9067/Vocalion 3587	Crying Holy Unto The Lord	1927	Victor 20959/Bluebird B-5264/Montgomery Ward 4841/Sunrise 3345
There's A Man That Comes To Our House	1937	Columbia 20345/Columbia 37768/Conqueror 9443/Vocalion 3766	Dixie Bo-Bo	1927	Victor 20852
			Hallelujah Side	1928	Victor 38520
			Hide You In The Blood	1928	Victor 38553
			I'm A Pilgrim	1927	Victor V-38029/Bluebird B-5386/Sunrise 3467
There's A Man Who Comes To Our House	1938	Conqueror 9066/Conqueror 9443 (1939)	I'm In His Care	1927	Victor V-38029
			I Shall Not Be Moved	1926	Victor 20183
They're Burning Down The House I Was Brung Up In	1937	Columbia 20344/Columbia 37767/Vocalion 3663	Join That Band	1926	Victor 20183/Bluebird B-5746
			Lead Kindly Light	1927	Victor 20185/Bluebird B-5368
Walkin' In My Sleep	1938	Vocalion 4010			
We're The Sweet Violet Boys	1938	Conqueror 9099Vocalion 4428	Mary Bowed So Low	1928	Victor 38520
What Would You Give In Exchange	1938	Vocalion 4010	Oh My Mother, You Got To Bow So Low	1927	Victor 20959/Bluebird B-5746
When It's Hop Pickin' Time In Happy Valley	1935	Vocalion 3219			
			Stop Dat Band	1926	Victor 20184
Widow's Lament, The	1939	Vocalion 5283	Then He Brought Joy To My Soul	1926	Victor 20185
Yip, Yip, Yowie, I'm An Eagle	1935	Vocalion 3218	Toot, Toot, Dixie	1927	Victor 20852
You Oughta See My Fanny Dance	1938	Columbia 20350/Columbia 37773/Vocalion 4528	**Taylor Trio**		
			Alice Where Art Thou	1916	Columbia A-2142
			Beauty's Eyes	1916	Columbia A-2013
			Believe Me, If All Those Endearing Young Charms	1916	Columbia A-1959
You're A Dog	1939	Vocalion 5283	Ben Bolt	1916	Columbia A-1959
You've Got To See Mama Every Night	1940	Vocalion 5498	Bring Back My Bonnie To Me	1916	Columbia A-1996
Syncopaters			Can't Yo' Heah Me Callin' Caroline	1916	Columbia A-2103
Mule Train	1949	National 9093			
River, Stay Away From My Door	1949	National 9095	Come Back To Erin	1916	Columbia A-1972
These Are The Things I Want To Share With You	1949	National 9093/National 9095 (1949)	Come Where My Love Lies Dreaming	1917	Columbia A-2279
			Darling Nellie Gray	1916	Columbia A-1934
T.C.I. Women's Four			Don't You Mind It Honey	1916	Columbia A-2103
I Got A Home In That Rock	1927	Paramount 12491	Drink To Me Only With Thine Eyes	1916	Columbia A-2142
That Great Day	1927	Paramount 12491			
Tampa Boys			Ever Of Thee	1916	Columbia A-1972
Hey Man! Hey Man!	1941	Decca 8586	Goodbye	1917	Columbia A-2234
Tampa Toppers, Rufus Beacham & the			Hearts And Flowers	1917	Columbia A-2463
Do You Know How To Boogie	1951	Jax 300	Home Sweet Home	1915	Columbia A-1866
Since I Fell For You	1951	Jax 300	I Love You Truly	1917	Columbia A-2180
			In The Gloaming	1915	Columbia A-1866
Taskiana Four			Massa's In The Cold, Cold Ground	1916	Columbia A-1934
Brightly Beams	1928	Victor 38553			
Creep Along, Moses	1926	Victor	My Dreams	1916	Columbia A-2013

My Old Kentucky Home	1916	Columbia A-1915
O Christmas Tree	1923	Champion 15044
Oh Loving Heart Trust On	1916	Columbia A-2049
Oh Promise Me	1916	Columbia A-2049
Oh, That We Two Were Maying	1917	Columbia A-2180
Old Dog Tray	1917	Columbia A-2279
Old Folks At Home	1916	Columbia A-1915
Parted	1917	Columbia A-2249
Silent Night Holy Night	1922	Champion 15041
Silver Threads Among The Gold	1916	Columbia A-2089
Sing Me To Sleep	1917	Columbia A-2234
Sweet Genevieve	1916	Columbia A-2089
Underneath The Stars	1915	Columbia A-1856
Violets	1917	Columbia A-2249
When You And I Were Young, Maggie	1916	Columbia A-1996
Whispering Hope	1917	Columbia A-2463

Temple Quartet

Come Ye Faithful People, Come	1927	Columbia 1125-D
Eternal Father, Strong To Save	1930	Columbia 2315-D
Few More Years Shall Roll, A	1931	Columbia 2412-D
Good Christian Men Rejoice	1927	Columbia 1125-D
Hark! Hark! My Soul	1930	Columbia 2227-D
Lead Kindly Light	1931	Columbia 2412-D
Now The Day Is Over	1930	Columbia 2315-D
Praise The Lord, Ye Heavens Adore Him	1932	Columbia 2623D
Rock Of Ages	1930	Columbia 2227-D

Texas Jubilee Singers

He's Coming Soon	1929	Columbia 14445-D
He's The Lily Of The Valley	1929	Columbia 14445-D

Thankful Quartet

Goin' To Shout All Over God's Heaven	1927	Okeh 8457
He Took My Sins Away	1927	Okeh 8493
I'm Troubled Lord	1927	Okeh 8493
Let The Church Roll On	1927	Okeh 8457

That Girl Quartette

Answer	1912	Victor 35192
Down At Mammy Jinny's	1912	Victor 17118
Haying Time	1911	Victor 16906
Hold Me Just A Little Closer	1912	Victor 16880
Honey Love	1911	Victor 16848/Columbia A-1128 (1912)
Honeymooning In Bombay	1910	Victor 16703
I'm Yours With Love And Kisses		Edison Blue Amberol 4730
In Dixieland With Dixie Lou	1912	Victor 17032
Make Me Love You Like I Never Loved	1911	Victor 16990
My Bombay Maid	1912	Victor 17146
My Little Persian Rose	1912	Victor 17270
Night Time's The Right Time	1911	Victor 16886
On San Francisco Bay	1911	Victor 16848
Peek-A-Boo Mr. Moon	1911	Victor 16886
Put Your Arms Around Me, Honey	1912	Victor 17267
Rosalie	1912	Victor 17219
Senorita	1912	Victor 17032
Silver Bell	1910	Victor 16695
We Have Much To Be Thankful For	1913	Victor 17409
When It's Springtime In Virginia	1913	Victor 17437

That Singing Four

Brown Eyes, Why Are You Blue'	1925	Edison DD 51648
Oh Say! Can I See You To-Night	1925	Edison DD 51601
Sweet Ramona	1925	Edison DD 51601
That Certain Party	1925	Edison DD 51657
Tomorrow Mornin'	1925	Edison DD 51648/Edison Blue Amberol 5085

Theremin Vocal Group

Lunette	1949	Capitol 872
Radar Blues	1949	Capitol 872

Thrasher Family

He Will Be With Me	1929	Columbia 15539-D
I Have A Friend	1929	Columbia 15717-D
It Was For Me	1929	Columbia 15717-D
My Saviour's Love	1929	Columbia 15396-D
Reapers, Be True	1929	Columbia 15396-D
This Is The Reason	1929	Columbia 15539-D

Three Admirals

Stormy Weather	1933	

Three Barons

Coffee And Kisses	1938	Vocalion 4030
Could Be	1939	Victor 26150
Dreamy Eyes	1937	Perfect 7-06-07
Good Mornin'	1937	Perfect 7-09-04
Iay Ovelay Ouyay (I Love You)	1938	Vocalion 4322
I'd Give My Life	1944	Savoy 527
I'm Laughing Up My Sleeve (Ha-Ha-Ha-Ha-Ha)	1937	Vocalion 3886/Perfect 8-02-09
Milkshake Stand	1944	Savoy 527
Milk Shake Stand	1948	Savoy 527
Night Before Christmas, The	1938	Victor 26104
One More Dream	1938	Victor 25884
Pippinella	1939	Victor 26238
Ruble A Rhumba, A	1939	Victor 26227
Shabby Old Cabby	1939	Victor 26298
Somebody Loves Me	1937	Vocalion 3932
So You Won't Sing	1937	Vocalion 3656
Stuttering In The Starlight	1939	Victor 26326
Swing And Sway	1937	Vocalion 3669
There's A Hole In The Old Oaken Bucket	1939	Victor 26157
Tinkle Song, The	1939	Victor 26243
Tu-Li-Tulip-Time	1938	Victor 26013
Umbrella Man, The	1938	Victor 26117

We Can Live On Love (We Haven't Got A Pot To Cook In)	1939	Victor 26273	Forever		Released in 1998 for the first time	
Why Should I Care'	1937	Vocalion 3700	Gee It's Rough	1952	Modern 881	

Three Barons (Three Riffs)

Poor Butterfly (recorded 1944)	1979	Savoy LP SJL 2241	Gloria	1948	Exclusive 703

Three Beaux, Ray Olson & the (with Ray Herbeck & his Music With Romance)

Trade Winds	1940	Okeh 5636	Groovy	1947	Aladdin 112
			How Blue Can You Get	1949	Camden LP 588
			How Could I Know	1949	RCA 22-0020

Three Bips And A Bop

Oop-Pop-A-Da!	1947	Blue Note 537	How Could You Be So Mean	1952	Aladdin 3139
			How Deep Is The Ocean	1946	Modern Music 139
			I Cried For You	1947	Exclusive 246

Three Bits Of Rhythm

Blow My Top	1947	Modern 523	If You Should Ever Leave	1946	Modern Music 154
Bronzeville Jump	1941	Decca 8553	I'll Get Along Somehow	1946	Modern Music 135
I'll Be True	1946	Modern Music 137	I Love To Make Love To You	1947	Exclusive 243
I'm Lonesome	1941	Decca 8572	In The Clay	1953	Hollywood 1001
I Used To Work In Chicago	1946	Modern Music 118	I Surrender Dear	1947	Exclusive 240
Man That Comes To My House, The	1947	Modern 539	It Had To Be You	1946	Modern Music 154
			It's Over	1947	Exclusive 257
			It's The Talk Of The Town	1946	Modern Music 131
Old Blues, The	1941	Decca 8553	I Was Wrong		Released in 1998 for the first time
Root Beer Sizzle, Sazzle, Sizzle	1947	Modern 539			
Signifying Monkey	1947	Modern 523	Jilted Blues	1948	Exclusive 40x
That's The Boogie	1946	Modern Music 118	Johnny Johnny	1953	Modern 888
This Is The Boogie, The Woogie, The Boogie	1941	Decca 8572	Johnny's Guitar Blues		Released in 1998 for the first time
Yas, Yas, Yas	1946	Modern Music 137	Juke Box Lil	1947	Exclusive 249

Three Blazers, Johnny Moore's

			Jumping Jack	1950	RCA 50-0095
Any Old Place With Me	1948	Exclusive 40x	Lonesome Train	1953	Modern 888
Baby Don't You Cry	1947	Aladdin 111/Aladdin 184 (1947)	Lost In The Night	1947	Exclusive 254/Exclusive 63x (1949)
Be Fair With Me	1946	Exclusive 233	Love Me Tonight	1949	Exclusive 86x
Better Watch What You Do	1947	Exclusive 243	Make Believe Boogie	1946	Modern Music 152
Blazer's Blues	1947	Aladdin 111	Mean Papa Blues	1952	Aladdin 3139
Blue Because Of You	1946	Modern Music 151	Melody	1950	RCA 50-0086
Blues For What I've Never Had	1949	RCA 22-0020	Merry Christmas, Baby	1947	Exclusive 254/Exclusive 63x (1949)/Hollywood 1021 (1954)
Bobby Sox Blues	1946	Exclusive 234			
Bop-A-Bye Baby	1949	RCA 50-0018			
Changeable Woman Blues	1947	Exclusive 251			
Christmas Eve Baby		Original 1045	Misery Blues	1950	RCA 50-0073
Christmas Every Day		Original 1045	Money's Getting Cheaper	1947	Exclusive 257
Citation		Released in 1998 for the first time	Moonrise	1947	Exclusive 249
			More Than You Know	1948	Modern 599
Cloudy Skies	1951	Aladdin 3106	My Song	1952	Modern 881
Competition Blues		Released in 1998 for the first time	My Sugar Is Sweet	1954	Hollywood 1012
			New Orleans Blues	1947	Exclusive 240
Cut Off The Fat	1949	RCA 50-0031	New Shade Of Blues, A	1949	RCA 50-0009
Diesel Drive	1954	Hollywood 1012	Now That You're Gone	1948	Exclusive 705
Dragnet Blues	1953	Modern 910	Pasadena	1947	Exclusive 246
Driftin' Blues	1947	Aladdin 112/Aladdin 183 (1947)/Modern 646 (1948)/RCA 50-0043 (1949)	Peek A Boo	1949	Exclusive 86x
			Playing Numbers	1953	Modern 910
			Race Track Blues	1947	Aladdin 129
			Rain-Chick	1950	RCA 50-0086
			Rocks In My Bed	1947	Aladdin 130
Fire, Fire, Fire		Released in 1998 for the first time	Rock With It	1949	RCA 50-0073
			Rosamay		Released in 1998

Sail On Blues	1946	Modern Music 151
Scratch Sheet	1947	Exclusive 259
Sleigh Ride	1954	Hollywood 1021
So Long	1949	RCA 50-0043/Modern Music 143
Someday You'll Need Me	1950	RCA 50-0095
Sooth Me	1947	Exclusive 259
St. Louis Blues	1948	Exclusive 703
Strange Love	1953	Hollywood 1001
Sunny Road	1946	Exclusive 233
This Is One Time, Baby (You Ain't Gonna Two Time Me)	1949	RCA 50-0009
Three Handed Woman		Released in 1998 for the first time
Till The Real Thing Comes Along	1947	Aladdin 130/Aladdin 183 (1947)
Too Late	1953	Modern 918
Travelin' Blues	1946	Modern Music 131
Walkin' Blues	1949	RCA 50-0026
Warsaw Concerto, Part 1	1946	Modern Music 134
Warsaw Concerto, Part 2	1946	Modern Music 134
Was I To Blame For Falling In Love With You	1946	Exclusive 234
What Does It Matter	1949	RCA 50-0018
What You Know About Love	1946	Modern Music 133
When I Meander In The Meadow		Released in 1998 for the first time
Why Is Love Like That	1947	Exclusive 251
Wrackin' My Brain Over You		Released in 1998 for the first time
You Are My First Love	1947	Aladdin 129/Aladdin 184 (1947)
You Can Go Feed Yourself	1949	RCA 50-0026
You Don't Have To Treat Me As A Stranger	1951	Aladdin 3106
You Left Me Forsaken	1946	Modern Music 143
You're Gonna Be Sorry	1953	Modern 918
You Showed Me The Way	1946	Modern Music 139
You Won't Let Me Go	1946	Modern Music 142

Three Blazers, Johnny Moore's, Floyd Dixon &

Bad Neighborhood	1952	Aladdin 3121
Blues For Cuba	1952	Aladdin 3121
Broken Hearted Traveler	1953	Aladdin 3166
Do I Love You	1951	Aladdin 3101
Empty Stocking Blues	1950	Aladdin 3074
Four Years	1951	Aladdin 3082
Girl Fifteen	1950	Aladdin 3069
Long Time Ago, A	1954	Aladdin 3230
Lovin'	1953	Aladdin 3196
Married Woman	1953	Aladdin 3196
Real Lovin' Mama	1950	Aladdin 3075
San Francisco Blues	1950	Aladdin 3074
Telephone Blues	1950	Aladdin 3075
Time And Place	1951	Aladdin 3101
Unlucky Girl	1951	Aladdin 3082
Walkin' And Talkin' The Blues	1950	Aladdin 3069
You Need Me Now	1954	Aladdin 3230
You Played Me For A Fool	1953	Aladdin 3166

Three Blazers, Johnny Moore's Three Blazers, Johnny Moore's

What Am I Gonna Do This Christmas'		Released in 1998 for the first time

Three Blue Notes

Adios, Americano	1938	Bluebird B-10581
Are You Lonesome Tonight'	194'	MGM 10628
Confucius Say	1938	Bluebird B-10548
Don't 'Sweetheart' Me	194'	Hit 7080
Get The Moon Out Of Your Eyes	1938	Bluebird B-10826
Honestly, I Love You	194'	MGM 10672
In A Little Dutch Kindergarten	1938	Bluebird B-7608
It's Time To Say 'Aloha' (with Glee Club)	1938	Bluebird B-7886
Little Red Fox, The	1938	Bluebird B-10581
Penny Wise And Love Foolish	194'	MGM 10628
Roller Skating On A Rainbow	1938	Bluebird B-10277
Sweet Genevieve	1938	Bluebird B-7605
Up-sy Down-sy	1938	Bluebird B-10537
Vamp, The	194'	MGM 10672

Three Cheers

How Can We Be Wrong'	1938	Bluebird B-7798
How Little I Knew	1938	Bluebird B-7811/Montgomery Ward M-7542
Simple And Sweet	1938	Bluebird B-7798
Someday Sweetheart	1938	Bluebird B-7827

Three Cheers, Betty Roth & the

Take A Number From One To Ten	1934	Brunswick 7303

Three Cheers, Bing Crosby & the

Dear Old Girl 1936 Brunswick 02341

Three Chips

Isn't Love The Grandest Thing'	1935	Melotone 5-12-05

Three Dynamites

Dig These Dynamites	1948	Columbia 30112
Dynamite Boogie	1947	Columbia 30096
Facing Life	1947	Columbia 30096
Jumpin' To The Boogie	1948	Columbia 30112

Three Earbenders

It's A Hap, Hap, Happy Day	1939	Columbia 35359

Three Esquires, Edythe Wright & the

Jamboree	1936	Victor 25496

Three Flames

Blue Moon	1946	Gotham 106

Chewing Gum Mama	1950	MGM 10741
Cling To Me Baby	1947	Columbia 37935
Cornelia Jones	1950	MGM 10853
Day Dreamin'		
Exactly Like You	1946	Gotham 107
Go Way Gal	1951	Columbia 39259
I Don't Want To Take That Chance	1950	MGM 10853
I'll See You By And By	1949	Harmony 1063
Johnny Take My Wife	1947	Columbia 37321
Milk Shake Stand		
Nicholas	1947	Columbia 37268
Open The Door Richard	1947	Columbia 37268
Please Stop Playing Those Blues, Boy	1949	Harmony 1063
Poor Butterfly		
Salt Peanuts	1947	Columbia 37935
Sky Full Of Sunshine	1950	Columbia 39078
Stick Around	1951	Columbia 39259
Succotash Baby	1950	Columbia 39078
Suffer	1950	MGM 10741
Susan Candy Ball		
Sweet Georgia Brown		
Them There Eyes		
Tiger's Blues	1946	Gotham 107
Viddle De Vop	1947	Columbia 37321
Your Issue Is Just Like Tissue	1946	Gotham 106

Three Georgia Crackers

Hannah, My Love	1930	Columbia 15653-D
I've Been Hoodooed	1930	Columbia 15630-D
Nothin' But The Blood Of Jesus	1930	Columbia
Pore Little Thing Cried mammy	1930	Columbia 15630-D
Whoa Buck Whoa	1930	Columbia 15653-D
Why Did They Dig Ma's Grave So Deep	1930	Regal Zonophone MR 504

Three Hokum Kids

Disconnected Mama	1929	
Toodle-Loo	1929	Brunswick

Three Horsemen

Don't Send My Boy To Prison	1930	Columbia 2364-D

Three Jacks

Spanish Shawl	1928	Okeh 41102
University Of California: Fight For California/All Hail	1930	Harmony 1222-H
University Of Harvard: Harvardian	1930	Clarion 5403-C/Harmony 1225-H
University Of Leland Stanford: The Cardinal Is Waving/Hail Stanford	1930	Harmony 1222-H
University Of Michigan	1930	Clarion 5401-C/Harmony 1166-H
University Of Princeton	1930	Harmony 1174-H/Clarion 5404-C
Washington And Lee Swing	1930	Clarion 5401-C/Harmony 1166-H
Without You, Emaline	1930	Harmony 1140-H

Three Jacks (as part of 'Hotel Pennsylvania Music' led by Lloyd Keating)

Alone With My Dreams	1930	Harmony 1126-H
Once Again Before We Part	1930	Diva 3120-G'Harmony 1120-H
So Sympathetic	1930	Harmony 1126-H
Stein Song (University Of Maine) (with Sid Garry)	1930	Clarion 5003-C/Harmony 1126-H/Publix 2019-P/Diva 3120-G

Three Jazz Aces, The (Porter Grainger's Three Jazz Songsters)

Ground Hog Blues	1926	Champion 15100
It Makes No Diff'rence To Me	1926	Champion 15100

Three Kadets

Modern Design	1941	Victor 27610

Three Kaufields

Daa Dee Dum!	1919	Columbia
Dardanella Blues, The	1920	Emerson 10215
Good Night Angeline (James Reese Europe, Noble Sissle & Eubie Blake)	1919	Emerson 10166
In Miami (Where Mammy's Waiting For Me)	1920	Emerson 1060

Three Kaufields (as the Kaufield Trio)

Just A Thought Of You	1919	Columbia

Three Kaufields (as the Kaufields)

I Know What It Means To Be Lonesome	1919	Columbia

Three Keys

Basin Street Blues	1932	Brunswick 6423/Vocalion 2744 (1934)
Fit As A Fiddle	1932	Brunswick 6411/Vocalion 2732 (1934)
Heebie Jeebies	1933	Vocalion 2523
I've Found A New Baby	1933	Vocalion 2569
(I Would Do) Anything For You	1933	Brunswick 6522/Vocalion 2755 (1934)
Jig Time	1932	Brunswick 6388/Vocalion 2730 (1934)
Mood Indigo	1933	Columbia 2706-D
Nagasaki	1932	Brunswick 6411/Vocalion 2732 (1934)
Oh! By Jingo!	1933	Brunswick

Rasputin	1933	Brunswick 6564/Vocalion 2765 (1934)
Somebody Loses - Somebody Wins	1932	Columbia 2706-D
Someone Stole Gabriel's Horn	1932	Brunswick 6388/Vocalion 2730 (1934)
Song Of The Islands	1933	Vocalion 2523
That Doggone Dog Of Mine	1933	Brunswick 6522/Vocalion 2755 (1934)
Wah-Dee Dah	1932	Brunswick 6423/Vocalion 2744 (1934)/Clanka Lanka CL-144.033
You Can Depend On Me	1933	Vocalion 2569

Three Little Maids

Across The Blue Ridge	1933	Conqueror 8158
Hear Them Bells	1933	Bluebird B-5860
I Ain't Gonna Study War No More	1933	Bluebird B-5860
I Hear The Voice Of An Angel	1933	Conqueror 8159
In The Harbor Of Home, Sweet Home	1933	Bluebird B-5336/Sunrise S-3417
It's Just A Tumbledown Shack	1933	Conqueror 8158
Since The Angels Took Mother Away	1933	Bluebird B-5336/Sunrise S-3417
When The Flowers Are Blooming In The Springtime	1933	Conqueror 8159

Three Melodians

Room With A View, A	1928	Columbia 1693-D
Song I Love, The	1928	Columbia 1702-D
What's The Reason'	1928	Columbia 1398-D

Three Minute Men

Let's Drift Away On Dreamer's Bay	1931	Brunswick 6188

Three Musketeers

At Night When The Sun Goes Down	1936	Bluebird B-6525
Bill Green	1936	
Goodbye To The Step Stones	1936	Bluebird B-6525

Three Peppers

Alexander's Ragtime Band	1937	Variety VA 523
Down By The Old Mill Stream	1938	Decca 2239 B
Duck's Yas, Yas, Yas, The	1937	Variety VA 590/Vocalion V 3803 (1937)/Okeh 3803
Fuzzy, Wuzzy	1938	Decca 2239 A
Get The Gold	1937	Variety VA 523
Good Old Tennessee	1947	Decca 48046
Hot Dogs	1940	Decca 3342 A
If I Had My Way	1937	Variety 630
It's A Puzzle To Me (So What!)	1939	Decca 2609 B
Just Because I Do	1947	Decca 48046
Love Grows On The White Oak Tree	1939	Decca 2557 A
Mary Had A Little Lamb	1940	Decca 8508
One Potato	1949	Gotham 189
One Too Many For Me	1949	Gotham 189
Pepperism (instrumental)	1939	Decca 2751 B
Serenade In The Night	1937	Variety 630
Swingin' At The Cotton Club	1937	Variety 650/Vocalion 3805 (1937)/Clanka Lanka CL-144.033
Swing Out, Uncle Wilson	1937	Variety VA 590/Vocalion V 3803 (1937)/Decca 2557 B (1939)/Okeh 3803
Three Foot Skipper Jones	1939	Decca 2609 A
Tom-Tom Serenade	1940	Decca 3342 B
Was That All I Meant To You'	1940	Decca 8508

Three Peppers, Sally Gooding & the

It Must Be Love	1938	Vocalion 4169
Midnight Ride Of Paul Revere	1937	Vocalion 3805 (1937)/Variety VA 650
Smile Up At The Sun	1937	Variety 554/Decca 2751A (1939)
Yours, All Yours	1937	Variety VA 554

Three Peters Sisters & Rhythm Boys

Everybody Step!	1938	Decca

Three Rascals

Did You Ever See A Dream Walking'	1933	Columbia 2852-D

Three Rascals (with Charlotte Murray)

Heat Wave	1933	Columbia 2821-D

Three Reasons

At A Little Hot Dog Stand	1939	Bluebird B-10183
Blue Evening	1939	Bluebird B-10234
Gotta Hit That Texas Trail Tonight	1939	Bluebird B-10274
Guess I'll Go Back Home (This Summer)	1939	Bluebird B-10327
Home In The Clouds, A	1939	Bluebird B-10272
I Can't Get You Out Of My Mind	1939	Bluebird B-10169
I Get Along Without You Very Well	1939	Bluebird B-10150
I'm Building A Sailboat Out Of Dreams	1939	Bluebird B-10183
I Paid For The Lie That I Told	1939	Bluebird B-10272

You		
I Promise You	1939	Bluebird B-10150
Little Lad	1939	Bluebird B-10144
Little Sir Echo	1939	Bluebird B-10169
Moonlight Serenade	1939	Bluebird B-10327
Penny Serenade	1939	Bluebird B-10144
Prairie Boy	1939	Bluebird B-10274
To You, Sweetheart, Aloha	1939	Bluebird B-10445
What Goes On Behind Your Eyes'	1939	Bluebird B-10335
Why Begin Again	1939	Bluebird B-10234
You're The Only Star (In My Blue Heaven)	1938	Bluebird B-10034

Three Rhythm Boys

Suzanne	1933	Victor 24235/Electrola EG 2785

Three Rhythm Kings

Grasshopper And The Ants, The	1934	Victor 24616
Love Thy Neighbor	1934	Victor 24604
Wise Little Hen, The	1934	Victor 24616

Three Rhythm Rascals

You've Got Me In The Palm Of Your Hand	1932	Victor 24061

Three Riffs

Ace In The Hole	1939	Decca 7634
Barbecued Ribs	1950	Apollo 1165
Cherry In My Lemon & Lime	1950	Apollo 1164
Don't Jump Off The Bridge		Pic 0007
Driftin'	1950	Apollo 1165
How Sweet Potatoes	1949	Jubilee 5003
I'll Be There	1949	Atlantic 871
It's A Killer, Mr. Miller	1939	Decca 7634
Jumpin' Jack	1950	Apollo 1164
My Baby And Lemon-N-Lime		Pic 0007
Pluto, You Dog	1949	Atlantic 871
Rev		Variety Music 339
Rock-A-Bye Boogie	1949	Jubilee 5003
Since The Day You Came Along		Variety Music 339

Three Riffs, Joe Medlin & the

Bewildered	1948	Atlantic 867
I'm Glad For Your Sake	1948	Atlantic 867
My Last Goodbye	1947	Atlantic 867

Three Riffs, Manhattan Paul & the

Go Long		Atlantic unreleased
Hard Ridin' Mama	1949	Atlantic 868
I'm So Good To You		Atlantic unreleased
I Wish I Didn't Love You So	1949	Atlantic 868

Three Ripples

I Must See Annie Tonight	1938	Bluebird B-10041

Three Scamps

Diga Diga Doo	1934	Victor
Jimmy Had A Nickel	1934	Victor
Pretty Polly Perkins	1934	Victor

Three Shades Of Rhythm, Herb Jeffries & the

At Least You Could Save Me A Dream	1944	Excelsior 100

Three Sharps & A Flat

I Ain't In Love No More	1939	Decca 7561
I Am, I Am, Am, Am (with Ethel Vick)	1939	Decca 7561
I'm Gettin' Sentimental Over You	1939	Decca 2278A
I'm Through	1938	Decca 7569
Poor Little Bug On The Wall	1938	Decca 7581
Skinny-Do	1939	Decca 2278B
Swinging In The Candy Store	1938	Decca 7569
That's No Lie	1938	Decca 7581

Three Sharps & Flats

Crazy And Worried Blues	1940	Okeh 05857
Hawaiian War Chant		Hamptone 518
Piccolo Stomp	1941	Okeh 05971
Rosie In The Garden	1940	Okeh 05857
That's That Rhythm	1941	Okeh 05971
Yes, Yes, Yes		Hamptone 519

Three Sharps And A Flat

Big Noise Of Winnetka	1947	Tower 1266
Sometimes I'm Happy	1947	Tower 1266

Three Songies

Troublesome Trumpet	1937	Variety VA 545

Three Star Singers

Darling	1928	Odeon 189186/Okeh
Don't Keep Me In The Dark, Bright Eyes	1928	Odeon A 189158/Odeon O-4075/Okeh
Sorry For Me	1928	Odeon A 189158/Odeon O-4075/Okeh
Too Busy!	1928	Odeon A 221083/Okeh

Three Toppers

We, The People	1938	Bluebird B-7666
Why'd Ya Make Me Fall In Love'	1938	Bluebird B-7595

Three T's

I'se A-Muggin'	1936	Victor 25273

Three Varieties, Billy Eckstine, Madeline Green & the

I Got It Bad And That Ain't Good	1941	Bluebird 11374

Three Varieties, Madeline Greene & the

Boy With The Wistful Eyes	1941	Bluebird 11394
I Never Dreamt	1942	Bluebird 11465
Sally Won't You Come Back	1941	Bluebird 11126/RCA 20-2635 (1948)
She'll Always Remember	1942	Bluebird 11512

Three Virginians

Carry Me Back To Old Virginny	1920	Okeh 4248

Three Voices

Clover Blossoms	1933	Bluebird 5120
Twelfth Street Rag	1933	Bluebird 5120

Three Wainwright Sisters
Got No Time	1925	Edison 51593

Three X Sisters
What Would Happen To Me (If Something Happened To You)'	1932	Victor 24162
Where (I Wonder Where)'	1932	Victor 24161
Just One Word Of Consolation	1936	Brunswick 02341/Decca 1044/Decca Y 5147/Brunswick A 81096

Tibbs, Andrew & the Dozier Boys
He's Got Her And Gone	1948	Aristocrat 1106
Holidays Are Over, The	1948	Aristocrat 1105
In A Travelin' Mood	1948	Aristocrat 1105
In Every Man's Life	1948	Aristocrat 1106

Tietge Sisters
Church In The Wildwood, The	1929	Victor 22265
Just Outside The Door	1929	Victor 22156
Kentucky Babe	1929	Victor
Lassie O' Mine	1929	Victor
Master, The Tempest Is Raging	1926	Victor 20515
My Wild Irish Rose	1926	Victor 20189
Name Of Jesus, The	1926	Victor 20515
O Master, Let Me Walk With Thee	1927	Victor 20980
Only A Flower	1927	Victor 21122
Only A Smile	1929	Victor 22156
Silvery Stars	1927	Victor 20980
Speak, Lord, We Hear	1929	Victor 22265
There's No-One Like Mother To Me	1926	Victor 20189
'Twas On A Cold And Stormy Night	1927	Victor 21122

Tolbert, Skeets & the Gentlemen Of Swing
Big Fat Butterfly	1941	Decca 8579
C.O.D.	1942	Decca 8641
Jumpin' Like Mad	1940	Decca 8528
W.P.A.	1940	Decca 7722

Tolbert, Skeets & the Gentlemen Of Swing (with Yack Taylor)
Those Draftin' Blues	1941	Decca 8516

Tom, Dick and Harry
All I Do Is Follow Butterflies	1929	Vocalion 15818
Home	1931	Victor
My Book Of Broken Dreams	1929	Brunswick
Save The Last Dance For Me	1931	Victor 22871
Then We Canoe-Dle-Oodle Song	1929	Vocalion 15818
When You're Counting The Stars Alone	1929	Brunswick
Where The Sweet Forget-Me-Nots Remember	1929	Brunswick

Tomcats
Daddy's Lullaby	1949	Capitol 15341
Honey, I'm Yours	1949	Capitol 15415
I Ain't Nowhere	1949	Capitol 15415
You Better Get Yourself Some Gold	1949	Capitol 15341

Tone Performers
Organ Grinder's Lament, The	1912	Columbia

Tones
Three Little Loves	1949	Baton 265
We	1949	Baton 265

Tones, Dusty Brooks & his
Cryin' Myself To Sleep	1950	Columbia 30236

Tones, Dusty Brooks & the
Heaven Or Fire	1951	Sun 182
Tears And Wine	1951	Sun 182

Toppers
If Money Grew On Trees	1948	Savoy 559
I'm All Alone	1948	Savoy 656
In A Palace Of Stone	1944	Savoy 559
Love Is A Many Splendored Thing	195'	Gilmar RX 114
Nat's Boogie Woogie		Regent 130
I'm Living For You	1944	Savoy 656/Regent 130

Toppers (as the Four Toppers)
Carry Me Back To Old Virginia	1940	Ammor 100

Toppers (Three Toppers)
I Take you	1941	Victor 27414
Jo-Jo, The Hobo	1941	Victor 27477
We Go Well Together	1941	Victor 27832

Toronto Rhythmaires
Son Of The Sea, A	1955	Decca 29237

Trail Blazers Male Quartet
Medley Of Stephen Foster Songs	1928	Trail Blazers W-116
Mighty Lak' A Rose	1928	Trail Blazers W-116
Ramona	1928	Trail Blazers W-115
Song Is Ended, The (But The Melody Lingers On)	1928	Trail Blazers W-115

Travelers
Feedin' The Horses	1935	Decca 448/Decca 5453
Ma	1936	Decca 5387
Raggin' The Fiddle	1935	Decca 449/Decca 5461
Toodle-Oo Rag	1935	Decca 449/Decca 5461
When The Pussywillow Whispers To The Catnip	1935	Decca 448/Decca 5453

Triangle Quartette
Doodlin' Back	1929	Broadway 5071/Paramount

She Done Quit Me Blues	1929	Broadway 5071/Paramount 12781 (1929)
Trinity Quartet		
All Hail The Power Of Jesus	1924	Victor 19499
Blest Christmas Morn	1923	Victor 19075
Break Thou The Bread Of Life	1924	Victor 19417
Bringing In The Sheaves	1924	Victor 19279
Christ The Lord Is Risen Today	1922	Victor 18873
Come All Ye Saints	1923	Victor 19222
Day Is Dying In The West	1924	Victor 19417
Full Surrender	1910	Victor 16709
God So Loved The World	1922	Victor 18873
Jesus Lives	1922	Victor 19004
Jesus Lover Of My Soul	1924	Victor 19499
O Sacred Head Surrounded	1922	Victor 19004
O Tender Loving Shepherd	1923	Victor 19067
Our Lord's Risen From The Dead	1922	Victor 18860
Saw Ye My Saviour	1923	Victor 19067
Shepherd Show Me How To Go	1923	Victor 19075
Silent Night	1929	Conqueror 7197
Some Time We'll Understand	1909	Victor 16414/Victor 19877 (1925)
Star Of The East	1929	Conqueror 7197
Strife Is Over, The Battle's Done, The	1922	Victor 18860
We Thank Thee O God	1923	Victor 19222
When The Mists Have Rolled Away	1912	Victor 17137
Troubadors (with Franklyn Baur, Lewis James, Elliott Shaw)		
Diane (I'm In Heaven When I See You Smile)	1927	Victor 21000
Troubadours (with Revelers)		
Tin Pan Parade	1927	Victor 21149
Trumpeteers		
Milky White Way	1948	Score 5001
Tuft's College Octette		
Tuft's Mosaic	1914	Columbia
Tune Twisters		
Hello 'Frisco	1940	Victor 26778
I'm Against Rhythm	1937	Liberty Music Shop L 224
I Saw Stars	1934	Decca 232
I Wish I Had You	1938	Vocalion 4257/Brunswick A 81831
On The Bumpy Road To Love	1938	Vocalion 4257/Brunswick A 81831
Pardon My Southern Accent	1934	Decca 232
Shine On Harvest Moon (with Anita Boyer)	1940	Victor 26779
Small Fry	1938	Vocalion 4212/Brunswick A 81769
Ten Easy Lessons	1938	Vocalion 4212/Brunswick A 81769
Triplets	1937	Liberty Music Shop L 224
'Way Back Home - Part 1	1935	Decca 473
'Way Back Home - Part 2	1935	Decca 473
Tune Twisters (with Evelyn Knight)		
It's My Lazy Day	1946	Decca 18902
My Fickle Eye	1946	Decca 18902
Tune Twisters, Hal Burke & the		
She's A Latin From Manhattan	1935	Decca 418
Zing! Went The Strings Of My Heart	1935	Decca 426
Tune Wranglers		
Buster's Crawdad Hole	1936	Bluebird B-6554
Drivin' The Doggies Along	1936	Bluebird B-6403
El Rancho Grande	1936	Bluebird B-6554
I Can't Change It	1936	Bluebird B-6365
I'm Wild About That Thing	1936	Bluebird B-6310
It Was Midnight Over The Ocean	1936	Bluebird B-6365
I Was Born Too Soon	1936	Bluebird B-6421
Lonesome Blues	1936	Bluebird B-6513
My Sweet Thing	1936	Bluebird B-6326
Ragtime Cowboy Joe	1936	Bluebird B-6438
Red's Tight Like That	1936	Bluebird B-6438
Ride On, Old Timer, Ride On	1936	Bluebird B-6403
She's Sweet	1936	Bluebird B-6326
Texas Sand	1936	Bluebird B-6513
They Go Wild Over Me	1936	Bluebird B-6310
Tune Wranglers (as the Chicago Rhythm Kings)		
Sarah Jane	1936	Bluebird B-6397
Tuskegee Institute Quartet		
Heaven's Song/Inchin' Along	1916	Victor 18075
Heidelberg Sten Song	1915	Victor 17899
Old Time Religion	1916	Victor 18075
Tuskegee Institute Singers		
Been Listenin' Good Lord	1918	Victor 18446
I Want To Be Ready/Get On Board	1918	Victor 18446
My Ways Are Cloudy/I'm Rolling Along	1918	Victor 18447
Nobody Knows The Trouble I've Seen	1917	Victor 18237
Roll Jordan Roll/I Want God's Healing	1917	Victor 18237
Tuskegee Quartet		
I Been Buked And Scorned	1918	Victor 18447
Steal Away	1915	Victor 17890
Swing Low Sweet Chariot	1915	Victor 17890

Umbrian Glee Club
Exhortation	1926	Vocalion 1013
Ma Honey	1926	Vocalion 1012
Rain Song	1926	Vocalion 1013
Swing Along	1926	Vocalion 1012

Unique Quartette
Mamma's Black Baby Boy	1893	Edison Cylinder 694
Who Broke The Lock (On The Henhouse Door)	1895	

University Male Quartet
Ann Arbor Days	1922	Brunswick 5074
College Days	1922	Brunswick 5073
When Night Falls, Dear	1922	Brunswick 5074
Yellow And Blue, The	1922	Brunswick 5073

University of Pennsylvania Quartet
Alma Mater	1914	Columbia A-1574
Dear, When I'm Gazing	1914	Columbia
Hail, Pennsylvania	1914	Columbia
Red White And Blue, The	1914	Columbia A-1574

University Singers
Deep River	1924	Cameo 531
Go Down Moses	1924	Cameo 530
Roll Jordan Roll	1924	Cameo 530
Swing Low, Sweet Chariot	1924	Cameo 531

Uptowners Quartet, Frances Langford with the
Hills Of Old Wyomin', The	1936	Brunswick 02242/Decca 783

Utica Institute Jubilee Singers
Watermelon	1928	Victor 21600

Utica Jubilee Singers
I Shall Not Be Moved	1932	Victor 24113
Swingin' On The Golden Gate	1932	Victor 24113

V-8 Vocal Ensemble
Bye Bye Baby	1936	Fred Waring Ford Dealers Program
Cross Patch	1936	Fred Waring Ford Dealers Program
Did You Mean It	1936	Fred Waring Ford Dealers Program
Double Trouble	1936	Fred Waring Ford Dealers Program
Honeysuckle Rose	1936	Fred Waring Ford Dealers Program
I Can Pull A Rabbit Outta My Hat	1936	Fred Waring Ford Dealers Program
I'd Rather Lead A Band	1936	Fred Waring Ford Dealers Program
I Know That You Know	1936	Fred Waring Ford Dealers Program
I'm Putting All My Eggs In One Basket	1936	Fred Waring Ford Dealers Program
Is It True What They Say About Dixie	1936	Fred Waring Ford Dealers Program
It's De-Lovely	1936	Fred Waring Ford Dealers Program
Jamboree Jones	1936	Fred Waring Ford Dealers Program
Let Yourself Go	1936	Fred Waring Ford Dealers Program
Rap Tap On Wood	1936	Fred Waring Ford Dealers Program
Robins And Roses	1936	Fred Waring Ford Dealers Program
Sing! Sing! Sing!	1936	Fred Waring Ford Dealers Program
Stompin' At The Savoy	1936	Fred Waring Ford Dealers Program
Stop Look And Listen	1936	Fred Waring Ford Dealers Program
Swing Mr. Charlie	1936	Fred Waring Ford Dealers Program
'Tain't Good	1936	Fred Waring Ford Dealers Program
There's Frost On The Moon	1936	Fred Waring Ford Dealers Program
Way Down Yonder In New Orleans	1936	Fred Waring Ford Dealers Program
Whirligig	1936	Fred Waring Ford Dealers Program
Why Do I Lie To Myself About You	1936	Fred Waring Ford Dealers Program
You Can't Pull The Wool Over My Eyes	1936	Fred Waring Ford Dealers Program

Vagabonds
At The End Of Sunset Lane	1933	Victor 23855/Bluebird B-5381/Sunset S-3462
Barbara Allen	1933	Bluebird B-5300/Electradisk 2171/Sunrise S-3381
Death Of Jesse James, The	1933	Bluebird B-5282/Electradisk 2043/Montgomery Ward M-4382/Sunrise S-3281
Do You, Don't You	1928	Brunswick
Drifting In A Lover's Dream	1933	Bluebird B-5588
Father, Mother Sister And Brother	1933	Bluebird B-5197/Electradisk 2087/Sunrise S-3287
For Ever And Ever More	1933	Bluebird B-5244/Electradisk 2127/Sunrise 3327
Four Thousand Years Ago	1933	Bluebird B-5315/Montgomery

Song	Year	Release
Give My Love To Mother	1933	Bluebird B-5588
How Beautiful Heaven Must Be	1933	Victor 23809/Bluebird B-5124/Electradisk 2034/Sunrise S-3205
In The Book Of Dreams	1933	Bluebird B-5989
In The Garden (a cappella)	1933	Bluebird B-6184
In The Little White Church On The Hill	1933	Bluebird B-6250
In The Sleepy Hills Of Tennessee	1933	Victor 23801/Bluebird B-5103/Electradisk/Sunrise S-3186
In The Valley Of Yesterday	1933	Victor 23855/Bluebird B-5315/Montgomery Ward M-4422/Sunset S-3396
In The Vine-Covered Church 'Way Back Home	1933	Bluebird B-5137/Electradisk 2043/Montgomery Ward M-4382/Sunrise S-3281
I Will Always Call You Sweetheart	1933	Bluebird B-5402
Leavenworth Jail	1933	Bluebird B-5472
Little Mother Of The Hills	1933	Bluebird B-5197/Electradisk 2087/Sunrise S-3278
Little Old Brick Church, The	1933	Bluebird B-5244/Electradisk 2127/Sunrise 3327
Little Shoes	1933	Victor 23801/Bluebird B-5103/Electradisk/Sunrise S-3186
Livin' On The Mountain	1933	Bluebird B-6184
My Pretty Quadroon	1933	Victor 23849/Bluebird B-5072/Electradisk 1995/Montgomery Ward M-4307/Sunrise S-3153
Ninety-Nine Years (Is Almost For Life)	1933	Victor 23820/Bluebird B-5072/Electradisk 1995/Montgomery Ward M-4422/Sunrise S-3396
Old Rugged Cross, The	1933	Victor 23809/Bluebird B-5124/Electradisk 2034/Sunrise S-3205
Old Sweet Song For A Sweet Old Lady, An	1933	Bluebird B-5381/Sunrise S-3462
Red River Valley	1933	Bluebird B-5297Electradisk 2168/Sunrise S-3378
Sourwood Mountain	1933	Bluebird B-5335/Sunrise S-3416
Sweetheart's Paradise	1933	Bluebird B-5989
That Little Boy Of Mine	1933	Victor 23820/Bluebird B-5072/Electradisk 1995/Sunrise S-3153
Waiting And Dreaming	1928	Brunswick
When It's Moonlight Down In Lovers' Lane	1933	Bluebird B-5137/Electradisk 2043/Montgomery Ward M-4382/Sunrise S-3281
When It's Time For The Whippoorwill To Sing	1933	Bluebird B-5402
When The Work's All Done This Fall	1933	Bluebird B-5300/Electradisk 2171/Sunrise S-3381

Valdese Quartet

Song	Year	Release
Just Over The Glory Land	1927	Okeh 45161
Waiting For The Boatman	1927	Okeh 45161

Valdosta Rotary Double Quartet

Song	Year	Release
Fishing Song	1925	Columbia
Medley Of Southern Melodies (Roll Them Bones, Uncle Joe, My Evaline)	1925	Columbia

Valentine Quartet, The Jimmie

Song	Year	Release
Walking With My Shadow	1948	Varsity 107

Valentine Trio, The Billy

Song	Year	Release
Baby, Please Don't Go	1951	Decca 48261
Clambake Boogie	1951	Decca 48297
Forever	1951	Decca 48243
It's A Sin To Tell A Lie	1951	Decca 48261
One Cocktail	1951	Decca 48202
Room I'm Sleeping In, The	1951	Decca 48202

She's Fit And Fat And Fine	1951	Decca 48243	His Love Waves Are Rolling	1930	Victor 40318
Tears, Tears, Tears	1951	Decca 48207	I Am Happy Now	1932	Victor 23597
Valley Inn Quartet			I'd Love To Go Down South	192'	Vaughan 1000
Blue Bonnet, You Make Me Feel Blue	1926	Champion 15123	If I Could Hear My Mother Pray Again	192'	Vaughan 775
Winding Trail, The	1927	Champion 15274	I'll Never Be Lonesome In Heaven	1929	Victor 40157
Van Brunt, Walter & the Peerless Quartet			I'll Take You Home Again, Kathleen	192'	Vaughan 725
Light Up Your Face With A Smile	1912	Edison 4mincyl 802			
Van Brunt, Walter with American Quartet			I'm In His Care	192'	Vaughan 900
I Want A Girl (Just Like The Girl That Married Dear Old Dad)	1911	Victor 16962	I Need The Prayers	192'	Vaughan 575
			In Steps Of Light	1928	Victor 40097
Let's Make Love Among The Roses	1910	Victor 16962	I See A Gleam Of Glory	1932	Victor 23769
			Is It Well With Your Soul'	192'	Vaughan 475
Varieteers			It's Just Like Heaven	1929	Victor 40202
Call My Gal Miss Jones	1954	Hickory 1025	It Will Make Heaven Bright	1932	Victor 23738
Deep Blues	1953	Hickory 1004	It Will Make Heaven Brighter	1929	Victor 23738
If You And I Could Be Sweethearts	1953	Hickory 1014	I Want To Go There	1928	Victor 40045
			Jesus Forgives And Forgets	192'	Vaughan 775
I'll Try To Forget I've Loved You	1951	MGM 10888	Jesus Leads To Victory	1930	Bluebird 5258
I Pay With Every Breath	1953	Hickory 1014	Juanita	192'	Vaughan 1000
I've Got A Woman's Love	1953	Hickory 1004	Just As Long As Eternity Rolls	1930	Victor 40333
Minnie, Come Home	1954	Hickory 1025	Keep My Hand In Thine	192'	Vaughan 500
You Don't Move Me No More	1951	MGM 10888	Kentucky Babe	192'	Vaughan 450
Variety Boys			Look For Me	192'	Vaughan 350
Chant, The	1941	Decca 8564	Lovesick Blues	192'	Vaughan 400
Harlem Fiesta	1941	Decca 8549	Magnify Jesus	192'	Vaughan 325
Tack Annie	1941	Decca 8549	Master Of The Storm	1928	Victor 21756
Uptown Jive	1941	Decca 8564	Mother And Home	192'	Vaughan 650
Variety Four Quartet			Music In My Soul	192'	Vaughan 625
I'm Coming, Virginia	1927	Brunswick 7025	My Heavenly Homecoming	1932	Victor 23738
Miss Annabelle Lee	1927	Brunswick 7025	My Loved Ones Are Waiting For Me	192'	Vaughan 525
Variety Girls, James Newell & the					
That's When I Cry Over You	1932		My Troubles Will Be Over	1928	Victor 40071
Vassar Girls Quartet			Naturalized For Heaven	1929	Victor 40289
Kentucky Babe	1907	Edison 9460 (black2mincyl)	O Happy Day	192'	Vaughan 925/Victor 23769 (1932)
Vaudeville Quartet & Billy Murray					
Lucia Sextet Burlesque	1912	Victor 17119	Old Fashioned Cabin, The	1924	Vaughan 675
Vaughan Quartet			One At Last	1929	Victor 40157
Beautiful Harbor Lights	192'	Vaughan 600	Only A Step	192'	Vaughan 650
Beautiful Life, A	1932	Victor 23597	O Such Wondrous Love	1929	Victor 23519
Better Than Gold	192'	Vaughan 550	Singing A Wonderful Song	1924	Vaughan 700
Bloom Brightly Sweet Roses	192'	Vaughan 800	Sittin' In The Corner	192'	Vaughan 1025
Couldn't Hear Nobody Pray	192'	Vaughan 300	Somebody Needs Just You	192'	Vaughan 375
Crossing The Bar	192'	Vaughan 425	Some Day	192'	Vaughan 325
Don't Forget The Family Prayer	192'	Vaughan 950	Steal Away	192'	Vaughan 300
Don't Forget To Pray	192'	Vaughan 500	Sunlight And Shadows	1928	Victor 40097
Don't You Love Your Daddy Too'	192'	Vaughan 975	Take Him With You	192'	Vaughan 875
Do You Know Him'	192'	Vaughan 375	That Little Old Hut	192'	Vaughan 750
Dreaming Alone In The Twilight	192'	Vaughan 425	They Left Him Alone	192'	Vaughan 675
Drifting Away	192'	Vaughan 475	This Charling Love	1928	Victor 40045
Echoes From The Shore	192'	Vaughan 575	Vaughan Quartet Medley	192'	Vaughan 400
Go To Jesus With It All	1924	Vaughan 700	Waiting At The Gate	192'	Vaughan 350
Happy Meeting, A	1929	Victor 40289	Wake America And Kluck, Kluck, Kluck	192'	Vaughan 825
His Charming Love	1928	Victor			

Walking With My King	1929	Victor 40202
We'll Live Again	192'	Vaughan 850
What A Morning It Will Be	1928	Victor 21756
What Is He Worth To Your Soul'	192'	Vaughan 950
When All Those Millions Sing	1928	Victor 40071
When Honey Sings An Old Time Song	192'	Vaughan 725
When Jesus Deems It Best	192'	Vaughan 525
When The Holy Ghost Comes Down	1930	Bluebird 5258
When The Home Gates Swing Open	1930	Victor 40318
When The Twilight Shadows Fall	192'	Vaughan 450
When We Lay Our Burdens Down	192'	Vaughan 750
Where Is God	1930	Victor 40333
Will The Gates Open For Me'	192'	Vaughan 800
Will You Be There	192'	Vaughan 900

Vaughan's Texas Quartet

Heaven All The Way For Me	1929	Victor 40231
I Walk With Jesus	1929	Victor 40174
King Needs Workers, The	1929	Victor 40174
That Beautiful Land	1929	Victor 40257
Walking With My King	1929	Bluebird 6039
Wayfaring Pilgrim	1929	Victor 40231
We'll Reap What We Sow	1929	Victor 40257/Bluebird 6039 (1929)

Velvetones

Ask Anyone Who Knows	1947	Sonora 2014
Can You Look Me In The Eyes	1947	Sonora 2015/Rondo 1554 (1949)
Cream Cheese And Jelly	1950	Columbia 30224
Don't Bring Me No News	1947	Sonora 2015/Rondo 1554 (1949)
Don't Say You're Sorry Again	1946	Coronet 4
Easy Baby	1946	Coronet 2
Find My Baby Blues	1947	Super Disc 1055
Georgianna From Savannah	1946	Coronet 4
Heyboblebip	1946	Coronet 1
Hole In My Pocket	1950	Columbia 30206
How I Miss You	1950	Columbia 30206
I'm Disillusioned	1950	Columbia 30224
I'm Gettin' Used To Love Again	1946	Coronet 5
It Just Ain't Right	1946	Sonora 3012
It's Written All Over Your Face	1946	Sonora 3010
I Want Some Bread, I Said	1947	Sonora 2014
Jason, Get Your Basin	1946	Coronet 3
One Day	1946	Coronet 1
Pittsburgh Joe	1946	Sonora 3010
Reverse The Charges	1946	Sonora 3012
Roberta, Get Out Of That Bed	1947	Super Disc 1055
Singing River	1946	Coronet 5
Sweet Lorraine	1946	Coronet 2
Swing Out, It Don't Cost Nothin'	1946	Coronet 3

Vernon Trio

Beautiful Faces	1920	Okeh 4235
Show Me How	1920	Okeh 4236

Vernon, Dolly & the Harmony Male Quartet

Star Of The East	1927	Harmony 518

Versatile Three

Chicken Rag	1926	Vocalion
Papa-De-Da-Da	1926	Vocalion

Victor Light Opera Company

Cocoanuts, The - Vocal Gems	1925	Victor 35769
Cossack Love Song	1925	Victor 19954
Countess Maritza - Vocal Gems	1926	Victor 35809
Dearest Enemy - Vocal Gems	1925	Victor 35766
Desert Song - Vocal Gems, The	1926	Victor 35809
Honeymoon Lane - Vocal Gems	1926	Victor 35811
Merry Merry - Vocal Gems	1925	Victor 35772
Princess Flavia - Vocal Gems	1925	Victor 35766
Song Of The Flame - Vocal Gems	1925	Victor 19954
Sunny - Vocal Gems	1925	Victor 35769

Victor Male Chorus (Revellers & the Peerless Quartet)

Faust - Soldier's Chorus	1925	Victor 19783
L'Africaine - Chorus Of Bishops And Priests	1925	Victor 19783

Victor Male Quartet

War Songs Of The Normans	1915	Victor 17725

Victor Salon Group (with Revelers)

Song Is Ended, The	1927	Victor

Victorians

Don't Break My Heart Again	1950	Specialty 411
I Guess You're Satisfied	1950	Specialty 411
Naturally Too Weak For You	1951	Specialty 420
Part-Time Sweetheart	1951	Specialty 420

Victory Four

Catastrophe, A	1920	Pathe 22272
Don't Forget To Pray	1928	Columbia
Little Tommy Went Fishing	1920	Pathe 22272
Look For Me, I'll Be There	1928	Columbia

Victory Quartet

Bringing In The Sheaves	1927	Broadway 8107
Jesus Is Precious To Me	1927	Broadway 8107

Vikings

Lonesome For You, Annabelle	1953	Decca 28829
When The Morning Glories Wake	1953	Decca 28828
When You're Smiling	1953	Decca 28828

Violet Harmony Singers

Lord, I Can't Stay Away	1927	Vocalion 1095
When All The Saints Go Marching In	1927	Vocalion 1095

Virginia Female Jubilee Singers

Go Down Moses Way Down In Egypt Land	1921	Okeh 4437
I've Been A Sinner All My Life	1921	Okeh 4482
King Jesus Is A Listening	1921	Okeh 4451
Lover Of The Lord	1921	Okeh 4430

My Time Ain't Long	1921	Okeh 4558
Old Ark's A Moverin', The	1921	Okeh 4482
O Mary, Don't You Weep, Don't You Mourn	1921	Okeh 4430
Revival Day	1921	Okeh 4558
Wait Until I Get On The Road Oh Yes! Oh Yes!	1921	Okeh 4451
When Jesus Christ Was Born	1921	Okeh 4437

Virginia Four

Comin' Down The Shiny Way	1930	Victor 38569
Don't Leave Me Behind	1929	Bluebird 5724/Victor 23376 (1933)
It'll Soon Be Over With	1929	Bluebird 5724/Victor 23376 (1933)
Since I Been Born	1930	Victor 38569

Virginia Four (Norfolk Quartet)

Dig My Jelly Roll	1939	Decca 7662
I'd Feel Much Better	1939	Decca 7808
Moaning The Blues	1939	Decca 7662
Queen Street Rag	1940	Decca 7808

Virginia Jubilee Singers (Norfolk Jubilee Quartet)

Crying Holy Unto The Lord	1924	Broadway 5077
Daniel In The Lion's Den	1927	Broadway 5051
Do You Want To Be A Lover Of The Lord'	1926	Broadway 5036
Ezekiel Saw De Wheel	1924	Broadway 5077
If Anybody Asks You Who I Am	1926	Broadway 5082
I'm Going Through	1927	Broadway 5066
I'm Gonna Build Right On Dat Shore	1924	Broadway 5074
Let The Church Roll On	1927	Broadway 5082
Louisiana Bo Bo	1926	Broadway 5011
Oh The Shoes That My Lord Gave Me	1926	Broadway 5036
Old Account Was Settled Long Ago, The	1927	Broadway 5051
Queen Street Rag	1926	Broadway 5011
Sinner You Can't Hide	1927	Broadway 5066
Sit Down, Sit Down, I Can't Sit Down	1925	Broadway 5002
Somebody's Always Talking About Me	1925	Broadway 5002
Swing Low Sweet Chariot	1924	Broadway 5000
Where Shall I Be'	1924	Broadway 5074

Virginia Male Quartet

I Am Wandering Down Life's Shady Path	1929	Okeh 45388
Light Of Life	1929	Okeh 45388
Looking This Way	1929	Okeh 45453
No Night There	1929	Okeh 45453

Virginians, Aileen Stanley with the

Don't Think You'll Be Missed	1920	Victor 19039

Vocal Quartet

Blind Tom	189'	Berliner 0851

Vocal Sextet

Floradora: Tell me Pretty Maiden	1908	Columbia A-0485

Vocal Trio

By The Camp Fire	1919	Okeh 1192
Since My Best Gal Turned Me Down	1935	Decca 453
T'aint Good	1936	Decca 960

Vocardians

My Little Grass Shack In Kealakekua, Hawaii	1934	Victor 24514/Electrola EG 3052

Voices Five

Brown Skin	1939	Vocalion 4739
Give Me Your Answer	1941	Okeh 6364

Voices Five (with Amy Amell and Don Brown)

(There'll Be Bluebirds Over) The White Cliffs Of Dover	1941	Okeh 6487

Voices Four

Where Do I Go From You'	1940	Vocalion 5505

Voices Four (with Don Brown)

Lazy River	1941	Okeh 6145

Voices Three

Bartender Polka	1940	Okeh 5717
Dog House Polka	1941	Okeh 6203
Ev'ry Sunday Afternoon	1940	Vocalion 5505
I Love You	1941	Columbia 37082/Conqueror 9629/Okeh 6145/Okeh 6633
I Love You (Oh! How I Love You)	1939	Varsity 8137
I Love You (Oh! How I Love You)	1948	Davis
It Happened In Kaloha	1940	Vocalion 5457
Mirrors Don't Tell Lies	1938	Vocalion 4228
Oceana Roll (with Amy Amell)	1940	Okeh 5861
Train Song, The	1941	Okeh 6487
When Your Old Wedding Ring Was New	1941	Okeh 6448
You Darling	1940	Vocalion 5543

Voices Three (with Amy Amell and Don Brown)

Conchita, Marquita, Lolita, Pepita, Rosita, Juanita Lopez	1942	Okeh 6698
Humming Bird, The	1942	Columbia 36638
Kille Kille	1942	Columbia 38247/Okeh 6698

Voices Three (with Amy Amell)

Ebb Tide	1937	Conqueror 8958/Vocalion 3680

Ev'rybody Ev'ry Payday	1942	Okeh 6701
I Don't Want To Set The World On Fire	1941	Okeh 6230
Lenny	1941	Okeh 6131
Would 'Ja Mind	1939	Varsity 8149

Voices Three (with Dan Brown)

Johnny Peddler (I Got)	1940	Okeh 5789
Moonlight Cocktail	1941	Okeh 6526
Shepherd Serenade	1941	Okeh 6353
Sometimes	1942	Okeh 6571
Walkin' Thru Mockin' Bird Lane	1940	Okeh 5973
Your Are My Sunshine	1941	Conqueror 9897/Okeh 6211

Volunteer Firemen with male quartet (Revelers)

Tie Me To Your Apron Strings Again	1926	Brunswick 3045

Wainwright Elkins Quartet

Silent Night, Holy Night	1927	Paramount 12418

Waldhorn Quartette, Heim & the

Post In The Forest, The		Edison 478 (4BA)

Walker, Esther & Male Quartet

All Alone Monday	1926	Brunswick 3349
Don't Be Angry At Me	1926	Brunswick 3348

Wallace Sisters

He's Just A False Alarm	1937	Decca 1624
Pork And Beans	1937	Decca 1624

Wallace Trio (Le Dandy Trio)

Call Me Darling (Call Me Sweetheart, Call Me Dear)	1931	Clarion 5359-C/Harmony 1381-H/Velvet Tone 2459-V/Okeh 41529
Everyone In Town Loves Little Mary Brown	1931	Clarion 5394-C/Harmony 1380-H/Velvet Tone 2458-V/Okeh 41524
It's The Darndest Thing	1931	Harmony 1380-H/Clarion 5394-C/Velvet Tone 2458-V/Okeh 41525
Who Am I'	1931	Harmony 1381-H/Clarion 5395-C/Velvet Tone 2459-V/Okeh 41523

Wanderers

Foot Warmer	1935	Bluebird 5994
Good Man Is Hard To Find, A	1935	Bluebird 5834
I Ain't Got Nobody	1935	Bluebird 5869
It's You I Adore	1935	Bluebird 5834
Nealski	1935	Bluebird 5921
No One To Say Goodbye	1935	Bluebird 5887
Thousand Miles	1935	Bluebird 5921
Tiger Rag	1935	Bluebird 5887
Wanderers' Stomp	1935	Bluebird 5869

Washington's Kentucky Quartet

I Will Be Da	1925	Gennett 3036/Gennett 5662/Silvertone 4016
Throw 'Way Dem Ole Shoes	1925	Gennett 3036/Gennett 5662/Silvertone 4016

Waters, Ethel & Her Ebony Four

Black And Blue	1930	Columbia 2184D
Brother, You've Got Me Wrong	1925	Columbia 433D
Do I Know What I'm Doing	1929	Columbia 1905-D
Harlem On My Mind	1933	Columbia 2826D
Heat Wave	1933	Columbia 2826D
Hundred Years From Today, A	1933	Columbia 2853D
I Got Rhythm	1930	Columbia 2348-D
I Just Couldn't Take It Baby	1933	Columbia 2853D
I've Found A New Baby	1926	Columbia 561-D
Loud Speakin' Papa (You'd Better Speak Easy To Me)	1925	Columbia 472-D
Maybe Not At All	1925	Columbia 14112-D
Memories Of You	1930	Columbia 2288D
My Kinda Man	1930	Columbia 2222-D
No Man's Mama	1925	Columbia 14118-D
No One Can Love Me (Like The Way You Do)	1925	Columbia 379-D
Pickaninny Blues	1925	Columbia 472-D
Please Don't Talk About Me When I'm Gone	1931	Columbia 2409-D
Porgy	1930	Columbia 2184D
River, Stay	1931	Columbia 2511-D
Second Hand Man	1929	Columbia 1871-D
Shake That Thing	1925	Columbia 14118-D
Shine On, Harvest Moon	1931	Columbia 2511-D
Shoe Shoo Bogie Boo	1929	Columbia 1905-D
Sweet Georgia Brown	1925	Columbia 379-D
Sympathetic Dan	1925	Columbia 433D
Tell 'Em About Me	1926	Columbia 561-D
Trav'lin' All Alone	1929	Columbia 1933D
True Blue Lou	1929	Columbia 1871-D
Waiting At The End Of The Road	1929	Columbia 1933D
When Your Lover Has Gone	1931	Columbia 2409-D
Without That Gal!	1931	Columbia 2481-D
You Brought A New Kind Of Love To Me	1930	Columbia 2222-D
You Can't Do What My Last Man Did	1925	Columbia 14112-D
You Can't Stop Me From Lovin' You	1931	Columbia 2481-D
You're Lucky To Me	1930	Columbia 2288D

Watson Sisters
China We Owe A Lot To You	1917	Columbia A-2375
I Always Think I'm Up In Heaven	1919	Okeh 1216
If I Can't Have Him All The Time	1917	Columbia A-2375
Lead Me, Jim	1919	Okeh 1252/Okeh 4075 (1920)
Never Let One Man Worry You	1920	Okeh 4075
When The Bees Make Honey In Sunny Alabam'	1919	Okeh 1213

Watson, Deek & 4 Dots (Brown Dots, Deek Watson & the)
Saturday Night Function	1948	Castle 2006
Strange As It Seems	1948	Castle 2006

We Girls Quartette
Glow Worm, The	1919	Edison DD 80469/Edison Blue Amberol 3765
Good-Bye, My Baby	1918	Edison DD 50944/Edison Blue Amberol 4570

Weary Willie Trio
Sons Of Mother Earth	1915	Edison BA 2830/Edison DD 50329-L (1915)

Weavers
Across The Wide Missouri	1951	Decca 27515
Around The Corner	1948	Decca 28054
Bay Of Mexico, The	1952	Decca 28542
Clementine	1952	Decca 28434
Down In The Valley	1952	Decca 28542
Gandy Dancer's Ball	1948	Decca 28054
Goodnight Irene	1950	Decca 28272
Hard Ain't It, Hard	1950	Decca 28228
Midnight Special	1950	Decca 28272
Rock Island Shuffle	1954	Decca 28919
Roving Kind, The	1951	Decca 27332
Run Home To Mama	1950	Decca 28228
Sylvia	1954	Decca 28919
Taking It Easy	1953	Decca 28637
True Love	1952	Decca 28434
Wreck Of The John B	1951	Decca 27332

Weber Four (Weber Male Quartette)
Jesus, Lover Of My Soul	1922	Vocalion 14311A
Still, Still With Thee	1922	Vocalion 14311B/Edison 915 (4BA)

Werrenrath, R. with Haydn Quartet
Old Nassau	1911	Victor 16860

Werrenrath, Reinald & Quartet
Lord Geoffrey Amherst	1911	Victor 16873

West Trio, Ray
Love Is Like That	1930	Columbia 2190-D
When The Sun Goes Down	1930	Columbia 2190-D

Wheat Street Female Quartet
Go Down Moses	1925	Columbia 14067-D
My Way Is Cloudy	1926	Okeh 8428
Oh, Yes!	1925	Columbia 15021-D
Religion Is A Fortune	1926	Okeh 8428
Wheel In A Wheel	1925	Columbia 15021-D
When The Saints Go Marching In	1925	Columbia 14067-D

Wheeler, Frederick & the Haydn Quartet
Mary ('Our Miss Gibbs')	1911	Victor 16828

Whippoorwill Four
Central Georgia Blues	1930	Brunswick 7150

White Way Quartet
Come Along	1922	Brunswick 2320
Georgia Cabin Door	1922	Brunswick 2373
My Dixie	1922	Brunswick 2331
No Wonder I'm Lonesome	1922	Brunswick 2331
Tomorrow Morning	1922	Brunswick 2349

White Way Quartet, William Reese (Billy Jones) & the
Nellie Kelly, I Love You	1923	Brunswick 2364

Whiteman, Paul and his Orchestra with vocal refrain by the American Quartet
Why Did I Kiss That Girl'	1924	Victor 19267

Whiteman, Paul and his Orchestra, with American Quartet
Last Night On The Back Porch (I Loved Her Best Of All)	1923	Victor 19139

Whitewater Trio
Holy Ghost With Love Divine	1923	Champion 15043

Whitney Brothers
Home Of The Soul (flip is	1909	Victor 16372
Jesus Savior, Pilot Me	1910	Victor 16441
Kitty McGee	1909	Victor 16373
Light Of Life	1910	Victor 16441
Light Of The World Is Jesus, The	1910	Victor 16465
Lord's Prayer, The - 23rd Psalm	1909	Victor 16362
Old Folks At Home	1910	Victor 16454
Remember Me Oh Mighty One	1909	Victor 16430

Whitney Brothers Quartet
Eternity	1909	Victor 16362
Galilee	1909	Victor 16430

Whitney Quartet
Sally In Our Alley	1909	Victor 16401

Wiedoft-Wadsworth Quartet
Moon, The	1920	Vocalion 14091A
Tell Me Little Gypsy	1920	Brunswick 2042

Wilkins Quartet
Glory For The Faithful	1930	Columbia 15592-D
I Am So Glad	1930	Columbia 15592-D

Williams Jubilee Singers
My Lord Is Riding All The Time	1930	Brunswick 7191

Williams Jubilee Singers, Famous
When The Love Comes Trickling Down	1930	Brunswick 7211

William Blevins Quartet
I Done Done	1937	Conqueror 8932
Wasn't That A Mighty Day'	1937	Conqueror 8932

Williams Brothers Quartet (with Bing Crosby)
Swinging On A Star	1944	Decca 18597

Williams Brothers Quartet, Bing Crosby & the
Going My Way	1944	Decca 18597/Decca 10170/Brunswick 03534/'Decca 24544/Decca 27605

Williams Brothers, Kay Thompson & the
Jubilee	1947	Columbia 38101

Williams Jubilee Singers
Angels Roll The Stone Away	1929	Columbia 14431-D
Gospel Train Is Coming, The	1929	Columbia 14457-D
He's Got His Eyes On You	1929	Columbia 14457-D
Oh! Didn't It Rain'	1929	Columbia 14431-D
Reign Massa Jesus, Reign	1930	Brunswick 7174
Walk In Jerusalem Just Like John	1930	Brunswick 7211

Williams Jubilee Singers, World Famous
Ding Dong Bells	1930	Brunswick 7174
Po' Mona	1930	Brunswick 7191

Williams' Trio, Clarence
Santa Claus Blues	1925	Okeh 8254

Williams, Billy Quartet
After I Say I'm Sorry	1952	MGM 11172
Ask Me No Questions	1953	Mercury 70271/Mercury 71187 (1957)
Azur-Te (Paris Blues)	1952	Mercury 5866
Baby, Baby	1958	Coral 61932
Begin The Beguine	1960	Coral 62230
Between The Devil And The Deep Blue Sea	1952	MGM 11249
Busy Line	1951	MGM 11117
Butterfly		
Callaway Went Thataway	1952	MGM 11145
Cattle Call	1953	Mercury 70210
Confetti	1952	MGM 11184
Crazy Little Palace, A	1956	Coral 61576
Cry Baby	1956	Coral 61576
Date With The Blues		
Don't Cry On My Shoulder	1956	Coral 61730
Don't Grieve, Don't Sorrow, Don't Cry	1952	MGM 11184
Don't Let Go	1958	Coral 61932
Don't Worry 'Bout Me		
Follow Me	1956	Coral 61751
Fools Rush In	1955	Coral 61346
For You	1960	Coral 62230
Gaucho Serenade, The	1951	MGM 10926/MGM 12537 (1952)
Glory Of Love, The	1955	Coral 61462
Go Home, Joe	1954	Mercury 70376
Good Night Irene	1959	Coral 62101
Got A Date With An Angel	1957	Coral 61886
Go To Sleep, Go To Sleep, Go To Sleep	1959	Coral 62131
He Follows She	1955	Coral 61346
Honey Dripper, The	1954	Coral 61264
I Cried For You	1960	Coral 62218
I Didn't Slip, I Wasn't Pushed, I Fell	1950	MGM 10764
I Don't Know Why (I Love You Like I Do)	1952	Mercury 70012
If I Never Get To Heaven	1953	Mercury 70271
I Guess I'll Be On My Way	1956	Coral 61684
I'll Close My Eyes	1954	Mercury 70324
I'll Get By	1958	Coral 61999
I'll Never Fail You	1951	MGM 11117
I'm Gonna Sit Right Down And Write Myself A Letter	1957	Coral 61795
In The Cool Of The Evening		
It Hurts So Much	1958	Coral 62029
It's A Miracle	1953	Mercury 70094
It's Best We Say Goodbye	1952	Mercury 5884
It's No Sin	1951	MGM 11066
It's Over	1951	MGM 11066
It's Praying Time	1958	Coral 61999
I've Got An Invitation To A Dance	1954	Mercury 70324/Mercury 71187 (1957)
I Wanna Hug You, Kiss You, Squeeze You (with intro by Alan Freed)	1955	Coral 61363
I Wonder	1959	Coral 62140
I Won't Cry Anymore	1951	MGM 10926
Just A Little Bit More	1955	Coral 61498
Learning To Love	1955	Coral 61498
Little Boy, The		
Longing	1950	MGM 10764
Lord Will Understand, The	1957	Coral 61795
Love Me	1954	Coral 61264
Lover Of All Lovers	1960	Coral 62218
Mad About'Cha	1952	Mercury 70012
Music For The Angels	1951	MGM 10857
Nola	1958	Coral 62069
No Other Love	1952	MGM 11145
Over The Rainbow		
Pied Piper, The	1957	Coral 61795
Pour Me A Glass Of Teardrops	1953	Mercury 70094
Pray	1956	Coral 61639
Pretty Eyed Baby	1951	MGM 10967
Red Hot Love	1959	Coral 62101
Room I'm Sleeping In, The	1951	MGM 10857
Shame, Shame, Shame	1956	Coral 61730
Sh-Boom	1954	Coral 61212
Sin	1951	MGM 11066

100 Years of Harmony: 1850 to 1950

Smack Dab In The Middle	1959	Coral 62140
Smile For Suzette, A	1953	Mercury 70210
Smoke From Your Cigarette	1955	Coral 61363
So Long	1958	Coral 62029
Some Folks Do Some Folks Don't	1952	Mercury 5902
Stay	1952	Mercury 5866
Steppin' Out Tonight	1958	Coral 61961
Stormy	1956	Coral 61751
That's What I'm Here For	1952	Mercury 5902
There, I've Said It Again	1958	Coral 61961
This Planet Earth	1956	Coral 61684
This Side Of Heaven	1953	Mercury 70180
Tied To The Strings Of Your Heart	1959	Coral 62069
What Can I Say After I Say I'm Sorry'	1952	MGM 11172
What You Don't Know Of Love	1952	MGM 11249
Wheel Of Fortune	1952	MGM 11172
Whenever, Wherever	1954	Coral 61212
Who Knows	1952	Mercury 5884
(Why Did I Tell You I Was Going To) Shanghai	1951	MGM 10998/MGM 12537 (1952)
Wonderful, Wonderful One	1955	Coral 61462
Wondrous Word (Of The Lord), The	1951	MGM 10998
You Don't Know		
You'll Reach Your Star	1956	Coral 61639
You Made Me Love You	1951	MGM 10967
You're The Only One For Me	1953	Mercury 70180
You're The Only One I Adore	1954	Mercury 70376
Williams, Irene & Male Trio		
Aloha Oe (Farewell To Thee)	1922	Brunswick 2701
Williams, Irene & the Crescent Trio		
Whispering	1921	Brunswick 5044
Willing Four		
Naaman	1943	Manor 1069
You've Got To Move	1943	Manor 1069
Wilson Quartet		
How I Love You Dear	1930	Clarion 5229-C/Velvet Tone 2294-V
Till I See You Again	1930	Clarion 5258-C/Velvet Tone 2324-V
When I Get Kisses From Mary	1930	Clarion 5197-C
Wilson Quartet (with Ted Wallace & his Campus Boys)		
Get Happy	1930	Columbia 2140-D
Windy City Four		
Oh Monah	1931	Vocalion 1681
Tiger Rag	1931	Vocalion 1738
Winkfield Sentimental Singers		
Going To See My Friend Again	1928	Paramount 12696
Oh Judgment	1928	Paramount 12696

Wisdom Sisters		
Amazing Grace	1923	Columbia 15093-D
Charge To Keep, A	1926	Columbia 15112-D
Children Of The Heavenly King	1926	Columbia 15129-D
Hide Thou Me	1927	Columbia 15153-D
I Saw A Way-Worn Traveller	1926	Columbia
Jesus Is All The World To Me	1926	Columbia 15112-D
O For A Closer Walk With God	1926	Columbia
Old Time Power, The	1926	Columbia 15129-D
Prayer	1927	Columbia 15309-D
Saviour's More Than Life To Me	1926	Columbia 15129-D
Sitting At The Feet Of Jesus	1923	Columbia 15093-D
Why Not Say Yes'	1927	Columbia 15309-D
Wonder State Harmonists		
My Castle On The Nile	1928	Vocalion 5346
Petite Jean Gallop	1928	Vocalion 5346
Wonder State Harmonizers		
Memory	1928	Vocalion 5275
Turnip Greens	1928	Vocalion 5275
Wonder Street Harmonizers		
El Menio	1928	Vocalion 5291
On The Wing	1928	Vocalion 5291
Wood, Gloria with Bachelors		
In Brazil It's The Nuts		Mastertone 3
Rhumba At The Matzo Ball		Mastertone 2
Woodlawn Quartet		
Juanita	1927	Gennett 6347
Old Oaken Bucket, The	1927	Gennett 6347
Wood's Jubilee Singers		
Bright Brown Crown	1925	Paramount 12316
Little Wheel Is Rolling In My Heart, The	1925	Paramount 12365
Lord I'm Troubled	1925	Paramount 12315
Lord's Prayer, The	1925	Paramount 12341
Oh Lord Have Mercy	1925	Paramount 12341
One Morning Soon	1925	Paramount 12365
Run To My Lord	1925	Paramount 12316
Seek And Ye Shall Find	1925	Paramount 12340
This Train Is Bound For Glory	1925	Paramount 12315
You Must Be Converted	1925	Paramount 12340
Wright Brothers Quartet		
God's Message To Man	1929	Columbia 15402-D
Mother Is With The Angels	1929	Columbia 15587-D
Somebody's Boy	1929	Columbia 15587-D
What A Glad Day	1929	Columbia 15402-D
Wynken, Blynken and Nod		
Ya Comin' Up Tonight, Huh' (with Harold Stokes)	1929	Victor 21889
X-Rays		
Charmaine	1951	Coral 65069
I'll Always Be In Love With You	1948	Savoy 681
I've Got A Pocketful Of Dreams	1951	Coral 65069
Today's Dream	1948	Savoy 681
Walking In The Sunshine	1952	Coral 65083

While We're Young	1952	Coral 65083

X-Rays, Brownie McGhee & the
Feed Me Baby	1950	Savoy 760
You've Got To Love Me Baby Too	1950	Savoy 760

Y.M.C.A. Quartet
I've Found A Friend	1918	Columbia
Still, Still With Thee	1918	Columbia

Yacht Club Boys
Ain't That Too Bad	1926	Brunswick 3405
Do You' That's All I Want To Know!	1927	Brunswick 4113
Every Little While	1926	Brunswick 3270
Great American Tourist, The	1934	Columbia 2908-D/Columbia DB 1356/Columbia FB 1238
How Could Little Red Riding Hood (Have Been So Very Good And Still Keep The Wolf From The Door')	1926	Brunswick 3270
I Fell Head Over Heels In Love	1927	Brunswick 3671
I Love That Girl	1927	Brunswick
I'm Wild About Horns On Automobiles That Go 'Ta-Ta-Ta-Ta'	1929	Brunswick 4118
Madman's Lullaby	1933	Columbia
Mahatma Gandhi/Shut The Door	1932	Columbia
Monte Carlo Song, The	1929	Brunswick 4118
Nobody's Baby But Mine	1926	Brunswick 3409
Oogel, Oogel, Oo (The Monkey Song)	1926	Brunswick 3269
Sing-Sing Isn't Prison Any More	1934	Columbia 2908-D/Columbia DB 1356/Columbia FB 1238
Spain	1933	Columbia
Super Special Picture Of The Year, The	1934	
Vulgar Boatman, The	1926	Brunswick 3269
We All Love To Sing In The Bathtub	1933	Columbia
We Own A Salon	1934	Columbia 2887-D/Columbia DB 1357/Columbia FB 1237
Will You Think Of Me'	1926	Brunswick 3405
Ya Gonna Be Home Tonight' (Oh, Yeh! Then I'll Be Over)	1926	Brunswick 3409
You Can't Walk Back From An Aeroplane	1927	Brunswick 3671

Yale Trio (of Yale University)
Dream House	1928	Brunswick 3981
Sweet Ella May	1928	Brunswick 3981

Yellow Jacket Four of 1925
Ramblin' Wreck From Georgia Tech	1925	Columbia 488-D

Yellow Jackets
Alma Mater Of Georgia Tech	1930	Brunswick 4773
Rambling Wreck From Georgia Tech	1930	Brunswick 4773

Yerkes Jazzarimba Orchestra (vocal refrain by the American Quartet)
Mammy O'Mine	1919	Columbia A-6108

Young Trio, Sterling
Peter Piper	1936	Melotone 7-01-02
Who Is My Baby Gonna Love All Winter Now That Summer Is Gone	1936	Melotone 7-01-02

Zonophone Male Quartet
Sleigh Ride Party, The	1906	Zonophone 373/Zonophone 5430 (1915)

Zonophone Quartet
Barnyard Medley	1906	Zonophone 364/Zonophone 5430 (1915)

Technology and Vocal Groups

Given the technology that we live with and can't live without in the twenty-first century, it must be difficult for all but the oldest among us to fully grasp the period covered by this book - 1850-1950. Today's media provide us with prodigious amounts about famous people. Probably more than we want to know. Certainly more than we can digest. Back then only the most famous of citizens, usually politicians, generals and the occasional scientist got the royalty treatment. Most people lived and died in obscurity.

Contrast that with a person who is roughly 50 years old today. He or she probably has several dozen photographs of his or her childhood, maybe half a dozen of his parents' early life, and several hundred (perhaps add another zero) of his children. His grandchildren are recorded on hours of videotape or digital media and themselves chronicle their own existence on social network websites or blogs. Today, everyone is special. One hundred years ago, no one was. Even the old photos that survive are posed, studio shots. Photos of early recording artists are rare, because the artists themselves didn't achieve the degree of fame that is accorded the artist of today. And the degree of fame achieved by anyone was limited by the technology of the day.

For example, in 1850, formal photography existed, but not much else. Recorded music wasn't available until 1890-1900 and the telephone did not attain popular usage until around 1900. Electric lights for the home and the widespread use of automobiles arrived around 1910; movies and radio in the twenties, personal photography in the 1930s. Widespread availability of television, air conditioning and transistor radios didn't occur until after the end of the period covered by this book. What this means is that there is very little in the way of historical documentation of these early years. We say "early years," but at the same time realize that these times happened only around 100 years ago, as of 2011.

The net effect should not be surprising, but is nonetheless profound. A great deal has been written, heard and seen about the artists of the last half of the 20th century, such as the Beatles, Michael Jackson and Elvis. But going back 100 years creates quite a contrast. Not many people remember a guy by the name of Billy Murray. Yet he was the leading recording artist of the first two decades of the twentieth century. He can be heard on over 1000 78 r.p.m. records as lead singer or vocal group member. And 1000 records was a significant portion of the number of records issued back then. Mr. Murray made good money for his time, but he wasn't enormously wealthy. Today, a number one male singer (Sinatra, Billy Joel, Kanye West or Justin Bieber) is/was/will be rich.

Why was Mr. Murray relegated to obscurity? Because when he recorded, he was primarily a studio artist, singing over and over into those old horns to create sound that was mechanically transferred to records. In fact his voice was "piercing" and came out crisp and clear through the mechanical recording process. When electrical recording of sound took over in the mid-twenties, Murray's voice didn't sound as good and he quickly faded into obscurity (just as stars of silent movies had trouble transitioning into talkies). And since he was yoked to the studio to record, and recorded so many times over a twenty year period, he had little time to travel and appear in front of live audiences. Also, because there was no ability to do the kind of public relations that today spawns famous people (no radio or television, only sheet music and records), recording artists weren't larger than life. His face wasn't even on many pieces of sheet music.

So as the reader examines the vocal group music of the period under study, he or she would be advised to consider the ways that technology shaped and channeled the music, affected the careers of the men and women that produced it, limited the speed and scope of cross-pollination of musical styles and, unfortunately, relegated some beautiful works of art to obscurity.

Sheet Music and Vocal Groups

Sheet music has played an important part in the history of music, including that of vocal groups. Before recording and the radio, sheet music was the primary way that that music travelled. Sheet music, simply, is music written in a standard format using a system of symbols and lines to inform the reader of what notes to play, when and for how long.

While music notation in some form likely dates back about 4000 years, printed sheet music goes back to the late 15th and early 16th centuries and hand-written sheets were produced before then. Before the invention of the recording, it was the only way to distribute music other than in live performances.

More modern sheet music came about beginning with Gutenberg's invention of the printing press in 1440. But, it is in the period covered by this book, with pianos being in many houses, that sheet music became extremely popular. It not only enabled pianists to be able to play the songs they loved; it also served as a great advertisement for the recordings of those songs and others by the same publisher.

Once recordings became available in the very latter part of the nineteenth century, sheet music had some real competition. But the sheets were far cheaper than the recordings and, also, if people heard a recording that they liked and wanted to play it on their piano, sheet music enabled them to do that. Few of us can simply sit down at a piano and play a song "by ear." One of the earliest successes in the sale of sheet music was "After The Ball" in 1892. It was the first popular music sheet to sell one million copies. A later version of the sheet appears above.

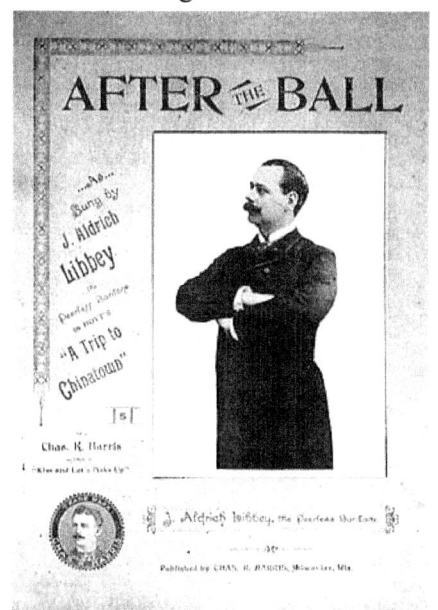

As recordings became less expensive, sheet music lost some of its popularity. The proliferation of radios in households in the 1920s further diminished sheet music sales.

Sheets from the mid-18th century had minimal designs and either no image of the artists or a simple drawing. Likenesses of singing groups were common on covers from about 1840 on. Here, for example, on

Hutchinson Family

the left is a sheet from 1843 depicting the Hutchinson Family. The drawing of the quartet is rather large and as we go through the years, the size of the drawing or photo would decrease and then increase again. Also shown here left below is an 1852 sheet from the Christy's Minstrels of the classic Stephen Foster song, "Massa's In De Cold Ground." Again, a very simple design with no illustration of the minstrel company. From 1851, we have the Harmoneons at right with ornate designs on the cover and likenesses of the six members.

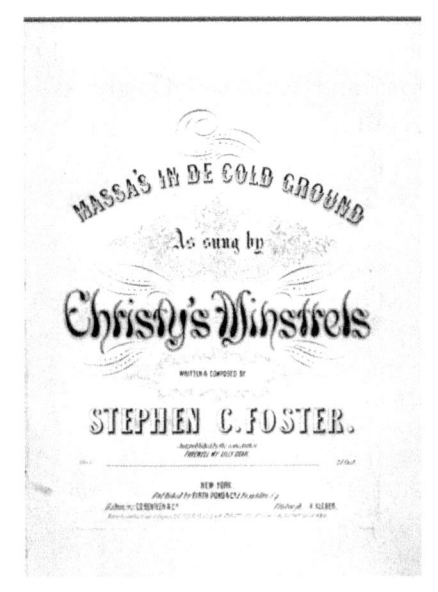

Christy's Minstrels

Harmoneons

The artwork became more elaborate as the century progressed and photos of single artists and groups appeared on the covers as advertisements towards the end of the 1890s. These changes all helped to sell copies. By the late 1800s we also find more elaborate backgrounds and photos of the groups appearing on the cover. For example here from 1899 is "The Girl I Loved In Sunny Tennessee" by the Knickerbocker Four.

Some sheets had very small photos of the group and much more elaborate artwork. For example, see "My Sweet Little Eskimo" (next page) by the Empire City Quartette from 1904. This group appeared on at least eight sheet covers, the most of any group at that time, yet they never made the pop charts, likely because they were a vaudeville group. (It is not always clear if a grouping of

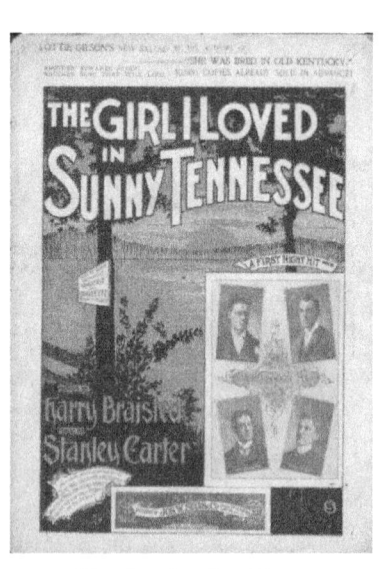

Knickerbocker Four

Empire City Quartette

individuals on a cover is an actual vocal group or just three or four members of the cast of a revue.)

The size of each element on the sheet was indicative of the importance of those elements. For example, at various times the song was more important than the artist and, at other times, the artist was more important than the song.

Around the turn of the twentieth century, music publishers in the United States were concentrated in New York where there were more of them than in the rest of the country combined. Some of those New York publishers were Chappell & Co., Shapiro, Bernstein & Co., T.B. Harms Company, Feist & Frankenthaler, Jerome H. Remick & Co. (also in Detroit), Jos. W. Stern & Co. (also in London and Chicago) and Harry Von Tilzer Music Publishing (also in Chicago, San Francisco, Sydney and London). The next largest concentration of publishers was located in Chicago. They included Calumet Music Co., Forster Music Publisher, Harold Rossiter Music Company and Milton Weil Music Co

Not surprisingly, Southern California also became a mecca for music publishers as the twentieth century wore on, given that it was the center of the film industry and entertainment people naturally gravitated there. Some of the companies located there were Hill and Range, Owens-Kemp Music, American Music Inc. and Schumann Music Co.

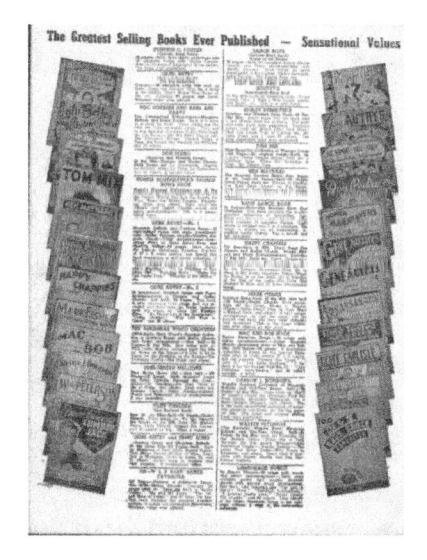

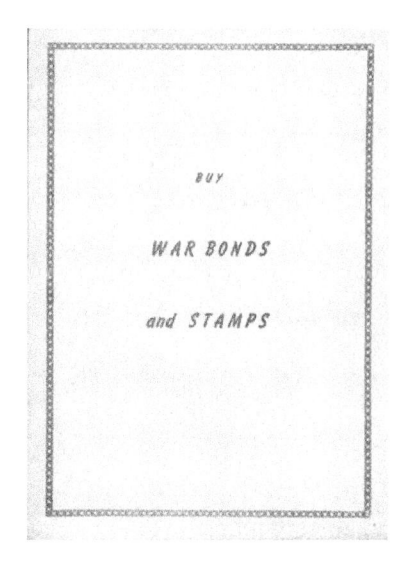

The back covers of sheets were usually reserved for advertisements for the publishers' other offerings. Below left is a sample from Calumet Music Co. of Chicago in 1938. During

the Second World War, some back covers had patriotic messages such as the one shown on the previous page on the right.

Major sheet music collections can be found in places such as the University of South Florida, Miami Campus, Brown University, the Center for American Music at the University of Pittsburgh, the Lester Levy Collection at Johns Hopkins University (more than 29,000 pieces), Middle Tennessee State University Center for Popular Music, the University of California at Berkeley California Sheet Music Project, the University of North Texas Catalog of Music Special Collections, University of Colorado, Duke University, Harvard Theatre Collection, University of Illinois at Urbana-Champaign Music Library, Lilly Library at Indiana University, University of Michigan, the Templeton Music Museum at Mississippi State University and the University of North Carolina at Chapel Hill.

Major non-university collections of early sheet music can be found at the Library of Congress, National Museum of American History's Archive Center in Washington, D.C. and the Bagaduce Music Lending Library in Blue Hill, Maine

Probably the best known name in early sheet music publishing was Harry Von Tilzer. When he was 14, he left home to join the circus. There he played piano and wrote music for the shows. Following that he wrote for burlesque and vaudeville. His first hit was "My Old New Hampshire Home" in 1898. Over two million copies of the sheet music of that song were sold. Von Tilzer then joined Shapiro, Bernstein Publishing Company in New York before forming his own company in 1902 with his brother Albert. Among Von Tilzer's hits are songs still heard today, particularly among barbershoppers, such as "A Bird in a Gilded Cage," "Wait 'Til The Sun Shines Nellie" and "I Want A Girl (Just Like The Girl That Married Dear Old Dad)."

Beaux and Belles Octette

Boswell Sisters/Mills Brothers

Another form in which sheet music appeared was as a "Music Supplement" to newspapers such as the *New York Journal and Advertiser*. Here (previous page, left) is one of "My Magnolia Maid" by the Beaux and Belles Octette from 1901. Some sheets contained more than one artist on the cover. The sheet for "Here Lies Love" from 1932 (previous page on right) contained photos of the Boswell Sisters and Mills Brothers as well as several solo artists.

Race

The first sheet found with a photo of a black group was the Windom Quartette in 1898 with "You'se Just A Little N*****, Still You'se Mine, All Mine" which is shown in the main text of this book. The offensive word is actually spelled out on the cover and this was far from unusual at the time.

The first sheet we found with a black female vocal group on the cover did not appear until 1946 with the Ginger Snaps' "Too Many Irons In The Fire." A mixed-gender black group appears on the cover of "Hunky-Dory" from 1900, but this is likely just four cast members from a revue.

Ginger Snaps   *Hunky-Dory*

Gender

The earliest sheets found with photos of a male vocal group on the cover are "Swingin In De Sky" by the Bison City Quartette (below left) and the Newsboys' Quintette with "My Honolulu Lady," (below right) both from 1895.

Bison City Quartette    *Newsboys' Quintette*

The first example of a sheet with a female group on the cover is the 3 Sisters Hawthorne with "They All Love Nellie Tracy (This Dainty Girl Of Mine)" from 1897. Next, in 1898, we had the Angela Sisters with "Susie-ue" ("A High Class Darkey Ballad") and the Original Dunbar Sisters, a trio pictured on "Tillie Tootie (The Coney Island Beauty)."

3 Sisters Hawthorne    *Angela Sisters* 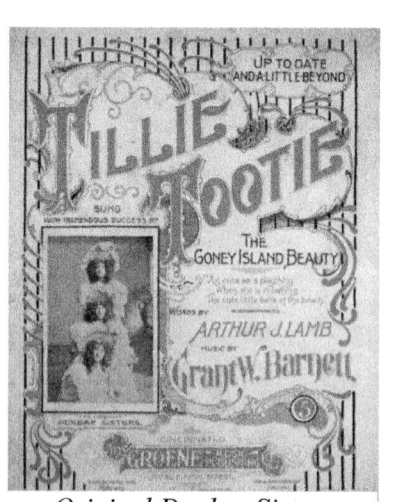   *Original Dunbar Sisters*

The earliest mixed-gender group found was the Bon-Ton Trio, two men and a woman who appear on the 1899 sheet music of "The Song That My Mother Sang To Me" (at right).

Politics

A sheet featuring the Euterpean Quartette from 1901 (below left) shows the late President William McKinley with pictures of the four women arranged below. It states that the sung was sung at McKinley's funeral. The Woods Bros. G.O.P. Quartette appeared on sheet music titled "Republican Rally Song: Republicans Will Win This Fall" in 1934 (below right). The sheet says it is from "Republican State Convention, Sprinfield [sic], Ill. Aug, 9. 1934." Finally, the Home Town Coolidge Club Quartette appeared on sheet music of "Keep Cool And Keep Coolidge" 1924. The picture on front has The Home Town Coolidge Club Quartette of Plymouth, Vermont, presenting to the President and Mrs. Coolidge the first certificates of membership in the Home Town Coolidge Club.

Bon-Ton Trio

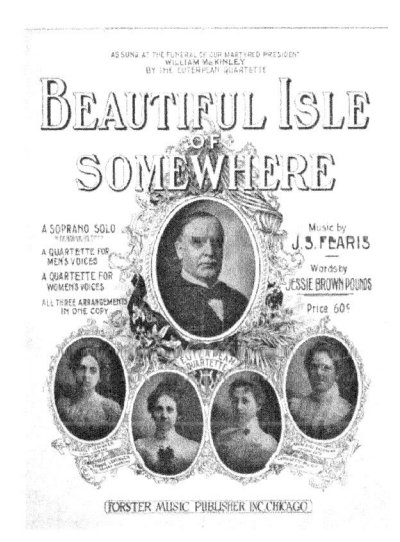

Euterpean Quartette

Woods Bros. G.O.P. Quartette

Home Town Coolidge Quartette

Sources for collections of and further information on sheet music:

Bagaduce Music Lending Library
http://www.bagaducemusic.org

Baylor University
http://contentdm.baylor.edu/cdm/

Brown University
http://library.brown.edu/collections/sheetmusic/

University of California at Berkeley
California Sheet Music Project

University of California, Los Angeles
http://unitproj.library.ucla.edu/music/mlsc/apam.cfm

California Sheet Music, 19th Century
http://people.ischool.berkeley.edu/~mkduggan/neh.html

Center For Popular Music, Middle Tennessee State University
http://popmusic.mtsu.edu/

University of Colorado, Boulder
http://libcudl.colorado.edu/sheetmusic/browse.asp?

Dreams of the past: 19th Century Color Lithographic Sheet Music Covers

Florida Atlantic University
http://wise.fau.edu/library/depts/spc/Music%20Scores/simple_search.php

Harvey's Sheet Music Collection
http://harveyssheetmusic.mazit.com/

Historic American Sheet Music-
http://library.duke.edu/rubenstein/scriptorium/sheetmusic/glossary.html

University of Illinois at Urbana-Champaign
http://www.library.illinois.edu/mux/about/collections/specialcollections/uiucsheetmusic.htm

Indiana University
http://webapp1.dlib.indiana.edu/inharmony/welcome.do

Johns Hopkins University, Lester S. Levy Collection
http://levysheetmusic.mse.jhu.edu/

Library of Congress African American perspectives
http://memory.loc.gov/ammem/aap/aaphome.html

Library of Congress, American Memory Project
http://memory.loc.gov/ammem/index.html

Library of Congress American Variety Stage
http://lcweb2.loc.gov/ammem/vshtml/vshome.html

Maine Music Box
http://mainemusicbox.library.umaine.edu/

University of Michigan
http://www.umich.edu/libraries.php

Minneapolis Public Library
http://www.libraryasincubatorproject.org/?p=5747

University of New Hampshire
http://www.library.unh.edu/special/index.php/sulloway-collection

University of North Carolina at Chapel Hill
http://www.lib.unc.edu/dc/sheetmusic/

University of North Texas
Catalog of Music Special Collections

University of Oregon
http://boundless.uoregon.edu/digcol/sheetmusic/

University of Pittsburgh
Foster Hall collection, Center for American Music,

San Francisco Public Library
http://sflib1.sfpl.org:84/

Santa Cruz Public Library
http://www2.santacruzpl.org/sheetmusic/

Sheet Music Consortium
http://digital2.library.ucla.edu/sheetmusic/

Smithsonian Institution
http://amhistory.si.edu/archives/d5300.htm

University of South Florida
http://www.lib.usf.edu/special-collections/arts/sheet-music-collections/

University of Wisconsin
http://uwdc.library.wisc.edu/collections/MillsSpColl/PopularMusic

Geography

<u>New York</u>
ABC Music Corporation
Broadcast Music, Inc. 194 (Will Von-Tilzer)
Broadway Music Corp.
Capitol Songs, Inc.
Chappell & Co.
Chas. K. Harris Music Pub. Co.
Crawford Music Corporation
Criterion Music Corp.
Davis, Coots & Engel
DeSylva, Brown and Henderson, Inc.
Edward B. Marks Music Corporation
Edwin H. Morris & Company
Exclusive Publications
Famous Music Corporation
F. W. Miller 1915
Feist & Frankenthaler 1900
Firth, Pond & Co. 1843
Geberak Music Publishing Company
Geo. W. Meyer Music Co.
George Pincus Music Corp.
Harold Dixon In.
Harry Von Tilzer Music Publishing New York-Chicago-Frisco Sydney-London 1907

Harry Warren Music
Henry Waterson Inc.
Hollis Music Inc.
Irving Berlin, Inc.
Jack Gold Music Co.
Jerome H. Remick & Co. (also Detroit) 1912 1925
Jerry Vogel Music Co.
Joe Morris Music Co.
Johnstone Music Inc.
Southern Music Pub. Co.
Jos. W. Stern & Co. (London, Chicago) 1899
Keit-Engel Inc.
Laurel Music Corporation
Leeds Music Corp.
Leo Feist Inc.
Leslie Music Corporation
Liscols Music Corp.
Ludlow Music Inc.
Manhattan Music Publishers
Massey Music Company
M. Witmark & Sons
Miller Music Corporation
Mills Music Inc.
Milsons Music Publishing
Paramount Music Corporation
Plymouth Music Co.
Radio Music Company
Regent Music Corporation
Robbins Music Corporation
Sam Fox Pub. Co.
Santly-Joy, Inc. 1944
Shapiro, Bernstein & Co.
Shapiro, Bernstein & Von Tilzer
Sheldon Music Corporation
Southern Music Pub. Co.
Supreme Music Corporation
T.B. Harms Company
Theron C. Bennett Co. (also Memphis, Omaha and Denver) 1911
Watersom, Berlin & Snyder Co.

California
Hill and Range 1951
Owens-Kemp Music
American Music Inc.
Schumann Music Co
Sherman, Clay & Co. (San Francisco)

Chicago
Calumet Music Co.
Boston Frazier
LaSalle Music Pub. Co. 1914
Forster Music Publisher
Harold Rossiter Music Company
Will Rossiter 1914
Ted Browne Music Co.
Milton Weil Music Co.
E. O. Excel 1901
Herb Morris' Songwriters

Boston
Daly Music Publisher
O. E. Story Music Publisher

St. Louis
Weile Pub. Co.
Stark Music Co.

Scranton
Whitmore Music Pub. Co.

Poughkeepsie
Song Hit Music Co.

Oklahoma
Ben Tillson Music Publishing Company

Hawaii
Harry Nordmark

Cleveland
Davies & Keating

Philadelphia
Emmett J. Welch Music Publishers

Postcards and Vocal Groups

American society that existed approximately a hundred years ago was, to be kind, primitive compared to what exists today. In 1904, 95% of people were born at home, life expectancy was 47 and the three leading causes of death were pneumonia/influenza, tuberculosis and diarrhea. There were only 8,000 cars in the whole country and 144 miles of paved roads. Our country did not yet include Arizona, Oklahoma, New Mexico, Hawaii or Alaska, and California had fewer people than Alabama, Mississippi, Iowa and Tennessee. This was the American society that existed when a European fad came to America; the use of postcards.

Almost all of the pictures we have of the early vocal groups appear on pieces of sheet music. Most are professional units posing for professional photographers. Most lived in or near big cities (though they may not have been born there) because that's where the sheet music publishers and the rest of the music industry resided. Postcards provide another perspective on singing groups for the last half of the time period covered by this book; 1900-1950. While the quality of the pictures that appeared on sheets was less than excellent, postcards were often merely photographs backed by cardboard, yielding sharp, clear images. And unlike the sheets, the geography of postcards was unlimited. The reader may find it interesting to keep track of the number of states from which the groups themselves came, or the locales to and from which the cards were mailed. (We count references to 25 states.)

Postcards caught the attention of Americans at the turn of the twentieth century, when the recording industry was beginning to thrive. "Real Photo" postcards appeared around 1900, and in 1906 Eastman Kodak came out with the affordable "Folding Pocket Camera," which allowed the printing of photographs onto cardboard. Some of these were used for advertisements or as trading cards, while others were pictures of real people, including a variety of vocal groups. After WWI, the telephone took over much of the purpose of postcards, though an interest in them continues to a lesser degree to the present day.

But what do postcards have to do with our topic of vocal groups between 1850 and 1950? The photos of many vocal groups appeared on postcards beginning in the early 1900s. By collecting these cards, we can learn much about the importance of vocal groups to American society and how ubiquitous they were, especially in the early years of the twentieth century. The real photo cards of groups that we have collected represent all strata of society, all geographical regions of the country, and rural as well as urban locales.

100 Years of Harmony: 1850 to 1950

The record industry, which was growing at the same time, was initially the province of the well-off because of the cost of playing machines and recordings, and was centered in the cosmopolitan areas of our country such as New York, Chicago, Philadelphia and Boston. Not so postcards. They come from all over and it is refreshing to see pictures of groups from Ohio, Iowa, Kansas and Wyoming as well as the larger metropolitan areas. They also represent many different genres of popular music, different delivery systems (minstrelsy, vaudeville, Chautauquas, radio, churches) and also provide an insight into the way people lived back then.

Local and Amateur Groups

The first group of cards represents local, small town and amateur groups. These early cards furnish the geography, the language, the styles and lifestyles of men and women who sang together. There is an implication that groups were formed and sang everywhere; from the towns and villages of the Midwest to the cities of the east coast.

The "Folding Pocket Camera," allowed local and amateur singers to put their pictures on post cards. The two cards below are from the "undivided back era," since the writing is on the front and only the addressee appears on the back. The Crescent Ladies Quartette (1906), from the postmark and address, hail from Angola, Indiana (northeast corner of the state) so we assume the Crescent Male Quartette (1907) comes from the same town.

Crescent Ladies Quartette *Crescent Male Quartette*

Scranton Quartet

Silver City Harmony Four

The reverse of the card above left, a picture of three women and a man, says "Kindest regards from 'The Scranton Quartet' to yourself and 'The Phila. Four.' Luna Park Sept 24, 1906." Luna Park is a name that has been given to many amusement parks since 1903. Frederick Ingersoll, a designer of roller coasters and scenic railroads, opened Luna Parks in Pittsburgh and Cleveland in 1905, the first of his chain of 44 parks. Given the writing on the reverse, this Luna Park is likely to be referencing the one in Pittsburgh. Above right, the Silver City Harmony Four (probably from Michigan, circa 1910).

Below, the Sunbeam Quartette (sent from and to Indiana, postmarked 1916) features hats and cigars.

The card at the right was sent from West Liberty, Ohio to Fayetteville, Kentucky (1910), and reads, "Hello Old Man. The bunch on the other side were caught killing sheep and snapped for the 'Rogue's Gallery. 'This constitutes the 'Big Brothers Male Quartet,' a wonderful organization." The names are listed on the back, and the guy second from the right, H. B. Foughty, has a wonderful head of hair.

Big Brothers Male Quartet

The group in the car, "The Westminster Quartet Enroute through Catskills," was on a card sent from Pittsburgh to New Wilmington, Pennsylvania in 1910, and the back refers to their picture being taken in New Castle, PA. Both cities are north of Pittsburgh near the Ohio border. The car they sit in is a Cadillac circa 1912.

Westminster Quartet

The last card in this category, the Telestrom Quartet, was sent to Eleva, Wisconsin, circa 1910. Eleva is a village of approximately 635 people as of the 2000 Census. It was originally called "New Chicago," but the grain elevator was only painted with the letters ELEVA before winter set in, and visitors assumed that was the name of the town, and it stuck.

Telestrom Quartet

More Professional Groups

Ionian Male Quartette

The second group of cards represents more professional groups of singers. Most are based in large cities, all are quartettes and most advertise their talents on the card itself. The Ionian Male Quartette of Toledo, Ohio was "Available for every sort of an engagement where a high grade of music is desired."

The Bostonian Quartette played instruments and sang, probably at the Seattle World's Fair in 1909 (as shown by the postmark). Another Boston group appearing below, the Lotus Male Quartette, promised "Music for all occasions" about 1910.

Bostonian Quartette

Lotus Male Quartette

532

Metropolitan Four

And finally, the Metropolitan Four, "Vocal and Instrumental Soloists & Harmony Singers," advertise their appearance at the Hotel Euclid, in Cleveland, Ohio. Part of the note on the back reads, "I've seen the latest. Gentleman's slashed trousers! Ornament at top of slash. Brilliant colored hose worn with them."

Minstrelsy

The story of the origins of minstrelsy is told elsewhere in this book. Around the turn of the twentieth century, minstrelsy was still popular, and the practice of "blacking up" was used by blacks and whites, by small and large groups of performers, and by professionals and amateurs alike. Our first postcard presents Vilsack's Famous Minstrels, in 1913, posing in front of the Hotel Bartlett in Cambridge Springs, PA, a small resort town in northwest Pennsylvania known for its mineral springs. The members of the troupe, most of whom are dressed in white, number over fifty people.

Vilsack's Famous Minstrels

The next card presents a large group of white men — the Post Office Clerks Minstrels (50 in number) from Buffalo, NY in 1913. The back proclaims, "The Minstrel success of the Season: Grand Minstrel Performance... Tuesday Eve., April 22, 1913... General Admission 50 cents, Reserved Seats 75 cents."

Post Office Clerks Minstrels

Proof that amateurs got into minstrelsy and blackface appears in the two postcards below. The one with the sign that says "Vaudeville" appears to be a home-made stage. Four performers, three in blackface, stand on the stage and four more stand in front of them. A small audience, which seems to include children, turns to stare at the camera. The second card presents four white performers, one of whom is "blacked up." The setting appears to be a porch in a small town neighborhood. Both cards are thought to be from 1910-1920.

Last, the card below is labeled "The Cake Walkers - Young's Pier, Atlantic City, U.S.A." The card is an early one (1901-1907), and the fifteen cakewalkers, mugging for the camera, are all black.

100 Years of Harmony: 1850 to 1950

Schools

Four-part harmonizing was common in educational institutions. Below are the Alexandrian Quartet (circa 1910) from the Bluefield, West Virginia high school and the Belle Plain, Iowa, Senior Double Quartette from 1907.

Alexandrian Quartette

Senior Double Quartette

Groups were also singing in colleges and seminaries. Below left is a 1906 postcard of a Campus Male Quartet from a Kansas college. Below right is "The Jamison House Quartette," from Ohio Northern University in Ada, Ohio. The back reads, "We are the only musical ones in the house so they have branded us the "Jamison House Quartette."

Campus Male Quartet

Jamison House Quartette

535

Even seminarians got into the act. At right is the Euphonia Quartet of Eden Seminary, St. Louis, Missouri, sporting big hair around 1920.

Early Black Singers

Black groups appear on early postcards, most of them jubilee singers following in the footsteps of the famous Fisk Jubilee

Euphonia Quartet

Singers of the nineteenth century. At left are the Original Canadian Jubilee Singers, composed of three men and three women from around 1900 and below the American Jubilee Singers who billed themselves as the "Successors to the Original Fisk Co," comprised of three women and four men (and a manager who claimed to have once sung tenor for the Original Fisk

Original Canadian Jubilee Singers

Singers, Daniel W. Brown, although works on the Fisk Singers contain no reference to him). This group toured Great Britain in the first decade of the twentieth century. They sang as a mixed octette for some songs and in quartets for others.

American Jubilee Singers

Williams Jubilee Singers

The Williams Jubilee Singers (1911), above, advertised their services in color and touted themselves as "...the World's Greatest Harmonizing Octet. A company of Colored Artists selected from American Colleges who have delighted millions of people in the leading cities of the world. Their repertoire includes all classes of music from the old Negro Melodies to Grand Opera." Based in Chicago and touring Europe frequently, the group was black-owned and operated.

Last, a secular group, the Poincinia Quintette, at right, appearing "In the Ladies' Grill at Reisenweber's," a famous jazz club and upscale eatery near Columbus Circle in New York City in 1912. On the reverse another group, "That Scandless Trio," is advertised as entertaining at the Brighton Beach Casino (Brooklyn, NY) which offered a "Genuine Old-Fashioned Beefsteak Dinner."

Poincinia Quartette

Chautauquas

Another early set of cards deals with the Chautauqua and rival Pantages circuits. The card below is subtitled, "A Redpath-Vawter Chautauqua crowd homeward bound."

Chautauqua Tent

The next card features the Chicago Boys Choir (four young men) on the front and advertises on the back, "Hey there, The Albert Lea Chautauqua will open Monday, July 5th [1909] and continue 7 days. Get a Season Ticket. You can't afford to miss. Tickets only $1.50 now - $2 at gate." Last in this category is the Wyoming Trio (bottom right), billed as "Wild West Warblers and Rope Twirlers," who toured on the Pantages Circuit during the 1920-21 Season.

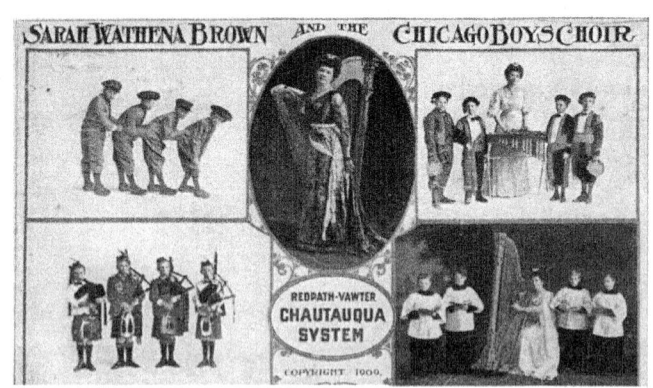

Chicago Boys Choir

Wyoming Trio

The Sons of the Range    *Doc Williams and his Border Riders*

Country & Western

This genre of music appeared on postcards in the 1930s. A few typical ones appear above. On the left is "The Sons of the Range" (likely modeled after the Sons of the Pioneers) with autographs of the four singers on the back of the card. To the right, Doc Williams and his Border Riders mug for the photo. The back of this advertisement gives the names of the group members, with "Doc" Williams the rightmost standing male, and "Froggie" holding the group's monkey mascot, "Jo-Jo" while lying on the bass viol.

Radio

Radio became widespread in the 1920s and postcards representing stations and artists soon followed. The interior of the studio of WGN in Chicago is shown here, the performers

Radio Station WGN

Breakfast Four

appearing before an audience of 600. The card was issued in the 1930s and several groups of singers appear on the left side of the stage. "The Breakfast Four" appear at left, as "featured artists of Westinghouse Stations WBZ-WBZA" on a card from around 1940. Less sophisticated performers are represented below by the Natural Quartette, who performed for KFEQ in St. Joseph, Missouri in the mid-1920s, and Boots, Jim and Bobby, "KWTO Entertainers" in 1942.

Natural Quartette

Boots, Jim and Bobby

Comedy Quartets

National Comedy Four

Comedy groups are represented here by two early cards. The National Comedy Four appears on the left on a 1907 card. They are "Up-To-Date Comedians and Vocalists" as well as performing "Crisp Single Turns and Dialect Sketches." They traveled well — a reference to them appears in *The Toronto World* newspaper in 1912.

On the right is the Imperial Quartette from the same era. There were several groups of this name and an advertisement for one appears in The Daily Tropical Sun in West Palm Beach Florida in 1912 and says that they "will sing your favorite song by request."

Advertisements

Although vocal groups advertising their own performances came early in the postcard era, it seems product ads were not common until around 1930. Below left is a picture of Tom, Dick & Harry, plugging Fels-Naptha Soap. Below right, is The Smiling Shell Quartet for Shell Service Stations.

Imperial Quartette

Tom, Dick & Harry

The Smiling Shell Quartet

On the right is the Olinger Quartet, appearing for the Olinger Mortuary in Denver Colorado. It was the 'home" of Buffalo Bill Cody's body for several months in 1917 during a burial dispute between Colorado and Wyoming. Colorado won.

Olinger Quartet

Armed Services

Servicemen in the armed forces in WWII are also saluted on post cards. Below is a group of entertainers throwing a "Servicemen's Radio Party" which went on the air each Wednesday night on a Chicago radio station. The second card below is extremely interesting; it appears to be set in a U.S.O. club on an armed forces base, and a quartet of black seamen seems to be in the act of entertaining men in khaki On the back is written one word, "KWAGALEIN," or "KWAJALEIN." Both refer to the same place, an atoll in the South Pacific, part of the Marshall Islands, which was the site of an American invasion on January 31, 1944.

Servicemen's Radio Party

U. S. O. Club

Children

Groups of child singers performed and appear on postcards. The first is Hurtt's Juvenile Quartette. A living descendant of the family puts the picture at about 1880, based on the apparent age of the children, whose names are written on the back.

The next family presents us with a quiz. Pictured are four brothers, ranging in age from 15 to mid-twenties. The card was mailed to a fan from Cincinnati, OH to North Vernon, IN. What is the name of the group? Who came out of this group to become an international star? (Answer: The Williams Brothers Quartet and Andy Williams)

Hurtt's Juvenile Quartette

Williams Brothers Quartet

Professionals

Many professional singing groups advertised and reached their fans by postcard. Two are featured here. The first is of the Andrews Sisters, the card posted in 1944 from Universal City, California. They appeared in 17 films overall. In one, *Argentine Nights*, they were required to dance, but Universal refused to

Andrews Sisters

The Encyclopedia of Early American Vocal Groups

pay for dance lessons. Fortunately, their co-stars, The Ritz Brothers, were more generous and taught the Sisters the steps.

The second card, at right, is a publicity card for the King Sisters put out by their record label, Victor. The reverse of the card contains a brief bio of the group that reads: "FOUR KING SISTERS . . . famous and attractive rhythm group . . . their dad taught them that mellow harmony . . . started as kids in family act on West Coast . . . several seasons with Horace Heidt . . . the favored feature with Alvino Rey's orchestra . . . regular sustaining and television broadcasts . . . big click on Victor label . . . S.R.O. sign on theatres from coast to coast when they appear."

At left is an autographed card of the Deep River Boys inscribed to "Gordy."

King Sisters

Deep River Boys

And finally, at right, a card from the Billy Williams Quartet.

Billy Williams Quartet

Lists

Twenty-Three Great Groups
Fisk Jubilee Singers
Dinwiddie Colored Quartet
Haydn Quartet
American Quartet
Peerless Quartet
Revelers
Boswell Sisters
Rhythm Boys
Dixie Hummingbirds
Comedian Harmonists*
Merry Macs
Mills Brothers
Andrews Sisters
Four Vagabonds
Ink Spots
Golden Gate Quartet
Delta Rhythm Boys
Charioteers
Modernaires
Cats and the Fiddle
Pied Pipers
Ravens
Orioles

Notable Lead Singers

Patti Andrews	Andrews Sisters
Connee Boswell	Boswell Sisters
Carl Jones	Delta Rhythm Boys
John Jordan	Four Vagabonds
Paula Kelly	Modernaires
Bill Kenny	Ink Spots
William Langford	Golden Gate Quartet
Billy Murray	American Quartet
Jo Stafford	Pied Pipers
Sonny Til	Orioles
George "Bon-Bon" Tunnell	Three Keys

Ira Tucker	Dixie Hummingbirds
Billy Williams	Charioteers/Billy Williams Quartet

Notable Bass Singers

Oscar Broadway	Four Knights
Otha Lee Gaines	Delta Rhythm Boys
Steve Gibson	Five Red Caps
William F. Hooley	Haydn Quartet
Orville "Hoppy" Jones	Ink Spots
John Mills, Sr.	Mills Brothers
Jimmy Ricks	Ravens
Len Williams	Norfolk Jazz/Jubilee Quartet
Orlandus Wilson	Golden Gate Quartet

Some Great Songs You Might Know

Sweet Adeline	Quaker City Four (1903)
Roll Jordan Roll	Four Harmony Kings (1919)
Them There Eyes	Rhythm Boys (1930)
The Object Of My Affection	Boswell Sisters (1934)
Java Jive	Ink Spots (1940)
Boogie Woogie Bugle Boy	Andrews Sisters (1941)
Didn't It Rain	Golden Gate Quartet (1941)
Take The "A" Train	Delta Rhythm Boys (1941)
Juke Box Saturday Night	Modernaires (1942)
Jersey Bounce	Deep River Boys (194?)
Mairzy Doats	Merry Macs (1943)
Paper Doll	Mills Brothers (1943)
Dream	Pied Pipers (1945)
For Sentimental Reasons	Brown Dots (1945)
Georgia On My Mind	Four Knights (1945)
I Sold My Heart To The Junkman	Basin Street Boys (1946)
P.S. I Love You	Four Vagabonds (1946)
Summertime	Ravens (1947)
It's Too Soon To Know	Orioles (1948)

A Kiss And A Rose	Charioteers (1949)
Marie	Four Tunes (1953)

Some Great Songs You May Not Have Heard

I Didn't Raise My Boy To Be A Soldier	Peerless Quartet (1915)
Red Hot Mama	Brox Sisters (1924)
Fit As A Fiddle	Three Keys (1932)
I Heard	Mills Brothers (1932)
If I Had A Million Dollars	Boswell Sisters (1934)
Anytime, Anyday, Anywhere	Five Jones Boys (1937)
Yours, All Yours	Sally Gooding/Three Peppers (1937)
Just Dream Of You	Norfolk Jazz Quartet (1937)
Well All Right (Tonight's The Night)	Andrews Sisters (1939)
My Walking Stick	Golden Gate Quartet (1940)
Someone's Rocking My Dreamboat	Ink Spots (1941)
Call It Anything, It's Love	Charioteers (1941)
Cheatin' On The Sandman	Merry Macs (1942)
Just For You	Five Red Caps (1943)
Rose Ann Of Charing Cross	Four Vagabonds (1943)
Honey, Honey, Honey	Deep River Boys (1946)
I Know	Jubalaires (1946)
I Wonder, I Wonder	Four Aces (1946)
Voot Nay On The Vot Nay	Basin Street Boys (1946)
I'm In Love With A Gal (Who's In Love With A Guy Who Looks Like Me But Ain't)	Delta Rhythm Boys (1947)
You're The Dream Of A Lifetime	Bill Johnson & Musical Notes (1947)
Don't Look Now	Ravens (1949)
Whirlpool	Cabineers (1949)
A Dream Is A Wish Your Heart Makes	Jubalaires (1950)
Mary Jo	Four Blazes (1952)

Some Songs That Influenced The Music

Mamma's Black Baby Boy Good	Unique Quartette (1893)
Down On The Old Camp Ground	Dinwiddie Colored Quartet (1902)
The Picture Turned Toward The Wall	Manhansettt Quartette (1902)

Sweet Adeline (You're The Flower Of My Heart)	Haydn Quartet/Peerless Quartet (both 1904)
Swing Along	Afro-American Folk Song Singers (1914)
Go Down Moses	Southland Singers (1919)
Coney Island Babe	Excelsior Quartette (1922)
Dinah	Revelers (1926)
Sweet Mama Tree Top Tall	Birmingham Quartet (1926)
When I Take My Sugar To Tea	Boswell Sisters (1931)
Tiger Rag	Mills Brothers (1931)
Wah-Dee-Dah	Three Keys (1932)
Ohne Dich (Stormy Weather)	Comedian Harmonists (1933)*
I Miss You So	Cats & the Fiddle (1940)
I Had The Craziest Dream	Four Vagabonds (1943)
Just A-Sittin' And A-Rockin'	Delta Rhythm Boys (1945)
It's Too Soon To Know	Orioles (1948)
Count Every Star	Ravens (1950)

* Not American, but included because of their influence

Most Songs On Pop Charts (Only those whose first chart hit was prior to 1950)

Peerless Quartet	108	1904 to 1926
Andrews Sisters	90	1938 to 1951
American Quartet	66	1910 to 1924
Haydn/Hayden Quartet	62	1898 to 1914
Mills Brothers	61	1931 to 1954
Ink Spots	46	1939 to 1951
Ames Brothers	29	1948 to 1954
Andrews Sisters/Bing Crosby	23	1939 to 1951
Boswell Sisters	20	1931 to 1938
Shannon Four	14	1917 to 1925
King Sisters	13	1941 to 1945
Revelers	13	1926 to 1930
Sterling Trio	13	1916 to 1922
Merry Macs	12	1939 to 1946
Pied Pipers	12	1944 to 1948**

Columbia Stellar Quartet	11	1912 to 1922
Lyric Quartet	11	1911 to 1917
Heidelberg Quartet	8	1911 to 1915
Charioteers	7	1940 to 1949
Orpheus Quartet	7	1914 to 1919
Modernaires	6	1945 to 1954***
Brox Sisters	5	1922 to 1926
Sportsmen	5	1943 to 1948
That Girl Quartet	5	1911 to 1913

** Plus 12 with Tommy Dorsey and two with Jo Stafford
*** Plus ten with Glenn Miller

Groups That Sang With Bands

Group	Band
Admirals	Gus Arnheim
Ames Brothers	Russ Morgan
Andrews Sisters	Larry Rich, Leon Belasco
Aragon Trio	Wayne King
Babs And Her Brothers	Fred Waring
Bachelors (Four Bachelors)	Ted Lewis
Barry Sisters	Wayne King
Bea And The Bachelors	Fred Waring
Beachcombers	Johnny Long
Bennett Sisters	Clyde McCoy
Biltmore Rhythm Boys	Bert Lown
Biltmore Trio	Bert Lown
Blue Notes	Blue Barron Band
Bob-O-Links	Bob Crosby
Bodyguards	Orrin Tucker
Boswell Sisters	Benny Goodman, Bunny Berigan, Dorsey Brothers, Eddie Lang, Joe Venuti, Mannie Klein
Campus Kids	Kay Kayser

Charioteers	Eddie Duchin
Clubmen	Freddie Rich
Crew Chiefs	Tex Beneke
Danford Sisters	Ben Selvin
Debutantes	Ted Fio Rito
DeMarco Sisters	Eddie Duchin
Dipsy Doodlers	Larry Clinton
Donna & Her Don Juans	Horace Heidt
Downe Sisters	Ray Miller
Four Kings	Horace Heidt
Four Recorders	Henry Busse
Freshmen	Ray Noble
Foursome	Roger Wolfe Kahn, Smith Ballew-Glenn Miller
Galli Sisters	Art Mooney
Gay Sisters	Russ Morgan
Ginger Snaps	Jimmy Mundy
G-Noters	Gene Krupa
Happy-Go-Luck Boys, Mark Kel's	Nat Shilkret
Heartbeats	Russ Morgan
Kassel Trio	Art Kassel
Kaydettes	Sammy Kaye
Keep Shufflin' Trio	Jimmie Johnson
Keller Sisters & Brother Lynch	Vincent Lopez, Jean Goldkette
Kim Loo Sisters	Ina Ray Hutton
King Sisters	Alvino Rey, Artie Shaw, Horace Heidt
King's Jesters	Paul Whiteman
King's Men	Paul Whiteman
Lane Sisters	Fred Waring
LeBrun Sisters	Glen Gray
Lee Sisters	Vaughan Monroe
Lunceford Trio	Jimmy Lunceford
Masters Voices	Frankie Masters
Mello Larks	Glenn Miller

Modernaires	Charley Barnet, Fred Waring, Glenn Miller, Paul Whiteman
Moon Maids	Vaughan Monroe
Moon Men	Vaughan Monroe
Moonlight Serenaders	Tex Beneke
Moreing Sisters	Anson Weeks
Morganaires	Russ Morgan
Mullens Sisters	Enric Madriguera
Murphy Sisters	Vaughan Monroe
Norton Sisters	McFarland Twins, Vaughan Monroe
Pastels	Stan Kenton
Pied Pipers	Tommy Dorsey
Radiolites	Ben Selvin
Revelers	Jean Goldkette
Rhythm Boys	Gus Arnheim, Paul Whiteman
Rhythmaires	Bob Chester, Ziggy Elman, Lew Raymond, Billy May, Les Brown, Tommy Dorsey, Spike Jones, Russ Morgan
Rollickers	Ben Selvin, Freddie Rich
Romancers	Paul Whiteman
Rondoliers	Ben Selvin, Paul Whiteman
Royal Hawaiian Sweethearts	Harry Owens
Satisfiers	Charlie Barnet, Tommy Dorsey
Sentimentalists (Clark Sisters)	Blue Barron Band, Tommy Dorsey
Sherry Sisters	Dean Hudson
Singing Serenaders/Four Harmony Kings	James Reese Europe
Skylarks	Harry James, Jimmy Dorsey, Russ Morgan, Woody Herman
Skyliners	Ray Anthony
Smoothies	Hal Kemp
Snowflakes (A Pair Of Pairs)	Claude Thornhill
Songopators	Red Nichols
Songsmiths	Victor Young

Sonnysiders	Sonny Dunham
Sophisticates	Bernie Cummins
Sportsmen Quartet	Gus Arnheim
Stardusters	Charlie Spivak
Starr Sisters	Paul Page
Stella And The Fellas	Fred Waring
Swing Masters	Frankie Masters
Three Barons	Sammy Kaye
Three Blue Notes	Blue Barron Band
Three Earbenders	Eddie Duchin
Three Esquires	Tommy Dorsey
Three Girl Friends	Fred Waring
Three Kaydets	Sammy Kaye
Three Melodians	Ben Selvin
Three Moaxes	Charley Barnet
Three Rhythm Rascals	Gus Arnheim
Three Songies	Red Nichols
Three Star Singers	Sam Lanin
Three Strikes	Henry Busse
Three Top Hatters	Jon Savitt
Three Toppers	Jon Savitt
Three Waring Girls	Fred Waring
Topper Trio	Jon Savitt
Town Criers	Bob Crosby, Earl Hines, Jimmie Lunceford, Kay Kyser, Les Brown, Lionel Hampton, Tommy Dorsey
Twin Tones	Jan Garber
V-8	Fred Waring
Voices Four (Voices Three)	Tommy Tucker
Williams Trio	Griff Williams
Wynken - Blynken - Nod	Jean Goldkette

Bibliography

'Do Thyself a' no Harm': The Jubilee Singing Phenomenon and the 'Only Original New Orleans University Singers,' in the Journal of the American Music Research Center, Volume 6 (1996)

Abbott, Lynn and Doug Seroff. *Ragged But Right*: *Black Traveling Shows, "Coon Songs," and the Dark Pathway to Blues and Jazz*. Jackson: University Press of Mississippi, 2007

Atlanta Historical Bulletin, The. Atlanta's Music: 1837-1977. Special Issue. Vol. XXI No. 2, Summer 1977

Averill, Gage. *Four Parts, No Waiting: A Social History of American Barbershop Harmony.* New York: Oxford University Press, 2003

Bean, Annemarie, Hatch, James V. & McNamara, Brooks (eds.). *Inside The Minstrel Mask: Readings In Nineteenth Century Blackface Minstrelsy*. Hanover: Wesleyan University Press, 1996

Booth, Mark W. *American Popular Music: A Reference Guide*. Westport, Connecticut: Greenwood Press, 1983

Brooks, Tim. *Lost Sounds*: *Blacks And The Birth Of The Recording Industry 1890-1919*. Urbana and Chicago: University of Illinois Press, 2004

Carpenter, Bil, Mavis Staples and Edin Hawkins. *Uncloudy Days: The Gospel Music Encyclopedia.* Backbeat Books, 2005

Clarke, Donald. *The Rise And Fall Of Popular Music*. London: Penguin Books, 1995

Cuney-Hare: Cuney-Hare, Maud. *Negro Musicians and Their Music*. New York: Da Capo, 1974

Czada, Peter and Günter Grosse. *Comedian Harmonists: Ein Vokalensemble erobert die Welt*. Berlin: Edition Hentrich, 1993, 1998

Dawson, Jim & Propes, Steve. *What Was The First Rock 'N' Roll Record?* Boston: Faber and Faber, 1992.

Diamond, Jared. *Guns, Germs, And Steel: The Fates of Human Societies*. New York, NY: W. W. Norton & Co., 1997, page 243

Dumont, Frank. *The Golden Days of Minstrelsy.* "New York Clipper," December 19, 1914

Dumont, Frank. *The Younger Generation in Minstrelsy and Reminiscences of the Past.* "New York Clipper," March 27, 1915

Encyclopedia of American Gospel Music, W. K. McNeil, Editor, Rutledge, Taylor & Francis Group, 2005

Ewen, David. *All The Years Of American Popular Music.* Englewood Cliffs, NJ: Prentice-Hall, 1977

Fletcher, Tom. *One Hundred Years of the Negro in Show Business.* New York: Burdge & Company Ltd., 1954, pp. 9-14

Friedman, Douglas E. *The Comedian Harmonists: The Last Great Jewish Performers In Nazi Germany.* West Long Branch, New Jersey: HarmonySongs Publications, 2010

Friedwald, Will. *Jazz Singing: America's Great Voices From Bessie Smith To Bebop And Beyond.* London: Quartet Books, 1990

Friedwald, Will. *Stardust Melodies, A Biography Of Twelve Of America's Most Popular Songs.* New York: Pantheon Books, 2002

Gillett, Charlie. *The Sound Of The City.* New York: Da Capo Press, Inc., 1996

Goldberg Marv. *More Than Words Can Say: The Ink Spots and Their Music.* Lanham, Maryland: Scarecrow Press, Inc., 1998

Gospel Music Encyclopedia, Robert Anderson and Gail North, Sterling Publishing, 1979

Gracyk, Tim. *Popular American Recording Pioneers: 1895-1925.* Binghamton, NY: The Haworth Press, 2000, pages 15-16

Gregory, Hugh. *A Century of Pop: A Hundred Years Of Music That Changed The World.* Chicago: A Cappella Books, 1998

Gribin, Anthony J. & Schiff, Matthew M. *The Complete Book of Doo-Wop.* Iola, WI: Krause, 2000

Hamm, Charles. *Yesterdays: Popular Song In America.* New York: Norton, 1979

Hardy, Phil and Dave Lang. *The Da Capo Companion to 20th-Century Popular Music*. New York: Da Capo Press, Inc., 1990, 1995

Harrison, Harry P. & Detzer, Karl. *Culture Under Canvas: The Story Of Tent Chautauqua*. New York: Hastings House, 1958

Hoffman, Frank, Carty, Dick & Riggs, Quentin. *Billy Murray*. Lanham, MD: Scarecrow Press, 1997

Homer, Charles F., *Strike the Tents, The Story of Chautauqua*. Philadelphia: Dorrance & Co., 1954

Kenrick, John. "History of the Musical Stage 1700-1865: Musical Pioneers." http://www.musicals101.com/1700bway.htm

Klamkin, Marian. *Old Sheet Music: A Pictorial History*. New York: Hawthorn Books, 1975

Meigs, Henry Benjamin. *Record of the Descendants of Vincent Meigs*. Baltimore: J. S. Bridges & co., 1901

Morgan, Thomas L. & Barlow, William. *From Cakewalks To Concert Halls: An Illustrated History Of African American Popular Music From 1895 To 1930*. Washington: Elliott & Clark Publishing, 1992

Nicholson, Stuart. *Ella Fitzgerald: A Biography of the First Lady of Jazz*. New York: Da Capo Press, New York, 1993

Ostergaard, Erik. "The History of Nipper and His Master's Voice." http://www.erikoest.dk/nipper.htm

Pafik, Marie-Reine & Guiheen, Anna Marie. *The Sheet Music Reference & Price Guide. Second Ed.* Paducah, KY: Collector Books, 1995

Paymer, Marvin E., General Editor. *Facts Behind The Songs: A Handbook Of American Popular Music From The Nineties To The '90s*. New York & London: Garland Publishing, Inc., 1993

Rice, Edward LeRoy. *Monarchs of Minstrelsy, 'Daddy' Rice To Date*. New York: Kenny Publishing Co., 1911

Rockwell, John. *An Instant Fan's Inspired Notes: You Gotta Listen.* Previously unpublished liner notes on the Comedian Harmonists (written in 1981). *The New York Times*, September 5, 1999

Sanjek, Russell & Sanjek, David. *American Popular Music Business in the 20th Century.* New York: Oxford University Press, 1991

Schlesinger, Joseph. *Turn Of The Century Quartets.* SWD Roundup. Volume 46, Number 3, August 1999

Schoener, Allon. *Harlem On My Mind: Cultural Capital Of Black America 1900-1968.* New York: Random House, 1968

Sforza, John. *The Andrews Sisters Story - Swing It!.* Lexington: The University Press of Kentucky, 2000

Short, Marion. *Covers Of Gold: Collectible Sheet Music.* Atglen, PA: Schiffer, 1998
Simon, George T. *The Big Bands.* New York: The Macmillan Company, 1967

Southern, Eileen. *Biographical Dictionary of Afro-American and African Musicians.* Westport: The Greenwood Encyclopedia of Black Music, Greenwood Press, 1982

Spaeth, Sigmund. *A History Of Popular Music In America.* New York: Random House, 1948

Tawa, Nicholas E. *High-Minded And Low-Down: Music In The Lives Of Americans, 1800-1861.* Boston: Northeastern University Press, 2000

Walker, Leo. *The Big Band Almanac.* New York: Da Capo Press, 1989

Ward, Andrew. *Dark Midnight When I Rise.* New York: Farrar, Strauss and Giroux, 2000

Warner, Jay. *The DaCapo Book of American Singing Groups, A History 1940 – 1990.* Cambridge: Da Capo Press, 2000

Waters, Mary M. *800 Pounds Of Harmony: The Big Four Quartette.* Bushnell, IL: McDonough Democrat, 2000

Joel Whitburn's Pop Memories, 1890-1954. Menomonee Falls, Wisconsin: Record Research, Inc., 1986

Whitburn, Joel. *Top R&B Singles 1942-1988*. Menomonee Falls, WI: Billboard, 1988

White: White, Charles. *Negro Minstrelsy*: *Its Starting Place Traced Back Over Sixty Years, Arranged and Compiled from the Best Authorities*. "New York Clipper," April 28, 1860

White's Male Quartette Book. New York: White, Smith & Co., 1884
Yanow, Scott. *Classic Jazz: The Essential Listening Companion*. San Francisco: Backbeat Books, 2001

Photo Credits

Unless otherwise indicated, all photos and other illustrations in this book are believed either to be in the public domain or are publicity photos. Any other use is unintended.

Front Cover
Back to Front, Hutchinson Family, Williams Colored Singers, Andrews Sisters, Ink Spots with Ella Fitzgerald, Orioles

Back Cover
The Sunbeam Quartette, Pickens Sisters

Chapter One Collage
Top left, Meigs Sisters Vocal Quartette; top right, American Jubilee Singers; bottom left, Amphions Quartette; bottom right, Boston Minstrels; center, Hutchinson Family

Chapter Two Collage
Top left, Dolce Sisters; top center, Lovenberg Sisters And Neary Bros.; top right, Four Musical Colby's; bottom left, Jersey City Police Quartet; Bottom center, Knickerbocker Four; bottom right, unknown

Chapter Three Collage
Top left, Four Belles; top right, Song Spinners; bottom left, Tasty Yeast Jesters; bottom right, 4 Aalbu Sisters, center, Mills Brothers

Chapter Four Collage
Top left, Parker Sisters; top right, James Quintet; bottom left, Escorts and Betty; bottom right, Ross Sisters; center, Beale Street Boys

Index

A Kiss And A Rose, 75
A Slip Of the Lip Can Sink A Ship, 68
Abbott, Lynn, 12
ABC Network, 69, 78
Abrams, Lawrence, 86
Aeolian-Vocalion, 28
Afro American Folk Song Singers, 32
Alabama Four, 56
Alabama Moon, 34
Albers, Ken, 93
Alford, Gene, 89
All Coons Look Alike To Me, 26
Alleghanians, 4
Allen, Lynn, 76
Alpine Minstrels, 4
Amazing Grace, 61
American Federation of Musicians, 66
American Four, 11
American Lyceum, 8
American Quartet, ix, 28, 29, 31, 32
American Society of Composers, Authors and Publishers (ASCAP), 35, 66, 67, 90
Ames Brothers, 83
Ames, Ed, 83, 84
Ames, Gene, 83
Ames, Joe, 83
Ames, Vic, 83
Amos and Andy, 59, 78
Andrews Sisters, ix, x, 46, 48, 49, 67, 68, 74, 75, 82
Andrews, La Verne, 48
Andrews, Maxene, 48, 49, 75
Andrews, Patty, 48, 49, 75
Anthony, Susan B., 8
Any Bonds Today, 68
Apollo Male Quartette, 32
Apollo Records, 90
Apollo Theatre, 41, 55
Arbuckle, Fatty, 39
Archer, J. "Buddie", 52
Aristocrat Records, 90
Armstrong, Harry, 27
Armstrong, Louis, 26, 40, 60
Arnheim, Gus, 45, 85
ASCAP. *See* American Society of Composers, Authors and Publishers
At Night, 91
Atkins, Essie, 59
Avon Comedy Four, 34
Axelrod, Mark, 27
Babs and her Brothers, 51
Bailey, Mildred, 45, 59
Bailey, Pearl, 59, 75
Baker Family, 5
Bands, sweet, 42
Barbershop, 25, 26, 27, 54, 83
Barbershop Harmony Society, 26, 27 (SPEBSQSA)
Barbour, Don, 93
Barbour, Ross, 93
Barker Family, 5
Barksdale, Chuck, 79
Barnes Orchestra, Walter, 80
Barnet, Charlie, 52
Barraud, Francis, 16, 17
Barraud, Mark, 16
Barris, Harry, 45
Basin Street Boys, 87
Battle Hymn Of The Republic, 31
Baur, Franklyn, 44
Baxter, Lex, 84
Bea and the Bachelors, 51
Beach Boys, 94
Beat Me Daddy Eight To The Bar, 74
Beaupre, Walter J., 71
Beautiful Isle Of Somewhere, 23
Beaux And Belles Octet, 23

559

Beavers, 57
Because, 20, 23
Beecher, Henry Ward, 8
Beedle De Beedle De Bop Bop, 53
Bei Mir Bist Du Schoen, 49
Belasco, Leon, 48
Bell label, 33
Bell, John, 76
Belmont, Joe, 20
Belmonts, 30
Benny, Jack, 85
Benson, Al, 88
Berle, Milton, 79
Berlin, Irving, 35
Berliner, Emil, 16, 17
Berry, William H., 33
Best, Pat, 87, 88
Beveridge, Betty, 84
Biberti, Robert, 63
Bieling, John, 23, 28, 31
Big bands, 40, 50, 69, 90
   Demise of, 66
Big Broadcast, The, 73
Big Four, 11
Big Four Quartet, 20
Bill Bailey, Won't You Please Come Home?, 22
Billboard, 19, 72
Birmingham Jubilee Singers, 56
Bison City Quartet, 20
Black groups of the late 1940s, 87
Black Patti. *See* Jones, Matilda Sissieretta
Black Swan label, 33
Blackface, 5
Blaine, Jerry, 91
Blake, Eubie, 59
Blakeley Family, 5
Blanc, Mel, 85
Bland, James, 10
Blenders, 57, 94
Bleyer, Archie, 83

Block, Martin, 41
Blue Barron Band, 83
Blue Chip Chatter, 27
Blue Room, The, 44
Blue Tail Fly, 6
BMI (Broadcast Music Incorporated), 35, 67, 90
Bobo, Willie, 62
Bon Bon and his Buddies, 58
Bones, 6
Boogie Woogie Bugle Boy, 67, 74
Booth, Mark, 25
Bootz, Erwin, 63
Born To Be With You, 83
Bossard, Henry, 86
Boswell Sisters, ix, x, 30, 46, 47, 48, 49, 78, 82
Boswell, Connie (Connee), 30, 46, 47
Boswell, Helvetia (Vet), 46
Boswell, Martha, 46
Bower, Frank, 6
Braden, Tommy, 80
Bremer, Fredericka, 10
Brent, Royale, 80
Brewster, Ralph, 51, 52
Bridges, Charles, 56
Brill Building, 36
Broadway, 60
Broadway, Oscar, 89
Brooks, Theodore, 81
Brooks, Tim, 20, 33, 34
Brown Dots, 75, 87, 88
Brown, Romaine, 82
Browning, Ivan Harold, 33
Brownlee, Archie, 86, 87
Brox Sisters, 35, 46
Brox, Eunice
   (Lorayne) Brox, 35
Brox, Josephine
   (Dagmar), also Bobbe, 35

Brox, Kathleen
    (Patricia) Brox, 35
Bruster, T. L., 62
Bryant, Hugh, 59, 78
Bryant, William Cullen, 8
Bryant's Minstrels, 6
Buck Privates, 67, 75
Buckley, George Swayne, 2
Bundesen, Jane, 83
Burr, Henry, 29, 31
Buschmann, Alice, 83
Butler, Arthur, 80
Buttons And Bows, 83
By The Light Of The Silv'ry Moon, 23
Cabaliers, 57
Caesar, Sid, 76
Cakewalk, 7, 25
Call and response, 21, 22, 26, 33, 56
Callender-Haverly Colored Minstrels, 10
Callender's Consolidated Spectacular
    Colored Minstrels, 10
Calloway, Cab, 57
Cambridge Sisters, 46
Camp meetings, 10
Campbell, Albert, 29, 31
Camptown Races, 7
Capehart, Homer, 41
Capitol Records, 90
Caravan, 43, 54
Cardinals, 94
Carnegie Hall, 61
Carolina Hayride, 89
Carry Me Back To Old Virginny, 7, 11
Carson, Johnny, 84
Carter, Benny, 69
Casey Jones, 28
Cats & The Fiddle, 79, 80
CBS Radio, 54, 59
Chalmers, Donald, 28
Charioteers, ix, 32, 34, 58, 68, 71, 75, 76, 91

Charmaine, 94
Chattanooga Choo Choo, 77
Chautauqua, 3, 8, 9
Chessler, Deborah, 90, 91
Chinatown, My Chinatown, 28
Chocolate Dandies, 33
Chordettes, 83
Christian, Ruth, 89
Christy Minstrels, 6
Christy, Edwin, 6
Churchill, Savannah, 88, 90
Clark Sisters, 83, 88
Clark, Ann, 83
Clark, Jean, 83
Clark, Lillian, 83
Clark, Mary, 83
Clark, Peggy, 83
Clarke, Donald, 34
Clinton, DeWitt, 8
Clovers, 94
Cocoanuts, The, 35
Colden, Melvin, 52
Cole Brothers, 58
Cole, Nat King, 89
Collin, Erich, 63
Collins, Arthur, 29, 31
Columbia Broadcasting System, 36
Columbia Male Quartet, 29, 30
Columbia Records, 29, 30, 31, 66
Columbia Stellar Quartet, 31
Come Josephine, In My Flying Machine, 28
Comedian Harmonists, x, 43, 44, 45, 63, 64, 84
Comedy Harmonists, 64
Comin' In On A Wing And A Prayer, 68, 85
Comstock, Bill, 93
Coney Island Babe, 33
Continental Four, 11
Continental Vocalists, 11

Conway, Bill, 51, 52
Cooke, Sam, 30, 62
Coon songs, 22, 25
Coon, Zip, 25
Corns For My Country, 68
Cotton Blossom Blues, 80
Cotton Blossom Singers, 86
Cotton Club, 50
Count Every Star, 93
Country and western, 63
Crawford, Traverse, 59
Crazy Blues, 39
Creole Love Song, 43
Criterion Quartette, 9
Crosby, Bing, 30, 45, 49, 50, 58, 59, 68, 70, 75, 76
Croxton, Frank, 29, 30, 31
Cruder, Harry B., 21
Crying In The Chapel, 92
Cunningham, Tinker, 82
Cycowski, Roman, 63
Cylinder, 15, 16, 17, 18, 19, 20, 21
Dale, Charles, 34
Dance bands, 42
Dandridge Sisters, 50
Dandridge, Dorothy, 50
Dandridge, Vivian, 50
Daniel, Howard, 58
Daniels, Jerry, 55
Daniels, Tom, 29, 31
Darktown Strutters' Ball, 34
Davis, James, 62
Davis, Richard, 82
Day By Day, 94
De Marco Sisters, 46
Dearborn, Kate, 5
Dearie, 23
Decca Records, 49, 66, 90
Deep River, 12
Deep River Boys, 58, 59, 71, 77, 78, 79
Deep River Singers, 9

DeKnight, Rene, 59
Delta Rhythm Boys, ix, 42, 43, 45, 58, 59, 71, 77, 78, 79, 84, 93
DeLuxe Records, 90
Deutsche Grammophon, 16
Dickens, Doles, 82
Dickinson, Hal, 51, 52, 77
Did You Ever Hear A Dream Walking, 48
Didn't It Rain, 62
Dillard University, 59
Dinah, 43, 44, 57, 58
Dinning Sisters, 82
Dinning, Ginger, 82
Dinning, Jean, 82, 83
Dinning, Lou, 82
Dinning, Tootsie, 83
Dinwiddie Colored Quartet, ix, 21, 22
Dion, 30
Disc, 18, 19
Dixie, 6, 62
Dixie Hummingbirds, 62, 86
Dixieaires, 81
Dixon, Clarence, 89
Dixon, Eugene, 76
Do I Worry, 75
Dominion label, 33
Dominoes, 30, 94
Don McNeil's Breakfast Club, 81
Don't Get Around Much Anymore, 75
Don't Sit Under The Apple Tree, 68, 77
Donahue, Al, 76
Don't Ask Me Why, 59, 78
Don't You Think I Ought To Know, 88
Doo-wop, 43, 80, 85, 94
Doring Sisters, 46
Dorsey Brothers Band, 47
Dorsey, Thomas, 61, 86
Dorsey, Tommy, 69, 77, 83, 88
Douglas, Harry, 59, 60
Down By The Old Mill Stream, 31
Down On The Old Camp Ground, 22

Downbeat Magazine, 66
Dozier Boys, 88
Drayton, Charles E., 33
Dream, 77
Dream Of A Lifetime, 88
Drifters, 30, 72
Du Droppers, 81
Duchin, Eddie, 59, 75
Dudley, S.H., 23, 31
Dunbar Male Quartette, 9
Economics of the music industry, 66
Ed Sullivan Show, 7
Edison label, 20, 23, 28, 29, 31, 33
Edison Male Quartette, 20, 21, 23, 29
Edison, Thomas Alva, 15, 16
Elkins, Alfred, 80
Ellington, Duke, 40, 57
Emerson label, 33
Emerson, Ralph Waldo, 8
EMI, 16
Emmett, Daniel Decatur, 6
Emperors of Song, 33
Empire City Quartette, 20
Errair, Ken, 93
Ertel, Janet, 83
Ethiopian Serenaders, 4
Europe, Jim, 33
Euterpean Quartette, 4, 23
Ewen, David, 10, 19
Exactly Like You, 91
Excelsior Quartette, 33
Exhortation, 33
Farewell Ladies, 6
Farley, Jesse, 62
Farr, Hugh, 63
Ferryboat Serenade, 74
Finkelstein, Harvey, 34
Fisk Free Colored School, 11
Fisk Singers, x, 11, 12, 71, 86
Fisk, Clinton Bowen, 11
Fit As A Fiddle, 58

Fitzgerald, Ella, 47, 59
Fitzgerald, John "Honey", 28
Five Aces Of Rhythm, 80
Five Blazes, 80
Five Blind Boys of Mississippi, 86
Five Keys, 61, 72, 94
Five Locust Sisters, 46
Five Red Caps, 68, 81, 87
Five Scamps, 89
Flamingos, 32, 72, 88
Flanigan, Bob, 93
Floradora Girls, 20
Floyd, Troy, 39
Follow The Boys, 75
For Sentimental Reasons, 87
Ford Motor broadcasts, 51
Ford, Charles, 89
Forever And Ever, 83
Forrest, Helen, 85
Forty Whites and Thirty Blacks, The, 21
Forty-Five RPM Records, 69
Four Aalbu Sisters, 46
Four Aces, ix, 79
Four Blazes, 80
Four Buddies, 94
Four Chicks And Chuck, 51
Four Dusty Travelers, 57
Four Freshmen, ix, 93, 94
Four Harmony Kings, 33, 86
Four Hits And A Miss, 85
Four Kings of Harmony, 54
Four Knights, ix, 71, 89
Four Lads, ix, 62
Four Pods Of Pepper, 57
Four Sharps, 78
Four Toppers, 81
Four Tunes, ix, 88
Four Vagabonds, ix, 43, 57, 58, 68, 71, 80, 81
Frederick Hall Quintet, 59
Freed, Alan, 94

Friedwald, Will, 45, 47
Friend, Stella, 51
Frommermann, Harry, 63
Fuqua, Charles, 55
Fuqua, Harvey, 55
Gaines, Otha Lee, 43, 59, 78, 93
Gaither, Tommy, 92
Gardner, Vernon, 60
Garfield and Arthur Campaign Songs, 13
Garnes, Sherman, 93
Gasoline Alley, 39
General Jumped At Dawn, The, 68
German Minstrels, 4
Gibbons, Paul, 51
Gibson Family, 5
Gibson, Steve, 81, 87
Giersdorf Sisters, 46
Gillett, Charlie, 92
Ginger Snaps, 89
Ginyard, Caleb "J. C.", 81
Give My Regards To Broadway, 31
Givens, Cliff, 75
Glenn, Wilfred, 32, 44
Glow Worm, 73
Go Down, Moses, 12, 34
Godfrey, Arthur, 81, 83, 89
Goldberg, Marv, 55, 64, 79, 88, 93
Golden Gate Gospel Train, The, 61
Golden Gate Quartet, ix, 11, 43, 61, 68, 71, 78, 81
Goldstein, Chuck, 51, 52
Good-Bye, Dolly Gray, 20
Goodman, Benny, 42, 50, 69, 90
Goodwin, Harry, 34
Gordon, Jimmy, 88
Gospel, 52, 60, 61, 62, 85, 86, 87, 89
Gospel and spiritual group singing, 60
Gracyk, Tim, 18, 20, 22, 24
Graduation Day, 94
Gramaphone, 16
Gramaphone Company, 17

Gram-o-Phone label, 23
Grand Central Station, 82
Grant, Ray, 80, 81
Graves, Randall, 24
Great American Broadcast, The, 75
Gregory, Gerald, 93
Griffin, Terrence, 89
Griffin, Wyatt, 89
Grofe, Ferde, 39
Gross, Jason, 78
Gypsy Love Song, 31
Gypsy, The, 75
Hall Negro Quartette, 57
Hall, Frederick, 59
Hampton College Singers, 13
Hampton Institute, 59
Hampton Institute Quartet, 59
Hamtown Students, 11
Hann, Will, 33
Harewood, John, 58
Harlan, Byron G., 20, 31
Harlem Hit Parade, 72
Harmony Four, 58
Harney, Ben, 25
Harper, Ethel, 89
Harptones, 72
Harris, Norman "Crip", 52
Harris, Phil, 81
Harris, R. H., 62
Hart, Charles, 32
Haverly's Minstrels, 6
Hawaiian Trio, 34
Hawkins, Coleman, 40
Hayden Quartet. *See* Haydn Quartet
Haydn and Handel Society of Boston, 3
Haydn Quartet, 20, 22, 23, 28, 29, 31, 32
Haymes, Dick, 85
He Just Hung His Head And Died, 53
Hee Haw, 83
Heidelberg Quintet, 29
Heidt, Horace, 48

Hemingway, Leona, 89
Henderson, Fletcher, 40
Henderson, Jimmie, 79
Henry, Dr. Jim, 26
Herbert, Victor, 35
Herman, Woody, 69
Hickman, Art, 39
Hicks-Sawyer Colored Minstrels, 10
Hiett, June, 82
Hi-Lo's, 74, 78
Hip Hip Hooray, 68
HMV (His Master's Voice), 16
Hobbies Magazine, 19, 30
Hogan, Ernest, 26
Holbrook, Josiah, 8
Holiday, Billie, 58
Holland, Clinton, 59
Hollins, Delrose, 52
Holman, Benny, 80
Holmes, Oliver Wendell, 8
Holt, Paul Lindsley "Jelly", 80
Hooley, William F., 23, 28, 31
Hopper, Hal, 77
How Would You Know, 88
Howe, Julia Ward, 8
Huddleston, John, 77
Hughes Family, 4
Human Orchestra, 43
Hummitzsch, Dorothy, 83
Husch, Richard Gerard, 27
Hutchinson Family, 4, 5, 94
Hutchinson, Abby, 4, 5, 94
Hutchinson, John, 4, 5
Hutchinson, Joshua, 5
Hutchinson, Judson, 5
Hutton, June, 77
Hyer Sisters, 11
I Can Dream, Can't I?, 75
I Cover The Waterfront, 91
I Didn't Raise My Boy To Be A Soldier, 30

I Don't Want To Set The World On Fire, 75
I Get So Lonely When I Think About You, 89
I Know, 81
I Learned A Lesson I'll Never Forget, 82
I Miss You So, 80
I Sold My Heart To The Junkman, 87
I Understand Just How You Feel, 88
I Want To Be Loved, 88
I Want To Cry, 88
I Wonder Who's Kissing Her Now, 83
I'll Be With You In Apple Blossom Time, 74
I'm Afraid the Masquerade Is Over, 94
I'm Making Believe, 75
I've Been Workin' On The Railroad, 7
(I've Got A Gal) In Kalamazoo, 77
If I Didn't Care, 55, 75
If I May, 89
I'm Getting Sentimental Over You, 83
I'm Gonna Sit Right Down And Write Myself A Letter, 76
In A Travelling Mood, 88
In Bamville, 33
In The Good Old Summertime, 22, 23
In The Navy, 75
Ink Spots, ix, x, 32, 53, 55, 56, 58, 69, 71, 75, 87, 91
Instrument imitation, 43, 44, 57
Instrument replacement, 42
Instruments, Influence on the sound of vocal groups, 42
International Sweethearts of Rhythm, 86
Into Each Life Some Rain Must Fall, 75
Invincible Four, 30
Invincible Quartet, 29
It Can Happen To You, 80
It Can't Be Wrong, 81
It's A Long Way To Tipperary, 28
It's Too Soon To Know, 90, 91, 92, 93

Italiano, Ronnie, 92, 93
It's Love-Love-Love, 78
Jackson Harmoneers, 86
Jackson, Mahalia, 61
James, Harry, 69
James, Lewis, 44
Jammin', 49
Jarvis, Al, 41
Java Jive, 75
Jazz, 25, 26, 38, 42, 44, 47, 50, 51, 87
Jeanie With The Light Brown Hair, 7
Jennings, John, 81
Jericho Boys, 62
Jeter, Claude, 86
Jim Crow, 6
Jingle Jangle Jingle, 76
Jive Bombers, 57
Johnson, Hall, 57
Johnson, William, 81
Johnson, Willie, 61
Jones Boys Sing Band, 82
Jones, Carl, 59, 78
Jones, Etta, 50
Jones, George, 33
Jones, Matilda Sissieretta, 13
Jones, Ollie, 92, 93
Jones, Orville "Hoppy", 55, 75
Jones, Randye, 60
Joplin, Scott, 25
Jordan, John, 58, 80
Jubalaires, 62, 71, 81
Jubilee, 61, 86
Juilliard School of Music, 48
Juke Box Joe, 89
Juke Box Saturday Night, 77
Jukebox, 16, 41, 66, 68, 69, 73
Jumpin" With A G.I. Gal, 68
Just A Gigolo, 30
Just A Kid Named Joe, 74
Just A-Sittin' And A-Rockin', 43, 59, 78
Just Between You And Me, 83

Just For You, 82
Just To See You Smile Again, 94
Kapp, Dave, 48
Kaufman, Irving, 34
Keep Movin, 21
Kelly, Paula, 76
Kemp, Hal, 51
Kenny, Bill, x, 55, 75, 77, 85, 87
Kenny, Herb, 55, 75
Kenton, Stan, 93
Keys, Harriet, 29
King Cole Trio, 79
King Records, 90
King Sisters, 48, 77
King, Alyce, 48
King, Donna, 48
King, Luise, 48
King, Maxine, 48
King, Wallace, 11
King, Yvonne, 48
Knickerbocker Quartet, 29
Kraft Music Hall, 59, 68, 75
Kratzsch, Hal, 93
Lane, Ken, 51
Langford, William, 61
Larks, 94
Laughing At Life, 80
Laughing On The Outside, 76
Lawson, George, 60
LeBrun Sisters, 46
Lee Sisters, 82
Lee, Maree, 82
Leitch, Craig, 51
Leschnikoff, Ari, 63
Let Me Call You Sweetheart, 30
Let's Dance broadcasts, 42, 50
Lew Quartet, 11
Lewis Bronzeville Five, 80
Lewis, Ted, 57
Library of Congress, 19
Lights Of My Home Town, The, 30

Lincoln, Abraham, 8
Linda Brown, 80
Lockard, Jinny, 83
Lollipop, 83
London Palladium, 79
Lonesome Road, The, 57
Long playing records, 69
Loomis Sisters, 46
Lopez, Vincent, 39
Loves Me Like A Rock, 62
Lowry, Chuck, 77
Lubers, George, 58
Luca, John, 11
Lundy, James, 59
Lyceum, 8, 9
Lymon, Frankie, 30
Lyric Quartet, 29, 32
Macdonough, Harry, 23, 29, 31
Mahoney, Jere, 23
Mairzy Doats, 76, 77
Major Bowes Amateur Hour, 59, 60
Make Believe Ballroom, 41, 52
Mama Put Your Britches On, 68
Mamma's Black Baby Boy Good, 20
Manhansett Quartette, 19, 32
Manhattan Transfer, 78, 94
Maple City Four, 46
Marie, 88
Marion, J. C., 90
Marshall, Maithe, 93
Marx Brothers, 35
Mary Jo, 80, 82
Massingill, Rudy, 89
Master disc, 16, 18
Maybe, 75
McFadden, George, 81
McGuire Sisters, ix
McKay, Cheri, 50
McKinley, William, 23
McMichael, Joe, 50, 76
McMichael, Judd, 50

McMichael, Ted, 50
McPhatter, Clyde, 30
McQuade Sisters, 46
Medlock, James, 62
Meet Me In St. Louis, Louis, 31
Meistersextett, 64
Mellomen, 85
Melody Kings, 81
Meltones, 84
Menuhin, Yehudi, 69
Mercer, Johnny, 59
Meredith, Clarence, 21
Merrily We Roll Along, 6
Merry Macs, 50, 76, 78
Meyer, John, 29, 31
Microphone, 40
Milkman's Matinee, The, 52
Miller, Elmaurice, 59
Miller, Glenn, 50, 52, 76, 77
Miller, Lewis, 8
Miller, Polk, 24, 46
Mills Brothers, ix, x, 32, 33, 43, 46, 53, 54, 55, 56, 58, 61, 71, 73, 74, 75, 80, 81, 91
Mills, Billy, 54
Mills, Donald, 54
Mills, Harry, 54
Mills, Herbert, 54
Mills, John, Jr., 54, 80
Mills, John, Sr., 54
Minoco, 70
Minstrelsy, ix, 2, 4, 5, 7, 10, 13, 25
Miss Otis Regrets, 74
Mississippi Fire Blues, 80
Mister Jefferson Lord) Play That Barbershop Chord, 27
Mobile Four, 56
Modern Records, 90
Modernaires, 50, 51, 52, 76, 84
Monarch Jazz/Jubilee Quartet, 56
Monroe, Vaughn, 82

Moon Maids, 82
Moonglows, 32, 55, 72
Moonlight Bay, 28
Morgan, Corrine, 23, 29
Morgan, Russ, 83
Morin Sisters, 46
Morton, Jelly Roll, 26
Movie, First black vocal group in, 39
Mullin, Jack, 70
Mundy, Jimmy, 89
Murray Quartet, 28
Murray, Billy, 23, 28, 30, 31
Music Box Theater, 35
Music Performance Fund, 66
Musical Notes, Bill Johnson & his, 88
My Adobe Hacienda, 83
My Little Grass Shack, 74
My Magnolia Maid, 23
My Old Kentucky Home, 7, 20
My Walking Stick, 43
My Wild Irish Rose, 31
Nabbie, Jimmie, 88
Natchez Mississippi Blues, 80
Nation, Opal Louis, 43
National Broadcasting Co. *See* NBC
National Records, 90
Naughty Lady of Shady Lane, The, 83
NBC, 36
   First radio network, 40
NBC Radio Blue Network, 69
Nelson, George, 92
New Jersey label, 20
New Orleans Quintet, 59
Newport Jazz Festival, 62
Nichols, Slumber, 63
Nipper, 16, 17
Noble, Ray, 52
Nobody's Sweetheart, 54
Norfolk Jazz and Jubilee Quartet, 52
Norfolk Jazz Quartet, 53, 56
Norfolk Jubilee Quartet, 53

Oakland, Will, 29
Object of My Affection, The, 47
Obrecht, Jas, 24
O'Connor, Ginny, 84
Oh Baby Mine, 89
Oh Dem Golden Slippers, 11
Oh Johnny, Oh Johnny, Oh, 29
Oh Susanna, 7
Oh! Mabel, Oh!, 80
Oh, Didn't He Ramble?, 22
Oh, You Beautiful Doll, 28
Ohne Dich, 64
Old Acquaintance, 30
Old Black Joe, 7
Old Piano Roll Blues, The, 81
Old South Quartette, 24, 46
Olio, 7
Oliver, King, 26
On The Banks Of The Wabash, 31
O'Neal, Robert, 80
Orchestrions, 73
Orioles, ix, 34, 61, 88, 90, 91, 92, 93, 94
Orpheus Quartet, 29
Ossian's Bards, 4
Over There, 29
Owens, Danny, 88
Owens, Henry, 61
Owens, Paul, 86
Ozark Sisters, 46
P.S. I Love You, 81
Pack Up Your Troubles in Your Old Kit Bag (And Smile, Smile, Smile), 29
Palmer Brothers, 57
Palmer, Clarence, 57
Palmer, Dick, 57
Palmer, Earnest, 57
Panoram, 70
Paper Doll, 73
Paramount label, 33
Pardon My Sarong, 75
Parke, Bernie, 84

Pathe label, 33
Patillo, David, 81
Patti, Adelina, 13, 28
Paul, Les, 70
Peerless Minstrels, 30
Peerless Quartet, ix, 29, 30, 31, 32
Pelham, Dick, 6
Penny, Dave, 80
Perfect Woman, 80
Petrillo, James C., 66, 68, 69, 90
Pharr, Kelsey, 59
Philadelphia Academy of Music, 24
Phonograph, 15, 16, 19, 71, 72
Pickens Sisters, 46, 47
Pickens, Helen, 47
Pickens, Jane, 47
Pickens, Patti, 47
Pickert Sisters, 46
Picture Turned Toward The Wall, The, 19
Pied Pipers, 30, 50, 76, 77
Pilgrim Travelers, 86
Pillars, Hayes, 39
Plantation Boys, 87
Please Send Her Back To Me, 80
Pollack, Ben band, 50
Pope, Peggy, 48
Porter, Steve, 28, 29, 31
Powell, Austin, 79
Praise The Lord And Pass The Ammunition, 76
Premier Quartet, 28
Premier-American Quartet, 28
Pretty Kitty Blues Eyes, 76
Price, Ernie, 79
Price, Gene, 87
Prince's Male Quartet, 30
Promenade, 7
Puzey, Leonard, 92
Quaker City Four, 28
Race records, 39, 72

Radio, 39, 51, 54, 56, 61, 66, 67, 68, 69, 71, 85, 90
Radio Corporation of America. *See* RCA
Radio station, First commercial, 39
Radio Transcription Service, 71
Radio, First band on, 39
Radio, Records played on, 40
Radios in the home, 42
Ragtime, 25, 38
Rain Song, The, 32, 33
Rainer family, 4
Rainey, Ma, 11
Rainwater, Arthur, 87
Ravens, ix, 91, 92, 93, 94
Ravenscroft, Thurl, 85
Ray Hutton, Ina, 69, 77
RCA, 17, 36, 66, 69, 72, 90
RCM Productions, 70
Recess In Heaven, 79
Record player, 15
Recording bans, 66, 68, 85, 90
Recording, electronic, 40
Records, materials used in making, 42
Red Caps, Steve Gibson and The, 82
Red Hot, 89
Redpath Lyceum Bureau, 8
Reed, Johnny, 92
Revelers, ix, 26, 31, 32, 43, 44, 45, 52, 63, 84
Rex, Sterling, 21
Rey, Alvino, 48
Rhythm and blues, 55, 67, 72, 85, 87, 90
Rhythm Boys, ix, 30, 45, 47, 51, 59, 77
Rhythm Club fire, 80
Rice, Thomas Darmouth, 6
Rich, Larry, 48
Ricks, Jimmy, 92, 93, 94
Riddick, Claude, 76
Right Quintette, 33
Ringwald, Roy, 51
Rinker, Al, 45, 51

Robins, 88
Robinson, Bill "Bojangles", 59, 78, 79
Robinson, Earl, 89
Rock and Roll, 47
Rock and roll, Birth of, 65
Rogers, Roy, 63
Roll Jordan Roll, 33
Rolling Stone magazine, 64
Romanowski, Ken, 56
Rose Ann Of Charing Cross, 68
Rosenfeld, Monroe H., 35
Rosie The Riveter, 43, 68
Royal Harmony Quartet, 81
Rum And Coca-Cola, 75
Ryan, Babs, 51
Ryan, Charlie, 51
Ryan, Little, 51
Rycroft, Fred, 23
Ryder, Noah, 59, 60
Sad Blues, 53
Sally In The Alley, 19
Saunders, Reuben, 87
Savitt, Jan, 58
Savoy Records, 90
Say Si, Si, 74
Says My Heart, 49
Scamps. *See* Five Scamps
Schoen, Vic, 48
Schuberts, 9
Seeburg Piano Co., 73
Sensational Nightingales, 86
Sentimentalists. *See* Brown Dots, *See* Clark Sisters
SESAC, 35
Sforza, John, 49, 67
Shannon Four, 31, 44
Sharp, Alexander, 92
Shaw, Artie, 48, 58, 77, 84
Shaw, Elliott, 32, 44
Sheet music, 14, 15, 22, 46, 56, 66, 72
Sherman, Jimmy, 58

Shoe Shine Boy, 74
Shoo-Shoo Baby, 68, 74
*Shrine Of St. Cecilia, T*he, 74
Shuffle Along, 33
Side Kick Joe, 74
Simon, George T., 77
Simon, Paul, 62
Simplex record changer, 41
Sinatra, Frank, 59, 75, 90
Singing Serenaders, 33
Sissle, Noble, 33, 34
Six Brown Brothers, 34
Six Hits And A Miss, 84, 85
Skelton, Red, 89
Slye, Leonard, 63
Smalle, Ed, 31
Smedburg, Johnny, 51
Smith and Dale, 34
Smith, Bessie, 11
Smith, Joe, 34
Smith, Mamie, 39
Smith, Raymond, 52
Smoothies, 51
Sometimes I Feel Like A Motherless Child, 12
Song Spinners, 68, 85
Songs, War-related, 68
Sons Of The Pioneers, 63
Soul Stirrers, 30, 62, 86
Soundies, 70, 89
Southern, Eileen, 62, 87
Southernaires, 56
Southland Jubilee Singers, 89
Southland Singers, 34
Spaeth, Sigmund, 27
Spaniels, 93
Sparrows, 57
SPEBSQSA. *See* Barbershop Harmony Society
Specialty Records, 90
Spencer, Tim, 63

Spirits of Rhythm, 57, 80
Spirituals, 60
Spivak, Charlie, 77
Sportsmen Quartet, 85
Spotlight Talent, 88
Springs, Jimmy, 81
Stafford, Jo, 30, 77
Stamper, James L., 24
Standard Quartette, 21
Stanley, Frank, 20, 29, 31
Stardusters, 77
Starr Sisters, 46
Stella and the Fellas, 51
Stepin Fetchit, 82
Sterling Trio, 30
Stevenson, Elise, 29
Stewart Sisters, 46
Stick To Your Knittin' Kitten, 68
Stinson's Jubilee Singers, 54
Stormy Weather, 64
Story songs, 73
Strip Polka, 74
Sullivan, Arthur, 16
Sullivan, Ed, 79
Summers, Helen, 29
Suntan Baby Brown, 53
Suttles, Warren, 93
Swain, Bea, 51
Swallows, 94
Swan Silvertones, 86
Swanee Quintet, 62
Sweet Adellne, 23, 27, 30, 31
Sweet Adelines International, 28
Swing Along, 32
Swing Era, 50
Swing Low, Sweet Chariot, 12, 32, 58, 60
Swingin' The Dream, 60
Syncopation, 25
Taborn, Norval, 80
Take Me Out To The Ballgame, 23, 31
Take The A Train, 78

Tambo, 6
Tape recorder, 70
Tasty Yeast Jesters, 54
Teagarden, Jack, 69
Technology, Effects on music, 69
Teen Angel, 83
Teenagers, 30, 93
Tell Me Pretty Maiden, 20
Tell Me So, 90, 92
Temple Quartette, 9
Tennessee Jubilee Singers, 13
Tessie (You Are The Only, Only), 31
That Girl Quartet, 29
That Moaning Saxophone Rag, 34
That Old Gang Of Mine, 31
(There'll Be A) Hot Time in the Town of Berlin, 68
Thomas, Allie, 29
Thomas, James Mantell, 21
Thomas, Mary Jo, 82
Thompson, Beechie, 62
Thompson, Kay, 51
Thompson, Precis, 29
Three Blazers, Johnny Moore's, 79
Three Dennis Sisters, 46
Three Keys, 58
Three Little Maids From Pixie, 47
Three Ormand Sisters, 46
Three Peppers, 57
Three Sharps And A Flat, 57
Three Smoothies, 51
Three Waring Girls, 51
Three X Sisters, 46
Tiger Rag, 54
Til, Sonny, 91, 92, 94
Tilghman, Erlington. *See* Sonny Til
Till Then, 73
Tin Pan Alley, x, 35, 36
To Each His Own, 75
Tom the Tattler, 26
Tonight Show, The, 84

Torme, Mel, 84
Townes, Clyde, 80
Transcriptions, 68, 71
Trent, Alphonso, 39
Trolley Song, 77
Tucker, Ira, 62, 86
Tunnell, George "Bon Bon", 58
Turkey In The Straw, 6, 7, 26
Tuscaloosa, 82
Tuskegee Institute Singers, 13
Tuskegee Quartet, 13
Tutson, Otto, 52
Two Loves Have I, 91
*Two Many Irons In The Fi*re, 89
Tyrolese Minstrels, 4, 6
U.S. Minstrels, 30
Under Western Stars, 63
Unique Quartette, 20, 21
United In Group Harmony Association, 92
United States Gramophone Company. See RCA
Up On A Cocoanut Tree, 31
Utica Institute Jubilee Singers, 56
V-8, 51, 52
Valencia, 44
Van Heusen, Jimmy, 35
Vaudeville, 7, 13, 27, 34, 35, 54
Vaudeville theater, 7
Vawter, Keith, 8
V-Discs, 69
Vibra-Naires, 90, 91
Victor label, 21, 22, 23, 28, 29, 30, 31, 34
Victor Minstrel Co., 30
Victor Talking Machine Company. See RCA
Victor Vaudeville Co., 30
Victrola and 78 Journal, 24
Vincent, John Heyl, 8
Vincent, Lt. George Robert, 68
Virginia Female Jubilee Singers, 56

Virginia Minstrels, 6
Vocalion label, 33
Voot Nay On The Vot Nay, 87
Walk-around, 7
Walker, James, 62
Walking bass technique, 53
Wallace, John, 89
Walsh, Jim, 19, 30
War and music industry, 65
Ware, Edward, 60
Waring, Fred, 51, 52
Warner, Jay, 26, 74, 76, 78
Washboard Rhythm Kings, 57
Washington, Booker T., 13
Washington, Dinah, 90
Watermelon Party, 24
Watson, Ivory "Deek", 55, 75, 87, 88
Watson, Leo, 57
We Three, 75
We'll Meet Again, 68
Werrenrath, Reinald, 23, 29
Wexler, Jerry, 72
Wheat Street Female Quartet, 56
When The Swallows Come Back To Capistrano, 75
Where Have We Met Before?, 49
Whispering Grass, 75
Whitburn, Joel, 19
Whitcomb, James, 89
White, George, 12
White, Josh, 62
White's Male Quartette Book, 13
Whiteman, Paul, 39, 45, 51
Whitlock, Billy, 6
Why Do Fools Fall in Love, 93
Wilberforce University, 58
Wiley, Cornell, 88
Williams Jubilee Singers, 23
Williams, Billy, 58, 75, 76, 77
Williams, Billy Quartet, 76
Williams, Charles, 23

Williams, Len, 52, 53
Wilson, Billy, 77
Wilson, Carter, 60
Wilson, Jackie, 30
Wilson, Oliver "Toy", 57
Wilson, Orlandus, 61
Wilson, Ormand, 87
Windom, W.H. and his Quartette, 21
Windom, William "Billy", 21
Winner label, 33
Witherspoon, Harvey, 32
WNEW Radio, 41
Woodard, Lloyd, 86
Woodpecker Song, The, 74
Woody Woodpecker, 85
World War II, Effects on music, 67
Wurlitzer, 41, 73
Yanow, Scott, 47
Yocum, Clark, 77
You Oughta Be In Pictures, 47
You're Just A Little N****r, Still You're Mine, All Mine, 21
You've Been A Good Old Wagon, 25
You'd Be So Nice To Come Home To, 85
Young, John, 28
Your Show Of Shows, 76
Ziv, Frederic, 71